NORTHERN CALIFORNIA'S WATER INDUSTRY

The Comparative Efficiency of Public Enterprise in Developing a Scarce Natural Resource

Figure 1

"Southern California has demonstrated the value of irrigation. Northern California illustrates its latent possibilities. When one considers the vast area of the Sacramento and San Joaquin Valleys, with a surface shaped by nature for the easy spreading of water, with soil of great fertility and a marvelous climate, there is no doubt that it is to be during the twentieth century a great field of activity, not of the farmer alone, but the engineer, the lawyer, and the student of social and economic questions."

Elwood Mead (1901)

NORTHERN CALIFORNIA'S WATER INDUSTRY

THE COMPARATIVE EFFICIENCY OF PUBLIC ENTERPRISE IN DEVELOPING A SCARCE NATURAL RESOURCE

By Joe S. Bain, Richard E. Caves & Julius Margolis

Published for
Resources for the Future, Inc.
by
The Johns Hopkins Press, Baltimore

RESOURCES FOR THE FUTURE, INC.,
1755 Massachusetts Avenue N.W., Washington, D.C. 20036

Resources for the Future is a non-profit corporation for research and education in the development, conservation, and use of natural resources. It was established in 1952 with the co-operation of the Ford Foundation and its activities since then have been financed by grants from that Foundation. Part of the work of Resources for the Future is carried out by its resident staff, part supported by grants to universities and other non-profit organizations. Unless stated, interpretations and conclusions in RFF publications are those of the authors; the organization takes responsibility for the selection of significant subjects for study, the competence of the researchers, and their freedom of inquiry.

This book is one of RFF's water resource studies, which are directed by Allen V. Kneese. The research was done under an RFF grant to the University of California, Berkeley, where the senior author, Joe S. Bain, is professor of economics. Richard E. Caves is professor of economics at Harvard University, and Julius Margolis is professor of economics at Stanford University. The manuscript was edited by Virginia D. Parker. The maps and charts were drawn by Adrienne Morgan.

Director of RFF publications, Henry Jarrett; *editor,* Vera W. Dodds;
associate editor, Nora E. Roots.

Printed in the United States of America
Library of Congress Catalogue Card Number 66-266-88

PREFACE

This study derives its organization and purpose from one elementary proposition: In any major water-producing and water-using region, all public and private agencies that develop and manage water resources, use them to generate electric power, and capture and distribute water for consumptive uses, comprise a water industry; and this water industry is a meaningful unit for significant economic analysis. Embracing this postulate, we have made a thoroughgoing analysis of the water industry of Northern California.

Our analytical purposes are generically similar to those of numerous studies of conventional private industries. An ultimate aim is to measure or appraise the composite performance of the industry's members with respect to the level of development of water resources, the timing and sequence of this development, the allocation of water among uses, and the technical efficiency they attain in fulfilling their functions—and to evaluate this performance in terms of appropriate criteria of optimal economic efficiency. A closely connected goal is to explain how the quality of industry performance is related to crucial aspects of the structure of the industry and of the behavior of industry members, establishing if possible causal connections between the industry's structure and the behavior of its members on the one hand, and its performance on the other. A final aim is to draw upon any findings concerning these causal relationships in order to identify feasible alterations either in industry structure or in water-agency behavior which should improve the performance of the industry. Such an identification should serve as a guide to those formulating public policies affecting water-resource development.

The close resemblance of this study of a water industry to conventional industry studies, however, does not go much beyond a similarity in general orientation and purpose. The water industry of Northern California is populated mainly by public enterprises which are not profit-seekers; it operates substantially without markets for water; its performance thus emerges from the quasi-insular policies and actions of many agencies serving captive constituencies. For these and related reasons that are developed in the introductory chapter, the established methodology of industry analysis has perforce been modified and adapted to fit the case in hand. The aspects of industry structure that are most important in our water industry differ from those considered crucial in private industries; the familiar market conduct of private firms is replaced by public-enterprise conduct on quite different planes; and more numerous aspects of performance require evaluation because practically no facet of performance is automatically and predictably regulated by market forces. A water industry study is therefore not only different from but more complicated than conventional industry studies. Nonetheless, the industry-study approach to economic problems of water-resource development seems generally promising, and has the merit of emphasizing a dispassionate appraisal of the actual behavior of public enterprises in one of the spheres of production in which they are most important.

Despite the peculiarities of a water industry, it has been useful to adhere to the broad analytical format previously developed for conventional industry studies. That is, we consider in successive parts of this volume the structure, the conduct, and the performance of Northern California's water industry, turning in a final part to suggestions concerning public regulation of the industry. Analyzing empirical evidence in this sequence facilitates observation of the ways in which water-agency conduct is influenced by the structure of the industry, and of how the industry's performance is codetermined by its structure and the conduct of its members. The organization of the study and its rationale are discussed in detail in the introductory chapter.

Attributing credit to individual authors for various parts or chapters of the volume may be misleading, since every segment that was initially drafted by one author was repeatedly revised in response to suggestions of the others, and on occasion rewritten by another; throughout, the work product is thus in considerable part a collaborative one. Subject to this caveat, it may be indicated that Bain was primarily responsible for Part One, and Caves and Margolis for the substantive chapters (9 through 14) of Part Two, with Margolis generally covering urban water agencies and Caves all of the rest. Of Chapter 8, Bain drafted the first two main sections, Caves the third, and Margolis the fourth. Part Three emerged from a fully collaborative effort by Bain and Caves (though each contributed some individual statistical analyses), substantially assisted by Margolis' cost-benefit calculations for the Feather River Project. After the semi-final version of the manuscript had been circulated to readers, Caves did most and Bain a minor part of a general editing and rewriting of the volume to compress and unify its content.

The findings of the study of course emerged from a huge effort in primary research and in assembly and processing of statistical and other information from numberless sources. And although all authors were personally engaged in the research effort, they depended heavily over a period of over three years on the assistance of a research staff. The contributions of a number of graduate students who worked as junior research assistants for relatively brief periods are gratefully acknowledged. We wish also to express our gratitude to Mrs. Adrienne Morgan, cartographer, for the high quality of her professional work in constructing and drafting all maps included in this volume. One research assistant, Mr. Richard Ernst, who worked with us during the entire research undertaking and assumed major responsibility for a number of statistical and other analyses, deserves especial thanks. Finally, we recognize our indebtedness and express our gratitude to Miss Inge Kaiser, who served full time as chief of the research staff and executive secretary to the project for the whole three and a half years while research was under way. Bringing to the project a considerable background in the water-resources field, she was invaluable in many ways—as office manager and staff administrator, as indefatigable accumulator of elusive source materials, as field interviewer on important assignments, as liaison representative to principal water agencies—as well as performing admirably the more routine duties of a senior research assistant.

The general plan for the present study emerged from discussions of a faculty seminar on public water-resource development, meeting in Berkeley during the Spring of 1958 and sponsored by Resources for the Future, Inc. Regular seminar members, in addition to the authors of this volume, included Professors Albert Lepawsky and Michael F. Brewer of the Berkeley faculty; their ideas contributed measurably to the development of plans for this study. A number of outside experts met with this seminar as consultants at that time, including L. B. Christiansen and R. J. Shukle of the Bureau of Reclamation; R. L. Hill, N. B. Sturm, and J. W. Thursby of the California Department of Water Resources; B. L. Smith, Secretary of the Irrigation Districts Association of California; J. D. Worthington, Chief Engineer of the Pacific Gas and Electric Company; and Professor J. W. Milliman. We wish to acknowledge the help provided to us by all of these people, who contributed considerably to our education in the area of California water.

The authors were greatly assisted in their last revision of the manuscript by the criticisms and suggestions of a number of readers of a semi-final draft. Readers to whom we are grateful include Irving K. Fox and Allen V. Kneese of RFF, Professor Brewer, the U.S. Army Corps of Engineers, and the California Department of Water Resources, all of whom commented on the whole manuscript. Especial thanks go also to Professor Sho Sato of the School of Law at Berkeley, for a detailed critical reading of and commentary of Chapter 3 of this volume, and to Eugene M. Prince of San Francisco, eminent attorney in the field of water law, for reading earlier draft material on the law of water rights. Professor Milliman also read and made comments on some chapters. By indicating simultaneously that the authors benefited from the suggestions of all of these readers but followed their suggestions only in a selective fashion, we absolve each of them of any responsibility for any of the content of the book.

Our study was supported by a generous grant made by Resources for the Future, Inc., to the Regents of the University of California, in an amount which defrayed substantially all salaries of research and other staff, salaries for released and summer time of the authors, and project office and travel expenses. The authors express their gratitude to RFF, and also to Joseph L. Fisher, its president, and Irving Fox its vice president, for their continuing personal advice and encouragement throughout the course of the study project. We wish further to thank Henry Jarrett, director of publications at RFF, and Mrs. Virginia D. Parker, who edited the final manuscript, for their efficient and cooperative handling of the editorial process.

We also gratefully acknowledge three sources of supplementary support of the project. The Institute of Business and Economic Research at Berkeley assumed financial responsibility for the huge volume of typing of draft and semi-final manuscript produced by the authors over several years, and also served as immediate accounting and hiring office for project funds and research assistants. The continually valuable cooperation and assistance of Miss Virginia Q. Brainard, executive secretary of the Institute, is especially appreciated. In addition, the Institute of Governmental Studies on the Berkeley campus paid a part of staff salaries during the closing stages of project research, and the Water Resources Center of the University of California defrayed part of the cost of preparation of a set of working maps of all Northern California water agencies.

The views expressed and findings reported in this volume are solely those of the authors, and do not necessarily reflect the views of Resources for the Future, Inc., or of any of the other supporting agencies, or of any of the officers or staff of any of them.

Berkeley, California
August, 1966

J.S.B.
R.E.C.
J.M.

CONTENTS

PART TWO: CONDUCT

8

9

10

13

14

PART THREE: PERFORMANCE

15

16

17

18

PART FOUR: SUMMARY AND POLICY PROPOSALS

19

20

APPENDICES

TABLES

FIGURES

ANALYTICAL APPROACH AND FRAMEWORK OF THE STUDY: ITS LOGIC AND PURPOSE

Northern California, an area which encompasses about two-thirds of the state, is a region with a water problem. This geographically complex area is made up of mountain ranges, huge areas of fertile agricultural land in one major and several lesser interior valleys, and three or four modest-sized coastal basins, one containing its principal metropolitan area. Annually, the region receives substantial amounts of precipitation, but much is in the mountains and nearly all occurs in the winter. It is traversed by many rivers carrying water supplied by winter falls of snow and rain from the mountains both through its valleys and basins and more directly to the sea. To serve agricultural and urban demands for water supply within the area, natural sources of water must be "developed," or transferred in time and place within the region: this is the physical task that confronts Californians. The economic and political tasks are those of creating institutions to facilitate these transfers in time and space. The analysis of such institutions is the subject of this study.

Northern California's physical problem differs from that of Southern California. There a vast desert land contains on its western edge an extensive semi-arid and largely metropolitan coastal basin which receives only light annual rainfall and is traversed by no stream that the average man would call a river. Given the volume and pattern of economic activity in the area, Southern California necessarily must reach into neighboring regions for large-scale water transfers to make up some portion of its water supply.

Nor is Northern California's water problem that of most regions of the eastern part of the United States, where local water supplies typically appear adequate in quantity but often present difficulties because of deficient quality. The water problem in the East usually is not one of inadequate quantities of water available within a region, or adequate quantities requiring transfers in time and place, but rather one of pollution and other externalities that create conflicts of interest in the management of water quality.

The development of water supplies in Northern California generally requires several related activities: (1) diverting the region's streamflows for irrigation during the usually dry growing season of crops as well as for urban uses; (2) harnessing these flows with dams and reservoirs so as to hold much of the winter precipitation for summer use and some of the precipitation of wet years for use in dry years; (3) transporting some of the flows from areas with relatively abundant river water to areas with relatively deficient local water sources; and (4) sinking and operating wells to recover winter precipitation from underground aquifers into which it percolates. It also involves, more than incidentally, the complementary use of harnessed streamflows to generate hydroelectric power, and is intermixed with, or constrained by, endeavors to control floods, facilitate navigation, conserve recreational values, and repel intrusion of saline waters into river estuaries.

The large number of organizations which develop water supplies in Northern California can be roughly lumped together as an "industry" on the basis of their generally similar economic functions. Every populous region contains a water industry, but not ordinarily one of comparable relative and absolute importance. The water industry in Northern California is relatively more significant because the region's economic activity is largely agricultural or dependent on agriculture (leading to a very high rate of consumptive use of water per capita); the bulk of the agricultural water supply must be developed as irrigation water; and the sources of regional water supply—and thus the productive activity required to develop them—are contained within the region. In contrast, many regional water industries mainly supply water for urban use (because their regions are not agricultural or their agriculture has sufficient natural precipitation), or they draw primarily on water imported from other regions. The greater absolute importance of the water industry in Northern California results mainly from the huge area of its irrigable agricultural land and its very large regional water supply available for irrigation. Only one or two figures are needed to illustrate this point. In recent times, from 20 million to 30 million acre-feet of water annually have been diverted from streams and recovered from wells for consumptive use within the region; of this, about 90 per cent is still used for irrigation, despite a doubling of the urban population of the region in the past twenty years. The regional output of hydroelectric power is correspondingly great.

The numerous functions performed in the development of water supplies in the region are undertaken by a multitude of separate bodies. Among these are agencies of the state and federal governments, various types of local public agencies, departments of local governments, mutual water companies, privately owned firms operating under public utility regulation, and a very large number of individuals or businesses that develop water for their own uses. Obviously, many differences in legal form, ownership, and function separate these from one another as well as from the enterprises in a conventional industry. Even so, it may be instructive to view all as members of a regional water industry, much in the same sense as crude oil producers, oil pipeline and tankship operators, oil refiners, and wholesalers and retailers of refined oil products operating in the Pacific Coast states may be viewed as members of a Pacific Coast petroleum industry.[1] There is, first, a distinct similarity on the level of physical function. Members of each group are engaged in

[1] Compare Joe S. Bain, *The Economics of the Pacific Coast Petroleum Industry* (3 vols.; 1944–47). (This and other footnote references are cited in brief form when they are also included in the Bibliography.)

capturing a natural resource, transporting it to localities of use, and delivering it to users. The major differences as regards physical function is that members of the petroleum industry do much more in the way of processing the natural raw material to separate and convert it into different end products delivered to customers, but this difference is essentially incidental. Second, in a fundamental sense, there is a comparable similarity of economic functions performed by the water industry and the petroleum industry. Each group, in its own way, determines or influences the total output of the resource which will be supplied to users; the allocation of the resource output among different uses, users, and places of use; the efficiency with which the output is produced and transported; the prices which the users of the output pay (or the costs they incur) to secure resource outputs; and the relationship of the costs of supplying the resource output (or derivative outputs) to its values to users. Private firms in the petroleum industry do not actively concern themselves with the allocation of their combined resource output among uses and users, other than by establishing or influencing a set of market prices for various specific outputs as delivered at various specific locations and thereafter permitting allocation to be determined by customers as they make their purchases in the light of these prices. Compared to petroleum firms, members of the water industry depend much less on markets or market prices to allocate and ration water. Again, however, this difference does not reflect a basic difference in economic function.

Each group in its own way—the member firms of the petroleum industry and the member entities of the water industry—generates a set of economic results, or an economic "performance," which is measurable ultimately in the dimensions of total output, of technical efficiency, and of allocation of output. Herein lies the root of the economist's common concern with the two sets of economic entities. Economic theory provides general criteria for evaluating the allocation of resources that are subject to alternative uses, no matter what processes may have given rise to the allocation prevailing at the moment. Entities in the water industry and those in the petroleum industry may form their policies and accommodate them to each other in very different ways, but economic analysis applies the same set of principles to assess the allocative results and suggest the substance of needed changes.

The analogy between the water and petroleum industries may hold for one further important step. Sometimes the economic performance of a collection of units forming an industry can be shown to result from specific categories of decisions of the entities in question, environmental elements influencing these decisions, and interactions of the decisions of separate units. When such conclusions are established, economic analysis may be able to do more than identify deficiencies in performance and indicate the direction and magnitude of desirable changes. It may also be able to point out imputed causes of the particular deficiencies and thereby suggest specific reforms. This goal would seem to be the ultimate one for normative economics. Economists differ over the extent to which it has been attained for an industry such as petroleum; they no doubt would differ even more widely over the chances of achieving it for Northern California's water industry.

THE INDUSTRY STUDY

A major research method that has been developed to answer questions concerning the performance of conventional industries and its determinants is generally known as the "industry study." Since we are using this experimental device for analyzing the Northern California water industry, a brief review of its genesis, nature, achievements, and limitations is in order.

Much of the progress of applied economics in getting beyond purely descriptive treatments of industries and markets derives from the advances in theories of imperfect competition that have been made since the late 1920's. Prior to that time, theories of pure competition and pure monopoly (plus a few engaging novelties masquerading as theories of duopoly) had supplied little basis for the effective empirical study of the significant determinants of industry performance. Such works as Edward H. Chamberlin's *The Theory of Monopolistic Competition* pointed in a new direction. This volume, first published in 1933, not only presented its well-known namesake model of a determinate market situation lying between pure monopoly and pure competition, but also set forth a new way of looking at situations of oligopoly. Chamberlin's method of analyzing oligopoly built upon the limiting case of full mutual dependence recognized and emphasized the critical role of various factors that may prevent the "small group" from fully attaining a pure monopolistic price-output result.[2] From these suggestions, and those of other contemporary writers, has emerged a taxonomic approach to the theory of market structures. It rests mainly upon the traditional ingredients of market models: firms, motivated by some form of profit maximization, interacting within the framework of a more or less elaborately described set of environmental constraints. But an acknowledgment of many possible sources of significant differences among markets is substituted for the traditional view that any market could, by and large, be viewed as some mixture of monopoly and competition.

The extensive literature of post-Chamberlin oligopoly theory contains two relatively distinct analytical strands. One stresses the formation of conjectures by market rivals and their interaction in an implicit or explicit bargaining process. The other focuses upon the elements of the environment or structure of a market that can perceptibly influence the decisions of the member firms. It is the latter line of oligopoly theory, emphasizing the determining force of the relatively stable elements of market structure, which in the 1930's supplied the basis for several important new lines of research in the applied field of industrial organization.

The industry study takes as its frame of reference the structural taxonomy of market models. It generally accepts a restatement of the explanatory, or cause-and-effect, hypotheses of the contemporary theory of markets in terms which make it possible to confirm or reject them on the basis of measurements made of the attributes of an actual market or markets. That is, the hypotheses must predict that potentially measurable effects will be associated with potentially measurable causes.

[2] Edward H Chamberlin, *The Theory of Monopolistic Competition: A Re-orientation of the Theory of Value* (8th ed.; 1962), especially pp. 46–54 and 100–04. See also Bain, "*The Theory of Monopolistic Competition* after Thirty Years: The Impact on Industrial Organization," *American Economic Review,* LIV (May 1964), 28–32.

The hypotheses must not be empty: the causal factors must be observable with tolerable ease and frequency; the predicted consequences must be distinctive enough that they might not occur in the cases under examination.

This restatement of market theory employs many specific concepts, but it emphasizes a general classification under the headings of market structure, conduct, and performance. "Market structure" encompasses those elements of the common environment of firms in a market which theoretical reasoning identifies as having a possible significant influence on their behavior. Elements of market structure that are customarily identified as theoretically significant include the number and size distribution of buyers and sellers in the market, the extent of barriers to the entry of new buyers and sellers, the presence or absence of product differentiation, the magnitude of fixed costs in the short run, the rate of growth of demand, and the presence of any special governmental regulations affecting the behavior of firms in the industry. "Market conduct" refers to the economically significant aspects of the behavior of buyers and sellers in a market—that is, to the formation of policies toward the market by the individual participants and the mutual accommodation and interaction of these policies. Principal types of policies include those for setting and adjusting the price and the quality (or range of qualities) of the product, and those aimed at coercing rivals or otherwise directly affecting their bargaining strength in the market. Finally, "market performance" designates those allocative outcomes of the conduct of entities in a market that theory designates as significant for economic welfare. These include level of output, the relationship of price to cost, the technical efficiency of the organization of production, the amount of expenditure on sales promotion, the extent of economic progress arising within the market, and the like.[3]

An industry study thus tests a set of hypotheses taking the following general form: a given constellation of elements of market structure generates a certain range of patterns of market conduct which, in turn, give rise to certain qualities and defects of market performance. It is not an exercise in unstructured description. Nor does it "test" the axiomatically true—or, at least, irrefutable—hypothesis that the behavior of human beings can somehow be explained by the environment in which they live. Rather the industry study tests refutable hypotheses drawn from economic theory.

Lending confirmation to some portion of the set of hypotheses drawn up for a particular industry tends to accomplish two things. First, it provides an opportunity for policy recommendations indirectly to improve the performance of that particular industry, based upon the imputed associations between deficient aspects of performance and the elements of structure and conduct giving rise to them. Second, it helps confirm the predictive power of the body of price theory that generates the successfully tested hypotheses. Thus, a series of industry studies may tend to confirm an association between the height of barriers to the entry of new sellers and the quality of price-output performance. If so, the economist can predict with increasing confidence that this association will hold for industries that have not been subjected to detailed investigation. Thus, a "successful" industry

[3] For a more detailed account, see Bain, *Industrial Organization* (1959).

study not only tends to demonstrate the explanatory power of theoretical reasoning for that particular industry, but also aids in identifying a set of cross-industry associations among market structure, conduct, and performance that can be assumed with some degree of confidence to apply to new situations and policy problems.

This is the research agenda for the industry study as an application of the theory of market structures. What about the success to date of this branch of applied economics? While no detailed appraisal is appropriate here, we can offer a few generalizations. The list of successful industry studies is not particularly long, but these seem to confirm the fruitfulness of the technique, and their paucity probably reflects problems of locating empirical information as much as it does inherent difficulties with the method itself. The successful studies identify at least rough logical relations between major elements of market structure and dimensions of the quality of performance. Furthermore, they not only tell a consistent story about the industries examined one by one, but also make some contribution in determining the role of such major aspects of market structure as concentration of sellers, barriers to entry, and differentiation of products on a cross-industry basis. The demonstrated reliability of these structure-performance connections on a cross-industry basis remains, however, somewhat lower than many economists would wish, and improvements are likely to come slowly.[4] In the social sciences, as in other sciences, both the rejection and the confirmation of hypotheses contribute to intellectual progress, and the extant body of industry studies seems to rule out some relations. So far, the indications are that patterns of conduct do not possess much predictive power for performance independent of the market structure in which they are imbedded. For example, collusive pricing arrangements may frequently fail to yield monopolistic price-output performance in a relatively atomistic industry because the level of recognized interdependence is low, and the arrangements cannot be consistently and effectively enforced by the participants.

While the success of economists in locating stable cross-industry relations between structure and performance is admittedly limited, it is perhaps not so low as is implied by their disarray when making recommendations for antitrust and related policies. Economists differ a good deal in their appraisals of the relative importance of the various dimensions of market performance. The accumulation of empirical evidence may serve better for predicting the quality of some one aspect of performance than for rendering an optimal recommendation when, for example, optimal efficiency and optimal progress seem to conflict.

An "Industry Study" Approach to Water Supply

The reasonable success of the industry study in the terrain of conventional markets and the clear importance of its potential policy conclusions seem amply to justify asking whether it can be applied in other areas. After all, private industry is not the only setting in which important functional aspects of resource allocation are determined by the interaction of independent decision units working within a

[4] Compare Carl Kaysen and D. F. Turner, *Antitrust Policy: An Economic and Legal Analysis* (1959), pp. 60–61.

common environment. There are many others, including regulated public utilities in the United States; industries containing a mixture of public and private enterprises in Western Europe and elsewhere; state enterprises in Yugoslavia; and, for that matter, government enterprises in the United States. Certainly, the varied groups competing for water in Northern California clearly fulfill some of the requirements for standing scrutiny as an industry. They are numerous and act without the direction of any central authority capable of coordinating their behavior to attain some preordained set of economic results. While they do not participate in what an economist would call a continuous market, they are actual rivals at many points for supplies of water, and are at least potential rivals for customers. And their joint allocative performance is a candidate for behavioral, as well as purely normative, analysis.

Furthermore, the voluminous existing literature on water problems contains no systematic analysis of the structure of existing systems of related agencies for water development, their prevailing patterns of conduct, or the sorts of economic performance they generate. And neither are there structural and behavioral explanations of why the performance of such agencies deviates from a socially optimal pattern. Shelves have been filled with analyses of planning for river basins—of how a central superagency should develop the water resources of a region—and libraries with engineering studies of conceivable ways of developing all the rivers, creeks, and rivulets of most regions of the United States. The questions of what should be done, from an economic standpoint, and what could be done, from an engineering standpoint, in developing water resources have received a great deal of attention, both generally and with particular reference to California. We propose, instead, to emphasize, with reference to Northern California as a case study, the rather different questions of what has been and is being done and why—and what is likely still to be done unless the rules are changed.

In dealing with these questions, we do not endeavor directly to assist the U.S. Bureau of Reclamation in planning its Central Valley Project or the California Department of Water Resources in its parallel endeavors. Both organizations will be viewed simply as central governmental agencies with projects for water development which have been superimposed on a number of developments of local agencies. We will look at them as agencies which, in a common environment with the local agencies, form and carry out policies that merit behavioral examination along with examination of the policies formed or pursued by the local units themselves. Thus, we commit ourselves to an industry study of Northern California water development—of necessity, primarily retrospective—in which we will try to adapt to our immediate purpose the analytical constructs and techniques that have been employed in the economic study of conventional private industries.

In summary, we are presenting a case study of a regional water industry, examining from a clinical point of view the actual structure, conduct, and performance of this industry, with twin aims of explaining observed performance and ultimately of deriving proposals for public policy affecting development of water resources and the agencies engaged in it. There is no novelty in making a case study as such; several recent books on water development have included condensed case studies of planning problems in various river basins. Some features of our study are novel, however. There is novelty in the scope of this case, which embraces all water agencies in a major region; in the examination of all agencies as interdependent members of an industry; in the emphasis on diagnosing actual conduct and performance in such an industry, as distinct from the analysis of planning possibilities; and in the attempt to learn the extent to which observed performance can be explained by characteristics of industry structure and conduct.

At this point, it is premature to predict how much of a contribution the approach, method, and viewpoint embodied in this particular pilot study can make to the understanding of water resource problems and of public policies that deal with them. We felt before undertaking the study that this approach and method had possibilities for enlarging the knowledge of a specific region and also for developing generalizations applicable to numerous regions. On concluding the study, we feel that it has yielded a distinct pay-off in terms of increased understanding of the character of water resource development in the region and its rationale. Furthermore, we believe that a series of comparable case studies of various regional water industries would fill similarly broad gaps in knowledge concerning water development in other regions, would help provide the basis for certain explanatory generalizations applicable to regional water industries generally, and would contribute significantly to the development of public policy. We recognize, however, that regional water industries have differences at least as important as their similarities and so discount the general exportability of our conclusions concerning Northern California's water—no matter how much they may illuminate current problems in the area. Therefore, it seems likely that the principal potential importance of our study may be found in the fruitfulness of its approach and methods as applied in studying other regions.

Distinctive features of the water industry

The process of adapting conventional methods to the study of a water industry necessarily is not a simple or routine matter. In spite of basic similarities, there are also fundamental dissimilarities between the conventional industry of privately owned profit-seeking firms and a water industry like that of Northern California. This water industry is different from conventional industries in at least six major ways: (1) the relationship between water suppliers and users, which is typically geared to the provision of maximum advantages for the user; (2) the influence of regulatory restraints on actions of the public utilities which operate as one of the entities of the water industry; (3) the competition for supplies of water rather than for customers; (4) the allocation of some water to benefit the public generally rather than special groups of direct users; (5) the inflexibility of long-term allocations of water supplies and the imperfections of the competitive process in meeting changing patterns of demand for water; and (6) Northern California's legal encouragement of bargaining processes as substitutes for markets in allocating water and water rights.

In the conventional private industry, the relationship of the member entities to the users of whatever final outputs they produce is the arm's-length association of independent sellers to independent buyers. The industry members produce to sell to others, not to use what they produce, and those to whom they sell have separate and conflicting aims; the seller seeks to sell dear, the buyer to buy cheap. On the other hand, the predominant type of member entity in the Northern California water industry is either a self-supplying user of water or a local public water agency which acts as a "users' cooperative" in developing water for a specific group of users. The self-supplying user (typically a farmer operating his own wells or diverting water from a stream) unites the functions of developing water and using it in a single entity, so that no supplier-user relationship exists. His motive presumably is to develop water in a quantity and at a cost which will help maximize the profit from his own water-using productive activity.

The public water agency acting as a users' cooperative for a particular group is not an independent entity, nor does it have with the users an arm's-length relationship of seller to buyer. Rather, it is an instrumentality created by a group of users to act in ways most advantageous to them. Its presumed motive is to secure water in such a quantity and at such a cost as will permit its constituents as a group to maximize their profits from the productive activities in which they use water, or their economic advantage as consumers of water. There is necessarily a nominal seller-buyer relationship between the agency and its user-constituents since the constituents assume the costs of agency operations by paying charges for water delivered and special taxes. But the agency's motive clearly is not to make a profit for itself by supplying water to the users.

In a considerable number of instances, principally having to do with urban water supplies, the supplier is not an independent public water agency, but a department of a local government or of an agency with a number of special functions. As a result, there is no direct line of relationships and responsibility between the water agency and water users. This characteristic also holds for the wholesalers and rewholesalers that are important members of the water industry, most of which are agencies of federal, state, and county governments. In these situations, the wholesalers' relationship to users generally is that of a public enterprise created by a government representing a broad constituency of citizens (all of those in the United States, all in California, all in a county) to a fraction of this constituency made up of certain groups of water users, each generally represented by a local public agency. They are not users' cooperatives created by specific groups of water users, though their ostensible purpose is to serve the needs and enhance the economic advantage of such groups. But what begins as a set of arm's-length relationships between wholesalers and their buyers usually is converted with reasonable rapidity into semipermanent alliances cemented by long-term contracts between the wholesalers and the customer agencies. In this way, the wholesaler's basic motivation becomes in some degree comparable to that of the users' cooperative, although the wholesalers are not instrumentalities created by the user groups they ultimately serve. This means a single general motive—maximization of water users' economic advantage—may be roughly assigned to the entire complex of entities in the water industry.

The one major category of private corporate enterprise operating in the Northern California water industry is subject to severe constraints upon its putative desire to maximize profits: the public utility which produces and supplies hydroelectric power. Other private enterprises supplying water are not an important segment of the industry; but they, too, are subject to the same constraints upon profit-seeking activities. The public utility not only has very different purposes from those of the users' cooperative; it also diverges from the motive imputed to the firm in the conventional industry as a result of the regulatory constraint. Furthermore, the law concerning the responsibility of public utilities for public service requires them to continue service to a given group of customers once service is begun. Hence, they become to some degree captive instrumentalities of particular groups of users, and have a relation to such groups somewhat resembling that of the local public water agency to its user-constituents.

As might be expected from the predominance of public agencies motivated as users' cooperatives in the Northern California water industry, overt rivalry among entities takes the form of competition for sources or supplies of water, and only rarely that of competition for customers. Important features of California water law join with the motives of users' cooperatives in producing this result. The important cases of rivalry for customers arise from the actions of water wholesalers. At the time when these wholesaling agencies develop new projects, they often are not under a rigid statutory obligation to make the new water supply available to a particular group of users, and rivalry among wholesalers for the favor of customer agencies may ensue. This picture of the predominance of backward-reaching rivalry for supplies contrasts sharply with that in most conventional industries, where a forward-reaching rivalry for customers is either much more, or equally, important.

A number of uses derived from, or related to, surface water supplies are not regularly represented by "buyers" or other "customers" in influencing the allocation of water. Navigation, flood control, and in-stream fisheries are examples. These interests are served, if at all, by indirect means and not by private enterprises or public agencies directly representing the beneficiaries. These indirect means largely consist of requirements imposed by regulatory agencies and allowances made for these useful purposes as components of the public interest by higher governments charged with serving that general objective. Again, this situation differs from that of the typical market, wherein persons or groups capable of deriving value from the product are typically free to register their willingness to purchase stipulated quantities at various prices.

In the water industry, markets—active alternative sources of water for the user, or alternative uses for the supplies—are not continuous in either time or space. Typically, the competition for scarce natural water supplies is not a rivalry for day-to-day or year-to-year supplies, but for long-term or perpetual legal rights to continuing streamflows and the water yield of underground aquifers. The result of such competition is to establish rigid and inflexible allocations of water rights among different users, which once established are effectively perpetual at law. In this industry, there is no live and continuing competitive process which operates to reallocate water supplies in the light of changing technologies and patterns of demand for water. It is rather an episodic historical process reflected in a series of events, each dated in time. Thus, competition for water sources turns out to be a very imperfect mechanism for allocating water supplies among users, and especially for reallocating them in the light of changing economic circumstances.

Furthermore, because of high transportation costs and other factors, such market alternatives as do arise in the distribution of water cannot be said to extend throughout Northern California. From this point of view, also, there is no organized and continuously functioning general market for current water supplies or for long-term water rights. Within the bounds of the service areas of individual water agencies, internal markets exist in the sense that the individual agency sells water to its user-constituents as a means of collecting their contributions to the cooperative enterprise. But of general open markets, in which either current water supplies or long-term rights to supplies from given sources are regularly bought and sold, there are none. And, in fact, there are only very few transactions among member entities of the water industry in which water supplies or water rights are sold or contracted for. The only markets which operate in the industry are essentially very limited temporary markets that are opened when a water agency—generally a major developmental or wholesale agency—develops an added water supply for a particular area. The agency, in such cases, declares itself open to offers by local agencies to enter into long-term contracts to purchase water on stipulated or negotiated terms, but the market is closed when all of the added water supply has been committed under long-term contracts. Such market episodes accomplish certain reallocations of water supply; those arrangements then become at least semi-permanent and are not effectively subject to alteration by subsequent purchases and sales of water or water rights.

Various legal processes operate in effect as substitutes for markets in determining the allocation of water and water rights among competing users in Northern California. The legal framework conspicuously permits and promotes the use of bargaining processes to determine allocations, in much the same sense that some types of imperfect market situations can be viewed as generating processes of implicit or explicit bargaining. Elements of strength and weakness in driving these bargains can be identified for the participants, as in conventional situations of bilateral oligopoly and other imperfect market models, but there is no a priori assumption that the elements will be the same in the two cases.

In addition to these six basic differences between Northern California's water industry and conventional private industries, one distinctive feature of water industries generally sets them apart as different in degree—if not in kind—from most other industries. This salient characteristic is the importance of "externalities" in water industries; that is, the use of water by various individuals and groups for a variety of purposes has notable "external effects" upon the value or cost of water to other users. Since this fact has been emphasized in most recent works on the economics of water resources, we need to comment on externalities only briefly here.

There will be "external effects" when the use or capture of water by one or more users or agencies (1) reduces or increases the value of water used by others, (2) reduces or increases the costs of using water to these other entities (alters their production and cost functions), or (3) damages or benefits third parties who are not themselves water users. Externalities can be classified as either "benefits" or "disbenefits." Examples of important external benefits are those which irrigators, users of navigable rivers, and residents of localities otherwise threatened by floods reap from streamflow regulated by others operating upstream storage reservoirs to support electric power production; or another example might be downstream power producers benefiting from such regulation by upstream reservoirs of other power producers or irrigators. Typical external disbenefits include the reduction of the value of water (or an increase in the cost of using it) to downstream irrigators, domestic users, or recreational users because of upstream pollution by other users; the loss of recreational or commercial values from fishing because power producers, irrigators, or urban users adversely alter streamflow patterns through reservoir operations or by diverting water for irrigation or domestic use; and losses to third parties who incur costly drainage problems because of irrigation by others.

External effects in water use occur only when two types of condition exist. The first of these elements is found in technical conditions, mainly of four kinds: (1) There are numerous uses of water, and many pairs or groups of uses from stream sources are economically "joint" (strictly "common"), or at any rate complementary. (2) Some uses of stream water by initial users affect the net value of the same water in subsequent downstream uses, or may injure third parties. (3) Ground water, recovered from wells, partakes of some of the characteristics of a common-pool fugacious resource, the antagonistic exploitation of which will result in group losses. (4) The character and quantity of surface water use tend to influence the availability of ground water.[5] The second necessary condition for the incidence of externalities is that water from given sources is used by more than one independent user or agency (typically by numerous independent units), so that one entity's actions can affect the net value of water to another. In such a case, an individual user can generate some, or many, external economic effects on water value—either bestowing benefits or imposing disbenefits on another independent user—without itself gaining or suffering equivalently from the effects. With a large number of users drawing water from a common source, externalities may be rife. If only a single agency developed and used water from one source, or a complex of physically interrelated sources, the only external effects would be the possible impacts on third parties who used no water. The sole developer would, or should, "internalize" nearly all externalities by adjusting its multiple uses in the light of all technical and value interrelationships of all water uses from the source.

Given the numerous uses of water and their complex technical relationships, externalities have particular economic importance in a water industry. This is precisely because most sources of water supply are drawn upon by numerous independent individuals or agencies who use the water in various complementary and substitute ways, but tend to neglect external effects in designing their separate operations. As a consequence, these independent water users do not adjust their rates and modes of use to take proper account of the external benefits or disbenefits they may engender. The result is that the allocation of water among uses and users

[5] Strictly, external effects do not arise simply from the fact that water has alternative uses, and that if more is used for one purpose, or one user gets more water, there is correspondingly less for another. However, the resultant competitive effects are sometimes difficult to distinguish from externalities, and some effects are concurrently competitive and external.

may be seriously distorted from what would be ideal economically in the light of all costs and benefits. Independent entities tend to overlook the external effects of their decisions for two reasons. They find it impractical to collect rewards for the external benefits they bestow on others; and they usually cannot be forced to make compensation (fully or at all) for the external disbenefits they impose on others. Where appropriate rewards and penalties for external effects can be awarded or assessed, users responsible for them will tend to take externalities into account.

As already noted, a water industry differs from most other industries in significant degree, rather than in kind, by being subject to important and complex externalities. In fact, various externalities are significant in most extractive industries, and not entirely absent from many others. Certainly, close attention must be given to the problems of external effects in the Northern California water industry, but not at the expense of the six somewhat more fundamental differences of the water industry from conventional private industries, which have been enumerated and discussed in this section.

Adapting the theory of markets

These differences between the water industry and a conventional industry are undeniably substantial. They raise questions on such fundamental matters as the appropriate maximization objective to impute to the member units and the degree to which allocative decisions are worked out in what are nominally nonmarket settings. In order to apply the methodology of an industry study in this environment, it is necessary to go back to the beginning and, to some extent, rewrite the underlying theory of markets. Only with the underlying theory adjusted to include the motivational assumptions and major unique structural features of the water industry can we set up the necessary hypotheses concerning the elements of structure that may stand as significant determinants of the quality of the water industry's performance.

It is not feasible to spell out the whole chain of reasoning in advance of the exposition of such matters as the legal environment of the water industry and the detailed consideration of the "users' cooperative hypothesis" concerning the motivation of public water agencies. We can, however, describe the general character of the hypotheses that result, particularly as they affect the organization and content of the subsequent chapters.

The users' cooperative hypothesis does not, of itself, require any fundamental revision of the existing body of market theory. Such a cooperative organization, optimizing its internal arrangements, would demand any input in such quantities that its marginal cost to the organization is equal to its net marginal value product to each and every member using it. The principle of derived demand governing the input purchases of the rational cooperative organization transferring its output to its member-customers is thus equivalent to that of a firm selling its product in a competitive product market. A market for an input in which a large number of users' cooperatives appear as buyers should not produce different allocative results from one in which a large number of conventional private firms appear as buyers. Furthermore, the introduction of imperfections in the form of an element of oligopsony or monopsony would have the same qualitative effect in both cases: a restriction of the level of input purchases, *ceteris paribus,* if the input is sold under conditions of rising market supply price.

The parallel between the conventional theory of derived demand and the theory of users' cooperatives can be pushed one step further. If a number of cooperatives secure an input from a common physical source by a process of establishing rights or perpetual legal claims to its flow, the allocative results will still be the same as those that private enterprise purchasers would attain if all parties are rational about employing the physical yields of their legal claims to the resource. "Rationality" in both cases would imply selling the yield of one's resource claim to the extent that its market value exceeds its marginal value product (within a conventional competitive firm) or its net marginal value product (within a users' cooperative).

The users' cooperative hypothesis begins to yield valuable and distinctive theoretical predictions only when more assumptions are added to introduce some of the organizational and legal traits of public agencies in the water industry and the legal constraints and opportunities within which they operate. For instance, a profit-maximizing firm in static equilibrium would make no necessary distinction between "regular customers" and "other customers," and would charge prices so as to receive the same marginal revenue from each group. A cooperative maximizing its members' welfare would charge outsiders the (generally higher) price warranted to equate marginal revenue from outside sales with the marginal value of its output to members. When we add assumptions to cover certain legal constraints on water sales by local districts, such as the risk that adverse rights might be created, we reach the prediction that sales of water by retailing districts to nonmembers would occur infrequently and would carry a higher price than the average unit charge to members. This same process of prediction will be employed in many different instances: always to anticipate the kinds of decisions which users' cooperatives can be expected to make about particular policies (such as pricing and investment) in the face of various environmental conditions (water law, cost characteristics of physical facilities, number and size of rivals for water, and so on).

This kind of modification of conventional price theory can be extended to the other differences so far enumerated between Northern California's water industry and the conventional industry. Consider, for example, the proposition that some uses of water or utilities related to it are for institutional reasons not represented in the market, either by users' cooperatives in the guise of public agencies or by ordinary private enterprises. Instead, they are protected mainly by the regulatory or administrative actions of high-level governments. The economic link between the marginal value product of water or water management facilities in these uses and the demand expressed on their behalf is severed, in the sense that no specialized users' cooperatives or private enterprises exist to claim water or build facilities for these purposes. Competing claimant uses which are so represented would thus tend to leave too little for the unrepresented uses, unless the latter are adequately protected by actions taken in the general interest by high-level governments. Thus, we can make the conditional prediction that the adequacy of allocations to uses not directly represented in the competition for water will depend on patterns of regulation and the preference functions of general government agencies empowered to recognize and protect these uses.

Another theoretical adaptation is needed for these special conditions because Northern California's water industry does not encompass one reasonably continuous market but, at best, embraces a number of sporadic ones. Conventional economic theories of markets deal, obviously enough, with the continuous market and the entities populating it as the subject of analysis. Furthermore, the typical study of a conventional industry can proceed on the assumption that it deals to an acceptable degree with a single market. In practice, the market in which a conventional industry sells or buys is often segmented geographically, but the presence of an adequate number of either sellers or buyers operating in more than one segment serves to link the segments into what can be viewed as one market. In the water industry of Northern California, high transportation costs plus a series of legal constraints tend to maintain a considerable amount of geographic segmentation. The number of kinds of links between these segments is large and growing, but their aggregate weight is small, and must certainly be counted as negligible among some segments of the industry.[6] Therefore, the guidance of economic theory tells us that our examination of the water industry must comprehend a number of separate markets and not pretend to face a single, if segmented, market.

Our unit of analysis, then, must typically be the local area in which physically feasible alternatives exist in (1) sources of water to satisfy a given use or (2) uses of water to employ a given source or supply. We shall on occasion refer to these localities as "markets" or "submarkets" even though they are only the possible, rather than the actual, sites of continuous transactions under efficient conditions. These latent markets are the loci of two principal kinds of rivalry for a common supply of water. The first is actual or implicit rivalry for the water flowing in a river or interconnected river system; the second is rivalry for the net yield of a ground-water basin. The latter type of supply will receive a relatively small amount of our attention—not because it lacks importance in Northern California, for it is important. The extraction of ground water from a common basin is an activity undertaken by many small and independent proprietors subject to little public regulation. It is a very simple economic process, although it involves some externality problems. Because of this greater simplicity, we shall have little to say about it except for the interrelation between the availability of ground water and the demand made upon surface supplies.

Conversely, the rivals for surface water in local common sources will receive the bulk of our attention. The waters of many, though not all, rivers and streams in Northern California can serve such a range of uses that if more of their flow is devoted to any one use there will be less for others. This is true for many streams at particular times during the year, and for some rivers it is true for the annual flow as a whole. The alternatives take two forms: diverting the flow for out-

[6] This geographic segmentation is, of course, further complicated by the segmentation in time that was mentioned earlier. Within local areas where physical alternative uses or sources of water are found, actual transactions or allocative changes may, but seldom do, occur.

of-stream users or leaving water in its natural channel for in-stream uses; and diverting the streamflow (whether natural flow or from storage) into aqueducts serving one group of users or another.

In examining these local market rivalries, we shall make certain adaptations of the theory of markets which conform to analytical procedures that are traditional in the study of water problems but run counter to the apparent dictates of general economic analysis. One of these practices is to distinguish between "consumptive" and "nonconsumptive" uses of water. The former traditionally refers to uses that require the diversion of water from a stream for agricultural or urban water supply; the latter, to in-stream uses such as recreation, navigation, and power generation that do not themselves significantly alter the location, quantity, or quality of a stream's flow. The point has properly been made that the so-called "consumptive" uses often put a significant return flow (polluted, perhaps) back into the channel, while the "nonconsumptive" uses may require that the water be passed downstream beyond the economic reach of out-of-stream uses, so that, in effect, such water is consumed.[7] An interrelated theoretical criticism is made of placing any emphasis on gross, rather than net, demands for water, since the over-all adequacy of water supplies depends on the net consumption occurring in any given use and what impairment (if any) is made in the quality of return flows from that use.[8]

We shall refer to consumptive uses and focus upon gross flows and diversions in our examination of local markets. The detailed reasons why this procedure is appropriate for our study will emerge later, but some of them may be mentioned here. Out-of-stream users of surface water in Northern California typically either act directly in their own interest to divert water or are represented by local government agencies that can be viewed as users' cooperatives. Most of the in-stream users, by contrast, are not represented, and in place of taking direct action are more in the position of taking what water comes their way. (The conspicuous exception to this, among in-stream users, are public utility companies which generate hydroelectric power. However, the exceptional status of this use is sharply mitigated by the fact that it often has a complementary, rather than competitive, relation with out-of-stream uses.) Furthermore, the geography of Northern California and the technology of canal and aqueduct systems are such that return flows come back to many rivers only at elevations or locations that render them largely useless either to support further diversions for consumptive use or to serve in-stream uses in critical stretches of the channel. To state the proposition in the reverse form, only in selected and distinct segments of Northern California's stream network does the water problem take the form of adequate quantities of polluted water rather than inadequate quantities of unimpaired water. Thus the appropriate theoretical market model for many parts of the Northern California water industry is one that evaluates the proximate allocation of gross flows, in that each contender who appropriates an acre-foot of water tends (as a first approximation) to exact the opportunity cost of a full acre-foot from some rival.

[7] Jack Hirshleifer, J. C. De Haven, and J. W. Milliman, *Water Supply: Economics, Technology, and Policy* (1960), chap. 2 and pp. 66–73.

[8] Compare Edward A. Ackerman and George O. G. Löf, *Technology in American Water Development* (1959), Part III.

The multiplicity of local markets for water has both advantages and disadvantages for the student. On the one hand, it greatly complicates the construction of an appraisal of the industry's performance, since its quality may vary greatly from one local area to another within the region. On the other hand, it creates a valuable research opportunity by greatly increasing the degrees of freedom we possess in testing our hypotheses concerning the industry. An industry study that centers on a single market in a single period of time can do no more than show a pattern of conduct and quality of performance consistent with what theory predicts for the particular set of structural forces surrounding that market. The extensibility of these hypotheses to other markets remains in doubt. But when the case study comprehends a number of local market situations, the testing of hypotheses takes on a comparative character that potentially adds a valuable new dimension to understanding. In simplest terms, our proposition is that the hypothesis that "a lot of *A* in Xanadu implies a lot of *B*" tends to be inherently less precise than the hypothesis that "more of *A* (in Xanadu than in Oz) implies more of *B*" and, once confirmed, it is less easily extended to Cibola. This advantage should not be overstressed, since the variety of cases that turn up in our study, and the difficulties of securing information in the detail needed to analyze them, offset much of this potential gain. Nonetheless, some of our conclusions can be based upon this type of comparative analysis of local market situations. Furthermore, they can be supplemented by another sort of comparative appraisal based upon changes wrought by the growth over time of the scarcity of water supplies relative to demands in the typical local area of Northern California. Therefore, cross-sectional observations, to some extent, can be taken over time as well as over areas.

Theoretical Predictions of Conduct and Performance

The preceding section has given a sample of the sorts of adjustments required of conventional market theory as the logical prelude to an industry study of Northern California's water industry. The second stage of the process is to identify the important observable elements of the structure or environment of the industry that may have economic significance for explaining the character of its behavior and the quality of its performance. These hypotheses must be extracted from market theory as interpreted for the special conditions of this particular industry. In outlining the critical elements of market structure, we shall emphasize the diversity of conditions surrounding particular local areas within Northern California in order to pave the way for our comparative analysis of local situations. There is a paucity throughout this industry of the kind of interactions among entities that would be called "market conduct" in a conventional industry, and a corresponding insularity of decisions by the typical individual entity. As a result, our hypotheses will not take solely the conventional form of predictions running from elements of structure to the character of conduct and thus the quality of performance. Some aspects of structure are important for explaining the insularity of the typical water agency and the reasons for the dominance of public enterprises in this particular form of economic activity. Still other features of structure are significant for governing the size and duration of misallocations within the industry, however they may arise.

A basic set of structural factors includes the geography and hydrology of Northern California. The leading position of irrigation among the uses of water that involve diversion from natural channels emphasizes the importance of relating the location of irrigable land to the location of such features as precipitation, natural surface runoff, and ground-water basins. These relationships tend to govern the supply-demand balance of claims on water in the various parts of the region. Geography also affects the costs of transporting water between local areas or basins, and thus the potential amount of linkage between local markets for water. Of similar, although slightly less permanent, importance is the existing network of physical facilities for the storage, diversion, and transport of water. These help to determine the existing pattern of allocations of water among uses, users, and places of use, as well as the potential degree of rivalry for the flows of surface runoff occurring at various times of the year and in various places. All of these natural and man-made physical features are described in Chapter 2, and some of the implications they raise for conduct and performance of the industry are indicated.

Another structural element, one of overwhelming significance, is the whole legal environment of the industry, which is taken up in Chapter 3. This environment determines the powers, opportunities, and obligations pertaining to each of the several types of public water agencies operating in Northern California, and defines the property right to the use of a supply of water. Finally, it creates a series of regulatory agencies that play a vital role in the allocation of water among uses and users. All of these elements of water law and regulation give rise to many hypotheses about the response of water agencies to their economic and physical environments and the quality of the resulting performance.

The number and size distribution of entities in the water industry, the subject of Chapter 4, constitutes another important element of structure—although not for the same reasons as in the conventional industry, except for seller concentration among nonintegrated wholesalers. The relative prevalence of different types of local districts and other entities in the industry needs to be considered because of the significant differences in their legal powers and in the range of interests of their constituencies. The degree of vertical integration matters because large wholesalers differ significantly in both motivation and powers from the typical vertically integrated local district; local markets in which large wholesalers play a significant part show somewhat different allocative performance from those containing only vertically integrated local producers of water. The number, distribution by size, and legal form of agencies competing for the individual source of water also matters, though not for the same reasons as those identified by conventional market theory. Because of the nature of legal allocation processes prevailing in California currently and in the past, the larger the number of would-be claimants to a particular source, the more cumbersome do the proceedings typically become, the greater is the amount of "tenure uncertainty,"[9] and the more likely is the outcome to reflect the

[9] Useful distinctions, including this one, among the types of uncertainty facing entities in the water industry are made by S. V. Ciriacy-Wantrup, "Concepts Used as Economic Criteria for a System of Water Rights," *Land Economics,* XXXII (November 1956), 295–312.

economic and legal bargaining strength of the parties. The size distribution and the mixture of types of agencies contending over a particular source of water also influence these elements of bargaining position. Finally, since economies of scale are important in the construction of certain facilities for water storage and distribution, the level of concentration may be related to performance in the attainment of efficient scales.

Conventional price theory marks one aspect of the demand for a commodity—its price elasticity—as an important structural feature. This parameter reveals the size of resource misallocations that will be associated with any given discrepancy between the marginal cost and marginal value of resources in their current uses, a familiar normative proposition that carries over unchanged into our present framework of analysis. Chapter 5 deals extensively with measuring the elasticity of demand for various groups of final users of water in Northern California. Otherwise, our analysis of the determinants of the demand for water mainly serves the function of providing background information to help in sorting out the influence of human institutions on water allocation from that of the natural environment.

Some aspects of the cost characteristics of the water industry, just like the price elasticity of demand, are important for reasons identified by conventional price theory. Given the presence of significant economies of scale, an atomistic organization of entities engaging in some phase of the industry can result in inefficiencies of small scale and the inflation of total costs. Conventional industry studies also typically examine scale economies as a source of barriers to entry and the extent to which costs are fixed in the short run as an inducement to price rigidity and associated pathological aspects of conduct. The users' cooperative hypothesis attributes little significance to barriers against entry into the water industry. However, this hypothesis does allot to high fixed costs their conventional power to bias the conduct of entities toward possibly undesirable arrangements for restricting the flexibility of resource allocation in order to cut private uncertainty. In fact, it suggests that the water industry might substantially outdo a conventional industry in trying to avoid the private uncertainties associated with high fixed costs. Cost characteristics and their consequences are discussed in Chapter 6.

As we move to Part Two, where we take up market conduct, it turns out that the categories of analysis do not differ radically from those appearing in a conventional industry study. When a study deals with a more conventional market, concern with conduct centers upon the policies chosen by the individual enterprises and the way in which these are reconciled and adjusted with one another. The policies in question are principally those affecting the price offered or demanded and the level of transactions associated with it. In recasting the industry-study methodology to suit the Northern California water industry, we have found at least two major differences for the analysis of conduct. First, because of the substantial insularity of the typical enterprise in the industry—the lack of continuous interactions with market rivals—the range and power of hypothetical influences of market structure upon conduct are naturally less than in the conventional industry. Nonmarket elements of the industry's environment correspondingly ascend in importance. Furthermore, the water agency's relative freedom from market pressures allows it substantial scope to adopt fixed policies of its own choosing. Such policies tend to lack the status of a fixed force in a conventional industry because they must either conform to pressures resulting from the market environment or else undergo changes; in the water industry, they possess an independent life and therefore deserve a direct, systematic analysis.

Another major difference in the anlysis of conduct in the water industry concerns the classes of agency policies and decisions that are most significant. Here the important policies are those relating to the quantity of water that the agency seeks to secure and the size and type of the associated physical facilities that it seeks to construct. This results from the relative scarcity of effective short-run allocative mechanisms in the industry, other than among the member-customers of a particular district or agency. The agency's investment plans and demands for water rights are reconciled and adjusted to one another in various ways—a major way is by judicial and regulatory bodies. Bargaining elements play an important part, as they do in the more conventional marketing of water supplies by wholesaling agencies to "retail" customer agencies. The chapters of Part Two explore various features of these interrelated policies concerning the appropriation of water and the construction of physical facilities.

In order to facilitate drawing inferences about performance directly from the record of conduct set forth in Part Two, Chapter 8 sets forth some simple norms for the allocation of water among various alternative uses and for making optimal investment decisions. Chapter 8 also provides a full statement of the users' cooperative hypothesis and suggests how the organizational structure of such agencies will affect their economic decisions, particularly the investment decision.

Chapters 9 and 10 are concerned with the "internal decisions" of water organizations and their normative implications. Chapter 9 explores the factors which govern the decision of a group of water users to form such a supply organization and the establishment and alteration of its boundaries. Chapter 10 discusses the pricing practices employed by various types of retailing organizations in transferring water to their member-customers. It also evaluates the probable allocative efficiency of these observed pricing systems and rules, and suggests how the resulting short-run allocative patterns might influence the agencies' decisions on such matters as investments and long-run water supply contracts with wholesalers.

Chapter 11 examines in detail another set of decision rules and practices: those relating to the investment decision. The investment criteria employed by local, state, and federal agencies in planning additional water storage and transportation facilities essentially provide another structural element of the industry's environment, on account of their constancy over time and independence of other structural elements.

Chapters 12 through 14 are concerned with the interaction of the decisions made by individual water agencies in the market place, before courts and regulatory agencies, or at bargaining sessions in small groups. These chapters set forth the equivalent of the market conduct of a conventional industry. Chapter 12 explores the rivalry for water, or rights to water, from various natural sources (unmodified streamflow, interseasonal storage of streamflow, ground water) and in various legal settings. Chapter 13 analyzes the bilateral relations between water wholesaling organizations and local retailers. The aim there is to explore such central questions as the effect of the number of market participants and their objectives or decision rules on the economic outcome. Finally, Chapter 14 studies relations of competition and complementarity among functionally differing types of uses of water. In it, we consider the extent to which problems of external effects have an influence on the allocation of water and the patterns of conduct which determine the resolution of these problems. A number of different uses of water must be considered, and the operation of several different decision mechanisms (bargaining, regulation at state levels, and the like).

Our analysis of the water industry's performance in Part Three also shows both similarities to, and differences from, the analysis of performance in a conventional industry. We curtail the range of performance dimensions investigated, concentrating on the allocative issues of price-cost performance and technical efficiency, and neglecting such matters as equity and progressiveness dealt with frequently (if unsuccessfully) in studies of ordinary industries. The measurement and evaluation of allocative performance in the water industry turns out to be a very complicated matter. It is necessary to examine separately the allocation of water and the allocation of physical facilities built to put water to various uses. Furthermore, it is necessary to distinguish between (1) the over-all level of water usage and the total quantity of water development facilities, and (2) the rationality with which water and facilities are allocated among various uses, users, and times of use. The conventional industry study essentially addresses itself to this simple question: are there too many, or too few, resources in the industry? Here we must investigate a large number of allocative frontiers. Furthermore, because of the great durability of physical facilities and water rights settlements, we must review the industry's past as well as present allocative performance.

The chapters of Part Three assemble two kinds of evidence to answer these many allocative questions. One consists of direct measurements, including a retrospective benefit-cost analysis of the so-called "basic features" of the Central Valley Project of the U.S. Bureau of Reclamation and a prospective evaluation of the state of California's Feather River Project. The other kind of evidence amounts to normative interpretations of the conduct patterns and decision rules identified in Part Two.

Following the four chapters assessing the industry's performance, a general analytical chapter summarizes the structure-conduct-performance hypotheses developed in the volume and evaluates the extent to which they have been confirmed or rejected. The volume closes with our suggestions for policy—changes in laws, regulatory practices, decision rules, and other structural forces within the scope of human relations—to improve the industry's performance.

PART ONE: STRUCTURE

GEOGRAPHY, HYDROLOGY, AND STORAGE AND TRANSPORT FACILITIES

This chapter considers what might be called the natural setting of Northern California's water industry: some of the elements of its physical environment that influence the character and intensity of local competition for water; and some of the long-lived physical facilities that determine the range of short-run alternatives in the allocation of water. The first group includes those factors of geography and hydrology which affect what we shall call the local demand-supply balance for surface water. This means, in practice, the relation between on-the-land uses that a given stream can conveniently serve and the volume of water flowing in the stream at various times of the year. Also important is the relative availability of ground and surface water supplies in different regions of Northern California, because of its obvious relation to the balance of demand for surface supplies, and because of the important differences between the types of enterprises that typically engage in the extraction of ground water and the capture of surface supplies.

The position of mountains and the average annual volume of precipitation lie largely outside of human control; the size and location of reservoirs and canals do not. Nonetheless, the obviously long physical lives of these works make them almost as permanent a part of the natural setting of the competition for water. Dams and reservoirs hold a place of special importance for this competition because they can be designed and operated to augment any of a number of uses relating to water. Thus the distribution of control of these facilities in Northern California has implications for the efficiency of the allocation of water among such uses as the generation of hydroelectric power, in-stream recreation, and consumption. Also, the relation between reservoir storage capacity and the volume of flow on various rivers is an economically significant factor on account of the imputed productivity of such storage on a river when the demands for its water exceed the natural flow. Another group of man-made works, canals and aqueducts, forge the link between consumptive uses and the demand-supply balance on particular rivers. In addition, the scale and location of such transport facilities affect the extent of potential competition for water and the magnitude of external effects in the form of pollution problems.

Geography and Physiography

The state of California borders the Pacific Coast of the United States from the forty-second parallel south to the Mexican border. As shown in Figure 2, it is about 775 miles long on an axis plotted roughly from north northwest to south southeast, and from about 215 to 280 miles wide. It is often thought of as being divided into two sections, Southern California and the rest of the state. This remaining region, dominant in area if not in population, is most accurately designated as "northern and central California," a cumbersome term; for the sake of brevity we refer to it as Northern California.

The natural dividing line between Northern and Southern California is formed by the Tehachapi Mountains, which cross the western part of the state in a southwest to northeast direction toward the southern end of the Sierra Nevada range, and by some loosely defined eastward extension of the Tehachapi line corresponding roughly to the northern border of the Mojave Desert. Southern California thus occupies approximately the southern third of the state, and Northern California the rest. The Tehachapi Mountains in the past have effectively isolated the water industry of Southern California from that to the north.

The land area of Northern California includes the great Central Valley, adjacent mountain ranges bounding it on the east, west, and north, several generally narrow coastal valleys, and a few coastal basins of modest size. For purposes of this study, we largely omit from consideration that part of Northern California which lies east of the divide of the major mountain ranges on its eastern border, a narrow band of land consisting mainly of the steep eastern slopes of these ranges and connected foothills and plateaus.[1]

The topography of Northern California, depicted in Figure 3, is dominated by two mountain chains which run roughly from north to south, with a moderate eastward tendency as they proceed southward. On the eastern border, the great Sierra Nevada range extends from the southern limit of the region to the far northern part of the state, where it joins the Cascade Range of Oregon and Washington. Its height at the divide varies roughly from 8,000 to 13,000 feet (with some higher peaks), generally decreasing from south to north. It has an extremely steep eastern slope, rising approximately from the eastern border of the state, and a more gradual western slope which descends in a succession of mountain ridges and then of foothills to the Central Valley. The width of the Sierra range from east to west within California varies from 80 to 100 miles, with the preponderance of this span being occupied by the western slope.

Near the seacoast border of the state, the Coast Ranges more or less parallel the Sierra Nevada and have a similar north-to-south extent. The crests of these ranges, with altitudes typically from 3,000 to 5,500 feet, generally lie from 120 to 150 miles

[1] The omitted area, the Lahontan region, includes principally the eastern slope of the Sierra Nevada range, from which the minor streamflows drain generally eastward into the state of Nevada. But also included are the Owens River Valley, which parallels the eastern slope of the Sierra for about 100 miles at the southern extremity of the range, as well as parts of the White, Amargosa, and Panamint mountains, which rise east of the Owens River within California.

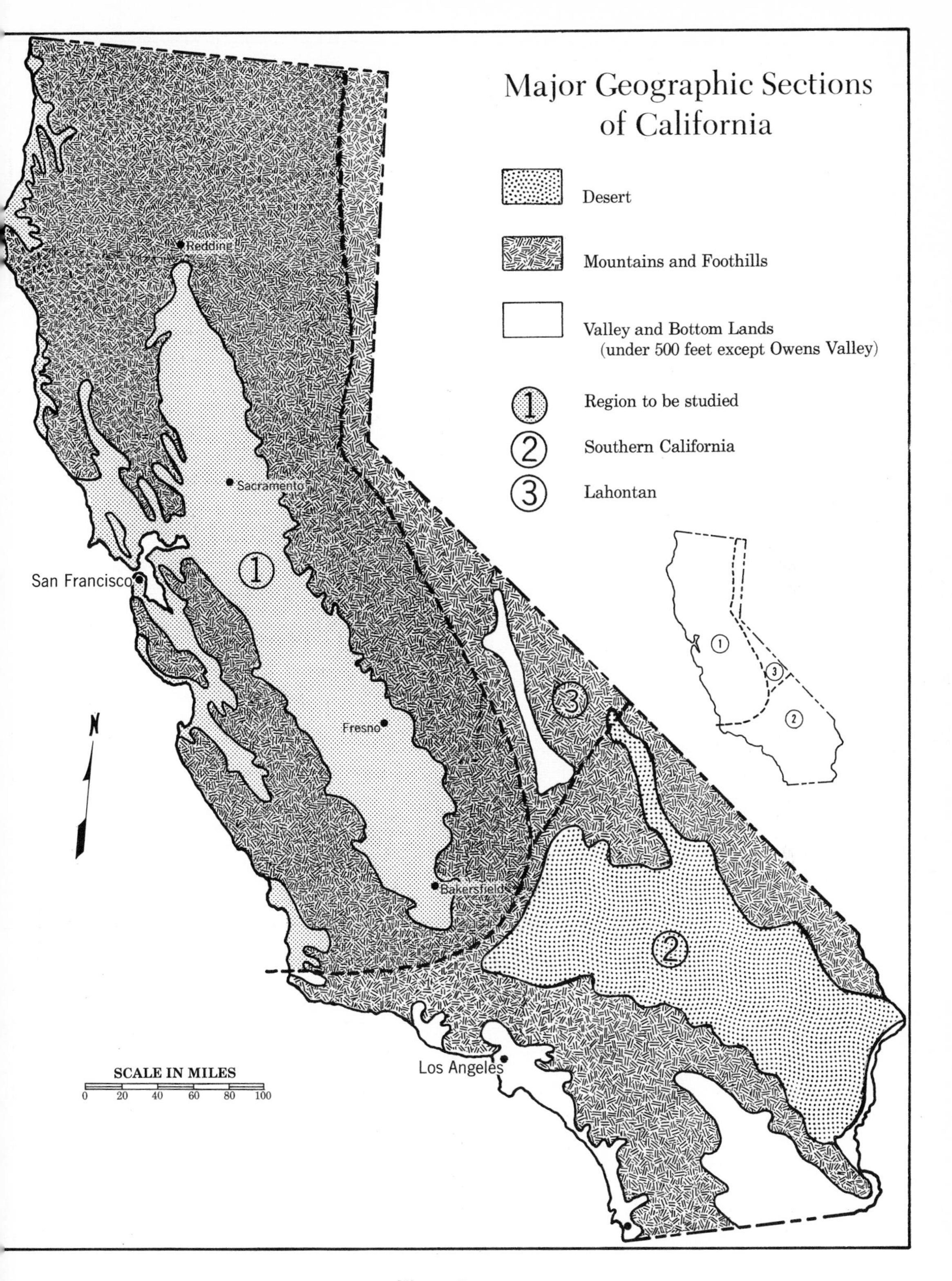
Major Geographic Sections of California
Desert
Mountains and Foothills
Valley and Bottom Lands
(under 500 feet except Owens Valley)
1
Region to be studied
2
Southern California
3
Lahontan
Redding
Sacramento
San Francisco
Fresno
Bakersfield
Los Angeles
N
SCALE IN MILES
0
20
40
60
80
100

Figure 2

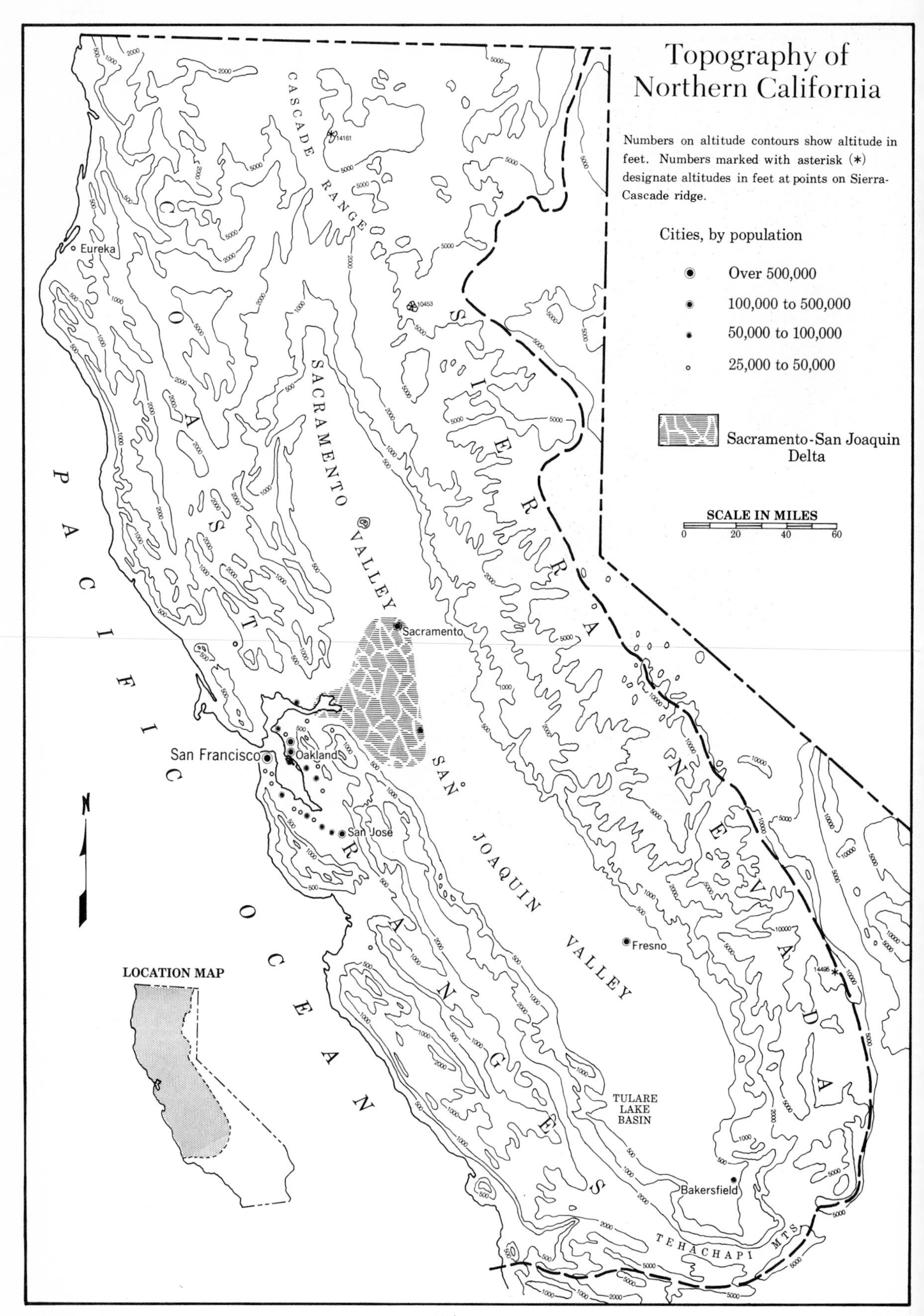
Topography of Northern California
Numbers on altitude contours show altitude in feet. Numbers marked with asterisk (*) designate altitudes in feet at points on Sierra-Cascade ridge.
Cities, by population
Over 500,000
100,000 to 500,000
50,000 to 100,000
25,000 to 50,000
Sacramento-San Joaquin Delta
SCALE IN MILES
0
20
40
60
LOCATION MAP
CASCADE RANGE
COAST RANGES
SIERRA NEVADA
SACRAMENTO VALLEY
SAN JOAQUIN VALLEY
PACIFIC OCEAN
TULARE LAKE BASIN
TEHACHAPI MTS
Eureka
Sacramento
San Francisco
Oakland
San Jose
Fresno
Bakersfield
14161
10453
14495

Figure 3

west of the crest of the Sierra. Their lower altitude causes much of their precipitation to occur as winter rains, by contrast to the heavy snows of the Sierra; this is an important factor in making the flow of the coastal streams much more variable. The Coast Ranges slope in a moderate incline westward to, or almost to, the sea, leaving only patches of relatively narrow coastal plain, and eastward to the Central Valley.

The two north-south mountain chains are joined at their northern and southern extremities by ranges crossing from west to east—at the southern end of the area by the Tehachapi Mountains and at the northern end by a mountain mass including the Klamath Mountains and the southern part of the Cascade Range. The mountain mass on the north, which extends from the coast to the eastern border of the state, reaches about 75 miles south from the Oregon border; the Tehachapis are narrower and mark the northern border of the Southern California area.

The eastern mountain chain, including the Sierra and its northern extension, is not broken by any stream flowing from east to west except the Klamath River. The Klamath originates in southern Oregon east of the divide, enters California, and proceeds generally westward through mountainous country to reach the sea near California's northern border. The Coast Ranges are broken, aside from the crossing of the Klamath River on the extreme north, only by the waters of the Sacramento River running southward and San Joaquin River running northward. The two rivers join roughly east of San Francisco and flow through a gap in the Coast Ranges into San Francisco Bay and on into the Pacific Ocean. Thus, the opportunities for exchange of water by way of natural channels between the coastal areas and the Central Valley watershed are sharply limited.

The Northern California mountain complex surrounds the elongated and continuous expanse of valley land known as the Central Valley of California. This basin is nearly 450 miles long and from about 30 to 60 miles wide, becoming generally broader toward the south. The valley floor occupies nearly 16,000 square miles, most of them arable and fertile. Most of it is quite flat, and both its northern and southern parts have only slight gradients toward the sea. The altitude is about 500 feet at its northern end and 300 feet at its southern end; from these extremes it descends to only a few feet above sea level at the confluence of the Sacramento and San Joaquin rivers. Terrace lands, covering an added area of about 6,000 square miles, lie between the valley floor and the surrounding mountains; their adaptability to cultivation varies but most are suitable at least for pasturage. The Central Valley is made up of three parts:

1) The Sacramento Valley comprises roughly the northern third of the Central Valley. It borders the Sacramento River as it flows southward after entering the valley at its northern end.

2) The San Joaquin Valley occupies approximately the southern two-thirds of the Central Valley. Its northern half borders the San Joaquin River as it proceeds northward on a course west of the center of the valley, after entering from the Sierra on the east. Its southern half is divided from the northern half by a low ridge of river sediment deposited by the Kings River, and mountain streams south of this barrier drain into a closed basin generally designated as the Tulare Lake Basin.

3) The Delta surrounds the confluence of the Sacramento and San Joaquin rivers, where they join and turn westward to flow to the sea. This very low region is composed of the terminal deltas of the two rivers, which are crisscrossed with tidal sloughs as well as main and subsidiary river channels. The land area is about 700 square miles, much of it reclaimed from swamp and overflow lands; toward the center much of the land has subsided below sea level and is protected by levees bordering the rivers and sloughs.

The Central Valley and the mountainous areas surrounding it include the bulk of the land area of Northern California, most of its agricultural land, and most of its forests. What remains? The remainder is made up principally of the western slopes of the Coast Ranges, of intermittent coastal basins and narrow patches or strips of coastal plain, of minor valleys along streams flowing west from the Coast Ranges, and of a few long narrow valleys which straddle rivers that flow south-to-north or north-to-south between ridges on the western slope of these ranges. This area is conveniently divided into the north coastal region, the San Francisco Bay region, and the central coastal region.

The north coastal region extends from the Oregon border about 250 miles south to a point approximately 40 miles north of San Francisco. It is bounded on the west by the ocean and on the east by the ridge of the Coast Ranges. For purposes of hydrologic classification, it is construed to include also a mass of mountains extending about 110 miles eastward from the coast along the Oregon border. The area is largely mountainous, and is traversed by many major and minor rivers. It contains some inland agricultural valleys of modest size, such as those of the Scott River and the Shasta River, but these lands comprise a very small portion of the north coastal area. Furthermore, because of physical isolation they have limited significance for the allocation of water in Northern California.

The San Francisco Bay region includes a land area with a radius of 30 to 60 miles from the city of San Francisco. It is bounded generally on the east by spurs of the Coast Ranges and by the Delta, through which the Sacramento River successively enters Suisun Bay, San Pablo Bay, and San Francisco Bay, and on the north and south by very low east-west divides. Although there are no large rivers within the region, there are a number of small valleys in the north, south, and east through which creeks or creek systems drain into the bays. Primarily, the area is a metropolitan complex, including several major cities in addition to San Francisco, and numerous suburbs.

The central coastal region extends for about 170 miles south of the San Francisco Bay region along the western slope of the Coast Ranges, with an average width of about 50 miles. Although largely mountainous, it includes some level coastal plains and terraces, a few minor river valleys, and one major valley—that of the Salinas River. This valley, with an average width of over 5 miles, extends from south to north for nearly 100 miles between mountain ridges.

The patterns of land use in the various regions have been suggested by the descriptions of their terrains. The extensive mountainous areas bordering the Central Valley on the east and north, and the Coast Ranges north of San Francisco, in general are heavily forested and support a major lumbering industry. In addition, the bulk of these mountain regions are important recreational areas and also support an appreciable amount of grazing. They are sparsely populated, with small towns far apart and oriented mainly to lumbering and the recreation trade.

The Central Valley is primarily agricultural. Most of it is intensively cultivated under irrigation wherever the requisite water is available; some of it is dry-farmed. A wide range of crops—including cotton, grains, alfalfa, citrus and other fruits, nuts, sugar beets, and truck crops—are grown, and cattle-raising is important. Industrial plants distributed through the Valley are largely devoted to processing and packing agricultural products. In the southern part, there are important oil and gas fields, and natural gas fields also are found farther north. The Central Valley contains several cities of moderate size and numerous towns, nearly all primarily oriented economically to servicing the surrounding agricultural area.

In the San Francisco Bay region, the major metropolitan area of Northern California, the pursuits of the population are primarily commercial and industrial. These reflect an intensive industrial development along the shores of the San Francisco, San Pablo, and Suisun bays, seaport activity, and the function of the city of San Francisco as the major commercial center of the northern two-thirds of the state. The several small valleys approaching the bays support an intensive agriculture featuring mainly fruit and nut orchards, truck crops, poultry, dairies, vineyards (with wineries), and pasturage.

The central coastal region is dominated for agricultural purposes by the Salinas Valley, which specializes in truck crops and, particularly, in lettuce. Also, there are minor agricultural valleys along smaller streams, and some productive coastal plains in the northern part of the region. Truck crops, orchards, and vineyards predominate in these areas. The small cities and towns of the region largely support food processing and packing industries, and service adjacent agricultural areas.

Hydrology and Hydrography

With this general description of the geography of Northern California, we turn to the hydrology and hydrography of the area and its subregions. Attention naturally focuses on the Central Valley and on the San Francisco Bay region, the two principal areas of economic activity, and it will center also on the balance of water demands and supplies by regions and the relative availability of ground and surface supplies for consumptive use. In analyzing the availability and use of water in Northern California, we must consider precipitation, surface runoff of water in streams, and subsurface or ground water. Runoff and ground water, of course, are ultimately derived from precipitation, but not all precipitation reaches streams or underground deposits, as some of it evaporates directly and some is assimilated by plants where it falls on the land surface.

Precipitation

The over-all precipitation pattern in Northern California might be characterized roughly as follows: It rains more in the north than in the south, more in the mountains than in the lowlands, and more on the western than on the eastern slopes of the mountains; it does not rain in the summer and rains mostly in the winter; rainfall on most of the lowlands is light and poorly timed for many uses, so the lowlands depend on the mountains and on underground aquifers for most of the water they use. If to the expression "it rains" we add "and snows" when referring to the higher mountains, this is a good general picture of precipitation in the area.

Both generally and by regions, the fall of rain and snow in Northern California is irregular from year to year. Short cycles in precipitation embodying the alternation of wet and dry periods of several years each occur in the area as a whole, but these cycles are more accentuated in some regions than in others—being more marked in the southern half or two-thirds of the area than in the north. In addition, there is some evidence of long cycles in precipitation in the area (upon which the short swings are superimposed), with a duration from peak to peak of 30 to 35 years. Data on mean annual precipitation must be interpreted accordingly, since there is a substantial variance around any mean.[2] Figure 4 provides a general depiction of the long-term average precipitation pattern in Northern California.

The largest region to be considered includes the Central Valley and the mountain chains which surround it. On the floor of the valley, mean annual precipitation over most of the land area varies from 10 to 20 inches annually, with extremes at its northern and southern ends of about 40 to 5 inches respectively. On about 10 million acres of valley floor an average of between 12 and 15 million acre-feet of rain water falls annually, to be assimilated by crops and other vegetation, to evaporate, to seep into deposits of ground water, and, to a minor extent, to run off on the surface.[3] This water supply is important but not sufficient on the average to support intensive cultivation of most of the valley floor. It may be compared to an average total annual runoff within the watershed (primarily from the mountains) of about 34 million acre-feet of water.[4] Of this total, about 13.5 million acre-feet are presently diverted for irrigation and other uses and an undetermined, but substantial, amount seeps through the valley floor to replenish ground-water reservoirs. From these figures, it appears that the Central Valley is dependent on the surrounding mountains for over 70 per cent of its potential natural water supply and for over half of the water currently applied to use.

The mountains to the east and north which drain into the Central Valley—the long western slope of the Sierra and the southern part of the mountains at the Valley's north end—receive a heavy average annual precipitation over a very large land area. The amounts increase from the valley floor through the foothills until precipitation reaches 60 to 70 inches at altitudes above 5,000 to 6,000 feet. At the higher elevations, the precipitation occurs mostly in the form of winter snowfall, and maximum snowpacks of from 10 to 20 feet in depth are common in average years. This snowfall is usually released as runoff rather gradually in the spring and early summer months, becoming available for irrigation during the growing season for crops. The eastern slope of the Coast Ranges is much less extensive in area

[2] California State Water Resources Board, *Water Resources of California,* Bulletin No. 1 (1951), pp. 32–36. (This and other footnote references are cited in brief form when they are also included in the Bibliography.)

[3] *Ibid.,* pp. 308–44.

[4] *Ibid.,* p. 407.

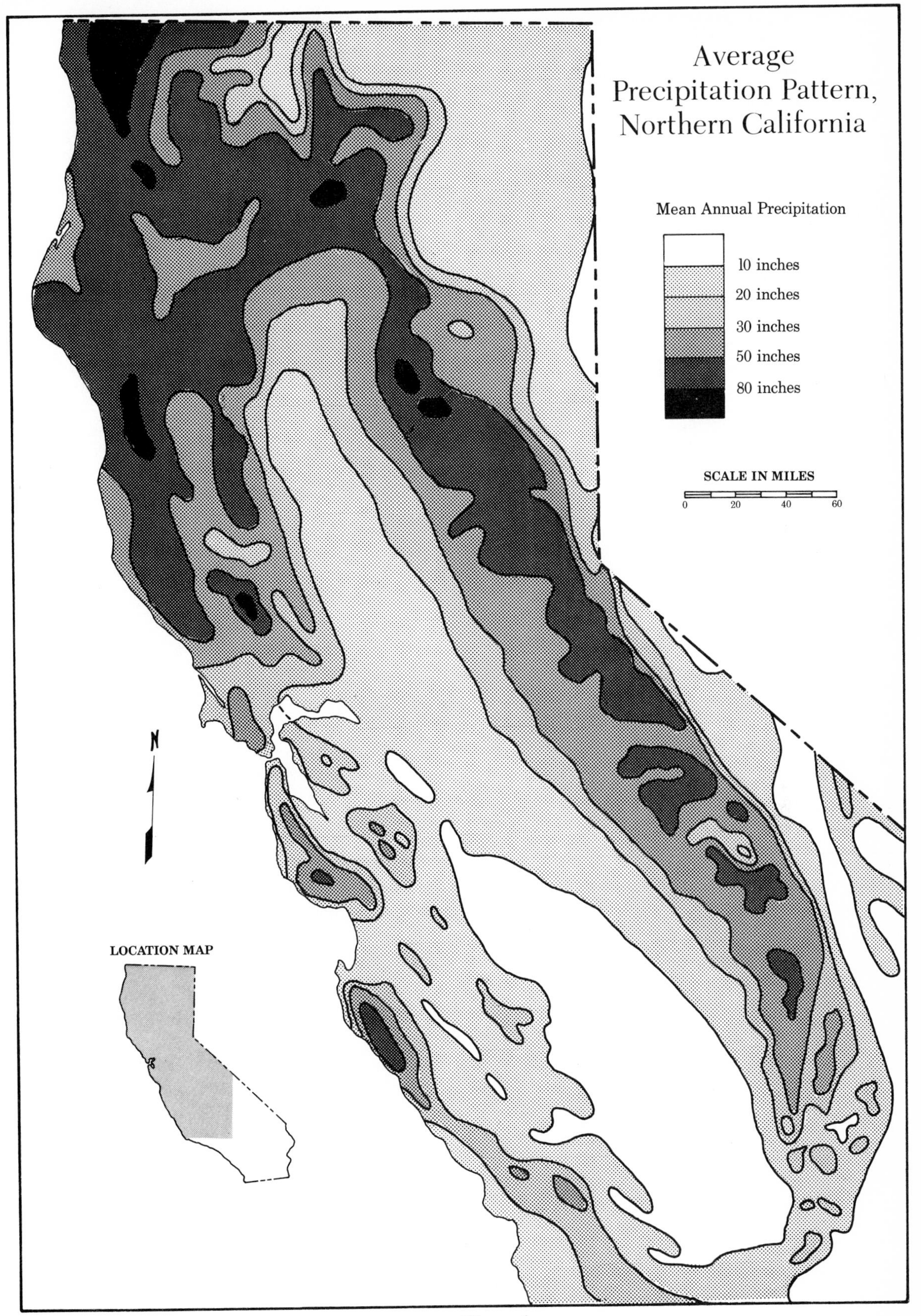
Average
Precipitation Pattern,
Northern California
Mean Annual Precipitation
10 inches
20 inches
30 inches
50 inches
80 inches
SCALE IN MILES
0
20
40
60
N
LOCATION MAP

Figure 4

and receives much lighter precipitation, but rainfall averages perhaps 20 inches annually, with up to 40 inches toward the divide. While the rainfall on this slope is generally insufficient to support major streams, it is unquestionably the source of some ground water for the Central Valley. The total precipitation falling on all mountains with streams tributary to the Valley is not easily measured, but their mean annual runoff of about 34 million acre-feet, primarily from the mountains on the east and north, suggests its magnitude.

The San Francisco Bay region has an average precipitation over most of its small area of 15 to 20 inches annually. The adjacent slopes of the Coast Ranges, though limited in area, receive much heavier rainfall, reaching 50 inches at the crests.[5] Usually the local rainfall and resulting runoff have been sufficient to support intensive agriculture in the several small valleys of the region, but much of the large demand for water for urban and industrial purposes has had to be met by importations from other regions.

As a whole, the north coastal region (including the mountainous area along the northern border of the state) receives very heavy precipitation—with minor exceptions never below 40 inches annually, and along a large part of the mountain slopes 60 to 80 inches. Most of this is rainfall, as snow occurs only at the higher elevations.[6] This precipitation results in very large runoffs which are not put to consumptive use, since valley lands are limited and population is sparse.

The central coastal region in general receives light rainfall—typically from 10 to 15 inches per year inland and about 20 inches along the coast; the higher parts of the western slopes of the Coast Ranges have heavy precipitation, ranging up to 70 inches, and this is an important source of runoff for adjacent cultivated areas. However, this runoff, resulting mostly from rainfall, is rapid and concentrated in the winter, as is also the case in much of the north coastal and San Francisco Bay regions.[7]

Ground-water reservoirs

Direct precipitation is an immediate source of water for use if it falls on cultivated land when needed by crops or on useful native vegetation, and is assimilated by plants before running off or seeping into underground reservoirs. In Northern California, it is much more important as a source of runoff in streams and in replenishing subsurface reservoirs of ground water.

Ground water collects in aquifers with physical structures which are adapted to holding, transmitting, and yielding water. One large aquifer, or several interrelated ones, may compose a ground-water basin or reservoir capable of storing a substantial amount of water. Water reaches such reservoirs from direct seepage of precipitation, from underground inflow of precipitation that infiltrated the ground elsewhere in a general drainage basin, from infiltration through stream channels

[5] *Ibid.*, pp. 99–105 and 111–12.
[6] *Ibid.*, pp. 55–69.
[7] *Ibid.*, pp. 135–53.

and in irrigation canals, from deep penetration of excess irrigation water, and from artificial spreading of water to induce percolation.

The quality of ground-water basins varies considerably through Northern California. The Central Valley is endowed with very large subsurface reservoirs. Under the Sacramento Valley, ground water is found largely in alluvial plain and alluvial fan deposits and most is of good quality.[8] A more complex system of aquifers underlies the San Joaquin Valley, providing a huge storage capacity at depths between 10 and 200 feet. The quality of this water varies among areas and by depths (some is high in mineral content or brackish), but most of it is usable.[9] These aquifers in the Central Valley are tapped by wells ranging in depth from a few feet under the surface (10 or 20 feet, for example) to over 400 feet. In the San Joaquin Valley, where over four-fifths of all withdrawals of ground water in Northern California are made, the depths of wells commonly range between 100 and 250 feet, and are sometimes greater. In the Sacramento Valley, the average depth is somewhat less.[10]

In both the San Francisco Bay and central coastal regions, the major agricultural valleys lie over substantial ground-water basins into which relatively large amounts of surface runoff percolate, and agriculture in these areas depends heavily upon pumping from ground water. The terrain of the north coastal region does not favor the development of important ground-water basins;[11] because of their spotty occurrence, plus the relatively small amount of land suitable for irrigated agriculture, little use is made of ground water in the area. In water-surplus areas of the coastal regions, very shallow wells—often not exceeding 20 or 30 feet in depth—are typical, but significantly greater depths prevail in important local areas where an overdraft of ground water has occurred.

Surface streamflows and diversions

The economic significance of elements of geography, hydrography, and hydrology lies in their impact on the net balance of supply and demand for water in the various regions of Northern California. Since water pumped from underground basins is jointly used with water diverted from surface streams in most agricultural sectors of the area, the concept of "balance of supply and demand" is not simple. Nonetheless, the facts readily permit some comparative judgments of how the relative pressure of the demand for surface water against available supplies varies from region to region. A summary description of the size of surface flows in the various major regions of Northern California, together with the portions diverted

[8] U.S. Department of the Interior, Geological Survey, *Geologic Features of Ground Water Storage Capacity of the Sacramento Valley, California* (1961).

[9] U.S. Department of the Interior, Geological Survey, *Ground Water Conditions and Storage Capacity in the San Joaquin Valley, California* (1959).

[10] California Department of Water Resources, *Ground Water Conditions in Central and Northern California, 1957–58*, Bulletin No. 77–58 (1960), plates 5 and 6.

[11] U.S. Department of the Interior, Pacific Southwest Field Committee, *Natural Resources of Northwestern California, Preliminary Report* (1958), appendix on water resources, pp. 19–89.

for agricultural and urban uses, and the degrees to which these flows are supplemented with ground water is given in Table 1. Figure 5 presents a general map of the rivers of Northern California and assists in placing the more detailed maps of rivers within the area's five regions, presented in Figures 6 through 10.

The first column in Table 1 presents our rough estimate of the mean annual natural surface runoff in streams flowing into or through Northern California's major regions.[12] Column 2 of the table shows estimates of the current gross diversions in a normal runoff year within each region for local uses, but does not include gross exports or imports. The figures in column 2 were based on reported 1957–58 diversions adjusted to the level of runoff in a normal year; by and large, they represent conditions prevailing in the early 1960's. Column 3 shows the balance of net imports to, or net exports from, each region; and column 4 gives estimated gross withdrawals from ground-water basins. The last two columns assist in making some crude interpretations on the basis of the data preceding them. Column 5 shows the portion of a region's streamflow diverted for local use within that region, and thus reflects the intensity with which a region utilizes its local surface water resources.[13] Column 6 indicates the extent to which ground water is used to supplement surface supplies. If we assume provisionally that surface supplies available by gravity diversion are typically less costly than ground water that must be pumped, then this column also contains potential evidence on the state of water development in the various regions of Northern California.[14]

Additional comments may shed further light on the information contained in Table 1. In comparing the two major portions of the Central Valley, it is often noted that the Sacramento Valley receives two-thirds of the total runoff, but contains only a quarter of the Central Valley's level land area and 22 per cent of its irrigated acreage. A relatively small portion of local runoff is diverted for local use, and ground-water resources are not heavily utilized. Conversely, the San Joaquin Valley and the Sacramento-San Joaquin Delta (counted in with the San Joaquin Valley except for major diversions made from the Sacramento for interbasin export) draws heavily upon its surface runoff and supplements this source with substantial drafts upon its ground water. Unlike the Sacramento Valley, an overdraft of the ground-water basin has increased pump lifts in substantial portions of the San Joaquin Valley in the past three decades.

[12] It should be stressed that these figures (drawn from *Water Resources of California*, Bulletin No. 1, *op. cit.*) are not just measures of recorded streamflows, but rather reconstructed figures for full natural flows that allow for consumptive uses upstream from gauging points. Furthermore, these figures were constructed for a 1951 publication, and the years since 1951 have seen less than the long-run average volume of precipitation in Northern California. Therefore, the figures in column 1 somewhat overstate long-run averages calculated from data running up to the present.

[13] Figures for net diversions would be significantly smaller than for gross diversions for agricultural, though not for urban uses, in Northern California. The geography of the area is such, however, that substantial rediversion of return flows occurs only in the San Joaquin River basin and Delta; thus the figures for gross diversions include little double counting.

[14] The factual assumption is certainly not correct for all areas. For instance, in the central coastal region's most important agricultural valley, the Salinas, natural conditions favor pumping from ground-water basins that are replenished by substantial percolation from the Salinas River. Thus, the values in both columns 5 and 6 for the central coastal region are deceptively low in comparison with other regions.

TABLE 1

SURFACE WATER SUPPLIES, DIVERSIONS, AND GROUND-WATER EXTRACTION IN A NORMAL YEAR, BY REGIONS

(In millions of acre-feet)

Region	Total natural surface runoff (1)	Diversions for local use (2)	Net imports (+)[a] net exports (−) (3)	Withdrawals of ground water (4)	Portion of runoff diverted (2 ÷ 1) (5)	Portion of local supplies from surface sources (2 ÷ [2 + 4]) (6)
Sacramento Valley	22.4	4.4	−1.1	1.3	20%	78%
San Joaquin Valley and Delta	11.3	8.0	+0.8	9.7	70	46
Rivers draining into Delta	1.5	0.6	−0.1	—	35	—
Rivers draining into San Joaquin River Basin	6.5	4.9	−0.1	—	75	—
Rivers draining into Tulare Lake Basin	3.3	2.5	+1.0	—	80	—
San Francisco Bay area	1.2	0.3	+0.3	0.3	24	48
Central coastal region	2.3	0.1	0	0.5	3	13
North coastal region	28.9	0.6	0	0.1	2	86

[a] Pattern for a normal year in the late 1950's; other interbasin transfers have since begun or are under construction. One of these is a large diversion from the Trinity River (north coastal region) to the Sacramento River (Sacramento Valley) which was not in operation at the cutoff date for our figures, although Trinity Dam, built to effect this diversion, was completed and appears in subsequent tabulations of dams.

SOURCE: Column 1 from California State Water Resources Board, *Water Resources of California*, Bulletin No. 1 (1951); columns 2, 3, and 4 from the variety of sources cited in note 6 of Chapter 4 (columns 2 and 3 are computed from data in those sources).

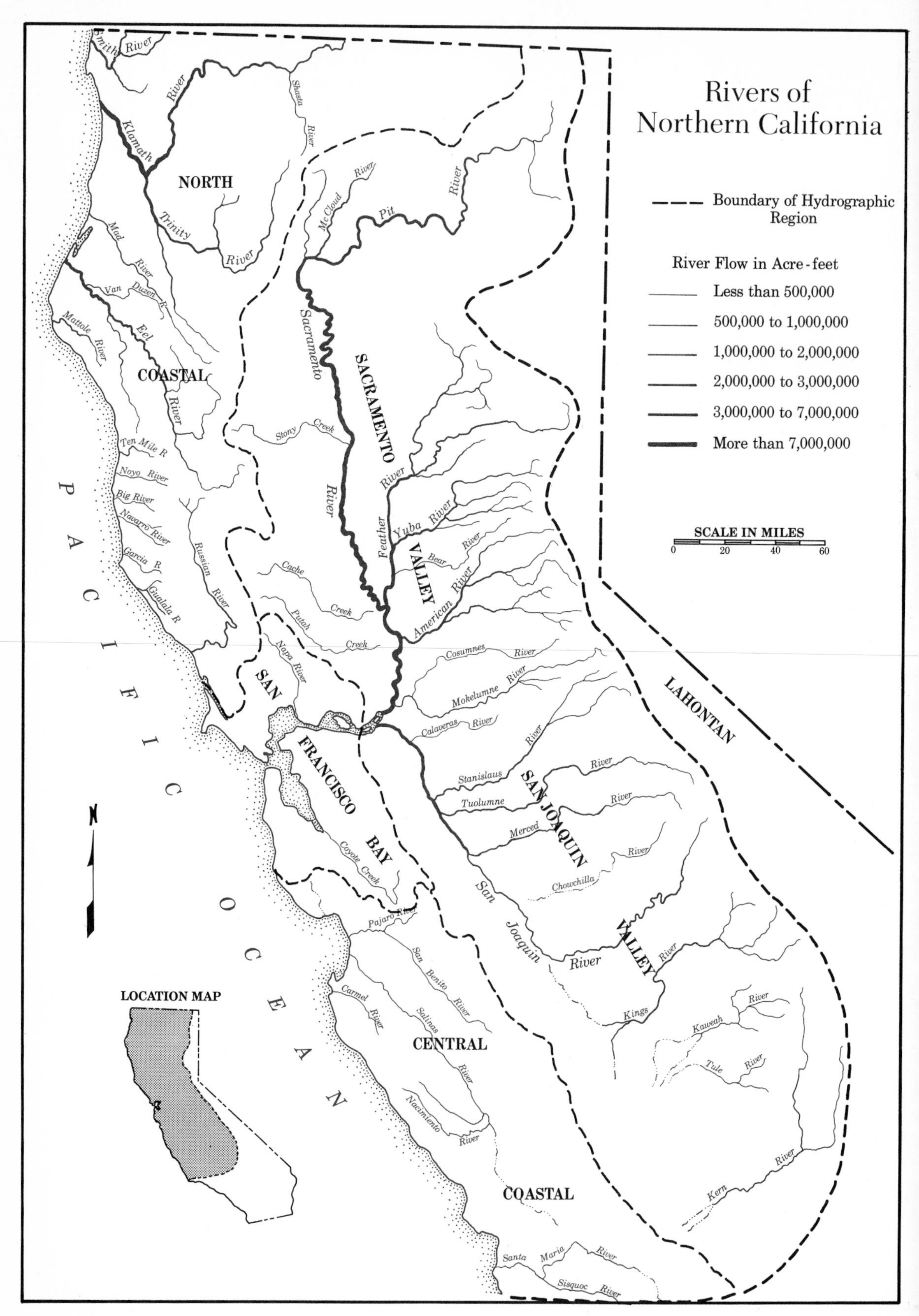
Rivers of Northern California
Boundary of Hydrographic Region
River Flow in Acre-feet
Less than 500,000
500,000 to 1,000,000
1,000,000 to 2,000,000
2,000,000 to 3,000,000
3,000,000 to 7,000,000
More than 7,000,000
SCALE IN MILES
0 20 40 60
LOCATION MAP
NORTH
COASTAL
SACRAMENTO
VALLEY
SAN FRANCISCO BAY
SAN JOAQUIN
VALLEY
CENTRAL
COASTAL
LAHONTAN
PACIFIC OCEAN
Smith River
Klamath River
Shasta River
Trinity River
Mad River
Van Duzen R
Eel River
Mattole River
Ten Mile R
Noyo River
Big River
Navarro River
Garcia R
Gualala R
Russian River
McCloud River
Pit River
Sacramento River
Stony Creek
Cache Creek
Putah Creek
Napa River
Feather River
Yuba River
Bear River
American River
Cosumnes River
Mokelumne River
Calaveras River
Stanislaus River
Tuolumne River
Merced River
Chowchilla River
San Joaquin River
Kings River
Kaweah River
Tule River
Kern River
Coyote Creek
Pajaro River
San Benito River
Salinas River
Carmel River
Nacimiento River
Santa Maria River
Sisquoc River

Figure 5

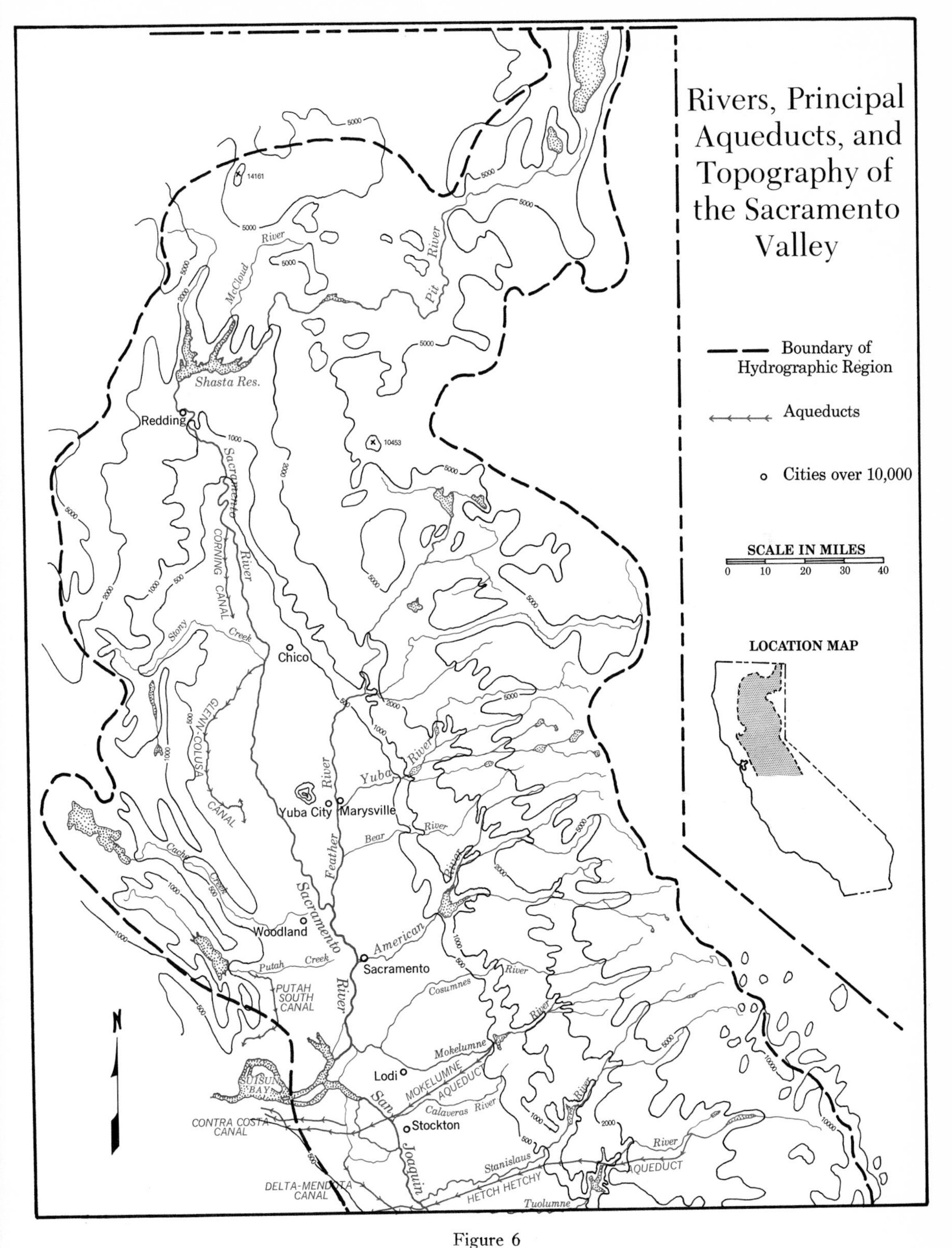

Rivers, Principal Aqueducts, and Topography of the Sacramento Valley
Boundary of Hydrographic Region
Aqueducts
Cities over 10,000
SCALE IN MILES
0 10 20 30 40
LOCATION MAP
Redding
Shasta Res.
McCloud River
Pit River
Sacramento River
CORNING CANAL
Stony Creek
Chico
GLENN-COLUSA CANAL
Yuba River
Yuba City
Marysville
Feather River
Bear River
Cache Creek
Woodland
American River
Sacramento
Putah Creek
PUTAH SOUTH CANAL
Cosumnes River
Mokelumne River
MOKELUMNE AQUEDUCT
Lodi
SUISUN BAY
CONTRA COSTA CANAL
Calaveras River
Stockton
San Joaquin
DELTA-MENDOTA CANAL
Stanislaus River
HETCH HETCHY AQUEDUCT
Tuolumne
14161
10453
N

Figure 6

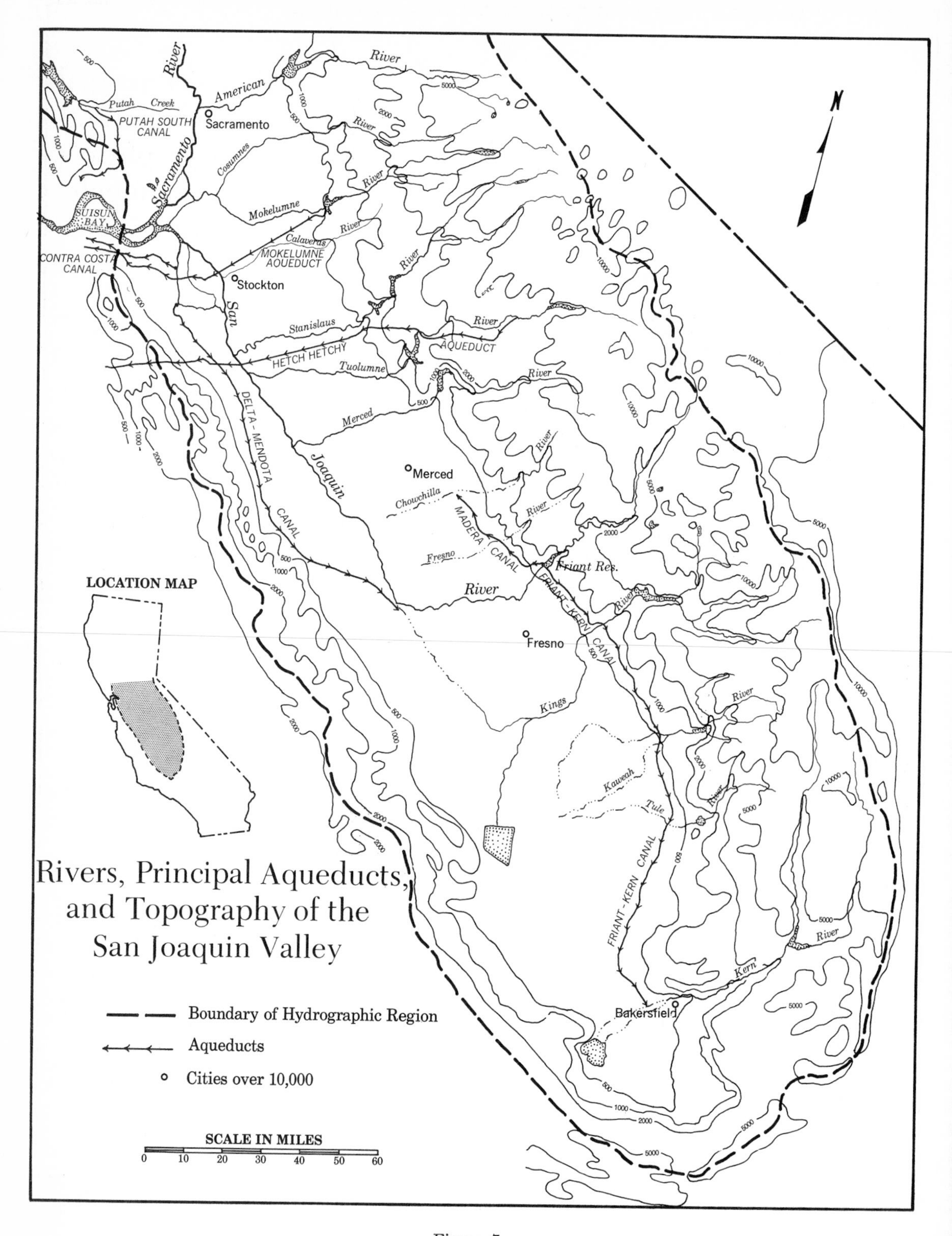
Rivers, Principal Aqueducts, and Topography of the San Joaquin Valley
LOCATION MAP
Boundary of Hydrographic Region
Aqueducts
Cities over 10,000
SCALE IN MILES
0 10 20 30 40 50 60
N
Sacramento
Stockton
Merced
Fresno
Bakersfield
American River
Sacramento River
Putah Creek
PUTAH SOUTH CANAL
SUISUN BAY
CONTRA COSTA CANAL
Cosumnes River
Mokelumne River
Calaveras River
MOKELUMNE AQUEDUCT
Stanislaus River
HETCH HETCHY AQUEDUCT
Tuolumne River
Merced River
San Joaquin River
DELTA-MENDOTA CANAL
Chowchilla River
MADERA CANAL
Fresno River
Friant Res.
FRIANT-KERN CANAL
Kings River
Kaweah River
Tule River
Kern River

Figure 7

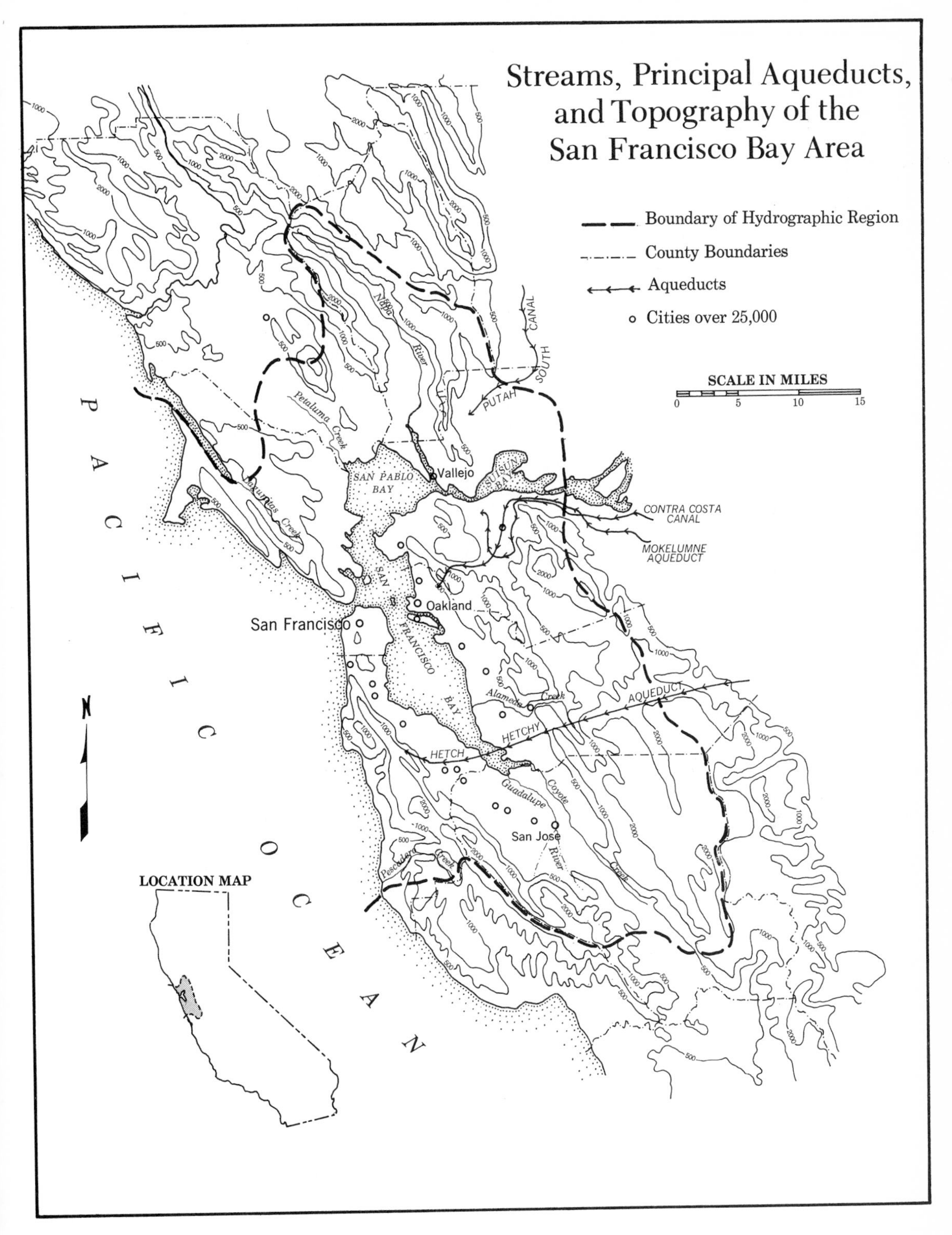
Streams, Principal Aqueducts, and Topography of the San Francisco Bay Area
Boundary of Hydrographic Region
County Boundaries
Aqueducts
Cities over 25,000
SCALE IN MILES
0
5
10
15
PACIFIC OCEAN
LOCATION MAP
SAN PABLO BAY
SUISUN BAY
SAN FRANCISCO BAY
Vallejo
Oakland
San Francisco
San José
Napa River
Petaluma Creek
Putah
South Canal
Contra Costa Canal
Mokelumne Aqueduct
Hetch Hetchy Aqueduct
Alameda Creek
Guadalupe River
Coyote Creek
Pescadero Creek

Figure 8

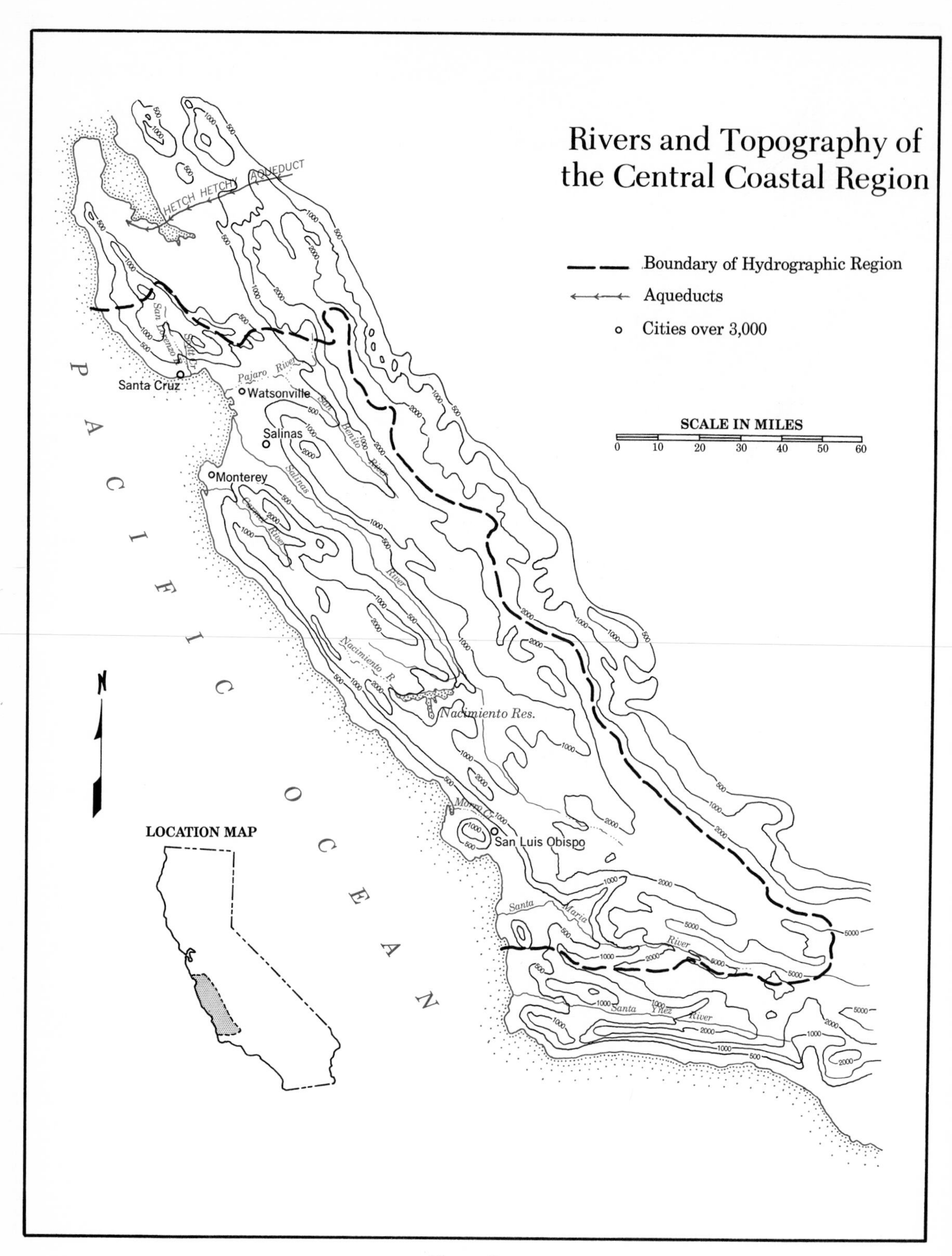

Rivers and Topography of the Central Coastal Region
Boundary of Hydrographic Region
Aqueducts
Cities over 3,000
SCALE IN MILES
0 10 20 30 40 50 60
HETCH HETCHY AQUEDUCT
PACIFIC OCEAN
Santa Cruz
Watsonville
Salinas
Monterey
San Luis Obispo
Pajaro River
San Lorenzo
San Benito River
Salinas River
Carmel River
Nacimiento R.
Nacimiento Res.
Morro Cr.
Santa Maria River
Santa Ynez River
LOCATION MAP

Figure 9

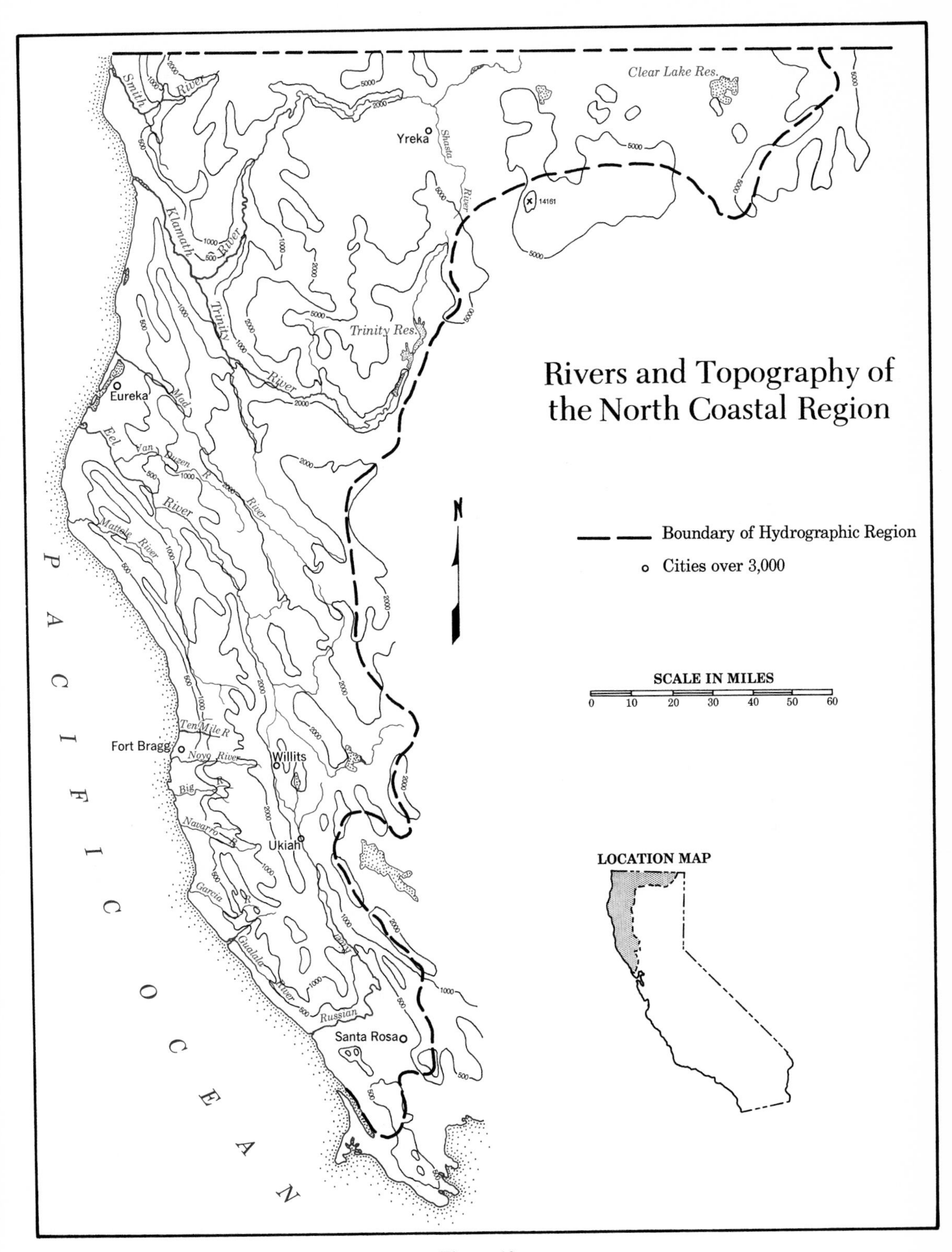

Rivers and Topography of the North Coastal Region
Boundary of Hydrographic Region
Cities over 3,000
SCALE IN MILES
0
10
20
30
40
50
60
LOCATION MAP
PACIFIC OCEAN
Clear Lake Res.
Yreka
Shasta River
14161
Smith River
Klamath River
Trinity River
Trinity Res.
Eureka
Mad
Eel River
Van Duzen R
Mattole River
Ten Mile R
Fort Bragg
Noyo River
Willits
Big R
Navarro R
Ukiah
Garcia R
Gualala River
Russian
Santa Rosa

Figure 10

Since patterns of water utilization differ within the San Joaquin Valley, we have divided the region into three parts. Moving from north to south, they are lands served by streams draining directly into the Delta (mainly the Consumnes, Mokelumne, and Calaveras); the San Joaquin River and streams draining into it; and the closed Tulare Lake Basin fed principally by the Kings, Kaweah, Tule, and Kern Rivers. As Table 1 shows, the extent of utilization of surface water increases significantly in the southern portions of the San Joaquin Valley. While technical factors are partly responsible for this (the closed nature of the Tulare Lake Basin and the rediversion of return flows in the San Joaquin basin), a difference in the balance between demands and supplies clearly has some responsibility.

A major system of interbasin transfers of water has been developed to assist in offsetting these differential scarcities. Those operating in the late 1950's were mainly the result of projects of the U.S. Bureau of Reclamation. The principal works are the Friant-Kern Canal, transferring water from the San Joaquin River into the Tulare Lake Basin, and the Delta-Mendota Canal, offsetting the Friant-Kern transfer by imports from the lower Sacramento River to the San Joaquin basin. In addition, column 3 of Table 1 also reflects smaller transfers from the Central Valley to the San Francisco Bay area: approximately 60,000 acre-feet annually from the Delta via the Contra Costa Canal (of the Bureau of Reclamation) and roughly 200,000 acre-feet annually from the Tuolumne and Mokelumne rivers via aqueducts serving San Francisco and the East Bay cities respectively.

Much of the supply of water for urban uses in the San Francisco Bay area is imported from other regions, and these imports will increase sharply in the coming years. (As will be seen, problems of water quality, as well as the availability of local supplies, underlie this fact.) The total surface runoff of local streams appears quite adequate relative to the amount of agricultural land remaining in the Bay area, but melting snow does not serve to regularize the flow of these streams as it does most of those flowing into the Central Valley, and their flows typically undergo greater seasonal and annual variations. These factors help to explain the relatively heavy dependence of the area on ground water. This same pattern of abundant, but irregular, local runoff holds in the central coastal region, where the bulk of water supplies for agriculture are secured by private pumping. Water resources of the mountainous north coastal region are extremely abundant relative to the small population and small quantities of arable land in the region.

Finally, the regional river patterns shown in Figures 6 through 10 can be better understood in the light of the volume and distribution of runoff in the major rivers of each region. The figures for the mean annual natural surface runoff for each region given in column 1 of Table 1 are further broken down by major rivers in Table 3. As one might expect, the rivers with great average annual runoffs flow in regions with relatively large annual runoffs. The Klamath, Trinity, and Eel rivers in the north coastal region and the Sacramento and Feather rivers in the Sacramento Valley carry flows substantially in excess of any other rivers in Northern California. Several rivers in the San Joaquin Valley have much less runoff. The Sacramento Valley and north coastal regions are drained by a few rivers of very substantial size, while their other streams carry flows of much smaller magnitude. The San Joaquin Valley, by contrast, contains a number of rivers of roughly the same size. This difference may contain an important implication for the conduct of water agencies in these regions. The maximum number of potential alternative sources of surface water in the Sacramento Valley is necessarily small for a potential large-scale diverter. In the San Joaquin Valley, a larger number of rivers may be able to sustain a given scale of diversion. Patterns of rivalry for surface flows in the two regions could be correspondingly affected.

Dams and Reservoirs

We now turn from the natural to the man-made elements of the structural environment of the water industry. A principal influence of the natural elements is to set the basic relation between local supplies and demand for surface water in the various regions of Northern California. The present stock of engineering features, such as dams and canals, records man's efforts to alter the natural distribution of flows of water in time and space. They constitute the fixed factors within which any short-run allocative options must be chosen. Furthermore, in connection with established water rights, they strongly influence the productivity of any new construction.

Dams and reservoirs can accomplish a number of familiar physical functions. They can store water and, by varying the amount in storage, alter the rate of flow below the dam over the hours of the day, the seasons of the year, or even from year to year. They can generate hydroelectric power from released flows. They can accomplish the diversion of stream-flow into canals or aqueducts to serve out-of-stream uses. They can provide recreational facilities. The size and location of dams and reservoirs, and the rules by which natural streamflows are depleted or supplemented by storage or diversion, are thus crucial in determining the actual and short-run potential distributions of water among uses, users, and places of use. Furthermore, what matters is not just the range of potential economic effects of the operation of a dam and reservoir—its contribution (not necessarily positive) to agricultural and urban consumptive uses, flood control, hydroelectric power generation, and stream and reservoir recreation—but also the results of its actual operation. Those depend, naturally, upon who operates it, and the kind of governmental regulations which affect operations. Therefore we shall distinguish between the familiar concept of a multipurpose reservoir and that of a multiproduct installation. The operation of a dam and reservoir may often have effects on the levels of utility or product associated with certain uses of water that are a matter of indifference to the owner-operator of the facility, and thus are essentially external effects in relation to his decisions. In that case, the operation of a dam and reservoir may be said to have more "products" than "purposes."

To clarify later discussion, we should note that a multiproduct dam and reservoir may often be designed to produce several different outputs, so that the investment is one that creates a joint-product facility. The outputs possess a complementary relation to one another. Nonetheless, by varying the operating rules of the same reservoir, or by varying its design at the time of construction, the combination of its outputs can be altered, and in that respect they stand in competitive relation to one another.

Purposes of dams and reservoirs

There appears no neat way to extract from published information a precise tabulation of either the purposes or the products of the many dams and reservoirs in Northern California; nor could such a tabulation be readily summarized if it were made. Consequently, we shall focus upon a tabulation of the sixty largest reservoirs (in terms of storage capacity), for which the ostensible purposes can be discovered from ownership data and other information. These top sixty, as of 1962, included all reservoirs with storage capacities in excess of 40,000 acre-feet. Table 2 shows the distribution of these dams and the proportions of total storage capacity that they account for in each of Northern California's regions.[15] Figure 11 shows their location and other information about them.

TABLE 2
REGIONAL DISTRIBUTION OF THE SIXTY LARGEST DAMS IN NORTHERN CALIFORNIA, BY NUMBER, STORAGE CAPACITY, AND PERCENTAGE OF TOTAL REGIONAL STORAGE CAPACITY, 1962

Region	Number	Reservoir capacity (millions of acre-feet)	Capacity as percentage of total regional capacity
Central Valley	49	15.3	86%
Sacramento Valley	19	9.7	90
San Joaquin Valley	30	5.6	80
North coastal region	6	3.6	95
San Francisco Bay and central coastal regions	5	0.6	35
Northern California total	60	19.4[a]	84%

[a] Detail may not agree with totals because of rounding errors.
SOURCE: California Department of Water Resources, *Dams Within Jurisdiction of the State of California, January 1, 1962*, Bulletin No. 17 (1962).

Only a small number of dams in the area can be classed as serving a wide range of multiple purposes: at a minimum the regulation of streamflows to enhance the supply of water for consumptive use and for electric power generation, and the provision of flood control. Such dams are also frequently operated to regulate downstream flows for the enhancement of navigability, preservation of fish habitat, and to check saline intrusion into river estuaries. There are six large dams in Northern California that are said to be managed for the attainment of so wide a range of economic purposes, including those with the first, second, and fifth largest

[15] As of the beginning of 1962, there were under construction, in addition to a number of lesser dams, seven major dams with a total planned reservoir capacity of 4.15 million acre-feet. Of this total capacity, about 3.97 million acre-feet will be on streams feeding the Sacramento Valley, including about 3.5 million acre-feet behind Oroville Dam, being built as part of the Feather River Project of the California Department of Water Resources. About 110,000 acre-feet of new capacity will be in the north coastal region, and about 70,000 acre-feet in the San Francisco Bay area. None of this capacity is included in Table 2 or subsequent tabulations.

individual reservoir capacities, and two more with individual capacities of 250,000 acre-feet or more. Five of these are operated by the Bureau of Reclamation, whose Central Valley Project has a definite multipurpose orientation in the development of the water resources of the region.[16]

A number of the remaining fifty-four of the sixty largest dams can also be classed as multiproduct, but essentially they have only dual purposes. These include twelve dams operated by several irrigation districts and the two principal agencies supplying the San Francisco Bay area with urban water—among them some dams built as joint ventures by electric utility companies and irrigation districts. All of these are operated with dominant emphasis on both production of electric power and the seasonal storage of water for irrigation or urban use. Although designed as dual purpose dams, they typically are multiproduct by virtue of regulations setting release patterns for wildlife conservation, operating arrangements with local parties of interest, or merely the existence of uncompensated external effects. Eleven other dams among the largest sixty also have dual purposes, but they combine the storage of streamflow for consumptive use with flood control functions, and do not support production of electric power. Six of these are controlled by the Corps of Engineers and three by the Bureau of Reclamation.

The most important dams having a single purpose (but with dual or multiple products) among the sixty largest are nineteen dams owned and operated by public utility companies producing electric power. These dams, together with the twelve dual purpose dams also supporting power production, account for about 40 per cent of the reservoir capacity of the region. The large contribution which they make to the regulation of streamflow suggests that to an important extent diverters of irrigation water freeload on reservoir storage capacity paid for by others instead of sharing its cost. The remaining single purpose dams among the largest sixty include nine which function mainly to accumulate water for irrigation, and three that provide local storage and terminal basins for water imported to supply the San Francisco Bay area. In brief, a majority—thirty-one—of the sixty largest dams in Northern California are not necessarily utilized to achieve an optimal economic balance even among the major products obtainable from such works,

[16] This and the following information on dam capacities and characteristics is drawn from these sources: California Department of Water Resources, *Dams within Jurisdiction of State of California, January 1, 1962,* Bulletin No. 17 (1962); California State Water Resources Board, *Water Utilization and Requirements of California,* Bulletin No. 2 (1955), Vol. II, Appendix H, "Major Reservoirs in California"; U.S. Department of the Interior, Bureau of Reclamation, Region 2, *Annual Project History, Central Valley Project, 1960, 1961* (1961 and 1962). Also consulted were the *Annual Report to the Public Utilities Commission* (for recent years) by Pacific Gas and Electric Company; an unpublished list supplied directly by Pacific Gas and Electric Company entitled "Reservoirs, Pacific Gas and Electric Company System"; the *Annual Report to Stockholders, 1961,* of Southern California Edison Company; and U.S. Army Corps of Engineers, South Pacific Division, *Water Resources Development in California* (1961). The Northern California region to which the reservoir data refer excludes lands east of the Sierra Nevada divide, in the so-called Lahontan region. The dams included are all those shown as completely constructed by January 1, 1962, plus one large dam which was nearing completion at that time. Not included as reservoirs are two valley-bottom basins in the San Joaquin Valley: Tulare Lake, a natural basin with a huge capacity, and the Mendota Pool, a valley basin contained by some damming which serves mainly as a storage reservoir for water imported to the San Joaquin Valley through the Delta-Mendota Canal.

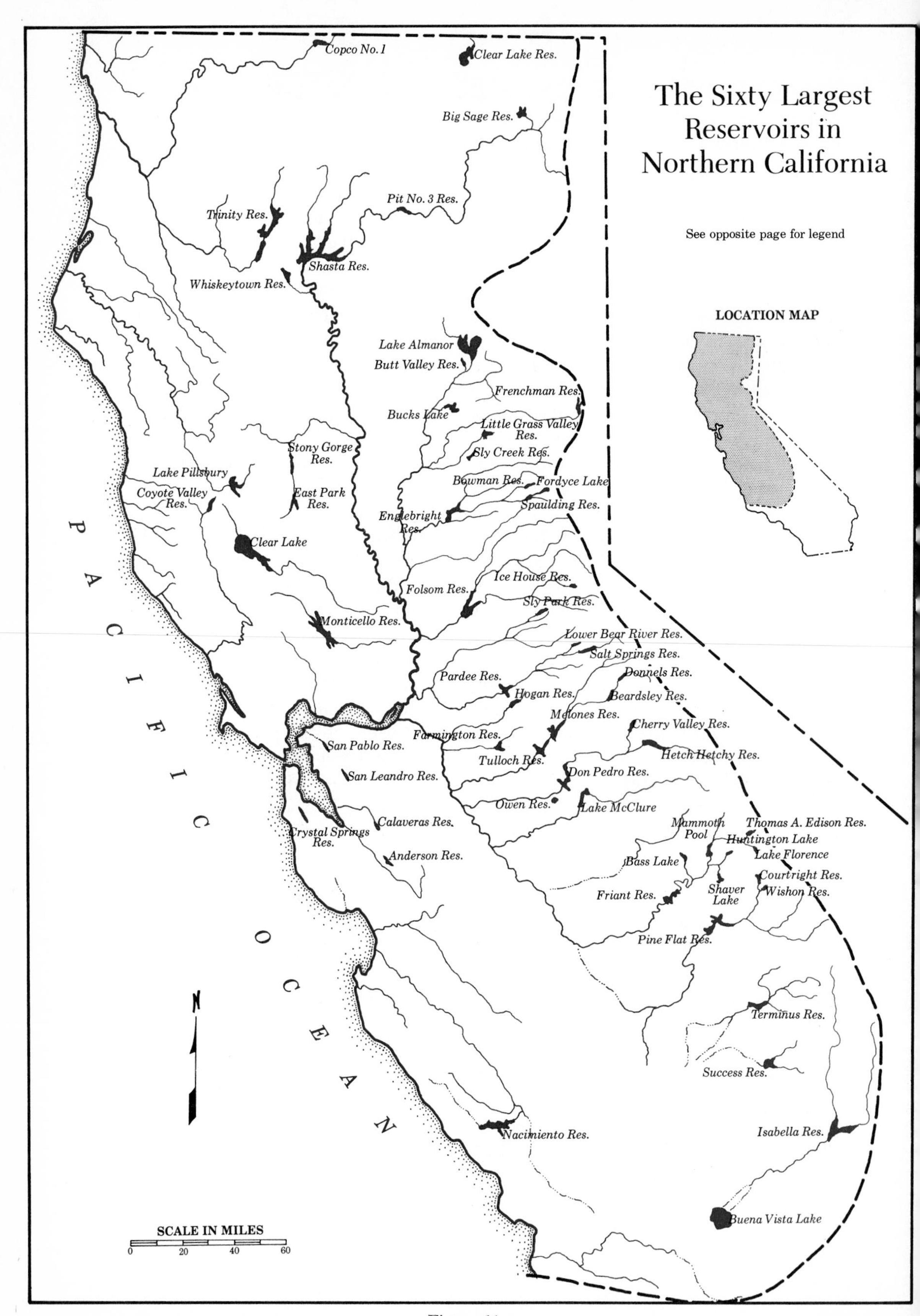

The Sixty Largest Reservoirs in Northern California
See opposite page for legend
LOCATION MAP
PACIFIC OCEAN
SCALE IN MILES
0
20
40
60
Copco No. 1
Clear Lake Res.
Big Sage Res.
Pit No. 3 Res.
Trinity Res.
Shasta Res.
Whiskeytown Res.
Lake Almanor
Butt Valley Res.
Frenchman Res.
Bucks Lake
Little Grass Valley Res.
Sly Creek Res.
Stony Gorge Res.
Lake Pillsbury
Coyote Valley Res.
East Park Res.
Bowman Res.
Fordyce Lake
Spaulding Res.
Englebright Res.
Clear Lake
Ice House Res.
Folsom Res.
Sly Park Res.
Monticello Res.
Lower Bear River Res.
Salt Springs Res.
Donnels Res.
Pardee Res.
Hogan Res.
Beardsley Res.
Melones Res.
Cherry Valley Res.
Farmington Res.
San Pablo Res.
Tulloch Res.
Hetch Hetchy Res.
San Leandro Res.
Don Pedro Res.
Owen Res.
Lake McClure
Mammoth Pool
Thomas A. Edison Res.
Huntington Lake
Lake Florence
Calaveras Res.
Crystal Springs Res.
Anderson Res.
Bass Lake
Courtright Res.
Friant Res.
Shaver Lake
Wishon Res.
Pine Flat Res.
Terminus Res.
Success Res.
Nacimiento Res.
Isabella Res.
Buena Vista Lake

Figure 11

Legend for Figure 11

Reservoir	Storage Capacity (Millions of acre-feet)
Bureau of Reclamation	
Shasta	4.49
Trinity	2.50
Monticello	1.60
Folsom	1.00
Clear Lake Res.	.53
Friant	.52
Whiskeytown	.25
East Park	.05
Stony Gorge	.05
Sly Park	.04
Pacific Gas and Electric	
Lake Almanor	1.31
Salt Springs	.14
Wishon	.13
Courtright	.12
Bucks Lake	.10
Lake Pillsbury	.09
Spaulding	.07
Butt Valley	.05
Lower Bear River	.05
Fordyce Lake	.05
Bass Lake	.05
Pit No. 3	.04
Corps of Engineers	
Pine Flat	1.00
Isabella	.55
Terminus	.15
Coyote Valley	.12
Success	.08
Farmington	.05

Reservoir	Storage Capacity (Millions of acre-feet)
Southern California Edison	
Shaver Lake	.14
Thomas A. Edison	.13
Mammoth Pool	.12
Huntington Lake	.09
Lake Florence	.06
Other	
Clear Lake	.42
Hetch Hetchy	.36
Nacimiento	.35
Don Pedro	.29
Lake McClure	.29
Cherry Valley	.27
Pardee	.21
Buena Vista Lake	.21
Melones	.11
Calaveras	.10
Little Grass Valley	.09
Beardsley	.09
Copco No. 1	.08
Big Sage	.08
Hogan	.08
Anderson	.08
Sly Creek	.07
Bowman	.07
Englebright	.07
Tulloch	.07
Donnels	.06
Crystal Springs	.05
Owen	.05
Frenchman	.05
Ice House	.05
San Pablo	.04
San Leandro	.04

although most of them provide dual or multiple products. Another eleven (heavily oriented to flood control) have dual purposes but do not produce electric power. Regulatory pressures may impose the consideration of added products in part of the thirty-one cases,[17] but they are not the primary concern of the owner-operators of the facilities.

Aside from the sixty largest dams, a number of somewhat smaller reservoirs with individual capacities ranging from 20,000 to 40,000 acre-feet fall in various categories. They have dual or single purposes and dual or multiple products. Among these are dams owned and operated by power companies, some for irrigation storage, and some for flood control. In addition there are a great many small dams

[17] See our Chapters 12 and 14.

in the region with no significant storage capacity, including those for power plants or irrigation storage and diversion weirs.

These figures on dams with single and limited multiple purposes raise questions concerning the extent to which they are operated to achieve the optimal mix of products, when these outnumber, or diverge from, their direct purposes. The great majority of storage dams in Northern California are owned and operated by electric utility companies, by local public water agencies interested primarily in securing irrigation or urban water supplies, or by coalitions involving local water agencies and electric utilities. In these cases, the dominant principle guiding streamflow regulation may be, respectively, maximization of power revenues; maximization, within economic limits, of irrigation or urban water supplies; or some sort of joint maximization of gains from power generation and the consumptive use of water. In any event, the controlling organizations are not motivated to create balanced time patterns of streamflow regulation which respond to the needs of all classes of users of the water.

Relation of storage capacity to runoff

The relation of the storage capacity of reservoirs to the mean annual runoff of streams in the major regions of Northern California holds the same sort of structural significance for the industry as the relationships developed in connection with Table 1. The ratio of storage capacity to runoff provides a rough index of the current physical potential for altering the natural time shape of this runoff. The greater the relative storage capacity, other things being equal, the greater is the alteration that can be made in the pattern of streamflow. Or, in the case of a reservoir storing water to be diverted, the more can the pattern of diversions differ from that of the natural inflow. Although simple statements of this sort are precluded as soon as inequalities are recognized among watersheds in variability coefficients of runoff and in evaporation from reservoirs, they nonetheless provide serviceable, although general, guidance.

Table 3 shows the relationships of reservoir capacities to annual runoff for each major region and for selected major streams within regions. We shall focus upon storage capacities contained behind the sixty largest dams, but regional storage capacities in all reservoirs are also shown as a check. Certain regional differences stand out in the table. Storage has been developed much more extensively in the San Joaquin Valley than in the Sacramento Valley, a reflection of the difference between the demand-supply balances already identified in the two areas. (The seasonal patterns of demand and natural runoff in the two valleys are relatively similar.) The San Francisco Bay and central coastal regions show a relation of aggregate storage capacity to runoff similar to that of the Sacramento Valley (although the capacity of the Bay and coastal regions is not behind large dams). But the much greater variability of flow of the coastal streams means that an equal relative capacity will accomplish less regularization of streamflows. Furthermore, about one-third of the capacity of the San Francisco Bay area serves as terminal reservoirs for imports of water and does not regulate local runoff to a significant degree. Finally, reservoir construction in the north coastal region has been pushed to a lesser level than in other regions. This is a clear reflection of the lower level of local consumptive demands.

TABLE 3
RESERVOIR CAPACITY IN RELATION TO MEAN ANNUAL RUNOFF, BY REGIONS AND SELECTED MAJOR STREAMS, 1962

Region and selected streams	Mean annual runoff (millions of acre-feet)	Reservoir storage capacity relative to mean annual runoff (percentage) 60 largest	All reservoirs
Sacramento Valley	22.4	43	48
Sacramento River[a]	5.7	81	
Feather River	4.6	36	
Yuba River	2.4	21	
American River	2.8	38	
Putah Creek	0.4	400	
Clear Lake inlets	0.5[b]	84	
San Joaquin Valley and Delta	11.3	50	62
Cosumnes River	0.4	11	
Mokelumne River	0.8	51	
Calaveras River	0.2	40	
Stanislaus River	1.2	29	
Tuolumne River	1.9	51	
Merced River	1.0	29	
San Joaquin River	1.8	62	
Kings River	1.7	72	
Kaweah River	0.4	38	
Tule River	0.1	80	
Kern River	0.7	109	
North coastal region	28.9	12[c]	13[c]
Klamath River[d]	9.0	7[c]	
Trinity River	3.9	70	
Eel River	6.3	2	
Russian River	1.6	8	
San Francisco Bay and central coastal regions	3.5	16[e]	46[e]
Total Northern California regions	66.1[f]	29%	35%

[a] Sacramento, Pit, and McCloud rivers at, and above, Shasta Dam.
[b] Maximum estimate of an uncertain total flow.
[c] Does not include important storage dams on Klamath River in Oregon.
[d] Excluding Trinity River, which joins the Klamath near its mouth.
[e] About one-third of the reservoir capacity of these regions is in terminal storage reservoirs, and about 20 per cent of the capacity stores water imported from the Central Valley.
[f] This figure is the sum of regional totals, which include runoff from rivers not listed in this table.

SOURCE: California State Water Resources Board, *Water Resources of California*, Bulletin No. 1 (1951); California Department of Water Resources, *Dams Within Jurisdiction of State of California, January 1, 1962*, Bulletin No. 17 (1962).

More surprising than the variation of relative storage capacity among regions is its variation among streams within the regions. The Sacramento River (augmented by the Pit and McCloud rivers) is rather fully controlled by major reservoir capacity equal to 81 per cent of the mean annual flow at the point of entrance to the Central Valley. But, in 1962, the almost equally large Feather River was controlled by major reservoir capacity equal to only 36 per cent of its flow, and the comparable ratios for the large American and Yuba rivers were only 38 and 21 per cent respectively. With the completion of the Oroville Dam, the ratio of major reservoir capacity to annual flow on the Feather River will rise to about 90 per cent. Nevertheless, a distinct imbalance in the degree of reservoir control of annual runoffs as among major rivers in the Sacramento Valley will still remain.

A similar imbalance is observed in the San Joaquin Valley. The rivers of this region, all flowing westward from the Sierra, are listed in north-to-south order in Table 3, from the Delta to the south end of the Tulare Lake Basin. Proceeding southward, there is both a general tendency toward an increasing degree of reservoir control of streamflows and a considerable variance in the degree of control of the five major adjacent rivers—the Stanislaus, Tuolumne, Merced, San Joaquin, and Kings.

Thus, while the broad patterns of regional development of storage capacity conform to the broad facts of the balance of demand and supply for surface water, the details of a river-by-river comparison may not. It is possible, of course, that such differences in the development of adjacent rivers might be consistent with a rational allocation of resources. The local concentration of demand might prove to vary more within each region (among rivers) than between regions, or differences in the cost characteristics of dam sites might explain the pattern. On the other hand, the possibility is raised by this evidence that important random elements or discontinuities have entered to create significant differences in the marginal productivity of storage capacity on adjacent rivers, and thus an inefficient allocation of resources. We are thus alerted to watch for patterns of conduct in the industry that might explain this allocation of storage capacity among rivers, as well as for patterns that might result from or reflect this imbalance.

Facilities for Transporting Water

In addition to dams and reservoirs, the other major man-made structures that are fundamental to the competition for water in Northern California are canals and aqueducts. The existing pattern of these works shows, more precisely than that for dams and reservoirs, the geography of competition in the water industry. The large scale of major canals and aqueducts relative to the rivers that they tap suggests what will be brought out more fully in Chapter 4: the relatively small number of water agencies drawing upon the typical surface source of water supply in the area. Furthermore, the length and layout of the major canals, and their dependence upon the force of gravity for conveyance, support our argument defending the traditional distinction between consumptive and nonconsumptive uses of water. The return flows from water that has been diverted for "consumptive" uses have little economic significance because the main aqueducts carry the diverted water such long distances from the natural channel and restore it to most streams so far below other competing diversion points.

Most of Northern California's water transportation facilities up to the present time have been located in the Central Valley. About 93 per cent of all diversions from surface flows and 91 per cent of all recoveries of ground water in Northern California occur in the Central Valley. Similarly, about 92 per cent of all man-induced transportation of water in the whole area originates in that region. Almost 91 per cent of it also terminates in the Central Valley; the only significant exports of water from the Central Valley are about 250,000 acre-feet a year which are carried to the San Francisco Bay area.[18]

The man-made media for the transport of water include very large and long canals or other aqueducts; local main canals and local feeder or lateral canals branching from them; users' irrigation ditches; and pipes of various diameters used to bring urban (and sometimes irrigation) water supplies to vicinities of use and to accomplish local distribution of such water supplies to users. The motive force employed to move water through all of these carriers is predominantly that of gravity. Diversion points on streams and the placement of wells are generally calculated so that they make as much use as possible of land surfaces sloping down toward areas of delivery. Some pumping, however, is employed in initiating and carrying out water transportation.

The costs of transit pumping can be high relative to other costs of capturing and carrying water, with the pumping costs mounting as the lifts increase. The costs of delivered water are thus significantly greater where substantial pumping lifts are necessary in the course of transporting water to points of use than where the main reliance is on gravity flows. For example, the delivered cost of water in the San Joaquin Valley tends to be higher on the western slope of the valley, which is appreciably elevated above the valley floor and not traversed by streams, than in the valley bottom or east of the bottom. And, on the average, a significant portion of the delivered costs of municipal water supplies is for local pumping.

The principal canals and other aqueducts of the area are shown in Figure 12. In the category of long aqueducts and those with large capacities, the two largest in Northern California are the Delta-Mendota Canal and Friant-Kern Canal, both operated by the Bureau of Reclamation as facilities of its Central Valley Project. The former extends for 113 miles from the Delta to the Mendota Pool, a major holding reservoir near the southern end of the San Joaquin River basin and close to the valley bottom. The Delta-Mendota, with an intake capacity of 4,600 cubic feet per second or 3.3 million acre-feet per year if it were operated continuously, carries about 1 million acre-feet of water annually from the Delta into the San Joaquin River basin, most of which may be viewed in the net as Sacramento River water. Approximately 85 per cent of this water arrives at the Mendota Pool for further distribution, the remaining 15 per cent being diverted to lesser canals en route. The movement of water in Delta-Mendota Canal involves a pump lift of

[18] Information supplied by the City and County of San Francisco and the East Bay Municipal Utility District. These figures do not take account of the planned diversion (not accomplished as this was written) of Trinity River water of the north coastal region into the Central Valley, which will amount on the average to roughly 1 million acre-feet a year.

about 200 feet from the Delta to higher lands draining into the San Joaquin basin, after which gravity takes over as a motive force.[19]

The Friant-Kern Canal, extending 153 miles southward along the eastern edge of the San Joaquin Valley from Friant Dam, has an intake capacity of 4,000 cubic feet per second or 2.9 million acre-feet per year, and also carries about 1 million acre-feet of water annually, from the San Joaquin River to the Tulare Lake Basin. Its gravity-actuated flow is spread through the Basin by about thirty main canals (and their laterals), which divert from it south of the Kings River. The Friant-Kern and Delta-Mendota canals together accomplish a major movement of water between sub-regions of the Central Valley, in which water of the San Joaquin River which would otherwise serve its basin is exported to the Tulare Lake Basin and is replaced by an equivalent amount of water imported from the Delta.

Other major canals operated by the Bureau of Reclamation include the Madera, Contra Costa, and Putah South. The Madera Canal, which runs for 36 miles north from Friant Dam, with an intake capacity of 1,000 cubic feet per second or 700,000 acre-feet per year, feeds part of the eastern side of the San Joaquin Valley with about 250,000 acre-feet of water annually. The Contra Costa Canal, which runs 48 miles from the Delta to the easternmost part of the San Francisco Bay region, has an intake capacity of 350 cubic feet per second and, in 1960, carried about 70,000 acre-feet of water. The Putah South Canal, which originates at the Monticello Reservoir in the southwest corner of the Sacramento River basin and can carry up to 200,000 acre-feet of water per year southward, largely irrigates land on the southwest corner of the Sacramento Valley and supplies urban water north of Suisun Bay. As this is written, the Bureau also is constructing Corning Canal in the upper Sacramento Valley, with a planned length of 26 miles and an intake capacity of 500 cubic feet per second (probable annual water diversion above 250,-000 acre-feet), and it proposes construction of a Tehama-Colusa Canal, which would parallel the Sacramento River on its west side for 121 miles and have an intake capacity of 2,000 cubic feet per second, suggesting an annual water diversion of perhaps half a million acre-feet. Both of these canals are designed to divert water directly from the Sacramento River.[20]

In addition to these Bureau of Reclamation canals, there are in the Central Valley a number of large "local" main canals, most operated by large irrigation districts. These canals, with individual capacities in excess of 1,000 cubic feet per second, are larger than all existing Bureau canals except the Delta-Mendota and Friant-Kern and are quite long. Details on such canals are shown in Table 4.[21]

[19] Bureau of Reclamation, *Annual Project History, Central Valley Project, op. cit.* (various years).

[20] *Ibid.* See also U.S. Department of the Interior, Bureau of Reclamation, *Delta-Mendota Canal, Technical Record of Design and Construction* (1959), and *Friant-Kern Canal, Technical Record of Design and Construction* (1958).

[21] Data underlying Table 4 and the related discussion have been drawn from a wide variety of sources. These include recent Annual Reports of the Central California Irrigation District, Fresno Irrigation District, Modesto Irrigation District, Richvale Irrigation District, and Turlock Irrigation District. They also include publications issued either by the California State Department of Public Works, Division of Water Resources, or by the California Department of Water Resources, as follows: Department of Public Works, *Report on Irrigation Districts in California, 1944–1950,* Bulletin No. 21–P (1951). Department of Water Resources, Division

Not listed in Table 4 are many other main canals, most in the Central Valley, which have smaller capacities and are frequently, but not always, somewhat shorter. There are about twenty such canals with intake capacities ranging between 250 and 1,000 cubic feet per second; annual diversions between 50,000 and 200,000 acre-feet; and length roughly from 10 to 30 miles. Distributed throughout the Valley, they are most heavily concentrated in the area of the Tulare Lake Basin, where they draw on the Kings, Kaweah, Tule, and Kern rivers. And, added to these are several hundred smaller and shorter main canals, including many with very small carrying capacities.

TABLE 4
CAPACITY AND LOCATION OF MAJOR IRRIGATION DISTRICT CANALS, CENTRAL VALLEY REGION

Operating irrigation district	Water source	Intake capacity (cubic feet per second)	Average annual diversion (acre-feet)	Approximate length (miles)
Glenn-Colusa	Sacramento River	1,700	750,000	65
Central California	San Joaquin River	n.a.	500,000	60
Modesto	Tuolumne River	2,000	250,000	45
Turlock	Tuolumne River	2,200	450,000	30
Merced	Merced River	1,700	400,000	17
Fresno	Kings River	1,500	250,000	30
Alta	Kings River	1,450	70,000	25

n.a. Not available.
SOURCE: Reports and documents listed in note 21 of Chapter 2.

Despite wide variations among regions and subregions of Northern California, we can make a few generalizations about the typical patterns of local canal systems. Where local main canals draw on streamflows or reservoirs on streams, as is usually the case, it is common for the canals to tap these flows upstream and upgrade from the principal intended vicinities of water use; to diverge from the stream; and then more or less to parallel any river tapped over distances usually ranging up to 60 or more miles. The canals usually are located from 2 or 3 to 15 miles away from the river, with distances between the canals and rivers either

of Resources Planning, *Report on Irrigation and Water Storage Districts in California, 1951–55, 1956–58, 1959, 1960,* Bulletin No. 21 (1956, 1959, 1960, and 1961); *Surface Water Flow for 1956, 1957, 1958, 1959, 1960,* Bulletin No. 23–56 through No. 23–60 (1957 through 1961); and *Kaweah River: Flows, Diversions, and Service Areas, 1955–60,* Bulletin No. 49–C (1961). Also, the Department's *Northeastern Counties Investigation,* Bulletin No. 58 (1960); *Land and Water Use in the Tule River Hydrographic Unit,* Bulletin No. 94–1 (1962); and *Colusa Basin Investigation,* Bulletin No. 109 (1962). Department of Public Works, *Report on 1956 Cooperative Study Program, Vol. 1* (1957); *Sacramento River Basin, 1931,* Bulletin No. 26 (1933); and *San Joaquin River Basin, 1931,* Bulletin No. 29 (1934). Among other sources are: California State Department of Engineering, *Water Resources of the Kern River and Adjacent Streams and Their Utilization, 1920,* Bulletin No. 9 (1921); U.S. Congress, House Committee on Interior and Insular Affairs, *Sacramento Canals Unit, Central Valley Project, California,* 83 Cong. 1 sess. (1953); and detailed large-scale maps drawn for use in preparation of this study by C. E. Erickson and Associates.

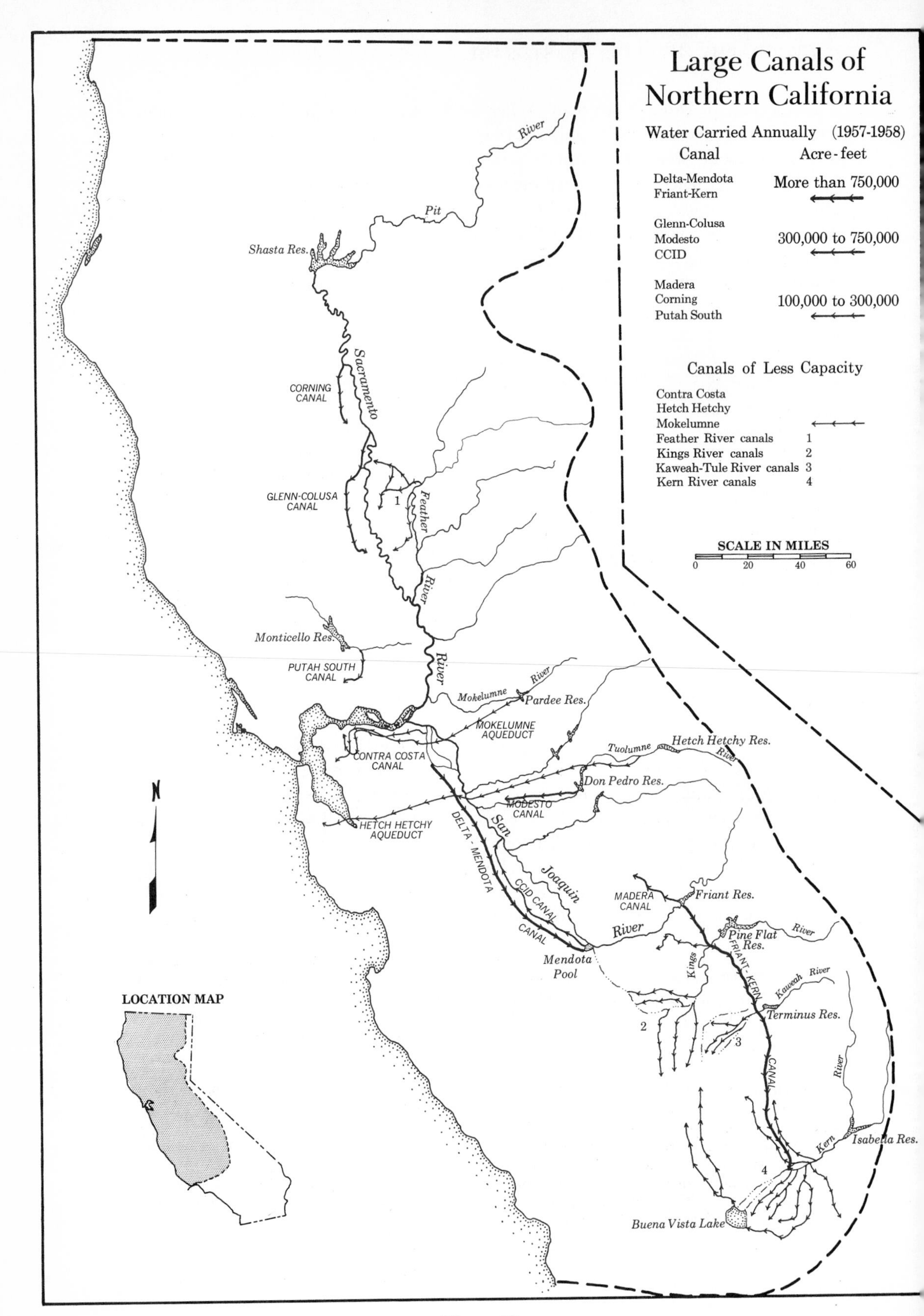

Large Canals of Northern California
Water Carried Annually (1957-1958)
Canal
Acre-feet
Delta-Mendota
Friant-Kern
More than 750,000
Glenn-Colusa
Modesto
CCID
300,000 to 750,000
Madera
Corning
Putah South
100,000 to 300,000
Canals of Less Capacity
Contra Costa
Hetch Hetchy
Mokelumne
Feather River canals 1
Kings River canals 2
Kaweah-Tule River canals 3
Kern River canals 4
SCALE IN MILES
0 20 40 60
Pit River
Shasta Res.
Sacramento River
CORNING CANAL
GLENN-COLUSA CANAL
Feather
Monticello Res.
PUTAH SOUTH CANAL
Mokelumne River
Pardee Res.
MOKELUMNE AQUEDUCT
CONTRA COSTA CANAL
Tuolumne
Hetch Hetchy Res.
River
Don Pedro Res.
MODESTO CANAL
HETCH HETCHY AQUEDUCT
DELTA - MENDOTA CANAL
San Joaquin River
CCID CANAL
MADERA CANAL
Friant Res.
Pine Flat Res.
Mendota Pool
Kings
FRIANT-KERN CANAL
Kaweah River
Terminus Res.
Kern
Isabella Res.
Buena Vista Lake
LOCATION MAP
N

Figure 12

increasing or remaining relatively constant as the canals proceed downstream. If a river flows into a closed basin or sink—as do the Kings, Kaweah, Tule, and Kern, for example—there is an added tendency to develop a radiating system of main canals which originate fairly near the lower end of the river and convey water in several directions toward the lower lands of the basin, and also perhaps to overflow or collecting pools in the basin's bottom. Where main canals divert water from principal aqueducts, such as the Friant-Kern and Delta-Mendota canals, their geographical pattern is generally influenced by the fact that big aqueducts are usually built to run at appreciable elevations above stretches of irrigable valley lands. Therefore, most local main canals that tap them will run downhill toward valley land, diverging from the aqueducts that feed them.

These patterns of distribution canals in the Central Valley go far toward explaining why the Northern California water industry can be viewed as a collection of entities competing for a scarce natural resource. As the typical river emerges from the foothills into the Central Valley, it encounters major canals with enough diversion capacity to intercept the whole streamflow during those parts of the year when a significant demand exists for agricultural water. The length of these canals, plus the extent of the local distribution systems which, in turn, divert water from the canals, means the water is carried substantial distances away from the natural river channel. Furthermore, whatever flows pass back into the channel often return some distance downstream—in many cases below the point where further significant diversions occur. The principal exceptions to this generalization, the lower San Joaquin River and Delta, by the same token, constitute the one portion of the Central Valley in which the water problem is rightly viewed as one of quality rather than quantity.

The foregoing discussion has centered on major aqueducts and main canal systems used primarily to transport irrigation water, with emphasis on the Central Valley. Some attention should also be devoted to the means for transporting urban water supplies. For most of the cities and towns of the area, such supplies are transported by pipelines from reservoirs or diversion points on nearby rivers or creeks, from local wells or well fields, and from aqueducts built by wholesale suppliers. Most of these pipelines are relatively short (5 to 10 miles up to 50 miles in length) and, compared to irrigation canals, relatively small in capacity.

The metropolitan San Francisco Bay region, however, depends for much of its urban water supply on two major aqueduct systems which transport water over long distances from rivers of the Sierra Nevada. One of these systems is operated by the City and County of San Francisco, and brings water to San Francisco and suburbs south of it from the Tuolumne River, a distance of about 150 miles. This system has a present capacity of about 180,000 acre-feet of water per year, or roughly 250 cubic feet per second, and as this is written is delivering about 100,000 acre-feet a year. (A proposed additional set of parallel pipelines would increase the present capacity by over 80 per cent.)[22] The other system is operated by the East Bay Municipal Utility District, and brings water from the Mokelumne River to

[22] City and County of San Francisco, Public Utilities Commission, *Annual Report, Fiscal Year 1961–62* (1962).

the east side of San Francisco Bay over a distance of about 94 miles. Its two aqueducts have a combined capacity of about 128,000 acre-feet per year under gravity flow and 205,000 acre-feet per year with pumping (or 177 and 282 cubic feet per second). Current deliveries of water are about 100,000 acre-feet per year. (A third aqueduct is under construction which will add about 94 per cent to total capacity under gravity flow, and about 77 per cent to capacity with pumping.)[23] The only additional imported urban water supply received in the San Francisco Bay area is part of the water carried in the Contra Costa Canal—one of the canals operated by the Bureau of Reclamation which was described above.

In addition to the major water transport facilities of Northern California, which have been referred to above, three new major aqueduct systems are planned or under construction as this is written. One is an aqueduct which will carry water from the new dams on the Trinity River through the Coast Ranges to the Sacramento River, in the amount of about 1 million acre-feet anually. Second is an aqueduct which will carry water southward from the Folsom Dam Reservoir on the American River to the east side of the San Joaquin Valley. Both of these are to be built by the Bureau of Reclamation as part of its Central Valley Project. The third is a major aqueduct system being built by the California Department of Water Resources. It will transport very large volumes of water from the Feather River via the Delta (upon completion of the Oroville Dam on the Feather) to the west side and south end of the San Joaquin Valley and to Southern California, and lesser volumes to such other areas as the San Francisco Bay area. The ultimate design and route of this aqueduct system is at present not yet fully determined, though most of the needed financing has been authorized and construction has begun. Therefore, at this time, any description of the transport facilities of Northern California's water should be viewed as an interim report.

This pattern of canal and aqueduct facilities raises certain questions about the structure of the water industry to be dealt with in subsequent chapters. It is evident that a very high concentration of sources of supply exists, in that few areas can receive water from more than one such means of conveyance. The significance of this concentration in the setting of the water industry will be considered in Chapter 4. Whether or not the observed large size and high concentration of long-distance transport facilities can be explained by economies of scale will then be considered in Chapter 6.

[23] *Official Statement of the East Bay Municipal Utility District, Alameda and Contra Costa Counties, Water Development Project for the East Bay Area Bonds* (Jan. 16, 1959).

3 

THE LEGAL FRAMEWORK OF THE INDUSTRY

An important part of any industry's structure consists of the framework of law within which it operates. This framework includes, first, the general law of the land concerning such things as the rights, powers, and freedoms of individuals; general constraints on individual actions; definition and content of private and public property; contracts; rights to incorporate and powers of corporations; private monopoly and restraint of trade; and so on. The second component specifically applies to the operations of the industry in question, including laws governing acquisition and use of the natural resources employed by industry; those establishing a public utility or other special regulation of firms operating in the industry; and those providing for public agencies to operate in the industry, conferring powers on them, and placing limitations on their activities.

In writing about an industry, we may ordinarily view the general law of the land, federal and state, as a part of its environment, and simply assume general knowledge of such law by the reader. But the special legal framework, if any, within which the industry operates deserves examination as a part of its particular structure. The legal framework, as a dimension of industry structure, may be a significant determinant of the conduct and performance of the producers and sellers of the industry. This is especially true in a water industry because the legal framework also contributes to the emergence of other aspects of the structure of the industry. In particular, it contributes to development of the public enterprise formed as a users' cooperative as the dominant form of producer organization; to the predominance of full vertical integration in such organizations; and to the substantial lack of markets through which these organizations can deal regularly with each other or with customers outside of their own constituencies.

In the United States, various regional water industries operate within special and complex legal frameworks. These frameworks are complicated because they are concerned with three interrelated matters: (1) property rights in the use of water, the definition and determination of which are intrinsically intricate; (2) the mode of creation and powers of public and private agencies which may engage in using, making available for use, and purveying water, and limitations on such agencies; and (3) public regulations of the use of water, including regulations governing the type and character of water resource development projects which may be undertaken. They are complex also because in any region they consist of an interrelated maze of federal, state, and local laws, including constitutional laws, statutes, administrative laws, judicial interpretations of various laws, and of common law as applied by the courts.

In California the legal framework of the water industry is especially complex. This results partly from the development in the state of an unusually complicated and somewhat ambiguous law of water rights, and from state laws which have permitted and encouraged the proliferation of a substantial variety of types of local public water agencies with a roughly corresponding variety of powers and purposes. Another complexity arises from a rather unusual role which the state of California has assumed in the water industry. The state legislature has since 1927 granted authority to a state administrative agency to file applications to appropriate rights to all surface water in the state to which proved rights have not previously been established by private parties or by other public agencies. This administrative agency has the right to hold such filings in trust for possible release or assignment to such parties and agencies in a manner consistent with a systematic and planned development of the water resources of the state.[1] California has also established a major state operating agency which—using water rights obtained under state-filed applications—captures, stores, transports, and sells water to local agencies, and also generates hydroelectric power and performs functions of flood control. This agency operates more or less parallel to the principal federal agency engaged in developing, using, and wholesaling water in California—the Bureau of Reclamation of the U.S. Interior Department.

Our discussion of the legal framework of the industry is necessarily brief. Applicable California statutes alone occupy a few thousand pages of fine print; a large number of federal statutes are involved; the number of state and federal court decisions interpreting or making relevant law is large and growing; and treatises have been, or could be, written on each of several main parts of the totality of law involved. We will attempt only to characterize the legal framework of the California water industry in broad terms, emphasizing the major outlines of that water law which has economic relevance, but neglecting much in the way of detail with respect to such law, as well as omitting reference entirely to numerous provisions of water law which have little significance for our analysis. Our emphasis, moreover, will be on the contemporary configuration of the law; only occasional and incidental reference will be made to subsequently altered historical configurations and to their past and present consequences.

This chapter will discuss, in turn, four major parts or bodies of contemporary law having a direct bearing on the water industry of Northern California: (1) the law of water rights; (2) the law affecting the establishment and operation of local public and private water agencies; (3) the law establishing and defining the powers of water development agencies of the federal and state governments; and (4) law regulating the use of water and governing the undertaking of water resource development projects. These four categories of law certainly are not mutually exclusive. For example, the full content of the California law of water rights is affected by the law governing the powers of local water agencies as holders of water rights, by congressional grants of powers to federal water agencies under

[1] California *Statutes* (1927), ch. 286. This power and its exercise are discussed further below.

the interstate commerce clause of the Constitution, and by regulations which attach conditions to the granting of water rights required for new water development projects. The existence of such interrelationships among the several categories of law will appear throughout the chapter, and also means that the treatment of the law of water rights will be incomplete until the end of the four main sections of this chapter. A fifth section will deal briefly with issues concerning the extent of servitude of federal water agencies to the California law of water rights and to connected regulatory law.

The Law of Water Rights

The most fundamental aspect of the law of water rights in California[2] is affirmed in basic constitutional and statute law and in applicable common law. This is that private individuals and companies, public agencies acting for and serving specific and limited constituencies of individuals, and municipal and state governments and the federal government acting for part or all of the general public of the region—all may acquire vested and perpetual property rights to the beneficial use of available surface waters and subsurface or ground waters wherever they may occur in their natural environment.[3] Such rights may be acquired most significantly for consumptive uses of water (such as for irrigation, industrial processes, or urban purposes), which involve the removal of water from its natural streams or underground basins and its employment so as to deplete the quantity available (or to cause deterioration of its quality) for some or all further immediate uses. Rights may also be acquired by private or public agencies for nonconsumptive uses of water such as the generation of hydroelectric power on streams, but rights to other nonconsumptive uses, such as recreation, generally cannot be acquired by private individuals except so far as their landholding may permit them to exclude others from enjoying such use.

In establishing rights to the consumptive use of any given water flow or supply of ground water, or to the nonconsumptive use of a flow for power generation, both private individuals and concerns and public agencies have the privilege of establishing water rights on certain alternative grounds and subject to certain conditions or specific restrictions. Given the necessary grounds and the fulfillment of the requisite conditions, all classes of potential claimants are *ab initio* equally privileged to secure water rights. There are, however, certain rules concerning the order of precedence of competing claimants for the same water. This order is determined primarily by the character of the grounds on which the claim is made. Private interests are inferior to public, in the main, only in that their rights may be condemned for public purposes. And within classes generally, members of any class

[2] This section draws heavily on the definitive work by Wells A. Hutchins, *The California Law of Water Rights* (1956). (This and other footnote references are cited in brief form when they are also included in the Bibliography.)

[3] See, for example, California *Constitution,* art. XIV, § 3; California *Civil Code* (1872), § 1422; California *Water Code* (1963); div. 2, pt. 2; *Lux* vs. *Haggin,* 69 Calif. 255 (1884); *Hewitt* vs. *Story,* 64 Fed. 510 (C-C-A. 9th, 1894); and *Katz* vs. *Walkinshaw,* 141 Calif. 116 (1902).

are subject to some rules of precedence among competitors who have equal privileges. Subject to these rules of precedence, private individuals have equal footing as claimants *inter se,* and the same applies to local public agencies and municipalities as a group. The federal and state governments have a special status, primarily by virtue of being able to acquire water rights on somewhat different and broader grounds; the federal government, however, has not often elected to exploit its special status in this regard in California.

These general precepts of law have operated in California throughout the historical development of the contemporary water industry, and their operation has had a fundamental and lasting influence on the present structure of the industry. To understand this influence, we must look first at the general grounds upon which it has been possible for the various categories of potential claimants to acquire water rights, and at the conditions they were required to fulfill and restrictions to which they were subject in acquiring them. At the same time we should give special attention to one aspect of the historical process of building the existing structure of water rights—the relatively recent points in time at which the federal and state governmental bodies undertook active roles in acquiring and exercising water rights, and at which the pattern of distribution of water rights in the state began to be appreciably less than completely dominated by an earlier accretion of a multitude of more or less autonomous individual and local actions to acquire and use water.

Water rights may be secured with respect to any water in its natural environment, as in streams and underground basins; but not to water that has been reduced to private possession and control, as through impoundment in a reservoir or having been taken into an aqueduct. Under California law, there are two basic types of water rights: (1) Rights are obtained by gaining ownership of land which is contiguous to (that is, bordering or overlying) a natural water supply. (2) Without need to rely on the preceding sort of land ownership, rights are obtained (a) by simply drawing water from a natural source of supply and regularly or continuously applying it (or delivering it for application) to a beneficial consumptive use, or (b) by using natural water for nonconsumptive purposes on a regular basis, as through the use of a streamflow for power generation. The first type are called "riparian rights" and "correlative ground-water rights"; the second, "appropriative rights." The fact that California recognizes two doctrines—the riparian and the appropriative—as governing water rights, and that these exist simultaneously and are often conflicting, has been the basis for describing the state as having a "dual system" of water rights.[4]

Riparian rights and correlative ground-water rights

Riparian rights are usufructuary rights to water inherent in a tract of land which borders on any stream or lake. They are primarily rights to capture and divert the waters of such stream or lake for beneficial consumptive use on the riparian tract of land, for private gain and without payment to others for the use

[4] See Hutchins, *op. cit.,* pp. 40–41.

of water.[5] Correlative ground-water rights comparably accrue to any owner of a tract of land which overlies a ground-water basin of "percolating waters" from which water may be drawn through wells, and, presumably, are rights to put such waters to beneficial consumptive use on the overlying land, again for private gain and without payment.[6] There are no special procedures to be followed or conditions to be met to secure and maintain riparian and correlative ground-water rights, other than the ownership of the requisite lands; they simply exist at law and may be protected against infringement by recourse to the courts. Owners of riparian and overlying lands thus enjoy a superior status in the hierarchy of those who may secure water rights.[7]

The extent of individual riparian and correlative ground-water rights—as measured in terms of the amount of water which the holder of a right may withdraw from the water source for consumptive use, and of the times of withdrawal during a year—is limited to the withdrawals of available supply required for reasonable beneficial use on the riparian or overlying tract.[8] In the event that there are competing holders of riparian or correlative ground-water rights to the same water source and that there is less than enough water available (in total quantity and at the desirable times) to satisfy the lawful claims of all holders of rights to the common source, any individual right is further limited by the requirement that all holders of rights must share equitably in the common water supply.[9]

The sum of all the minimal riparian rights for reasonable and beneficial water use of the waters of a given stream, or the correlative rights of overlying landowners to the waters in a given underground basin below their lands, generally has legal priority over appropriative rights which may be asserted to the waters of the same stream or underground basin.[10] That is, appropriative rights generally cannot be exercised to deprive the holders of riparian or correlative ground-water rights of waters required for reasonable and beneficial use on their riparian or overlying lands. If such adverse appropriations are made, the affected holders of riparian or ground-water rights can secure relief in the courts. In this sense, holders of riparian and overlying land rights, on the one hand, and appropriators, on the other, are unequal claimants for rights to water for consumptive use. The former generally enjoy superior status; the latter in general can legally establish and defend rights only to "surplus" waters of any stream or ground-water basin which are not required for

[5] *Lux* vs. *Haggin,* 69 Calif. 255 (1884). See Hutchins, *op. cit.,* pp. 178–256, as a general source on riparian rights in California.

[6] *Katz* vs. *Walkinshaw,* 141 Calif. 116 (1902). See Hutchins, *op. cit.,* pp. 418–514, as a general source on correlative ground-water rights in California.

[7] A public body, such as a city, owning riparian or overlying land can exercise a riparian or correlative right to use water on the land in question, but not to secure water to serve other lands lying within its jurisdiction. *Antioch* vs. *Williams Irr. Dist.* 188 Calif. 451 (1922).

[8] The limitation to "beneficial" use has applied over any relevant historical period, but riparian rights have been restricted to water required for beneficial uses which were also "reasonable" only since 1928 (by California *Constitution,* art. XIV, § 3), and even thereafter the added restriction has been subject to ambiguous interpretation by the courts.

[9] *Seneca Consolidated Gold Mines* vs. *Great Western Power Co.,* 209 Calif. 206 (1930); *Prather* vs. *Hoberg,* 24 Calif. (2nd) 549 (1949); *Hudson* vs. *Dailey,* 156 Calif. 617 (1909).

[10] The only clear exception is that appropriative rights established by diverting from a stream *on public lands* prior to the passage of competing riparian lands on the same stream to private ownership are superior to riparian rights derived by this passage.

reasonable beneficial use by the holders of riparian or overlying rights to the same water sources.[11]

Riparian and correlative ground-water rights may be "sold" independently of the land to which they attach to buyers who will use the water acquired on lands which are not adjoining the stream or overlying the ground-water basin in question, only in the sense that the seller waives objection to the buyer taking his water. The water to which a right is so acquired ceases to enjoy a correlative status with competing riparian or overlying rights to the same source of supply, the latter gaining priority over it and any non-riparian use being wrongful to other riparian owners.[12] Similarly, the holder of a riparian right may not use water secured under the right on non-riparian land, or sell water so secured for such use, without trespassing upon the rights of other riparian proprietors on the same stream.[13]

Because of the characteristics of riparian and correlative ground-water rights, the holders of such rights turn out mainly to be private owners of riparian and overlying lands. Intermediary agencies which engage in delivering water to constituencies or customers for use on lands which do not border or lie over the source of water ordinarily find the acquisition of riparian or overlying land a poor course in securing the requisite water rights. This is because of legal disabilities encountered with respect to the right if the water is not used on such land. Local public water agencies and private water companies perforce rely mainly on appropriative rights which are not subject to such restrictions, or on "prescriptive" rights (discussed below).

The federal government is potentially a powerful holder of riparian and comparable rights by virtue of its ownership of public lands. However, its public land policy as based on federal statutes has been not to assert or exercise such rights. Instead, the federal policy has been to permit the establishment of private riparian rights by disposing of public lands to others—generally private parties—and also freely to permit the establishment by private parties and public agencies of appropriative rights to waters flowing through public land. In acquiring water rights in California essential to its own operations in the water industry, the federal government has relied primarily on securing regular appropriative rights consistent with state law, on purchasing or condemning existing private water rights, or on entering

[11] Before 1928, the prior rights of riparian landholders were limited only to beneficial use ("reasonable" use not being required until that year) and "surplus" waters available for appropriation were consequently smaller and often potentially nonexistent. (A divergent line of case law held that a riparian holder could enjoin a non-riparian use irrespective of injury to him.) See *Herminghaus* vs. *Southern California Edison Co.*, 200 Calif. 81 (1926); *Miller and Lux* vs. *Madera Canal and Irrigation Company*, 155 Calif. 59 (1907). While the amendment to the state constitution in 1928 (see reference in note 8 of this chapter) restricted the extent of prior riparian rights to waters required for reasonable beneficial use, the term "reasonable" has an elastic meaning. The courts, in interpreting and applying this law in subsequent litigations, have frequently sought "solutions" to conflicts between riparian and appropriative rights which afforded holders of riparian rights access to some excess of water above what have appeared to be minimum reasonable amounts, or compensation if they were deprived of such an excess. See *Peabody* vs. *Vallejo*, 2 Calif. (2nd) 351 (1935); *U.S.* vs. *Gerlach Livestock Co.*, 339 U.S. 725 (1949).

[12] *Spring Valley Water Co.* vs. *Alameda County*, 88 Calif. App. 157 (1927); *Gould* vs. *Eaton*, 117 Calif. 539 (1897).

[13] *Moore* vs. *California Oregon Power Co.*, 22 Calif. (2nd) 725 (1943).

into contracts to exchange waters from different sources with the holders of existing rights. The government of the state of California does not occupy a significant position as a holder of riparian lands, but in recent decades has assumed a major role by reserving from appropriation rights nearly all otherwise unappropriated public waters in the state.

The great bulk of riparian and correlative ground water rights in the state are thus held by private landowners who usually exercise them for irrigation of their own riparian and overlying lands. The number of such owners, their identities, and the sizes of their individual holdings at the present time are necessarily the result of an accretion of autonomous historical incidents through which such titles have been acquired and subsequently transferred by sale or bequest. As a group, such owners enjoy a privileged status in being able to secure, without payment other than through land purchases, liberal use of a naturally free but economically scarce good in the form of the water, and in being able to exclude all others from the use of the water to which they hold rights.

The status of such owners is a matter of some consequence in an area where much of the arable land is naturally semiarid, and where the natural supply of water which may feasibly and economically be transported to most potential sites of use is clearly scarce relative to existing and prospective economic needs. One special category of landholders is placed in a superior position compared to other categories with respect to their ability to convert natural wealth into private wealth or income. Even more important, a system of water rights giving priority to owners of riparian and overlying land has a tendency to induce an inefficient or uneconomic allocation of the water supply. Scarce water may be used on riparian and overlying lands when it might be more beneficially used on the great remainder of lands. However, this tendency is partly mitigated by appropriations of water which is in surplus supply on the land for which rights are held. Owners of riparian and overlying lands are entitled to water (though frequently in liberally adequate quantity) only for use on their own riparian or overlying land—their riparian and correlative ground-water rights do not extend to water which they might sell or otherwise transfer to other landholders for use on dry lands. They are thus unable to distribute water claimed under such rights more widely over the land through selling it to owners of dry lands. Also their ability to transfer such water by selling their riparian or ground-water rights to others is impeded because they can transfer only a waiver of objection to the use of this water and not a correlative right as against competing holders of riparian or correlative ground-water rights to the same stream or ground-water basin. In this circumstance, they are enabled, and inclined, to retain more liberal allotments of water for their lands than appropriators can usually secure for dry lands.

Furthermore, neither they nor others can water more land on the basis of riparian or correlative ground-water rights by placing the tract of land for which rights are held under the same ownership as physically adjacent dry land; the quantity of water running to a riparian or ground-water right is not increased by adding dry land to the size of the continuous tract of land owned by the holder of the right. The area of land for which a riparian or correlative ground-water right is held cannot be increased by this or comparable means, from the time that the right initially came into being through establishment of private ownership of a riparian or overlying tract. However, the area covered by rights may be reduced if the holder of riparian rights sells parts of his land not physically adjacent to the stream. In the preceding context, it may be said that the tract for which riparian rights are held must be the smallest tract held in any single ownership in the chain of title leading to the present owner.[14]

In summary, there are limitations on extending the area of land covered by riparian or correlative ground-water rights, limitations on the sale of water secured under these rights or of the rights themselves, but a relatively bounteous apportionment of water to riparian and overlying lands. As a result, it seems likely that the operation of this system of rights favors the allocation of more water to use on riparian and overlying lands and less water to use on some other lands (primarily in agriculture) than would be ideal from the standpoint of securing a maximum net productivity from all available water. This is an arbitrary and undesirable result of arbitrary law. The tendency toward this misallocation of water has been mitigated in the past by the ability of owners of the other lands to secure water on the basis of appropriative rights (in part because surpluses remain after riparian and overlying claims are satisfied) or by establishing prescriptive rights. It may be further mitigated by other appropriations in the future; but, so far, it appears to be appreciably less than fully checked. Comparable misallocations of water as between the lands of holders of riparian rights on different streams—especially adjacent ones—may also be engendered by the exercise of the law of riparian rights if the riparian landowners on one river are more bounteously endowed with water than those on the other. The same applies to the allocation of water between owners of overlying lands which draw on different ground-water basins, and very definitely as between the owners of riparian lands and those of overlying lands.

Appropriative rights

Appropriative water rights, as already noted, have never been obtainable on the basis of ownership of riparian lands or lands overlying ground-water basins. Rather, they are obtained simply by the process of appropriating water for a reasonable beneficial use by reasonable methods, and then continuously or regularly applying the water, or delivering it for application, to such use. These appropriations, however, are subject to certain procedural requirements and minimal substantive regulatory conditions.

Appropriative rights to streamflows may be established in California by private persons or companies, by a variety of types of local public water agencies, by municipalities, and by the state and federal governments.[15] As established by private parties to water for their own use, appropriative rights become their own private property. If established by most intermediaries, such as local public agencies and private water companies, for the purpose of obtaining water for delivery to con-

[14] *Rancho Santa Margarita* vs. *Vail,* 11 Calif. (2nd) 501 (1938).
[15] California *Water Code* (1963), div. 2, pt. 2.

stituencies or customers, such rights are nominally the property of the intermediary agencies or companies. But the users to whom the water is delivered—whether the constituent voter-users who have established and control a public agency, other customers of such an agency, or the customers of a private company—acquire beneficial interests in the appropriative rights held by the agency or company, and these rights are considered to be appurtenant to the lands on which they use the water. Appropriative rights to surface water thus run ultimately to the users of appropriated water (typically private individuals or companies) and to the owners of the lands on which they use such water. Any appropriative rights established by the federal or state governments when acting as intermediaries in capturing water and delivering it to users are potentially subject to the same rule, depending upon the terms of contracts between the intermediaries and their customers. But filings of applications to appropriate made by the state, to be held in trust for unspecified future use, simply reserve rights in which only the citizens of the state as a whole hold a possessory interest.

The physical requirements for establishing an appropriative right to surface water are essentially the existence of an unfulfilled need for the reasonable beneficial use of water; the ascertainment of a source from which water can feasibly be diverted and transported to the location where this need for use occurs; the establishment of access to a site at which the water may be diverted from the source; the acquisition of a right-of-way for transporting the water; the construction of necessary facilities; and the delivery and application to use of the diverted water.

For the appropriation of streamflows, the legal procedures in essence are as follows. An application for the right must be filed with the California State Water Rights Board, describing the source of water to be appropriated, the site of diversion, the site of intended use, the nature or purpose of this use, the quantity of water to be used, the location and character of facilities, and so on. Public notice must be given of the application, and hearings held if there are any protests.[16] If the Rights Board grants the application, it issues a permit to begin construction of needed works.[17] Upon satisfactory completion of the construction project and the initiation of use of the water in question, the Board issues a license which confirms the appropriative right of the applicant to divert such quantity of water as is being applied to beneficial use.[18] Approval by the state authority is required at each stage of the procedure. To maintain the right, the appropriator must continuously or regularly use the water to which the appropriative right applies; failure to use the water for a period of three years results in loss of the right.[19]

The principal substantive legal conditions which must be fulfilled to secure a license to appropriate water are essentially that: (1) the claimed need for reasonable and beneficial use of water in a stated amount exists; (2) the project is feasible and not illegally injurious to others, except so far as they may be compensated for injury; (3) there is apparently a "surplus" supply of water from a

[16] California *Water Code* (1963), §§ 1300–1380.
[17] *Ibid.*, §§ 1375–1464.
[18] *Ibid.*, §§ 1600–1677.
[19] *Ibid.*, § 1241.

specified source to which prior rights do not exist, in sufficient quantity to satisfy the reasonable needs of the appropriator.[20] That is, appropriations may be made only of water in excess of the requirements (for reasonable beneficial use, as judicially construed) of the holders of existing riparian and appropriative rights (but existing permits or licenses to appropriate which are not being exercised through beneficial use or preparation therefor are not deducted in determining this excess). In addition, the project must meet such terms and conditions as in the judgment of the State Water Rights Board will best serve the public interest.[21]

In granting an appropriative right, however, the state does not generally determine in detail the aggregate of existing prior rights or the existence and size of a surplus supply of water. Consequently, any appropriative right it grants does not guarantee immunity to all adverse claims. Holders of prior riparian rights or prior appropriative rights may proceed for relief in the courts to upset an appropriative right which they claim would deprive them of water to which they are legally entitled, and their claims are subject to adjudication.[22] Riparian rights are generally superior to appropriative rights;[23] and senior (earlier) appropriative rights, to junior ones.[24]

Some crucial questions concern the transferability of an appropriative right to surface water to effect a change in the place of use of the water acquired under the right—particularly a change in the land to which such water is applied for irrigation. Such questions arise in cases where the holder of the right attempts either to shift the water to use on other lands while still retaining the right or to sell the right, or the water secured thereunder, to another party for use on other lands. Each license to appropriate surface water specifies, in addition to a quantity of water, a point of diversion and a place and type of use, and the licensee is correspondingly restricted in exercising his appropriation. Moreover, the appropriative right, as noted earlier, becomes appurtenant to the land on which the use of water is made under the right,[25] and an appurtenant water right passes with sale of the land to the buyer as an appurtenance thereto.[26]

Despite the numerous legal impediments to transferring water secured under an appropriated right to another place of use, such a right is not strictly inseparable from a given tract of land. The law provides that a licensee may change the point of diversion, place of use, or purpose of use of water secured by appropriation only with the permission of the State Water Rights Board. To do so, the licensee, as a petitioner, must establish, and the Board must find, that the change will not

[20] *Ibid.*, §§ 1200–1203, 1240–1242, 1300–1355.

[21] *Ibid.*, § 1253.

[22] *Ibid.*, §§ 2000–2900.

[23] Excepting appropriative rights established on public land prior to the emergence of competing riparian rights through the conversion of riparian lands to private ownership.

[24] Prior to 1872 in California, appropriative rights to water were acquired by fulfilling simpler but similar procedural requirements under the common law, and the substantive requirements for establishment and successful defense of such rights against prior or superior claimants were essentially the same, except that then (and until 1928) riparian rights were not limited to water required for "reasonable" beneficial use.

[25] *Senior* vs. *Anderson,* 138 Calif. 716 (1903); *Cave* vs. *Crofts,* 53 Calif. 135 (1878); *Crooker* vs. *Benton,* 93 Calif. 365 (1892).

[26] *Alta Land & Water Co.* vs. *Hancock,* 85 Calif. 219 (1890).

operate to the injury of any other water user who depends on the same watershed.[27] This is more than a nominal requirement in the light of the typically interrelated interests of diverters from the same stream. Thus there is potentially a significant legal impediment to changing the place of use of water secured under appropriative right. If the hurdle can be surmounted, the appropriator can shift water obtained under his right to use on other land, either while retaining title to the water or by selling or exchanging it.

Similar impediments stand in the way of the sale of an appropriative water right to a buyer for use on other land. The holder of a water right may sell part of the land to which the right is appurtenant without the water right, and still reserve the entire right to obtain water for use on the unsold part of the land.[28] But, apparently, he can effect a sale of part or all of his appropriative water right for use on other land only through a process in which the State Water Rights Board grants to the purchaser a new license; and the new license would be granted only on the Board's finding that the change in place or type of use, plus any related change in point of diversion, would not injure any other water user dependent on the same local source. Moreover, sale of a water right by verbal agreement has been held to effectuate an abandonment of his right by the appropriator, leaving him nothing to sell.[29] At the least, sales of appropriative water rights, or of water secured under such rights for use on other lands, are very difficult to accomplish.

There are other reasons why there is not a generally free and continuous process of reallocation of appropriated water among different lands, even though such reallocations are made discretely and sporadically over time. Development of this process is impeded because the application for an appropriative right is initially made by, or for, a specified group for use on specified lands; because the needs of these lands for the appropriated water are likely to persist over time, unless substitute water supplies are secured; and because the original users and their successors have beneficial interests in the appropriative rights held by an intermediary serving them with appropriated water (and cannot be deprived of such water without their consent unless compensated). All act as impediments to the emergence of a process of continued reallocations of appropriated water "to the highest bidders" or toward lands where its net productivity is greatest, and they prevent the development of anything approximating an open market for appropriative water rights. Whereas water acquired under appropriative rights is not quite so fully tied to given tracts of land as is water secured under riparian rights, it is so bound in substantial degree.

In the preceding discussion of appropriative rights to streamflows, the express or implicit reference has been to appropriations for consumptive uses away from streams, such as irrigation and domestic and industrial use. Appropriative rights may also be acquired, and usually are, for the essentially nonconsumptive use of streamflows in transit for the generation of hydroelectric power. Irreconcilable conflicts between the exercise of rights held for power generation and of those held

[27] California *Water Code* (1963), §§ 1700–1706.
[28] *Stanislaus Water Co.* vs. *Bachman,* 152 Calif. 716 (1908).
[29] *Griseza* vs. *Terwilliger,* 144 Calif. 456 (1904).

for the consumptive use of the same water do not ordinarily arise, since power generation usually is not strongly adverse to consumptive uses. However, restrictions may be placed on the way appropriative rights to use water for power are exercised in order to protect downstream interests. For example, power producers may be required to schedule releases of impounded water so that streamflows will be maintained in a manner which does not impair the rights of downstream users—the latter being afforded administrative and judicial protection of their rights as against the power producers.[30]

The operation of hydroelectric facilities may also impair the rights of the general public to the nonconsumptive use of streamflows for fishing and other recreational purposes. If this is the case, individual citizens do not have the right to assert competing claims against the appropriations of power generators. The state and the federal government, however, can intercede as representatives of the general public in protesting such appropriations or in insisting on limited restrictions on the manner in which they are exercised,[31] on the ground that the public has prior rights to the nonconsumptive use of streamflows which would be unduly infringed by proposed appropriations.

The legal requirements and restrictions applying to the appropriation of ground water for use on lands which do not lie over the ground-water basin are similar to those described above for streamflows. Ground waters may be appropriated for use on such lands by persons, companies, public agencies, and governmental bodies. Both the general physical requirements and implied legal requirements are the same as in the case of streamflows, and the substantive legal conditions in large part are the same. Overlying landholders have prior rights to the waters of an underground basin, to the extent of their needs for reasonable beneficial use; only waters which are surplus after these needs have been fulfilled may be appropriated. The appropriator must serve himself or others on lands not overlying the basin, and the appropriated water must be put to reasonable beneficial uses. The appropriator is restricted in the quantity of his appropriation to the amount of water required for such uses.[32]

The major difference between the establishment of appropriative rights to streamflows and to ground water is that for ground water there are no procedural requirements at law, such as for applying to a state authority, publishing notices, and securing licenses. All an appropriator of ground water need do is withdraw water from an underground basin; convey it to a location of use; and apply it to reasonable beneficial use or deliver it for such application by others. He thus

[30] This protection is afforded in provisions for protests (and hearings thereon) of applications to appropriate water filed with the California State Water Rights Board, and by similar protest and hearing procedures prior to the licensing of projects by the Federal Power Commission, as discussed in a later section of this chapter dealing with regulation of the use of water.

[31] See California *Fish and Game Code,* §§ 5901, 5931, 5933; California *Water Code* (1963), § 1243; 48 U.S. *Statutes* 402 (1934); 72 U.S. *Statutes* 563 (1958)—as discussed below in the section on public regulation of water use.

[32] *Katz* vs. *Walkinshaw,* 141 Calif. 116 (1902); *Pasadena* vs. *Alhambra,* 33 Calif. (2nd) 908 (1949); and see Hutchins, *op. cit.,* pp. 418–76.

acquires an appropriative right, subject to action in the courts by owners of overlying lands, who may allege that he is depriving them of water to which they have prior right. An appropriative right to ground water is thus more or less firmly established only after the appropriator has successfully defended himself against all actual and possible valid court actions of the holders of correlative ground-water rights with whom he may compete for water. If he is unsuccessful in such defense, he loses, or does not have, his appropriative right.

Because of this situation, in a context wherein appropriative rights are unsupported by any administrative approval or licensing, the amounts of water to which ground-water appropriators have rights (as well as the amounts to which overlying holders have correlative rights) remain continually undetermined in the great bulk of cases. Thus, although appropriative ground-water rights may be sold, and locations of water use changed with or without sale, the development of markets in which ground-water rights are sold or exchanged is very seriously impeded because appropriators and prospective buyers typically are not sure of the extent of the right which might be conveyed. This limitation operates to a degree also on the salability of appropriative rights to water of any stream, which, though licensed, are not proved until an adjudication in the courts of all rights to the stream, or until all rights are settled by agreement.

Prescriptive rights

We have seen so far that water rights are obtained in California primarily in two basic ways—by the ownership of riparian land or land overlying ground-water basins, and by the appropriation of water for beneficial use. In these, we find a basic dichotomy of rights—with riparian rights and correlative ground-water rights being generally prior and superior to appropriative rights. These are the only basic water rights obtainable, aside from "pueblo rights" derived from Spanish law, which have minor and unimportant application in California.

There is, however, a third way to obtain water rights. And the rights so obtained make up a broadly significant category of water rights—one which has been important in the historical development of the contemporary structure of the Northern California water industry. These rights are called "prescriptive rights." The manner in which such rights are obtained is by the "prescription" of waters belonging to others under riparian, correlative ground-water, or appropriative rights through the "adverse use or possession" of such waters for a period of five years. The use or possession must be adverse in the sense that such use has deprived the original holders of rights of the use of their waters to an appreciable extent, by excluding the right holders from using these waters during the times at which they have had the right to use them (and this—at least until 1928—regardless of whether the original right holders attempted to exercise their rights to such an extent as to experience actual deprivation during the period of time in question). While prescriptive rights are significant, we have not classified them as "basic" because they are in essence obtained by capturing and converting to new ownership existing basic water rights.[33]

The physical requirements for establishing a prescriptive right to water (involving access for diversion, rights of way, works and, so on), as well as the legal requirements implied by the physical ones, are comparable to those involved in establishing appropriative rights. There are no procedural legal requirements. The substantive legal requirements are: (1) that the diversion and use of the waters to which the prescriptive right pertains be adverse to parties which have prior rights to the water; (2) that the use be actual, open, and notorious, without attempt at concealment; (3) that the use continue for five years, whenever needed by the adverse user; (4) that the party developing a prescriptive right openly assert his right to the use of the water; (5) that he pay any taxes that may be assessed against the water rights he is infringing; and (6) that the rightful owner does not interrupt or proceed to interrupt his use of the water being diverted over a five-year period by physical means, by successfully demanding interruption, or by bringing court action. If these requirements are fulfilled by the prescriptive claimant, then the diversion and use of water (which were unlawful for the five years during which this took place) cease to be unlawful as against the injured parties; the prescriptive claimant acquires a prescriptive right as against the parties whose rights he has invaded, and this right is superior to theirs. Essentially, the riparian, correlative ground-water, or appropriative rights of others have changed ownership and become the prescriptive right of the adverse claimant. This prescriptive right then is entitled to full satisfaction from the available water before the displaced holders of other rights can claim water from the source invaded.

Prescriptive rights cover specific quantities of water, rather than correlative shares. The quantity of water which can be claimed under a prescriptive right is limited to the amount used throughout the statutory period of five years, and also to the amount which can be put to reasonable beneficial use.[34] If the amount claimed is enlarged during the period or subsequently, the added amount must itself be used for five years before a prescriptive right to it is obtained. Prescriptive rights can be obtained both to streamflows and to ground water, although prescriptions of streamflow have been historically much the more important in California, and prescriptions of riparian rights much more important than those of appropriative rights.[35]

The adverse claimant who obtains a prescriptive right may be in essence a sort of unlicensed appropriator, who fulfills the conditions for obtaining a prescriptive

[33] Prescriptive water rights are secured under the general common law of adverse possession, as construed specifically with respect to water in statutes and court decisions. See Hutchins, *op. cit.*, pp. 298–348, and especially California *Code of Civil Procedure,* § 325; *Crandall* vs. *Woods,* 8 Calif. 136 (1857); and California *Civil Code,* § 1007.

[34] *California Pastoral and Agricultural Co.* vs. *Madera Canal and Irrigation Co.,* 167 Calif. 78 (1914); *Northern California Power Co., Consolidated* vs. *Flood,* 186 Calif. 301 (1921); *Pabst* vs. *Ferrmand,* 190 Calif. 124 (1922).

[35] The condition that an appropriative right must be exercised in order to be retained (not applicable to riparian rights) operates to encourage action by appropriators which will automatically forestall prescription.

right without necessarily fulfilling all legal requirements for establishing an appropriative right. But the adverse claimant may well be, and historically often has been, one who has fulfilled all legal conditions for claiming an appropriative right, and whose asserted appropriative right "ripens" into a prescriptive right through open and adverse use for a period of five years or more of waters to which others might rightfully lay claim. Historically, this process of converting asserted appropriative rights into prescriptive rights has been active, and has affected access to a very important share of natural streamflows in Northern California.[36] It has been, moreover, a rather automatic process, wherever the holders of basic riparian rights did not intervene during the statutory five-year periods over which prescriptive rights were established, because of the similarity of legal procedures and conditions for appropriation and for prescription.

That appropriative rights could be, and in very numerous instances were, converted to or ripened into prescriptive rights has historical importance for two reasons. First, the ultimate status of an appropriative right is uncertain until fully tested in the courts, in the sense that it can be upset by the court action of holders of prior riparian rights, correlative ground-water rights, or senior appropriative rights by establishing the fact that their prior rights have been infringed by the contested appropriation. In California prior to the amendment of the state constitution in 1928, moreover, it was clearly open to question whether most asserted appropriative rights to streamflows could be perfected by successful defense in the courts. Until then, the prevailing judicial view was that holders of riparian rights on any stream had a superior claim to all waters of the stream needed for beneficial use, without the condition that the use, or method of use, be reasonable. This generally was equivalent to saying that the holders of riparian rights were entitled to the use of the full natural flow of the stream to any extent required for beneficial use on riparian lands.

Because the extent of these requirements, as judicially construed, could be very large relative to natural streamflows, appropriations of substantial amounts of water from streams could be, and if contested would be, viewed as infringing riparian rights; appropriative rights very often probably could not be defended fully, if at all, against the court actions by holders of riparian rights. The appropriation of streamflow for use on lands not contiguous to the stream thus faced serious, if not precisely defined, legal barriers. But by having their asserted appropriative rights ripen into prescriptive rights, appropriators obtained legally secure rights, and could assure themselves or the users they served of a continuity of supply of water. Many asserted appropriative rights in effect became prescriptive rights in the historical process of the development of water use in Northern California. The recognition of the prescriptive doctrine by California courts provided a broad avenue for circumventing the barrier which their co-recognition of the priority of riparian rights placed in the way of distributing water widely over non-riparian lands; and it is credited with facilitating a much more balanced early

[36] See Hutchins, *op. cit.*, p. 323; Lucien Shaw, "The Development of the Law of Waters in the West," *California Law Review*, X (September 1922), 443–60.

development of agricultural and other economic activity in the region than would otherwise have been obtained.[37]

There is a second advantage from converting appropriative into prescriptive rights, assuming that both cover the same amount of water and are equally valid and defensible at law. The prescriptive right is superior to competing riparian or correlative ground-water rights, and is entitled to satisfaction in the allocation of water ahead of such competing rights, but appropriative rights are not. This advantage was rather widely exploited by appropriators prior to 1928, and that exploitation is fully reflected in the contemporary structure of historically accumulated water rights in California.

Prescriptive rights to surface water are subject to substantially the same requirements and limitations affecting changes in place of use or point of diversion, and affecting sale for this or other purposes, as those, described in the previous section, that govern appropriative rights.[38] A special restriction, however, is that prescriptive rights may not be obtained against public agencies, whose appropriative rights (and others, if any) are thus better protected by law than are water rights in general.[39]

The law's impact on allocation of water rights

From what has been said so far about the historical development of the water-using economy in Northern California and the operation of the law concerning riparian and correlative ground-water rights, some misallocation of water might be expected. Misallocations between riparian and overlying lands, on the one hand, and dry lands, on the other, as well as among different tracts of riparian and overlying lands, would result both from the comparatively generous water rights attached to particular parcels of land settled in the early days and from legal barriers to change. This tendency to misallocate rights evidently has been considerably mitigated, but not entirely overcome, by the establishment of appropriative and prescriptive rights to water for use in watering lands in general. We now look at some consequences of the historical operation or application of the California law of water rights as a whole, including the law pertaining to appropriative and prescriptive rights.

[37] Since the adoption of the 1928 state constitutional amendment, the ability of appropriators to obtain prescriptive rights has been somewhat less important. Not only did that amendment restrict the rights of holders of riparian rights to waters needed for reasonable beneficial use, but also water "surplus," after satisfying these needs, was defined (though not measured) and declared subject to legal appropriation. Furthermore, though rights to waters not in surplus can still be obtained by prescription, surplus waters are evidently subject to prescription only after the party asserting prescription has obtained a permit and license to appropriate the same waters from the State Water Rights Board. See Gavin M. Craig, "Prescriptive Water Rights in California and the Necessity for a Valid Statutory Appropriation," *California Law Review,* XLII (May 1954), 219–42. This point is still debated, however, as indicated by *obiter dicta* in *Hudson* vs. *West,* 47 Calif. (2nd) 823 (1957).

[38] *Cheda* vs. *Southern Pacific Co.,* 22 Calif. App. 373 (1913); Hutchings, *op. cit.,* pp. 335–38.

[39] California *Civil Code,* § 1007.

As noted in the preceding sections, rights to water obtained by appropriation and prescription are more or less attached to particular parcels of land. They are attached to the lands of those who acquire the rights in order to secure water for their own use; or of the water users served by intermediary firms or public agencies acquiring such rights initially. Any such right is ordinarily appurtenant to the lands of the initial users of the water secured under the right; and, in addition to several legal impediments to transferring the rights to other lands, a further deterrent is that such users must generally surrender their claim to beneficial interests in the right before some or all of the water secured may be shifted to use on other lands. There are definite legal and natural obstacles to breaking the bonds which attach appropriative and prescriptive rights to particular tracts of land. And these ties are reinforced when the intermediary agency holding the rights, as is very often the case, is a local public agency representing a limited constituency of landholding water users.

Historically, the law of water rights in California, including that which concerned appropriative and prescriptive rights, provided a congenial framework for the local development of local water resources for local uses. In each of a great many localities in Northern California, individual holders of riparian and overlying land put local streams and ground water to their own use. Similarly, and more important, many individual holders of dry or under-watered lands appropriated local waters for their own use and established appropriative or prescriptive rights to such waters; numerous private companies secured similar rights to serve water users in various localities; and numerous groups of individual landholders in such localities formed public agencies to secure appropriative and prescriptive rights to water for use by members of the groups. Since neither the federal or state governments nor massively financed private enterprise intruded into the field of water development, for a long time these resources were mainly developed by a large number of local interests for local uses. Correspondingly, rights to the uses of a substantial proportion of locally available natural waters in many areas with good agricultural lands were distributed among numerous individuals and intermediary public and private agencies, with each right either firmly or quasi-firmly attached to a particular local tract of land.

The acquisition of appropriative and prescriptive water rights by progressively increasing numbers of individuals and local firms and agencies went on at random through a long series of mutually autonomous local moves to acquire water and water rights. This process took place, moreover—and still does—in the absence of any efficacious regulatory power to control the allocation of water in the interests of economic efficiency, or to limit individual water rights so as to direct incremental supplies to uses with the highest productivity.

Given the potential rigidities we have identified in allocations of water rights under California law, we might expect this historical process of "settlement" upon the region's water resources to result not only in their development, but also in fixing their allocations for long and sustained periods of time. Thus, we would expect that the uses and places of use which were the first claimants to water in Northern California would tend eventually to become "overwatered" as the rigidities of water law discouraged transfers to subsequently developing uses and places of use, even though the productivity of water were higher for such new uses and locations. Because of their greater resistance to transfer, we would expect riparian and correlative ground-water rights to place a special stumbling block in the way of correcting allocative distortions, and appropriative rights to erect a somewhat smaller, but substantial, barrier. We would expect relatively little resistance to transfers of water from one use to another when it remains appurtenant to land that is simultaneously transferred—as when suburbs take over land formerly devoted to agriculture. But there would be a tendency for all other types of transfer to face substantial impediments, and transfers to uses for which independent water rights cannot be legally established (for example, navigation and in-stream recreation) would be blocked in the absence of intervention by public regulatory authority. Finally, because transfers of water rights are subject to legal protest by third parties threatened with external effects associated with changes in places of use, we would expect greater difficulty to be encountered in effecting transfers of rights to water from a source drawn upon by many users than from one serving few users. These predictions will be tested in Chapters 9 and 12.

The Law Affecting Local Water Agencies

The essential exercise of water rights to bring surface and ground waters to consumptive users and to make nonconsumptive use of water by power generation (as well as the regulation of water flows and their destinations) is accomplished in California, as we have emphasized, by many public and private organizations. It is carried on preponderantly, except for hydroelectric power generation, by a variety of types of public agencies; and their formation is provided for in a large number of legislative enactments—most those of the state of California.[40] A body of statutory and common law defines and limits the powers and functions of the several significant types of private water agencies.

These laws, taken together, form an integral part of the total legal framework of the water industry of the region. Such laws not only determine who can do what to make water available to users; also, by granting powers to, and imposing limitations on, various types of private and public water agencies, they implement the basic law of water rights, give it operational content and meaning (or complete its meaning in practice), and sometimes modify it by either intensifying or ameliorating its restrictive impact on the allocation of water among uses and users.

In briefly considering here the law affecting all types of water agencies, we first turn to all types of local agencies, public and private, which are established, and possibly regulated, under state law. We do not undertake here a detailed description of their functions; this is done in Chapter 4. However, we draw two broad functional distinctions, by classifying the agencies according both to the types of

[40] The state laws are usually general ones providing for the formation of different classes of local agencies, but some types of local agencies are established individually by specific pieces of legislation, as was the California Department of Water Resources and predecessor agencies. The principal federal legislation establishing water agencies and granting them powers is that concerning the Bureau of Reclamation of the U.S. Department of the Interior and the U.S. Army Corps of Engineers.

water users they supply (agricultural, urban, or both), and to their general degree and pattern of vertical integration. These distinctions appear especially relevant in the consideration of the economic impact of applicable law.

The multiplicity of the types of California's local water agencies and their specific or primary functions, and the corresponding multiplicity of different statutes providing for their establishment and differing powers, make it especially difficult to prepare a satisfactory condensed description of the law affecting water agencies in the state. Our broad-brush depiction of the general framework of the law in question emphasizes not only generalizations covering numerous different types of agencies (though these generalizations may be subject to exceptions in the case of individual types of agencies), but also the broad provisions of the law having widespread economic implications rather than legal technicalities concerning precise powers of, and limitations on, agencies.

At present, general enabling statutes in California provide for the formation of fourteen classes of local public districts which have, or may have, the supplying of water for use as a primary function; in addition, special statutes providing for the formation of specific districts have created in effect two main classes of local districts similarly engaged in water supply. Added to these are numerous municipal water departments, and, outside the public realm, there are a great many private water suppliers in the form of individual proprietorships, mutual water companies, and privately owned public utility companies. This listing omits, moreover, ten more classes of "water" districts, provided for by general statutes, which are not engaged at all, or are only incidentally engaged, in supplying water, and three similar types of district that have been created individually by special statutes—none of which are considered in the following discussion.[41]

Classifying agency types according to the water service they provide is difficult and may be misleading because each of most types has some members which provide only one specific kind of service, and others which provide only one different kind of service, and, perhaps, still others which provide two or more types of service. Thus, if an agency type is classified as supplying both irrigation water and urban water, this may be taken to mean that the category includes some agencies which specialize in one sort of water service and some in another, or that all or most agencies in the category provide two or more sorts of service, or both. With this brief caveat, we offer the following classification of types of local water agencies in California according to the nature of predominant water service offered; there is no distinction of agency types according to whether or not they generate electric power:[42]

[41] The districts so omitted from discussion here include the following provided for as classes by general statutes: county drainage districts, levee districts, protection districts, reclamation districts, recreation and park districts, resort districts, soil conservation districts, storm drain maintenance districts, storm water districts, and water replenishment districts. Special enactments have created individually numerous county flood control districts, and a few county storm drainage districts and conservation districts, which we also will not discuss. (See California Department of Water Resources, *General Comparison of California Water District Acts* (1958); and California *Water Code* (1963), divs. 11–20.)

[42] Information drawn from California *Water Code* (1963), divs. 11–14, 16, 20, providing respectively for irrigation districts, county water districts, California water districts, water storage districts, county waterworks districts, and municipal water districts; California

A. *Types of agencies predominantly or entirely engaged in supplying irrigation water*
   1) Irrigation districts
   2) California water districts

B. *Types of agencies engaged to significant degree in supplying both irrigation water and urban water*[43]
   3) Individual proprietorships
   4) Mutual water companies
   5) Privately owned public utilities
   6) Water storage districts
   7) Water conservation districts
   8) Water storage and conservation districts
   9) County water districts
   10) Flood control and water conservation districts
   11) County flood control and water conservation districts
   12) County water authorities
   13) County water agencies

C. *Types of agencies predominantly or entirely engaged in supplying urban water*
   14) Municipal water departments
   15) County waterworks districts
   16) Public utility districts
   17) Community service districts
   18) Municipal water districts
   19) Municipal utility districts
   20) Metropolitan water districts.

The nomenclature used in giving a title to a type of local public agency is sometimes an accurate indication of the general kind of service it predominantly supplies (for example, municipal water department, irrigation district, municipal utility district); sometimes an ambiguous indication of agency service (California water district, county water district, public utility district); and sometimes mis-

---

Government Code, Title 6, div. 2, § 61,000 ff., providing for community services districts; California *Statutes* (1943), ch. 545, providing for county water authorities; California *Statutes* (1931), ch. 641, providing for flood control and water conservation districts; California *Statutes* (1927), ch. 429, providing for metropolitan water districts; California *Public Utilities Code,* div. 7, §§ 15501 ff., providing for public utility districts; California *Statutes* (1927), ch. 91, providing for water conservation districts; and California *Statutes* (1941), ch. 1253, providing for water storage and conservation districts. County water agencies and county flood control and water conservation districts are provided for in numerous individual legislative acts, such as the Contra Costa County Water Agency Act [California *Statutes* (1957), ch. 518], and the Marin County Flood Control and Water Conservation Act [California *Statutes* (1953), ch. 666]. Proprietorships, mutual water companies, privately owned public utility companies, and municipal water departments are established under the general laws of the state, and utility companies and some mutual companies are subject to general regulatory provisions of the California *Public Utilities Code.*

[43] Numbers 11 and 13 in this listing are individual districts established by individual legislative enactments.

leading (county flood control and water conservation district—often significantly involved in wholesaling or re-wholesaling water for consumptive use and, to some extent, in capturing water for use).

Technical provisions of laws affecting local water agencies

The laws governing private water agencies are relatively simple. Individual proprietors operate as such under the general law governing such proprietorships. Privately owned public utilities engaged in the water industry are established under general laws governing private corporations in the state; they are especially restricted in that (1) they generally must acquire franchises to provide service to defined areas (or to generate and distribute hydroelectric power to such areas) and (2) the rates they charge for customer services are regulated by the California State Public Utilities Commission. Mutual water companies can be formed as nonprofit cooperative enterprises by any number of landowners as a means of banding together to secure and distribute a common water supply; they are governed by their shareholders (usually the landowners in question). These mutual companies are not subject to public regulation unless they regularly supply water to customers who are not members, in which case they may be regulated as public utilities.[44] None of these three types of private agencies is governed by public elections, though mutual companies are governed by the votes of their shareholders, and none has any taxing power. Of the group, only privately owned public utilities (plus individuals in some cases) have powers of eminent domain, as well as the general powers to issue bonds granted to private corporations as a group; the bonding power granted to mutual companies is limited because they cannot mortgage the lands of their shareholders.

The laws governing the establishment of local public water agencies, their powers, and the limitations placed on them—or their customers or constituencies—contain provisions touching on numerous matters. Many of these provisions are more or less technical, routine, and legalistic, and have little economic significance except so far as they furnish legal implementation for the creation, financing, control and management, and operation of public water agencies. Some broad patterns of technical legislative provisions which apply to such local public water agencies as a group, or to subgroups thereof, are shown in this rough summary:[45]

1) All types have been granted general corporate powers (to enter into contracts to construct works, to buy and sometimes sell water, make purchases and sales, carry out their own construction programs, operate their works, sue and be sued, and so on). The grant is usually by general legislative enactment providing for a type of agency, but occasionally by specific enactments establishing specific agencies, and in the case of municipal water departments runs from the powers of the municipality.

[44] *Yucaipa Water Co. No. 1* vs. *Public Utilities Commission,* 54 Calif. (2nd) 823 (1960).
[45] See California *Water Code* (1963), divs. 11–20; also other statutes listed as sources in note 42 of this chapter.

2) Practically all types have powers of eminent domain and can condemn property as needed for designated uses, subject to a few limitations.[46]

3) All types have the power to incur bonded indebtedness, by issuing either general-obligation bonds or revenue bonds or both. In all cases, the floating of a bond issue must be approved at an election by the member landowners or other eligible voters of the district, by a simple majority or by a two-thirds majority, as is usual in the case of general-obligation bonds.

4) All types have, directly or in essence, the power to levy taxes on their constituencies—generally, both for servicing and retiring bonded indebtedness and to cover other expenses; in a few cases, only to service and retire bonds; and, in two cases, only if revenues are inadequate in spite of a general mandate to try to cover all costs from charges and tolls. Establishment of, and changes in, tax rates may require approval by the eligible electorate.

5) Nearly all types have the general power to fix charges or tolls for the delivery of water or of other services.

6) In all but four of the types noted, there are provisions in general laws for elections at which the member landowners or other eligible voters approve or disapprove establishment of proposed districts, elect boards of directors, approve or disapprove bond issues, approve or disapprove annexations to districts or consolidations with other districts, pass on tax rates, and so on. The usual rule in election is that of one vote per eligible person in the district and simple majority rule, but there are exceptions. The two principal exceptions are a common provision for a two-thirds vote to approve a general-obligation bond issue, and, in several types of districts, the basing of voting power on the assessed value of lands owned in the district. Also some types of districts—mainly large "overlay" organizations with important intermediary functions in purveying water to smaller local public agencies or widely dispersed landholders, and including county flood control and water conservation districts and county water agencies—are established to date individually by individual legislative enactments. Even in the case of these districts established by special legislation, however, bond elections generally must be held.

7) Operating control of most types of districts is vested in elected boards of directors or trustees or supervisors of specified numbers. In three types of agencies (county waterworks districts, county flood control and water conservation districts, and county water agencies), county boards of supervisors exercise direct control; municipal water department managements may be appointed. In most types of districts, board members are elected at large within any district; but in several types of agencies, including overlay agencies, the board of directors is elected so as to give representation to each geographical division or constituent agency which the district serves.

8) Provisions for both voluntary and involuntary dissolution of most types of agencies, under specified circumstances, are contained in the various general laws establishing agency types. California water districts are not permitted voluntary

[46] No specific provision for eminent domain is made in the legislation providing for county waterworks districts.

dissolution, and the dissolution possibilities for particular types of agencies established by special legislative enactment are not clear.

9) As to supervision of agencies, the bond issues of irrigation districts must be approved, after investigation and analysis, by the Districts Securities Commission; other types of agencies in general may voluntarily seek certification of their bond issues by the Commission.[47] Most types of local districts engaged in retailing water to users (as well, perhaps, as in capturing and transporting it) operate under the general overseeing powers of county boards of supervisors. Such boards must examine and approve plans for delineation and establishment of the districts, plans for works, later exclusions, inclusions, consolidations, and so forth. In the case of municipal water departments, the city government is the overseeing or controlling instrumentality. The California Department of Water Resources exercises certain supervisory functions (parallel to those ordinarily exercised by county boards of supervisors) in the case of several types of agency. Four types of districts—municipal utility districts, metropolitan water districts, county flood control and water conservation districts, and county water agencies—enjoy a large measure of autonomy from control at a higher level once established.

10) There is a wide variety of provisions concerning the functions which different types of agencies may legally perform in capturing or delivering water or both for consumptive use and in doing things indirectly connected, or totally unconnected, with purveying water for use. Hydroelectric power generation and/or distribution (in some instances limited to wholesaling) is permitted to municipal water departments, irrigation districts (only a few produce power), county water districts (wholesale only), public utility districts, community service districts, municipal water districts, municipal utility districts, water storage districts, and possibly some others—in every case in conjunction with the purveying of water for use. As to other related and auxiliary functions of agencies purveying water, irrigation districts can engage also in reclamation, drainage, and flood control; county flood control and water conservation districts in addition to their more obvious functions (plus water wholesaling), can manage ground-water basins and engage in ground-water replenishment programs. The widest range of powers is afforded to two types of utility districts—public utility districts and municipal utility districts. Such districts not only can purvey water and supply electric power; they generally can provide telephone, transportation, heat, sewer, and other services (all usually to urban users). Community service districts have a comparable range of powers, except that they cannot supply electric power or heat.

Substantive provisions of laws affecting local water agencies

In addition to the technical provisions of the law affecting local private and public water agencies, other provisions have, or may have, significant direct economic impacts on the allocation of water among uses or users and different areas of land,

[47] California *Water Code* (1963), div. 10.

as well as on the efficiency with which available water supplies are exploited. These substantive provisions establish and constrain the manner in which water agencies implement the law of water rights and imbue it with operational meaning. They deal with such matters as the following:

1) Procedures employed in, and especially substantive rules governing, the delineation of districts or the service areas of private concerns or individuals at the time districts are formed or service areas established, with emphasis on the type and flexibility of criteria for inclusions and exclusions of territory and water users.

2) Procedures and substantive rules affecting additions of territory to a district or service area, as well as exclusions of that which was previously included.

3) Procedures and rules affecting consolidations of public agencies.

4) Restrictions or conditions placed on water agencies, or on their constituencies or members in the case of public districts, with regard to supplying water to "outsiders"—that is, to persons and lands which are not included in given districts or service areas.

5) Scope of sources of water supply, with emphasis on the distinction between integrated supply secured by obtaining water rights and purchases of water from others.

These provisions, as applied and observed in practice, are crucially important in the industry's primary undertaking: capturing and distributing water for consumptive use. In the context of the existing law of water rights, they strongly influence the range within which economic misallocations of water may occur and be perpetuated, the extent to which misallocations that are hypothetically possible under the law of water rights may be reduced or ameliorated, the degree to which maximum efficiency in the exploitation of available water is attained, and, finally, the extent to which development of a free market is precluded while insularity among different water agencies and user groups is encouraged.

The first four kinds of legal provisions are most significant for their effects on fully integrated water agencies engaged in obtaining water rights, capturing water, performing all intermediate functions prior to retailing, and finally delivering water at retail to given lands and given users. As such, these agencies are typically intermediaries in conveying water to, and in exercising water rights for, designated constituencies or customers and designated land areas; in the case of public agencies, they act in a way similar to users' cooperatives for given user groups. Thus, the delineation of the areas they are established to serve, the possibilities for altering such areas, and any limitations on their supplying outside areas are all quite important influences on the allocation of water among users as well as on efficiency in exploiting available water.

This and the following propositions hold more for agricultural than for urban agencies, more for integrated retailers than for local wholesalers or re-wholesalers, and least of all for nonintegrated retailers. Nevertheless, all types of water agencies other than individual proprietorships—including the so-called local agencies—clearly have the generic attribute of providing devices for local groups of users to cooperate in order to secure both water rights (generally of an appurtenant variety) and water supplies derived from these rights or rights held by others for common use. And they do this in situations where individuals acting separately ordinarily could not accomplish such aims. Broadly construed, therefore, water agencies are ameliorative devices affecting the operation of the law of water rights, in that they make it possible to obtain rights for development and distribution of water among the memberships of numerous local groups of users who would be ineffective if not banded together for joint action to attain a common goal. Some hypothetically possible extreme strictures on access to water inherent in the law of water rights are thus by-passed through the use of water agencies; in addition, the cooperative efforts implemented by water agencies make possible financing, construction, and operation of various physical facilities which could not be done by the ordinary individual user or landowner.

As already noted, the preceding is true not only of all types of public districts, but also of private agencies other than individual proprietorships. Privately owned public utility water companies act for customers in service areas in acquiring water rights and providing works, and must dedicate the water they purvey to public use—generally the use of a given constituency of landholders or residents of a defined service area.[48] And mutual water companies could certainly be classed as nonprofit cooperatives of individual persons or landholders banded together primarily to secure rights for, and provide common water supplies to, memberships of shareholders.

The ameliorative effects of water agencies generally in exploiting the law of water rights deserves emphasis. This, however, is only one side of the coin. For, although local water agencies generally are required to dedicate the water they secure to public use, the dedication need not be, and typically is not, to the public at large—that is, to all citizens of California. Ordinarily the dedication is primarily to some part of the public—some designated constituency or customer group or land area—and there are generally no legal obligations for the water agency to serve the public at large, nor to broaden its constituency except at the discretion of its directorate and constituency.[49] Limited constituencies acquire senior beneficial interests in the water supplies, and in effect, the equivalent of water rights appurtenant to their lands where agencies hold rights. As a result, within broad limitations, they may preclude outsiders (on other lands, in other areas) from sharing in the water supplies secured by their representative agencies.[50] In addition, in the case of many types of agencies, there are significant legal barriers to the transfer of water supplies to outsiders, either by the water agency or by its constituent members.[51] Thus, these ameliorative effects often are severely tempered by

[48] 53 Calif. Juris. (2nd) 38–39.

[49] *Ibid.*

[50] This is made clear with respect to the constituencies of irrigation districts, for example, in California *Water Code* (1963), §§ 22259–22261, even though the *Code* provides that district members and other customers do not actually acquire water rights (§ 22262). It is true generally for the customers of public and private agencies, under the California law of utility responsibility and under comparable *Code* provisions protecting constituent customers of other classes of public water agencies.

[51] As regards irrigation districts, see California *Water Code* (1963), §§ 22251, 22259, 22261. These restrict the sales of water to outsiders to "surplus" water, limit powers of assignment of water by member-customers to assignment within the district, and provide that "nothing in this article authorizes the sale of any water right."

the operation of the appurtenant rights doctrine, by a restricted judicial definition of dedication to public service, and by various legal restrictions of varying degrees of severity on conveyance of water outside the district. This general legal situation favors insularity on the part of numerous different local agencies and is unfavorable to the development of a free market in water. By the same token, the creation and perpetuation of economic misallocations of water and of inefficiencies in exploiting available water supplies are engendered.

In the light of this general background, we may now turn to an examination of these substantive and procedural provisions as they relate to specific sectors in the water industry.

In the irrigation sector, there are three main types of public agency and two of private organization which are primarily, or to an important extent, engaged in retailing water. In the public sector, irrigation districts are by far the most important type in the region, and almost entirely engaged in supplying irrigation water; California water districts also specialize in irrigation water, and county water districts supply both irrigation and municipal water in significant volume. In the private sector are privately owned public utilities and mutual water companies; both, as types, supply urban as well as irrigation water, though the latter in larger total volume.

To these five types of public and private agencies, a general motif of law applies, expressly or in effect, to the initial delineation of territories and customers served, to the revision of initial delineation by subsequent inclusions and exclusions or by consolidations, and to the ability of an agency to sell to outsiders. In brief:[52]

1) The proposal for the formation of a public district, for the delineation of the territory it should serve, and for the water it should provide is originated by petition of self-organizing local groups of landowners or citizens, subject to no important restrictions on the size of the group or on the location or size of the territory to be served. It is only necessary that the citizen petitioners represent a specified minor percentage of the eligible electorate or of the assessed land value within the proposed district. In the private sector also, local initiative is not subject to important restrictions. A privately owned public utility may simply take the initiative in offering water to a service area it designates and apply for a franchise from the Public Utilities Commission of the state; and any group of landowners may voluntarily band together to form a mutual water company, subject to no particular restrictions. A sort of catch-as-catch-can local initiative, relatively unrestricted, is relied upon to set in motion the process of forming the agencies which are to retail the bulk of irrigation water sold in the region. Proposals for forming agencies or providing works to supply irrigation water at retail are thus voluntary on the part of local landowner groups or private firms. In addition, such groups or firms are implicitly vested with broad discretion in proposing delineation of the territories and customers to be included in their districts or service areas.

2) Petitions to form public districts of this sort must be reviewed—generally

[52] As regards public districts, see California *Water Code* (1963), div. 11, pts. 2, 11, 12, applying to irrigation districts, and comparable parts of div. 12 and div. 13, applying to county water districts and California water districts.

by county boards of supervisors and, in some cases, also by the California Department of Water Resources; and, for initial approval and submission of the proposal to the electorate, certain conditions must be met. But these conditions are rather loose and imprecise, allow considerable latitude in the permissible delineation of districts, and vest broad discretionary powers in the reviewing authorities. Thus, those forming an irrigation district are required mainly to include a body of land susceptible of irrigation by the same set of (proposed) works from a common source,[53] and to exclude lands which would not benefit from water purveyed by such works.[54] The same general rule applies to California water districts, and to county water districts (which need not include the whole territory of a county). Mutual water companies may be formed and delineated without review by higher authority or subsequent regulation, unless they provide public utility service to outsiders. Privately owned public utilities seem to be restricted in delineating areas for water service (by the Public Utilities Commission) mainly in having to identify some area needing water, showing it has water to supply the area, and demonstrating the feasibility of the works plan.

Local initiative, combined with loose rules for delineation of districts or service areas and with the implicit grant of broad ranges of discretion to local landowner groups or firms and to reviewing agencies, thus can lead to the development of a haphazard or capricious pattern of local agencies supplying irrigation water—a pattern with probable adverse effects both on the allocation of water among lands, uses, and users, and on the efficiency of the exploitation of water resources. This is particularly true for types of local retailing agencies which typically rely for most, or all, of their water supplies on their own water rights, which are fully integrated from capture of water through retail delivery, and are in various ways restricted from supplying water to users outside their districts or service areas. And this retailing group includes most irrigation districts and almost all mutual water companies and privately owned public utilities. County water districts and California water districts, to the relatively minor extent that they engage in integrated operations, are similarly affected.

3) Subsequent inclusions and exclusions of territory are provided for all three types of public districts in the irrigation sector. But these changes are voluntary, originate through local initiative (usually by landowners seeking inclusion or exclusion), and are largely discretionary on the part of the boards of directors of districts and their constituencies. Local voluntarism and broad ranges of local discretion are thus reiterated in the matter of revising boundaries of these public districts. In the private sector, mutual water companies apparently are free to extend their territories if this does not infringe on the vested interest in water rights of existing mutual shareholders, and they may implement exclusions, both without higher supervision. Privately owned public utilities are permitted to extend their water service areas only if the extension would not shorten the water supply of users within the existing service areas. Exclusions require approval of the California Public Utilities Commission, and good cause must be shown.[55] In general,

[53] California *Water Code* (1963), § 20700.
[54] *Ibid.*, §§ 20840-20846.
[55] See, for example, 57 *PUC Opinions and Orders* 586 (1957).

for these agencies retailing irrigation water, inclusions and exclusions, under the law, are sharply restricted, as a device for rationalizing the allocation of water among lands and users or for securing enhanced efficiency in exploiting water resources—although in some degree they may be able to accomplish these things.

4) Provisions for consolidations of public districts or private companies follow the same general pattern, except for California water districts, for which consolidations are not provided. The permitted consolidations of public districts are voluntary on the local level and subject to the discretion of district boards of directors. Mutual water companies evidently can consolidate with each other, as can privately owned public utilities, but again the pattern of local voluntarism and discretion is prominent. Thus, no positive device for rationalizing allocation of irrigation water or improving efficiency is provided by consolidations either, though they have occasionally accomplished something along this line.

5) For both public and private agencies retailing irrigation water, there is a general pattern of legal restriction on the ability of an agency or its members to sell water (or transfer water rights) to users outside the given district or service area, or to other districts. These restrictions are especially significant impediments to the development of free water markets as devices for rationalizing water allocation so far as fully integrated agencies holding water rights (as distinct from agencies which purchase water at wholesale) are involved. This applies to most irrigation districts, mutual companies and privately owned public utilities, and for some part of the operations of California water districts and county water districts.

The general pattern of legal restrictions on outside sales by public districts is set forth in the law governing irrigation districts. They exist primarily to supply water only to members, being empowered to sell the outsiders only "surplus" water, and then on contracts running for no more than three years.[56] The members of the district in essence acquire preferential rights in a public service, which is to say that the water rights held by a district become effectively appurtenant to its members' lands. District members cannot assign their water rights to outsiders.[57] The property, including water rights, of an irrigation district is held in trust for the membership, and the district has been created primarily for the improvement of lands within its boundaries. Aside from delivering water outside the district to fulfill obligations incurred in acquiring water rights,[58] the definition of surplus water which an irrigation district can sell to outsiders is sufficiently flexible that a district is easily discouraged from selling water to other individual users or other districts which would be willing to pay more than its marginal value to the district's own members. Rules of the same general sort apply to California water districts and county water districts. Moreover, there is one strong major deterrent to regular sales of water by a district—whether surplus or not—to outsiders: if it continues to do so it incurs a public-service responsibility to continue water service to these outsiders indefinitely, thus impairing the water rights of its members in a way which may be hazardous in the face of instability in annual water supplies.

[56] California *Water Code,* §§ 22250–22257, 22259.
[57] *Ibid.,* § 22251.
[58] *Ibid.,* § 22258.

Privately owned public utilities purveying water legally provide a service dedicated to the public use of the customers in an initially established service area. The recipients of water in such an area may demand continued performance of this service, and essentially acquire vested rights to service from a public supply. The utility thus cannot make outside sales or extend its service area at the expense of reducing the water supply of established customers, nor can it sell its water rights without their consent. Again, effectively, only surplus water may be sold outside an established service area.

Mutual water companies may occupy either of two positions with respect to outside sales. Often, mutuals have charter provisions which make their water rights appurtenant to the parcels of land held by the shareholders, and these rights are transferable only by sale of the land along with the water shares. Outside sales are effectively precluded. Frequently, however, mutuals are set up in which the shareholders may sell their water outside within some limited service area, or in which the mutual company itself may sell to outsiders. But in the latter instance, the mutual is exposed to being declared a public utility, and as regards its outside sales becomes subject to the limitations imposed on privately owned public utilities.[59]

Viewing the restrictions on outside sales by retailers of irrigation water as a whole, it is clear that there are very substantial legal impediments to the development of free water markets as devices for rationalizing the allocation of such water among lands and users. Arbitrary misallocations resulting from the processes of delineation and redelineation of districts and service areas under the governing laws are not easily corrected by the outside sale of water by districts retailing water. These impediments are very important so far as fully integrated operations are involved, either entirely or in part. It is not suggested that these barriers are theoretically or legally insuperable; but, in practice, they seem sufficient in combination with other considerations[60] to preclude the development of anything approximating free markets for the irrigation water secured under rights held by and captured by retailing agencies.

In the foregoing discussion, insularity, in contrast to water transfers through free market dealings, is emphasized—this insularity being combined with a rather haphazard pattern of delineation of districts and service areas which is not readily self-correcting. None of the preceding, however, should be construed as discounting the substantial contribution of the agency types in question as devices for exploiting the law of water rights to secure common irrigation water supplies for numerous groups of local users and for apportioning such supplies equitably within such groups.

Of some interest, in the light of the significance of the integration (as opposed to nonintegration) of water rights and capture by irrigation-water retailers, is their ability at law to purchase water at wholesale. They may buy the water either from several types of local "overlay" agencies or from very large water-supplying agencies such as the U.S. Bureau of Reclamation, the Army Corps of Engineers, and

[59] *Yucaipa Water Co. No. 1* vs. *Public Utilities Commission,* 54 Calif. (2nd) 823 (1960).

[60] Important contributing considerations, but in themselves not sufficient considerations, include the disparate locations of water sources and of service areas, the specialization of transport facilities to given routes, and the high cost of transporting water.

the California Department of Water Resources. All three types of local public agencies—irrigation districts and the California and the county water districts—are empowered to purchase water from the Bureau or the Corps, and generally also from local overlay agencies. (All of the local overlay agencies act in part as re-wholesalers of Bureau, Corps, or Department water.) At present irrigation district operations are in large part fully integrated. However, a significant minor proportion of the irrigation districts in Northern California contract to acquire their entire water supplies at wholesale from the Bureau, and a number of others supplement their integrated supplies with similar contract purchases from the Bureau or from other wholesale suppliers. California water districts and county water districts, on the other hand, rely mainly on purchases from the Bureau, the Corps, or local overlay agencies—thus assuming the role of nonintegrated retailers of purchased irrigation water. As a result, the manner of delineation and the strictures on outside sales of these two types of water districts are of greatly reduced importance as influences on irrigation water allocation. It is their wholesale suppliers to a considerable degree which dominate the allocation of irrigation water for nonintegrated retailing. By the same token, attention appropriately shifts to the laws governing wholesale suppliers and the policies they pursue.

Privately owned public utilities and mutual water companies are not legally eligible in general to purchase water at wholesale from federal, state, and local public wholesale suppliers, and depend mostly on their own integrated supplies.

A word may be said in conclusion about individual proprietors and other water users who are self-suppliers. There are multitudes of these—they are, in the great bulk of cases, quite small operators—engaged in supplying themselves either with irrigation water or domestic water. Their operations, by definition, are fully integrated, and usually they depend on their own riparian or ground-water rights. As a class, they apparently have the common-law rights of proprietors to expand or contract and to consolidate with others; but generally they are limited to self-service and cannot sell to others (mainly because of strictures in the law of water rights). In the agricultural sector, these users include many farms, both large and small, which adjoin streams or overlie ground-water deposits; as a whole, they account for an appreciable share of the total irrigation water supply and one which, added to agency-supplied water, is arbitrarily allocated and not readily subject to transfer by sale. Many farmers are, of course, simultaneously individual self-supplying proprietors (especially as pumpers of ground water) and members or customers of public districts or privately owned public utilities. In addition, a great many individuals, commercial establishments, schools, and others in rural or ex-urban areas supply water for their own domestic use.

The major types of local overlay agency supplying smaller public districts with irrigation water are: water conservation districts, water storage districts, county flood control and water conservation districts, and county water agencies. The first two types mainly supply irrigation water; types three and four supply water both for irrigation and for domestic and municipal purposes, though with greater emphasis on irrigation water. The first two types of overlay agencies most heavily emphasize integrated wholesaling; they have only a secondary interest in re-wholesaling of water from the very large supplying agencies and only a minor interest in integrated retailing. The water conservation districts have been formed primarily to develop conjunctive use by smaller local districts of the surface or ground-water supplies of given basins (surface supplies often coming from several small streams); the water storage districts, formed generally to provide supplementary supplies to smaller local districts serviceable by a single large complex of works, are generally closely comparable to water conservation districts in functional emphasis. The second two types, aside from performing functions other than the purveying of water, emphasize re-wholesaling most heavily, and integrated wholesaling to a somewhat lesser extent; they do not engage in retailing. Significant provisions regarding (1) delineation, (2) redelineation, (3) ability to sell to outsiders, and (4) sources of water (other than integrated sources) for all four types of overlay agencies may be summarized briefly as follows:[61]

1) Initial delineation—Water conservation districts and water storage districts—the first two types of agencies—are proposed by local petitions which are reviewed by county boards of supervisors and also, recently, by the California Department of Water Resources. The rules governing their delineation have been suggested in the description of their functions above, and are rather broad and general. They originate because of local initiative, and in the approval of their delineation a broad range of discretion is vested in the reviewing agencies. Allocational issues regarding irrigation water are not paramount. This is partly because they serve fairly large areas and generally apportion water among several smaller agencies, and partly because, as re-wholesalers, some of their supply is allocated by larger agencies farther up in the hierarchy of water suppliers. Both the county flood control and water conservation districts and the county water agencies are established individually by special legislative acts and are delineated to serve entire counties. Again, allocational issues are not paramount, generally for the same reasons mentioned in connection with water conservation and water storage districts. Flood control and water conservation districts, of course, have a primary responsibility for functions suggested in the title, and may secure water for distribution by impounding flood waters.

2) Redelineation—Water conservation and water storage districts may make exclusions and inclusions subsequent to formation under rules similar to those governing districts that retail irrigation water. Such alterations of territory are voluntary and broad ranges of discretion are vested in the boards controlling the agencies. For these districts, the picture with respect to consolidations is not clear. As county-wide districts, the county flood control and water conservation districts and the county water agencies are not generally empowered to make inclusions and exclusions after formation; consolidations do not seem to be entirely barred to them, but would evidently require special legislative acts.

3) Outside sales—Water conservation and water storage districts are empowered to sell outside the district water or water rights not needed by member agencies of the district. Again, the definition of the term "surplus water" becomes

[61] See California *Water Code* (1963), div. 14; California *Statutes* (1927), ch. 91; and provisions of numerous individual laws establishing county water agencies and county flood control and water conservation districts.

important. It is not evident in the various special legislative acts establishing them that county flood control and water conservation districts and county water agencies can generally sell water outside of county limits. This, of course, impedes market processes and their possible remedial effects on water allocation to some extent, but the primary function of these agencies as re-wholesalers mitigates this tendency considerably.

4) Sources of water—All four types of overlay agencies are empowered to contract with the Bureau of Reclamation, the Corps of Engineers, and the California Department of Water Resources for water supplies needed for re-wholesaling to small constituent districts or other public agencies. Exercise of this power by such agencies has increased greatly in the past fifteen years and is definitely on the increase.

In general, although some restrictions are imposed on district delineations and powers to make outside sales, the four types of overlay agency can potentially help in reducing the insularity of retail supplies, redressing the imbalance in allocations of irrigation water, and creating limited markets for water within their respective territories. On the whole, however, their legal powers do not encourage engagement of two, or several, such agencies in selling water competitively in a common market, and rivalries are more likely to express themselves, and to be worked out, on a political level.

So far, we have discussed the law governing types of agencies which are important purveyors of irrigation water or both irrigation and urban water. Here we will turn to the law affecting types of public agencies that specialize in urban water supply. Again, a distinction may be drawn between local agencies engaged in retailing integrated or purchased water and local overlay agencies which emphasize wholesaling to smaller local public districts or municipalities.

The retailing agencies specializing in the delivery of urban water—all public organizations—have varied forms and functions. The simplest forms are public utility districts, community service districts, and county waterworks districts; all three may be established to serve either unincorporated territories alone or unincorporated plus incorporated territories. Each type is engaged primarily in nonintegrated retailing of water purchased at wholesale, and secondarily in fully integrated operations to supply such water, though individual members of each type may specialize in one direction or the other. Their process of formation and the rules governing their delineation are similar to those described for comparable districts supplying irrigation water. Formation is proposed by local initiative through petition; there are regularized reviews of petitioners' proposals; the rules governing their delineation are general and loose; and in the determination of district delineations a great deal is left to the discretion of the petitioners and the reviewing county boards of supervisors. Subsequent exclusions and inclusions are provided for under the same general conditions as apply to districts supplying irrigation water; consolidations are possible for county waterworks districts but not for the other two types. Public utility districts may make outside sales, but not in excess of 50 per cent of their total deliveries; the powers of county waterworks districts and community service districts in this area are not clear. All three types are empowered to acquire water at wholesale from federal agencies and from local overlay agencies, which would include county flood control and water conservation districts and county water agencies as well as municipal water districts and metropolitan water districts. In the region generally there is an adequate supply of water at acceptable costs for such districts to distribute to their constituencies, either from local sources which they exploit as integrated operators or from a variety of water wholesalers. Therefore, the law governing their delineation and their powers does not in general seem to be such as to favor creation or perpetuation of misallocations of water among different groups of urban users or between agricultural and urban use.

The public agencies engaged primarily in retailing urban water to incorporated cities and towns are municipal water departments and municipal utility districts. The former are created by actions of city governments. Municipal water departments may not extend their official territories for retailing except as cities merge or municipal boundaries are extended, and the same sort of rule applies to consolidations, though this limitation is strongly mitigated by the ability of such departments to sell water at wholesale to other municipalities. The municipal utility districts emerge from the familiar petition-review-election system, under loose rules, with organization through local initiative, and with wide ranges of discretion as to delineation vested in the petitioners and the reviewing authorities. The final delineation of a municipal utility district is limited in two ways—its territory may not exceed that proposed by the petitioners and approved by reviewing agencies, but will include only that part of this territory in which the citizens of individual component municipalities vote for inclusion at elections.[62] These municipal utility districts may undertake inclusions and exclusions under the general sort of rules and conditions described for agricultural water agencies; the situation regarding consolidations is not clear. As in the case of the municipal water departments, these districts may make water sales outside their proper territories, generally at wholesale. Both these types of retailers thus can exercise considerable flexibility in apportioning water supplies they acquire among urban users within and outside their boundaries, although outside sales are undertaken voluntarily and at the discretion of the boards governing such agencies.[63]

Both types of urban retailers can purchase water from a variety of wholesalers, including federal agencies and local overlay agencies, and many do, particularly cities or towns of moderate and small size—though the latter frequently are fully integrated for part or all of their water supply. In general, these smaller agencies are not significantly engaged in outside sales. In the large metropolitan area of Northern California, two agencies supply the bulk of the domestic water supply—the Public Utilities Commission of the City of San Francisco, and the East Bay Municipal Utility District. Both are fully integrated in all their operations, drawing water by aqueduct from the Sierra Nevada and supplementing this with the capture of local runoff; both large suppliers of urban water have a primary emphasis on retail sales, but a significant engagement in outside wholesaling of such water.

[62] See California *Public Utilities Code,* div. 6, §§ 11501–14509.

[63] See California *Water Code* (1963), div. 16; California *Public Utilities Code,* div. 7, §§ 15501–18004; California *Government Code,* Title 6, div. 2, §§ 1600 ff.

The San Francisco Commission supplies the city with water at retail, and wholesales water to a number of suburban municipalities in the peninsula area south of San Francisco. The East Bay Municipal Utility District retails water to most urban and suburban areas on the eastern edge of San Francisco Bay and in the immediate hinterlands. In general, the law governing municipal water departments and municipal utility districts is not such as to interfere with an economically rational allocation of domestic and municipal water. On the contrary, there are significant instances when such agencies serve as important instruments for making possible the exercise of water rights by, and apportioning water equitably among, very large groups of domestic and municipal users spread over large territories.

Another kind of agency supplying urban water—municipal water districts—as a type has hybrid functions.[64] These districts can operate, and often do, both as fully integrated retailers of domestic and municipal water, and as retailers of water acquired at wholesale from other agencies—and they generally supply broad areas including a number of municipalities. They may also act either as integrated wholesalers or as re-wholesalers supplying numbers of municipalities. Their formation stems from local initiative and their delineation is subject to loose rules which vest wide ranges of discretion in the cities or petitioners initially proposing them and in the reviewing agencies. Subsequent annexations and exclusions are provided for under the usual rules; but it is not clear that they are empowered to enter into consolidations or to make sales outside their district limits, which are generally defined to include a number of not necessarily contiguous municipalities. They are clearly empowered to acquire water at wholesale from primary overlay agencies, such as metropolitan water districts, and from other wholesale suppliers. Although they are important devices for implementing the exercise of water rights by, and apportioning water among, very large groups of urban and suburban residents, they do not meet in a common free market as rival suppliers.

Finally, metropolitan water districts (of which the Metropolitan Water District of Southern California to date is the only example) are entirely overlay agencies which may operate separately or jointly as integrated wholesalers or as re-wholesalers of water purchased from the very large-scale supplying agencies.[65] They are to be formed to provide wholesale water for two or more (in the single instance mentioned, many) municipal water districts (which may act as intermediate re-wholesalers to supply smaller agencies), municipal water departments, municipal utility districts, public utility districts, and county water districts.[66]

[64] See California *Water Code* (1963), div. 20.

[65] See California *Statutes* (1927), ch. 429.

[66] The Metropolitan Water District of Southern California supplies water to numerous subsidiary agencies serving a very large geographical area and a huge population with domestic and municipal water, and stands at the apex of a pyramid including two or more tiers of re-wholesaling and retailing agencies. The metropolitan water district as a type is formed to acquire water rights, purchase water, store and transport it, and deliver to smaller agencies. Such districts may be proposed by the passage of an ordinance by any municipality, and their delineation (subject to approval at elections by the individual proposed customer agencies) is not closely restricted, much being left to local initiative and discretion. Subsequent annexations, exclusions, and consolidations are provided for under the usual rules. Surplus water not needed by customer-member agencies may be sold for other than domestic purposes and to outsiders, but with preference to uses within the district. Metropolitan water districts may contract to purchase water from the California Department of Water Resources and from federal agencies, as well as developing their own supplies.

The metropolitan water district can be an important peak agency for spreading the exercise of water rights and supplying water to very large urban and suburban populations, via smaller water agencies which collectively control its policies and management. There is no evident tendency for it to misallocate water among its member-agencies or their customers. But as a huge unit, bargaining with a very large-scale water supplier such as the state's Department of Water Resources, it may drive bargains and enter into contracts which have very significant, and possibly adverse, impacts on the allocation of water from the point of view of different regions of the state, and of urban as opposed to agricultural uses. For further exploration of this possibility, we look at the laws governing the major water supplying agencies—especially the California Department of Water Resources. Whatever the allocational impact of the bargaining and contracting activities of the Metropolitan Water District of Southern California, they are accomplished on the political level rather than in a free water market.

Laws Governing the Federal and State Water Agencies

Three large water agencies, each established to undertake major projects for water resource development and to supply water to local agencies, operate in California. They include two federal agencies—the Bureau of Reclamation of the U.S. Department of the Interior, and the Corps of Engineers of the Department of the Army—and one state agency, the California Department of Water Resources. Their emergence has represented the major phase to date in the development, still in minor degree, of a separation of functions among water agencies. As this separation develops, three tiers of agencies emerge, emphasizing respectively: (1) multipurpose river basin development, including streamflow regulation, flood control, and power generation, together with the large-scale capture, long-distance transportation, and wholesaling of water; (2) re-wholesaling of water; and (3) local distribution and retailing of water. This vertical structure is being superimposed on a pattern of self-sufficient local agencies, or complexes thereof, which accomplish fully integrated retailing of water.

The Bureau of Reclamation was created by Congress to implement a national land policy directed toward reclaiming arid and semiarid lands of the West through providing irrigation water for agricultural purposes. The Bureau has been operated to this end in California and other states, assuming through time other functions relating to water. These extend to multipurpose river basin development, interbasin transfers of water, and large-scale wholesaling of water. The Corps of Engineers, since the rivers and harbor acts began in 1824, has been the chosen instrument of Congress for surveying, improving, and maintaining inland waterways in the interests of navigation, and it has been further charged with constructing works for flood control. In the process of performing these duties, the Corps has emerged in California and elsewhere as a major agency engaged in constructing reservoirs to capture and store water and in making water available for consumptive use, primarily for irrigation, as well as in the generation of hydroelectric power. The California Department of Water Resources (and its predecessor agencies) has developed extensive plans of its own for undertaking large-scale water developments, in which it emphasizes capture and storage, transportation between areas and regions, and the wholesaling of water, and has begun construction of its first major project.

The functions and operations of the Bureau of Reclamation and Corps of Engineers are now fairly well assigned and coordinated under federal laws, though there was serious inter-agency rivalry over assignments in the past. The California Department of Water Resources, in its role as a major water supplier, appears to have two primary aims: supplying very large amounts of water for the use of an expanding urban population, mainly by transmitting water from Northern California to the southern part of the state, and supplying irrigation water in volume to large areas in the central and southern parts of California which are not currently served by the Bureau or Corps. Some degree of cooperation between the Bureau and the California Department of Water Resources has emerged and will undoubtedly continue. However, there are evidently intrinsic elements of inter-agency competition for service areas, as well as a differentiation of function with regard to the relative emphasis placed on agricultural, as opposed to urban, water supplies. The major elements of the legal framework within which the three agencies operate, with special reference to California, can be outlined quite briefly.

The Corps of Engineers

The Corps of Engineers of the Army of the United States, traditionally charged with responsibility for maintaining and improving navigation on inland waterways, had its attention directed to California by the Rivers and Harbors Act of 1880, in which Congress ordered a survey of mining debris impeding navigation in the Sacramento and San Joaquin rivers. Subsequently, in 1886, Congress appropriated funds for use by the Corps in improving navigation in these rivers, and granted it powers to regulate hydraulic mining operations. Thereafter, strategic congressional legislation affecting operations of the Corps in California and elsewhere has included the following:

1) The rivers and harbors acts of 1890 and 1899, in which Congress generally asserted jurisdiction over the protection of all navigable waters in the country by prohibiting impairment of navigation by dams, wharfs, or other structures or by dumping refuse, without the approval of the Corps.

2) An act of 1892 establishing the California Debris Commission as a regulatory, planning, and operating agency within the Corps, and empowering it to regulate hydraulic mining practices, to construct reservoirs to the end of controlling mining debris, to tax miners benefiting from these reservoirs, and to improve the navigability of the two major rivers.

3) The Flood Control Act of 1917 (applying to the Mississippi River as well as to the California rivers), which provided for general watershed studies, works construction to improve navigation and to control floods, and the use or disposition of water stored in pursuit of these duties to generate hydroelectric power and for other related uses.[67]

[67] 39 U.S. *Statutes* 948 (1917).

4) The Rivers and Harbors Act of 1927, which authorized the Corps to conduct a series of surveys of all navigable streams and their tributaries in the country where hydroelectric development seemed feasible, and to formulate plans for improved navigation, flood control, and irrigation. (This led to the development of a large body of reports, known generally as the 308 Reports, comprising an inventory of possible water control and storage projects, designed not only for improved navigation and flood control but also for power generation and developing supplies of irrigation water.)

5) The Flood Control Act of 1936,[68] which declared the constitutional powers of the federal government to improve rivers in general and their watersheds for flood control purposes. This extended the sphere of operations of the Corps to include the many non-navigable streams of California (and elsewhere) along with navigable streams and their tributaries. (It was at that time, during the Great Depression, that the Corps extended its California operations from those concerned mainly with the regulation of debris and flood control in the Sacramento and San Joaquin river systems to a greatly expanded flood control program on non-navigable streams, involving multipurpose water storage projects in the Tulare Basin and in several coastal valleys.) The same Flood Control Act was also significant in its provision that federal improvements for flood control could be undertaken "if the benefits to whomsoever they may accrue are in excess of the estimated costs. . . ."[69] This provision effectively subjected at least all flood control projects of the Corps to trial by benefit-cost analysis, and made an excess of benefits over costs a requirement for authorization of a project.

6) The Flood Control Act of 1944,[70] which expressly provided for designing flood control projects by the Corps with due attention to the joint and alternative uses of water, and to the end of preserving river waters for all purposes. It also contained two other important provisions. First, in addition to providing for coordination of Corps plans with Bureau plans, it stated that the Corps should deliver to the Bureau both its hydroelectric power and its irrigation water for transmission and distribution by the Bureau, though this provision did not apply retroactively to Corps projects already in operation. This confined future Corps operations (aside from maintenance of navigation and flood control) largely to the capture and storage of water and power generation; its wholesaling operation shifted to the Bureau, which thus assumed a more or less centralized control over federal allocation and wholesaling of irrigation water and hydroelectric power. Second, the act significantly provided that in connection with the operation of flood control works in states west of the 98th meridian, use of water for navigation should be only such "as does not conflict with any beneficial consumptive use."[71] The operations of the Corps in the West thus officially ceased to be oriented primarily to navigation.

7) The Water Supply Act of 1958[72] (extending a provision of the Flood Control Act of 1944), which provided generally for the development of domestic,

[68] U.S. *Statutes-at-Large* 1510 (1936).
[69] *Ibid.*
[70] 58 U.S. *Statutes* 887 (1944).
[71] *Ibid.*
[72] 72 U.S. *Statutes-at-Large* 319 (1958).

municipal, and industrial water, and water quality control in connection with flood control, irrigation, or multipurpose projects. Provisions of this Act apply equally to projects of the Corps of Engineers and Bureau of Reclamation.

8) The Fish and Wildlife Coordination Act (last amended in 1958), which provides for consultation by the Corps with federal and state fish and game agencies, and ultimately for a report by the Secretary of the Interior, which may require inclusion in project plans of such justifiable means and measures for the preservation and enhancement of fish and wildlife resources as the Secretary deems necessary "to obtain maximum overall project benefits."[73] These provisions apply equally to Bureau of Reclamation projects.

In the contemporary scene, the Corps appears to be a federal agency with a rather complete range of powers in the regulation and development of water resources, since its main restriction is that the functions of transmitting and distributing the irrigation water it impounds and the electric energy it produces are passed to the Bureau of Reclamation (on projects completed after 1944). However, it is limited very importantly in powers in that each individual project undertaken by the Corps requires congressional approval at every significant stage: authorization of surveys and estimates, re-studies, project authorization, and appropriation of project funds. It is thus very much an agency of Congress in planning and constructing specific public works, except for small flood control projects for which general grants are usually made. In the words of the Corps, local interests initiate, Congress authorizes, and the Corps constructs. The Corps thus does not appear as a superagency for planning national or regional water development.

The Bureau of Reclamation

The Bureau of Reclamation was created as an agency (a branch of the Department of the Interior) to develop and reclaim arid western lands, and especially public lands, primarily by irrigation. Performance of this function involved it from the outset in the development of water resources. Since the middle of the 1930's, the Bureau has expanded its functions by emphasizing multipurpose water projects, operating in part parallel to, and in part cooperatively with, the Corps of Engineers.

Unlike the Corps, which has more or less backed into the water business by undertaking a series of specific congressional assignments, the Bureau was created by an act of Congress which both included a general definition of its intended program and policies and provided a general mode of financing its continuing operations. The Reclamation Act of 1902[74] provided that the Secretary of the Interior should secure funds (to be paid into a Reclamation Fund) from the sales of western public lands (lands including and westward of the Dakotas, Nebraska, Kansas, and Oklahoma), in order to finance the development of irrigation works and to reclaim arid and semiarid lands in the states named. The Secretary of Interior was required to survey sites for irrigation projects, draw plans for them, and construct works. In the course of so doing he was to report annually to Congress on contemplated

[73] 72 U.S. *Statutes* 563 (1958).
[74] 32 U.S. *Statutes* 388 (1902).

projects and their costs. The Secretary, to perform functions spelled out in the Act, first established the Reclamation Service in the Geological Survey, but later removed it from the Survey and subsequently changed the name to Bureau of Reclamation—a name used throughout this discussion for the sake of simplicity.

Two policy principles of some importance were introduced in the basic act of 1902. First, private entry under the homestead law on public land reclaimed by the Bureau was limited to 160 acres per entrant. The entrants were to pay over time for assignable reclamation costs, and after payment had been completed, the operation of the irrigation works in question, excepting reservoirs and connected facilities, was to pass to the landowners. Second, the Bureau was instructed to adhere to, observe, and be governed by the law of water rights of any state within which it undertook projects—effectively, it could not commandeer water rights on its own motion, and could not infringe upon or acquire established private (or state) water rights except as provided for under the laws of the state in question. This latter provision, however, has been subject to attrition by judicial interpretation.

The principal subsequent revisions of, or additions to, the law governing powers and policies of the Bureau of Reclamation are the following:

1) An amendment in 1906 of the Reclamation Act[75] empowered the Bureau to develop municipal, as well as farm, water supplies, and, importantly, to develop hydroelectric power as a coordinate aspect of any water project. It was also provided that power revenues were to go to the Reclamation Fund, but that on any project "surplus" power and other revenues received after all project construction costs had been amortized (and in excess of current operating costs) should go to the general funds of the Treasury rather than to the Reclamation Fund.

2) An amendment passed in 1910 provided that no irrigation project could begin without recommendation by the Secretary of the Interior and direct approval by the President.[76]

3) An amendment passed in 1914 provided that Congress must authorize expenditures from the Reclamation Fund.[77]

4) The Reclamation Project Act of 1939[78] authorized the Secretary of the Interior to take into account a variety of joint and alternative uses in the development of any reclamation project, including irrigation, power production, urban water supplies, flood control, navigation, and other miscellaneous purposes; and required that he consult with the Corps of Engineers on flood control and navigation features of projects and secure special congressional appropriations for such features.

This 1939 Reclamation Project Act, moreover, contained two new provisions of more far-reaching importance. First, it empowered the Bureau of Reclamation to enter into long-term contracts of a utility type for the wholesale delivery of water to landowners whom it supplied, in lieu of contracts to repay the cost of irrigation

[75] U.S. *Statutes* 116 (1906).
[76] 43 U.S. *Code*, § 413.
[77] 43 U.S. *Code*, § 414.
[78] 53 U.S. *Statutes* 1187 (1939).

facilities. This has permitted the Bureau to establish itself as a continuing management and operation agency with respect to substantially all features of its projects, instead of being restricted to the role of a planning and construction agency which ultimately passes control of its irrigation works to its customers.

Second, it required the Secretary of the Interior to estimate the total benefits and the total costs of every project, and required that the sum of the benefits from a project must at least cover the total project costs if congressional authorization for a project is to be secured. This provision subjected Bureau projects, like those of the Corps of Engineers, to trial by benefit-cost analysis. Significantly, however, it left the appraisal of benefits and costs essentially to the agency which would sponsor, propose, and construct them, rather than to a disinterested arbiter—as is also the case with such appraisals of Corps projects. (The manner in which administrative latitude has been employed in the implementation of this provision will be discussed in Part Two.)

There has been a considerable change in the policies of the Bureau and extension of the scope of its activities since its inception, most supported or encouraged by congressional legislation and occurring since 1932. From 1902 through 1932, the Bureau operated almost entirely with moneys accumulated in the Reclamation Fund, and engaged principally in projects of small or moderate scale. Beginning in 1933, Congress began making special appropriations for specific projects to be carried out by the Bureau—including large and expensive multipurpose projects such as the Central Valley Project in California.[79] The Bureau thus became engaged in valley or river basin planning and development on a large scale.

In so doing, it increasingly came to have as customers, instead of new entrants on public lands, established private landowners, many of whom had already developed various local irrigation works after forming local public districts. And in connection with large and complex projects like its Central Valley Project in California, the Bureau has shifted from accepting contractual commitments from individual landowners to contracting with local public water-user agencies such as irrigation districts, with re-wholesaling overlay districts, and so forth. At the same time, it generally shifted from accepting contracts for repayment for its facilities (which, after repayment, would pass to water users) to providing water on a utility basis—simply charging for water delivered to a local district under long-term contracts. Its charges were supposed to be set to cover an appropriately allocable share of total project costs. This sort of utility-contract arrangement for water delivered from long-distance transmission facilities of the Bureau may be coupled with contracts under which local districts repay the costs of local distribution systems built by the Bureau and then assume control of them.

The provisions of the Reclamation Act of 1902 concerning water rights still stand without significant amendment, asserting that in constructing intrastate projects the Bureau is bound by state laws concerning water rights (presumably placing certain constraints on the Bureau's ability to acquire requisite water rights).

[79] It was authorized as a project of the Bureau of Reclamation finally in the Rivers and Harbors Act of 1937. The dams and reservoirs of the Central Valley Project thus authorized were to be operated to give first priority to river regulation, navigation, and flood control; second priority to irrigation and domestic use; and third priority to power generation.

It implies that the lands, or landowners, being served by Bureau-supplied water acquire appurtenant rights to the use of this water under the doctrine of public service responsibility, thus constraining the Bureau to continue a water service to a particular customer group once it is begun under contract provisions that are not temporary. The extent of the servitude of federal water agencies to state laws governing water rights and regulating their appropriation by attaching conditions to the approval of projects for which rights are sought, nevertheless, has been seriously questioned in a series of relatively recent Supreme Court decisions. As a result, there is little question that, under prevailing judicial doctrine, this servitude is significantly qualified, and, according to contentions of the Bureau of Reclamation, erased. As a result, remedial legislation is currently before Congress.

The California Department of Water Resources

There were a number of forerunners with some of the functions now handled by the California Department of Water Resources (a department of the Resources Agency of California) which was created by statute in 1956. This relatively new Department is headed by a Director of Water Resources appointed by the Governor subject to the approval of the state senate.[80] It was designated to succeed in matters pertaining to water and dams to the powers, duties, and purposes previously vested in the Department of Public Works, the State Engineer, and a defunct Water Project Authority (in the planning, construction, and operation of water facilities); to some powers of the Department of Finance in filing applications to appropriate water;[81] and to planning powers of the State Water Resources Board.[82] It is given broad investigatory powers with respect to water resources and their development,[83] and condemnation powers over real property needed for any project authorized by the state legislature.[84] None of its plans or proposals for water projects shall be submitted to the state legislature, however, unless they include comments and recommendations of the Department of Fish and Game, and provisions for such recreational facilities and for the preservation and enhancement of fish and wildlife as the Department of Water Resources deems justifiable in the statewide interest.[85]

The water projects which the Department of Water Resources is authorized by currently effective legislation to construct constitute an overlapping series, and many of the features of some of them have already been constructed by the Bureau of Reclamation. Included among these are the following:

1) The Central Valley Project (state of California version), as authorized in the Central Valley Project Act of 1933 and in subsequent amendments to that Act.[86] A Central Valley Project had been proposed and planned by Californians for many years prior to 1933. As authorized, the California Project is defined as a

[80] California *Water Code* (1963), 120.
[81] *Ibid.*, §§ 10500–10507.
[82] *Ibid.*, §§ 123, 125–129.
[83] *Ibid.*, §§ 225–231.
[84] *Ibid.*, §§ 250, 251.
[85] *Ibid.*, § 233.
[86] The authorization is now covered in full by California *Water Code* (1963), div. 6, pt. 3, § 11125 ff.

single unit, and it includes all basic features of the federal Central Valley Project constructed to date except the Trinity Division works of the Bureau of Reclamation, plus two Sacramento Valley canals now planned by the Bureau, a couple of minor dams, and one canal unit of the Feather River Project.[87] Since most or all of the Central Valley Project thus authorized by the state of California either has been built, or is evidently to be built, by federal agencies, the significant content of the authorizing legislation in the California Water Code is found in detailed provisions defining the powers and responsibilities of the Department of Water Resources with respect to the Project. These provisions have been incorporated by reference in legislation authorizing other projects assigned to the Department of Water Resources. These include the indication that the Department shall carry out all governmental functions in relation to the Project[88] subject to watershed-of-origin protections,[89] and shall have full charge of construction and maintenance of the Project and of the collection of revenues from it.[90] They also confer on the Department the powers to design the Project works, to make contracts, and to fix rates for Project water,[91] and include numerous bonding, financial, and general implementing provisions.[92] All such provisions apply specifically to the Feather River Project, which is separately authorized as a part of the Central Valley Project.

2) The State Water Plan, authorized in 1941 pursuant to a plan set forth by the Division of Water Resources of the California State Department of Public Works in a report to the legislature of 1931.[93] This plan, still authorized, covers the Central Valley Project, or a version thereof, plus a Colorado River aqueduct and other Southern California works. Since the authorizing legislation did not repeal any provisions of the Central Valley Project Act of 1933, and in the case of inconsistencies the provisions of the 1933 Act were to prevail, this legislation seems redundant.

3) The Feather River Project, added to the Central Valley Project by statute in 1951.[94] The statute was subsequently amended and the authorization now appears as a section of the division of the California Water Code authorizing the Central Valley Project.[95] The current authorization provides that units of the Project set forth in the 1951 *Report on Feasibility of the Feather River Project*, as modified in the 1955 *Program for Financing and Constructing the Feather River Project as the Initial Unit of the California Water Plan*,[96] as further modified by

[87] California *Water Code* (1963), § 11200.

[88] *Ibid.*, § 11127.

[89] *Ibid.*, §§ 11460, 11463, for specifications of these protections.

[90] *Ibid.*, § 11451.

[91] *Ibid.*, §§ 11551, 11453–11455.

[92] *Ibid.*, div. 6, pt. 3, chs. 3–10 and §§ 11135–11141.

[93] The report is California State Department of Public Works, Division of Water Resources, *Report to the Legislature of 1931 on State Water Plan*, Bulletin No. 25 (1930). The authorizing legislation was Calif. *Statutes* (1941), ch. 1185, now contained in California *Water Code* (1963), div. 6, pt. 1.

[94] California *Statutes* (1951), ch. 1441.

[95] California *Water Code* (1963), div. 6, pt. 3, § 11260.

[96] Division of Water Resources of the California State Department of Public Works (1951 and 1955).

a 1959 report of the Department of Water Resources,[97] and subject to further modifications as may be adopted by the Department of Water Resources, shall be constructed, operated, and maintained by the Department of Water Resources as units of the Central Valley Project—*apart from all other units thereof* to such an extent and for such a period as the Department deems desirable.

This language leaves the precise scope of the authorization less than perfectly clear, even to one who has carefully read all of the reports and documents referred to in the legislation. Even so, it seems plain that the Feather River Project, whatever it turns out to consist of or contain, may be constructed and operated apart from the rest of the California version of the Central Valley Project. The Feather River Project is somewhat more circumstantially described, however, in the Water Resources Development Bond Act of 1959,[98] which authorized a bond issue, subject to popular referendum, to finance the project. This act defined the project for which bond funds were to be provided as State Water Facilities including: (a) a multipurpose dam at Oroville on the Feather River, plus smaller dams upstream in Plumas County; and (b) an aqueduct system to transfer water (1) to termini in Marin, Alameda, Santa Clara, Santa Barbara, Los Angeles, and Riverside Counties, and (2) en route in Solano, Napa, Sonoma, Contra Costa, San Benito, Santa Cruz, Fresno, Tulare, Kings, Kern, Ventura, San Bernardino, Orange, San Diego, San Luis Obispo, and Monterey counties.

The project thus authorized evidently includes by implication all contemplated dam and storage facilities of the Feather River Project other than supplementary storage on the Eel River (which has been subsequently proposed or planned), and all basic aqueduct facilities (with connected pumping works) currently planned. These aqueduct facilities include the North Bay Aqueduct and South Bay Aqueduct from the Delta to areas north and south of San Francisco Bay; the main project aqueduct from the Delta through the San Joaquin Valley to the Tehachapis; the West Branch and East Branch aqueducts carrying water from there into Los Angeles and across the Mojave Desert and down to the vicinity of San Bernardino in the South Coastal Basin; and the Central Coastal Aqueduct tapping the main project aqueduct. A spur aqueduct from the East Branch Aqueduct to the vicinity of Palm Springs is supposed to be constructed and operated by the local contracting agencies. The 1959 act also makes an adequate allowance for alternates and additions, since the aqueduct system generally described embraces, and by implication goes beyond, the basic system planned for the Feather River Project, and beyond the service capacity of Oroville Dam. (The basic features of the Project as currently planned are shown on Figure 32, page 565.)[99]

[97] California Department of Water Resources, *Investigation of Alternative Aqueduct Systems to Serve Southern California,* Bulletin No. 78 (1959).

[98] California *Statutes* (1951), ch. 1441. Codified in California *Water Code* (1963), §§ 12931–12934.

[99] The 1959 Bond Act provides that the Feather River Project shall be constructed, operated, and maintained pursuant to Water Code provisions governing the Central Valley Project, thus incorporating the provisions of the Central Valley Project Act by reference for a second time. California *Water Code* (1963), § 12931.

The California Water Plan

The preceding list of actual authorizations for major projects of the Department of Water Resources to date reveals that, at present, there is just one big authorization which is effective—namely that for a somewhat elastically defined Feather River Project. We also need to look briefly at general plans for projects which have not been specifically authorized.

An investigation of the water resources of California, aimed at solving problems of water conservation, control, and use for the greatest public benefit, was authorized by the state legislature in 1947, to be carried on by the California State Water Resources Board.[100] This investigation culminated in the publication of three detailed reports: Bulletin No. 1 in 1951; Bulletin No. 2 in 1955; and Bulletin No. 3 in 1957.[101]

Bulletin No. 3 contained "a master plan to guide and coordinate the planning and construction by all agencies of works required for the control, protection, conservation, and distribution of California's water resources for the benefit of all areas of the state and for all beneficial purposes."[102] It went on to give detailed plans (including alternates) for the locations, sizes, purposes, service areas, and costs of all dams needed for the ultimate full development of all water resources of the state, and similar plans and costs for all aqueduct systems needed in connection with such development. It did not attempt to estimate project benefits or to compare these with costs, adhering to a "requirements" approach to water demand and value. The 1957 bulletin containing the California Water Plan was published just after creation of the Department of Water Resources, but it had many antecedents in old plans drawn by federal and state agencies. The Plan included the Feather River Project as one main feature or as an alternate to a main feature. It recognized existing works as finished and went far beyond the Central Valley Project plus the Feather River Project to propose intensive development for interbasin transfer of all of the principal undeveloped rivers of the north coastal region. (The broad outlines of the California Water Plan are described in Appendix D.)

The California Water Plan is recognized in the Water Code,[103] which declares that the plan for the orderly development of state water resources given in the three bulletins, with such supplements and additions as may later be necessary, "shall be known as the California Water Plan." It provides further that amendments of and supplements to the plan made by the Department of Water Resources shall become effective when reported to the legislature, which may also amend the plan.[104] Given this, the Code states that it is the policy of the state that the California Water Plan, with necessary supplements and amendments, "is accepted as the guide" for orderly development of water resources in the state, but that this declaration does not constitute approval of specific projects or routes of transfer

[100] California *Statutes* (1947), ch. 1541.

[101] California State Water Resources Board, *Water Resources of California,* Bulletin No. 1 (1951); *Water Utilization and Requirements of California,* Bulletin No. 2 (1955); and *The California Water Plan,* Bulletin No. 3 (1957).

[102] *Ibid.,* Bulletin No. 3, Introduction.

[103] California *Water Code* (1963), div. 6, pt. 1.5.

[104] *Ibid.,* § 10004.

of water for construction or financial assistance without further legislative action.[105] The California Water Plan is thus recognized as a guide or blueprint for future water development, but no part of it is authorized except so far as it may have been in the Central Valley Project Act or in the authorization of the Feather River Project.

The other main legislative reference to the California Water Plan is found in the Water Resources Development Bond Act of 1959.[106] It says that the object of the bond issue is to provide funds to assist in construction of "a State Water Resources Development System," consisting of the Feather River Project, and such added facilities as may now or hereafter be authorized by the legislature as a part of (1) the Central Valley Project, or (2) the California Water Plan, and including such other facilities as the Department of Water Resources deems necessary for local needs. This bond act not only fails to authorize the California Water Plan beyond the Feather River Project, but provides no financing for it in fact, since the bond proceeds will be more than fully expended on the Feather River Project. Thus, commendable legislative prudence has been displayed in declining to authorize a multibillion dollar grab bag of projects—almost none of which has been analyzed with respect to either economic or financial feasibility.

Public Regulation of the Use of Water

The aggregate of public regulation to which the California water industry, or any regional water industry in the United States, is subject is actually rather small. In fact, it seems surprisingly small since a very substantial group of suppliers and users of water operate in quasi-insular fashion without participating in any real market for water, with the result that their policies and actions are not market-controlled, or "governed by the invisible hand of the market." The bulk of the entities in the industry are not even subject to public-utility regulation of the sort customarily applied to enterprises which are the sole suppliers of given groups of customers.

The reason for—or better, the explanation of—the relative immunity of the water industry from public regulation is that the bulk of suppliers in the industry are not private enterprises but public agencies or departments of government. It is assumed, and in most instances correctly, that these public enterprises do not seek profits, and that regulation of their rates to protect water users is not necessary. It is correlatively assumed, more or less correctly, that public agencies—as servants of the public subject to political control by the public that they serve—will be diligent without regulatory pressure in providing adequate services to their constituent-customers. What is overlooked is that there is no good reason to believe that a large number of quasi-insular public agencies, whose policies and actions are not coordinated and controlled by a market, will tend to generate a socially optimal, or even a reasonably workable, industry-wide performance in determining the level of development of water resources, the timing of this development, and the allocation of water among uses and users. Thus, it may be regrettable that the water

[105] *Ibid.*, § 10005 from California *Statutes* (1959), ch. 2053.
[106] *Ibid.*, § 12931.

industry in California and elsewhere is not subjected to a more effective and comprehensive system of regulation by public bodies other than water-supplying agencies themselves.

There is some regulation of the industry by general regulatory bodies now in effect, however, and the principal types of this regulation (not all of equal importance) fall under three headings: (1) regulations governing the type and character of water resource development projects which may be undertaken; (2) regulations to protect streamflows as a means of preserving public benefits derived from recreation and fish and wildlife resources, and also for protecting the navigability of waterways; and (3) regulations to control pollution and quality of water. In addition, there is a miscellany of regulations of lesser import. In this section, we will consider in turn, with special reference to California, state and federal regulations falling under the three main headings, and thereafter describe very briefly a miscellany of other regulations.

The authorization of water resource development projects

Most of California's water projects are authorized by the electorate, or segments thereof, or by their duly elected legislative representatives. Such authorization may be through municipal and local public district bond or other elections, by actions of the state legislature possibly followed by statewide referenda, or by action of the federal Congress. These authorizing groups or bodies supply a sort of case-by-case regulation of water resource development, though not of an expert, highly informed, or very well coordinated sort. Private public utility companies authorize their own projects, subject to the approval of the Public Utilities Commission of the state. The regulations which we consider here are not those thus automatically imposed, but are those imposed by independent boards and commissions prior to submission to the final authorizing bodies—these regulations serving potentially to screen out undesirable projects and to attach to the approval of projects specifications and conditions which must be met before they are eligible for approval by the final authorizing bodies.

Regulations so imposed have frequently been characterized as controls designed to secure or implement "a comprehensive and coordinated plan of development" of the water resources of the state. At least one plan which might be so characterized, and was given legislative recognition, is the California Water Plan which has already been described. The Bureau of Reclamation has a comparable plan or set of alternate plans for the state. But the term "regulation to secure comprehensive and coordinated development" is likely to be misleading. The California Water Plan and competing plans are comprehensive enough, in that they generally contemplate so full a stage of development of the water resources of the state that almost no drop of fresh water would reach the sea without having been first put to some commercial use. But they are less cogent, unified, and really coordinated plans than they are descriptions of large assortments of water projects intended to exploit all previously unexploited surface water. Although comprehensive and possibly in some sense coordinated, they most definitely are not plans which have passed even rudimentary tests of economic feasibility or desirability, or demonstrably optimal plans from an economic standpoint. Correspondingly, boards and commissions regulating water development by screening and attaching conditions to the approval of water projects usually have no reliable master plans to guide their decisions, and employ *ad hoc* and common-sense judgments in the context of overdefined engineering blueprints for future development as supplied by state and federal water agencies.

The regulatory powers of the higher governmental bodies are based on two main governmental powers. In California, regulations by a commission and a board are imposed under the power of the state to attach conditions to the securing of appropriative rights to surface water for the purpose of constructing and operating water development projects—under the asserted power of the state to control appropriations of intrastate surface waters.[107] By attaching such conditions, the state commission and board are in a position to control the location, size, design, and mode and purpose of operation of all new water projects, and even to deny approval of projects by refusing to grant appropriate water rights needed for them.

Federal regulation is based on powers over navigable waters reserved to the federal government by the interstate commerce clause of the Constitution, and powers over federal reserved lands under the property clause, as implemented by congressional legislation requiring all citizens, corporations, states, municipalities, and other local governmental bodies (but not agencies of the federal government) to secure licenses from a federal commission for constructing dams and appurtenant works on any stream over which Congress has authority.[108] By attaching conditions to its licenses, the federal commission can control the design of the in-stream features of practically all nonfederal water projects, and approve or reject them, in accordance with broad statutory criteria.[109]

We first consider regulation of project authorizations by the state of California. There is a policy declaration in the state constitution to the effect that the general welfare requires beneficial use of the waters of the state to the fullest possible extent and that the right to use surface water shall be limited to the requirements of reasonable beneficial use.[110] Other than this, the basic policy declarations of the state regarding water development and water rights are statutory, and to the effect (1) that all water in the state is the property of the people of the state, but that the right to use it may be appropriated,[111] and (2) that the state shall determine what surface and underground water can be converted to public use and in what way such water should be developed for the greatest public benefit.[112]

This policy assertion, however, is only one of the two legs on which California regulatory authority over water projects stands. The other leg is supplied by the fact that, under 1927 state legislation authorizing it to do so, the state of California has filed applications to appropriate practically all previously unappropriated sur-

[107] California *Water Code* (1963), §§ 102–105.

[108] 17 U.S. *Code* 797 (e).

[109] 16 U.S. *Code* 803.

[110] California *Constitution,* art. XIV, § 3 (adopted by amendment in 1928).

[111] California *Water Code* (1963), § 102. The federal water agencies, and the Supreme Court of the United States, have not accepted this declaration without reservations.

[112] *Ibid.,* §§ 104–105. Again, reservations have been expressed concerning the servitude of federal water agencies to California regulation, a matter to be discussed in the next section of this chapter.

face water in the state, these applications retaining priority over all subsequent applications for the same water even though the state does not proceed with due diligence actually to appropriate and use the waters on which its filings of applications to appropriate have been made.[113] The state thus holds in trust the equivalent of prior rights to practically all previously unappropriated surface waters of California. The same law also provides that the state is empowered at its discretion to release or assign its filings of applications to appropriate the water to persons, corporations, and public agencies which wish to appropriate the water for the purpose of developing water projects, and that it may do so for water projects "not in conflict" with a comprehensive and coordinated plan of development of the water resources of the state.[114] Therefore, in order to acquire water rights to support development of a new project, the developing agency must almost always secure approval of its project from a state commission in order to get a release or assignments of state filings on the water. The agency is thus subject to such conditions concerning project design and operation as the commission may impose in order to assure consistency of the project with a comprehensive and coordinated plan of development; it is also potentially subject to rejection of the project.[115]

The state of California is thus in a position to control the authorization of intrastate water projects at two successive stages and on two legal bases. The stages are: first, that of attaching conditions to the release or assignment of state filings on unappropriated water; and, second, that of attaching conditions to permits and licenses to appropriate once the applicant for water has secured a release and can make its own application to appropriate water. The two legal bases are: first, the holding of prior filings on nearly all unappropriated surface water by the state in the name of the people of California and for the purpose of securing a comprehensive and coordinated system of development of the state's water resources; and, second, the state's statutory assertion of its power to determine what water in the state can be appropriated and in what way. The regulatory institutions of the state charged with authorizing water projects, and the substantive law which instructs them, conform to the pattern just outlined. To carry out these responsibilities, the legislature has created two state agencies—the California Water Commission and the California State Water Rights Board.

The California Water Commission is appointed by the governor of the state subject to approval of the state senate.[116] It holds in trust all state filings of appli-

[113] California *Statutes* (1927), ch. 286.

[114] *Ibid.*, codified in California *Water Code* (1963), § 10500. Filings of applications to appropriate were initially made by the Department of Finance; in 1956, this function was transferred to the California Department of Water Resources. The initial legislation placed a terminal date on the priority of the state filings, but subsequent amendments have regularly postponed the date in order to maintain the priorities in effect.

[115] This applies to projects of federal agencies as well as to others, except so far as the agencies may successfully assert nonservitude to the state's prior filings or to regulations attached to the release or assignment thereof.

[116] The Commission has nine members appointed to four-year overlapping terms, to be qualified by general education, business experience, interest in or experience with water, and engineering experience, and to represent all parts of the state. See California *Water Code* (1963), §§ 150–155. The Commission does not have its own expert staff, and draws upon the Department of Water Resources for technical advice and staff assistance.

cations to appropriate surface water[117] and is empowered to release from priority or assign any portion of any application when the release is for the development of water resources and not in conflict with a general and coordinated plan of water development.[118] This "not in conflict" provision is almost its only statutory instruction, and the character of the general and coordinated plan referred to in the statutes is not described or defined specifically, generally, or in terms of essential attributes. The other principal legislative instruction is that no priority shall be released or assignment made that would deprive a county of origin of any water necessary for the development of the county.[119] In addition, recipients of releases or assignments of filings must comply with all regulatory requirements affecting all appropriations of water as provided in the Water Code and as administered by the State Water Rights Board.[120] Assignees are to include both federal water agencies and the Department of Water Resources.[121]

The foregoing description of the powers of the California Water Commission might suggest that its functions are mainly ministerial, or would be unless it attempted to implement the "not in conflict" proviso with extensive staff work and a substantial body of administrative law, which it has not done. However, the Commission is instructed to,[122] and does, (1) issue public notice of applications for the release or assignment of state filings, and (2) hold hearings on these applications. In so doing, it provides a forum for the registration of protests by parties with conflicting interests, by federal and state water agencies, and by other departments of the state government, and thus provides a forum for resolution or compromise of conflicting interests—resolutions which may shape the conditions attached to ultimate releases of filings. It is not clear, however, that the Commission's procedures lead strongly toward project selection or approval on the basis of appraisal in terms of economic efficiency. Moreover, its interpretation of the county-of-origin protection has come to involve some very substantive issues. In general, it provides the first of two forums before which the merits of projects (for which applications for appropriation of water are made) may be debated, the second being provided by the State Water Rights Board.

The California State Water Rights Board is also appointed by the governor of the state subject to the approval of the state senate;[123] and it is empowered to enforce the regulations of the Water Code governing the issuance, denial, or revocation of permits and licenses to appropriate surface water.[124] The Water Code which it administers specifies that all water in streams is public water subject to appropriation, except so far as it is being used or is needed for beneficial purposes

[117] California *Water Code* (1963), div. 6, pt. 2.
[118] *Ibid.*, § 10504.
[119] *Ibid.*, § 10505.
[120] *Ibid.*, § 10504.
[121] *Ibid.*
[122] California *Water Code* (1963), § 10504.1.
[123] The State Water Rights Board is established within the Resources Agency of California, and has three members appointed to four-year overlapping terms, these members to include an attorney admitted to the bar of the state and an engineer licensed in the state. See California *Water Code* (1963), §§ 175, 177.
[124] *Ibid.*, § 179.

on riparian lands, or except as it has otherwise been appropriated.[125] Water may be appropriated only through a process of application to the State Water Rights Board, and thereafter by securing from the Board permits (to proceed with construction of works) and licenses (issued upon the approved completion of works).[126]

The statutory rules for granting a permit (and ultimately a license) for appropriation of water to an applicant are limited to the following:

1) The appropriation must be made for a useful or beneficial purpose.[127]

2) The Board shall allow appropriation under terms and conditions which in its judgment will best serve the public interest in the water sought to be appropriated, and may reject applications which would not best serve the public interest.[128] The statute is silent, however, with respect to any general or specific attributes or properties which projects must have, or analytical or other tests they must pass, in order to qualify as serving the public interest.

3) In determining the public interest, the Board shall give consideration to any general and coordinated plan for state water development and conservation, including the California Water Plan or any predecessor or modification thereof adopted by the Department of Water Resources or by the state legislature.[129]

4) In acting on appropriations, the Board shall consider the relative benefits to be derived from all beneficial uses (enumerated in detail) and may subject appropriations to such terms and conditions as will best conserve, develop, and utilize water in the public interest.[130]

5) The use of water for recreation and for preservation of fish and wildlife is declared to be a beneficial use, and in determining the amount of water available for appropriation for other beneficial uses, the Board shall take account, when in the public interest, of the amounts of water required for recreation and for the preservation of fish and wildlife.[131] (This is the only provision of the Water Code which bears directly on the preservation of streamflows for the purposes mentioned.)

6) The Board shall be guided by the policy that domestic use is the highest use of water, and that irrigation is the second highest use.[132]

7) Reservations to protect counties of origin attached to California Water Commission releases or assignments of state filings of applications to appropriate must be carried forward in the terms of the permits and licenses for appropriating the same water as issued by the Board; also, all other conditions for release or assignments of filings by the Commission must be carried forward.[133]

The State Water Rights Board is thus ostensibly given a very broad discretionary power over the authorization of water projects proposed by all types of agencies,

[125] *Ibid.*, §§ 1200–1203.

[126] *Ibid.*, § 1225. The authority of the State Water Rights Board stems ultimately from powers granted to a State Water Commission in 1913 in California *Statutes* (1913), ch. 586; and, further, by later legislation in California *Statutes* (1917), ch. 133, and (1921), ch. 329, etc.

[127] California *Water Code* (1963), § 1240.

[128] *Ibid.*, §§ 1253, 1255.

[129] *Ibid.*, § 1256.

[130] *Ibid.*, § 1257.

[131] *Ibid.*, § 1243.

[132] *Ibid.*, § 1254.

[133] *Ibid.*, § 1254.

including the power to reject them as not in the public interest and to attach conditions without limit as to location, size, design, and mode of operation if it finds these conditions to be in the public interest. (Its decisions may be appealed to the courts in mandamus proceedings.) At the same time, it is provided with only the broadest and most general statutory instructions, which conspicuously omit any criteria for determination of when projects are, or are not, in the public interest. Like the California Water Commission, but perhaps in greater degree, the Board could be a powerful regulatory authority which had developed a substantial body of administrative law. But, by and large, it has not done this, and it has not exercised latent powers of establishing rigorous criteria for the economic evaluation of water projects prior to issuing permits for appropriation of water in support of them.

The Water Code contains elaborate provisions for the filing of applications before the Board, their required content, publicity concerning applications to appropriate and hearings on them, and so forth.[134] Through its hearings, the State Water Rights Board provides a forum for, and acts as mediator with respect to, protests of competing or injured parties; it provides a device whereby conflicts of interest may be reconciled or compromised, and where interested government agencies may be heard. In fact, it acts as a second-stage forum in which many protests raised before the California Water Commission in connection with hearings on the release of state filings may be raised once again.

We turn now to federal regulation involving the authorization of water projects —a regulation which very heavily overlaps state regulation, with the exception that the federal water agencies are not subject to a federal commission's regulation or control over the authorization of their water projects. Federal regulation is exercised by the Federal Power Commission (FPC) under the provisions of the Federal Power Act of 1920.[135] Since 1950, the FPC has been made up of five commissioners appointed to five-year overlapping terms by the President with the approval of the Senate. Its procedures are analogous to those of the State Water Rights Board, in that it receives applications and issues licenses for projects, but its licenses are authorizations rather than instruments conferring water rights. As noted above, it has jurisdiction to license all nonfederal water resource developments that involve damming any streams over which Congress has authority under the Constitution.[136] All exploitable rivers in California are thus effectively covered.

The basic statutory criterion for granting an FPC license is that the Commission should select—among alternative projects for a given site or sites on a given river, once an application for a project has been made—the project which is best adapted to a comprehensive plan for improving or developing the waterway, for improving and utilizing development of water power, and for other public use, including recreational use.[137] The Commission is empowered to require modification of any project and of the specifications for its works in order to secure the best project;

[134] *Ibid.*, div. 2, pt. 2, ch. 1, arts. 2, 3, and chs. 3–9.

[135] Provisions of the 1920 act are now Part I of the current Federal Power Act; later legislation has given the FPC jurisdiction over electric power companies in interstate commerce and over the transportation and sale of natural gas in interstate commerce.

[136] 17 U.S. *Code* 797–e.

[137] 16 U.S. *Code* 803.

and detailed maps, plans, and specifications are made part of an FPC license. In implementing these powers, the Commission can require the applicant to provide, in addition to evidence of the nature and ownership of water rights to be used, the following information: a description of the proposed annual pattern of release flows from reservoir storage; an exposition of the proposed use of the project for the conservation and use of water for power, navigation, irrigation, reclamation, flood control, recreation, preservation of fish and wildlife, and urban water supplies; and a plan for full public utilization of project waters and adjacent lands for recreational purposes, so far as consistent with the other purposes.[138]

It stands out, however, that the statutory instructions themselves supply no criteria for selecting "best" or "acceptable" projects or for project evaluation generally, or any indication of the general or specific desirable characteristics of a comprehensive plan for developing a river. Furthermore, the language of the legislation suggests that the FPC will perforce evaluate projects serially on a case-by-case basis over time, and is not established as a comprehensive planning agency. The freedom of the federal agencies from FPC jurisdiction is also significant, and tends to become more so to the extent that these agencies succeed in asserting their freedom from servitude to state regulations.

As to the relationship of FPC regulation to that imposed by such state agencies as the California Water Commission and the State Water Rights Board, the law provides that an applicant to the FPC must show evidence of compliance with state laws affecting power development and related functions of water projects.[139] However, although the FPC requires the applicant to submit such evidence of compliance with state laws, it apparently needs to require compliance only with those state requirements which the FPC finds appropriate to effect the purposes of a federal license. State laws must give way to contrary FPC requirements, and state requirements are not added to federal requirements. The FPC rulings to the preceding effects, as sustained in decisions of the Supreme Court, have strongly suggested that the jurisdiction of state authorities to regulate the authorization of projects for the in-stream use of intrastate navigable waters or of waters on federal reserved lands (including dams and reservoir storage, power generation, and streamflow regulation) is strictly subordinate to that of the FPC.[140]

One further power of the FPC deserves mention in relation to the conflict-of-laws question just raised. The Commission has the power to determine whether or not a project proposed by a nonfederal applicant should instead be developed by a federal water agency, and if it determines that the development should be made by federal agencies, it must deny the nonfederal application for a license.[141] This provision must be read in the context of the provision mentioned above to the effect

[138] Federal Power Commission, *Regulations Under the Federal Power Act* (1959), § 4.41, as amended in 1963.

[139] 16 U.S. *Code* 802 (b).

[140] See, for example, *First Iowa Hydro-Electric Cooperative* vs. *Federal Power Commission,* 328 U.S. 152 (1946); *State of Washington Department of Fish and Game* vs. *Federal Power Commission,* 207 Fed. 2nd 391 (1953); *Federal Power Commission* vs. *Oregon,* 349 U.S. 435 (1955).

[141] 16 U.S. *Code* 800 (b).

that federal water projects are not subject to the licensing and regulatory powers of the FPC.

The law establishing the authority of the FPC to license water projects also contains the usual complement of procedural provisions, including those concerning publicity concerning applications, protests, and public hearings—comparable to procedural provisions affecting the State Water Rights Board. Such law also specifically provides that, upon the filing of applications for licenses, the FPC must give notice to the affected state or states and municipalities, and must submit applications for review by the secretaries of the Army, of the Interior, of Agriculture, and of Health, Education, and Welfare, as well as clearing any contemplated impediments to navigation with the Corps of Engineers. Any of these governments or departments or officers may protest applications and be heard at hearings on these applications. The FPC thus provides a third and perhaps broader forum before which the merits of the usual water project may be argued.

Protection of streamflows

A second general category of regulations affecting the use of water includes laws designed to protect streamflows, primarily in the interest of the preservation of public benefits derived from recreation and from fish and wildlife resources, and—in the modern context—secondarily in the interest of preserving the navigability of waterways. Such regulations are in some degree interwoven with regulations of the authorization of water projects, but we have set them aside for separate discussion here.

It has already been noted that the statutory instructions to the State Water Rights Board regarding conditions for authorizing water projects stipulate that the use of water for recreation and preservation of fish and wildlife is a beneficial use and that the Board should, when in the public interest, take into account the water required for these in-stream uses in determining the amount available for appropriation for commercial uses.[142] All further state regulatory provisions bearing on this matter are contained in the Fish and Game Code of California. These, few in number and limited with respect to the protection they afford to the noncommercial in-stream uses of water, may be described briefly as follows:

1) The California Department of Fish and Game is empowered to establish, in specifically designated fish and game districts, certain streams as sanctuaries in which any structures tending to impede the movement of fish up and down stream are prohibited.[143] This provides selective protection to runs of anadromous fish in certain minor streams.

2) The Department must examine all existing dams on streams naturally frequented by fish; if there is obstruction to the free passage of fish around any dam, it may order the construction of suitable fishways of such form and capacity as it

[142] California *Water Code* (1963), § 1234.
[143] California *Fish and Game Code,* § 5901.

determines, and also may itself construct such additional fishways as it deems necessary.[144]

3) When an application for a new dam or an enlargement of an old one is filed with the State Water Rights Board, the Fish and Game Commission (a political body), having under mandate received a copy of the application, may require the construction of fishways if they are necessary for the protection of fish and also practicable. If fishways are deemed impracticable, the Fish and Game Commission may order the operator of the dam to construct and equip a fish hatchery in lieu of a fishway, to be operated by the Department of Fish and Game at state expense, the owner of the dam being required to furnish enough water to operate the hatchery. There are similar requirements for fish screens on diversion works in general.[145]

4) The Department of Water Resources, the Department of Fish and Game, and the Department of Natural Resources are charged with the responsibility, in connection with state water projects, for developing recreational facilities and enhancing fish and wildlife resources. Furthermore, they are instructed to coordinate planning with federal and local water agencies in an endeavor to arrive at a master plan of multipurpose use of the streams of the state, which plan embraces developing a system of public recreational facilities and a program for enhancing fish and wildlife resources.[146]

In spite of the reflection of growing concern for the preservation of streamflow for noncommercial in-stream uses in the relatively recent legislation described above, it would be fair to characterize the approach of the state of California to this regulatory problem as one still based on the assignment of a high cardinal priority to the commercial uses of streamflows without much regard to quantities of water involved. Further, it is an approach that emphasizes primarily measures aimed at ameliorating or mitigating the adverse effects of commercial dams on recreation and on fish and wildlife, rather than modifying dam location, size, and design in the light of recreational needs and considerations of fish and game.

Federal regulations to protect streamflows for recreational purposes and to preserve fish and wildlife are somewhat more positive and far-reaching. The most stringent regulation requires that the Federal Power Commission—having filed any application for a license with the U.S. Department of the Interior (among other agencies, as required by law)—as a condition of the license sought must require fishways as prescribed by the Secretary of the Interior. Further, the federal water agencies, not regulated by the FPC, are required to include in their water project plans such justifiable means and measures for the preservation of fish and wildlife as the Secretary of the Interior finds should be adopted to obtain maximum over-all project benefits.[147] These regulations are contained in recent amendments to the

[144] *Ibid.*, § 5931.

[145] *Ibid.*, §§ 5931, 5933.

[146] *Ibid.*, § 11900. Mention may also be made of the Davis-Grunsky Act (*ibid.*, § 12880), which provides for state grants to local projects to defray costs of project features designed to enhance fish and wildlife resources.

[147] 72 U.S. *Statutes* 563 (1958).

Fish and Wildlife Coordination Act, first passed in 1934.[148] The basic act applies both to dams built under FPC license and to federal water projects. It now requires that the federal water agencies consult the U.S. Fish and Wildlife Service and the counterpart department in the affected state, and that these agencies give consideration to fish and wildlife protection and enhancement in designing their projects. The U.S. Fish and Wildlife Service is also automatically a party at interest at hearings before the FPC on applications for licenses for dams by nonfederal agencies, wherein the FPC must consider the use of water for the preservation of fish and wildlife as one of the beneficial joint and alternative uses of water.[149]

In the net, with respect to federal water projects, the federal agencies are subject to much advice and persuasion from the U.S. Fish and Wildlife Service and from state departments of fish and game, and subject to regulatory control of the Secretary of the Interior at his discretion, in a context wherein that Secretary is head of the federal department of which the main federal water agency, the Bureau of Reclamation, is a subdepartment. Nonfederal agencies are regulated effectively at the discretion of the Secretary of the Interior and of the Federal Power Commission, as advised by federal and state fish and wildlife agencies. The pertinent legislation nowhere provides substantive rules to guide the Secretary or the FPC in their decisions.

The general power of the federal government to regulate works and activities affecting the navigability of rivers was asserted in Rivers and Harbors Acts of 1890 and 1899.[150] They provided that the creation of any obstruction to the navigable capacity of any waters of the United States is prohibited unless affirmatively authorized by Congress (as it is in any congressional authorization of a federal water project). Other provisions specifically name bridges, dams, dikes, causeways, breakwaters, and excavations and fills, as prohibited except as authorized by the Secretary of Army upon recommendation by the Corps of Engineers. As to intrastate waters developed under state legislation, any works affecting the navigability of streams require approval of the Corps. The full power of the federal government in this respect has been affirmed in a recent Supreme Court decision.[151] With respect to California and other western states, however, this federal power is qualified by a provision of the Flood Control Act of 1944 to the effect that, in states west of the 98th meridian, the use of water for navigation in connection with the operation of federal water agency project works shall be subordinated to all beneficial consumptive uses. All subsequent Flood Control and River and Harbor acts contain this provision.

Pollution control and maintenance of water quality

Regulation of stream pollution and water quality in California as yet is not very advanced, largely because the pollution problem has not become widespread and acute—and this mainly because industrial developments on inland streams, as dis-

[148] 48 U.S. *Statutes* 402 (1934).
[149] 72 U.S. *Statutes* 563 (1958).
[150] The 1899 Act is identified as 30 U.S. *Statutes* 1121, 1151, § 10 (1899).
[151] *U.S.* vs. *Republic Steel Corporation,* 362 U.S. 482 (1960).

tinct from tidewater, are still relatively unimportant. Nevertheless, the pollution of streams by return flows from irrigation is emerging as a major problem in the lower San Joaquin Valley and the Delta, and general pollution problems are becoming more acute in the estuary of the Sacramento River and in the Suisun, San Pablo, and San Francisco bays into which the river empties.

The relevant regulatory law in California at present is a patch-work, divisible nevertheless into two main parts: (1) law providing direct regulatory powers by state and municipal authorities, as contained in the Health and Safety Code; and (2) law providing for more or less voluntary solutions to regional pollution problems through regional water pollution control boards, as contained in the Water Code.

The basic and direct regulatory processes are vested primarily in the State Department of Public Health, and in subsidiary fashion in local public health officers and in private citizens who may seek injunctive relief in the courts. There are three principal substantive provisions of the law thus enforced. The first is prohibition of the dumping of garbage into navigable waters (including the ocean) and various acts polluting water "used to supply" any inhabitants of the state—including drainage of water closets, privies, cesspools, septic tanks, and slaughterhouses into these waters, as well as the contamination of such waters by livestock, bathing, and laundering. Such acts may be penalized as a misdemeanor, and are subject to summary abatement. (Exceptions are provided for fishing in reservoirs.) These regulations apply to waters drawn upon for human consumption.[152] Second, distinctions are drawn among "contamination" of water, defined as impairment of water quality by sewage or industrial waste which creates an actual hazard to public health; "pollution" of water, defined as impairment by the same means which does not create an actual public health hazard, but which adversely and unreasonably affects waters for any beneficial uses; and "nuisance," such as generation of undesirable odors. Contamination is made subject to summary abatement by the State Department of Public Health or by public health officers; and that department is instructed to report pollutions to appropriate regional pollution control boards for their handling as provided in the Water Code.[153] Third is the so-called "pure water law" which provides that any person, utility, municipality, or other sources can supply water for domestic use only with a permit from the State Department of Public Health; and that permits shall be granted only subject to accepted standards of purity, wholesomeness, potability, and lack of menace to human health and life.

In sum, the mandatory direct regulation of pollution and water quality in California applies almost entirely to the prevention of contamination of waters used for domestic water supplies and of other contamination which creates an actual hazard to public health—is mainly a limited sort of human and industrial sewage control—and to the control of the purity of domestic water supplies as delivered at the faucet.

The other structure of administrative control of water pollution is provided by a State Water Quality Control Board and nine regional water pollution control

[152] California *Health and Safety Code,* §§ 4453 ff.
[153] *Ibid.,* §§ 5410 ff.

boards (one for each of nine designated regions of the state).[154] The powers of the regional pollution control boards are to obtain coordinated regional action for the abatement, prevention, and control of water pollution and nuisances as defined in the Health and Safety Code and the Water Code, by means of formal or informal meetings of the parties involved. The regional boards are to encourage and assist self-policing waste disposal programs for industry. They are to formulate long-run regional plans for pollution control, and may recommend programs for pollution reduction to the state board if they are eligible for financial assistance. And they may request enforcement of laws governing pollution by the appropriate federal, state, and local agencies, and must report uncorrected contamination to the State Water Quality Control Board and to local health officers having jurisdiction.[155]

In addition, the regional boards have somewhat firmer powers. The law requires any party discharging, or proposing to discharge, sewage or industrial waste into waters in a region to file a report on the actual or proposed discharge with the regional board having jurisdiction. Or the regional board may require such a report. After hearings, a regional board may prescribe requirements affecting the nature, quantity, and location of such discharges, and the persons notified of these requirements must provide facilities to meet them. If requirements so issued are violated, a regional board may issue cease-and-desist orders, and if such orders are not complied with, it shall refer them to the district attorney of the county in question for the securing of injunctive relief in the courts. And, if the county district attorney then refuses to act, the State Attorney General may take the proper court action. In addition, there are provisions in the law for civil actions for summary abatement of pollutions or nuisances which are transitory in nature or short in duration but periodic in occurrence, such actions to be brought by a county district attorney at his discretion, or by mandate if a regional board so requests.[156]

The State Water Quality Control Board is empowered to require reports on water pollution, and to assist in the formation of local public districts for the correction of pollutions and nuisances. It is supposed to formulate a statewide policy for pollution control, taking cognizance of the California Water Plan. It administers a statewide program for pollution research, and also a statewide program of financial assistance to regions or localities for pollution control. And it may direct the appropriate state agency to correct a pollution or nuisance, either on its own initiative or if a regional board fails to request such action. If contamination exists and is not being corrected, the state board must refer it to the state agency having

[154] It is notable that the nine appointive members of the state board must be chosen to represent seven designated "fields" of interest in water, by reason of the nature of their occupations. These are (1) supply of domestic water, (2) irrigated agriculture, (3) industrial water use, (4) production of industrial waste, (5) public sewage disposal, (6) city government, and (7) county government. Similarly, the seven appointive members of each regional pollution control board must include one each associated with urban water supply, irrigated agriculture, industry producing industrial waste, a municipality, a county, a fish and wildlife organization, and the public at large. Self-policing of pollution by polluters is thus rather heavily emphasized in the required composition of the state and regional boards. California *Water Code* (1963), §§ 13010, 13040–13042.

[155] *Ibid.*, § 13052.

[156] *Ibid.*, §§ 13054, 13054.1, 13054.3, 13060, 13063, 13080.

jurisdiction.[157] The law does not appear to contain, however, any substantive instructions as to when proceedings against pollution (as distinct from contamination) must be taken by any state or local agency; to supply any statutory criteria for determining when pollution abatement proceedings should be undertaken; or to provide any penalties for polluting waters other than those that might be imposed for contempt of court under an injunction, following the discretionary issuance of orders by the regional or state pollution control boards.[158]

The powers of the State Water Quality Control Board and of the regional water pollution control boards are only supplementary to the other state powers previously enumerated. No provision of the legislation establishing these boards and defining their powers is a limitation on the power of any city or county to adopt and enforce further regulations (not in conflict with the Water Code provisions) which impose further restrictions on the disposal of sewage or industrial waste or on other polluting activity, or on such power to prohibit and abate nuisances. Further, no provision of this legislation is a limitation on the power of any other state agencies to enforce any law which it is permitted or required to enforce, or on the right of persons to seek judicial relief against nuisance, pollution, or contamination.[159] It has further been determined that negotiated settlements of regional pollution problems arrived at through the offices of regional water pollution control boards are not immune from other provisions of the law, such as that contained in the Health and Safety Code or in local laws.[160]

The federal government has also entered the field of water pollution control with legislation providing support to state control efforts, and further asserting the power of the federal government to impose pollution regulations on interstate waters under certain conditions.[161] Specifically, with respect to interstate and navigable waters, the Secretary of Health, Education, and Welfare is empowered, if state measures to secure pollution abatement fail or are inadequate, to request the Attorney General to bring suit in the federal courts in the name of the United States to secure abatement. Since nearly all California streams are intrastate, this legislation would not seem to have broad applicability within the state. However, there has been public discussion of the need for encouraging the federal government to invoke its powers to secure abatement of pollution of the waters of Lake Tahoe (interstate between California and Nevada), as endeavors to arrive at a pollution control plan by agreement between the states have dragged on interminably while the problem becomes more acute.

Other regulations

The preceding pages do not cover every facet of public regulation of the use of water in California, and most minor aspects of regulation will remain undiscussed. Two further items of regulatory law, however, deserve brief mention.

[157] *Ibid.*, §§ 13020–13025.
[158] *Ibid.*, div. 7 as a whole.
[159] *Ibid.*, § 13001.
[160] *People* vs. *City of Los Angeles,* 160 Calif. App. 2nd. 494 (1958).
[161] 33 U.S. *Code* 466.

The first is the famous 160-acre limitation contained in federal reclamation law, which provides that to be eligible for irrigation water supplied by the Bureau of Reclamation, no landowner shall hold more than 160 acres in a service area, nor any husband and wife jointly more than 320 acres. This applies to water received from the Bureau under utility service contracts, including contracts with irrigation districts, as well as to water supplied through irrigation works of which the water users ultimately take possession. Under administrative regulations implementing the statutory law, moreover, in order to become eligible for Bureau water under service contracts, landowners must dispose of "excess lands" (beyond the 160-acre or 320-acre limit) within ten years of entering into a contract for Bureau water. Furthermore, they must do so under anti-speculation provisions which are designed to prevent the seller of excess lands from securing for himself any increment in the land value which is attributable to its being supplied with Bureau water.[162] The regulation is evidently designed to implement broad sociological objectives not having to do with economic efficiency, and has tended to reduce the potential customers of the Bureau of Reclamation appreciably in an area where large landholdings are common.

The second sort of regulation bears on a quite different matter. Under the California Water Code, all irrigation districts (the most important of the numerous forms of local public water districts) are required to file annual reports with a California Districts Securities Commission, and further to secure from the Commission certification of any proposed district bond issue, which the Commission may issue after finding that the project to be financed is economically sound and financially feasible. The total outstanding general obligation bond issues of any irrigation district shall not have a principal value exceeding 60 per cent of the value of the property owned by the district, including property to be acquired with bond proceeds. (This limitation does not apply to revenue bonds.) All certified bonds are declared to be legal investments for trust funds, insurance companies, commercial and savings banks, trust companies, state school funds, and any funds which may be invested in municipal and school-district bonds. The Commission is also charged with supervising the expenditure of irrigation-district bond funds.[163] All the preceding is mandatory only with respect to irrigation districts. The other numerous types of water districts may voluntarily seek and secure certification of their bond issues, but they are not required to do so.[164] This omission in the law occasionally has proved unfortunate, as the purposes of the laws providing for other types of water districts have from time to time been perverted through the formation of local water districts for the benefit of a few landholders, with uncertified general obligation bonds thereafter being issued and sold to unsuspecting investors.

[162] The basic statute, subsequently amended, is the Reclamation Act of 1902, 32 U.S. *Statutes* 388 (1902); administrative law is found in U.S. Congress, House Committee on Interior and Insular Affairs, *Central Valley Project Documents, Part 1,* 84 Cong. 2 sess. (1956). Powers under the law described are affirmed in *Ivanhoe Irrigation District* vs. *McCracken,* 357 U.S. 275 (1958).

[163] California *Water Code* (1963), div. 10, §§ 20000–20107.

[164] *Ibid.,* § 20003.

Servitude of Federal Water Agencies to California Law

A matter of considerable importance in evaluating the public regulatory system affecting the use of water—and in particular that part of it governing the authorization of water projects—concerns the extent of the servitude of the federal water agencies to state water laws. This is important, especially, because the proposals and project plans of the federal Bureau of Reclamation and Corps of Engineers are not subject to the licensing authority of the Federal Power Commission or to critical scrutiny by another independent federal agency. Rather, their projects are subject at the federal level to scrutiny only by the Secretary of the Interior and Secretary of the Army, who are simply the executive superiors of the heads of the Bureau and the Corps, by the Bureau of the Budget, which has not generally been organized or staffed to undertake detailed analysis and scrutiny of proposed projects, and by Congress and its committees, where detailed project evaluation is not generally undertaken or emphasized. Therefore, the federal water agencies are substantially self-regulating, and more or less exclusively evaluate their own projects, except so far as they are subject to the review powers and licensing authority of the individual states. It is thus essential to inquire whether the Bureau and the Corps—especially the Bureau—are subject to the jurisdiction of the California Water Commission and the State Water Rights Board (as the nonfederal agencies are) in the matter of obtaining authorizations of intrastate projects in California, and in other ways are obliged to operate subject to the common-law content and statutory provisions of the California law of water rights.

The question thus posed should be distinguished from the related question referred to above—whether the California Commission and Board can really exercise regulatory authority bearing on the authorization of nonfederal water projects, at least as regards dams and in-stream uses, independently of the Federal Power Commission, except so far as the FPC chooses to honor rulings of the state authorities. The latter is indeed a separate question, though judicial rulings on it may have some relevance to the question concerning the servitude of the federal water agencies to California water law.

The problem is simplified by first noting that the Corps of Engineers, not being subject to any federal statutory requirement to conform to state water laws, exercises federal prerogatives under the commerce clause of the Constitution in undertaking projects for flood control and improvement of navigation, and is under no obligation to procure water rights under state laws in support of its projects. However, the supplying of water for consumptive use and the generation and distribution of electric power as parts of Corps projects are always undertaken by the Bureau of Reclamation, by a nonfederal licensee of the FPC, or by a state or local agency under contract with the Corps; and these agencies are, or may be, required to perfect water rights under state law.

The question of servitude of federal agencies to state water laws thus concerns almost entirely the Bureau of Reclamation. At present, there is a clear difference of opinion between the Bureau on the one hand, and the regulatory authorities of California on the other. In 1960 pleadings before the California Water Commission on a request by the Bureau for approval of proposed amendments to pending Bureau applications for the appropriation of water for a project, the regional solicitor contended that:

> While the Department of the Interior reaffirms its desire to abide by State water laws and to construct and operate projects in cooperation with State and local interests, the State in this instance is without authority or jurisdiction to control, limit, or prescribe the manner, method, or extent of operations of it, or the method by which it will perform its functions, or to impose conditions relative to such construction, operation, or performance of functions.[165]

In opposition to this contention, the chairman of the State Water Rights Board stated on a later occasion that "there is a basic difference between conditions that delineate the extent of water right granted and provide for the protection of vested rights, and conditions that hinder or interfere with the Federal Government's use of the water right so granted. . . . The State may impose conditions in limitation and delineation of the right to be granted the United States in the first instance, but may not impose conditions hindering or interfering with the delivery and distribution of the *water so granted.*"[166] This statement may be construed to assert that requirements affecting project design and construction by the Bureau of Reclamation can indeed be imposed by California authorities as conditions for granting water rights, which the federal agency must legally secure under state law in order to proceed with a project.

In the context of these opposing views of the law, it is worthy of note that the Bureau of Reclamation in the past has observed, and continues to observe, all the procedural and substantive requirements of California law affecting project authorization in connection with granting rights to appropriate water—applying to and securing releases of state filings from the California Water Commission and, in turn, applying to and securing permits and licenses from the State Water Rights Board. The real issue is whether this apparent recognition of servitude to California law is merely a formality which the Bureau is willing, though not required, to observe because the discretionary powers vested in the California Commission and Board habitually have not been exercised to subject federal projects to real critical scrutiny or to requirements much at variance with the applicant's wishes, or whether any more vigorous exercise of their powers by the state authorities could in fact be made binding on the Bureau of Reclamation.

The question is posed in the context of Section 8 of the Reclamation Act of 1902 (the act that established the Bureau of Reclamation and its mission), which is still in full force and effect. This section subordinates the administration of the reclamation program to servitude to state water law and to water rights acquired under state law in the following language:

[165] *Answer of the United States to the Petition by the Sacramento River and Delta Water Association for Reconsideration of the Decision and Order Made by Resolutions 82 and 83 by the California Water Commission, August 5, 1960.* Several Supreme Court decisions were cited in support of this view.

[166] Kent Silverthorne, "State-Federal Water Rights Facts," address (mimeographed) to the Irrigation Districts Association of California, Coronado, California, Nov. 8, 1962.

> . . . nothing in this Act shall be construed as affecting or intended to affect or to in any way interfere with the laws of any State or territory relating to the control, appropriation, use or distribution of water used in irrigation, or any vested right acquired thereunder, and the Secretary of the Interior, in carrying out the provisions of this Act, shall proceed in conformity with such laws, and nothing herein shall in any way affect any right of any State or of the Federal Government or of any land owner, appropriator, or user of water in, to or from any interstate stream or the waters thereof: *Provided,* that the right to the use of water acquired under the provisions of this Act shall be appurtenant to the land irrigated and beneficial use shall be the basis, the measure, and the limit of the right.[167]

The real issue raised here concerns the extent to which the Supreme Court has since qualified, modified, and restricted this statute by interpretation, or the extent to which the Court has interpreted it or "superlegislated" it out of existence.

Actually, decisions of the Supreme Court bearing directly on the extent of servitude of the Bureau of Reclamation (as distinct from nonfederal FPC licensees) to state water laws have by no means entirely stricken the servitude established by federal statute, though they have restricted it significantly. For the sake of an abbreviated discussion, we list the principal pertinent rulings and comment on them briefly as follows:

1) The claims of the Bureau of Reclamation that the United States owns all unappropriated waters in the West by virtue of cession of waters along with lands to the United States by France, Spain, and Mexico has not been directly ruled upon by the Supreme Court; it has been ruled that the federal government was the initial proprietor of these waters and that state claims derive from this title, as the federal government has relinquished its interests by grants or by statute. On the other hand, in one of the cases in point it was further ruled that the United States takes water from a river (which it claimed to own) like any other appropriator, under state law and the Reclamation Act of 1902.[168]

2) The most extreme restriction on federal servitude to state water laws is found in a ruling that the United States is not liable for depriving another proprietor of the opportunity to use the flow of a navigable or non-navigable stream to produce power, and need acquire no state right to appropriate water for in-stream uses by virtue of its powers under the commerce clause of the Constitution.[169]

3) On the other hand, with respect to the operation of the Bureau in diverting and delivering irrigation water, it has been ruled (and not subsequently overruled) that the Bureau is a storer and carrier of water, and that its customers become holders of appropriative rights to the water carried to them by the Bureau (rights appurtenant to their lands), under state water laws and under the Reclamation Act of 1902.[170] The thrust of the rulings so far enumerated is that the Bureau is

[167] 32 U.S. *Statutes* 388 (1902).

[168] *U.S.* vs. *Grand River Dam Authority,* 363 U.S. 229 (1960); *Nebraska* vs. *Wyoming,* 325 U.S. 589 (1945).

[169] *U.S.* vs. *Grand River Dam Authority, supra.*

[170] *Ickes* vs. *Fox,* 300 U.S. 82 (1937); *Nebraska* vs. *Wyoming, supra.*

subject to state laws of water rights in appropriating water for diversion and delivery for consumptive (other than in-stream) uses, either in general or to the extent that state laws define the interests that must be compensated when water is taken by the Bureau.

4) There have been several rulings to the effect that the Bureau is not subject, as an appropriator of water, to provisions of state water law which are in conflict with federal reclamation law, and in effect that whereas the acquisition of water rights by the Bureau is subject to state control, the operation of federal projects is not. Thus, water users supplied by the Bureau are not eligible for indiscriminate service, and can be made subject to the 160-acre limitation; and California state law giving preference to domestic use over irrigation use of water is not binding on the Bureau.[171] In the light of these rulings, it is unlikely that the Bureau can be required, if it wishes to protest, to observe county-of-origin and watershed-of-origin protections now contained in the state law.

5) It has been held that the Reclamation Act of 1902 does not permit state laws to prevent the United States from exercising powers of eminent domain to acquire the water rights of others, and also that the California courts cannot use physical solutions as forms of judicial remedy against the United States in water rights conflicts in which the Bureau is involved.[172]

The restrictions on federal servitude to state water laws in connection with Bureau of Reclamation projects outlined above evidently stop well short of erasing this servitude altogether, or of constituting a judicial repeal of Section 8 of the Reclamation Act of 1902. On the other hand, it would appear unlikely that the Supreme Court would find the Bureau of Reclamation subject to any rigorous and detailed conditions for project authorization which the state might try to impose through the California Water Commission, the State Water Rights Board, or successor agencies.

Some students of recent court decisions have gone much further, and concluded that the Bureau is no longer subject to any sort of servitude to state water laws, and can now proceed to commandeer unappropriated water for any legitimate project purposes. And it has been reported that the current instructions from the Department of Justice to the Bureau of Reclamation are that it should notify the state board of federal intentions, but must not recognize the right of California to limit or control its use of water.[173] It would appear that this extreme interpretation of the current state of the law, as espoused by agencies of the federal government and by others, rests heavily upon drawing implications from several cases in which the superiority of the licensing power of the Federal Power Commission over state regulatory authorities with respect to nonfederal applicants for licenses to build dams has been rather firmly established, both under the commerce clause as applied to navigable waters and under the property clause as applied to federal reservations

[171] *Ivanhoe Irrigation District* vs. *McCracken,* 357 U.S. 275 (1958); *City of Fresno* vs. *California,* 372 U.S. 627 (1963).

[172] *City of Fresno* vs. *California, supra; Dugan* vs. *Rank,* 372 U.S. 609 (1963).

[173] Burnham Enersen, attorney, address to the Commonwealth Club of San Francisco, as reported in *The Commonwealth* (San Francisco), July 13, 1964.

(including national forests).[174] Since in none of these cases has the Bureau of Reclamation been a party at interest, nor has the construction of the Reclamation Act of 1902 been at issue, these projections of judicial doctrine to cover the issue of servitude of the Bureau of Reclamation to state water laws involve an element of speculation, regardless of the Bureau's wishes. Nonetheless, several pieces of legislation have been introduced in Congress which would declare that the withdrawal or reservation of public lands would not affect state-created water rights or affect state jurisdiction over water rights as conferred upon admission to the Union, and in addition would clearly subordinate the use of water for navigation to consumptive uses in all federal projects in the West.[175] The passage of these bills, however, would not remove all areas of conflict and ambiguity in the laws in question.

In concluding this discussion, comment may be added concerning the servitude to regulatory authority, especially regarding project authorization, of the California Department of Water Resources. It is, of course, fully subject to the licensing power of the Federal Power Commission. It is also formally subject to the jurisdiction of both the California Water Commission and the State Water Rights Board. However, as the state's primary water development planning agency and the sole instrument of the state in constructing large-scale water projects, the Department occupies a political position which modifies its exposure to requirements that may be established by the state regulatory agencies. This is the case in considerable part because the state legislature can, and does, authorize projects recommended by the Department (as parts of the California Water Plan) without first securing authorization from the Commission or Board. Therefore, in fact and probably in law, the Department of Water Resources is substantially immune to the powers of the state regulatory bodies, even though as a matter of form it makes applications for appropriation of water to these bodies.

Summary

We make no attempt here to give a general resume of the legal framework of the Northern California industry, but restrict this summary to what appear to be the principal economic implications of this framework for the structure, conduct, and performance of the industry. Seven points seem to deserve particular emphasis.

First, the law of water rights has permitted private and public agencies to acquire perpetual property rights to the use of streamflows and ground water, in amounts per acre of land irrigated or per urban user served upon which only very loose and general restrictions are placed. Given this permission, an unplanned historical process has resulted in the allocation of rights to the use of economically scarce water among users, uses, and sites in a haphazard fashion which could only by unlikely coincidence approximate an economically efficient allocation.

Second, the law affecting water-using organizations has encouraged the develop-

[174] *State of Washington Department of Fish and Game* vs. *Federal Power Commission*, 328 U.S. 152 (1946); and *Federal Power Commission* vs. *Oregon*, 349 U.S. 435 (1955)—the so-called Pelton Dam case, involving federal reserved lands.

[175] U.S. Congress, S. 101 and S. 1275, 88 Cong. 1 sess. (1963).

ment of an institutional structure in which most of the available surface water is developed and most of the water rights to it are held by a great many fully integrated local public and private agencies, each of which acts as an agent for a particular group of users and their lands in securing water rights, and each of which has a public-service responsibility only to its particular constituency or group of customers. The laws concerning the delineation and re-delineation of the service areas of these agencies are sufficiently loose that uncoordinated and independent local groups of water users are given wide discretionary power over the manner in which the supply of available water will be allocated as among potential users and sites of use as a whole. Thus, these agencies serve as relatively unregulated independent instrumentalities for exploiting the law of water rights in such a way as to make possible significant economic misallocations of the available water supply.

Third, the legal doctrine that water rights become appurtenant to the lands on which water claimed under rights is used, together with numerous legal restrictions on the ability of integrated public and private water agencies to sell water or water rights, has been sufficient, taken with other considerations,[176] to preclude the development of anything approximating organized and continuous markets in water or water rights. As a result, no process of market exchanges has developed to correct misallocations of water created through the pattern of initial acquisition of water rights. Nor does the legally available, but by no means compulsory, process of expanding agency service areas and consolidating agencies accomplish much in the way of needed reallocations.

Fourth, local producer-wholesaler agencies, of the numerous types provided for by law to supply nonintegrated retailing water agencies, are in general more or less tied by law to securing water rights for limited constituencies and serving them to the exclusion of others. They are less likely to be responsible for significant misallocations of water to the degree that their constituencies are larger than those of most fully integrated agencies.

Fifth, the large federal and state agencies which produce and wholesale water, together with local "overlay" agencies which re-wholesale some of this water, are not tied from the beginning to serving specified and limited groups of users, and may pursue policies which are aimed at redressing existing misallocations of the regional water supply. Their effectiveness in so doing has been necessarily limited, however, since together they supply less than 10 per cent of all water put to consumptive use in Northern California. Moreover, the laws establishing them do not generally permit them to operate as water sellers in a continuous water market. The supplies that they develop from individual projects are committed to particular user groups under long-term contracts. Once this is done, market mechanisms for reallocation of their water supplies are as conspicuously absent as they are for the reallocation of supplies to which local integrated agencies hold rights.

[176] The legal impediments to the development of water markets may not be considered theoretically sufficient to explain the failure of such markets to develop, but in a context where water users wish to be water users and not water merchants, in which potential purchasers desire long-term commitments to deliver water and potential sellers are unwilling to give them, and in which transport costs are high and transport facilities specialized, they do suffice.

Sixth, the legal characteristics and responsibilities of local water agencies, public and private, are such that they may be viewed broadly as users' cooperatives, having motivational patterns of the general sort attributable to such cooperatives rather than to profit-seeking producer-sellers.

Finally, the system of the regulation of the use of water is weak and inadequate, particularly in the absence of market forces to serve as an automatic regulator. Most important, perhaps, is the fact that state and federal authorities charged with authorizing water projects operate under vague and general statutory standards and perforce do not evaluate projects in terms of their economic desirability and feasibility or of their impact on the allocation of water among uses and users. Moreover, both the federal water agencies and the California Department of Water Resources are legally or in fact relatively immune from the regulation of these authorities and operate largely as self-regulating bureaucracies. As to other types of regulation, the protection of streamflows for recreational purposes tends to be weak—heavily subordinated to commercial uses of water but according to no valid economic criteria—and based on an inadequate grant of real regulatory powers. And the powers granted, and the institutions established, for the control of water pollution and water quality also appear to be weak and inadequate. Furthermore, there is currently a state of confusion concerning the respective jurisdictions of federal and state regulatory agencies, and concerning the extent of the Bureau of Reclamation's servitude to state water laws.

4

MEMBER ENTITIES AND THEIR ORGANIZATION

The physical environment surrounding the water industry, as well as the legal framework governing water rights and the powers of various classes of water agencies and imposing regulation on water resource development, have been described. We now consider the prevalence of these agencies in the industry and certain aspects of their industrial organization—those aspects likely to be economically significant in the physical setting of Northern California.

In the conventional industry study, the number and size distribution of firms typically stands out as the highest peak in the range of structural elements. In the present case, the upward thrust of this element will be somewhat less. Conventional price theory readily identifies seller and buyer concentration as structural elements of great potential significance in influencing the conduct and performance of an industry. When theory is adapted to the circumstances of the water industry, significant hypotheses still emerge concerning the influence of the number and size distribution of buyers and sellers and the degree of vertical integration, both in the industry as a whole and in its more cohesive local segments. Furthermore, they call for roughly the same sort of measurement and appraisal of these structural elements as in the conventional industry study. But these hypotheses, aside from being rather different from the conventional ones, generate a significantly weaker set of predictions about the industry's conduct and performance.

Economic Significance of the Organization of the Water Industry

To begin on a negative note, in the institutional setting of the water industry, seller concentration among retail agencies can be expected to have no appreciable influence on the degree of competition in markets of water-supplying agencies for water-using customers. This is because there are no markets in which customers can shop for offers among competing sellers. Most individual water-supplying organizations (excepting wholesalers in some degree) are the captive suppliers of various groups of water users, with each organization fairly firmly tied to its own group of users. This is true of local public agencies which are generally established by given user groups, essentially as users' cooperatives for securing water supplies; of mutual companies which are similarly established by user groups; and of private water companies which become the captive suppliers of given areas under the law of public service responsibility. Given their status and relationships to groups of water users, various water-supplying organizations supply their insular service areas and do not compete as sellers in general markets for customers. A rational users' cooperative will expand its sales under certain circumstances, but, as noted in Chapter 3, legal elements are very likely to stifle this impulse.

Similarly, no significant effect of seller concentration seems likely on the rivalry of organizations for long-term relationships with additional customers, principally because there is little such rivalry to be affected. Public agencies in the process of formation conceivably may clash in laying out prospective service areas, and going agencies with reasons for expanding their service areas similarly may have conflicts, but the occasions of such rivalry appear rare. So far as they may occur, the likelihood might be somewhat influenced by the existing degree of agency concentration in an area, in that the fewness of agencies reduces the number of possible contenders for service areas. But since this sort of rivalry does not seem to be an important type of competition in the Northern California water industry, we hesitate to attribute much importance to concentration in this context.

Thus, the asserted prevalence of the users' cooperative motivation in the water industry, coupled with other institutional traits, precludes the existence of retail sellers' markets, and thereby knocks out the conventional hypotheses concerning the effect of seller concentration on resource allocation. As if this were not adversity enough for the significance of ordinary measures of concentration, we have also noted that alternative uses of water are not linked in continuous fashion throughout the whole Northern California area. The flow of a given river may be economically usable in potentially competing, alternative ways, but the choice made among them may have no impact—either actually or optimally—upon allocations elsewhere in the area. In short, not only do no markets for water at retail exist, but if they did arise in those basins or sub-basins where alternative uses of water can be detected, they would be local and fragmented, rather than area-wide. Any hypotheses we can devise concerning the market impact of the organization of the water industry, then, are likely to call for investigations and measurements of local, rather than general, conditions.

Having identified these important limitations on the economic significance of concentration in the water industry, let us turn to a positive quest for hypotheses indicating those traits of the industry's organization which forecast an impact upon conduct and performance. Several important groups, somewhat overlapping, can be found. Their total rationale cannot be explained in some cases prior to some of the discussion presented later, in Part Two; for the present, we need only to indicate the measurements of industrial organization they dictate.

1) As indicated in Chapter 3, agencies taking different legal forms and performing different economic functions in the water industry vary greatly in the opportunities for action open to them and extent of constraints impelling them to take into account the external consequences of their actions. These opportunities and constraints can be identified as raising the possibility of certain defects in the allocative performance of the water industry. Thus, we need to know the relative prevalence of different types of legal entities in the industry in order to evaluate the threat of the kinds of misallocation to which they may be susceptible. Such hypotheses call for area-wide measurements, rather than measurements of the

concentration of different types of agencies in particular basins or "latent markets" —although the distribution of types of entities in a particular basin may affect conduct and performance there in other ways.

2) For somewhat overlapping reasons, the degree of vertical integration attained in the Northern California water industry as a whole may hold considerable significance. A water user who supplies himself from a well or stream is completely integrated (in the industrial sense of that concept); he comes into market contact with other water users, if at all, only in rivalry for water at the natural source. The public water agency that gathers water from a natural source and transmits it to retail customers attains a lesser degree of integration, even though in theory the users' cooperative internalizes relations between the organization and its member-customers. Finally, the existence of one or more layers of wholesalers between the retailing agency and the source of water represents a further reduction in the amount of integration. Because of the differing legal powers of entities showing differing degrees of integration, differences in the cost characteristics of the various stages and types of integration (to be discussed in Chapter 6), and the motivational differences that can arise because wholesaling agencies generally represent higher levels of government than retailing agencies (to be taken up in Part Two)—because of all of these, considerable differences may arise in both the behavior and performance of various segments of the water industry that are related to variations in their degrees of integration. Some of these contrasts will appear as we compare, in Chapters 12 and 13, the conditions of rivalry for water in its natural sources with the conditions of rivalry in transactions between wholesalers and retailers. These possible consequences of integration call for data on the degree of integration, both in Northern California as a whole and in its component regions.

3) Wholesaling agencies, especially those not integrated forward into retailing to any significant degree, find themselves acting in the role of arm's-length sellers, whether or not their legal frameworks place them in the role of acting as users' cooperatives of their retailing-agency customers. Thus the seller concentration of wholesalers may be significant for relatively conventional reasons relating to the greater freedom of action (together with its allocative consequences) for the seller not faced with market rivals. Wholesaling activities tend in practice to be affected with much more substantial economies of scale than do retailing activities in the water industry; in partial consequence, the geographic scope of activity open to a wholesaler is significantly wider. Therefore, we shall be concerned with the concentration of wholesaling activities in Northern California as a whole and in its major regions because of the potential impact of concentration on market performance, although that impact may affect local basins as well.

In connection with this type of measurement, we underline the freedom of the monopoly wholesaler in the water industry not just to monopolize, but rather to respond to any of a number of possible whims and motives. The major disadvantage of monopolized wholesaling of irrigation water is probably that most of the power to plan for large-scale development of storage and of interbasin transfers is vested in a single decision-making body, and is subject to influence by such caprice, error, or bureaucratic bias as may influence the decisions of this body. Monopolized wholesaling reverses the safety in numbers secured when numerous independent agencies with separate decision-making bodies are engaged in a common pursuit—when the fittest of alternative schemes has a chance openly to prove itself, and users are provided with alternative plans and alternative sources of supply. A heavy weight is thus placed on the wisdom of those guiding the policies of the single agency. On the other hand, the likelihood that scale economies have a good deal to do with the rise of wholesaling agencies in the first place suggests that concentration in wholesaling may also be related to technical efficiency. Furthermore, a wholesaler with activities that are larger in scope and geographic range than another wholesaler may potentially do a better job of taking into account external economies and diseconomies stemming from its actions. Thus, there are potential gains to increasing the absolute size of wholesaling organizations that may come into conflict with the gains from decreasing seller concentration. In any case, measures of both the concentration and absolute size of wholesaling activities in Northern California are clearly indicated.

4) The seller concentration of retailing agencies in basins or latent markets may be relatively unimportant, as was suggested above, but not their concentration when viewed as "buyers" vying for a single source of water. Their number, size distribution, and absolute size may all be quite significant in this context. (The word "buyers" is purposely placed in quotation marks here, because the rivalry for water among fully integrated retailing agencies occurs mainly over the establishment of water rights and the construction of physical facilities, not over the purchase of water itself. The term "buyer" concentration is retained because it correctly designates the measurements of industry structures to be made, and because no more apt expression seems available.) A principal reason why "buyer" concentration may affect behavior and performance in a particular river basin is the cumbersome character of some of the legal processes employed in defining water rights. Increasing the number of parties seeking to establish overlapping claims to a given supply of water augments enormously the complexity and cost of making a full adjudication. It may thereby predispose the parties to certain compromise solutions that affect not only the allocation of water among them, but also the total quantity and efficiency of physical facilities built for the storage and transportation of water.

Turning these possible effects of "buyer" concentration of retailing agencies into firm predictions, however, is a difficult matter. Episodes of rivalry for water rights or facilities in a particular basin may well cause changes in the number of agencies and their degree of integration, so we must be rather cautious about framing hypotheses running from market structure to resulting allocation. An observed pattern of concentration may be either the setting in which a rivalry for water sources takes place, or the outcome of some complex historical process of rivalry. So far as an observed pattern of concentration is a setting for such rivalry, one would not necessarily expect the rivalry to be less intense because of the existence of high concentration. It might be expected, on the one hand, that with a typical concentration pattern in which the principal organizations are of distinctly varying sizes, the odds might favor the larger and financially stronger organization in securing more water rights, and that an undesirable bias in water allocation might result. On the other hand, all sorts of misallocations can occur when a large number of small organizations are rivals for water supplies, and there is no solid ground for holding that with a concentrated structure of organizations the allocations attained among organizations tend to be worse than with a more atomistic structure. About the most that can be said is that whatever misallocations emerge from a process of rivalry for water sources, they will tend to occur in a simpler pattern, involving fewer but absolutely larger individual misallocations, as the number of rivals is smaller.

A further question relating to "buyer" concentration concerns whether or not concentration among agencies in a sub-basin will much affect the freedom of access of potential water users to surface water supplies, either by being included in the service areas of existing water-supplying organizations or by participating in the formation of new organizations for the purpose of securing water rights and water supplies. We would tend to support the a priori hypothesis that concentration would have little effect on such access. Each of a few large organizations generally serves many users, and each of many smaller ones serves fewer users; in either case, the legal possibilities for artificial barriers to membership in the public agency or mutual company or to inclusion in the service area of a private company are about the same. Certainly, equal access to water service from established suppliers by all equally eligible potential customers does not exist, and misallocations of water result. But it is not apparent that the situation is appreciably bettered or worsened by a high degree of local concentration of organizations when all such organizations are effectively captive suppliers of given groups of water users. Nor is the opportunity of excluded potential users to secure water supplies by forming their own agencies or mutual companies apparently much influenced by the existing degree of concentration of control of surface supplies by existing organizations. In regard to the access of added users to water supplies in general, moreover, it would appear to make relatively slight difference whether the dominant organizations in a concentrated structure are public agencies, mutual companies, or private water companies with public utility status—although the private forms of organization within narrow limits may be able somewhat more easily to accommodate new customers.

5) A final group of hypotheses concerns the relation between agency concentration in basins or latent markets and several aspects of performance involving the technical efficiency with which water is supplied to a given group of final users. Examples of technical inefficiency include diseconomies of small scale, duplicated facilities, excess capacity, and the like. Whether or not these problems arise is likely to depend more on the absolute sizes than the relative sizes of supplying organizations. As a useful shorthand, we can think of these hypotheses as concerning the effects of fragmentation of the supplying agencies on the efficiency of water supply to a given area. To test them, we require measurements of the absolute size of agencies serving individual basins or latent markets, since the question is one of technical efficiency within a given potential market. Let us review this fifth group of hypotheses and some related matters in somewhat more detail.

Large organizations supplying large service areas may allocate available water more or less equally among all the tracts within these areas; or, if unequally, may allocate it in a manner that provides all users in the area access to water on equal terms. The large organization with a large service area is thus likely to eliminate or greatly reduce the misallocation of water as among small tracts within its service area which would tend to occur if the same area were supplied instead by a number of smaller independent organizations. This is because the rivalry for water rights among such smaller organizations would almost inevitably produce a patchwork of local misallocations, which the large agency could wipe out by treating customers in a large area equally in the matter of access to water. The large agency is thus a deterrent to a good deal of local patchwork misallocation of water. Its contribution in this direction would appear to be only slightly offset by the tendency of large organizations to support some misallocations within the service area by failing to charge differential prices to customers whose costs of delivered water differ significantly. On the other hand, it should be emphasized that misallocations of water among large agencies in a sub-basin may emerge from their rivalrous pursuit of water sources, and that these misallocations may be long-lasting if the large agencies are all strong and stubborn. Thus, large agencies are no panacea for misallocations of water, but they do simplify the form of such misallocations and perhaps tend to reduce the aggregate of misallocations.

There appear, moreover, to be several clear advantages of large over small water supplying organizations, where largeness implies a concurrently large service area, diversion of large quantities of water, and large financial resources or borrowing capacity. First, the large organization usually should be able to exploit some economies of large-scale transportation of water and large-scale storage of stream water which are not available to smaller organizations.[1] Smaller organizations might conceivably achieve the same economies by making cooperative use of joint transportation or storage facilities, but it seems unlikely that they will do so often because of the many stumbling blocks in the way of making arrangements mutually satisfactory to several or many parties.

Second, large agencies are more likely than many small ones to be able to supply themselves with adequate storage reservoir capacities, since they are individually large enough to use and finance them. Small agencies not only cannot use or finance reservoirs of efficient size individually, but there are numerous impediments to working out cooperative arrangements for building jointly used facilities. The fact that the small agencies may tend to freeload on reservoir capacities built by electric utility companies or federal agencies, possibly with some private financial advantage, should not obscure the fact that the large agencies, on the average, will probably secure economically more efficient reservoir operations. They are assisted in so doing in that, as large organizations with adequate financing, they can much more easily arrive at cooperative arrangements with electric utility companies for construction and joint dual-purpose operation of efficient storage reservoirs.

A final advantage of large agencies is that, having large service areas, they are more likely to incur internally the side-effects of their primary operations, and to adjust their operations accordingly, rather than disregarding them as external effects impinging on outsiders. Two illustrations of such effects are those involving drainage and the recharge of ground-water basins. The small agency in its primary operations may create costly drainage problems for other agencies, but disregard them because it does not bear their costs. The large agency is more likely to create

[1] Such economies are discussed in Chapter 6.

drainage problems within its own service area, and adjust its primary operations so as to achieve an economically more desirable over-all result. Similarly, the small agency may have little interest in spreading part of its surface diversions for percolation into efficient storage in ground-water basins, because it is small enough that the water it spreads is likely to be recovered by others. But the large agency may often be so large that it can expect to recover much of the water it spreads for percolation, and thus have an inducement to engage in more efficient over-all practices in water use. Because it tends to internalize effects which would be external to the small agency, the large agency tends to act more efficiently in using water.

Integration and Concentration of Self-Suppliers and Retailers

Among the potentially significant aspects of the organization of the water industry, we first consider the extent of integration and concentration of agencies in Northern California as a whole. This section develops these measurements of industrial structure for the self-supplying users and organizations retailing water for consumptive use. The section that follows sets them forth for water wholesaling and related activities that employ or regulate water in its natural channels or basins.

The conjecture that vertical integration can exist to varying degrees in an industry implies that its economic function can be broken down into a series of physically separable phases. The functions involved in getting water from natural surface sources to users can be broken into a number of stages, and we can observe these stages being carried out in only a small variety of alternative sequences. Thus, for some applications of irrigation water, the sequence involves mainly, in the following order, these stages: reservoir storage, streamflow regulation, diversion, long-distance transport, wholesaling, medium-distance bulk transport, local transport, and retailing. For a much larger part of irrigation water, we would find the same sequence, except that long-distance transport and wholesaling would be omitted. For simple nonconsumptive use of water to generate power, the essential sequence may involve only storage, in-transit use to drive turbines, and regulation of downstream flow. In practice, to what extent are these separable physical functions integrated within the operations of single organizations in the industry?

Nearly 90 per cent of all the water that is directed to consumptive uses in Northern California is handled by organizations or persons which individually integrate all necessary functions—from initial capture of water through delivery to immediate localities of use, possibly including retailing to final users, and also possibly adding storage of streamflows, their regulation, and their use in transit.

One very significant category of these "fully integrated" entities is made up of numerous farmers who pump ground water from wells and transport it locally so as to apply it to their own uses. Since ground water so captured and applied to irrigation constitutes about 45 per cent of all water applied to consumptive uses in Northern California, this simple pattern of complete integration clearly looms large in the water industry of the area. This sort of pattern is also formed by some industrial users who pump from wells, or divert and locally transport water from streams for their own uses, and by numerous farmers who also divert and transport individually small, but in the aggregate appreciable, volumes of stream waters for the irrigation of their own lands.

Another very important category of fully integrated organizations is composed of the numerous public agencies and private firms which perform complete sequences of functions, beginning with capture of water (or before) and extending through the retailing of water for final use. Such public agencies and private firms capture about four-fifths of their water from streamflow diversions and one-fifth from wells, and proceed through transportation of various sorts to the retailing phase. They usually undertake medium-distance bulk transport—up to 60 miles—of the water they handle. In a minority of cases, the fully integrated water agencies undertake storage of streamflow in reservoirs upstream from diversion points; if so, they frequently use reservoir capacities to support generation of hydroelectric power as well as to regulate downstream flows available for diversion. In a substantial majority of cases, such agencies begin their operations with diverting either unregulated streamflows or flows regulated by the reservoir operations of other agencies or firms. The organizations thus involved include a majority of local public water agencies and most private water companies.

The remaining retail organizations in the water industry are not fully integrated and they typically perform only one or two functions in the essential sequence involved in getting water from source to user. First among these is a group of public agencies (which have been increasing in number during the several years while this study was being made) that purchase water at wholesale, most of it from the Bureau of Reclamation; perform some intermediate transportation function; and then re-wholesale the same water to lesser public agencies which thereafter generally distribute the water and retail it to users. This group includes agencies that engage in some capture of water and in some retailing,[2] and is thus included in the category of retailers as well as in that of wholesalers.

In a second group, there is a considerable number of public agencies which purchase water wholesale from the Bureau or from other public agencies (including re-wholesalers) and which then transport the water over medium distances or locally and retail it to users. Such agencies fall into two subclasses—those which are solely dependent on the wholesaled water, and those which capture some water themselves and depend on wholesaled water for only part of their supplies.

In the first subclass are numerous public agencies, composed of irrigation districts and other public water districts, which take water at wholesale or through re-wholesalers, predominantly from Bureau of Reclamation canals, and then perform the functions of medium-distance or intermediate transportation, local distribution, and retailing of the water secured for irrigation purposes.[3] Also numerous small municipal districts or departments and some private water companies rely

[2] The category includes the Flood Control and Water Conservation Districts in Solano, in Sonoma, and in Santa Clara counties; the Contra Costa Water District; the Sacramento County Water Agency; and the Kern County Water Agency.

[3] U.S. Department of the Interior, Bureau of Reclamation, Region 2, *Water Service Repayment—Review Statement, 1959* (1960), pp. 38–40. (This and other footnote references are cited in brief form when they are also included in the Bibliography.)

entirely on water sold to them by wholesalers—predominantly the City and County of San Francisco,[4] the Bureau, and re-wholesalers—and distribute and retail the water received for urban use.

In the second subclass, there are approximately 60 public agencies and private companies which draw mainly on the same principal wholesale suppliers—the Bureau, re-wholesalers, and the City and County of San Francisco. These transport over medium distances, distribute, and retail aggregates of water including some which they have captured and some which they have bought. Agencies in the second subclass are fully integrated, from capture through retailing, with respect to part of the water they deliver; but they are relatively nonintegrated (being only transporter-retailers) with respect to the remaining part.[5]

Table 5 provides an overview of the pattern of integration in those activities involving the collection and transportation of water for so-called consumptive uses, focusing upon the sources of water handled in 1957 by self-supplying users and all retailers. The data underlying the table have been drawn from a wide variety of sources. Those describing diversions of water for consumptive use refer to 1957—a year in which annual stream runoffs were moderately below normal, but the closest to a normal year in runoff for which recent data were available when our compilation was made. They should be viewed throughout as only approximately accurate, both with reference to quantities of water diverted and to numbers of entities of various types. This is because the census of entities we have compiled is not entirely complete, because some of the data secured are not unqualifiedly reliable or unambiguous, and because the period reported as "1957" is in different sources variously the calendar year 1957, the water year of November 1956 through October 1957, and the fiscal year 1957–58. In addition, 1957 data for some relatively unimportant categories of agencies have been estimated from 1958 data because data for the earlier year were not accessible. Except for a few aggregates calculated as residuals from over-all totals, the data tend, on the average, to err slightly in the direction of understatement. We do not feel, however, that any of the total errors in the principal subaggregates exceeds 10 per cent, or that for most of them it exceeds 5 per cent.[6]

[4] City and County of San Francisco, Public Utilities Commission, *Annual Report of the Commercial Division, 1958–59* (mimeographed); and California State Comptroller, *Annual Report of Financial Transactions Concerning Cities of California, Fiscal Year 1958–59* (1960), Table 6.

[5] Similarly, it appears that although the City and County of San Francisco is fully integrated through retailing with respect to slightly over half of the water it delivers, it is integrated only through wholesaling with respect to the remainder of its deliveries.

[6] The principal sources of data concerning diversions and deliveries and agencies making them are: From California Department of Water Resources, *Ground Water Conditions in Central and Northern California, 1957–58,* Bulletin No. 77–58 (1960); *Directory of Water Service Agencies in California,* Bulletin No. 114 (1962); and from the Department's Division of Resources Planning, *Report on Irrigation and Water Storage Districts in California, 1956–58,* Bulletin No. 21 (1960); and *Surface Water Flow for 1957,* Bulletin No. 23–57 (1958). From U.S. Department of the Interior, Bureau of Reclamation, Region 2, *Water Service Repayment—Review Statement, 1957* (1958); and *Water Deliveries and Revenues, Central Valley Project, Calendar Year 1957* (1958). And from the following: California State Comptroller, *Annual Report of Financial Transactions Concerning Cities of California, Fiscal Year 1957–58* (1959); Kings River Water Association, *Water Master Report for the Year 1957* (1958);

TABLE 5
PERCENTAGES OF DIVERSIONS OF WATER MADE BY, OR ON BEHALF OF, VARIOUS CATEGORIES OF RETAILERS AND SELF-SUPPLYING WATER USERS, NORTHERN CALIFORNIA, 1957

Category of retailers	Percentages of total diversions		
	Ground water	Surface water	Total water
Integrated:			
Self-supplying water users	38.2	8.2	46.4
Fully and partly integrated retailers of irrigation water[a]	5.2	28.6	33.8
Fully and partly integrated retailers of urban water[a]	2.4	2.5	4.9
Total integrated	45.8	39.3	85.1
Nonintegrated:			
For partly integrated and nonintegrated retailers of irrigation water[b]	0	8.7	8.7
For partly integrated and nonintegrated retailers of urban water[b]	0	0.4	0.4
Losses and spillages of wholesalers[c]	0	2.5	2.5
Total nonintegrated	0	11.6	11.6
Other[d]	0	3.3	3.3
Total percentages for all categories	45.8	54.2	100.0

[a] Only the integrated diversions of partly integrated retailers are included.
[b] Only the water purchases of partly integrated retailers are included.
[c] About one-fourth of this amount represents water spread for percolation by nondistributing agencies which receive this water from wholesalers, and another one-fourth represents losses of water diverted by the Bureau of Reclamation pursuant to exchange agreements.
[d] The other potentially includes uncounted integrated and nonintegrated retailing, uncounted losses, and miscellaneous omissions and errors.
SOURCE: See note 6 of Chapter 4.

In the water year 1957, total gross diversions of water for consumptive use in Northern California amounted to about 24 million acre-feet, including 13 million acre-feet diverted from streams and 11 million acre-feet of ground water pumped from wells. The general apportionment of these diversions—between those which were integrated in the sense of having been made by water retailers and self-supplying users, and those which were nonintegrated in that they were made by water wholesalers and sold to and resold by water retailers—is suggested by Table 5.

This table presents information in such condensed form that it deserves some interpretation as well as recapitulation of the different categories of integrated and

U.S. Department of the Interior, Geological Survey, *Surface Water Supply of the United States, 1957,* Water Supply Papers No. 1515 and 1565 (1959). Additional sources are annual reports to the California Districts Securities Commission by county water districts and California water districts; annual reports of private water companies to the California Public Utilities Commission; data supplied by East Bay Municipal Utility District and Pacific Gas and Electric Company; numerous interviews with personnel of regulatory and operating commissions and agencies.

nonintegrated suppliers. Included in the table as integrated retail suppliers of water are: self-supplying users, who make their own diversions; fully integrated retailers, which capture all of the water they deliver and are fully integrated from diversion to retailing, but in many cases do not also undertake storage and streamflow regulation; and partly integrated retailers—those who capture part of the water they deliver and purchase part from wholesalers—to the extent of their integrated operations (by showing the quantities of water they capture for retail delivery). As nonintegrated retail suppliers of water, we include retailers who purchase all of their water from wholesalers, and also partly integrated retailers to the extent of the quantities they purchase at wholesale for retail delivery. All data referring to retailers include losses and spillages of water diverted or purchased (including deliberate spillage to recharge ground-water basins). These losses and spillages amounted to about 24 per cent of diversions and purchases by fully and partly integrated retailers, and 5 per cent of purchases by nonintegrated retailers.[7] Included in the category of integrated suppliers are agencies receiving water from Bureau of Reclamation facilities without wholesale charge, pursuant to an exchange agreement that the Bureau replace river water to which the recipients had prior rights but to which they were denied natural access by dam construction and diversions of the Bureau. The water thus received amounts to about 3.3 per cent of all diversions, 3.7 per cent of all integrated diversions of water, and 8 per cent of all integrated surface water.

Subject to these definitions, Table 5 shows that in the year reported about 88 per cent of all water captured for consumptive uses in Northern California was captured by fully integrated retailers and self-supplying users, and that about 12 per cent or more was captured by wholesalers and sold at retail by nonintegrated retailers. Fully integrated entities captured practically all of the ground-water supply and about 77 per cent of the surface supply from streams. The pattern of full integration of functions, from capture to delivery for final use, was thus dominant among the entities supplying water in the area.

Of the supply captured by integrated entities, about 55 per cent was captured by self-supplying users (dominantly farmers) and 45 per cent by public agencies and private companies serving various groups of users—which we may generally refer to as water agencies. Within the group of water agencies, as distinct from self-supplying users, about 77 per cent of the water diverted was captured by integrated retailers, and 23 per cent was purchased from wholesalers. Integrated agencies captured substantially all of the ground water extracted by agencies as a whole, and about 73 per cent of all streamflows captured by agencies. If it is assumed that nearly all self-supplied water went to agricultural uses, only about 6 per cent of all water captured was applied to urban uses.

Another relevant consideration is the number of integrated and nonintegrated retailers and of integrated users of water in the area. With respect to the integrated users (private pumpers and private diverters), detailed and systematic data are not available. However, we do know that annual withdrawals of ground

[7] Losses and spillages of wholesalers are shown separately; such losses have not been estimated for self-supplying users.

water made by private pumpers as a group constitute about 38 per cent of the annual water supply; that probably another 8 per cent of the supply is secured by private individuals or companies which divert surface water for their own use; and that in both cases most of the water captured is put to irrigation uses. We estimate that roughly 30,000 to 40,000 individual farmers or farm companies and several industrial concerns are engaged in private pumping, with no more than one accounting for over 1 or 2 per cent of total private pumping, and nearly all being much smaller. We estimate also that there are at least several hundred private diverters, almost all agricultural, none large enough to account for more than 2 or 3 per cent of private diversions, and that nearly all account individually for less than 1 per cent. Concentration among entities in the private pumping and diverting sector, as measured by volumes of water captured, is thus very low, and the population of capturing organizations and individuals is large. The preceding figures apply to entities capturing almost half of all water put to consumptive use in Northern California.

The integrated retailers of irrigation water comprise the next most important category of entities engaged in the process of making water available for consumptive use. In Table 6, we summarize their retail deliveries of water, including deliveries made from water purchased by them at wholesale in 1957.

The integrated retailers of irrigation water, including both public agencies and private firms, range in size from minuscule to quite large—each of two of the public agencies, for example, annually performs over 2 per cent of total area diversions. The general size distribution of the population, as represented by the relation of the percentage of the number of firms to the percentage of total integrated retail deliveries, is J-shaped. We will defer consideration of specific concentration measures until we have a larger aggregate also including the nonintegrated retailers of irrigation water.

The nonintegrated retailers of irrigation water, who purchase all of their water from wholesalers (principally from the Bureau of Reclamation), are all public agencies, and are described in Table 7. The size distribution of this group of nonintegrated retailers is roughly comparable to that of the group of integrated retailers, but none in the nonintegrated group is very large.

Some notion of the degree of concentration in all retailing of irrigation water in Northern California may be developed by comparing the annual retail deliveries plus retailers' losses of the largest public agencies and private firms with those of all such agencies and firms—in this case combining integrated and nonintegrated retailers for purposes of comparison. The results of this sort of comparison for 1957 are as follows:

Public agencies and private firms: number	*Percentage of all retail deliveries for irrigation*
2 largest	10
8 largest	29
20 largest	43
248 (or more) making up total	57

TABLE 6
NUMBER OF INTEGRATED RETAILERS OF IRRIGATION WATER AND RETAIL DELIVERIES AS PROPORTION OF TOTAL AREA DIVERSIONS, NORTHERN CALIFORNIA, 1957

Type of retailer	Number of active entities	Retail deliveries as percentages of total diversions
Public agencies:		
Irrigation districts	59	21.07%
California water districts	6	0.88
Reclamation districts	6	0.71
Water storage districts	2	0.50
County water districts	5	0.13
Public utility districts	3	0.04
Subtotal, public agencies	81	23.33%
Private firms:		
Commercial water companies	30	1.67
Mutual water companies	100[a]	4.17[b]
Subtotal, private firms	130	5.84%
Total, public and private	211	29.17%
Add calculated losses and spillages of all entities		10.0[c]
Total captures and purchases by integrated retailers		39.17%[d]

[a] Numbers are approximate only for mutual water companies.
[b] Data on mutual water companies, almost all very small, are incomplete; the figures presented here reflect nothing better than informed guesses.
[c] This does not include losses incurred by wholesalers prior to wholesale delivery.
[d] Includes water purchased from wholesalers in an amount equal to 5.4 per cent of total area diversions.
SOURCE: See note 6 of Chapter 4.

TABLE 7
NUMBER OF NONINTEGRATED RETAILERS OF IRRIGATION WATER AND RETAIL DELIVERIES AS PROPORTION OF TOTAL AREA DIVERSIONS, NORTHERN CALIFORNIA, 1957

Type of retailer	Number of active entities	Retail deliveries as percentages of total diversions
Irrigation districts	11	1.66%
California water districts	25	1.00
Municipal utility district	1	0.46
Total	37	3.12%
Add calculated losses and spillages of all entities[a]		0.17
Total purchases by nonintegrated retailers		3.29%

[a] This does not include losses incurred by wholesalers prior to wholesale delivery.
SOURCE: See note 6 of Chapter 4.

The largest eight organizations are all public agencies; two of the largest twenty are private companies. Top-level concentration in the retailing of irrigation water in the area is evidently moderately high. This suggests that much may be learned about the conduct and performance of irrigation-water retailers in the area by examining the operations of the largest ten or twenty of them.

The next category of retailers to be considered are the suppliers of urban water, integrated and nonintegrated. Table 8 contains information on the water deliveries from both captures and purchases of integrated domestic retailers in 1957. These individual public agencies and private firms again range from minuscule to quite large. However, there is a higher degree of top-level concentration in this category than for integrated retailers of irrigation water. Two public agencies retailing much of the urban water used in the San Francisco Bay area account for about 35 per cent of all retailing of urban water in Northern California. And these two, together with four public agencies and private firms supplying urban water to the cities of San Jose, Sacramento, Fresno, and Bakersfield, account for about half of all such retailing. Among the private firms is one which operates a number of systems serving numerous smaller cities or towns. After we have passed the largest ten

TABLE 8
NUMBER OF INTEGRATED RETAILERS OF URBAN WATER AND RETAIL DELIVERIES AS PROPORTION OF TOTAL AREA DIVERSIONS, NORTHERN CALIFORNIA, 1957

Type of retailer	Number of active entities	Retail deliveries as percentages of total diversions
Public agencies:		
City water departments	50	1.75%
East Bay Municipal Utility District	1	0.63
Irrigation districts	15	0.29
County water districts	25	0.13
Public utility districts	37	0.08
Municipal water district	1	0.08
County waterworks districts	55	0.04
Community service districts	52	0.04
Subtotal, public agencies	236	3.04%
Private firms:		
Commercial water companies	240	1.04
Mutual water companies	100	0.42[a]
Subtotal, private firms	340	1.45%
Total, public and private	576	4.50%
Add calculated losses of all entities		0.50[b]
Total captures and purchases by integrated retailers		5.00%

[a] This is a rough estimate, based on inadequate data.
[b] This does not include losses incurred by wholesalers prior to wholesale delivery.
SOURCE: See note 6 of Chapter 4.

organizations, we come quickly to units of small or very small size which comprise the remaining 560-odd agencies and firms. The integrated retailers of urban water as a group rely (aside from purchases) about equally on diverting surface water and pumping ground water, with ground water on the average being a much more important source of supply for the multitude of smaller agencies. Wholesale purchases of water by this group are rather small.

While the group of nonintegrated retailers of urban water is quite unimportant, its composition in 1957 is described in Table 9 to round out the picture. These retailers are supplied almost entirely by surface water conveyed by wholesalers.

TABLE 9
NUMBER OF NONINTEGRATED RETAILERS OF URBAN WATER AND RETAIL DELIVERIES AS PROPORTION OF TOTAL AREA DIVERSIONS, NORTHERN CALIFORNIA, 1957

Type of retailer	Number of active entities[a]	Retail deliveries as percentages of total diversions
City water works	11	0.21%
County water districts	10	0.08
Commercial water companies	12	0.04
Public utility districts	5	[b]
Total nonintegrated retailers and their purchases	38	0.33%

[a] Minimum estimates based on incomplete count.
[b] Negligible.
SOURCE: See note 6 of Chapter 4.

The preceding description of the organization of water retailing in Northern California is based on data referring to a period around calendar year 1957. Since then, the organization has evolved in some respects. However, it has not undergone any significant general changes, other than a very modest increase in wholesaling agencies and the volume of water wholesaled, and a corresponding increase in purchases of irrigation water by nonintegrated public agencies.

INTEGRATION AND CONCENTRATION IN WHOLESALING, STREAMFLOW REGULATION, AND POWER GENERATION

To complete our description of patterns of integration and concentration in the water industry, we now approach it by way of the original source rather than the final user. This section assesses the degree of integration and concentration in wholesaling, streamflow regulation, and power generation—by organizations which gather or utilize water, primarily streamflow, in its natural channels.

Public agencies and private firms of the Northern California water industry that engage in storage and regulation of streamflows, generation of hydroelectric power, and wholesaling of water for consumptive use fall into three categories: (1) those which specialize in one or two functions and exclude retailing; (2) those which perform a larger variety of functions and exclude retailing; and (3) those which are integrated retailers but which also perform the functions of regulation of streamflows, wholesaling, and power generation to a significant extent. In the third group, we find some organizations which are primarily oriented to integrated retailing; one for which retailing and wholesaling are side lines to power generation; and one in which wholesaling and retailing are relatively balanced as primary functions, but which also make significant contributions to power generation and streamflow regulation. This third group thus is made up of organizations already mentioned as integrated retailers.[8]

Table 5 has already indicated the relatively small role of wholesaling in relation to the total volume of annual diversions of water in Northern California. We now turn to consideration of the number of agencies performing this function. In 1957, roughly 78 per cent of all wholesale water deliveries in the area (excluding in-transit losses and spillages and excluding re-wholesaling) were made by three organizations. The Bureau of Reclamation alone accounted for about 75 per cent, and the remaining 25 per cent of wholesale deliveries was made by integrated retailers. All of the wholesaling involved (re-wholesalers being excluded) was of water captured and transported by the wholesalers in question. About 4 per cent of the wholesaled water went to domestic uses, and approximately 96 per cent to irrigation (including some spreading of water for percolation into underground reservoirs). The annual wholesale deliveries of all agencies and firms involved are analyzed in Table 10.

This table suggests the highly concentrated nature of water wholesaling in Northern California, the small number of the organizations engaged in such wholesaling, and the preponderant emphasis in wholesaling on agricultural water. It probably modestly understates the average position of the Bureau of Reclamation as a wholesaler, which has contracts to deliver "surplus" water in varying quantities as it becomes available in wetter years. On the other hand, it fails to reflect the beginning, since 1957, of small-scale integrated wholesale operations of several local public agencies, such as flood control and water conservation districts.

The organizations engaged in the regulation of streamflow, and thus in the storage of these flows in "on-stream" reservoirs,[9] deserve special attention in an evaluation of the extent of concentration. The types and functions of storage reservoirs in Northern California, their numbers and aggregate capacity, their distribution among regions, and the high degree of concentration of total reservoir capacity in the sixty largest reservoirs were discussed in Chapter 2. There we indicated the range of possible functions that a storage reservoir might fulfill and distinguished the products, or potential effects inherent in the operation of a given reservoir, from its purposes, the effects consciously sought by the agency operating it. We con-

[8] We have taken care in such cases to avoid double counting with respect to wholesaled or retailed water.

[9] "On-stream" reservoirs are located on or adjacent to natural river or creek beds, and if large enough can perform significant regulation of downstream flows. Most reservoirs in Northern California are of this type, but others, not classified here as on-stream, include terminal storage reservoirs for urban water supplies and in-transit reservoirs on aqueducts. (Some small terminal storage reservoirs are located on and primarily fed by local creeks, but impound their flows for diversion from the reservoirs and cut off all or most downstream flows.)

TABLE 10

NUMBER OF INTEGRATED WHOLESALERS AND WHOLESALE DELIVERIES AS PROPORTION OF TOTAL DIVERSIONS, NORTHERN CALIFORNIA, 1957

Agency or type of agency	Approximate number of wholesale customers	Wholesale deliveries as percentages of total diversions
Bureau of Reclamation	80	6.67%[a]
City and County of San Francisco	25	0.29
Pacific Gas and Electric Company	15	0.21[b]
Irrigation districts (several)	n.a.	1.96[c]
Total	120[d]	9.13%
Add calculated losses and spillages of wholesalers		2.50[e]
Total diversions by integrated wholesalers		11.63%

n.a. Not available.

[a] This figure excludes large exchange deliveries by the Bureau made without wholesale charge to organizations and individuals to compensate for the closure of their access to streamflows to which they had prior legal rights, such closure resulting from the construction of facilities by the Bureau. (Such exchanges have already been accounted for under the heading of integrated retailers.) The figure does not include any wholesaling by the Bureau from the east slope of the Sierra Range.

[b] This figure excludes exchange deliveries by PG&E. It is a rough approximation, and for any particular year may include some nonrecurrent wholesale deliveries.

[c] This total may include a significant amount of water involved in exchange deliveries; for this category, precise data distinguishing wholesale sales from exchanges are not available.

[d] That is, 120 plus the number of irrigation districts included.

[e] About one-fourth of these losses and spillages are estimated to be incurred in connection with exchange deliveries by the Bureau of Reclamation, and another one-fourth represent water spread for percolation by nondistributing agencies that receive water from the Bureau. (The latter might be viewed in large part as an addition to Bureau wholesaling which is not reflected in retailing.) Correspondingly, the grand total of wholesaling and wholesale losses is perhaps overstated by an amount equal to 0.6 per cent of annual area diversions.

SOURCE: See note 6 of Chapter 4.

cluded that, although most of the sixty largest reservoirs are multiproduct, most seem to serve no more than two purposes. Here we can supplement those conclusions somewhat by showing the specific patterns of ownership of the sixty largest, deleting from that list four reservoirs which have only terminal storage among their significant functions.[10]

In Table 11, we summarize information concerning the organizations which own or control these fifty-six reservoirs; the reservoir capacities controlled by individual organizations or groups thereof; the rivers on which the reservoirs are located; the functions that the reservoirs primarily perform, listed in the order of their importance; and the extent of engagement of the organizations in the diversion of water for consumptive use. In column 5 we use the symbols *C*, *P*, and *F*, to refer, respectively, to regulation to support diversion for consumptive use, to support power generation, and to control floods. In addition, symbols are employed in column 6

[10] Their combined storage capacity is about 234,000 acre-feet. The total capacity of the sixty largest reservoirs (19.4 million acre-feet) and their regional distribution were shown in Table 2.

TABLE 11

OWNERSHIP, CAPACITY, LOCATION, AND FUNCTION OF THE FIFTY-SIX LARGEST ON-STREAM RESERVOIRS IN NORTHERN CALIFORNIA, 1962

Controlling organization or type of organization	Number of organizations (1)	Number of reservoirs with capacities over 40,000 acre-feet (2)	Total storage capacity of designated reservoirs (millions of acre-feet) (3)	Rivers or major creeks on which reservoirs are located[a] (4)	Principal functions of reservoirs, in order of importance[b] (5)	Diversion activities of controlling agencies[c] (6)
Bureau of Reclamation	1	10	11.04	Sacramento, American, Cosumnes, San Joaquin, Trinity, Klamath, Stony, Putah[d]	All, especially *C,P*	D_i, D_u (major)
Pacific Gas and Electric Company	1	12	2.17	Feather, Yuba, Pit, Mokelumne, San Joaquin, Kings, Eel[e]	*P,C*	D_i (minor)
Corps of Engineers	1	6	1.95	Tule, Kaweah, Kings, Kern, Russian, Littlejohn[f]	*F,C*	0
City and County of San Francisco	1	2	0.63[g]	Tuolumne	*C,P*	D_u (major)
Southern California Edison Company	1	5	0.54	San Joaquin	*P,C*	0
Irrigation districts	8	11	1.29	Merced, Tuolumne, Stanislaus, Yuba, Feather, Pit[h]	*C,P*	D_i (major)
Other public agencies	7	7	0.88[i]	Salinas, Calaveras, Feather, Yuba, American, Mokelumne, Coyote	*C,P*	D_i, D_u (major)
Other private companies	3	3	0.70	Kern, Klamath, Cache	*C,P*	D_i (major and minor)
Total	23	56	19.20	—	—	—

[a] Tributaries and forks of rivers are designated by the names of their main rivers.

[b] The symbols indicate the primary functions supported by reservoir operations: *C* is for consumptive use; *P*, for power generation; and *F*, to control floods.

[c] The symbols indicate diversions are made for consumptive use. D_u indicates the diversion is at the reservoir; D_i, that it is downstream from the reservoir.

[d] All of these rivers and creeks except the Trinity and Klamath rivers naturally feed the Central Valley. The Trinity developments are designed mainly to divert water to the Central Valley.

[e] All of these rivers except the Eel naturally feed the Central Valley.

[f] All of these rivers except the Russian naturally feed the San Joaquin Valley, and four feed the Tulare Lake Basin.

[g] This excludes two terminal storage reservoirs with a combined capacity of 150,000 acre-feet.

[h] Six of the eleven large irrigation district reservoirs are on the Stanislaus and Tuolumne rivers. All are on rivers feeding the Central Valley.

[i] This excludes two in-transit or terminal storage reservoirs with a combined capacity of 84,000 acre-feet.

SOURCE: California Department of Water Resources, *Dams Within Jurisdiction of the State of California, January 1, 1962*, Bulletin No. 17 (1962), and other sources cited in note 6 of Chapter 4.

to indicate that the organization, or group of organizations, is making diversions for consumptive use—D_u to indicate the diversion is at the reservoir; D_i, that it is downstream from the reservoir.

The high degree of concentration of control of reservoir capacity in the area is notable. Of all reservoir capacity in Northern California, 74 per cent is controlled by the largest three organizations; 79 per cent, by the largest five; and a total of only 23 organizations control about 91 per cent of all reservoir capacity. Roughly the same pattern of concentration is found in the control of on-stream reservoir capacity. The regulation of most streamflows in the area rests in very few hands—far fewer than are engaged in diverting streamflows. Accordingly, the regulation of streamflows is subject to the judgment, principal interest, and caprice of a very few decision-making bodies, plus such limitations as may be imposed by regulating agencies. Table 11 not only confirms the pattern of high concentration prevailing in the ownership of on-stream reservoirs, but also provides information to elaborate on several other trends and patterns noted in Chapter 2. Nearly all of the fifty-six largest reservoirs are on streams which naturally feed the Central Valley or whose water is to be diverted to the Central Valley region. The exceptions to this pattern involve two reservoirs on the upper Klamath River, one on the upper Eel River, one on the Russian River (the Eel and the Russian mainly serve the southern part of the north coastal region), and one on a tributary on the Salinas River. If these fifty-six reservoirs are viewed as an aggregate, the primary functions are control of downstream flows, mostly for the benefit of diverters, and support of power generation. The next most important function is probably flood control. Preservation of commercially navigable streams is of minor importance in Northern California except on the Sacramento River. Preservation of fish habitat is generally an auxiliary function, or a constraint on the performance of primary functions, more important for federal agencies than for other organizations. Among different organizations, of course, the functional emphasis vis-à-vis the use of reservoir capacities varies.

The largest fifty-six reservoirs described in Table 11 have a combined reservoir capacity equal to about 84 per cent of all on-stream reservoir capacity in Northern California. To account for the remaining 16 per cent, we must look to about 600 smaller reservoirs, and to a comparable but smaller number of controlling entities (including some of the large ones just discussed). These smaller reservoirs have individual capacities up to 40,000 acre-feet of water. Their average capacity is about 6,000 acre-feet, but the dispersion among sizes is very great, as is suggested by the fact that only about 115 have individual capacities above 1,000 acre-feet.

The major functions of the smaller reservoirs vary among regions. In the central coastal region and the San Francisco Bay area, the smaller reservoirs most frequently support the diversion of water for urban uses rather than for irrigation. In the Central Valley region, where most of the smaller reservoirs are found, the major function is to facilitate diversions of irrigation water, although four or five of the larger ones and a great many smaller ones support facilities for power generation; a modest number supports the diversion of urban water and local flood control. In the north coastal region, most of this group of smaller reservoirs are particularly small; they are primarily used to support irrigation diversions, but a few are used to support power generation or diversions for domestic uses. For this group of smaller reservoirs in Northern California as a whole, support of irrigation diversions is probably the primary function; support of electric power generation ranks second; support of diversions of urban water is third; and any other functions are usually fringe benefits.

Tables 10 and 11 have dealt (in reverse order) with the distribution among agencies of control over reservoir capacity and over one of the major functions utilizing that capacity—the wholesaling of water for consumptive uses. We now look at another function physically based upon the possession of dams and reservoirs—the generation of hydroelectric power. Ten organizations, listed as owning such capacity in Northern California in 1961, are taken up in Table 12, which indicates also the quantity and location of this capacity, and the number of power plants.[11]

One thing which stands out in this tabulation is that in 1961 nearly all of the hydroelectric power generated in Northern California originated on rivers and creeks feeding the Central Valley—the only exceptions involved relative traces of power originating on the Klamath, Trinity, and Eel rivers. This is understandable in view of precipitation and snowmelt patterns, the geographical distribution of population over the area, topography, and the alternative of electric power generated by steam. Much, but not most, of this hydroelectric power serves regions outside the Central Valley.

The table also directs attention to the high degree of concentration among entities supplying hydroelectric power. Pacific Gas and Electric Company (PG&E) controlled about 55 per cent of the generating capacity in the area; PG&E and Southern California Edison together had approximately 70 per cent; and these two private firms plus the Bureau of Reclamation had about 87 per cent. After these three, the next largest generator of hydroelectric power could claim about 6 per cent, leaving about 7 per cent to be accounted for by the six remaining organizations.

Actually, the degree of concentration in the sale of electric power generally is higher than an inspection of generating capacities of these ten entities would indicate. The Bureau of Reclamation, in effect, consumes a significant portion of the power it produces (to pump water over hills), and PG&E owns at least as much steam generating capacity in the service area in question as it does hydroelectric capacity. However, both PG&E and Southern California Edison are regulated public utilities, so that a monopoly problem in the usual sense does not arise.

In this section, we have so far established the identity and concentration of agencies engaged in several major physical activities drawing upon water at the source—reservoir storage operations, wholesaling, and hydroelectric power generation. The description of wholesaling activities, when taken in conjunction with Table 5, also covered the degree of vertical integration of wholesalers forward into the retailing of water to final customers. What is now needed to complete this section

[11] It might be noted that the Pacific Gas and Electric Company has many small power plants, associated usually with correspondingly small reservoirs, which often depend on major upstream reservoirs held by the Company, and that, on a smaller scale, the Southern California Edison Company follows roughly the same pattern. Installed generating capacity in kilowatts is used throughout, instead of kilowatt-hours of energy delivered, as a measure of the sizes of entities. No power from the east slope of the Sierra is included.

TABLE 12
OWNERSHIP, LOCATION, AND SCALE OF HYDROELECTRIC POWER GENERATING CAPACITY IN NORTHERN CALIFORNIA, 1961

Organization	Stream location[a]	Number of power plants	Total generating capacity (kilowatts)
Private firms:			
Pacific Gas and Electric Company	Pit, Feather, Yuba, American, Mokelumne, Stanislaus, Merced, San Joaquin, Kings, Tule, Kern, Trinity, Cox, Battle	62	2,015,700
Southern California Edison Company	San Joaquin, Kaweah, Tule, Kern	8	500,000
Pacific Power and Light Company	Klamath	4	50,000
Subtotal, private firms		74	2,565,700
Public agencies:			
Bureau of Reclamation	Sacramento, American	4	629,500[b]
City and County of San Francisco	Tuolumne	2	215,000
Oakdale and South San Joaquin irrigation districts	Stanislaus	3	80,000
Sacramento Municipal Utility District	American	1	66,000
Turlock and Modesto irrigation districts	Tuolumne	2	30,900
Merced Irrigation District	Merced	1	25,000
East Bay Municipal Utility District	Mokelumne	1	15,000
Subtotal, public agencies		14	1,061,400
Total, private and public		88	3,627,100

[a] Tributaries and forks of rivers are designated by the names of their main rivers.
[b] This excludes 384,000 kilowatts of planned generating capacity on the Trinity River, not installed by the end of 1961.
SOURCE: California State Water Resources Board, *Water Utilization and Requirements in California, Vol. II*, Bulletin No. 2 (1955), Appendix G; Federal Power Commission, *Hydroelectric Power Resources of the United States, Developed and Undeveloped* (1960); and data furnished by agencies listed in the table.

is a review of the degree of integration among the various physical activities associated with using and regulating water at the source. Because of the limited number of agencies involved, this is best provided by a brief textual review of each agency. Reference to the geographical pattern of each agency's activities is included.

1) The Bureau of Reclamation—As regards control of reservoir capacity, the Bureau of Reclamation is dominant in Northern California, with about 57 per cent of the total capacity of the largest fifty-six on-stream dams and 48 per cent of all

reservoir capacity in the area in 1962. It tends to emphasize large-scale river basin development and large dual or multiple purpose dams and reservoirs which combine storage and regulation of streamflow with hydroelectric power generation in quantity, and with large-scale diversions of water for transport over long distances. All but one of the Bureau's developments in Northern California (excluding the east slope of the Sierra) primarily serve the Central Valley,[12] though they include two dams with reservoirs on the upper reaches of the Trinity River, from which water is to be diverted to the Central Valley. By 1962, it had constructed and controlled nine large dams (with reservoirs above 40,000 acre-feet in capacity) as parts of its Central Valley Project—six of them very large, with individual reservoir capacities ranging between 250,000 and 4.5 million acre-feet. It also had two medium-sized dams and four diversion dams in the Valley.

The Bureau also operates major works not connected with large dams, such as the Tracy Pumping Plant at the northern end of the Delta-Mendota Canal. As regards its own principal diversions of water, it emphasizes long-distance or medium-distance bulk transportation of the diverted water in large aqueducts (such as the Delta-Mendota, Friant-Kern, Madera, Contra Costa, and Putah South canals, and the major aqueducts which are to originate from the Trinity and American rivers), in several cases implementing massive transfers of water between regions or subregions. The Bureau's transportation of water generally terminates when the water is wholesaled to local public agencies; it is not a retailer nor does it provide medium-distance or local transport after its water has been diverted from its few large aqueducts.[13]

The Bureau's operations are multipurpose, not only in that it performs several functions, but also in that performance of one function serves another. Thus, its diversion of Sacramento River water from the Delta to the San Joaquin River basin via the Delta-Mendota Canal is implemented by its generation of electric power for pumping at Shasta Dam and elsewhere; at the same time, Shasta Dam permits the regulation of downstream flow in the Sacramento River for irrigation and other purposes. All things considered, the Bureau has four major functions: diversion of water for long-distance transport, regulation of streamflows for downstream diversions for irrigation, power generation, and flood control. Navigation in the Sacramento-San Joaquin river system is incidentally assisted, as is repulsion of saline intrusion into the river estuaries; and preservation of fish habitat has met the minimum required by regulatory agencies.

2) The Army Corps of Engineers—In 1962, the Corps controlled reservoir capacity in Northern California totalling about 2.03 million acre-feet, contained in six large reservoirs with individual capacities above 40,000 acre-feet and six smaller ones with a total capacity of about 75,000 acre-feet. It thus controlled about 9 per cent of all reservoir capacity in the area, and 10 per cent of the total capacity of the largest fifty-six on-stream dams. Four of its large dams lie on rivers feeding the Tulare Lake Basin of the Central Valley, but it also has large dams on Little-

[12] The exception is an installation in California on a tributary of the upper Klamath River.

[13] The Bureau does, however, finance the building under contract of local distribution systems for customer agencies.

john Creek (feeding the Delta region) and on the Russian River.[14] In its operations of large reservoirs, the Corps emphasizes flood control and the regulation of downstream flows, largely for the benefit of irrigators. To say which function is dominant would be difficult offhand, though the reservoirs have been justified primarily on the basis of flood control benefits. Its reservoirs do not yet provide a base for water wholesaling, but contractual arrangements are made by the Bureau of Reclamation for payment for irrigation benefits resulting from its streamflow regulation. The Corps' operations of small reservoirs are mainly oriented toward flood control. Though one of its major duties as outlined in federal legislation is to support navigation, its placement of dams in California is not such that it contributes much to navigability. In its Russian River operations, at least, the Corps has given considerable attention to the preservation of fish habitat and the enhancement of the utilization of a major sport fishery.

3) The Pacific Gas and Electric Company—The reservoir capacity of PG&E, amounting to about 4 million acre-feet, represents 17 per cent of all capacity in Northern California. Most of its dams support slight individual reservoir storage, and serve almost entirely small power plants. The smallest 262 of the PG&E reservoirs, with individual capacities less than 40,000 acre-feet, had an average capacity of about 7,000 acre-feet. But twelve PG&E reservoirs were among the fifty-six largest on-stream reservoirs in the area, with an aggregate capacity of about 2.17 million acre-feet, and accounted for over 11 per cent of the total capacity of these fifty-six reservoirs.

The company regulates streamflows primarily as a producer of electric power. Its major reservoirs usually are located well upstream on rivers, where they can provide important service to downstream power plants. The general patterns of streamflow regulation that it emphasizes are designed for power production first, and anything else second, except as it is constrained by regulatory agencies. The Company is only incidentally engaged in diverting, wholesaling, and retailing water for consumptive use. However, the streamflow regulation accomplished by its major reservoirs confers, if only incidentally, substantial benefits on downstream diverters for irrigation, and these reservoirs—whether so designed or not—are dual product in character. Its involvement in irrigation benefits stems mainly from several important ventures in constructing dams and reservoirs in collaboration with local water districts. (These projects, largely of recent inception, are discussed in Chapter 11.) The Company's streamflow regulation also is generally conducive to the preservation of fish habitat, and it contributes to flood control.

4) Southern California Edison Company—Operating mainly in the southern part of the state, the Southern California Edison Company also owns some facilities in the San Joaquin Valley basin. These lie mainly upstream on the San Joaquin River, where in 1962 its five large reservoirs accounted for about 2.8 per cent of the total reservoir capacity of the largest fifty-six on-stream dams of Northern California. The Company is more specialized functionally than PG&E, having no direct or indirect involvement in the sale of agricultural water. So far as is known,

[14] U.S. Army Corps of Engineers, South Pacific Division, *Water Resources Development in California* (1961).

its reservoirs were installed and are operated entirely for power generation, although incidental benefits of other sorts have been provided, including that of general streamflow regulation on the San Joaquin River above Friant Dam.

5) The City and County of San Francisco—In 1962, the City and County of San Francisco had a total reservoir capacity of about 780,000 acre-feet (or about 3.4 per cent of all reservoir capacity in Northern California). This includes an on-stream reservoir capacity of 630,000 acre-feet on the Tuolumne River (in two large reservoirs), which accounts for about 3.3 per cent of the total capacity of the largest fifty-six on-stream dams in Northern California. The reservoirs are operated primarily to support regulated diversions of water for long-distance transportation to the San Francisco Bay region and to generate power, but they also contribute to regulation of downstream flows, which is beneficial to irrigators.

6) East Bay Municipal Utility District—Included in Table 11 with "other public agencies," the East Bay Municipal Utility District conducts a similar operation on the Mokelumne River, oriented to supplying water to the eastern part of the San Francisco Bay area and to producing power. In 1962, its total on-stream reservoir capacity was substantially smaller (210,000 acre-feet) than that of the San Francisco agency (though new capacity was under construction), as was its total reservoir capacity (294,000 acre-feet), though it delivered a roughly comparable amount of water.

7) Irrigation districts—In 1962, eight irrigation districts owned eleven on-stream reservoirs with individual capacities above 40,000 acre-feet. The eight reservoirs had a total capacity of 1.29 million acre-feet, or 6.7 per cent of the aggregate capacity of the largest fifty-six on-stream reservoirs. Three-fourths of this capacity was owned by five districts, including two pairs which shared common facilities, and all eight reservoirs were on streams entering the Sacramento Valley or the San Joaquin River basin. These reservoirs are operated primarily for regulation of streamflows to facilitate diversions for irrigation, but most also support facilities for power generation. In a few instances, these power facilities are owned by the districts; in others, by the Pacific Gas and Electric Company, operating under arrangements whereby it underwrites all or part of the cost of dam construction. They are thus usually dual purpose, and the patterns of streamflow regulation they impose are influenced accordingly.

It is remarkable that so few irrigation districts—as a group the largest single category of diverters of water for consumptive use in Northern California—own reservoir storage capacity. It is not only that so few districts own large reservoirs; also, only about one-fourth of about sixty active irrigation districts in the area control any reservoir storage capacity. As a group, the districts' proportion of all stream diversions is about six times as great as their proportion of all on-stream reservoir storage capacity. They are thus, as a group, heavily dependent in their diversion operations on streamflow regulation provided by other agencies—predominantly by the Bureau, the Corps, and the Pacific Gas and Electric Company. An important question thus arises about the relation between payments made for this regulation and the marginal cost of providing it.

8) Other public agencies and private firms—The remaining on-stream reservoirs with individual capacities in excess of 40,000 acre-feet were owned by nine public

agencies and private companies in 1962. These included two water conservation districts (one with a reservoir on the Salinas River in the central coastal region and one in the southern part of the San Francisco Bay region); one municipal utility district (serving Sacramento); one city (Stockton); two state agencies; two private water companies; and one private electric power company. As a group, they are primarily devoted to streamflow regulation to support diversions for consumptive uses (both agricultural and urban) or to facilitate spreading of water for percolation into underground aquifers.

The role of major governmental agencies engaged in water storage and wholesaling will be increased by completion of projects now planned or under construction. Beginning in the 1960's, the California Department of Water Resources started construction to support large-scale operations comparable in type to those of the Bureau of Reclamation, and including major storage and streamflow regulation, long-distance transportation of water, wholesaling, and power generation. Its first major project is in the early stages of construction at this writing. The Bureau also has major new projects planned or under construction. In view of this prospect of rapid development of wholesaling, the preceding discussion gives an exaggerated impression of the degree of vertical integration likely to prevail in the industry during the coming decades if the percentages shown in Table 5 are mechanically extrapolated. On the basis of present estimates of the deliveries to be made by wholesaling projects now fully planned (but not necessarily fully financed by appropriations), and assuming no increase in integrated diversions, we can provide a maximum estimate of the portion of gross diversions to be made by wholesalers for transmission to nonintegrated retailers. The estimated ultimate annual deliveries in Northern California of projects planned by the Department of Water Resources and the Bureau of Reclamation total 5.82 million acre-feet annually.[15] This quantity would raise the nonintegrated portion of total annual diversions from 11.6 per cent to approximately 25 per cent, and the nonintegrated portion of annual surface diversions from about 21 per cent to about 40 per cent.[16]

Industry Organization in the Major Regions of Northern California

So far, several aspects of the structure of the water industry have been described in terms of the distribution of entities and activities within Northern California as a whole. This whole, however, is not a homogeneous, compact, and unified geographic area. As was shown in Chapter 2, it can readily be divided into five

[15] The figure includes 1.48 million acre-feet to be delivered by the Department (Feather River Project Aqueduct to Kern County, etc., 1.18 million; South Bay Aqueduct, 188,000; North Bay Aqueduct, 67,000; Feather River local deliveries, 38,500) and 4.3 million acre-feet to be delivered by the Bureau (Eastside Canal Project, 1.5 million; Folsom South Canal, 850,000; extended Tehama-Colusa Canal, 400,000; West Sacramento Canal, 340,000; federal service area of San Luis Project, 1.25 million). These figures, drawn from various recently released estimates, are distinctly subject to change.

[16] These calculations assume that losses and spillages of wholesalers will also increase proportionally, an assumption which should be viewed as a maximum estimate.

widely separated regions possessing distinctive topographic, hydrologic, and economic characteristics. They also differ substantially with respect to the organization of entities supplying water for consumptive use.

It cannot be said that each region comprises a separate market for water, as there are no continuous, developed markets for water in Northern California in the customary sense. Nonetheless, latent markets, in the sense introduced in Chapter 1, do exist within regions. In some cases, they knit together the bulk of the water users in a given region through chains of potential economic alternative uses for particular sources of water. As we indicated above, where such alternatives exist in river basins and sub-basins, patterns of integration and concentration may significantly affect important decisions concerning the allocation of water, even though these influences operate through nonmarket channels and are not identified in the customary economic theory concerning enterprise concentration. To pave the way for testing these hypotheses in Parts Two and Three, this section outlines some significant differences among regions in the organization of the industry.

Table 13 shows some of the major traits of the organization of water supply in Northern California's regions, and textual comments will develop others. In the

TABLE 13
SOURCE, CHARACTER OF END-USE, AND DEGREE OF INTEGRATION IN WATER SUPPLY PATTERNS, BY MAJOR REGIONS OF NORTHERN CALIFORNIA, 1957

Region	Percentage of local supplies from surface source (1)	Percentage of irrigation water self-supplied (2)	Sources of retailed irrigation water[a]: Percentage captured by integrated retailers (3)	Percentage purchased from wholesalers (4)	Percentage of water captured from all sources for urban use[a] (5)
Sacramento Valley	78	25–30	97	3	4
San Joaquin Valley	46	50–55	81[b]	19	2
San Francisco Bay	48	Almost all[c]	77[d]	23[d]	69
Central coastal	13	Predominant share	Almost all	Almost none	n.a.
North coastal	86	Substantial share	(150,000 acre-feet)[e]	Small fraction	n.a.

n.a. Not available.

[a] Includes both locally captured supplies and gross imports.

[b] This figure would be 71 per cent if we excluded supplies provided to certain retailers served by the U.S. Bureau of Reclamation under an exchange arrangement whereby the retailers have given up supplies originally developed from the San Joaquin River on a fully integrated basis.

[c] A portion of ground water pumped by self-supplying users in the Santa Clara Valley is deliberately percolated by the Santa Clara Valley Water Conservation District, and thus might be construed as originating with a wholesaler.

[d] These figures pertain to urban, not irrigation, supplies. Practically all irrigation water is captured by fully integrated retail agencies or self-supplying users.

[e] Includes water secured pursuant to contractual arrangements with the Bureau of Reclamation not involving wholesale purchases.

SOURCE: See note 6 of Chapter 4.

table, column 1 indicates the portion of local supplies derived from surface sources —significant in the present context because of the much greater importance of large-scale organizations in the capture of surface water than in the extraction of ground water. Column 2 presents a necessarily rough estimate of the portion of irrigation water in each region that is supplied or secured by the irrigator himself. Columns 1 and 2 are closely related, in that about 85 per cent of all ground water recovered in Northern California is pumped by self-supplying users, and the self-supplying users depend on pumping for over 80 per cent of their water supplies. Columns 3 and 4 show the proportions of water distributed for irrigation purposes[17] by retailing agencies that are drawn respectively from supplies developed by the retailer and from wholesale purchases. Column 5 indicates the portion of retail water deliveries going to urban customers. All of the estimates are approximate, and in some cases we can provide only a general verbal indication.

Broadly speaking, the table indicates the regional degrees of vertical integration in the water industry. Column 2 indicates the extent of complete vertical integration from the water user back to the source of natural supply. Columns 3 and 4 show the extent of integration back to the source by retailing agencies, and thus the relative potential importance of rivalry for natural sources of water and bargains struck between wholesalers and retailers. It is immediately clear that wholesaler rivalry (actual or potential) is mainly confined to the San Francisco Bay and San Joaquin Valley regions, and that organized retailing takes on significance only in these areas plus the Sacramento Valley. Let us now review some specific features of the major regions.

Sacramento Valley

About 70 per cent of the integrated irrigation retailing in the Sacramento Valley is undertaken by about twenty-five public agencies, roughly two-thirds of them irrigation districts; the remainder is performed by about fifteen to twenty mutual water companies and commercial water firms. The dominant enterprises in urban retailing, which accounts for only 4 per cent of total retailing in the area, are the Sacramento City Water Department and the Citizens' Utility Company serving, respectively, Sacramento and its suburbs.

The relatively insignificant amount of water wholesaling done in the region is carried on by the Bureau of Reclamation, the Pacific Gas and Electric Company, and two irrigation districts. All except the Bureau also are fully integrated through the retailing of water. The PG&E is the largest wholesaler; the Bureau and irrigation districts wholesale only negligible amounts.[18] The Bureau's wholesale operations in the Sacramento area are expanding—or will expand substantially with the completion of the Putah South and Corning canals—but even with these additions water wholesaling will be comparatively unimportant in the Sacramento Valley. A

[17] Except in the case of the San Francisco Bay region.

[18] Bureau of Reclamation, *Water Service Repayment—Review Statement, 1957, op. cit.;* data supplied by Pacific Gas and Electric Company; and California Department of Water Resources, *Report on Irrigation and Water Storage Districts in California, 1956–58, op. cit.*

major development of water wholesaling in the region apparently awaits completion of the Trinity River diversion works and the building of the Tehama-Colusa Canal.[19]

San Joaquin Valley

As Table 13 shows, self-supply plays a greater role in the San Joaquin Valley than in the Sacramento Valley (or in Northern California as a whole, for which the figure is 46 per cent). Even so, wholesaling plays a more important role than in any of the other regions, and many self-supplying irrigators in the San Joaquin Valley also make substantial purchases of surface water. This region, therefore, possesses a relatively complex structure of institutions for the capture and distribution of water for irrigation use. It will be noted that 10 per cent of retail supplies can be viewed as neither captured by integrated retailers nor purchased from wholesalers. This amount constitutes supplies transferred by the Bureau to retailers on the lower San Joaquin River through the Delta-Mendota Canal on an exchange arrangement, through which the Bureau has secured rights to the retailers' original claims to the natural flow of the San Joaquin River. (The Bureau's wholesale sales in the Valley are about one and a half times as large as its imports—excluding exchange deliveries—to the Valley through the Delta-Mendota Canal.) The percentage of retail sales which are from fully integrated retailers (inclusive of retailing of water received on exchange contracts) varies between the Valley's northern and southern halves (San Joaquin River basin and Tulare Lake basin), being roughly 90 per cent in the north and 65 per cent in the south. If self-supplying users and integrated retailers are combined, from 86 to 91 per cent of irrigation water used in the San Joaquin Valley is supplied by fully integrated operations.

Involved as integrated, partly integrated, and nonintegrated retailers of irrigation water are about thirty-five irrigation districts, twenty-one water districts, a few other public districts, a large number of mutual water companies, and a smaller number of commercial water companies. Irrigation districts account for about 70 per cent of the total irrigation retailing, and for a somewhat larger portion in the northern than in the southern part of the Valley. In the retailing of urban water (which accounts for about 2 per cent of the total supplied in the valley), the California Water Service Company is important, serving Bakersfield, Stockton, Visalia, and several smaller communities. The Fresno Water Department, serving the city of Fresno, is the largest public agency purveying urban water in the Valley. About 90 per cent of the Valley's urban water supply comes from wells, and nearly all is delivered by fully integrated organizations.

The sizable amount of nonintegrated retailing of irrigation water in the San Joaquin Valley (about 19 per cent) is matched by a comparable amount of water

[19] It may be noted that, since the construction of Shasta Dam by the Bureau of Reclamation, summer diversions from the Sacramento River have increased so that they considerably exceed the natural summer flow of the River, the dam-regulated summer flow being much larger. Thus the Bureau, as a wholesaler, is making available for diversion a large quantity of water for which it has been unable to collect any payment. (See Chapter 13.)

wholesaling, predominantly by the Bureau of Reclamation. It wholesales approximately 500,000 acre-feet of water annually in the San Joaquin River basin—about half from the Delta-Mendota Canal and half from the Madera Canal—and roughly 1 million acre-feet per year in the Tulare Lake basin from the Friant-Kern Canal. In addition, the Bureau delivers about 800,000 acre-feet per year from the Delta-Mendota Canal under exchange agreements, and about 50,000 acre-feet is diverted for the preservation of wild-life. Minor wholesalers in the area are the Pacific Gas and Electric Company and Merced Irrigation District; wholesaling by other irrigation districts is sporadic and the amounts are not large.

San Francisco Bay region

Of the rather small locally captured water supplies of the San Francisco Bay region (about 630,000 acre-feet a year), slightly more than half is ground water, and slightly less than half, surface runoff. About 57 per cent of these supplies are used for irrigation and 43 per cent as urban water. Nearly all of the irrigation water is captured by self-supplying users through private diversions and private pumping, though the pumping is assisted by deliberate water spreading by such public agencies as the Santa Clara Valley Water Conservation District. The capture of irrigation water by integrated retailers is relatively unimportant. There are no integrated irrigation districts, but a number of public water districts intermittently purvey some irrigation water, and some small mutual water companies do so on a regular basis. In one way or another, practically all the region's supply of irrigation water is captured by fully integrated users or water-supplying organizations.[20]

The local supply of urban water (about 270,000 acre-feet a year) is supplemented by imports of about 250,000 acre-feet annually by the City and County of San Francisco, the East Bay Municipal Utility District, and the Bureau of Reclamation. Of the total annual supply of about 520,000 acre-feet, about 120,000 acre-feet are wholesaled for nonintegrated retailing by local city water departments and other public agencies. The entire 50,000 acre-feet imported by the Bureau through the Contra Costa Canal are wholesaled and then re-wholesaled (by the Contra Costa Water District) to five or six nonintegrated retailers in the Suisun Bay area. And the City and County of San Francisco wholesales about 70,000 acre-feet a year of its combined supply from imports and local captures to approximately a dozen suburbs south of San Francisco. These customers of San Francisco and of the Contra Costa Water District are the principal nonintegrated and partly integrated retailers of urban water in the region; their retail sales of purchased water comprise about 23 per cent of the urban water supply of the San Francisco Bay region.

The remainder of the urban water supply—about 77 per cent, or 400,000 acre-feet annually—is sold by integrated retailers. The largest of these (in terms of integrated sales) are the East Bay Municipal Utility District (about 150,000 acre-feet per annum, two-thirds from imports); the City and County of San Francisco

[20] One irrigation district retails water which it purchases from a wholesaler.

(about 80,000 acre-feet per year of retail sales, from imports plus local captures); the San Jose Water Works Company (about 40,000 acre-feet per year, locally captured); and the Marin Municipal Water District (about 20,000 acre-feet, locally captured). These organizations serve, respectively, communities on the east side of San Francisco Bay, the City of San Francisco, the City of San Jose at the south end of the Bay, and the west side of the Bay north of San Francisco. About forty-five commercial water companies and a few public agencies, all fully integrated, supply the remainder of the urban water delivered in the region.

It is apparent that the San Francisco Bay region differs greatly from the Central Valley with respect to the proportions of the water supply going to urban and agricultural uses, the degree of dependence on imported water, and the institutional structure for capture and delivery of both irrigation and urban water.

Central coastal and north coastal regions

The limited water supply of the central coastal region (about 550,000 acre-feet a year) is about 87 per cent ground water and only 13 per cent surface runoff. Capture by self-supplying users through pumping and diversions is the dominant motif for irrigation water, with the pumping assisted in the Salinas River valley by the water-spreading operations of the Monterey Flood Control and Water Conservation District. Small integrated mutual companies supply most of the other irrigation water, which is thus almost entirely handled by fully integrated agencies. Water wholesaling is almost nonexistent. A fairly large number of integrated private companies, plus some public agencies, retail the rather small aggregate urban water supply. A difference in institutional pattern from the Central Valley is again notable.

The north coastal region, by contrast, also uses a small total water supply (about 660,000 acre-feet a year), but about 86 per cent of it is from surface sources and only 14 per cent from ground water. Diversions by self-supplying users of irrigation water evidently account for a substantial portion of the water used. Six integrated irrigation districts and two small integrated mutual companies together supply about 150,000 acre-feet of water annually, most of it in the area of the upper Klamath River and its tributaries. Some of the irrigation districts take their water pursuant to contractual arrangements with the Bureau of Reclamation which do not involve wholesale purchases. One nonintegrated irrigation district in the region purchases a small amount of water annually. The pattern of urban water retailing is similar to that found in the central coastal region. Water wholesaling is as yet practically undeveloped. But the Sonoma County Flood Control and Water Conservation District, drawing upon the Russian River below Coyote Dam, is developing as a water wholesaler on the northern fringe of the San Francisco Bay region, and should become a significant wholesaler in time. Also, the Humboldt Bay Municipal Water District, serving the City of Eureka and adjacent towns, is beginning to wholesale water. While the maximum potential for wholesaling is not yet known, it is not large.

Concentration of stream diversions in sub-basins of the Central Valley

Table 14 shows data on the relative and absolute size of fully integrated retailing agencies diverting from selected major rivers and river groups in the Central Valley, listed in north-to-south order. (Figures 6 and 7 assist in locating these streams.) In column 2 of Table 14, concentration ratios are presented for varying numbers of the largest diverters in each sub-basin; the number in the array for each sub-basin is allowed to vary to reflect somewhat the differences in the absolute size of agencies among sub-basins. Column 5 shows the importance of the various sub-basins in terms of gross diversions in 1957, and columns 3 and 4 provide measures of the absolute size of diverting agencies in terms of water diverted and acreage irrigated. The sub-basins covered in the tables do not include quite all of the Central Valley. The Delta and rivers descending from the mountains to its eastern border, as well as some minor rivers and creeks, are omitted. However, the table includes the great bulk of streamflows and diversions in the Valley and should adequately depict the variety of local situations encountered.

TABLE 14
PROPORTION OF DIVERSIONS MADE FROM MAJOR RIVERS AND RIVER SYSTEMS FOR LOCAL USE BY LARGEST DIVERTERS, NORTHERN CALIFORNIA, 1957

River	Number of diverters (1)	Share of diversions (per cent) (2)	Size range of diversions (thousand acre-feet) (3)	Acreage irrigated (thousand acres) (4)	Total local diversions (million acre-feet) (5)
Sacramento	5	60	100–600	7–70	2.1
Feather	6	90	95–150	10–15	0.75
Yuba, Bear	6	95	20–140	2–20	0.4
Stanislaus, Tuolumne, Merced	7	95	270–565	24–169	2.06
Lower San Joaquin[a]	9	75	30–535	7–122	1.25
Kings	5	75	100–390	53–210	1.35
Kern	3	95	n.a.	n.a.	0.38

n.a. Not available.
[a] Below Mendota Pool; sources of river flow include water provided under exchange contract at Mendota Pool by the U.S. Bureau of Reclamation and inflows from tributaries.
SOURCE: See note 6 of Chapter 4.

The five largest diverters from the Sacramento River, which take 60 per cent of diversions, include three irrigation districts, one reclamation district, and a mutual company, with the largest irrigation district taking 30 per cent of the total. If the next six largest public agencies were added to these five, another 10 per cent of diversions from the Sacramento would be accounted for. A large number of small private diverters take the remainder. The majority of water is thus captured and distributed by organizations that have very extensive service areas and individually divert very large absolute amounts of water. This general picture is repeated, though sometimes in accentuated or attenuated form, in most of the other sub-basins examined.

Diversions from the Feather River mainly serve an area on its west bank, between it and the Sacramento River. The six leading diverters, including five public agencies and PG&E, take a significantly higher share of total diversions than do a corresponding number of Sacramento River diverters. The sizes of the largest organizations on the two rivers are in the same range if we overlook the largest single agency (Glenn-Colusa Irrigation District) on the Sacramento. The Yuba and Bear rivers, tributary to the Feather, have (mainly for topographic reasons) a quasi-separate service area lying east of the main stem of the Feather. The six organizations accounting for 95 per cent of diversions include four irrigation districts, one mutual company, and PG&E. Concentration of diversions is comparable to that found on the Feather, and the average size of the largest agencies is somewhat smaller. If the Feather-Yuba-Bear service areas are considered as a unified sub-basin, we find over 90 per cent of all diversions in the basin controlled by eleven organizations.

The next major river complex consists of three major tributaries which flow from the east into the lower part of the San Joaquin River—the Stanislaus, Tuolumne, and Merced rivers. These parallel each other over a span of about 45 miles, and have as a mutual service area their adjoining or overlapping alluvial plains or fans on the east side of the San Joaquin. In 1957, annual diversions from them in the San Joaquin Valley were, respectively, about 510,000, 950,000, and 600,000 acre-feet. Diversions from each individual river were highly concentrated. Two irrigation districts and one private company accounted for nearly all of the diversions from the Stanislaus; two irrigation districts made almost 90 per cent of the valley diversions from the Tuolumne, and three over 90 per cent; and one irrigation district made about 95 per cent of all diversions from the Merced. The individual rivers actually serve separate service areas, but they can be viewed as potential suppliers of a quasi-unified sub-basin, in which seven organizations accounted for over 95 per cent of all diversions made in 1957 from the three rivers combined. Concentration of diversions in these sub-basins is substantially higher than in the Feather-Yuba-Bear sub-basin, and on the individual rivers extremely high. Moreover, the average size of the largest organizations, as measured in terms both of annual diversions and of service areas, is greater than in the sub-basins of the Sacramento Valley reviewed above.[21]

A related sub-basin is that of the lower San Joaquin River, which flows northward in the San Joaquin Valley from Mendota Pool to the Delta. Fed from the east along this course by the three rivers just mentioned, its flow is augmented both by their undiverted waters and irrigation return flows. Its service area—lying generally on its western side—is separated from those of these tributaries by a belt of land of poor quality. Most or all of the natural flow of the San Joaquin River, of course, is diverted at Friant Dam before it reaches the Valley, to serve the Tulare Lake Basin region through the Friant-Kern Canal and some lands east of the upper part of the lower San Joaquin River through the Madera Canal. But its flow is augmented at Mendota Pool by importations through the Delta-Mendota Canal as

[21] See California Department of Water Resources, Division of Resources Planning, *Lower San Joaquin Valley Water Quality Investigation,* Bulletin No. 89 (1960).

well as by its east-side tributaries. One irrigation district took about 50 per cent of gross diversions in 1957, and the nine largest organizations (including six irrigation districts and three large mutuals) took about 75 per cent. Most of the rest of the diversions were made by about eight public agencies and six private water companies or large ranches, and the remainder by many small private diverters. In the lower San Joaquin River sub-basin, we observe a degree of concentration of diversions slightly higher than that found on the Sacramento River, and a very similar concentration pattern. It is notable that one very large agency occupies a dominant position (accounting for half of all diversions), just as one large agency does (with 30 per cent of diversions) on the Sacramento.

The five largest water-supplying organizations drawing upon the Kings River took about 75 per cent of 1957's total diversions. Most of the remainder was captured by five public agencies and four private companies, with service areas ranging in size from 6,400 to 38,000 irrigated acres. A rather high degree of concentration of diversions is thus noted, as is the fact that the agencies accounting for the bulk of diversions are all of substantial absolute size.

A sub-basin of the Kaweah and Tule rivers (the Tulare Lake Basin narrowly construed) is omitted from Table 14, for reasons implicit in the following brief description. In this sub-basin, which lies south of the sub-basin of the Kings, most irrigation needs are supplied by ground water pumped from wells and by surface water imported in the Friant-Kern Canal (which furnishes about 70 per cent of the local supply of surface water). Diversions from the local rivers are relatively unimportant, amounting to only about 310,000 acre-feet in 1957. Both wholesale purchases of water from the Bureau of Reclamation and local diversions are made by a large number of public agencies and private companies (including mutuals), with the private companies depending mainly on local diversions and the public agencies on Bureau water. Low concentration of diversions and wholesale purchases is notable, and most individual organizations are quite small in terms both of water used and of irrigated acreage. The largest diverter of local surface water, an irrigation district, makes about 10 per cent of all local surface diversions, or about 31,000 acre-feet a year. (Its 64,000 acres are served primarily by water from other sources).[22] The degree of concentration of local stream diversions is thus not only atypically low, but of reduced economic significance.

In the Kern River sub-basin, about 55 per cent of 1957 diversions were made by several subsidiaries or dependencies of the dominant landholder in the region, the Kern County Land Company. Another 40 per cent were made by two public water storage districts, but at least half of these also went to the Kern County Land Company or its dependencies, as members of the districts. Nearly all water imported via the Bureau's Friant-Kern canal—100,000 acre-feet—was purchased by one municipal utility district. We thus find in the Kern sub-basin not only extremely high concentration of control of local diversions, but an ever higher concentration of use of locally diverted water in the hands of one land company. The land company apparently irrigates in excess of 200,000 acres, and all other users

[22] See California Department of Water Resources, Division of Resources Planning, *Kaweah River: Flows, Diversions, and Service Areas, 1955–60,* Bulletin No. 49–C (1961).

of irrigation water in the area less than 50,000 acres.[23] This is the only sub-basin in the Central Valley in which a high degree of concentration of control of diversions of local stream water is matched by a comparably high concentration of ownership of irrigable land. In most sub-basins, each of the large water-supplying agencies serves numerous independent landowners and water users.

If we take an overview of the major sub-basins of the Central Valley discussed above, two things stand out with respect to concentration among water supplying organizations and the sizes of such organizations. First, in every sub-basin except that of the Kaweah and Tule rivers either a high, or a very high, proportion of all local stream water is diverted by a few, or a very few, water-supplying organizations. (Most of these are public agencies; the rest are largely private water companies and mutual companies.) Only minor fractions of the available supplies are handled by somewhat larger numbers of smaller organizations, or diverted by users. This tendency toward concentration reaches its apex in the Stanislaus-Tuolumne-Merced sub-basin; is quite strong in the sub-basins of the Kings and Kern rivers and in the Feather-Yuba-Bear sub-basin, and somewhat less strong in the service areas of the Sacramento River and the lower San Joaquin River. In none of these sub-basins (the Kaweah-Tule area being excepted) does the availability of imported water at wholesale alter this concentration picture appreciably.

The second thing that stands out is more or less a corollary of the first, though it may have independent importance. In all the sub-basins reviewed, save that of the Kaweah and Tule rivers, most of the surface water is supplied by organizations which individually have very large service areas and which divert correspondingly large absolute amounts of river water. Nearly all of the thirty-nine organizations, which make about 85 per cent of all surface diversions in the seven sub-basins in which concentration is high, have individual service areas larger than 10,000 irrigated acres and divert annually in excess of 30,000 acre-feet of water apiece. Twenty-one of them have service areas of over 20,000 irrigated acres and each of ten serves an area of from 65,000 to 270,000 irrigated acres. A great majority of all thirty-nine agencies diverts individual volumes of surface water in excess of 100,000 acre-feet annually, with the four largest individually handling roughly between 400,000 and 600,000 acre-feet a year. The possible economic implications of the fact that much of the surface water diverted in the Central Valley is thus captured and delivered by agencies that individually serve very large areas of irrigated land and divert very large absolute quantities of water require examination.

[23] See California State Department of Engineering, *Water Resources of the Kern River and Adjacent Streams and Their Utilization, 1920,* Bulletin No. 9 (1921).

5

THE DEMAND FOR WATER: GENERAL DETERMINANTS AND RELATION TO PRICE

The activities of the entities engaged in the water industry anywhere are directed broadly toward satisfying the total demand for water in the area, or, more specifically, toward satisfying each of numerous component demands which make up this total. The total water demand consists of two broad parts: demands for consumptive and for nonconsumptive uses. Demands for consumption, in turn, are composed of demands for irrigation, domestic, municipal, commercial, and industrial uses; demands for nonconsumption are those for generating hydroelectric power, for recreation, and for navigation. Each of these smaller components may be broken down geographically into demands expressed in particular regions or localities, and still further into demands expressed by individuals or organizations who are actual and potential water users.

Theoretical analysis of the characteristics of total water demand or any of its major components—such as the demand for irrigation water in the Sacramento Valley—must begin with a consideration of the demands of the actual and potential individual water users that are members of the designated user group. Here we are interested primarily in the general characteristics of the demands for water by the major components of consumptive use in Northern California—water needed for irrigation, for general urban purposes, and for industrial activities. But consideration of individual demands comes first in the process of analyzing and interpreting these broad components of water demand.

The demand schedule for water of any individual or group of individuals for any use of course generally reflects the quantities of water which the individual or group is willing and able to purchase, or otherwise pay for, at each of a range of different prices. We have some general indications of the extent of current consumptive demands actually expressed at the going prices in Northern California from statistics on the annual volume of water used in the late 1950's. In 1957, water was captured for consumptive use in the amount of about 24 million acre-feet; of this, almost 94 per cent was directed toward agriculture and a little over 6 per cent toward domestic, municipal, commercial, and industrial uses combined. If allowance is made for a greater percentage of losses in transit to points of use for agricultural water, the proportions of water actually used were probably closer to 92 per cent for irrigation and 8 per cent for the other consumptive purposes. These quantities should be fair measures of the aggregate expressed demands for water for consumptive use, except so far as offers to purchase water went unfulfilled (meaning that water was rationed to some degree and in some way other than by price).

At the theoretical level, we can identify a large number of determinants of the quantity of water demanded by members of each of these classes of users. The substance of this chapter concerns those determinants which can be denoted a priori as significant aspects of the water industry's structure, capable of affecting its economic conduct and performance in a discernable way. While a number of causal factors holding this power will be mentioned, one will receive the bulk of the attention: the price of water. Price elasticity of demand, as in the case of a conventional industry, holds considerable potential significance for both the performance and conduct of the water industry. Its normative significance stems from the economic criteria identifying an allocative optimum with the equation of the marginal cost of resources placed in any given use to their marginal value, the latter measured by the price paid in a free market. Any discrepancy between marginal cost and marginal value tends to signal an excess, or deficiency, in the quantity of resources employed in the activity in question. The elasticity of demand indicates the size of the misallocation associated with a given gap between marginal cost and marginal value.

If water demands were generally almost totally inelastic to water price over relevant ranges of price, the allocative impact of water prices would be slight and the magnitude of misallocations of water and other resources engendered by economic pricing errors would be small. This is because substantial variations in various prices over the relevant range would induce only small changes in the patterns of water use—whether geographical or other patterns—and in the allocation of non-water resources to water development. The impact of pricing errors would then be primarily on the distribution of income among various segments of the populace (on what they paid for water), and only slightly on resource allocation (how much water they got).

If, however, some or all important component water demands display an appreciable price elasticity—even though they are inelastic in the sense that a given proportionate price change will produce a somewhat smaller proportionate change in demand—the allocative impact of water prices will be quite significant; the possibility of a very appreciable misallocation of water and other resources will be distinctly present. With an even more elastic water demand, the allocative impacts of water prices will be very strong, and huge misallocations may result from economic pricing errors.

The price elasticity of demand also has significance in separate, but related, ways. It is involved, for instance, in determining the economic justifiability of any water project that is designed to supply water in volume to a previously unwatered area, or to substantially augment the water supply in an area which is currently under-watered in comparison to some others or promises to become so with expected increases in population—all at a determinable added cost per unit of added water supplied. In such advance consideration, there must be a definite allowance for the effect of a price of water sufficient to cover this added cost on the amount of water which will be demanded from the new supply. This is particularly essential where introduction of the new supply entails higher water costs and prices than those previously experienced in the area. If due allowance is not made for the effect on demand of elevated water prices, a project may be undertaken which is designed to supply more water than would be economically most desirable for the area. Furthermore, in such a case, the revenues will not cover costs, and the project is likely to be operated in the long run with water prices below costs and an economically undesirable subsidy provided to water users in the area. This is to say that too large a quantity of non-water resources may be allocated to water development in the light of the greater over-all productivity of such resources if some or all of them were allocated to other lines of production.

The price elasticity of demand may also affect the conduct of the water industry, especially the viability of bilateral bargaining situations. In an atomistic market, a low aggregate elasticity does not have much direct effect on conduct, since each decision unit tends to see itself as facing a highly elastic demand. When a low elasticity of demand combines with fewness of sellers, it implies a lack of alternatives for the buyer (whatever the seller's situation). Given the institutional environment of the water industry, such a lack of alternatives may mean that the bargaining situation is not politically viable.

Other determinants of demand for water are large in number and vary from one kind of consumptive use to another. Like demand elasticity, they may affect either the performance or the conduct of the water industry. For example, the extent to which variations appear in the quantity of water demanded at different times for urban domestic uses governs the size of misallocations that may result from a lack of intertemporal variations in the price charged in those cases where it would be appropriate. Demand determinants that vary from region to region in Northern California may help to explain observed variations in the conduct of water agencies among these regions. Rather than citing a number of hypothetical possibilities, we turn to the evidence, first for agricultural and then urban demand.

Environmental Determinants of the Demand for Irrigation Water

A great many physical and economic factors could be listed that can influence whether or not irrigation water is demanded for a particular tract of land and, if so, in what quantities at various prices. In addition to the most important influence on demand for the purposes of this study—the price of water—some of the interesting determinants are those which explain important interregional differences in irrigation demands in Northern California. Even if they possess no special significance for our policy conclusions, they must be considered so that we can sort out, in later chapters, their influence from those other factors holding immediate and direct policy significance. To put the matter more vividly, it matters whether alkali soil or peculiarity of the water rights situation precludes a particular tract from being irrigated, even if only the institutions of water rights are capable of change by human endeavor.

Soil characteristics

"Soil type" is a complex concept because any soil possesses several significant properties, and its type may be measured in each of several dimensions. Principal soil characteristics which are frequently listed by soil technologists include:[1] texture, measured by relative percentages of silt, sand, and clay, or by the percentage of soil particles having less than a certain diameter; compactness or density; structure, whether cloddy, granular, fibrous, layers, etc.; permeability by water; available nutrient capacity; chemical properties, such as acidity, alkalinity, calcareousness, salinity; and gravel content. Other important characteristics—not, strictly speaking, soil properties—might be mentioned, such as depth of the surface soil to bedrock or to a subsoil of a different type. These soil characteristics might help to explain variations in the patterns of demand for irrigation water from one region of Northern California to another.

First, we will consider their effects on the "irrigation efficiency" obtainable with a soil. This can be measured by the percentage of the irrigation water applied to the soil which will be retained by the soil within the root zones of plants being grown and thus be available for consumptive use by the crops—as opposed to the percentage lost by surface runoff and by deep percolation. This efficiency will clearly affect the amount of irrigation water required to obtain a given irrigation result. Also, to the extent that irrigation efficiency is lower, the costs of water will be higher (with any given price of water) for producing a given crop, and the soil with lower irrigation efficiency will suffer a virtual disadvantage compared to soils with higher efficiencies. Among the soil characteristics listed above, irrigation efficiency usually is jointly determined by several: texture, compactness, structure, and permeability. Their interrelations cannot be described in any simple way.

Variations in irrigation efficiency (as we pass from an area of one soil type to an area of another) may impose several economic effects. The annual demand for irrigation water to support a given crop may vary greatly. Thus, statistics show that, in three Central Valley irrigation districts, rice was grown with applications of irrigation water ranging annually from 7.8 to 15.8 acre-feet per acre, and, in five irrigation districts, cotton was grown with applications ranging annually from 1.4 to 2.4 acre-feet per acre.[2] Other things being equal, farmers will be influenced to grow crops with lower requirements for consumptive use of water on soils with lower irrigation efficiencies, so that the net effect of variations in irrigation efficiency from place to place may be either to increase or decrease the demand for irrigation water per acre.

One soil characteristic of particular importance in explaining variations in

[1] Compare Harry F. Blaney, "Use of Water by Irrigated Crops in California," *Journal of the American Water Works Association,* XLIII (March 1951), 189–200; David Weeks and J. Herbert Snyder, "Soil Variables for Use in Economic Analysis," *Hilgardia* (April 1957), 497–520. (Most footnote references in this chapter are cited in brief form when they are also included in the Bibliography.)

[2] California Department of Water Resources, Division of Resources Planning, *Report on Irrigation and Water Storage Districts in California, 1956–58,* Bulletin No. 21 (1960). (Hereinafter cited as Bulletin No. 21 with the date covered in parentheses.)

agricultural patterns and water demands from one segment to another of the Central Valley is the chemical properties of soils. Slightly acid and neutral soils are readily adaptable to the production of a wide range of crops, but soils which are appreciably alkaline or saline are not so adaptable, and provide distinctly inferior environments for the growth of many crops. Many such soils, however, are quite adaptable—and in California are so adapted—to the growth of rice (a heavy user of irrigation water); barley and some clovers (light users); and pasture (light to heavy user). Since more than 20 per cent of the acreage of the Central Valley is significantly saline or alkaline, this restriction on crop pattern imposed by alkalinity and salinity has a significant impact on demands for irrigation water in the region. The impact, however, is mixed, since some such lands are very heavily irrigated and some slightly or not at all. Topography being favorable, as it is for the bulk of saline-alkaline lands which are also very flat bottom lands, the demand for irrigation water for use on many such lands tends to be very responsive to price. If the water price is, or becomes, quite low, the cultivation of rice, requiring very large annual applications of water per acre, is generally encouraged; with distinctly higher water prices, there may be a shift to the growth of pastures and small grains, which have much smaller requirements for consumptive use of water and may be irrigated slightly or not at all.

The conditions of natural drainage of soils has great general importance in the determination of demands for irrigation water. They are especially important in the Central Valley. In addition to lands with saline and alkaline soils, the majority of which are also poorly drained bottom lands, another fifth of the acreage of the Valley is in basin lands that are imperfectly drained under natural conditions, although the soils are not appreciably alkaline or saline.[3] If these lands are not artificially drained, they provide an inferior environment for the production of a wide range of crops; in the Central Valley, their use for the growth of rice, other cereals, or pasture is favored, with the choice of crop depending, again, strongly on the price of water. Thus, the effects of imperfect drainage on the demand for irrigation water are roughly the same as those attributed to salinity and alkalinity of soil. In particular, the two sets of characteristics combine to influence and restrict irrigation patterns in a large portion of the trough of the San Joaquin Valley.

Land characteristics—topography

The topography of the land which soils overlie is generally significant in influencing demands for irrigation water, and especially in determining—assuming that soil characteristics are reasonably favorable—whether or not irrigation will be undertaken in various localities and on various tracts. In Northern California, the relevant broad topographic categories are the following:[4]

[3] Some of these lands, however, are calcareous.

[4] R. Earl Storie and Walter W. Weir, *Generalized Soil Map of California,* Manual No. 6, California Agricultural Experiment Station, Extension Service, Berkeley, n.d.

1) Valley basin land—in valley bottoms, nearly flat, and, in this region, nearly all at quite low altitudes, ranging from sea level to around 500 feet.

2) Valley land—gently sloping and smooth, and usually adjoining valley bottom lands at slightly higher altitudes than such adjoining lands, but not exceeding 1,000 feet in altitude for a preponderance of acreage so classified.

3) Terrace land—gently to moderately sloping and frequently undulating, very frequently but not always adjoining valley lands as fringes between valleys and foothills, and at somewhat higher altitudes than adjoining valley lands.

4) Upland—rolling, from hilly to steep, and at various altitudes, ranging from sea level (where hills or mountains meet the sea) through moderately low altitudes (where foothills fringe valleys and valley terraces) to the higher altitudes (which are typical of much of the vast mountainous regions of the area).

Northern California has roughly 5 million acres of valley basin land and 6 million acres of valley land, with about 90 per cent of the total 11 million acres lying in the Central Valley. (Nearly all of the valley basin land of the region is there, and about 85 per cent of the valley land.) Terrace land, the bulk of which adjoins the Central Valley, amounts to about 5 million acres; and there is in the neighborhood of 45 million acres of upland—hills, foothills, and especially mountains.

The principal influences of topography on the demand for irrigation water are through its effects on cultivability and cultivation costs, and on the physical feasibility and cost of applying and getting net benefit from irrigation water. Valley basin and valley lands, being smooth and relatively flat, are ideally suited topographically to cultivation and, other things being equal, can be cultivated at a minimum cost. They can also be most easily and cheaply irrigated in the sense that simple and inexpensive ditch facilities for spreading water can be employed without encountering appreciable soil erosion and excessive grade-induced runoff losses. Terrace lands, in varying degrees according to the kind of undulation and slope encountered, generally can be cultivated at slightly to moderately higher costs. Uplands in Northern California generally are not suitable to cultivation or irrigation.

The net advantages for irrigated crop production of Northern California lands of different topography are influenced by the fact that certain soil characteristics associated with topography may either increase or reduce the economic advantage or disadvantage which inheres in the topography. It is notable, for example, that the area's lands in the valley category not only have a nearly maximum topographic advantage, but also generally have deep, fertile, and friable soils with moderately good to good irrigation efficiencies, and are not afflicted with appreciable salinity or alkalinity. With minor exceptions for valley lands having very sandy soils (that is, "sandy wind-modified soils"), valley lands in general have a combination of topography and soil type which favor a maximum likelihood that irrigation water will be demanded at any given level of water prices.

The situation is different for nearly all of the valley basin lands of the region (except about a third of a million acres with peaty soils), which also have a maximum topographic advantage for irrigation. These soils either are saline-alkaline to a significant degree, and often poorly drained as well, or they are imperfectly drained under natural conditions—the two limiting soil characteristics affecting about equal amounts of valley basin acreage. On these acres, the disadvantages of soil characteristics tend to offset, in part or entirely, or to overbalance topographic advantages. As a result, the lands involved may be—and frequently are—close to, at, or below the margin as candidates for irrigation; may be specialized as to crop in the case of saline-alkaline soils; and may support demands for irrigation water which are fairly sensitive to appreciable changes in water prices or in the ratio of crop prices to costs in general.

In the case of Northern California's terrace lands, slight or moderate topographic disadvantages for irrigation are typically conjoined with various disadvantages of soil type. Somewhat more than half of the roughly 5 million acres of terrace lands have iron hardpan soils or shallow surface soils with dense clay subsoils—mostly the former. These soils tend to limit the terrace lands to pasture and shallow rooted crops. Although such crops may be profitably irrigated given existing water prices, most frequently they are not. Most of the remaining half of the terrace lands, however, have loamy surface soils and only moderately dense subsoils, and are generally respectable candidates for irrigation for the growth of a broader variety of crops. Even so, they are at some economic disadvantage compared to valley lands.

The general distribution of Northern California lands by topographic type is shown in Figure 13, which should be interpreted in the light of the preceding comments on the distribution of soil types by topographic areas.

Climate

A final economically significant physical factor influencing the demand for irrigation water is Northern California's climate. The pattern of precipitation, described in Chapter 2, involves limited rainfall on the region's agricultural lands, coming almost entirely in the late fall, winter, and very early spring months; about 80 per cent of precipitation occurs from November through May. Thus, although the growing season is quite long because of annual temperature patterns, precipitation does not supply the bulk of the water required by most crops grown during their cultural periods and primary reliance for water is placed on irrigation.

The great interior Central Valley always experiences long hot summers and mild winters. During the coldest part of the year, generally November through February, average daily high temperatures usually range from 45 to 60 degrees, but night-time lows are periodically freezing except in certain thermal belts on the eastern fringe of the San Joaquin Valley. Other interior valleys—closer to the coast but sheltered from the ocean—have climates similar to that of the Central Valley but generally experience somewhat less intense summer heat.

What are the major impacts of this combination of climatic characteristics on the demand for irrigation water in the area? Over the great bulk of the agricultural regions in the Central Valley and other interior valleys—with the relatively great length of the growing season and mild winter conditions which permit

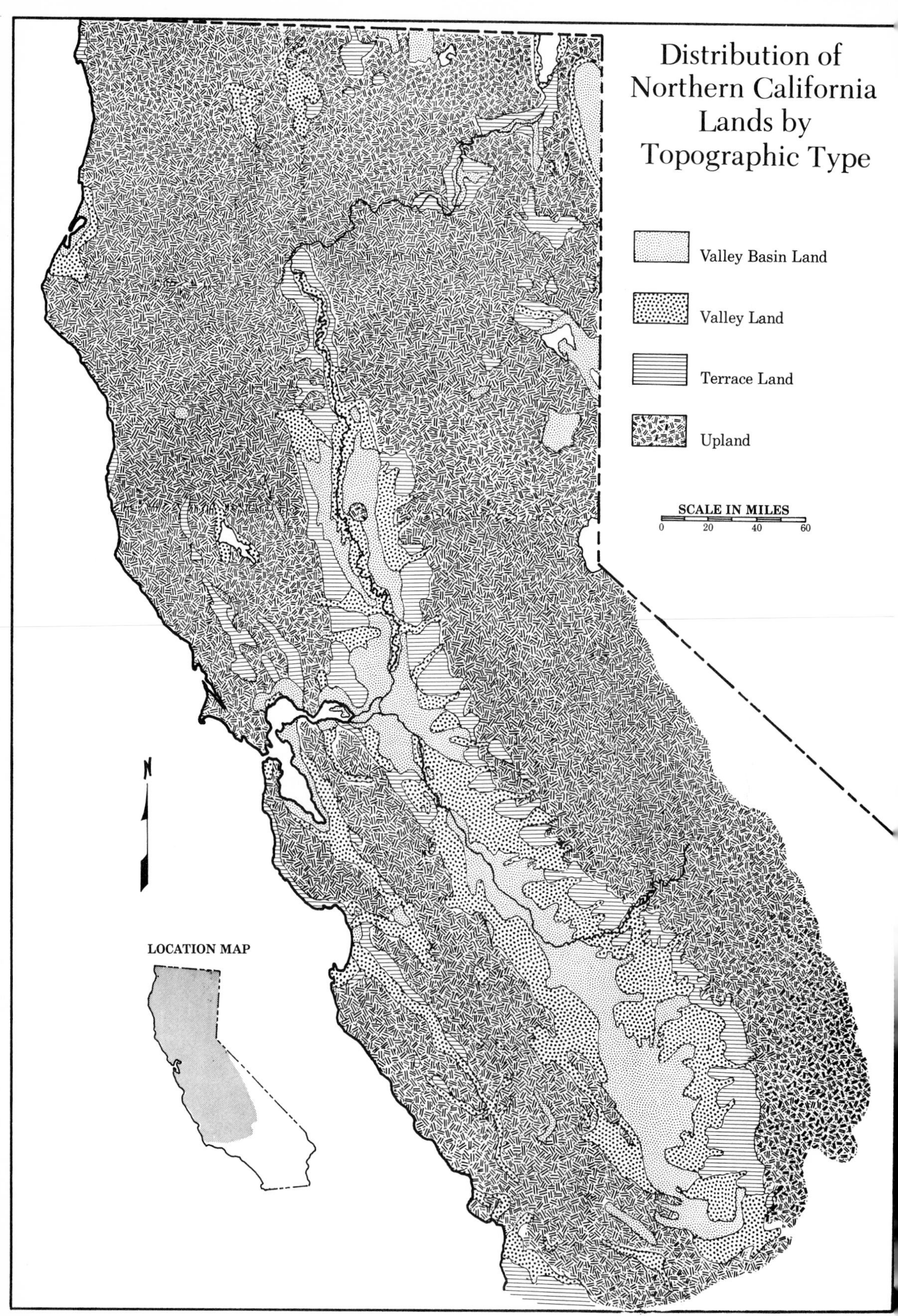
Distribution of Northern California Lands by Topographic Type
Valley Basin Land
Valley Land
Terrace Land
Upland
SCALE IN MILES
0
20
40
60
N
LOCATION MAP

Figure 13

cultivation and planting at almost any time of year except when limited rainfall intervenes—a very wide range of crops, with both long and short cultural periods, can be grown. These range, for example, from cotton to small grains, and include some subtropicals such as oranges in certain thermal belts. Not only does this climatic condition generally provide farmers in the area with a wide range of crops among which they may choose and with a correspondingly substantial range of water requirements. It is also favorable to considerable sensitivity in the response of farmers' demands for irrigation water to differences or changes in water prices or in cost-price ratios for crops. And it permits, especially in the more southerly part of the Central Valley, the growth of two successive crops of types with short cultural periods within a single growing season. So far as this opportunity is exploited, the demand for irrigation water per acre is generally increased.

Technical Determinants of the Demand for Irrigation Water

The preceding section has discussed selected environmental determinants of the demand for irrigation water in Northern California—those which play a significant part in explaining patterns of conduct or interregional differences in conduct within the area. Now we consider briefly two important classes of technical determinants of demand, both identified with familiar concepts of economic theory. The first class concerns the impact of varying the quantity of water combined with given quantities of other inputs to produce a given crop: the marginal productivity function for water. The second reflects losses in the productivity of water caused by deficiencies in its quality: the marginal disutility of pollution as quantities of various types of pollutants are increased.

Varying water quantities combined with other inputs

One of the most familiar constructions of economic theory is the marginal productivity function, showing the variations in quantity of a given output in response to variations in the quantity of one input, all other inputs being held constant. In the case of irrigation water, we conceive it as showing the variations in the yield of a particular crop in response to variations in the amount of irrigation water applied to a given quantity of land and other farm inputs.[5] What is at issue is the extent of technical substitution possible between water and land in the growing of particular crops. This factor has obvious significance in determining the general price elasticity of demand for irrigation water.

Empirical evidence on the shape of the marginal productivity function for water in producing various California crops is a good deal less than one would wish. In earlier years, serious attention was occasionally given to the problem by conducting crudely constructed, but sensible, experiments to determine a marginal

[5] Such a relation might be conceived or measured either with all non-water inputs held constant, or with land held constant and other inputs varying along with water in some defined way.

productivity function for irrigation water as used within a year in growing given crops.[6] Recent literature bearing on the general issue at hand has tended to emphasize more complicated subsidiary issues, while losing sight of—or dismissing—the central issue of water-land substitutability. After extensive analyses of such various matters as soil moisture tension and its relationship to crop yield, numerous authors have concluded: (1) that the relationship of the annual quantity of water used per unit of land area to crop yield is not simple; (2) that crop yield depends very heavily on the frequency and time pattern of individual applications of irrigation water and the size of individual applications (as well as on soil type); and (3) that (apparently) the relationship of crop yield to variations in individual irrigation frequencies and amounts deserves emphasis up to the point that the relationship of total annual amount of water used per acre to crop yield may be expediently forgotten or put aside.[7] Without discounting at all the considerable importance of recent findings concerning the complexity of the relationship of crop yield to water input, it must be emphasized that the central issue remains, that it is important, and that it deserves more analysis than it has been getting. For, assuming that every alternative total quantity of water applied to given land to grow a given crop is applied with optimal irrigation frequencies and in optimal individual amounts—however difficult it may be to determine such optima—there still must be a determinable marginal productivity function for total water used annually (with other variable factors), just as there must be determinable limits on the economical ratio of total water used annually to land.

We thus return to the central problem, without too much assistance from contemporary irrigation and soil specialists, and will have to rely on some relatively ancient studies and some indirectly relevant indications in arriving at a guess-estimate type of answer. One somewhat helpful guide is provided by old studies of the marginal productivity of water under arbitrary experimental conditions, such as that cited in note 6 above. Another is found in data concerning the variability in requirements for consumptive use of water for various crops in the Central Valley (showing a generally narrow range of variability for most crops).[8] A third guide, or perhaps a consolation in arriving at a conclusion, is the apparent willingness of various specialists studying water demands in general to assume for purposes of calculation essentially fixed annual coefficients of land to water in raising most crops on given land, in spite of substantial changes in water prices.[9]

[6] See, for example, California State Department of Engineering, *Investigations of the Economical Duty of Water for Alfalfa in Sacramento Valley, California, 1910–1915*, Bulletin No. 3 (1917). For a scattering of more recent data, see Earl O. Heady and Luther G. Tweeten, *Resource Demand and Structure of the Agricultural Industry* (1963), pp. 115–17.

[7] See, for a random sample of recent literature, Christopher Beringer, *An Economic Model for Determining the Production Function for Water in Agriculture*, Giannini Foundation Research Report No. 240 (1961); Weeks and Snyder, *op. cit.;* and Charles V. Moore, "A General Analytical Framework for Estimating the Production Function for Crops Using Irrigation Water," *Journal of Farm Economics*, XLIII (November 1961), 876–88.

[8] See Blaney, *op. cit.*, especially p. 194.

[9] See, for example, Trimble R. Hedges and Charles V. Moore, *Economics of On-Farm Irrigation Water Availability and Costs, and Related Farm Adjustments—1. Enterprise Choices, Resource Allocations, and Earnings on 640-Acre General Crop Farms on the San Joaquin Valley Eastside*, Giannini Foundation Research Report No. 257 (1962), especially p. 54.

The impression given by this evidence is also supported largely by information obtained in interviews conducted (in connection with Part Two of this volume) with numerous officials of irrigation districts and others in close touch with actual agricultural practices in the Central Valley. Their opinions presumably reflect what farmers think marginal productivity functions look like, a relevant datum even if it should be shown to conflict with experimental evidence. For most crops, variations in water applications above the wilting point are felt to have no significant influence on output. Certain crops are significant exceptions, however; yields of irrigated pasture and alfalfa substantially with the amount of water applied, and rice shows some variability.

On the basis of available evidence and of inferences drawn from it, we are willing to guess that on a given quality and quantity of land the substitutability of water for land within economic limits is quite poor for most crops. Furthermore, this conclusion probably would not change appreciably if we added to the picture the possibility of substitution between water and other inputs than land. Field interviews suggest that some substitutability for labor may be possible, in that more labor-intensive methods of irrigation result in less waste of water.[10] But, again, that relatively fixed proportions prevail among land, water, and other inputs for a given crop seems to be the best general statement that can be made.

Varying quality of irrigation water

In certain portions of Northern California, notably in the lower San Joaquin Valley and the Delta, irrigators face a recurrent problem of deficient quality of irrigation water drawn from local surface sources. In other areas, mainly the west side of the San Joaquin Valley, ground water sometimes presents the same problem.

Such deficiencies in water quality are of two main sorts. First, the water may contain, generally in solution, chemicals which on impact are toxic to various plant species. This is the case, for example, with water containing even minute traces of boron—such water generally being ground water which has absorbed the element from the rock and earth structures in which it is contained. It is also the case for waters in river estuaries which, because of tidewater intrusion, have become sufficiently brackish with sodium chloride and other chlorides that many, most, or all plants will not survive irrigation with them. And the same may apply to some ground-water deposits which have become brackish through the prolonged percolation of surface waters in which natural chlorides have been concentrated through evaporation (or through subsurface seawater intrusion).

In the second type of deficiency, the water may contain relatively small quantities of chloride and bicarbonate ions (the latter producing exchangeable sodium) as

[10] Sprinkler irrigation is sometimes suggested as a significant method of economizing the use of water through more intensive use of other inputs; but since it is little employed in Northern California, we have not investigated this possible form of input substitution in detail. See Guy O. Woodward, ed., *Sprinkler Irrigation* (2nd ed.; 1959), especially p. 279.

well as sodium and salts. These are not generally toxic to plants on impact, but over a period of years they accumulate in the soil to which water is applied for irrigation—producing "slow poisoning" of the soil as salts accumulate in the soil profile, and also affecting the structure of the soil and, in particular, its permeability. Natural river water or ground water may produce these effects over a period of years when overly "efficient" irrigation practices result in insufficient leaching of the soil of accumulating chemicals, or when high ground-water tables deter efficient leaching. In such cases, however, the cumulative effects on the soil are at all pronounced only with the culture of perennial crops (orchards, alfalfa, etc.); they are minimal with the culture of annual crops. In addition, the quality of water flowing in a river, such as the lower San Joaquin, may itself deteriorate in quality over time because return flows from irrigation, admixing in river flows, become more heavily laden with chemical pollutants than the river's natural flow. This occurs partly because return flows are concentrated by evaporation and partly because chemical fertilizers, soil additives, and pesticides are dissolved in the return flows. It can happen some times also if irrigators try to reverse the cumulative process of soil deterioration by increasing water applications for leaching, and thus cause previous accumulations of salts in the soil to be returned in concentration to the river. (The same, in general, may apply to deterioration of ground waters.)

The effects of these two types of deficiency of water quality on the demand for irrigation water are likely to be somewhat different. For water which is toxic on impact to all plants there will be no irrigation demand, unless purer water is economically available with which to dilute it and make it less than generally poisonous to vegetation. For water which contains enough of boron, salts, or other chemicals to be toxic on impact to many crops, but not all, there will be a tendency to induce its use in special resistant crops. Whether or not the water is used for these resistant crops will depend on its cost and on the price elasticity of demand for irrigation water to grow these crops. It is not logically necessary that the demand for such water should be smaller at any price, or more price elastic, than better water. It appears, in fact, that in many cases the crops in California which will tolerate such water, and even thrive when irrigated with it, are large water-users and have highly price-elastic demands for irrigation water. When this is taken in conjunction with the generally low price of the water in question (in the lower San Joaquin River and in Delta and Sacramento River water made somewhat brackish by tidewater intrusion), net demands for it are not reduced. They would be reduced, however, at higher prices for the same water.

As to water of a quality which slowly but progressively tends to result in soil deterioration when applied for irrigation unless countermeasures are taken, the responses of demand for irrigation water may vary. One possibility is that irrigators will adapt to deteriorating soil by shifting to tolerant crops, such as sugar beets or rice. Depending on the crop selected and the price of water, demand may either decrease (as in the case of sugar beets) or increase (as in that of rice). Another possibility is that farmers, taking the long view, may increase irrigation in order to increase leaching, and thus retard or check soil deterioration. This policy should tend to result in larger demands for poorer water, and a greater price elasticity of demand. A related possibility, also connected with foresight, is that irrigators may shift from perennial to annual crops; the result would be either a decrease or increase in the demand for water or in its price elasticity. A final possibility is that the soil-deteriorating effects of poor water may be offset by the use of soil additives, or by improved drainage or other agricultural practices. This should reduce the marginal productivity of given quantities of water, but may correspondingly open opportunities for crops with more price elastic demands for water, so that the effect on demand is not uniquely predictable. Beyond this, and lacking detailed probing of the matter, there is little more of a general nature to be said of the effect of inferior water quality on irrigation water demand.[11]

Price Elasticity of Demand for Irrigation Water

Having considered the effect on the demand for irrigation water of its more significant environmental and technical determinants, we now turn to the question of demand elasticity, a matter basically of the purchaser's economic choice in the face of the environmental and technical conditions.

The price elasticity of demand for irrigation water—relation of quantity purchased to price paid—can be conceived and measured in various fashions. What is mainly relevant for our purposes is the elasticity of demand for irrigation water sold by retailing organizations to individual farm enterprises. This elasticity can differ for a number of reasons from the "pure" theoretical concept of the elasticity of the derived demand for irrigation water as an input in the production of crops. Despite these sources of difference, it is convenient to start from the more familiar theoretical concept and then, as we discuss measurements of the empirically relevant one, indicate the sources of difference between them.

One group of determinants of the pure elasticity of demand for irrigation water—namely the technical possibilities of substitution between water and other inputs in growing a given crop—was considered in the preceding section. It was suggested that, for most crops raised in Northern California, the possible substitutions are quite limited. On the basis of this factor alone, one would predict a very low elasticity of demand for irrigation water, but other important determinants remain to be considered. In Appendix A we show the effect of shifts in the crops grown resulting from changes in water prices on the elasticity of demand for irrigation water. It is there demonstrated that, on a priori grounds, crop substitution can give rise to a substantial elasticity of demand. An increase in the price of irrigation water tends to cause shifts toward the production of less water-intensive crops. These shifts do not depend on crops that make heavy use of water becoming absolutely unprofitable,[12] but merely upon a re-ordering of profitability between

[11] For some detailed examination of problems of water quality as they affect irrigation, see California Department of Water Resources, Division of Resources Planning, *Lower San Joaquin Valley Water Quality Investigation,* Bulletin No. 89 (1960), especially pp. 160–63 and 179–85.

[12] This conclusion is contrary to a view often stated or implied in material relating to the water industry. For example, both state and federal government agencies on occasion calculate the "payment capacity" of a local water district planning to undertake some major commitment

more and less water-intensive crops in consequence of the input's price change. In Appendix A, we also explore the effect of certain constraints upon this crop-substitution process. One source of constraints is governmental and related restrictions upon the maximum acreage that a farmer can devote to a given crop. Others include natural restrictions on the timing of deliveries of irrigation water and the various factors in farm management which tend to induce the growing of a number of crops rather than simply the one apparently yielding the greatest excess of expected revenue over long-run costs. The effect of these qualifications and constraints is somewhat to weaken the earlier a priori finding that crop substitution may generate a high elasticity of demand for irrigation water. Nonetheless, in an area such as the Central Valley, where a great number of crops can be and, in fact, are grown, crop substitution must certainly have some significance as a source of price elasticity.

Before setting forth the empirical evidence of the elasticity of demand faced by sellers of irrigation water in Northern California, we need to examine two of the factors that make this elasticity different from a pure elasticity of demand for water, for they create problems in the construction of empirical measurements and interpretation of the results. First, farmers in many parts of the Central Valley own wells capable of supplying large quantities of water for irrigation. This source is available to them as an alternative to any supplies derived from surface sources purchased from a retailer.[13] The existence of this alternative source for the irrigator could be expected to make the demand for surface supplies more elastic than otherwise, at least in certain price ranges. We are potentially concerned both with the pure elasticity and with the net elasticity of demand for surface supplies when ground water is available. The latter hybrid elasticity is the one relevant to decisions of the retailer of surface water, but the former is relevant to some of our normative concerns.

The second special factor in the sale of irrigation water concerns the method of levying charges used by the public districts that are the dominant retailers. A two-part charge is frequently employed, one part taking the form of an assessment that does not vary with the quantity of water taken, the other a "toll" or quantity charge that does.[14] Should we expect the quantity of water taken by the typical irrigator to be adjusted to the level of the tolls that he pays, or to the average

to purchase water or to install facilities for storing or distributing water. The figure for the "payment capacity" of a crop is essentially calculated by deducting the average cost of non-water inputs from the assumed average revenue, thus yielding a rough estimate of the net value of the average product of water applications, stated per unit of water applied. The implication is left that the crop pattern could and would stay unchanged in the face of water charges that absorb most of the payment capacity of at least some crops. This contradicts the theoretical finding of our Appendix A, as well as a Hedges-Moore study discussed below, to the effect that shifts in the crop pattern toward less water-intensive crops can occur without the payment capacity of the more water-intensive crops being exhausted. These studies of payment capacity, which are discussed more extensively in Appendix C, thus implicitly underestimate the price elasticity of demand for irrigation water.

[13] In practice, wells are often used to supplement surface supplies when the latter are exhausted before the end of the irrigation season.

[14] Assessments are set in many different ways, and tolls sometimes vary with the quantity taken so that average and marginal tolls to the irrigator may differ. The range of practices and their respective prevalence are discussed in Chapter 10.

price of water including both toll and tax? An economist is prone to answer immediately that the toll alone is the appropriate parameter, since profit maximization by the irrigator requires equating the marginal value product of water to its marginal (not average) cost. When we recall our hypothesis that public water districts can be viewed as users' cooperatives, however, this answer is thrown into doubt. Suppose that irrigators feel a collective responsibility for the total costs of their district's operations and, furthermore, that they believe it to operate under conditions of constant (or increasing) cost in the long run. In that case, even if the district's management chooses to collect only a portion of its revenues from tolls, members would be conscious that the expected unit cost of water exceeds the toll. They might conceivably adjust their purchases to what they think is the true marginal cost of water, measured by the average of all charges that they pay, rather than just to the short-run marginal price that they incur. Thus, it is not obvious whether a statistical investigation of the demand elasticity faced by users' cooperatives that retail water to their members should take as the independent variable the toll per unit of water or the average total charge per unit. Furthermore, we have in the theory that an agency's customer-members might look behind the direct tolls levied upon them a "strong" test for the basic users' cooperative hypothesis itself.

The available literature does not contain a great deal of statistical or similar evidence concerning the price elasticity of demand for irrigation water, although a number of horse-back estimates can be found. Yet, since the relevant predictions of a theory of demand for irrigation water are entirely qualitative in nature—identifying sources of some price elasticity, showing that it should be negative in sign, and guessing whether it will be appreciable or negligible—some quantitative estimates of the price elasticity of such demand are clearly needed.

The development of adequate and representative measures of the price elasticity in question, as it is found in an area such as Northern California, is no easy task. Desired data are not generally available in adequate number or in the most useful form, and difficult statistical problems are encountered because demand for irrigation water has so many determinants in addition to the price of water, not all of which are readily measurable on a quantitative scale. Numerous problems of interpretation arise because demands are determined subject to some constraints on water availability, and because the degree of such constraints may have some correlation with water price; and the price elasticity may be expected to differ appreciably among localities within the area. Because of the last difficulty, any statistical elasticity measure developed from data referring to various parts of the area will refer to a somewhat heterogeneous universe, for which some sort of an average tendency will be shown; conversely, elasticity measures developed for limited and relatively homogeneous areas cannot be taken as generally representative of other areas in the region.

Faced with these difficulties, and at present unable to overcome many of them, we will offer here the results of two studies of the price elasticity of the demand for irrigation water in the area. One is our own statistical analysis of the relationship of demand for irrigation water to water price in a single year for thirty-eight irrigation districts in California, nearly all of them scattered through the Central

Valley. The other is based on "engineering estimates" of the expected reaction of such demand to changes in the price of water for "typical" farms of various sizes in one relatively homogeneous area in the Tulare Basin section of the east side of the San Joaquin Valley. These estimates were prepared by Hedges and Moore in works which will be cited below.

Our analysis explored the relationship of price to demand for irrigation water by comparing deliveries by irrigation districts with different water prices in the same year, 1958. As a measure of price for any district we used total annual payments for water made to the district, divided by the annual quantity of water in acre-feet delivered by and within the district. The average water price for each district is thus a delivered price per acre-foot equaling the sum of its total annual water income and its annual income from tax assessments (both general-fund and bond-fund) on district members, divided by the annual total of acre-feet of water it delivered within the district. The demand for irrigation water in each district was stated in terms of acre-feet of district-supplied water used per irrigated acre annually, calculated as total acre-feet of water delivered annually by and within the district, divided by the number of irrigated acres in the district.[15] The total number of irrigation districts in the state for which the requisite data were reported was eighty-two. Of these, forty-four were eliminated from our sample because the sales of water outside the district or sales for domestic use within the district exceeded 5 per cent of total water sales.[16] Of the remaining thirty-eight districts which comprise the working sample, thirty-four are well scattered through the Central Valley, two lie in the eastern part of the north coastal region (north and east of the Central Valley), and two are in Southern California.

With the data converted into logarithmic form, the following regression equation was calculated:

$$\log q = 1.74 - 0.641 \log p.$$

The price elasticity of demand for irrigation water is correspondingly about −0.64. About 48 per cent of the variance in the quantity of water demanded is explained by differences in water prices among districts—and surprisingly this percentage is high in view of the large number of other determinants of demand which differ in value among the irrigation districts. The confidence interval is such that there is a 95 per cent chance that the price elasticity lies between −0.42 and −0.87.

We also investigated the relation between the quantity of water delivered per irrigated acre by many of these irrigation districts[17] and the average level of

[15] All data for water quantities and irrigated acreage are taken from Bulletin No. 21 (1956–58), *op. cit.;* all data for water charges are taken from California State Comptroller, *Annual Report of Financial Transactions Concerning Irrigation Districts of California for the Calendar Year 1958* (1959).

[16] This seemed necessary because incomes from domestic sales were not stated separately from incomes from sales of irrigation water, incomes from outside sales were not separately stated, and because the outside acreages supplied and the uses to which water sold outside was put were unknown. Thus, feasible calculations of average delivered prices and use of irrigation water per acre could be significantly biased for districts with appreciable outside or domestic water sales.

[17] Several of the thirty-eight districts had to be omitted because of deficiencies in available data.

district water revenues per acre-foot of all types except taxes. In this case, no significant relation was found, either between water deliveries and average tolls for the sample of districts in general, or between deliveries and the portion of revenue derived from tolls for districts collecting about the same total revenue (tolls and taxes) per acre-foot delivered. These findings are consistent with the hypothesis that demands for irrigation water tend to be determined by members of irrigation districts generally on the basis of long-run calculations oriented to maximizing the joint welfare of the total group of members. They also suggest that a regression of quantities demanded on total price is about as reliable a statistical measure of the demand-price relationship for irrigation water as we can get. Barring a statistical mirage, the users' cooperative hypothesis would seem to receive substantial support.

We mentioned above that our calculated demand elasticity for water delivered by irrigation districts is, for several reasons, not equivalent to an estimate of a pure price-elasticity of demand for irrigation water. More disturbing for our immediate purposes is that it may also suffer some biases in estimating the demand elasticity typically faced by sellers of irrigation water in Northern California. Several possible sources of bias require particular attention.

1) The dependent variable in our calculations in all cases was water deliveries per irrigated acre. This definition has the effect of excluding one of the possible types of adjustment to variations in the price of irrigation water—namely, the movement of land into and out of irrigated cultivation (see Appendix A). The resulting elasticity measure thus tends to pick up only those differences in water demand, induced by price differences, which are attributable to different intensities in the watering of given crops and to differences in the choice of crops. The general elasticity of demand for irrigation water furnished by retail suppliers thus tends to be underestimated.[18]

2) The charges levied by a public water district cover not only its wholesale cost of water (if any), but also all of its long-distance and local transportation costs and the costs of any related services furnished by the district to its member-customers. There appears to be some tendency for districts to provide, in those areas where relatively high-value crops are grown, a service of higher quality—such as installing and operating a pressurized pipe distribution system rather than one utilizing open ditches, thus reducing the labor inputs required of the irrigator. If the higher charges collected by irrigation districts partly cover such additional services to member-customers, rather than higher costs of providing water itself, then we would not expect the quantity of water purchased necessarily to be reduced by the higher price. Our data do not permit a formal test of the hypothesis that districts charging a higher total price per acre-foot delivered supply a wider range or higher quality of services, but casual observation suggests that such a

[18] Available statistical data did not permit us readily to perform these same computations using water deliveries divided by total acreage, rather than irrigated acreage. Even if they had, the problem would not have been solved, for land that cannot be irrigated profitably at the going charges levied by a public district tends sooner or later to be excluded from the district boundaries—or not to have been included at the time of its formation.

relationship exists. Other things being equal, its result is to cause our calculation to underestimate the price elasticity of demand faced by sellers of irrigation water.

3) Calculations of demand elasticity of this cross-sectional type assume that purchasers are permitted to take whatever quantities they wish at the going price. It is clear, however, that rationing is employed to a significant degree in the allocation of irrigation water, both to restrict its availability at particular times of the year and to restrict the quantity available to irrigators over the whole of the irrigation season. If the incidence of rationing (the percentage curtailment of demand for the whole season) were approximately the same for districts collecting different levels of average revenue, then the estimate of elasticity would not be biased. If rationing imposes a greater proportionate restriction where prices are lower, then an underestimate results. Again, quantitative data on rationing could not be assembled to permit its inclusion in a multivariate analysis, and we must resort to qualitative impressions. Among the districts levying low charges per acre-foot of delivered water, we find both some with excellent water rights which apparently impose no rationing and some with limited sources of supply which appear to ration severely. No net tendency can be established for the probable direction of bias due to rationing.

In summary, an examination of three possible sources of bias in our estimate of the price elasticity of demand facing sellers of irrigation water identifies two pointing to an underestimate and one that is inconclusive. The net bias is thus presumed to be an underestimate.

In the "engineering estimates" of the demand-price relationship and price elasticity of demand for irrigation water in Northern California, Trimble R. Hedges and Charles V. Moore studied farms of a particular type in one area on the east side of the San Joaquin Valley during the period 1956–60.[19] The findings are referred to here as "engineering estimates" because Hedges and Moore derive the demand for irrigation water by calculating an optimized crop mix for each hypothetical water price on the basis of cost data for "cotton-general crop" farms situated in the east-central section of the Tulare Lake Basin.[20] Typical levels of technology and patterns of local soil types are assumed, and a range of farm sizes typical of those in the area is investigated. Constraints imposed by federal agricultural programs or other output-control schemes are assumed to limit the maximum portion of a farm's land that could be planted to most crops, with alfalfa as the

[19] The findings are given in three parts of their report on *Economics of On-Farm Irrigation, Water Availability and Costs, and Related Farm Adjustments, op. cit.* Their work is summarized in *3. Some Aggregate Aspects of Farmer Demand for Irrigation Water and Production Response on the San Joaquin Valley Eastside,* Report No. 261 (1963). This summary draws for primary data on *2. Farm Size in Relation to Resource Use, Earnings and Adjustments on the San Joaquin Valley Eastside,* Report No. 263 (1963). A detailed description of a study of the demand-price relationship for a single typical farm of a given size is contained in the first volume, *op. cit.* See also Hedges and Moore, *Some Characteristics of Farm Irrigation Water Supplies in the San Joaquin Valley,* Report No. 258 (1962); and Moore, "Economics of Water Demand in Commercialized Agriculture," *Journal of the American Water Works Association,* LIV (August 1962), 913–20.

[20] Crops that might be cultivated on such farms are assumed to be cotton, black-eyed beans, sugar beets, cantaloupe, alfalfa, barley, and grain sorghum. Excluded are other crops important in the area, such as citrus, deciduous, and vine fruits.

only truly unrestricted crop. An aggregate water demand curve is derived for the area under investigation, representing the distribution of farm sizes actually found there. The arc elasticity calculated over the whole experimental range of water prices is −0.65, quite close to our own estimate derived by a very different procedure.[21] Nonetheless, the potential usefulness of the Hedges-Moore finding apparently is not as a representative irrigation-water demand schedule for the San Joaquin Valley, the Central Valley, or Northern California as a whole.[22] Rather, it is as a dramatic indicator of the potential variability of water demand schedules and price elasticities of water demand among limited areas and among types of farms in the region, and of their sensitivity to soil types, institutional restrictions, and relative crop prices.

In summary, the evidence suggests that the elasticity of demand for irrigation water is low, but perhaps not so low as a superficial view of the matter would suggest. Our own statistical estimate, which is probably on the low side, puts it at −0.64. The Hedges-Moore study—which includes a number of empirically applicable constraints on the value of the elasticity, but assumes an atypical land-quality and crop-choice situation and does not include the influence of competing ground-water supplies—indicates −0.19 in the range of prices actually observed in most of the Central Valley, but a significantly higher figure for higher prices.

The Demand for Water for Urban Uses

In Northern California, about 6 per cent of all fresh water captured and delivered for consumptive use is devoted to uses other than irrigation. These other uses fall into several general categories and are not easily described by a single brief term. "Municipal and industrial" use and "urban use" are the designations most frequently employed, though both may be somewhat misleading, because the component uses referred to (both nonindustrial and industrial) are not entirely confined to cities and towns. We have adopted the term "urban use" because of its brevity.[23] The broad components of urban use for water are principally:

1) Domestic or residential uses by individuals for the direct satisfaction of their needs or desires. These include at-home uses of water for drinking, cooking,

[21] When arc elasticities are calculated for shorter stretches of the Hedges-Moore demand curve, very different figures result. For water prices between $30 and $16.50 per acre-foot the estimate is −0.70, but for the range between $16.50 and zero (typical of that actually prevailing in the area) the estimate is only −0.19.

[22] The particular findings would appear to result from an atypical concomitance of composition of crop opportunities, breadth of difference in net returns from growing different crops, formal and informal acreage limitations on various crops, and specific dichotomy of acreage as between two soil types of distinctly different general productivity in growing the crops considered. It is worth noting, moreover, that the relatively limited area studied would appear to have been assigned for purposes of calculation about half of recent total federal cotton acreage allotments made to the entire Central Valley. The area is thus far more cotton-dominated in its determination of crop choices and water demands than is most of the irrigated farming in the valley.

[23] In addition, available data concerning the several component uses of water in question refer almost entirely to urban areas.

sanitary facilities, bathing, washing and cleaning, watering of lawns and gardens, swimming pools, some types of home air-conditioning, and so on.

2) Public uses by municipalities and other public agencies, for washing streets, watering public parks, public swimming pools, fire control, and so on.

3) Commercial uses of a variety of sorts, including two main uses: those comparable to domestic uses (drinking, sanitary facilities, washing, and cleaning) which are incidental to the operation of commercial establishments such as stores, offices, and service depots; and those in which water is a significant, if minor, input employed in producing such saleable services as those provided by laundries, restaurants, and automobile-washing establishments.

4) Industrial uses in which water is an input employed in producing other goods. Examples of these numerous and varied industrial applications are the use of water as a coolant in industrial processes, for washing operations involved in such processes, for generating steam to drive turbines, for cooking (as in canneries), as a component of the final goods produced (as in canned goods and bottled beverages), as well as for drinking and for sanitary facilities in industrial plants.[24]

A corresponding classification of urban demands for water may be established, and the determinants of each category can be investigated theoretically and statistically. A general analysis is complicated, however, because a single theoretical explanation is not applicable to all four types of urban demand. As we turn to statistical analysis of urban water demands, moreover, our efforts are hampered because available data as to quantities of urban water use in various localities in most cases do not distinguish quantities applied to the separate component uses. In practice, the measurable relationship of urban water demand to its determinants is thus typically that of an aggregate of the four component demands to these determinants. The statistical relationship derived is thus ordinarily a sort of over-all average. Moreover, it may be distorted, so far as the comparison of urban demands in different communities is involved, by the fact that the relative importance of the various component demands varies significantly among communities.

General determinants of urban demand

The most important single component of urban demands for fresh water in California is the domestic demand—not only in the state as a whole but also for the great bulk of communities, excepting only a few cities or suburbs with unusually intensive industrial or commercial development. In the large and moderately industrialized cities on the coast and in their suburbs, domestic demand for water generally accounts for from 55 to 65 per cent of all demands for fresh water from public water works; commercial demand, from 20 to 30 per cent; demand for public use in the neighborhood of from 3 to 7 per cent; and industrial use, less

[24] The line between industrial uses and the second sort of commercial uses is necessarily somewhat indistinct.

than 5 per cent.[25] In cities and towns of the interior agricultural areas of the state, on the average, domestic water demand plays a somewhat more important role, and commercial and industrial demand a somewhat smaller one.

The general manner of the determination of the demand for domestic water is distinctly different from that for irrigation water (and of commercial and industrial demand as well). A somewhat different order of theoretical explanation of its determination is therefore required. The difference stems from the fact that domestic water is essentially a consumer's good, acquired by individuals for their personal consumptive uses and for the satisfaction of their personal needs and desires. The demand for it is thus not a derived input demand, and cannot be studied in terms of water's objective dollar value in production processes.

The determinants of domestic water demand in any locality include numerous aspects of the environment of domestic users which influence their needs or desires for differing amounts of water. Various dimensions of climate may evidently exercise this sort of influence, including precipitation, temperature, humidity, the proportional incidence of sunshine hours, wind conditions, and so forth. Precipitation and temperature are perhaps the most important, and will be emphasized in the following discussion. Another environmental determinant of evident importance is the amount of land space occupied per person for residential purposes. This may be measured roughly for a group of users in an urban area by the density of population relative to land area—that is, by the number of residents per square mile of built-up urban area. The state of household technology is a further environmental determinant, especially perhaps as it is reflected in the proportion of residences equipped with automatic machines for washing clothes and dishes, with air conditioners using water as a coolant, with swimming pools, and so on.

In addition to environmental determinants of domestic water demand, there are two monetary variables which may be expected to influence this demand: (1) the incomes of users, as measured, for example, by annual income per capita in any locality (income being closely associated with ability to pay for goods in general); and (2) the price per unit of domestic water.

So far as domestic uses are concerned, precipitation and temperature are primarily influences on the quantity of water demanded for watering lawns and gardens. The precipitation pattern as interrelated with temperature over the year will influence this need and demand for water. In California, there is essentially

[25] These are modal observations based on a scattering of available data, and in some extreme instances the proportionate importance of the four components is appreciably different. This is true in a few incorporated areas in which a very large portion of the land area is occupied by industrial plant and the residential population is rather small; in dormitory suburbs with negligible industry and disproportionately small commercial development relative to the resident population; and also in the city of San Francisco proper, where commercial development is disproportionately large relative to the resident population. Some data referring to the composition of urban water use in California cities are found in the following documents: Los Angeles Department of Water and Power, *Statistical Reports, Fiscal Years 1950–59* (1959); City of San Diego, "Water Service Statistics, Fiscal Year Ending 6/30/60" (worksheet of the San Diego Utilities Department); San Francisco Water Department, *Annual Report, Commercial Division, Fiscal Year 1958–59* (1959); California State Comptroller, *Annual Report of Financial Transactions Concerning Cities of California, Fiscal Year 1959–60* (1961).

a twelve-month growing season for gardens in all coastal areas, and only a slightly shorter one in the interior valleys. The actual importance of the precipitation pattern in explaining differences in domestic water use among different areas in the state is simplified by the fact that in all populous areas there is a substantially rainless "summer" period of about five months, during which the peak requirements of lawns and gardens for water naturally occur.[26] As to temperature levels and time patterns, considerable statistical experimentation suggests that the average daily high temperature for the summer months is in California more strongly related to urban water use than any other measure of temperature. There are quite significant differences in average summer temperatures among three major areas of California, with the Central Valley being the warmest, the Southern California coastal area less warm, and the coastal area in the vicinity of the San Francisco Bay the coolest. Population density relative to land area influences domestic water demand primarily because of a negative association of density to the area of lawns and gardens per person in a locality, and possibly also to the number of home swimming pools per capita. There is probably some inverse association between population density and per capita income.

Income per capita is expected to be positively associated with domestic water demand per capita. Similarly, an inverse relation is expected between the price of water and the quantity demanded per capita. The influences of differences in climate, population density, and income, however, may be such as to negate or override the virtual influence of the price of water.

Commercial water demand is of course a derived demand, determined principally in a city or suburban area by (1) per capita income of the city or suburb and (2) the extent to which the city or suburb provides less or more commercial services than are purchased by its own population. Precipitation and population density would not appear to be significant influences on commercial water demand, but temperature may be a factor so far as it influences the rate of use of air-conditioning facilities in commercial establishments. The effect of water price on such demand has not been studied very much, but it would appear that commercial water use is unlikely to respond much to appreciable price changes. There is in general a very low degree of substitutability (if any) of water for other factor inputs used in providing commercial services. Furthermore, changes in the price of a single input (like water) are not likely to induce appreciable shifts in the pattern or volume of commercial activity; and water costs are so small a portion of the total costs of providing commercial services that changes in price would induce no appreciable change in per capita demand for commercial water.

The demand for water for public use by municipalities typically is not demand by a purchaser from a separate supplier, but a diversion of self-supplied water by the municipality to various public uses. Although internal accounts may be kept

[26] Moreover, as we approach a statistical analysis of the relationship in California of domestic water demand to its determinants, it should be noted that along the extended coastal area of California there is a significant negative correlation between two climatic determinants: precipitation and temperature. As among coastal communities in southern, central, and northern California, there is a tendency for the level of temperature to be higher (and the number of relatively warm months greater) in the areas where annual precipitation (and the number of months with appreciable rainfall) is smaller. This circumstance makes it difficult to isolate statistically the separate influences on domestic water demand of precipitation and temperature.

in which charges for water are made to street, park, recreation, school, fire, and other municipal departments, the price or cost of water as such does not seem likely to be a major factor determining over-all demand for municipal use. Principal determinants probably are the proportion of the city area devoted to public parks and recreation areas (as determined by topography, historical development, and governmental decisions), and temperature and precipitation.

Industrial demand for fresh water supplied by municipalities or other public or private water-supplying agencies does not generally constitute a very large proportion of all urban demands for water so supplied in Northern California. This is partly because California is not heavily industrialized and because much of its industrial development involves industries which are not heavy users of water.[27] In the case of industrial plants which are heavy users of water—petroleum refineries, steel works, smelters, chemical plants, pulp mills, fiberboard plants, etc. —there is a strong general tendency toward self-supply, and, in the San Francisco Bay area, toward self-supply with salt water from the San Francisco Bay and connected bays, or with brackish water from the lower reaches of the Sacramento and San Joaquin rivers.[28] Industrial self-supply of fresh water is generally from wells, and there is available no good measure of the total quantity of industrial water thus secured in the area. Similarly, adequate data on the regional volume of self-supply with salt and brackish water are not available, though inquiries concerning use of water by a sample of industrial plants in the San Francisco Bay area suggest that this volume is quite substantial.

The quantity of some sort of water demanded by an industrial plant depends on the industrial processes involved and the design of the plant. These things also determine the proportion of total water requirements which must be fulfilled with fresh water. Cooling water, which accounts for almost 60 per cent of industrial water intake in the area,[29] generally can be salt or brackish instead of fresh, though the choice of water dictates some differences in facilities. Fresh water used for cooling will generally be recirculated, and recirculating facilities will be required; salt and brackish water will generally require different treatment facilities to control the quality of the effluent to conform to water pollution regulations. Process water may or may not have to be fresh; boiler water generally must be fresh and very pure.

Though no sweeping generalization is applicable to all industries in the area which are in the category of heavy water users,[30] there is a general tendency for purchased fresh water and self-supplied salt or brackish bay or river water

[27] Industrial use of water is highly variable. Industries like jewelry, communication equipment, and apparel use less than 10 cubic feet of fresh water per employee per working day, while sugar and sawmills use more than 1,300. See California Department of Water Resources, *Water Use by Manufacturing Industries in California, 1957–59,* Bulletin No. 124 (1964), pp. 66–73.

[28] *Ibid.,* pp. 58–60. In California as a whole almost half of all the intake of industrial water is composed of brackish water, while in the Bay area brackish water accounts for over 60 per cent.

[29] *Ibid.,* p. 65.

[30] *Ibid.,* pp. 52–57. Four industries dominate the industrial demand for water in Northern California: lumber and wood products; food and kindred products; petroleum refining, chemicals, and allied products; and paper and allied products. In the state as a whole they employ 25 per cent of the workers engaged in manufacturing, but use 82 per cent of industrial water.

to be workable substitutes for the bulk of water used. There may thus be, among a variety of industries and industrial operations using large amounts of water, a corresponding variety of critical prices for purchased fresh water of a given quality (or different critical prices for different qualities) below which purchased fresh water will be used for various industrial purposes and above which self-supplied salt and brackish water will be used. This circumstance seems likely to create a quite appreciable price elasticity of demand for purchased fresh water for industrial use. However, the response of the demand to a change in the price of fresh water may take place rather slowly over time, because replacements of existing plant facilities to facilitate the use of a different type of water may be deferred until existing facilities are nearing their normal replacement dates. The price of water may thus have a significant influence on the demand for purchased fresh water (or for fresh water in general) for industrial uses. Other possible determinants of industrial demand—such as climate, local per capita income, and the various additional determinants of domestic water demand—do not appear to have significant influences on the industrial demand.

Summarizing the determinants of the urban demand for fresh water, we conclude that the four major components of total urban demand probably are not equally responsive to each of the several major determinants of this total demand. Domestic demand per capita may be expected to be significantly responsive to the largest number of determinants, including temperature, precipitation, population density, per capita income, and water price. Commercial water demand per capita, on the other hand, would not be expected to be appreciably sensitive to climatic factors, population density, or water price, though it should be related to income per capita and to the ratio of the volume of commercial activity to the resident population. Demand per capita for water for public use would appear to be influenced by random factors and also by climate, but not very much by water price. Demand per capita for industrial use would not appear to be appreciably sensitive to the determinants mentioned above other than the price of fresh water, but will clearly be influenced in any locality by numerous other considerations bearing on the determination of industrial plant locations.

Statistical evidence

The preceding relationships which hypothetically determine the quantity of water demanded by urban users are obvious candidates for investigation by multivariate statistical analysis. A number of practical pitfalls stand in the way of securing satisfactory results, however.

The task of finding a demand-price relationship is made more difficult by the fact that for most cities published sources do not state separately quantities of water demanded for the four main types of urban water use. Domestic, commercial, industrial, and public demands are usually lumped in a single aggregate. Only aggregate urban demand per connection or per capita can thus be associated to water price in comparisons of cities with different water prices which are designed to reveal the response of urban water demand to a change or difference in the price of water.[31] But the responsiveness of water demand to price change or difference is predictably different for each of the four component demands contained in the aggregate, and the most that could be ascertained from analyses using aggregate urban demand data would be an average response for the four components combined. Even this, however, cannot be unambiguously determined. As among different cities, the proportionate importance of each of the four components in the aggregate urban demand varies significantly. Therefore, a comparison of the aggregate urban demands for water per connection or per capita in a number of cities having a number of different water prices will reflect not only the response of aggregate water demands of a single given composition to water price differences. It also will show the effect on aggregate demands of differences among them in the relative importance of the several components, and of differences in the responsiveness to price differences among the several components.

Nor are these our only statistical problems. Within the usual city, different types of buyers, or different buyers of a given type, do not all pay the same price per unit of water. Different buyers pay different prices as determined by the quantity of water they purchase and by the structure of the rate schedule applicable to the city, and also perhaps by class-pricing practices which favor some categories of buyers over others. Statistical evidence does not permit one to break out the consumption of groups of users all of whom pay the same price per unit. Any price variable chosen to represent a determinant of the average quantity of water consumed by users in a city must thus serve as a proxy for a structure or distribution of rates actually paid. Since this distribution is known to vary from city to city, no simple parameter will suffice to describe it. Two devices are customarily employed. One is the use as a price measure of the charge made in each city for a specified quantity of water taken per month by a residential buyer, the quantity presumably being chosen to correspond roughly to the modal monthly quantity taken by water buyers in general. The difficulty with the use of this sort of measure of water price in an analysis of demand-price relationships through a comparison of cities is that the actual prices paid per unit in any city by different buyers will be dispersed around the reference price, and the shape of this distribution will differ among cities.

Second, we may choose as a price measure the simple average price per unit for all water sold in a city. Although this average price is unsatisfactory in that it is one which no buyer pays, it does have the advantage of reflecting in a general way both the level and structure of rates. The major difficulty is that the average price, as a determining variable, is not strictly independent of the variable it determines, namely the aggregate quantity of water purchased. This is because the response of the purchases of water buyers to the quantity discounts offered in a rate structure influences the average price obtained with that rate structure. And as rate structures differ among cities, it might be argued that in some degree larger aggregate urban demands per capita or connection are not the result of lower average water prices, but that lower average water prices are the result

[31] This is true if the comparison is to include a sufficient number of cities to support a meaningful statistical analysis.

of purchasers' taking advantage of rate structures offering more attractive quantity discounts. This is an undoubted difficulty, logically and from the standpoint of statistical analysis, but it seems unlikely that differences in rate structures among cities are sufficient to vitiate the meaning of average water price as a determinant of water demand and as a useful reference or indicator price to be used in approximating statistically some sort of average demand-price relationship.

Some of the difficulties enumerated above are also encountered in analyzing statistically the relationship of urban water demand to determinants other than water price. In addition, there are some problems, especially in the case of complex variables like temperature and precipitation, encountered in choosing the most appropriate indicators or reference measures of the values of these nonprice variables. Most of the statistical results which we can cite concerning the relationship of urban water demand to water price and to other variables are thus not entirely satisfactory, particularly because they refer to heterogeneous aggregates of demand and to averages of prices charged to different individual water purchasers in different water-use categories.

We first concern ourselves with measures of the price elasticity of urban water demand. In an early effort, Metcalf calculated a simple regression of average consumption of water per capita on average price of water (all types of uses being aggregated), for twenty-nine waterworks systems. He used average quantities and prices for the years 1920–24, and fitted a straight line to the logarithms of the quantities and prices. The price elasticity of the urban demand for water appeared as −0.65, but the significance of the statistic was doubtful.[32]

Much later, a somewhat more sophisticated statistical analysis of urban water demand in metropolitan areas in 1955 was made by Louis Fourt, using two samples of large cities and two different sets of determinants in multiple regression equations. In both cases, all types of urban water demand were aggregated and the aggregate was stated in per capita terms. For forty-four cities in 1955 (all with metered water delivery), the quantity of water delivered per capita (x_1) was related to the following determinants: price for the first 1,000 cubic feet of water delivered through a meter within a month (x_2); number of days of rainfall in June, July, and August (x_3); average number of persons served per meter (x_4); and total population served (x_5). The equation derived, employing the logarithms of all numbers, was as follows:

$$\log x_1 = 5.81 - 0.386 \log x_2 - 0.037 \log x_3 - 0.309 \log x_4 + 0.00003 \log x_5.$$

The value of the coefficient of determination (R^2) was 0.683, and the price elasticity of demand per capita appeared as approximately −0.39. The signs of the other coefficients are not contrary to theoretical expectations; but, aside from price, the only determining variable included in the analysis which appeared to have a statistically significant influence on urban water demand per capita was the number of persons served per meter, which might be taken as a rough indicator of population density.

[32] L. Metcalf, "Effect of Water Rates and Growth in Population upon Per Capita Consumption," *Journal of the American Water Works Association,* XV (January 1926), 1–22.

For a sample of thirty-four cities in 1955, Fourt related the quantity of water delivered per capita to these determinants: price for the first 1,000 cubic feet of water delivered through a meter within a month (p); per capita income (y); and percentage of dwellings with three or more units per dwelling (d). The regression calculation, employing the logarithms of all numbers, developed the following equation:

$$\log q = a - 0.387 \log p + 0.277 \log y + 0.006 \log d.$$

The value of R^2 was only 0.303. Price elasticity appears as approximately −0.39 again. The only other variable included which appears to have a significant influence on urban water demand per capita is income per capita. The general indication of the two calculations is for a price elasticity of aggregate demand for urban water per capita of roughly −0.4 in large cities.[33] The extent of the influence on this finding of the arbitrary choice of the price for the first 1,000 cubic feet of water taken per meter per month, of intercity differences in rate structures, and of the varying composition of urban water demands by types of use cannot be readily ascertained.

A recent study by Gottlieb of demands for urban water centers on small cities and towns in Kansas, in which from 80 to 90 per cent of all urban water sales are residential or commercial. Thus, total consumption of urban water is advanced as a proxy for domestic or residential consumption (though the proportion of commercial consumption to the total is not indicated).[34] The demand quantity was measured as gallons delivered per capita for all uses and the price as the average price per 1,000 gallons for all water sold (as affected by all minimum charges and bulk rates in effect). A simple linear regression of quantity demanded per capita on price (employing the logarithms of both numbers) revealed a price elasticity of demand of −1.02 for sixty-eight Kansas water systems in 1952 and of −0.69 for eighty-four Kansas systems in 1957.[35]

Gottlieb also calculated three multiple regressions of quantity demanded on average water price and income per household for Kansas, one for Illinois, and one (like Fourt's analysis of thirty-four cities) for large cities in the United States—employing the logarithms of all numbers throughout. The Kansas results for price elasticity are more or less in line with those derived from simple regressions calculated for the same state, showing price elasticities of −1.24 for 19 systems in 1952, −0.68 for 24 systems in 1957, and −0.66 for 24 systems in 1957.[36] For twelve systems in Illinois in 1947–49, however, the same sort of multiple regression yielded a price elasticity of +0.27.

[33] Louis Fourt, "Forecasting the Urban Residential Demand for Water" (Unpublished seminar paper, University of Chicago, 1958).

[34] Manuel Gottlieb, "Some Characteristics of the Urban Demand for Domestic Water" (Unpublished paper, University of Wisconsin, 1961); another version of this paper appeared as "Urban Domestic Demand for Water: A Kansas Case Study," *Land Economics*, XXXIX (May 1963), 204–10.

[35] The range of water charges covered was from \$2 to \$8 per 10,000 gallons per month. The values of R^2 were 0.71 and 0.78 respectively.

[36] In the first two calculations, demand was measured as quantity per connection, and in the third as quantity per capita. The values of R^2 in the three calculations were 0.69, 0.72, and 0.69.

The combined results of these various tests might create the impression that in small midwestern towns and cities the price elasticity of demand per capita for urban water is probably in the neighborhood of −0.7. This compares with Fourt's findings of a corresponding price elasticity of about −0.4 in large cities, which is corroborated almost exactly by Gottlieb's finding of an elasticity of −0.39 for eighteen large cities in 1955. The difference between large and small cities with respect to price elasticity of water demand is generally attributed by Gottlieb to differences in population density and in the area of lawns and gardens per capita, the underlying notion apparently being that the part of domestic water used for watering lawns and gardens is more sensitive to water price than are other components of urban water demand.[37] (The relationship of urban water demand to determinants other than price, alluded to above in passing, will be discussed later.)

All of the studies noted above have referred to the United States as a whole or to regions other than California. We sought to analyze the price elasticity of demand for urban water in California, working primarily with a sample of forty-one cities that are supplied by municipal waterworks or other public water agencies. The sample was obtained by eliminating from a list of ninety-one cities, for which data pertaining to water rates had been assembled in a study in 1955, all cities for which adequate data covering both prices and quantities were unavailable or which charged flat rates per month for water to residential users.[38] The 41 cities include 21 in Southern California (all but one in the South Coastal Basin); 5 in the central coastal area (extending from just north of the Los Angeles Basin to just south of the San Francisco Bay area); 12 in the San Francisco Bay area (including contiguous coastal valleys); and 3 in the Central Valley. Large and small cities, cities with and without considerable industrialization, industrial suburbs, dormitory suburbs, and resort towns are all included. Among cities within the sample, there are substantial variations in temperature (as measured in various dimensions), precipitation, and population density, but in general rather small variations in per capita income. Within the sample also, rates per 1,000 cubic feet of water per month (for the first 1,000 cubic feet) varied from $1.30 to $3.60 in 1955 and from $1.30 to $5.20 in 1960; in the fiscal year 1955–56, annual water use per capita ranged from about 14,000 gallons to about 154,000 gallons (1,880 to 20,530 cubic feet).[39] Average urban water rates per 1,000 cubic feet per month were between 40 and 45 per cent higher in the San Francisco Bay area than in Southern California and in the Central Valley, and rates in the

[37] One other scrap of information may be mentioned. In an unpublished study of thirty-six water service systems, Edward F. Renshaw developed estimates (from simple arithmetic linear regressions) of the price elasticities of demand for urban water in different uses, which interestingly enough placed the elasticities at the mean price at −0.45 for residential use, −0.80 for industrial use, and −1.04 for commercial use. See "The Demand for Municipal Water" (Unpublished paper, University of Chicago, 1958).

[38] The basic source of the sample was "Water Rates in California Cities," Parts I and II, *Western City Magazine,* XXXI (October and November 1955).

[39] These price data are drawn from City of Redding, *A Survey of Water Rates and Related Data for 86 Municipal Systems in California as of January 1, 1960* (1960); data on water quantities sold by cities are contained in California State Comptroller, *Annual Report of Financial Transactions Concerning Cities of California, Fiscal Year 1955–56* (1957). Data on climate are from U.S. Department of Commerce, Weather Bureau, *Climatological Data,* Vols. LIX and LX (1955 and 1956). Data on income per capita were taken from U.S. Department of Commerce, Bureau of the Census, *County and City Data Book* (1961).

central coastal area on the average about half way between Southern California and San Francisco Bay rates.

Unfortunately, it proved possible to extract very few conclusions from this sample. First of all, the set of cities contained in the sample proved unsatisfactory. The Central Valley was underrepresented, because many of its cities are served by private water companies or joint urban-agricultural agencies, or else charge flat monthly rates for water to residential users. In the San Francisco Bay area, the enormous East Bay Municipal Utility District had to be dropped because some data could not be secured for either individual cities served or the district as a whole. Southern California cities thus had to be included to secure a sample of reasonable size.

The inclusion of these cities, however, created a statistical problem which precluded a satisfactory multivariate analysis of the determinants of urban water demand in California. As a minor problem, the variation of income per capita within the sample was too small to reveal a significant income elasticity. As a major problem, the observations in the sample contain a very high fortuitous negative correlation between two independent variables—the price of water and average temperature. The reason for this is that pricing policies of water agencies in the warmer Southern California area result in systematically lower water charges than in cooler Northern California. The simple correlation between temperature and price was higher than the simple correlation of either variable with the dependent variable—the average quantity of water consumed. As a result, the influence of temperature and price could not be separated, and any simple relation estimated between quantity and either independent variable inevitably contains the influence of both. A simple price elasticity estimated from these data would thus tend to be overestimated. Thus, one simple regression of the logarithms of quantity per capita on the logarithms of average price gave a statistically significant elasticity of −1.099, a value that looks high in relation to those estimated in the other studies cited above.

Let us turn next to the relationship of urban water demand to income. The principal body of systematic findings on this relationship has been assembled by Gottlieb[40] in connection with his presentation of measures of the price elasticity of urban water demand. He presents measures of the income elasticity of urban water demand derived for five samples of cities, for each of which a multiple regression of quantity demanded on average price and income per household was calculated, using logarithms throughout. Two national samples of Standard Metropolitan Areas in 1955 gave income elasticity estimates of 0.34 and 0.28 respectively. Three samples of Kansas water systems in 1952 and 1955 provided estimates of 0.28, 0.45, and 0.58; and a single Illinois sample for 1947–49 indicated an income elasticity of 0.89.[41] Giving more weight to the national samples, this study would tend to support an estimate of income elasticity of about 0.3. Our own analysis produced no significant relation between income and the quantity of water demanded, no doubt due to the small variation of income per capita among California cities. But we note that two very rich communities, among twenty-eight communities, for which data were available proved to be the heaviest users of

[40] Gottlieb, "Urban Domestic Demand for Water," *op. cit.*
[41] *Ibid.*, p. 210. No evidence on statistical significance is provided.

water per capita. A study of cities in the San Francisco Bay area by Headley, which also gives somewhat unsatisfactory results, can be broadly interpreted as confirming Gottlieb's findings of a low but significant income elasticity.[42]

We also analyzed the relationship of temperature to urban water demand per capita in California. Average daily high temperature for the summer months was the dimension of temperature most highly associated with urban water use. Our statistical analysis of demand-temperature relationships for urban water involved a comparison of thirty cities (of our basic sample of forty-one for which temperature data were available). The measure of temperature chosen for regression analyses was the average daily high temperature for the months of July, August, and September in 1955. In this period, the average daily high in the thirty cities ranged from 66.0°F. to 102.2°F. The measure of quantity was water used per capita (in thousands of gallons) in the fiscal year 1955–56. A simple arithmetic regression of quantity on temperature was calculated, yielding a coefficient of +2.48. This may be interpreted as indicating that, among the cities sampled, annual water use per capita increased by 2,480 gallons with each increase of one degree in average summer temperature. It proved not significantly different from zero at the confidence level of 5 per cent. Furthermore, because of the high inverse correlation between price and temperature in the sample, and probably a high inverse correlation between temperature and precipitation as well, the implied elastic response of water consumption to a temperature increase is probably an overstatement due to inclusion of a simultaneous response to a lower price, and lower precipitation.

In sum, the disappointing character of our own and others' investigations of the determinants of urban water demand in California forces us to rely largely on studies dealing with other parts of the country. These support low, but significant, elasticities of demand for water with respect to both price and income. It also seems likely that the price elasticity of nonindustrial demand is significantly increased by a reduction in the density of residential population, holding other influences constant, because of the quantitative importance of the watering of lawns and gardens.[43] This conclusion will take on importance for performance when we consider the pricing systems used by urban agencies which supply water in Chapter 10.

[42] J. Charles Headley, "The Relation of Family Income and Use of Water for Residential and Commercial Purposes in the San Francisco-Oakland Metropolitan Area," *Land Economics*, XXXIX (November 1963), 441–49. Headley studied fourteen cities in the Bay area. Ten purchase water from a single utility district, and all fourteen charge very similar rates. Temperature and precipitation are also similar, but population density varies significantly. Headley estimated income elasticities both from time series data for 1950–59 and from cross-section data for 1950 and 1959. The cross-section elasticities, 1.49 and 1.124, appear to be substantially over-estimated due to a strong inverse correlation between income and population density. The time series results range more sensibly between 0.165 and 0.404, with a median estimate of 0.256 and a population-weighted mean of 0.1886. None of the individual time series elasticities is significant at the level of 5 per cent.

[43] Most of the urban-suburban population of Southern California lives under conditions of substantially lower density relative to occupied land than that of other metropolitan areas. This presumptive evidence of high demand elasticity is relevant to evaluating demands for, and benefits from, large new water-import projects to serve that area.

6 

THE COSTS OF SUPPLYING WATER: LEVEL, COMPOSITION, AND RELATION TO SCALE OF FACILITIES

In a conventional industry, the level and structure of costs may exert many influences upon the setting and kind of competition. A cost structure involving substantial economies of scale can assure high barriers to entry into an industry, and thus preclude the possibility of atomistic competition. A cost structure heavily weighted with short-run fixed costs can render firms' profits highly sensitive to variations of market price, and thus promote market conduct aimed at the avoidance of competitive price reductions. Costs can flavor the environment of an industry in many other significant ways, such as the creation of situations of effective local monopoly by the presence of relatively high transportation charges. Finally, costs possess a great normative significance as a potential measure of the value of product foregone by the allocation of resources to any given use; and studies of conventional industries regularly concern themselves with the accuracy with which reported costs perform this measuring function and the judgments they support about the correctness of resource allocation within the economic sector in question.

Costs as a Structural Element in the Water Industry

As with the aspects of concentration discussed in Chapter 4, there can be little doubt that costs are a significant structural feature of the water industry; similarly, the reasons for this significance are rather different from those affecting the conventional industry. Their significance as a direct determinant of patterns of rivalry in the industry is apparently limited to a few special features. Aspects of costs discussed in this chapter, however, fulfill two other important functions in the general design of our study. First, they supply an important part of the explanation for the near absence of private enterprise from Northern California's water industry (absence, except for a few urban retailers and for self-supplying users of irrigation water). Second, problems of evaluating reported costs as measures of foregone opportunities in other lines of production, as a preliminary step in drawing conclusions about the water industry's performance, are much more severe than those arising in the conventional industry. Therefore, we must seek at least some preliminary indications of the gaps between accounting and economic costs in the industry.

Succeeding sections will document two significant features of the water industry's cost structure: moderate to substantial economies of scale in the construction of storage reservoirs and water transport facilities that persist up to very large scales; and fixed costs comprising a very high proportion of total costs in all activities except the extraction of ground water. These features, occurring in tandem, would tend to discourage workable competition among private enterprise units in any industry. They would assure relatively high concentration of sellers or buyers, plus a cost-structure incentive for the sellers or buyers to avoid price competition. Without tracing the theoretical arguments involved or citing case studies, we note that a situation of this kind can lead to such performance deficiencies as price rigidity, excess capacity, and various sorts of bargaining stalemates in markets characterized by fewness of both buyers and sellers. While it is not a matter of central concern, some of the material developed later in Part Two will suggest that these problems actually arose in earlier decades when private enterprise played a much more substantial role in the Northern California water industry.

With regard to the present industry in which public enterprises behave in general as users' cooperatives, the presence of scale economies and high fixed costs generate some important hypotheses. We would expect substantial incentives to exist for the formation of coalitions among agencies to carry out functions involving major scale economies; failing the formation of these, significant performance deficiencies are suggested. The presence of high fixed costs can induce defensive actions in a public district just as readily as in a private enterprise; we are led to watch for the erection of rigid allocative arrangements, unresponsive to changing resource productivities, as a defense against reductions in revenue that threaten the ability to meet fixed charges. When the fixed costs are not only high in the short run, but also relate to capital goods of great durability so that the "short run" is in fact long, then the possibility arises that induced misallocations relating to high fixed costs can persist over a long period. The outcomes of bilateral bargaining situations may become heavily colored with a quest for assurances relating to the usefulness and productivity of facilities in the distant future, at the cost of concern for issues of possibly greater (discounted) present allocative significance.

The combination of scale economies with high fixed costs suggests the problem named "absolute-cost barriers to entry" in the conventional industry: total capital costs for important new facilities that are very large in relation to the funds a given agency or class of agencies can attract in the financial market place. In Part Two, we watch for evidence of capital rationing; and when we find it in ample measure, we consider the resulting effects on the efficiency of investments in major types of facilities in Part Three.

Certain other features of the structure of costs to be explored carry implications of their own for the industry's conduct and performance. We have already remarked upon the prevailing economic insularity of the typical entity in the water market. One possible explanation for this condition—a vital one—is the relative significance of transportation costs as a portion of the total costs of delivering water for various consumptive uses. Evidence presented below will show the general relation of the costs of long-distance water transport to prevailing levels of total retail water cost. Another feature developed below is the comparative level and structure of the costs of drawing water from ground and surface sources. In Chapter 2 we suggested the extent to which the rivalry for surface supplies operates in the context of ground-water availability and the use made of it, especially by private pumpers. Here, we consider the comparative levels and structures of costs for these two sources of supply in order to define their relation more exactly.

Throughout this chapter, we shall be pointing to gaps between the recorded costs of various entities in the water industry and the true economic cost of the water they supply or the services they perform. While the assessment of these divergences and their meaning for the industry's performance are taken up in Part Three, a preliminary view of the nature of the difficulty comprises essential background for Part Two. In a market economy, we can usually take the market value of resources used to supply a particular good as an approximate measure of their value-producing power in alternative uses. The measure often includes nothing more complex than the money payments made to purchase resources employed in supplying the good, plus the imputed market value of any resources similarly employed which, though not purchased, are provided by the supplier. The main deficiency of such a measure lies in its omission of added costs to, or losses incurred by, the general populace or by specific individuals or groups (including other producers) because of external effects of the process of supplying the specified good. Such external effects may include polluting the atmosphere with smoke and gases from industrial processes; despoiling natural flood control devices by the indiscriminate cutting of trees or other clearing of natural vegetation on watersheds; polluting streams, lakes, and bays through the discharge of sewage and industrial contaminants into natural waters; and so forth. They may also include external diseconomies to other producers, imposed by increasing their costs of production or reducing the net value of some productive input to them.[1] A common characteristic of items in this category of costs is that they are social losses or disbenefits. And the suppliers who cause them generally are not required to make payment or compensation, even though laws may require the suppliers to take certain measures and incur certain direct costs aimed at reducing such losses.

The market value of resources employed in supplying water provides a first-approximation measure of the full cost of supply. As in the general case, this measure fails to include uncompensated external losses and diseconomies incurred as effects of supplying water. The latter category of costs, in fact, is of appreciable importance in the case of water supply. As we turn to the task of measuring water costs, or of evaluating various dollar amounts reported as costs by water suppliers, however, one additional fundamental issue and a number of complications are encountered.

The basic issue is the following: Aside from uncompensated external losses and diseconomies, should the costs of supplying water be measured to include, in addition to the costs of storing, transporting, and delivering it, a value or price for water as such, in any case in which a positive value can be imputed to it? This question is of more than hypothetical interest, since it would appear that in many regions, including important parts of Northern California, water is a scarce resource. It is in demand for competing uses and by competing users; in many locali-

[1] In addition, of course, there may be external positive benefits to society or external economies resulting from producing a given output of a good, and these are properly regarded as deductions from its net costs.

ties, water from relatively proximate sources could command a total price greater than all the costs of making it available for use; and a great many water rights could command substantial prices. Despite these facts, it is general practice among public water agencies, privately owned public utilities, and mutual water companies to sell water to their constituencies at prices which do not include a value for the water. Furthermore, there are numerous legal and institutional barriers to selling water or water rights in an open market; and pressures to develop open markets in water or water rights in areas of scarcity are ameliorated by the importation of water from distant sources for sale at prices below the cost of capture and importation.

In the accepted vocabulary of economic analysis, the answer to the question of whether a price for water itself should be included in its cost is affirmative. The economic cost of supplying a quantity of water for a given use in any locality properly includes (aside from uncompensated external losses and diseconomies) any payment which the water thereby made unavailable for alternative uses could command if sold in an "open market"—this market being one in which all potential beneficial users of the water were bidders expressing demands based on the net value of marginal units of water supplied to them. In arriving at the economic cost of water delivered by a particular supplier of stream water for consumptive use, we should add to his costs for storage, capture, and transmission a figure representing the net streamside "open market" value (actual, if there is such a market, implicit, if there is not) of the water captured. To the costs incurred by a supplier of well water, we should add the excess of the open-market wellhead value of pumped water over his allocable costs of establishing and operating his wells. By calculating water costs in this manner, we would conform—except so far as uncompensated external losses and diseconomies are omitted from costs—to the principle of measuring costs in terms of all foregone benefits.[2] Determining the rate of use of water by placing costs so measured against values in use to the customers of particular suppliers would tend to result in an economically more appropriate allocation of water among uses and users than if the net value of water (and the costs of supplying it not incurred by the immediate suppliers) were not recognized as costs.

If we have added to the private costs of supplying water for consumptive use or power generation the net open-market value of water made unavailable for other use, at streamside or wellhead, we have thereby included a substantial portion of what are often loosely denoted as the external effects of the diversion of water for consumptive use. Certain true externalities, however, would still be omitted from the calculated costs of water supply. They would arise when the activity of any

[2] In the case of suppliers of water for nonconsumptive on-stream use, a net value of water is properly included in the economic cost of supply only to the extent that, because of on-stream use, the supply of water having a net value in other uses is reduced. (If the value of such a supply is reduced without reducing its quantity, the reduction should be added to cost as an external loss or diseconomy.) Such losses in quantity or value are properly included in the economic cost of supplying water for on-stream use (for example, electric power generation), but are not necessarily matched by revenues which the on-stream supplier-users could obtain if they did not reduce either the supply of water for other uses or its value; and would forego, if they do. To the extent that they are not so matched, they do not represent private economic costs to the suppliers.

water user or supplier results in an increase in the cost of securing a given quantity of water or a reduction in the value of a given quantity of water to other users or suppliers drawing on the same source and also expressing demands for water. External effects may also take the form of losses inflicted on (or benefits provided to) users who cannot be construed as expressing an actual or hypothetical demand for water in the market place.

In practice, however strong may be the case for calculating the costs of specific water supplies to include the net open-market value of water as such, the supply costs which are not borne by the immediate supplier, and the external losses and diseconomies inflicted in securing the supplies, these inclusions are seldom made. The costs which are reported by suppliers represent, or reflect predominantly, their own direct non-water costs of bringing the water to use—costs of storage dams, diversion dams, wells, canals and ditches, pumps, power for pumps, connected equipment and paraphernalia, pipes and tunnels at hydroelectric installations, purification facilities and distribution facilities for urban water supplies, plus the labor, capital, and materials costs involved in operating, maintaining, and administering all facilities. Even these reported costs are generally deficient in handling capital charges. Where retail or intermediary suppliers purchase water from wholesalers, and count the purchase prices as costs, the non-water costs of supply of the wholesalers are in general roughly reflected in the purchase prices, and thus in the supply costs of their customers. There is considerable evidence, however, that the principal wholesaler in the region, the Bureau of Reclamation, usually does not charge its customers enough to cover fully its own non-water costs of supply.

The Cost of Retail Supplies of Irrigation Water

Some features of the level and composition of the costs of supplying irrigation water are analyzed in this section. It is convenient to consider one by one the costs of the various physically separable phases of this supply activity, both because the cost characteristics differ from one phase to another and also because they are sometimes, if not always, carried out by separate legal entities. We take up, first, such functions typically performed by irrigation districts as diversion, local transportation, and distribution of water captured from either ground or surface sources. Then we turn to the specific costs of ground-water extraction, of water-wholesaling operations, and finally of reservoir storage.

Water costs of irrigation districts

The wide variety in the types of public districts retailing irrigation water in Northern California was reported in Chapters 3 and 4. The physical traits of these different retailers' operations may vary greatly, depending on the nature of the water distribution system, the pattern of the terrain, transport distances involved, and many other features. But, although these differences lead to great variations in costs, the several major legal forms of districts often possess about the same sorts of physical plant. Thus we can assume that irrigation districts, on which considerable information is available, produce a reasonable sample of the cost characteristics of several classes of irrigation retailers, including California water districts, mutual irrigation companies, and certain water storage and municipal utility districts.

Irrigation districts in California must systematically report their annual expenses for current operations, their capital outlays, and other financial information to the State Comptroller; and must report operating information—including the annual quantities of water diverted and delivered and the source of diversions and destinations of deliveries—to the California Department of Water Resources. The data surveyed here refer to the calendar year 1960, and are drawn from the published annual reports of these agencies.[3] The costs which the agencies report are the "private contractual costs" of the irrigation districts. As a result, they exclude any amounts reflecting the net value of water itself, the value of services received without payment from the reservoir operations of other agencies, and the value of external disbenefits or losses inflicted without compensation on others. In addition, private capital costs are reported only as incurred, and are not prorated among the years of service of capital equipment acquired, so that no calculated depreciation figures appear (this omission evidently results in part from the general use of fund accounting by irrigation districts). Estimates of annual depreciation costs on capital equipment must thus be calculated through a time-consuming process; and we have done this for a sample of the agencies covered in the published reports. Similarly, annual interest costs on investment are not reported; although annual interest payments on outstanding bonds and time warrants are reported, these in general are not acceptable approximations to the annual economic interest costs on total investments. Reported interest payments have thus been disregarded in our calculations of annual costs. For the sample of districts for which estimated depreciation costs have been calculated, however, imputed economic interest costs can be estimated from data used in arriving at depreciation estimates.

We survey first the reported current expenses of operation in 1960 (excluding depreciation and interest) for fifty-nine irrigation districts in Northern California, stated as expenses per unit of water delivered. These fifty-nine include all except eight districts in the region operating and reporting sufficient data for 1960, with six of the excluded districts supplying all or a substantial proportion of their diverted water to urban users, and two directly engaged in the production and sale of electric power.[4] The current expenses described here include all general-fund expenditures for current operations as listed under the headings: "Administrative

[3] California State Comptroller, *Annual Report of Financial Transactions Concerning Irrigation Districts of California for the Calendar Year 1960* (1962); and California Department of Water Resources, *Report on Irrigation and Water Storage Districts in California, 1960*, Bulletin No. 21–60 (1961). (This and other footnote references are cited in brief form when they are also included in the Bibliography.)

[4] The first six were omitted because irrigation water was not being supplied or because the separable cost of irrigation water, as distinct from urban water, could not be determined, in a context where the cost of urban water was appreciably higher than that of irrigation water; the latter two were omitted because costs of power supply could not be distinguished from costs of water supply.

and General" (salaries and wages and other), and "Maintenance and Operation" (salaries and wages, materials and supplies, water purchases, electrical energy for pumping, and other). As such, they represent a fair approximation to the total annual private costs of water minus allocable costs of depreciation of capital goods and of interest on investment.

Table 15 shows the median level and range of these costs. It reveals that differences among districts in unit costs per acre-foot delivered are rather clearly associated with differences among the areas in which districts are located and with differences in the type of source of water on which they draw. Current expenses per unit are on the average substantially lower for districts depending primarily on surface diversions of water than for districts depending mainly on purchased water or on pumping from wells (the costs of water from the latter two sources are not greatly different); and among districts depending primarily on their own surface diversions, such expenses are on the average substantially lower for districts drawing on streams in the Sacramento Valley than for those drawing on streams in the San Joaquin Valley.

Depreciation costs for irrigation districts cannot be directly obtained from published records of agencies of the state of California, as noted, and the great majority

TABLE 15
CURRENT EXPENSES OF WATER DELIVERY FOR FIFTY-NINE IRRIGATION DISTRICTS, BY LOCATION AND SOURCE OF WATER SUPPLY, NORTHERN CALIFORNIA, 1960

Item	Current expenses (dollars per acre-foot delivered)		
	Median	Quartile	Range
12 Sacramento Valley irrigation districts with over 75% of water from surface diversions	$1.09	$0.91–$ 1.43	$0.35–$ 5.35
7 Irrigation districts outside of Central Valley with over 75% of water from surface diversions	3.29	0.39– 3.79	0.27– 4.13
15 San Joaquin Valley irrigation districts with over 75% of water from surface diversions	4.40	2.26– 6.33	0.76– 30.85
3 San Joaquin Valley irrigation districts with mixed sources of supply[a]	5.07	—	3.80– 5.73
17 Irrigation districts with over 75% of water obtained by purchases[b]	7.90	5.57– 10.74	4.89– 31.27
5 Irrigation districts with over 75% of water from wells	7.43	3.02– 13.99	2.31– 15.83

[a] These districts did not obtain as much as 75 per cent of their water from any single source, but depended on two or three of the types of source: surface diversions, pumping from wells, and purchases.

[b] Fifteen of these districts are in the San Joaquin Valley.

SOURCE: California State Comptroller, *Annual Report of Financial Transactions Concerning Irrigation Districts of California for the Calendar Year 1960* (1962); California Department of Water Resources, *Report on Irrigation and Water Storage Districts in California, 1960*, Bulletin No. 21–60 (1962).

of irrigation districts do not calculate depreciation on the bulk of their capital assets. They either calculate no depreciation at all, or they calculate it only for types of short-lived equipment which ordinarily account for about 15 per cent of total capital investment. Irrigation districts do, however, report the value of their capital investment to the California Districts Securities Commission. Using this information, supplemented by inquiries to individual districts, we constructed for each of a random sample of eighteen districts a measure of annual depreciation, depreciated value of capital equipment at the beginning of the year, and annual rate of return on investment for the years 1952 through 1960.[5] An imputed interest cost for each district in 1960 (the same year as that for the current-expense figures shown in Table 15) was calculated at a very conservative 4 per cent of the depreciated value of its capital assets as of the beginning of 1960.

Table 16 shows for seventeen members of our district sample[6] a set of constructed figures for total costs per acre-foot of water delivered, including reported current-expense figures from Table 15 and our own calculated values for depreciation and interest costs. As can be seen by comparing the column headings of Table 16 with the line headings of Table 15, our random sample of districts proved reasonably representative of the geographical and functional categories shown for the larger population.[7] Table 16 also contains (in lines 5-7) some measures of the composition of costs—that is, estimates of the portion that can be construed as fixed.

[5] The depreciation data were derived as follows. The reported value of capital assets for each district as of the end of 1951 was converted to an original-cost basis by adding to it any depreciation which had been previously deducted in arriving at the figure. Where no depreciation had been deducted, as was true in the majority of cases, the 1951 reported value was taken to represent original cost. Since in all cases the great bulk of assets had been acquired prior to the war and postwar inflationary period, a rough general price-level adjustment was applied to all 1951 original-cost values of capital assets by multiplying them by two. (The lack both of accurate information on the original date of construction and of appropriate price indices precluded a more refined procedure.)

In succeeding years, the value of capital assets for each district at the beginning of each year was increased by the amount of current capital outlays of the preceding year, these new outlays being subjected to no price level adjustment. Annual depreciation was then calculated for each district at the rate of 2 per cent per annum on undepreciated total capital investment equaling twice the original cost of assets reported on hand at the end of 1951 plus the actual capital outlays accumulated since 1951. (The over-all average rate of 2 per cent per annum for depreciation was chosen in the light of the extreme longevity of the basic facilities, which accounted on the average for about 85 per cent of total investment, and of the relatively short useful lives of the remainder of capital equipment.)

The depreciated value of capital assets for each district at the end of 1951 was taken as twice the original cost of the assets minus depreciation at 2 per cent per annum from the assumed average date of acquisition of the assets to the end of 1951. For each district, the average date of acquisition of assets on hand in 1951 was assumed to be midway in time between the date of formation of the district (or of a predecessor agency it had acquired) and 1951. For each of the years following 1951, the depreciated value of capital assets at year's end was arrived at by adding subsequent capital outlays and deducting depreciation at 2 per cent per annum on the undepreciated value of pre-1952 "old" investment in capital assets (price-level-inflated) and of post-1951 "new" investment in capital assets (not adjusted for price-level change).

[6] One of the eighteen districts in our sample had to be omitted because of failure to report its volume of water deliveries in 1960.

[7] By coincidence, only one of the seventeen districts sampled reported owning any reservoir capacity, so that in appraising capital costs of irrigation districts we are dealing in effect with the physical functions of transportation and distribution of irrigation water, but not storage.

TABLE 16
LEVEL AND COMPOSITION OF COST OF IRRIGATION WATER PER ACRE-FOOT DELIVERED, SAMPLE OF SEVENTEEN IRRIGATION DISTRICTS, NORTHERN CALIFORNIA, 1960

Category of costs		Districts securing more than 75% of supply from surface diversion		Three districts securing more than 66% of supply from wells (3)	Four districts securing more than 75% of supply by purchase (4)
		Four Sacramento Valley districts (1)	Six San Joaquin Valley districts (2)		
1. Current expenses:	Median	$0.95	$3.59	$5.50	$9.25
	Range	0.90–1.05	0.76–6.36	2.31– 8.46	5.70–16.00
2. Depreciation:	Median	0.32	1.00	1.04	6.36[a]
	Range	0.17–0.52	0.28–1.75	0.58– 1.37	6.17– 6.54
3. Imputed interest:	Median	0.30	0.75	0.98	11.08[a]
	Range	0.09–0.51	0.14–1.39	0.76– 1.17	10.43–11.73
4. Total unit costs:	Median	$1.57	$5.32	$7.52	$24.87[a]
	Range	1.16–1.93	1.26–8.82	3.65–10.65	22.67–27.07
5. Depreciation and interest as % of total unit cost:	Median	40%	33%	27%	70%[a]
	Range	22–53	19–53	21–37	66–75
6. Other fixed costs as % of total unit costs		27	30	27	5(23)[b]
7. All fixed costs as % of total unit costs		67	63	54	75(93)[b]

[a] Capital costs shown only for those two of the four districts which had contracted with the U.S. Bureau of Reclamation for the construction of a distribution system. Figures in the "median" rows are means.

[b] Alternative estimate reflecting contractual obligation to purchase water at wholesale; see text.

SOURCE: Calculated from California State Comptroller, *Annual Report of Financial Transactions Concerning Irrigation Districts in California for the Calendar Year 1951* through *1960* (1952–61); data taken from files of California Districts Securities Commission and secured directly from irrigation districts.

Besides the calculations of depreciation and interest costs described above, the preparation of Table 16 also entailed some tactical decisions in the construction of line (6) and of the final column, relating to districts which purchase water wholesale. An economic concept of "fixed costs" to the individual enterprise requires us to look beyond accounting categories. Depreciation and interest reflect contractual costs that cannot be avoided by the enterprise in the short run (except in those cases when its capital assets can quickly be disposed of on a perfect market through sale or rental); the distribution of water obviously does not fall under this exception. Other costs may also be fixed, however, even the expenses of inputs used by the enterprise in physically variable quantities per period of time, if contractual or technical limits restrain the extent to which the quantities taken can be varied. It is clear from a general knowledge of irrigation district operations that administrative and general expenses are largely fixed over a short-run period of a year, and that maintenance and operation expenses contain some fixed elements. If we assume on the basis of judgment that all of the former, and one-third of the latter, category are fixed, then the percentages of total unit costs indicated in line 6 of Table 16 can also be designated as fixed. Even these additional fixed costs fail to cover all the fixed elements of costs for the districts securing more than 75 per cent of their supplies by purchase. Their contracts for purchase of water with the U.S. Bureau of Reclamation specify minimum quantities to be purchased annually at a stated price, and so their reported wholesale water payments cannot be counted as variable costs except by invoking the possibility of ready resale of the water to other districts. Furthermore, these payments compensate the wholesaler for costs of reservoirs and bulk-transport canals that are largely fixed. Because of this doubtful element, two mean estimates appear in lines 6 and 7 of column 4. The first includes only those elements of current expenses assumed as fixed for the other categories of irrigation districts, and thus parallels the other entries in lines 6 and 7. The percentages in parentheses give a maximum estimate of the fixed component of current expenses by assuming that all wholesale water costs are contractually fixed.

Another problem also arose in connection with column 4 in that two of the four districts sampled had recently contracted for the construction of local water distribution systems by the U.S. Bureau of Reclamation, and reported as capital costs only those contract payments made to date. Our estimates for depreciation and interest in column 4 are based on the reported total contractual obligations incurred by these two districts for the construction of distribution systems. They exclude entirely the data reported by two other districts in the sample which were securing their supplies primarily from a wholesaler in 1960.[8]

Finally, column 4 must be qualified because the costs included do not cover a range of physical activities involved in the capture and distribution of water precisely comparable with those of other districts. The others enjoy the benefit of no reservoir regulation of their water supplies and perform any long-distance transport themselves. The districts purchasing at wholesale pay a charge for both of these services, performed for them by the Bureau of Reclamation. On the one hand, one could argue that payments to the Bureau should be subtracted out, to permit a comparison of the local distribution costs of the various retailers. On the other hand, the physical location of retail purchasers is such that they clearly could not secure water unless long-distance transportation were provided by someone. This interpretive problem can be cleared up somewhat when we consider below the costs of wholesale transportation recorded by the Bureau.

A number of features stand out in Table 16. San Joaquin Valley districts diverting from surface sources continue to show substantially higher costs than Sacramento Valley districts performing the same function, but the margin of excess in depreciation and interest costs is not quite so great as the margin in current expenses noted above. Districts securing their supplies from ground-water basins

[8] The elements of fixed costs reported by these two districts, whose distribution systems are not of recent construction, are much lower than those of the districts with systems recently built by the Bureau of Reclamation, despite our adjustment for changes in the price level. In one case, the numbers are too low to be believable, and so the exclusion has been made on the grounds of a presumptive reporting error.

exhibit higher costs than those depending on surface diversion, but the ones purchasing surface supplies from a wholesaler are much higher. The portion of costs that are fixed must be called high in all cases, but it is significantly lower for districts depending on ground water than those depending on surface supplies, and highest of all for districts purchasing surface supplies from a wholesaler. The figures showing the range of reported and calculated costs in each column reflect great variations even among districts performing relatively similar functions. Furthermore, when we compare individual districts within the small sample included in each column, the correlation between the level of current expenses and the level of depreciation and interest costs is clearly low.[9] In short, substantial fixity and great variability among districts are the main traits of irrigation district costs.

Certain obvious considerations from economic theory suggest that, in view of the great variation in costs that apparently exists among irrigation retailers, a good deal of economic insularity must exist among them. This phenomenon—a lack of continuous markets—has been mentioned before, and will be developed further in Part Two. Although we cannot explain all of this interdistrict variation, some of the causes may be mentioned. One cause—of particularly great normative significance—is the difference in the extent to which districts' recorded costs reflect all of the economic costs of their inputs. Water captured without financial charge may nonetheless bear opportunity costs, or its capture may inflict external diseconomies. Surface diverters who freeload upon the regulation provided by upstream storage dams owned by other agencies clearly receive a service at less than its economic cost. The same can be said of purchases from wholesalers in those cases where wholesale charges do not cover all allocable costs.

Other cost variations among districts may stem from differences in their physical situations, and thus in the array of inputs necessary to supply water to their member-customers. For those districts which pump from ground-water basins, the depth of the wells directly influences the level of pumping costs.[10] So does the extent to which water must be lifted from the point of diversion (streamside, wellhead, or wholesaler's canal) to points of delivery to the district's customers. An important source of variation among districts lies in the length of haul of water, since its canals are the principal capital good for the typical district, which does not own reservoir storage capacity.[11] There is a wide variation among the districts studied with respect to the distances over which they transport water, ranging from 2 or 3 miles to over 50 miles, as a study of detailed maps showing districts and canals reveals. Another important influence on canal construction costs is the slope

[9] On the other hand, calculated interest and depreciation costs are rather highly correlated and relatively similar to each other for most districts in the sample. This results from a common interest rate and lifespan of facilities being assumed for all districts, plus the fact that individual district assets, in the great bulk of cases, were not less than 40 per cent, or more than 60 per cent, depreciated as of 1960.

[10] The behavior of pumping costs is discussed in detail below.

[11] Under current conditions, an earth canal large enough to transport 100,000 acre-feet of water annually under moderately good load-factor conditions would have a basic construction cost for excavation of about $14,000 to $140,000 per mile as constructed on a variety of terrains, ranging from lowest cost to medium-high cost. Thus, an annual interest charge of 4 per cent on investment in canal excavation alone could readily amount to from $0.30 to $0.50

of the land at a 90-degree angle to the axis of the canal.[12] And there is the important matter, considered below, of the extent to which scale economies are attained.

Still other differences among the costs of districts might stem from differences in the method of their operations. For instance, some districts arrange to operate their water-conveyance facilities at a higher load factor than others, and thus tend to achieve lower average expenses (perhaps at some cost in convenience to their members). Some districts consciously take action to encourage the percolation of water to ground-water basins, thus tending to inflate their costs per unit of water delivered to their customers via surface conduits. Finally, cost variations among districts in a particular year may reflect varying deviations from normal of the amount of water available that year in different parts of Northern California. Even if interannual rainfall variations are highly correlated among regions of Northern California (as they in fact are), the observed and calculated costs for one year may not be typical of those for years with a different amount of annual surface runoff.[13]

Water costs of private pumpers

The costs involved in extraction of ground water should be reviewed along with those of irrigation district operations, because the member-customers of districts retailing irrigation water can often resort to ground water as an alternative supply. Just as in the competition between road and rail for freight shipments, the comparative cost levels of ground and surface water are the basic determinant of the outcome of implicit rivalry between these sources of supply. Also like the competition between road and rail, cost structures may rival cost levels in importance because of their effect on choices affecting allocation in the short run. If the source of supply with the higher long-run costs offers the lower variable costs in the short run through incurring a heavier burden of fixed costs, then a variety of conduct patterns may come into play, and significant problems of efficient allocation may result.

The foregoing evidence on irrigation districts that depend substantially on ground-water supplies appears unambiguous: ground water typically costs more,

---

per acre-foot of water for carrying it ten miles in a main canal of relatively efficient capacity. Calculated from V. F. Smirnovsky, "A Report on the Effect of Canal Capacities on Cost of Canals on Irrigation Systems" (Unpublished B.S. thesis, College of Civil Engineering, University of California, Berkeley, 1930); Ivan E. Houk, *Irrigation Engineering* (1956), Vol. II, chaps. 5 and 6; and current estimates of canal excavation costs released by the Estimates Section of the U.S. Army Corps of Engineers, San Francisco District.

[12] According to Smirnovsky, *op. cit.,* the excavation cost per mile for an earth canal of given cross section is five times as great when constructed all-incut on a 4:1 side slope as when constructed with a balanced section on level land.

[13] As between a "wet" year (annual runoff about 125 per cent of normal) and a "dry" one (annual runoff about 75 per cent of normal) in the 1950's, average costs per acre-foot of water delivered by eleven San Joaquin Valley irrigation districts differed only moderately, with cost for the "dry" year on the average only about 13 per cent above costs for the "wet" year. See Trimble R. Hedges and Charles V. Moore, *Some Characteristics of Farm Irrigation Water Supplies in the San Joaquin Valley,* Giannini Foundation Research Report No. 258 (1962), pp. 40–41.

and a larger fraction of the costs are for current expenses. As a general proposition about the cost of ground-water supplies, however, this finding is clearly suspect. It is manifestly more expensive to pump ground water from 200 feet beneath the earth's surface than from 20 feet below the ground. Specifically, a large, if diffuse, body of evidence suggests that the cost of ground-water extraction (holding constant its other determinants) increases about proportionally with the height of the pump lift. To put the same finding another way, pumping costs can be described in terms of a relatively constant number of cents per acre-foot per foot of lift, the constant being not much influenced by the height of the lift, although it may vary on account of other factors.

As in the case of distributing surface water, those "other factors" can be quite numerous. Some economies of scale result from increases in pump capacity. The load factor attained in the use of a well is clearly a matter to be considered, since some fixed costs are assuredly present. Finally, soil conditions affect the costs of ground water, both because of the varying difficulty of drilling through different materials to the underlying aquifers, and because varying characteristics of the aquifer determine the rate at which water can be pumped out and the drawdown in the process of continuous use.

The costs of obtaining irrigation water from wells incurred by self-supplying operators in Northern California are not regularly recorded and reported by any public agency. Thus, satisfactory empirical knowledge of the behavior of ground-water costs in the area is hard to obtain. A number of specific estimates can be found for various locations, but they often are not sufficiently explicit about the method of treating depreciation, the assumed load factor, inclusion of taxes, and other significant matters.[14] The structure of electric power rates can exert an important influence. Nonetheless, the general impression that emerges is that moderately large pumping installations (pump capacity of 800 gallons per minute or more) typically attain long-run average costs of five to seven cents per acre-foot per foot of lift. As was suggested above in examining irrigation districts dependent upon ground water (Table 16, column 3), half or slightly less of this long-run average cost level may consist of costs that are variable in the short run.

These estimates take on significance for determining water costs in conjunction with the levels of water tables in various parts of Northern California and the resulting total costs of ground water per acre-foot. The best available evidence on the combined effects of pump lifts and pumping costs per foot of lift appears to have been developed by Hedges and Moore in their recent study of the San Joaquin Valley region, where the bulk of ground water used in Northern California is captured. They have worked out systematic estimates of the cost per acre-foot of well water (at the wellhead) for twenty hydrographic areas covering almost all of the San Joaquin Valley.[15] These estimates are based on detailed assumptions descriptive of actual operating conditions and referring to recent years. They show that, among areas studied, the average total cost per acre-foot of water pumped

[14] Furthermore, like the reported costs of irrigation districts, they include no allowances for opportunity costs of the water itself or the value of externalities stemming from its use in such cases as would be appropriate.

[15] *Op. cit.*, p. 30.

ranged from $2.39 to $22.64. Among areas, there was a similar disparity in average pump lifts, and the rank correlation between average pump lift and average cost per acre-foot of water was high. The median cost for the twenty areas was $4.99, and the quartile costs $3.58 and $12.25. These costs, which do not include costs of distribution from well to field, compare to mean total unit costs, including distribution (shown in our Table 16), of $7.52 for 3 irrigation districts sampled which obtained two-thirds or more of their water from wells. The data available are insufficient to support any observations on the comparative costs of well water supplied by irrigation districts and by private pumpers, other than that they are evidently subject to comparable degrees of variance, and that the height of the pump lift has the strongest influence on the level of unit costs in both cases.

The costs of private pumpers in the twenty areas, according to definitions used by Hedges and Moore, were generally from 55 to 70 per cent fixed costs, and 45 to 30 per cent variable costs, with a median tendency at about 60 per cent for fixed costs. In arriving at these percentages, they include depreciation, interest on investment, taxes, and the flat service demand charges made by electric power suppliers in fixed costs, and treat only repair and maintenance and the variable energy charge for electricity as variable costs. If the service demand charges were considered variable (strictly they are, since they would not be incurred at zero output), costs would appear on the average slightly less than half fixed and slightly more than half variable, and would lie generally within the limits of a 60-40 and a 40-60 division between fixed and variable costs.

Given the substantial variability both of ground-water costs and the costs of irrigation districts which are representative of retailers of irrigation water in Northern California, we would expect a variety of local situations with regard to the competitive relation between the two sources of supply. In Chapter 10 we shall note the effects of these varying situations on pricing and other institutional arrangements made by irrigation districts, and their implications for the efficient choice between sources of irrigation water.

Water costs of wholesale agencies

Just as any discussion of the cost structure of irrigation districts covers a somewhat heterogeneous mixture of physical facilities and processes, so must a review of the cost characteristics of the wholesaling of irrigation water. In this case, the typical facilities include reservoir storage (usually large-scale and with a substantial multipurpose element) and long-distance transportation. And at present, the "typical" irrigation wholesaler in Northern California must be selected from a sample of one: the U.S. Bureau of Reclamation. As we indicated in Chapter 4, however, the coming years will see the rise of another wholesaler of comparable scale—the California Department of Water Resources—and local re-wholesaling of irrigation water is now developing in a significant number of areas. Here, we will limit ourselves to estimating the costs of the Bureau's main operation in the region—the importation and wholesaling of water in the San Joaquin Valley—and of one lesser operation centering around the Contra Costa Canal.

The Bureau's project in the San Joaquin Valley involves regulation of the flow of the Sacramento River through the operation of the reservoirs behind the Shasta Dam and the related Keswick Dam; the diversion of water from the Delta through the Delta cross channel and the Tracy pumping plant into the Delta-Mendota Canal (the Delta water supply being augmented in times of need by the effects of the Shasta Reservoir operation on the flow of the Sacramento River); and the delivery of a major portion of the water carried in the Delta-Mendota Canal into the Mendota Pool to replace water diverted from the San Joaquin River into the Friant-Kern and Madera canals, and of a minor portion to wholesale purchasers. It further involves the operation of the Friant Dam and Reservoir to store and divert the flow of the San Joaquin River, and of the Friant-Kern and Madera canals to transport major and minor portions of this flow, respectively, southward and northward from Friant Dam along the east side of the San Joaquin Valley for wholesale delivery to irrigation districts along the routes of the canals. A further feature of the project involves the generation of hydroelectric power at the Shasta site and its transmission for use at the Tracy pumping plant. The net wholesale delivery of water by the Bureau in the San Joaquin Valley is best measured by the total of deliveries from the Friant-Kern, Madera, and Delta-Mendota canals, less that large portion of Delta-Mendota deliveries (about 850,000 acre-feet in a normal year) which is made to replace water diverted from its natural course in the San Joaquin River. The net addition to the total San Joaquin Valley water supply is about the same as the replacement.

Clearly assignable as capital costs of net wholesale deliveries by the Bureau in the San Joaquin Valley are most of those of the Tracy pumping plant and connected works, and all of those of the Delta-Mendota, Friant-Kern, and Madera canals, and of the Friant Dam. These costs, as measured in terms of 1959 prices, total at least $187 million dollars. High and low estimates of average annual net wholesale deliveries from the system over the life of the facilities range roughly from 1.38 million to 1.63 million acre-feet per year, depending mainly on the extent of further development of use of the Delta-Mendota Canal. Capital costs per acre-foot per year should thus range from about $115 to about $135. Of these amounts, about 82 per cent are for the transmission facilities and 18 per cent for the Friant Reservoir. If the combined annual interest and depreciation charge were 4 per cent of the original investment (equivalent roughly to depreciation at 2 per cent per annum and interest at 4 per cent on depreciated value of investment), the average capital cost would be between $4.60 and $5.40 per acre-foot of water delivered over the life of the project. If the combined charge were 3 per cent per annum on original investment (equivalent roughly to depreciation at 1 per cent per annum and interest at 4 per cent on depreciated investment), the average capital cost per acre-foot of water delivered would be between $3.45 and $4.05. With a slightly higher interest charge (5 or 6 per cent might be considered as appropriate by many), capital costs per acre-foot of water would be appreciably higher. It should be noted that these capital costs are calculated exclusive of any portion of the costs of Shasta and Keswick dams (about $242.6 million in 1959 prices), although some portion of their costs should probably be considered allocable to the San Joaquin Valley operation. Because of the complex multipurpose character of the Shasta-

Keswick activities and related operations, we have not attempted any such allocation here; as a result, our estimates of capital costs of wholesaled water are on the low side.

The current operating and maintenance costs of water delivered through the system in question is calculated at about $1.60 per acre-foot, again in 1959 prices, and is not significantly altered as the alternative volumes of delivery noted above are considered. Of this cost, about 95 per cent is for transmission and 5 per cent for reservoir storage. Total capital and current costs should thus average from $6.20 to $7.00 per acre-foot with a 2 per cent depreciation rate and a 4 per cent interest rate, and from $5.05 to $5.65 with a 1 per cent depreciation rate and a 4 per cent interest rate (all costs omitting any charge for the Shasta and Keswick operations). These costs compare to a flat-rate wholesale price of the same water of $3.50 per acre-foot in the area. We will not endeavor here to distinguish differences in costs among different points of delivery in the area.[16]

The Contra Costa Canal delivers water from the Delta to areas west of the Delta and south of the San Joaquin and Sacramento rivers as they flow westward toward the sea. Allocable capital costs for the pumping plant and the Canal lie between about $120 per acre-foot of water delivered per year and about $80, depending on the estimate of the average volume of deliveries over the life of the facilities. This suggests a capital cost per acre-foot of water delivered of from $4.80 to $3.20 if the combined annual interest and depreciation charge is 4 per cent of original investment. Operating and maintenance costs should be approximately $1.00 per acre-foot, and total costs thus from $5.80 to $4.20 per acre-foot of water delivered. These costs again omit any allocation of the Shasta and Keswick installations.

It will be noted that, on both projects, capital costs represent dominant proportions of total costs. The proportions would appear higher if it were recognized that an appreciable fraction of current operating and maintenance costs, as recorded, effectively represent capital costs incurred at Shasta and Keswick and for transmission lines to generate and deliver electric power for pumping. Also, the costs of wholesaled irrigation water described above refer generally—and especially in the case of San Joaquin Valley water—to water which is transported over long distances; and this entails high transmission costs. Transmission costs, which comprise the bulk of all these costs, should increase more or less with the distance over which wholesaled water is carried, though perhaps less than proportionally if shorter hauls may on the average tend to involve smaller quantities of water and canals of smaller and less efficient capacity.

Reservoir-storage costs of irrigation water

The costs of reservoir storage allocable to irrigation water diverted from streams by irrigation districts and other agencies supplying irrigation water are not reflected in the cost data for districts discussed above. As noted previously, these costs are difficult to determine because of the nature of reservoirs providing the bulk of

[16] The preceding estimates are calculated from data presented in Appendix C.

storage capacity on streams in the region. The reservoirs are either primarily constructed and operated for generation of electric power, with streamflow regulation as a sort of by-product; or they have dual or multiple purposes, with streamflow regulation and either electric power generation or flood control or both included among the purposes. In either event, even if typical figures of dam-reservoir construction costs per acre-foot of storage capacity can be established, we are forced to make essentially arbitrary allocations of joint costs among such functions as power generation, streamflow regulation resulting in an augmentation of irrigation water supply, and others.

Even after some such allocation is made, and a dam-reservoir cost allocable to irrigation water is attached to a known reservoir storage capacity for each of a number of reservoirs, there are additional difficulties. It is necessary to know, if reservoir storage costs per unit of irrigation water are to be estimated, how much additional water is "produced" by each reservoir for irrigation purposes—that is, how much is made available in seasons when needed over and above the supply which would be available if there were no reservoir. With California precipitation patterns, this annual addition is unlikely to exceed the storage capacity, and will probably fall short of it by varying and often substantial percentages. But by how much? Unfortunately, no systematic data are available on this point for reservoirs of the region as a group, and we are reduced to making cost estimates based on alternative arbitrary suppositions.[17]

What we say here on reservoir-storage costs of irrigation water, therefore, is of a very rough and ready character. First, the reported gross construction costs of reservoir storage per acre-foot of capacity vary widely from project to project. For eleven large reservoirs built in the region since 1956 (with storage capacities between 50,000 and 128,000 acre-feet of water), construction costs were reported to range from $32 to $154 per acre-foot; four (with capacities from 268,000 to 2.5 million acre-feet) cost from $13 to $50 per acre-foot of storage, with the lowest cost associated with a 350,000 acre-foot reservoir.[18] There is believed to be some tendency toward declining costs per unit of water stored with increase in reservoir capacities, other things being equal. However, numerous other influences on costs—including site, type of construction, and range and emphasis of purpose—in combination are stronger, and result in a wide dispersion of reservoir construction costs per acre-foot of water storage among reservoirs of the same size, as well as among reservoirs generally. For smaller reservoirs, construction costs per unit of storage show even wider variations. Six reservoirs built since 1956, with capacities ranging from 4,000 to 10,000 acre-feet, for example, had construction costs per acre-foot of storage ranging from $6 to $229; the intermediate observations were $9, $26, $71, and $91. It is thus misleading to rely on any one average figure for costs of reservoir storage capacity in endeavoring to estimate the storage-cost component of irrigation water costs. A very detailed study of the reservoir complex on each of a

[17] Various figures are quoted in Chapter 11 for the yield of "new water" from storage reservoirs, but the controversies over these estimates suggest that different parties can predict wildly differing yields from a given project.

[18] California Department of Water Resources, *Dams Within Jurisdiction of State of California, January 1, 1962,* Bulletin No. 17 (1962).

considerable number of rivers from which diversions are made would be required to support even reasonable guesses at the reservoir storage costs incurred on individual rivers from which various districts draw water.

For these reasons, we retreat to rather broad generalizations regarding average costs. There are available estimates of the average level of reservoir costs for sizes varying from 20,000 to 5 million and 10 million acre-feet of capacity for the region based on actual experience of the Bureau of Reclamation and the Army Corps of Engineers. These are shown graphically on smooth curves, and readings at many capacities must be regarded as interpolations, but the general showings are indicated in Table 17. There is a substantial discrepancy between the estimates of the two agencies for reservoirs with capacities between 20,000 and 500,000 acre-feet (which would include most in the region), with the Corps, but not the Bureau, showing progressive diseconomies of reduced scale for reservoirs progressively smaller than 500,000 acre-feet in storage capacity. Since the Corps' estimates refer to an area much larger than Northern California, we are inclined to regard the Bureau's estimates as more relevant to our problem.

TABLE 17
VARIATIONS IN UNIT CONSTRUCTION COSTS OF DAMS AND RESERVOIRS AS REPORTED BY U.S. BUREAU OF RECLAMATION AND ARMY CORPS OF ENGINEERS
(Dollars in 1959 prices)

Capacity (acre-feet)	Construction costs per acre-foot of storage	
	Bureau of Reclamation, "Central Pacific" region	Corps of Engineers, "Pacific Coast" region
20,000	$50	$127
100,000	50	81
500,000	50	50
1,000,000	40	45
5,000,000	35	28

SOURCE: U.S. Congress, Senate Select Committee on National Water Resources, *Water Resources Activities in the United States: Water Supply and Demand*, 86 Cong. 2 sess. (1960), pp. 60–61.

Taking into account reported costs on individual dams built in the region since 1956, as well as Bureau and Corps estimates, we would guess that, in terms of current dollars, the construction cost per acre-foot of storage for the great bulk of on-stream reservoir storage in the region averages between $60 and $75. Most of this storage capacity is found in dam reservoirs which have dual or multiple purposes. We have not formulated allocations of such costs among functions for most of these dams, and any allocation will be in a considerable degree arbitrary. Attempting to err on the conservative side, let us suppose that one-third of all reservoir construction costs are on the average allocable to the augmentation of the effective supply of irrigation water. Then the construction costs allocable to irrigation water produced would lie between $20 and $25 per acre-foot of storage capacity. The next question concerns how fully this storage capacity is on the average "worked" to augment irrigation water supply—what is the ratio of additional water provided annually to the storage capacity? A fairly high estimate, according to various field reports and guesses, would place the annual yield of added water at 75 per cent of storage capacity. If this were the case, the allocable reservoir storage construction cost per acre-foot per annum of added water, on the average, would be from about $27 to about $33.

On this construction cost, the annual capital charge would be made up of depreciation costs plus charges for interest on investment. Supposing an interest charge of 4 per cent per annum on a declining investment and a depreciation charge of 2 per cent per annum, the average annual charge for both interest and depreciation over a 50-year period would amount to about 4 per cent of the original construction cost, or to from $1.08 to $1.32 per acre-foot. Neglecting reservoir operation and maintenance costs, this would be the average cost per acre-foot of water produced by the reservoir storage capacity on streams in the region—an average about which there would be a very considerable dispersion of costs for individual rivers. Since the preceding estimates emerge from a compound of several rough estimates, and two or three weakly supported suppositions, they could very easily be in error by at least 25 per cent in either direction—though we may hope for offsetting errors.

These costs would, of course, be the average costs of the incremental water supplies provided by storage reservoirs for surface diversion. They thus provide an estimate of the incremental fixed costs per unit involved in augmenting in-season natural supplies of irrigation water with water retained from the period of winter runoff. These costs can be viewed either as an addition to the fixed costs per unit incurred by a fully integrated irrigation district (compare Table 16) or as a component of the costs of a wholesaling operation.

Economies of Scale in Supplying Irrigation Water

Of the numerous factors which influence the cost of irrigation water and account for the wide range of differences in the costs per acre-foot of water delivered by different supplying agencies, one may be the existence of economies of large-scale plant. That is, if a single "plant" for supplying irrigation water is enlarged in capacity, and correspondingly delivers a larger volume of water, the costs per unit of water delivered may be reduced, other things being equal.

The process of supplying irrigation water is essentially very simple, involving the performance of only a few main functions. Moreover, it is generally a capital-intensive process; the original cost of capital equipment, plus the materials and non-human services used to maintain and operate it, account for a predominant share of all costs, and labor a quite minor share. In this operation, the only important economies of large-scale plant stem from the use of items of capital equipment of larger unit capacity. And the principal items which provide greater efficiency at larger capacity are canals, storage reservoirs, wells, and pumps.

Not much evidence is available with respect to the extent of economies of size realized with wells and pumps. It is generally held, and seems reasonable, that appreciable economies are obtained by increasing the gauge and capacity of wells (if water recovered can be increased proportionately with capacity). But the extent of these economies is difficult to ascertain because various analysts of pumping costs have not isolated the effect of well gauge from those of other determinants of the cost of well water.[19] It is similarly held that modest economies are obtained by increasing the capacity of pumps and the horsepower of pump motors (provided the capacity can be utilized); but, again, the net effects on costs of such increases are not readily isolated.

Because of their evidently greater over-all importance, and also because more data concerning them are available, we will center attention here on economies of large-scale plant realized through increased carrying capacity of canals and storage capacity of reservoirs. Other things being equal, systematic scale economies occur for both canals and storage reservoirs per unit of capacity as their respective capacities are increased over a substantial range.

Economies of large capacity in canals

Economies of scale realizable in the costs of irrigation canals relate to the construction costs per unit of carrying capacity for any given length of canal. Not only must length be held constant to isolate the desired relationship, but also two other factors which influence a canal's carrying capacity in complex ways. One of these factors is the presence or absence of canal lining, since a hard-surface lining in a canal permits a greater velocity of flow, and thus a greater carrying capacity than in the identical unlined canal. The other factor is the grade or slope of the canal, since a steeper grade results in a higher velocity of flow, and thus a greater carrying capacity for a given canal cross section.[20] Various other factors (for example, the canal's design, and the "side-hill" grade of the land at a 90-degree angle to the axis of the canal) also influence its unit costs of construction, although not necessarily the relation of cost to scale.

Taking these other influences as given (that is, with given dollar costs of excavation and lining, given grade or imposed grade variation with scale, and given side-hill slope and excavation design), construction costs per unit of the canal's carrying capacity for a unit length will decline as the capacity of the canal increases, for both earth and lined canals. The physical reasons for this are as follows. First, for both types of canal, successive increases in the carrying capacity of the canal on a given grade are accomplished by less than proportional increases in the area of the cross section of the canal. Thus, other things being equal, carrying capacity increases

[19] We refer here to the scale of a well as measured by its gauge (diameter or area of cross section) and corresponding capacity, and not by its depth, since increase in well depth in itself involves constructing a larger quantity of (more "units" of) a facility of the same scale or capacity, just as does building a longer canal of the same carrying capacity. Costs of recovering water from wells increase more or less proportionately with increase in depth of the well.

[20] The returns to hard-surface lining of a canal are related to its grade, as well as to its scale. The possibilities of increasing the velocity of flow in an earth canal by increasing its grade are sharply limited if "scouring" is to be averted.

with less than proportional increases in the volume of excavation per unit length of canal. This is principally because, as the area of the canal cross section increases, the velocity of flow on a given grade increases, with a diminution of the net "drag" effect of the wetted perimeter. It is also because of a declining ratio of the free-board of the canal to its total depth as the canal is made larger and deeper. These physical factors permit scale economies in canal construction through declining excavation costs per unit of carrying capacity. For lined canals, the area of the lining for a unit length of canal (and the cubic volume of lining material) increases less than proportionally with increases in the area of the cross section of the canal, because of the operation of a derivative of the general law that the volume of a container (or the area of its cross section) increases as an exponential function of its circumference as the circumference increases. Thus, the canal's lining area increases proportionately with the square root of the canal's cross-section area multiplied by a constant, for any given shape of canal section.[21]

To secure an empirical estimate of canal construction costs and the extent of scale economies, we can employ data assembled by Houk on canal capacities and related characteristics reflecting average experience for canals on Bureau of Reclamation irrigation projects.[22] The data as presented associate a series of ranges of canal cross sections with a corresponding series of ranges of canal capacities. We have processed this information by associating the mean cross sections for each of a series of cross-section ranges with the corresponding mean capacities. Dividing the second series into the first provides a measure of the square feet of canal cross section per second-foot (that is, cubic foot per second) of a canal's carrying capacity. If we assume that excavation costs are proportional to the cross section of a canal, then this result also yields an index of relative excavation costs per unit of capacity for a canal of any given length.

Table 18 shows such indexes for both earth and hard-surface lined canals. As column 2 indicates, modest scale economies in excavation costs accrue in the construction of earth canals. (There should be somewhat comparable economies in maintenance and operation costs, which as a component of total unit costs usually may be as large as, or larger than, interest charges on investment per unit of water carried. We lack data, however, on the precise level of operation and maintenance costs and on scale economies in such costs.) Column 3 shows that economies of large capacity in excavation costs are substantially greater for hard-surface lined canals than for earth canals. As noted above, such canals can be built to exploit much more fully the increases in velocity of flow which are attainable on a given grade with increases in the area of the cross section of a canal, because scouring at higher velocities is not encountered as it is with earth canals. Grades do not have to be diminished as cross sections increase. Finally, substantial scale economies also accrue in lining a canal, no matter which of the possible lining materials is em-

[21] Smirnovsky, *op. cit.*, and Houk, *op. cit.*

[22] Houk, *op. cit.*, drawing upon U.S. Department of the Interior, Bureau of Reclamation, "Canals and Related Structures," *Reclamation Manual*, Vol. X, Supp. 3 (1952); and its *Hydraulic and Excavation Tables* (10th ed.; 1950). These data clearly reflect an adaptive diminution of canal grade with increase of canal capacity for earth canals, evidently undertaken to maintain velocities of flow within permissible limits, but are based on the assumption of a constant grade for all sizes of lined canals.

ployed. Column 4 provides an index of total construction costs, including lining a canal, assuming the use of an unreinforced concrete lining which does not vary in thickness with changes in canal size. The apparent economies of scale are very great.

TABLE 18
INDEXES OF CONSTRUCTION COST PER UNIT OF CAPACITY IN RELATION TO SCALE, EARTH AND HARD-SURFACE LINED CANALS

Capacity of canal (cubic feet per second) (1)	Earth canals: Index of excavation cost per unit of capacity (2)	Hard-surface lined canals: Index of excavation cost per unit of capacity (3)	Hard-surface lined canals: Index of total construction cost per unit of capacity (4)
20	100	100	100.0
100	90	66	43.
300	85	50	26.
600	82	43	20.
1,000	80	38	15.
2,000	76	31	10.0
3,000	72	28	9.2
4,000	71	26	8.4
5,000	70	24	7.8
10,000	70	21	5.9
15,000	70	20	5.3

SOURCE: Calculated from Ivan E. Houk, *Irrigation Engineering* (1951), Vol. I, pp. 130–31; V. F. Smirnovsky, "A Report on the Effect of Canal Capacities on Cost of Canals on Irrigation Systems" (Unpublished B. S. thesis, College of Civil Engineering, University of California, Berkeley, 1930).

Generally speaking, it pays to switch from an earth canal to a hard-surface lining at some point as canal capacity is increased under given conditions. A composite total cost index could be constructed to reflect this switch, but it would require a number of particular assumptions about grade, type of soil, and the like. The choice between earth canals and those with hard-surface linings, of course, depends on other considerations than initial construction costs. Those with hard-surface linings generally have lower maintenance costs and avoid or greatly reduce losses from leakage or seepage, but linings depreciate (requiring replacement about every fifty years) in ways that canal excavations do not. In the light of these considerations and the preceding data, it would appear that only a very small minority of irrigation districts in Northern California divert enough water annually to justify the use of hard-surface lined canals, even if each carried its total diversion initially through one main canal. This estimate is consistent with the observed behavior of districts in selecting canal designs, and with the fact that irrigation water is transported in concrete-lined canals mainly by the large-scale wholesaler, the Bureau of Reclamation. Low-cost linings used primarily to avoid leakage and seepage losses have a somewhat wider range of use, and are employed in canals of medium gauge with increasing frequency in recent years, especially where such losses would be high. For irrigation districts in general, the moderate scale economies found for earth canals are generally the relevant ones, rather than the more dramatic scale economies for hard-surface lined canals.

To permit comparison with the unit costs of agencies retailing irrigation water, we have estimated the dollar costs per unit of capacity of an earth canal with a given length and the ensuing annual interest costs on this investment. Confining ourselves to excavation costs alone (the bulk of all costs for earth canals), we determined the cubic yardage of excavation that would be required for constructing canals with various cross sections and a given length and assigned a dollar cost to a cubic yard of excavation. In Table 19, we show in column 2 excavation costs per acre-foot of water carried yearly for a ten-mile canal of varying delivery capacity.[23] Here, the scale of the canal is not measured in flow capacity (second-feet), but rather in annual delivery capacity on the assumption of a 33⅓ per cent load factor.[24] In column 3, we convert these excavation costs into annual interest costs using an interest rate of 4 per cent. Because of the very long prospective physical life of earth canals, annual depreciation charges would be relatively small, and annual interest costs thus do not fall too far short of total annual fixed costs per unit of water delivered. The variation of unit costs with scale is thus shown to be small for the type of main canals typically used by Northern California irrigation districts, especially when compared with the estimates of their total unit costs presented in line 4 of Table 16.

TABLE 19
EXCAVATION AND ANNUAL INTEREST COSTS PER ACRE-FOOT OF ANNUAL CAPACITY FOR 10-MILE EARTH CANALS IN RELATION TO DELIVERY CAPACITY

Capacity of canal (acre-feet carried annually) (1)	Excavation cost for 10 miles of canal per acre-foot carried annually (2)	Annual interest charge per acre-foot carried in 10-mile canal, at 4% on investment (3)
5,000	$17.00	$0.68
10,000	16.50	0.66
25,000	15.40	0.62
50,000	14.90	0.60
100,000	14.20	0.57
250,000	13.60	0.54
500,000	12.80	0.51
750,000	12.30	0.49
1,000,000	12.00	0.48
Above 1,000,000	12.00	0.48

SOURCE: See text.

[23] Using data from Smirnovsky and Houk, *op. cit.*, we have assumed all-incut excavation on a relatively steep 2:1 side-hill slope. Excavation is priced at $1 per cubic yard on the basis of current estimates by the Corps of Engineers.

[24] To permit comparison of Table 19 with Table 18, we can provide the following associations between the second-feet capacities listed in column 1 of Table 18 and acre-feet delivered annually at a load factor of 33⅓ per cent: 20 cubic feet per second corresponds to 4,820 acre-feet annually; 100 cfs to 24,100 ac.-ft.; 600 cfs to 144,600 ac.-ft.; 1,000 cfs to 240,100 ac.-ft.; 5,000 cfs to 1,205,000 ac.-ft.

Optimal design of irrigation canal systems

The presence of scale economies, especially in the case of lined canals, might seem to imply that a given territory could be most efficiently supplied by irrigation water (from a single source) if a single main canal is employed, in order to maximize the extent to which water is carried in large-scale canals. A few agencies retailing irrigation water in Northern California employ multiple diversions through more than one main canal and, in a few other cases, a single main canal is shared among several districts. However, the general practice is for every agency drawing upon surface diversion to employ a single main canal. If we take this as the typical case, then the economies of scale in the construction of canals would seem to indicate that a multiplicity of districts supplying an area constitutes an inefficient arrangement if it could be served from a single main canal owned by a single district.

While this argument correctly identifies a relation between patterns of efficient design of canal systems and the organization of irrigation water retailing, it neglects another important set of forces. These forces govern the optimal capacities of individual irrigation canals, the optimal size of territory to be served by a single main canal, and the optimal degree of concentration of the main canal's capacity in fewer and larger, as opposed to more and smaller, irrigation canals. The problem of determining these optimums is complex. Rather than simply being carried from predetermined point to predetermined point, irrigation water is distributed from various sources over land areas economically serviceable from those sources, under conditions in which numerous spatially disparate origin or diversion points on the same source may often be used either alternatively or concurrently. Furthermore, it must be distributed under conditions in which the water carried in main canals from the source must ultimately be delivered to a large number of spatially disparate small plots of land, composing together the total land area served from a source or related sources. And these plots lie at different distances from each other, at different distances from any given origin or diversion points on a source, and at different distances from other alternative origin or diversion points on the same source. Moreover, the various plots will have certain elevations relative to the source in general, to given origin or diversion points on the source, and to each other. These relative elevations are reflected usually in a certain pattern of the slope or slopes of the land in the total service area away from or toward the source (generally and relative to specific diversion points), and in its slope or slopes parallel to the source, where the source is a river. And this slope pattern will definitely influence the solution for the number and sizes of main canals which is optimal for carrying water to a given service area.

In this general setting, it must be recognized that the bulk of the task of transporting water from a source to destinations will usually be accomplished by the following type of canal system: Each "unit" consists of a "main canal" which leads water from a source to and through the service area, and of "lateral" canals which tap the main canal at regular intervals as it passes through the service area in order to carry water through successive segments of the area served by the main canal. The laterals, in turn, are tapped by a series of sublaterals or ditches, which begin the task of purely local distribution of water to particular plots of land. Since such canal systems are usually designed to employ gravity as the primary force in moving water, main canals will be positioned (on side-hill slopes or, occasionally, on ridges) so that their laterals can run downslope through their service areas. For our discussion, we shall ignore alternative organizations of distribution systems which use pumping to supplement gravity flow.

Appendix B discusses and illustrates some of the considerations governing the optimal design of distribution systems in this setting. It deals with cases that can be viewed as involving the provision of water either (1) from a river course (a line, geometrically) to a service area consisting of a strip of land that parallels the river, where diversions to the service area can be made at many points all along the line; or (2) from a "pool" (a point, geometrically) on a river[25] to a service area consisting roughly of a semicircle of land around and downgrade from the pool. The distribution of water by gravity flow entails moving it first away from the line or point of origin and then either parallel to the line (river course) of origin or in concentric circles around the point. In these settings, two general forces are shown to influence the efficient design of a canal system for the service of a given total land area.

First, a reduction in the number of main canals carrying water away from the source (outhauling water) permits the concentration of water transport in canals of larger and thus more economical scale. Consequently, consolidating outhauls from a river or pool in one main canal instead of two or more such canals running parallel and adjacent to each other to the same destination—or consolidating in one main canal the outhauls to two or more service areas that lie successively farther from the source and are serviceable from a single canal route—obviously results in net economies of scale. The outhauled water is carried in a canal of larger capacity, while at the same time the distance over which water is outhauled is not increased. By the same token, there is a virtual economy, when outhauling water to a strip of land that parallels a river or to a semicircle of land around a pool, in concentrating the outhaul in the smallest number of main canals which is consistent with maintaining gravity flows in lateral (or main) canals that parallel or circle the source—and thus in spacing the outhauling main canals as far apart as possible, consistent with this constraint.

Second, however, consolidating hauls of water running parallel to a river course or around a pool—whether in main canals or in laterals—and therefore having fewer and longer parallel or concentric canals rather than more numerous shorter ones, results in the virtual economies of larger-capacity canals (reflected in lower costs per mile for carrying a unit of water) being progressively offset by diseconomies that result from increases in the distance over which water is carried. That is, more canal capacity multiplied by canal length is required per unit of water delivered. These diseconomies set a distinct limit on the optimal length of parallel or concentric main or lateral canals. Further, they place a corresponding limit on the optimal width of spacing of outhauling canals from a river course or

[25] The pool may be one at which water naturally gathers or is gathered, or a point on a river at which diversion is topographically favored—the latter often occurring on a distributary of a river entering a closed basin.

pool—on the degree to which outhauls should be concentrated in fewer canals—because wider spacing of outhauls results in increased distance of carriage of water in parallel or concentric canals. The cost-minimizing compromise between savings from enlarging and reducing the number of outhauling canals, and cost increases due to the consequent lengthening and increasing of the capacities of parallel or concentric canals, will in general be struck where decreases in the cost per unit of water delivered for its outhaul are offset by increases in the unit cost for carrying water greater distances parallel or concentric to the source.

From these generalizations, a few simple corollaries may be drawn. First, the optimal degree of concentration of main canal capacity hauling water away from the source into fewer and larger canals increases—the optimal spacing of outhauling canals is wider—the greater the distance is from the source to the service area. Second, service areas which lie successively farther away from a source and are all serviceable from a single main canal route are always more economically served by one main canal than by two or more. Third, any two or more very closely adjacent and parallel canals traveling the same route could have their task performed more efficiently by a single canal regardless of whether one is longer than another and regardless of whether their hauls are out from, parallel to, or concentric to the source on which they draw. In addition, it might be noted that where the scale of irrigation deliveries warrants the use of hard-surface lined canals, a higher degree of concentration of canal capacity in fewer canals should be more economical (other things being equal) than where only the use of unlined canals is economically justified.

From a consideration of these factors governing the optimal design of distribution systems, we may draw inferences concerning the desirability of enlarging the service areas of various irrigation districts, mutual water companies, and so forth, in cases where enlargement is a prerequisite to securing larger service areas for individual main canals. Such opportunities for improving the efficiency of canal systems are by no means absent, especially so far as a series of adjacent districts sometimes lies progressively farther from a common water source, and where parallel outhauling in separate canals might economically be avoided. But in the great bulk of cases, the limitations on economic extension of individual main-canal service areas are such that enlarging district service areas could not clearly be justified by savings in water transport costs. This matter is explored further in Chapter 17.

Economies of large-scale reservoirs

The economies of large-scale storage reservoirs are again economies of large-size individual items of capital equipment—principally of larger and higher dams built to retain water on stream courses. In this case, unit capital costs are appropriately measured as dam-reservoir construction costs per acre-foot of storage capacity, and economies of large scale are reflected mainly in the decline of these unit capital costs as the size of the reservoir increases. Capacity, in turn, is most meaningfully measured as "active" or usable storage capacity; that is, the quantity of water retained which actually may be withdrawn from a full reservoir, excluding any base amount that in effect cannot or should not be withdrawn. Unfortunately, various sources of data on reservoirs do not indicate whether stated dam capacities are gross or active capacities.

Before setting forth evidence on economies of scale in water storage, we must emphasize that economies in constructing large-scale storage capacity do not necessarily indicate similar scale economies in relation to the imputed value in use of this storage capacity. First of all, the volume and time distribution of streamflow in the river in question may or may not allow use to be made of any given quantity of storage capacity during a year. For example, a basic given capacity may permit usable intra-annual regulation of the flow of a river, and any increase would have utility only for interannual carryover and regulation. Second, even if we assume a proportional relation between storage capacity and the volume of water produced in the form of regulated streamflow, we must keep in mind the variable relation between the volume of flow and its marginal productivity in the various uses to which the regulated flow can be put. Besides augmenting the supply of irrigation water, on-stream storage is also employed to maintain regular and regulated flows of water through turbines for generating hydroelectric power, to control floods, to repel the intrusion of saline waters into river estuaries, to maintain navigability of major rivers, and to secure a regular flow of stream water to cities for urban use. A hypothetical marginal-productivity function could serve to relate the net value of product attributed to each of these functions to the net regulation of streamflow accomplished by a given dam and reservoir. There is no reason to suppose that these marginal productivities would be constant. As a consequence, scale economies in enlarging the storage capacity of time do not necessarily signify increasing returns in the average productivity of a dam's various functions.

Any universally applicable relation of the construction costs of reservoirs to their capacities is essentially impossible to derive because of the extremely wide variations among individual reservoir sites and because site has strong influences not only on the level of costs for any given capacity but also on the relationship of cost to capacity. Both the cost level and the relationship of unit cost to capacity will be influenced by topographic, soil, and rock conditions at the available dam site in a river ravine and by topography upstream from the dam site. Together these determine what types of dam (earth, earth and rock, rock fill, gravity, arch, etc.) are feasible, what type is most economical, and what sizes of dams will impound reservoirs of various alternative capacities up to some practical maximum. No single formula will apply to the relationship of dam-reservoir costs to reservoir capacity at all sites; we are closer to needing a different formula for every site.

Nevertheless, there are sound reasons for supposing that on most sites reservoir capacity will tend to increase more than proportionally with the height, volume, and cost of the dam as the latter are increased up to some limit. This is because the dam's wall is ordinarily a small fraction of the surface of a container, and the cubic capacities of containers generally increase as exponential functions of the total surface of the containers. Thus, even allowing for the necessary increase in the average thickness of the dam as its height is increased, economies of scale in creating reservoir storage should be encountered on most sites, over a substantial range of alternative reservoir capacities. This supposition is supported both by some engineering estimates referring to alternative reservoir sizes on given sites, and by statistical data relating reservoir capacity to average actual construction cost per unit of capacity for numerous dams built on different sites. Furthermore, spillway costs appear to increase much less than proportionally with the total cost of a dam on a given stream, and may even decline. For any size of dam, the spillway must be of sufficient capacity to avoid the loss of the dam, and the capacity needed for this purpose may decline as the storage capacity of the reservoir itself increases.

Two estimated relationships of a reservoir's storage capacity to cost on given sites were developed in connection with planning a dam and reservoir for storing water of the San Joaquin River and diverting it into the Friant-Kern and Madera canals on the east side of the San Joaquin Valley. One was a reservoir at the Friant site (ultimately chosen); the alternate site was at Temperance Flat. The indexes of estimated costs per acre-foot of storage for reservoirs of various capacities on the two sites are shown in Table 20. On each of these sites, significant scale economies of about the same relative magnitude are realized at a decreasing rate as reservoir capacity is increased from 100,000 to 500,000 acre-feet, and slight further economies to 700,000 acre-feet on one site. The decreases are followed by a slight upturn in unit costs as capacities are further increased to the largest considered. These sites, however, probably are not typical, in that the impounded water was to be side-tracked by diversions at the reservoir rather than dropped through electrical generation facilities.

As we turn to data on costs of reservoirs of different capacities on different sites, we must remember that site characteristics probably shift systematically in some ways with shifts in reservoir size, and that the recorded association of reser-

TABLE 20

INDEXES OF ESTIMATED CONSTRUCTION COST PER ACRE-FOOT OF ACTIVE STORAGE CAPACITY FOR VARIOUS RESERVOIR SIZES, FRIANT AND TEMPERANCE FLAT DAM SITES

Active storage capacity of reservoir (acre-feet)	Cost indexes	
	Friant site[a]	Temperance Flat site[b]
100,000	100.0	100.0
200,000	72.5	73.6
300,000	65.0	66.0
400,000	62.8	63.5
500,000	62.5	62.2
600,000	63.0	61.7
700,000	64.1	61.5
800,000	n.a.	61.7
900,000	n.a.	62.0
1,000,000	n.a.	62.5

n.a. Not available.

[a] Cost at the 100 level was $78 per acre-foot of storage capacity.

[b] Cost at the 100 level was $61 per acre-foot of storage capacity.

SOURCE: California State Department of Public Works, Division of Water Resources, *San Joaquin River Basin, 1931*, Bulletin No. 29 (1934), p. 247.

voir capacity to costs per unit of capacity probably reflects the influence of site changes as well as that of capacity changes. Also, choices of sites, among alternatives on given rivers, are not necessarily oriented toward minimizing the cost of storing water available for irrigation use. For example, where multipurpose reservoirs are designed to support power generation, a competing consideration in site choice is placement of the dam and reservoir at a point on the river from which a fairly long steep fall of water to turbine installations can be obtained. So far as this consideration is influential in site choices, both the level of costs of storage and the relationship of storage capacity to unit cost of storage may be different than if power generation were not one of the purposes of most medium-sized and large-sized reservoirs.

Subject to the preceding cautions regarding interpretation, Table 21 shows the associations of relative costs per unit of storage to reservoir capacity for reservoirs on different sites. These are suggested by smoothed curves fitted to actual data reported by the U.S. Bureau of Reclamation and the Army Corps of Engineers for reservoirs, respectively, in the "Central Pacific" region and the "Pacific Coast" region, and by the Bureau for reservoirs in "all regions" (Central Pacific, Colorado River, Upper Missouri, and Pacific Northwest). Costs for a reservoir of 100,000 acre-feet are assigned an index of 100 in order to facilitate comparison with single-site data presented in Table 20.

TABLE 21
INDEXES OF CONSTRUCTION COSTS PER ACRE-FOOT OF STORAGE CAPACITY FOR RESERVOIRS OF VARIOUS SIZES, BASED ON AVERAGE EXPERIENCE OF U.S. BUREAU OF RECLAMATION AND ARMY CORPS OF ENGINEERS

Active storage capacity of reservoir (acre-feet)	Index of construction cost per acre-foot of active storage capacity		
	Bureau of Reclamation, Central Pacific[a]	Corps of Engineers, Pacific Coast[b]	Bureau of Reclamation, all regions[c]
20,000	100	157	128
50,000	100	121	105
100,000	100	100	100
200,000	98	81	83
300,000	98	74	75
400,000	98	68	67
500,000	98	64	58
600,000	92	62	50
700,000	89	59	46
800,000	82	57	40
900,000	78	56	42
1,000,000	74	54	38
2,500,000	73	42	35
5,000,000	68	34	33

[a] Cost at the 100 level was $51 per acre-foot of storage capacity, based on 1959 prices.
[b] Cost at the 100 level was $81 per acre-foot of storage capacity.
[c] Cost at the 100 level was $60 per acre-foot of storage capacity.
SOURCE: U.S. Congress, Senate, Select Committee on National Water Resources, *Water Resources Activities in the United States: Water Supply and Demand*, 86 Cong. 2 sess. (1960), pp. 60–61.

Significant economies of large-capacity reservoirs are generally indicated, but the considerable difference in the shapes of the three scale curves constitute adequate evidence of the very considerable independent influence on costs of variations in sites. Thus, in the Central Pacific region (roughly Northern California), the Bureau of Reclamation appears to have been able to adapt site to reservoir size to keep costs per acre-foot of storage relatively uniform at a comparatively low level for reservoirs with capacities ranging from 20,000 to 500,000 acre-feet. In contrast, on the Pacific Coast as a whole, the Corps roughly matches Bureau costs only after capacity is expanded to 500,000 acre-feet, and experiences serious diseconomies of smaller scale as reservoir capacities are reduced below this point. Beyond the 500,000 acre-foot level of storage capacity, both experience significant scale economies, but between the levels of 1 million and 5 million acre-feet, the Corps experiences much greater scale economies on the Pacific Coast than does the Bureau in the Central Pacific area.[26] The curve representing the Bureau's experience in all regions incorporates a still different pattern, in which appreciable scale economies are realized throughout the range of capacities, but at different rates in various capacity ranges than realized either by the Corps on the Pacific Coast or by the Bureau in the Central Pacific region.

We are reluctant to conclude much more from these showings than the following. First, on any practicable dam-reservoir site, significant economies of scale in storing water are likely to be realized as the reservoir is enlarged from some minimal size up to a size that minimizes average costs of storage capacity on that site. Further increases in size beyond this point are likely to encounter some diseconomies of scale; and, finally, there will be a practical maximum scale which cannot be exceeded on the site. Second, the reservoir capacity at which lowest costs are reached will differ widely among sites, as will the shape of the scale curve (the rate of decline of unit costs with increases in reservoir size) as capacity is increased toward the point of lowest cost. Third, the lowest attainable cost per unit of storage capacity will also differ widely among sites, and there is a tendency for this to be smaller on sites where the lowest cost capacities are larger than on sites where the lowest cost is for a smaller capacity. This tendency, combined with the availability of scale economies on given sites, accounts in large part for the relationship of construction costs per unit of storage capacity to reservoir storage capacity suggested by Bureau and Corps data referring to different sizes of reservoirs on different sites.

The apparent presence of rather substantial scale economies in dam and reservoir construction implies that important deficiencies in the performance of the industry might arise if reservoirs are constructed at less than optimal scales.[27] One important question is whether the sizes of agencies engaged in supplying irrigation water (as measured by quantities of water delivered) are in any way related to the sizes of the on-stream storage reservoirs which they construct. The existence

[26] The comparison of construction costs per acre-foot between Corps and Bureau projects may not be entirely appropriate. Generally, the cost of spillway construction for the Corps' projects is substantially greater than that for the Bureau of Reclamation.

[27] In making the following conjectures, we assume provisionally that the effect of scale economies in the construction of storage capacity is not washed out by the effect of diminishing marginal productivity of its use for various purposes.

of such an association is not so automatically apparent as is the relation of agency size to the capacities of canals employed. Though such individual agencies as irrigation districts typically construct their own canal systems, they often do not construct the storage reservoirs which augment their water supplies, and reservoir sizes are thus most often determined more or less independently of the sizes of individual districts. However, the following may be suggested.

First, to the relatively limited extent that irrigation districts do construct their own storage reservoirs—either individually or in cooperative arrangements involving two or three districts—the sizes of the reservoirs are likely to be keyed to the quantities of water the districts have rights to and can deliver, and to the sizes of their service areas. This may result in the construction of individual reservoirs of inefficiently small capacity when stream runoffs and reservoir sites are taken into account. If several districts at different points in time construct their own reservoirs on a single river, the result may be inefficient for at least two reasons. A large number of unduly small reservoirs will be constructed on a river, or the total reservoir capacity will be increased by building new reservoirs on inferior sites, rather than larger reservoirs on superior sites. Further, the preemption of several sites to build a number of reservoirs of substantial aggregate capacity on a river may block future development of the most efficient reservoir system on the river by a large-scale development agency such as the Bureau of Reclamation, the Corps of Engineers, or the Department of Water Resources of the state. Such results are only possibilities; whether these possibilities are realized or not will depend heavily on the characteristics of individual rivers as regards types of available reservoir sites, the sizes of districts, the extent of interdistrict cooperation in reservoir construction and so forth. Other things being equal, however, it would appear that in cases where irrigation districts—or similar agencies depending on water from stream diversions—construct their own storage reservoirs, the enlargement of individual agencies drawing upon a single river source should provide conditions more favorable to the best exploitation of scale economies in reservoir construction and the best use of superior reservoir sites.

Second, to the extent that storage reservoirs augmenting supplies of irrigation water are built by agencies other than irrigation districts or similar agencies engaged in diverting streamflows and retailing water, the degree to which economies of scale in reservoir construction will be exploited will depend both on the sizes of these other agencies and their primary purposes. Where the primary purpose of such other agencies is to generate electric power—as is true of the two dominant privately owned public utility firms in the region—attainment of maximum economies in reservoir storage is in general not fully consistent with the most efficient production of electric power. Site selections will be other than those best suited for economical multipurpose reservoir storage, and reservoir capacities generally will not be chosen to attain the lowest cost per unit of water storage. Where the primary purpose of the other agencies is to impound and divert an urban water supply, similar deviations from the ideal are likely. Reservoir capacities tend to be tailored to the needs of individual municipal water systems and, even for the largest urban water suppliers in the region, tend to fall short of the scales which would be optimal if all uses of the reservoirs were considered. In contrast, where the primary purpose of the other agencies is to effect balanced multipurpose development of rivers —to supply irrigation water as well as to generate power, control floods, and so on—there is probably a tendency to seek optimal reservoir capacities which exploit more or less fully the scale economies in reservoir storage available at given sites, and also to emphasize the selection of sites on which optimal reservoir capacities will be relatively large.

A third and final point is that the full exploitation of economies of large capacity at the limited number of sites where site and river runoff make practicable very large reservoirs (in the range, for example, of 1 million to 5 million acre-feet) may be a course open only to very large organizations with huge financial resources, which are in addition able to arrange for serving very large areas with irrigation water.

Before leaving the matter of scale economies in reservoir construction, some mention should be made of an element in reservoir costs so far neglected—namely, the losses or disbenefits they may impose on other parties or on the public generally. Important among these disbenefits are deterioration of fish habitat in general, and the destruction or diminution of runs of migratory fish (principally salmon and steelhead). Such disbenefits must be included among the social costs of any dam-reservoir, subject to off-sets for any virtual improvements in fish habitat they may create. These social losses may be imposed by both small and large reservoirs. In Northern California, the upper reaches of the two major rivers of the Central Valley (the Sacramento and the San Joaquin) have been blocked to migratory fish runs by two very large dam-reservoirs, Shasta and Friant. But perhaps equivalent or greater damage to such runs has been inflicted by an assortment of smaller dams on tributary rivers downstream from the major dams—such as the Feather, Yuba, American, Mokelumne, Stanislaus, Tuolumne, Merced, and others.

In the context of the discussion of performance in Part Three, the main question that arises is whether increases in the capacities of reservoirs lead to increasing social losses through the destruction of migratory fish runs and the deterioration of fish habitat generally, so that, if these losses are counted as costs, the over-all economies of large-scale dam reservoirs are appreciably less than appears if such losses are neglected. By and large, as larger reservoirs tend to be created by higher dams, there would seem to be a tendency in this direction. As the height of the on-stream dam becomes greater, the practicability and efficiency of fish ladders decreases until at some critical height their installation is omitted from project plans and migratory fish runs are completely blocked. It thus seems fair to say that the over-all economies of increasing dam heights and reservoir capacities beyond some moderate limit are appreciably less than the cost figures reviewed above would suggest. A revised evaluation of the costs of dam-reservoir developments which gives full weight to the social losses inflicted may be critical as decisions are made concerning the desirability of projects which, when only private costs to the developing agency are counted, are close to marginal.

As regards effects on fish habitat generally (aside from effects on migratory fish runs) it is not apparent that larger dam-reservoir units have more unfavorable effects than smaller ones. The effects on habitat depend more strongly on the manner in which downstream flow from the reservoir is regulated over the year. Here, a better preservation of fish habitat seems likely to result from the operation of large reservoirs for a multiplicity of purposes than from the operation of smaller reservoirs with the predominant purpose of maximizing the supply of irrigation water in the growing season for crops.

The Cost of Supplying Urban Water

Organizations that supply urban water have many physical similarities to their rural counterparts and resemble them broadly in the structure of their costs. Because roughly the same conclusions about the composition of costs and their behavior in relation to scale hold for urban districts as for irrigation suppliers, and because satisfactory data for a thorough study of urban water costs in Northern California are not available, we shall confine ourselves to a description of some general traits of urban water costs in the area, including such crude conclusions as can be drawn from the available data.

In applying the preceding conclusions about scale economies to the distribution of urban water, we should remember that only a handful of urban water agencies in Northern California deliver as much water to an urban area annually as is delivered by a medium-sized irrigation district in the region. The largest two, it will be recalled, are the City and County of San Francisco, which is engaged in wholesaling water to a number of nearby suburbs as well as in retailing water in San Francisco, and the East Bay Municipal Utility District, which supplies water at retail to sixteen cities and towns on the east side of San Francisco Bay. Each of these two agencies delivers between 150,000 and 200,000 acre-feet of water annually, whereas each of seven irrigation districts deliver substantially more and a number of them roughly equivalent amounts. A very few principal cities not served by these two agencies—including Sacramento, Stockton, and Fresno in the Central Valley and San Jose in the Bay area—are served by agencies delivering to them in the neighborhood of 50,000 acre-feet apiece annually (about a modal volume for irrigation districts in the region), but substantially all others of the very numerous cities and towns of Northern California are supplied by water systems delivering from less than a thousand to 10,000 or 15,000 acre-feet of water apiece annually—volumes corresponding to those handled by the smallest third of irrigation districts in the region. In general, urban water is supplied by agencies with systems delivering smaller quantities of water annually than is delivered by agencies supplying irrigation water, and thus by agencies which operate at smaller scales.

In part at least as a result of their individually small water requirements, very few medium-sized and small-sized municipal water agencies which divert stream water undertake large-scale on-stream reservoir storage on major rivers, nor are they dependent on such storage. Some of them simply divert relatively unimportant amounts of water from major rivers and are only tenuously dependent on upstream reservoir storage facilities of other agencies. A considerably larger number employ minor reservoirs or catch-basins to impound the flows of local creeks and the general runoff of local basins. Only a very few large agencies, including the two major ones serving the San Francisco Bay area, are seriously engaged in damming principal rivers to create large on-stream reservoirs. A further phenomenon, which is in part the result of the relatively small individual water requirements of most urban water agencies, is that a very substantial majority depends entirely, or primarily, on local wells for water supplies. Wells are more important as a source of water supply to urban water agencies as a group than to irrigation districts and kindred agencies as a group.

Other physical differences affect the cost structures of urban water agencies differently from those of agricultural agencies in a variety of ways. On-stream storage reservoirs, as operated by or for suppliers of irrigation water, are usually employed to regulate flow downstream from the reservoirs, with most diversions of water for use taking place at downstream points. As operated by urban water agencies, such reservoirs more typically serve either as diversion points from which aqueducts are run, or—in the case of local creeks and basins—as both diversion points and terminal storage reservoirs. In choosing sources of water, the two types of agency differ in that urban water suppliers tend to be more selective in order to secure water relatively free of impurities in suspension or solution and of contaminants. Urban water as delivered must meet certain purity specifications imposed by the Department of Public Health of the state, and the supplier must either secure a relatively pure natural water supply requiring a minimum of filtration and chemical treatment or incur substantial expense in treating impure or contaminated water. The choice is most frequently in the direction of getting relatively pure water from other than the least expensive source and thereby reducing treatment costs. Such a choice may be to minimize costs, but other considerations are also influential. Water users tend to place a premium on water without undesirable odor or taste and without much dissolved mineral content. Therefore, the supplying agency may in many cases incur substantially higher costs than necessary to secure legally passable water in order to draw a water supply from a mountain stream or from a well field providing particularly pure water. Practices in this regard, however, vary considerably among cities and towns in the region, as does the potability of municipal water supplies.

A final important physical difference lies in the distribution facilities used for the local processing and distribution of water. Not only must urban water be treated for purity and potability. Also, it is always available to the user on demand (that is, by turning a tap), while agricultural supplies typically are not—a difference which requires local storage capacity and other features. The complexity of local distribution facilities, as well as the much greater number of customers typically served by an urban agency as compared to an irrigation district handling a comparable volume of water, renders the urban agency's local distribution costs much higher than those of the irrigation district. The extent of their short-run variability may also differ, although this is not apparent from the available evidence.

For all of these reasons, the cost per unit of water delivered to urban users tends to exceed very substantially that of water delivered to irrigators. As is true of the costs of agencies supplying irrigation water, however, the costs per unit of water delivered vary considerably as among different suppliers of water for urban use. Unfortunately, producing economically appropriate cost estimates on a comparable basis for a sample of urban agencies large enough to show these variations precisely has proved impossible. The only source of publicly collected data covers only cities with municipal water agencies, excluding those served by private utilities or other forms of public district (such as the important East Bay Municipal Utility District).[28] They present many major difficulties. The extent to which depreciation costs are included in those reported and recorded usually is unclear, and different agencies have apparently distributed comparable costs among several functional categories established in the reports which they file according to a large variety of different, but unidentified, principles. As a result, relatively little meaning can be attached to the recorded compositions of total costs of various agencies or to differences among them regarding composition of costs. In addition, no interest costs are recorded, nor any values of investment on which imputed interest charges might be calculated.

Recognizing these limitations, the following general observations on the levels of water costs and on cost composition may be offered. The highest level of apparent costs is noted in the San Francisco Bay region, for the city of San Francisco and for adjacent cities which purchase water wholesale from that city. For its combined wholesale and retail operations (about 60 per cent retail and 40 per cent wholesale), San Francisco reports total costs per unit of water "into the system" (sold, used, or lost) at about $68 an acre-foot. Costs of retailed water alone must be appreciably higher. A sample of three suburban communities purchasing all of their water wholesale from San Francisco show costs of "source of water supply" from $67 to $81 per acre-foot (evidently mostly purchase costs), and total costs of from $118 to $143 per acre-foot of water into the system. All these costs apply to a water supply imported in large part from the Sierra; all include directly or indirectly depreciation costs of reservoirs and long-distance transport.

Generally second in rank as regards level of apparent total unit costs are cities of the San Francisco Bay area depending on local supplies—either wells, creeks, or the San Joaquin-Sacramento river estuary. Six of these that were sampled reported total costs per acre-foot of water ranging from $39 to $55—well below costs for water carried in the San Francisco system.[29]

Urban water costs in the Central Valley appear to be appreciably lower. A representative sample of six cities, dispersed throughout the area and obtaining their own water from wells or from the Sacramento or San Joaquin rivers, reported total costs of water ranging from $18 to $49 per acre-foot, with five under $35. It seems likely that the total cost per unit of urban water supplied is significantly lower in most of the Central Valley than in the San Francisco Bay area, but the data described do not indicate the actual cost difference, even with approximate accuracy. Part of the apparent variance in costs among cities in the Central Valley, moreover, is probably attributable to differences in the proportions of actual full costs reported.

In four cities sampled in the coastal areas north and south of San Francisco

[28] California State Comptroller, *Annual Report of Financial Transactions Concerning Cities of California, Fiscal Year 1958–59* (1961); California State Department of Public Health, *California Domestic Water Supply Statistics* (1958).

[29] However, only two of the six reported any cost under depreciation (and this substantial), but they did not report higher total unit costs than the average of those reporting no depreciation. Depreciation may have been included under other cost categories by the latter, and also may be underreported generally.

(three drawing on local streams for water and one on wells), costs per acre-foot of water ranged from $43 to $76, on the average somewhat higher than in cities in the Bay area drawing on local supplies, but lower than those for retail water from the San Francisco system. The preceding may serve to impart only the roughest idea of the general level of urban water costs in the region, and of interarea and other interagency differences in the level of costs. Aside from the fact that interest costs on investment are nowhere included, the data in general probably tend to understate total costs to a significant degree except in the case of San Francisco and its wholesale customers.

The broad explanations for these interregional differences are clear enough. The two major high-cost systems serving the San Francisco Bay area engage in long-distance transport and undertake large-scale storage to serve their populations. Selection of such sources was made, in part, because the population in the metropolis was, or was becoming, so dense that available local water supplies were inadequate to fulfill current or prospective needs for urban water; and, in part, because of a preference for pure mountain water over that available closer from the muddy and polluted water of the Delta. Thus, San Francisco and cities purchasing water from it report little or no treatment costs, but very high costs must be imputed to the capture and transport of water supplied to the Bay area.

Urban water suppliers drawing on the lower courses of the Sacramento and San Joaquin rivers, in both the Bay area and the Central Valley, incur substantial treatment costs, which account for their relatively high rank; and, in some of these cases, cost of bulk transport may also be important. Cities located in the coastal regions and the remainder of the Central Valley attain low total costs through dependence on local ground or surface supplies. Pumping costs as reported (evidently largely energy costs if depreciation is not included) are important fractions of total costs for agencies securing water from wells, and run generally in the range of $5 to $15 per acre-foot; most of these users avoid significant costs for either treatment or bulk transport. The relatively few cities in the Central Valley and coastal regions depending on surface diversions in most cases have a convenient source at hand requiring relatively little treatment. The relatively large city of Sacramento, lying immediately adjacent to a large river carrying usable water, reports relatively low costs. Thus, contrary to the impression given by the reported costs of the large cities of the Bay area, large size does not seem to involve substantially increasing average unit costs,[30] unless it is associated with the exhaustion of local supplies and the need to undertake long-distance transport.

Some of the gross intercity cost differences will be shown to have a significant impact on recent patterns of wholesale water marketing in Northern California, especially differences among the cities in the Bay area. Nonetheless, finer characterizations of cost levels or cost structures has proved impossible. The available picture of urban water costs in Northern California is incomplete and blurred, and considerable primary investigation would be required to clarify it.

[30] There is not much variation in one category of costs that might be expected to reflect diseconomies of scale—the aggregate of distribution costs (other than pumping) and customer account, sales, and administrative and general expenses. As reported to state agencies, they appear to range generally from $15 to $20 per acre-foot for the San Francisco Bay area and from $10 to $15 for the Central Valley cities.

7

SALIENT ASPECTS OF THE STRUCTURE OF THE INDUSTRY

The preceding chapters have reviewed in some detail various significant dimensions of the structure of the Northern California water industry. Together, they should have provided a general picture of main structural determinants of the economic conduct and performance of public agencies and private firms and individuals that are members of the industry. They have also sought to identify and describe the *dramatis personae* with the actions of which Parts Two and Three of this study will deal, and to establish some important contrasts among regions and basins within the area. In this chapter, we will not attempt a general summary of the information presented in the preceding chapters. Instead, we will reconsider briefly the more salient aspects of the structure of the industry which have determined its organizational form, which point to the identity of the more crucial aspects of its conduct and performance, and which condition and help determine such conduct and performance.

Let us give initial attention to those structural characteristics of the industry which explain its rather unique properties as an industry. It was suggested in Chapter 1 that, compared to conventional private industries, the water industry of Northern California had several distinct peculiarities. First, most of the member entities of the industry bear an unusual relationship to water users or customers, and are evidently guided by unusual motives. In brief, most of the entities are not independent sellers to water users who are their customers, but are in essence users' cooperatives, each acting as a representative of a particular and limited group of water users. And, occupying this position, their presumed and observable motivation is not to maximize their own profits. Rather, it is to supply water to their customer-constituent groups in such quantity and on such terms as to maximize the joint profits (or other measure of joint welfare) of these water-using groups, as calculated after deducting the cost of securing water. This is clearly true of most local water agencies and mutual companies. It also holds, to some extent, for the large-scale federal and state agencies which act as producer-wholesalers of water, although their ties to groups of water customers are less distinct and firm and their statutory and bureaucratic motives are somewhat unique.

Second, the water industry is different in that there is substantially no competition among water agencies for customers. Their rivalry with each other is rather for rights to natural water supplies from which they may serve their respective customer-constituencies. At any rate, this is predominantly true of all local water agencies; the federal and state agencies operate with powers and within limits such that their rivalry with each other or with local agencies is rather subdued.

A third difference is that there are in the Northern California water industry no continuous organized markets for water or for water rights. Although markets for water may be absent, however, competing uses for it are generally present, so that the allocative problems of the industry can be viewed as the selection among market alternatives, rather than as compensation for externalities. As Part Two will show, cumbersome and devious substitutes for market transactions replace the working of a market as devices for resolving the rivalries and coordinating the actions of various water agencies—whose actions remain in large part insular and uncoordinated—and for allocating water among uses and users.

What basic characteristics of industry structure seem to explain these interrelated peculiarities of the industry? Several seem to contribute to an explanation:

1) Given the fact that the climate of the area is such that a major dependence will be placed on diversions of stream and ground water for irrigation, the location of sources of water has been favorable to the development of water resources by a large number of local agencies for local use. Most of the stream runoff feeding the Central Valley is dispersed among a substantial number of relatively minor rivers, well-spread through that Valley—so that each of numerous spatially disparate localities has a separate natural source of water. This same natural push toward dispersed local development also can be observed in the lesser agricultural regions of the area.

2) The law of water rights in California, to the extent that it tends ultimately to attach water rights to particular tracts of land rather than to producer-sellers of water, provides a strong inducement to the development of institutional arrangements whereby water users tend to become directly involved in the business of supplying water to themselves.

3) This tendency to become self-suppliers is implemented and encouraged by the California law providing for the establishment of local public water agencies with the general institutional form of users' cooperatives, each acting for an individual and limited group of users, and providing that such agencies may essentially be formed by local initiative under rather loose governing rules.

4) The characteristics of water-using activities are such, especially in agriculture, that water users have strong incentives to devise organizations which will assure long-term supplies of water; captive local agencies which secure water rights appurtenant to their lands provide users with the desired types of organization.

5) The local public district is controlled by a group of water users whose lands and the tax yields from them may be pledged as security for the repayment of loans. This form of organization provides a superior means of providing investors in water development with captive groups of customers and with assurance of repayments of principal and interest with the minimum attainable risk. The local public district, therefore, has prevailed in an evolutionary process in which the private water-selling firm has become a vanishing species.

6) The law of water rights and the law of water-supplying organizations (in a context wherein the bulk of water supply is undertaken by local agencies) together clearly discourage the development of markets in water or in water rights. This is done by making the sale of water by agencies to nonmember outsiders very difficult at best, and by placing many impediments in the way of transactions involving transfers of water rights. This complex of law also encourages the vertical integration of local agencies from capture through retailing of water (as an adjunct to securing firm water rights), and widespread integration reduces considerably the pressure to develop water markets and encourages insularity of actions by individual agencies.[1]

7) The statutory law and bureaucratic rules or practices which govern, or can be observed in the large-scale federal and state water agencies generally have the following characteristics: (a) confine them to wholesaling water, thus not disrupting the pattern of quasi-insular local water agencies; (b) deter them from profit-maximizing pricing, and from using actual or implicit market prices of water as the primary guides in allocative and developmental decisions; and (c) predispose them toward tying up the water they supply under very long-term contractual commitments, thus avoiding the development of continuous markets in wholesaled water.

These seven structural characteristics of the industry together provide a fairly complete explanation of the major peculiarities of the Northern California water industry, in the general respects mentioned at the outset of this discussion. Their ability to explain these basic peculiarities, however, is not the only aspect of their significance. The characteristics of structure alluded to above, as well as a number of additional structural characteristics, have further implications; they are important in explaining conduct and performance within this peculiar framework. Let us review several of the more important of these implications.

Regarding geographical dimensions of industry structure, it is noteworthy that the precipitation pattern of the area (in which nearly all of the annual precipitation is concentrated in a few winter and spring months) tends to induce a very heavy reliance on reservoir storage on all principal rivers feeding the main agricultural areas. It thus encourages a highly capital-intensive development of water resources involving the use of long-lived facilities. As a result, water development in the area makes allocative commitments of water which, if they were not optimal when made or subsequently prove not to be optimal, cannot be economically reversible for very long periods of time. Therefore, very great importance is placed on the initial correctness of investment decisions in the industry. It is further noteworthy that there is heavier precipitation in the drainage basins feeding the Sacramento Valley than in those feeding the San Joaquin Valley, and heavier precipitation yet in the north coastal region. This fact provides a natural inducement to undertaking long-distance interbasin transfers of water within Northern California (and also away from it). And, in turn, this inducement has provided the principal

[1] It may also be noted that the implementation of initial allocations of water with investments in long-lived fixed facilities for delivering water to particular sites of use constitutes a virtual impediment to reallocations through market transactions.

occasion for large-scale intervention in Northern California water development by federal and state agencies.

With reference to the legal framework of the industry, four facts warrant special attention: First, the law of water rights in California propagates an inbuilt disposition toward the development of misallocations of water among users of a given class and among classes of use; and such misallocations are not readily remedied because of a general lack of markets for water or water rights and the rigidity of long-term investment commitments associated with given initial misallocations. Second, the law governing the establishment of local water agencies confers a wide range of discretion on self-appointed local groups of water users in arriving at the definition of service areas of local agencies and in determining the pattern of access (or lack of access) to available local water supplies. Capricious determinations of service areas and exclusions of potential users from access to water may result, and there are no effective devices, through markets or laws, for remedying the possible misallocations and other economic irrationalities. The existing law of water agencies, moreover, has probably tended to encourage the proliferation of inefficiently small local agencies, even though a rather large share of all water is purveyed by a relatively few large ones. Third, the legal limitations on the powers of local agencies, and legal provisions affecting their means of financing investments, are usually such as to produce rather ubiquitous budgetary constraints. These constraints—together with the institutional orientation of local agencies toward developing water to serve a predetermined and limited local group of users—generally favor development of reservoir storage and transport facilities at less than optimal scales, except in the case of fairly large agencies in rather fortuitous natural circumstances.

The fourth fact in connection with the legal framework of the industry has to do with the peculiar triangular legal-political relationship among federal agencies, the federal legislature, and local groups of water users wanting subsidized water. This relationship creates an opportunity, and perhaps an incentive, for excessive or unwise investment in water development, as well as for misallocations and subsidies. (A similar triangular relationship finds the California Department of Water Resources at one of its corners.) More generally, water at the federal or state level is a political football, whatever the virtues of these governments' potential abilities to take account of effects external to the actions of local agencies.

The structure of water agencies reflects the play of a number of the forces just discussed, and several comments on it seem appropriate in passing. First, the pattern of vertical integration from capture through retail delivery, which is dominant among agencies supplying water for consumptive use, is inimical to the development of organized and continuous markets in water and water rights; so also are law and policy governing federal agencies acting as wholesalers. Second, independent electric power companies follow policies which tend to implement a movement away from a more desirable development of dual or multiple purpose reservoirs on rivers. (As we shall see in Chapter 11, however, this tendency has been ameliorated by the increasing use of cooperative arrangements involving power companies and agricultural water districts.) Third, many otherwise fully integrated local water agencies depend for water supplies on storage reservoirs they neither pay for nor own. This lack of direct responsibility provides an incentive for over-use or misallocation of water to irrigation, as opposed to in-stream use; and this tendency may be compounded by excessive interseasonal transfers of water by federal agencies. Fourth, the use of legal substitutes for market allocation of water and water rights suggests that the concentration of agencies may be significant if it affects the workability and outcome of these legal processes. Their use tends to grow more complicated, the greater is the number of rivals, and thus, in the absence of conventional markets, low concentration may actually worsen performance.

Several characteristics of the demand for water for consumptive use seem strategic. One is that the demand for both irrigation and urban water appears to be moderately price-elastic. This being the case, it is not very difficult for the industry to commit serious allocational errors by making water available to different users or regions at prices bearing different relationships to the marginal costs of delivered water. Another is the heavy influence on particular demand-price relationships for water by such artificial interventions as acreage limitations on growing particular crops, marketing agreements, and price supports. In addition, the level of agricultural water demand is significantly elevated by price supports coupled with government purchases of surplus crops—especially of cotton grown in Northern California. And, finally, demands for water are not generally expressed as an aggregate, but in insular slivers that reflect the institutional organization of local water agencies and implement their tendencies toward misallocation and toward undertaking projects of less than optimal scale.

As to the costs of supplying water, a matter worth reiteration concerns the fact that most water going to consumptive uses comes from sources in which water is a scarce good, but that agencies widely disregard its opportunity costs in making investment and related decisions (partly because of the lack of water markets), just as they tend to disregard external diseconomies and disbenefits. Such disregard bulwarks or implements misallocations of water, especially so far as contractual costs of water vary more widely than total costs inclusive of opportunity costs. It is also significant that a high proportion of the total non-water costs of supplying water for consumptive use represents fixed costs of long-lived facilities. This consideration not only places great importance on the correctness of investment decisions in the water industry, but it also poses some problems of coordinating long-run investment decisions with short-run pricing and rationing policies. Another aspect of the costs of water lies in the considerable economies of large scale that are attainable through the use of large-capacity canals and reservoirs, though their economic exploitation is subject to geographic and topographic limitations. The existence of such economies poses a problem of whether a pattern of water development by insular local water agencies (each devoted to its individual service area and possibly faced with budgetary constraints) will be compatible with the optimal exploitation of these economies, although the scale economies due to service being provided to a given territory by a single agency are less pronounced than those present in the water-transport process taken by itself. The high fixed costs and great longevity of most of the capital equipment used in the water industry underlines the importance of those allocative biases which affect the investment decision. The quantitative importance of various sources of deficient performance is bound up in their power to influence the investment plans of entities in the water industry.

PART TWO: CONDUCT

8 

CONDUCT OF WATER AGENCIES: ORGANIZATIONAL MOTIVES AND NORMATIVE CRITERIA

The investigation of conduct in the course of an industry study normally fulfills two functions. It establishes the record from which the social performance of the industry is in part assessed. It also examines the relation between the economic environment of the members of an industry and their decisions. Thus it comprises an essential bridge in linking structure to performance and testing theoretical hypotheses which identify presumed critical elements of the industry's structure and predict their impact on behavior and performance.

Conduct is analytically significant mainly because of its possible relation to the performance of an industry, and then primarily as a reflection of structural factors. Moreover, many hypotheses concerning the influence of structural elements can be tested empirically without reference to conduct. Granting this, a systematic investigation of conduct still remains essential for at least two reasons. First, although it is most reliable to evaluate performance by direct measurement, it is often necessary in practice to infer the level of some attribute of performance by the essentially indirect method of deduction from observed patterns of conduct. Second, where the quality of performance can be measured directly, the analysis of aspects of conduct underlying such performance aids in understanding why such performance comes out as it does, and in evaluating possible reforms that might make it come out better.

These statements, pertaining to industry studies in general, also hold for our rather special exercise. While we have had to adapt the normal hypotheses of the economic theory of markets to the circumstances of the water industry, we have still been engaged in developing hypotheses linking aspects of structure with either conduct or performance or both. Thus the functions of the chapters on conduct contained in Part Two differ relatively little from those dealing with conduct in any conventional industry study. Furthermore, since the categories of performance to be investigated in Part Three are those designated by general economic theory (and not some special set indigenous to the water industry), the categories of conduct reviewed below also constitute a relatively familiar list.

The first principal aspect of conduct to be studied concerning suppliers of water for consumptive use is the determination of the group of potential water users an agency will serve (this may or may not be determined concurrently with the formation of the agency), the annual quantity of water it will supply to this group, the time pattern of its deliveries, and the way in which this quantity will be allocated among various users whom it supplies. A correlative aspect of its conduct is the determination of the price or schedule of prices which it will charge its customers. Implementation of its decisions in these regards involves making consistent decisions regarding the purchase of numerous non-water factor inputs required to construct and operate the facilities necessary for supplying water; in particular, decisions regarding the quantity of funds to be invested in facilities and the design of investment projects. Comparable aspects of conduct also are primary for the water agency in its role as a supplier of electric power or other utilities or services derived directly from the use of water.

In sum, one principal aspect of the conduct of the individual water agency involves output-price-investment determination, together with the determination of the scope of the group of customers to be served. This aspect heads the list in the conventional industry study. Further, the essential character of this conduct is judged by familiar tests concerning the principles which effectively guide the agency's decisions on these matters, or the goals it seeks as measured in terms of the relationships of the costs of the outputs it supplies to their values in use.

Price-output decisions of agencies in the water industry, however, include some special aspects not encountered in the usual industry. The actions of many agencies affect the welfare of parties other than their direct customers. An example is the incidental benefit from streamflow regulation provided by a reservoir operator to independent parties downstream, such as in-stream users of these flows or of those subject to losses from floods. The significant price-output conduct of the reservoir operator includes, first, his recognition, or lack of recognition, of these effects and, second, if the agency does pay such heed, the principles governing determination of the manner in which it will adjust operations to preserve the benefits, or reduce the disbenefits, accruing to in-stream users of water or holders of land subject to floods. Another example rests on the agency's status as a users' cooperative. The water agency, unlike the conventional private firm, must effectively make a decision on the scope of its markets or group of customers, rather than offering its product to the public for what it will bring. Thus the formation of agencies by, or for the benefit of, particular groups of customers becomes another special element of the price-output decisions of water agencies not found in the conduct of conventional private enterprises.

A study of conduct in the conventional industry typically moves from the principles governing the price-output decision of the individual enterprise to the process of coordinating these decisions in the market place. At this point, the analogy with the water industry grows much weaker. And for this reason, the principles guiding the conduct of water agencies with respect to output, price, investment determination and related matters require special attention.

As individual water agencies within a group pursue their own ends, they come into competition with each other, occasionally in the pursuit of customers and frequently in the pursuit of sources of water. Further, as some water agencies are essentially producer-wholesalers and others are retailers of water (or power), they enter into long-term contracts, in which prices are established and quantities of water to be transferred are determined, together with the areas of use which certain parts of the total water supply will serve. By and large, however, the individual output-price-investment determinations or decisions of the general populace of water agencies do not come into competitive conflict in any single organized market or set of submarkets for water, wherein they could be reconciled and coordinated by a general market-price mechanism. For various legal and institutional reasons, no such general organized market or set of submarkets for water exists. Instead, substantially insular agencies pursue substantially insular policies, with the only important counterpart of a market emerging in sporadic economic and legal contacts between agencies.

There are, however, substitutes for such market-oriented conduct which serve to impose some limitations on the unbridled insular output-price-investment decisions of numerous individual water agencies. These include extra-market legal and political skirmishes between water agencies for rights to sources of water, negotiation of legal agreements among contesting agencies regarding the sharing of given water sources, and intervention of regulatory bodies to place various constraints on the actions of agencies—in the interest of better over-all industry performance—which a market might otherwise impose. They also include the actions of large agencies of higher governments—such as the Bureau of Reclamation of the U.S. Department of the Interior and the California Department of Water Resources. In planning a coordinated and balanced development of water resources and entering the industry as large-scale developers and wholesalers of water, such agencies can ameliorate, through strategically planned contracting to supply water, the misallocations of water among uses and users which develop from the uncoordinated actions of local agencies.[1] A pressing question, as we view the behavior of the Northern California water industry, concerns the general character and working of this complex of substitutes for market-oriented conduct (or for markets), and its probable efficacy as a means of securing socially acceptable performance from the industry. This side of conduct is at least as important as that which concerns the decision-making principles of individual water agencies.

The following chapters will describe some principles and patterns of conduct followed with reasonable regularity by water agencies. From the observed patterns of conduct, it becomes possible to predict a certain sort of industry-wide economic result or performance as regards the quantity of water supplied to the regional economy, its allocation among uses and users, the volume of investment undertaken to develop water resources, and so on. Knowledge of the conduct pattern and its predictable economic consequences, however, is information with little meaning in itself unless the pattern and its results can be measured against some norms or ideals representing what conduct and resultant performance would be optimal from the standpoint of over-all economic welfare. Comparing actual performance with the optimal performance will be the function of Part Three. Nonetheless, to interpret evidence on conduct patterns, we must first provide a translation of some of the general principles of economically efficient conduct and performance into propositions reflecting the special circumstances of the water industry. That will be

[1] Such large agencies attempt through their projects also to create some balance in the totality of activities involving water so as to protect the public interest in such matters as flood control and preservation of streamflows for recreation, navigation, and other purposes.

the task of the first two main sections of this chapter—one dealing with the efficient allocation of water as between uses and users, the other with the principles for the optimal investment in fixed facilities relating to the supply of water.

The chapter's two concluding sections also provide analytical background for the remainder of Part Two in the form of behavioral hypotheses concerning the organizational motives and constraints influencing the conduct of the typical water agency. We stressed in Chapter 1 the proposition that water agencies, while they clearly cannot be viewed as profit-maximizing enterprises, can be characterized by an equally strong motivational hypothesis as users' cooperatives organized for the benefit of fixed groups of profit-maximizing or utility-maximizing member-customers. This hypothesis was employed throughout Part One in generating further hypotheses about the elements of structure or environment which would influence the conduct and performance of entities bearing this organizational stamp. In the third section of this chapter, we seek to validate the users' cooperative hypothesis by relating it formally to the legal structures of important classes of water agencies. Because of the general significance of the investment decision as an aspect of conduct, the fourth section deals with hypotheses about the investment behavior that might be predicted theoretically for enterprises organized as users' cooperatives.

The Shadow Prices and Optimal Allocation of Scarce Water

Conflict among agencies over water—some of it taking the forms of market rivalry and bargaining, but most being registered through other channels—has emerged because water in Northern California has become, at least in the major localities of use, a scarce good or resource. Moreover, it is becoming increasingly scarce relative to demands for it, so that ever-increasing importance attaches to the mode of conduct through which water agencies resolve conflicts and establish relations with each other. For this reason, it seems appropriate to explore the general meaning of water scarcity, and its influence on interagency conflict and interdependence. Exploration of these matters, moreover, will lead naturally into the development of rudimentary norms for the socially optimal allocation of scarce water among uses and users, and of derived norms for socially optimal conduct by water agencies.

Free and scarce goods and water

A "free" good in economic analysis is one which is in such abundant supply that all persons wishing to use it can as much as they wish—that is, use it in such quantities that its marginal utility or net value of its marginal product to them is zero—without exhausting the supply. If this is the case, a process of competitive bidding for the good by all potential users, expressing their demands for it, would result in its having a zero price, since the total supply would equal or exceed all demands at a zero price.

The economist, casting about for examples of a free good, often chooses air and water. Air obviously qualifies. Water is also often cited as a free good "at the source"—that is, at stream or wellhead—in the sense that it is sufficiently abundant that a process of competitive bidding for it by all potential users would result in a zero price for water.[2] It is recognized that most users of water have to incur the costs of capturing, transporting, and distributing it to points of use (so that delivered water has a positive price), and that the need to incur these costs reduces the effective demands of most users for water at any source. (These effective demands are derived by deducting from the values at sites of use of the marginal utilities or net marginal products of various alternative quantities of water the marginal costs of capture, transport, and distribution.) But the sum of these effective demands at any source are thought to be insufficient, relative to natural supply at the source, to result in a price of water at the source greater than zero. A corollary of the existence of a zero price for water at the source would be that it had no opportunity cost.

Despite this belief, water, in many parts of the United States and particularly in California, generally is a scarce good rather than a free good as defined above. In the developed agricultural and urban areas of Northern California, total demands for water from most sources typically exceed total supplies; if all demands on each of these sources were expressed in competitive bidding for the use of water, some positive price for water would be established at each source. Even if the bidding were restricted to that of users who are institutionally organized to bid (thus excluding the bids of unorganized individuals who use water in streams for recreational purposes, of shipping companies using water for navigation, and so forth), a somewhat lesser positive price for water would ordinarily emerge.[3] Correspondingly, the last acre-foot of water taken from a natural source by any user typically has an opportunity cost measured by the marginal value of the water in alternative uses.[4]

[2] This is on the assumption, of course, that there would be no monopolistic control of water sources which would permit any owners of the rights to use water to withhold some of the natural supply in order to create an artificial scarcity and establish a positive price for water.

[3] In fact, these unorganized groups are represented in the competition for water by governmental agencies which secure some degree of preservation of streamflows for recreational and navigational purposes, thus effectively reserving some of the supply of stream water for in-stream use by the public, restricting the supply of water available to users who might be organized to bid, and raising the price of water which bidding by such users would establish.

[4] Different measures of the opportunity cost of water, viewed as a marginal value in alternative uses or as a marginal value lost in other uses because of its devotion to a particular use, may be derived. It would differ according to whether or not all uses are counted in calculating the opportunity cost, and according to whether or not "external effects" of the use of water by one user on the net value of water to other uses are recognized in the calculation. This matter will be explored in the succeeding analysis. In any event, it will appear in this analysis that, to the individual user, the gross opportunity cost of water at the source (streamside or wellhead) is properly its marginal net value in alternative uses, and that the net opportunity cost to the user (if different) is the gross opportunity cost minus any marginal cost for non-water productive inputs which the user incurs to make the water he uses available at the source. In other words, it is the gross opportunity cost minus any marginal storage-reservoir costs he incurs to make stream water available at streamside, or minus the marginal cost he incurs to make well water available at the wellhead. This net opportunity cost is thus a kind of measure of the sacrifice in income which the user would make by keeping water for his own use rather than selling it in a competitive market, if there were such a market.

The shadow prices of water

In spite of the status of water as a scarce good in much of Northern California, it is true, if superficially puzzling, that organized markets for water or for rights to water at the source have not developed in the region. Correspondingly, there has not developed in any explicit form a market price, or set of prices, for water at its source or sources—for "raw" water itself, net of the costs of capturing and delivering it. And even the explicit delivered prices of water at various destinations charged by water agencies do not usually include, in addition to costs of capture and transmission, the implicit or "shadow" price of the raw water in these "latent" markets where it would be positive. This failure of water markets and prices for water as such to emerge in explicit fashion is partly attributable to a variety of institutional impediments which include importantly the law of water rights and the law governing the operation of public water agencies. And it is partly attributable to the historical development of entrepreneurial units in the water industry in the form of consumer cooperatives representing specific groups of water users, rather than in the form of private enterprises capturing and selling water and sufficiently unregulated so that they could establish water prices which include an implicit net value of water as such.

Nevertheless, "shadow prices" of water do exist at many sources, and their existence, and more generally their emergence and increase over time, continue to influence indirectly the conduct of water agencies. A shadow price for water in any source is generally a price it would command at the source if it were regularly offered for sale in an organized market, if actual and potential water users were present in the market as buyers, and if those owning or holding rights to the water (including water users) were present in the market as sellers. More specifically, we will use the term "shadow price" (unmodified) to refer to a competitive price for water, such as would be established in an organized market if there were many small buyers in the market, none possessing any monopsony power to depress the price of water by restricting his purchases, and also many small sellers, none possessing any monopoly power to elevate the price of water by withholding water from the market.[5]

For any individual water source such as a river, moreover, it is quite possible to envisage several alternative measures or versions of even the competitive shadow price for water. Here we will center attention on only two major choices between sets of alternative assumptions. First, we either may assume that the participants bidding for or offering water in the hypothetical market are limited to all commercial users of water (those who divert water for consumptive use or use it in-stream for power generation); or, alternatively, may assume that the participants in the market include all members of all classes of water users (not only commercial users, but also those who use streamflow for recreation, navigation, repelling intrusion of salt water into river estuaries, and so on).[6] Second,

[5] Or if, regardless of numbers and sizes of sellers and buyers, none exercised any monopoly or monopsony power he might possess.

[6] In either case, we would also include among those offering water any "third parties" who do not use water but do hold rights to water in the source.

we either may assume that every participant in the hypothetical market, in determining how much water he will retain for use, disregards all external effects of his operation on the net value of water to all other users or on the welfare of other affected parties; or, alternatively, we may assume that all participants adjust the opportunity costs determining their rates of use to reflect the external effects of their water use on the welfare of all other users and affected parties—thus reducing their own water use in appropriate degree if it imposes external diseconomies or disbenefits on others, and increasing it appropriately if it confers external economies or benefits on others.

Although these assumptions can be combined in several different ways, we need for later reference to put convenient labels on two particular combinations. One is a "commercial" shadow price, one that would be determined in a perfectly competitive market by the bidding of actual and potential buyers of water for consumptive and power uses. The other is an "ideal" shadow price, set in a perfectly competitive market in which users not normally organized in institutions capable of making such bids are also present, and all bidders (commercial and other) take into account any external economies or diseconomies resulting from their purchase or use of water. The exact nature and status of the "noncommercial" bidders will be discussed in Chapter 14; here we can identify them in effect, if not in substance, with the status of "public goods" as defined in the theory of public finance. It should be clear from the familiar propositions of welfare economics that the "ideal" shadow price would correctly measure the social opportunity cost of water at the margin for any user, and thus reflect an optimal allocation of water. To bring it into actual being, however, would require not only the establishment of perfect competition among the commercial bidders but public interference of two sorts: governmental bidding on behalf of the noncommercial users calculated to express the net value of the marginal product of water to them (adjusted for externalities); and a tax and subsidy arrangement to force commercial bidders to take external effects into account correctly. A "commercial" shadow price would result from the removal of restraints on bidding by the commercial users (including the elimination of all market imperfections), but without the governmental bidding and tax-subsidy policies just mentioned. The corresponding allocation would provide excessive water to commercial users relative to noncommercial users as well as containing biases of indeterminate sign as a result of externalities.

The usefulness of the concept of "ideal" shadow price as a tool for stating normative conclusions is clear. The usefulness of the "commercial" concept arises mainly in the analysis of historical patterns of market conduct. The emergence of positive shadow prices for water from various sources, and of different shadow prices for water from different sources—in the absence of organized markets—activates commercial water users or agencies serving them to undertake various extra-market courses of conduct, responsive to water scarcity generally and to differentials in water scarcity among sources. So far as shadow prices play this role, commercial shadow prices which would emerge in unregulated commercial water markets within the context of existing governmental regulations are probably the most relevant in explaining observed extra-market conduct. Such commercial shadow prices come closer than any others to reflecting the private opportunity costs of water agencies and the scarcity values of water to them. Although the hypothetical commercial markets that make shadow prices into actual prices literally do not exist, commercial shadow prices are quite real and do exert influences on conduct, even though their magnitudes are not precisely measured. Commercial shadow prices also possess limited usefulness in drawing normative conclusions by indicating the direction of distortions resulting from a lack of the institutional arrangements necessary to cause a fully ideal shadow price to be determined.

Shadow prices and patterns of water allocation

Because of the significance of shadow prices, both for explaining historical patterns of conduct and facilitating normative judgments, we shall describe briefly the sorts of allocative patterns that would emerge in various hypothetical markets and the associated marginal conditions of equilibrium. In all of the succeeding cases, we assume that none of the participants in any hypothetical market exercises any degree of monopoly or monopsony power, and that the shadow price established is a competitive price. In general, no distinction is made between short-run and long-run situations.

Consider first the simple situation in which the water from a given source, a fixed quantity of which is available per period of time, can be put only to consumptive commercial uses. In the absence of external effects, the identical commercial and ideal shadow prices assume a value that clears the market of the available supply of water, with each commercial user purchasing a quantity such that the net value of the marginal product of water to him at the source equals the shadow price. In turn, this shadow price is the opportunity cost of water to all users. The derived demand functions of the commercial users can be thought of either as associated with optimizing adjustments of the quantities of their other variable inputs and outputs (and only the prices of these inputs and outputs held constant) or as derived in a setting where the quantities of some other inputs and outputs are held constant. Furthermore, this case is consistent with any number of institutional patterns of ownership of rights to utilize the source of water, so long as a large number of actual and potential sellers are present. These sellers might be entirely separate parties from the set of actual and potential buyers, or the buyers might hold the rights among themselves so that the only arm's-length transactions are the net sales or purchases of those users who employ less or more water respectively than the yield of their rights. If the agencies bidding for water as "users" are actually retailers selling at arm's-length to final consumers, then the optimal retail price of water would equal the sum of its shadow price (also its opportunity cost) at the source plus the change in the total cost of non-water inputs (for transportation, delivery, etc.) associated with the last unit of water sold. A price covering only the change in the cost of non-water inputs would, of course, be too low and would tend to lead to excessive use of water.

Various changes can be made to elaborate this simple model of the determination of a commercial (and ideal) shadow price. One modification would allow for the return flow of part of the diversions made for some consumptive use to the water source. As a first approximation, supposing that no problems of pollution of the return flow arise, the shadow price can be determined by treating the demands of various actual and potential users as net of return flows, rather than gross.[7] Another modification, very important for our subsequent analysis, drops the assumption that demands and supplies of water can be viewed as constant over the relevant period of time. While a number of actual cases of intertemporal variation in demands and supplies occur in the industry, that of variations between the winter and spring period of heavy runoff and light irrigation use and the summer period of heavy use and light runoff will serve as a prototype. Intertemporal variations in the shadow price obviously occur in this situation; the interesting case for analysis, however, is that in which on-stream dams and reservoirs are constructed to accumulate "winter" water for "summer" use.

This case is complex enough to warrant graphical analysis. Let us consider the determination of the shadow price for water from a single source when storage reservoir operations are involved, and where all bidders in the hypothetical market are still competing consumptive users of water (power generation being neglected). The typical function of on-stream reservoirs is to store the flow of water in periods of maximum natural runoff (which are generally also periods of minimum aggregate demand) and to release it for use—both consumptive use such as irrigation (here considered) and substantially nonconsumptive use such as power generation (here neglected)—in periods of lesser natural runoff (which are also generally periods of greater aggregate demand). The reservoirs thus essentially shift part of the available supply of water from some time periods to others, in order to make a given flow of water available in such a time pattern that it has the greatest net value in use. We ignore variations of demand and flow within the respective seasons and concentrate only on differing seasonal rates.

In Figure 14, let us suppose that the sum of all summer streamside demands for water from a given river is represented by line D_s, and that they are all demands for consumptive use which will generate no return flows to the stream. The purpose of reservoirs is then only to increase the supply of water for consumptive use in the summer. Let us suppose also that the natural supply in the

[7] This situation is characterized as a first approximation because, in fact, water returned to a river is either unavailable to bidders upstream of points of return, or available to them only at substantial extra cost for carrying it back upstream. The situation may thus arise in which downstream bidders are faced with a sufficiently abundant downstream flow that they effectively express no demand for upstream water, or for the natural flow of the river, or at any rate no demand at the price established for such water by upstream bidders. In this event, more than one shadow price for streamside water may develop, and upstream and downstream bidders may find themselves in separate markets, for natural flow and return flow respectively. The complex analysis which demonstrates the determination of water prices and allocation in such a situation will not be presented here. Where our simplified analysis is applicable (where downstream bidders face a sufficiently short downstream flow that they effectively enter the market for upstream or natural flow), it is clear that downstream returns to the river which are economically available to no further bidders should not be included in the total available supply, and that demands for water of bidders generating such returns should not be measured net of these returns.

summer period (the natural summer flow without storage reservoirs) is OQ_n. The corresponding summer streamside shadow price of water will then be P_n, and interbidder transactions in a hypothetical market should allocate this supply so that all bidding users attain the same streamside net value of marginal product of water, equal to P_n. In this situation, it should be profitable (and socially desirable) for any bidder (or independent entrepreneur who can sell water) to extend the summer supply at the expense of the winter supply if he can do so at a cost less than the price P_n, and to continue extending it until the marginal cost of increasing the summer supply equals the marginal streamside value or shadow price of water in the summer market.

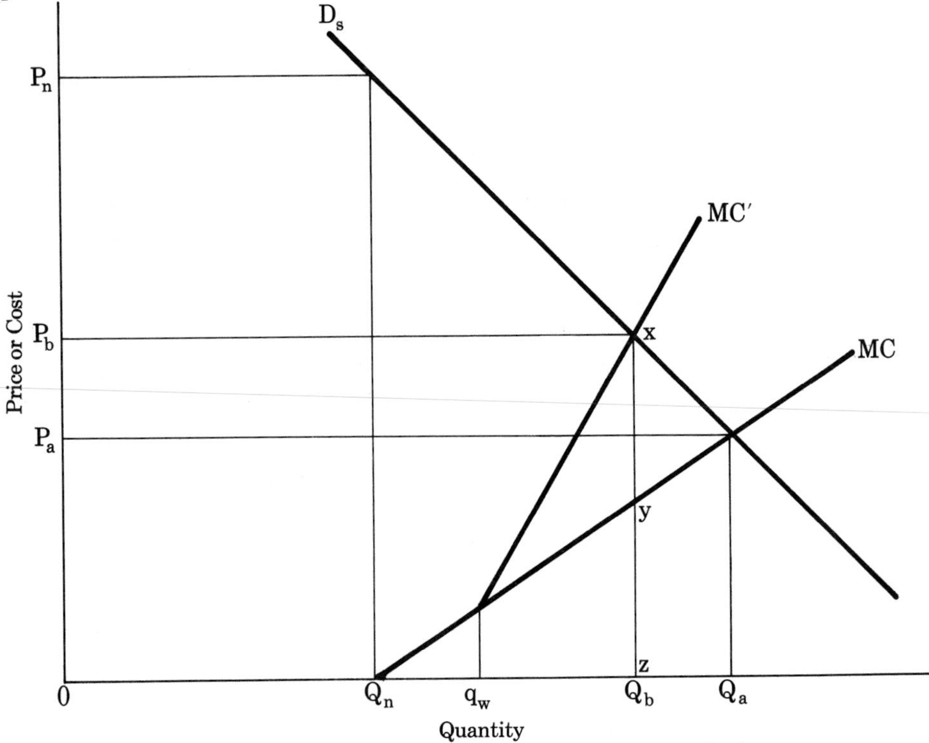

Figure 14. Optimal interseasonal transfer of water for a single use.

This extension will involve constructing and operating storage reservoirs, and thus incurring costs for these facilities. Water supply beyond the natural flow, therefore, unlike the natural flow, will have a cost in terms of non-water inputs, rather than merely a scarcity value. Let us suppose that the summer supply of water can be increased continuously by augmenting reservoir capacity (and operating it) at increasing marginal costs for non-water inputs as shown by the line MC. The quantity OQ_n is available without cost in terms of non-water inputs; added quantities can be secured at marginal costs for non-water inputs shown on MC. If these are the only costs to be reckoned (as they would be if water in the winter market remained a free good after subtracting Q_nQ_a from the winter supply), investment would be justified in reservoir capacity sufficient to extend summer supply to OQ_a, with which total supply of summer water would have a streamside shadow price of P_a.

Before analyzing this equilibrium, however, let us consider another possible element in cost—namely, the streamside shadow price in the winter market of water transferred to the summer market, or the opportunity cost in the winter market of the transferred water. This may not remain at zero as successive amounts of water up to Q_nQ_a are transferred from the winter market. In that case, we must add to the marginal cost of each unit of transferred water (as measured by costs of non-water inputs) its marginal opportunity cost in the winter market. This addition begins at that level of transfer at which a positive shadow price for winter water emerges; and increases as the quantity of transfer increases. In Figure 14, let us suppose that a positive shadow price for winter water emerges as transfers exceed the quantity Q_nq_w, and the shadow price increases as transfers increase thereafter. Then the marginal cost of non-water inputs plus the opportunity cost in the winter market of transferred water could be represented by MC up to the supply Oq_w and by MC' at larger supplies.

With the opportunity cost of transferred water in the winter market included in the cost of supplying summer water, a process of investment in storage and bidding for water by both summer and winter users would establish the price P_b for streamside water in the summer market and the total summer supply OQ_b. At this equilibrium point, the opportunity cost of transferred water in the winter market would be xy, and this would also be the streamside shadow price of water in the winter market. This opportunity cost and winter price would be equal to the summer price of water p_b (xz) minus the marginal cost for non-water inputs of supplying the added summer quantity Q_nQ_b, or minus yz. Given the assumptions, the hypothetical process of price determination just outlined should result in an optimal allocation of water as between bidders in the winter market and bidders in the summer market, and as among bidders in each separate market.

We can now develop another model of the determination of a shadow price by adding the production of electric power to the uses represented in the bidding for the water supply of a given river. The consideration of power producers as bidders for water introduces a new element into the analysis of commercial shadow prices for water from a single river source. Whereas all consumptive users of water drawing on a source are generally putting water to competitive uses (except in the case of usable return flows), so that the water taken by one user reduces the amount available to others, power producers using the source often do not compete significantly with each other or with consumptive users. Rather, power producers often tend to be complementary *inter se,* in the sense that use of the water of a river by one power producer does not tend to reduce appreciably the amount of water available to other power producers on the same river. Similarly, power production often tends to complement consumptive uses on the same stream, in that it does not appreciably reduce the supply of water available for consumptive uses, so long as the power is produced upstream of the diversion points of all consumptive uses—and this is typically the case.

Consider the use of a given river flow (run-of-the-stream water unregulated by storage) by assorted power producers and consumptive users. Suppose that all power producers have demands for water which are strictly complementary with each other; that all consumptive users have demands which are entirely competitive with each other; and, further, that all demands of the power producers are strictly complementary with all consumptive demands. For each of the component power-producer demands there would be a corresponding individual shadow price (but not an opportunity cost), which a party "owning" the river or its power sites could collect as a rent from the producer in question. The price that could be collected from all power producers together would be determined by the conjunction with the total water supply of an aggregate power-producer demand obtained by adding *vertically* the several demands of the separate producers. The aggregate demand of the competing consumptive users would be obtained by adding *horizontally* their separate demands for water, and the conjunction of this aggregate demand with total water supply would establish a shadow price and opportunity cost for water for consumptive use. The shadow prices for power uses and consumptive uses would be established independently and would not tend to coincide.[8]

When we consider the case of interseasonal transfers of water in the setting of seasonal variations in demand and supply, the assumption that power uses are fully complementary with each other and with consumptive uses is no longer tenable, even as a first approximation. Winter power use becomes competitive with summer power use; and consumptive use in either season becomes competitive with power use in the other, even though our earlier complementarity assumptions hold within each season. Then further there is a logically unique pairing of complementary uses: the vertical aggregate of total summer consumptive demands and total summer power demands competes with a comparable aggregate of winter demands. And in terms of Figure 14, both the summer demand (D_s) and the winter demand (the difference between MC and MC') can be viewed as vertical summations of power generation and aggregate consumptive demands in the separate seasons. Price p_b continues to designate the appropriate shadow price in the summer market, including the marginal costs of storage, yz, and the marginal opportunity costs of water in the winter market, xy, vertically aggregated for the complementary winter demands.

The case of interseasonal transfers and independent demands merits a more complete analysis in terms of Figure 15. The problem is that of determining interseasonal transfers and commercial shadow prices for water when both consumptive users of water and power producers are participants in a hypothetical market for water in a single source. In this case, any reservoirs built for storage and interseasonal transfer of water will be used by, or serve jointly, both consumptive users and power producers. If the summer demands for power and consumptive use are strictly complementary (which we will assume in this example), it is appropriate to add vertically the aggregate summer demand for consumptive use, D_c (itself a horizontal aggregation of all individual summer demands for con-

[8] For a more formal analysis of this and other cases, see Robert Dorfman, "Mathematical Models: The Multistructure Approach," in Arthur Maass, *et al.*, *Design of Water-Resource Systems* (1962), chap. 13. (This and other footnote references are cited in brief form when they are also included in the Bibliography.)

sumptive use), and the aggregate summer demand for power use, D_p (itself a vertical aggregation of all individual summer power demands if they are independent of each other), to arrive at a total aggregate summer demand for water in the two uses, ΣD in Figure 15. In this figure, let us also suppose that the natural summer supply of water is OQ_n, and that the marginal cost of transferring further water from the winter to the summer season for use, *inclusive of the opportunity cost of water in the winter market,* is represented by MC'.

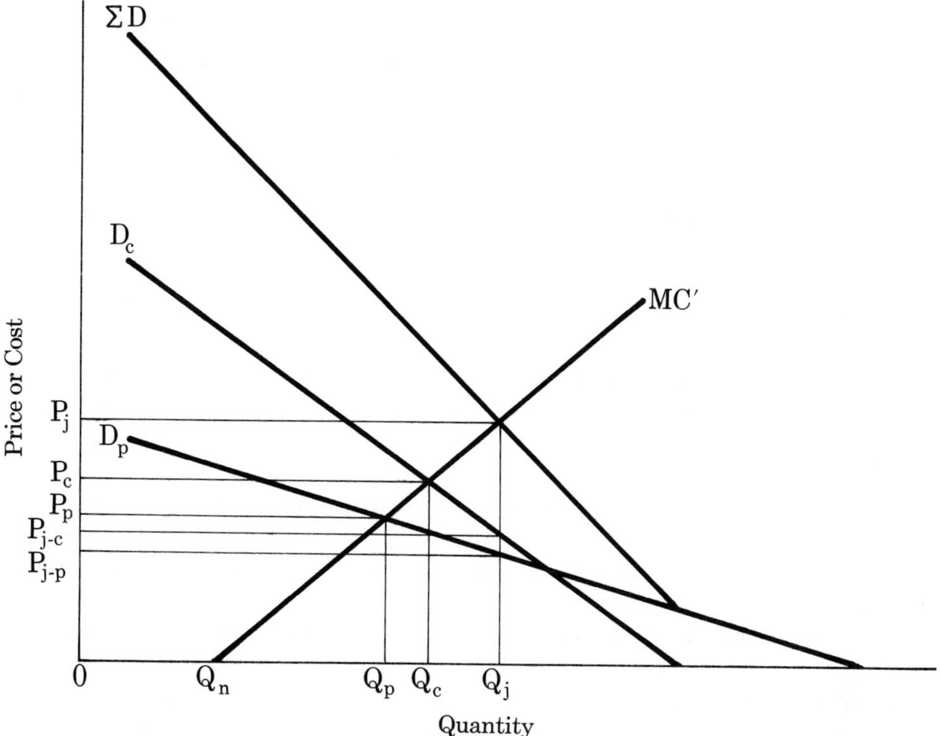

Figure 15. Optimal interseasonal transfer of water for joint uses.

In this situation, an optimal interseasonal allocation would require that consumptive users and power producers undertake a joint or cooperative venture in reservoir storage construction, adjusting reservoir capacity and interseasonal transfer in the light of joint benefits from summer water, as reflected in ΣD, and of the costs of transfer including the opportunity cost of transferred water in the combined uses in the winter market. They should expand joint reservoir capacity to transfer water until MC' equals the combined marginal value of transferred water as shown on ΣD, and thus transfer the amount of water Q_nQ_j to the summer market. At this point, the general criterion of extending investment for use until all marginal costs, inclusive of opportunity costs, equal total marginal value would be observed. The total shadow price for water in the summer market would be P_j, the shadow price for water for consumptive use in the summer market $P_{j\text{-}c}$, and the shadow price for water for summer power generation $P_{j\text{-}p}$. Both consumptive users as a group and power producers as a group would use the total quantity of water in the summer OQ_j, of which Q_nQ_j would be transferred water. The shadow prices $P_{j\text{-}c}$ and $P_{j\text{-}p}$ would be established by market transactions among consumptive users and among power users, and water allocated so that the respective marginal values were equated to the shadow prices. Moreover, the total summer shadow price P_j would equal the opportunity cost of water in the winter market (in power plus consumptive use), or the total shadow price for winter water, plus the marginal cost in terms of non-water inputs of transferring water to the summer market.

An inferior allocation would result if power producers and consumptive users did not undertake joint ventures, and if instead either group acted independently. Independent development of transfers oriented to power demands alone would in a hypothetical market tend to result in transferring only Q_nQ_p of water, and establishing a summer shadow price for water for power use of P_p (and a summer shadow price greater than $P_{j\text{-}c}$ for water for consumptive use). Independent transfers oriented to consumptive demands alone would result in transferring only Q_nQ_c of water, and establishing a summer shadow price for water for consumptive use of P_c (and a summer shadow price greater than $P_{j\text{-}p}$ for water for power use). Either result would be less than optimal. It should be noted, moreover, that the two independent transfers of the magnitudes indicated neither should be or would be undertaken simultaneously, since either one partly serves the water transfer needs of the other use. Any combination of independent developments other than one accomplishing the transfer Q_nQ_j would involve inferior inter-seasonal allocation of water.

The scarcity of water relative to demands on rivers and other sources of supply has developed slowly in Northern California. At the outset, water was a free good in most or all sources; progressively, first a few, then many, and finally nearly all water supplies from sources feeding the Central Valley and those in the urban and agricultural areas of the coastal basins and valleys became scarce, and proceeded to become more scarce over time. (At present, the only sources where commercial water scarcity does not exist is in the rivers of the north coastal region, where streamflows are great and local population and agricultural and industrial activity small, and even in that area there is evidently some scarcity value of water for in-stream recreational uses.) The study of the conduct of water agencies in a situation of water scarcity thus necessarily assumes the form of a historical study, covering many decades, of evolving conduct in response first to an emerging scarcity and then to an increasing scarcity of water.

With local scarcities of water, from given sources drawn upon to supply local users, emerging at various times and developing at various rates, different shadow prices have prevailed in the many local markets (including zero shadow prices in some markets) at any given time. The differences in shadow prices can persist because water demand and water supply are not distributed over the land in the same pattern, and because the costs of transporting water have been, and remain, quite high relative to its net marginal value. Thus, substantial differences may prevail among the shadow prices of water in various local areas without the differentials growing large enough to overcome the cost of transporting water from any one to another.

During a historical process in which local scarcities of water emerge and grow, therefore, there will be a period during which individual localities depending on individual water sources remain insular, since no differences in shadow prices have developed among them which will economically justify the transfer of water from one local market to another. But as local scarcities increase in a situation in which the geographical patterns of water demand and supply are distinctly different, a point will be reached where there is economic advantage to transporting water from some local sources to the relatively nearby localities of others. And the number of such advantageous opportunities for transferring water will increase as water becomes scarcer. At some stage in the historical process of developing scarcities, moreover, some interregional transfers of water involving very costly transportation over long distances tend to become economically advantageous. As this process occurs, local latent markets for water tend to merge more and more into larger subregional latent markets, and subregional latent markets into latent regional markets. Within these regional markets, the shadow prices in various latent submarkets differ, but all tend to be systematically interrelated in a pattern established by relative degrees of local water scarcity and by the costs of transporting water. Ultimately, all latent submarkets in a large region may tend to be included in a single latent water market, with water having some positive shadow price in each of them.

It is thus useful to supplement the preceding analysis dealing with the allocation of scarce water from a single source with a brief analysis of the manner in which market forces would hypothetically tend to allocate water from different sources within a broader market. For a hypothetical submarket with access to water from an alternative source, the marginal cost of importing it will include, along with non-water costs, the net opportunity cost of the water at the source from which it is brought, adjusted for any differences in the costs of local delivery between imported and local water. In this hypothetical submarket, the general principle is that water should be imported whenever its marginal cost is less than the market price for local water at the source in the absence of imports; and it should be imported in such a quantity that the marginal cost of the total supply (including local water) is made equal to the net marginal value of water for all users in the importing submarket.

The application of this principle is most simply illustrated in Figure 16. There it is supposed that a given local streamside supply is available without "production" costs of storage, and that an imported supply can be brought in at a certain constant marginal cost of transport from a source where it has no opportunity cost in any quantity demanded. In this figure, ΣD represents the aggregate local streamside demand, made up of the component demands of two local bidders, the demands D_1 and D_2. The local supply is OQ_1 and MC represents the marginal transport cost of any supply of imported water.[9] If no imports were made, the local market price would be established at P_1, at which bidder 1 would use the

[9] Reduced by any excess of the unit cost of local delivery of local water over the unit cost of local delivery of imported water, or increased by any opposite excess. For purposes of simplification, we will assume that any such local delivery-cost differential applies equally to all local users.

amount Oq_1 and bidder 2 the amount Oq_2 (the two amounts adding to the total local supply OQ_1). If imports could be made available at the relevant cost level of MC, a proper market adjustment would involve the importation of the amount cc' and the establishment of the price of all water (local and imported) at P_g, with an aggregate supply of OQ_g. At this price, bidder 1 should use the quantity Oq_1' and bidder 2 the quantity Oq_2'.

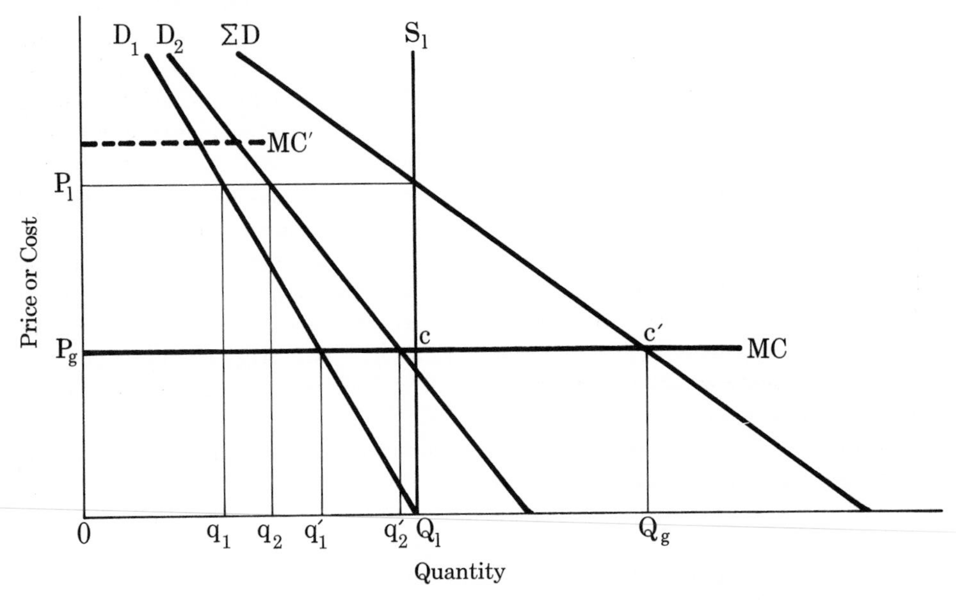

Figure 16. Optimal water import volume with constant costs of import.

Suppose that bidder 1 held rights to the whole local water supply. It would be definitely uneconomic—disadvantageous to bidder 1, and of no advantage to bidder 2—if bidder 1 were to keep all of the local water, OQ_1, for his own use and if the larger quantity Oq_2' were imported to satisfy the demands of bidder 2 at the price P_g. Bidder 1 would under this arrangement gain less value product in using the incremental water $q_1'Q_1$ than he could gain cash by selling it; bidder 2 would be no better off; and the "excess" import $q_1'Q_1$ would effectively cost more than it added to the value product of water. This simple observation should be underlined, because important allocative errors may be made in determining the quantity of interbasin transfers of water (in the direction depicted in Figure 16 by the importation of Oq_2' of water rather than cc') due to the unwillingness of holders of abundant local water rights to sell part of their water at the market price it would command to local holders of insufficient local water rights.

Stubborn holders of dominant local water rights who refuse to sell water to other users at its opportunity price can (and, we shall argue, do) set the stage for an economically excessive importation of water to satisfy the demands of local users with inadequate local water rights. Indeed, imports can occur where none at all is justified. In Figure 16, for example, if bidder 1 utilized all of the local water, bidder 2 would be willing to pay a cost for some imported water which was in excess of what a free local market price would be in the absence of imports. Thus, he would be willing to pay for imported water at a cost higher than P_g, such as MC' (receiving a quantity of imports corresponding to the point where his demand curve intersects MC'). Such imports would tend to occur in the absence of intervention by a higher government to rationalize the local allocation. This case illustrates the significant way in which local misallocations can distort the economic environment of investment decisions in interbasin transfer facilities.

Summary and conclusions: rules for optimal conduct

To summarize the preceding models for determination of shadow prices in particular cases, we shall set forth a simplified statement of the rules that would have to be followed by all decision units in the water industry in order for ideal shadow prices to prevail in long-run equilibrium. Such a summary provides the requisite background for the following chapters on actual patterns of conduct by affording a quick indication of the nature and direction of the resource misallocation presumptively associated with any given departure of actual from optimal conduct. We shall assume throughout the following summary that no decision units face problems of uncertainty, or of information being limited or costly. We shall not assume, however, that each local agency is motivated to take into account externalities and effects on the public good when making its decisions; and shall make specific provision for rules governing the optimal intervention by higher governmental regulatory bodies to deal with these problems.

Given such governmental interference, the main guideline for any water agency making long-run plans is that it should supply water to a particular group of users, or put water to a particular use, only in such an amount that the long-run marginal cost of supply is equal to the long-run marginal value of water in use. This long-run marginal cost should be measured to include not only the agency's private non-water costs, but also the net opportunity cost of water to the agency, as measured by the excess of the implicit commercial-market value of marginal units of water taken over its private non-water marginal costs. This net opportunity cost at any margin is measurable generally as the streamside commercial-market value (or shadow price) of water used less the agency's marginal private costs of storage, or as the wellhead open-market value of water less the agency's private costs of pumping ground water. Fulfilling this principle exactly would be difficult in practice because, lacking organized markets, the shadow price or opportunity cost of scarce water can only be guessed. But failing to fulfill it is easy (and such failure can be identified more or less easily), for to do so the agency only needs to disregard the marginal net opportunity costs of water and determine the quantity of scarce water it will supply or use at the excessive level at which its private non-water marginal cost is equal to its marginal value in use.

There are, in addition, two subsidiary rules for the water agency to follow. First, in undertaking development of reservoir storage for interseasonal transfer of water, it should always make optimal cooperative arrangements for joint development of storage with other parties where joint and complementary use of storage and water transfers is economically feasible. By this means, it can equate long-run marginal cost to marginal value when the latter is defined as combined value to joint users of the storage. Second, the agency, having determined the total quantity of water it will supply to a number of users, should allocate it among users so that the net marginal value of water to each user supplied (net of separate costs of distribution) is the same. If distribution costs vary among users, the agency may accomplish this by differential pricing, or by direct rationing under a regime in which prices are used only to collect revenues sufficient to cover agency outlays.

The way in which the water agency accomplishes this allocation may not be a matter of indifference, however. The agency supplying water to consumptive users should also properly determine its service area, so that the area includes only those users which it can supply more cheaply than any other agency (which may draw water from another source)—but the area must include all of the users it can supply more cheaply. This determination could be made by a separate calculation process, but it could also be arrived at by a system of differential pricing under which each user paid a price for water equal to the full marginal cost of supplying him, all users being left free to change suppliers in order to obtain the cheapest water.

Where water agencies hold rights to the use of water from a natural source, similar rules apply to the decision about making net sales (or purchases) of water or water rights. All agencies and self-supplying users holding rights to scarce water in excess of the amounts they should supply according to the principles stated above should sell the excess to other bidders. These sales may be accomplished by selling either water or water rights. The sale price should be competitive, determined under a system in which agencies with excess supplies simply offer them on the market to all bidders, and in which bidders do not restrict their offers in order to depress the price of water; users should freely transfer their custom among agencies in order to secure the lowest price for water.

These rules for optimal conduct by water agencies would establish "ideal" shadow prices, and correspondingly optimal allocations, only if higher governmental units intervened optimally to eliminate sources of discrepancy between commercial and ideal prices. The types of interventions in question are those identified in the general literature of welfare economics as appropriate to deal with external effects and the presence of "public goods." Briefly, the form such optimal interventions would take in the setting of the water industry is something like this:

1) Commercial bidders should be forced to recognize external effects on other bidders, whether adverse or favorable, by taxes or subsidies that alter their marginal costs. If *A*'s applications of irrigation water create problems of an excessively high water table for user *B*, then *A*'s applications should be taxed by an amount equal to the estimated marginal disbenefits to *B*, thereby reducing *A*'s use of water to an extent determined by the elasticity of his derived demand. The total demand for water from the source in question would thereby be reduced

at any given price and, if *A* is a significantly large user, the commercial shadow price would fall. Another important example of such externalities arises in the case of ground-water mining; in this case, the opportunity costs of water extracted by a particular pumper are perhaps most easily viewed as an external diseconomy in the form of increased pumping costs for other users of the same ground-water basin. Whatever theoretical view is taken of this case, appropriate governmental intervention requires a tax on water pumped to offset the discounted present value of the increase in marginal costs of pumping occasioned for all other users.[10]

2) Governmental units should intervene to reserve or bid for water to supply uses or groups of users which institutionally cannot be organized to bid correctly on their own behalf. The situation of these uses—principally flood control, navigation, recreation, and salinity repulsion—is that of a "public good." The demand curve for water to serve such uses can be constructed hypothetically by a vertical aggregation of the functions showing the net value of marginal product to individual complementary users. Although we shall argue in Chapter 14 that some of the significance of "public good" status among the uses for water in Northern California results from public policy and not from economic necessity, the proposition remains that government must intervene to see that such uses are supplied with water to the extent that the value of the appropriately defined net value of marginal product equals its opportunity cost.[11] If the demand function imputed to the public good is known, government can act either by bidding on the basis of this function or reserving a quantity of water that would be optimal in light of the function and of competing demands for the water supply.

3) Government should employ taxes, subsidies, or equivalent quantitative regulations to offset externalities that result from, and are related to, the method of use or the facilities associated with the water's use, rather than the quantity of water taken by commercial users. Two empirically significant examples will illustrate this rule. First, return flows of irrigation and industrial process water to streams are often polluted to some degree in relation to the needs of downstream users. If we regard the "commodity" being sold or allocated as "water" of natural quality, then the pollution must be viewed as an external diseconomy. What needs to be discouraged in this case is not the use of the water by the party who pollutes, but rather the act of polluting itself.[12] Second, a similar problem may arise in the construction of physical facilities for the storage and diversion of water, especially dams. A major example is found in the effect of dams on fish habitat and their tendency to destroy migratory fish runs. Direct intervention of public authority would seem to be indicated in such cases, and could involve restricting heights and sites of dams, requiring that effective fish ladders be included in dam designs to help preserve migratory fish runs, and so forth. Such

[10] See J. W. Milliman, "Commonality, the Price System, and Use of Water Supplies," *Southern Economic Journal,* XXII (April 1956), 426–37.

[11] The calculation of taxes and subsidies to offset external effects, as specified in the preceding rule, should of course include those external effects impinging upon water uses with the status of public goods.

[12] A tax on water use by the polluter could achieve optimal results only if the extent of pollution bears a fixed relation to the gross or net quantity of water diverted. See Allen V. Kneese, *Water Pollution: Economic Aspects and Research Needs* (1962), chap. 2.

intervention would tend to raise the cost and price of summer water (and to restrict the degree of shifts from winter to summer markets), the added costs being appropriately paid by the consumptive users and power producers involved. Intervention should be so limited, however, that it would not proceed beyond the point where added costs of water to commercial users would exceed added benefits to users who do not bid on or consume the water.

If these rules for optimal governmental intervention were followed, as well as the rules for optimal commercial conduct by the bidders for water from a single source, then an "ideal" price would prevail in the market in question, as well as an optimal allocation of water.

In concluding, we can briefly extend the optimal commercial rules to those agencies contemplating or engaging in interbasin transfers of water. Where a single export source and a single import destination are involved, water transfer should be made in such quantity that the marginal cost of the total supply in the import area (including local supply) is equated to the marginal value of water in the import area, marginal cost being calculated to include the net opportunity cost of imported water at the export source. With multiple export sources and multiple import destinations, a general over-all rule is to allocate so as to maximize the excess of the aggregate value of exported water over the aggregate costs of exported water (the latter being measured to include aggregate net opportunity costs of water at the export sources).[13] Some corollaries of this rule are the following:

First, if there are alternative export sources which can supply water imports to a single locality at marginal costs below the local shadow price of water without imports, the source or combination of sources of exports should be chosen which affords the greatest excess added aggregate values over added aggregate costs, the marginal cost of imports in any event being equated to the local shadow price that prevails when the total supply includes local as well as imported water. Scale economies in transportation from a single export source may influence the determination of the optimal source pattern. Ordinarily, the optimal choice of source or pattern of sources will be such as to secure the lowest attainable local shadow price after imports, marginal cost of water being equated to this price. But with significant scale economies in transportation and certain constraints present, it is conceivable that securing the lowest attainable shadow price would not be optimal.[14]

Second, assume that water from a single export source is demanded by two or

[13] These aggregates are properly measured diagrammatically as areas under the relevant ranges of marginal value and marginal cost functions.

[14] Suppose that either source *A* or source *B* can supply a locality with substantial scale economies in transport, so that each has a markedly declining marginal cost curve as its exports increase, and that the marginal cost curve for supply from *A* lies significantly below that for supply from *B*. But suppose also that *A*'s supply is exhausted at a point slightly short of the quantity at which its marginal cost would equal marginal value in the importing submarket. In this case, it may be optimal for the market to take all of *A*'s supply, and then a remainder from *B* at a marginal cost which, because the remainder is small, is above the shadow price which would be established if *B* were the sole supplier. A higher-than-attainable shadow price will then be established, but the addition to aggregate net benefits will be maximized. A planning commission rather than a market would probably have to be relied upon to produce the solution. Other special cost conditions resulting from limits on the supplies from specific sources may also result in the emergence of similarly atypical optimum conditions for allocation.

more competing importing localities, either of which it can supply at a marginal cost below the local shadow price without imports, and either so as to produce a greater aggregate net advantage than if an alternative export source were used. In this case, the exports should generally be allocated between or among the submarkets so as to equate the marginal cost of imported water to the shadow price after imports in each submarket, *provided* that as this is done its total export supply is not so expanded that it becomes a more costly source than alternative export sources because of elevated net opportunity costs at the source (the height of which is determined by the combined volume exported to all submarkets).[15] If this proviso is not met, the export source should supply less than all, and perhaps only one, of the competing submarkets, but still according to the same allocational principle. This is to say that the indicated allocational procedure may cut out one or more competitive importing localities as importers of water from the source; it would certainly do so if they have alternative sources; and would do so, even if they do not have alternative sources, if their transport costs are relatively high and the net opportunity cost of water from the export source rises continuously as its total exports increase. If scale economies in transport are important, moreover, the gains from leaving some importing localities to be supplied by higher-cost sources or not supplied at all are increased.

Third, any source which can supply water for export to any localities at a marginal cost which is below the local shadow prices without imports and also below the effective marginal costs of supplying them from alternative sources (such alternative costs being established after all demands are brought into play, and including net opportunity costs at sources) should export to such localities in a volume such that it equates marginal cost to local shadow prices after imports in each (subject to restrictions stated in the second rule outlined above). This third rule of course does not imply that, even with water scarce in many localities of use, every distant available source of water for import should be tapped.

In a multisource, multimarket complex, most, but not all, of the conditions established for choice by a single import area among alternative export sources and for the choice by a single export source among alternative import areas can (with generality) be simultaneously satisfied. A complex simultaneous solution is required to find the optimum optimorum of over-all allocations. This circumstance is the basis of some doubts as to whether an unregulated market process would automatically produce the best results.

Investment Criteria

In the foregoing pages we have set forth some norms which should govern the allocation of water among uses, users, and places and time of use, and have derived certain rudimentary criteria which should guide a water agency in determining the quantity of water to be supplied in the long run. These criteria have so far been stated in terms of the static analysis of conventional price theory, wherein the passage of time and the fact that long-run costs and long-run marginal

[15] And provided, of course, that it does not run out of water.

values are not incurred or realized simultaneously are not explicitly taken into account.

In the water industry as in other industries, however, many costs of supplying outputs (water services) are incurred at times well in advance of those when outputs and their values will be realized. Investments involving current cost outlays for capital facilities result in the yield of outputs of goods or services at future times, together with the incursion of other connected costs at such future times. Thus, the realization of the net values which accrue from investments are deferred in time from the dates of the original investments. This tendency is especially marked in the water industry; in it, most of the costs of supplying water are investments in durable facilities, and these facilities are exceptionally long-lived, so that returns from a major investment will typically be recovered over a period of from fifty to a hundred years. Investment decisions therefore predominantly determine water outputs. Once capital facilities for supplying water are put in place, moreover, the major long-run outlines of the level of water development and the allocation of water among uses and users have been determined in a semipermanent fashion, and are only subject to modification over long periods mainly by added investments. Further, any initial set of investments makes a large range of alternative investments uneconomic thereafter for a long time, and narrows the range of economic alternatives for further investment.

Since investment in long-lived facilities plays a dominant role in the water industry, time lags between cost outlay and value realization are long and important. It then becomes essential that we translate the "timeless" criteria for the determination of water supply by an agency, developed in the preceding section, into criteria taking time into account for the determination of the amount and type of its investment in capital facilities for supplying water.

The entry of time into calculations to determine the socially optimal quantity of water that should be supplied for given uses and users in the long run has two main consequences. First, a rate of interest or discount should be employed in the process of determining the relationship of costs incurred at an earlier time to net value yields which are realized at a later time. This rate of interest or discount should effectively be that rate of "time preference" for present as compared to future income which is appropriate both in the light of the psychology of investors and marginal rates of return available on alternative investments. Second, because the magnitudes of future net returns to be realized from present investments are generally never known with certainty, appropriate means of allowing for uncertainty must be incorporated into the calculations of optimal investments.

Given an appropriate rate of interest and an acceptable means of allowing for uncertainty, a rudimentary criterion for optimal investment in water resource development is readily derived. Formulating a reasonably adequate operational criterion, however, requires more. First, because numerous alternative possible rates of interest or discount may be suggested as appropriate in discounting future returns and costs, some reasoned selection of the most appropriate rate of interest must be made. Second, the same in general applies to selection of the most appropriate means of allowing for uncertainty in calculating yields from investments. Third, an operational criterion for investment must be elaborated sufficiently to take account of at least two peculiarities of the natural setting and technology of the water industry which complicate the problem of determining the optimal level and type of investment. These are: (a) the fact that the sizes of investment projects can frequently be varied only by substantial discontinuous increments, so that "ideal" conditions of marginal equality cannot be achieved; and (b) the frequent availability of mutually exclusive alternative project designs (or project technologies which would accomplish the same general function and all be economically feasible) among which the investing agency should make a rational choice. Finally, some attention must be given to the proper selection among both mutually compatible and alternative investment projects, all economically feasible, by a water agency which operates with an effective budgetary constraint.

Because of these complexities, we will proceed here to develop investment criteria in several stages, considering in turn:

1) The determination of the optimal size or scale of investment in an individual water project (including determination of when it should not be undertaken at all) with a given rate of interest or discount, in the absence of uncertainty about future net yields from the project, and without budgetary constraints. This will be done for two situations: (a) where the scale of investment may be varied continuously; and (b) where the scale of the investment may be varied only by discontinuous increments.
2) The optimal selection among mutually exclusive investment projects, again assuming a given interest rate, no uncertainty, and no budgetary constraints.
3) The optimal selection of mutually compatible investment projects and of alternative projects subject to budgetary constraints.
4) The appropriate choice of a rate of interest or discount.
5) The appropriate treatment of uncertainty concerning future yields and costs.

Before considering these matters, however, we offer a few remarks concerning some terminology to be employed in the analyses.

The uses of the term "benefits"

An initial task in formulating investment criteria is to establish a measure of the value of yields from an investment in each of a series of future years. This value of yields in each year will be an aggregate amount derived by multiplying the physical quantity of yields in that year by an appropriate unit value.[16] Consistent with our reasoning in the preceding section, this appropriate value in any year should be the marginal value of output in that year, and the aggregate for any year j should be $(q_j \cdot mv_j)$. If the output of each year were sold at a price equal to its marginal value (which is the price it would command in a competitive market), the value $(q_j \cdot mv_j)$ could be simply designated as an annual total revenue from the investment.

The "revenue" designation is generally unsatisfactory, however, for two reasons: first, because some of the yields of water projects are not sold or easily saleable, so that their marginal values are not matched by revenues collected by the invest-

[16] Several quantities and several values will be involved in the calculation if several different water services are supplied.

ing agency or anyone else; or second, because some saleable yields are sold to users at prices below their marginal values. In this event, revenues collected from the sale of services are not a good measure of the value $(q_j \cdot mv_j)$, and the term "revenues" is inappropriate for designating this value aggregate. Faced with this problem, analysts of water resource development have widely adopted the term "benefits" to refer to the aggregate values of yields of water projects. Correspondingly, the adoption of the term benefits to designate these values *may* signify only that we are counting the aggregate values of all services provided by a project—whether sold or not, and regardless of price if sold—and moreover are valuing the output of any service in any year at its marginal value, so as to arrive for any year j at an aggregate value or benefit of $b_j = (q_j \cdot mv_j)$.

This terminological innovation has turned out not to be a simple one, however, because the use of the term "benefits" in formulating investment criteria is frequently intended to indicate not only that the value of nonreimbursed water services are included, but also that all services in any year are valued not at their *marginal values* but at their *average values* to users, the latter including so-called buyers' surpluses.

The difference between marginal value and average value is illustrated in Figure 17. There the marginal value of the physical yield of a given water service to a group of users in a given year is represented by the line *MV,* relating this marginal value to the quantity of service supplied. (To simplify, we will suppose arbitrarily that marginal value declines continuously as the output of the service is increased from zero.) Suppose that the water service is supplied in the quantity *Oq.* The marginal value of *Oq* is *qm,* and the aggregate benefit from the service, if all units are valued at the marginal value of the quantity supplied, is *Oqmb,* the equivalent of $(q_j \cdot mv_j)$.

In a sense, however, the total value of *Oq* to users is greater than *q* multiplied by *mv,* because although the marginal unit supplied has a value of *qm,* the inframarginal units have higher marginal values as shown along *MV* between *d* and *m.* If each unit of the quantity *Oq* is measured at its own marginal value, the "total value" of *Oq* is measured by the area *Oqmd* (including in addition to the area *Oqmb* a "buyers' surplus" measured by *bmd*). This is the total value in the sense that the buyers, if faced with an all-or-nothing bargain, would be willing to pay as much as *Oqmd* for *Oq* rather than get no water at all. The same total value, inclusive of buyers' surplus, may be arrived at by calculating for each alternative quantity of water supplied the average of the individual marginal values of all units included in that quantity—in this sense an average value of each quantity. This average value is shown as *AV* in Figure 17. Then the total value of *Oq,* including buyers' surplus, is alternatively measured as *Oqac,* which is equal to *Oqmd.*[17]

[17] The simplifying condition supposed in Figure 17 that *MV* declines monotonically as output is increased from zero will not hold in many cases, as where the water service in question is a factor used in further production. It may rise and then fall as *q* is extended, and with it *AV* will also rise and fall. In this case, the same principle of measurement applies, but it is necessary to incorporate *AV* in calculations applying to any segment of *MV* under analysis if all of *MV* is not shown or known, in order to assure a correct measurement of total value. For this reason, measures such as *Oqac* are preferred to measures such as *Oqmd.*

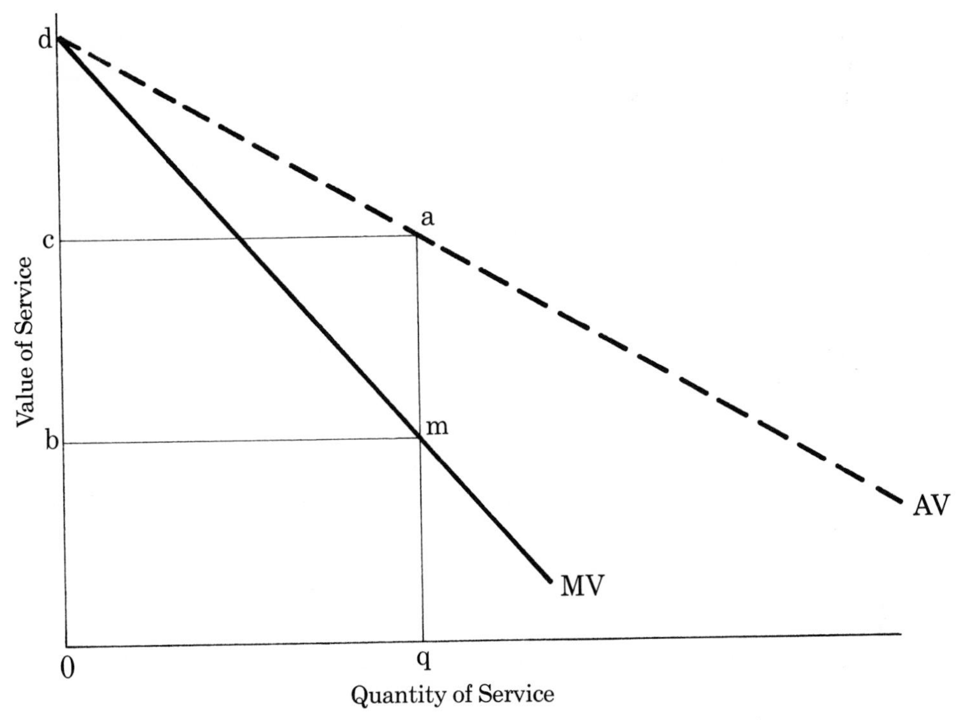

Figure 17. Marginal and average benefits of water supply.

We thus have two alternative measures of the value of aggregate benefits derived from a given quantity of water service:

1) Quantity of service multiplied by the marginal value of service—designated as $b_j = (q_j \cdot mv_j)$ for any year j—as represented by *Oqmb* in Figure 17.
2) Quantity of service multiplied by the average value of service—which we may represent as $b'_j = (q_j \cdot av_j)$ for any year j—as represented by *Oqac* or *Oqmd* in Figure 17.

The former measure excludes, and the latter includes, buyers' surplus in the aggregate value of benefits. For some analytical purposes we will wish to refer to the first measure and for others to the second, but clarity will be enhanced if we consistently designate which measure is being used in formulating investment criteria.

The optimal scale of a single investment project

A general rudimentary norm for the amount of water an agency should supply to a given group of users in an appropriately defined service area, as developed in our "timeless" long-run analysis above, was that it should supply such a quantity that the long-run marginal cost of supplying it (inclusive of the net marginal opportunity cost of water) should equal the long-run marginal value of the water to users. In converting this norm into a criterion for investment in the absence of budgetary constraints, we will suppose initially that the agency has optimally selected a water source, dam site (if any), diversion point, transport route, and general technique; that it views with certainty or assigns unquestioned magnitudes to future physical yields, costs, and marginal and average values; that it has adopted a satisfactory rate of interest or discount for comparing present and future values; and that the size of its investment and the quantity of water it supplies can be varied continuously by small increments over any relevant range.[18]

In this situation, the agency accepts the following fixed magnitudes:

1) i, the applicable rate of interest or discount per annum, and
2) n, the number of years during which the contemplated project will provide service.

And it must determine the following variable magnitudes:

3) I_o, the initial investment in capital equipment for the project, made at time zero;
4) A series of quantities of water service supplied in each of the years from year one to year n, with the quantity designated as q_j for any year j, and the series as: $q_1, q_2, q_3 \ldots\ldots q_n$.
5) A corresponding series of marginal values of water service supplied in each of the same years, with marginal value designated as mv_j for any year j, and the series as: $mv_1, mv_2, mv_3 \ldots\ldots mv_n$.
6) A derived series of the aggregate value of benefits from water service in each of the same years, as valued at the marginal value of water in each year, with the benefit designated as b_j for any year j, and the series as: $b_1, b_2, b_3 \ldots\ldots b_n$, where $b_j = (q_j \cdot mv_j)$.
7) A corresponding series of the average values of water service supplied in each of the same years, with average value designated as av_j for any year j, and the series as: $av_1, av_2, av_3 \ldots\ldots av_n$.
8) A derived series of the total value of benefits from water service in each of the same years, as valued at the average value of water in each year, with the benefit designated as b'_j for any year j, and the series as $b_1', b_2', b_3' \ldots\ldots b_n'$, where $b_j' = (q_j \cdot av_j)$.
9) A corresponding series of operating and maintenance costs in each of the same years, with such costs designated as o_j for any year j, and the series as: $o_1, o_2, o_3 \ldots\ldots o_n$.
10) A corresponding series of the net opportunity costs of water supplied in each of the same years, with such costs designated as p_j for any year j, and the series as: $p_1, p_2, p_3 \ldots\ldots p_n$.

The agency must now consider various possible magnitudes for I_o, subject to the general conditions that as I_o increases, q_j will increase; mv_j and av_j will decrease over the relevant range; b_j will either increase or decrease; b_j' will in-

[18] Further, all dollar magnitudes, present and future, are assumed to be stated in terms of dollars of equal purchasing power.

crease over any economically relevant range;[19] o_j will increase; and p_j will increase. It should choose the scale of investment for which "marginal cost" is equal to "marginal value." In this setting of early outlays and deferred returns, this is equivalent to selecting that size of investment for which the marginal increment in the discounted present value of all costs is equal to the marginal increment in the discounted present value of total benefits (which is equivalent to saying that the marginal rate of return on the last increment of investment should equal the interest rate).

For any investment, I_o, there will exist two corresponding series of future benefits, both based on the same series of quantities of service. One will value these quantities at the marginal value of service, and the other at the average value of service in each year. The discounted present values at time zero of these series may be designated respectively as B and B', where

$$B = \frac{b_1}{(1+i)} + \frac{b_2}{(1+i)^2} \cdots + \frac{b_n}{(1+i)^n} = \sum_{j=1}^{n} \frac{b_j}{(1+i)^j}$$

and

$$B' = \frac{b_1'}{(1+i)} + \frac{b_2'}{(1+i)^2} \cdots + \frac{b_n'}{(1+i)^n} = \sum_{j=1}^{n} \frac{b_j'}{(1+i)^j}.$$

For the same investment, there will exist a corresponding series of future costs, the discounted present value of which may be designated as Φ, where

$$\Phi = \frac{(o_1+p_1)}{(1+i)} + \frac{(o_2+p_2)}{(1+i)^2} \cdots + \frac{(o_n+p_n)}{(1+i)^n} = \sum_{j=1}^{n} \frac{(o_j+p_j)}{(1+i)^j}.$$

The discounted present value of all costs (C) of the project may be represented at time zero as

$$C = I_o + \Phi.$$

To equate marginal cost to marginal value, and thus choose the optimal scale for the project, the agency should extend I_o to the point where $\Delta B' = \Delta C$, subject to the condition that at smaller values of I_o, ΔC is less than $\Delta B'$, and that at larger values of I_o, ΔC is greater than $\Delta B'$. This is the best possible scale for the project; it is in addition an economically feasible project if where $\Delta B' = \Delta C$, B' is greater than C. A word of explanation is perhaps required as to why the optimal scale is found where $\Delta B'$ equals ΔC rather than where ΔB equals ΔC. This is because

$$\Delta B' = \frac{\Delta q_1 \cdot mv_1}{(1+i)} + \frac{\Delta q_2 \cdot mv_2}{(1+i)^2} \cdots + \frac{\Delta q_n \cdot mv_n}{(1+i)^n}$$

and thus directly measures (in terms of discounted present value) the marginal value of the increment to output associated with a small increment to I_o. On the other hand, ΔB measures (in discounted present value terms) the marginal

[19] That is, as long as mv is positive.

revenue from the same increment to output, or its marginal value minus the associated decline in $(mv_j \cdot q_j)$ in each year for all inframarginal outputs.[20]

If the scale of the project is continuously variable, the conditions just specified for determination of optimal project scale may be stated as:

1) $\delta B'/\delta C = 1$, subject to
2) $\delta^2 B'/\delta I_o^2 < \delta^2 C/\delta I_o^2$, and with the project economically feasible if
3) $B' \geq C$.

The condition that $\delta B'/\delta C = 1$ should definitely not be confused with the erroneous condition sometimes stated that $B' = C$; ordinarily, B' will be greater than C at optimal scale, and its relation to C does not furnish a scale criterion, but only a test of whether, at its best scale, a project is economically feasible.[21]

These criteria for the determination of an optimal scale or project are applicable to cases involving all types of relation of long-run marginal cost of output to scale—to cases in which marginal cost increases, is constant, and decreases with the increase of scale. If for a project we have measures only of the aggregates B' and C, however, and do not have information on $\triangle B'$ and $\triangle C$, as is frequently the case, it is difficult to determine if the project is of approximately optimal scale. B' may exceed C at suboptimal, optimal, and excessive scales with all types of relationships of long-run marginal cost to scale, so that the existence of an excess of B' over C provides no assurance that the project is not uneconomically large or uneconomically small. Only if B' is less than C can a definite judgment be made; then the project either is of the wrong scale or is not economically feasible at any scale.

Does any comparison of aggregate benefits with aggregate costs provide a clue to whether or not a project approximates optimal scale? It should be noted that a comparison of B (aggregate benefits valued at their marginal values rather than at their average values) with C may provide some clues in the context of other information. In particular, $B = C$ when $\triangle B' = \triangle C$ *if long-run marginal costs are constant* with expansion of scale of the project, since with B equal to C average cost equals marginal value and average and marginal costs are the same with constant long-run marginal costs.[22] With increasing long-run marginal costs with increasing scale, B will exceed C when $\triangle B' = \triangle C$, and with decreasing marginal costs B will be less than C when $\triangle B' = \triangle C$. In the latter case, average cost exceeds marginal value, but the project is justified if average value exceeds average cost (if $B' > C$). A comparison of B (rather than B') with C for a project, in

[20] See Maass, *et al.*, *op. cit.*, pp. 104–09.

[21] See J. R. Hicks, "The Foundations of Welfare Economics," *Economic Journal,* XLIX (December 1939), 696–712. It will be noted that the second-derivative condition in equation 2 above specifies that $\triangle C$ be less than $\triangle B$ short of optimal scale and greater than $\triangle B$ beyond that scale. It should also be noted that the scale criterion described holds strictly only if the prices of factor inputs to the investing agency are invariant to the scale of its project; otherwise we should substitute for $\triangle C$ a $\triangle C'$ which is not affected by induced changes in the prices of inframarginal factor inputs, and reflects only physical increments in further inputs multiplied by their marginal costs.

[22] Then also, the average rate of return on investment is equal to the interest rate used in discounting, *i*.

the context of a knowledge of roughly how important for the project in question are economies or diseconomies of scale, may thus provide some clue to whether or not the project has been built to optimal scale.

We have referred so far to determination of optimal scale for a project in cases where the scale is continuously variable. Suppose instead, as is not infrequently the case, that the scale of the project can be increased from zero outward only by large discrete or lump increments. Thus the relevant increments, $\Delta B'$ and ΔC, will be large rather than small; let us designate these lump increments as $\triangle B'$ and $\triangle C$. The same general rule for determining optimal scale which has already been developed applies here. Scale should be extended by adding lumps to the project if at some stage in their addition B' will exceed C (otherwise the project is not economically feasible); and, a scale at which B' exceeds C having been reached, lumps should be added to long as $\triangle B'$ for the last lump increment exceeds $\triangle C$. But no further increment should be added for which $\triangle B'$ is less than $\triangle C$. (It should be noted that although this scale criterion for projects which can be increased in scale only discontinuously closely resembles that developed for continuously variable scales, it actually does not imply comparison of marginal values and marginal costs, but rather of lump additions to total value, B', and lump additions to costs C. As a result, the marginal value may be below the average cost of the last lump increment which is justified, although average value for that lump will exceed its average cost.)

Proper application of this criterion requires that any project considered should be analytically "disaggregated" into as many successive lump increments as technology and natural conditions permit, and then by justifying each successive lump increment by showing that for it $\triangle B'$ exceeds $\triangle C$ once a range where B' exceeds C is reached. This discussion suggests the dangers inherent in the common practice of making an *a priori* decision on the scale of a project and then simply inquiring if at this scale B' exceeds C. Such an excess may conceal the fact that the project incorporates detachable increments which are not economically justifiable because for them $\triangle B'$ is less than $\triangle C$.

The preceding provides criteria for whether or not an investment project should be undertaken at all, and for its optimal scale if it should be undertaken. With unconstrained budgets, water agencies presumably should undertake all economically feasible projects (for which B' can exceed C) which are mutually compatible (having eliminated from consideration all but the best of mutually exclusive alternative projects), and build them to optimal scales. It does not provide a criterion, however, for *when* individual projects should optimally be undertaken.

Any project which may be constructed "now" can also be built later, and there is thus a general problem as to what is the best time for each project to be built, in the context of optimal "dynamic investment programming." It is quite possible, for example, that as of the present year zero, a given project X will have a larger net capital value $(B' - C)$ as discounted to this year zero if it is built ten years hence than if it is built now. This may be because C is reduced by deferring construction (since there is compound discounting for ten extra years), whereas B' is not equivalently reduced by discounting because the services of the project will not be much in demand and will not generate significant benefits for the first ten years beginning now. The solution to the problem of timing of project construction in the absence of budgetary constraints is simple. Each project should be constructed in that year (and thus built at once or deferred, as the case may be) in which its construction will result in the greatest excess of B' over C as discounted to the present year zero. Thus not all projects for which B' would exceed C if constructed immediately should be built immediately. Some, and perhaps many, should have their construction deferred so as to maximize their present net capital values. If the rule stated is followed, there will be an optimal allocation of investment over time as well as among alternative uses. This rule is a very simple one when investment budgets are unconstrained, but it becomes indefinitely complicated when investment is undertaken subject to budgetary constraints.[23]

Choice among mutually exclusive investment alternatives

In the determination of investment policies, a water agency planning to supply water or water services to a given area or group of customers often is not limited to a single given project and project design, but must choose the best of mutually exclusive alternatives. It often has options between or among two or more projects that will perform the same general function or set of functions. Such options involve choices among river sources and dam sites, between high and low dams and on-stream and off-stream storage, between lined and unlined canals, and so on.

Application of the criterion for optimal choice in the absence of budgetary constraints requires that the agency make two kinds of calculation. First, it should analyze each available project alternative (including as a separate alternative each major permutation of a general type of alternative) and determine its optimal scale, in the manner described above. All alternatives should be considered as designed at optimal scale, and all for which B' exceeds C at optimal scale should be considered as active candidates.[24] Second, as among the active candidates, that project should be chosen for which the excess of B' over C is the greatest. If this principle of choice is followed, the greatest attainable net addition to economic welfare should be accomplished.

A special, but not rare, case of project selection involves the choice among mutually exclusive alternatives providing total packages of water services which are significantly different. Such a choice might be among a project which would provide irrigation water alone; one which would provide irrigation water and electric power; and one which would provide water and power plus streamflow control which repelled saline intrusion in a river estuary. The same general rule

[23] See Joe S. Bain, "Criteria for Undertaking Water-Resource Developments," *American Economic Review*, L (May 1960), pp. 317–18; Stephen A. Marglin, *Approaches to Dynamic Investment Planning* (Amsterdam: 1963), pp. 9–36. In analyzing optimum construction timing, possible variation of optimum scale of a project with variation in time of starting must be taken into account.

[24] But no single alternative should be included that provides services which could be provided with a greater combined excess of B' over C by two or more smaller projects. This condition is necessary to avert improper determination of project service areas.

of choice among such projects still holds, though the measurement of benefits becomes more difficult when a project supplies several different types of service, each with its own marginal and total values. The preceding may make the selection process in such cases sound easier than it is, however, since the initial determination of the optimal scale of a multipurpose project actually involves the determination of its scale in each of several dimensions (of the proportions and amounts in which it will supply various complementary and substitute water services), and the computation problem involved is complex.

Project selection subject to budgetary constraints

The discussion of investment criteria to this point has all referred to situations in which water agencies operate with effectively unlimited supplies of funds for investment and operating costs—funds obtainable by taxation of constituencies, by borrowing against future taxation, or by legislative appropriation of public funds secured by taxation or borrowing. All the investment criteria so far suggested are thus criteria for "unconstrained maximization," in situations where the undertaking of investment projects, the determination of their sizes, and the choice among mutually exclusive investment projects is not in any way constrained by an arbitrary shortage of funds for investment.

Actually, however, water agencies frequently may operate subject to budgetary constraints. They may have less funds to invest than the exploitation of all economically desirable projects they might undertake would require; or, worse yet, less than required for the best of mutually exclusive alternative projects; or, still worse, less than required for any desirable project of optimal scale. In these cases, the agency may be able to obtain "too little money" to allow it to operate in an economically optimal fashion. Also, it may on occasion be able to obtain too much money, enabling it, if it chooses, to undertake projects of excessive scale, or projects for which B' falls short of C, or to undertake projects prematurely.

We will here simply deplore any occasions in which agencies are oversupplied with funds, and consider the essential problems faced by agencies which can secure "too little" money. When under budgetary constraints, how should agencies dispose of funds available for investment? This general problem may be broken into two major subproblems: (1) that of the large federal or comparable agency which is supplied with enough funds to undertake a number of "optimally scaled"[25] and selected projects, but less than all of the projects it might undertake which would be economically justified; and (2) that of the local agency which is supplied either with insufficient funds to permit it to adopt the best one of several mutually exclusive alternative projects, or insufficient funds to permit it to build any alternative project to optimal scale.

The problem of the large agency with more good projects available for construction than it can finance may be attacked with the aid of drastic simplifying

[25] That is, projects at scales which would be optimal in the absence of budgetary constraints.

assumptions, or on the basis of assumptions more likely to result in a meaningful solution. The former approach is most familiar in recent economic literature, where the problem is simplified by assuming that the *scales* of all available projects are given (at what would be optimal with unconstrained budgets, or in other ways arbitrarily), and that all available projects are arbitrarily considered as equally eligible candidates for construction in a single current time period. Thus, with this approach, the problem of codetermining the best sets of projects in a sequence of time periods, including the present and a number of future ones, is assumed away along with that of finding an optimal construction date for each project undertaken. Then, if the budgetary constraint is in the nature of a fixed annual budget for initial capital outlays, with no restraints on future operating outlays (or opportunity costs), the appropriate ranking of projects would be in the descending order of $(B' - \Phi)/I_0$, and the agency should move downward from the top of the list in undertaking projects until its annual capital-outlay budget is exhausted. If the constraint takes the form of a fixed annual budget to cover both initial capital outlays and the operating costs of projects undertaken in the past (opportunity costs presumably being unconstrained) the ranking of projects should be in the descending order of $(B' - P)/(C - P)$ (where P is the unconstrained present value of opportunity costs), or simply B'/C if opportunity costs are absent or disregarded. Therefore, under these simplified assumptions, the agency should follow this ranking in choosing the projects on which it will spend that part of its annual budget which is available for additional capital outlays.[26]

Criteria in this form, however, embody such brutal oversimplifications that their utility, even as rough-and-ready guides to policy, is seriously in doubt. They could be improved somewhat by modification to recognize the problem of timing of project construction in the context of multiperiod planning (with project scales still assumed to be given), to arrive at a definition of an optimal group of project sets for a succession of years such as would maximize the present value of all future $B' - \Phi$ for a given constrained I_0 stream continuing over a period of years, or the present value of all future B' for a comparable C stream. Even then, however, it is fundamentally unreasonable to assume project scales to be given, since scales of projects as well as number of projects undertaken will be influenced by budgetary constraints if welfare is to be maximized, and scales must be codetermined (generally at less than unconstrained optima) along with the number of projects to be undertaken. Moreover, freeing scale and then applying the criteria outlined above for single-period maximization with timing of construction disregarded—ranking by $(B' - \Phi)/I_0$ or by B'/C—will lead in the direction of nonsensical results. Agencies following these rules would tend to build an excessive number of projects of excessively suboptimal scale in early periods to an extent which would reduce the project opportunities of future periods enough that total gains for a series of periods would not be maximized. A multiperiod criterion for selecting and timing the construction of projects from

[26] See Bain, *op. cit.;* Otto Eckstein, *Water-Resource Development: The Economics of Project Evaluation* (1958), chap. 3; and Roland N. McKean, *Efficiency in Government through Systems Analysis* (1958), chap. 2.

a time stream of constrained budgets is thus a "must" if codetermination of project scales is to be incorporated, as it should, in the criterion.

This general criterion problem, as outlined here, has been attacked by Stephen Marglin, who concludes by suggesting certain complex iterative calculating procedures through which optimal solutions to the planning of investment over time can be approximated.[27] There is still a need to extract from work of this sort something simpler as a guide to selecting projects subject to budgetary constraints than directions for programming a computer.

The problem of the local agency which wishes to construct only a single project now, and will undertake further projects not at all or only at some indefinite time in the future, is somewhat simpler. Assuming in general that the agency's budgetary constraint will operate on the size of the capital outlay for the project (I_0 is limited), it should determine for each mutually exclusive project the value of $B' - \Phi$ when I_0 is expended on that project; and this should be done even though this $B' - \Phi$ may be for a scale of project smaller than the unconstrained optimum for some or all of the projects, and conceivably even larger than the unconstrained optimum for some. It should then select the project (and corresponding scale of the project) for which $B' - \Phi$ is the greatest, unless an even greater $B' - \Phi$ can be obtained by spending less than all of I_0 on some project. It effectively faces a budgetary constraint if it selects a different project (or a smaller scale for the same project) than it would have in the absence of budgetary constraints. In this context, projects of unconstrained optimal scales have no premium position; the agency may find it more advantageous to build a project that has a large unconstrained optimal scale to a suboptimal scale than to build a project which has a small unconstrained optimal scale to that scale.

One thing may be said in general of budgetary constraints of both sorts mentioned above: they tend to reduce economic efficiency by inducing a suboptimization rather than a full optimization of economic welfare.

The choice of a rate of discount

Throughout the preceding discussion of criteria for investment in water projects, we have assumed that an "appropriate" rate of interest was being used in discounting future returns from, and costs of, any project. We must now turn our attention to the essential problem of what is the appropriate rate of interest or discount, in general or for particular categories of projects. Variations in the rate used can alter many dimensions of an optimally designed project. Employment of higher rates of discount in appraising water investment projects will generally result in finding as optimal (1) smaller total investment in water resource development, (2) the undertaking of fewer projects, (3) the construction of smaller-scale projects, and (4) selection among mutually exclusive alternatives of projects of

[27] Marglin, *op. cit.,* chaps. 3–8.

lower capital intensity, shorter lives, and earlier payoffs in the form of yields. Employment of lower rates of discount will generally have opposite results.

Just what is the appropriate rate to employ in implementing criteria for optimal investment in water development has been widely debated. This is largely because many considerations bear on the choice of such a rate and because there is a variety of existing interest rates and rates of return on other investments which might be thought to approximate the best rate for the purpose at hand.[28]

We will not attempt here to summarize this debate, or to develop fully and defend our own analysis of the appropriate rate. Briefly, however, it would appear that, in order to secure the optimal or best attainable suboptimal allocation of resources to water development (given existing organization and performance in the private sector, including the organization of markets for funds), the appropriate rate of discount should be roughly equal to the *marginal* rate of return in marginal long-term investment in the private sector, and also equal to the marginal rate of time preference of the taxpayers or agency constituents who ultimately finance the bulk of investment in water projects. These two rates tend generally to coincide, and to be approximated by the going net rate of interest on private savings invested in real estate—at this writing in the neighborhood of 5 to 6 per cent. Given the selection of such a rate, water agencies should be supplied with budgets large enough (but not larger) to undertake all projects which are economically feasible when evaluated at this rate of discount—but only if budgets over time are so controlled that individual projects are constructed at optimal times, with appropriate deferment of construction of projects which would be worth more if built later and the corresponding avoidance of premature investment.

A somewhat more sophisticated choice of rates would involve two steps: The private time preference rate just referred to would be used in determining the aggregate volume of investment in water resources in any year (together with budgetary regulation to forestall premature investment). And a lower social time preference rate, especially applicable to social decisions concerning very long-lived investments which will serve future generations, would be used in calculating the allocation of this aggregate among alternative investment projects. If such a social rate of time preference can be guessed with some reliability, this procedure would seem to be the most appropriate. Both the simpler and the more complicated choice of discount rates may be kept in mind as we proceed to evaluate investment projects of water agencies.[29]

[28] See, for example, Otto Eckstein, "A Survey of the Theory of Public Expenditure Criteria," in National Bureau of Economic Research, Special Conference Series 12, *Public Finances: Needs, Sources, and Utilization* (1961).

[29] The choice of interest or discount rates suggested here is essentially the same as that proposed by Otto Eckstein in his *Water-Resource Development, op. cit.*, pp. 94–104, which should be referred to for elaboration of the more complex interest rate criterion. In making the preceding choice of interest or discount rate, we expressly reject as alternatives, for reasons which are demonstrable by analysis, the interest rate on government bonds, the interest rate on local water agency bonds, and the average rate of return on private investments or any multiple thereof. Coincidentally, of course, interest rates on government bonds could correspond to social rates of time preference because such bond rates are lower than our preferred indicator of the private marginal rate of time preference, but they cannot be accepted on their own merits.

Uncertainty concerning future yields and costs

A related matter to be considered is that of the treatment of uncertainty concerning the future yields and costs of investment projects. For each investment project which may be evaluated to determine whether it is economically justifiable, what its size should be, and whether or not it is superior to alternative projects, there are associated magnitudes to be determined, for each alternative size at which it may be built, including original cost, a series of future benefits, and a corresponding series of future costs. In general, though in varying degree, the knowledge of the investing agency about these relevant magnitudes is imperfect—they are not precisely known but must be estimated.

Even the original cost of the project, as built to any given size, may not be exactly known at the time it is planned. The best that a water agency can do about this is to accumulate all relevant information on the engineering features of the project and on the prospective prices of construction materials and services; and then make the most "realistic" possible estimate of the original cost, or alternative original costs of different sizes of project, avoiding both unjustified optimism and unjustified pessimism.

The other essential magnitudes can be estimated with much less certainty, since they refer to a series of future quantities of output of water service, a series of future marginal and average values of such services, and a series of future operating and opportunity costs. Each of these series can conceivably assume any of a considerable range of average values and time-shapes, depending on future events which are not foreknown. This uncertainty concerning essential future magnitudes raises a complex problem, and its treatment in evaluating investment projects requires special attention.

Proper treatment of this problem may be more easily understood if we distinguish two general types of uncertainty. The first type involves future events which are individually unpredictable but which as a group can be expected, on the basis of long past experience, to behave in a fashion which can be predicted with considerable accuracy. In the water industry, this sort of risk arises with respect to such things as the annual runoffs of streams, as affected by annual precipitation; the quantity of water demanded per year by farmers and other water users, as affected by year-to-year variations in temperature and other weather patterns; and the quantity of water needed annually by a city in reserve storage to quell fires. Each of these magnitudes is known to have been variable from year to year for a long time, and may be expected to continue to be variable. The value of any of them in any specified future year cannot be predicted with much certainty. But each is known to have had a certain mean annual value, and also a certain pattern of variation around the mean, which can be described by a frequency distribution showing the proportions of a large number of years in which the annual value assumed each of a number of alternative magnitudes. Thus, projecting past experience, both the probable mean annual value and the probable variance of annual values around the mean can be predicted with some accuracy.

Where this is the case, the agency making calculations may assume as a first approximation that the future annual value of the variable in question will always be the mean of past annual values over a long period of years, and calculate the return on the investment on this assumption. This operation alone in some cases may lead to erroneous valuations of the investment, however, because variance around a given mean may influence either the present total value of the mean (in the case of series of benefit-producing outputs), or the costs of supplying a given aggregate of benefits over the life of the project, and in these cases the mean values should be correspondingly adjusted.[30]

The second type involves uncertainty concerning the mean values and variances of benefit and cost streams associated with investments. Such uncertainty arises because the frequency of occurrence and impact of possible events which would influence these values cannot be fairly predicted on the basis of long past experience—such events reflecting no known periodicities of nature or human behavior and being generally, but unpredictably, nonrandom in their occurrence.[31] Such events would include the rate of growth or decline of a population demanding water from a project, changes in technology which change the demand per acre or per capita for water or for hydroelectric power, changes in consumer tastes directly or indirectly influencing the demand per capita for water, changes in the profitability of agricultural production, or the discovery of unknown and un-

[30] The case of benefit-producing outputs is illustrated by predictable variance in the annual flows of water available for diversion from rivers. Suppose each of two rivers has the same mean annual flow available for diversion by an agency, but that one experiences relatively moderate year-to-year variations in flow and the other wide swings in annual flow. Other things being equal, any variance around the mean reduces the total value of flows because an increase above the mean in any year adds less to the total value of water (marginal value of water decreasing as the quantity supplied increases) than an offsetting decrease below the mean subtracts from the total value of water (marginal value of water increasing as the quantity supplied is restricted). In addition, if there is a significant variance in the annual supply of water available, users will tend to develop less efficient processes and equipment for handling water than if there were no variance, and this will tend to reduce the marginal value of water to them generally. The greater the variance in annual flow, the greater will be the reduction in the total value of benefits obtainable from a given flow, and the river with a widely fluctuating flow will therefore yield smaller over-all benefits than one with the same mean flow but lesser fluctuations in flow.

This being so, agencies undertake added costs to reduce interannual fluctuations in available flows of rivers (by building dams and storage reservoirs) up to some margin, but some variance in available flow generally remains. In seeking an optimal design for a project, an agency must take into account not only the known historical variance of the flow of a river, assumed to persist into the future, but also the way in which marginal increases in the scale of its reservoir and dam will affect the project's benefits through reducing the variance of water service made available to final users. Simulation techniques are in common use for this purpose.

The case involving costs of supplying a given aggregate of benefits is illustrated by predictable interannual variance in the quantity of water demanded by users. If a given mean annual demand for water is subject to relatively wide interannual variance, the cost of facilities to supply this demand will necessarily be greater than if the variance were less, since the facilities will need to supply larger peak or near-peak annual demands, and the load factor over the lives of facilities will be reduced. This elevation of costs should be recognized, and should tend to induce a reduction in quantity of water supplied and in net benefits from a project.

[31] The distinction between variable outcomes drawn from a distribution with known parameters and variable outcomes drawn from a distribution with unknown parameters harks back to Frank H. Knight's distinction between risk and uncertainty in *Risk, Uncertainty, and Profit* (1921), chap. 7. We shall employ Knight's terms in some of the following discussion, but shall also speak of "uncertainty" in the general case for which incomplete information is available on the parameters of the distribution.

anticipated properties of irrigable land which an investment project is supposed to supply with water.

About such future events, the investing agency is in a state of relative ignorance. And it is correspondingly reduced to guesswork in predicting in what direction and by how much future benefits and costs may be influenced by such events, or caused to deviate from what they would be in the current situation. The degree of uncertainty concerning future costs and benefits, moreover, increases as they are farther away in future time. The agency is faced with a substantial variance of possible future benefit and cost outcomes, widening as the outcomes are farther in the future, but is in a poor position to assign a reliable mean probable value to either sort of outcome.

In this sort of situation, what is the proper response of the water agency in evaluating current investment projects? An offhand answer might be that the agency should simply make the best estimates it can, on the basis of the best relevant information attainable, of the mean probable levels and time shapes of future benefit and cost streams; then proceed with its calculations just as if these estimated magnitudes were known with certainty, implicitly assuming that its actual future net returns have the same chance of being above as below estimated returns, and gambling "at even odds" that its estimates are correct. In effect, it should be willing to invest on the assumption that the present value of future net returns will be $1 million if it feels that there is a one-third chance they will be $800,000; a one-third chance they will be $1 million; and a one-third chance they will be $1.2 million.

In fact, this sort of a procedure has often been recommended for a large agency, such as the Bureau of Reclamation, which over a period of time undertakes a large number of projects. The recommendation is based on the grounds that since the large agency rolls the dice a large number of times, the laws of probability will have a chance to operate, and that on a large number of projects it will "win" (that is, will generate higher than estimated net benefits) as often as it "loses" (generates lower than estimated net benefits). In this case, the procedure would clearly appear to have strong justification, provided that the agency does not have an institutional bias toward making patently optimistic or pessimistic estimates.

But the procedure has been questioned for the smaller agency which undertakes, at the most, only one or two investment projects every two or three decades. Questions are raised on the principal ground that one or two rolls of the dice by the small agency may easily turn up unfavorable results (it may roll a two or a three instead of a six or a ten or a twelve), that if it is unlucky it will lose heavily or be wiped out, and that it cannot afford to take this chance. This is to say that it cannot afford to be an even-odds gambler; when it estimates a future benefit return to be worth $1 million, the fact that it has a one-third chance of reaping a benefit of only $250,000 is not really compensated for by the fact that it also has a one-third chance of reaping a benefit of $1.75 million. "Unfavorable surprise" and "favorable surprise" are unequally weighted, and a small gambler should therefore always err on the side of caution.

If the preceding line of argument actually reflects the psychology of water agency (and other) investors, it is unfortunate from the standpoint of one who would wish to see a maximum net return eventually realized from all investments, and thus we cannot recommend investments based on estimates which deliberately err on the side of caution. If a bias toward caution is to be introduced into the calculation of the worth of investments, there are several available devices for doing so: (1) increasing the rate of discount employed to include a factor for "risk"; (2) making "safety allowances" by arbitrarily reducing estimates of future benefits by arbitrary percentages; and (3) placing arbitrary time horizons on investment calculations by disregarding all costs and benefits beyond some chosen number of years, such as fifty years. If one of these devices must be chosen, it can be demonstrated that increasing the rate of discount to include a risk factor is probably the least undesirable, because it has the fewest undesirable side effects.[32]

The only general justification for introducing a "risk allowance" of one sort or another into investment calculations would be that some or all water agencies seem to have shown a propensity to make unjustifiably optimistic estimates of future benefits of projects; thus, reducing their estimates by such a means as increasing the rate of discount by two or three percentage points would compensate for their optimistic bias in estimating. Such congenital optimism is perhaps discernible in the history of the large federal water agencies—the Bureau of Reclamation and the Corps of Engineers—and in the California Department of Water Resources, if one examines in detail their bases for estimating future benefits (see Chapter 11). That a similar optimism exists in local water agencies generally is not clear, though instances of this sort of optimism can be found. We conclude with the observation that general uncertainty is properly allowed for in evaluating investments in water development in the case of agencies which evidence a propensity toward apparently optimistic estimates of future benefits accruing from such investments.

An alternative manner of dealing with uncertainty is to reduce it by postponing investment in various separable features of a total investment project as long as possible, and building it in a sequence of steps according to a determined time schedule, subject to the constraint that the stretch-out of the total construction undertaking should not greatly increase the present value of total costs. This procedure has the advantage of reducing the average interval between increments to investments and the realization of benefits from these increments, and thus of reducing uncertainty. The sort of procedure outlined seems in the net preferable to dealing with uncertainty through risk discounts, time horizons, and safety allowances. It is thus recommended that the planning staffs of water agencies should employ sequential planning models in designing and evaluating proposed projects, a procedure which modern computer techniques now make entirely feasible—if congressional and other legislative procedures in authorizing projects and making appropriations for them can be adapted accordingly.

The Motives of Water Agencies

The two preceding sections establish the normative criteria needed in the succeeding chapters for a running appraisal of the conduct of agencies in the water industry, as well as for the statement of systematic conclusions about

[32] See Eckstein, *Water-Resource Development, op. cit.*, pp. 80–90.

performance in Part Three. We now consider the problem of stating predictive hypotheses about the motivation of the main classes of actors in the industry.

It is clear on the surface that no single or simple motive guides the behavior of all public water agencies. They take many legal forms, ranging from fiscally independent special district governments with very restricted functions through independent districts empowered to perform numerous functions, through agencies that are departments of county and municipal governments, and to agencies of the state or federal government which are empowered to devise and implement comprehensive plans of state or regional development. Since it would be unreasonable to assume that the same simple motive or principle of conduct should serve as a guide to all of these types of agencies, it is necessary to distinguish among agency types in speaking of agency motivation. Here, without neglecting any important types, we will give the largest amount of attention to local agencies, including independent districts and departments of local government, which from the start have been the basic entrepreneurial units of the regional water industry. Less space will be devoted to the consideration of motivations in agencies of the federal and state governments, though because of their increasing importance as entrepreneurial participants in the industry they should not be neglected.

Internal motives of local water agencies

Local water agencies in the form of public districts engaging in essentially business operations may obviously pursue or have a variety of objectives or internal motives. These objectives may relate to the price or quality of the service provided to customers, or the price paid to suppliers. They may encompass the welfare of persons who are not customers of the enterprise but are somehow affected by its operations. The enterprise may serve an electorate including factions which would impose a number of competing motivations upon it, so that some balancing process is involved; or it may be controlled by a group single-minded in its objectives. The local public district always faces some constraints on the relation between its financial receipts and disbursements, with the exact nature of the constraints depending on legal access to taxation, borrowing, and assorted subventions. These constraints establish a substantial, though limited, range within which the agency's economic behavior can diverge from that consistent with profit maximization. Within this range, it retains considerable freedom to act differently from the "model" hypothetical firm of economic theory.

Our central hypothesis about the dominant motivation of the bulk of the agencies in the water industry holds that such agencies seek to make the maximum contribution to the economic welfare of a relatively fixed group of member-customers. They can thus be identified as "users' cooperatives." Some of the evidence supporting this hypothesis was established in Chapter 3, where we described its basis in the location of political authority over the decisions made by these agencies. Chapter 4 showed the prevalence of public agencies and self-supplying users in the industry and, conversely, the narrow range of activities undertaken by privately owned utilities and large state and federal government agencies which are subject to at least somewhat different motives. Most local government units supplying irrigation water are independent special districts, usually formed at the initiative of some of their members-to-be and typically requiring approval at the polls by a majority of these members. Major investment decisions, territorial changes, and alterations in the district's legal relations with other agencies also typically require electoral approval. Day-to-day decisions are made by a board of directors popularly elected for short terms.[33]

In the case of some agencies which are not agricultural retailers, the linkages supporting the application of the users' cooperative hypothesis are somewhat less direct. Urban water agencies are often departments of general city governments. While the extent and nature of electoral control over urban water supply are usually the same in principle as over single purpose retailing agencies, nonetheless water service is a joint product provided by the city along with other services of local government. The quantities of water supplied and the terms under which it is offered to urban residents can be affected by other objectives of city government, such as the promotion of new industry or the incorporation of additional territory.

In addition to local agricultural and urban retailing organizations, the water industry includes a number of important local agencies performing the functions of wholesaling or re-wholesaling, or other water management activities not directly related to retail sales of water. Frequently these agencies are organized at the county level. Single or special purpose agencies with their own elected boards of directors are subject to the same *pro forma* control by water users as are irrigation retailers, although wholesaling agencies are occasionally controlled in principle, and often in practice, by their retailing-agency customers. Frequently water agencies at county levels are directly controlled by the county supervisors. The users' cooperative hypothesis remains appropriate in this case, but the possibility arises of "joint product" effects similar to those cited in connection with city water departments.

In the case of nearly all local public agencies, the financial arrangements are consistent with the users' cooperative hypothesis. No holder of equity is present to claim the excess of receipts over expenditures, nor any equity capital to make up the shortfall. While the financial risks associated with particular projects or activities of local water districts are sometimes insured against or otherwise passed

[33] In some types of districts, suffrage in elections reposes in all citizens residing within the district's boundaries. In others, such as water districts and water storage districts, voting is on the basis of assessed valuation. Districts also vary in the extent to which suffrage extends to persons who are not directly customers for the district's water or water-related services. Some districts include amounts of land which cannot be irrigated or land that is riparian to streams and thus not served by the district; owners of such land often pay taxes to the district without receiving immediate or direct benefits from it. Some important irrigation districts include towns at the centers of their crop marketing areas—especially the older districts, whose boundaries were often drawn so that sentiment favoring irrigation in a town could force irrigation upon owners of surrounding dry-farmed land. Frequently towns are included because city water is drawn from wells replenished by percolation from the irrigation district's applications of imported surface water. City water users thus are the definite, but indirect, beneficiaries of the district's activities. Nonetheless, this fact may not be realized by the city dwellers, who often vote in irrigation district elections but feel they have no direct economic interest in district activities.

on to others, the general residual obligation to provide the revenue necessary to cover a district's contractual costs lies with its member-customers. Some local agencies, especially county-wide organizations, constitute partial exceptions in that their members and customers do not entirely coincide, and cross-subsidy to benefit particular interest groups becomes a more likely possibility.

Internal motives of federal and state agencies

The motivations of and constraints on water agencies established by the federal and state governments in order to augment local water supplies and manage regional water resources are much more difficult to characterize than those of local water agencies. The state and federal agencies are not supported by electorates coterminous with their service areas. They are responsible to legislature and administrations which perform many other functions and to electorates far larger than the populations of areas they serve with water. These agencies, in contracting to supply water, usually deal with local water agencies as customers or intermediaries rather than dealing directly with final users. Typically, therefore, their final customer-users are voter-controllers in two capacities: as constituents of the local intermediary agencies, and as electors of a few representatives in the state and federal legislatures and of the chief executives of the state and federal governments.

Formally, the federal and state water agencies are under the control of cabinet members, and thereby are subject to some obligation to heed the "general interest," as well as being guided and constrained by the requirement of legislative authorization for projects of the agency and appropriation of funds to finance them. Informally, as we shall argue in Chapter 11, state and federal agencies collaborate with local users' organizations in designing and managing projects on behalf of the users; thus they acquire the character of users' cooperatives one step removed from the final customers. The state and federal agencies may also be subject to other motivations. They may derive bureaucratic satisfaction and prestige from the growth of their agencies through undertaking many and large projects for the development of water resources. Since they are primarily engineering groups in terms of composition of personnel and functions performed, a bias favoring technical achievements may hold sway.

Thus, the motivation of the federal and state agencies must be viewed as a sharply qualified users' cooperative outlook. This view is supported by their financial arrangements. They do not have to be self-financing, earning sufficient revenues from sales of their products to cover their costs. They secure revenues from local intermediary agencies for some types of benefits provided to them, but a sizable part—sometimes a major part—of the funds which finance their operations comes from the treasuries of the federal or state governments. The federal and state water agencies which design projects and give leadership to local agencies in organizing local support for projects are not fiscally responsible for their actions, and do not share in the gains or suffer the losses of a well or poorly designed project. Local support for a project is gained if the local agencies bear costs less than the benefits they receive, and legislative support is gained if legislatures consider the project to be a desirable part of a governmental program (according to mixed criteria of desirability). Legislative support is likely to emerge from a process of vote trading in a legislative logrolling process,[34] and to depend on many things in addition to an evaluation of the project's consequences for the national welfare.

Normative and organizational theory of cooperative enterprises

A small but relatively adequate literature deals with the economic theory of cooperative enterprises.[35] It contains two distinct branches, each useful for the purpose of this study. One concerns the normative theory of optimal allocation of resources located in a cooperative firm, and the structure of agreements among members which, if perfectly adhered to under static conditions, would bring this optimal allocation into being. The other branch concerns the organizational problems of the cooperative enterprise arising from a divergence in interests and circumstances among members and especially from the fact that individual members may reap short-run gains by violating the normative rules for general joint maximization.

The central conclusion of the normative analysis holds that the cooperative enterprise should be viewed as a joint plant integrated with the enterprises of each of the members. Each member contributes to the cost of the joint plant up to the point where the return to the marginal dollar he invests in the cooperative enterprise equals the return to the marginal dollar in his individual enterprise. That is to say, the decision on allocating resources to the common plant resembles the allocation of resources by a multiple plant firm to its individual plants. In terms of physical inputs, for each participating firm, the marginal productivity of a resource contributed to the cooperative plant must be the same as its marginal productivity in the individual plant.[36] Each participating firm then sets its own level of activity, including the level of the productive input it draws from the common plant, by "considering its separate activities *plus* its proportionate share of the joint activity as an integrated production unit."[37]

[34] For a theoretical analysis with attention to the normative economic implications, see J. M. Buchanan and Gordon Tullock, *The Calculus of Consent: Logical Foundations of Constitutional Democracy* (1962).

[35] See Richard Phillips, "Economic Nature of the Cooperative Association," *Journal of Farm Economics,* XXXV (February 1953), 74–87; Paavo Kaarlehto, "On the Economic Nature of Cooperation," *Acta Agriculturae Scandinavica,* VI (No. 4, 1956), 3–114; Peter G. Helmberger and Sidney Hoos, "Cooperative Enterprise and Organization Theory," *Journal of Farm Economics,* XLIV (May 1962), 275–90; Peter G. Helmberger, "Cooperative Enterprise as a Structural Dimension of Farm Markets," *Journal of Farm Economics,* XLVI (August 1964), 603–17; and references cited in these articles.

[36] Phillips, *op. cit.,* 74–76. This analysis holds generally with respect to either a buyers' or a sellers' cooperative. The equilibrium conditions discussed here will deal with technical transformations and assume constant market prices. The case of a buyers' cooperative operating to exploit a resource monopsonistically, or a sellers' cooperative exploiting a product market monopolistically, falls within the same analysis by writing it in terms of marginal revenue products rather than values of marginal products.

[37] *Ibid.,* 76.

It follows that the users' cooperative plant can be thought of as vertically integrated with the plants of the individual members, and the usual conclusions about vertically integrated enterprises under static conditions become relevant. The vertically integrated firm is interested in the profits for the whole chain of operations. Under conditions of independence between the cost functions of the members and the central cooperative plant, the setting of optimal output by each member requires the equating of the marginal revenue product of the final member firm with the sum of allocable marginal costs from all of the earlier stages, including the cooperative plant. The "transfer price" placed on an output going from the cooperative enterprise to serve as an input into members' plants is arbitrary unless it plays a role in encouraging the use of the factor to develop the maximum profits for the entire system.

Suppose these principles are followed by a large number of water users, joining in random groupings to organize a number of users' cooperatives to supply themselves with water. Suppose also that every final user operates under identical cost and revenue conditions, as does every possible cooperative plant. Then all aspects of resource organization relating to the "industry" of cooperative plants will be identical to the results of organizing the same activity as an industry of independent, purely competitive firms. If all cooperatives are of the open-membership type, so that users can shift their membership freely among them, it can be shown that the same congruence between a conventional competitive industry and an industry of cooperatives will hold even if the cost curves of all units are not identical (so that elements of rent accrue here and there), so long as the large-numbers assumptions are maintained. Thus the normative theory of the cooperative enterprise shows that cooperative organization of an industry would have the same optimal properties as private enterprise organization when both operate in environments consistent with the existence of pure competition.

Because the cooperative, by definition, exists as a joint venture requiring the coordination of members' separate decisions, the arrangements needed to bring about a joint optimization of resource allocation for the cooperative and its members take on a good deal of significance. Assume that the cooperative includes enough members so that none takes into account the influence of variations in his own activity on the level of marginal costs for the cooperative plant. Then the simplest set of optimizing agreements would require each member to pay into the cooperative treasury a sum equal to the cooperative plant's long-run marginal cost for each unit of input taken from the cooperative. The members could then view the cooperative plant in practice as an arm's-length seller, and still set their own production levels consistent with the essential vertical relation that exists.

If a cooperative association rests upon such a structure of agreements among its members revolving around long-run marginal cost, members' payments will just cover the cooperative's total costs if it operates under conditions of constant average costs, so that average and marginal costs are equal.[38] With rising or falling long-run average costs, marginal costs will, respectively, exceed or fall

[38] With constant costs, all input costs of the cooperative plant would be shared by the member-customers in proportion to the plant output which they take. This case is stressed by Phillips, *ibid.*, 77–78.

short of average costs and the cooperative's receipts will exceed or fall short of covering its total costs. The members will then need some arrangement for absorbing or making up this difference in the form of a rebate or tax which is not directly proportional to the output they take from the cooperative plant. A tax per capita or per unit of assessed valuation would satisfy this requirement.

Such a set of agreements would permit the cooperative plant and its members to co-exist from day to day at arm's length, but it would not change the essential vertical integration between them. Thus, with regard to optimization conditions, no distinct entrepreneurial role would exist for the cooperative, because all of its input and output decisions would be determined by the sum of the allocative decisions of the members. It has thus been said that the cooperative association creates a separate plant but not a separate firm, and consists only of "the sum of multilateral agreements among the firms participating in the joint activity, in order that these firms may function coordinately through their common plant."[39] Once the structure of cooperative agreements is known, then a maximization function for the cooperative plant can be stated in terms of the output decisions of the members in their individual plants.[40]

While this analysis seems to cover satisfactorily the basic normative properties of resource allocation within a cooperative enterprise, it assumes away a great range of problems concerned with setting the rules of association necessary for an efficient cooperative enterprise and maintaining them in the face of changing conditions. For predicting the responses of the cooperative to external changes, or the internal arrangements it will make under more complex conditions than those discussed above, the normative theory must be supplemented. In particular, the conclusion that no distinct entrepreneurial element resides in the cooperative, as distinct from its members, must be modified in order to develop a behavioral analysis.

> The participating member of a cooperative association cannot in general be assumed to manage the cooperative plant and operations. Through membership, he commits himself to abide by group decisions. . . . In brief, the frame of reference espoused by [a purely normative theory] does not reflect the emergence of a new decision-making unit upon the organization of a cooperative.[41]

As usual, surrounding a normative theory with an organizational one does not result in a unified or clear-cut set of predictions, but rather in the identification of possible sources of conflict within the organization and their impact on its internal allocations and external behavior. Let us consider a series of these which seem likely to assume importance for local agencies that supply water to their

[39] *Ibid.*, 75–76.

[40] Helmberger and Hoos (*op. cit.*, 281–90) develop such functions for a sellers' cooperative in the short run with a fixed amount of the input provided by members, and in the long run with either open or closed membership. The functions for a buyers' or users' cooperative are essentially symmetrical.

[41] *Ibid.*, 276–77.

member-customers. Some empirical evidence relating to the Northern California industry will be developed in passing, but most of it will appear in the remaining chapters of Part Two.

1) Equilibrium conditions in the normative model run in terms of the resources which each individual member places within the cooperative plant and within his own separate plant. In practice, of course, the scale of the cooperative plant and its levels of resource inputs and outputs are set proximately by collective action of its members. All sorts of discontinuities and uncertainties may be present to prevent the collective allocations within the cooperative from being simply the sum of those desired by the members.[42] When this situation exists, the management of the cooperative takes on an independent life in making allocative decisions for the association, and the institutional arrangements underlying the political control pattern in the district determine how the resulting conflicts are settled. This problem of political organization exists for any cooperative, and is merely brought to the fore when the organization is *pro forma* a governmental unit. A special aspect of the political problem in this case is that a public enterprise usually requires support by a consensus in the political community that ultimately controls it—support by an overwhelming majority rather than bare constitutional majorities.[43] Thus the agency's officials must try to form and maintain a consensus through the equitable treatment of all groups, and many possible pressures for less than optimal arrangements may come into play.

2) Efficient allocative arrangements may not be attainable to the local district because they do not seem equitable to its membership as a whole, and solutions which seem "fair" and acceptable may, in fact, result in less than optimal allocations, both for the membership and for the economy as a whole. For example, an irrigation district may have access to a costless, but fixed, water supply. This supply may be so small that a unit price which effectively restricts its members' demand to the available supply will yield a great surplus of revenue over financial expenses. It may not be possible politically to get support for the optimal solution of imposing the charge and giving a rebate which is not proportional to water use from those innocent of economic theory, and a rationing scheme of lesser efficiency is likely to evolve in its stead.[44] As another example, cooperative managements supplying water, with the greatest good will, may seek to supply water to their member-customers at the lowest possible average cost. It can be shown that this practice will lead the agency to supply the optimal quantity of water only if it

[42] To mention the obvious problem, few government units or enterprises manage to function through accepting voluntary contributions of capital inputs from their member-customers in return for an assured stake in the economic outcome of their operations.

[43] We cannot fully explore the reasoning behind this view, but shall cite some specific elements. One obvious reason for needing a consensus in support of a local water agency is the necessity of having a stable governing board for the agency. Farmers' investment decisions subjectively require assurance of a firm long-term supply of water. Manufacturers design plants on the basis of an assumed pricing policy by the water agency. Residential areas are developed with an understanding that water will be supplied at a stated pressure and of guaranteed quality. Upsetting the established programs of an agency would cause great disturbance and tend to lead to a quest for some other organizational solution.

[44] The relevant evidence will be examined in Chapter 10.

operates under conditions of constant cost; too much, if it operates under increasing cost; and too little, if it operates under decreasing cost.[45]

3) It seems likely that equitable arrangements that serve to maintain a consensus among an agency's member-customers may diverge more from joint welfare maximization, the more heterogeneous are the needs and interests of the members of its electorate.[46] For instance, an irrigation district supplying lands of sharply differing productivity at the same marginal cost would properly charge farmers in both areas the same price, but the community consensus may accept discrimination in favor of the poorer group. Similarly, marginal costs of delivering water in the typical system may vary from customer to customer, but an acceptably "equitable" pricing system may decline to penalize users in hard-to-serve locations. The wider the range of each difference among customers, and the more numerous the types of difference, the greater become the chances that the maintenance of community consensus will require less than optimal arrangements, especially when memberships are "closed" and a member, once in, cannot readily opt out.

4) Both the constitutional arrangements for control and the political system actually prevailing within a local government cooperative may create opportunities for special interests to benefit at the expense of joint optimization for the community. That is, normative equilibrium requires certain definite types of arrangements for sharing inputs and outputs of the cooperative plant. But one member may feel that he can better his position by some maneuver that raises the output which he receives from the cooperative relative to the quantity of inputs which he contributes. Where output of the cooperative plant lacks complete homogeneity, and when particular inputs do not contribute proportionally to the outputs available to every member, then differences over appropriate allocations may legitimately arise among the members. Urban water systems may be more prone to policy manipulations by special interests than agricultural agencies. On the one hand, the water bill constitutes a small charge upon the city's residential user, both in relation to total consumer expenditures and to the maximum he would be willing to pay for at least a "subsistence" quantity of water. On the other hand, some users in the city may be more sensitive to water costs and be willing to expend the political effort required to secure favorable treatment.[47] The price of

[45] The prescription of supplying water at the lowest possible average cost can presumably be interpreted as involving the transfer of a quantity such that average cost and average revenue are equated. Average revenue to the agency corresponds in the simple case to the value of the net marginal product of water to its members, but average cost corresponds to marginal cost for the cooperative enterprise only when average cost is constant. If average costs are rising, then they lie below marginal costs, and the equating of average costs and revenues will lead to excessive deliveries. Conversely, if average costs are falling in the relevant range, marginal costs lie below them, and deliveries will be deficient. If an industry of open-membership cooperative enterprises operates under conditions that would be consistent with the emergence of a conventional purely competitive industry, it can be shown that each cooperative unit would be forced to set a charge equal to minimum average costs, and thereby marginal costs as well, and the pursuit of an objective of equating average costs and average revenue would not lead to allocative inefficiencies. See Helmberger, "Cooperative Enterprise as a Structural Dimension of Farm Markets," *op. cit.;* Kaarlehto, *op. cit.,* 34–50.

[46] Kaarlehto, *op. cit.,* 71–75.

[47] Price discrimination in favor of industrial users is the most likely result. Evidence will be discussed in Chapters 9 and 10.

irrigation water, however, holds greater importance to the typical farmer, and the farm enterprises within the service area of the typical irrigation district are relatively homogeneous in size. Thus, allocative distortions due to pressures from special interests seem relatively unlikely within this sector.[48]

5) Compounding the two preceding problems of equitable treatment and influence by interest groups as forces acting upon the allocative decisions of a water users' cooperative, some members of the association may not participate as immediate profit maximizers. Actions of the cooperative may affect their private economic welfare in indirect ways which alter their interest in allocations occurring within the cooperative plant. For example, a city water system may serve a public which includes commercial interests wishing to exploit the water supply as a means of promoting local economic growth. They may urge policies which are inconsistent with their own short-run profit maximization, as well as the optimal allocation for the community as a whole, in the hope of securing future gains stemming from general urban growth. In this case, the output level of the cooperative enterprise would be greater than optimal. The same problem may arise when the water agency is not a single product cooperative but an arm of a general local government (or "joint product" cooperative). It may be called upon to make its contribution to the attainment of the local government's plans for such things as development or annexation, to assist in local recreation plans, and often to earn profits on water sales which will permit a reduction of property taxes.

6) Efficient organization of a cooperative requires that the member-customers perceive and voluntarily acknowledge their benefit from the cooperative's actions. Even when public-good problems are absent and close study can impute the benefits of the cooperative's activities separately to individual members, the member as an average citizen may fail to recognize his benefit. Districts serving private households, for which water plays a seemingly small part in the total bundle of services purchased, may face this problem. The function performed may be purely technical and not widely understood. The benefits may be roundabout—as when the main result of enlarging the district's water-supply capacity is the reduction of fire insurance rates. When a district's output takes on some of the characteristics of a public good, as does ground-water replenishment, the achievement of optimal allocation within the agency becomes organizationally difficult for exactly the same reason that public goods tend to be marketed in less than optimal quantities by an industry that is conventionally organized. In addition to ground-water replenishment, such activities as drainage, reclamation, and levee maintenance are examples of other services supplied by water agencies which have public-good characteristics.

7) The cooperative enterprise formed to provide specific inputs for its members may discover that it can also provide services to outside customers. The character of optimal behavior of the cooperative in dealing with its members may be quite different from that of maximizing behavior in dealing with nonmembers. The cooperative is concerned with maximum profits to its members and not with

[48] All in all, local agricultural districts certainly deserve their reputation for democracy at the grass roots. The voters constitute an informed electorate. Though turnouts at irrigation district elections are often small, they can become very large when serious issues have split a district. Recall elections for recall of district directors have not been uncommon in the past.

maximum profits to the sum of cooperative members and nonmember customers. The insular cooperative enterprise may well have some degree of monopoly power in dealing with nonmembers, and under these conditions it will charge a price to the nonmembers which is greater than its marginal costs and therefore greater than the price charged to members. The possibilities of the output of the cooperative enterprise entering on the market and becoming a source of profits may create an entrepreneurial center within the structure of the enterprise which may be beyond the control of the members. On the whole, water agencies do not develop this market-oriented entrepreneurial spirit, but price discrimination against outsiders is the general rule (see Chapter 10).

8) Closely related to the preceding proposition that the cooperative enterprise, by the nature of its organization, can be expected to maximize profits in its dealings with outsiders is the proposition that the drawing of political boundaries between "us" and "them" will itself create a resistance to such switches of member-customers among agencies as might be required for optimal allocation. The normative theory of cooperative enterprises declares that, if the cost functions of the members' separate plants are independent of each other and members can freely switch agencies, the scale of each cooperative plant would tend to be expanded or contracted to the point where minimum long-run average costs are achieved.[49] In terms of the typical retail water district, this mobility would involve a tendency to annex or exclude territory until optimal scale is attained. But the maintenance of political consensus is rendered very difficult in any such fluid situation, and this fact—plus innate hostility toward "outsiders"—would tend to make boundaries rigid. Thus, we would expect relatively little redrawing of boundaries of water districts once agencies become firmly established (this prediction is confirmed in Chapter 9), and so could expect suboptimal performance in the form of inefficient scales of organization so far as average costs vary significantly with scale. This prediction is made independently of the legal rigidities restricting exclusion and inclusion that were identified in Chapter 3.

9) The management of a cooperative enterprise involves not only a political coordination process (whether the unit be a governmental or a private organization) but also a technical coordination process of managing its inputs and outputs. The quality and productivity of this management may be affected by the local water agency's cooperative, governmental status. The cooperative's management would have the same incentive to minimize the cost of producing any given output as would the management of a private enterprise. In the context of American attitudes toward government expenditures, however, this "efficient" objective may well be converted into the fallacious view that the cheapest input is always the best. A large amount of casual evidence assembled in the course of this study suggests that agricultural districts in particular may make less than

[49] The actual attainment of optimum scale for every cooperative enterprise would require identical cost curves for all cooperatives plus certain large-numbers assumptions. More generally, the scales of all cooperative enterprises would be adjusted through the unrestricted mobility of member-customers so that no further switch would reduce the total cost of supplying a given quantity of water.

optimal expenditures on skilled management[50] and may provide service of a lower quality (and cost) than would be optimal in the interest of member-customers of the joint enterprise. The possibility of significant performance deficiencies arising in the water industry from this source is augmented because the efficient managerial unit seems significantly larger than the typical local water agency; the common practice of spinning off elements of management to outside consultants[51] does not remove the concern that deficiencies may exist. Urban water agencies in Northern California seem to suffer less from a lack of professionalism in their management, though this judgment may reflect a concentration of the urban water supply function in the large agencies in the San Francisco Bay area rather than any systematic difference between agricultural and urban conditions. The political leadership of urban agencies tends to be drawn from the economic elite of the city in question; although its members are likely to possess abstract qualities of entrepreneurship in ample measure, they are also likely to be imbued with objectives of urban growth and expansion that may conflict with efficient water supply.

In conclusion, this review of the organizational aspects of users' cooperatives not only is built upon the legal characteristics of local water supply organizations, but also reinforces a number of performance predictions stated in our review of the industry's legal framework in Chapter 3. The water agency not only holds its water rights in trust for its closed membership, but also has as its main managerial task the development of a policy consensus among its membership on the course of action giving the greatest communal benefit. This communal benefit is built up from the preferences of individual member-customers on the basis of the agency's formal voting structure and its informal political system. In maximizing members' welfare, the agency is not constrained by considerations of the economic welfare of the state or nation as a whole (except as regulation intervenes), and indeed acts as a profit-maximizer in dealing with outsiders. Legal rigidities tending to impose a "closed membership" character on these agencies are compounded by organizational considerations which demand a stability that is

[50] For example, in 1958 a leading management consulting firm made a study of California's largest irrigation district which confirmed previous charges that its management suffered from a few dedicated individuals thriftily attempting to do excessively large jobs. The report recommended a substantial expansion of the district's managerial staff.

[51] In several cases, the management of a contiguous group of districts is pooled and carried out by one of them. (See U.S. Department of the Interior, Bureau of Reclamation, Region 2, *Sacramento River Service Area: Investigations of Glenn-Colusa, Jacinto, Provident, Compton-Delevan, Maxwell Irrigation Districts and Related Areas* [1953], pp. 9–10.) Many consulting facilities are available to perform some management functions of public water districts. Specialized engineering firms design and develop projects. A number of California attorneys and law firms specialize in water law, and these attorneys often play an important role in guiding a district's political decisions regarding the exercise of its legal rights. Many public agencies also give assistance. The California Districts Securities Commission, which must approve of investment projects of those districts under its authority, makes an independent engineering and economic evaluation of each project and frequently suggests modifications or raises questions for the district's management. The California Department of Water Resources and the Bureau of Reclamation similarly dispense a good deal of counsel to public districts on technical managerial problems.

not necessarily consistent with free mobility of members into or out of an organization.

Investment Planning and the Structure of Local Governments

In the opening sections of this chapter, after first stating normative guides to the appropriate allocation of resources within the water industry, we developed the specific applications of these criteria to the all-important investment decision: "all-important" because of its crucial role in determining the degree to which the industry attains optimal performance. In this section, we again engage in a hypothetical analysis of the investment decision, now in the context of the users' cooperative hypothesis and its implications about organizational behavior. Governmental units in the water industry face many external or constitutional constraints on their power to undertake investment projects. They reach their investment decisions through a political process which registers the individual and collective preferences of their member-customers and the institutional mechanism by which these are reconciled into a common decision. Here, we seek to explain how these internal decision patterns and external constraints may affect the scale, design, or timing of investment projects, in terms of causing departures from the norms outlined above. These hypotheses rest upon characteristics which we have found empirically significant for some range of public water agencies. We shall not try to indicate the extent of their descriptive validity at present, however, and so the discussion should be taken for the time being as entirely theoretical. We shall emphasize the traits of local government units rather than state and federal agencies; the small number of the latter involved in Northern California allows them to be covered on a case-by-case basis in Chapter 11.

Benefits, costs, and political decisions

Investment planning within an agency can be schematized to two stages: management proposes, the voters dispose. Into the design and timing of a proposed investment go various biases which may be held by the appointed or elected officials of a public water agency. The resulting proposal must typically win approval, at some stage, from the unit's electorate, and must also survive a series of constraints and win the express or tacit approval of a number of external entities. At each of these stages of an investment project's progression toward construction, allocative bias may be introduced, and the final outcome for a project actually constructed must clearly constitute the net result of a string of distortions, plus and minus, from optimality.

We note first that leaders of water agencies are elected officials whose function is to lead. They play their roles in a setting where economic growth is viewed as an unquestioned virtue, and where many local governments are expected to make all reasonable efforts to promote it. This atmosphere creates an inducement to build with a long time-horizon and, in the process, to take a rosy view of the area's economic future. Furthermore, people in the western states tend to view abundant water supplies as a catalyst that promotes local economic development, reasoning perversely that the best way to adapt economic activity to the relative scarcity of resources is to make the most scarce resource abundant. The bias injected by these views tends, of course, to promote overestimation of the benefits stemming from a water investment, unfortunate unless it counterbalances some undesirable constraint on growth.

Growth optimism does not affect all local governments alike. A farmer has no great interest in promoting the formation of more farms, whereas a retail merchant holds a definite personal stake in the rise of more factories and suburbs. A general government, feeling responsible for the whole economic future of its territory, will be moved more profoundly than one responsible only for special functions. We should expect "growth optimism," therefore, to hold greater sway among municipal than agricultural agencies, and among county-wide or other general governments than among special purpose water districts. Furthermore, investments which involve expansions of a going public service may offer less scope for clairvoyant optimism than those which anticipate a major qualitative change in the character of local economic activity, such as the conversion of land from dry farming to irrigation.

Other attitudes and practices of officials of water agencies could also inject bias into the planning of investment decisions. Some of these concern how the need or demand for an investment is inferred from the interests of the agency's customers. A consumer of water, untutored in the fine logic of short-run and long-run marginal cost, may expect his water agency to provide him with "enough" water at the going price. He is not likely to understand that a rise in his water rate is justified because augmented service should not be provided unless he is willing to pay a rate that covers the elevated long-run marginal cost at an expanded scale of operation. Therefore, short-run pricing disequilibria may affect the estimation of the benefits from an expanded supply; specifically, quantities of water demanded at prices below the relevant marginal cost may be taken as an index of the "requirements" which an expanded supply must meet. In the same vein, water users are unlikely to accept automatically a pricing scheme which raises charges at times of peak use ("when they need water the most"), and so the best-intentioned water agency management may lack the opportunity to test the relation between the value and cost of expanded supplies. The impact of these conditions on investment planning may be to promote investment in excessive fixed capacity or premature investments.

Still other attitudes and practices of water agency officials may reflect differences between true social opportunity costs and those "local" opportunity costs seen by the managers. The interest rate used to discount estimated future benefits and costs may not be that nominated above, a marginal rate of time preference of about 5 to 6 per cent, but rather the actual borrowing rate of the agency in question. Local agencies borrow under rather diverse terms in the capital markets, but some are able to secure funds at rates significantly below the 5 to 6 per cent range while none is observed to go above it. Furthermore, capital and operating costs of a proposed project are always estimated in terms of expected money costs to the district and not social opportunity costs. The differences may run in both directions, but money costs conspicuously omit such factors as any opportunity costs of additional water captured through a new investment, or the rising opportunity cost of urban land occupied by water system structures as an urban area grows.

The control of a district's electorate over its investment decision comprises both the informal expression of wishes and desires and formal powers exercised in electing district officers and balloting on any investment project which requires an increase in the agency's bonded indebtedness. At the formal level, California local officials are elected for short terms and are subject to recall. Ballots are often crowded with special measures introduced by initiative. Especially in agricultural water districts, elections are often fought over issues relating to investment decisions. There is no doubt that these decisions by local agencies tend strongly to conform to the wishes of politically dominant member-customers.

We wish to focus, however, not upon this general responsiveness of local public investment decisions to the popular will, but rather upon the typical specific requirement that bond issues be authorized by the voters at the polls. For a project to win approval by majority vote—frequently a two-thirds majority under California law—it may have to satisfy requirements for the distribution of its anticipated benefits and costs among the voters which have little to do with the total relation of the present value of benefits to the present value of costs. Let us examine this problem in detail, making the following assumptions which are broadly suitable to an irrigation district:

1) All of the benefits of the project are received, and the costs paid, by residents of the service area.

2) The project is financed by the sale of water and an ad valorem property tax, set so that revenue from water sales covers expected annual operation and maintenance costs and net opportunity costs of water, while the property tax covers debt service.

3) Each voter casts his ballot on the basis of his judgment about whether or not the project's benefits to him exceed its costs to him.

4) The voter identifies the project's net benefits to him with the increased personal income he derives from the project (net of increases in his operating costs and in his payments for purchase of water). He identifies the project's other costs to him with the increases in property tax payments associated with it.

5) The aggregate of individual voters' assessments of the benefits of the project equals that estimated by the district's officials (and their expert consultants).

6) A two-thirds majority is required to approve a bond issue.

Let us designate the present value of the increased income[52] derived from the project by the *i*th voter as B'_i, the present value of his anticipated future increases

[52] Net only of increases in operating costs other than increases in payments for purchase of water.

in water-purchase payments as Φ_i, the present value of his net benefits derived from the project as R_i, and the present value of his anticipated increase in annual tax payments as T_i. Then, for every voter, $R_i = B'_i - \Phi_i$; by the second assumption, $\sum_i \Phi_i = \Phi$ and $\sum_i T_i = I_o$.[53] By the fifth assumption, $\sum_i B'_i = B'$. The rational ith voter will favor a project if, and only if, $R_i - T_i \geq 0$.

These assumptions lead directly to the conclusion that a project may be rejected at the polls even if $B' > C$ (where $C = I_o + \Phi$) because for no subset consisting of two-thirds of a district's voters do personal benefits exceed personal costs for every member of the subset. Some voters may receive large benefits, the sum of which may exceed the small negative benefits of the larger number of voters who do not expect to benefit. A redesigning of the project which redistributes its benefits, a change in the system of taxation, or other such strategies may prove necessary to produce the required majority for a project with a favorable benefit-cost ratio.

Our interest lies, however, not in these expedients but in the probable bias in the scale of investment projects which occurs when a voting requirement must be met. Consider what happens to the benefits and costs to individual voters as a project is hypothetically expanded toward its optimal scale, at which $\triangle B' = \triangle C$. One can argue that the portion of negative votes will increase because of the way in which $B' - \Phi$ $(= \sum_i R_i)$ is distributed as compared to the way in which the debt service payments for I_o $(= \sum_i T_i)$ are distributed. R_i is distributed among individual voters according to the productivity of water on land. T_i is distributed among individual voters according to the total value of some component of their existing property. As the project's scale is expanded, for each voter $\triangle R_i$ will fall and $\triangle T_i$ will be constant.[54] The rate of consumers' surplus (R_i/T_i) will fall. Since T_i is not based on water productivity, nor is it perfectly correlated with any increase in property values due to water, it will be high relative to water productivity for some users and low for others. Units with relatively high tax payments will probably be as numerous as those with relatively low tax payments. As scale increases, $R_i - T_i$ will become negative for an increasing number of units, those for which R_i/T_i happens to be low. This process creates negative votes. Since a negative vote offsets two positive votes (by our sixth assumption), a one-third opposition will develop even though it may still be true that $\sum_i \triangle R_i > \sum_i \triangle T_i$, or $\triangle B' > \triangle C$.

Thus we conclude that the requirement for a two-thirds majority to authorize bond financing will tend to result in projects of inefficiently small scale. This argument obviously depends critically upon its many assumptions. The conversion of the two-thirds majority assumption to a simple majority destroys the presumption for a suboptimal scale, unless the distribution of R_i/T_i can be shown to be

[53] Aggregate variables without subscripts are those defined above in the discussion of the optimal scale of a single investment project. In discounting to arrive at present values, the discount rate must equal the rate of interest on the debt increase to invest I_o if $I_o = \sum_i T_i$.

[54] It is assumed that T_i increases proportionally with I_o, and that assessed valuations do not change in response to changes in the quantity of water used.

skewed.[55] Furthermore, if the character of the project is such that the excess of B' over B is substantial in the neighborhood of the optimal scale, the chances are increased that $B'_i - \Phi_i - T_i > 0$ for the typical voter, and the expected favorable vote increases.[56]

Nonetheless, we wish to emphasize the effect of altering one of the assumptions in a way which strengthens the presumption that voter approval may be obtainable only for suboptimal scales of investment. Let us alter our fifth assumption which equates B' estimated by expert consultants with $\sum_i B'_i$ as appraised subjectively by the individual members. We retain the assumptions that the individuals and the district agree on the expected costs (and employ the same discount rate). Now, $\sum_i R_i$ perceived by individual voters may fall short of $B' - \Phi$ estimated by the district's experts. Two major reasons for this might be the disutility to individuals of changing their patterns of economic activity, and attitudes toward uncertainty which may diverge from those held by the district's management. A major expansion of agricultural water supplied in an area assumes, and is justified by, the expectation that a significant amount of land will be converted from dry farming to irrigation. Expert appraisal, based on statistical studies, may show that farmers can clearly increase their profits by shifting crops, preparing new land, purchasing new machinery, and so on. These shifts to new technology are not costless to the farmer and are fraught with uncertainty. This uncertainty and the disutility of what amounts almost to a change in occupation may well cause farmers to write down the value of R_i. Problems of transitional periods and learning curves may also arise.

Uncertainty of a purer and more general sort may affect the valuation of R_i because a district investment adds a sure cost (T_i) and a benefit ($B'_i - \Phi_i$) which will be subject to uncertainty. It is of the essence of a users' cooperative that member-customers bear the role of holder of equity in the face of any shortfall of revenues as against fixed costs. So far as members wish to avoid the increase of risk associated with an expanded investment by the district, their voting behavior will tend to compel scales of investment which are suboptimal by the test of expected returns calculated by the district's management.[57]

On balance, our review of the institutional pressures on the investment decision operating within the public district boils down to this: the interests of officials, in some types of districts, may tend toward excessive scale or longevity of projects, or premature construction. The voice of the member-customers, heard in particular

[55] A case of such skewness would be found in an irrigation district whose voters include a number of town residents. For them, R_i/T_i tends to be very small, but so does the absolute value of T_i. They may well be numerous in comparison to the number of farmer-voters, for whom both R_i/T_i and the absolute values T_i tend to be high. There would be a tendency for majorities to be obtainable only for projects for which $\Delta B' > \Delta C$.

[56] One might argue, with logical validity, that if R_i and T_i are perfectly correlated for any scale of I_o the problem is disposed of. Nonetheless, the many sorts of slippage which render this correlation imperfect, even where conscious efforts are made to adjust T_i in this direction, seem to warrant exploiting the implications of our third assumption.

[57] In this case, some ambiguity creeps into the notion of optimal scale. Some might argue that the voters are perforce right, and that in this institutional setting it is their attitudes toward uncertainty which should be controlling.

at the bond-authorization election, may tend to impel suboptimal scale or project life, especially in those cases where more than a simple majority must give consent. Let us now consider how the impact of these countervailing pressures[58] may be further modified by pressures from without the agency.

External influences and constraints

At the level of hypothetical discussion, we can usefully consider two sets of external factors which affect the optimality of investment decisions made by local agencies. One of these concerns the types of capital rationing imposed on these agencies. The other set of forces relates to the fragmentation of local government units, whereby some kinds of benefits and costs accrue to "outsiders" and are not taken into account by officials acting in the rational interest of their own electorate.

It is fair to say that all local governments operate under some sort of limitation upon the maximum indebtedness which they may incur. This limit is often statutory. In the absence of a formal requirement, it will be applied by lenders or regulatory agencies. Whatever the merit of such a restriction, it clearly may inflict a cost in economic efficiency.

The normative criterion for investment stated above essentially calls for investment by a public district whenever the net productivity of the community's factors of production can be enhanced thereby. Whenever $\triangle I_o < \triangle(B' - \Phi)$, the real wealth of the community is increased by investing. Yet a debt limit, or its equivalent in informal capital rationing, restricts the amount of investment in relation to current wealth, whatever may be the long-run prospects of return associated with a particular investment opportunity. A debt limit is set in terms of some fraction of the assessed value of land or of real property in the district, typically from 5 to 25 per cent. Assessed values are always a small fraction of market value, often one-fourth or less, so that the agency is typically restricted to possessing at any one time unamortized investments equal to 5 per cent or less of the market value of the land or real property which constitutes its tax base.[59] In short, debt limits and other forms of capital rationing regularly affect the investment decisions of local governments. As was shown in the preceding section, the agency best adjusts to the constraint by ranking different available projects (including alternative scales of given projects) in the order of $(B' - \Phi)/I_o$ and selecting the design-scale combination which maximizes $B' - C$ attainable with an

[58] We have not sought to consider the relative strength of the pull of management toward excessive scale versus the pull of the member-customers toward deficient scale. It might be noted, however, that control over the range of alternative investment proposals discussed and evaluated lies strongly in the hands of the officials. Furthermore, voters are seldom in the position, while considering one proposal, of knowing that its rejection will cause an alternative to be placed upon the ballot in a subsequent election. Thus they often find themselves substantially in the position of being confronted with an all-or-nothing offer.

[59] Furthermore, it would be a rare investment project which had sufficient effect on land values to be in any way self-financing through increasing assessed values and thus the absolute value of the debt limit; in any case, this relaxation of the capital constraint on the agency would come only after any particular investment causing it had been financed.

investment not exceeding the constrained I_0. Nonetheless, this procedure simply makes the best of the constraint and does not blunt its impact of imparting a bias toward investments too small in scale and too late in timing of construction.

The other main group of external influences upon a local district's investment plans stems from the very fact that it is local. Our previous assumption that all benefits and costs accrue within the investing district in many cases may be wrong on both counts. Two broad classes of external spillovers of benefits and costs arise: (1) elements of cost may be neglected which constitute opportunity costs to economic entities located outside the district; (2) elements of benefit, either positive or negative, may be ignored because they stem from external economies or diseconomies affecting others. Much of Chapters 12 and 14 will deal with the institutional substitutes for a market mechanism which have (or have not) arisen to force recognition of these external effects. The possibilities are reviewed here briefly in terms of their implications for the optimality of investment decisions.

A fragmented economy is the economy of everyday life. Every action by a private business enterprise tends to spill over and affect the profits of many other firms in the economy. There is nothing wrong in general with the initiating firm failing to take these effects into account, for indeed they constitute the signals through which the market mechanism works.[60] It works correctly, however, only if money costs to one firm are opportunity costs to another. At this point, a difficulty arises in the water industry because shadow prices for water at the source usually are not recognized.

Another problem arises from fragmentation because a water district calculating the optimal scale of a project may consider only the marginal benefits attainable to its present member-customers. Although districts can expand their territories to utilize efficiently the outputs of projects subject to significant scale economies, or cooperate with other districts in undertaking such projects jointly, evidence reviewed in Chapters 3 and 9 suggests that these processes are likely to operate imperfectly. To the extent that they do, suboptimal projects will result. In practice, this problem arises in the form of projects being designed to serve some given "need," based on current economic conditions within a district's boundaries, rather than being scaled in terms of marginal costs and benefits attainable with an ideal rearrangement of boundaries and service areas.

The failure of the sponsoring agency to count external economies and diseconomies of an investment has an obvious influence upon the correctness of the scale and timing of a project or, indeed, the question of whether or not it should be undertaken at all. We shall argue in Chapter 14 that these external effects are extremely pervasive in the water industry. The plausibility of this conclusion appears clear when one realizes that external effects are incapable of neat analytical separation from the phenomenon of joint products, widely associated with water projects. The degree to which externalities spill beyond the horizon of a particular agency depends upon some of the physical circumstance of that agency. A general government dealing in water but holding a constitutional interest in the general

[60] See Tibor Scitovsky, "Two Concepts of External Economies," *Journal of Political Economy,* LXII (April 1954), 143–51.

welfare of its member-customers may be relatively alert to externalities; a special purpose district, or one subject to political control reflecting a special interest, may not. A distinction is thus suggested between the behavior of municipal governments and county-wide agencies, on the one hand, and the special purpose districts common in agricultural water service, on the other. The size of an agency, relative to the physical size of the water service area it inhabits and the topographic and hydrographic characteristics of the area, also influences the chances of its perceiving the full range of external effects. An agricultural district serving all lands within economic reach of a given river thus might score better than one covering only a fraction of this service area. Finally, it may matter whether the physical works of a project are all located within a district's boundaries, or whether dams, power plants, and conduits reach out to great distances. Most externalities resulting from a dam and reservoir presumably accrue in the immediate vicinity of the damsite and upstream and downstream on the river. A city in a different hydrographic area might be less concerned with these than, say, a county agency developing a river whose basin lies largely within the county's boundaries.[61]

Let us carry the analysis of external effects one step farther, asking about the chances that those effects which fail to enter directly into the utility function of an investing agency will be abruptly placed there by the action of affected outsiders. We present the following general hypothesis: the chances that an investing agency must compensate others for external diseconomies are greater than the chances of its being compensated for external economies. Although this hypothesis does not hold for all types of externalities, it does have an important basis in the institutions of the water industry. Adjusting the balance of externalities is largely the task of judicial and regulatory processes, and the law is more ready to redress damages than to force the seizure of neglected opportunities. Furthermore, the beneficiary of an external economy often optimizes his position not by speaking up and offering to pay an amount equal to its marginal worth to him, but rather by offering no compensation and quietly enjoying whatever benefits come his way without fussing over an inappropriate marginal adjustment. If external benefits take a directly saleable form (such as hydroelectric power), if they are so distributed that the beneficiaries accurately perceive them and can be organized to offer compensation, or if a government at a higher level undertakes to offer compensation, then the problem of neglected external benefits of an investment may be solved, and optimal scale and timing may be attainable by the investing agency. Otherwise, desirable investments may be foregone entirely, or their scale and timing may be suboptimal.

While not all external diseconomies are perceived with equal precision by their victims, forms of legal redress generally tend to become available for those which are detected. The chances of the investing agency having to answer for them are thus increased over the chances of its being apprised of external benefits which it creates. It does not follow, of course, that external diseconomies are correctly taken into account. They may be undercompensated—for example, if

[61] Similar conditions might be stated for the location of a water agency relative to the location of externalities resulting from its use of water, such as stream pollution resulting from return flows, or the raising of ground-water tables.

the investing agency successfully upholds the position that a major economic undertaking is threatened and "progress is being blocked." On the other hand, forcing an investing agency to quiet all objectors may give the latter undue bargaining power in some settings, and a judicial process which enjoins an agency from damaging other parties may force the defendant to incur costs far in excess of any damages inflicted.

In summary, the external forces operating on the investment decisions of local agencies may have the following types of effects: (1) Capital rationing may restrict investment below optimal scale and timing. (2) The ignoring of opportunity costs, particularly those of water itself, will have complicated results, depending on whether the apparent yield of the project thereby gains or suffers. (3) Investing to serve only arbitrarily defined service areas tends to cause adoption of suboptimal project scales. (4) External effects neglected by an investing agency may bias its investment decision in either direction from optimal, but the asymmetry between external economies and diseconomies suggests a net tendency toward suboptimality.

Investment Behavior of State and Federal Agencies

The policies of the three state and federal water agencies which carry on extensive operations in Northern California—the California Department of Water Resources, the Bureau of Reclamation, and the Corps of Engineers—are discussed in detail in Chapter 11. Here we confine ourselves to noting some important contrasts between the hypotheses developed above concerning the institutional traits and investment behavior of local agencies and the conduct which we might on *a priori* grounds expect of state and national government agencies.

There is no reason to expect the optimistic bias of state and national governments in planning projects for water development to be any less pronounced than that of local agencies. Indeed, it may be stronger. In particular, the federal agencies in their nature are primarily construction agencies. As such, they would naturally tend to develop an engineering bias in favor of proceeding with physically feasible construction and achieving "full utilization" of all available water supplies, a bias threatening to extend projects to the point where marginal costs exceed marginal benefits. The state agency, tied to a government with a notable faith in economic growth, would presumably tend in the same direction. Local agencies, by contrast, may settle for building capacity to provide some desired average level of output, even if a larger project would return marginal benefits in excess of marginal costs.

When we consider the relation between the planning process of the state and national governments and the consent of citizens, a sharp contrast with the local district arises. Apart from peripheral questions of the distribution of payments, the same persons pay the costs and receive the benefits of a local unit's project. Federal agencies require the consent both of those who pay and those who benefit, but these two groups may overlap little if at all. Except when the agencies seek to impose on project beneficiaries charges for use in the neighborhood of allocable costs, or social policies which the beneficiaries find not in their personal interest, the latter can be expected to register enthusiasm for proposed construction. Restrictions on the scale or timing of investments due to the beneficiaries' doubts about the net benefits are most unlikely.

On the other hand, the consent of those who will pay the costs of federal programs (in excess of user charges) comes from Congress, and from the State Legislature and voters of California, in the case of the bond-financed California Water Plan. Approval of federal projects comes subject to the requirement of some showing of benefits in excess of costs, and indeed the federal government has pioneered in developing and applying benefit-cost calculation techniques. But political processes are also involved, and measures of benefits used in benefit-cost analyses are distressingly elastic, so that these procedures serve as a dubiously efficient filter of inefficient projects.

Capital rationing, which acts as an external check upon the behavior of local agencies, becomes an internal constraint upon the state and federal governments, which can borrow with little difficulty once such action is authorized.[62] Capital rationing can still be said to operate, but in the form of a budgetary rather than a borrowing restriction. Apart from the particular incidence of the rationing, it becomes a constraint of lesser order than that binding the local agencies because it limits investment in a given time period rather than the total cumulative indebtedness which the investing agency incurs. An effective financial constraint upon a state or federal agency is perhaps more likely to delay the construction projects than to restrict their ultimate scales. An effective restriction upon a local agency may permanently block a project of optimal scale.

In short, the investment decisions of state and federal agencies seem subject to weaker internal offsets to any congenital optimism of their managements than do those of local government units. Furthermore, in view of the considerations stated in the preceding paragraphs, it would seem difficult to accept an argument that the amounts of funds appropriated to these agencies via the political process are "right" by any economic or normative political test. They are determined by decision processes that cannot be said to reflect the democratic weighting of the preferences of a well-informed electorate.

As we consider the other external forces governing the investment planning of local agencies, an obvious difference for the state and federal agencies arises in that their political boundaries are far more likely to contain all of the external effects of any construction which they undertake. If externalities are not considered in estimating benefits and costs, then, the reason should not be because governments at higher levels act in the interests only of their own citizens and not those of some other jurisdiction. But the problem of ignoring externalities does not thereby disappear. Instead, it turns into a problem of pressures by interest groups within the complex political networks of the state and federal governments.

[62] The conspicuous historical exception to this statement is the inability of the state of California, in the depths of the depressed 1930's, to manage bond financing of the Central Valley Project.

9

FORMATION AND EVOLUTION OF WATER AGENCIES

In Northern California, as indicated in Chapter 4, water agencies develop and purvey nearly all water supplies from surface sources (such supplies comprising about 55 per cent of the total). The entry of an area's water users into the market for surface supplies is thus normally presaged by the formation of public water agencies of various types to purchase or capture such supplies. Further, agencies that wholesale water normally secure retail distribution by encouraging the formation of local public districts with which they can contract. (The case is different with respect to ground water supplies, since this water is captured almost entirely by a multitude of small private pumping plants operated by individual water users.)

This chapter provides a major part of the evidence underlying the users' cooperative hypothesis by showing the regularity with which changes in water allocation result not from sellers seeking buyers but from users organizing cooperatively to seek sources or sellers. As we explore the circumstances surrounding the formation of agencies, moreover, this hypothesis helps to explain the range of motives governing their behavior. It suggests the scope for competition of one kind or another, as agencies are created and their legal forms altered in response to actual or incipient rivalries. Such findings about the conduct patterns of water agencies, moreover, lead to inferences concerning the performance of the industry. Are the motives of agencies, revealed in the process of their formation, compatible with behavior which seeks to utilize water where and when the net value of its marginal product exceeds its marginal cost? Are the scales at which agencies are formed, and any changes occurring in those scales, consistent with an efficient scale of their economic activities?

Throughout this chapter, we must keep in mind the determinants of the pattern of agency formation and their significance for market performance. Particularly significant here are water law and the law of water agencies, obviously major influences on the creation of districts. Physical features of the region having economic significance, ingrained attitudes of local water users, and the policies of state and federal regulatory agencies are also environmental features which stand as candidates for the role of determining the pattern of district formation.

The following sections review in turn the causes of the formation of districts, of major changes in their legal form, and of their disappearance. We emphasize the relation of these events to the economic transformation of water from a free to a scarce good. Finally, we deal with the determinants of the physical size of districts in relation to the efficiency of their distributive operations and of the allocation of water.[1]

Causes of the Formation of Organizations

In the most basic sense, water organizations are formed because of the marked indivisibilities in the physical facilities used to store and transport water. The unit costs of wells, pipes, canals, and reservoirs all decrease over a large range of scales. In most cases an individual user can efficiently provide for his own supply only if he transports the water over a relatively small vertical or horizontal distance. In a city some large firms may find it economical to draw water from adjoining rivers or pump from wells, but few households, stores, or offices will prefer this mode of supply. An organization to provide water service to an area will be necessary.[2] In agricultural districts the relative efficiency of organization is not always so great. If a stream runs through or by a farmer's land, or if ground water lies at a moderate depth, individual self-supply proves relatively efficient. But to serve a farm in the arid West which lacks easy access to ground or surface water requires more extensive operations—operations which can be carried on efficiently only with an organization to serve a community of farmers.

Entrepreneurship in district formation

In the early years of the development of irrigation in California, the technology of pumping water from underground basins remained relatively primitive. The conversion of the lands of the Central Valley from dry farming and ranching to irrigated agriculture thus necessarily involved a search for surface supplies, and this almost always entailed some form of communal organization. Land promotion enterprises played an important part in the settling of the Valley and the development of irrigated agriculture. A promoter often constructed a water system based on gravity diversion from some adjacent river, distributing shares in a mutual water company along with the sale of each parcel of land. Though these mutual companies often gave way later to more complex forms of organization with greater legal powers, they sufficed at first for operating simple water systems. Furthermore,

[1] Many of the conclusions set forth in this chapter and those following in Part Two depend heavily upon numerous interviews carried out between 1960 and 1963 and upon files of local newspaper clippings made available by the Irrigation Districts Association of California and the Water Resources Center Archives, University of California. Because of the detailed and specific character of the evidence drawn from these sources, it will be discussed only in a general way in the following pages, and footnotes will cite only especially important sources of information. We recognize that evidence of this sort has relatively low initial reliability and can easily become out of date. We have tried to cross-check all data and to avoid basing conclusions upon small numbers of cases or dubious documentation, but this caution could not be exercised as thoroughly as when carrying out a study based upon less fugitive sources of information.

[2] Usually taking a form of larger scale than the burro and water cart which in the days of the forty-niners made the rounds of San Francisco streets with water drawn from springs and from barges ferried across the Bay from Marin County. See Ray W. Taylor, *Hetch Hetchy* (1926), p. 10. (This and other footnote references are cited in brief form when they are also included in the Bibliography.)

mutual systems offered the advantage to promoters that they were easily dissolved in case the ventures failed.[3]

Public water agencies were also formed by the cooperative action of established settlers. In the 1880's, a major political issue in the state was whether or not the great landholdings in the valley should be broken up and placed under irrigation. The first irrigation district statute, the Wright Act of 1887, aimed at accomplishing this by allowing the formation of districts by popular sovereignty. It permitted the citizens of a town having five hundred or more electors to propose and approve by election the formation of an irrigation district upon a large tract of dry-farmed land. If the district were successfully organized, its assessments would force the conversion of this land to irrigation and, it was hoped, its subdivision into relatively small tracts. The prototype of districts thus formed is the Modesto Irrigation District, for which the Wright Act was largely written.[4] Formed in this way, the early districts inevitably faced built-in internal opposition from ranchers wishing to continue with dry farming. This contributed heavily to their mortality rate. Though failures substantially outnumbered successes among the early districts seeking to bring dry land under irrigation, the few successes had important demonstration effects.[5] Thus, social policy, plus the enthusiasm of town dwellers for irrigated agriculture as a means to raise the scale of local commerce and the potential population of the state, speeded the displacement of dry farming. The subsequent formation of agricultural districts lacks such important entrepreneurial elements, and can be explained largely from the objective causes discussed below.

The pattern of entrepreneurship in forming urban water agencies has been relatively routine at all times. The vast systems serving the San Francisco Bay area have grown from simple beginnings in small companies formed to serve a nascent urban area. One way or another, they grew with the area. Numerically speaking, the great bulk of urban water agencies realized their early expectation of remaining small-scale water suppliers to compact areas of urban settlement, operating either as private enterprises or as mutual water companies. Where such units have been combined into large systems, either an incremental process has been involved, or entrepreneurship at some more general level of government has entered the picture. This relatively routine process of forming urban agencies continues to this

[3] Charles F. Lambert, "Land Speculation and Irrigation Development in the Sacramento Valley, 1905–1957" (Typescript, University of California General Library, Berkeley, 1957), p. 314.

[4] California State Department of Public Works, Division of Engineering and Irrigation, *Irrigation Districts in California, 1929,* by Frank Adams, Bulletin No. 21 (1930), p. 180. This publication was the first of a series identified as "Bulletin 21" which is continuing to the present. The California State Department of Public Works, Division of Water Resources, under the title *Report on Irrigation Districts of California for the Year 1929* began its publication of annual developments with Bulletin No. 21–A and continued through Bulletin 21–O for 1943; its Bulletin No. 21–P covered the years 1944–1950. The California Department of Water Resources, Division of Resources Planning, continued the series under the title *Report on Irrigation and Water Storage Districts in California for 1951–55,* and has since issued its Bulletin No. 21 for the periods 1956–58, and 1959–60, and annual reports beginning with 1961. [Hereinafter all issues of Bulletin No. 21 cited in this chapter will be by number and, if necessary, date; the original will be cited as Bulletin No. 21 (Adams).]

[5] Bulletin No. 21 (Adams), *op. cit.,* pp. 163 and 177; and Sol P. Elias, *Stories of Stanislaus* (1924), pp. 155–56.

day in areas lacking large water suppliers possessing an expansionist outlook, but where unconstrained suburban expansion continues. The process of suburban expansion has turned some agricultural water districts into urban suppliers—but this role invariably has been thrust upon the districts and accepted only reluctantly.[6]

Since the need of organization for urban water supply is transparently clear, the interesting questions of entrepreneurship and objectives deal much more with the succession of types of organization. In agriculture, where self-supply of water by the final user is more feasible, the causes of organization are both more interesting and less obvious.

Inadequacy of ground water

In contrast to the pioneer irrigation districts of the nineteenth century, the formation of most public districts to secure agricultural water supplies has not been complicated by real estate promotion and motives of driving dry-farmed land into irrigation. At least through the 1920's, most districts were formed as a result of local landowners' anticipations of sufficient profits from irrigated agriculture to warrant cooperation in seeking external water supplies[7] or improving the facilities and services of struggling private or mutual companies. In the last three decades, different factors have assumed great importance in the formation of districts. One, following the development of private pumping, is community action to halt the depletion of ground-water resources. Another is the formation of a district as a step in doing business with wholesalers of water, or to ward off competition for natural or wholesaled supplies. Now it is the exception for agencies or districts to be formed in "empty" unirrigated territory to tap unclaimed sources of water; most of the scattered examples lie in foothill areas.[8]

By the end of World War II, nearly all parts of the Central Valley that were reasonably promising for irrigated agriculture had undergone some development. However, as early as 1920 most land that could be watered by gravity with unregulated streamflow from adjacent rivers had already come under irrigation. The agricultural boom of World War II pushed the frontier of cultivation into large areas where only ground water was available. And, except for a few favorably situated tracts, the development of irrigation from ground-water sources came to involve withdrawals from the underground basins in excess of natural replenish-

[6] R. T. Durbrow, "Use of Irrigation Water for Domestic Purposes," *Journal of the American Water Works Association,* XLI (September 1949), 771–76.

[7] Even before 1920, the quest of agencies for surface supplies in some areas had become both complex and fruitless. For example, the Corcoran Irrigation District was formed in 1919 on the fringe of the Kings River area and east of Tulare Lake, embodying "the efforts of landowners . . . to gather up such scattered waters as are available and apply them to a fertile belt of land that thus far has not been highly developed." The District's main hope was the construction of a dam on the Kings River, but in the meantime it sought "scattered waters" by buying shares in a mutual canal company, purchasing the surplus water of an adjacent district with a strong water right, gathering the flood flows of the Kaweah River and Tule River, and planning for district pumping from the underground basin. See Bulletin No. 21 (Adams), *op. cit.,* pp. 257–58.

[8] See Bulletin No. 21–E (1933), *op. cit.,* pp. 14–19, and Bulletin No. 21 (1956–58), *op. cit.,* p. 16.

ments; the consequence was more or less rapidly falling water tables and increasing pumping costs. Levels of ground water reflect the prosperity, and hence the rate of expansion, of irrigated agriculture. They also reflect the rainfall cycle; and these contributed to severe declines in water tables in the early 1930's and again in the 1950's, but during the later 1930's and up to the end of World War II, some areas under irrigated development enjoyed a recovery of ground-water levels.

Ground-water tables have declined secularly in much of the Central Valley during the past three decades—in nearly all of the southern San Joaquin Valley and parts of the Sacramento Valley. Declining ground water in turn has furnished a strong incentive to farmers to seek surface sources of water. A falling water table means increased operating costs, since the costs of pumping increase about proportionally with the pump lift. Farmers must eventually incur large capital costs to deepen wells and install larger pumps. Worst of all, in attempting to deepen wells, the farmers may encounter connate brines or reach impervious strata too thick to penetrate economically, putting an end to the availability of ground water in excess of natural replenishment. Such developments give a major stimulus to the formation of public districts as means of securing supplementary supplies. In the past few decades, unsatisfactory ground-water conditions have influenced the formation of the great majority of public water districts in California. Depending on the local situation, public action has usually sought to provide surface water for direct application—as in the case of the Central Valley irrigation and water districts—but sometimes to replenish ground-water basins through percolation.

Table 22 illustrates the influence of falling ground water on the formation of districts. It lists chronologically the irrigation districts formed to purchase water from the Friant-Kern Canal of the U.S. Bureau of Reclamation during the years 1937-49, along with ground-water conditions prevailing at and before the time of

TABLE 22
CHARACTERISTICS OF GROUND-WATER SUPPLIES IN SELECTED IRRIGATION DISTRICTS FORMED TO RECEIVE WATER FROM THE FRIANT-KERN CANAL

Year of formation	District	Depth to ground water, time of formation (feet)	Average rate of decline	
			Feet per year	Period of observation
1937	Orange Cove	80–100	3–8	1917–37
1937	Exeter	75–130	3–5	1921–37
1937	Lindmore	200 & over	7–9	1921–36
1937	Shafter-Wasco	75–100	3.5	1921–37
1938	Delano-Earlimart	150–280	15.0	1921–36
1941	Saucelito	120	4.0	1921–39
1948	Ivanhoe	75	1.8	1921–48
1948	Stone Corral	44	3.2 2.6	1921–35 1942–48
1949	Lower Tule River	83	1.3 5.5	1921–43 1943–48
1949	Porterville	55	0.6 4.3	1921–43 1943–48

SOURCE: California Department of Public Works, Division of Water Resources, *Report on Irrigation Districts in California for the Year 1937, 1938, 1941,* and *1944–50;* Bulletin No. 21–I, 21–J, 21–M, and 21–P (1939–1953).

their formation. Lands in those irrigation districts which came into being before World War II incurred the costs of significantly greater pump lifts than those formed later. The recently formed districts generally did not suffer serious declines in ground-water supplies until agricultural activity boomed during World War II. This pattern suggests that farmers are sensitive both to rapidly rising ground-water costs (which they expect to persist into the future) and to costs that are high relative to those of other areas. Both conditions seem to create an interest in organized efforts to stabilize or reduce these costs.

Arrival of wholesale suppliers

A very important element in the formation of public water districts recently has been the appearance of potential wholesalers. A major wholesaler, the Bureau of Reclamation, has transformed the organizational pattern of a large portion of the Central Valley since its arrival in the 1930's. Before that time, wholesale agencies were of little ultimate significance, despite an occasional local impact.

The first large-scale moves to form irrigation districts aimed at dealing with a large cooperative wholesale supplier were seen in the Kings River area. Around 1920, local interests were discussing plans for the construction of Pine Flat Dam on the Kings, and a Kings River Conservation District was formed. A number of new irrigation districts appeared in territory having poor or impeded rights to the Kings River, or no rights at all—and some of the land was far removed from the river. As hope for Pine Flat faded, several of the districts became inactive. Others sought to "buy into" the available natural runoff of the Kings, either by purchasing shares which conveyed a partial entitlement to the water yielded by the rights of established mutual water companies (a successful move), or by establishing well fields to capture percolation from the river (unsuccessful because of legal opposition).[9]

New local wholesalers continue to spur the formation of districts as water distribution in Northern California takes on more and more vertical articulation. Several cases involve the organization of suburban territory around cities or towns in response to the creation of an area-wide wholesaler or rewholesaler. In at least one such case the local fire-prevention district has encouraged this development in the expectation that a water system of higher capacity drawing upon wholesale supplies would permit the reduction of fire insurance rates in outlying areas.[10] The organization of retail districts is sometimes tinged with rivalry for water when the wholesaler's proposed water supply taps the same source as that of the integrated retailer.[11]

[9] Bulletin No. 21 (Adams), *op. cit.*, pp. 217, 218, 224–30, 260–63.

[10] *Sonoma Index-Tribune,* Dec. 10, 1959; *Santa Rosa Press-Democrat,* Dec. 18, 1959; Bulletin No. 21–P (1944–50), *op. cit.*, pp. 9–10, 15–16.

[11] For example, Linden Irrigation District was formed along the Calaveras River in 1930 with the goal of arranging for storage behind Hogan Dam, under construction by the city of Stockton. But the District also feared that, unless it acted, the dam's operation would impair its existing rights to the flow of the Calaveras. Bulletin No. 21–P (1944–50), *op. cit.*, pp. 16–18.

The great majority of agricultural water agencies formed in California since the late 1930's has arisen from the stimulus of a potential major wholesale supplier—either the Bureau of Reclamation or the California Department of Water Resources. Of the thirty-seven irrigation districts, water districts, and municipal utility districts holding permanent contracts in 1960 for service from the Bureau's Contra Costa, Delta-Mendota, Madera, and Friant-Kern canals, only six were organized before the prospect of a wholesale supply appeared. The Friant-Kern area illustrates the pattern clearly. When it became clear in the mid-1930's that the project would be built, districts began to form here and there in the immediate service area of its canals in anticipation of contracting for supplies. As indicated above, the first districts to organize in the San Joaquin Valley were those with the most unsatisfactory ground-water conditions. This process continued as the canals were built, with districts forming to fill the "holes" among organized agencies until the lands which could be economically served by the canals were fully covered. Even after the Bureau of Reclamation had entered into contracts for all of its available supplies, new districts kept forming in the hope that supplementary facilities would be built to serve the area. The Bureau of Reclamation has maintained a priority list of late applicants for any supplies becoming available in the future, and surface water may occasionally be available to them in wet years. Several districts, such as Pixley and Ducor Irrigation Districts, have proceeded with formation on this basis.[12] Such districts have the hope of being supplied through the Bureau's East Side project, a complex plan with the purpose of serving scattered territory on the east side of the San Joaquin Valley which failed to place timely requests for service from the Friant-Kern or Madera canals, or which lies at too high an elevation.[13]

On the lower west side of the San Joaquin Valley and in Kern County at the south end, lands in large ownerships and with relatively less irrigation development from ground-water sources have been forming very large water districts and water storage districts in the general hope of eventually contracting for supplies from the East Side project, the Bureau's San Luis project, or the Feather River Project aqueduct of the California Department of Water Resources. Many of these districts not only formed in anticipation of wholesale supplies, but also worked vigorously to help the potential wholesaler over the political barriers to the construction of this project.[14]

Where customer organizations have not appeared autonomously, wholesalers often have encouraged the formation of local units—sometimes retail agencies, sometimes local re-wholesalers to sell to retailing units. The Bureau of Reclamation has steadily promoted the formation of retail agencies, especially in the San Joaquin Valley during the 1930's[15] and in the service area of the Sacramento canals during the 1950's. The more passive policies of the East Bay Municipal Utility District

[12] Bulletin No. 21 (1956–58), *op. cit.*, pp. 5–16.

[13] U.S. Department of the Interior, Bureau of Reclamation, Region 2, *East Side Division, Central Valley Project, California: A Discussion of the Need for a Supplemental Water Supply and Facilities for Providing It* (1960), pp. 1–2, 6.

[14] See Chapter 11.

[15] U.S. Congress, Senate Committee on Public Lands, *Exemption of Certain Projects from Land-Limitation Provisions of Federal Reclamation Laws,* Hearings on S. 912, 80 Cong. 1 sess. (1947), p. 1310.

have had the same result. Perhaps the most thorough plan for district formation to deal with an emerging wholesaler is found in the blueprints of the Yuba County Water Agency. Organized in 1959 to develop the Yuba River and safeguard its waters for use within the county, this county-wide agency has promoted the complete filling in of all empty spaces within the county borders with new agencies, as customers for its contemplated wholesale supply. Two considerations may have motivated this policy of the county supervisors: (1) to obtain county-wide coverage, and thereby co-extensive political and financial support, which are of great importance in this small, relatively poor county; (2) to insure fair treatment of areas in the county not already supplied or represented by water districts, in order to minimize possible jealousy among the various regions which, again, might impair political support for the county agency.

Other large wholesalers, however, prefer to deal with larger local agencies which in turn sell to retailers, and their arrival in an area sets forth a different pattern of moves in the formation of local districts. The Sonoma County Flood Control and Water Conservation District was formed in 1949 to contract with the Army Corps of Engineers for the water conservation benefits of the Coyote Dam on Russian River; the Corps had been intermittently studying this project for some time, and an arrangement for local contributions was necessary before construction could begin. Similarly, the county-wide Kern County Water Agency was formed in 1961 to contract with the state of California for a large portion of the water from the Feather River Project. It will transmit its purchases to the large water storage districts covering the county's agricultural lands. The Water Agency was promoted both to offer a single entity for dealing with the state and to give access to the tax base of urban Bakersfield and of Kern's extensive oil properties to subsidize water for the agricultural users.

Rivalry for water

Competition for water often accompanies the causes already discussed for the formation of public water agencies. Action by irrigators may reflect not only fear for the adequacy of the ground-water supplies, but also the fear that potential surface supplies might be captured by others. The widely recognized rigidities of the allocation of water rights in California create active fears that water supplies must be appropriated at the first hint of rivalry, even if the day of need lies well in the future. The anxieties of cities about water to serve future enlarged populations also are increased by the possibility that other cities may get the water—and the population—first. The efficiency of water allocation in California, and thus the performance of the water industry, depend vitally on the way these rivalries affect the actual use of water. Rivalrous actions involving the formation of agencies in turn reflect many facets of water law, the law of water agencies, and the physical circumstances surrounding the capture and use of water in California. We will seek to show the role of these environmental forces.

An element of rivalry often enters in the formation of districts seeking contracts with wholesale suppliers. The formation of agencies to purchase water from the

Bureau's Friant-Kern Canal proceeded for a time, and then remained at an impasse for several years as the Bureau insisted on contractual terms which the districts vigorously opposed. By 1950, however, a period of years of high rainfall was passing, water tables were continuing to drop sharply, and the existing districts were coming to terms with the Bureau and progressively placing its available water under long-term contracts. The realization that the end of this supply was in sight had a strong influence on previously unorganized territory. The existing empty spaces rapidly filled in. The Bureau's waiting list soon included not just these latecomers but also districts downstream on rivers crossed by the Friant-Kern canal. Previously, the latter had by and large resisted any plan for interchange or coordinated operation between the Friant-Kern system and such rivers as the Kings and Kaweah. Officials of the Bureau of Reclamation have said that representatives of late-coming districts offered to pay more than the posted price; the Bureau flatly rejected such competitive pricing.

A different, but related, pattern appears in the area of the Bureau's San Luis project. The development of irrigation on these lands since World War II has entailed rapidly increasing water cost and serious problems of water quality, and as already noted newly formed districts were probably instrumental in promoting the project's authorization. Still another case is Kern County where, partly because of the very large units of land ownership in the region, the limited waters of the Kern River were long allocated without the appearance of any public districts. Recently, however, when the prospect of large new transfers of water to this area by the state of California and the Bureau of Reclamation led to rather quick organization of most of the county into a number of large water storage districts, the Semitropic, Rosedale-Rio Bravo, and Wheeler Ridge-Maricopa districts were added to the previously organized Buena Vista, Arvin-Edison, and North Kern.

Another type of rivalry for water which leads to the organization of districts appears when an existing district plans to expand its consumption from external sources. Neighboring areas thereupon form new districts to demand a share. One of the reasons for the frequency of this sequence of events has been a quirk of California's political geography. Along the state's eastern border lies a row of "mountain counties" whose western boundaries follow a relatively straight line drawn through the lower foothills of the Sierra Nevada. To the west of this line lies another row of counties which stretch at least part way across the agricultural lands of the Central Valley. The latter counties contain the rich land to be irrigated; upon the former fall the snows that yield the irrigation water. The mountain counties hold a legal card in the state's "county of origin" legislation, and sometimes the necessary dam sites as well. The mountain counties are thinly populated and usually contain only small scattered agricultural valleys which will seldom support independent water supply systems. As a result of these conditions, almost every mountain county in the central part of California has created some type of public district or commission—mainly to protect its interest in the plans of water agencies in the Central Valley. At a minimum, this protection can be accomplished by virtue of the county-of-origin legislation, which restricts any water rights handed over by the state to agencies developing supplies for downstream use so that enough water remains to meet the requirements for "ultimate development" in the mountain counties. Once stirred into action, the mountain counties may go beyond this to promote water projects for their own use and development.[16]

One example of actions by the mountain counties is the formation of the Mariposa County Water Agency in 1959 by special act of the State Legislature. The Merced Irrigation District in Merced County, immediately west of Mariposa County, is an old and highly successful district diverting water from the Merced River. In 1926, the Merced District built Exchequer Dam on the Merced River in Mariposa County. By the late 1950's, increasing demands for irrigation water within the district, together with the fear that the Merced watershed would be invaded by the state or the Bureau of Reclamation to export Merced waters to other areas, had stirred the Merced Irrigation District to enlarge Exchequer Dam and plan the building of two new dams, Bagby and Snelling, on the Merced River. An engineering firm found this construction to be feasible in 1958, and the district went about meeting the requirements for beginning construction. The following year, the Mariposa County Board of Supervisors, after having protested Merced's application before the State Water Rights Board, secured legislative formation of the Mariposa County Water Agency. Mariposa County had no immediate use for irrigation water, but the agency soon succeeded in extracting a large payment from the Merced Irrigation District in return for withdrawing its objections.

During the last few years, especially in 1959, the State Legislature has authorized the formation of numerous special county water agencies or authorities for many of the mountain counties. In the majority of cases, any hopes of these sparsely inhabited counties to finance and construct water projects of their own are probably illusory; the primary objectives of the new agencies are to form more perfect unions and more effective tools for the defense of the counties' water supplies against intruding downstream developers. However, several attempts to organize these mountain agencies into joint defense groups including more than one county's agency have not succeeded. When one of the participating county agencies begins to formulate development plans of its own—plans which almost of geographic necessity change its defensive role to that of an aggressor against its neighbors—the loose group disintegrates.

The defensive formation of water agencies can occur in many different settings and reflect tenuous and complex chains of causation. The activity of a power company developing hydroelectric generation on a stream can stimulate the organization of downstream irrigation users.[17] In at least one case, a water district was organized in an area served largely by mutual water companies whose shares were being bought outside the area; local water users feared that the export of some of the mutuals' diversions was reducing the amount of water percolating to the groundwater basin, and they therefore hoped somehow to terminate or offset this export.[18]

[16] These rivalries are discussed at length in Chapter 12. On the county-of-origin reservation, see Chapter 3.

[17] Bulletin No. 21 (Adams), *op. cit.*, pp. 123–24, 174; Lambert, *op. cit.*, pp. 198–99; William Durbrow, "William Durbrow, Irrigation District Leader" (Typescript, University of California General Library, Berkeley, 1958), pp. 92–106.

[18] *Hanford Sentinel*, April 1, 1952; *Fresno Bee*, Nov. 18 and Dec. 3, 1952, Feb. 25, 1953; *San Francisco Examiner*, Feb. 19, 1952. See also Senate Committee on Public Lands, *Exemption of Certain Projects from Land-Limitation Provisions of Federal Reclamation Laws, op. cit.*, pp. 292–93.

No case shows better the ways in which the formation of districts can be interrelated, often through accidental events, than that of the Glenn-Colusa area of the Sacramento Valley in the period before 1925. The facts are more than a little complicated. The legal history of the organization of water agencies in the area began in 1887 with the formation of the giant Central Irrigation District west of the Sacramento River. (Figure 18 shows the districts presently serving the area.) It began construction of a long canal to divert from the river, but internal opposition brought an end to construction work in 1891 and the district became inactive. In 1903, a private group organized as Central Canal and Irrigation Company leased the District's entire property, established a right to Sacramento River water, and began commercial water service to the northern part of the old Central District and to a substantial area outside of the District to the east, between it and the river. In 1909, the Central Canal Company's properties passed into the hands of another group that later organized them as the Sacramento Valley Irrigation Company and Sacramento Valley West Side Canal Company. The former was a land enterprise which bought up large amounts of land along the existing canals for speculative purposes. The West Side Canal Company intended to confine its service to lands controlled or sold by it and thereby avoid the status of a public utility with its associated obligations and controls, but in this it was not successful. Farmers in the old Central Irrigation District, but not in the Canal Company's service area, brought suit to establish that the Canal Company was a public utility and that it had a first obligation to serve lands lying within the Irrigation District, whose properties it leased. In *Byington v. Sacramento Valley West Side Canal Company,*[19] the plaintiffs established these claims, bringing the Canal Company under the regulation of the State Railroad Commission and potentially requiring it to move a portion of its service area back inside the Central Irrigation District boundaries. A case simultaneously brought before the Railroad Commission resulted in a parallel finding of the company's public utility status and a requirement that it revise its rates. Even before these decisions were finally affirmed, the Irrigation Company and Canal Company were thrown into bankruptcy through the failure of the parent interests owning them.

This event plus the Byington decision left local landowners in a variey of predicaments which set the scene for the formation of a number of public districts. Some lands within the Central Irrigation District but not in the Canal Company's service area now had a water right but no service. Other lands outside the District had service from a bankrupt company and possibly no water right. Areas of both types soon grasped the greater collective legal powers of the public district. The first districts were formed in those lands lying outside of the Central District which were threatened by the Byington decision with a loss of water rights—Jacinto, Provident, and Princeton-Codora-Glenn irrigation districts. Jacinto Irrigation District, formed in 1917, immediately entered into an agreement with the Sacramento Valley West Side Canal Company to purchase a right in the Central Canal for $70,000; later, when the Central system was transferred to another district, the transfer was subject to this agreement. Provident Irrigation District, formed the following year, was in about the same situation as Jacinto. Its area

[19] 170 Calif. 124 (1915).

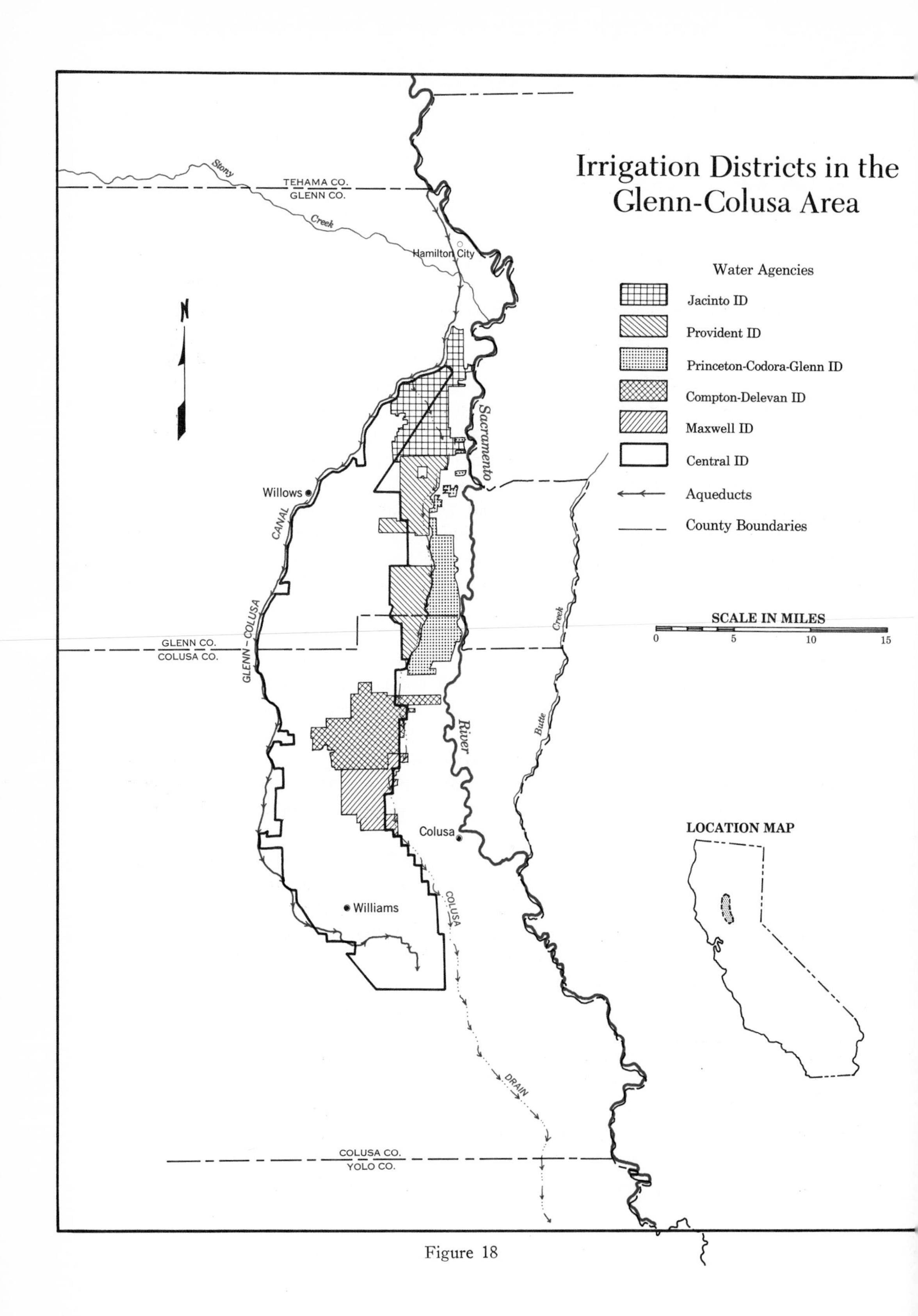
Irrigation Districts in the Glenn-Colusa Area
Water Agencies
Jacinto ID
Provident ID
Princeton-Codora-Glenn ID
Compton-Delevan ID
Maxwell ID
Central ID
Aqueducts
County Boundaries
SCALE IN MILES
0
5
10
15
LOCATION MAP
N
Stony
Creek
TEHAMA CO.
GLENN CO.
Hamilton City
Willows
CANAL
GLENN-COLUSA
GLENN CO.
COLUSA CO.
Sacramento
River
Butte
Creek
Colusa
Williams
COLUSA
DRAIN
COLUSA CO.
YOLO CO.

Figure 18

covered mainly lands which had belonged to the Sacramento Valley Irrigation Company at the time of its bankruptcy in 1914. They passed to another syndicate, and then to a group called the Provident Irrigation Syndicate which constructed irrigation works independent of the Central Canal in order to capitalize on the boom in rice production during World War I. The Provident District was formed by members of the Syndicate to reimburse themselves for their personal expenditures on the distribution system. The Princeton-Codora-Glenn Irrigation District, like Jacinto, was organized in 1916 to buy out a portion of the Central Canal works supplying it from the receivers of the Sacramento Valley West Side Canal Company. Instead of continuing to depend on the Central Canal, this district transferred its point of diversion directly to the Sacramento River. In this way it avoided further litigation with interests within the Central Irrigation District over water diverted through the Central Canal.

These districts accounted for most of the lands outside the Central Irrigation District served by the Sacramento Valley West Side Canal Company. Most of the territory common to both areas went into the Glenn-Colusa Irrigation District, which was formed in 1920. Here the problem of securing a legal claim on the water supply was less urgent; and undoubtedly the rice boom served as an extra incentive for organization of the District to clean up the tangled legal affairs left by the bankruptcy of the Canal Company.

The remaining lands of the old Central Irrigation District, which had never received water from either of the subsequent canal companies, were organized into districts only when spurred by the rice boom. Maxwell Irrigation District occupied territory where irrigation had been developed by large private interests during World War I, and the district was organized in 1918 to take over these private works. Land promoters had constructed a surface distribution system in the area of Williams Irrigation District, despite the lack of an assured source of water. Formation of the District was rushed in 1920 to assist in acquiring a temporary supply of water in the trough of Colusa Basin in order to take advantage of the rice boom. The District suffered extremely high operating costs, and was nearly shut down by 1923 as the rice boom ended. The Williams District arranged the following year to merge with Glenn-Colusa Irrigation District. The Colusa Basin water supply had proved inadequate, and the only route to long-term development was this merger which foresaw a return to a pattern of distribution works very similar to that planned for the original Central Irrigation District.[20]

Though the same urgency in regard to undisputed access to supplies of water exists in the urban sphere, rivalry usually has not expressed itself through the formation of agencies. Private or public organizations are developed to supply water as soon as settlements start to approach urban density, and so conditions of scarcity simply raise controversies between existing agencies. In the San Francisco Bay area, the formation of districts has, if anything, related more to rivalry for customers than to rivalry for supplies of water, a phenomenon unknown among retailing agricultural agencies.

[20] Bulletin No. 21 (Adams), *op. cit.*, pp. 77–101; U.S. Department of the Interior, Bureau of Reclamation, Region 2, *Sacramento River Service Area: Investigations of Glenn-Colusa, Jacinto, Provident, Compton-Delevan, Maxwell Irrigation Districts and Related Areas* (1953), pp. 9–12.

Part of the absence of rivalry in formation of districts in the Bay area relates to the long-standing status as wholesaler of the San Francisco Water Department and its private predecessor, the Spring Valley Water Company. Before becoming part of the local government, the Company had sold wherever it could profitably and legally move. In particular, it supplied on a commercial basis all of the communities lying in the watersheds of the streams it had dammed or near the wells it pumped. Many of the cities in the area took over their water systems earlier than San Francisco, but continued to purchase from the Spring Valley Water Company as well as to sink their own wells. When the city of San Francisco purchased the Spring Valley system, it also took over the Company's wholesale contracts. Its construction of an aqueduct to the Sierra eliminated for both itself and its customers the possibility of rivalry over inadequate local sources. However, the Spring Valley Company's Calaveras Reservoir in Alameda County had already threatened the replenishment of ground water used by agricultural users in the area, and they responded with the formation of the Alameda County Water District in 1914.[21]

Rivalry for water sources may not have been a major factor in the formation of districts in the Bay area, but it has strongly affected the functions of some agencies. In the San Jose area, neither the Santa Clara Valley Water Conservation District nor the Santa Clara Flood Control and Water Conservation District was founded with the intent of importing water or developing a distribution system, but both have sought to undertake these functions. Their aspirations reflect not only the quest for growth normal to bureaucracies, public or private, but also the sense of urgency now common in California to put water to beneficial use before another agency can lay claim to it. This urgency has become more intense in recent years as the massive state program of water transfer supplements the existing federal works. The Santa Clara Valley is a principal marketing area for the state's South Bay Aqueduct, and state representatives sought either the formation of a special large contracting agency or, barring that, adaptation of some existing unit. Both Santa Clara districts responded. The Santa Clara County supervisors and their agency, the Santa Clara Flood Control and Water Conservation District, particularly pursued this opportunity. They kept reminding residents of the need for expeditious action in order to keep all water from being tied up under contract to Southern California, and urged action with the determination of an entire county, rather than through the limited jurisdiction of the competing Santa Clara Valley Water Conservation District.[22]

These urban and agricultural cases show some typical patterns of the formation of districts as an element in the competition for water. The legal and physical linkages which can bring about such patterns are enormous in number and they multiply as the ultimate scarcity of water is more commonly felt and the statewide water transfer networks become more prominent in the total water industry.

In summary, both the existence of a collective demand for water in an area and the availability of a feasible source of supply lie behind the formation of the typical

[21] It was only after World War I, as urbanization came to the part of Alameda County south of Oakland, that this district was transformed into an urban supplier.

[22] Robert R. Lee, *Local Government Public Works Decision-Making,* Project on Engineering-Economic Planning, Report No. EEP–9 (1964), Part II.

water agency. The creation of a district registers some desire or intention of its citizens to make a transaction or investment to obtain water, and no barriers hamper the formation of a district to attempt such action. However, not every possible type of transaction has proved an effective instrument. No important cases appear of the purchase of water from neighboring retail districts, or of the purchase of water rights, except from moribund holders. Nonetheless, the typical circumstances surrounding the formation of irrigation districts have changed as water has moved more firmly into the category of a generally scarce resource, and as some rudiments of an economic market for it have begun to appear. These trends become clearer as we consider what causes an area to switch from one form of organization to another or to seek association with an existing water agency.

Changes in Forms of Organization: Private to Public Enterprise

The citizens of an area often experiment with more and more elaborate forms of organization, or overlay one district with another, in order to deal with successive problems of water supply. The available forms of organization, public and private, vary considerably in degree of formality, legal powers and obligations, patterns of administration and control, and ease of dissolution in case of failure. Thus an area may often find advantage in switching from one form to another, and these changes in the water supply agency serving an area often reflect important changes in its posture in the competition for water in California. In fact, changes in the form of organization have a significance that is parallel to the organization of districts in virgin territory.

Sometimes the replacement of one form of agency by another reflects a need for broader powers to deal with outside agencies, but the more common case has been dissatisfaction with the internal performance of an existing agency. By and large, this is the story of the failure of private enterprise to retain its once dominant position in the California water industry, since this is the most conspicuous single type of change in organization. Among the suppliers of agricultural water, only one private enterprise of significant scope is still operating in Northern California. Pacific Gas and Electric Company maintains certain small operations inherited from predecessor companies, but not on account of commercial profitability. The private municipal supplier is not quite so near to extinction, and indeed, the revenues of private water companies have been increasing rapidly in the past two decades[23] and their absolute number has been rising.[24] Their aggregate size, however, remains relatively small.

[23] Despite a dramatic increase in the number and size of public water organizations, the revenues of the large private water utilities in California increased over sixfold in the period 1940 to 1962, a rate of increase slightly less than that of the large private electric utilities. See California State Public Utilities Commission, *Annual Report 1962–1963* (1963), pp. 48, 59. The gross investment (at original cost) of private water utilities increased at an annual rate of 8 per cent in the period 1953–63 while the value of plant for electrical utilities increased at a rate of 7.6 per cent. *Ibid., Annual Report, 1963–1964* (1964), p. 39.

[24] *Ibid.*, p. 59. The year 1963–64 was the first time in the last decade that the number of water utilities under the jurisdiction of the Public Utilities Commission decreased. While 22

Although they are somewhat shrouded in history, some of the reasons for the decline of the private water industry can be identified. From the 1870's to the 1920's, large sums of money were invested in private irrigation companies in California, usually as joint ventures with land promotions. Some of these enterprises were better planned than others, but all were highly speculative, and many failed or went through reorganization before they had even completed the construction of their physical plants. Of those which completed construction, hardly any proved profitable. On the surface this might seem paradoxical for a water company is a "natural monopoly" facing a demand that is sure to be inelastic in the short run, at least over a substantial range. However, the company's marketing position normally holds disadvantages as well as advantages. First, although it is the only feasible supplier of its customers, they are also its only feasible customers once the works are constructed; the marketing of water by the private companies often resembles bilateral more than simple monopoly. Second, the private water company normally carries a substantial burden of risk; it is caught between customers who insist upon regular service and uncertain sources of natural supply.[25] Third, the State Railroad Commission, the predecessor of the Public Utilities Commission, was often hostile to the earning of significant profits by rural water companies.[26] Fourth, California farmers, though otherwise loyal to the institutions of capitalist enterprise, often took the view that it is unfair for a profit to be taken on the distribution of water, a sentiment usually activated when a private water company raised its rates.[27] Fifth, the capital rationing imposed on private water companies and their limited legal powers compared to public districts often led to their replacement when their customers became convinced of the need to construct reservoir storage capacity or other large works.[28] Indeed, private water companies, particularly when under pressure from regulatory authorities to fulfill public utility obligations, have often seen the handwriting on the wall and taken an active part in encouraging the formation of public districts to buy out their investment.[29]

Many of the same factors have been operative in the municipalization of the private water utilities in urban areas. In these cases, however, the economic and technological factors are sometimes supplemented by such ideological factors as mu-

---

new systems were established, 34 left their jurisdiction for the following reasons: transferred in ownership to other utilities, 14; sold to municipalities, 4; sold to county or public utility water districts, 12; service discontinued, 4. The net decline of 12 systems still left 521 private water utilities in operation.

[25] Elwood Mead's sixty-year-old analysis of the unworkability of private enterprise in agricultural water service still repays study. "The result of [Mead's] experience shows that attaching water to land makes for peace; attaching it to the ditch owner makes for war. So long as ditch owners are the appropriators, they have to maintain a dual conflict. They must strive with other ditch owners for control of the stream and with water users over the quantity and price of the water delivered. On the other hand, where ditches are made carriers of water and appropriations attached to the land, the expense of the struggle over a fair division of streams does not fall, as it does in California, solely on the owners of canals." See U.S. Department of Agriculture, Office of Experiment Stations, *Report of Irrigation Investigations in California,* by Elwood Mead *et al.,* Bulletin No. 100 (1901), p. 41.

[26] Lambert, *op. cit.,* pp. 241–54.

[27] For examples, see Bulletin No. 21 (1951–55), *op. cit.,* p. 11; *Mendota Advance,* March 26, 1953; Bulletin No. 21 (Adams), *op. cit.,* pp. 204–05, 222.

[28] Bulletin No. 21 (Adams), *op. cit.,* pp. 190–91.

[29] *Ibid.,* pp. 135, 231–33; Lambert, *op. cit.,* pp. 241–54.

nicipal pride and such municipal goals as tax reduction, annexation, and city planning—in line with our earlier characterization of city governments as joint-product cooperatives. The private water systems serving San Francisco and the East Bay area underwent many corporate changes within the private sector before finally becoming public. The story could be repeated in every sector of the Bay area. Almost all of the elements of the succession of private companies and then municipalization can be seen, however, in the operations of the California Water Service Company.[30]

This Company is an amalgamation of what had been many independent companies. For example, its Petaluma system had been originally founded by the Petaluma Water Company and bought by the Sonoma County Water Company and then by the Petaluma Power and Water Company, before being added to the California Water Service Company in 1928. Its Stockton division was purchased from Pacific Gas and Electric Company in 1927. In succeeding years the company bought out six more systems in the San Francisco area. California Water Service Company's pattern of operations seems to be to purchase systems throughout the state and to integrate the operations of adjacent systems. Although the Company has grown over the years, partly reflecting the rapid growth of the suburbs and cities which it serves, there have been changes in its pattern of growth as the march of municipalization has continued to erode the system. In recent years it has sold water systems to Fresno, Redding, Hanford, Hillsborough, and Petaluma, while other cities have studied the procedures to purchase further parts of the system.

The drive of municipalization arises from the two general causes indicated earlier: a feeling of dissatisfaction with the existing private system and possible advantages to the community of a publicly operated system. Though both factors are often present, the latter is frequently sufficient ground for the move to develop a municipal agency. The major dissatisfactions with private water systems voiced by city officials have been over inadequate facilities and services (especially with regard to fire protection) and reluctance of private companies to expand into newly urbanized areas. Another source of dissatisfaction has been variations between the service of companies supplying different portions of an urban area; the co-existence of several small companies in fast-growing California cities has tended to implant the idea that public action could bring the service to all areas up to the standard of the best.

The private urban water system is often indicted not for inadequate service but from fear that it will not act in a sufficiently grand manner to serve an expected boom in municipal population or to avert the depletion of its ground-water resources. Thus, the North Marin County Water District was organized to replace the Novato Water Company, dependent upon a declining ground-water supply, in anticipation that the public agency would go farther afield to develop sources of supply.[31] The

[30] This firm, with nineteen scattered urban systems, is the largest private water utility in the state, and except for the San Jose Water Works, it has the largest private service area in the San Francisco metropolitan region. The San Jose firm is the largest "independent" private urban system in the state, but its independence is questionable because five of the nine directors of the California Water Service Company were among the seven directors of the San Jose Water Works in 1961.

[31] North Marin County Water District, *Water Supply and Distribution Report,* by T. C. Brinkley (1960), p. 1.

larger private water companies have undertaken investment projects of substantial absolute size,[32] but they have lacked the organizational resources and access to capital necessary to undertake large-scale investments of great durability, in facilities condemned by scale economies to long initial periods of excess capacity. Neither the privately owned Spring Valley Water Company of San Francisco nor the East Bay Water Company proposed to lay an aqueduct from the Sierra Nevada to the Bay area—the repeated suggestion of the consulting engineers that was later carried out by public bodies. Only the power of taxation and other legal resources of governmental units could allow the risk of such ventures to be undertaken.

The predominance of higher governmental units in the major water transfers within California often tempts city governments into the business of water supply to assure representation for their areas in the public planning and bargaining which shapes these large projects. Indeed, the Army Corps of Engineers and Bureau of Reclamation and the California Department of Water Resources—all of which have initiated vast storage and distribution schemes—either prefer or insist on contracting with local governmental agencies for the disposition of their water, and thus impel the municipalization of private water companies. Furthermore, when these large wholesalers seek to contract with as few agencies as possible, they often give birth to two separate layers of local public agencies—local re-wholesalers and municipal retailers, which in turn seek to exercise their political influence on the operations of intermediate wholesale agencies.[33]

Another group of factors in the replacement of private urban water companies by municipal departments lies outside of the physical arrangements for water supply and in the area of other municipal policy goals which can be served through public control of the water system. Some of these other goals possess a clear utilitarian character for the city. The municipal purpose of zoning may be served through municipal control of the water supply, although this has not commonly been done.[34] Another significant goal is that of adding to the city's revenue base; the city can make a gross addition to its revenues by using the water bill in effect as an instrument of taxation supplementing property taxes.[35] But this practice is

[32] The Spring Valley Water Company of San Francisco developed a reservoir in southern Alameda County, miles from its service area—partly in order to frustrate proposals for municipalization by San Francisco.

[33] Attitudes voiced by the city of Los Altos show these pressures at work. The Mayor's Water Study Committee felt that a municipal water department had to be established in order to give the city "a flexibility which will permit it to participate effectively in the area-wide planning and action which surely lies ahead. The City of Los Altos cannot and should not be relegated to the position of an outsider looking in while major decisions are made affecting its lifeblood." (Mayor's Water Study Committee, *Water for Los Altos* [1960], p. 30.) The city sits on a county-wide water commission which has sought to shape the importation plans of Santa Cruz County for water from California's South Bay Aqueduct, but has felt its debating effectiveness seriously reduced by its lack of a public water system.

[34] The city of Hayward has been reluctant to accept an offer of water service from, with the corollary annexation to, East Bay Municipal Utility District, despite the offer of attractive water rates, because it now restricts access to water service in an attempt to control suburban development. In a number of instances, it has rejected applications by subdividers who wish to develop properties in areas which the city plans to restrict to industrial use.

[35] This policy is discussed in Chapter 10 in connection with the pricing decisions of water agencies.

not necessarily connected with any net saving to the community as a whole from transferring the water supply function to the public domain. The major clear net savings from the perspective of the water consumers are the income-based taxes which the private utilities pay to federal and state governments, with lesser gains in reduced ad valorem taxes to other political jurisdictions. Estimates of the total tax savings of a municipally operated utility for the local community have been placed at 29 per cent of gross revenues for Stockton, 23 per cent for the Contra Costa County Water District, and 17 per cent for San Jose.[36] The other major net saving from municipal operation, at least in the short run, comes from the profits realized by private water companies. The net income after taxes of the San Jose Water Works, which has been threatened with municipalization, is approximately 17 per cent of the operating revenue and around 8 per cent of net worth.[37] Although part of this net income would be retained by either private or public agencies as a source of investment financing, clearly a substantial share could be allotted to the lowering of prices or supplementing of city revenues if the system were municipalized.[38]

Outside of these tangible goals of municipal government policy lies a vague but powerful motive for municipal ownership—a desire for home rule. The ideology which rates water as too important to be left in private hands may make it a matter of pride for a city to control this vital service. But there is no doubt that management of the water supply can in fact serve as an adjunct to a city's long-run plans. The provision of water, like streets or sanitation facilities, is a necessary condition for any urban settlement. The operating rules under which water is supplied affect the pattern of development of the city. The distribution of reservoirs and the size of pumps and mains dictate the density of settlement and the feasibility of opening up new areas. The rate structure influences the establishment of business firms. Quality characteristics of the water supply affect the location decisions of some types of industries. Since urban governments often pursue planning goals related to these features of urban development, it is understandable that they should try to control an instrument which assists in attainment of these goals.[39]

[36] Stone and Youngberg, *Financing Water System Acquisition: City of Stockton* (1960), p. 16; *idem, Contra Costa County Water District* (1959), p. 20; *idem, City of San Jose* (1961), p. 23.

[37] San Jose Water Works Co., *Annual Report, 1964.*

[38] Although the studies of citizens' committees, city councils, and consultants all stress the pecuniary savings of municipalization, these depend on the utility failing to capture their capitalized value in the condemnation proceedings. Utilities often prove to be effective campaigners, however, and the following ratios of purchase price to book value of the utility's plant suggest that significant portions of the cities' desired financial gains are lost: Arcade County Water District, 1.20; Hanford, 1.64; Vacaville, 1.23; Lakewood, 1.30; Petaluma, 1.56. See Stone and Youngberg, *City of San Jose, op. cit.;* California State Public Utilities Commission, *General Report of the Results of Operation of California Water Service Company, 1959 Adjusted and 1960 Estimated* (1960), pp. 3–4.

[39] Such objectives lie behind the repeated sparring between the city of San Jose and the well-established private San Jose Water Works over policy in regard to extension of service to outlying areas. The extension of water service takes on special importance for San Jose since it, like many other cities in the Bay area, pursues a policy of aggressive annexation of suburban territory. The supply of water is one of the inducements that a city can hold out to desired areas.

The desire for home rule explains also the limited size of many systems. A city is just as reluctant to allow another government as a private firm to control its water supply. This attitude promotes the emerging pattern of the large wholesaler or re-wholesaler (which may be a city department, a county agency, or a district) formed to contract with a state or federal wholesaler and a multitude of small units coterminous with city boundaries retailing the water and setting the rules for its distribution. It is a pattern that generally prevails in the San Francisco Bay area; the San Francisco Water Department, for example, which serves as a major wholesaler, has accelerated the municipalization of local private systems. The one major exception is the East Bay Municipal Utility District (EBMUD); as a normal policy it induces, first, the transfer of local private water facilities to a public district, and then the dissolution of the local public district into EBMUD. Local districts are formed for the sole purpose of floating bond issues to purchase existing distribution systems and to make contributions to EBMUD for the cost of improvements to bring them up to EBMUD's standards. Once purchased, a system is turned over to EBMUD, and the local public district continues in existence only until its bonds are paid off.[40]

In summary, many factors can tempt a city into an effort to transform its water supply to municipal operation. While we have not attempted to rank these in importance, those relating to broad goals of local governmental policy appear to rival strongly those relating to the improvement of the water supply. However, actual municipalization campaigns have been less successful where the private utility was financially strong and professionally managed.[41]

Disappearance of Water Districts

Public districts can pass into inactivity or disappear through consolidation, annexation, or dissolution (voluntary or involuntary).[42] Inactivity often precedes disappearance, as when a district fails to achieve its initial plans for construction or contracting. Bankruptcy, the terrible problem of California's public water districts in the 1930's, may or may not lead to disappearance. Since the taxes of water districts constitute a lien on all included lands, the bankruptcy of a district normally corresponds to a situation in which much of the included land has either reverted to the district or is on the verge of doing so. Bankruptcies themselves have never been the result of interdistrict rivalry, only of internal conditions. Inactivity or disappearance resulting from frustrated plans or the denial of access to water, however, often grows out of rivalry among districts.

The only cases of consolidations are very rare instances in which similar, adjacent districts combine. Their aim is almost always to secure economies of scale

[40] This policy naturally can create some local resentment. Bickering among the founding cities marked EBMUD's early years, but the only recent rebellion has been the formation of the Southwest Contra Costa Water District within EBMUD's territory as a device to bargain better prices for industrial water supplies. (This case is discussed in Chapter 10.)

[41] In San Jose, the campaign has been defeated, although further efforts are being made. In Stockton, the proposition was defeated; and several elections were required in San Francisco.

[42] Legal provisions for these actions vary somewhat among types of districts (see Chapter 3).

in management. This feature is important, but the potential gains can come through a contractual arrangement as well as actual merger, and this less formal procedure seems to be the normal one. Agreements to contract for managerial services, purchases of the shares of large mutual companies by other districts, and cooperative investment projects—all of these are substitutes for the gains which could theoretically be obtained through mergers. Glenn-Colusa Irrigation District and its smaller neighbors illustrate these conditions. Two of them have actually merged into Glenn-Colusa, while several others have sought to get major services performed by the larger district.[43] One of the exceptional cases in which these kinds of advantages were sought through outright merger was the formation of the East Contra Costa Irrigation District in the late 1920's. The core of this district was an elaborate and successful speculative development laid out by the Balfour, Guthrie Company in 1912 and 1913. Balfour followed the common practice of turning the management of its water system over to a mutual company. The development of the surrounding lands was also taking place. The area immediately to the south first formed a mutual company, then a public utility water company in order to acquire the power of eminent domain. Landowners to the east organized the Knightsen Irrigation District in 1920 and at first proposed to obtain an independent water supply. To the north, the Lone Tree Irrigation District was formed in the same year. It was clear that the original Balfour water system could readily be developed to serve the whole area, and an understanding to that effect was reached. The Knightsen and Lone Tree districts purchased large holdings of stock in the Balfour mutual in 1921 and 1922. In 1923, the lands originally in the Balfour development formed the Brentwood Irrigation District. Following several years of negotiations among these three districts with regard to the merging of their indebtedness, the whole area consolidated into the East Contra Costa District.[44]

In addition to occasional consolidations, there are also converse cases of splitting districts into independent parts; usually this results from internal political disputes. The example that has received the most attention recently is the splitting of Chowchilla Water District from the Madera Irrigation District (located on the east side of the San Joaquin Valley). It has not been possible to construct a completely satisfactory account of what happened, but apparently the split occurred at the time of the construction of the Madera Canal by the Bureau of Reclamation. Factions in the district differed sharply over plans for a distribution system. One group wished to contract with the Bureau to build a system; the other group, the core of the Chowchilla District, felt that it could secure a system more quickly and cheaply by contracting independently. Also, one group wished for a district area that would lie firmly within its political control.[45]

In urban water supply, the process of suburban expansion sometimes involves

[43] William Durbrow, *op. cit.*, pp. 84–85.

[44] Bulletin No. 21 (Adams), *op. cit.*, p. 149.

[45] The Chowchilla District's distribution system is a modification of the distributaries of an existing stream network. The farmers themselves have done much of the work of constructing laterals. Statements by the District's leaders have always shown great pride in its low average cost and the degree to which construction and improvement has been undertaken locally. See *Chowchilla News*, March 9, 1950, Feb. 28, 1957; *Madera News-Tribune*, Sept. 20, 1955, Sept. 18, 1956.

the formation of small mutual companies or waterworks districts to serve individual tracts or developments and their subsequent consolidation into the system serving the urban center.[46] The economics of water supply usually has less effect on whether or not this process occurs than the political objectives of the central city regarding suburban expansion, the relation of the general city government to channels of policy formation in the city's water agency, and expansionist interests (if any) of the urban agency. Without the entry of such political interests, there seems to be little economic pressure for consolidation or annexation of atomistic suburban systems.[47]

In short, consolidations and dissolutions among public districts are conspicuous by their absence. Once lands are incorporated into a public water district, their fate in the market for water tends strongly to be tied to the success of that particular district. Any errors in the scale and layout of physical facilities can be rectified only by action within the district, unless another district overlapping the same territory can come to the rescue. Any transactions involving water or water rights must, with some exceptions, come through arm's-length dealings with other organizations and not by "buying into" agencies with claims to abundant water. Once a given district has exhausted its legal and economic powers without success, its only alternative is to lapse and permit a fresh start with some other organizational form.

Size of Public Water Organizations

Given the geographical area within which water can economically be distributed and the legal and technical barriers to overlapping retail service areas, the number of retailing agencies has to bear an inverse relation to their average size. Since the number of agencies influences the pattern of rivalry and the allocation of resources, it is worth asking whether the patterns of conduct in district formation offer any explanation of their actual sizes. Topography and hydrology are, of course, important determinants of the pattern of district boundaries, as is the legal requirement for most types of agricultural districts that the district's territory must all be serviceable from a single source. County boundaries and local town marketing areas, largely unrelated to conditions of water supply, also exert an obvious influence on the boundaries of public water districts. However, a few degrees of freedom remain, and the history of California's water agencies yields some insight into the way conduct can influence the scale of organizations and thus the structure of the industry.

We may recall the implications of the users' cooperative hypothesis for the determination of an agency's scale of operations. Assuming that we can identify a

[46] Philip F. Walsh, "Problems of Service Extension to Fringe Areas," *Journal of the American Water Works Association,* LI (March 1959), 348–53.

[47] That such insularity and stability can prevail in the organization of urban water retailing without economic inefficiencies becoming painfully evident is due to the flexibility of larger (often county-wide) organizations in undertaking wholesaling, ground-water management, and other such activities involving manifest scale economies. Legal restrictions on the inclusion of a given piece of land in a number of different districts generally do not cause problems.

basic nucleus of membership sharing the agency's costs under something approaching a correct normative allocation, it would be to their interest to expand membership if the long-run average cost of the agency's function is decreasing, and to contract membership if it is increasing. For instance, the existing membership of a district would benefit by declining to accept new members, when it faced marginal costs of water in excess of average costs (as an example, if increased supply required supplementing diversions of a river's natural flow by constructing a storage reservoir). When we add organizational elements to the theory, other possibilities arise. The going rules for allocating charges among members may be such that the addition of certain types of members increases the revenues of the cooperative enterprise relative to its costs—as when new water users possess more taxable property relative to their water consumption than the average of the existing membership.

Because the determinants of size in agricultural districts are more complex and reflect economic interest more than those in urban systems, we will consider them first, confining the discussion to retailers and local wholesalers.

Determinants of size of agricultural districts

Little can be said, unhappily, about what determines the size of a district when it is first established, beyond the obvious factors of physical characteristics of the land and of the prospective water supply and of the boundaries of other districts. The boundaries of some types of districts are the subject of hearings held by the county supervisors, in which the interest or disinterest of various landowners can be ascertained as well as the likelihood of benefit to all included areas. For other types of districts, such as special districts established by the State Legislature, the law provides no such opportunity for review and consent by the members-to-be. Normally the founders of a district which will undertake to supply water have only a general idea of the maximum supply capacity it can attain or the shape of the cost curve upon which it will operate. Probably for this reason we have found practically no evidence of a district's founders consciously reducing its proposed area in order to insure themselves a more adequate water supply. Many older districts, formed to develop natural water supplies, have continued for many years to provide water only to a portion of their members. The rest either dry-farm or irrigate from ground water; as Chapter 10 will show, districts generally have been able to devise taxation and pricing systems that provide acceptable treatment to all members under these conditions.[48]

The more telling evidence of behavioral factors determining the size of agricultural districts stems from their experience after formation. Then, the distribution of benefits as among members and the extent of benefit to members over adjacent nonmember lands become apparent, and responsive efforts of landowners to seek

[48] When a retailing district is formed to purchase water from a wholesaler, the quantity is usually adaptable to the demands of the customer, and the problem of the adequacy of the water supply to the district's area does not arise.

inclusion or exclusion may occur. Furthermore, factors relating to the organizational characteristics of water districts, although not necessarily to their economic costs and benefits, may come into play. It is true that most changes in the size of agricultural water agencies after their formation usually are small,[49] and those which occur often serve to correct small errors in estimating areas of benefit from a district's works and patterns of physically feasible construction. Nonetheless, those changes which have occurred provide insight into the pressures affecting the size of districts, and the forces which limit changes in the size of districts after they have been organized hold interest in themselves.

A very conspicuous factor of the organizational type restricting the size of retailing districts is the poor political viability of very large districts, except in areas where individual landholdings are correspondingly large. Some of the examples in this connection are old and reflect the weaknesses of early legislation on irrigation districts as much as the problems of large scale. The districts formed under the Wright Act of 1887 were typically much larger than those of recent times. Most of them either were broken up into smaller districts or lapsed into inactivity for substantial periods of time. More recent examples suffice, however, to show that the high mortality rate of large districts was not caused solely by the defects of early legislation.[50] Furthermore, a very high proportion of those large overlay districts formed to effect a reconciliation of conflicting interests in a local basin or latent market have failed conspicuously.[51] For example, the 550,000-acre San Joaquin Water Storage District, formed in 1924, included both the Madera area, in which the landowners wished to build a dam to store the flood waters of the San Joaquin River, and lower San Joaquin interests which customarily used these same flood flows for irrigating pasture land. The large district brought the parties no closer to agreement, and was dissolved in 1929.[52] The inability of local water users to agree upon such apparently beneficial joint projects logically implies a tendency to resort to higher governments for mediation and assistance. The San Joaquin example is instructive in that the Central Valley Project of the Bureau of Reclamation can be viewed as just such an outcome. Opposite cases of successful large-scale districts generally involve either relatively enormous internal benefits for all parties or a clear need for action to deal with a common enemy.

[49] One tabulation made in 1955 showed that, since 1930, 43 irrigation districts in California had gained or lost 100 or more acres by inclusions or exclusions; 26 districts showed a net gain of 473,469 acres while 17 reported a net loss of 147,949 acres. These totals would amount to only a low percentage of the total acreages involved. See University of California, Bureau of Public Administration, *Irrigation District Movement in California: A Summary,* by J. F. McCarty, a report prepared for Assembly Interim Committee on Conservation, Planning, and Public Works (1955).

[50] See, for example, Bulletin No. 21 (Adams), *op. cit.,* p. 166.

[51] The failure of the Kern River Water Storage District provides an instructive case because of its elaborate plans to rationalize the use of the Kern River's waters—plans which at least superficially appear likely to have benefited some users without injuring any others. See Kern River Water Storage District, *Report to State Engineer on Feasibility of Project* (1928); and *Digest of Report on Modified Plan of Development Recommended by Board of Directors* (1928).

[52] Senate Committee on Public Lands, *Exemption of Certain Projects from Land-Limitation Provisions of Federal Reclamation Law, op. cit.,* pp. 1121–22. This failure also led to a reduction by half of the area of the Madera Irrigation District, which originally had been 350,000 acres. The original area included both lands without a water right, whose owners were vitally

Cases of the scaling down of newly formed districts from what would superficially appear to be an efficient size have also occurred among smaller retailing organizations. Sometimes these have resulted in smaller, but still homogeneous, territories being served; sometimes they have led to the clear-cut inefficiency of a distribution system built to supply a patchwork service area.[53]

This tendency toward the breakdown of large districts, then, is the main observable effect upon the size of agricultural water agencies of pressures in the on-going pursuit of water. Specifically, there does not seem to be much pressure upon small districts to expand or unite. Several elements underlie this lack of strong tendencies for small districts to increase in size. First, once a district has established its distribution system, its chances of attaining scale economies through expansion are very slight. Second, a range of legal and contractual problems tends to make the inclusion (or exclusion) of territory a rather complicated matter. Third, where there is a choice territory outside, a district often prefers the home rule gained by forming its own agency to joining an existing one.

A district supplying agricultural water might wish to expand under two different sets of circumstances: It is developing (for example, constructing storage facilities) a greater water supply than that demanded by present members; or it sees some prospective gain from integrating with an adjacent territory having its own source of water. Both motivations appear occasionally. Because of the discontinuities and scale factors influencing the capacities of water storage and transport facilities, the construction of such works by or for a district often leads to territorial changes to adapt to the new supply.[54] Inclusions of new territory or consolidations with existing districts are at times undertaken when a sale of water by one district to another would be a simple alternative. The reluctance of retailing districts to make water sales to other districts or outside individuals is almost absolute, however, for reasons discussed in Chapter 3, and so the more cumbersome procedure of a change of legal form is undertaken instead.

Occasionally, retailing districts also show interest in expanding to overcome some disadvantage of small scale. Sometimes the objective is to obtain scale economies in skilled management. Technological change, such as alterations in pumping technology, may render districts suboptimal in scale some time after they have begun operation. Expansion may be pursued to capture payment for an external benefit, particularly the recharge of underground aquifers drawn upon by private pumpers outside a district. Economies in the joint operation of interconnected diversion or distribution systems may furnish yet another reason.

---

interested in the construction of Friant Dam, and lands owned by the Miller and Lux interests holding controlling rights to the San Joaquin River. After the dissolution of the San Joaquin Water Storage District, litigation resumed between the Madera District and Miller and Lux, culminating in the so-called "Haines decree" of 1931, which enjoined the District from diverting water from the San Joaquin except under limitations that rendered it infeasible. Anticipating this defeat, the District in 1930 reduced its area to 170,000 acres of the more readily irrigable lands. See Madera Irrigation District, *History of Madera Irrigation District* (Mimeographed, n.d.).

[53] Bulletin No. 21–P (1944–50), *op. cit.*, pp. 11–12.

[54] See, for example, Tudor-Goodenough Engineers, *Feasibility Report on Merced River Development for Merced Irrigation District* (1958); *Placerville Mountain Democrat,* Nov. 3, 1955; *Sacramento Bee,* Sept. 27, 1959, June 12, 1960, May 11 and June 15, 1961.

These motives for expansion were often expressed in our interviews with officials of water districts, yet such expansions are rare in practice. Both legal and organizational factors tend to preclude them. In the legal category, a district with outstanding bonded debt must impose on any included territory some obligation to share in the district's preexisting debt, and exclusions by such districts are practically impossible.[55] Territorial changes by districts holding contracts with the Bureau of Reclamation require the Bureau's permission, and thus may be precluded as an indirect result of the Bureau's water marketing policies. Some types of districts are limited as to the inclusions which they may make: territory may have to be contiguous, or all included territory may have to be served from a single source of water. Even where none of these legal prohibitions intervenes, the district and owners of the land considering inclusion often have trouble coming to terms. Acrimonious disputes over inclusion fees occasionally block apparently logical annexations of territory. As a result of these restrictions and difficulties, both inclusions and exclusions are typically small and generally occur shortly after a district has been formed.

Among the many cases in which the adjacent territory prefers to organize on its own, rather than to join an expanded district, a preference for local sovereignty is part of the explanation. Landowners in an unorganized area often show an acute consciousness that they will not control the decisions of a larger district following their inclusion into it. They feel that the existing district's board is attuned to the problems of its own territory and that they as newcomers will not receive equal treatment. Beyond a preference for local autonomy, a newly organizing area frequently has economic reasons for preferring an autonomous agency. Organizers of a new district often cherish the hope that they can produce water more cheaply than neighboring districts. Farmers may hold back on the prospect that a future source of supply might be cheaper than that currently offered to them.

In conclusion, we observe ample motives for existing agricultural water districts to make changes in the size of their operations involving territorial expansion, but not much interest in pursuing these motives and many pressures precluding the pursuit. On the other hand, would-be buyers in the water market often seek annexation to existing districts fruitlessly unless a major change in wholesale supplies is occurring. These patterns hold two major implications for performance. First, relatively easy annexation could serve as a substitute for external water sales by districts holding established water rights as a means to attain optimal allocation of water. But the absence of such annexations and of interdistrict sales assures the persistence of significant misallocations of water between districts or between in-

[55] The Oroville-Wyandotte Irrigation District furnishes a conspicuous example of how a district's indebtedness prevents annexation of territory to yield a more contiguous district area. Made up of two large and several smaller segments, not wholly contiguous and of quite irregular shape, this District lies in southeastern Butte County, south of the Feather River. When it took over two ditch systems (Palermo Ditch and Forbestown Ditch) from private owners, quite a number of the "prior users" of water preferred not to join the District. Oroville-Wyandotte, however, is obligated to continue to serve these prior users, and most of them are located in the interstices between segments of the District. Some years later, these prior users sought admission to the District, but then the bonded indebtedness incurred by district members constituted an effective barrier to their inclusion. The prior users have still not been admitted, yet they receive 40 per cent of all district water deliveries.

cluded and excluded territory. Second, there is not much pressure for adjustment of the actual sizes of districts to optimal cost-minimizing scales. This second defect is probably the less important because scale problems can be handled in other ways. When a small district wishes to build a large project, it can sometimes manage through a cooperative venture with other districts or by inducing some wholesaler to take over.[56] When a small district suffers legal inadequacies, it can sometimes correct the trouble merely by changing its legal form. But the forces tending to increase the size of retailing agricultural water districts are relatively weak and frequently frustrated. Finally, special functions such as ground-water recharge, drainage, and the conjunctive use of ground and surface water, which may require larger scale organization than the provision of surface water alone, can be looked after either through the formation of large overlapping districts or through the activities of the state and federal governments acting as water wholesalers or merely as superior political bodies.

These normative conclusions pertain largely to the "extensive margin" in the application of irrigation water—the extent of the territory served by a given supply organization. A parallel list of normative questions could be drawn up concerning the relation between the factors determining the size of districts and the "intensive margin"—the quantity of irrigation water combined with the average bundle of non-water agricultural inputs. The relevant behavioral evidence is unfortunately slight. The founders of districts that are formed to supply water on a fully integrated basis seldom know at the start what the delivery capability or average cost of the district will be. An important random element is thereby contributed to the determination of the intensive margin and the opportunity cost of water as between districts. Those agencies formed to contract with a wholesaler, on the other hand, usually enjoy some consciously determined relation from the start between the size of the water supply and the amount of territory to be watered. But whether this relation is calculated to satisfy the normative tests for correct allocation proposed in Chapter 8 is another question. In general, our normative findings on the intensive margin of water application will have to depend on direct measurements made in Part Three.

Scale in urban water supply

Urban retailers usually furnish water to areas determined by the sizes of the cities which they serve, and all other influences on their scale of operations are sharply subordinated to this one. Among the subordinate influences, however, no tendency appears for large agencies to break down, and some elements of conduct seem to favor the growth and consolidation of independent agencies.

Like very large agricultural districts, large urban agencies serve areas with differ-

[56] Examples of the respective alternatives would be the cooperation of Oakdale and South San Joaquin irrigation districts, and the Madera Irrigation District's substantial efforts to get the Bureau of Reclamation to construct the dam at Friant on the San Joaquin River which its own efforts had not accomplished.

ing water requirements and costs of supply. However, the possibilities of price discrimination among classes of consumers, coupled with the relative indifference of the numerical bulk of urban customers to the price of water, keep internal friction to a minimum. Low-elevation residents do not seek to form an agency which would exclude the higher cost, high-elevation residents, and they rarely even insist on lower rates. Most urban customers show more interest in the high-quality water and continuous service which can be provided by larger systems with excess capacity and sufficient capital to go to distant sources of higher quality water. The East Bay Municipal Utility District charges the same rates throughout its sprawling area, and so does the San Francisco Water Department along the long stretch of its aqueduct from the Sierra. Only once was EBMUD threatened with dismemberment, and this rebellion was quelled by a price adjustment. The question arises whether some of the large agricultural districts might have survived if they could have relied more on tolls and less on property taxes.

Not only are large urban agencies viable, but also a willingness to expand seems somewhat more common among urban than among agricultural suppliers. It appears as an outright preference among some public suppliers, while private companies often are prodded into expanding by the cities they serve. Some cities use such tactics as requiring that suburban subdividers install water systems and dedicate them to the cities. Then the private water company serving a city has no choice but to convey water to the city at wholesale rates for sale to the home buyer.[57] In less extreme cases, there has merely been perennial bickering between the city and the water utility over the latter's expansion.[58]

Some public urban water suppliers, without acting as wholesalers, have become completely adjusted to a policy of steady expansion. An excellent case study is the East Bay Municipal Utility District, an Oakland-based supplier which freely crosses city and county boundaries.[59] Shortly after its founding in 1923, EBMUD marked out an ultimate service area of 400 square miles, permitting it "to plan its transmission and distribution system more thoroughly" and to obtain the necessary water rights. Its initial system occupied only 92.5 square miles, and in 1961 it had risen only to 245 square miles. It settled on a standard method of expansion: the annexation of the companies or districts already serving fringe areas. Armed with relatively low prices and much better service than the typical small agency, it has generally stood by passively to await requests from residents or owners in the territory desiring annexation. This approach has provided satisfactory public relations at the same time that it has permitted a relatively steady rate of expansion.

[57] Walsh, *op. cit.*, 351.

[58] The aspirations of cities for growth and independence can, of course, cut in the other direction. Small cities in a metropolitan area may maintain small inefficient water systems rather than submit to pressures toward absorption into a larger government. When Oakland's East Bay Municipal Utility District was proposed in the 1920's, it was approved in a second election in 1923, but defeated in an earlier attempt. Part of the political opposition has been attributed to the fear of some Oakland leaders that an East Bay district would lead to the consolidation of East Bay cities and eventual area-wide consolidation under the hegemony of San Francisco. See Louis Bartlett, "Memoirs" (Typescript, University of California General Library, Berkeley, 1957), pp. 98–102.

[59] See H. Buford Fisher, "Problems of System Expansion by Annexation," *Journal of the American Water Works Association,* LIII (April 1961), 388–96.

The District has developed standard pricing and integration procedures for its inclusions, requiring that a new area form a county water district or improvement district to bring its distribution system up to EBMUD's standards, and setting a charge for the new area calculated to cover EBMUD's additional operating costs—and some but not all of its incremental capital costs—over a fifteen-year period.

In using this mode of expansion, EBMUD allegedly has been somewhat choosy about the territory that it annexes, to the annoyance of a neighboring water agency with more general responsibilities. The Contra Costa County Water Agency has accused EBMUD of selectively annexing territory which would make a relatively substantial addition to its tax base, and has urged it "to stop picking off the cream" of valuable territory in south Contra Costa County.[60] Such behavior on EBMUD's part would, of course, constitute a rational policy for a users' cooperative acting in the interests of its existing membership.

Recent legal decisions involving districts in Southern California have apparently made it easier for an expanding city to absorb special purpose water districts which lie in its path. The decision in a case involving the Downey County Water District and the city of Downey affirmed the doctrine that a special purpose district is automatically dissolved when it is totally annexed by a city. Piecemeal annexations without the consent of the dismembered district have also been approved.[61] Thus, cities with a zeal to expand, whether or not related to the function of water supply, face no blocks from the existence of special purpose districts. No substantial exercises of these powers of general municipal governments have occurred in Northern California, however.

In summary, both agricultural and urban water districts show some tendencies to adapt their scales of operation to the crude determinants of optimal scale at the time of their formation, with agricultural districts perhaps more sensitive to such forces than urban agencies, which are typically tied down by city limits. Neither type of agency shows much tendency to adapt its scale to secure maximum efficiency in the face of changing economic conditions, although both agricultural and urban agencies have responded properly in some cases. In the case of agricultural—but not urban—agencies, these rigidities also contribute to denying some would-be buyers access to local markets for water. Some political pressures seem to operate on the scales of both urban and agricultural agencies, although in opposite directions: agricultural agencies, at least in earlier years, appeared to lack political viability at large scales; urban agencies show some tendency to expand along with the general geographic extension of municipal governments.

Conclusions

The organization of agencies in the water industry, changes in their legal form, and changes in their boundaries all respond broadly to changes in supply (cost) and demand (productivity) conditions relating to water.

[60] *Oakland Tribune*, July 26. 1963.

[61] For a brief summary of these cases, see *Western Water News*, May 1963, pp. 1–2. Compare Irrigation Districts Association of California, *Minutes of Semiannual Convention, San Francisco, California, April 25–27, 1962* (1963), pp. 13–28.

The long history of the formation of districts caused by deteriorating groundwater conditions, the availability of wholesale surface supplies, and the perceived rivalry of other lands for available natural surface supplies closely identifies the organization of agricultural water districts with changing allocation and increased scarcity of surface water supplies.

Changes in the legal form of districts and the disappearance of some unsuccessful districts confirm the fundamental role of these economic factors. And the failure of private enterprise in much of the industry reflects structural traits and attitudes affecting transactions in water which are violently hostile to private-market workable competition.

The same economic forces operate, but in a very loose way, upon the size of individual districts. The location of irrigation district boundaries, like the expansion of urban water agencies, may often be determined by noneconomic goals of local governments and historic accidents in the location of other political subdivisions—factors bearing no relation to the economics of water supply. These forces are important because of the relative rigidity of agency boundaries once they are first officially established, and the many constraints on the expansion, contraction, and dissolution of districts tend strongly to perpetuate any inefficiencies created at the time of their formation.

Some economic transactions that are not associated with changes in the population of districts, or in their boundaries, may be more significant than changes which are so associated. Retailing agricultural districts do not compete for new customers (inclusions), and urban agencies seldom do so for reasons related to the economics of water supply. The owners of unorganized territory seeking to augment their water supplies normally form an entirely new district rather than seek access to an existing one. Newly formed districts contemplate a range of strategies to gain a supply of water, but one which they contemplate only rarely is the purchase of water rights from another district. These gaps in the range of alternatives under consideration in the water industry, along with the many rigidities affecting those changes and reallocations which do occur, give preliminary warning of some of the problems of economic performance to be discussed in Part Three.

10

PRICING AND WATER ALLOCATION WITHIN RETAIL AGENCIES

The conduct of water agencies in determining the prices charged for water distributed to their customers is reviewed in this chapter. We shall be dealing with short-run situations in which the water supply of the agency is not altered by building a new dam or enlarging a canal. The agency must choose some means of allotting available water among its customers and, in the process, covering its own costs of operation. Supplemented by various rationing practices, retail pricing decisions determine the short-run efficiency of the allocation of water within districts. More important, they also exert a major influence on the investment decisions made by and on behalf of water retailers. Wholesale pricing, of similar significance but considerably less insular in character, is discussed in Chapter 13 as one facet of wholesaler-retailer relations.

The Setting and Significance of Retail Water Pricing

The bulk of Northern California agencies supplying water to final users are public districts, including special districts or general units of local government. Our hypotheses developed in Chapter 8 suggested that the economic behavior of these units might best be viewed as that of cooperative organizations serving the economic interests of their regular customers. This analogy provides both a framework for making a normative appraisal of the performance of these units and a source of detailed hypotheses about their conduct.

The decision on pricing water to member-customers should provide a major test of the effects of the organizational traits of public water agencies on their operations. The pricing decision affects all customers and raises all possible issues of equity as among them. In the deliberations of agency management, issues of equity in fact dominate the setting of prices. The political nature of a public body necessitates a broad community support for its operations. A price structure which is thought to embody exploitation may create insurmountable barriers to political consensus and frustrate other plans.

Agricultural water agencies, being largely single purpose organizations, normally prove to be directly responsive to the wishes of their electorates in setting prices, as in other matters. Irrigators see their chief interest, in the short run, in minimizing the supply price of water; the main legal restriction on the district's charges to them is that revenues cover all current financial obligations. Putting these organizational features together, the dominant objective of short-run pricing by agricultural water districts is predicted, and turns out to be, setting charges to cover current money costs of a fixed supply of water. Many other objectives, however, can also affect agricultural water prices, and the relatively complex structure of these charges provides a vehicle for reflecting them within the general framework of covering costs.

Urban water service is often provided by a department of a general municipal government, although special districts and private water companies retain a significant role. Municipal governments comprise, in a sense, users' cooperatives providing a collection of goods and services to their citizens. In contrast to agricultural districts, the pricing of water is less important both to most customers and as an element in the range of decisions made by local city governments. The level of water prices is usually set primarily to cover costs, as in agricultural agencies; the structure of charges is used to promote other objectives, especially where wholesale charges to other governmental units occur.

A demonstration of the principles employed in the retail pricing of water in the short run provides a vital basis for appraising the efficiency of the water industry. In Chapter 8, we outlined some of the basic normative rules for the allocation of water between both competing and independent uses. For example, water districts diverting the water of a particular river should divide it among themselves in such a way that the marginal value of water taken, net of transport and distribution costs, should be the same for all districts. This common marginal value becomes the net opportunity cost of water to each agency. Within a district, essentially the same principle operates. Let us suppose, first, that the long-run marginal costs per acre-foot of the district's operations are the same for service to any member-customer. Then the price charged by the district to customers should in general equal the sum of the opportunity cost of water to the district plus its own long-run marginal costs of operation. And each user should be permitted to take a quantity of water which equates this retail price to the net value of marginal product of water in his own operation. Such a retail pricing pattern in all districts, combined with a correctly calculated opportunity cost, would be consistent with optimal commercial allocation of water throughout the river basin in question. If the resulting revenue failed to cover total costs for the district, a charge independent of the quantity of water taken should be levied upon users to make up the difference.

Typically, a water agency does not incur the same long-run marginal costs to serve all customers at every time, so that a single price to all members will not suffice. Customers will be located at varying distances from the agency's wholesale source of water or diversion point, and the greater length of canals or mains required to serve the more distant users are reflected in higher long-run marginal costs of serving them, and a higher appropriate unit charge. Some residences or farmlands may lie at higher altitudes than others, so that greater unit costs are incurred to sustain a given water pressure or delivery rate. Where the groundwater basin underlying an agency's lands serves as a natural storage basin, replenished by the agency's operations and drawn upon by the pumps of its members, prices must be adjusted to insure efficient conjunctive use of the ground-water basin.[1] Finally, when we take into account the timing of customers' demands for water, a distinction between long-run and short-run marginal cost arises, and the criteria developed in the literature on peak-load pricing must be built into the normative structure of charges.[2]

These factors influencing the appropriate retail pricing pattern direct attention to many features of the tolls, assessments, block rates, and the like used in pricing California water. They also point to the importance of water rationing devices, which frequently supplement the use of tolls in allocating water among alternative final users in agricultural districts, and occasionally do so in urban supply. A pricing system that is optimal without rationing cannot be optimal if rationing is introduced with other factors constant. On the other hand, rationing practices could conceivably be used to amend the allocations induced by an inefficient pricing system or provide a serviceable alternative when a "sophisticated" pricing system is too expensive to operate, given the size of the allocative errors which it might avert.

Water pricing practices gain additional normative significance because they indirectly influence aspects of allocative efficiency other than the distribution of water among a district's customers. Consider the major behavioral connection between short-run pricing and the investment decision. The normative rules for pricing, when stated in terms of long-run marginal costs, subsume the problem of investment criteria and essentially suppose that problem to be solved along with the determination of an optimum pricing pattern. In practice, of course, water industry investments occur in highly discontinuous fashion, and the pricing decision for all agencies, both agricultural and urban, is sharply divorced from decisions relating to changes in capacity. And in the appraisal which follows, those limited and qualified statements which we can make about levels of marginal costs and their differences will relate mainly to short-run costs. In abstract theory, and ignoring discontinuities, optimal pricing and investment decisions can be made by setting prices equal to short-run marginal costs and expanding the fixed plant whenever short-run marginal costs (and price) exceed long-run marginal costs. One can indeed conceive of correct investment decisions being made even if inappropriate pricing rules are in force when the investment decision is made, assuming that the inefficient pricing is due to some cause other than lack of information. In fact, the evidence reviewed in Chapter 11 suggests that decisions of water districts to expand their storage and distribution capacity often rest (within the limits of financial feasibility) upon relatively simple tests of the "adequacy" of the existing water supply. In this case, links between the efficiency of short-run pricing and the efficiency of investment become extremely important. If excess demand for water appears because of pricing below short-run marginal costs, not only will current water use be too great (in the absence of rationing) but also the inducement to invest may look stronger than it should. In appraising the efficiency of short-run

[1] This complex case is discussed more fully below.

[2] See Ralph K. Davidson, *Price Discrimination in Selling Gas and Electricity,* Johns Hopkins University Studies in Historical and Political Science, Series LXXII, No. 1 (1955), chaps. 2, 4; Peter O. Steiner, "Peak Loads and Efficient Pricing," *Quarterly Journal of Economics,* LXXI (November 1957), 585–610. (Most footnote references in this chapter are cited in brief form when they are also included in the Bibliography.)

pricing, we must keep in mind the possibility that the short-run tail could wag the long-run dog.

The following sections deal first with the typical structural traits of retail water pricing systems; then they turn more formally to the objectives which apparently underlie these characteristics and to the normative implications. Agricultural and urban agencies by and large are treated separately, since the differences between urban and agricultural pricing are greater than their similarities. Whereas most agricultural districts charge a unit price for water that is invariant with the quantity taken, urban price schedules almost always contain a "taper" or declining marginal price. Though most agricultural districts levy a tax on land to supplement their tolls, most urban water systems do not employ taxes.[3] Agricultural districts seek to use associated activities (power principally) as a means to reduce the price of water, whereas urban systems sometimes divert their water revenues to cover part of the costs of other public services. In many agricultural districts, the irrigator usually has access to supplies other than those from the district, such as pumping from the ground-water basin or, occasionally, diverting from a river. This choice is not open to the urban consumer except for large industrial firms.

Patterns of Water Pricing

The charges levied by a Northern California water agency consist of one or more components, depending on the type of agency, its financial requirements, the wishes of members or customers, and less tangible considerations that may include both economic and political elements. The major division of payments is between those which vary with the quantity of water purchased and those which are independent of quantity. The latter charges may take the form of taxes, and therefore be levied on both water users and nonusers. They may consist of a rate for a meter connection, minimum delivery charge, or a fixed toll per crop-acre. Quantity charges may be based on a metering of the volume of water delivered, or some cheaper method may be used to relate the charge to the quantity taken.

Water tolls and quantity charges

Most agricultural water districts employ a charge containing two components, a water toll proportional to the amount of water sold and a tax levy proportional to the assessed value of the property within the district.[4] The water toll is based directly on the number of units delivered or indirectly in other ways. The unit of water measurement varies a good deal; the acre-foot is the most common unit for irrigation service. However, some districts retain charges based on a measurement of the rate at which water flows during the season rather than the volume delivered.

A number of districts approximate a water toll by a charge per irrigation under

[3] This proposition holds for urban systems in Northern California but not Southern California.

[4] Where a more complex system of pricing is employed, it has usually been devised to meet some special problem of equity or allocative efficiency affecting a particular district.

a rotational delivery system or a charge based on the number of acres of each crop a farmer raises.[5] Such substitutes for prices per unit of water are used because they avoid the need for measuring water delivered, and making accurate measurements of the amount of irrigation water delivered is fairly expensive relative to the cost of the water itself. Also, in some types of soil the amount of water a farmer can apply to any given crop is more or less technologically fixed. Unless this condition holds, of course, these approximations to a water toll will alter both the water-use incentives for the irrigator and the quantity he actually purchases, for the marginal cost to him becomes zero. When one divides the charges set on a crop-acre basis by the approximate number of acre-feet applied per crop, the price per unit of water frequently turns out to vary significantly from crop to crop. In some cases, the variation from crop to crop seems to be random; in others, a district has a conscious policy of either favoring or discouraging particular crops. The districts which cast their water tolls in the form of charges per crop-acre are not randomly distributed over the state. They concentrate in areas where water is relatively abundant and cheap, principally the Sacramento River valley. The average unit cost of water to irrigators in these districts appears to be less than half of the average for the whole Central Valley.[6] This pattern tends to confirm the suggestion that measuring water consumption precisely becomes inefficient when the cost of the water itself is very low, at least from the viewpoint of the district seeking to set charges in relation to its costs. In general, water tolls used by agricultural districts in the Central Valley vary considerably in absolute level, and these variations are not random.[7]

Although a number of cities in the Central Valley, such as Fresno, employ a fixed charge and do not meter water consumption, some kind of two-part tariff is the most common arrangement in urban water pricing. This usually consists of a fixed meter charge (sometimes including a minimum quantity of water monthly) and a toll which usually declines significantly as the user's monthly consumption increases. Tables 23 and 24 show the structure of these charges for a sample of cities in the San Francisco Bay area. Table 23 shows the meter charge and the toll pertaining to the first and to the largest blocks of water purchased, along with total costs to the consumer of 1,000 and 50,000 cubic feet per month. Table 24 converts columns 2 and 3 of Table 23 into average costs per 100 cf, to facilitate comparison of the charges to large and small consumers.

The tables show declining marginal water tolls for all but two cities—Fairfield and San Bruno—and declining average unit costs to the customer for all. As column 3 of Table 24 shows, the rate of taper is far from uniform. Although cities usually do not set different schedules for different types of users, the quantity discounts are primarily for the benefit of selected industrial users. Special rates are typically established for standby capacity to fight fires (sprinklers in buildings or fire hydrants) or for special customers, including public users (schools, parks, and the like), and sometimes for special supply conditions such as service to shipping from common hydrants on open docks.

[5] See Irrigation Districts Association of California, *Water Use and Water Costs in Some Typical Irrigation Districts in California* (1960) for examples.

[6] See Chapter 6, section on The Cost of Retail Supplies of Irrigation Water.

[7] *Ibid.*

TABLE 23
RESIDENTIAL WATER CHARGES AND THEIR COMPONENTS, SELECTED SAN FRANCISCO BAY AREA CITIES, 1960

City or district	Minimum charges 5/8″ or 3/4″ meters (1)	Total cost of water per month on 5/8″ meter: 1,000 cf (2)	Total cost of water per month on 5/8″ meter: 50,000 cf (3)	Minimum charges 2″ meter (4)	Toll for first 100 cf over minimum delivery (5)	Toll per 100 cf of largest delivery (6)
Antioch	$1.75	$2.35	$ 77.85	$ 1.75	$.20	$.15
Burlingame	1.50	3.00	123.00	6.00	.30	.23
Daly City	0	3.70	113.95	0	.295	.225
East Bay Municipal Utility District[a]	1.60	3.00	81.64	15.86	.20	.09
Fairfield	3.00	3.20	52.20	5.00	.10	.10
Hayward	0.50	4.00	109.42	3.50	.35	.18
Hillsborough	2.00	5.20	147.00	5.00	.32	.23
Napa	1.50	3.07	42.50	3.50	.262	.133
Palo Alto	1.35	2.70	111.10	5.10	.27	.20
Pittsburg	2.65	3.33	96.78	7.00	.225	.19
Redwood City	1.80	3.30	131.08	9.00	.33	.22
San Bruno[b]	1.25	2.00	75.50	1.25	.15	.15
San Francisco	0.70	3.29	107.35	4.85	.259	.135
Santa Clara	1.35	2.20	68.60	5.25	.22	.13
Sunnyvale	2.00	3.35	95.56	7.50	.335	.18
Vallejo	1.50	3.00	108.05	1.50	.30	.177

[a] Cities of the East Bay area in the San Francisco Bay region.
[b] For delivery from the city's wells. Higher tolls pertain to water purchased from the San Francisco Water Department.
SOURCE: City of Redding, *A Survey of Water Rates and Related Data for 86 Municipal Systems in California as of January 1, 1960* (1960).

TABLE 24
RELATION OF UNIT WATER COSTS FOR LARGE AND SMALL CONSUMERS, SELECTED SAN FRANCISCO BAY AREA CITIES, 1960

City or district	Costs per month for 1,000 cf 5/8″ meter (per 100 cf) (1)	Costs per month for 50,000 cf 2″ meter (per 100 cf) (2)	Col. 2 as % of col. 1 (3)
Antioch	$0.235	$0.1557	66%
Burlingame	.300	.237	79
Daly City	.37	.2279	62
East Bay Municipal Utility District[a]	.30	.1931	64
Fairfield	.32	.1044	33
Hayward	.40	.224	56
Hillsborough	.52	.30	58
Napa	.307	.186	61
Palo Alto	.27	.222	82
Pittsburg	.333	.1926	58
Redwood City	.33	.2696	81
San Bruno	.20	.151	76
San Francisco	.329	.223	68
Santa Clara	.22	.137	62
Sunnyvale	.335	.2021	60
Vallejo	.30	.2161	72

[a] Cities of the East Bay area in the San Francisco Bay region.
SOURCE: Columns 2 and 3 of Table 23, calculated.

Tax levies

Tax levies, the other major component of water charges, are somewhat restricted by state laws setting the powers of various types of districts. Irrigation districts can levy annual ad valorem taxes on land exclusive of improvements sufficient for certain fixed obligations and other special purposes. There is a statutory maximum on the rate of taxation for operation and maintenance and for other general purposes. Taxes can be levied according to benefits, where payments must be made to the United States or where separate improvement districts are established and operate within irrigation districts. Other types of districts are subject to slightly different provisions. Municipal utility districts assess all taxable property, not just unimproved land. So-called California water districts have an omnibus right to assess land when other sources of revenue are inadequate.[8] These provisions leave a good deal of flexibility to the districts. Except for generous limitations on the amount that can be collected by levies for certain purposes, they can select any mixture of charges they wish.

Assessment practices vary a good deal from district to district. A flat assessment, often $100 per acre, is common where an agricultural district's works serve the whole of a relatively homogeneous territory. Assessments differ from ownership to ownership, however, where land differs in quality or where some of it receives manifestly less benefit from the district's activities. Some irrigation districts have recently adopted land valuations directly relating to soil productivity by using information provided by the Bureau of Reclamation. When the Bureau executes a contract for permanent water service to a district, it issues a report on the district's ability to pay for water that includes a detailed soil classification map. This map sometimes becomes the basis for the district's assessments,[9] so that the tax component of water charges contains a relatively precise value-of-service element.

Assessment practices vary a good deal from district to district. A flat assess-nicipal Utility District (Oakland and nearby cities) levies a tax on all land and improvements in its jurisdiction, accepting the county assessor's estimation of the value of property. County water districts and conservation districts are the other major water agencies levying taxes in the urbanized San Francisco Bay area. The county water districts employ all property in their area as a tax base and similarly accept county assessors' appraisals. Conservation districts must usually restrict their assessments to land only. The benefits which they confer, frequently controlled ground-water recharge, are widely dispersed, and many residents may gain only slight benefits. Restricting the tax base to land only then becomes a political necessity. Unlike irrigation districts, such conservation districts as the Santa Clara Valley Water Conservation District accept the county assessor's appraisal of unimproved land as the base for their taxes.

[8] California *Water Code* (1963), §§ 20500–29978, 34000–38501, and others. For a convenient summary, see California State Legislature, Assembly Water Committee, *Water District Laws of California: An Analysis Report Prepared for Assembly Interim Committee on Conservation, Planning, and Public Works*, Vol. 13, No. 5A (1955), pp. 74–87, and Chapter 3 above.

[9] Michael F. Brewer, *Water Pricing and Allocation with Particular Reference to California Irrigation Districts* (1960), p. 51.

Objectives in Pricing Agricultural Water

This discussion of the pattern of retail water charges in use in Northern California suggests that decisions on water prices may be affected by a wide variety of circumstances prevailing within and about the water agency in question. It does not, however, tell anything about the principles employed in setting these charges, which is the crucial matter for drawing conclusions about the performance of the industry. At the risk of slight simplification, we shall give separate consideration to principles governing the average level of charges (whatever the structure may be) and to the practices followed in adjusting the components of the structure of rates used to attain any given level of gross returns. Agricultural and urban agencies require separate treatment. The normative implications will be suggested from time to time, and then drawn together in a subsequent section.

Principles governing the level of rates

The conscious pricing policy of management in public water agencies in the agricultural sector, reflected in interview after interview, is to set tolls and tax rates so that current financial outlays will be covered, or occasionally to cover these costs plus a contribution to a "safe" surplus. Small increases or decreases in districts' tolls and taxes are explained in terms of changes in current costs.[10] However, public water districts frequently increase their revenues in anticipation of higher future expenditures, partly to keep the year-to-year change in charges small, partly through a strong conservatism in financial matters. This explains some of the available facts about aggregate cost and revenue data for California water districts which would otherwise seem inconsistent with the hypothesis of pricing to cover current outlays. Not only have some districts built up substantial surpluses, but the rate at which total revenues of California irrigation districts have exceeded total expenditures has been as much as 10 per cent in recent years.

Is this consistent with a reigning motivation of pricing to cover current costs? Part of the answer lies in the failure of irrigation districts to record the depreciation of assets as a cost. Some assets which must be occasionally replaced or subjected to extensive maintenance operations are not formally depreciated, but districts allow reserves to build up an anticipation of these expenditures. When the aggregate volume of district activities expands from year to year, these accumulations on balance will add to their total reported surplus. Another part of the explanation

[10] The following explanation made for a tax increase ordered by the Merced Irrigation District provides a sample of the typical reasoning: "The new rate was the lowest possible to provide for continued improvements to the facilities and services of the district. Withdrawal from surplus funds in order to make capital improvements to the water distribution system during the last 10 years has amounted to almost $1,000,000 or a little more than one-half of the reserve funds held by the district 10 years ago.

"To deplete remaining reserve funds would endanger the district's financial stability in the event of a series of subnormal power years. About one third of these funds must be held to fulfill legal obligations to bondholders. Withdrawal from the balance of the reserve will need to be made in subnormal years." (From *Merced Express,* Sept. 8, 1955.)

is a conservatism in the financial decisions of water districts' boards of directors. There is a very strong aversion to being caught short and having to issue warrants or take other emergency actions; what an irrigation district manager calls a price set to cover costs, an ordinary businessman might call a price set to yield a modest profit. Still another possible explanation for apparent "profits" among the water agencies is the terms of bond financing agreements, which often compel the borrowing district to build up its cash surplus to a certain point. In any case, public districts make no distributions from their accumulated surpluses to any holder of equity. When "profits" are earned on annual operations they are either windfalls (a result of deferred price adjustments) or the fruit of some conscious policy of managing the accrued surplus of the district. There is abundant evidence of the conscious management of surpluses, whether to build them up or to draw them down.

Whatever pricing pattern is chosen, many districts prefer to keep taxes and tolls stable for as long a period as possible. Changes come seldom and are small when they do occur, unless there is a major change in the water supply or distribution system. This practice is possible because most of a public water district's costs are fairly stable, either in total amount or relative to the amount of water distributed, and because rather substantial liquid financial reserves are often maintained.

To consider in a preliminary way the normative significance of this pricing principle of covering "costs," there is serious question about the relation between these financial outlays and the economic costs of a district's operations. Indeed, the only close matching of economic and financial costs is likely to be in payment for variable inputs other than water. Capital costs are covered through amortization rather than depreciation. Any marginal net opportunity cost associated with the use of water itself is largely ignored; this hypothesis was suggested in Part One and will be explored empirically in Chapter 12. No economic function of riskbearing is undertaken within the district (that is, within the cooperative plant) as distinguished from its members' contingent obligations, and indeed no equity function is rewarded. If average unit costs of the district remain approximately constant when the size of the territory which it serves changes, and if these assorted accounting biases should happen to offset one another, then the over-all level of financial return to the agricultural retailing district would be appropriate. This conditional conclusion will be considered further below.

Principles governing the structure of rates

The principles employed by districts in setting the structure of rates, mainly as between tolls and taxes, involve a rather rich variety of issues of economic analysis and raise a corresponding number of normative issues. We will review these in some detail, beginning with the more casual factors affecting the rate structure and proceeding to some more complex cases.

The mixtures of tolls and taxes chosen by districts often depend strongly on local history. Irrigation districts in relatively prosperous areas, or districts which are themselves wealthy through sales of hydroelectric power generated at their storage dams and need only minor water revenues to cover costs, often use a moderate tax levy but no toll on water.[11] The long-established districts in the Kings River area because of local custom employ only taxes, but the practice makes some economic sense in the light of the low direct marginal costs associated with their run-of-stream diversions and simple distribution systems.[12]

A different pattern appears in some of the districts of the eastern Sacramento River Valley. Many of this area's districts went through painful bankruptcies in the 1930's. These left their mark on long-time residents who lost their lands to the irrigation districts for delinquent taxes. Assessments are still feared as a "lien on the land," and several districts therefore either avoid them entirely or use them only from time to time. Of the dozen districts on the east side of the Sacramento Valley, three collect no taxes at all.

Many more districts use some combination of tolls and taxes than depend on either alone. Where the toll-tax balance does not seem to be arbitrary, a good many things can determine the actual pattern chosen. Some districts seem to set their levies at a rate which will just meet scheduled payments on their bonded indebtedness. Other districts buying water from a wholesaling agency often set the toll to cover the wholesale price and load the other variable costs and all fixed costs onto the tax. Generally speaking, a relatively large number of districts set tolls and levies in such a way that the toll approximates the average variable or marginal cost of water to the district, while fixed costs are covered by tax levies. One statistical study has shown a high correlation between irrigation districts' revenues from water tolls and their administrative and operation and maintenance expenses,[13] costs which are largely variable in relation to the volume of water distributed. This type of pattern is frequently chosen unless some other conspicuous factor influences the setting of the toll-tax balance—usually one of the considerations of equity or incentives discussed below.[14]

Another major motive governing pricing by irrigation district managers is to provide an appropriate set of incentives for the use of district water by irrigators. To a large extent, this is the same thing as taking into account the position and elasticity of the aggregate demand curve of the district's member-customers, for the incentives are those regarding the amount of water pumped by individual irrigators from ground-water basins, the timing of demands made upon the district's surface supplies, the construction and maintenance of conveyance facilities, the crops grown, and so forth. Some of the incentives manipulated by adjustments of the rate structure also concern aspects of water use which are the source of external effects.

[11] Examples of these wealthy types are the Modesto and Turlock irrigation districts, located on the east side of the San Joaquin Valley. Modesto imposes no water charges of any kind; Turlock uses a low tax levy only as backing for an incentive program to cause farmers to maintain their local portions of the distribution system.

[12] The area is one, however, in which positive marginal opportunity costs of the water at the source clearly exist, and these typically are not taken into account.

[13] Brewer, *op. cit.*, p. 71. Correlation coefficients for all California irrigation districts in six separate years lay between 0.738 and 0.919.

[14] Of course, some districts' tolls (perhaps a large minority) are set per acre or per crop-acre rather than per acre-foot of water, and so would not vary directly with the volume of water distributed.

The pricing practice of one important organization, the Lower Tule River Irrigation District, exemplifies this tendency. Its policies reflect not only the adjustments mentioned above made by districts to the terms of water supply offered by a wholesaler (the Bureau of Reclamation), but also the principle typically employed in setting the rate structure by districts whose irrigators have ready access to privately pumped ground water. The District is one of many holding long-run contracts for San Joaquin River water delivered by the Bureau through the Friant-Kern Canal. Such districts are largely assured a certain minimum annual supply of "Class 1" water for which they pay $3.50 an acre-foot at canal-side. Also, in all but very dry years they may receive some additional supply of "Class 2" water, in uncertain quantities up to a maximum, at $1.50 an acre-foot. The contract deliveries to the Lower Tule River District are 61,200 acre-feet of Class 1 water annually and a maximum of 238,000 acre-feet of Class 2; the total supply bought from the Bureau of Reclamation can thus range from 61,200 to 299,200 acre-feet each year. The average unit cost of the water is lower the more is taken. The District's annual average "wholesale" cost of water could range from a maximum of $3.50 an acre-foot (no Class 2) down to $1.91 an acre-foot (maximum Class 2).

The District normally varies its water toll between $2.40 and $3.20 an acre-foot with the supply of surface water available, raising it in dry years and lowering it in wet years. This achieves two objectives for the District. First, it controls the amount of water demanded by irrigators from the Lower Tule River District. The pump lifts for the District's irrigators vary from 60 to 200 feet, so that the out-of-pocket costs of pumping (roughly 4 cents per acre-foot per foot of lift) are from the shallower wells within the range of variation of the water toll. Many farmers are near the margin of indifference between surface and ground-water supplies, making the demand elasticity for surface water very high over this range, and small toll adjustments strongly affect the quantity demanded. A second desired result of this pricing policy is to cause the District's revenue to vary with its total costs as between dry and wet years. Thus, changes in the District's financial obligation to the Bureau of Reclamation can be met without changes in assessments or wide variations in the District's surplus. In 1958, a year when irrigation water was particularly abundant, the Lower Tule River District resorted to shifting from a water toll per acre-foot to a charge per irrigated acre. This maneuver reduced the marginal cost of surface water for the irrigators to zero, except for their own labor. It caused a considerably greater quantity of water to be applied, as two crops that are widely grown in the District, alfalfa and permanent pasture, yield outputs that are quite responsive to the amount of water applied. On the highly permeable soils covering much of the District, 9 to 10 acre-feet of water could be applied during the year to permanent pasture. From the District's point of view, this had the desirable results both of causing considerable surface water to percolate through the root zone to the underground basin and of encouraging the growth of pasture grasses which loosen the soil and increase its permeability for further percolation.[15]

[15] Interview with William A. Alexander, engineer and manager, Lower Tule River Irrigation District, Aug. 26, 1960, and his report for the District, *Lower Tule River Irrigation District: History and Operational Report, 1950 to 1957* (1957). Also see Brewer, *op. cit.*, pp. 97–102, 114–22.

Practices of the Lower Tule River District are typical of those of many irrigation districts. The adjustment of water tolls to affect farmers' incentives for choosing between surface and pumped ground water is common throughout the important districts on the east side of the San Joaquin Valley. There are at least three reasons for this. First, the pump lifts for irrigators in much of this area are such that the average variable (and marginal) cost of securing ground water is in the same neighborhood as the average total unit cost to public districts of providing surface water. Second, nearly all irrigated farms in the area retain their own pumping plants and wells, either because the receipt of surface water is relatively recent or because surface supplies have never been sufficient to last through the whole irrigation season. Third, the requirement of the Bureau of Reclamation that its contract customers pay for their total contractual supplies (after a development period), whether they take them or not, compels the districts to develop pricing methods which induce farmers to use surface water when available and thus accomplish cyclical storage of water in the underground aquifers.[16]

Several other districts, such as the Madera Irrigation District and Chowchilla Water District, both located north of Fresno, similarly set their water tolls equal to the average cost of private pumping in the district. In the Chowchilla District, this policy is coupled with the decision of the directors to serve only about 60 per cent of the District's lands by the surface distribution system, the rest depending on pumping at all times. On top of the necessity for setting a water toll low enough to induce farmers within reach of the surface distribution canals to use them, there is the problem of equitable treatment of district farmers who can and those who cannot use surface water. Under these policies, the farmer who operates his own pumps lays out about as much as one who depends on the District's supply, and no inequities are felt.[17] In the adjacent Madera Irrigation District very similar conditions exist—a moderately high water table and a distribution system that has not been extended to serve all farms in the district. The water toll, set at $2.50 or $2.60 in recent years, serves the same double purpose of manipulating incentives to secure use of surface water and achieving equity between those who can and those who cannot use surface supplies. Defining appropriate normative criteria for appraising pricing practices in these cases of conjunctive ground-water utilization raises complex, separate questions; the appraisal of these practices is undertaken below.

The price structure of water districts often discriminates among different crops. Although sometimes unintentional, these differentials often reflect conscious policy. The adjacent James and Tranquility irrigation districts, located on a distributary of the Kings River, both set their toll structures to serve rice at a lower toll per acre-foot than other crops. Rice is more tolerant of alkali than other crops, and this fact, plus the effect of heavy water applications to rice of leaching alkali from the soil, makes it an excellent crop for reclaiming alkali land. Another reason is that rice farming would be unprofitable in this area if rice growers paid as much per acre-foot of water as do growers of other crops; an element of value-of-service

[16] Brewer, *op. cit.*, p. 94.

[17] Irrigation Districts Association of California, *op. cit.*, p. 6; and interview with Francis C. Adair, resident engineer, Chowchilla Water District, Aug. 17, 1960.

pricing is thus involved. Other districts impose a rising marginal charge as irrigators take increasing quantities per acre, in order to combat excessively high ground-water tables.[18]

Many irrigated areas of the Central Valley lack storage facilities and so do not have equally good access to surface water through the irrigation season. Thus, water has an increasing imputed scarcity value as the season goes on. Some districts recognize this by setting the water toll lower in the early part of the season. For example, the Chowchilla Water District charges $2.00 an acre-foot after June 1, but $1.50 before. Chowchilla is a customer of the Bureau of Reclamation, which makes Class 2 water available at $1.50 to the District only early in the season, so that the District's costs and revenues vary together.

As we have seen, providing equitable treatment to various classes of citizens or customers of a district is a major factor governing pricing policies. Often this is a matter of providing acceptable treatment to parties who are located within a district's boundaries and subject to its assessments but are not direct customers for its water. One district, constrained by this limitation on its taxes and a limitation on tolls created by the prevailing level of ground-water costs, has chosen to add a third element to its rate structure: a demand charge, such as urban systems often employ. In times past it was common to include city lands within irrigation districts, and agricultural lands are still included which potentially could be served by the district but for one reason or another are not. Many districts adjust their tolls and assessments to these conditions, and those which do not make such adjustments often seem to suffer chronic internal controversies.[19]

Some types of pricing considerations seen by the districts as issues of equity may simply amount to recognizing differences in costs of service. Some districts serve a portion of their territory by gravity distribution but have to pump water to other users. Several districts along the Bureau's Friant-Kern Canal are bisected by its right of way. They can provide gravity service to users below (west of) the Canal, but must pump to those above (east of) it. The common practice of these districts is to charge the customers served by pumping more per acre-foot than the others, with the margin set to cover the cost of electric energy used in pumping. The standard explanation offered for this practice is that a difference based on energy costs of pumping seems "fair." Sometimes this problem is solved by forming separate "improvement districts" in areas where extra costs must be incurred and levying improvement district charges to cover them. This device is used by many irrigation districts for financing the capital costs of particular segments of the distribution system through taxes on the beneficiaries, but is not commonly employed for a comparable allocation of current costs.

[18] For older examples of these practices, see California State Department of Public Works, Division of Engineering and Irrigation, *Irrigation Districts in California, 1929,* by Frank Adams, Bulletin No. 21 (1930), p. 80; *idem,* Division of Water Resources, *Report on Irrigation Districts in California for the Year 1929,* Bulletin No. 21–A (1931), p. 25.

[19] For example, the Oroville-Wyandotte Irrigation District faced serious financial problems in the early 1950's due to high operating costs and heavy expenses for planning a large new project. Increases in taxes fell upon a number of residents of the District who were actually served by a private water company. A recall movement succeeded in recalling or defeating a majority of the District's board of directors, and further revenue increases were obtained by raising the water toll.

Pricing by water districts is seldom clouded by issues of equity among growers of different types of crops, large versus small operators, or other such personal distinctions among direct customers of the district, but a few examples exist. Discrimination in favor of rice growers, was mentioned above; it sometimes seems to rest on a recognition of the rice growers' lesser ability to pay. The Glenn-Colusa Irrigation District, however, discriminated against rice production in the 1920's because political control of the district lay with the small-scale general farmers rather than the large-scale rice growers.[20] The James Irrigation District in the San Joaquin Valley has set taxes and tolls so that each covers half of the District's expenses including a return to surplus. The reason is that much of the District's land is rented; the renters bear the ditch expense of irrigation, and the tax is levied to put half of the burden upon the owners of the land.

Price discrimination against outsiders

One final objective frequently seen in the retail pricing of agricultural water is to charge district customers who are not citizen-members whatever the traffic will bear. The users' cooperative hypothesis about district behavior predicts that charges to nonmembers would be set to maximize profits to the cooperative plant, and the available examples seem consistent with this prediction. Most public districts operate under legal restrictions on retail sales outside of their official territory, but these are far from being prohibitive, and districts often serve a few customers outside of their borders for one reason or another. The most common reason is that the public district has taken over some older physical irrigation works which served some territory outside its boundaries. Sometimes honoring pre-existing water rights on a stream brings a district into retail distribution to outsiders. Occasionally, this distribution occurs under the terms of a court decree which prevents any charge being made for the water; but often there is no such legal requirement, and the district can set its own price.

The nearly uniform practice in this case is to charge outsiders more than residents of the district. The Fresno Irrigation District serves some customers outside of its borders who hold legal rights stemming from an old ditch company. The Fresno District charges them a water rental set at 50 cents higher per $100 valuation than the tax rate for district members. Since the Fresno District imposes no toll, the average cost of water to outsiders is higher in the same proportion.[21] Outside irrigation customers of the Nevada Irrigation District pay nearly twice as much per miner's inch for irrigation water during the irrigation season as farmers within the District, and outside domestic customers pay a premium of 50 per cent.[22]

A similar pricing problem arises for districts which produce and sell hydroelectric power. When the power goes to an outside electric utility, it is generally

[20] William Durbrow, "William Durbrow, Irrigation District Leader" (Typescript, University of California General Library, Berkeley, 1958), pp. 78–80.

[21] *Fresno Bee,* Sept. 5, 1956.

[22] Nevada Irrigation District, *Charges for Water Service Established by Board of Directors Effective April 1, 1961* (1961).

sold at a price that will allow irrigation water to be distributed very cheaply, or even free of charge, to district members. This is true not just when power is sold to a utility, such as Pacific Gas and Electric Company, but also when the district retails electricity to its own residents (including urban households). One example is found in the policies of Turlock Irrigation District. In 1959, the maintenance and operation costs of its irrigation works were $446,000 more than its cash receipts from taxes, the only charge falling on irrigators. Its sales of electricity, however, brought in $1,627,000 more than maintenance and operation expenses for its electrical system.[23] The adjacent Modesto Irrigation District goes one step further by placing no charges at all upon users of irrigation water. As we shall see, water districts undertaking investments in dual purpose water and power projects regularly seek to maximize their net revenue from power sales in order to reduce the charge for irrigation water.

Nonprice allocation of agricultural water

The practices and objectives of agricultural water agencies in setting retail prices and the tax-toll balance have a number of implications for allocative efficiency. However, it is necessary to avoid the temptation to leap to these directly, for price is often not the sole device used to ration available water supplies among competing users in a district. Some irrigation districts ration water as a regular arrangement; in this case, water tolls have no direct normative significance as an allocative device. We must assess the character and prevalence of rationing as a prelude to considering the efficiency of the pricing systems used.[24]

The types of rationing used by agricultural districts depend on the nature of their physical facilities. Those diverting streamflows regulated by their own storage reservoirs or the reservoirs of wholesalers can distribute their total supply through the season in response to demand variations (subject to the capacity of the distribution system); they may ration the total quantity taken, but need not ration as to time of use. By contrast, districts which capture uncontrolled stream runoff or runoff controlled by other parties must either ration as to time or use or vary their tolls continuously over the irrigation season. Another significant physical feature is the presence or absence of excess capacity in the distribution system. A system without excess capacity must either vary its tolls by time of day, day of week, and so on, or employ some form of short-run rationing. In fact, the open-ditch and low-pressure pipe systems used by most agricultural districts lead to the use of short-run rationing by which irrigators take turns in using the full flow of some segment of the distribution system. This is called the rotation method.

Because summer irrigation water in the Central Valley derives primarily from the melting of winter snowfall, districts with access to storage capacity know in ad-

[23] Turlock Irrigation District, *Seventy-first Annual Report—Year of 1959* (1960). See also *Turlock Journal,* Dec. 20, 1958.

[24] Water rationing is employed only as a rare emergency measure by urban water agencies in California. They normally maintain substantial excess capacity at all times, so that direct rationing is not needed to control either the total level of demand or its variations over time.

vance of the planting of most annual crops how much water will be available. The districts served by the Bureau of Reclamation's Madera and Friant-Kern canals are largely in this position. Their guaranteed supplies of Class 1 water can be drawn at any time in the season; the amount of Class 2 water is known in advance and is somewhat variable in delivery time. These districts require their customers to place orders for water early in the season. In many cases, tolls and taxes are juggled in ways described above to achieve at least a rough balancing of demand and supply over the season. Some districts, however, ration by cutting back all orders proportionally when they add to more than the anticipated supplies.

Districts which draw upon uncontrolled streamflow ration over-all demand more frequently. A common practice, especially in the southern parts of the Central Valley, is for a district to distribute by rotation whatever water its rights permit it to capture for as long as it is available. This gives each irrigator a proportional share over that period. As supplies grow short, the cycle of rotations may be stretched out. Those districts without storage facilities which do not ration usually have strong water rights which permit them to view water as a free good if they disregard opportunity costs. Irrigators apply all they wish, and in these cases no water toll would be appropriate from the viewpoint of the district except to cover variable operating costs.

Like pricing policies, a district's rationing policies can become an issue in internal disputes. In 1952, the Merced Irrigation District's board of directors decided to close the irrigation season with 92,000 acre-feet of water remaining in the district's Exchequer Reservoir. A group of clover growers pleaded strongly for a continuation so that they could get an extra crop, but the board insisted on holding the remaining water from the wet year of 1952 as insurance against the possibility that 1952-53 precipitation would prove insufficient to fill the reservoir.[25] State water legislation requires that in the event of water scarcity, public districts prorate available water in proportion to assessments collected. But this was enacted at a time when tolls were not legal; when the use of tolls gained approval, the directors were given power to make a reasonable distribution among those applying for its use. The element of reasonableness in distributing short supplies particularly affects some of the rice-growing districts in dry years, where it is customary to provide adequate water to perennial crops such as orchards and alfalfa, cutting down on others accordingly. Lump-sum losses to the districts' farmers are thus minimized.[26]

Considering these patterns, to what extent does rationing override the influence of water tolls on irrigators' demands for water? The practice obviously has substantial significance in adjusting the short-run timing of demand for water within an irrigation season, but this is not particularly important. Its role in constraining total demand over an irrigation season holds much greater significance, and this also seems substantial. The general inclination of water districts to set tolls and taxes so that current financial outlays are covered cannot be fully compatible with

[25] *Stockton Record,* Oct. 3, 1952. The directors pointed out that Exchequer Reservoir had failed to fill in six of the preceding twenty-six years.

[26] Charles F. Lambert, "Land Speculation and Irrigation Development in the Sacramento Valley, 1905–1957" (Typescript, University of California General Library, Berkeley, 1957), pp. 318, 321.

the use of price as the sole rationing device in many cases. Because of the discontinuous nature of investments and the legal constraints precluding expansions of any kind for some districts, a price which bore the sole responsibility for rationing scarce water to competing final users would yield sustained surpluses for more districts than actually show such financial results. This conclusion directs attention to the financial obligations of districts, and points to the sort of district which might be unwilling to accumulate a large surplus in the process of using tolls as a rationing device. The older districts with no owned storage capacity and no contracts with major wholesalers fill this requirement. Their investments are either fully amortized or of insignificant scale relative to the quantity of water distributed, and thus their current operating costs per unit of water are quite low. For them, rationing is probably important in allocating water, and the water toll (if any) often understates the marginal value product of water. For those districts having recent major investments or contracts with wholesalers (or both), it is possible that tolls may serve to perform the bulk of the rationing function.

Granted that rationing is important, is it predominantly important? Although we can make no precise estimate, the bulk of agricultural water distributed by public districts in the Central Valley is probably not subject to regular, systematic, and substantial rationing over the irrigation season. To turn the proposition around, in most cases the marginal price of water to the irrigator can wield some influence on the quantity which he uses. What about the probable impact of rationing in those districts where it clearly does play an important allocative role? For several reasons, it may not cause much short-run misallocation of water within the district, whatever its effect on the district's over-all demand for water and its investment plans. First, lands within a district are often of relatively homogeneous physical and economic character. With a rationing scheme in force that provides the same quantity of water to each crop-acre (the typical pattern), differences in marginal products of water between ownerships are likely to be small. Second, ground-water conditions typically are also relatively homogeneous within districts, so that any irrigator denied surface water at the going toll faces about the same cost of an alternative underground supply. Third, since district managements usually know in advance of annual planting decisions the season's prospective water supply, it is possible to induce the same crop substitutions in dry years by direct notification to irrigators as would occur in response to a higher posted price. For instance, the water requirements of rice differ so much from other crops that farmers in rice-growing districts of the Sacramento Valley are readily induced to switch to those with lower water requirements when a dry year is foreseen. Tomatoes, corn, sugar beets, and commercial seed crops serve this function in some areas near the Sacramento River.[27]

In short, the allocative effect of rationing on the distribution of water within districts does not seem conspicuously serious in the short run. Undoubtedly, some irrigators waste water in the absence of a price incentive, but distortions as between users are likely to be moderate for the reasons listed. As we shall suggest below, however, rationing may combine with certain pricing practices to give mis-

[27] *Ibid.*, pp. 269–70. Compare Brewer, *op. cit.*, pp. 82, 87.

leading impressions about the demand of an area for additional water supplies, and thus it contains important implications for the efficiency of capital allocation and of the water rights system in the industry.

Pricing of mutual water companies: a special case

The preceding discussion of agricultural pricing and rationing has omitted one type of agency which plays an important role in a few parts of the Central Valley—the mutual water company. A mutual may be a small and informal group cooperating to maintain a single ditch; but some mutual companies are enterprises as large and as well-run as many irrigation districts. We discuss them separately here because the pricing of their services differs in an essential way from the various types of public district. Mutual companies issue shares, each entitling the owner to some portion of the water which the company can capture through its water rights and physical works. Normally the companies impose tolls or annual assessments (against shares) to cover current expenses, but the shares themselves can be traded or rented on the market, so that the total price of water service by mutual companies can be competitively determined.[28]

The terms under which mutual water company shares are issued vary from company to company, and these variations affect their marketability. The most important feature is the presence or absence of a restriction on the transfer of shares to a specific geographic service area. Usually, when a company's by-laws restrict its service area narrowly, the company itself takes the responsibility for delivery ditches to the individual farmer's property. When shares are freely transferable geographically, the owner must himself make connections with the company's ditches. Of two mutual companies whose shares otherwise convey similar benefits, the shares which do not appertain to a particular area of land can be traded more widely and usually bring a higher price.[29] On the other hand, land bearing appurtenant mutual water shares sells at a higher value reflecting the water endowment.[30]

All of these characteristics appear in the major mutual water companies operating in the Central Valley. Nearly all mutuals in this area collect their revenue by the assessment of shares, either furnishing the irrigator with as much water as he

[28] The best treatise on the operation of mutual water companies is U.S. Farm Credit Administration, Cooperative Division, *Mutual Irrigation Companies in California and Utah,* by Wells A. Hutchins, Bulletin No. 8 (1936). See also Raymond L. Anderson, "Operation of the Irrigation Water Rental Market in the South Platte Basin," *Journal of Farm Economics,* XLII (December 1960), pp. 1501–03.

[29] Nonappurtenant shares of important mutuals in the Kings River and Kaweah River areas of Northern California have undergone substantial movement over time in response to relative shifts in the marginal value productivity of water on different parcels of land in these areas. For an interesting case study of the Kaweah area, including the role of mutual companies, see Mason Gaffney, "Diseconomies Inherent in Western Water Laws: A California Case Study," in *Economic Analysis of Multiple Use,* Proceedings of Western Agricultural Economics Research Council, Tucson, Arizona, January 23, 1961, 55–81.

[30] U.S. Farm Credit Administration, *op. cit.,* p. 63.

wishes when the supply is adequate, or prorating water equally among the outstanding shares when it is not. Most of the companies are old and have good water rights, so that the cost of water on the basis of assessments alone is quite low. Correspondingly, the shares command a substantial market value, one which fluctuates markedly with the fortunes of irrigated agriculture.

In summary, although mutual water companies do not comprise a large segment of agricultural water distribution in Northern California, they provide an interesting contrast of competitive, if thin, markets to the organizational allocations which result within the predominant public districts. Furthermore, the considerable movement of the service areas of mutuals whose shares are not appurtenant to narrowly defined tracts reflects the fact that this is often the one way in practice for a would-be irrigator to secure water via a market transaction.

Agricultural Water Pricing and Economic Efficiency

The pricing patterns of some agricultural water districts reveal no apparent economic logic. The majority, however, seem to have built their charges on the basis of numerous considerations of equity and efficiency as seen from within the district. There is a vital question of the performance of these pricing systems, in terms of the level and timing of water use which they tend to induce and the allocation of water within districts. The evidence on conduct developed so far bears on these questions of performance, but not on a range of other performance features considered in later chapters. Whether a district appropriates the right amount of water, given its opportunity cost in other uses, depends on evidence not yet developed.

Let us begin with the observation that a majority of districts use both a toll and a tax as sources of revenue. This combination of charges, when properly used, has certain optimal properties. When an enterprise operates with a constant marginal cost and some fixed costs, it will normally incur losses if it sets a single price for its product equal to the marginal cost. It is a familiar proposition of public utility pricing theory that in such cases only a two-part tariff can both return normal profits to the enterprise and permit customers to buy at a price equal to marginal cost. If the enterprise operates under conditions of increasing returns, then the two-part tariff is needed to insure optimal scale consistent with normal returns. If it operates with excess capacity, then the two-part tariff can allow optimization with regard to short-run marginal cost, but the effect of such a practice on the desired level of capacity (that is, the investment decision) may be called into question.

To what extent do actual rates in Northern California's water districts meet the exact requirements for an efficient two-part tariff? Although numerous exceptions were noted above, in a significant portion of the districts studied taxes are set to cover the district's bond interest and redemption requirements and some portion of the general administrative expenses,[31] leaving maintenance and operations expenses plus the wholesale cost of water, if any, to be covered by the water toll. Probably a majority of the irrigation water purchased at retail in Northern California is sub-

[31] Lambert, *op. cit.*, pp. 316–17.

ject to this pricing system; much of the remainder is not subject to any toll, and only for a minority are all charges on the basis of tolls.[32] Michael Brewer's statistical finding of good correlations between changes in irrigation districts' administrative and maintenance and operations costs and their revenue from water tolls confirms this as the dominant method of handling two-part charges.[33] If districts' variable costs—principally operation and maintenance plus any wholesale costs of water—are a relatively constant linear function of the volume of water delivered, then water pricing would seem to come close in many cases to the theoretical norm —at least in the short run.

This conclusion must be qualified in a number of different ways. First of all, statistical results discussed in Chapter 5 detected a stronger relation between water use by irrigators and average, rather than marginal, charges paid to the district. Taken literally, this conclusion implies that member-customers of irrigation districts persistently take a long-run view in their decisions about the quantity of water to employ, acting as if the extra cost of taking another unit of water were the average cost of the district rather than the average variable cost typically covered by tolls. So far, so good, one might say. Our discussion of the cost structures of irrigation districts in Chapter 6 suggested relatively insubstantial long-run economies of scale with regard to territorial expansions. Irrigation districts should construct storage and distribution capacity to serve additional farmers only to the extent that the farmers are willing to pay prices approximately equal to long-run average costs. If the pricing systems employed by typical agricultural districts are not conspicuously successful in achieving short-run optimization, they nonetheless may be rated well for their impact on investment decisions.

At this point in the argument, the favorable interpretation of the normative quality of agricultural water pricing practices must largely come to an end. Too many further qualifications serve to question much of the optimality that might be hoped for in the light of either the long-run or short-run possibilities outlined above. The biases typically prevailing due to irrigation districts' accounting practices could lead to an average price for water that exceeds long-run marginal cost if the district's amortization requirements exceed economic depreciation of its capital. A deficient price would tend to be charged, however, as a result of at least two more important distortions: the failure to include price-adjusted depreciation on fully amortized facilities; and the failure to include a charge for the marginal net opportunity cost of the water itself. The net effect of these accounting biases is

[32] No precise tabulation could be made to demonstrate these propositions without interviewing every agricultural water district in Northern California, since no general source of pricing information exists.

[33] Brewer, *op. cit.*, p. 71. Another historic fact consistent with water tolls approximating marginal costs appears in Brewer's Figure XIII (p. 72), which shows that during the 1930's average water sales receipts per acre-foot stayed about constant in real terms while assessment receipts per acre-foot fell by more than half. During those years, many districts went into default and many acres of land passed to the districts for nonpayment of assessments. The pattern of receipts is consistent with a policy of maintaining tolls to cover constant marginal (and average variable) costs and extracting what was available through levies. The pattern is also consistent, however, with simple price rigidity. On irrigation district pricing during the depressed 1930's, also see Murray R. Benedict, *The Merced Irrigation District: An Economic Survey of Farm Incomes, Expenses, and Tax-Paying Abilities* (1933), pp. 23–30.

probably to understate the economic costs of water which provide the basis for calculating both the tolls and taxes collected by the typical district, and thus lead to an understatement of these charges. This conclusion is supported by the further bias introduced by the presence of rationing, since districts are not known to collect a financial surplus by collecting charges in excess of their costs for the purpose of restricting demand for water to the available supply.

A normative analysis of prices is really a convenient shorthand for a normative analysis of the allocation of quantities. In translating these results into quantities of water and associated inputs, we should first recall the findings of Chapter 5 concerning the price elasticity of demand for irrigation water: while the elasticity of demand for water to grow a given crop on a given acreage may be negligible, the shifting of the crop mix (including dry farming as an alternative) can give rise to a substantial over-all elasticity. Therefore the price of water does matter for the total pattern of economic activity. The price distortions in the industry would thus be consistent with excessive gross diversions of water for irrigation use within any district which can capture the requisite rights. As stated, this conclusion is independent of the incidence of rationing; the effect of that practice is rather to create uncertainty about the maximum excessive diversions that might be associated with the observed structure of water prices. Rationing, together with the agricultural districts' pricing practices, is probably more important for its impact on investment decisions to expand an area's total water supply. It helps to preclude a test of irrigators' willingness to pay a charge in excess of the long-run marginal cost of additional supplies. So far as such investments occur because "we run out of water down here," excessive capital may be put into place;[34] this problem is considered in Chapter 11 and Part Three.

Among subsidiary allocative problems raised by the pricing principles described above, the joint management of ground and surface water supplies provides the most important. This is because the two sources are alternatives for the bulk of Central Valley irrigators, and many of the districts' take this into account in setting tolls. Some simple and "unrealistic" theorizing becomes helpful. Assume first that the ground-water basin underlying a district is essentially a tank with fixed capacity, and without autonomous inflows or outflows. Assume that spreading operations (undertaken at some cost by the district) can replenish the ground-water basin, but no water applied to crops by irrigators percolates to the basin. The district buys water from a wholesaler at a fixed price per acre-foot in the summer, and at a fixed and substantially lower price in the winter and spring when no irrigation demand exists (sales by the Bureau of Reclamation from the Madera and Friant-Kern canals are subject to such an arrangement). In the long run, the district will minimize water costs to its members by purchasing winter water and causing percolation to "fill up" the ground-water basin, if the winter-summer differential in

[34] So far as irrigators set their water purchases in the light of the marginal charge they pay rather than the average, this can be another possible cause for demanding excessive levels of fixed facilities and excessive diversions. Our analysis does not, however, support any general condemnation of the use of a mixture of tolls and taxes. With proper accounting practices and investment criteria, that system could indeed assure correct short-run allocation; without them, there is little likelihood of straightening things out just by dropping the two-part charge.

wholesale prices exceeds the costs of percolation plus pump retrieval per acre-foot.[35] In the irrigation season, the more expensive summer water should be purchased by the district only to the extent necessary to prevent the marginal costs of ground water (district cost of winter water plus incremental spreading and pumping costs) from exceeding the marginal cost of surface water (district cost of summer water plus incremental costs of surface distribution).

Achieving this optimization would require some special tactics for the district because of an institutional quirk: irrigators are never charged for private ground-water extractions in Northern California, and so the private cost of ground water (marginal pumping costs) falls short of collective costs to the district (irrigator's pumping costs plus the district's wholesale price and marginal spreading costs). If the district set a toll on surface water equal to the higher marginal cost, ground water would be used excessively. The optimal solution in this case would be a pumping tax to equate private and total costs of ground water. If the pumping tax is ruled out, then the next best solution would be to lower the charge on surface water (loading the uncovered costs onto a tax) and to use rationing (if necessary) to prevent overintensive use of water.

If we relieve part of the unrealism of this case by supposing the district to overlie a large ground-water basin, so that its recharge activities have only a small influence on the water table, the problem is not essentially changed. A difference still exists between the private and collective cost of pumping, but when ground water is not viewed as a fixed inventory this difference is best identified as the discounted present value of all future increases in pumping costs for district water users that result when the extraction of one acre-foot lowers the water table slightly.[36] Again, efficient pricing by the district must take into account this difference between private and collective costs of ground-water use.[37]

In the actual circumstances faced by agricultural water districts in the San Joaquin Valley the amount of percolation to ground water is more or less technologically fixed, and the supply of summer water to a district purchasing water from a wholesaler is rationed. These facts, plus assorted uncertainties, make the common practice of keying tolls on surface water to the level of private pumping costs look reasonably sensible. This practice seems to avoid the question of an

[35] How full the underground basin can be kept depends on maintaining the water table sufficiently low so that the roots of crops are not damaged. In many areas of the San Joaquin Valley, our assumption that winter water stored underground and recovered would be cheaper than summer water delivered directly is factually correct.

[36] Other circumstances which make the conjunctive use of ground and surface water supplies economically efficient lead qualitatively to the same conclusion about a difference between private and collective costs of ground water. For instance, we might focus attention on inter-annual, rather than interseasonal, differences in the availability of water, or upon summer rationing of wholesale supplies to the district under the terms of a water right. In short, any difference in the shadow price over time creates the same problem for retail pricing by the district.

[37] We have avoided the usual terms "private" and "social" cost to call attention to the fact that this appraisal centers, so far, only on rational action by the district within a given environment and not on the general social welfare. If the wholesale prices which the district must pay for water do not equal the opportunity cost of water elsewhere, or if ground-water extraction causes disutilities outside the district's boundaries, efficient pricing must satisfy additional criteria.

optimal level for the ground-water table in the long run, but the technical determinants of water-table behavior are themselves inadequately known.[38]

Happily, most other questions about districts' tax-toll adjustments are simpler to analyze. We noted a number of features of the use of tolls which run in the right allocative direction. We cannot generally be sure that they are used correctly by the districts which employ them, nor that all districts which should use them do so. Where a district's marginal cost of service to one group of customers significantly differs from that to another, the difference usually shows up to some extent in the tolls charged. Pumping services of the district are often put in at their incremental cost. Seasonal variations normally bear a close correlation to changes in the shadow price of water at the source and within the district. Irrigators located farther from a district's diversion point often pay part of the cost of longer canals through improvement district assessments.[39] On the other hand, many opportunities for appropriate differentials in tolls are undoubtedly missed, and our appraisal generally tends to the conclusion that while the efficiency of agricultural water pricing at retail is low, it could be worse.

Pricing Municipal Water: Objectives and Pressures

Urban water price structures are more complex than those for the agricultural districts just discussed. The range of influences playing upon them and the possibilities for success or failure in equity and efficiency in designing pricing systems are greater. Nonetheless, water prices hold a good deal less significance for the urban economy than do agricultural water prices for irrigated farming. Partly as a consequence, we can tell less about the behavioral objectives underlying urban water pricing systems. Even so, we examine here some of their properties, concentrating on the San Francisco Bay area.

Objectives of urban water pricing

In studying the principles governing the pricing of urban water supplies, we cannot employ the same distinction between the average level and the structure of charges which was utilized in discussing agricultural water pricing. Many city water agencies are parts of municipal governments that levy taxes, but not for the specific purpose of supporting the water department, which depends primarily on some structure of tolls or water charges. Thus the important normative question becomes whether revenues of water departments just cover the costs of the water system, fall short of them and require subsidy from general revenues, or exceed them and thus effectively contribute to covering the costs of general city government.

[38] On the one hand, excessively high ground-water levels often eventually plague heavily irrigated lands; on the other hand, ground-water basins in much of the area are widely interconnected, so that the benefits of one district's percolation spill over to other districts.

[39] These assessments do not enter into marginal water costs, but then the variation of short-run marginal cost of district operations with the length of canals is probably quite small.

In Northern California, water departments are rarely supported by tax funds. Either they seek to cover financial costs (as the agricultural districts do) or, more typically—at least in the San Francisco Bay area—water profits are used to support other municipal functions. Where water departments are used as instruments of taxation, the purpose may be either to overcome political resistance to expanding revenues via property taxes or to shift the tax burden among, or away from, the residents of the area. To the extent a profit-making water department sells outside of the city limits, it shifts the burden of local public services to nonresidents. Within the city, the shift from property tax to water utility revenues probably means a more regressive fiscal structure and a windfall to holders of commercial property, since commercial users, offices and stores, are light water consumers compared to industrial and residential users.[40] To shift tax incidence within a city by water pricing probably is seldom a conscious policy of its political leaders. At least this was never suggested in our extensive interviews in the San Francisco Bay area. These shifts are probably a by-product of water profits sought for another reason: there is less resistance to this means of financing increased city expenditures. Commercial interests are often vocal in organized opposition to government expansion, and low-income property holders are reluctant to support any increases in property tax rates. An "indirect-tax illusion" probably inhibits the low-income group from seeing the possible relation between taxes and water rates, and the way in which water rate increases can work to their relative disadvantage.

Although some cities with integral water departments have used water revenues as a substitute for property taxes, those urban water agencies organized as independent districts have generally followed the contrary policy. Their financing practices closely conform to those of agricultural districts, analyzed above. The reason most frequently given for this practice is that of equity. Spokesmen argue that the benefits of water are widely dispersed throughout the community, and some of the greatest beneficiaries, like stores, are among the lightest users. The evidence of the benefits to stores is that their profits are based upon the growth of the community which, in turn, is dependent upon the provision of water. This specious argument is repeated by agency after agency, and happily coexists with the use of municipal water departments as taxation devices. In essence, it is similar to treating the total income of adjoining towns as indirect benefits of irrigation works.

Certain specific advantages accrue to agencies from the use of taxes to supplement water tolls. The interest costs on general obligation bonds are lower than on revenue bonds, but the former can be used only by agencies which employ general taxing power. The use of taxes thus permits lower interest costs and slightly lower water rates than if all revenues came from tolls. Furthermore, the presence of taxes set to pay off general obligation bonds tends to protect water districts against inroads by competitive suppliers. Even if an alternative supplier can offer a price lower than the average cost for an established agency, the presence of an irremovable tax can make the incremental cost to water users of the competitor's service

[40] The regressivity among households is due to the compound reasons that, although the property tax is generally regressive and water consumption increases with income, the elasticity of water consumption with respect to income is less than the elasticity of property valuation with respect to income.

higher than the incremental cost of water from the resident agency. Any shift between suppliers must then take the cumbersome form of controversial and costly referenda to leave one district and to join another.

This discussion of the relation of urban water departments' costs and revenues is subject to the same sorts of qualifications for accounting biases as were suggested for agricultural districts. Although depreciation accounting is perhaps used to a greater extent, and financial reserves thus gathered in anticipation of at least some replacements, a historical-outlay concept of cost is employed throughout. Opportunity costs can diverge from actual outlays for urban agencies in even more complex ways than for irrigation districts.

For example, a city administration recognizes with commendable foresight that it should reserve reservoir sites while they are easily available, before the expanding urban area blankets all sites and makes them "too expensive." The land procurement program is financed along with a construction program through a bond issue. The "costs" of the land for the next twenty years are measured by the procurement expenditures, and after the bond issue has been retired no further "costs" are associated with using the land for reservoirs. But in reality the expansion of the city, horizontally and vertically, makes the reservoir sites more valuable. The opportunity costs of keeping the land for reservoirs increase as city population is forced to spread out more and to incur higher transportation costs. The historical costs of land procurement give no clue to the value of the resource being used in water supply. And water prices to cover the costs of "cheap" land would be too low and lead to a wasteful use of resources.

Urban water rate structures

The complicated structures of charges employed by urban water agencies were indicated in Tables 23 and 24. A number of principles of price determination having both organizational and normative significance may be in operation; here, we shall emphasize pricing discriminations between members and outsiders, and the structure of rates provided to differently situated members.

The practice of setting a price differential between those who are residents of the territory of the relevant government and those outside the area is even more prevalent than among agricultural districts, and we are reminded of the characterization of public water agencies as cooperatives. But in the urban sphere more is at stake than just the economic welfare of member-customers. Except for the East Bay Municipal Utility District, the bulk of urban water in the San Francisco Bay area is supplied by city governments. Although their policies in regard to charges to outsiders differ markedly, almost all of them discriminate. Sunnyvale charges outside customers three times the internal rates.[41] Antioch and Martinez charge outsiders twice the price to insiders, while Daly City's outside prices are only 25 per cent higher than those for insiders. Santa Rosa adds a flat $3 per meter more bimonthly. The facts of differentials are clear but the reasons are not.

[41] Unless noted to the contrary, all references to prices are taken from the printed schedules of rates of each city or water agency.

Three justifications are commonly given for the inside-outside differential. The one which would seem to be the most specious is that it costs more to service those outside the city limits. Though this might be true occasionally, it is equally true that substantial differential costs within a city are rarely matched by differential prices. A second reason given is that the residents of the city pay taxes to support the municipal government, and therefore the outsider must pay a higher price to compensate for his lack of tax liability. But urban water systems usually are not tax supported, and in fact may collect revenues for the general funds.[42] A third reason which is unofficially but widely accepted is that a differential is a device to encourage annexation. Some cities in the San Francisco Bay area have aggressive plans for territorial expansion, and water is one of their instruments. As noted in Chapter 9, the municipalization of water is often fostered by a desire to extend services to outlying areas, unattractive for private water companies, on the condition that they be annexed to the city. Rate differentials against unannexed territory are a further club to encourage annexation.

Generally, outside sales are too small a part of the revenues of a water department to give rise to a serious charge that the city is acting as an entrepreneur vis-à-vis the outside world. But this charge has been leveled in regard to San Francisco, a city not afflicted with a passion to annex. More than two-fifths of its sales are at wholesale to cities in the Bay area located near its pipeline from the Sierra or near its vast storage and catchment reservoirs located in counties south of San Francisco —and in time far more than two-fifths will be sales of this kind. We shall examine the economics of San Francisco's outside sales below.

Like agricultural districts, urban water departments create a few price differentials between customer groups because a sense of fairness indicates that substantial cost differences should be reflected in prices. Except for fire protection, however, such price differentials are small and probably more rare than in the pricing of agricultural water. San Bruno charges different rates in the parts of the city which are served from its own wells and those served by purchases from the San Francisco Water Department. Vallejo charges a lower price for untreated water. But the more common pattern is for a city to establish a single rate structure which, on the average, covers all the costs of water distribution. The result of this averaging is a subsidization of the use of the high-cost water. For many cities located along southern San Francisco Bay, high-cost water is a seasonal phenomenon, since they use San Francisco water to supplement their supplies only during the dry period. It would be appropriate for them to charge seasonally differentiated prices to reflect the cost differentials, with the expectation that they would thereby reduce the demand for more expensive water. But none of the urban systems interviewed uses seasonal price variations.

Differentiation by height of pump lift would be another basis for varying prices with costs. Burlingame justifies its higher rate outside the city by the extra pump-

[42] Occasionally the capital funds for a water system are raised by means of general obligation bonds, so that the tax revenues of the city provide security for the water bonds. Some differential in prices might be equitably charged to offset this risk factor, but certainly it would not justify differentials of 25 to 100 per cent. Some cities which have extreme differentials, such as Sunnyvale, have financed their capital improvement programs through revenue bonds, and the taxpayers have assumed no obligations.

ing facilities required for outside users at higher elevations. The Menlo Park Municipal Water District uses three rate structures: inside the city, the residential hill area south of the city, and the industrial area north of the city. Both outside areas pay rates higher than inside, and in both cases the differentials are probably justified by differences in costs. Despite these isolated instances of rate differentials justified by costs, the general practice is a uniform rate structure independent of elevation, distance from reservoirs, or other sources of cost differences.

The two major deviations from a uniform retail price for urban water are fixed monthly charges for connections and tapered tolls or commodity charges. The connection charges increase with the size of connection, and the commodity charges decline with the volume of water taken. Water departments apparently create these structural elements in water charges because they believe that a more suitable relation of prices to costs results. The trouble lies not in the motive but in the achievement: as we shall see below, these pricing structures typically rest upon faulty analyses.

Finally, one objective in setting retail water prices which plays an important role among agricultural agencies holds sporadic importance in the urban sector. That is the adjustment of charges to manipulate the incentives for individual users to draw upon the ground-water basin. Within the Bay area, this problem becomes acute in an organizational sense for parts of Alameda and Santa Clara counties in which substantial use is made of ground water and specialized agencies exist for the sole or major purpose of ground-water replenishment. Plans for the joint management of ground and surface supplies have been undergoing major changes in the last few years, and so the allocations ultimately to result cannot yet be appraised. Pumping taxes, generally the most efficient device for optimal ground-water management, have not been used in the past but are now authorized or in force in important areas. The relation of these taxes to other water charges is entangled with complex patterns of rivalry among water organizations, particularly in Santa Clara County. Therefore we reserve discussion of these issues for Chapter 13.

Urban water pricing and competition

An element significantly affecting urban water pricing which is not present in the agricultural sector is potential or actual competition. Much of this occurs at the wholesale level in bargaining between rival wholesale suppliers for retail agency customers; these cases will be considered below in Chapter 13. But competition also operates at retail when a group of a water agency's customers threatens to defect to an adjacent retail agency or to establish its own source of supply. In a sense, the access of irrigators to ground water through private pumping plants comprises a parallel, but our review of agricultural water pricing showed little tendency for this alternative to produce toll differentials among an agency's customers. The reason for this is certainly that most irrigators in a district tend to have access to ground water on about the same economic terms, so that any pricing adjustments by the district must occur in its over-all toll-tax balance. In urban areas, however, the access of customers to alternative sources usually varies sharply, and so its influence is likely to affect the advantages which the rate structure offers to different customer groups. Furthermore, geographically overlapping districts with equivalent legal powers to provide retail water supplies seem more common in urban areas than in the agricultural sector—although not because of difference in the legal forms of water agencies available.

The water users most likely to employ competitive threats against their supplier are those to whom water rates or quality may make a large economic difference. Only commercial or industrial customers could conceivably fulfill these requirements and, of these two, industrial customers are typically much heavier water users. One case of successful pressure of industrialists upon the water rates has involved the East Bay Municipal Utility District (EBMUD). The overt political struggle of this case is atypical, but it may explain why large quantity discounts to industrial water purchasers generally prevail even without such hard bargaining.

The city of Richmond, at the northern end of the East Bay urban area, became an industrial boom town during World War II. When the conclusion of the war caused sharp cutbacks in many defense-based industries, efforts to establish a peacetime industrial base included plans for providing cheap water supplies. But Richmond was located within EBMUD, and the District could not be persuaded to reduce industrial water rates. The industrialists, including the largest customer of EBMUD, Standard Oil Company of California, decided to develop a competitive supply.

In 1949 the voters of Richmond approved the formation of the Southwest Contra Costa County Water District (SWCCWD), lying almost completely within the territory served by EBMUD, and efforts were made to initiate a Bureau of Reclamation reconnaissance survey on the feasibility of a conduit leading from the Contra Costa Canal to serve Richmond industrial plants through the SWCCWD. The only prospective customers would be less than fifty industrial plants which presumably could use the raw water from the canal with only a minimal treatment, yet the proposal was highly popular within the area, and the vote to form the District carried by a margin of eight to one. The Bureau initiated an investigation; but, after one year of study, EBMUD's arguments before the appropriation committees in Congress induced the inclusion of provisions in the Department of Interior appropriation bills which forbade any further work on surveys for the conduit. During the period of the survey, EBMUD cut its water rates to the large industrial users by 25 per cent.

Despite this setback in Congress, the SWCCWD drafted a proposed service contract with the Bureau of Reclamation and submitted it to the voters for approval. This contract had not been seen by the Bureau, but the voters authorized the SWCCWD to offer it by a majority of five to one. The contest between the two districts extended into the campaign over this referendum. Both rivals bought advertising space in the local newspapers, provided speakers, and sought endorsement of their positions by private civic associations. The premature election on a contract which had not been negotiated was undertaken in the hope "that if a contract for water service is approved by more than a two-thirds majority of the electors of the Southwest District . . . the Congress of the United States will make a new appropriation to continue the Bureau's work on the project."[43] The SWCCWD was successful in its strategy. A second round before the Appropriations Committee of the U.S. Senate resulted in the authorization of funds to complete the survey on the feasibility of the conduit from the Contra Costa Canal to Richmond.[44] Authorization was given despite EBMUD's plea that competition would lead either to a decline in revenues or to the fracturing of the water supply of the area into many smaller agencies, to higher total costs, and, of course, to the embarrassment of EBMUD.[45]

The temporary success of SWCCWD in Congress was an empty victory for the District, but not for the industrial firms. The Bureau of Reclamation received its funds and completed the study. It estimated a cost of $38 per acre-foot to bring untreated water to industrial plants in Richmond; and treatment would increase the costs somewhat.[46] This figure was only one dollar less per acre-foot than the reduced EBMUD price to Standard Oil. With this finding, SWCCWD became inactive, but was kept in readiness as a potential source of harassment in case the Richmond industrialists feel it necessary to give battle to EBMUD again.

Urban Water Pricing and Economic Efficiency

Given this review of pricing patterns typical in Northern California urban water distribution and the pressures which shape them, let us consider their probable economic efficiency. Unlike the pricing systems of agricultural water agencies, urban pricing systems generally rest on formulas and procedures which are well-known and widely used within the public utility industries; and large quantities of relevant (and irrelevant) cost data are available.

Against the background of our basic normative propositions concerning resource allocation in terms of marginal adjustments, we may examine some of the basic cost characteristics of the two major urban water systems in the San Francisco Bay area—the San Francisco Water Department and the East Bay Municipal Utility District. The bulk of their costs are the fixed costs of storage, treatment, and distribution systems. Some of the annual maintenance costs of the aqueducts, tanks,

[43] Southwest Contra Costa County Water District, *Reply to Statement of East Bay Municipal Utility District, Before the California Districts Securities Commission* (Typescript, Jan. 28, 1952), p. 9.

[44] The debate indicated the devious paths that competition must take within the political forum. On the floor of Congress, speakers took sides based upon their attitudes toward the Bureau of Reclamation. To the opponents, the proposed conduit represented an attempt on the part of the Bureau to break the no-new-starts policy of the Eisenhower Administration and to extend its province into urban and industrial water sales. To the proponents, the proposed survey was a necessary part of developing the water resources of the West—the historic mission of the Bureau of Reclamation. The issues as formulated by the contesting districts were broadened to reflect general positions held by members of the Congress bearing no relation to the issue at hand. See *Congressional Record,* March 27, 1952, 3104–10.

[45] U.S. Congress, Senate Appropriations Committee, *Interior Department Appropriations for 1953,* Hearings on H. R. 7176, 82 Cong. 2 sess. (1952), pp. 1007 ff.

[46] U.S. Department of the Interior, Bureau of Reclamation, *Report on the Feasibility and Estimated Cost of the Southwest Contra Costa County Water District System* (1953), pp. 46, 48.

reservoirs, and pipes vary with the quantity of water handled, but most of them depend on the size and age of structures. The appropriate scales of dams to capture and store water in the Sierra Nevada and of major aqueducts are a function of both the volume of water used and the seasonality of water supply. The capacities of the distribution system, including local reservoirs, are a function of peak demands on the system and of the local topography. Generally the increments in costs near the source of water can be attributed to the growth in total quantity of water delivered over the year, while the capital costs incurred near the final users are those related to daily and seasonal peaking. In addition to the costs associated with the capacity of the system and its maintenance, there are those associated with the number of customers (billing, meter-reading, collections, and so on) and the volume of water delivered (including such things as purification and pumping).

If the physical plant of an urban water system can be viewed as continuously variable in scale, so that incremental costs are defined for each aspect of the output or capacity of the system, then rules can be stated for an efficient pricing system as an elaboration of the marginalist principles developed in Chapter 8 and in the preceding appraisal of agricultural water pricing. The components of an urban water pricing schedule for the individual customer should include: (1) a fixed charge per period of time to cover customer costs and a proportional share of fixed costs not otherwise allocated; and (2) a quantity charge which covers only incremental operating costs, if none of the capacities of the system is being fully used, or operating costs plus the incremental capital cost of any capacities which are fully utilized.

Rules of this type have often been proposed for the pricing of water and related municipal utility services, yet have obviously made little headway in practical application. Two economic phenomena clearly stand in the way of their acceptance: costs that are incurred jointly in serving more than one customer; and units of fixed plant that can be built only at one scale or added only in large discontinuous units. The latter factor was touched upon in our discussion of the relation of short-run and long-run marginal cost. The former, which we have not discussed, is a phenomenon of special importance in urban water service.

The bulk of an urban water agency's facilities obviously contain some element of jointness, in the sense that the water output which a given facility can supply to one user depends upon the amount being supplied to others. Only the pipes connecting an individual user's establishment to a water main would be exempt from elements of jointness. If facilities subject to joint use can be varied continuously in scale and the proportions of output going to different users can be freely varied, their presence does not significantly change the applicability of the marginal pricing principles suggested above. They do cause the marginal cost of supplying a given quantity of water to one customer to depend on the amounts taken by others, so that a shift in the demand of the others can shift the marginal-cost function of serving the one, and thus the appropriate price to be charged to him.[47] Apart from this effect, the basic rules for efficient pricing are not altered by the existence of joint costs in continuously variable facilities, although the interrelation of the marginal-cost

[47] Sune Carlson, *A Study on the Pure Theory of Production* (1956), chap. 5. Technically, these conclusions hold for any total-cost function that is partially differentiable at all points.

functions for different users of a joint facility might be felt to raise issues of equity. These conclusions hold considerable importance for the pricing of water at retail because of the large but variable role of joint costs in the different physical components of an urban water system. Increases in demand for service through one part of a system may often require the enlargement of central mains, terminal reservoirs, and the like, and these investments may reduce the incremental cost of providing service to other parts of the system. Prices to the latter group would appropriately be lowered.

More destructive of the marginal approach to pricing is the existence of facilities which are fixed in scale or can be varied only discontinuously. In the extreme case of facilities that are truly joint and can be built only at a single capacity, their costs are presumably best allocated proportionally among all users of the facility. In any case, the distribution of such costs becomes a matter of equity and not of efficiency, and it should be handled so as to avoid interfering with any other components of charges which are designed to secure some objective of marginal adjustment.[48]

Even if units of physical plant are variable in scale, such variations may perforce occur in sufficiently discontinuous fashion or under such constraints that maintaining a pricing system related to incremental costs, aside from operating costs, becomes impractical. The most reasonable approximation to a correct pricing system may then reflect a separation of capital and current overhead costs into two classes: (1) separable and common costs which can reasonably be allocated to particular users or groups of users, and (2) truly joint costs. Prices can then be set to cover the average costs imputable to each user plus a proportional share of the truly joint costs. Such a relatively simple procedure would produce the same result as pricing according to marginal-cost principles if costs are approximately constant. Furthermore, if operating costs are covered by a charge proportional to the amount of water purchased by each consumer, the allocated joint and separable costs are appropriately added on as a fixed or demand charge, and a two-part tariff again remains the best form of pricing.[49]

[48] Consider a water system based upon a fixed plant of an invariable capacity, in the sense that it cannot be enlarged or rebuilt to a different scale. Its short-run output of water can be increased, however, subject to rising short-run marginal costs. Optimally, all users should be charged a price per unit of water equal to its short-run marginal cost. So far as the revenues derived from this charge fail to cover the fixed joint costs of the facility, the latter should be distributed among customers in some proportional fashion. If proportional to the amount of water taken by the customer, the proportionality should bear on historic use and not be affected by shifts in the current level of consumption, or else the adjustment of consumption in relation to short-run marginal costs will be disturbed.

[49] One qualification to these propositions about pricing in relation to marginal costs and the proportional allocation of joint fixed costs comes from the theoretical case in which price discrimination may be justified. Under certain conditions, the use of price discrimination may permit the construction of a joint facility subject to decreasing costs to a larger scale than if each group of customers is charged a sum equal or proportional to incremental costs. The effect of the discrimination is to favor groups with a relatively more elastic demand and increase the average revenue attainable from the sale of any given output. The expansion of the fixed plant thus warranted may reduce unit costs and permit a lower charge to each group than if discrimination were not used. See Joan Robinson, *The Economics of Imperfect Competition* (London: 1933), chaps. 15 and 16; D. A. Worcester, Jr., "Justifiable Price 'Discrimination' under Conditions of Natural Monopoly: A Diagrammatic Representation," *American Economic Review,* XXXVIII (June 1948), 382–88.

Demand and quantity charges

Are the urban water pricing systems of the San Francisco Bay area consistent with these principles? The answer is clearly negative. Since data on the costs of the systems broken into the appropriate analytical categories are not available, we cannot test the efficiency of the pricing systems directly. Their structures, however, appear to bear little relationship to any pattern that would lead to the efficient use of existing capacity or the proper incentives for its expansion. Taking the rates of the San Francisco Water Department as a case study (its rate structure is shown in Table 25), let us consider some of the problems involved.

Almost all Bay area systems employ a fixed charge per customer that may or may not be related to customer costs. In 1958-59, the meter service charges of the San Francisco Water Department were not too far below what the Department's

TABLE 25
SAN FRANCISCO WATER DEPARTMENT RATES, 1960[a]

Rate component	Within city	Outside of city
1. *Service charge per month:*		
Size of meter (inches)		
5/8	$ 0.70	$ 0.80
3/4	1.10	1.30
1	1.60	1.90
1½	2.70	3.20
2	4.85	5.70
3	8.65	10.20
4	13.50	15.90
6	27.00	31.80
8	43.20	50.80
10	62.00	73.00
12	86.40	101.60
16	172.80	203.20
2. *Quantity charges per month*[b] *(cents per 100 cubic feet):*		
Quantity (cubic feet)		
0–3,300	25.9¢	30.5¢
3,301–33,000	22.7	26.7
33,001–333,000	18.0	21.2
333,001 and over	13.5	15.0
3. *Demand charge:*[c]	None	$0.01 for each 100 cf delivered. Minimum is 75 per cent of highest charge levied in last two months.

[a] For residential, commercial, industrial, and general use. There are special rates for fire service, dock and shipping supply, and builders and contractors supply. There are also installation charges.

[b] There are minimum billings by size of meter; that is, 1 in., 800 cf; 2 in., 2,400 cf; 16 in., 86,400 cf. These minimums are higher for users outside the city.

[c] Only applicable to purchasers who resell water, therefore to all other cities which purchase water from San Francisco.

SOURCE: San Francisco Public Utilities Commission, *Rate Schedule for Water Service* (1960).

consultant estimated as its customer costs. Since the customer costs were most likely overstated, the fixed monthly charges may have been a reasonable estimate of the costs of connections, billing, meter maintenance, and the like.[50]

The other component of charges to the main classes of consumers—residential, commercial, and industrial—is a commodity charge with a declining block rate. One may justify a declining block rate as a device for covering the total costs of the system while charging a price for the last unit of water taken equal to its marginal cost. But in practice the block rate does not work out that way, nor is it usually justified in those terms. For example, 98 per cent of San Francisco residents purchase 90 per cent of the residential water without going beyond the first block. However, only 12 per cent of the commercial and industrial water is bought in monthly quantities within the first block, and 25 per cent is bought at the lowest block rate, which is less than one-half of the initial block rate.[51] Therefore a substantial price differential prevails by type of customer. Unless these differentials are related to cost differentials, there will be an inefficient allocation of water among customers, and possibly excessive investment.

The demand of large industrial consumers is said to fluctuate less than that of residential users, requiring relatively smaller reserve capacity in the system. This may hold for some cities, but it does not for San Francisco. The ratio of average to maximum daily demand is almost the same for residential as for commercial and industrial consumers.[52] To take another example, in the Alameda County Water District most large industrial users have drilled their own wells and use the District's supplies as a supplemental source. A higher ratio of peak to average consumption prevails for industrial than for other customers, despite the low price to the former group. Of course, the relevant factor is not the variation in demand of the respective classes but the demands placed by each group at the time of peak utilization. If residential demand during the peak demand period were far more uncertain than industrial demand, requiring greater reserves to be held against it, then costs could justify a price differential. But this differential would not extend to nonpeak periods, in which a uniform price should be exacted from both groups unless other cost differentials are present.

Distributional economies probably exist for serving large industrial consumers compared with small residential consumers, although the distributional reservoirs and pipelines systems of most water systems provide integrated service to these two customer groups and the costs of serving them cannot be separated. Some of this cost differential is built into the structure of San Francisco's meter charges: despite the fact that the commercial-industrial group pays average charges 25 per cent below those imposed on the residential group, it pays only 11 per cent of the total as meter service charges, compared to 22 per cent paid in this form by the residential group.[53]

[50] San Francisco Water Department, *Annual Report, Commercial Division, Fiscal Year 1958–59* (1959); Roy A. Wehe, *Cost and Rate Analysis, San Francisco Water Department, for City and County of San Francisco* (1958), Table 17.
[51] Wehe, *op. cit.,* Appendix D.
[52] *Ibid.,* Table 8.
[53] San Francisco Water Department, *Annual Report . . . 1958–59, op. cit.*

Price differentials among areas

Cities typically impose higher water charges for service outside their boundaries. Although claims of cost justification often possess some merit, the differentials seldom seem to rest upon a satisfactory economic analysis. Such a case is the demand rate charged to the suburban division of the San Francisco Water Department. As Table 25 shows, suburban customers pay an additional .01¢ for each 100 cubic feet delivered (subject to a minimum charge) over the quantity charges built into the regular schedule. This surcharge has proved a steady bone of contention between San Francisco and the cities which purchase water from it for local distribution. These cities are served not by a special extension of San Francisco's aqueducts, but by tapping the main aqueduct from the Sierra to San Francisco's catchment reservoirs. They therefore argue that their rates should lie below those prevailing within San Francisco, because they add nothing to the costs of the San Francisco distribution system while providing their own local distribution systems. San Francisco counters with the claim that the cities do not support its wholesale distribution system, since they purchase water at the lowest block rate. San Francisco also claims that the greater variance of the demand of the suburban purchasers has meant that the costs of supplying them exceed the costs of supplying the city, so that the rate of return realized by the city is less for suburban sales than for sales within the city.

The cities are clearly correct in their contention that large portions of San Francisco's system are attributable to consumption within the city and do not constitute joint costs of serving the suburban division. No appraisal can be made, however, from available data of the amount of costs that might be separable and imputable to the suburban customers. San Francisco's major document justifying the existing structure of charges is not based on such a cost analysis, but upon the fallacious if widely used method of nonsimultaneous demand.[54] This method of allocating the total fixed costs of a water system is based on the variability of demand for individual classes of customers, measured by a ratio of peak to average demand. It is fallacious in ignoring whether or not the periods of peak use of the separate customer groups coincide. Only if they do, so that all groups contribute proportionally to the maximum demand on the system, would the method give a reasonable allocation of fixed costs. Otherwise, it imputes to at least one customer group an excessive responsibility for the peak demand in the system as a whole, since that group's own peak demand occurs when the system as a whole is not operating at its peak utilization. A correct procedure, consistent with the principles outlined above, would impute the fixed costs of the system's joint facilities (whether computed as average or long-run incremental costs) in proportion to demands registered by various groups at the period of peak usage of the whole system.

Just this problem appears in the application of the method of nonsimultaneous demand to allocate the costs of San Francisco's water system. The maximum demand for San Francisco's suburban division occurs in June; the maximum demand

[54] For an exposition, see Davidson, *op. cit.*, chap. 7, especially pp. 133–34. The document justifying San Francisco's structure of charges is Wehe, *op. cit.*

for the central division and the system as a whole occurs in September. Thus the method of nonsimultaneous demand overstates the fixed costs assignable to the suburban division, and a misallocation of water away from it tends to occur.

Peak demand problems

The problem of proper pricing in relation to peak demands arises, generally, not only for cities in the Bay area but for those in other locations. Peaks in urban water use are very substantial; one survey of 206 cities showed peak-day demands exceeding average-day demands by 62 per cent, and peak hours exceeding average hours by 157 per cent.[55] The relative sizes of peak demands reported by cities in the San Francisco Bay area lie close to these average figures. The San Francisco Water Department reports peak-day deliveries 53 per cent above those for the average day. Palo Alto has recorded a peak day that is 70 per cent in excess of the average day, and a peak hour that is 183 per cent in excess of the average hour.[56]

Lawn sprinkling can comprise 80 per cent of water use during the year's peak hour, and 75 per cent of the peak day's use. It is clear that an urban pricing system which charged the marginal costs of capacity against the sprinkling demand might cause a significant change in use patterns and an increase in the water system's load factor, since lawn sprinkling seems clearly to be a price-elastic element in the demand for water. But neither Northern California cities nor those elsewhere have welcomed the time-of-day metering necessary to impose this charge correctly. The possibility cannot be ruled out that the extra cost of sophisticated metering would more than offset the net gain in real resource cost.

Discrimination through special rates

Certain urban water rates quoted to special types of users often constitute a possible source of inefficient pricing. Most cities provide free water to their own governmental agencies. Some of these departments—parks and playgrounds, fire, street cleaning and maintenance—are heavy consumers of water. This practice not only loads the cost of general governmental services on the water user, but it also tends to encourage inefficient water use. Fire protection involves slight consumption of water but imposes a substantial cost on the system in the form of extra capacity, a cost which is rarely related to the payments exacted from the beneficiaries. Such costs are for capacity to provide heavy flows of water under pressure at the hours of peak consumption and also for ability to shift supplies of water if there are failures of pumps, breaks in pipes, or other mishaps. These precautions require

[55] This and other studies by J. B. Wolff are summarized by J. W. Milliman, "Policy Horizons for Future Urban Water Supply," *Land Economics,* XXXIX (May 1963), 120–26.

[56] Worksheets supplied by San Francisco Water Department; Brown and Caldwell, *Study of Water System Improvements: A Report Prepared for the City of Palo Alto* (1957), p. 26.

increases in size of terminal and distribution reservoirs, size of mains, number of pumps, interconnections, and so on.

Most cities levy charges upon the owners of private sprinkler systems, and upon public fire hydrants where fire protection is provided by a fiscally independent special fire district. The revenues collected from the provision of the hydrants are probably well below the costs of providing the service. The Belmont County Water District collects 2 per cent of its revenue from fire protection facilities but estimates that 6 per cent of its costs are assignable to fire protection.[57] This cost assignment will be higher for most cities, since the Belmont system is small and takes all of its water from San Francisco, relying on the city's excess capacity to fulfill extraordinarily heavy consumption needs. In Palo Alto, a city with a larger system but also reliant on San Francisco for supplemental supplies, it has been estimated that as much as one-fourth of the total investment in the water system is chargeable to the fire protection function.[58] However, only 2 per cent of its operating revenues came from hydrant rentals.[59]

The underassessment of direct fire protection costs means that these come to rest on the water purchases of general consumers. The practice tends both to shift the incidence of the costs of fire protection and to render the community unaware of them. Expenditures on an improved water system are often justified with the argument that it will cost the community little or nothing, since the outlay for extra storage, pumps, or distribution capacity will be offset by the reductions in fire insurance rates. For the city of Santa Ana an improvement program involving annual expenditures of about $211,000 was held to have brought annual insurance savings of about $244,000 to property owners, since the city was raised from a class 5 rating to a class 3 rating.[60] Other studies express the same theme,[61] or point out how the necessity to satisfy fire protection requirements affects the estimates of water requirements.[62]

Since the fire protection costs consist mostly of maintaining augmented capacity, they would best be financed through a property tax levied by the fire district. In this vein the East Bay Municipal Utility District partly justifies raising approximately 20 per cent of its revenues from the general property tax as a payment for fire protection.

Summary

The pricing systems of urban water agencies resemble those of agricultural districts in having certain features appropriate to ideal resource allocation. City systems employ two-part or even three-part tariffs (if a tax is used along with demand

[57] *Report on the Results and Operations and the Costs to Serve of the Belmont County Water District* (Belmont, 1958), p. 40.

[58] Brown and Caldwell, *op. cit.*, p. 27.

[59] California State Comptroller, *Annual Report of Financial Transactions Concerning Cities of California, Fiscal Year 1958–59* (1960), Table 6.

[60] Engineering Science Inc., *Water Requirements of the City of Fremont, California* (1960), p. 16.

[61] George S. Nolte, *Milpitas County Water District Study, Milpitas, California* (1960), pp. VII–14 and 15.

[62] Alameda County Water District, *Report on Bond Sale No. II* (1960), pp. 22–23.

and commodity charges), and in some cases set price differentials where marginal cost differentials clearly exist. In the cases which we have examined, however, such formal structures of charges seem to be applied largely without any basis in a correct economic analysis of their relation to costs. Furthermore, the use of tapered rates and special rate schedules for a few users creates significant possibilities for price discrimination among user groups in relation to the long-run marginal costs of serving them. Distortions of water allocation among classes of urban consumers thus may have greater relative importance than those among agricultural users. But for both groups of agencies deficiencies in retail pricing practices and resulting allocational distortions are varied and important.

The major distortion seems to lie in prices too low to reflect the long-run marginal costs of the typical system. This conclusion rests upon the failure of urban pricing systems to differentiate between demands expressed at the system's peak demand and at other times; and upon the accounting practices and the use of rationing to restrict peak demands among irrigation agencies. In addition, neither class of retailer makes allowance for any external marginal opportunity cost of the water it sells (unless a wholesaler's unit charge should accurately approximate this), and another source of underpricing is thus identified. In general, retail water pricing tends toward excessive use of water for these consumptive purposes, particularly so far as excessive investments are made in water development facilities. Because of the crucial role which the investment decision may play in effecting this misallocation, we now consider it in detail.

11

THE INVESTMENT DECISION

The norms which should guide water investment decisions if optimal allocation is to result were outlined in Chapter 8. There we also discussed the implications of the users' cooperative hypothesis for the procedure employed by public agencies in making such decisions. Here, as underpinning for the over-all normative appraisal in Part Three, we propose to test these behavioral hypotheses against the conduct of agencies in the water industry, seeking to identify the actual normative biases that this behavior implies.

When a public agency undertakes to invest in such major works as dams and aqueducts, it casts up a great deal of information on the technical and physical side of its plans. To a less and varying extent, it also reveals the criteria employed in selecting the project, the anticipated benefits, and the expected costs. As it nurtures and promotes the project in the face of regulatory constraints, and perhaps opposition of other agencies wishing to undertake the same project or utilize the same water, more information on the project's costs and consequences becomes available. Most of the following analysis is based on such evidence of the plans made for water investments in Northern California during the past decade or two. Retrospective study of the results of investments in place long enough for their actual costs and benefits to be apparent will appear in Part Three.

Behavioral evidence on the investment decision will be organized around the following schematic view of the process. First, the management of an agency decides to investigate the feasibility of a project designed to establish or extend its functions in the water industry. This general objective is transmitted to technical planning personnel, along with a more or less explicit criterion for picking the best way to attain it. The resulting proposal, as accepted by the agency's management and its member-customers, generally implies significant reallocations within the water industry. These must be cleared with assorted regulatory agencies and competing users or would-be users of water. While the acceptability of some of these reallocations is anticipated through constraints imposed in the initial planning process, many of them are considered only at later stages, when they have a discernible impact upon the design, scale, or timing of the project. Thus the definition of the internal objective and the imposition of the external constraints tend to be a literal sequence of events in gestation of a project, and will be treated as such below.

Our previous consideration of the legal powers and economic objectives of water agencies (Chapter 3 and Chapter 8) suggests that one species of local district will not make its investment decisions in just the same way as another, and that local districts as a group will differ significantly from state and federal organizations. On pragmatic grounds we group all major investors into three categories for discussion: local urban agencies; local agricultural districts; and arms of higher governments. In a concluding section we summarize the major allocative biases detected in their investment behavior.

Water Investments by Urban Agencies

Our study of investment decisions by urban water agencies will focus on the large cities of the San Francisco Bay area. Not only do they account for a dominant portion of the urban population in Northern California, but also their water supply facilities assume a far more complex physical form and have involved them in much more violent rivalries for water than those of any of the Central Valley cities. Most of the latter supply themselves through wells, a method which removes the complexities of discontinuities of scale from the investment decision. They have, however, come into conflict with surrounding agricultural areas over supplies of ground water, and these controversies are considered in Chapter 12.

Present-day investment decisions in the Bay area involve not only large and small local organizations, but also the three large-scale wholesalers operating in the state: the Bureau of Reclamation of the U.S. Department of the Interior, the U.S. Army Corps of Engineers, and the California Department of Water Resources. The full story of investment in the area and its attendant pressures and rivalries thus can be completed only after we have examined the investment decisions of these wholesalers below, and the effects of wholesaler competition in Chapter 13.

Environment of investment decisions

Table 26 shows the water supplies used in various hydrographic sectors of the Bay area in 1960—a reflection of the accumulation of past investments. In addition, it shows one forecast of supply patterns in the year 2020 which gives a general indication of the character and relative size of investments to come. Well over a third of the water used in this highly urbanized area still serves agricultural purposes, but this fraction is expected to decline over the coming sixty years to 5 per cent. Thus a significant volume of urban supplies will result from bidding land and water away from agricultural uses.

Local sources of water in the area are quite fully developed. A little less than half of the reservoir capacity is used to store the extremely variable local runoff, serving in part to support percolation to recharge ground-water supplies and in part to supply conventional surface distribution systems. Ground-water recharge operations are important in those parts of the area where agriculture remains a heavy user of water, supporting increased water use in an economy of irrigated farms drawing their water through individual wells. Some important cities also depend on ground-water supplies, and a substantial portion of current investment plans reflect the fact that percolation operations using local supplies have not managed to keep up with growing ground-water extraction.[1]

Municipal water distribution through surface mains is dominated by two large suppliers, San Francisco Water Department and East Bay Municipal Utility District (EBMUD). Both systems include local catchment reservoirs inherited from predecessor systems which were consolidated many years ago. These reservoirs now serve prominently as terminal reservoirs for aqueducts drawing upon distant sources in the Sierra. The relative decline in the role of private and small municipal water systems is clearly related to the completed development of local supplies and the rise of interbasin transfers involving great economies of scale. Major investment programs of the current and coming decades, as Table 26 clearly shows, will consist of expanded interbasin transfers. Some expansion will occur in the existing plants of San Francisco and EBMUD; new aqueducts of the major wholesalers—the Bureau, Corps, and Department of Water Resources—are being built into the area to connect with the expanding distribution systems of a number of local water agencies.

This sketch highlights certain important environmental forces affecting Bay area investment decisions. First, major investments for urban water supply have occurred relatively late compared to the development of the state's water for agricultural use, and have competed with established irrigation agencies for both "old" and "new" water. Both the transfer of local water sources to urban use and the design and execution of interbasin transfers reflect this rivalry. Bay area cities have felt forced to go far afield for their water imports, and even so have become entangled with prior agricultural claimants to their chosen sources of water.

Another major environmental feature is the multiplicity of governments in the Bay area. In 1957, the nine-county area included 650 units of local government, of which 87 were municipal or county governments of general jurisdiction and the rest were special districts performing a variety of functions.[2] These units tend to maintain a relatively stable legal complexion in the face of changing economic forces. One of these forces is the redistribution of population within the area. Today, San Francisco remains the central city of the Bay area but has only one-fifth of the population of the nine counties. In 1900, just before the major water systems of the area were designed, San Francisco contained over one-half of the population. Its share will continue to decline, and the Department of Commerce estimates that by 1990 the city's population will be one-eighth of the nine-county total.[3] In 1900, San Mateo County, lying immediately south of San Francisco, had less than 4 per cent of San Francisco's population, and was a rural hinterland in which the private water company serving San Francisco developed a large watershed to supply the city. When San Francisco municipalized the private system, it became a supplier to several small public systems which had been contracting with the private utility. This fortuitous acquisition of the role of wholesaler helped to shape the city's later

[1] Additional information is provided in Chapters 2 and 4.

[2] U.S. Department of Commerce, Bureau of the Census, *Census of Governments, 1957* (1958–59), Vol. VI:4, Table 36. (This and other footnote references are cited in brief when they are also included in the Bibliography.)

[3] U.S. Department of Commerce, Office of Area Development, *Future Development of the San Francisco Bay Area, 1960–2020* (1959).

TABLE 26

WATER SUPPLIES OF THE SAN FRANCISCO BAY REGION IN 1960 AND ESTIMATED SUPPLIES IN 2020, BY AREA

(In thousands of acre-feet)

Region of use	Local supplies		Coyote Valley Project[a]		Cache Slough Diversion		Solano Project[b]		Contra Costa Canal[b]		Moke-lumne Aqueduct[c]		Hetch Hetchy Aqueduct[d]		State Water Plan Aqueduct	
	1960	2020	1960	2020	1960	2020	1960	2020	1960	2020	1960	2020	1960	2020	1960	2020
Marin and Sonoma counties	25	40	5	154												
Napa Valley	20	26			13	23		15								
Solano County	7	7					31	172								
Contra Costa County	16	16							64	146	44	102				
Livermore Valley	14	14											2	15		46
Alameda County (bayside)	41	73									109	263	5	59		64
Santa Clara County	185	185											8	94		88
San Mateo County (bayside)	20	20											53	228		
San Mateo County (coastal)	6	6											4	44		
San Francisco	0	0											83	130		
Total	334	387	5	154	13	23	31	187	64	146	153	365	155	570	0	198

[a] U.S. Army Corps of Engineers.
[b] U.S. Department of the Interior, Bureau of Reclamation.
[c] East Bay Municipal Utility District.
[d] San Francisco Water Department.

SOURCE: U.S. Army Corps of Engineers, South Pacific Division, *Appendix C to the Technical Report on San Francisco Bay Barriers* (1963), Table 15.

water-marketing role in the area, as San Mateo County and other suburban areas have gained greatly in population relative to the city of San Francisco.

Still another changing economic force which has pressed against a stable structure of governments has been the changing scale economies of water supply for the area. The relative decline of local supplies, which could be economically developed by small governments or private companies, has compelled either the integration of water supply units or the development of a wholesaler-retailer structure. Both trends are apparent in the Bay area. But this has not been a painless or automatic process among governments affected with fraternal rivalries, interests in annexation and expansion, and the like. Water investment decisions, like the decisions on pricing urban water, reflect governmental motives quite unrelated to water.

Against these background elements, we first consider the internal aspects of investment decisions made by cities of the Bay area and the formal criteria employed, and then the external constraints and restrictions on carrying out these decisions.

Internal decisions and investment criteria

Urban agencies typically seem to make investment decisions within the framework of investment criteria that bear little relation to maximizing the excess of benefits over costs. The following list of "requirements," provided by one agency, gives an indication of the sort of approach taken: (1) the supply must arrive by a fixed date; (2) capital outlays must be substantially financed through revenues; (3) the supply must be adequate to meet long-term needs; (4) the water must be of good quality; (5) the project should minimize the cost of water delivered to a common point.[4] In general, this approach tends to substitute constraints upon the project for any straightforward maximization rule. Insofar as a maximization rule can be detected, it consists of picking the lowest-cost method of meeting an assumed fixed demand.

Local agencies often employ this sort of approach, not so much from ignorance of the full optimizing rule as from a lack of any ready means to evaluate benefits. Feeling unable to measure the value of their product to users, they cannot very well apply a rule which seeks to maximize the difference between the value of the product and its cost. A fixed forecast of the level or growth rate of demand is substituted instead, and the agency chooses among alternative scales, designs, sources of water, and the like, on the basis of minimizing the costs of meeting this requirement.

Such an approach might yield the same results as a more sophisticated treatment of benefits, particularly if the marginal benefit function should be highly inelastic at the level of demand forecast. But there is no reason why this need be the case, particularly in view of the pricing practices used by most municipal water systems. Predicted demand levels normally run in terms of peak-period demands, associated

[4] North Marin County Water District, *Water Supply and Distribution Report,* by T. C. Brinkley (1960).

with an assumed distribution of demand over time.[5] Yet prices of water are not adjusted to reflect its higher marginal cost at the time of peak use, nor is any qualitative judgment made about the urgency or postponability of demands occurring at that time. Thus, water agencies are often without a clue as to the size of marginal benefits to users at the time of peak demand. In general, the preference of agencies for uniform pricing leaves them with no information about the willingness to pay of differently situated customer groups, and thus about the returns to expanding or improving various features of their distribution systems.

The sort of investment criterion used by the city of San Francisco is much less clear. This is because of the complexity of its existing system (including power generation as well as water), its wholesale marketing activities, its special problems of water rights, and its objectives involving political goals unrelated to water—such goals as maintaining political and business leadership in the metropolitan area. For example, it probably cannot both maximize its profits on water sold at wholesale to suburban customers and still expand suburban business at a sufficient rate to retain its unusual water right (which requires continuing development to avoid permanent forfeiture of rights to further development). How these considerations fit together is not clear, but the fact that San Francisco's water sales seem to some degree aimed at yielding a profit for the city suggests that incremental benefits may exceed incremental costs, so far as the price received measures incremental benefits.

The discount rate

The choice of a discount rate in planning a project seldom takes on major concern for local governments, and they typically select their own borrowing rates, usually ranging between 3 per cent and 4.5 per cent.[6] The investment is almost always financed by a bond issue, and a city can normally secure a reliable estimate of the interest rate which it would have to offer at any given time. This borrowing rate is used in the typical engineering analysis for comparing the costs of alternative proposed systems or designs. It is seldom applied, however, in appraising benefit streams because the "requirements" approach to benefits neglects alternative time streams of benefits and, indeed, neglects all variability in the total amount of benefits attainable. Sometimes a discount rate is employed that even lies below the agency's borrowing rate.[7] Only rarely are the effects of alternative interest rates on the choice of a project discussed at all,[8] and the conclusions of such comparative

[5] For a typical illustration, see Brown and Caldwell, *A Study of Water System Improvements: A Report Prepared for the City of Palo Alto, California* (1957).

[6] For example, see Brown and Caldwell, *ibid.,* p. 32, and North Marin County Water District, *op. cit.,* p. 39.

[7] The engineering staff of the Alameda County Water District used a discount rate of 4 per cent in computing the average annual cost of alternative projects, while a financial analysis of the District's concurrent improvement program indicated that an interest charge of 4½ per cent was being paid. See Alameda County Water District, Engineering Staff, *Comparison of Supplemental Sources of Water Supply* (Fremont, 1961), p. 68; and its *Report on Bond Sale No. II (1960) for Improvement District No. 1 Bonds Authorized March, 1956* (1960), Table 6.

[8] For example, Engineering Science, Inc., *Water Requirements of the City of Fremont, California* (1960), p. 81.

analyses are sometimes not controlling even after the analyses have been performed.[9] Yet engineering studies show that the feasibility of projects studied by water agencies in the Bay area is dramatically affected by the choice of discount rate.[10]

The treatment of uncertainty

Like the discount rate, the amount of uncertainty can be shown to have a powerful influence on the investment choices made by urban agencies. Only a few examples are needed to show the extent of the effects of uncertainty.

The East Bay Municipal Utility District has a long record of investment choices which forego the lowest-cost source of design because of elements of uncertainty. In the years when large-scale water imports to the Bay area were first planned, EBMUD chose not to work with San Francisco in its Hetch Hetchy development because that project was proceeding too slowly and the date of its availability was too uncertain. At the time of the first major expansion of its own Mokelumne Aqueduct system, a purchase of water from the Folsom South Canal of the Bureau of Reclamation would probably have proved a less costly source than the additional dam on the Mokelumne which was actually chosen. When this was done, however, Folsom South had not been authorized by Congress for construction. Although EBMUD's proclaimed interest could certainly have helped to secure and speed congressional approval, the District felt the attendant delay too risky.

Yet another example concerns EBMUD's choice of the Camanche over the Middle Bar reservoir site on the Mokelumne River. The latter's advantage lay in revenues from power generation, attainable because the District's demand for water, competitive with securing maximum revenues from power, would not for some time absorb the full water output of the new project. An underestimate of the growth of the District's demand for water, however, would threaten the power revenues and lend an element of uncertainty to the superior status of the Middle Bar alternative. The consultants' report found that if this and other contingencies came out adversely, Middle Bar would cost $6 million more than Camanche. The consultants were "not certain that ultimate resolution of all of the factors would be so extreme in their effect on the economic comparisons as indicated," but the negotiations necessary to determine the precise numbers would have meant a delay which itself would increase the cost of Middle Bar above that of Camanche.[11] This means of

[9] Bechtel Corporation, *Report on Mokelumne River Development Investigations, East Bay Municipal Utility District* (1960).

[10] Consultants for EBMUD investigated the economic feasibility of uprating the turbines in the District's existing Pardee power plant. The ratio of discounted revenues to construction costs for the uprating at various interest rates was: 3½ per cent, 1.20; 4 per cent, 1.10; 4½ per cent, 1.01; 5 per cent, 0.94. Computed from Bechtel Corporation, *Report on Economic Feasibility of Pardee Turbine Uprating, East Bay Municipal Utility District, Oakland, California* (1960), Table A.

[11] Bechtel Corporation, *Report on Mokelumne River Development Investigations, op. cit.*, p. IX–9.

treating uncertainty is unconventional, but essentially correct in assigning extra costs to the alternative affected by uncertainty. The assignment is not tailored to the degree of uncertainty, however, nor is that degree carefully evaluated.

These cases indicate the power of uncertainty, and efforts of urban water agencies to avoid it, over the shape and timing of investment decisions. Let us now consider more systematically the different types of risk and uncertainty which may arise, with main stress upon the following elements: (1) hydrologic risk concerning the volume of precipitation; (2) uncertainty concerning the possibilities of major damage to the water storage and distribution system—for example, by a violent earthquake; (3) uncertainty about variations in the level of demand, in particular due to fire-fighting requirements.

In terms of the classic distinction between risk and uncertainty, hydrologic uncertainty is really a type of risk. Long-standing and reasonably accurate records of precipitation and runoff exist for California's major watersheds, and a water agency planning an investment has quite an accurate knowledge of the relevant parameters of the distribution of possible supplies. The usual method of incorporating this knowledge into investment plans is through computer simulations used to indicate the minimum storage capacity that would supply target water requirements in the driest period on record. The procedure essentially aims to eliminate risk on the basis of historically known contingencies; no calculations investigate the cost saving and the size and frequency of supply reductions which would result from taking some chance of a short-fall. This practice gives another example of the use of a "requirements" approach to investment planning rather than marginal benefits and costs.

The choice of large reservoir capacities to permit carryover storage in the case of a prolonged drought is one reaction to hydrologic risk. But the "wet" tail of the runoff distribution also influences storage capacities in order to permit flood control. All of the systems importing water into the Bay area incorporate storage space for flood control purposes. The Sonoma County Flood Control and Water Conservation District draws water from Coyote Dam, constructed by the Corps of Engineers, while the other state and local systems have received federal grants to finance excess capacity for floodwater storage. Again, flood control capacity is designed in terms of achieving some predetermined level of safety, not subject to a marginal benefit-cost analysis. The level of safety sought would seem, in many cases, to eliminate all possible flood hazards.[12] The incremental benefits and costs of attaining complete precaution are unknown, but a $\Delta B'/\Delta C$ ratio as large as unity seems quite improbable.

The reactions to hydrologic risk probably create a bias toward excessive scale in reservoirs, and the "true" uncertainty concerning the possibility of major interruptions of service may work in the same direction. The San Francisco earth-

[12] Camanche Dam of EBMUD is required by the Corps of Engineers to insure that the city of Lodi "is protected against a flood equal to 90 per cent of the standard project flood." The standard flood is defined as having a peak flow which is 400 per cent of the maximum flood ever recorded on the stream and a five-day volume of flow which is 250 per cent of the maximum recorded volume for such a period. See U.S. Congress, House of Representatives, *Camanche Reservoir, Mokelumne River, California,* H. Doc. 436, 87 Cong. 2 sess. (1962), pp. 17, 26.

quake of 1906 disabled the city's water distribution system and permitted the catastrophic fires which followed it to rage unchecked. The fear of a recurrence of this disaster pervades the design of local water transportation and storage facilities in the Bay area. The EBMUD maintains terminal storage sufficient to supply its service area for 90 days of normal consumption, even if an earthquake wrecked its aqueduct and gave rise to sweeping fires in its cities. Storage capacity within the distribution system itself is over four times that considered normal by cities elsewhere. For the same reason, the San Francisco Water Department maintains even greater excess capacity in terminal and distribution storage. Again, these precautions are subject to no marginal benefit-cost analysis. In emergencies, cities develop *ad hoc* methods of rationing water, and their experience gives little insight into the benefits of converting nonfirm to firm supplies. No doubt the marginal cost and benefit functions would be extremely hard to establish.

Yet another source of true uncertainty in the supply of water lies in the future availability of water rights. Water agencies often feel that the availability of water rights by purchase from an existing holder at some future date cannot be counted upon, and that unappropriated streamflow will become progressively encumbered with rights at a pace that is hard to foresee. Sometimes an agency can choose between an investment of moderate scale (say, in the development of local sources of supply) which will serve its requirements in the near future, and a large-scale investment (say, an interbasin transfer) which will suffer heavy excess capacity for a long time. Agencies fear that the large-scale investment may become ultimately necessary, but might be blocked by the water rights situation unless it is undertaken promptly. Avoidance of this form of uncertainty produces a strong pressure toward premature construction or the inflation of project scales.

Investment planning also faces elements of risk and uncertainty concerning future demand: average rate of growth and changes which may occur in the distribution of periods of peak utilization. Almost all urban water agencies expect to serve rising populations, but they are uncertain about the rate and pattern of growth and, therefore, the appropriate timing of added capacity. They are uncertain about future consumption per capita, which will reflect both the changing pattern of water consumption by given types of users and the changing pattern of land use.

The investment planning of most Bay area agencies is based on the same type of crude demand estimate, but practices differ with respect to the future time period considered. Consumption per capita is estimated for each type of consumer: residential, commercial, and industrial. These amounts are projected into the future by adopting the estimates, prepared by some independent planning agency, of population and economic activity for a distant future year. Current use per capita is then inflated by some trend factor. Trends in the peaking pattern of annual demand are also frequently analyzed. Single-valued trend projections of use are normally made for specific years in the near future; long-run estimates typically take the form of demand under conditions of "ultimate" urban saturation of the area in question, without dating this state of completion. Although the agencies seem inclined to employ very long time horizons in view of the demand uncertainty involved, they are often precluded from acting on this inclination. The location of population growth or the pattern of future supply alternatives may be too uncertain,[13] or capital rationing may impel attention to investment projects that make some supply available quickly and cheaply.[14] Because the variations in patterns of peak consumption (given the pricing schedule) are very small, uncertainty about them comprises only a minor problem. There is an exception, however, in the case of fire-fighting requirements; capacity for this purpose can account for as much as one-fourth of the total investment in the water system.[15] Investment plans generally adhere mechanically to the standards of fire flow set by the National Board of Fire Underwriters, employing storage in the distribution system and a scale of pumps and pipes far in excess of those required for ordinary consumptive use in order to qualify for minimum fire insurance rates.[16] The marginal benefits may not meet the marginal costs involved,[17] yet the calculations do not seem to be made. On the other hand, many cities receive low grades on fire insurance standards and, by not choosing to make investments to meet the highest standards, implicitly judge the costs to exceed the benefits.

In summary, investment decisions by urban agencies take account of a number of forms of uncertainty, unless precluded by capital rationing or other constraints. The avoidance of uncertainty is given a heavy and relatively mechanical weight in making the investment decision, with the result of a substantial increase in the capital-intensity of water development facilities.

Adjustments for future price changes

Investment decisions of local governments depend on forecasting real magnitudes related to benefits and costs, copying with uncertainties about these forecasts, and selecting an appropriate discount rate to convert these to comparable present values. Project studies for local governments also occupy themselves with another forecasting exercise: estimating future money price and cost trends. Typical cost analyses estimate future costs of construction and of operation and maintenance in current prices, and then adjust by projecting an inflationary trend in the prices of construction goods. Two justifications are offered for this procedure. One is an apparently persistent upward trend in construction costs; the other is a common bias toward an underestimate of real costs by engineering staffs.

Local agencies consider this allowance a wise and conservative procedure, a reasonable view in terms of their own financial situations. Their investments are financed by current borrowing. They seek to provide water services at the lowest

[13] See, for example, North Marin County Water District, *op. cit.*, introductory letter.

[14] See Arthur P. Davis, *Additional Water Supply of East Bay Municipal Utility District: Report to the Board of Directors* (1924), p. 63.

[15] Brown and Caldwell, *op. cit.*, p. 27.

[16] National Board of Fire Underwriters, *Standard Schedule for Grading Cities and Towns of the United States with Reference to Their Fire Defenses and Physical Conditions.*

[17] Water supply accounts for only about one-third of the factors determining a city's fire insurance rating, and so the savings in insurance (apart from savings in fire losses themselves) may not in all cases promise marginal benefits warranting the costs of the "safest" level of fire-fighting capacity.

prices that may be charged while covering the money costs of debt servicing and operating expenses. Neglect of rising future prices of inputs (capital or current) tends to cause the postponement of expenditures to times when greater debt or operating expenses would have to be incurred, and higher prices would result. Indeed, this view is quite rational in the light of their member-customers' interests, if market interest rates do not fully anticipate inflationary trends.

Investment decisions that take inflation into account favor present over deferred construction, and favor designs involving relatively large amounts of current costs over those requiring relatively large amounts of future costs. In plain words, agencies tend to build ahead of demand and use more capital-intensive designs.[18] The usual method of taking price trends into account is simply to add an unexplained cost allowance for contingencies. In one case in which an explicit comparison was presented of alternative investments subject to assumed price trends, it can be shown that their inclusion was responsible for the choice of the more capital-intensive design.[19]

What is the normative significance of this practice? If dollars are to be used as the basis of measuring value, care must be taken that the dollars used in measurement have equal significance. If dollar measurements relate to different years, then an adjustment must occur because a dollar today provides the holder with more opportunities than does the prospect of a future dollar. This adjustment is properly handled through the discounting procedure. When the money price of an item (along with all other goods) is expected to rise from $1.50 this year to $2 next year, however, it has not become more costly in that the opportunity cost in the form of other goods foregone is presumptively the same in the two cases. The same sacrifice of real resources is involved. Federal government agencies in their analyses of benefits and costs abstract as much as possible from general inflationary movements.[20] Local agencies, for the behavioral reasons indicated above, have followed the opposite course. Only under special conditions in which all other transactors and all market prices (including the rate of interest) have adjusted to a common expected rate of inflation will this practice fail to produce an investment pattern in which designs are too capital-intensive and construction too early.

A different issue from trends in the general level of prices and costs is raised by foreseen changes in relative prices. These are considered in federal evaluative procedures and should be, but generally are not, taken into account by local agencies. Take, for example, the particularly important case of land. Often a city plans land-using water facilities well in advance of the growth of population, so that the relative value of land occupied by reservoirs and the like will increase as time goes on. These increasing opportunity costs should be taken into account in setting the

[18] For a more general discussion of the economic effects of adjustments to anticipated inflation, see Reuben A. Kessel and Armen A. Alchian, "Effects of Inflation," *Journal of Political Economy,* LXX (December 1962), 530–35.

[19] The choice was between building a large-diameter aqueduct and building a smaller one, with the smaller one subject to higher operating costs because of greater pumping requirements. See East Bay Municipal Utility District, Water Resources and Planning Division, *Mokelumne Aqueduct No. 3: Determination of Size of Future Water Supply* (1957).

[20] U.S. Interagency Committee on Water Resources, *Proposed Practices for Economic Analysis of River Basin Projects* (1958), pp. 16–20.

design of projects. San Francisco's storage and catchment reservoir in adjoining, suburban San Mateo County is equal in acreage to the city of San Francisco itself, and EBMUD's terminal storage reservoirs cover over 40 square miles. No small amount of resources is involved.

By the same token, changes over time in the relative scarcity value of water are typically ignored (as is, for that matter, the absolute level of its shadow price), whereas its effect on the appropriate combination of water and nonwater inputs should be taken into account. Also ignored are any foreseeable changes in the relative price of water which the agency shall charge to its customers, and the impact which that might have on the estimated growth of demand. Local agencies are in the perverse position of taking into account those price trends which, from the viewpoint of general economic welfare, they should ignore, and ignoring those which they should take into account.

External forces affecting investments

Investment is more than the construction of facilities to increase an agency's water deliveries. It is also a means to establish or augment water rights, or to counter the plans of rivals or potential rivals. Admittedly premature construction of water projects may be undertaken by agencies fearful that neither water nor water rights may be available at the appropriate future time. Thus the efficiency of investment in the water industry and the efficiency of the allocation of water itself are closely interrelated questions.

The absence of a market for water means that the establishment of rights occurs through judicial, legislative, and administrative procedures. Any agency undertaking investments in the industry—whether local, state, or federal—must run a gamut of administrative proceedings as well as deal with the threat of lengthy court procedures. In the course of these encounters, water rights are established, external economies and diseconomies of the proposed project are to some degree taken into account, and a variety of statutory or administrative requirements are imposed on the project. The proposed project itself may be considerably altered in the process. In Chapters 12-14 we outline the substance of these rivalries and the forces determining their outcomes, and the procedural stages involved are conveniently deferred to the following section of this chapter. Here we shall look only at the results for the investment decision. Do the political, judicial, and administrative processes which determine the allocation of water cause bias in the normative character of the investment decision? Do they help to offset or avert errors which the investing agencies would make on the basis of their internal planning practices? For answers, we consider San Francisco's experience at length, that of EBMUD more briefly.

At the turn of the century, the city of San Francisco filed for water rights on the Tuolumne River, seeking to locate a storage reservoir in the river's Hetch Hetchy Valley, within the boundaries of Yosemite National Park. A debate broke out in Washington over granting the city permission to construct a reservoir within the park, and controversy spread. At first, only the private water company serving San

Francisco and the Turlock and Modesto irrigation districts,[21] competing for the waters of the Tuolumne, were involved, but subsequently conservation spokesmen from coast to coast were drawn into the fray. San Francisco finally won its grant, but the city's investment plans were completely altered in the process; a small project became a large multiple purpose project, committed to continuing growth. The final outcome was the Raker Act of 1913, containing provisions which have continued to dominate the investment plans of the San Francisco Water Department to this day. The provisions of the act reflected the interests of a number of groups, not just the city's direct rivals:

1) The city could develop the Hetch Hetchy site only on condition that it maintain continuous development of the Tuolumne River. All rights to further development would be forfeited if the city ceased such development for three consecutive years.

2) The city could not sell power generated at the site to any private party for resale. Unable to gain voter approval for municipal distribution of electricity within San Francisco, the city blatantly defied this clause for many years and sold power to Pacific Gas and Electric Company. This practice was finally terminated by Supreme Court action.

3) The city was required to recognize the extensive water rights to the Tuolumne held by the Turlock and Modesto irrigation districts, located downstream in the San Joaquin Valley. If the districts wished to purchase additional supplies from San Francisco, the Secretary of the Interior would approve the price.

4) San Francisco was to sell electric power to the irrigation districts at cost, for any purpose.

5) Water could not be exported from the San Joaquin Valley until San Francisco had made full use of its locally available supplies. This provision blocked any competition with the Spring Valley Water Company, San Francisco's local private supplier, and forced the city to buy out the company.

6) Among ancillary provisions, the city would be required to maintain park facilities and to make regular lease payments to the Secretary of the Interior to be used for park improvements.

Thus, although the conservation interests were fundamentally defeated in their effort to maintain Yosemite National Park unspoiled, all of San Francisco's opponents were granted some satisfaction, with the Turlock and Modesto irrigation districts gaining what turned out in the long run to be the most valuable concessions. Furthermore, the scale and character of the project were changed completely.

Although San Francisco's early plans to undertake the Hetch Hetchy development concerned merely the city's own needs,[22] by the time of the Raker Act when the final plans were formulated, the scale of the project had increased almost sevenfold to 448,000 acre-feet annually and the market area had been extended to all of the Bay area cities. A preliminary decision by the Secretary of the Interior had

[21] These districts and the general features of the Tuolumne watershed are shown in Figure 21, Chapter 12.

[22] City and County of San Francisco, Board of Supervisors, *Report on the Water Supply of San Francisco* (1908), p. 123.

only suggested that "adjacent cities . . . may join with [San Francisco] in obtaining a common water supply,"[23] but later reports and studies confidently assumed that all Bay area cities would band together. Power generation, only an incidental function in the early plans, later grew to considerable importance. It seems clear that this enlargement grew out of the more intensive study and broader appraisal of alternatives made by San Francisco under pressure of the controversy prior to the Raker Act. Additional consultants were retained, and more alternatives were examined than would have been without the pressure of opposition.[24]

The influence of the settlement embodied in the Raker Act has been firmly imprinted on all subsequent investment decisions of the city of San Francisco. This is clearly apparent in the main investment currently being planned for the Tuolumne River, an enlargement of the downstream Don Pedro Dam belonging to the Turlock and Modesto irrigation districts, to be financed in part by San Francisco.

A few facts about the Tuolumne River and the demands upon its waters further an understanding of this proposed project. The only major users of its waters at present are San Francisco and the two irrigation districts. The city has built its power plants, reservoirs, diversion channels, and pipelines in the headwaters high in the Sierra Nevada. The power plant, reservoirs, and distribution network of the districts lie in the foothills and on the valley floor. These parties have cooperated for many years on the operation of their facilities, subject to the terms of the Raker Act, and their present common investment program reflects its terms and the opportunities which it creates.

The Raker Act guaranteed the Turlock and Modesto irrigation districts a continuous flow of 2,350 second-feet, almost exactly 1,700,000 acre-feet annually. Since the average flow of the river is 1,842,000 acre-feet annually (ranging from a recorded high of 3,750,000 to a recorded low of 542,000), the two districts were essentially granted rights to the whole natural flow in most years, with San Francisco possessing clear title mainly to what it could save from the years that were wetter than average. In fact, the actual average annual diversions of the districts have been a good deal smaller than those to which they are entitled—only 845,000 acre-feet—allowing the city to draw its current diversion of less than 200,000 acre-feet without extensive storage capacity to carry water over from unusually wet years.

Electric power is an important output of San Francisco's operations, and in 1961-62 it supplied two-thirds of the revenues earned by the Hetch Hetchy Project Division of the San Francisco Water Department.[25] Water releases from San Francisco's reservoirs to satisfy the claims of the downstream irrigators in dry years, plus the normal growth of the demands of the city's own water customers, tend to cut sharply into attainable power revenues. These financial losses induced the city

[23] U.S. Department of the Interior, Office of the Secretary, *Proceedings in Re: Use of Hetch Hetchy Reservoir Site in the Yosemite National Park by the City of San Francisco* (1910).

[24] Ray W. Taylor, *Hetch Hetchy* (1926), pp. 111–18.

[25] Water revenues attributed to the Sierra storage and diversion works of the Department are essentially based on an arbitrary transfer price, but since this price bears some relation to the cost of the works after power revenues are taken into account, the figure given above has some general significance as a rough indicator.

to plan an enlargement of the downstream Don Pedro Reservoir, belonging to the irrigation districts, so that its storage capacity could regulate releases for them and permit the city's upstream reservoirs to be operated more profitably for power generation.[26]

Economically, if not legally, an alternative to the enlargement of Don Pedro Reservoir would be a reduction in the use of water by the irrigation districts. Hence its marginal productivity to them takes on importance for appraising the investment project. Most of the revenues of Turlock and Modesto irrigation districts stem from retail sales of electric power, either generated in their own power plant or purchased from San Francisco at cost, according to the terms of the Raker Act. In 1962, Modesto irrigators paid no water tolls and their land tax averaged only $1.20 an acre. Water applications are around 4 acre-feet per acre annually,[27] with surface supplies supplemented to some degree by private pumping. This amounts to a heavy application of water to the sort of crops raised in Turlock and Modesto. That fact plus the zero marginal cost of water to irrigators suggest that the value of marginal product of water would be low, and therefore that the New Don Pedro could not have substantial water conservation benefits for the districts. The same conclusion holds for the project's power benefits.[28] Although we have not sought to compute a full benefit-cost ratio for the project, including flood-control and recreational benefits, a favorable appraisal seems unlikely.

Whatever the actual state of benefits and costs from New Don Pedro, it is unlikely that the project would have been built by the districts without the participation of San Francisco, and that San Francisco's participation was in a sense pressed upon it by its obligations under the Raker Act. San Francisco's contribution to the cost of New Don Pedro is $45 million. With this, it intends to buy the freedom to divert a maximum quantity of 448,000 acre-feet of water annually and to release water from its own reservoirs in a pattern optimal for power generation. We can test this investment decision crudely against a hypothetical alternative: If San Francisco's operating pattern were freed of the obligation to serve the downstream irrigation districts, would the present value of the benefits lost to the districts exceed $45 million?

Suppose that San Francisco were to buy out a portion of the land located in the irrigation districts—enough so that their remaining acreage could enjoy the same level of unit benefits after San Francisco optimized its own operations as do the whole of their lands when the city observes the Raker Act's requirements. A generous estimate of the value of irrigated land in the two districts, using a price of $500 per acre, would be $135 million. The sum of $45 million would buy out one-third of their acreage and permit a one-third reduction in their water consumption

[26] "Under present conditions of diversion, the City requires about 450,000 acre-feet of New Don Pedro storage to firm up the use of the upstream City reservoirs for most advantageous operation for the generation of power. Without New Don Pedro, the City would have to release this amount of water to the Districts as the flow occurred and would be unable to use a large portion of it in the City power plants." Bechtel Corporation, *New Don Pedro Project, Report on Project Operation Studies* (1961), pp. 23–24.

[27] Modesto Irrigation District, *Annual Report, 1962;* Bookman, Edmonston, and Gianelli, *Investigation of Supplemental Water Supplies for Modesto Irrigation District* (1961).

[28] *Brief of the Commission Staff Before the Federal Power Commission, Project No. 2299* (Mimeographed, Jan. 14, 1963), pp. 33–36.

with no decline in unit productivity. Since one-third of their current annual diversion of 845,000 acre-feet exceeds the 213,000 acre-feet by which San Francisco's annual intake is expected to increase over the next fifty years,[29] the view is reinforced that New Don Pedro's justification lies in institutional constraints affecting the use of waters of the Tuolumne: the terms of the Raker Act plus the general absence of financial compensations in California as a means to change the allocation of water.

East Bay Municipal Utility District is now constructing Camanche Dam on the Mokelumne River, to allow it to satisfy other established rights on the Mokelumne and still enlarge its diversions to meet the rapidly growing demand in its service area. This investment has not in any direct sense been undertaken or changed on account of rival demands on the Mokelumne, but the different settlements which EBMUD had to make in order to get the project under construction show the effects which external rivalries may have on the process of undertaking water investments.

The EBMUD's rivals for water are relatively numerous. The headwaters of the Mokelumne River lie in Amador and Calaveras counties, which thus possess county-of-origin status under the California Water Code, although their present state of development does not involve any demand for substantial quantities of water. Downstream lies the Woodbridge Irrigation District. Its rights to the Mokelumne predate those of EBMUD, but were undefined until a 1938 legal proceeding between the two parties detailed Woodbridge's prior rights at different times of the year and for various levels of runoff.[30] After 1938, but before 1949 when EBMUD filed for increased diversions, Woodbridge and other downstream users made filings on their own behalf, and the additional claims on the river resulting from these have not been settled. Finally, the California Department of Fish and Game has sought substantial releases from any new project of EBMUD to sustain and enhance fish life.

In proceeding with its project, EBMUD has had to reach a final settlement with each of these interests except Woodbridge, in which case negotiations are not concluded. The agreement with Calaveras and Amador counties resulted from EBMUD offering them various combinations of money and water for the withdrawal of their objections. They chose mainly money: a payment of $2 million went to each county, along with a reservation of 27,000 acre-feet for Calaveras and 20,000 acre-feet for Amador. The agreement with the Department of Fish and Game called for less sacrifice of water than the Department had originally sought in the form of fish releases, but committed EBMUD to expend around a million dollars to provide a fish hatchery, spawning channel, and related facilities. These extensive compensations, and others which might come in the future, meant that the Camanche investment constituted a substantial risk for EBMUD since it might or might not yield the desired amount of water. That it seems likely to do so seems due to an ad-

[29] *Ibid.*, p. 20.

[30] *Agreement Between East Bay Municipal Utility District and Woodbridge Irrigation District*, Jan. 7, 1938; also see California State Department of Public Works, Division of Engineering and Irrigation, *Irrigation Districts in California, 1929*, by Frank Adams, Bulletin No. 21 (1930), pp. 145–47.

ventitious favorable circumstance: a flood control contribution to Camanche from the Corps of Engineers covering 28.9 per cent of the construction cost and providing an extra 200,000 acre-feet of reservoir space. The operating rules for this flood control storage are such that EBMUD can in most years fill it up by the end of the spring runoff, gaining that much more effective storage and facilitating the payoffs in water and cash indicated above.

As with the case of San Francisco's contribution to New Don Pedro, the Camanche project is significant for what was not considered as well as for what was. If water rights of the Woodbridge Irrigation District had been partly bought out, would the total cost have been less? Do the flood control or other benefits of the extra 200,000 acre-feet of capacity warrant the cost of the federal flood control contribution? These are the sort of performance uncertainties created by external forces bearing on water investments by urban agencies.

Water Investments by Local Agricultural Districts

Most active irrigation districts and other types of agricultural water districts possess substantial physical plants, including at least distribution systems of ditches or pipelines connecting a district's water source with the irrigation systems of individual farms. Some districts also have invested in dams and reservoirs to retain the winter runoff for summer use (often producing electric power as a joint output). Here we focus upon investments in dams and reservoirs. Not only do these typically involve larger capital sums, but also they possess a much greater significance for the allocation of water than do present-day investments in improvement of distribution systems.

Agricultural districts usually apply their investment criteria with practices and abuses similar to those of local urban agencies. As a result, the range of issues concerning investment criteria will receive a relatively small amount of attention here. The more interesting aspect of agricultural water investments is the influence of external forces upon the scale and timing of projects. The opportunity of joint ventures in production of electric power and the threat of rival claimants to available water supplies have exercised a much stronger impact upon agricultural agencies than upon urban agencies.

During the past decade or more, internal and external pressures and opportunities have stirred a number of districts located on the east side of the Central Valley to undertake major investments in dams, power plants, and reservoirs. The Feather, Yuba, Bear, American, Mokelumne, Tuolumne, and Merced river systems have each been eyed by at least one agency as a potential site for a project; the large urban agencies of the San Francisco Bay area of course also operate in part of this territory. Our investigation has focused upon these current cases of investment planning, especially on the east side of the Sacramento Valley, and the associated interagency rivalries. This concentration runs little risk of generalizing from a special case, since the area includes the sites of not only the bulk of such projects now being planned in Northern California, but also a significant portion of those constructed by local water agencies in the past.

While projects currently planned or under construction will add substantially to the reservoir storage capacity on these rivers, it is important to keep in mind that storage for consumptive use and power generation is already well developed in the area. Indeed, reservoir sites constitute as scarce a resource in the area as does water itself, in that the remaining sites entail higher construction costs per unit of output or capacity than those utilized in the past. Another important historical fact is that both electric power companies and agricultural water districts have been active in the area for many years, so that both naturally maintain an active interest in further development. Much of the following story will concern a pattern of joint ventures developed by water agencies and the Pacific Gas and Electric Company (PG&E) for the production of electric power and regulation of streamflows, the relation of these projects to the competition for water, and the efficiency of the resulting project scales and designs.

A few facts about the current round of projects planned by local agencies on the east side of the Central Valley both provide useful background and raise important behavioral questions.[31] While ostensibly "owned" by water supply agencies, most of these projects by any test are designed importantly or predominantly to produce electric power. They appear to vary substantially in their unit costs, in the sense that some exhibit estimated construction costs per unit of both water and power output that are considerably lower than others. The estimated costs of the projects tend to be quite high relative to the assessed valuations of the lands lying within the agencies constructing them. Each observation raises important normative or behavioral questions: Are water and power outputs correctly balanced at the margin? Does the insularity of water agencies lead some to construct inefficient projects? Does capital rationing depress the number of projects or affect the scale and efficiency of project designs?

Internal needs, opportunities, and the decision to invest

In the case of the urban agencies considered in the preceding section, we could characterize the investment criterion simply in terms of minimizing the average unit costs of facilities designed to provide an independently chosen level of capacity. No such simple recipe can be found for agricultural districts. Although we shall argue that most of those biases operating upon local urban agencies also affect agricultural districts, the investment decisions of irrigation districts respond to a much wider variety of forces and evidence greater reaction to external opportunities and threats. Thus, before we can describe the process of choosing a project and pressing forward with construction, we must consider the general forces bearing on the decision to invest: the internal signals which identify benefits to be won, and the external pressures and opportunities which powerfully influence the design and timing of projects.

[31] The following propositions and many subsequent generalizations in this section are based on information collected from engineering studies and sundry other sources for thirteen projects which were in the planning or construction stage during roughly the period 1959–63. These sources are cited below in connection with other points.

Agricultural districts do not share the tendency of their urban cousins to treat the amount of water provided as a matter of "requirements" based on the assumption of a perfectly inelastic marginal benefits function. The evidence on demand elasticity reviewed in Chapter 5 suggested that the "true" benefit function is quite elastic for agricultural districts. They in fact take a more flexible view of their water needs than do urban agencies. Certain obvious facts tell of marginal benefits to be obtained. A district which can irrigate only part of the irrigable lands with available supplies has a constant incentive for expanding operations. In some areas, double-cropping or the planting of more profitable water-intensive crops becomes possible with enlarged water applications. Declining ground-water tables point directly to a rising productivity of supplemental surface supplies.[32]

Districts on the east side of the Sacramento Valley have experienced most of these conditions, especially a desire to irrigate more land or to stop the decline of ground-water tables and, in several cases, to provide for an influx of residential population. For instance, in southern Sutter County,[33] when ground-water levels dropped, with the result that irrigation costs increased, landowners responded by looking for a supplemental surface supply, forming a new district to handle planning and construction. A similar condition motivated the farmers across Feather River to the east, in the Wheatland Water District.[34] Districts feel the inadequacy of their water supplies in different degrees. Some, such as the Nevada and Oroville-Wyandotte irrigation districts, employ rationing of water; others, as in the case of the Richvale Irrigation District, could expand irrigated acreage with no apparent reduction in average benefits. In major parts of the area in question, ground water does not provide a suitable alternative to surface supplies.

The users' cooperative hypothesis predicts that an existing district would seek to expand its "plant" to provide an increment of benefits in excess of costs to its members; or that districts would be formed in unorganized territory to construct water development facilities where economic circumstances are favorable. It also predicts an interest in reducing the net cost of existing supplies, whether by a direct cost-reducing investment in storage or transport facilities, or by securing additional supplies at a marginal cost less than the district's going average cost.[35] The motive of cost reduction is significant only if the opportunity to reduce costs is

[32] These propositions are consistent with important features described above of the users' cooperative interpretation applied to agricultural water districts. The statistical evidence reviewed in Chapter 5 suggested that water utilization by irrigators was more responsive to the level of districts' average total unit costs than to their marginal price to water users. Furthermore, in Chapter 10, we noted the role of rationing in dampening the response of water use to "price" in the conventional sense. This evidence implies that, on balance, irrigators are relatively sensitive to the long-run incremental cost of water supplies in relation to the productivity of water at various margins—a conclusion consistent with the propositions stated in the preceding paragraph.

[33] Most agencies, places, and projects mentioned in this chapter can be located in Figures 23 and 24, presented in Chapter 12.

[34] T. H. McGuire and Son, Consulting Engineers, *Camp Far West Project, Feasibility Report* (1958), pp. II-1 and II-2.

[35] Because of the rigidities of district boundaries discussed in Chapter 9 and the typical pricing systems discussd in Chapter 10, the membership presently supplied with "expensive" water by a district could definitely expect to benefit if the district secures a "cheap" supplemental supply that goes to users not previously served.

present, of course, and it has appeared for the eastern Central Valley districts in two important forms. The first, and probably lesser, of these is the opportunity to substitute a reservoir-regulated flow delivered through an efficient distribution system for an unregulated flow delivered through an inefficient system.[36] The second, and greater, opportunity is to exploit the joint product of electric power. A standard form of cooperative venture has emerged between the local districts and Pacific Gas and Electric Company that provides the cooperating districts with what they view as "free water." An agency designs its water project in such a way that it will generate the largest possible amount of hydroelectric power as a complementary product. It next contracts to sell this power to Pacific Gas and Electric Company for a series of uniform, firm semiannual payments sufficient to meet bond interest and redemption requirements, thus covering the total capital cost. A revenue bond issue can then be marketed by the district on the strength of the power purchase contract and the financial standing of PG&E.

The pattern for this procedure came from the Tri-Dam Project, built by two irrigation districts on the Stanislaus River in the San Joaquin Valley and financed by PG&E in this manner. The contract for the power sale was signed on July 9, 1952 (although construction on Tri-Dam Project did not begin until 1955), and it proved to districts elsewhere the model way to finance their own projects, some of which had been languishing for lack of demonstrable financial feasibility.[37]

A few districts have released data on the water-rate effects of new developments of this type now under way. Early expectations on the part of the Oroville-Wyandotte Irrigation District pointed to a retail price of water at $3 an acre-foot to the irrigator, contrasted with the then prevailing rate of $9.[38] This substantial reduction was strongly desired because the $9 rate has allowed the economical application of water to only a small portion of district lands for the cultivation of olives and oranges. The Yuba County Water Agency merely concedes that water will cost whatever the operation and maintenance charges on the major new conveyance channels will require.

Not only do these projects offer the member-customers of local districts the prospect of cheaper water in the short run, but also they provide the enticing prospect of pure profit from the sale of electric power after the bonded indebtedness is paid off (in forty or fifty years). At such a remote point in time, these revenues could substantially exceed financial outlays for operation, maintenance, and replacement of project facilities. Copious political maneuvering for a slice of these far-distant (and uncertain) profits testifies to their importance in motivating the local districts.

"Internal" motives for undertaking water projects, such as benefits from increased water applications and profits from exploiting power generation, probably would not have produced the current upsurge of interest without external pressures in the form of rivalry for ultimately scarce supplies of water and dam sites. Latent or semidormant interest in new water development in many instances has received a jolt from the reports and studies of the California Department of Water Re-

[36] Some of the districts in question, located in the Sierra "gold rush" country, have utilized old mining flumes as transport networks, with very high operating costs as a result.

[37] Tudor-Goodenough Engineers, *Summary Report on the Tri-Dam Project, Stanislaus River, California* (1959).

[38] *Oroville Mercury-Register,* Nov. 22, 1952.

sources (and its predecessor agencies) during the past fifteen years. Dealing with available water resources, their utilization, and with the ultimate requirements of the several sections of the state, these studies aimed toward the design of an official California Water Plan.[39] The first of a series of three major state-wide bulletins based on these investigations appeared in 1951. It drew attention to the need for "redistribution" of water from areas of surplus to areas of deficiency as "the greatest challenge" in water planning.[40] The notion of exporting "surplus" water from the northern part of the state into the south was nothing new, having received serious thought and study since the 1920's and having been put into effect with the construction of the initial features of the Bureau of Reclamation's Central Valley Project. But the renewed attention by the state to this redistribution of water aroused the people on the east side of the Sacramento Valley and farther south. Wherever "surplus" water seemed available for potential export, they stood to lose it to water-hungry Southern California.[41]

At the same time, the Bureau was completing the initial features of the Central Valley Project and had additional plans of its own for water transfers. These plans involved, at one time or another, waters from the Yuba, American, Consumnes, Mokelumne, and Stanislaus rivers (not to mention the largely unused streams of the north coastal region, which it expected gradually to be diverted south and eastward to augment Central Valley water flows and transfers).[42]

To safeguard their surplus for local use many agencies, counties, and individuals in the early 1950's filed applications for water with appropriate state and federal agencies, though in many instances they had only the vaguest of plans for its utilization.

At Christmas time in 1955, a great deal of this surplus water came rushing down the Feather and Yuba rivers, inundating vast stretches of the Sacramento Valley floor, including the twin cities of Marysville and Yuba City. That event reinforced some development plans and gave birth to others, especially those which included flood control components, such as Yuba County's plan for the Yuba River. And the state of California, the Corps of Engineers, and the Bureau of Reclamation dusted

[39] These studies were authorized by the State Water Resources Act of 1945 and were begun in 1947. See California State Water Resources Board, *Water Resources of California*, Bulletin No. 1 (1951), pp. 17–18.

[40] *Ibid.*, p. 22.

[41] To quote the chief engineer of Merced Irrigation District for instance: "Someone is going to make further development on the Merced River; it is only a question of when and by whom." If we "proceed with the development of the Merced River as rapidly as possible," then there will be no fear of losing water to outside interests, because "little or no water will be available for export." (*Merced Sun Star*, July 26, 1956.) In the Yuba River basin, spokesmen advocating local project development cited "fear [that] the state or federal government will step into the picture with a flood control project" which "could cost the five Yuba River Basin counties . . . the water." They also feared it might cost these counties the profits needed to finance irrigation works. (*Sacramento Bee*, Oct. 17, 1958.)

[42] See U.S. Department of the Interior, Bureau of Reclamation, *Central Valley Basin: A Comprehensive Departmental Report on the Development of the Water and Related Resources of the Central Valley Basin, and Comments from the State of California and Federal Agencies*, S. Doc. 113, 81 Cong. 1 sess. (1949). In the 1949 hearings on the American River project, Bureau officials keep referring to their need for more reservoirs to get enough water for the San Joaquin Valley and mentioned the Yuba and Bear rivers as sources. See U.S. Congress, House Committee on Public Lands, Subcommittee on Irrigation and Reclamation, *The American River Basin Project*, hearings, 81 Cong. 1 sess. (1949), pp. 20, 29.

off studies and plans to seek some means of preventing a recurrence of such extensive flood damage.

Their actions, however, brought a reaction on the part of local water agencies and related groups which preferred to build their own projects. The Bureau of Reclamation had been embroiled in protracted negotiations and conflicts with various water users, especially in the San Joaquin Valley, which had generated distrust of and animosity toward this federal agency.[43] Then, on June 23, 1958, the U.S. Supreme Court unanimously reversed the California Supreme Court and confirmed applicability of the Reclamation Act's acreage-limitation provisions in California. This gave "local initiative" a giant shot in the arm.[44] As evidence of this reaction, the year 1959 brought more authorizations by the State Legislature of new county-wide water agencies than any year before or since then. Most of them involved counties enclosing east-side streams with surplus water, as yet unappropriated and undeveloped.[45] To be sure, some of the counties newly equipped with water agencies had no plans for immediate developments of their own and merely sought to protect themselves from inroads of their neighbors or to improve their bargaining position to obtain compensation for such inroads.

Granted the popular assumption that a water export once begun will never cease, California water law encourages—nay, demands—what amounts to premature construction of "defensive" projects. A local agency cannot protect its logical source of water for its own future development merely by a declaration of intent. Water law requires that in order to retain a permit for the appropriation of water (or to be finally granted a license) the applicant must proceed with "due diligence" to put the water to use. "Due diligence" means that unless the holder of a water-use permit proceeds with the planning and construction of a project to put the water to beneficial use, he loses his permit, and the water becomes available to other applicants.[46] Only a positive commitment of resources will assuredly ward off potential competition.[47]

Criteria and constraints affecting investments

With these forces which impel an agency to plan a project for water development in mind, we now show how the objectives of the entrepreneurial agency are trans-

[43] See below, Chapter 13.

[44] *Ivanhoe Irrigation District* vs. *McCracken,* 357 U.S. 275 (1958). Following this decision, for instance, the Yuba County Board of Supervisors reversed its unanimous endorsement of federal development on the Yuba River, which it had agreed to only two months before. The Board instead decided to try to undertake this development itself and, moving with something akin to lightning speed in such endeavors, signed a contract with a major engineering firm to design a Yuba River development plan of its own. *Marysville Appeal-Democrat,* April 14, June 27, Sept. 10, and Oct. 22, 1958.

[45] These included the following counties, all except one of which are mountain counties: Amador, El Dorado, Mariposa, Nevada, Sutter, and Yuba.

[46] California *Water Code* (1963), §§ 1396 and 1410.

[47] McCreary-Koretsky-Engineers, *Feasibility Report, Placer County Water Agency, Middle Fork American River Project* (1961), p. 2.

lated into specific design criteria, and how the external constraints and opportunities affect the scale and design of the project and the timing of construction.

The instructions of water districts to their engineering staffs give some insight into the investment criteria employed. At the very least, they specify the constraints upon the maximum physical scale of project which the agency wishes to undertake. The constraints often stand out more clearly than the objective which they limit. The ceiling imposed on the size of the proposed project may be stated in terms of the ability of the agency or its present or potential constituent members to use water at some time in the future,[48] or to develop those water resources available within the agency's boundaries.[49] Often the agency's ability to finance a project, or some related agency-oriented parameter, will be set as a constraint upon the project.[50]

The underlying goal to be pursued is usually stated with less clarity. Sometimes maximum profits for the agency are specified. More often the sponsor indicates a level of unit water costs and asks for the largest project compatible with this cost level. This prescription might with charity be taken as calling for marginal costs to be equated to marginal benefits with an elastic marginal-benefit function, but it could equally well refer to average magnitudes. Sometimes the objective is stated in terms of the "full development" of a particular source of water, a concept with primarily physical connotations and no perceptible relation to marginal benefits and costs. Finally, in some cases, agricultural districts seem to follow the practice of urban agencies and specify the provision of a given quantity of water at minimum cost as the desired objective. None of these rules necessarily coincides with equating marginal benefits with marginal costs, although any of them could do so in an imaginary case. Probably the most important and prevalent of these objectives is that of securing the maximum attainable quantity of water at a given cost level. In the context of joint ventures between local districts and PG&E, this objective becomes one of finding the project with the largest yield of irrigation water for which PG&E will agree to pay the capital costs. The costs which remain to be met by the local district are typically the fixed costs of designing and promoting the project and of any improvements in the distribution system needed to put its water output to use, plus associated operation and maintenance costs. This would seem to imply an arbitrary and quite low level of assumed marginal benefits to the agricultural district.

Whatever the maximization rule employed, the power of various constraints over the maximum scale of the project seems notably strong in the case of agricultural agencies, whether they result from evaluating only benefits to accrue within a specified area, sticking to the development only of water within district's boundaries, or restricting capital costs to its borrowing ability. Only one case has emerged of a district investigating a project having benefits well beyond its own boundaries. This was a proposal by Wheatland Water District (later Johnson Rancho County Water District) of a vast development plan for the Yuba River which would make water

[48] See, for example, Gillett-Harris & Associates and Woodward-Clyde-Sherard & Associates, *Feasibility Studies of Extensions to Irrigation Facilities for Browns Valley Irrigation District* (1958), pp. 1–3.

[49] See International Engineering Company, Inc., *Report on Development of Water Resources of Yuba River* (1961), p. II–2.

[50] See Bechtel Corporation, *Preliminary Feasibility Report on Yuba River Development* (1959), p. S–2.

available for export beyond the boundaries of Yuba County.[51] Oroville-Wyandotte Irrigation District, which became embroiled in a long conflict with Yuba County Water District (not to be confused with the county-wide Yuba County Water Agency), considered building a project large enough to meet the claims of this competing agency. The Yuba District, similarly, explored the possibility of designing a development to meet the needs of both agencies. Both failed for lack of sufficient financial capability. The Oroville-Wyandotte Irrigation District ended with a project reduced in some respects (although augmented in others), because the constellation of bond interest rates and contractors' bids did not cover the facilities earlier proposed for inclusion.[52] The Yuba District received a pay-off and a part of the water, a combination which may eventually permit it to supply its water needs.

Some concern for the efficiency of project designs emerges from this strong evidence that characteristics of the sponsoring agency impose constraints upon the scale of the project. Abundant descriptive evidence suggests that serious capital rationing and capital-market imperfections affected the investment decisions of local districts before World War II.[53] Such evidence of capital rationing still exists, along with a marked prevalence of other agency-oriented parameters influencing the design of projects, and these factors can impair the efficiency of the investment process in ways indicated in Chapter 8. This fear of the effect of agency-oriented constraints should not be overemphasized, however, for two reasons. First, large-scale projects throughout California receive ample attention from the Bureau of Reclamation, Corps of Engineers, and California Department of Water Resources. Where an agency-oriented constraint would prove serious, a higher level government will sometimes step in. Second, county-wide agencies, less affected by such constraints than small districts, have taken on a major role during the past decade.

Beyond the prevailing maximization rules and constraints, the design practices of agricultural districts seem largely to parallel those of urban agencies on such matters as the choice of a discount rate and the treatment of future prices. The implications for performance are the same in both cases. The two groups diverge only in the handling of uncertainty. For agricultural districts, the avoidance of physical uncertainty in water supplies becomes a relatively expensive luxury that cannot be afforded. The avoidance of economic uncertainty relative to the ability of the entrepreneurial agency to meet its financial obligations, however, holds great importance. Let us turn, then, to the steps through which an agency must go in shepherding its project toward the construction stage.

[51] L. Cedric Macabee, Consulting Engineer, *Feasibility Report on the Yuba River Development for the Wheatland Water District, Yuba County, California* (1954), p. I–1; also see Kaiser Engineers, *Engineering Review of Yuba River Development for Johnson Rancho County Water District* (1961).

[52] *Oroville Mercury-Register*, Jan. 30, 1953, June 15, 1960; *Marysville Appeal-Democrat*, Oct. 28, 1955, June 9, 1956, Aug. 31 and Sept. 7, 1959; *Sacramento Bee*, May 6, May 21, and Nov. 8, 1959, April 15, 1960.

[53] For example, J. Rupert Mason, "Single-Tax, Irrigation Districts, and Municipal Bankruptcy" (Typescript, University of California General Library, Berkeley, 1958), pp. 25–98, which describes the evolution of the local government bond market in California from 1914 on; and Harry Erlich and P. H. McGauhey, "Calaveras River Case Study," *Economic Evaluation of Water: Part II. Jurisdictional Considerations in Water Resources Management* (1964), pp. 115–70.

Designing a joint project

The first stage in bringing to completion a joint project of a local district and PG&E is for the district to interest the utility in such a venture and get agreement on its tentative design. (Such agreement is in the form of PG&E's "letter of intent" to purchase the anticipated power output.) At this stage, the "mixture" of joint products—electric power and irrigation water—undergoes an initial determination, along with the scale of the project. The district's interest in bargaining is clear: to secure the maximum yield of irrigation water for which PG&E will pay the capital costs. The utility's motivation is harder to interpret. Ostensibly, it procures power through these joint ventures up to the point where the marginal cost equals the cost of alternative steam generation facilities. The utility's goals may cut on either side of this norm, however. Since the districts retain title to the projects, they do not enter into the utility's "rate base," and thus fail to increase its allowable profits in the eyes of the Public Utilities Commission. On the other hand, the Company may be interested in undertaking these projects for their public relations value or in order to preclude their construction by the Bureau of Reclamation or other government agencies.[54]

Negotiations between the parties over the design of a proposed development can continue for years, often concurrently with proceedings before the various state regulatory authorities. There is no way of telling how the bargaining power lies in these negotiations. The extent to which either party has what it considers acceptable alternatives is subject to widely varying interpretations.[55] Futhermore, the calculations upon which PG&E's offers are based are made available neither to the partner-to-be nor to the general public. The trend of adjustments in the project plans is clear, however. Installed power capacity tends to gain and planned irrigation water deliveries to be reduced in the early years in favor of water releases designed to yield more energy, but often coming in the wrong place and at the wrong time for irrigation. Facilities that can remotely be considered frills or nonessentials are lopped off a project or at least postponed (usually beyond the repayment period). For the first fifty years, many of these plans turn out to be primarily power projects.[56]

In view of the small irrigation benefits to their sponsors which some of these projects yield over their pay-out period, one can only believe that local districts derive significant utility from merely having their nameplates on projects. Other explanations, however, may also reconcile this interest of water districts in undertaking power projects. The Nevada Irrigation District, with much of its land un-

[54] These normative issues are considered in Chapter 15.

[55] On the one hand, most of these projects probably would not be feasible for the water districts without PG&E's participation; on the other, assistance from federal or state agencies might well be forthcoming. The bargaining elements are considered further in Chapter 14.

[56] "The recommended Development provides sufficient storage to regulate unappropriated water available to the Agency to meet its ultimate requirements. However, during the 45 years of its indebted life, regulation will be influenced by power requirements at some sacrifice to a firm water supply. In view of the need for power revenue to support the financing of the development, it would not be economical to regulate streamflows to obtain a maximum firm water supply with undue curtailment of usable power generation." International Engineering Company, Inc., *op. cit.*, p. ix.

irrigated, has continued to design additions to its water supply chiefly to provide new power revenues, rather than maximum supplies of irrigation water.[57] This District suffered serious financial hardships beginning with its early days in the middle 1920's, especially when the depression and a simultaneous five-year dry period reduced revenues far below bond service requirements on its first power project. In its present plans, the Nevada District has shunned taking the risk of variable power revenues and aimed at an assured self-financing project at the expense of water yield. In other cases, not risk avoidance but uses for profits may explain the emphasis on power generation. Lower costs to existing water users, at the expense of potential benefits from the irrigation of now unirrigated land, may suit the water users in control of a district. A county water agency, with broader horizons, may find many uses for its profits. The Placer County Water Agency has pushed to develop what is largely a power project, in the hope of sufficient revenues to pay for the construction of irrigation structures elsewhere in the county.

Whatever the motivation of the local districts, the role of PG&E is pervasive: without the Company's power payments, projects could not be built at all (under present circumstances and conditions, including costs, institutional patterns, etc.), at least not at the time and by the agencies now undertaking them. The Pacific Gas and Electric Company is very influential in determining the design of projects, the sequence of construction, and who, among competitors, succeeds. Indirectly, therefore, PG&E determines the future schedule and pattern of water sales for both domestic and agricultural purposes. The utility, in turn, gains through the local districts' powers to issue tax-exempt securities and the freedom of the works from property taxes. And, as noted earlier, it also averts the threat of competing power sales either by local public bodies or by state or federal agencies which might otherwise lay claim to the dam sites.

Engineering firms may have less effect, but still significant influence, in a project's early stages. The financing of engineering studies often proves quite difficult for a district, especially if it plans to add a project to a small base of existing facilities. Relatively large taxes must be extracted from the prospective beneficiaries, the district's member-customers, without the directors being able to promise a definite return in the form of a successful project. Therefore, the practice has developed in some cases of hiring engineering firms with payment to be made only if a viable project results. Once a district completes the major financing for construction, engineering costs can be easily met.

One also wonders whether engineering firms play a significant role, in that the character and scale of the project chosen may depend on which engineers plan it. This question is hard to answer, since most projects receive a full investigation by only one firm. In those cases where different engineers prepare designs for a given project according to the same given maximization criterion, they essentially emerge with the same project. Differences in planned sizes of particular reservoirs and

[57] One historical Sacramento irrigation promoter referred to Nevada as a "power district"—usually a somewhat derogatory term. See Charles F. Lambert, "Land Speculation and Irrigation Development in the Sacramento Valley, 1905–1957" (Typescript, University of California General Library, Berkeley, 1957), pp. 198–99.

power installations are not likely to exceed 15 per cent,[58] although there may be variations on finer points, such as safety factors. When different agencies are involved, however, using different criteria, substantial engineering differences may emerge. The Bureau of Reclamation has the reputation of being very conservative in its specifications, and PG&E reveals conservatism in some respects.[59]

Establishing and protecting financial feasibility

Once the preliminary design is complete, a project must go through a series of stages before construction. Each stage may offer enemies of the project a chance to undermine it. Each disappointment in clearing these hurdles may threaten the political solidarity for the project among the sponsoring district's constituency. The various stages of project planning may interact in complicated ways, so that changes or delays in a project may be compounded. The fact that the local government units seldom have experience in entrepreneurial activities of this magnitude makes their task no easier. Here we shall emphasize two of the many aspects of this sequence: (1) the activities undertaken to establish and protect the financial feasibility of a project; and (2) the ways in which the policies of regulatory agencies and the opposition of other agencies may affect the design and timing of a project.

From an analysis of these stages of planning one gains insight into the strength of different constraints imposed on local districts, and also their rationality in terms of correct allocative decisions. Does the restraining hand of the capital market impose inefficient rationing, or does it stay the enthusiasm of local promoters for projects with subnormal benefit-cost ratios? Do the forms of special financial assistance from the state and federal government offset restrictions on the ability of local agencies and compensate for external benefits of their projects, or does this assistance simply promote inefficient construction? Do the many opportunities for intervention which arise in regulatory proceedings give an adequate hearing to the prospective external diseconomies of a project, or do they merely provide a channel for harassment and bureaucratic rivalry?

Establishing the financial feasibility of a project involves implicit investment criteria just as important as those considered above. Once a project has been designed, the capital markets must be convinced that the agency can repay all financial obligations that must be incurred. Governmental sources of financial assistance must be sought so far as they are available and necessary. The member-customers of the agency must be induced to provide full support to produce the necessary majorities in bond elections.

[58] Three or four agencies studied Bullard Bar Reservoir on the Yuba River, and all recommended a storage capacity between 900,000 and 1,000,000 acre-feet.

[59] In some ways, PG&E's alleged conservatism relates to extracting the maximum power output from a project. That means, for instance, avoiding friction in power feed tunnels through smoother excavation methods and more lining. The utility, when dealing with public districts, also presses for investment features which will economize on its later maintenance costs, such as designing power houses so that access can be had to turbines without first removing the generators.

Once a district and PG&E have reached agreement upon a project, the debt-service costs of which are to be met by firm payments by PG&E, the district need anticipate no serious difficulty in selling its bonds. Revenue bonds can be issued, marrying the advantages of PG&E's credit rating with the tax advantages of local government securities. In the rare case of a project lacking a joint arrangement with PG&E, general-obligation bonds must usually be issued, and they are clearly restricted in relation to the current assessed valuation of the district. Thus, the typical project involving PG&E's participation is not afflicted by capital rationing at such scale as the utility is willing to finance; but those without such joint participation (including a number constructed in the past) clearly encounter this constraint.

Whatever type of bond financing is employed, a local election is normally required to approve it. The mobilization of the support of an agency's member-customers for a project focuses upon this election, which constitutes the only formal expression of the membership (as distinguished from elected leaders) on the project. All the fine arts of local public relations are brought to bear in these election campaigns, since an outcome much short of unanimity may threaten the salability of the bonds. The electorate generally goes along, but internal dissent may arise when a project is long delayed or altered by external forces.

The planning process for an ultimately successful project moves toward a definitive establishment of its financial feasibility. The first phase ends with the completion of these related activities: (1) the basic feasibility report, containing a description of project features considered to have engineering feasibility, together with operating schedules to show how much water and—if applicable—power it will yield; (2) a cost analysis of a fairly routine variety, often including large contingency components to cover possible construction problems cloaked by present uncertainties; and (3) estimates of anticipated revenues and suggestions for financing sufficient, if possible, to meet annual costs of construction, operation, maintenance, and replacement. Even in the absence of the external influences on cost to be discussed below, the project's feasibility may face many further tests and threats.

As geologic and hydrologic surveying commences in the field, older, perhaps generalized, information may prove inaccurate. The dam location may have to be moved, or it may be possible to build it larger, or necessary to build it smaller, than initially contemplated. In the case of earth and rockfill dams, the distance to adequate sources of fill material becomes crucial. It may determine the final composition of the dam. When tunnels and canals are involved, the material through which they are to be cut usually is not tested sufficiently until just before—or even during—construction to ascertain whether or not they will require lining or realigning. Similarly, the design of the spillway may require modification as the result of further investigation or, in some instances, at the request of the Supervision of Dam Safety Office.

The resolution of these uncertainties more often than not increases the apparent financial cost of the project. This trend (plus any fortuitous rise in interest rates which may occur while a project is being planned) often threatens the financial feasibility of the initial design. Agencies are often forced to revise their initial plans by reducing the scales of their projects, shaving the design, or postponing separable features. At the financial end, they may seek additional sources of financing or try to renegotiate the contract with the power customer (PG&E). Agencies have resorted to all of these, often in combination. Renegotiation, or an attempt to enlarge power revenues, is standard procedure for all agencies planning to generate power whenever any event occurs that raises, or threatens to raise, costs or requires their reduction.

Similarly, agencies customarily explore further sources of financing which may be available at a lower cost, or no cost, whenever doing so promises to enhance the feasibility of their project. These are available in several forms. Since 1958, federal loans up to $5 million have been available (interest-free except to the extent that lands in excess of 160 acres in one ownership are to be served) for financing the whole of a small project or supplementing a larger one.[60] These loans under P.L. 984 have been utilized by several Northern California districts. Acceptance of one of these loans from the Bureau of Reclamation, pursuant to congressional appropriation, requires submission to various Bureau rules and regulations, ranging from design of structures to keeping of accounts. Districts find the interest-free feature attractive but not these requirements. From the federal government, pursuant to congressional authorization and appropriation, it is also at times possible to obtain an outright contribution commensurate with the flood control benefits which a local development would contribute. Every agency now studying a development has sought to obtain a federal contribution to any flood control benefits it could claim, but few have been successful.

In addition, the state of California has set up a Local Project Assistance Fund of $130 million in connection with the State Water Fund, from which it will loan up to $4 million, or grant up to $400,000, to local agencies for project construction, feasibility reports, and fishery or recreation enhancement under the provisions of the Davis-Grunsky Act.[61] Loans carry interest at the prevailing rate paid by the state. A number of agencies have taken advantage of these funds, sometimes in combination with a federal loan. These moneys are designed specifically to help those agencies which cannot obtain loan funds from other sources, and may be disbursed even when repayment is dubious.[62] Furthermore, the State Legislature has appeared willing to amend the program whenever an applicant could not qualify under its existing terms, and amendments have been numerous. The varied sources of state and federal funds available to local districts clearly help to combat the impact of capital rationing and, in some cases, compensate for external benefits

[60] Small Reclamation Projects Act, P.L. 984, 84 Cong. 2 sess.

[61] California *Statutes* (1959), ch. 1752, as amended in *Statutes* (1961), chs. 520, 1286, 1348, and 1723. Loans or grants in excess of these ceilings can be made, but only by special authorization of the Legislature. Further amendments to the program in 1963 liberalized the degree to which feasibility reports could be financed through Davis-Grunsky loans and otherwise increased the types of projects which could be financed through loans and grants and the freedom of the state to enter into joint planning and construction of projects with local agencies. See *Western Water News* (October 1963), p. 3.

[62] In the case of a loan to the South Sutter Water District, the Department of Water Resources cited a number of contingencies which might have an adverse bearing on repayment, but declared that this "element of risk . . . is within the intent of the Davis-Grunsky Act." California Department of Water Resources, *Report of Findings on Formal Application for a State Loan for Camp Far West Project* (1962), p. 2.

which local districts would otherwise ignore. Indeed, their easy terms and low or nonexistent interest rates raise the possibility that projects thereby reach construction despite deficient benefit-cost relations.[63]

Influence of external regulators and rivals

A project proposed for construction must run a whole gamut of state and federal agencies or authorities for assorted approvals, permits, licenses, and other formal or informal arrangements. These cover the water to be utilized, the land to be occupied, the safety of structures to be built, relations with and protection of other claimants of water, arrangements for recreation facilities and for fishery protection or enhancement, safeguarding of assorted federal interests (relating primarily to public lands and to navigable rivers), consistency with the California Water Plan and with "a comprehensive plan" (under the Federal Power Act), as well as the financing plans related to the payment capacity of prospective water users, security for bond holders, and feasibility of the proposal. Prior plans of the Corps of Engineers or the Bureau of Reclamation or both may have to be considered and reconciled. When federal or state funds are required in aid of construction, still other considerations come into play.[64]

In the course of these proceedings, elements of rivalry for water, dam sites, or other scarce resources or opportunities are thrashed out. Some of the approvals for a project by higher governments thus merely place a seal of approval upon the results of economic bargaining or legal maneuvers among competing local agencies. At other procedural stages, however, state or federal agencies impose constraints or criteria of their own upon the project. Some of the criteria, especially those spelled out in state laws, are fairly well known and understood; others may be far more elusive until the agencies enforcing them have been consulted. We consider these regulatory agencies in turn, reviewing the criteria they employ and the opportunities they provide for a project's opponents.

The Department of Water Resources essentially undertakes only auxiliary staff functions, performed for and at the request of the California Water Commission, which employs only a small staff of its own, and for the Districts Securities Com-

[63] See *ibid.*, pp. 6–7; Stone and Youngberg, *Financial Analysis, Camp Far West Project, South Sutter Water District* (1958); T. H. McGuire and Son, *op. cit.* This Camp Far West Project of South Sutter Water District is a good illustration of the problem. No evidence proves that its benefits will fall short of its costs, but the excess of benefits is clearly no better than slight, and the Project has made heavy use of special financing. The Project is estimated to provide water to the District at a cost below current ground-water costs, but definitely above the prices paid for agricultural water in similar surrounding territory. The mixture of financing sources first proposed, including a loan under P.L. 984 and some general-obligation bonds, was found by the South Sutter District's bond consultants to be extremely risky, since the general-obligation bonds would constitute 65 per cent of the District's assessed valuation. As a result, a special loan to the District was approved by the State Legislature (*Statutes* [1959], ch. 2163). When the special loan and the P.L. 984 funds proved insufficient to meet the lowest bid for construction of the project, another loan from the state under the Davis-Grunsky Act was secured.

[64] The legal background of these regulatory proceedings has been summarized in Chapter 3.

mission, which does some of its own engineering review work. Nevertheless, even in this secondary capacity, the Department's view may be influential in shaping a development. Its main function tends to be to guide the California Water Commission in determining whether projects are in conflict with a general and coordinated plan of development of California's water resources,[65] of which the California Water Plan may serve as a model.[66] Entrepreneurial agencies tend to shape their proposals accordingly, or assert that their own plans will not interfere with further implementation of a general and coordinated plan of development. The Department, not so much under specific legislation as in its over-all role as guardian and promoter of state water development, has also assumed at times a strong role in trying to compromise conflicts among competing agencies. Here again, it has acted as an adjunct, in part, to the California Water Commission.

The Water Commission is frequently the first state body with which a would-be builder of a water development has formal dealings. It is the guardian of the filings of applications to appropriate unappropriated water first executed in 1927 by the State Department of Finance.[67] Inasmuch as most large-scale sources of currently available water are covered by these state filings,[68] a project planner must apply to the Commission for assignment to him of the relevant state filing or a part thereof, or of release from priority of the state filing in his favor. The Commission performs these assignment or release functions under two criteria: (1) a proposed project must not impair the future water requirements of the counties of origin; (2) it must not be in conflict with a general and coordinated plan of development of the state's water resources.

Since the Water Commission is largely guided by the Department of Water Resources in its findings as to consistency with a coordinated plan, an agency will shape its project and conduct its negotiations with the Department's staff, but possibly under guidance of the Commission. To anticipate the claims of the counties of origin, the promoting agency will usually ascertain the wishes of these counties and attempt to compromise with them. The Commission will accept agreements as an indication that the interests of the counties of origin have been satisfied as required by law.

When agreement is impossible, or when an agency designs a development plan without apparent regard for the upstream claimants, the Water Commission will allocate shares of the water in its approval of the assignment or release from priority of state filings. It is probably correct to say that if the conflicts can be

[65] California *Water Code* (1963), § 10504.

[66] California State Water Resources Board, *The California Water Plan,* Bulletin No. 3 (1957). The California Water Plan, however, is not mentioned in the legislation as a model for a general and coordinated plan of development.

[67] A 12-page list of these and subsequent state filings can be found in California State Legislature, Senate Fact Finding Committee on Water, *Budgets, Reports, Local Assistance for State Water Development,* Report No. 2 (1961), pp. 81–93.

[68] Unappropriated streamflow in California not covered by existing water rights or pending water rights applications as of 1960 is estimated to range from zero in the average of the three driest years to 2.8 million acre-feet per annum for the long-term average (of the 50-year period 1894–95 through 1946–47 for the north coastal area, and of the 30 years preceding 1954–55 for the Central Valley area), to 16 million acre-feet per annum for the average of the three wettest years. All of the long-term average and almost one-half of the average of three wettest years occurs in the north coastal area. (*Ibid.,* p. 80.)

compromised easily, the parties will usually anticipate Commission action with stipulations, shaping their projects accordingly. If the conflicts are irreconcilable, and if the Commission considers them to fall within its jurisdiction, it will attempt to decide the issues or, alternatively, to pass them on to the California State Water Rights Board. In arriving at such decisions, the Commission makes a special effort to leave the entrepreneur agency with a feasible project.

The Water Rights Board has jurisdiction over all applications for permits to appropriate unappropriated water (except percolating ground water), so that it will pass on a somewhat greater number of cases than the Water Commission. In the words of the Board:

> The intended use must be beneficial and there must be unappropriated water available. . . . The board is authorized to issue permits upon such terms as in its judgment will best develop, conserve, and utilize in the public interest the water sought to be appropriated . . . [and to] reject an application when in its judgment the proposed appropriation would not best conserve the public interest.[69]

Private, local public, and all other agencies, including those of the state and the federal governments, come to the Water Rights Board under California water law to apply under those terms, or to contest other applications.

To anticipate the Board's action, an applicant will first of all design his project to use what he believes to be unappropriated water. The criterion of beneficial use is combined with the Board's duty to protect the interest of domestic or agricultural customers on the one hand, and proper provision for other water uses, such as fishery protection, recreation, on the other. Would-be builders, for instance, usually obtain from the Department of Fish and Game at the very outset of their studies those releases which that Department considers necessary to maintain fish life below proposed structures, and take them into account in calculating the details of construction and output. (This does not mean that differences of opinion about and modifications of these release patterns do not occur.) As far as the "public interest" is concerned, it is probably difficult to anticipate what the Water Rights Board may see as its function and to design that into the project in advance. Its standards do include the safeguarding of existing projects, such as the Bureau of Reclamation's Central Valley Project, against later claims for water.[70]

The Water Commission and the Water Rights Board also play vital roles in the process of settling the conflicts which embroil the agencies proposing to develop projects. Upon the filing of the application with the Commission and/or the Board and publication thereof, interested counterclaimants ask to be heard, intervene, protest, or otherwise make themselves known. To satisfy the statutory criteria of the Water Commission, an agency must usually negotiate with existing water

[69] California State Water Rights Board, *Second Annual Report, Covering Period July 1, 1957–June 30, 1958* (1958), p. 8.

[70] California State Water Rights Board, Decision No. D 935 (San Joaquin River), June 1959; Decision No. D 990 (Sacramento River), February, 1961; also see U.S. Congress Senate, Joint Subcommittee of Committee on Appropriations and Committee on Interior and Insular Affairs, *Bureau of Reclamation, Interior Department,* Hearings on the Solano Project in California, 82 Cong. 2 sess. (1953), pp. 34, 42.

agencies or county governments located upstream from the applicant and thus having county-of-origin protection. In addition, protests may come from agencies sponsoring a competing plan, irrespective of county-of-origin rights or consistency with the California Water Plan. Such competing proposals constitute the strongest form of intervention, even though their standing before the Water Rights Board depends on their ability to claim priority as to time of filing or some other basis of water rights.

The protests of competing local agencies reflect sometimes an honest concern with protecting opportunities for local development, but sometimes merely a desire to garner for themselves a share of the implicit profits likely to accrue to the entrepreneur agency.[71] Typically, the protestant claims that the applicant's project, if built, would deprive him of needed water. The protestant has a price at which he is willing to withdraw his objection, and the sponsor must either meet it or bargain it down in order to secure the desired actions from the Water Commission and Water Rights Board. While the "price" is usually stated in terms of a quantity of water to be reserved for the protestant, this water often appears convertible into dollars. If the protestant really wants to foil the sponsor's plans, he can effectively do so by holding out for too high a price in either water or money, but such an attitude is uncommon. Most projects under construction or under consideration for the east side of the Central Valley are not so feasible financially as to be able to withstand much of a payoff. These facts, plus the difficulty of determining what the implicit profits from a project really are, tend to promote extensive negotiations.[72]

When one of the opponents or interveners is promoting a definite development plan of his own, scarce water supplies become definitely the bone of contention, and the pattern of compromise tends toward a reduction in the scale of competing projects. Occasionally the intervening agencies do not possess an active competing demand for water, but instead possess a right to potential use in the form of prior filings for water rights, county-of-origin status, and the like. In such cases, compromise may result in a cash payoff, such as the $4 million given by East Bay Municipal Utility District to Amador and Calaveras counties. These are rare, however, because only municipal agencies tend to be able to afford this means of settling protests.

Another equally ubiquitous claimant is the California Department of Fish and Game, which has taken an increasingly vigorous stand in order not only to protect and maintain existing fisheries, but to eke out measures for their enhancement. The Department usually intervenes with the Water Commission, the Water Rights Board, and the Federal Power Commission, where it may be joined by the U.S. Fish and Wildlife Service of the Department of the Interior. In some instances, agreement—and, hence, stipulation and withdrawal of objections—may be reached

[71] These protests and the substance of the resulting conflicts are discussed more fully in Chapter 12.

[72] To take a few cases in the Sacramento foothills: Oroville-Wyandotte Irrigation District spent six years in negotiating with Yuba County opponents until a price was reached. Then suddenly, adverse financial conditions forced it to renegotiate to save its project. Richvale Irrigation District has faced conflicting demands for water without which its proposed project is believed to be infeasible. Yuba County Water Agency declared itself willing to meet claims to water asserted by counties of origin, but not to accede to monetary claims in lieu thereof.

before the Water Commission approves an assignment, but in really obstinate situations, such as one involving the Richvale Irrigation District plan for the Middle Fork of Feather River, the Water Commission passes the unresolved conflict on to the Water Rights Board. Depending on the importance of the fisheries in the particular stream to be developed and on the extent of the anticipated damage thereto by the applicant's plan, the fisheries negotiations may be relatively simple or bitter, extended, and costly.

The actual procedure before the Water Commission and Water Rights Board consists largely of registering disagreements and reporting compromises. The two agencies seek strongly to minimize the conflicts remaining for formal resolution and devote considerable effort to reconciling conflicts which would disqualify an application under their respective criteria. Both agencies avoid making active determinations themselves, One tool for promoting compromise is simply the postponement or, alternatively, the timely scheduling of hearings.

At various stages of investment planning and execution, many agencies also have to satisfy the requirements of the Districts Securities Commission. Born of the many defaults of irrigation districts during the depression of the 1930's and the simultaneous critical seven-year drought, this agency aims to make district bonds safe and attractive for buyers and thus to facilitate district financing. Also it seeks to protect districts in the negotiation of contracts with other agencies.[73] In order to perform its functions, the Commission examines the feasibility of proposed projects, financing plans and proposed contracts with such water wholesalers as the Bureau of Reclamation, or with lenders or underwriters of funds. An irrigation district must have the Commission's approval before it may invest major sums, call bond elections, sell bonds, or sign contracts. A water agency therefore must submit its investment plans to the Districts Securities Commission and attempt to satisfy it of their soundness.

Federal Power Commission (FPC) jurisdiction relates to licensing projects proposed for construction on navigable waters and their tributaries or on public lands; the law requires that a project, to be licensed, be "best adapted to a comprehensive plan" for development of a waterway. The FPC also requires that an applicant for a federal hydroelectric license have his state water rights in order and satisfy various federal interests as to the lands to be occupied (especially national parks or national forests), as to fish protection, recreation resources or benefits, and financial feasibility of the project. On these points having to do with federal interests, applicants usually consider and largely honor the requests of federal agencies before completing their applications to the Federal Power Commission, although fisheries problems and land requirements sometimes remain for determination after a license is obtained. As far as the basic requirements of comprehensive development of water resources is concerned, agencies tend to do no more than bow in the FPC's direction in planning their projects. In collaboration with the California Depart-

[73] The District Securities Commission has statutory jurisdiction over irrigation and water storage districts only, but other public districts may avail themselves of its bond certification services. If they do so, they have to reciprocate by filing annual reports on their financial conditions and activities.

ment of Water Resources, they tend now to try to make a showing that any project which receives the Department's approval and that of the California Water Commission as consistent with a general and coordinated plan of development is *prima facie* best adopted to a comprehensive plan. This procedure ordinarily removes the burden for any additional showing to satisfy the Federal Power Commission, whose past performance in California indicates that it is easily satisfied.[74]

Inasmuch as the bias of the Federal Power Act tends to favor development of river basins as against their dormancy, it is perhaps plausible that almost any applicant with almost any kind of a project would receive favorable consideration if the alternative appears to consist of nondevelopment.

Water Investments by State and Federal Agencies

In Chapter 8, we contrasted the investment behavior which one might expect from agencies of state and federal governments in the water business with that hypothesized for local governments. The beneficiaries of particular investments by federal and state agencies typically constitute a small segment of those who will bear the costs, since the full costs are seldom if ever charged to local beneficiaries and some classes of benefits are declared entirely nonreimbursable. Whatever the merit of technical planning criteria used by the agencies at higher levels, their decisions to proceed with an investment are unlikely to meet with reluctance from the beneficiaries. The check which is imposed by Congress or the State Legislature, representing those who pay the residual costs, is essentially political and may or may not serve the interests of economic efficiency.

The investment practices of the federal agencies, the Bureau of Reclamation and Corps of Engineers, have been studied extensively at the national level in recent years.[75] We will not undertake an elaborate documentation of those aspects of their California activities which merely follow national practice. Instead, we shall investigate planning activities specifically related to California projects, including their relation to local clamor for construction by higher level governments and the actions of the latter in the context of local water rivalries. As between the two federal agencies, the Bureau has been far more active in Northern California and will receive the bulk of our attention. The enormous California Water Plan of the state of California has been evolving only during the course of our study, and we shall review the investment planning practices of the California Department of Water Resources only briefly.

[74] Indeed, it may be more easily satisfied than state water authorities, as indicated by the fact that in other states it has licensed projects which had been rejected by state authorities, or set aside requirements imposed by these authorities. (See Chapter 3.)

[75] See Otto Eckstein, *Water-Resource Development; The Economics of Project Evaluation* (1958); Alfred R. Golzé, *Reclamation in the United States* (2nd ed.; 1961). Among volumes dealing with the Army Corps of Engineers are one prepared for RFF by John V. Krutilla and Otto Eckstein, *Multiple Purpose River Development* (1958), and one by Arthur Maass, *Muddy Waters: The Army Engineers and the Nation's Rivers* (1951).

Investment criteria of federal agencies

The federal agencies have pioneered in moving toward the use of an investment criterion which closely parallels the normative ideal which we outlined in Chapter 8. Marginal benefits and costs are now calculated, in at least some cases, although a bias may remain to scale projects for full physical development of a resource, even if marginal benefits fall below marginal costs. Concepts of benefits have been refined to the point where many of the major types of economic confusion have been removed. Sometimes a wide range of alternative designs is considered for a given project.[76] Certain systematic errors remain, however, along with statutory or bureaucratic biases of the constructing agencies which make them unequally sensitive to different types of benefits or costs associated with projects.

The calculations of benefits differ favorably from those of local agencies in attempting to cover all types of benefits and to include them no matter where they accrue. Primary or direct benefits are usually measured by broadly reasonable procedures which test the surplus or net product attributable to the outputs of the project in question or, as an alternative, the lowest cost of securing equivalent outputs from some other source. Some practices of the Bureau and the Corps have been criticized for including in the estimated net product of their projects some elements which are really opportunity costs. This charge is particularly valid and significant for the calculation of secondary benefits; such benefits have been attacked as containing few if any items of imputed income which do not reflect an output foregone elsewhere.[77] Apart from errors of principle in calculating benefits, these agencies have been suspected of bias in the detailed estimations—either to overstate total benefits or to understate those particular types of benefits whose allocated costs, under federal law, must be collected from the beneficiaries.

Furthermore, the federal agencies commit some of the same errors in the handling of benefits and costs as do local governments. They incorporate the same biases in neglecting opportunity costs of water and such "disbenefits" as harm done to in-stream recreational resources. Estimates by the Bureau and Corps of the benefits of municipal water supplies make the same assumption of perfectly inelastic marginal benefits as do the plans of municipal agencies, incorrect in the light of evidence cited in Chapter 5.

[76] A good example of the consideration of alternative dam sites to provide water for a given service area appears in the planning of the Bureau of Reclamation's Folsom South Canal, designed for lands on the east side of the Central Valley. The Canal's proposed service area lies between the American River on the north and the Stanislaus River on the south. Between them it intersects the Consumnes, Mokelumne, and Calaveras rivers. Each of these rivers was considered as a possible basic source of water for the project, with the American on the north finally chosen. Though its water would evidently incur higher transportation costs, the American River offers a larger quantity of apparently unappropriated water and a large low-cost dam site. See U.S. Department of the Interior, Bureau of Reclamation, Region 2, *Folsom South Unit, Central Valley Project, California: A Report on the Feasibility of Water Supply Development* (1960), chaps. 4 and 10.

[77] On the other hand, it is not clear that the calculation of secondary effects has gone as far as it might in considering contributions to social welfare other than through increasing national real income. See U.S. Bureau of the Budget, Panel of Consultants, *Standards and Criteria for Formulating and Evaluating Federal Water Resources Development* (1961), chap. 3.

The most disturbing feature of the feasibility reports prepared for projects constructed in California by the Bureau and the Corps is the presence of manifest biases tending to inflate the resultant benefit-cost ratios. For example, the feasibility report for the Sacramento Canals (several proposed gravity canals running southwest from the Sacramento River) estimates primary irrigation benefits of $15.71 per acre-foot of water, not counting substantial water transmission losses and not deducting for the costs of constructing local distribution systems. Judging by our own estimates of agricultural benefits to much more productive soils in the San Joaquin Valley (see Appendix C), this estimate is overstated several times; indeed, local water users have been unwilling to commit themselves to pay the costs of distribution systems and a $2.75 charge for water.[78] Similarly inflated figures appear in the feasibility report for the Trinity Division of the Central Valley Project, which drops water from the Trinity River into the Sacramento at Shasta Dam. Electric power benefits from Trinity are placed at 8.6 mills per kilowatt-hour or more (depending on the output estimate), almost twice the figure which we calculate as appropriate in Appendix C.[79]

In other cases, where the basis of the calculations is clearer, benefits are valued by inappropriate alternatives, or costs are omitted. The Corps of Engineers issued a feasibility report for a flood control dam at Dry Creek Basin on the Russian River shortly after completion of its Coyote Valley Dam on the same river. As the most economical alternative source for valuing water from a Dry Creek multiple purpose dam, the Corps selected a single purpose water conservation dam at Dry Creek producing water at $14 an acre-foot. Yet it rejected the alternative of raising the existing Coyote Valley Dam, which would have produced water at only $4.13 an acre-foot.[80] The report of the Bureau of Reclamation on the San Luis unit of the Central Valley Project employs reasonable procedures throughout in estimating benefits; however, it acknowledges that the project will create a drainage problem and require the construction of major drainage facilities without including them as a cost in its evaluation.[81]

As we go back to Bureau projects receiving authorization in the 1940's, evaluation practices become still less satisfactory. The basic Central Valley Project itself was evaluated only after its major features were under construction or completed. Folsom Dam on the American River was authorized through a Senate floor amend-

[78] U.S. Congress, House Committee on Interior and Insular Affairs, *Sacramento Canals Unit, Central Valley Project, California*, H. Doc. 73, 83 Cong. 1 sess. (1953), pp. 9, 39. If we value marginal irrigation benefits of this project at $2 per acre-foot and include other classes of benefits and operating costs at values estimated by the Bureau, the canals would yield in perpetuity a rate of return of 1.93 per cent on the invested capital.

[79] *Idem, Trinity River Division, Central Valley Project, California*, H. Doc. 53, 83 Cong. 1 sess. (1953), reprinted in *idem, Central Valley Project Documents, Part 1: Authorizing Documents*, H. Doc. 416, 84 Cong. 2 sess. (1956), pp. 865, 868.

[80] *Idem, Russian River, Dry Creek Basin, California*, H. Doc. 547, 87 Cong. 2 sess. (1962), pp. 29, 45, 46, 52. The Corps offered the spurious justification that the Coyote enlargement would eventually be built in any case, so it did not constitute a true alternative. Recalculation would pull the reported benefit-cost ratio from 1.2:1 to below unity.

[81] U.S. Department of the Interior, Bureau of Reclamation, Region 2, *San Luis Unit, Central Valley Project, California: A Report on the Feasibility of Water Supply Development* (1955), p. 22. The cost of a major drainage facility for the area, serving more than the San Luis service area, has been quoted at $34 million.

ment to the Flood Control Act of 1944 without any benefit-cost appraisal; and it was built without any decision having been made on the nature or place of use of its water output.[82] The Solano Project was authorized on November 11, 1948, by the Secretary of the Interior under a procedure in accordance with the provisions of Section 9(a) of the Reclamation Projects Act of 1939, requiring no congressional action. A quick calculation of its benefits and costs, valuing benefits at their marginal worth, would attribute to it a perpetual yield on invested capital of about 1.25 per cent annually.[83]

The interest rates employed in federal investment criteria bear no necessary relation to market interest rates; and in this they are unlike rates in local districts which in fact borrow to finance their projects. Federal projects are financed through current appropriations. Nonetheless, prevailing federal practice calls for using the federal borrowing rate as a discount rate. The specific rate chosen is an average which includes long-term federal debt of ancient vintage. In view of the rising trend of federal interest rates, it is below current marginal borrowing rates. For example, the Solano Project of the Bureau of Reclamation was evaluated by a benefit-cost ratio computed with a discount rate of 2½ per cent and the Coyote Valley and Dry Creek Basin projects of the Corps were evaluated on the basis of rates of 3 and 2⅝ per cent respectively. Typically, no tests are presented of the sensitivity of investment decisions to the rate employed.

Whatever the appropriateness of discount rates commonly used by local agencies, they lie significantly above the federal rates in most cases. This spread of rates itself tends to preclude efficient allocation, with federal agencies undertaking capital-intensive designs and "premature" construction which local units would pass over. Clearly the practices of the federal agencies in choosing discount rates tend to reinforce any "engineering" bias toward the full development of resources. Furthermore, longer time horizons, sometimes one hundred years, are used by the federal agencies as against shorter periods related to the bond repayment period for the local districts.

Whether because of lower discount rates, longer time horizons, or other factors of bias in its design criteria, the Bureau of Reclamation clearly comes up with more capital-intensive designs than most California agricultural water districts would choose for themselves. Evidence of this difference comes from the federal program which provides interest-free financing to irrigation districts for water distribution systems built by the Bureau. Districts have foregone the interest-free feature in

[82] In its reauthorization of Oct. 14, 1949 (63 *Stat.* 852), Congress specified that: "Nothing contained in this Act shall be construed by implication or otherwise as an allocation of water and . . . the Secretary of the Interior shall make recommendations for the use of water in accord with State water laws." See House Committee on Interior and Insular Affairs, *Central Valley Project Documents, op. cit.,* chap. 5.

[83] Ultimately, minimum contract deliveries for the project will be 219,000 acre-feet annually, but demand has been developing very slowly. Putting average deliveries over a fifty-year project life at 150,000 acre-feet and valuing them at the price actually received by the Bureau (a measure of actual marginal value), the figure in the text was derived. We added a substantial allowance for recreation benefits from Lake Berryessa and neglected operating costs for the main features of the project. For a discussion of the demand for water in the area, see Stoddard & Karrer, *Solano County Water Resources and Requirements* (2nd ed.; 1962).

some cases in order to secure cheaper construction than the Bureau would provide. The Commissioner of Reclamation himself conceded, in hearings on bills to provide loans to irrigation districts wishing to build their own distribution systems, that they might desire simpler and less durable works than the Bureau constructs.[84] Although the Bureau has been accused of being a high-cost designer of small local projects because of heavy overhead, the more common cause of the reluctance of local districts to retain the Bureau's services has been their desire for systems with lower real capital costs per acre (and correspondingly higher operation and maintenance costs).[85]

The federal agencies show no marked tendency to avoid economic uncertainty in evaluating the benefits or in undertaking their projects. As we shall argue below, this attitude turns up in a willingness of the Bureau (at least) to undertake what has amounted to a substantial role of holder of equity in some California projects. It also tends to accept the distant future as relatively sure, as indicated by a willingness to build excess capacity into some of the features of the Central Valley Project on the chance that the cost of integrating future additions to the project would be reduced thereby. The Delta-Mendota Canal was constructed with 1,100 second-feet of capacity more than would be supplied from Shasta Dam.[86] The Bureau has described its East Side Project as drawing upon the waters of the Sacramento and American rivers to serve initially between 1.5 million and 2 million acres of land on the east side of the San Joaquin Valley. But the initial phase is being planned:

> . . . in such a manner that it can be extended or enlarged to import additional water supplies from the Yuba River and other areas of excess water as the need develops in future years. The service area studies now approaching completion on the Initial Phase are concentrated on compact blocks of irrigable land. Between these blocks are about 1,000,000 acres which will have a supplemental water requirement of possibly 1,000,000 acre-feet. Some of the latter areas have already expressed an interest in obtaining additional water.[87]

The evidence does not prove that these practices reflect either commendable foresight or improvident overbuilding. But neither does it show that serious calculations are made to test even crudely the marginal benefits and costs of such provisions for the uncertain future. However, fragmentary indications suggest that the Bureau of

[84] Q. "You would not insist that [local projects] meet the longer range standards which you normally follow yourself in a project?" A. "That is correct." U.S. Congress, House Committee on Interior and Insular Affairs, Special Subcommittee, *Federal Assistance for Small Reclamation Projects,* 84 Cong. 1 sess. (1955), p. 30.

[85] *Ibid.,* pp. 53–54. Usual differences include the use of pipelines or open ditches, the lining of ditches, and the accuracy of measuring devices employed.

[86] A Bureau representative explained: "Several other dams . . . have been authorized for federal construction. No one in California, and I am quite sure no one in the Bureau of Reclamation, feels that when the features now under construction are completed, that the project is going to end." U.S. Congress, Senate Committee on Public Lands, Subcommittee, *Exemption of Certain Projects from Land-Limitation Provisions of Federal Reclamation Laws,* 80 Cong. 1 sess. (1947), pp. 836–37.

[87] U.S. Department of the Interior, Bureau of Reclamation, *Estimates of Appropriations, Fiscal Year Ending June 30, 1962,* Part 1 (n.d.; n.p.).

Reclamation may be somewhat more willing to take a hopeful view of the distant future than the Corps of Engineers.[88]

Whatever their treatment of uncertainty of future benefits, the federal agencies in one sense incur less danger of misallocations associated with uncertainty than do local districts. They do not have to adjust to the same threat of financial uncertainty affecting each project. To the federal government, the economic failure of a particular project has no disastrous organizational consequences, since it is but one of many under federal sponsorship. If some care in planning has been exercised, the government can expect to realize its hopes on the average. With a normal central tendency in operation, some glaring failures will be offset by some glowing successes. Although the economic uncertainty surrounding a single project constructed by a local agency carries a grave risk for that agency, the federal agencies can depend on a normal distribution of returns over time and a pooling of risk. The avoidance of this effect of uncertainty concerning the individual project constitutes an economic gain of the same sort as removing the incidence of capital rationing.

Investment criteria of the Department of Water Resources

The detailed design and planning of the Feather River Project, the first unit of the California Water Plan being undertaken by the California Department of Water Resources, is still under way. For this reason we cannot present an appraisal of the practices used that is nearly so firm as that for the federal agencies. Nonetheless, certain major principles are now clear.

Economic analysis of the California Water Plan has come after its technical planning and after the electorate authorized a bond issue of $1.75 billion to finance its initial phase. Any official benefit-cost analysis thus necessarily becomes an ex post facto justification. In any case, the Department and the State Legislature have both consistently held that benefit-cost analysis does not furnish a proper guide to investment planning. In the eyes of the Department, it does not adequately reflect the public interest or "political and operational considerations."[89] Instead, justifications for the program have emphasized the policy of gaining commitments from water purchasers to repay the reimbursable costs of the project, substituting a test of reimbursability for one of benefit-cost relations. The main line of argument favoring this approach registers a general suspicion of "expert" benefit-cost calculations, implying that they include irresponsible and specious elements and that willingness to pay constitutes a better test of benefit than does an outsider's pencil work. No-

[88] One case involved the storage capacity proposed behind Monticello Dam on Putah Creek. In its 1949 report, the Bureau urged 2.2 million acre-feet; this was not justified by the Putah Creek runoff but by the possibility of a diversion at some later date from Cache Creek into Putah Creek. The Corps of Engineers recommended 980,000 acre-feet, still several times the stream's annual runoff, on the basis of excessive uncertainty about the Cache Creek diversion. See Bureau of Reclamation, *Central Valley Basin, op. cit.*, p. 343.

[89] California State Water Resources Board, *The California Water Plan*, Bulletin No. 3, *op. cit.*, pp. 223–24; California State Legislature, Assembly Water Committee, *Economic and Financial Policies for State Water Projects*, Vol. 26, No. 1 (1960), pp. 11–16.

where in this discussion is there a hint that water users might be coaxed into paying sums greater than benefits measured in terms of alternatives, although our own analysis in Chapter 15 and Appendix D suggests that exactly this is occurring.[90]

Despite this position, the Department of Water Resources has produced a benefit-cost ratio of 2.34 for its aqueducts to carry water from the Sacramento-San Joaquin Delta to Kern County and to Southern California,[91] and a later ratio for the entire Feather River Project, including dams as well as aqueducts, of 1.3.[92] As we shall argue below, it grossly overstates benefits in both calculations.[93]

In designing facilities to carry out some particular function, the Department of Water Resources has sought to minimize costs using an interest rate of 3.5 per cent. This is an inappropriately low rate. Furthermore, the Department's decisions on the initial size of certain aqueducts have been criticized for including substantial excess capacity and for building capacities adequate for anticipated demands in the year 2020 without testing for possible savings from the staged construction of transmission facilities.[94] Considering the federal and state agencies together, they seem at least as likely to overinvest as are local agencies to underinvest.

Local promotion of federal projects

Returning to the process of project formulation by the federal agencies, the strong and weak features of investment criteria used by the Bureau of Reclamation and the Corps of Engineers have been studied more than the extent to which their projects respond to the wishes of particular groups of would-be local beneficiaries. These wishes tend to define, and perhaps restrict or distort, the benefits sought in the design of federal projects. The Bureau and the Corps not only see themselves as responding to the voice of the public, but they depend heavily on such local

[90] Compare Jack Hirshleifer, J. C. De Haven, and J. W. Milliman, *Water Supply: Economics, Technology, and Policy* (1960), Chapter 11.

[91] California Department of Water Resources, *Investigation of Alternative Aqueduct Systems to Serve Southern California,* Bulletin No. 78 (1959), pp. 143–45.

[92] Unpublished office reports of 1960 entitled "Information and Data on Proposed Program for Financing and Constructing State Water Facilities."

[93] For example, the estimates of urban water benefits in the South Coastal Basin are based on costs for alternative sources. No alternative source of supply is recognized which is less costly than desalinization of ocean water. A benefit figure of $150 per acre-foot is set, representing a "cost somewhat less than the presently estimated minimum future cost of demineralizing ocean water. It is believed that could ocean water be converted for beneficial use at this cost, it would be within most municipal and industrial users' payment capacity." (California Department of Water Resources, *Investigation of Alternative Aqueduct Systems,* Bulletin No. 78, *op. cit.,* p. 144.) This figure may lie within the payment capacity of its prospective users, but "water requirements" are estimated on the basis of water demand at going or estimated prices of about $35 per acre-foot, a fraction of this estimated benefit level. An overestimate of benefits results from demand being appreciably elastic, apart from the inappropriateness of the assumed alternative source and cost at least from 1972 to 1990, and from an estimate of desalinization costs which is probably 50 per cent above prospective costs at the dates of reference.

[94] California State Legislature, Assembly Water Committee, *Economic and Financial Policies for State Water Projects, op. cit.,* pp. 17–21.

support to secure appropriations from Congress. Compared to the relative strength of local pressure and support, the relative benefit-cost ratios of the projects competing for congressional appropriations turn out to bear little weight. Therefore, the allocative results of federal construction programs for water projects depend at least as much on patterns of local promotion and support as they do on the principles of investment criteria just discussed. We consider first the pattern of local efforts to promote project construction in Northern California, and then the responsiveness of the federal agencies to this clamor. We cannot, unfortunately, draw many lessons from the initial features of the Bureau's Central Valley Project: Shasta Dam, the Delta-Mendota Canal, Friant Dam and its service canals. They were first planned long ago by the state of California and taken over by the federal government during the 1930's. The great scope of this project and the special pressures on the state's finances during the depression render impossible any concise discussion of the political forces that brought the project into being.[95] Later and smaller additions to the Central Valley Project as well as dams constructed by the Corps, however, have shown regular patterns of local promotion and support, from the initial plans of the constructing agency through the final appropriation by Congress.

No simple generalizations seem possible about the sources of local entrepreneurship in promoting projects, although owners of large landholdings naturally play a prominent role. The San Luis Project in the San Joaquin Valley was successfully promoted by a group of large landowners in the area, organized first as the West Side Land Owners Association and later as the Westlands Water District and San Luis Water District. The Bureau began investigating the San Luis Project in 1943 at the request of the Association, which put up $40,000 to finance the exploratory studies.[96] In the 1950's, the same group of landowners fought for the Project through a half-dozen congressional hearings. State authorities and Southern California water users opposed the Bureau's Project because the California Water Plan also contemplated the use of the San Luis reservoir site. The San Luis landowners promoted a series of meetings and compromises among the interested parties so that progressive removal of opposition could finally permit passage of the authorization. They worked tirelessly to promote a plan for joint federal-state use of the site and for federal control of the operation of the reservoir and the service canals, on the theory that the Bureau could probably offer a better price and more rapid construction.

Like the San Luis area, the Tulare Lake Basin (formerly the depository of flood waters from the Kings, Kaweah, Tule, and Kern rivers) is comprised of large landholdings, and the large-scale farm operators have devoted considerable effort to promoting flood control projects through the Tulare Lake Basin Water Storage District. Their efforts were less clearly related to favorable congressional action on the projects than in the case of San Luis, however, because other cities and water

[95] See U.S. Department of Agriculture, Bureau of Agricultural Economics, *History of Legislation and Policy Formation of the Central Valley Project,* by Mary Montgomery and Marion Clawson (1946).

[96] U.S. Congress, House Committee on Interior and Insular Affairs, Special Subcommittee, *San Luis Project, California,* 85 Cong. 2 sess. (1958), p. 83.

agencies had taken a more intimate interest in each of the rivers in question. The plans of the Corps of Engineers for dams on the Kaweah and Tule rivers lay fallow for lack of local interest until serious floods in 1955 caused the mounting of effective local campaigns for congressional approval and appropriations.[97]

Where large-scale landowners play a less prominent role, many different types of persons and groups take the lead in agitating for local projects. Local chambers of commerce, county supervisors, units of the American Farm Bureau Federation and the National Grange, agricultural extension agents, and, especially, state senators and assemblymen and members of the U.S. House of Representatives take the initiative in conceiving and promoting projects. Many motives and interests combine to give these campaigns the broad base and strong enthusiasm which they often show. Capital gains to landowners always play a part,[98] and this form of enrichment often seems to stir more enthusiasm than the higher profits available by shifting from dry to irrigated farming. Federal reclamation law contains the familiar land-limitation and antispeculation provisions which seek to spread the benefits conferred by the law's various subsidies to irrigation among at least a minimum number of farm families. Nonetheless, ranchers faced with making substantial sales of land to comply with the law have often chosen this course to having no project whatsoever.[99] Increased agricultural income and population due to reclamation projects create the expectation of increased profits for local retail and service businesses, giving them a self-interest to work for water conservation projects. Finally, these campaigns would not develop the wide base of support which they do without the popular desire to promote local economic growth.

[97] The State Water Resources Board considered pushing for federal appropriations in 1952 for Success and Terminus reservoirs on the Tule and Kaweah rivers, respectively, but dropped the idea on account of disagreement and lack of interest among local residents. After the 1955–56 floods, however, the Terminus-Success Flood Control Dams Association was formed and mobilized effective congressional support. The dams were included in the omnibus bill which was vetoed in 1956. The same fate struck in 1957, but authorization finally came in 1958.

[98] Various figures have been presented to suggest the land-value increment caused by reclamation projects. The Bureau of Reclamation estimated $200 an acre in a 1947 Senate hearing. Evidence for Kern County in 1957 suggested a gain of $300 an acre. For these and other figures, see the testimony of Dr. Paul S. Taylor in U.S. Congress, Senate Committee on Interior and Insular Affairs, Subcommittee on Irrigation and Reclamation, *Acreage Limitation (Reclamation Law) Review,* 85 Cong. 2 sess. (1958), p. 150.

[99] The willingness of large landowners in the San Luis service area to back the Bureau's San Luis Project has occasioned some surprise in view of the hostility to the Bureau of large holders elsewhere in the state. One experienced water lawyer, Harry Horton, offered the following interpretation, with reference to the late president of the Westlands Water District and leader in the campaign for San Luis: "I will give you my own opinion of Jack O'Neill's willingness to sign the 160-acre limitation. He thinks if he gets water for 10 years on there without having to sell [his excess land], he can make enough money out of it so he can afford to sell the land at any old price. That is my opinion of Jack O'Neill's willingness to back the San Luis project." (*Ibid.*, pp. 87–88.) Also relevant is Representative Clair Engle's statement: "I call your attention to the fact that in 26 years since the recordable contract provisions have been in the reclamation law, not in one single instance has the Secretary of the Interior ever set a price on land and sold the land under a recordable contract. . . . They find ways to get around it. They set up corporations and partnerships and every adult or child has 160 acres and if there are not enough of those they bring in the uncles and aunts and, as a consequence, they spread it around so that the pro forma title at least is within the limitation." See House Committee on Interior and Insular Affairs, Special Subcommittee, *Federal Assistance for Small Reclamation Projects, op. cit.*, p. 93.

The timing of these campaigns for projects is harder to explain than the basis of interest and support. Frequently the idea of a project lies in the public domain for decades before the forces combine to bring its actual construction. For instance, Pine Flat Dam on Kings River, built in the 1940's, was widely discussed by local interests around the time of World War I, but apparently failed because of inability to reach an agreement. Similarly, irrigators along the Sacramento River channel showed substantial interest in upstream storage during the rice boom immediately after World War I, but the construction of Shasta Dam awaited World War II.[100] The wave of interest in recent years, like that surrounding World War I, related in a general way to the sustained prosperity of agricultural operations in California. But beyond that little can be said. Another element explaining the timing of interest in federal projects, like those undertaken locally discussed above, has been the fear of future competition for local water supplies. The case of San Luis shows the role of incipient interregional competition for water in spurring local interest just as strongly as do the local projects on the east side of the Central Valley.

The heterogeneous patterns of local support and methods of local efforts to promote water projects have no clearer illustration than the campaign mounted to bring about the Sacramento canals, a series of gravity canals designed ultimately to bring water from the Sacramento River to dry-farmed lands in Glenn, Colusa, Tehama, Yolo, and Solano counties. (See Figure 19.) This case is atypical only in that the most serious obstacles did not arise in connection with initial authorization, but later in securing construction funds and clearing other roadblocks. Otherwise, it illustrates well the course of such campaigns and the sort of persons involved.

The general idea of the canals was conceived in 1948 by (then) Representative Clair Engle and others of the area. A group known primarily as the Sacramento Valley Irrigation Committee was immediately formed through Engle's efforts to work for authorization and construction of the canals as a part of the Central Valley Project. In 1950, James K. Carr, one of the employees of the Sacramento office of the Bureau of Reclamation (employees who were active as "technical advisers" of the Committee), was making speeches in the area urging that local water committees be organized to "follow closely the detailed irrigation plans for the Sacramento Valley as they are developed by the Bureau of Reclamation."[101] Congressional authorization for the project came in September 1950, even before the Department of the Interior could issue a feasibility report, when President Harry S. Truman signed the so-called Engle-Scudder Bill. Unanimous support for the project was noted among otherwise warring groups such as the Farm Bureau Federation, Grange, State Chamber of Commerce, California Water Project Authority, and the State Engineer.[102] The Irrigation Committee's secretary and Tehama County farm adviser, D. M. Smith, attributed the bill's passage to:

[100] Kings River Water Association, *Forty Years on Kings River, 1917–1957,* by Charles L. Kaupke (1957), pp. 57–58; Lambert, *op. cit.*, pp. 112–15.

[101] *Maxwell Tribune,* September 27, 1950.

[102] U.S. Congress, House Committee on Public Lands, Subcommittee on Irrigation and Reclamation, *Authorize Sacramento Valley Canals, Central Valley Project, California,* 81 Cong. 1 sess. (1949), p. 25 and *passim.*

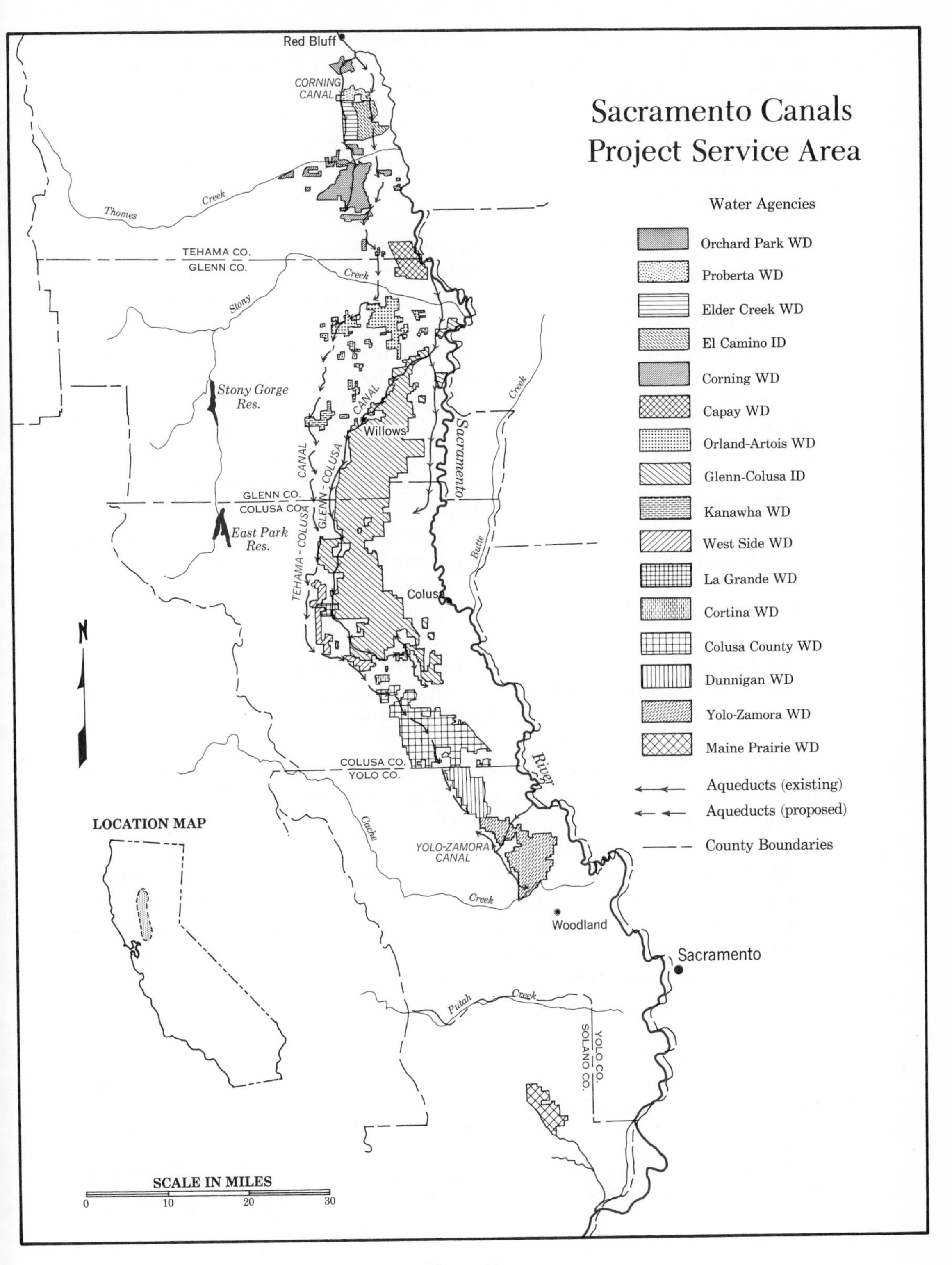
Sacramento Canals
Project Service Area
Water Agencies
Orchard Park WD
Proberta WD
Elder Creek WD
El Camino ID
Corning WD
Capay WD
Orland-Artois WD
Glenn-Colusa ID
Kanawha WD
West Side WD
La Grande WD
Cortina WD
Colusa County WD
Dunnigan WD
Yolo-Zamora WD
Maine Prairie WD
Aqueducts (existing)
Aqueducts (proposed)
County Boundaries
Red Bluff
CORNING CANAL
Thomes Creek
TEHAMA CO.
GLENN CO.
Stony Creek
Stony Gorge Res.
East Park Res.
Willows
CANAL
GLENN - COLUSA
TEHAMA - COLUSA CANAL
GLENN CO.
COLUSA CO.
Sacramento
Butte Creek
Colusa
COLUSA CO.
YOLO CO.
River
Cache Creek
YOLO-ZAMORA CANAL
Woodland
Sacramento
Putah Creek
YOLO CO.
SOLANO CO.
LOCATION MAP
SCALE IN MILES
0
10
20
30
N

Figure 19

> The fine support of the state legislature and administration, a sharp four county irrigation committee which by-passed controversial issues and kept its eye on the ball as far as valley water needs were concerned, the effective bi-partisan backing which the bill enjoyed in California and in both houses of Congress, the helpful cooperation of the U.S. Bureau of Reclamation, and finally to the heads-up Congressional leadership of Congressmen Clair Engle and Hubert Scudder.[103]

After passage of the bill, it became generally clear that the Sacramento canals as authorized would oversubscribe the water available in the Sacramento River. The backers of the Sacramento canals were thus forced to campaign for Bureau storage-reservoir projects which would make the needed water available. In so doing, they met sustained opposition from the established Irrigation Districts Association, which was seeking to oust the Bureau of Reclamation from the state; and the Sacramento interests undertook to form a rival organization of irrigation interests in alliance with the Bureau. Support crystallized upon the proposed Trinity Project as the most likely source of additional water. The Sacramento interests then formed an alliance with those areas of the San Joaquin Valley which would also benefit from Trinity's supplementation of water so that they too would campaign for the additional project. This campaign ultimately succeeded, as did efforts to secure appropriations for the construction of those portions of the canals for which sufficient water was already available.

In the late 1950's, the development of the Project once more was stalled because of the unwillingness of districts formed to retail water from the Sacramento canals to sign long-term contracts at prices asked by the Bureau of Reclamation. While not much local action was stirred toward proceeding to sign these contracts, the supporters were able to keep this stalemate from entirely blocking construction of the rest of the canals.

This case shows the pattern of local promotional activities which typically lies behind projects undertaken in Northern California by the Bureau of Reclamation. We have devoted less attention to the political forces behind the activities of the Corps of Engineers in the area. The Corps won congressional authorization for numerous projects in the area in 1944, but since then its role has been secondary to that of the Bureau and the California Water Plan. Evidence from other areas suggests from the Corps, at least as much as the Bureau, addresses itself to serving the demands voiced by local interests. Projects normally start from local agitation, which is communicated to Congress either directly or with the advice of the district engineer. Interested congressmen either prevail upon the chief of the Corps to begin an investigation or act directly to get an item included by the House Appropriations Committee.[104] The Corps has effectively promoted its willingness to heed the whims of local interests. Even more than with the Bureau, the demand for projects creates its own supply.

[103] *Corning Observer*, October 18, 1950.

[104] See Charles McKinley, *Uncle Sam in the Pacific Northwest: Federal Management of Natural Resources in the Columbia River Valley* (1952), chap. 2.

Congressional authorizations and appropriations

Projects of the Bureau of Reclamation and the Corps of Engineers generally require both authorization and appropriation by Congress to bring them into existence.[105] In principle, political forces operating in the congressional arena determine the choice and timing of projects to be constructed. Analyzing these pressures to explain what forces succeed in generating favorable legislative action is a substantial task, and the present study permits only a short-cut approach. We should note, first, that all California water projects thoroughly studied by the Bureau or the Corps and supported by local interests have ultimately received congressional approval and appropriations. The differences from case to case lie mainly in the time required to achieve these goals and, to a lesser degree, the compromises necessary along the way.

Apart from shifts in national political control, the factors which appear to influence the speed and ease with which congressional approval is won include mainly the degree of need expressed by local supporters and the presence or absence of local opposition. The Sacramento canals—with well-organized local support, evidence of inadequate local ground-water supplies, and no local opposition—were authorized, as noted above, even before a feasibility report emerged from the Department of the Interior. Similarly, the American River division of the Central Valley project won fairly easy authorization upon testimony of the need for the power and flood control benefits which it would confer. Conversely, the San Luis and Trinity divisions of the Central Valley project and the Solano project faced difficult fights on account of local opposition. The San Luis project ran into state-federal competition for the same reservoir site and hence conflict between the water users in the service areas of the respective projects. Four years of intermittent negotiation and compromise were needed to reduce the disagreement to tolerable levels and permit authorization. The Trinity project, to drop a portion of Trinity river some 1,500 feet through tunnels into the Sacramento River channel, ran into trouble over features of electric power generation. The Bureau needed the power, even more than the water, to support extensive pumping required by the San Luis project and other proposed developments in the San Joaquin Valley. Pacific Gas and Electric Company sought to invoke the Eisenhower Administration's partnership policy to secure the right to construct and operate the power features of the Trinity project. The utility's powerful political position delayed all federal construction for several years. Finally, the Solano project ran afoul of county rivalries. It involved the construction of a large reservoir in Napa County to serve lands and cities located in Solano County, and possibly Yolo County. The indifference of Yolo County and the bitter opposition of Napa County (as much to the loss of its tax base through the inundation of farm lands as to the loss of its water) forced a

[105] Strictly speaking, Bureau projects can be authorized by a finding of the Secretary of the Interior under the Reclamation Projects Act of 1939, but this route has been little used. Its requirements are relatively stringent and, more important, key congressional committees have shown a strong hostility to its use. See House Committee on Interior and Insular Affairs, *Trinity River Division, Central Valley Project, California*, *op. cit.*, p. 25.

scaling down of the project and the holding of a striking number of hearings for the size of the proposed reservoir.

Congressional hearings and floor debates on these projects reveal much about what conditions seem to draw strong support for proposed projects.[106] One which seems to make very little difference is the benefit-cost ratio reported by the agency proposing construction. Practically nothing is made of an unusually high or low ratio apart from other features of a project, and committee hearings rarely delve directly into the basis of this calculation. The issues of equity raised by witnesses for local interests receive the great bulk of attention. Congressmen tend to look favorably upon projects which relieve the plight of farmers whose ground-water supplies are failing. This problem was stressed in connection with the Friant-Kern Canal of the original Central Valley Project and the San Luis unit. This congressional sympathy seems to rest on two bases: a strong desire to assist in the avoidance of financial losses; and lip service to the objective of not encouraging the expansion of agricultural output in the face of farm surpluses. Nonetheless, the prospect of large expansion in the output of price-supported crops can be successfully glossed over by a project's promoters. Much interest, favorable or unfavorable, always attaches to the degree to which a project will promote reductions in the size of farm enterprises and increases in the supply of public power. Needless to say, the consequence of these traits for a project's chances of approval depends on the current balance of political sentiment in the legislative and executive branches.

Actual congressional voting records reveal the shifting patterns of log-rolling and personal relations and animosities long familiar in public works legislation. Trading relations among legislators come and go, are seldom stable for more than a few sessions because of the changing congressional personalities and the changing mixtures of projects which are brought up for authorization or appropriation. In this milieu, the fate of a particular project will depend on the bargaining strength held by the senators and representatives of beneficiaries. Their presence on key committees, especially the control of a chairmanship, makes a great difference in the speed with which a project receives authorization and appropriations. California legislators apparently often try to develop a package arrangement when several projects are due to come before a particular session.[107]

More broadly, direct interest in reclamation projects centers in seventeen western states and their legislative representatives, as does a large portion of the interest in flood control projects of the Corps of Engineers. These legislators often take the view that, when in doubt, favorable action on projects is to be preferred, and they commonly see the acquisition of new water supplies as preferable to disputes over the possession of those currently available.[108] This bloc offers a large field for political alliances, although broad ones covering large portions of the West are the exception. Many rivalries, such as those between California and the representatives of the Upper Colorado basin, exist within the region.

[106] For a general discussion, see Arthur A. Maass, "Congress and Water Resources," *American Political Science Review,* XLIV (September 1950), 576–93.

[107] See, for example, *Sacramento Bee,* January 7, 1962.

[108] Consider Representative Engle's statement concerning Folsom Dam on the American River: "The major question that remains unsettled is the distribution of the water. We

Political promotion and project design and efficiency

As we have suggested, projects of the Bureau of Reclamation in California are oriented strongly toward serving a demand voiced by a local group. This fact affects both the choice and the design of projects. For example, the groups and individuals behind the Sacramento Valley Irrigation Committee not only initiated the Bureau's investigation of the Sacramento Canals but also took an active hand at guiding their design.[109]

The vital corollary of the role of local sentiment in initiating projects is that the Bureau tends to seek feasible projects to provide a specifically desired bundle of benefits rather than (say) to design the project with the highest benefit-cost ratio using the unappropriated water of a particular stream. For example, the Bureau originally enjoyed a wide choice in the market area to be served by its southbound canal from Friant Dam on the San Joaquin River. Water could be carried in a canal along the east side of the Valley as far as the Kern River, serving primarily lands on the east side and at the south end of the Valley. Or it could be carried in a shorter canal, dropping its water into existing natural channels (the Kings, Kaweah, and Tule rivers) for delivery to lands farther to the west and not so far to the south. The Bureau's original proposal and its subsequent construction emphasized the former approach. The Friant-Kern Canal was constructed to carry water all the way to the Kern River, and the Bureau's 1949 report placed great emphasis on yet another canal to be constructed from the Kern River at a higher altitude around the south rim of the Valley. Kern water would then be transported farther to the south and replaced downstream by San Joaquin water imported through the Friant-Kern Canal.[110] Not only was this exchange emphasized as vital

---

haven't authorized a single canal to be built off of the Folsom project because we don't know yet where the water will go. It is rather unique to have a million acre-feet of stored water and no canals for the use of that water. . . . This is an example I think that could be intelligently followed in the planning and construction of some of the projects under consideration in California. The way to get them started is to start. It's a mistake to try to settle all of the questions. When there is a substantial agreement a project should go forward. If this kind of formula is followed, there will be less dilly-dallying around and more cement and steel in evidence in the solution of California's water problems." (*Chico Enterprise-Record,* May 9, 1956.) Also see U.S. Congress, House Committee on Interior and Insular Affairs, Special Subcommittee on Irrigation and Reclamation, *Central Valley Project, California: Water Rights, Supplies and Uses,* 82 Cong. 1 sess. (1952), *passim.*

[109] In 1960, the Bureau proposed a modification of the Tehama-Colusa "long canal" to substitute three separate distribution systems pumping from the Sacramento River for one very lengthy gravity canal. The Bureau's action grew out of the difficulty it had met in securing repayment contracts from local districts except at the lower end of the Tehama-Colusa service area. The Sacramento Valley Irrigation Committee preferred the original plan, in part because it avoided the danger of future increases in power rates. And it was able to mount an effective campaign against the counterproposal. See *Sacramento Bee,* October 6–13, 1960 (*passim*) and November 5, 1960.

[110] The Bureau declared: "It is believed that, for the coordinated plan of operation, agreements can be worked out to the mutual advantage of all local interests so that a considerable portion of the regulated Kern River run-off can be diverted into the high-line Kern Maricopa Canal, for irrigation of lands in the Arvin-Edison Water Storage District and ultimately other areas to the west, in exchange for water to be imported through Friant-Kern Canal for lands now irrigated from Kern River. *Without such exchanges, there would be small justification for continuing Friant-Kern Canal to Kern River.*" [Emphasis added.] Bureau of Reclamation, *Central Valley Basin, op. cit.,* p. 132.

for the feasibility of the Canal, but also local interests in the Arvin-Edison area south of the Kern apparently had taken a very active part in voicing their interest to the Bureau and urging appropriations for the work. No evidence shows that the Bureau determined that the Kern service area would afford greater relative benefits than one drawing upon a shorter, less costly canal from Friant. However, a decade later the Kern River interests had still not reached a solution of their internal difficulties which would permit the exchange declared necessary to justify the then existing extension of the Friant Canal to the Kern River, while the Bureau had standing orders for at least 1 million acre-feet of water from agencies nearer to Friant and having access to the Canal by natural channels.[111] Other projects show similar orientations toward local demands.[112]

Federal agencies and external constraints

In the competition for water and related inputs in Northern California, the Bureau of Reclamation has been heavily embroiled in the same network of conflicts and regulatory procedures as local agricultural water districts. Its role in these conflicts will emerge in the following three chapters. What we would point out here is the greater boldness with which the Bureau has been able to proceed in the face of these external constraints, a boldness reflected in frequent local resentment of the agency's "highhanded" tactics. The results, which have both their merits and their drawbacks, stem basically from a greater willingness of the Bureau to bear certain types of entrepreneurial risks in the construction of water projects.

Consider the Bureau's design and construction of projects in relation to the water rights situation on the streams in question. On the one hand, the Bureau has been willing and able to construct projects and put them into operation long before securing the water rights under state law necessary to operate them. The Bureau constructed Shasta Dam in the 1940's but made its first move to secure permits to divert and store water in the early 1950's, and these were granted only in 1961. Local interests have complained that, once the Bureau appears with plans and funds to construct a project, the state's water rights machinery never interferes—irrespective of the merits of competing applications of those not yet ready to go ahead with construction.[113] Furthermore, the Bureau in the last few years has taken a much more aggressive attitude toward the validity of restrictions placed upon its permits to appropriate water by the State Water Rights Board.[114] On the other

[111] Only in 1962 did Arvin-Edison Water Storage District finally reach a contract with the Bureau. An exchange arrangement on the Kern proved impossible, and the District finally resigned itself to a crosshaul arrangement, pumping Friant-Kern water uphill at least fourteen miles to its lands. See *Western Water News,* July 1962.

[112] See Bureau of Reclamation. *Folsom South Unit, op. cit.*, p. 13; and the Bureau's *Central Valley Basin, op. cit.,* p. 123. See also, U.S. Congress, House Committee on Public Lands, Subcommittee on Irrigation and Reclamation, *The Solano County Project, California,* 80 Cong. 2 sess. (1948), p. 119.

[113] "In California, it is not who files who gets the water, but who files and gets there first with the money and starts to use that money." Senate, Joint Subcommittee, *Bureau of Reclamation, Interior Department,* hearings [on the Solano Project], *op. cit.,* p. 43.

[114] Irrigation Districts Association of California, *Minutes of Semiannual Convention,* "Creek Law vs. Federal Paramount Rights," by Martin McDonough (April 26, 1962). Also see Chapter 3 above.

hand, the Bureau has shown some reluctance to tangle with difficult water rights situations. Officials have suggested that use of the American River for the Folsom South Canal's service area rather than several other local rivers bore some relation to differences in the water rights situations. Applications on file to store and divert from each of the rivers covered more than the whole flow. But, unlike the American, the largest rivers among the alternative rivers were dominated by local agencies with established works and at least tentative plans for future developments. Such concerted opposition was not to be found on the American River. Likewise, the dropping of Clear Lake and Cache Creek from the Solano Project on Putah Creek related not only to the lack of a ready market for Cache Creek water, but also to a complex tangle of court decrees affecting Clear Lake.[115] Possibly the Bureau finds it easier to operate on a large stream or one lacking concerted water rights opposition than on a small one or one with concerted local opposition.

As a general rule, the Bureau shuns the risk-bearing role of financial entrepreneurship—of obligating itself to absorb the difference between uncertain revenues and uncertain costs. Its bitter experience concerning a repayment contract for Pine Flat Dam on the Kings River led to insistence that repayment arrangements for reimbursable functions be in hand before construction is completed. But it cannot always maintain this position, particularly when local interests desiring a project control enough political support to secure on their own congressional appropriations to the Bureau for construction. The Sacramento Canals project has shown this situation in most acute form, with strong local pressure for construction but much less willingness to sign repayment contracts. In this case, the Bureau has been driven to take on an additional risk-bearing function in designing local distribution system contracts. Where districts have been able to secure only a checker-board membership pattern, rendering difficult the design of a financially feasible distribution system, the Bureau has agreed to assume provisionally some costs which landowners could only bear if additional land were added to the districts. To the same end of designing feasible distribution systems, the Bureau reallocated some pumping installations from the distribution systems to the main works of the canals, thus removing from local landowners the obligation to pay for them directly.[116]

Related to entrepreneurial discretion on the financial arrangements for a project, the Bureau and Corps possess some freedom in determining the reimbursement required for the benefits of their projects. The joint costs of multiple purpose projects now are customarily allocated against various classes of beneficiaries by the "separable costs-remaining benefits" (SCRB) method, originally developed for the Tennessee Valley Authority and adopted for general use by the Bureau at least a decade ago.[117] No information seems to be available to suggest how much flexibility adheres in the application of this formula to particular projects—that is, how broadly

[115] Senate, Joint Subcommittee, *Bureau of Reclamation, Interior Department, op. cit.*, p. 7. Also see Lambert, *op. cit.*, pp. 256–64.

[116] *Sacramento Bee*, Sept. 2 and 11, 1961.

[117] U.S. Congress, House Committee on Interior and Insular Affairs, Special Subcommittee on Irrigation and Reclamation, *Water Resources Development Criteria*, 84 Cong. 2 sess. (1956), pp. 17–18. The SCRB method was designated as preferable for general application by agreement among the Department of the Interior, Department of the Army, and the Federal Power Commission as of March 12, 1954. In some circumstances, the "alternative justifiable expenditure" and "use of facilities" methods may be used.

the resulting allocation may depend on matters of judgment or might vary with the person performing the calculation.

Even before the Bureau tests its ability to collect the calculated reimbursable costs of a project, the mere designation of certain classes as reimbursable may influence the design of projects. For instance, a major benefit anticipated from the Friant-Kern Canal in the San Joaquin Valley was replenishment of depleted ground-water basins in its service area. Thus there would seem to be a possibility that leaving the canal unlined would both reduce construction costs and increase the benefits stemming from ground-water recharge. Independent engineering or hydrological reasons may have existed for rejecting this possibility and lining the canal, but the Bureau's public statement on the question instead emphasized the revenue-cost side of the issue:

> The Bureau of Reclamation has the responsibility for getting this investment back, and unless we can measure this water out to [local irrigators] and have them pay for it, we will not get the money back. . . . Leakage from the canal would be quite effective, but how would we ever collect for it?[118]

In short, however good or bad the investment criteria used by the Bureau and Corps, and the methods of calculation used to apply them, the investment decisions of these agencies are sensitive to political forces of all kinds. Local interest often bestirs the initial investigation of a project, defines the type and geographic magnitude of benefits sought, and governs the timing of construction through its influence on congressional appropriations. The requirement of a showing of "financial feasibility" (as defined) for federal projects (apart from satisfying benefit-cost criteria) obviously affords some elastic check against rank overoptimism in estimating benefits, but it also puts the design and timing of projects somewhat at the whim of imperfect local perceptions of benefits.

Implications of Investment Patterns for Market Performance

At this stage, it may be helpful to summarize the implications of the motives and constraints operating on investment decisions for allocative efficiency. Pending discussion to come in the following chapters about the impact of interagency rivalry for water, the exploitation of joint products, and the like, does the typical method of reaching investment decisions in the water industry contain serious biases away from optimality? Several distinct frontiers of economic efficiency can be violated by the marching forces of capital formation: the scale of projects may be too large or too small; their designs may value the distant future too dearly or too cheaply; in the face of growing demand, construction may come too soon or too late; uncertain outcomes may be too heavily discounted or too openly risked. And projects that are totally unjustified economically may be undertaken. We shall try to indicate the

[118] U.S. Congress, House Committee on Public Lands, Subcommittee on Irrigation and Reclamation, *The American River Basin Project*, 81 Cong. 1 sess. (1949).

general behavior of the different types of agencies toward these major allocative frontiers.

A study of the form and treatment of investment criteria employed by urban agencies indicates inefficiently low rates of discount and mechanical treatment of benefits which essentially assumes that marginal benefits are inelastic at any level of the consumptive use of water. Taken in conjunction with the typical pricing practices of these urban districts—practices which probably inflate present consumption by charging users responsible for the system peak less than long-run marginal cost—this treatment probably tends toward an overestimate of marginal benefits. Thus it tends toward an excessive scale of investment, just as the low discount rate favors the distant future too strongly. The risk of variations in peak demand and in natural water supply is typically met by attempts to avoid this uncertainty entirely. Although cities do not always succeed ex post in avoiding all contingencies of deficient water supply, investment plans nonetheless do not compare the net benefits of going to various lengths in the avoidance of anticipated risk. Nor are pricing systems adjusted to penalize appropriately those elements of demand with relatively large random components. While these factors all point toward excessive scale or capital-intensity of urban water investments, the evidence does not suggest that the timing of investments has been markedly premature. The lead time actually achieved by San Francisco Bay area agencies has reflected their complex external encounters, and they do not seem to have made excessive allowances in planning for the administrative and procedural delays occurring between the proposal of a project and its timely construction in the face of growing demand.

The one major force running counter to this tendency toward excessive scale and capital-intensity has been capital rationing and the related agency-oriented parameters entering into the design of projects. Clear evidence of capital rationing exists for East Bay Municipal Utility District (EBMUD), not to mention smaller urban water systems and the local agricultural districts. Although we stressed in preceding chapters that some urban agencies serve as tools in the expansion of general municipal governments, in these cases it is expansionist desires that lead to growth of the water agency and not scale economies for the water agency that lead to expansionist desires. The typical urban water agency does not question the given scope of its service area. The over-all impact of agency-oriented parameters on investments is a tendency toward inefficiently small scale. One cannot say that this pull just offsets the forces tending toward excessive scale identified above. Furthermore, because of the many dimensions of fixed plant in the water industry wherein the actual might either exceed or fall short of the ideal, a given project might readily be "too much" in some ways but simultaneously "too little" in others.

Concerning external influences upon the investment decisions of urban agencies, we have so far shown only that such influences may occur and operate strongly. The existence of rivals with valid claims to the source of water means that their claims must somehow be satisfied, and a new set of efficiency tests must be applied to the alternative compensations which might be made. In the case of San Francisco, the city's obligations to its rivals under the Raker Act have been met through providing physical investments in some cases when financial compensation (such as EBMUD employed with Amador and Calaveras) might have been more efficient.

Yet such compensation is not typically considered, in this or other such conflicts in the industry. Another bias toward excessive investment would seem tentatively identified.

Local agricultural districts make their investment decisions under rather different circumstances from their urban cousins. Broadly similar practices prevail in the selection of an investment criterion, particularly with regard to the rate of discount, but arbitrary assumptions about the scale at which marginal benefits fall to zero are replaced by arbitrary assumptions about an assumed elastic marginal level of benefits. In the recent rash of joint ventures with the Pacific Gas and Electric Company, the scales of investments have been set by the arbitrary procedure of designing the maximum output of irrigation water which could be secured under the condition that PG&E would be willing to pay all of the capital costs. This formula might conceivably lead to excessive scales because of the discount rate employed and biases in taxation factors. But also it obviously might produce inefficiently small projects so far as districts do not consider the marginal benefits and costs of increasing the output of irrigation water if they themselves contributed to the capital outlays for construction. An overriding interest in far-future profits from sales of electric power, or in reducing the cost of water to existing irrigators, may explain this. The "payment capacity" apparent in the farm enterprises of the districts in question does not suggest that substantially larger projects would be warranted with appropriate calculations; but the possibility that they might does not seem to have had full consideration.

The external forces bearing on local agricultural water projects cause them to run through an elaborate series of procedural steps which, by their duration, affect the timing of projects, and which can produce substantial changes in project designs. The scale of projects tends to diminish, in at least some cases, and in contrast to the case of urban agencies. The composition of joint outputs tends to shift toward electric power. The trend in the scale of investments, as affected by external rivalries, would seem to be the opposite of that operating on the urban agencies, which tend to build larger projects to satisfy everybody. But this is a very tentative generalization based on a very few cases.

Agricultural water investments also show the mark of external forces in the conspicuous role of band-wagon effects and defensive investments. Surely the fact that water or water rights now claimed by another agency may never again come up for sale has proved a powerful stimulus for new investment projects. The allocative results of these forces are hard to appraise. Are inefficient projects built in order to keep the water at home? Or does the entrepreneurial interest in undertaking beneficial projects arise only when stirred by external rivalry? The evidence on these questions is hardly clear.

Local agricultural agencies tend to be limited by capital rationing and the short time horizons of their member-customers much more sharply than are urban agencies, and there is little doubt that this factor has restricted the scales of their investments in the past. The same bias results from the specialized character of many local agricultural districts, which removes from their purview those types of benefits other than irrigation water and salable joint outputs—principally electric power. A number of present-day factors are working to reverse these historic restrictions on the scales of investments by local agricultural districts. The federal government makes contributions to cover the cost of including provision for flood control benefits. Several "soft" forms of financial assistance are now available to offset the pressure of capital rationing. County-wide agencies, with presumably broader vision in contemplating all types of benefits, are playing a greater role. The net result of these forces is highly uncertain, but it would seem safe to guess that there has been a trend away from suboptimal scales and delayed timing in local agricultural investments.

Among the agencies of federal and state governments, the Bureau of Reclamation and the Corps of Engineers possess the theoretical advantage of employing investment criteria which, with proper use, could give better results than those used by local agencies. Furthermore, their cognizance of benefits is not restricted to one class of benefits, or to benefits accruing to a particular area, as with local and special purpose districts. The California Department of Water Resources shares the second of these hypothetical laurels, but not the first, on account of its foreswearing of any evaluation criterion other than reimbursability.

Unfortunately, difficulties start to appear as soon as we examine the actual use made of these investment criteria by the federal agencies. Inappropriately low discount rates are used throughout. Certain types of opportunity costs are systematically ignored. The calculation of marginal benefits and costs, rather than total or average figures, remains in its infancy. Furthermore, the examination of specific feasibility studies made by the Bureau and the Corps reveals frequent departures from the correct application of these methods of appraisal in devising particular estimates. Sometimes benefits seem by any reasonable test to have been grossly overstated. Sometimes the evaluation of benefits by the cost of the best alternative is abused by the choice of an inappropriate alternative. Sometimes costs which obviously should be assigned to a project are simply left out, either because some other party can be expected to incur them or because the agency responsible can justify them in some other way.

Partly to explain these undesirable practices, partly to identify still other biases, we have investigated the relation of investment planning by the Bureau of Reclamation to the expressed preferences of would-be local beneficiaries in the location. scale, and character of projects. This relation appears to be a strong and important one. Added to the traditional orientation of the Bureau toward reclamation benefits (and the Corps toward flood control benefits), these pressures tend to produce construction programs responsive to expressed political interest rather than economic benefit. They tend to produce inappropriate scales and designs related to the geographic extent of interested beneficiaries rather than to calculated marginal benefits and costs. They tend to bias project designs toward those classes of benefits destined for groups with active political organizations and spokesmen. Some of the abuses of benefit-cost analysis no doubt result from economic analysis being bent to the justification of decisions made essentially on political grounds. We have developed behavioral evidence on these points relating mainly to the Bureau of Reclamation because of its longer history of activity in Northern California. Nevertheless, evidence on the Corps' activity in other areas and the initial steps taken by the California Department of Water Resources suggests no better marks for them. The congressional processes of authorization and appropriation mainly balance equities among regions and interest groups and show little tendency to correct the distortions induced by the administrative agencies.

In closing, we can contrast the normative appraisal of the state and federal agencies with that of the units of local government. The investment decisions of the latter appear subject to a number of biases pulling this way and that. No strong net direction of bias is apparent, and a mixture of effects seems a strong possibility. The chances seem strong, though, that capital rationing and other agency-oriented parameters have promoted investments of deficient scale and deficient regard for diverse classes of benefits—especially among agricultural districts and especially in the past. By contrast, the net bias of the state and federal agencies seems clearly toward excessive scales of investment and premature investment, whether it is due to the political forces operating on their investment plans, to a bias toward the full physical development of water resources, or to purely bureaucratic factors. Furthermore, the very advantages of higher level governments in contemplating benefits of all types, and costs wherever they may accrue, seem to a serious extent to have been discarded. A final appraisal must await Part Three, where we place this behavioral evidence beside some direct measurements of the allocative efficiency of the state and federal dam-builders.

12

COMPETITION TO APPROPRIATE NATURAL SUPPLIES

Transactions occurring among units in the water industry of Northern California and the general economic relations which they maintain with one another are considered here and in the following two chapters. The number and character of interagency contacts having market implications show the extent to which perceived economic rivalry exists within the area: whether water is a scarce good only within particular river basins, or whether its scarcity casts a network of positive shadow prices over the resource throughout the area. Although the existence of some market-type transactions or allocations tells us that the allotment of water among alternative uses is not entirely random, a direct normative appraisal of the transactions or their results is necessary for weighing the quality of the performance. In making this appraisal, we must keep in mind comparisons among the industry's regions with respect to the demand-supply balance for surface water and user concentration (discussed in Chapters 2 and 4). Are there systematic relations between these structural traits and the quality of performance?

We shall divide market relations into three groups, recognizing throughout that a given transaction, agreement, or settlement between a pair of agencies may fall into more than one group. First of all, there is rivalry for water in its natural state or source: the summer flow of a river which can be diverted and put directly to use; the winter flow or spring runoff which can be stored and then diverted during the season of peak demand; and water in underground basins which can be extracted with pumps. This water is, in the first instance, no one's property. The process of rivalry for it stems from efforts to establish conditional or unconditional legal rights to make use of water. This process and its outcome is studied in the present chapter.

Once claims have been established to a particular flow of water, further transactions in water must involve either the sale or other transfer of water rights between agencies, or the sale or transfer of water itself. Transactions of this type can take the conventional buyer-seller form, although they need not do so. Within the California water industry, we can identify to some extent layers of agencies with essentially wholesaling and retailing functions in the distribution of water. Their classification reflects transactions of this type between units in these respective layers. Such "bilateral" transactions are considered in Chapter 13.

The use, management, regulation, and conveyance of water can provide many types of utilities. Consumptive uses for domestic, industrial, and agricultural purposes are joined by the generation of electric power, recreation, navigation, and flood control as sources of major types of benefits. Some of these utilities are complementary with one another, so that a given allocation of water can increase more than one of them simultaneously, whereas others are competitive. Some such relations are dispersed in space and nonproportional in amount, and are not readily distinguishable from what we customarily think of as external economies and diseconomies. In any case, certain transactions and relations in the water industry reflect the relations between these different types of water-related utilities. Chapter 14 reviews these relations.

Establishing a claim to the use of water essentially amounts to the creation of a property right. One might suppose that no economic transaction is involved beyond the appropriation of a free resource into the category of economic scarcity. Even if that characterization were apt, the creation of rights to water would have economic significance because of the impact of the pattern of established rights on subsequent economic relations among water users. But the characterization is not suitable for much of the present-day process of creating new water rights. Appropriative rights to most flows now unappropriated cannot by California law be established *in vacuo,* but can accrue only along with a physical investment plan for putting water to some beneficial use. Thus the establishment and definition of water rights is broadly interrelated with the investment process discussed in the preceding chapter.

Indeed, economic and litigatory conduct are thoroughly scrambled in the water industry. There is no large class of transactions involving the establishment or transfer of a water right that involves the exercise only of general powers to contract. Often the property rights themselves are defined only imperfectly, so that no substantial action can be undertaken involving water or water development facilities without judicial definition of rights. Even where rights are clearly defined, contractual arrangements affecting such allocations often encounter litigatory complications because external effects (real or imagined) are so common. But it is not only contractual transactions which often become entangled with litigation over the determination and protection of property rights. In addition, the legal machinery created for determining and protecting these rights affords many tactical opportunities that extend and complicate the dimensions of bargaining power bearing upon any given contractual transaction. Furthermore, these legal constraints and opportunities affect not only the positions of the primary parties to a transaction (and thus its economic outcome), but also those indirectly or incidentally affected who thus gain a chance to improve their position in the process. Litigatory action (before courts or quasi-judicial bodies) becomes a means by which to harass, deter, or displace, and not just a constraint upon making contracts.[1]

A major reason why the rivalry for water rights and water in its natural state assumes such great importance is the near absence of rivalry among retail distributors of water for final customers. We have indicated that the use of water

[1] One of the few major empirical studies to probe this sort of interrelation of law and economic conduct effectively is James Willard Hurst, *Law and Economic Growth: The Legal History of the Lumber Industry in Wisconsin, 1836–1915* (1964). (This and other footnote references are cited in brief form when they are also included in the Bibliography.)

by final customers is in effect attached to the location of these buyers on particular parcels of land, and these parcels cannot readily be attached to one water district or detached from another except in unusual circumstances. Only among urban water agencies have we uncovered any significant number of cases of rivalry between retailers to supply given groups of final customers. The nearly complete lack of rivalry for customers among agricultural water agencies reflects, in addition to legal barriers, their orientation toward minimizing the cost of water to existing members. It also reflects the attitudes of the irrigators themselves, since those in a district levying higher charges than neighboring units passively accept their fate rather than agitate for an adjustment of district boundaries.[2]

Of course, this absence of alternatives at retail would not necessarily preclude efficient allocation of water in Northern California. The fact that competitive conduct in the water industry "reaches back" toward sources of water rather than "reaching forward" toward final customers does not inevitably forestall such allocation. Therefore, if local districts, acting as users' cooperatives seeking water for their members, competed effectively for water and water rights, if no artificial restrictions precluded the entry of new districts, and if any water secured by a district were allocated optimally among its members, then optimal allocation could result at all stages of the distribution process.[3] But failure of fulfillment of any or all of these conditions is likely to result in the emergence of misallocations from the rivalry for sources of water.

The character of rivalry for water and water rights in Northern California has changed continuously over the past century. The earliest conflicts arose over the establishment and definition of rights to the late spring and summer flows of the major rivers, water which could be put to agricultural use through direct diversion alone. By the time of World War I, these flows had become fully appropriated in most streams passing through the Central Valley, and the locus of rivalry began to shift toward unappropriated winter and early spring runoff, where it could be retained for summer agricultural use through the construction of storage reservoirs. But because of the severe depression of California agriculture during the 1930's, relatively little rivalry of this type actually arose. Only since World War II has the competition for "out of season" water opened in earnest. Along with it has come a newly effective interest in transferring water from river basins where it is relatively abundant to areas where it is scarce. The on-going rivalry for water and rights now involves more far-flung claimants to a given source than ever before, and the rise of large wholesaling units to exploit the scale economies inherent in long-distance inter-basin transfers of water.

As important changes have occurred in the economic environment of the competition for water rights, so also have important changes taken place in the

[2] The fact or belief that land values seem only weakly to reflect differences in the quality of water rights and the cost of water service facilitates this attitude. Interviews with Bert L. Smith, secretary, Economics Committee, Irrigation Districts Association of California, August 5, 1960; and Charles L. Kaupke, consultant, Kings River Water Association, August 19, 1960. Compare Michael F. Brewer, *Water Pricing and Allocation with Particular Reference to California Irrigation Districts,* California Agricultural Experiment Station, Giannini Foundation of Agricultural Economics (1960), pp. 128–30.

[3] See Chapter 8, section on Shadow Prices and Optimal Allocation of Scarce Water.

legal environment. The 1928 "beneficial use" amendment, the state filings for unappropriated water, and improved official records of runoffs and diversions—all comprise important parts of the story. Both the changing extent and character of the competition for water and the changing legal environment afford additional degrees of freedom for determining the relations between the structural environment of the industry and the character and quality of its conduct.

To relate the subsequent discussion to this thumbnail sketch of historical development, the first section below deals with the process of establishing rights to water usable in agriculture by direct diversion alone. We then turn to the more recent competition for water in the "winter" markets, associated with the construction of water storage projects. The role of interbasin transfers by large wholesalers in the competition for rights and water is postponed to Chapter 13, because the pursuit of water by these wholesalers is inextricably tangled with bargaining for the sale or transfer of the water thus captured to retailing agencies. A final substantive section of this chapter discusses rivalry for water in underground basins.

Rivalry for Surface Supplies: Natural Flow

The most striking examples of conflict over unregulated streamflow go far back into the history of California irrigation. By the 1930's, control of the natural flow in rivers of the San Joaquin Valley had been fully determined through economic or judicial procedures. While parallel disputes over control of natural flow are scarce today, it is not because such allocations have been settled once and for all, but probably more because of the reluctance of user agencies to invoke such procedures. The sort of rivalry which typified the earlier period is illustrated by the struggles over water from the Kings River.

The Kings River

The forum of conflict for Kings River claimants before the 1920's was the county superior courts. At least 150 suits were filed between 1880 and 1910 in which one riparian or appropriative user sought to establish a prior right against another.[4] Appropriators based their claim on priority of filings; riparian users, after the decision in *Lux* vs. *Haggin* (1884),[5] had only to establish their riparian status. In principle, such judicial proceedings might lead to a complete ordering of claims to water of the Kings. In practice, the procedure proved clumsy and produced inconsistent results and peculiar side-effects. Economic elements of market conduct became very much evident. Part of the trouble with this adjudicatory process was that each decision settled the rights only as between two parties.

[4] Kings River Water Association, *Forty Years on Kings River, 1917–1957,* by Charles L. Kaupke (1957), p. 31.
[5] 69 Calif. 255 (1884).

A might establish a right to the first hundred second-feet of the river as against *B*, a similar right as against *C*, but a right to the first thousand second-feet as against *D*. The relative rights of *B*, *C*, and *D* remained completely undefined. *A* might gain an injunction forcing *E* to cease diverting and to fill in the head of his canal; but *E* might gain a prior right as against *F* and continue to operate on that basis. At best, any agency knew its rights to the river only as against those rivals with whom some legal proceeding had been joined.[6] Even the agencies which had gone through these proceedings had no assurance that the resulting decisions (often rendered by different courts) would be consistent. *A* could conceivably establish a right prior to *B*'s, *B* a right prior to *C*'s, and *C* a right prior to *A*'s.[7] No machinery existed to provide quick enforcement of existing decisions and injunctions, so that in dry years physical warfare often occurred as agencies sought to destroy upstream diversion works.

Court decisions at that time suffered from many drawbacks of inadequate information and inefficient procedure. Many notices on file of intention to appropriate were vague about the location of the diversion and inconsistent and extravagant in the amount of water claimed. Information on whether or not a proposed diversion had been diligently prosecuted was, naturally, even harder to secure. The courts lacked impartial technical aid to establish the facts.[8] As a final drawback, these court proceedings were widely felt to be very expensive relative to the discounted present value of the rights which they might establish.

The prominent actors in the strife over Kings River water at that time can be located with the aid of Figure 20. They included Laguna de Tache Rancho (a giant riparian territory including land now in the Laguna Irrigation District), a number of small canal companies downstream, and several larger canal companies diverting upstream near where the Kings River emerges from the Sierra Nevada foothills. Decisions affecting these parties set off a remarkable string of mergers, agreements, and transfers of rights which finally led in 1949 to a complete negotiated settlement of water allocation on the Kings. The first steps involved actions taken by defeated districts. Laguna de Tache Rancho had won a decision requiring the Fowler Switch Canal, an upstream channel, to cease diverting entirely. However, the Emigrant Ditch, another diversion serving a territory interlocked with that of Fowler Switch, established a modest right against the Rancho. (Both served lands now in Consolidated Irrigation District.) Fowler Switch and Emigrant reached an agreement whereby part of the Emigrant diversion would be taken through Fowler Switch, maximizing the lands benefiting through the diversions of the two canals jointly.[9] Likewise, two large and formerly competing upstream canal companies, Fresno Canal and Kings River and Fresno Canal (now Fresno Irrigation District), merged their properties as a result of

[6] U.S. Department of Agriculture, Office of Experiment Stations, *Report of Irrigation Investigations in California*, by Elwood Mead *et al.*, Bulletin No. 100 (1901), pp. 58–62. (Hereinafter cited as Bulletin No. 100.)

[7] *Ibid.*, p. 282. For an actual example, see California State Department of Engineering, *Use of Water from Kings River, California, 1918*, by Harry Barnes, Bulletin No. 7 (1920), p. 108.

[8] Bulletin No. 100, *op. cit.*, pp. 269–72, 282.

[9] *Ibid.*, pp. 277, 291.

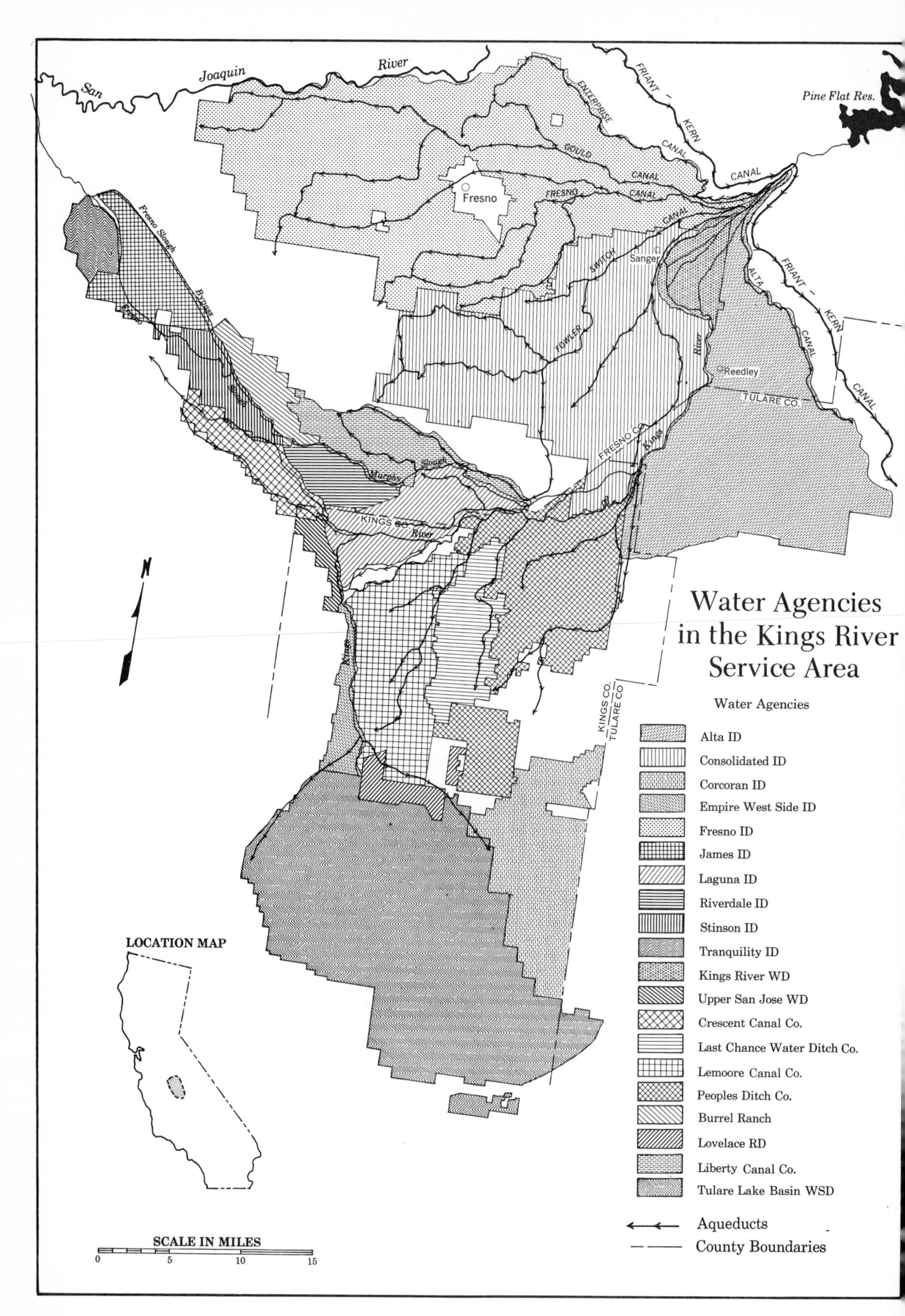
Water Agencies in the Kings River Service Area
Water Agencies
Alta ID
Consolidated ID
Corcoran ID
Empire West Side ID
Fresno ID
James ID
Laguna ID
Riverdale ID
Stinson ID
Tranquility ID
Kings River WD
Upper San Jose WD
Crescent Canal Co.
Last Chance Water Ditch Co.
Lemoore Canal Co.
Peoples Ditch Co.
Burrel Ranch
Lovelace RD
Liberty Canal Co.
Tulare Lake Basin WSD
Aqueducts
County Boundaries
San Joaquin River
Pine Flat Res.
FRIANT - KERN CANAL
ENTERPRISE CANAL
GOULD CANAL
FRESNO CANAL
Fresno
Sanger
SWITCH
FOWLER
ALTA CANAL
Reedley
TULARE CO.
FRESNO CO.
KINGS CO.
Kings River
Murphy Slough
Fresno Slough
Bypass
N
LOCATION MAP
SCALE IN MILES
0
5
10
15

Figure 20

court decisions. The latter canal had been ordered to cease diverting, but it was well located, both for effecting a diversion and for serving a large and fertile agricultural territory.[10] In addition to mergers and agreements approximating merger, many other agreements on sharing water were reached out of court.[11]

More extensive agreements grew from these beginnings. The Laguna de Tache Rancho was in such a strong position that the upstream canals could secure a water right only by buying it out. This was done by the best financed and potentially most profitable of the upstream companies, the Fresno Canal and the Kings River and Fresno Canal. After acquiring title to the Rancho, the owners of the canals quit-claimed some 3,000 second-feet of water. This action transferred no water right to the canals, but it did set aside the court decree and allowed the Kings River and Fresno Canal to divert to its full capacity.[12] The way was paved for an agreement in 1897 on the measurement and division of diversions made by the parties holding the strongest rights to the Kings River.

In the 1910's, the proposal to construct a dam at Pine Flat for irrigation and power development was being widely discussed. A group was formed to investigate its feasibility and to promote a broader negotiated diversion schedule, which was seen as a prerequisite to carrying out a storage project. By 1917, companies and irrigation districts had reached the point where they were submitting trial diversion schedules, which at least led to agreement on the need to employ a neutral engineer to make the necessary measurements.[13] The negotiations remained deadlocked on minor issues until the whole mare's nest of long-pending riparian suits was set for trial in 1921. The threat of a long expensive trial was enough to force the parties to accept arbitration by the State Division of Water Rights.[14] Eventually, under the pressure of interest in the proposed construction of Pine Flat Dam,[15] a diversion schedule was completed in 1927 covering all but flood flows (which were included only in 1949).

Taken by itself, the case of the Kings River suggests a number of conclusions

[10] *Ibid.*, pp. 286, 289. In 1901, the Fresno Canal interests expanded further by gaining control of Fowler Switch Canal. For a more extensive account of the growth of the Fresno Canal enterprise, including other mergers, see I. Teilman and W. H. Shafer, *The Historical Story of Irrigation in Fresno and Kings Counties in Central California* (1943).

[11] Bulletin No. 100, *op. cit.*, pp. 306–10.

[12] *Ibid.*, pp. 310, 321; Kings River Water Association, *Forty Years on Kings River, op. cit.*, p. 34 (quoting W. P. Boone, "Kings River Water Rights History, Litigation and Mutual Agreement of Settlement," unpublished manuscript, *ca.* 1935); California State Department of Public Works, Division of Engineering and Irrigation, *Irrigation Districts in California, 1929*, by Frank Adams, Bulletin No. 21 (1930), pp. 204–05. [Hereinafter cited as Bulletin No. 21 (Adams).] At the time of the purchase, the Rancho had gained court decrees against almost every major upstream canal company.

[13] Kings River Water Association, *Forty Years on Kings River, op. cit.*, pp. 6–10, 36–37, 72–74.

[14] *Ibid.*, pp. 18–21; California State Department of Public Works, Division of Water Rights, *Kings River Investigation*, by Harold Conkling and Charles L. Kaupke, Bulletin No. 2 (1923), pp. 8–15.

[15] Apparently the lack of a diversion schedule had previously forced the water users to reject an offer by the San Joaquin Power & Light Corporation to construct the dam in return for rights to the power it could generate therefrom. In addition, the irrigators suspected the utility's motives and assumed that, if San Joaquin Power & Light saw a profit in the venture, they could reap this same profit by proceeding alone. See Charles L. Palmer, *The Story of the Kings River* (1955), p. 40.

about the allocation of surface water among competing irrigation agencies. Prior appropriation and riparian status convey powerful advantages to their possessors in what is primarily a legalistic allocation process: to the extent that these primary generalizations make up the complete story, economic factors are absent from market conduct. However, economic factors were very much present, and not only as a result of the incompleteness and inefficiency of the judicial allocation process. The fixed cost of establishing and defending water rights is reflected in the more resourceful maneuvers of the larger and wealthier agencies and the collaborative arrangements of the smaller ones. In a few cases, lands denied access to water won access to a water right by merger or negotiated agreement, but this solution required direct proximity to an agency with satisfactory rights, and permitted only limited if desirable reallocations. The long-time uncertainty about rights to the Kings, reflecting in part the unwieldy legal processes of the time, greatly hampered efficient water allocations and investment decisions within the area. Finally, a number of factors biased the outcome of controversies over water toward negotiated rather than judicially determined settlements—principally the number of agencies and the imperfect character of historic records of flows and diversions.

Other San Joaquin Valley rivers

These events on the Kings River coincided with the ordering of water rights on most of the other rivers of the Central Valley. Each case shows sundry similarities to as well as differences from that of the Kings. Are these comparisons correlated with structural similarities and differences in the patterns of competing units? Do other rivers with large numbers of agencies show coalitions and negotiated settlements? A comparative study seems to show a pattern in the broader aspects of water rights determination on the various rivers.

First, consider three tributaries of the San Joaquin River—the Merced, Tuolumne, and Stanislaus rivers, shown in Figure 21. The Merced River has long been dominated by a single large agency; the Tuolumne and the Stanislaus each by a pair of large agencies in long-standing cooperation with each other. Since the early development of irrigation along the Merced River the one large unit operating near the foothills—now Merced Irrigation District—has always been the focus of litigation. Various downstream rights, mostly riparian, have been established against the District and its predecessors, but these are all relatively small and can be satisfied either by maintaining a minimum flow in the Merced River or transferring water directly through the District's canals. The District's rights situation allowed it to build its first major storage project in the 1920's, and the existence of a large diverter with a strong but not exclusionary water right has greatly simplified the establishment at law of the rights of other users by effectively eliminating the need for ordering all possible pairs of priorities.

The cases of the Stanislaus and Tuolumne rivers are similar except that the dominant units are pairs of large irrigation districts which have maintained

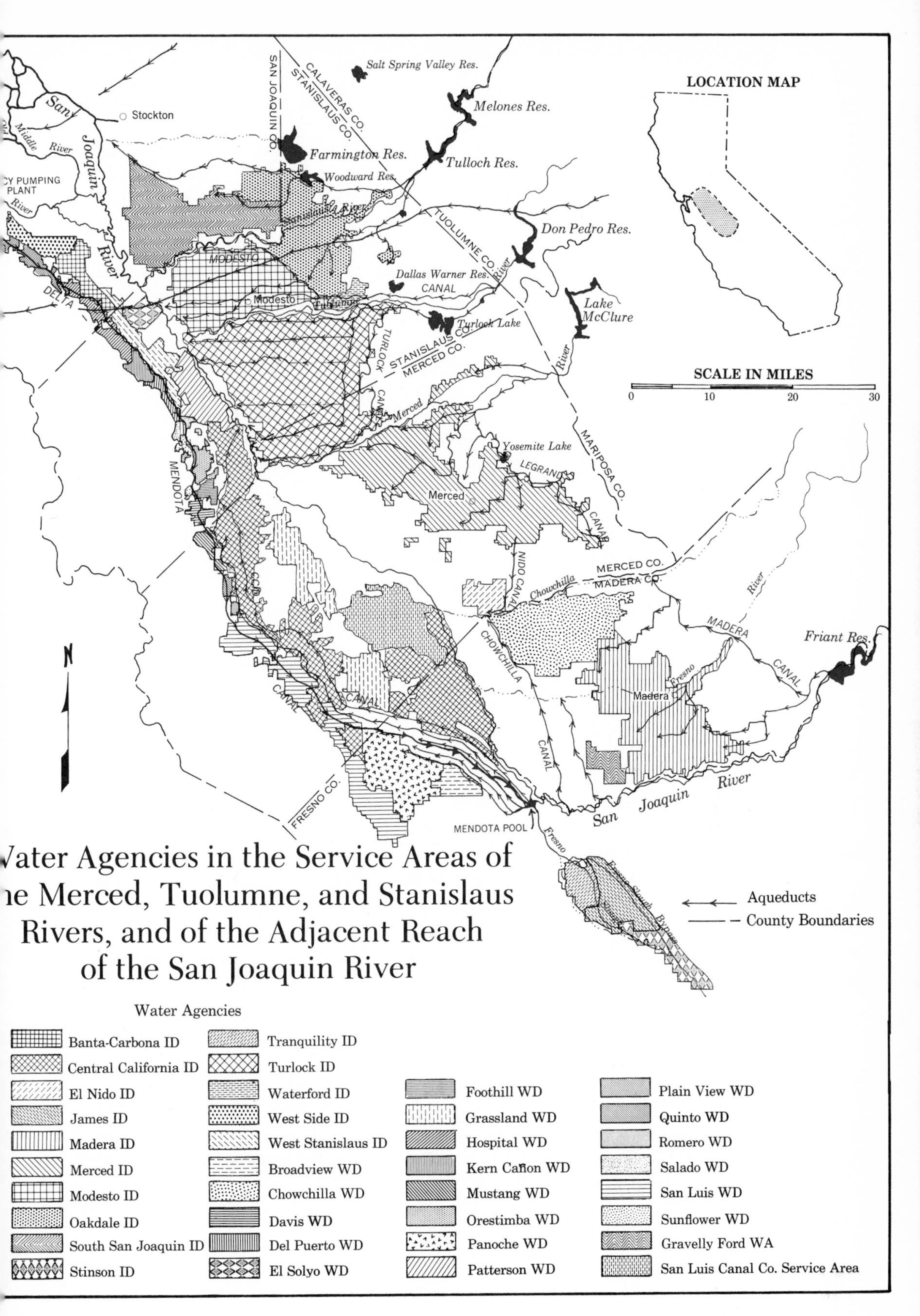

Salt Spring Valley Res.
Melones Res.
Stockton
San Joaquin River
Middle River
CALAVERAS CO.
STANISLAUS CO.
SAN JOAQUIN CO.
Farmington Res.
Woodward Res.
Tulloch Res.
PUMPING PLANT
Stanislaus River
Don Pedro Res.
TUOLUMNE CO.
MODESTO
Modesto
DELTA
Dallas Warner Res.
CANAL
Tuolumne River
Turlock Lake
Lake McClure
TURLOCK CANAL
STANISLAUS CO.
MERCED CO.
Merced River
MARIPOSA CO.
Yosemite Lake
LEGRAND CANAL
Merced
MENDOTA
NIDO CANAL
Chowchilla River
MERCED CO.
MADERA CO.
CHOWCHILLA CANAL
MADERA CANAL
Friant Res.
Fresno River
Madera
CANAL
FRESNO CO.
MENDOTA POOL
San Joaquin River
Fresno Slough Bypass
LOCATION MAP
SCALE IN MILES
0
10
20
30
N
ater Agencies in the Service Areas of
e Merced, Tuolumne, and Stanislaus
Rivers, and of the Adjacent Reach
of the San Joaquin River
Aqueducts
County Boundaries
Water Agencies
Banta-Carbona ID
Central California ID
El Nido ID
James ID
Madera ID
Merced ID
Modesto ID
Oakdale ID
South San Joaquin ID
Stinson ID
Tranquility ID
Turlock ID
Waterford ID
West Side ID
West Stanislaus ID
Broadview WD
Chowchilla WD
Davis WD
Del Puerto WD
El Solyo WD
Foothill WD
Grassland WD
Hospital WD
Kern Cañon WD
Mustang WD
Orestimba WD
Panoche WD
Patterson WD
Plain View WD
Quinto WD
Romero WD
Salado WD
San Luis WD
Sunflower WD
Gravelly Ford WA
San Luis Canal Co. Service Area

Figure 21

successful cooperation since their formation.[16] Here we will discuss only the Tuolumne.[17] In that case, the Modesto and Turlock irrigation districts were formed in 1887 and reached an early agreement to share water rights and supplies, with the Turlock District holding a 68.46 per cent interest.[18] The two districts had originally planned to draw on different rivers (with the Modesto Irrigation District going to the Stanislaus), but the greater runoff of the Tuolumne River and the economies of joint construction of diversion and storage dams quickly became apparent. These steps were accomplished without an unusual amount of litigation, although over occasionally severe internal opposition. Unlike the case of the Stanislaus, however, these districts were later joined by two other agencies competing for water in the face of the strong prior rights of Modesto and Turlock. Shortly after the turn of the century, the city of San Francisco fastened upon the Tuolumne River as a source of high quality water for large-scale export. While the city was willing to assure minimum flows to the still developing districts, the Modesto and Turlock districts opposed its filings and application for a permit from the U.S. Secretary of the Interior to develop the headwaters of the Tuolumne in Yosemite National Park. The compromise eventually embodied in the Raker Act[19] acknowledged the right of the districts to the natural flow of the Tuolumne at their diversion works up to 2,350 cubic feet per second, which is equal to or greater than the full natural flow in five to eight months of the year. Furthermore, they gained the privilege of buying water from San Francisco in dry years.[20]

The other late-comer to the Tuolumne was the Waterford Irrigation District, formed in 1913 adjacent to Modesto Irrigation District. Having initially friendly relations with Modesto, it succeeded in establishing a reasonably satisfactory water right by a series of moves. These were: the purchase of an old mining right to the Tuolumne; a filing for any unappropriated water at the Modesto-Turlock diversion works; and the purchase of a perpetual right to transfer the water it captured through the Modesto main canal.[21]

Uneasy relations between San Francisco and the irrigation districts on the Tuolumne continued despite the Raker Act compromise and subsequent amicable arrangements about water releases, water purchases, and common investment in dams. San Francisco's chief engineer reported that he was "starting tunnel work at the Early Intake aqueduct so as to make a stronger physical demonstration of our intent for diversion of water to protect us in our controversy with the

[16] Bulletin No. 21 (Adams), *op. cit.*, pp. 190–97. Compare, however, Merced's conflict with Mariposa County (described below under subsection on types of conflicts).

[17] The case of the Stanislaus River is documented in the following sources: California State Department of Engineering, *Irrigation Districts in California, 1887–1915,* by Frank Adams, Bulletin No. 2 (1916), pp. 66–74 [hereinafter cited as Bulletin No. 2 (Adams)]; Bulletin No. 21 (Adams), *op. cit.*, pp. 168–77; Tudor-Goodenough Engineers, *Summary Report on the Tri-Dam Project, Stanislaus River, California* (1959), pp. 13–16; and California Irrigation District Bond Commission, *Report on Oakdale Irrigation District* (1914), pp. 31–40.

[18] The gross area of the Turlock Irrigation District was 68.46 per cent of the gross area of the two districts together.

[19] For other features of the Raker Act, see Chapter 11.

[20] Bulletin No. 21 (Adams), *op. cit.*, pp. 180–83; California Irrigation District Bond Commission, *Report on Modesto Irrigation District* (1914), pp. 26–29.

[21] Bulletin No. 2 (Adams), *op. cit.*, p. 76; Bulletin No. 21 (Adams), *op. cit.*, pp. 177–80.

irrigationists. The Modesto directors have had a row in their camp and discharged their engineer, so they are not now in shape to go to court with us, and as time is working in our favor we are awaiting the proposed legal contest with interest but no anxiety."[22] The speed of construction of different facilities was affected by the competition over supply presumably settled by the Raker Act, in the belief that rights to floodwater could be secured that way.[23] Not only was speed felt to be necessary, but the antagonism encountered at Washington, and the obstructions offered by the districts of Turlock and Modesto, demanded a more expensive scale of activities and heavier expenditure for works in the Sierra watershed than necessary for actual immediate water supply needs, in order to underwrite and protect the city's water rights in its future needs for domestic water supply. Hence the city undertook the construction of a larger dam at Hetch Hetchy than was contemplated in the original reports, and the early diversion of waters of Cherry River and Eleanor Creek into the watershed of the main aqueduct at Early Intake.[24]

The Tuolumne River case shares with the cases of the Merced and Stanislaus rivers some characteristics associated with the control of rivers by a few large units. Prior appropriation by the two dominant irrigation districts basically settled the allocation of rights, and late-comers were forced, after more or less of a struggle, to use Tuolumne waters on terms which fully recognized these preexisting rights. The purchase of existing rights was a relatively common occurrence. Elements of oligopsonistic rivalry appear in the later relations between the irrigation districts and the city of San Francisco.

Several rivers dominated by a few large users show more extreme forms of interagency conflict and less of the cooperation found on the Stanislaus and Tuolumne, because of more fundamental disagreements between the dominant users. The Kern River was the scene of California's greatest legal battle over water rights, that between the Miller and Lux and the Haggin and Tevis interests. The Miller forces owned a large parcel of reclaimed swampland into which the Kern River, without outlet to the ocean, discharged its waters. Miller and Lux claimed riparian rights for this land to the flow of the Kern, as against the intention of the Haggin and Tevis interests to appropriate water upstream for use on non-riparian land. The State Supreme Court decision of 1886 favored Miller and Lux and affirmed the riparian right in California. But the final result was an agreement whereby Miller and Lux offered the Haggin interests two-thirds of the water of the Kern available to these parties (minus percolation losses) if they would build a downstream storage reservoir at Buena Vista Lake. The Miller-Haggin agreement of 1888 has ruled the allocation of the Kern, except

[22] M. M. O'Shaughnessy, *Hetch Hetchy: Its Origin and History* (1934), p. 76.

[23] *Ibid.*, p. 122.

[24] M. M. O'Shaughnessy, "Present Status of Hetch Hetchy," *Transactions of the Commonwealth Club of California,* XVII (May 1922), 420. For information on related political maneuvers, see Ray W. Taylor, *Hetch Hetchy* (1926), pp. 158–59; Benjamin Franklin Rhodes, Jr., "Thirsty Land: The Modesto Irrigation District, a Case Study of Irrigation under the Wright Law" (Unpublished Ph.D. dissertation, University of California, Berkeley, 1943), chap. 11.

for minor adjustments, to this day, despite some deconcentration in the landownership pattern and any differences which may have existed between the marginal productivity of water in the two areas.[25]

On the Kern River, the fewness of competing users finally proved compatible with an agreement being reached on some sort of division of water among them. The San Joaquin River (above the junction with its major tributaries) provides a striking contrast in the failure of two similarly large agencies, Miller and Lux and the Madera Irrigation District, to reach agreement. Miller and Lux once held great quantities of riparian land west of the San Joaquin and north of Mendota Pool (see Figure 21) and controlled much of the River's flow, using it partly for conventional irrigation and partly to water grazing or grasslands from winter and spring floodwaters. The Madera Irrigation District, formed in 1920 without a significant water supply of its own, then covered a giant block of 330,000 acres north and east of the San Joaquin River and capable of irrigation from its appropriated waters.[26] In 1922, the Madera Irrigation District and some of the Miller and Lux lands were drawn together into the San Joaquin Water Storage District, in an attempt to provide the basis for an agreement for the construction of a dam at Friant on the San Joaquin. This effort failed, the Storage District was dissolved in 1929, and the project was postponed until the Bureau of Reclamation reached an agreement with Miller and Lux a decade later.[27] Records do not show why the negotiations in the 1920's failed. Possibly the Miller and Lux interests, adjusted to using the floodwaters of the river, had little use for a dam. Possibly the Madera District was not able to offer what Miller and Lux considered reasonable compensation. In any case, the use of San Joaquin water for flooding grasslands was clearly a use of much lower productivity than that contemplated by Madera, and no objective economic circumstances seem to explain two major failures in four decades to reach an agreement.[28] The Kern and San Joaquin cases, taken together with the Merced and Tuolumne cases, suggest that a higher concentration of users along a river can lead to easy agreement, firm rights, and efficient development of storage and distribution facilities,

[25] Another agreement, the Shaw decree of 1895, affirmed rights on the basis of historic use between Haggin and smaller upstream diverters who had appropriated about one-third of the Kern water. See Edward F. Treadwell, *The Cattle King* (2nd ed.; 1931), pp. 78–94; California State Department of Engineering, *Water Resources of the Kern River and Adjacent Streams and Their Utilization, 1920,* Bulletin No. 9 (1921), pp. 36–37; California State Public Utilities Commission, *Report on the Results of Operation of Buena Vista Canal, Inc. . . . Year 1959 Recorded and Adjusted, Year 1960 Estimates,* Applications No. 41402–41407 for Authority to Increase Rates for Irrigation Service Near Bakersfield, County of Kern (1960).

[26] This discussion omits the role of numerous other downstream users of the San Joaquin, such as Chowchilla Farms and the Stevinson Corporation. Mostly riparian to the river and mostly grassland operators, these agencies were also embroiled in the courts with Miller and Lux. Without resort to county court records information on them has proved elusive.

[27] Bulletin No. 2 (Adams), *op. cit.,* pp. 25–27; Bulletin No. 21 (Adams), *op. cit.,* pp. 199–203.

[28] The Madera Irrigation District apparently was not the only agency to attempt to secure San Joaquin water through negotiations with Miller and Lux. An official of the Fresno Irrigation District has stated that this District in the 1920's acquired an option for 100,000 acre-feet annually, but it lacked storage facilities at the time and saw the option thrown out by the courts before it could be exercised. The city of Fresno filed applications in 1930 and 1931 to appropriate 175,000 acre-feet annually from a dam at Friant for both municipal and irrigation purposes; see California State Water Rights Board, Decision No. D 935, pp. 5–6, 21.

but the examples do not imply that it has consistently done so. They also indicate no systematic access of dry land to water by any of the various possible means. In none of these cases did significant amounts of dry land gain inclusion in agencies able to offer a water supply except by forming a separate agency and making some kind of compensation to prior claimants. Finally, and perhaps most important, the evidence linking firmly established rights and high concentration of agencies to reallocations of water in the direction of higher productivity is thin indeed. On almost all of the rivers discussed above, efficient allocation over the long run required transfers in water use from downstream grazing lands to upstream crop irrigation. Those transfers which occurred were large in scale, but their timing and character, as well as the failure of others to be accomplished, suggest that substantial friction impeded desirable reallocations.

A very different case is that of the Kaweah River, lying just south of the Kings and resembling it in the large number of agencies which have competed for its flows. In 1940, these included nineteen mutual water companies, two irrigation districts, one public utility company, and five private enterprises—a total of twenty-seven.[29] (See Figure 22.) The usual conflicts arose between riparians and appropriators but on the Kaweah riparian claimants also came into conflict—a problem not so evident on the Kings River. These conflicts promoted the extension and intermingling of the mutual ditch companies serving the area, as did the effect of repeated floods which shifted the flow of the Kaweah between its two distributary branches and forced the extension of ditches to tap the relocated stream.[30]

The same problems of uncertain physical facts and legal rights that affected the Kings River plagued the Kaweah, and the bickering agencies set forth upon the road to compromise in the 1890's only when the demand for surface water declined because of the agricultural depression and advances in pumping technology. With the aid of much negotiation and the services of a water master (again as in the case of the Kings), a series of agreements emerged which provided by the mid-1930's for a complete allocation of the Kaweah's flow between the distributary channels and to the diverters drawing upon each channel. These agreements were built up from the usual bilateral court decisions, records of appropriation and actual use, and voluntary compromises.[31]

Some flexibility of use in the Kaweah delta was permitted by the transferability of shares in the mutual ditch companies, allowing a long-term transfer of water use from north to south within the delta that corresponds with the apparent relative productivity of water. This type of transfer lacked the problems of minimum efficient scale involved in outright purchases of water rights and so could occur without the concentration of Kaweah users into a few large units. However, it involved significant inefficiencies in physical facilities. Furthermore, legal and technical conditions have conspired to prevent some transactions which clearly would have increased the efficiency of water use. Principal among these is the

[29] California State Department of Public Works, *Kaweah River Flows, Diversions and Service Areas,* Bulletin No. 49 (1940), p. 13.

[30] Bulletin No. 2 (Adams), *op. cit.,* pp. 28–30, 87–89; *Visalia Times-Delta,* June 25, 1959.

[31] California State Department of Public Works, *Kaweah River, op. cit.,* pp. 18–23.

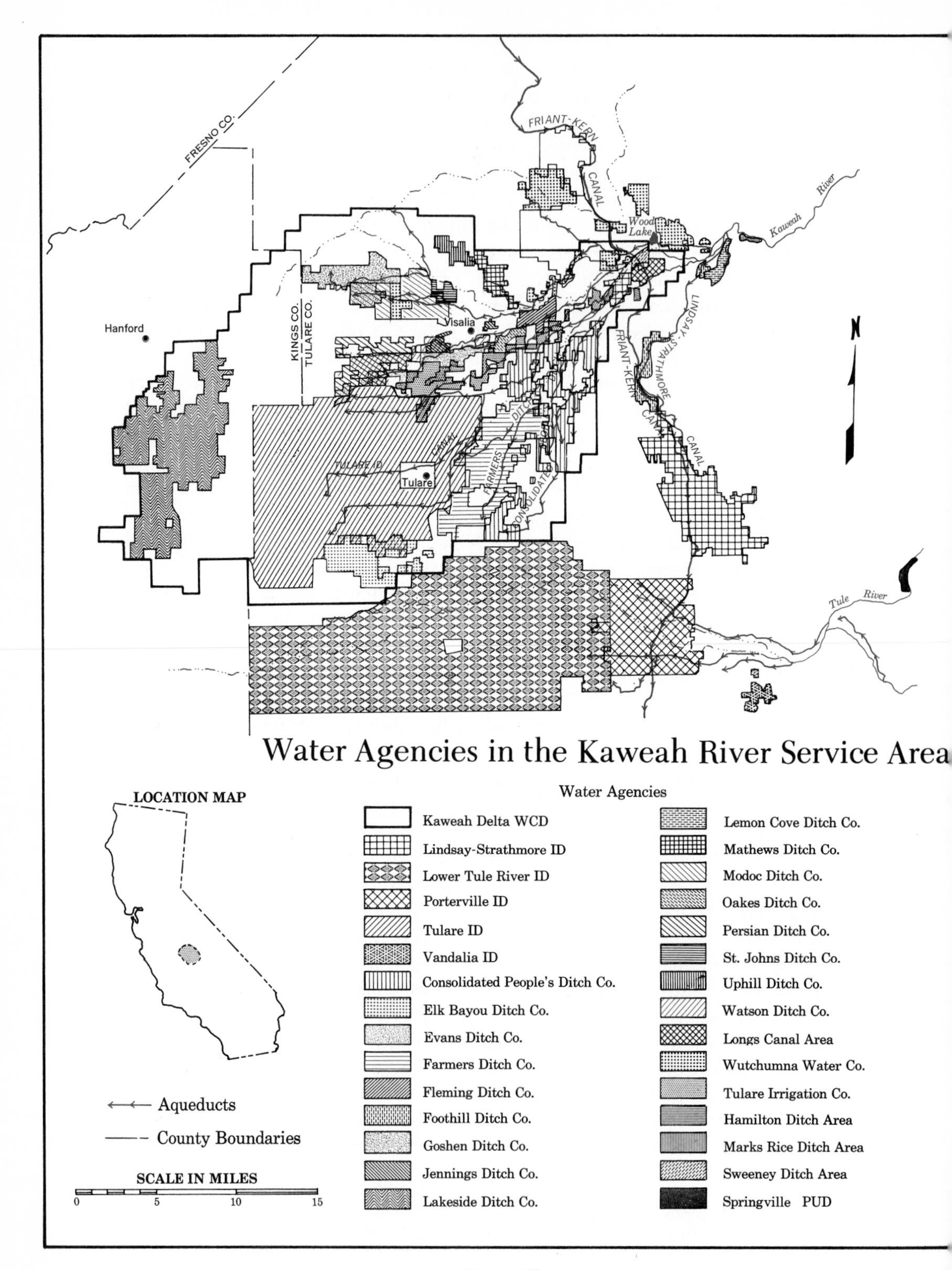
Water Agencies in the Kaweah River Service Area
FRESNO CO.
KINGS CO.
TULARE CO.
Hanford
Visalia
Tulare
Wood Lake
FRIANT-KERN CANAL
LINDSAY-STRATHMORE CANAL
Kaweah River
Tule River
TULARE ID CANAL
FARMERS DITCH
CONSOLIDATED
N
LOCATION MAP
Aqueducts
County Boundaries
SCALE IN MILES
0
5
10
15
Water Agencies
Kaweah Delta WCD
Lindsay-Strathmore ID
Lower Tule River ID
Porterville ID
Tulare ID
Vandalia ID
Consolidated People's Ditch Co.
Elk Bayou Ditch Co.
Evans Ditch Co.
Farmers Ditch Co.
Fleming Ditch Co.
Foothill Ditch Co.
Goshen Ditch Co.
Jennings Ditch Co.
Lakeside Ditch Co.
Lemon Cove Ditch Co.
Mathews Ditch Co.
Modoc Ditch Co.
Oakes Ditch Co.
Persian Ditch Co.
St. Johns Ditch Co.
Uphill Ditch Co.
Watson Ditch Co.
Longs Canal Area
Wutchumna Water Co.
Tulare Irrigation Co.
Hamilton Ditch Area
Marks Rice Ditch Area
Sweeney Ditch Area
Springville PUD

Figure 22

near-failure of the intensive efforts of the Lindsay-Strathmore Irrigation District, located to the south of the delta, to secure Kaweah water despite the clear-cut improvement in allocation which would have resulted.[32]

The Kaweah River replicates many features of the Kings River situation—the inefficiency of litigated settlements among a large number of claimants, the ultimate resort to mediation and compromise settlements based on beneficial use, the complexities and rigidities restricting transfers of use within the service area, and the use of suboptimal physical facilities for surface irrigation and control. One element of the Kings situation is lacking: the tendency toward the consolidation of users into large units in order to purchase water rights. A comparison of the main features of both the Kings and Kaweah cases to those rivers dominated by fewer and larger units shows that the latter have afforded more security in the tenure of water rights and more efficient (or at least more rapid) development of such physical facilities as dams and permanent diversion works. However, the evidence does not show that the allocation of water between competing large units in such cases has been any more efficient. Can the water distribution agreements on the Stanislaus (Oakdale-South San Joaquin) and Tuolumne (Turlock-Modesto), persisting for decades with utmost tranquility, have continuously equated the net marginal productivity of irrigation water between the member agencies? Where marginal productivity and prior appropriation have conflicted, the achievement of agreements raising the efficiency of allocation has depended strictly on the accidental circumstances of each case. The access of dry lands to water in the Kaweah basin was much better than along rivers controlled by a few agencies. This was a result not only of lower user concentration per se but also of the prevalence of mutual ditch companies along the Kaweah and geographic factors which allowed a ditch company's service area to change substantially without altering its diversion point from the river.

The cases of allocation of river rights discussed here have come from relatively ancient history. Are they still relevant to current conditions? Rivalry over natural flows is in fact less important now, if only because the natural flows of most streams outside the north coastal region have long been fully appropriated (although not fully adjudicated). Furthermore, the physical and legal uncertainties which colored this early history have been reduced in many ways. Other forces then operative remain, however, and affect the more recent competition to appropriate water through storage and for power generation. Constraints and discontinuities still affect the bargaining among rivals and the problems of externalities remain,[33] despite alterations in water law designed to encourage the development of water resources according to a comprehensive plan and to weaken the position of water uses having low productivity.

[32] Bulletin No. 21 (Adams), *op. cit.,* pp. 245–52; Mason Gaffney, "Diseconomies Inherent in Western Water Laws: A California Case Study," in *Economic Analysis of Multiple Use,* Proceedings of Western Agricultural Economics Research Council, Tucson, Ariz., January 23, 1961, 55–81.

[33] Consider, for example, the recent difficulties of the Bureau of Reclamation in dealing with the many riparians and appropriators along the Sacramento River, which will be discussed in Chapter 13.

Rivalry for Surface Supplies: Storage Projects

The present pervasive competition to appropriate water through storage takes a much different form from the older rivalry for surface flows. The legal and institutional process of acquiring water rights has greatly changed: riparian rights hold minimal significance in this competition; new sources of conflicting legal claims have arisen; and quasi-judicial procedures have effectively replaced county courts as the main forum for establishing new rights and defending old ones. Furthermore, since the competition for winter runoff is intimately bound up with investment decisions, water is not the only scarce resource subject to competition. As we have noted, dam sites of a given quality (measured by construction costs per unit of storage) are also scarce.

Still another scarce or critical element can arise because of the importance of electric power generation to many of these projects. That energy derives from falling water, which may not suffice to make feasible the projects of all agencies wishing to undertake them on a given river system. The importance of this consideration stems from the considerable apparent dependence on power revenues for the financial feasibility of most local projects.

Setting and stakes of conflicts

Recent rivalries over storage projects in California have involved conflicts over each of these scarce elements—storage sites, streamflow, and potential energy. As in the preceding chapter, we focus upon projects located along the east side of the Sacramento and lower San Joaquin valleys—a large and representative portion of all such projects developed by local agencies in Northern California.

Several factors of topography and hydrology (discussed in Chapter 2), local political organization, and California water law contribute to this series of conflicts. The whole flow of these rivers on the eastside arises in the high Sierra where only occasional mountain valleys are suitable for agricultural use. They flow in canyons of varying depth until they reach the foothills, where the fall may be retarded but where streambeds are still confined to narrow valleys. Only when emerging onto the Central Valley floor do the rivers traverse wide areas of level land suitable for irrigation. A river's source typically lies in one county, and the main stems of the river and the majority of land which it can irrigate in another. With one or two exceptions, a row of "mountain counties" covers the high ranges of the Sierra to the Nevada line or to the crest of the mountains on the east without including much irrigable land. As we have mentioned, these counties nonetheless have a strong interest in the revenues, prestige, or stimulus to industrial development that might result from a local hydroelectric project. The parties primarily interested in water for consumptive use are the irrigation districts or other local agencies lying in the valley and foothill counties, or occasionally county-wide agencies in these areas. The typical parties to a dispute over the construction of a storage project on a river are irrigation agencies downstream and adjacent to the river, and mountain counties astride its headwaters. Mountain county vs. mountain county and irrigation agency vs. irrigation agency are much less common types of conflict.

Yet another type of rivalry may join local and nonlocal agencies. The bulk of locally promoted projects are designed primarily, if not exclusively, to yield their benefits in areas immediately adjoining rivers. A state or federal agency sponsoring a competing project may represent a different clientele, and often proposes the export of water diverted from storage to some other hydrographic area. The two large urban agencies of the San Francisco Bay area—the San Francisco Water Department and the East Bay Municipal Utility District—are engaged in exporting water from local sources. From the standpoint of their Central Valley water rivals, they take on the properties of nonlocal agencies.

California water law generally encourages conflicts over projects not only by giving several different types of agencies some claim to rights to a particular stream; it also does so by containing some biases in favor of whatever agency is ready to proceed with construction of a project as against those who would protect their rights and wait. It is helpful at this stage to recall some conclusions drawn in Chapter 3 on the county-of-origin law. This law provides that, in releasing or assigning state filings for unappropriated water, those quantities of water required to meet the future needs of a county of origin shall be reserved for that county. In principle, the reservation of water to a county of origin does not preclude the present storage and diversion of water by some other user; it merely insures the mountain counties against frictions in the future market for water and water rights that might impede their access to water during some future period of development. To the irrigation agencies now seeking to construct projects, however, the reservation constitutes a threat to the returns from their proposed projects during the period of repayment of bonded indebtedness, with both the scale and the timing of the threat constituting additional sources of uncertainty.[34] Apart from county-of-origin status, an agency may base its claim on the obvious factor of temporal priority in filing for a permit to appropriate. But it also may depend on the hope of securing the release of a state filing (most bearing a priority due to the initial 1927 filing date), or base its hopes on the interpretation of the "public interest" by the several state and federal agencies holding jurisdiction.

These legal provisions show some of the opportunities open to an agency interested in the appropriation through storage of additional water. The defense

[34] The county-of-origin statute has been interpreted by the California Attorney General as permitting the recapture of water which has previously been exported from the area. It thus constitutes a clear-cut exception to the ordinary terms of the appropriative right. (See 25 Ops. Cal. Atty. Gen. 8 [1955].) The Watershed Protection Act (California *Water Code* [1963], § 11460) applies a similar prohibition to the water transfer facilities constructed by the California Department of Water Resources and (to the extent that it abides by state water law) the Bureau of Reclamation in the Central Valley. The Department adheres to this statute by building compensatory upstream works for those watersheds from which it plans to export large quantities of water under the California Water Plan; thus its effect *de facto* is to increase the volume of investment in water development facilities.

of such interests, however, can be accomplished by many other tactics than those leading to the positive establishment of a water right through the construction of a project. Agencies often have alternative strategies under more or less continuous consideration. It is useful at this point to set forth the main possibilities open to an agency.

1) It can proceed to develop available water resources if it has the requisite present and future market and the supply of funds necessary for a project of tolerably efficient scale.

2) If a project can be designed for a large yield of electric power, that output may justify immediate construction—even where the marginal benefits from the consumptive use of water are small. The power revenues may constitute a profit for whatever purpose, as well as the only accessible source of financing for projects aimed at local consumptive use of water.

3) An agency may be able to draw upon an outside wholesale source of water at favorable terms and forego developing its own resources. This alternative leaves unrequited the strong interest of a local agency in having a project of its own sponsorship.

4) In some cases, a joint project may be designed to serve the needs of contending agencies. State officials often support this approach, but it also runs against the pervasive desire for local control and for the sole claim to any profits expected from the development of hydroelectric generation.

5) An agency with county-of-origin status can hold its rights to future stream diversion without undertaking physical construction. Other agencies must actively pursue projects in order to protect and develop their claims to water.

These alternatives take on special importance because any new proposal (federal, state, or local) to store and utilize water directly affects the interests of every present or potential local water user on the same stream. It also affects the plans of would-be exporters, whether for near-by use or for major transfer. Water transfers are increasing in distance and complexity, and the Sacramento-San Joaquin Delta is being used as a major transfer point for water from north to south. The resulting interdependence of water activities is growing to such an extent that water users and water developers in all parts of the state tend increasingly to feel affected by water developments anywhere. This interdependence with its multiplication of parties in interest (real or fancied) leads, of course, to rather fantastic permutational potentials for conflicts over new projects.

Furthermore, the essential rigidity imposed upon water development by California water law, by long-term bond financing, and by high fixed costs of storage and transmission facilities implies that a project once built becomes and remains a rather immutable fixture of the landscape. Typically, water rights do not change hands; major facilities, once constructed, are not modified or substantially enlarged for three or four decades if at all. The time to assert claims against, or to contest, major water development projects is when they are being first formally proposed or, more specifically, when their promoting agency petitions the various regulatory and administrative authorities for the assorted permits, licenses, and approvals required.

Types of conflicts

Against this background, we can summarize those conflicts which have actually arisen among California water agencies in the last decade or so, along with the forums in which these conflicts have been threshed out. Three types of conflicts appear to predominate in the quest for storage projects. They can be classified by the relation of the parties to each other or by the relation of their respective objectives to each other. Figures 23 and 24 show the locations of two groups of competing agencies and the main features or general locations of their projects.

1) The first type of conflict involves two agencies (or groups of agencies) seeking to develop roughly the same resources (water, dam site, power drop) for similar purposes and for the same or similar service areas. The proposed plans may differ somewhat in size, purposes, or place of use, but they are fully mutually exclusive.

An outstanding case of this type of competitive planning involved Yuba County Water Agency and Johnson Rancho County Water District, both of which have sought to develop the Yuba River. Facing each other as rivals were a county-wide agency with a county-sized plan and a very small agency operating in a corner of the same county with a plan two to three times greater in both cost and output of water and power. The County Water Agency proposed to develop just enough of the Yuba River to serve water users in the county—to the extent that capital costs could be financed out of power revenues. The Water District proposed to serve not only this same group but, in addition, to export water not required by county users. Once built, it planned to turn over control of the project to the water users for administration.

A similar dispute has emerged over development of Stanislaus River in the lower San Joaquin Valley. Here the Bureau of Reclamation is one of the protagonists and the "Stanislaus River Basin Group" is the other.[35] The local agencies want to develop the river for use in their own area and for that purpose would design a project to the corresponding size: 1 million acre-feet of storage capacity in an enlarged New Melones dam and reservoir, plus half a dozen small upstream installations to serve needs in the associated mountain counties. The Corps of Engineers and the Bureau of Reclamation propose to enlarge the size of New Melones to 2.4 million acre-feet, to serve the function of off-stream storage for the proposed East Side Division of the Central Valley Project. The East Side project would serve valley and foothill lands just above those served by the Bureau's Friant-Kern Canal. Present Stanislaus River users, of course, would continue to obtain the same quantities of water as before, but they would probably have to purchase from the Bureau any additional supplies desired. Opposition to the federal project stems not only from the Stanislaus River Basin Group itself, but contains among its ranks a wide array of proponents of local

[35] This group consists of four agencies shown in Figure 24: two irrigation districts which have gradually developed Stanislaus River since 1909 (Oakdale Irrigation District and South San Joaquin Irrigation District) and two of the counties on the upper reaches of this stream (Tuolumne County Water District No. 2 and Calaveras County Water District).

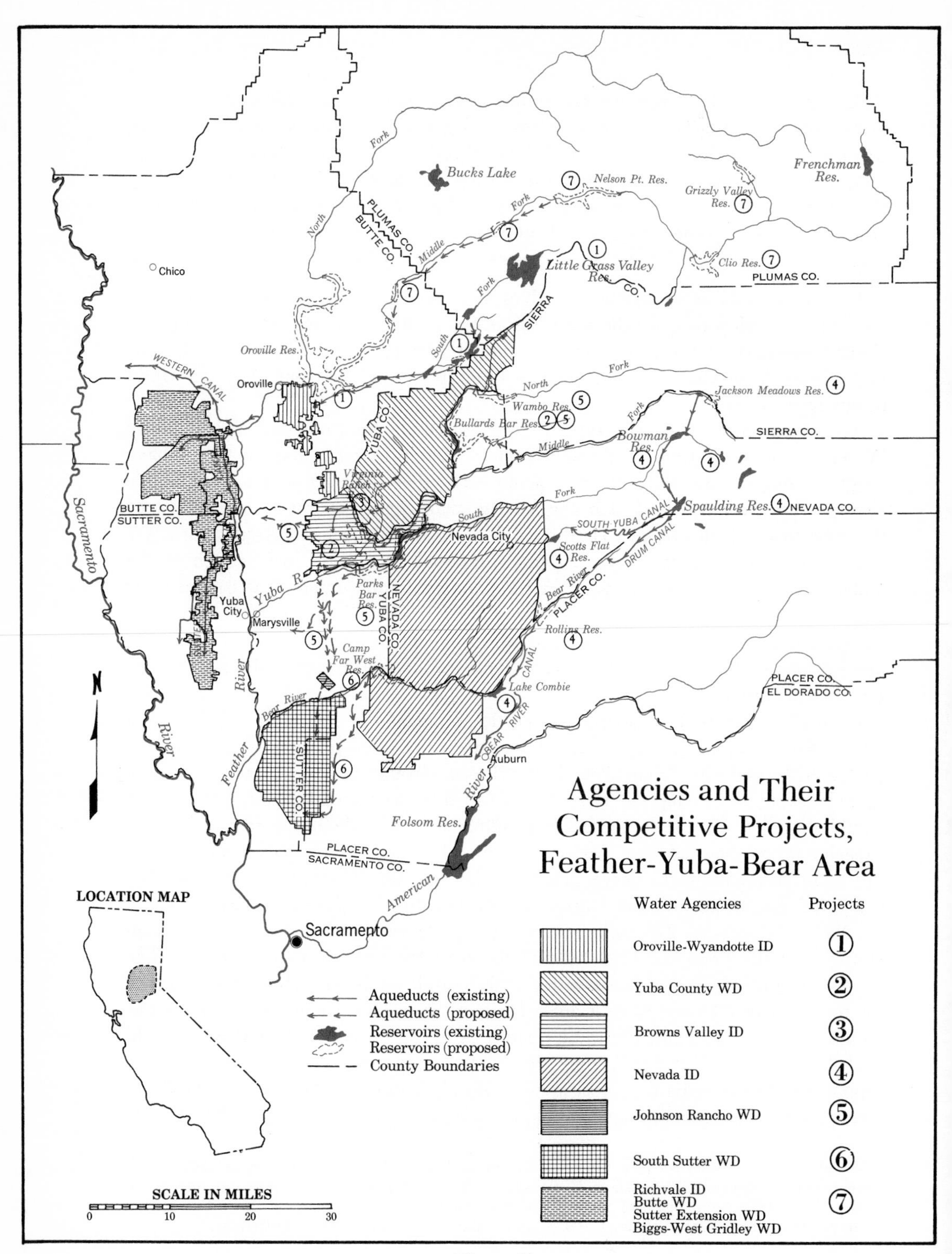
Agencies and Their Competitive Projects, Feather-Yuba-Bear Area
Water Agencies
Projects
Oroville-Wyandotte ID
Yuba County WD
Browns Valley ID
Nevada ID
Johnson Rancho WD
South Sutter WD
Richvale ID
Butte WD
Sutter Extension WD
Biggs-West Gridley WD
Aqueducts (existing)
Aqueducts (proposed)
Reservoirs (existing)
Reservoirs (proposed)
County Boundaries
LOCATION MAP
SCALE IN MILES
0
10
20
30
Chico
Oroville
Yuba City
Marysville
Nevada City
Auburn
Sacramento
Bucks Lake
Frenchman Res.
Nelson Pt. Res.
Grizzly Valley Res.
Clio Res.
Little Grass Valley Res.
Oroville Res.
Jackson Meadows Res.
Wambo Res.
Bullards Bar Res.
Bowman Res.
Spaulding Res.
Scotts Flat Res.
Rollins Res.
Lake Combie
Parks Bar Res.
Camp Far West Res.
Virginia Ranch
Folsom Res.
WESTERN CANAL
SOUTH YUBA CANAL
DRUM CANAL
BEAR RIVER CANAL
PLUMAS CO.
BUTTE CO.
SIERRA CO.
YUBA CO.
NEVADA CO.
PLACER CO.
SUTTER CO.
EL DORADO CO.
SACRAMENTO CO.
Sacramento River
Feather River
Yuba R.
Bear River
American River
North Fork
Middle Fork
South Fork

Figure 23

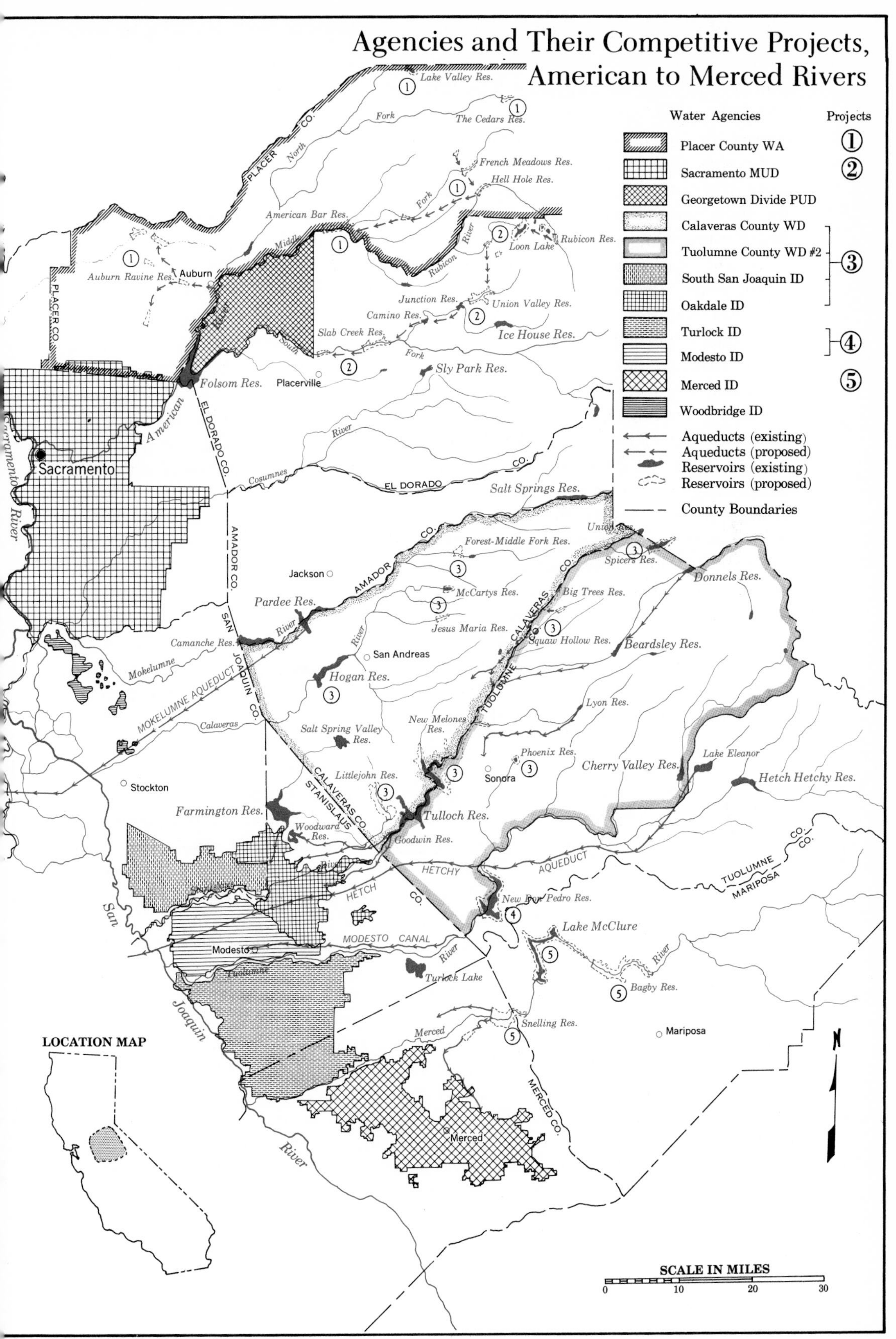

Agencies and Their Competitive Projects, American to Merced Rivers
Water Agencies
Projects
Placer County WA
Sacramento MUD
Georgetown Divide PUD
Calaveras County WD
Tuolumne County WD #2
South San Joaquin ID
Oakdale ID
Turlock ID
Modesto ID
Merced ID
Woodbridge ID
Aqueducts (existing)
Aqueducts (proposed)
Reservoirs (existing)
Reservoirs (proposed)
County Boundaries
Lake Valley Res.
The Cedars Res.
French Meadows Res.
Hell Hole Res.
American Bar Res.
Rubicon Res.
Loon Lake
Auburn Ravine Res.
Auburn
Junction Res.
Union Valley Res.
Camino Res.
Slab Creek Res.
Ice House Res.
Sly Park Res.
Folsom Res.
Placerville
Sacramento
Salt Springs Res.
Forest-Middle Fork Res.
Spicers Res.
Donnels Res.
Jackson
McCartys Res.
Big Trees Res.
Pardee Res.
Jesus Maria Res.
Squaw Hollow Res.
Beardsley Res.
Camanche Res.
San Andreas
Hogan Res.
Lyon Res.
MOKELUMNE AQUEDUCT
New Melones Res.
Salt Spring Valley Res.
Phoenix Res.
Cherry Valley Res.
Lake Eleanor
Hetch Hetchy Res.
Littlejohn Res.
Sonora
Stockton
Farmington Res.
Tulloch Res.
Woodward Res.
Goodwin Res.
HETCH HETCHY AQUEDUCT
New Don Pedro Res.
Lake McClure
MODESTO CANAL
Modesto
Turlock Lake
Bagby Res.
Snelling Res.
Mariposa
Merced
LOCATION MAP
SCALE IN MILES
0
10
20
30

Figure 24

control and local development. The Stanislaus Group, depending on the cost at which it could supply its own water, may stand to lose little other than local control and power revenues in the period after repayment of the bonds.

Another case in this first type of conflict, in which both contenders sought in some degree to develop the same resource (South Fork of the Feather River) for the same general service area, will be covered separately, because it turns more than the preceding cases upon the county-of-origin statute.

2) The second type of conflict has been the more prevalent numerically in recent years. The downstream development agency is pitted against one or more upstream counties or agencies which claim county-of-origin status but usually are unable to develop the water resources in question themselves.

For instance, Merced Irrigation District has sought to appropriate most of the remaining flows of Merced River for use during dry years on the District's lands and on new land to be annexed. Mariposa County, which straddles the upper reaches of the Merced River, entered the official proceedings to oppose the request unless its own future needs would be met by reservations of water and the construction of facilities to deliver it. Mariposa County was without a plan of its own and, despite the best efforts of the Department of Water Resources, none emerged before a compromise deal with Merced Irrigation District terminated the fight. Almost a decade earlier, the members of the Stanislaus River Basin Group were involved in a similar fight over the Tri-Dam project of South San Joaquin and Oakdale irrigation districts which was later completed.

Another such conflict involved a municipal water agency, East Bay Municipal Utility District, which beginning in 1949 sought to expand its use of Mokelumne River water. The two counties of origin in this case, Amador and Calaveras, intervened in 1955–56 and forced a compromise which permitted issuance of the release only in 1959.

The long fight over water of the South Fork of the Feather River and adjacent minor streams occupied the greater part of the 1950's. It contains some elements of the first category of contest—the conflicting plan—but the essential motivation of the upstream opponent reflected the traits of a county-of-origin protestant. Oroville-Wyandotte Irrigation District sought to add to its water supply by building a series of reservoirs on the South Fork of Feather River, on which it had already constructed a small dam in the 1920's. To augment the flows of South Fork (and thereby power revenues), it proposed to divert water from several of that stream's own tributaries and also from high small tributaries of the North Fork of Yuba River. Activation of the plan struck the people of upper Yuba County as a threat to their own sources, primarily some of the tributaries which Oroville-Wyandotte proposed to divert for use on its own lands in lower-elevation portions of Butte County. Forming themselves into Yuba County Water District, they filed for water permits of their own beginning in 1948, and before Oroville-Wyandotte had filed all the applications it would need for the plan of development initially proposed. This interlacing in time of filings, under the prevailing priority provisions of California water law, led to a particularly severe and drawn-out controversy. The parties themselves might never have resolved this conflict, had not Pacific Gas and Electric Company come to the rescue by agreeing to buy the power output from Oroville-Wyandotte's project at a rate high enough to permit satisfying the demands of the Yuba District.[36]

3) The third type of conflict relates to situations in which two parties are planning water projects more or less adjacent to each other and sufficiently proximate to give rise to actual or potential marginal interference. The term "marginal" indicates that the technological or economic conflict applies to only a portion of the resources needed by the projects—a portion small enough that both conflicting plans are capable of being constructed.

Some recent cases of this type have involved a federal agency as one of the parties. For example, the Placer County Water Agency began in 1958 to promote a plan for the Middle Fork of American River. A series of reservoirs would regulate the flow for electric generation in a series of power plants. The lowest of the power houses was designed for an elevation at which it would impinge on the water-surface level of a reservoir just below this point (Auburn dam and reservoir) proposed for construction by the Bureau of Reclamation. Furthermore, Placer proposed to divert more water in the future than the Bureau recognized as new yield attributable to Placer's reservoir operations. Placer's plans would thus reduce somewhat the water which the Bureau would have for sale from its Auburn project. Finally, to transport water to its proposed place of use in western Placer County, the Agency would have to divert from the very spot on which the Bureau's Auburn dam would some day rise. Eventually the Placer Agency decided to jettison its lowest power installation. Instead it planned to increase the generating capacity installed farther upstream to compensate for the loss and obtain compensatory water deliveries from the Bureau.

In this case, as in the many which are settled routinely in the course of project planning, design, and execution, the mutually incompatible or potentially threatening portions or aspects of the developments are sufficiently minor to permit solution without seriously jeopardizing either plan involved. In the first two categories of conflict, on the other hand, the large area of overlap, coupled with the slim economic feasibility of most projects even before rivalries are untangled, precludes such an outcome. Although some of these cases involve organizational competition rather than alternative uses in rivalry for scarce resources, none is without significance for allocation between ultimate uses and users.

Assets and strategies

The importance of rivalries between competing projects lies in the effect of the result upon resource allocation. Among mutually exclusive projects, does the best project win? Do the pressures for changing a project under fire increase its economic efficiency? In the remainder of this section, we explore the determinants of the outcome when projects conflict, in order to provide a basis for answering

[36] California State Water Rights Board, Decision D 907, May 29, 1958 (mimeo.), pp. 2–4; Frank E. Bonner, Consulting Engineer, *Report for Oroville-Wyandotte Irrigation District on Proposed Water and Power Development of South Fork of Feather River, California* (1958), pp. 1–2.

these questions about the performance of the industry. Not only the basic positions of the parties, but also their strategies and the choice of sequences of maneuvers, play a vital role in determining the outcome. What cards do the players hold in these games? Which are the high cards, the trumps?

Theoretically, the two most important cards are (1) claims of entitlement to a water right (used here in the broadest sense, including all the necessary permits, licenses, and approvals of assorted authorities), and (2) a source or method of financing a plan. No player enters the game with the first, and some enter with only a portion of the second. Part of the game consists of preventing one's opponent from acquiring the water right; without it he neither needs nor could obtain the money.

The best card, of course, is a water right consisting of a perfected license, rather than merely a permit. Licenses are issued only after water, under permit, has actually been developed by physical diversion and/or storage works. A right, thus firmly vested, must be reckoned with by any and all players in the game; and a right embodied in an existing diversion (or sometimes one granted a permit but not yet perfected) serves as a limit or constraint to future development by another agency. Any newcomer must either avoid any possible physical infringement of the existing right (sometimes an uncertain matter) or be prepared to make some kind of compensation.

In the case of rights not yet firmly acquired, whoever holds the application with the earliest date is theoretically closest to obtaining a water rights permit. Chronological priority is followed strictly in proceedings before the California State Water Rights Board. Yet the ensuing game may be a long time in the playing, and its outcome uncertain. All that can really be said is that the earliest filings are better than later filings. One important method of circumventing the potentially fatal lack of an early filing is to seek assignment of or release from priority of a state filing; many of these date back to 1927 and, hence, predate most actively pending applications by any other party. Assignment gives to the assignee a filing bearing the 1927 date; release simply removes the state's filing from the conflict.

The crucial role played by dates on applications revealed itself in the fight over the South Fork of Feather River. A series of about ten applications had been filed over a number of years. Yuba County Water District held the earliest and latest filings, Oroville-Wyandotte Irrigation District held a group in the middle years. Neither wanted to relinquish any filings in favor of the other. In the judgment of the State Engineer, to grant permits to each party based on its respective earliest filings would leave neither side with a feasible project.[37]

In order to forestall preemption of resources through early promiscuous filings by agencies unable to develop these waters, the State Water Rights Board now and then wipes the slate clean by canceling filings for permits not followed by further action within a few years.[38] In one such housecleaning, Placer County

[37] California State Engineer, *In the Matter of Applications 13676 etc., by Oroville-Wyandotte Irrigation District and Applications 12532 etc., by County of Yuba and Yuba County Water District,* Decision No. D 838, Oct. 27, 1955 (mimeo.).

[38] For example, decisions RD-1, RD-3, RD-4, issued in the spring of 1957.

Water Agency lost early filings dating from 1951 or 1952. This very withdrawal caused the agency to take action and to pursue, this time with "due diligence," filings for a new project on that part of the American River remaining available to it. Fortunately for the success of this move, no one had filed any intervening applications.

Under present law, state filings are designed to protect a general and coordinated plan of development of water resources and the rights of the counties of origin.[39] From this fact derive two other high cards. First, a project which is not in conflict with such a plan (usually interpreted as meaning one which has been described in the California Water Plan as set forth in Bulletin No. 3 or is reconcilable with a project described therein) would outrank a project which is in conflict with one already outlined in Bulletin No. 3 for eventual construction. In principle, this provision is intrinsically flexible, as conformity to the California Water Plan (or any other specific plan) is not officially required, and since the Plan itself is considered to be subject to refinement and adaptation to changing circumstances and increased technical study and information.[40] The Water Rights Board has been willing to accept projects which would be compatible with the "basic concept" of the Water Plan and to urge cooperation with the Department of Water Resources to enhance the compatibility.[41] And agencies with otherwise strong positions have secured the needed approvals from the state despite questionable conformance of their proposals with the California Water Plan. The authorizing agencies are rarely confronted with two different and comprehensive development plans for a river at the same time (the only recent cases have involved the Yuba and Stanislaus rivers). When the choice lies between starting a development now and waiting for one more in conformance with the Water Plan, the bias in favor of development of all California public authorities favors the cause of the current applicant despite some deviation from a "general and coordinated" plan.

A second card based on the state filings is held by the counties of origin, which automatically possess something tantamount to firm water rights even in the absence of any specific filings of their own. These cards themselves hold a certain safe minimum value when played defensively, and when adroitly handled they can acquire considerable offensive value for promoting projects or securing payoffs. Although the county-of-origin reservation applies specifically so far as the disposition of state filings is concerned, it extends in effect to the acquisition of surface water rights in general. Few important flows have remained uncovered by state filings, and furthermore the State Water Rights Board in granting permits to appropriate has tended to follow the Water Commission's disposition of state filings and to consider that such upstream reservations fall generally within the scope of the public interest which it is charged to guard.

Financing is another essential element in the card game of project construction.

[39] California *Water Code* (1963), §§ 10500–10505.

[40] California State Water Resources Board, *The California Water Plan,* Bulletin No. 3 (1957), p. 245.

[41] California State Water Rights Board, *In the Matter of Applications 14785 etc. of Pacific Gas and Electric Co.,* Decision D 978, Aug. 25, 1960 (mimeo.), p. 15.

Access to funds for the construction of storage works, appurtenant items, and the incremental water transmission facilities tends to rate high, whatever the rest of the hand. For the federal agency, it depends on congressional willingness to appropriate funds for the proposed project; and this is related to the economics of the project and especially to the character of local support for it in ways (and proportions) discussed in Chapter 11. For the local agency, financing must be secured through either general obligation or revenue bonds. Districts in partnership with PG&E can manage revenue bonds with minimal difficulty. Others must usually depend on general obligation bonds and face the associated problems of capital rationing by lenders and the maintenance of internal consensus. Lenders' risk for a given scale of project is inversely related to the agency's existing assessed valuation, conveying to the agency with a larger valuation base a virtual advantage in developing a given project. Lenders also seem highly sensitive to uncertainty over a district's water right, however, so that the water rights and financing positions of some districts are directly interrelated.

One rather intangible element which aids a contestant is public support, which expresses itself most effectively as political support. Public support can be measured roughly by the number of voter-beneficiaries a project may have. Alternatively, it may be gauged by how vociferous these beneficiaries may be, or by the effectiveness of an agency's educational campaign. In the contest between Yuba County Water Agency and Johnson Rancho County Water District, for instance, public support appears to have played a fairly crucial role in influencing the decision of the California Water Commission. The County Agency had marshalled endorsements from almost all operating water districts in the county, from civic and fraternal organizations, county officials, and assorted supporters. But Johnson Rancho, despite its larger plan with more ostensible beneficiaries, had been able to find few adherents.[42]

Sometimes a contestant for a water development project may garner something like public support by taking the role of an underdog. This appears to have been the case when Mariposa County tried to wrest water for its own use from Merced Irrigation District's project, and secured the aid of the Department of Water Resources.

No agency can take public support for granted, even when it has a sound project with numerous beneficiaries and few losers. Local agencies may enjoy some political support as agencies, apart from their current programs. But nonlocal agencies, notably the Bureau of Reclamation, must build support for each project separately. These campaigns enjoy uneven success. On the one hand, the weight of public pressure favored the Bureau over the Stanislaus group for construction of the New Melones project, as was effectively expressed in the promotion of the federal project by a bipartisan congressional delegation. But the

[42] "Germane to this, is the factor of public support. While not by itself dispositive, it must be given some weight in the case of public agencies such as those here involved. It is clear from the record that the [Yuba county water] agency has much broader acceptance by the residents of the river basin than has Johnson Rancho." California Water Commission, *Report of Committee Designated to Hear Requests of Yuba County Water Agency, Johnson Rancho County Water District and Nevada Irrigation District for Assignment and/or Release from Priority of State Applications 5631 and 5632 on the Yuba River,* May 4, 1962 (mimeo.), p. 6.

same delegation opposed the Bureau's attempt to enlarge its Auburn reservoir at the expense of the American River project of the Placer County Water Agency. The future beneficiaries of the Bureau's East Side project, for which its version of the New Melones reservoir would provide off-stream storage, obviously outnumber the as yet unknown beneficiaries of the larger Auburn project.

Another potentially important card lies in the amount of "users' surplus" attributable to a proposed project. Where payoffs of one kind or another must be made, a project with a greater surplus of expected benefits over costs is more likely to stand the tax. Furthermore, the extent of such surpluses clearly affects the evaluations of "public interest" made by the various regulatory bodies in reaching their decisions, although the relation is anything but a precise one.

The ace in the hole in most, if not all, of these contests appears to be the threat of extended litigation. Water rights and permits and assignments and releases from priority of state filings are tenuous claims. Injunctions against their execution seem readily obtainable. Water rights litigation in the past has often been lengthy and expensive. An agency anxious to begin construction of a water supply project would like to avoid it, to the extent of paying well for the privilege. In fact, the more an agency wishes to expedite proceedings, the more it exposes itself to the risk of delaying litigation instituted by a dissatisfied contestant, so a strong incentive is created for building ahead of demand. When one (or more) of the protestants lacks other cards of sufficient value to gain his desired objective, resort to litigation is always available. Frequently, the mere threat or opportunity to undertake legal action serves the same purpose.

Resort to litigation as a means of furthering his objective is rarely available to the successful, or more probably successful, of the applicants. Legal action initiated by him would not hinder his construction activities so far as state or federal authorities are concerned, but it might well jeopardize his standing with the banking fraternity and, hence, undermine his financial footing. That is tantamount to the very delay he wishes to avoid. This then is a one-sided device, available only to the apparent loser.

Outcomes of project rivalries

Since rivalries over projects are fought out in and around the regulatory and supervisory processes, an experienced agency, or one with experienced lawyers or engineers, will anticipate problems in the course of study, engineering, and design. Informal prenegotiation inquiries may be made with agencies concerned —for example, the Department of Water Resources. At the same time, public support is solicited inside and outside of the agency. All efforts are focused on welding a strong case for submission to the various regulatory agencies. That involves showing a project compatible with a general and coordinated plan of development and consideration of other water users' interests, and demonstrating a need for water, public support, financial feasibility, and access to sources of financing.

Once regulatory proceedings are begun and all protestants become known, the proponent of a project must undertake the hard bargaining involved in paying off interveners according to the apparent quality of the cards or claims they hold or their ability to strengthen actual hands by bluffing. The end result of this process is embodied in a stipulation leading to withdrawal of the protest. The ability to pay off, of course, varies. And claimants may be expected to know how far they can go in pressing their demands, regardless of the quality of their claims. If they attempt to exact more than the developer can afford to yield, the project may become infeasible. Some protestants, of course, may wish to accomplish that very result.[43] The counties of origin, on the other hand, usually feel that they stand to gain from construction as long as they can collect some benefits. Furthermore, at the point where the project would be pushed into the realm of infeasibility, the bias toward development held by state (and federal) agencies would come into play and would insist on the kind of bargain which would permit construction to proceed.

The settlements reached in this bargaining process take certain standard forms. They will be discussed below in roughly ascending order of the size of the concession made by the entrepreneurial agency, in the sense that paying off in water now, other things being equal, is more costly than paying off in water in the future. But, of course, a small present payoff may be preferable to a large or open-ended future obligation.

1) Recognition of prior vested rights—The majority of protestants to water rights applications seek no more than the protection of vested rights. Those protestants who request and settle for this safeguard usually are only concerned lest the new proposed storage and diversion infringe on or diminish their own established rights. Their claims are routinely covered by the inclusion in all permits granted by the California State Water Rights Board of approval "subject to vested rights" only; these rights exist by force of law and are not subject to the Board's discretion. Corresponding to statutory requirements, the Board uses this language even in the absence of protests to an application.

Although not a question of law, prior vested rights creep into many proceedings as a question of fact. In these cases, it is necessary to determine how the proposed new project operation might affect vested rights of downstream diverters—especially the Bureau of Reclamation, with its Delta-centered system of interbasin transfers, and the lower San Joaquin water users, who face deteriorating water quality from upstream projects. The Bureau, in at least one of many cases in which it intervened to protect its Delta water supply, negotiated for more than the routine protective language. The lower San Joaquin districts, uncertain how new storage projects will affect their water quality but painfully aware of its deterioration, are seeking more than the verbal protection. At this writing, they have been unable to obtain anything through bargaining.

2) Recognition of future depletions—Settlements involving future rights, compared to presently vested rights, heretofore have proved much more costly to

[43] Fisheries interests and sportsmen's groups are prominent among these, but their activities will be discussed below, in Chapter 14.

applicants proposing storage projects and vastly more uncertain. Protestants advancing claims of this type tend to operate upstream from a proposed project and to fall under the protection of the county-of-origin law. They include those who want to preserve a county's or an area's water supply for eventual future use without having any formal development plans as well as those who already have plans prepared.

Mountain counties of origin are entitled by law to those quantities of water "necessary for the development of the county" so far as assignment of state filings are concerned, and in most instances applicants take this fact into account in planning and designing their projects. Engineers for Yuba County Water District, for instance, claimed to have made "very liberal allowances" for future depletions by Nevada Irrigation District upstream on South and Middle Fork of Yuba River and by others.[44] Such allowances necessarily must include a fair amount of speculation as to the quantities and timing of potential future diversions upstream. If the developing agency delays anticipated depletions assumed in its operation studies beyond the period of bonded indebtedness, it can improve its showing of financial feasibility; at the same time, it may arouse fears and generate protests among would-be upstream diverters, leading them to demand more positive guarantee or benefits for their future water supply.

Quite routinely, assignments of state filings and the water rights permits based thereon are issued with what is called a "general reservation" of the water supply required for the development of counties of origin, whether or not the affected area enters a protest. In practice, areas of origin do not leave this to chance, but enter proceedings affecting their respective watershed to claim at least a general reservation, if not additional benefits from the applicant. Thus, such reservations sometimes become a matter of assiduous bargaining. Either the mountain counties encounter reluctance on the part of the developing agency to agree to a general reservation, or they look for something more than this routine guarantee[45] which, of course, does not contain any means of bringing about development of the reserved water resource.

A general reservation obviously constitutes a serious source of uncertainty for the agency developing a project, even more in the financial sense of threatening project revenues before the bonded indebtedness will be paid off than in the economic sense of increasing the uncertainty about the present value of future net benefits. Entrepreneurial agencies often bargain hard for specific rather than general reservations, but counties of origin naturally will not accept this limitation without some other compensation.

Consider the case of the Richvale project. The Richvale Irrigation District faced a complex problem in the reservation for the counties of origin of the Middle Fork of Feather River. Upstream depletions appeared somewhat more

[44] International Engineering Company, Inc., *Report on Development of Water Resources of Yuba River* (1961), pp. IV–2 through IV–10.

[45] For example, in the Water Commission proceedings on the project of Yuba County Water District, Nevada Irrigation District (located in a county of origin) sought and won assignment of a portion of the state filing rather than just a general reservation against it. See California Water Commission, *Release from Priority of Applications Nos. 5631 and 5632 etc.,* Resolution No. 145, Oct. 5, 1962 (mimeo.), App. A, p. 4; App. B, p. 4.

imminent, since one of the potential upstream developments—Grizzly Valley Reservoir—had already been authorized for construction as part of the Feather River Project division of the California Water Plan. The value of this site for the generation of salable electric power was so great to Richvale that it sought to undertake construction, but to make water therefrom available in the quantities demanded by the city of Portola. The counties of origin, however, rejected any such proposals, insisted on the general reservation and on construction, by the Department of Water Resources of Grizzly Valley Reservoir, hoping to obtain a surer and cheaper supply of water. Before issuing the assignment of a state filing to Richvale, the California Water Commission first ascertained that Richvale would be able to proceed without Grizzly Valley and with such a general reservation.[46] These terms were then imposed.[47]

3) Mutual nonaggression pacts—An applicant, with the planning of his project under way, will sound out the protestants to ascertain the nature of their claims and demands. Any who can be satisfied by the language protecting prior vested rights, or by mutual acceptance of the general reservation for counties of origin, are easily disposed of. But those opponents with active plans of their own and with either established or pending claims to water often require more costly compensation. This may take one or more of the following forms: the parties may reach some terms for the mutual withdrawal of protests to each other's projects; one party taking the initiative may pay the other off in water; outright cash compensation may take place.

Mutual nonaggression pacts between rival agencies are not possible without at least one party redesigning its proposed project. Furthermore, commitments not to attack future applications have not been tested in the courts, and lawyers tend to view dubiously the extent to which they are binding on anyone. But such a withdrawal did occur in connection with the Tri-Dam project on the Stanislaus River. Tuolumne County Water District No. 2 had pending applications for water permits and also could claim county-of-origin status vis-a-vis the Tri-Dam group (Oakdale and South San Joaquin irrigation districts) which was located downstream on the Stanislaus River. It obtained from them an agreement to allow a specified diversion subject to payment during the fifty-year period of the Federal Power Commission license of the project, but would be charged thereafter only for allocable operation and maintenance costs.[48] Also, the Tri-Dam districts agreed

[46] California Water Commission, *Report of Subcommittee Designated to Hear the Request of Richvale Irrigation District for a Release from Priority of State Applications,* March 16, 1962 (mimeo.), pp. 2–3.

[47] California Water Commission, *Re: Release from Priority of Applications Nos. 5629 etc.,* Resolution No. 131, April 6, 1962 (mimeo.), Exhibit "A," p. 3.

[48] Oakdale Irrigation District and South San Joaquin Irrigation District, *Supplemental Official Statement relating to $5,250,000 Oakdale Irrigation District Sixth Issue Tri-Dam Revenue Bonds* (Oakdale and Manteca, 1955), Exhibit A, p. 48. (Hereinafter cited as *Supplemental Official Statement.*) For every acre-foot taken by the Tuolumne District, Pacific Gas and Electric Company would reduce by $2.45 payments under its Tri-Dam project contract with the two irrigation districts. (See Sec. 15 of that contract as it appears in *Supplemental Official Statement,* p. 34.) In other words, the constructing districts would come out even financially, leaving their bond retirement ability undiminished by the water diverted by Tuolumne.

not to oppose future developments by Tuolumne or Calaveras County agencies on higher reaches of the Stanislaus (for which applications of both counties were then pending). The decision granting the permit for the Tri-Dam project, issued two years later, incorporated the substance of these agreements.

The counties of origin in this case attained freedom from interference with their own future development plans and, in addition, Tuolumne County Water District No. 2 obtained access to water without having to invest funds of its own except for transmission facilities. The irrigation districts yielded little, if any, present benefits—only a small quantity of water of limited utility, and that without revenue loss—but did yield by restricting somewhat the scope of future claims to water of the upper Stanislaus.

4) Yielding water to protestants—Where an agency's opponent seeks compensation in the form of water, either he already diverts water for beneficial use or has some project under way. Thus, payoffs in water often go along with the need for at least one of the rivals to redesign his project, thereby complicating his problems of keeping the project financially feasible. This occurred in the conflict over the South Fork of the Feather River, probably the most complex and durable in recent years. The parties were Oroville-Wyandotte Irrigation District, an established agency planning a joint water-power project to bolster its water supply, and Yuba County, the upstream county of origin.

Before Oroville-Wyandotte became active in developing its new project, Yuba County had decided that it must guard its local tributary streams as the only possible source of water supply against potential future irrigation needs. Oroville-Wyandotte, in the southern part of neighboring Butte County, thought in order to formulate a feasible plan it needed to reinforce the water supply available to it from the South Fork of the Feather River by diversions from various upper tributaries, including some of the Yuba River. Any feasible plan for either party would have to be financed from proceeds of a contract for power sales with the Pacific Gas and Electric Company. It seemed likely that initial partial development would threaten the feasibility of developing the remainder of the resource by the other party—a matter of interest to both the potential beneficiaries and to the state water agency.

The conflicting water rights applications came to a hearing before the Division of Water Resources of the California State Department of Public Works, which then had the jurisdiction later assumed by the State Water Rights Board. In order to find ways to "develop the water resources concerned to the best and fullest extent in the public interest," the Division undertook a comprehensive study of the case and concluded that a joint project for the two agencies was feasible and desirable.[49] Neither party involved showed any inclination to adopt the plan proposed by the state, and the State Engineer therefore issued a decision, stating

[49] *Supplemental Report on Applications 13676 etc., Oroville-Wyandotte Irrigation District and Applications 12530 etc., County of Yuba and Yuba County Water District* [author unknown, but probably prepared in the State Water Rights Board] n.d., (mimeo.), p. 2. (Hereinafter cited as *Supplemental Report.*) This report is embodied in California State Department of Public Works, Division of Water Resources, *Analysis of Plans for Development and Utilization of Water Resources of the South Fork of Feather River* (1954). (Hereinafter cited as *Analysis of Plans.*)

that because the applications involved physical conflict and were "intermixed" in priority, "to approve the applications strictly in order of their priority would have the effect of allowing neither applicant to proceed with its proposed project." Based on the impression that a joint project appeared mandatory, he ordered that action on the applications be deferred.

Any such solution required finding a way to satisfy Yuba's desires for water without ruining the feasibility of Oroville-Wyandotte's project, and at the same time reconciling the desires of both parties to build projects of their own.[50] Under the threat by the State Engineer to cancel all filings, Yuba requested an exchange of half-interests in the pending applications, but Oroville-Wyandotte refused this suggestion, and the boards of the two agencies could agree on no joint venture.

Oroville-Wyandotte had begun early to make occasional inquiries to Pacific Gas and Electric Company to ascertain what the Company might be willing to pay for the potential power output from the various proposals. But for several years, PG&E had remained rather aloof, wishing presumably to wait until the argument between the contending parties had been resolved in order to avoid antagonizing either. As the distance between the agencies remained large, PG&E apparently began to try to conciliate the parties. Some spokesmen are inclined to credit PG&E with introducing the first break in the logjam by offering to pay $2.5 million annually to Oroville-Wyandotte Irrigation District for the power from a specific project outlined by the Company and designed to furnish 15,000 acre-feet of water annually to the Yuba area.[51] This plan resembled previous plans of Oroville-Wyandotte, but included a reservoir (Brownsville) designed to serve Yuba interests.

This PG&E offer set the project off on a five-year course of renegotiation and revision, the matters at issue including joint versus single ownership and operation by Oroville-Wyandotte, the schedule of construction of irrigation features, and the division of power revenues after the pay-out period.[52] A power plant and a conduit were added to serve Yuba County areas, and Yuba was assured of definite flows of water.[53] Construction bids on the project proved to be higher than expected, and the project apparently would have foundered except for PG&E's willingness to raise the level of its annual firm payments to $3,128,000, compared to the initial offer of $2,500,000 and a later offer of $2,830,000.[54]

During these complex negotiations, the capacities and detailed features, although

[50] For instance, in its analysis of the plans offered until then, the Division of Water Resources of the Department of Public Works found "that the power and irrigation plan of development prepared by Yuba County Water District would not be desirable from financial and practical operational standpoints and that the plan of development proposed by Oroville-Wyandotte Irrigation District provides no water supply for the areas in upper Yuba County." *Analysis of Plans, op. cit.*, p. 39.

[51] *Supplemental Report, op. cit.*, Appendix A. See also Frank E. Bonner, *op. cit.*, p. 2: "A spur toward settlement of the controversy was supplied by the Pacific Gas & Electric Co. proposal . . . to lease the power facilities to be constructed by OWID for $2,500,000 annually."

[52] *Supplemental Report, op. cit.*, pp. 9–11.

[53] California State Water Rights Board, Decision D 907, *op. cit.*, p. 4; *Supplemental Official Statement, op. cit.*, p. 39; California Department of Water Resources, *Report on Proposed Oroville-Wyandotte Irrigation District Water and Power Development on South Fork of Feather River* (1958), pp. 33–34.

[54] *Sacramento Bee*, Nov. 8, 1959; May 26, 1960.

not the basic purpose, of the South Fork project underwent considerable changes. Pacific Gas and Electric Company increased its promised stream of payments without the prospect of getting proportionally more power from the project. If the design was optimal before the haggling began, it could not have been at its close, and vice versa. If PG&E's final payment offer equaled the discounted present value of the power yield to the utility, then its first offer must have been less. In short, conflicts over storage projects in California change both the efficiency of the resulting uses of capital and the distribution of spoils. No evidence suggests that the impact on resource allocation is necessarily for the better.

5) Yielding cash payments to protestants—At last and at most, an entrepreneurial agency can dispose of its opponents simply by buying them off. Sometimes financial compensation provides a sensible remedy when an existing small project must be destroyed in making way for a large one. Sometimes payment seems more like a bribe, when an agency with a claim to water but no current use for water development takes cash to quiet its objections.

The latter class of cases, usually concerning the counties of origin, obviously hold the greater interest. Amador and Calaveras counties extracted $2 million each from East Bay Municipal Utility District for the latter's Camanche Project. The counties used this lump-sum payoff with varying effectiveness to try to promote local water conservation projects of their own. Another conspicuous case involves the bitter dispute between Merced Irrigation District and Mariposa County, the county of origin for the Merced River.

Mariposa County had no plans or applications pending or outlined when Merced Irrigation District in 1954 first applied for water rights permits to enlarge its storage capacity on Merced River; nor did Merced, whose feasibility report was not completed until 1960.[55] Meantime, in June 1956, the Department of Water Resources, on behalf of the future water requirements of Mariposa County, had filed applications for a site upstream on the South Fork of the Merced River and was undertaking studies relating to its development.[56] Mariposa County undertook to enhance its own bargaining stature by obtaining legislative authorization in 1959 to establish a county water agency,[57] and proceeded to negotiate with Merced in an attempt to obtain a reservation of 100,000 acre-feet annually for use in the County. When Merced's counteroffers struck Mariposa as resting on too doubtful a contingency—the receipt of a federal flood control contribution—Mariposa entered a formal protest against Merced's application. It announced that "the County now feels compelled to take appropriate action to protect its right to Merced River water, and to proceed with studies of the full development of the Merced River Basin."[58] Such studies, of course, would take time and thus would delay construction.

In the following protracted negotiations, the Mariposa interests first sought the construction by Merced of special project features designed to serve the mountain

[55] Tudor Engineering Co., *Merced River Development* (1960).

[56] California State Legislature, Senate Fact Finding Committee on Water, *Budgets, Reports, Local Assistance for State Water Development,* Report No. 2 (1961), p. 89.

[57] *Fresno Bee,* March 23, 1959.

[58] *Mariposa Gazette-Miner,* June 4, 1959.

county, features which Merced claimed it could not afford. Eventually Mariposa offered a compromise which essentially amounted to a financial payoff: a total of $5 million over the fifty years Merced would need to settle its bonded indebtedness, plus a substantial diversion right and a part of Merced's net power revenues after fifty years.[59] Essentially this proposal was accepted and incorporated into the decision of the Water Rights Board.[60]

Organizational rivalry and allocation

We have viewed the competition for storage projects as a series of organizational encounters. In closing, we need to consider it as a process for allocating scarce resources among competing uses. Some organizational rivalries reflect competition for resources only to a limited degree. Two rival public agencies seeking to develop the same resources to serve the same customers engage in competition only in the same sense as rivals in a proxy fight for the control of a corporation. County-of-origin protestants in search of financial compensation tend to seek an income transfer without substantial resource reallocation, just as those asking a reservation for future diversions seek to assure future water supplies without paying a scarcity value but do not aim to affect current resource allocation directly.

Nonetheless, investment plans are delayed or altered by the proceedings which occur before and around the regulatory bodies. The resulting changes in the efficiency of resource allocation may be favorable in some cases, unfavorable in others; certainly no presumption can be drawn. The proceedings call attention to important external diseconomies of some projects and thus improve the chances that they will be taken into account. They force the consideration of differing scales of investment from that which the entrepreneurial agency first had in mind. In another situation, the holder of a high legal card may secure the construction of physical facilities which would not pass an independent benefit-cost investigation. Furthermore, some of the institutional blind spots in water allocation are not affected by the observed rivalries. Existing rights must be recognized, but apparently there is no increased tendency to consider buying them out wholly or in part. Scales of projects are altered subject to the constraint that the Pacific Gas and Electric Company remains willing to make firm payments to cover the capital costs, but districts do not look more fully into the merits of financing part of the capital costs themselves.

The cases reviewed show no large number of clear-cut choices between alternative projects, so we can reach no conclusion on whether or not organizational rivalry tends to make the best project win. All incidental evidence suggests, how-

[59] *Merced Sun-Star,* Dec. 29, 1959; California Districts Securities Commission, *Supplemental Staff Report on Merced River Development Proposed by Merced Irrigation District* (1961), p. 5.

[60] California State Water Rights Board, *In the Matter of Applications 16186 and 16187 of Merced Irrigation District to Appropriate from Merced River in Mariposa and Merced Counties,* Decision No. D 979, Aug. 25, 1960 (mimeo.), p. 13.

ever, that the relative strength of the rivals lies more in their organizational assets than in the relative economic benefits of their projects. The accident of temporal priority in filing for a permit to divert, the political strength of a local agency as related to its population base, its financial capability as related to its existing tax base: these factors carry weight before the regulatory bodies but bear no necessary relation to the economic efficiency of their proposed projects. These same organizational traits, as shown in Chapter 11, allow excessive scales or rates of investment by state or federal agencies or well-situated local bodies, and the process of rivalry between organizations appears to supply no corrective.

The allocative impact of the regulatory bodies seems clear from the preceding examples. The California Water Commission, as guardian of the state filings and thereby the county-of-origin preference, plays the key role unless it defers to the State Water Rights Board. The Commission's strong interests in promoting the construction of projects and gratifying the entrepreneurial wishes of the maximum number of agencies hardly promise optimal performance although (as we shall argue in Chapter 20) the basic function of the California Water Commission has an excellent potential. The State Water Rights Board, while charged with a general concern for the public interest, has not established clear-cut administrative standards for this preservation.

A few definite conclusions for performance stand out from this welter of possibilities. Payoffs in cash to holders of county-of-origin rights may be better than constructing inefficient facilities to serve them, since payoffs redistribute income along lines set (for better or worse) by social policy and do not necessarily cause any resource misallocation. The open-ended reservation for future depletions by the counties of origin has several drawbacks: it formally exempts them from paying a future price for water reflecting its prevailing shadow price; it creates additional uncertainty about the benefits obtainable by an agency from current construction; and thus, other things being equal, it can delay efficient construction plans or reduce their scale.[61] Finally, the process of interagency rivalry and the economic provincialism of long time horizons considered by the participants tend to reinforce one's fears that the resulting timing of investments may depart seriously from the optimum.

Rivalry for Ground Water

One reason why tactical elements are important in pursuing appropriative rights to surface water secured through storage is the absence, in many cases, of any full legal determination of riparian and senior appropriative rights to the same supply. Because of the expense and complexity of such determination, competing water users often either find some form of mutual nonaggression pact or com-

[61] Conversely, a justification can be made for the county-of-origin preference in view of the considerable rigidities in the transfer of water rights in California. If the hypothesis were actually correct that efficient future water allocations would direct increasing quantities to uses in the counties of origin, creating a reservation for them now might simply offset rigidities that might hamper such transfers at the proper future time.

promise an attractive alternative despite its uncertainty and vulnerability to the arrival of additional competitors. A study of the competition for ground water in Northern California confirms the significance of this connection, because ground-water rights in the area are much less subject to full legal ordering than are the rights to surface water, and *ad hoc* patterns of compromise are even more prevalent. As indicated in Chapter 3, correlative ground-water rights of land overlying a ground-water basin are somewhat analogous to the rights of owners of land riparian to a surface stream. Both rights entitle the holder to water which he can put to reasonable beneficial use on the land in question, subject to the adequacy of the water supply to meet the requirements of reasonable beneficial use by owners of other overlying lands. This qualification creates an important uncertainty about rights to any ground-water basin subject to overdraft. Furthermore, although appropriative rights to a ground-water basin can be established by ways analogous to the establishment of an appropriative right to a surface supply, no formal procedure (such as application to the California State Water Rights Board) exists in the case of ground water. Any appropriation that invades the entitlements of owners of overlying lands must be dealt with in the courts, or it may ripen into an established right. The owner of overlying land thus has an incentive to fight off efforts to pump from the common ground-water supply to serve owners of lands that are not overlying, but without a fully defined right of his own may be in a difficult position to do so.[62]

In the absence of special policy measures and actions based upon legal rights, economic forces would ultimately curtail the mining of ground-water reserves. In the case of competitive extraction by a large number of users or water agencies, a falling water table and rising pumping costs would eliminate the less valuable uses progressively until the water table stabilized, with the average rate of replenishment equal to the rate of extraction by the remaining users. With a smaller number of users (oligopsony), individual pumping units would recognize the increase of future pump lifts caused by their annual drafts, and extractions would be restricted to permit stabilization at a higher water table than without this recognition. The extraction patterns of individual pumpers in some ground-water basins display these competitive adjustments for extended periods.[63]

Patterns of rivalry among owners of overlying lands

Significant portions of the Central Valley and some smaller areas of Northern California have been subject to rapidly declining ground-water tables at one time or another during the twentieth century. In no substantial case has litigation been

[62] Recent cases in Southern California tend to discourage full adjudication, in that they have continued to prove cumbersome and costly, and have commonly resulted in all users of an overdrawn basin being cut back proportionally in their water use. See Wells A. Hutchins, "California Ground Water: Legal Problems," *California Law Review,* XLV (December 1957), 688–97.

[63] See J. Herbert Snyder, "On the Economics of Ground-Water Mining—A Case Study in an Arid Area," *Journal of Farm Economics,* XXXVI (November 1954), 600–10.

employed to stop an overdraft by owners of overlying lands, and the competitive extraction process has been allowed to run. Its main influence has been to encourage the action of large wholesalers (principally the Bureau of Reclamation) to import supplemental surface supplies.

Most active conflicts concerning overlying lands have occurred between cities in the Central Valley and surrounding irrigation districts. The issue has typically been whether or not the city's water supply, secured from wells, was benefited significantly by the ground-water replenishment activities of the district, and, if so, what charges the urban users should be made to bear. Agricultural water districts now commonly draw their boundaries to exclude urban areas, but many of the older and more important irrigation districts date their formation to days when towns were typically included. In several cases this has led to running controversies, with the included city unwilling to recognize any benefit from membership and the district unwilling to exclude it. In most cases nothing more than chronic grumbling has occurred. In some cases arrangements for compensation have been worked out after considerable haggling, but none seems to embody any precise assessment of the marginal costs and benefits involved—on account perhaps of the factual uncertainties involved if not for other reasons.[64]

The most dramatic case of conflict between rural and urban agencies overlying a ground-water basin in the Central Valley has been that between the city of Fresno and the surrounding Fresno Irrigation District. It has affected not only their relations with each other but also their separate searches for wholesale surface supplies. The physical situation resembles that of several other Central Valley towns. The Fresno Water Department draws its supplies entirely from the underground basin at the rate of about 60,000 acre-feet annually. Based on the city's geographical boundaries as of 1960, about 38,000 acre-feet of this constituted the "safe yield" of its ground-water basin—an amount which could be taken annually without lowering the water table. The Fresno Irrigation District, one of California's largest, entirely surrounds the city and includes some of its suburban areas, although not the central core of the city itself. (See Figure 25.) Direct water service to many new suburban areas comes from small, passive county water districts and private water companies serving individual subdivisions from wells. The only other significant water agency in the area is the Fresno Metropolitan Flood Control District, which covers both the central core of the city and its suburbs and overlaps some portion of the Irrigation District. Its functions reflect both the city's interest in disposing of flood waters and the Irrigation District's interest in encouraging percolation of water to the ground-water basin.

The Fresno Irrigation District's boundaries were drawn around the city of Fresno originally, but the District has not excluded territory subject to suburban expansion, and the usual problems involving double taxation of the suburbs

[64] Descriptive material on cases concerning the cities of Tulare and Stockton respectively is presented in Tulare Irrigation District, "Agreement between Tulare Irrigation District and City of Tulare, Aug. 18, 1954," Exhibit No. 6A, in California State Water Rights Board, *San Joaquin River Case*, Applications No. 234 *et al.*, June 2, 1959 (mimeo.); and Harry Erlich and P. H. McGauhey, "Calaveras River Case Study," *Economic Evaluation of Water, Part II. Jurisdictional Considerations in Water Resources Management*, Sanitary Engineering Research Laboratory, University of California, Contribution No. 42 (Berkeley, 1964).

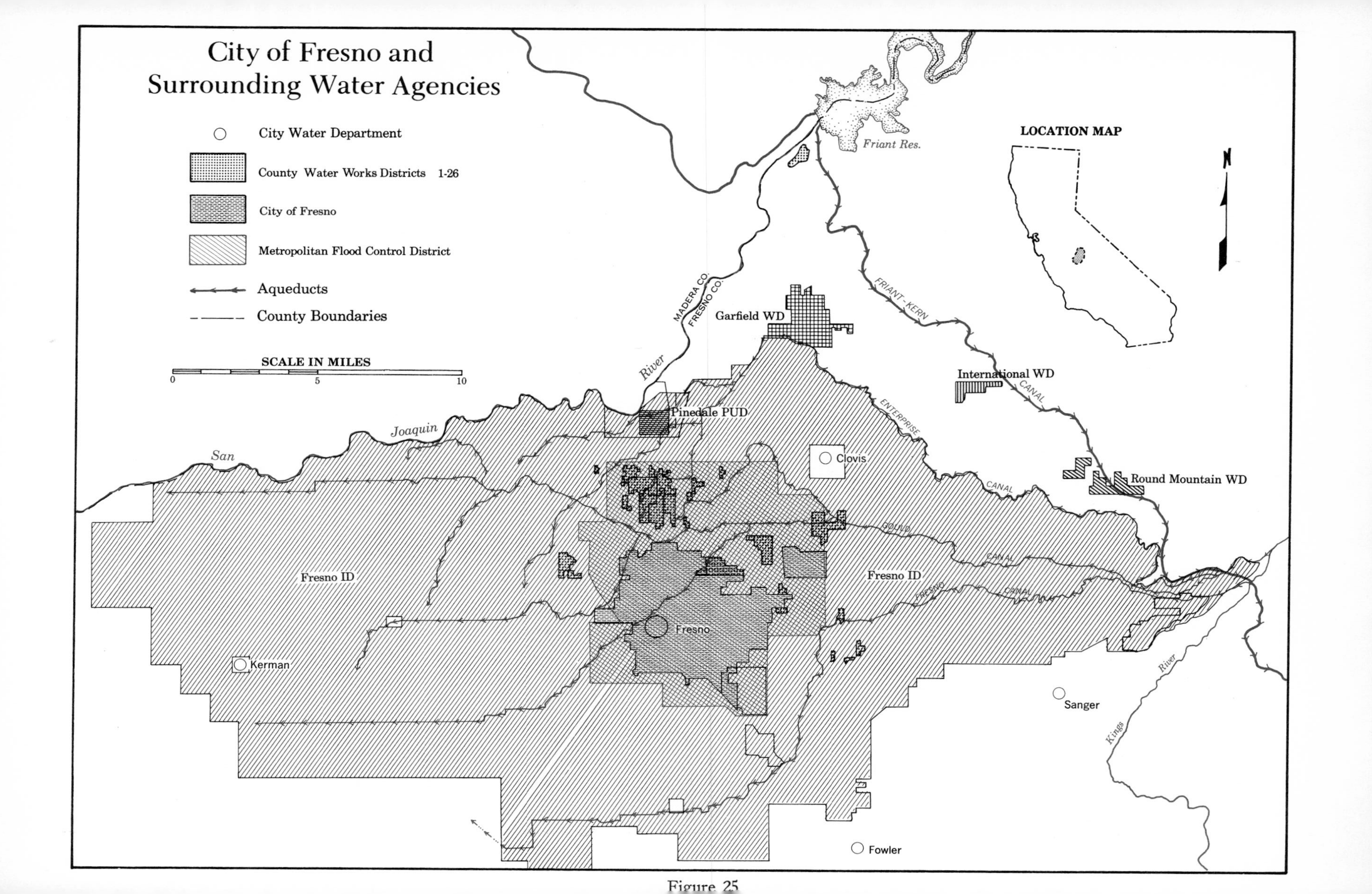
City of Fresno and
Surrounding Water Agencies
City Water Department
County Water Works Districts 1-26
City of Fresno
Metropolitan Flood Control District
Aqueducts
County Boundaries
SCALE IN MILES
0
5
10
LOCATION MAP
Friant Res.
FRIANT - KERN
MADERA CO.
FRESNO CO.
River
Garfield WD
International WD
CANAL
ENTERPRISE
Pinedale PUD
Clovis
Round Mountain WD
San
Joaquin
GOULD
CANAL
FRESNO
Fresno ID
Fresno
Kerman
Sanger
Kings
Fowler

Figure 25

have emerged. The city's draft upon the ground-water basin has also been a point of contention, though the city does not simply pump water which has percolated as a result of the Irrigation District's activities. To some degree, Fresno draws its water from deep confined strata historically replenished more from the San Joaquin River than from Kings River water imported and spread by the Irrigation District. Some of the area's agricultural pumping competes with the city in the confined strata; some draws upon shallow unconfined aquifers replenished by seepage from surface applications. In any case, local interests have perceived enough interdependence to behave as if the city and irrigation interests used the same ground-water basin.

In 1930 and 1931, the city of Fresno and the Fresno Irrigation District separately filed applications to construct a dam at Friant on the San Joaquin River and diversion works to serve their respective needs. The District planned a canal to transfer water from the San Joaquin to its own main canal. The city proposed a pipeline to connect with its own distribution system.[65] These quarter-century-old filings and applications came before the State Water Rights Board in its hearings on applications of the Bureau of Reclamation to divert water from its then completed Friant Dam. Neither the city of Fresno nor the Irrigation District succeeded in overturning the Bureau's application for a permit.

All physical and economic logic suggests that the city and the District, overlying the same ground-water basin, should have reached some joint plan for water importation and ground-water management. The area's opportunities for ground-water recharge and management of the underground basin are limited, but even so cooperative pilot efforts, as local interests have come to realize, are clearly justified. The city of Fresno lacks low-cost natural sites for water storage, off-stream or otherwise, and any hope of managing such storage depends upon cooperation with the district. Yet the city and the District have not only failed to pursue such joint efforts but also have worked at cross purposes in their legal actions. The lower-court decision in the *Rank* case stressed the strength of Fresno's claim upon water from the San Joaquin River, but the court was evidently puzzled by the contrast between the city's aggressive behavior in the courts and its lack of physical plans or facilities.[66] The decision of the State Water Rights Board contained the same attitude and even suggested a detail plan of cooperation.[67] Thus hostility resulting from rivalry for ground water between the Fresno Water

[65] California State Water Rights Board, Decision No. D 935 on Applications No. 234 *et al.*, June 2, 1959 (mimeo.), pp. 22–25.

[66] "Under the evidence the City of Fresno is in pressing present need of an additional supply of water for domestic and municipal purposes . . . *The United States and the defendant districts have no right to divert water at Friant which is presently needed by the City of Fresno* . . . But, under the evidence, the City of Fresno has not, as yet, enabled itself to receive any water from Friant; and, until it is in a position to take the water at a delivery point, it is entitled only to a declaration of its rights, but no decrees to enforce them." *Rank* vs. *Krug,* 142 F. Supp. 1 (1956), pp. 184–85 (italics in original). Also see *Fresno Bee,* Feb. 4, 1953, Feb. 10, 1953.

[67] Decision No. D 935, *op. cit.,* pp. 76–78. The State Water Rights Board urged that the Fresno Irrigation District provide its lands north and east of the city with a full gravity surface supply and serve areas south and west of the city from pumps (both areas presently receive a partial surface supply). Ground water would then percolate toward the city's pumps instead of away from them and out from under the District to the west.

Department and the District's farmers, among other factors, has led the two agencies into long-standing animosity and resulted in apparently inefficient water supply plans for the area as a whole.

Conflicts between owners of overlying lands and appropriators

Occasionally, individual enterprises or districts in Northern California have attempted to secure a water supply by purchasing territory overlying a ground-water basin, establishing a well field, and pumping water for use on non-overlying lands. In most cases, owners of overlying lands have taken action either to levy charges upon the appropriator or repel him entirely. Irrigation districts in a few cases have negotiated arrangements for charging ground-water appropriators operating within their boundaries sums at least equal to the marginal cost of the water taken.[68] The formation of several districts has been influenced by the desire of owners of overlying lands to gain an organizational device for dealing with appropriators.

Ground-water extraction, even along with pumping to supply non-overlying lands, can be carried out relatively efficiently at a small scale. Thus it constitutes a potential source of easy entry into the market for water. As such, it offers an important prospect in view of the weight of evidence developed so far to indicate a host of formidable rigidities in the transfer of water among uses, users, and places of use. Because of the potential significance of this market strategy, we shall examine at some length the twenty-five-year history of a complex and costly effort to make such a transaction—that of the Lindsay-Strathmore Irrigation District, lying south of the Kaweah River area, to secure a water supply by pumping from the Kaweah delta. This episode intertwines with Lindsay-Strathmore District's efforts to obtain surface water as well, and the case has been studied intensively with regard to the question of whether existing water law impedes desirable transfers of water.[69]

After its formation in 1915, the Lindsay-Strathmore District ascertained that its only possible source of water lay in surface diversion or underground pumping from the delta of the Kaweah River. (See Figure 22 above.) Prior users claimed it to be fully appropriated except for floodwaters, but the District went ahead to purchase the riparian Rancho de Kaweah and install pumps and pipelines to extract ground water from aquifers replenished by percolation from the Kaweah. This plan rested on legal advice that prior claimants were not making beneficial use of a large portion of the Kaweah River's flow. Action was predictably brought

[68] Tulare Irrigation District, Exhibit No. 8, in California State Water Rights Board, *San Joaquin River Case,* Applications No. 234 *et al.,* June 2, 1959 (mimeo.).

[69] Gaffney, *op. cit.;* Frank J. Trelease, "Water Law and Economic Transfers of Water," *Journal of Farm Economics,* XLIII (December 1961), 1147–52; Mason Gaffney, "Water Law and Economic Transfers of Water: A Reply," *Journal of Farm Economics,* XLIV (May 1962), 427–34.

against the District by various riparians and appropriators in the Kaweah delta, and the decision eventually went against Lindsay-Strathmore in 1925.[70]

Facing a decisive defeat in the quest to utilize its wellfield, the Lindsay-Strathmore District started in 1925 to search for a new method of getting Kaweah water. It spent approximately $165,000 for shares of various mutual water companies which serviced the delta and bought an easement in the Foothill Ditch, highest in elevation of the mutuals drawing upon the River, with the intention of taking the water in question through the Foothill Ditch. But this tactic was also enjoined by the delta agencies, and the State Supreme Court ruled against Lindsay-Strathmore's plans in 1928.[71] The District could take its proportionate share of water through the diversion works of the respective ditch companies, the Court said; but it could not transfer the point of diversion to a different (higher) ditch for easier transfer to its own bench lands. The decision rests partly on the negative reasoning that mutual-share ownership conveys no right other than the mutuality of a proportionate share of the water captured at the ditch company's intake. However, a separate reason, sufficient by itself, was that allowing any share owner to move his point of diversion "would result in a state of inextricable discord and confusion" among the holders of various rights to the Kaweah. How the Court could reach this conclusion becomes clear upon reference to the form of the diversion schedule which the Kaweah users had negotiated. It specified the division of the river at each diversion point in terms of the current rate of flow *at that point*. In this fashion, stream losses through seepage and evaporation were automatically shared without requiring special attention. Allowing any changes of diversion points would have forced either a complete redrawing of this compromise or a radical change in the implicit loss-sharing agreement. Thus Lindsay-Strathmore's effort to secure surface water was frustrated by the complex form of the Kaweah's negotiated rights settlement.

The Lindsay-Strathmore District pressed an appeal to the State Supreme Court from the 1925 decision enjoining the extraction of ground water from its wellfield, but lost in 1935.[72] Again, the decision holds great interest because of its implications for the transfer of water from one user to another. To simplify the complex decision considerably, the key issue remained that of whether riparians and prior appropriators were making reasonably beneficial use of their Kaweah supplies. The State Supreme Court found the evidence conflicting but nonetheless sided with the Kaweah delta parties. It conceded the existence of substantial inefficiencies in the Kaweah River's tangled pattern of diversion canals, but attributed them to the historic rivalries for water within the delta. The whole system was inefficient, but not to an unreasonable degree if the practices of individual ditch companies or irrigators were considered one by one. Lindsay-Strathmore had offered one physical solution: lining the channel of the Lower Kaweah River across the cone of depression created by its pumping. The Court found this in-

[70] Bulletin No. 21 (Adams), *op. cit.,* 248–49.
[71] *Consolidated People's Ditch Co.* vs. *Foothill Ditch Co.,* 205 Calif. 54 (1928).
[72] *Tulare Irrigation District* vs. *Lindsay-Strathmore Irrigation District,* 3 Calif. (2nd) 489 (1935).

adequate, although it encouraged a further quest for a physical solution which would permit Lindsay-Strathmore's diversions to continue without injury to other parties.

The 1935 decision left all parties sufficiently exhausted that they negotiated a settlement rather than resuming litigation with the riparians in the county superior court. Lindsay-Strathmore was allowed to keep operating its Kaweah wellfield, but only until water should become available from the Friant-Kern Canal. The vexing question remains of why Lindsay-Strathmore should have been unable to effect a transfer of ground or surface water from a use of lower marginal productivity to a higher use.[73] The parties spent between one and two million dollars on litigation (Gaffney's estimate). It seems a fair guess that this sum, spent by Lindsay-Strathmore in straightening and lining canals of the Kaweah delta users, would have permitted it to pump its wellfield without this use becoming perceptibly adverse to any of the parties to the case. Lindsay-Strathmore had proposed a physical solution, but the Court was clearly justified in finding it inadequate. More curiously, the evidence fails to show that Lindsay-Strathmore ever tried to bribe or compensate the Kaweah users to permit water transfers either from the wellfield or through ownership of the ditch-company stock. But given the number of users involved and the complexity of their own legal interrelations, there is no presumption that a policy of either type of compensation would have succeeded, even if Lindsay-Strathmore had offered sums several times the relatively small net productivities involved for the prior users. Apportioning the blame for this situation among the physical situation, water law, and the attitudes of the various parties must be postponed until our investigation of performance in the water industry.[74]

Considering the prevalence of declining water tables in the Central Valley, the absence of a greater number of cases of rivalry among buyers or pumpers over ground water presents a paradox. Yet this paradox quickly dissolves when one considers the political success which areas suffering from declining water tables have had at securing large-scale publicly financed water transfer and storage projects. Water users depending on declining ground-water supplies have had little trouble choosing among suffering rising pumping costs in silence, entering into expensive litigation likely to end in compromise, and joining hands to call for relief from a public wholesaling agency. First, deteriorating ground-water conditions were shown in Chapter 9 to supply the major cause for the formation of new local districts. Second, these districts and their promoters have enjoyed consistent success in winning public assistance. One can hardly follow committee hearings and congressional debates over projects of the Bureau of Reclamation

[73] Mason Gaffney, "Diseconomies Inherent in Western Water Laws: A California Case Study," in *Economic Analysis of Multiple Use,* Proceedings of Western Agricultural Economics Research Council, Tucson, Arizona, January 23, 1961, 55–81, demonstrates this difference convincingly.

[74] The Kaweah area, perhaps as a result of this experience, has now undertaken a more conscious management of its ground-water resources through the Kaweah Delta Water Conservation District.

without gaining the impression that a favorable benefit-cost ratio carries much less persuasive power than visions of abandoned farmsteads and impoverished towns.

Competition for Water and Resource Allocation

The three main sections of this chapter have considered the major types of rivalry for water and water rights in the California water industry—for surface flows usable by direct diversion, for the storage of surface water for later use, and for ground water. Each of these areas of conflict reveals a sort of "settlement" process placing previously unowned and largely unused resources under some private proprietary interest. The process constitutes the legal counterpart of the coming of economic scarcity for water which had previously been a free good with respect to those uses exercised through private appropriation.

In the diversion or storage of surface water and the capture of ground water, the rule of "first come, first served" plays a basic but not exclusive role. This rule certainly dominated the establishment of claims to the natural flow of Central Valley rivers during the irrigation season, a process largely completed before World War I. The riparian law in California was and is important, since it creates a right which does not depend upon temporal priority of use. Nevertheless, the economics of irrigated agriculture in nineteenth century California in any event placed riparians among the first claimants on those streams, and such claims have continued to hold great importance. The process of defining and ordering claims to the natural summertime flows of Central Valley rivers reflected, besides temporal priority, the tangled and uncertain legal processes in use at that time. Our review of the comparative water rights history of the rivers of the San Joaquin Valley neither affirms nor denies the rationality of water allocations established as much as a century ago. But whatever their rationality at the start, it is clear that they could not have remained optimal for long. Pressures for transfers of water use between areas and classes of users were built up well before the turn of the century, giving behavioral evidence of misallocation of water. Furthermore, the apparent inefficiency of the development of facilities for the diversion and use of water from certain rivers testify to the character and extent of the misallocations involved.

The process of appropriating winter and spring runoff through storage, the dominant feature of the competition for water since World War II, similarly has achieved a questionable success in placing a scarce resource in the most deserving hands. Many of the strictly legal deficiencies of older procedures for conferring title to water have been eliminated by the present roles of the California State Water Rights Board and California Water Commission. But a greater improvement has come in the procedure for establishing new rights than for formally defining those in existence. Both the Board and the Commission enforce standards of public interest in taking actions which eventually lead to an increased appropriation of water. How fully these standards and their mode of administration agree with an economic concept of the public interest, however, is another story. Priority of application retains some significance in the process, although any relation it holds to optimal allocation must be tenuous. Consistency with the California Water Plan, if used as a model of general and coordinated development, also has only little to recommend it as a test of the public interest, since the Plan represents a grandiose scheme for full physical development which is unproved by the yardstick of benefit-cost analysis. At best, it might call to attention the suboptimal scale of a proposed project. Finally, the apparent bias in favor of physical construction (and commercial use) may misallocate water as between in-stream uses and consumptive uses requiring storage and diversion upon the land. And among diverters, water tends to be misallocated between those agencies constrained by capital rationing and those not so constrained. Such biases would lead not only to a misallocation of water but also in all likelihood to an excessive level of investment in water facilities.

The definition of legal rights to ground water in Northern California has made so little headway that one must speak, not of the efficiency of the resulting allocations, but rather of the consequences of no formal rights or allocations having been established. As a process of resource exploitation by atomistic users, ground-water extraction logically contains an inefficiency in the failure of individual users to take into account the increased pumping costs to other users resulting from their own depletions. In the less atomistic situations, wherein ground-water rivals act directly to try to curtail one another's depletions, the results have been even less happy because of the apparent gaps in the range of solutions considered by the combatants. The Fresno and Lindsay-Strathmore cases may justly be viewed as isolated ones, but they do suggest a failure of the parties involved to consider arrangements for compensation, joint resource management, and the like, which might lead toward more appropriate allocation.[75]

As we have emphasized, the efficiency with which newly established claims to water are allocated among users causes concern only if their subsequent reallocation is subject to constraints. The preceding chapter does not contain all of our evidence on this score, but we can summarize the information developed so far. Outright transfers of water rights in Northern California have been few in number, large in size, and complex in legality. Consider two major cases: on the Kern River (Miller and Lux transfer to the Haggin interests) and on the San Joaquin River (Bureau of Reclamation purchases). Each covered a large portion of the flow of the river in question and involved nearly all of the dominant holders of rights. Each occurred only after a long history of complex negotiations and legal maneuvers in which many other solutions to the allocative problem at hand were considered. Each involved the transfer of riparian rights, essentially by quitclaim—a shaky procedure which can work at all only if the purchaser is legally "next in line." Those smaller transfers of rights which have come to light usually attach to the replacement of a small-scale resource development with a larger one. The party bought out is usually compensated in water as well as cash,

[75] A similar problem of deficient ground-water management is revealed in the case of the Santa Clara Valley, discussed in Chapter 13.

the goal of the process being a more efficient exploitation of water resources but no net transfer of end uses.[76]

The shortage of overt transfers of rights does not, however, necessarily imply either an absence of transfers among end uses or a massive inefficiency in the use of resources. End-use transfers occur without involving the sales of water rights. The sale and rental of shares in mutual water companies accomplish this result in areas where they operate. In Northern California extraction of ground water is an atomistic process with no restriction on transfers of use among owners of overlying lands. Inflexibilities in the transfer of ground water to non-overlying lands are significant but not crippling. Finally, water appurtenant to land can easily undergo an end-use transfer when the land itself makes the same switch: consider California's many suburbanized irrigation districts.[77] Another source of limited allocative flexibility lies in the activities of water wholesalers, the subject of the following chapter. In Part Three, below, we shall try to appraise both the role of these allocative processes or institutions and the extent to which the task of attaining optimal allocation remains undone.

[76] Compare the following conclusion from a survey of water rights taxation in California: "Because there is virtually no market for water rights, and because the rights themselves were acquired by the entities by virtue of beneficial use, not generally by the payment of any sum of money, the approach to valuation has been as varied as the counties making the assessment." C. Marvin Brewer, "Taxation of Water Rights in California," *Journal of the American Water Works Association,* LIII (May 1961), 619–24.

[77] Stephen C. Smith, "The Rural-Urban Transfer of Water in California," *Natural Resources Journal,* I (March 1961), 68–69.

13

WHOLESALE AGENCIES AND TRANSACTIONS

A producer-wholesaler in the water industry secures water rights and water; then contracts to deliver water to a re-wholesaler or retailer. Such an agency makes investment decisions in planning facilities to store and divert water and to transmit it to prospective users. It makes pricing decisions in proposing and negotiating the terms of contracts for the disposal of water to purchasers. Thus the wholesaler is an active participant in the conduct of the water industry and importantly influences its performance. Wholesalers are responsible for the bulk of interbasin transfers of water, and thus directly account for efficiency achieved in the interbasin allocation of water. And their pricing decisions affect the allocation of water among customer agencies within their chosen service areas, just as their investment decisions affect the allocation of water among types and times of use at the sources of water.

As was shown in Chapter 4, the Bureau of Reclamation of the U.S. Department of the Interior dominates the wholesale water transactions actually occurring at present, with other wholesalers accounting only for small volumes of transactions in local areas. However, the California Department of Water Resources is undertaking the construction of the Feather River Project and has negotiated contracts for the sale of its water in both Northern and Southern California. The Department's policies are still evolving as our study reaches completion in 1965. Because of this pattern of timing, much of the information in this chapter will concern the policies of the Bureau of Reclamation and their significance. But we shall also discuss the activities of the local wholesalers and consider the direction of development of the policies of the Department of Water Resources. The Department's role takes on special interest where it has come into rivalry with other wholesalers.

In reviewing these policies we emphasize, first, the process by which the price is calculated by the seller, and, second, the forces governing the reconciliation of sellers' and buyers' offers in the market place, hoping to conclude something about the efficiency of allocation as it is influenced by the price and other terms established in wholesale contracts. We shall also be concerned with the structural factors that appear to affect the outcome of these bargaining processes, including seller and buyer concentration, various aspects of law that govern the rights and obligations of the various parties, and the attitudes of local retailing agencies that result from their users' cooperative status and their trusteeship relation to the rights of their member-customers.

In the following sections we consider first the price determination principles used by wholesalers, then several cases of bilateral bargaining in a variety of structural settings.

Price Determination Principles of Producer-Wholesalers

Our description will move from the general statutory principles and agency practices governing the pricing decisions of the Bureau of Reclamation and the Department of Water Resources to the specific case of the Bureau's pricing of water delivered from Friant Dam.

General principles: Bureau of Reclamation

Reclamation law places a series of constraints on the pricing policies followed by the Bureau.[1] First of all, the total costs of a reclamation project must be allocated among the various classes of beneficiaries by some formula for allotting the joint costs of a multiple purpose project. The "separable costs-remaining benefits" method of cost allocation came into regular use during the 1950's. It levies against each class of beneficiaries the separable costs associated with serving them, plus a share of the remaining joint costs which is proportional to the excess of their expected benefits over the separable costs.[2] Reclamation law then designates these various classes of allocated costs as either reimbursable or nonreimbursable (repayment by beneficiaries obligatory or not), and the reimbursable benefits are further subdivided as to whether or not their repayment must include interest charges. Flood control, navigation, and recreation benefits are nonreimbursable; irrigation and salinity and sedimentation control are reimbursable without interest; power benefits and the benefits of municipal and industrial water supply are reimbursable with relatively low interest charges.

In broad principle, each class of recipients of reimbursable benefits is obligated to cover its share of costs. In practice, however, the Bureau's accounting of receipts for the reimbursable benefits of multiple purpose projects provides an extremely important qualification. While the repayment of costs allocated to power need be only sufficient to cover the calculated obligation, the Bureau in fact seeks to charge for power something closer to what the traffic will bear. Approximately the same statement holds for municipal and industrial water. Any "profits" in the form of power or municipal water revenues in excess of allocated costs can be used to reduce the repayment obligation computed for irrigation water.[3]

These policies set the general limits which affect prices set by the Bureau in

[1] See Alfred R. Golzé, *Reclamation in the United States* (2nd ed.; 1961), chaps. 9–11 and 17, for an extensive treatment of policies of the Bureau. (This and other footnote references are cited in brief form when they are also included in the Bibliography.)

[2] Or to the excess of the cost of providing these benefits through alternative facilities, if that should be less. Numerous other methods of allocating joint costs were in use before the separable costs-remaining benefits method came into ascendancy. See *ibid.*, chap. 9.

[3] The interest charges levied on power and municipal water benefits can also be so used.

negotiating contracts for the disposal of the water output of its projects. They obviously constitute very elastic limits. Experience suggests that the separable costs-remaining benefits method may be manipulated to give very different results for the same project, since revised allocations for a project often diverge significantly from their predecessors. Furthermore, the Bureau can vary the minimum revenue that it must seek from purchasers of irrigation water by its choice of a pricing policy for power and municipal water—at least in those cases where the power and municipal water enjoy a significant surplus of benefits over allocated costs.

Out of the clashes between the Bureau and the U.S. Army Corps of Engineers has come a division of labor which similarly places some constraints on the repayment obligations of local beneficiaries for projects constructed by the Corps. While at one time it was not obligated to make cost allocations, the Corps now employs the separable costs-remaining benefits method to allocate the costs of multiple purpose projects. And the Bureau undertakes to negotiate the repayment for irrigation benefits indicated by the allocation, under the terms of federal reclamation law. The Bureau has no authority to adjust the sum that it seeks to collect in such cases, but the Corps itself may well be subject to pressures to adjust its allocations to minimize reimbursable benefits, in order to secure local support for its activities.

In marketing the supplies of irrigation water generated by its own projects, the Bureau may employ several different types of contracts. It does not normally act as a retailer of water to individual proprietors, but rather transmits water to public districts which distribute it to their members. Such transfers can be made under three separate types of contracts. One is the utility type contract for the sale of irrigation water at specific prices per acre-foot over a maximum period of forty years. This is referred to as a "9(e) contract," after the authorizing section of the Reclamation Project Act of 1939. The "9(c) contract" is a similar one used for municipal water supply and miscellaneous purposes on the basis of utility type pricing. The "9(d) contract" is used for repayment by districts of the costs of surface water distribution systems constructed for them by the Bureau of Reclamation. As with other Bureau contracts, no interest is charged on irrigation service features. Under 9(d) contracts, the districts take over maintenance and operation of the distribution systems, and when repayment is completed take title to the works themselves.[4]

Certain special provisions of reclamation law concerning the terms of sale for irrigation water have generated enormous controversies in California since the late 1940's. These are the "excess land" and "anti-speculation" clauses, dating back to the establishment of the federal reclamation program in 1902. That statute restricted the application of water from reclamation projects to a maximum of 160 acres per person prior to the time when all repayment obligations on a project have been met. Later legislation permitted excess lands, thus defined, to receive water for a maximum of ten years provided the owner had signed a "recordable

[4] 43 U.S.C. 485. For discussion and examples of these contracts, see U.S. Congress, House Committee on Interior and Insular Affairs, *Central Valley Project Documents, Part 2: Operating Documents,* H. Doc. 246, 85 Cong. 1 sess. (1957), pp. 79–280.

contract" promising sale of the excess lands at a price involving no speculative gains.[5]

General principles: Department of Water Resources

Let us now consider briefly some of the directions in which policies of the California Department of Water Resources seem to be moving.[6] According to the Burns-Porter Act, which authorized the bond issue financing the Feather River Project, it is supposed to be financially self-supporting. There is, however, some ambiguity about the return of those funds drawn from the California Water Fund, which is built up by revenues derived from offshore oil and gas leases. And while total costs are to be covered by revenues, there is no requirement that each contracting agency or class of users must pay all costs imputable to its own supply of water. The Department of Water Resources also appears to have some discretion about the reimbursability of particular classes of benefits and as to the form of sale contracts and the period of repayment. In the early stages of planning the Feather River Project, the Department favored a system of pricing differentials to provide relatively cheap water for irrigation. That proposal threatened to raise the whole issue of acreage limitation as in federal reclamation law, however, since the theory behind acreage limitation stresses restricting the subsidy provided to individual farm families to a reasonable size. To avoid being embroiled in a controversy over land limitation, on the one hand, and to avoid committing itself to demanding a full payment of costs imputed to each contractor, on the other hand, the Department has adopted a policy of surcharges on water delivered to lands in large ownerships.

While the Department of Water Resources has by now placed under sales contracts most or all anticipated deliveries of water from the Feather River Project, its marketing practices and their allocative significance cannot be appraised in the same level of detail as those of the Bureau of Reclamation. The contracts do not specify a price which the purchaser is to pay, but rather they include a formula by which that price will be determined. Thus the terms of sale offered by the Department must be viewed as subject to some uncertainty.

Bureau of Reclamation pricing in practice

Probably the most important single pricing decision which the Bureau has made in California concerns water of the San Joaquin River, stored behind Friant

[5] The fine points of these provisions have been subject to extensive controversy. See 43 U.S.C. 485 *et seq.;* U.S. Department of the Interior, Office of the Secretary, *Excess Land Provisions of the Federal Reclamation Laws and the Payment of Charges,* Vol. I (1956); Paul S. Taylor, "The Excess Land Law: Legislative Erosion of a Public Policy," *Rocky Mountain Law Review,* XXX (June 1958), 480–504, and "The Excess Land Law: Execution of a Public Policy," *Yale Law Journal,* LXIV (February 1955), 477–514.

[6] As revealed, for example, in California State Legislature, Assembly Water Committee, *Economic and Financial Policies for State Water Projects,* Vol. 26, No. 1 (1960). (Hereinafter cited as *Economic and Financial Policies.*)

Dam and diverted into the Friant-Kern and Madera canals. This case is also stressed because we shall examine in some detail the subsequent negotiations over this price in the next section.

By the time general negotiations for San Joaquin water were opened in 1945, the Bureau had set its position on most of the terms of sale. It had decided it could safely market a total of 900,000 acre-feet of water as a firm annual supply. This is called "Class 1" water, its quantity "so established that deficiencies will not occur too often, or be of such severity as to result in loss of a crop." An average of 400,000 acre-feet of "Class 2" water would also be available annually—an uncertain supply in any particular year that would have to be taken in the months before the main irrigation season.[7]

The Bureau had also decided on its asking price for Friant water for irrigation uses—$3.50 an acre-foot for Class 1 and $1.50 an acre-foot for Class 2 to all users along the Friant-Kern and Madera canals. Unfortunately, in view of the importance of this price, there is no public account of the process by which it was set. The underlying calculations were made in Washington during World War II, when the prospects for the postwar economy were at best uncertain and the memory of the extensive defaults on repayment obligations for reclamation projects before the war was still fresh. These pricing decisions must have taken two major factors into account. One was the expected ability of farmers to pay for water supplies developed by the project, allowing for generous margins of error in computing their capacity.[8] The other was covering those costs of the project allocated to irrigation in all of its service areas taken together,[9] allowing for revenues from the sale of power and municipal and industrial water in excess of the costs imputed to them. In a recent recalculation, the Bureau's regional director indicated that the repayment obligations of irrigators would cover 72 per cent of the total costs of the Central Valley Project allocated to irrigation over the life of the Project.[10] There is no evidence that specific consideration was given to the expected incremental costs of storing and delivering water, or to the marginal value of this water in places of use other than the prospective service area.

In estimating the ability of irrigators to pay for water, the Bureau typically uses farm budget studies for the area in question to determine the net productivity of irrigation water for various crops and various grades of land. Once the crop pattern and the size of the average farm are estimated, the total net productivity of water is computed after subtracting all other costs, including normal profits under the guise of a "farm family living allowance." There is also an estimate of marginal productivity in the restricted sense of average productivity for the crop which has the lowest net productivity in the area. Normally, judgment is then

[7] U.S. Congress, Senate Committee on Public Lands, Subcommittee, *Exemption of Certain Projects from Land-Limitation Provisions of Federal Reclamation Laws*, 80 Cong. 1 sess. (1947), p. 702. (Hereinafter cited as *Exemption of Certain Projects*.)

[8] California State Legislature, Senate Fact Finding Committee on Water, *Contracts, Cost Allocations, Financing for State Water Developments* (1960), pp. 54–56. (Hereinafter cited as *Contracts, Cost Allocations, Financing*.)

[9] *Exemption of Certain Projects, op. cit.*, pp. 849–50.

[10] *Contracts, Cost Allocations, Financing, op. cit.*, p. 55.

used in setting a price for water that is above, but near, this average productivity for the marginal crop.[11]

There are several conservative factors in these calculations of net productivity as the Bureau normally makes them. They are based on "new land" and thus include full depreciation for buildings and equipment. The family living allowance apparently is supposed to contain an incentive factor and thus is probably above the minimum supply price of farm family units. Furthermore, the Bureau's regional director has testified that "irrigation water rates or annual repayment obligations are normally established so as not to exceed 75 per cent of the estimated payment capacity."[12]

Setting the charge for Class 1 and Class 2 Friant water was not the Bureau's only decision. There appears to have been a debate within the Bureau after 1945 over charging all users along any one of the Bureau's canals the same rate for Class 1 water, despite the substantial variations in transmission distance from Friant Dam. This dispute between advocates of "train ticket" and "postage stamp" rate systems was finally settled in favor of a uniform rate. Apparently the dominant argument was that the land in the service area nearer the Dam had a higher average payment capacity than that near the lower end of the Friant-Kern Canal in Kern County. A train-ticket rate built around an average price of $3.50 might have been out of reach of some lands in the Kern area that the Canal had been consciously designed to serve. Later, some train-ticket elements were built into the pricing of water by setting a price of less than $3.50 for Class 1 water in other portions of the Central Valley Project. A lower price for irrigation service in the Sacramento Valley and for water stored behind Folsom Dam on the American River could serve the dictates of cost-of-service and value-of-service considerations. Not only would the Bureau incur lower transport costs in delivering water to these lands than to those at the south end of the Central Valley, but also the average productivity of water in the north was clearly much less.

An additional important initial pricing decision also concerned Class 2 water. It was to bear a relatively mechanical relation to the price of Class 1 water. The theory of the relation between the two classes was that Class 2 generally would not be available during the irrigation season but only for "preirrigation," so that districts could use it only by first sinking it into the underground basin for their irrigators to pump up in time of need. To make water users largely indifferent between Class 1 and Class 2 and to permit cyclical underground storage of San Joaquin water, the difference would have to equal the average cost of pumping water from underground storage. The $2 difference between the two classes was set, in general, to do just this.[13]

[11] This can be done because it is normal practice for water districts to use both tolls and assessments. They can thus meet a price higher than that which their marginal customers can pay by using assessments to annex the "excess" profits to be made on nonmarginal crops.

[12] Statement before California State Legislature, Senate Interim Committee on Proposed Water Projects, Aug. 20, 1959, quoted from Sacramento River and Delta Water Users Association, Exhibit No. 11, *Sacramento River Case,* California State Water Rights Board, Applications No. 5625 *et al.* (mimeo.), pp. 3–4.

[13] U.S. Department of the Interior, Bureau of Reclamation, Region 2, *Factual Report, Lindmore Irrigation District* (1948), p. 20. For a discussion of this pricing problem in relation to irrigation district policies, see Chapter 10.

Bilateral Negotiations over Central Valley Project Water

Since negotiations opened in 1945 for the sale of water from Friant Dam, the Bureau has been in almost continuous negotiations with one or another group of prospective customers of the Central Valley Project. In each case until recently it enjoyed a monopoly wholesaling position, but factors other than seller concentration that have influenced these bargaining rounds have varied significantly from case to case. In no instance has the Bureau's basic price offer been substantially altered in the bargaining, but ancillary terms of the agreement have undergone considerable change in the market place.

Contracting for San Joaquin River water

The contracts for water delivered from Friant Dam took the Bureau almost a decade to negotiate. Although the supply was eventually placed (and a lengthy waiting list formed), the negotiations were complex and acrimonious. (The districts which signed contracts are shown in Figure 26.) The would-be buyers' objections were not so much to the Bureau's price as to the basic excess-land provisions of reclamation law and to the utility type 9(e) contract. The feeling about these provisions rose to tremendous heights, leading to several hostile congressional investigations of the Bureau, congressional denial of salaries to two Bureau officials, and an ambitious campaign to get the state of California to issue the enormous amount of general obligations bonds necessary to buy the Central Valley Project from the United States.

The substance of the issues concerning acreage limitation does not concern us here, except to note the extraordinary reluctance of districts in the San Joaquin area to accept it and the almost pathological political consequences.[14] Of greater significance for the allocation of water are objections raised to the utility service character of the 9(e) contract. It conveyed no water right and no title to the Bureau's physical facilities, and it contained no guarantee of renewal after a period of forty years.[15] Land values might tumble as the expiration date approached, and at any time mortgage loans would be hard to get for lands not possessing a firm water right. In addition, the districts objected to many administrative features of the 9(e) contract, largely because of the potential influence it gave the Bureau over their internal affairs.[16]

The water users called for a contract wherein they would obligate themselves

[14] For example, see *Exemption of Certain Projects, op. cit.*, and (Senator) Sheridan Downey (Dem., Calif.), *They Would Rule the Valley* (1947).

[15] California State Legislature, Joint Legislative Committee on Water Problems, *Report on Water Problems of the State of California* (1949), pp. 11–20; U.S. Congress, House Committee on Interior and Insular Affairs, Special Subcommittee on Irrigation and Reclamation, *Central Valley Project, California: Water Rights, Supplies, and Uses*, 82 Cong. 1 sess. (1952), pp. 260–68. (Hereinafter cited, respectively, as *Report on Water Problems* and *Central Valley Project: Water Rights, Supplies, and Uses.*)

[16] U.S. Congress, House Committee on Public Lands, Subcommittee on Irrigation and Reclamation, *To Amend the Reclamation Projects Act of 1939*, 80 Cong. 1 sess. (1947), pp. 126, 154–55. (Hereinafter cited as *To Amend the Reclamation Projects Act of 1939.*)

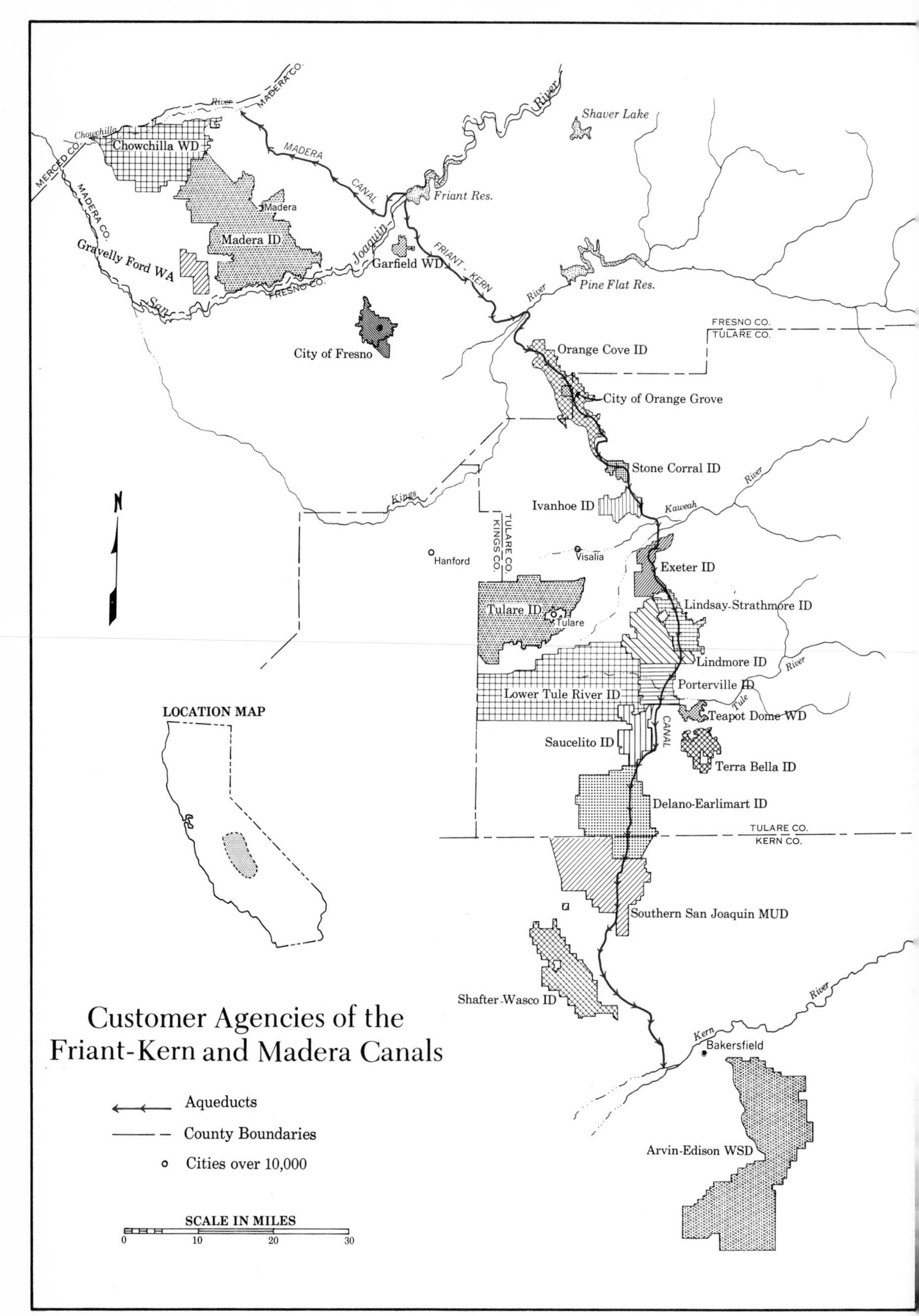
Customer Agencies of the Friant-Kern and Madera Canals
Chowchilla WD
Madera ID
Madera
Gravelly Ford WA
Garfield WD
Friant Res.
Shaver Lake
Pine Flat Res.
MADERA CANAL
FRIANT-KERN
City of Fresno
Orange Cove ID
City of Orange Grove
Stone Corral ID
Ivanhoe ID
Visalia
Hanford
Exeter ID
Tulare ID
Tulare
Lindsay-Strathmore ID
Lindmore ID
Porterville ID
Lower Tule River ID
Teapot Dome WD
Saucelito ID
Terra Bella ID
Delano-Earlimart ID
Southern San Joaquin MUD
Shafter-Wasco ID
Bakersfield
Arvin-Edison WSD
MERCED CO.
MADERA CO.
FRESNO CO.
TULARE CO.
KINGS CO.
KERN CO.
LOCATION MAP
Aqueducts
County Boundaries
Cities over 10,000
SCALE IN MILES
0
10
20
30

Figure 26

to pay for some fixed allocation of the costs of the Central Valley Project over forty years and take title to the physical facilities at the end. The Bureau's objections to this approach lay in the nature of the project. The complex physical facilities defied the conventional methods of allocating fixed costs in multipurpose projects. Because of the large numbers of public agencies to be served by the project, it was inconceivable that the physical works should be turned over for their separate operation. In any case, the Bureau contended that the Central Valley Project was a metaphysical unity including works on other rivers not yet constructed. Thus, the total costs and benefits would not be known for many years, and no definitive cost allocation could be made.[17]

To a small degree, the users' objections to the 9(e) contract represented a quarrel over the price. Declared one spokesman:

> There has been an insistent demand upon the part of those who are in these various irrigation districts . . . as to what [the Bureau's] costs are, how much they are, whether they include a lot of heavy overhead expenses, or whether they are going to be charged up with litigation that has been necessarily carried on by the Bureau. They want to know what their repayment charges are and what they can expect and some definite statement on that so they can know what they are going to pay and what they are going to get.[18]

However, the issue as seen by the irrigation district officials was not really one of the size of annual payments during the coming half-century. One irrigation district representative stated: "There is no question in the mind of anybody there that $3.50 [per acre-foot of Class 1 water] is all right." The Bureau's offers in terms of quality of water were also accepted without apparent dispute. The Bureau was concerned both with maximizing the area served and averting future groundwater problems. A representative declared: "We have a shortage of first-class, firm water and we believe that we should distribute that water where it is needed the most and in almost every case the district applications have been for more water than we think they should have."[19]

The issues in dispute instead were such long-term matters as the U.S. government's earning substantial profits from the proposed contract or, worse yet, switching sales to some other buyer of water in years well beyond the lifetimes of any of the current negotiators. These features of the districts' attitudes deserve emphasis, for they depict strikingly both outlook and behavior in the water users' organizations that one would hardly expect to find in a conventional industry. That the current price of water should be unimportant relative to the profits which might be earned at that price forty years hence, that the quantity of water currently purchased should receive less attention than contractual assurances of the opportunity to renew the contract for water four decades in the future—these attitudes give some impression of the objectives and the time horizons of the officials speaking for local water agencies.

[17] See *Report on Water Problems, op. cit.,* pp. 60–62; *Central Valley Project: Water Rights, Supplies, and Uses, op. cit.,* pp. 267–68.

[18] *Ibid.,* p. 162.

[19] *Exemption of Certain Projects, op. cit.,* pp. 634 and 1061.

These positions of the Bureau of Reclamation and the San Joaquin Valley water agencies remained largely fixed, although the Bureau made a number of minor changes in its basic contract over the period of the negotiations. The districts which eventually signed did so with most of their misgivings unassuaged. Nonetheless, the Bureau of Reclamation had to make some compromises. As an example, the first contract with the Southern San Joaquin Municipal Utility District did not state the maximum amount of Class 1 water which the Bureau proposed to market eventually. Because the availability of Class 1 water is not subject to an ironclad guarantee, a district would have a greater assurance of regular supply, the smaller the total quantity that the Bureau placed under contract. In its second contract, with the Lindsay-Strathmore Irrigation District, the Bureau included this assurance and lowered the maximum figure for Class 1 water to 800,000 acre-feet from the 900,000 acre-feet which had been mentioned earlier.[20] Later, the Bureau supported congressional action to allow it to include a renewal option clause in the 9(e) contract. In negotiating an agreement with Shafter-Wasco Irrigation District, one of the last to sign in the Friant-Kern area, the Bureau agreed to provisions protecting the District against accidental loss of water through the Bureau's negligence. Each of these changes, once agreed to, was made available to all contracting parties.

Contracting for Sacramento Valley water

In the northern part of the Central Valley, the Bureau of Reclamation has faced different problems in securing contracts for the sale of water to be delivered through the Corning and Tehama-Colusa canals, west of the Sacramento River, and from Folsom Dam on the American River. In the case of the Sacramento Valley canals, the Bureau's problems went beyond those of reaching agreement with existing districts to the necessity of getting the districts organized in the first place. The Bureau set a price for water from the canals of $2.75, largely with reference to the capacity of local lands to repay. It was clear that, in view of the low agricultural productivity in the area, this would be no bargain to water users. In congressional hearings on the canals, at least one independent spokesman suggested that a price of $2 might be more reasonable in comparison to the San Joaquin's $3.50, because of the shorter growing season and other factors.[21]

Despite an extremely effective campaign mounted by local leaders to get the canals built, popular sentiment seems to have taken the same view. Partly because of the experience with Pine Flat Reservoir (discussed below), the Bureau sought to enforce a policy of securing contracts before any construction took place. A year before the Corning Canal was started, a Bureau representative stated that a majority of the water to flow through the Sacramento canals would have to be contracted for before construction would begin. Progress was slow, however; and

[20] *To Amend the Reclamation Projects Act of 1939, op. cit.*, p. 575.

[21] U.S. Congress, House Committee on Public Lands, Subcommittee on Irrigation and Reclamation, *Authorize Sacramento Valley Canals, Central Valley Project, California,* testimony of James K. Carr, 81 Cong. 1 sess. (1949), p. 33.

the Corning Canal was started without signed contracts in 1954, and completed in 1957. However, work was then stopped before completion of the pumping plant necessary to draw water from the Sacramento River. This stemmed partly from the continued lack of contracts with the Corning and Proberta water districts, but also from a general halt of the Bureau's construction work in California because of legal uncertainties over reclamation law stemming from the Ivanhoe case concerning the applicability of acreage limitation. Supporters of the Sacramento canals in Congress were blocked by presidential vetoes of appropriations in 1956 and 1957 and insufficient congressional support in 1958. The Bureau itself refused to proceed with the construction of another of the canals, the Tehama-Colusa, for lack of contracts with its customers.[22]

These delays and difficulties put one of the local agencies, Corning Water District, in trouble both with the Bureau and from internal dissent. In 1958, the District was considering suing the Bureau to require completion of the Corning Canal. Corning spokesmen were particularly irked because they did not object to the acreage limitation, the uncertain legal status of which was the Bureau's official reason for delay.[23] The internal difficulties were caused by the wish of many local landowners to be excluded from the District. The result was a checkerboard pattern for the District which threatened to preclude the design of a distribution system which could be financed by the District. While not altering its basic price for water from the Sacramento canals, the Bureau eventually had to make other financial concessions by absorbing part of the cost of distribution systems for districts with checkerboard service areas and by constructing and operating canal-side pumps to deliver water from the main canals into the districts' distribution systems.[24] The attainable contracts with the Sacramento canals districts apparently promised to cover such a small portion of the costs allocated to irrigation for the project that the Bureau tried to recoup by charging a higher price to one district with relatively higher payment capacity, but the district mustered enough political strength to beat off the move.[25]

The bargaining problems which the Bureau faced in the Sacramento canals area contrast with those dominating the Friant negotiations. To the San Joaquin Valley farmers the Bureau offered a valuable commodity at a reasonable price, but with repugnant conditions attached. There was no question but that an excess demand existed at that price, only whether or not the conditions might be relaxed. In the Sacramento area, the auxiliary conditions caused little trouble, but the irrigators perceived little net surplus to be derived from purchasing water at the terms offered by the Bureau. The same situation has plagued the Bureau in negotiating the sale of American River water through the proposed Folsom South Canal, where irrigators complained that ground water cost no more than that which the Bureau was offering.[26]

[22] *Orland Register,* June 16 and July 14, 1958, Sept. 10, 1959; *Red Bluff News,* July 3, 1958; *Willows Journal and Glenn Transcript,* Feb. 3, 1959.

[23] *Redding Searchlight,* June 14, 1958; *Red Bluff News,* July 9, 1958.

[24] *Red Bluff News,* Nov. 4, 1959; *Sacramento Bee,* Nov. 15 and Dec. 18, 1962.

[25] *Sacramento Bee,* Jan. 26, 1959, March 9, 1960; *Woodland Democrat,* Feb. 17 and March 5, 1960.

[26] *Sacramento Bee,* Feb. 7, 1957; *Sacramento Union,* Nov. 21, 1958.

Compensation for incidental benefits to Sacramento River users

The Bureau of Reclamation has faced trouble enough in selling water to direct customers. It has encountered even greater difficulties in securing payment for incidental benefits which it could not readily withhold from those enjoying them. This experience is important because of the enormous role which external effects play in the transactions of the Northern California water industry. The technology of water is such that a major water project can produce incidental benefits and injuries to many parties other than those primarily involved. Under California water law, those who are, or may be incidentally, harmed can often claim compensation or block constructions and transactions. Also, collecting for incidental benefits, or taking them into account in estimating a benefit-cost ratio, will often make a substantial difference for the payoff to a project or transaction.

The Bureau stores water at Shasta Dam on the Sacramento River, theoretically to be released for diversion from the Sacramento-San Joaquin Delta through the Delta-Mendota and Contra Costa canals some 200 miles to the south.[27] Between Shasta and the Delta, these releases must run the gamut of the pumps and other diversion works of many channel riparians and appropriators. That such users might intercept water released by the Bureau during the dry season and destined for diversion from the Delta was foreseen when Shasta Dam was built during World War II. Channel users had taken a little less than 1 million acre-feet annually between World Wars I and II. The Bureau assumed that an extra 300,000 acre-feet allotted to these users would cover any foreseeable agricultural development along the Sacramento. They reckoned without the economic impact of World War II. Total diversions between Redding and Sacramento rose from 900,000 acre-feet in 1925 to about 2 million in 1951.[28] Along the critical stretch between Red Bluff and Knight's Landing, irrigated acreage increased by one-fourth between 1943 and 1954. Diversions in 1954 were much greater than they could have been without net releases from Shasta Dam, yet they were still significantly less than the rights claimed by the diverters.[29]

These developments raised for the Bureau a complex problem involving both water sales and water rights. Increased Sacramento channel diversions threatened the feasibility of the Bureau's exports from the Delta, for without Shasta's releases saline ocean water from San Francisco Bay would threaten the quality of water in the Delta. Increased use along the Sacramento channel had to be discouraged, or at least the Bureau felt a sum had to be collected for the benefits provided. To pursue either of these courses, however, the Bureau had to establish its rights to the water of the Sacramento River as against the channel diverters, and this had not previously been done.

Facing this dilemma, the Bureau concluded by 1944 that the rights of the channel users would have to be legally defined. The Sacramento had never been fully adjudicated, and merely to identify all users (especially riparians) was proving

[27] For the relation of these works to the rest of the Central Valley Project, see Chapter 4 and Figure 31.

[28] *Central Valley Project: Water Rights, Supplies, and Uses, op. cit.*, pp. 9–30.

[29] California State Water Rights Board, *Opinion by Board Member W. P. Rowe, Concurring in Part with, and Dissenting in Part from, Decision D 990,* Feb. 9, 1961 (mimeo.), pp. 63–68.

difficult and expensive.[30] The Bureau sought to organize them into negotiating committees to secure a voluntary settlement, but no acceptable basis for agreement was found and this effort was abandoned. However, in 1948 the users received an assurance from Secretary of the Interior Julius Krug that no water needed in the Sacramento Valley would be exported from it.[31] In 1951, the State Division of Water Resources took the opening steps in the procedure for considering the Bureau's applications to divert Sacramento River water, approval of which was required to legalize the operation of the Central Valley Project. The Bureau disclosed that it was considering a full adjudication of the Sacramento River which would involve all users.

The prospect of a full adjudication prompted Representative Clair Engle to hold a hearing in Sacramento of a subcommittee of the House Committee on Interior and Insular Affairs. Here the Sacramento users demanded rights not just to the amount of water which they had previously used but rather to the full natural flow of the river (unmodified by Shasta Dam). For example, one spokesman put it this way: "The natural flow—that is our right, that is our ancient heritage, and we think we are entitled to it, and we don't see any reason why the growth and development of the valley should be impaired by taking that water away from us."[32] The Bureau's engineer suggested that 60 to 75 per cent of the Central Valley Project's diversions from the Delta were to come from this natural flow of the Sacramento and only 25 to 40 per cent from storage behind Shasta Dam.[33] The hearings contained no evidence that a negotiated settlement was in the making or even considered feasible by either party. The only alternatives discussed were the initiation of a judicial determination of rights to the Sacramento water or construction of additional storage capacity (for example, diversion of the Trinity River into the Sacramento to increase the summer flow enough to eliminate the threat of scarcity).[34] The Engle subcommittee brought strong pressure to bear against the former solution, and it was dropped.[35]

Negotiations between the parties were again pressed and eventually yielded an understanding that the users were entitled to sufficient water for reasonable beneficial use, past or potential, and a cooperative program of measurement of flows and diversions was carried out. But no specific agreement had been reached when the California State Water Rights Board handed down its decision, in February 1961, on the Bureau's applications. There was no question of these being approved, especially since the Bureau would be subject, in any case, to such prior rights as might be established at law.[36] The Board thus could do no more than encourage some kind of solution to a problem of defining existing

[30] *Central Valley Project: Water Rights, Supplies, and Uses*, *op. cit.*, pp. 104, 199.

[31] *Ibid.*, p. 195; U.S. Department of the Interior, Bureau of Reclamation, Region 2, Exhibit Nos 92, 93, 94, 95, *Sacramento River Case*, California State Water Rights Board, Applications No. 5625 *et al.* (mimeo.).

[32] *Central Valley Project: Water Rights, Supplies, and Uses*, *op. cit.*, pp. 183–90.

[33] *Ibid.*, pp. 190–91, 217.

[34] *Ibid.*, pp. 80–81, 102, 220–21, 398–99.

[35] *Ibid.*, p. 10 and *passim;* U.S. Congress, House Committee on Interior and Insular Affairs, Special Subcommittee on Irrigation and Reclamation, *Report on Central Valley Project, California*, 82 Cong. 1 sess. (1952), pp. 4, 18–19.

[36] California State Water Rights Board, Decision D 990, Applications No. 5625 *et al.*, Feb. 9, 1961 (mimeo.), pp. 6–9.

rights, over which it had no jurisdiction. It chose to keep the door open for new Sacramento users to seek contracts with the Bureau and to encourage a negotiated solution with the existing users. "It is imperative," declared the decision, "that the holders of existing rights and the United States reach agreement concerning these rights and the supplemental water required to provide the holders with a firm and adequate water supply, if a lengthy and extremely costly adjudication of the waters of the Sacramento River and its tributaries is to be avoided."[37]

We shall not here concern ourselves with the subsequent economic and legal complications of this case, since they will not be disposed of for some time.[38] We might mention, however, that the price sought by the Bureau for water sold to the Sacramento users in excess of their rights bears no known relation to its opportunity cost or to the Bureau's marginal costs. The importance of the case lies in its showing of the extreme difficulty of defining rights as among a large number of claimants, a difficulty only partly solved by present licensing procedures. It also shows some of the biases which are built into the practicable means of settling such disputes: (1) the necessity for compromise solutions, with the compromise weighted by the general political strength of the contestants; and (2) the single solution capable of pleasing all parties, namely, providing enough additional water to avoid the need to define the rights of all claimants to a presently scarce supply. If the evidence of the San Joaquin Valley shows that local misallocations can prejudice the case toward the importation of (perhaps excessive) supplies to an area, the Sacramento Valley case demonstrates that the mere complexity of legal determination of rights can do the same.

Repayment obligation for Pine Flat Dam

The most famous and most acrimonious of the Bureau's various bargaining sessions in the Central Valley was over payment for water conservation benefits provided to local users by Pine Flat Dam, constructed on the Kings River by the Corps of Engineers. It holds relatively little importance for our investigation, however, and will be considered only briefly.[39] The background to this controversy includes an extended dispute between the Corps of Engineers and the Bureau of Reclamation over which agency should construct Pine Flat Dam. It was finally settled that the Corps would construct it and the Bureau would collect a repayment for the "incidental" water conservation benefits, with a figure of $14,250,000 eventually agreed upon for the value of the benefits. The Dam would be operated

[37] *Ibid.*, pp. 75–76.

[38] *Sacramento Bee*, Oct. 1962–Dec. 1963, *passim;* California Water Commission, *Agenda and Data for Meeting of April 5, 1963* (mimeo.); Irrigation Districts Association of California, *Minutes of Semiannual Convention*, "Creek Law vs. Federal Paramount Rights," by Martin McDonough (April 26, 1962), pp. 6–10.

[39] Sources include Arthur Maass, *Muddy Waters: The Army Engineers and the Nation's Rivers* (1951), chap. 5; U.S. Department of the Interior, Office of the Secretary, *Excess Land Provisions of the Federal Reclamation Laws and the Payment of Charges, op. cit.;* Paul S. Taylor, "The Excess Land Law: Pressure vs. Principle," *California Law Review*, XLVII (August 1959), 499–541.

by the Corps for flood control purposes only until arrangements for this contribution were completed.

Against this background, the Bureau of Reclamation began its long and bitter negotiations with the Kings River Water Association, which represented the user agencies on the Kings River. The rivalry between the Corps and Bureau made it plain to the water users that the federal government's attitude was malleable. Furthermore, the runoff pattern of Central Valley streams is such that operating a reservoir for maximum flood control comes to just about the same thing as operating it to maximize the value of its storage for irrigation use. Thus, as in the Sacramento case, the Bureau was negotiating for something it could not withhold, but in this case without even a credible threat of extended litigation available to strengthen its hand. As in none of the cases of negotiation discussed previously, the Bureau did not hold any substantial claims in the form of water rights, except for a minor right to floodwaters of the Kings River which had historically flowed into the San Joaquin River. Other rights to the River had been allocated by negotiation among the Kings River users themselves.

The position of the Kings River interests was that the Bureau's price was too high, that the acreage-limitation provisions of reclamation law were unacceptable, and that they would not tolerate integration of Pine Flat Dam into the Bureau's Central Valley Project. The parties were stalemated as a result of this position until 1952 when Pine Flat was actually in operation. Subsequently, a "temporary" contract was negotiated whereby the Kings River users paid a small sum to cover their share of the operating costs of the Reservoir and a larger one that was credited against their $14,250,000 repayment obligation (starting in water year 1955–56). With this routinely renewed annual agreement in effect, the Bureau was collecting some payments and the users were avoiding the acreage-limitation provisions. Pressures for a permanent settlement were thus sharply reduced. Eventually, in 1963, the parties agreed to a court test of an arrangement whereby one of the Kings River retailing districts paid off its remaining share of the repayment obligation in a lump sum and thereby avoided the acreage-limitation features of reclamation law.[40]

So far as the Kings River stalemate reflects a dispute over distributional questions and issues of social policy not directly connected with the allocation of water, it holds relatively little significance for the present study. What does matter, however, is the ease with which potentially superior allocative alternatives can be ruled out by such a dispute. The integration of Pine Flat with the Central Valley Project, proposed by the Bureau and violently opposed by the Kings River interests, might have meant two things. One is a "bookkeeping" integration lumping the revenues and costs associated with this project into the rest of the Central Valley Project works, with potential effects on future construction plans of the Bureau. The other is integration of the water service (and, potentially, power service) in the Kings River area. Through existing physical interconnections, this could permit equalizing the net value of the marginal product of water as between the Kings River area and other substantial portions of the San Joaquin Valley—

[40] *Western Water News,* November 1963, p. 2. A separate agreement was reached for the sale of the Bureau's floodwater rights to the Kings.

an integration that in principle could make all parties better off. That such interchange possibilities are readily ruled out by distributional and other issues is the main normative significance of the controversy.

Another lesson of the Kings episode concerns the position of the wholesaler in the California water industry. The Sacramento River case shows the unquestionable deterrents to the expansion or extension of transactions in water when rights are undefined. The Kings case suggests a somewhat more fundamental uncertainty, in that no sequence of steps will minimize uncertainty for the producer-wholesaler and his prospective customers together: On the one hand, if the wholesaler negotiates first and builds his facilities afterward, either his customers incur substantial risks from his nonperformance or he undertakes a great financial risk himself. On the other hand, if the wholesaler builds first and negotiates afterward, he creates a different sort of financial risk for himself and enters into a bargaining situation in which it is difficult to withhold the benefits of his facilities for want of payment. These considerations not only contribute further to explaining the absence of private enterprise in the industry, but also explain why the allocations attained by the entities actually present are so affected by elements of uncertainty and policy considerations not directly related to the use of water.

Rivalry among Wholesalers in the San Francisco Bay Area

A common denominator of the negotiations just discussed is that neither party had reasonable access to any alternative transaction. The Bureau negotiated service contracts for its canals only after they were firmly committed or under construction; canceling the construction plans or dealing with a totally different service area was never a serious alternative. Similarly, the prospective water users had no immediate alternative sources of surface water. The situation is now changing, however, for the Bureau's wholesaling activities in the Central Valley. There have been definite suggestions of competition for customers in the southern San Joaquin Valley between the Bureau's proposed East Side Division and the Feather River Project's west-side aqueduct, currently under construction. Rivalry between the state and federal governments arose over both the dam site and service areas of the San Luis project, now under construction on the west side of the San Joaquin Valley as a joint project between them. Finally, both the Bureau and authorized or proposed features of the California Water Plan may encounter fringe competition from the smaller projects on the Feather, Yuba, and American rivers which were discussed in Chapters 11 and 12.

These impending developments create great interest in any actual cases of economic relations between public wholesalers and retailers under conditions where either group enjoys market alternatives. This situation has emerged in vivid fashion in the San Francisco Bay area. Not only are three large wholesalers vying for customers in the counties at the southern end of the Bay, but also one area, Santa Clara County, offers a case of active rivalry between two would-be local wholesalers over the role of reselling water purchased from a large outside agency. Furthermore, in the less developed counties north of San Francisco Bay the first signs are emerging of similar rivalries which may develop over the next ten to twenty years. Does the presence of rival buyers and sellers have the virtues usually imputed of insuring the consideration of all alternatives? Of weakening positions of monopoly and securing better allocation thereby? Do agencies enjoy less freedom to follow parochial and bureaucratic motives in the face of opposition? These are the significant questions of conduct and performance to put to these situations.

Water rivalry in Santa Clara County[41]

The Santa Clara valley has the unusual fortune to lie over a large ground-water basin which in the past has been a munificent source of water. Hydrologically, the valley is divided into two sectors in terms of its underground aquifers: a forebay (outer rim of the valley) where water percolates into underground storage, and a pressure zone (center of the valley) where the ground water is confined. Both are pumped, but percolation occurs only in the forebay. Mining the ground-water supply has created problems beyond those of increased pump lifts: compaction of the underground aquifer and extraction of ground water from beneath San Francisco Bay.

So far, the main solution chosen for this problem of a declining water table has been percolation induced into the aquifer by the storage of natural runoff and its slow release into natural channels and artificial spreading ponds. Because of the heavy investment of both urban and rural residents in pumping systems, this solution has seemed the most reasonable; early plans which involved surface distribution encountered resistance because they entailed additional capital expenditures. The current program of percolation, however, has not halted the decline of ground-water supplies and probably cannot do so.

An unusually complex structure of water agencies attempts to deal with these problems. The agencies are shown in Figure 27. The largest consumer of water in the Santa Clara Valley is the San Jose Water Works Company, a private company which supplies the city of San Jose primarily from deep wells in the forebay

[41] In addition to interviews, newspaper clippings, and the like, the following reports are important sources for this section: Santa Clara-Alameda-San Benito Water Authority, *Report of Progress* (1958); Santa Clara-Alameda-San Benito Water Authority and Santa Clara County Flood Control and Water Conservation District, Board of Review, *Report on Supplemental Water Supplies for North Santa Clara Valley and Related Service in San Benito and Santa Cruz Counties* (1960), and *Materials Supporting Report on Supplemental Water Supplies for North Santa Clara Valley* (1960); Santa Clara County Flood Control and Water Conservation District (FCWCD), Special Water Committee, *Unified County Water Plan: Report to the Board of Supervisors* (1961); Santa Clara Valley Water Conservation District (WCD), *Report to the Honorable Board of Directors on Additional Conservation and Distribution Facilities* (1960); Creegan and d'Angelo, *North Santa Clara Valley Demand Study* (1960), and *Comparison of Cost of Importing Water to North Santa Clara Valley from Hetch Hetchy, South Bay Aqueduct and/or Pacheco Aqueduct* (1961); U.S. Department of the Interior, Bureau of Reclamation, Region 2, *A Report on the Feasibility of Water Supply Development: San Felipe Division, Central Valley Project* (1963).

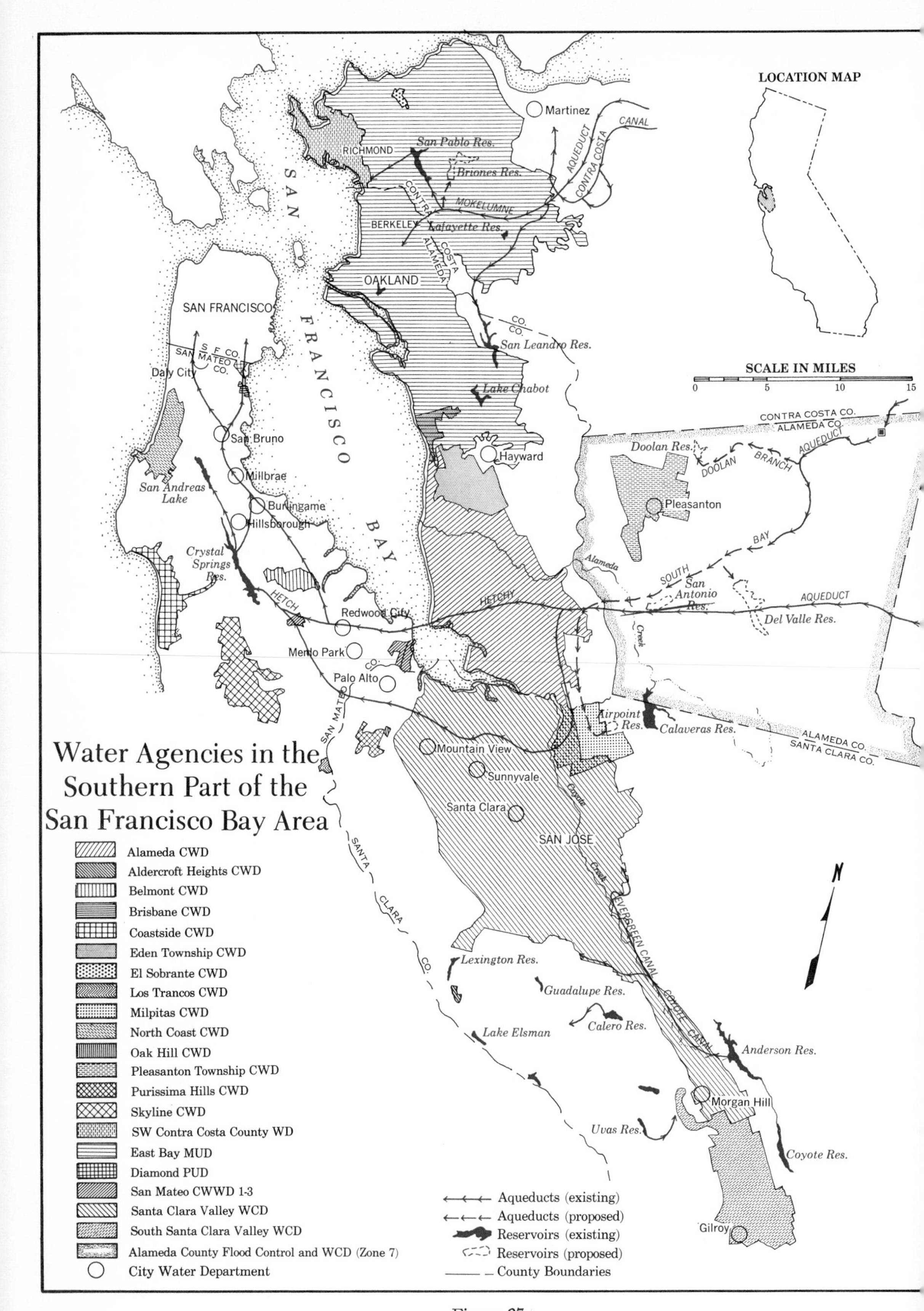
Water Agencies in the Southern Part of the San Francisco Bay Area
Alameda CWD
Aldercroft Heights CWD
Belmont CWD
Brisbane CWD
Coastside CWD
Eden Township CWD
El Sobrante CWD
Los Trancos CWD
Milpitas CWD
North Coast CWD
Oak Hill CWD
Pleasanton Township CWD
Purissima Hills CWD
Skyline CWD
SW Contra Costa County WD
East Bay MUD
Diamond PUD
San Mateo CWWD 1-3
Santa Clara Valley WCD
South Santa Clara Valley WCD
Alameda County Flood Control and WCD (Zone 7)
City Water Department
Aqueducts (existing)
Aqueducts (proposed)
Reservoirs (existing)
Reservoirs (proposed)
County Boundaries
LOCATION MAP
SCALE IN MILES
0
5
10
15
N
SAN FRANCISCO BAY
RICHMOND
BERKELEY
OAKLAND
SAN FRANCISCO
Martinez
San Pablo Res.
Briones Res.
Lafayette Res.
MOKELUMNE
AQUEDUCT
CONTRA COSTA
CANAL
CONTRA COSTA
ALAMEDA
CO.
CO.
San Leandro Res.
Lake Chabot
Hayward
S F CO.
SAN MATEO CO.
Daly City
San Bruno
Millbrae
Burlingame
Hillsborough
San Andreas Lake
Crystal Springs Res.
HETCH
HETCHY
Redwood City
Menlo Park
Palo Alto
SAN MATEO
CO.
Mountain View
Sunnyvale
Santa Clara
SAN JOSE
CONTRA COSTA CO.
ALAMEDA CO.
Doolan Res.
DOOLAN
BRANCH
AQUEDUCT
Pleasanton
SOUTH
BAY
San Antonio Res.
Del Valle Res.
Alameda
Creek
Airpoint Res.
Calaveras Res.
ALAMEDA CO.
SANTA CLARA CO.
Coyote
Creek
SANTA CLARA CO.
EVERGREEN CANAL
COYOTE CANAL
Lexington Res.
Guadalupe Res.
Lake Elsman
Calero Res.
Anderson Res.
Morgan Hill
Uvas Res.
Coyote Res.
Gilroy

Figure 27

zone of the aquifer. Its distribution system within the city draws from dispersed wells, not from a single large aqueduct. The other urban centers in the vicinity of San Jose (Palo Alto, Santa Clara, Sunnyvale, and Mountain View) are served by municipal water departments, and a county water conservation district indirectly contributes to their supply. In 1948, municipal use accounted for only 18 per cent of total water use in the Santa Clara Valley. By 1960, it had risen to 48 per cent, and one projection gives the figure of 89 per cent for the year 2010. Agricultural use, based on private pumping, makes up most of the large but declining balance of use.

There has been no shortage of outside wholesalers willing to serve the Valley. The city of San Francisco's Hetch Hetchy Aqueduct follows the Bay side of the Valley past the string of cities northwest of San Jose—Santa Clara, Sunnyvale, Mountain View, Palo Alto. Some purchase all or part of their supply from San Francisco, and San Francisco has sought to expand its sales to protect access to its rights to the Tuolumne River.[42] But San Francisco operates under constraints. By terms of the Raker Act, the city cannot export water from the San Joaquin Valley for irrigation purposes, and therefore it can only sell to cities. This constraint is becoming less significant as the Valley increasingly turns urban, but it has been important. Second, San Francisco does not aim to subsidize the consumption of water, and so its price is relatively high.

The California Department of Water Resources has already completed the crucial first section of its South Bay Aqueduct, designed to carry water from its projected Feather River Project aqueduct on the west side of San Joaquin Valley to the southern end of San Francisco Bay.[43] The state sought—and for some time unsuccessfully—agencies to contract for this water and applied pressure to Santa Clara Valley to share the costs of the project under construction. The state says it follows the same policy as San Francisco in offering water under contracts which require the recipients to pay the full allocated cost of supplying it. Also like San Francisco, the state has actively campaigned for customers and has threatened all-or-nothing offers to potential customers wishing to defer a decision.

The Bureau of Reclamation has studied the construction of an aqueduct from its San Luis Reservoir over Pacheco Pass. Although the Bureau's report on this project emerged only after the crucial decisions were made in Santa Clara, and the Bureau was not an active campaigner, its project was thought technically feasible at the time. And it was expected that the Bureau would, as usual, offer a price reduced by substantial elements of federal subsidy. Unlike the other two potential sellers, the Bureau's project would deliver water at the upper (south) end of the Valley, with easy access to the forebay; also, the earliest date for completion of the Bureau's project was thought to be six years later than for the state's South Bay Aqueduct.

Two local agencies stood between these outside wholesalers and the Santa Clara retail agencies and final users, contending vigorously for the role of water im-

[42] San Francisco's investment policies and its water rights situation are discussed in Chapters 11 and 12.

[43] The water is to be taken at first from the Bureau of Reclamation's Delta-Mendota Canal, later from the aqueduct built as part of the Feather River Project.

porter and local wholesaler. They are the Santa Clara Valley Water Conservation District (WCD) and the Santa Clara County Flood Control and Water Conservation District (FCD). These districts have in the past engaged in only trivial retailing functions. The FCD is relatively new and without water supply facilities. The WCD is older and well established in the activity of ground-water replenishment, but has retailed only a small part of its supplies directly. Each of these would-be local wholesalers has had certain logical preferences among the three equally competing outside wholesalers.

The prime function of the Santa Clara Valley WCD has been to construct dams to store the floodwaters of the Valley's creeks and rivers. These waters are then released down natural channels or into percolation ponds for underground replenishment, and canals and pipelines have been constructed where necessary to carry water to percolation areas. As Figure 27 shows, its territory includes only a portion of the county. Furthermore, in some parts of the Valley within the district's boundaries, no substantial benefits from its activities have previously been perceived, and these areas came to resent their tax payments to support it. The nature of the District's function makes its benefits hard to measure. The process of inducing percolation is simple in principle; in practice, ignorance of the hydrology of underground aquifers have made it very difficult to determine the benefits provided to specific areas. The incidence of benefits has clearly been uneven, since the aquifers do not underlie the area evenly. In particular, the cities in the northwestern part of the Valley received little benefit.

The major force in opposition to the Santa Clara Valley WCD was the governing board of Santa Clara County, the Board of Supervisors. They also serve as directors of the county-wide Flood Control and Water Conservation District. This agency was established by the State Legislature in 1951 with the power to perform almost any act in the area of water conservation and supply as well as flood control, and the Board of Supervisors believed that it "should be responsible for the construction, maintenance and operation of all new wholesale distribution facilities and water treatment plants." In the opinion of the county-wide FCD's Special Water Committee, the WCD, which expected to be the dominant local wholesaler, instead "should be responsible for the maintenance and operation of all existing water distribution facilities used for percolation and irrigation purposes within their respective areas."[44] The conflict between these two agencies as to which would do the importing, the contracting, and the wholesaling was primarily a bureaucratic rivalry. But the struggle encompassed more than primacy, and vitally affected the decisions made about the choice among supply and distribution alternatives.

The physical positions of the two agencies strongly affected their preferences as among the three competing outside wholesalers. The California Department of Water Resources proposed service to the Santa Clara area through the South Bay Aqueduct, planned with a capacity of 210,000 acre-feet annually, with 88,000 acre-feet assigned to Santa Clara County at the end of the line. The South Bay Aqueduct would terminate at a low altitude at the northeastern corner of the

[44] Santa Clara County FCWCD, *Unified County Water Plan, op. cit.*, p. 21.

Santa Clara Valley; the higher southern reaches could clearly be more efficiently served from a more southern crossing of the hills separating the coast from the Central Valley. The plans to construct the South Bay Aqueduct bestirred the initial rivalry within Santa Clara County over alternative imported supplies, since the capacity and length of the Aqueduct appeared contingent upon the completion of long-term contracts. The sense of urgency to influence the design of the South Bay Aqueduct became coupled with a fear that the state's potential supply for Santa Clara might go to the Metropolitan Water District of Southern California if no firm contract were signed; and the tactic subsequently used by the Department of Water Resources was, in fact, to secure a contract with the Metropolitan Water District to take all supplies not contracted for by other agencies.

This sense of urgency was promoted in Santa Clara County by the Board of Supervisors and their FCD, for they were the natural allies of the South Bay Aqueduct. The state's preference for contracting with as large and as few agencies as possible predisposed it toward dealing with the Supervisors. Furthermore, the Aqueduct would involve the use of facilities, such as surface distribution networks and treatment plants, unrelated to the Water Conservation District's storage and percolation works. The Supervisors were eager to control these new facilities.

In its negotiations with the Metropolitan Water District of Southern California, the Department of Water Resources developed the pricing principles applied to the South Bay Aqueduct. Contracting agencies would pay a two-part charge set with the general objective of covering the costs of the project to the state. Each South Bay Aqueduct contracting agency was to pay an annual fixed charge determined by its allocated share of the cost of the facilities from which it benefits, the share related to its separable costs plus a portion of the common costs estimated by the "proportionate use of facilities" method. Santa Clara County, at the end of the South Bay Aqueduct, would be charged for all fixed costs of the canal beyond delivery points in Contra Costa and Alameda counties, plus its share of the common costs. Thus, the annual fixed charge would be higher per unit, the smaller the portion of its water Santa Clara County took from the South Bay Aqueduct. This pricing system placed the County Board of Supervisors in a delicate position in contracting for South Bay water, because the fixed charge could make it quite expensive unless purchased in sufficient quantities to serve the whole of the County's needs.

The Santa Clara Valley WCD supported a different proposal which would place imported water within its own control, namely an aqueduct entering the county from the south via Pacheco Pass. This could be either a California Water Plan aqueduct or one drawing from the Bureau of Reclamation's San Luis project. The WCD was convinced that this route would be the most efficient, since water would be delivered at a point suitable for percolation through the District's existing facilities. Furthermore, the pricing policy of the Bureau, which had the project under study, contains subsidy elements which would work to Santa Clara's substantial benefit.

The third large wholesaler offering water to Santa Clara County was the city of San Francisco. Although already supplying part of the water used in the cities of Palo Alto, Sunnyvale, Mountain View, and Milpitas through its Hetch Hetchy

Aqueduct, nonetheless it lacked any strong natural allies in Santa Clara County. Its customers shared the common view that transactions between public bodies should be priced at cost. Thus they showed dissatisfaction with San Francisco's high price and apparent profits from water transactions, a dissatisfaction heightened by a lack of full access to the seller's cost accounts. They pay according to a rate schedule slightly higher than that for customers within the city of San Francisco. Since the Santa Clara cities already took a relatively large volume of water, however, they enjoyed substantial quantity discounts. Even if San Francisco's price was high in absolute terms and yielded a "profit" to the city in the eyes of its customers, it nonetheless retained the advantage of providing water of excellent quality in comparison to almost any conceivable alternative source.

The presence of the three competing wholesalers, each offering different sorts of advantages and each having different natural allies and enemies among the local water agencies, led to an extremely complex series of maneuvers; the end result was that each competing wholesaler claimed a share of the business. Although the presence of competition in this case obviously forced the consideration of several of the relevant alternative approaches to water supply, it seems clear in retrospect that not all of the relevant alternatives were considered. Nor can the lengthy series of engineering reports and studies prepared in the course of the conflict be said to have brought much rationality to the decision-making process. The self-interests of the local agencies, however, clearly did have a substantial impact on the outcome. Since the historical story of these organizational rivalries has been well told elsewhere,[45] we turn directly to the results.

The relatively weak position of the Santa Clara Valley WCD in the face of the Board of Supervisors' strong position and the state's ultimatum on the South Bay Aqueduct led it to take crucial action. Its reservoirs were dry in 1961 because of a season of very light rainfall, and it proposed immediately to build a temporary pipeline over Pacheco Pass to pump water from the Delta-Mendota Canal into the Valley. More important, it offered to pay the cities of the northwestern part of the Valley to abandon plans to draw water from the South Bay Aqueduct and instead purchase from San Francisco. The WCD signed an agreement with Sunnyvale that "for each acre-foot of water purchased by Sunnyvale from the City and County of San Francisco, District will contribute Twenty Dollars ($20) toward the cost thereof."[46] No specific justification was given for this figure, but it had been estimated that when the South Bay Aqueduct was used to full capacity the costs to the northwestern cities would be $50.80 per acre-foot as against $70.00 per acre-foot asked by San Francisco. This contract was extended to Mountain View, and those parts of Milpitas and Palo Alto which were within the WCD's boundaries.

This inducement, coupled with San Francisco's pressure for contracts for an assured twenty-years' supply of "pure" Hetch Hetchy water, was sufficient. All of the cities mentioned signed long-term contracts to purchase water exclusively

[45] Robert R. Lee, *Local Government Public Works Decision-Making,* Stanford Project on Engineering-Economic Planning (1964), pp. 108–272.

[46] *Agreement between the City of Sunnyvale and the Santa Clara Valley Water Conservation District,* May 23, 1961 (mimeo.), p. 2.

from San Francisco and eschew all other suppliers.[47] San Francisco had to make only small concessions in the process. It promised the cities that, as usage of its water system built up and indebtedness was liquidated, they would receive reductions in rates. But San Francisco was able to hold fast on its basic price and win, through the help given by the WCD.

San Francisco's success did not, however, deter the Santa Clara County Flood Control and Water Conservation District from proceeding with its contract for water from the South Bay Aqueduct. This agreement was signed in November 1961, for 88,000 acre-feet, the quantity originally allocated to the Santa Clara area in the state's planning. Deliveries were scheduled to begin in May 1965. The decision to contract for this water did not automatically resolve the conflicts over agencies' jurisdiction and methods of water delivery within the County. Indeed, to attain the consensus necessary to get a South Bay Aqueduct contract signed the supervisors had to agree to support plans for construction of the Pacheco Pass project by 1970. When the Bureau of Reclamation finally issued its feasibility report on this project in 1963, it contained a favorable benefit-cost finding and offered the expected low prices as a result of the various forms of user subsidy available to the Bureau. But it did no more than the many previous reports to provide a solid comparison of the various alternative arrangements for water supply in Santa Clara County, nor did it deal appropriately with the question of optimal timing for such a project.

Although no federal commitment has been made to undertake the Pacheco Pass project, we can draw some conclusions about the efficiency of this water marketing process and the issues of equity entangled with it. Taking, first, a general view of the competing outside wholesalers, the business has not gone strictly to the seller able to offer the largest amount of implicit subsidy to his customers, although the urgency of the local supply situation and the Bureau's tardiness alone may have prevented this. Indeed, correct accounting (subject to the uncertainties associated with joint costs) might show that San Francisco earns more than a normal return on capital associated with the delivery of water to its suburban customers. Our information does not, however, yield the converse conclusion that San Francisco would prove to be an efficient supplier if each wholesaler's costs and prices were optimally calculated. The city's success in wholesale competition in any case depended entirely upon the cooperation of the Santa Clara Valley WCD in providing what essentially amounts to an internal subsidy sufficient to make San Francisco's price attractive.

As between the Department's South Bay Aqueduct and the Bureau's Pacheco Pass conduit, a number of engineering studies made of the proposals during the period of active controversy showed sometimes one, sometimes the other, alternative to be superior. The issue was considerably complicated by the apparent problem of timing: in 1961, it appeared that supplementary imports would be needed in a few years, but the Bureau's project seemed no closer than 1970. In any case, what is disturbing about the various evaluations of these alternatives is Lee's demonstration that all employ more or less defective procedures in making cost

[47] See Santa Clara Valley WCD, *Report to the Honorable Board of Directors on Additional Conservation and Distribution Facilities, op. cit.*

comparisons, especially in handling costs incurred at different times. The range of alternatives available was never fully appraised, especially the alternative of additional short-run development of local sources instead of resorting posthaste to an outside wholesaler. Another omission, important for the same reason, was the evaluation of the marginal benefits of additional supplies in the short run; the "requirements" approach to benefits, typical of urban water planning, was followed throughout.[48] Lee's own evaluation strongly suggests the possibility that additional local supplies might have been a preferable short-run alternative, and clearly demonstrates that (1) given the selection of the South Bay Aqueduct, the construction of Pacheco Pass around 1970 would amount to building considerably ahead of demand; and (2) Pacheco Pass project offers a financially superior alternative for Santa Clara County but, if subsidy elements in the federal project are removed, comprises a higher-cost source of water than South Bay Aqueduct.[49]

The Santa Clara situation presents other performance deficiencies of equity and efficiency that bear some relation to interagency rivalry there. The WCD levies taxes on land exclusive of improvements. It concedes that urban areas pay far more than their share of its costs in terms of the portion of water used, but holds that the present tax structure constitutes a reasonable degree of subsidy to agriculture.[50] Despite its arguments that the entire District shares in the benefits of the percolation, whatever their initial incidence, the residents of the Valley perceive that the benefits and the costs have not been either equally or equitably distributed. Parts of the District are not efficiently supplied via percolation, while parts of the basin that are benefited lie outside the tax zone of the WCD. The WCD's decision to offer a rebate to cities on water purchased from San Francisco can be viewed in part as a response to the problems of equity in its tax structure, forced by competition from the FCD. The exact amount of the rebate, however, cannot be justified on grounds of equity, and was clearly designed to swing the balance between the prices for water from San Francisco and from the South Bay Aqueduct. From the viewpoint of the WCD's own operations, an equitable rebate to included territory paying its taxes but purchasing water from an outside source would at a minimum offset the excess of the wholesaler's charges over the cost of pumping from the underground basin. But this would call for a much larger figure than the $20 rebate actually offered.[51]

With regard to the economic efficiency of its charges, the WCD had shown little interest in the use of a pump tax prior to this settlement of wholesaling arrangements. Given the facts of ground-water management, however, this device is relatively essential, both for attaining the appropriate adjustment between the private and social marginal costs of ground water and for making an equitable distribution of the costs of ground-water management and replenishment, if these are to be proportional to the benefits received.[52] It was introduced into the area

[48] See Chapter 11, section on Water Investments by Urban Agencies.

[49] Lee, *op. cit.*, chaps. 7 and 8.

[50] Santa Clara Valley WCD, *Report to the Honorable Board of Directors on Additional Conservation and Distribution Facilities, op. cit.*, pp. 40–41.

[51] On the other hand, a rebate calculated to offset the taxes paid to the District by cities purchasing from San Francisco would have been smaller. See Lee, *op. cit.*, p. 243.

[52] The efficiency issues relating to ground-water management were discussed more fully in Chapter 10.

in 1963 only as a means of financing the costs of a local distribution system, and was apparently not calculated to attain any allocative optimum.

Water wholesaling in the North Bay area

The four counties rimming the San Francisco Bay complex on the north—Marin, Sonoma, Napa, and Solano—reflect some of the conditions found in the counties to the south at an earlier stage in their development. Urbanization has not reached the same degree in the north, and industrialization lags far behind. Agriculture still constitutes the major activity but, compared with the South Bay counties, it relies far less on irrigation and, where irrigated, experiences lower water requirements. One reason is the somewhat greater precipitation, another is a lack of the plentiful ground-water resources on which that valley's agriculture originally built so prosperously. Nor are surface sources sufficiently plentiful to lend themselves to extensive irrigation use. Two factors are now pressing on the available water supply. Population is growing, and many satellite communities of San Francisco commuters are springing up on subdivided cattle ranches; and interest in irrigation as a means of raising farm income is increasing.

The North Bay area has not become quite such a locus of active rivalry in the wholesale water market as Santa Clara County. Nonetheless, alternative wholesalers have begun to make their appearance. Several types of local agencies have come into being, some with ambitions to take an active role in local water wholesaling and development. In short, the water "market," like the economy of the area generally, appears as a less developed replica of the Santa Clara area.

The counties of the North Bay area and the main local water agencies now serving them are shown in Figure 28. In Marin County, immediately north of San Francisco, Marin Municipal Water District handles only about one-tenth the amount of water distributed by East Bay Municipal Utility District (shown in Figure 27 and discussed in Chapters 9 and 11). But it has followed a somewhat similar pattern of first buying out local private water agencies and then extending its service wherever new communities spring up. Engaged largely in retailing, again like EBMUD, the Municipal District has managed to remain abreast of its growing demand by developing its own watershed. Its local supply is estimated to meet requirements until 1975. Beyond that period, water imports will be needed, but where these will come from is not yet certain. The District feels that ample time remains to review the alternatives.

North Marin County Water District, the only other water agency in Marin County except for a few very small private systems in coastal towns, has already exhausted the possibilities of developing local surface runoff, on which it has relied. Serving a growing suburban area centering around the town of Novato, it has explored alternatives and has found a wholesale supply from an agency in neighboring Sonoma County to the north, in effect importing water from another hydrographic region.

The majority of other retailing agencies in the area—Sonoma, Napa, and Solano counties—consists of municipal water departments and small private water com-

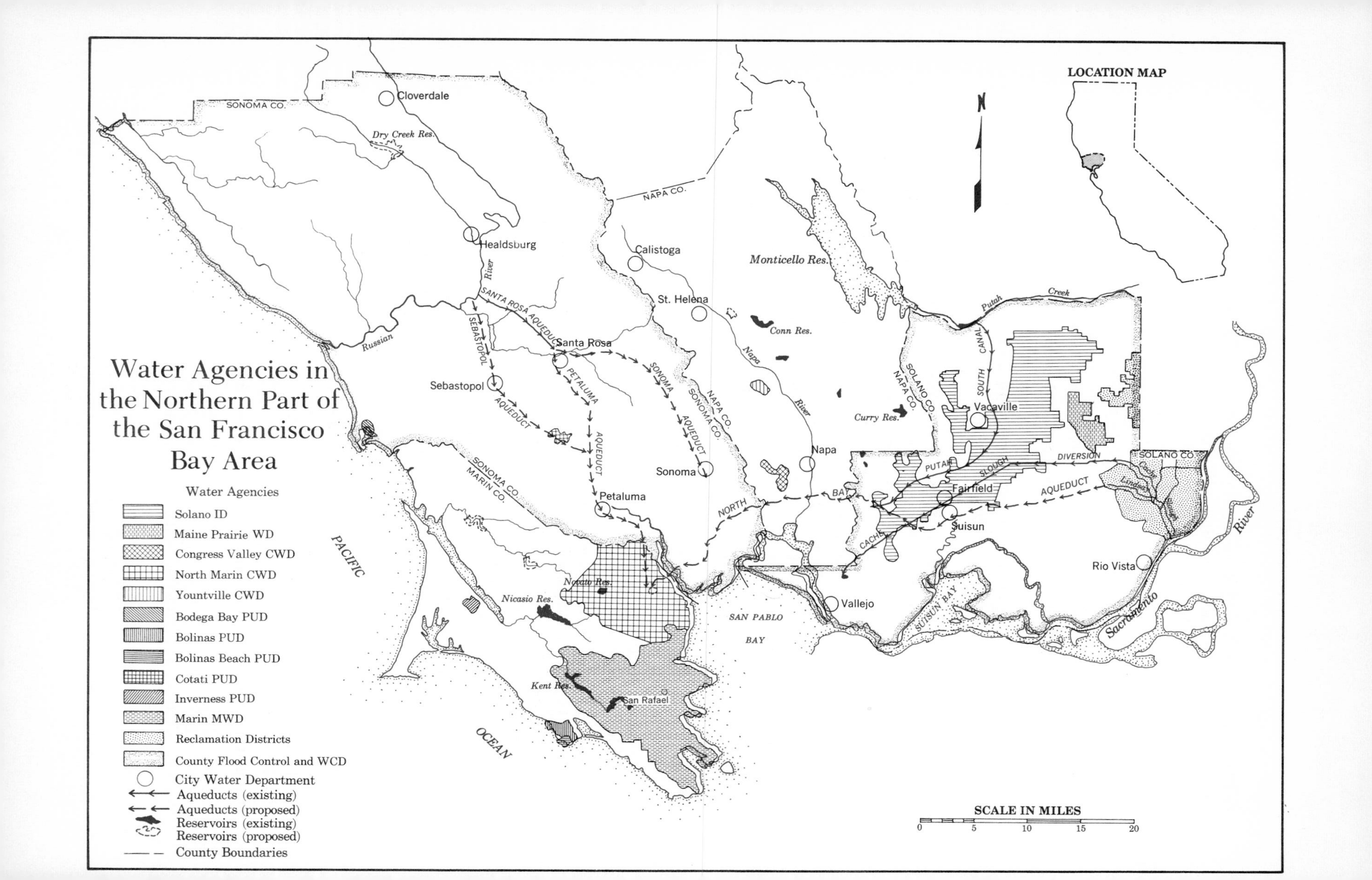
Water Agencies in the Northern Part of the San Francisco Bay Area
Water Agencies
Solano ID
Maine Prairie WD
Congress Valley CWD
North Marin CWD
Yountville CWD
Bodega Bay PUD
Bolinas PUD
Bolinas Beach PUD
Cotati PUD
Inverness PUD
Marin MWD
Reclamation Districts
County Flood Control and WCD
City Water Department
Aqueducts (existing)
Aqueducts (proposed)
Reservoirs (existing)
Reservoirs (proposed)
County Boundaries
LOCATION MAP
N
SCALE IN MILES
0
5
10
15
20
SONOMA CO.
NAPA CO.
SOLANO CO.
NAPA CO.
SONOMA CO.
MARIN CO.
Cloverdale
Dry Creek Res.
Healdsburg
Russian
River
SANTA ROSA AQUEDUCT
SEBASTOPOL
Santa Rosa
Sebastopol
AQUEDUCT
PETALUMA
AQUEDUCT
SONOMA
AQUEDUCT
Petaluma
Sonoma
Calistoga
St. Helena
Monticello Res.
Conn Res.
Napa
River
Napa
Curry Res.
Putah
Creek
SOUTH
CANAL
Vacaville
PUTAH
SLOUGH
DIVERSION
AQUEDUCT
Fairfield
Suisun
NORTH
BAY
CACHE
Lindsey
Slough
Rio Vista
Sacramento
River
Vallejo
SUISUN BAY
SAN PABLO
BAY
Novato Res.
Nicasio Res.
Kent Res.
San Rafael
PACIFIC
OCEAN

panies drawing from ground or surface sources. An exception is the city of Vallejo, which imports water from Cache Slough, one of the deltaic arms of Sacramento River estuary. Irrigation water is drawn primarily from farmer-owned wells.

In Solano County, the easternmost among the North Bay counties, almost one-quarter of the County's area is now included in the Solano Irrigation District. This District was formed in 1948 in anticipation of construction of the Bureau of Reclamation's Solano Project, which consists of Monticello Dam and Reservoir (Lake Berryessa) on Putah Creek (a tributary of the lower Sacramento River), and of Putah South Canal and associated facilities. The Project is designed to irrigate some 70,000 acres of previously dry-farmed land and to provide supplemental water for 20,000 additional acres. Ten per cent of the water yield is supposed to be sold to future municipal and industrial customers at the north shore of the Bay and to some military installations. The Solano Project began operations in 1959, and is not yet delivering much of its planned supply of 243,000 acre-feet per year. This quantity of water is greater than the total amount of water now used in the North Bay counties, but inasmuch as most of it is to be used to irrigate hitherto unirrigated land, its superimposition on the current water supply pattern is not supposed to cause major changes except in its immediate service area. But because of the Solano Project's large output and low cost, the impact of its presence on the attitude of potential water consumers within and without its service area is significant.[53]

Like agencies in the South Bay area, the North Bay agencies are—seemingly at least—in the fortunate positions of having alternative wholesale supplies from which to choose. In terms of the water sources involved, they include: (1) the Russian River, the southernmost of the rivers draining to the Pacific in the north coastal hydrographic region; (2) the Sacramento River system, its flow augmented by storage built under the California Water Plan; (3) coastal rivers farther north diverted either (a) into the Sacramento, (b) into and through Clear Lake and thence possibly through the Solano Project, or (c) directly southward by way of the Russian River system. The water agencies involved in the development of these various sources of supply roughly match them in number.

Let us first consider agencies involved in developing the Russian River. The Corps of Engineers built Coyote Dam on the Russian River for flood control purposes as the first stage of a major flood control plan. Sonoma County Flood Control and Water Conservation District obligated itself to pay that part of the cost (about one-third) allocated to storage for water conservation, and now wholesales a substantial proportion of the water available from the project. The District

[53] The construction of the Solano Project itself closed a wholesale rivalry between the Bureau of Reclamation and the Napa County supervisors. The latter objected to the construction by the Bureau of a large reservoir in their county for the benefit of neighboring Solano County and also offered to supply water themselves from small local projects to serve Solano's relatively small urban requirements. This offer was aired in several congressional hearings on the subject, as were doubts by the Solano interests of the long-term adequacy of Napa's supply and a general resentment against Napa County's alleged desire to derive a profit from Solano County's water needs. See U.S. Congress, House Committee on Public Lands, Subcommittee, *The Solano County Project, California,* 80 Cong., 2 sess. (1948), pp. 11, 37, 40, 57, 70–71.

has recently set its arrangements for the far distant future by contracting with the Corps to pay costs allocated to water storage benefits of the authorized Warm Springs Dam, to be completed in 1969. Payments for this supply will begin in phases and not be concluded until 2040. Matching these long-run plans to acquire water, it has successfully established a steadily expanding marketing network in the area and anticipates making wholesale sales farther afield in adjacent counties.

Because of the slim and deteriorating ground-water resources of Sonoma County's Santa Rosa Valley, the Flood Control District initially found a ready market for its water supplies. Indeed, the municipalities in the County had been engaged in an active search for supplemental supplies.[54] To serve them, the District follows a policy of building and financing aqueducts itself (rather than asking its customers to do so) because its greater bonding capacity permits the construction of aqueducts of larger capacity to serve expected future customers in addition to the initial contractors. This policy gives access to economies of scale in transmission and—incidentally—to greater political support. Its bond-issue authorization for the transmission system prevents the District from selling bonds until "revenues to be derived from sale of water delivered through the facilities to be constructed will be sufficient to pay substantially all costs of operation, maintenance, and bond service."[55] The aqueducts are thus self-supporting. By dealing largely with customers who themselves have taxing power—for example, city water systems and water districts—the District minimizes financial risks.

The Sonoma District follows the practice of most other public water distributors in setting its prices to cover costs. Charges per acre-foot to its wholesale customers are generally based on the specific cost components of the District's operation. All municipal and industrial customers are charged a uniform $7.50 "conservation charge" per acre-foot, designed solely to meet the bond service requirements on the District's payments for the Coyote project. Irrigation customers, who take only about 1 per cent of District water, pay only a $1.50 conservation charge. Other charges, calculated separately for each group of customers, cover operation and maintenance, depreciation on selected items, and bond interest and redemption on the aqueducts. While these municipal charges are clearly related to the costs of service for each of the separate aqueducts, there is substantial discrimination in pricing in favor of agricultural users, who pay total charges of $10 to $11.50, compared to a minimum of $44 for municipal service.

The major components of the total price are fixed charges divided by the current quantity of water distributed, and so the price charged per acre-foot is expected to decline significantly as deliveries rise. However, the "conservation charge" is not set to cover fully the service of the bond issue financing this pay-

[54] An alternative to Coyote Dam that had been investigated at their behest was the diversion of additional water from the Eel River into the Russian through a project of Pacific Gas and Electric Company, but the Flood Control District could not come to agreement with PG&E on this. The question seems an open one of which alternative would have been more efficient. See Stone and Youngberg, *Financing Report, Water System Acquisition, City of Petaluma* (1958), p. 6, and *Control and Use of Russian River Water, A Report on the Financial Feasibility of the Proposed Coyote Valley Reservoir and Utilization of Russian River Water in Sonoma County* (1954), pp. 106–07.

[55] Sonoma County Flood Control and Water Conservation District, *Official Statement in Connection with the Sale of $5,650,000 1955 Coyote Valley Dam Bonds* (1955), p. 7.

ment until 1970. To fill this gap, the District imposes a county-wide tax on real property.[56]

The Sonoma Flood Control District's expanding marketing activities have already led to sales in Marin County, to the North Marin County Water District, and it seems likely that in a decade it will supply the much larger Marin Municipal Water District. How much farther to the east the District will be able to sell its water without running into sales competition from the Department of Water Resources via its projected North Bay Aqueduct will probably depend primarily on comparative costs. Napa County has been approached on this basis. In any case, the development of the Flood Control District's marketing arrangements has followed a serene course. In contrast to the Santa Clara Valley Water Conservation District, its county-wide base permits it both to insure the financial security of its own operations and to impose tax burdens which may not be perfectly equitable but still fall lightly enough to avoid complaint. Unlike the San Francisco Water Department, the District concerns itself only with water-related activities, has not engaged in basic reservoir construction and operation, and has shown no inclination to extract a higher rate of return from one service territory than another. Its pricing system is not optimal unless the bond service charges it levies on customers can be shown to approximate the net marginal cost (including opportunity cost) of water captured by the Corps' Coyote Dam, but the divergence probably is not large.

A number of agencies are associated with the Sacramento River system and the North Bay Aqueduct. Construction of a North Bay Aqueduct as a feature of the California Water Plan was recommended by the Department of Water Resources in March 1957.[57] It would carry water from the Sacramento Delta some distance into the North Bay area. In 1957, the State Legislature adopted this recommendation and appropriated funds for the acquisition of lands, easements, and rights of way. But, as the Department of Water Resources cautiously phrased it, "As work proceeded . . . it became increasingly apparent [in 1958] that the attitude of the water users in the four north bay counties did not indicate unanimity of interest in the North Bay Aqueduct." The Department therefore suspended work on the project for more than a year. At a public meeting held in 1960, agreement was reached that the Department would re-evaluate its study to determine probable demand, costs, pricing and repayment policy, local water development alternatives, and the ability of local users to pay, primarily for irrigation water.[58] Talk of contracting deadlines had little effect.[59] According to the latest plans, the North Bay Aqueduct will carry water only to the middle of the Napa Valley.[60]

[56] Other sources of revenue available for this purpose include a tax levied on resort areas along the Russian River which benefit from the guaranteed minimum summer flow provided by Coyote Dam.

[57] California Department of Water Resources, *Interim Report to the California State Legislature on the Salinity Control Barrier Investigation*, Bulletin No. 60 (1957).

[58] California Department of Water Resources, *North Bay Aqueduct,* Bulletin No. 110 (1961).

[59] Summary statement by R. V. Moir, secretary, North Coastal Chamber of Commerce, and coordinator of local testimony at meeting of California Water Commission, Petaluma, April 6, 1962; *San Francisco Chronicle*, May 8, 1962; *Economic and Financial Policies, op. cit.*, pp. A121–28.

[60] See Figure 32.

The chief objection to the Aqueduct was to the water costs estimated by the Department, which range from $8.10 per acre-foot canal-side for delivery in Solano County through the largest capacity pipeline studied to $35.50 for water delivered in a fairly small line in Marin County. The range of anticipated costs for Sonoma County was $22.00 to $27.10, and for Napa County, $16.60 to $20.40.[61] To make this water usable for domestic purposes, it would have to be treated and put under pressure. A rough estimate of cost including treatment and pressurization arrived at by one of the engineer witnesses was in excess of $60 an acre-foot for service at Petaluma or Sonoma, not counting local distribution costs, barely competitive with average charges for Russian River water. Finally, after typically extended discussions, contracts have been reached with the state for urban water supplies to be delivered to flood control and water conservation districts of Napa and Solano counties. They call for deliveries of 67,000 acre-feet to begin in 1980, a sharp reduction from the 274,000 acre-feet originally allocated by the state.

We consider finally agencies potentially involved with direct imports from rivers north of the Russian. Imports from the north coastal region into the North Bay counties through a new Bureau of Reclamation project have been under study, so that local interests count the Bureau as a potential competing wholesaler. Water diverted by routes other than through the Delta area (Lindsay Slough) would probably be cleaner (requiring less treatment for domestic and industrial purposes) and come at higher elevations, making it available in the higher, northern portions of the counties where in some cases needs appear to be more critical. In addition, the Bureau has available the means to charge considerably less than the Department of Water Resources. Its agricultural water rates charged for water from the Solano Project are lower than those prevailing on other Bureau projects and far below estimated payment capacities on the basis of which the Project was "justified." These particularly low rates serve as ideals to which potential water purchasers naturally aspire.

Similarities and differences between the wholesale-retail conditions of the North and South Bay counties thus become clear. More urgent water needs, including large present requirements for irrigation but more rapidly developing urbanization, coupled with a much higher payment capacity have helped the state to market water through the South Bay Aqueduct. The constellation of local rivalries and ambitions has also played into the hands of the Department of Water Resources. The entrenched position of the city of San Francisco did it little good per se, especially in view of its high prices. The generally less costly water of the Sonoma County Flood Control and Water Conservation District has prevented the growth of strong interest in the North Bay in water from any other source in the immediate future. Like San Francisco, the Sonoma District has water of the highest quality to offer at the earliest time. Unlike San Francisco, Sonoma institutionally is more responsive to its customers' wishes; indeed, their political identities largely overlap. The lesser pressure of active demands on local supplies has also meant a greater local willingness to await subsidized offers from the Bureau of Reclamation than was displayed by South Bay interests.

From the standpoint of allocative performance, the North Bay situation also

[61] California Department of Water Resources, *North Bay Aqueduct, op. cit.,* Table 11, p. 31.

seems to score fairly well. The Sonoma County Flood Control and Water Conservation District's pricing practices might be criticized on several points of detail (for example, discrimination in favor of agricultural users and an improper balance of fixed and variable charges). However, its basic service facilities appear clearly to exploit a more efficient source of water than any of the larger and more remote sources of wholesale supplies. The latter would surely show highly adverse benefit-cost characteristics at the present time.

Wholesale Transactions: Patterns and Prospects

The progressive movement of water into the category of a scarce resource has by now firmly established its tendency to call large wholesaling agencies into existence and to create an increasingly complex network of wholesale-retail relations. Subordinate to the ultimate scarcity of water, numerous causes appear to operate. Economies of scale in dams, canals, and pumping plants play a critical role. Retailing districts of viable size[62] can generally distribute the natural flows of rivers to adjacent lands with passable efficiency and often can handle (individually or cooperatively) the problems of constructing moderate-sized storage facilities on "their" rivers. But the supply of unappropriated water and dam sites for efficient small projects is rapidly being exhausted. When storage dams on large rivers or interbasin water transfers come into consideration, economies of scale cause the water output of any economically feasible project often to exceed many times the demand of any single agricultural retail agency and most urban ones. Another encouragement to such wholesaling operations comes from the complex of factors tending to discourage local transactions in and transfers of water drawn from a surface-water source or ground-water basin—a complex including the attitudes of local agencies, the economic fact of the substantial external economies and diseconomies normally associated with transfers of water use, and certain features of water law.

The development of wholesale-retail relations to date reflects strongly the working of special motivations. The Bureau of Reclamation, committed to providing agricultural water cheaply to as much land as possible, has actively sought customers where water is available (for example, in the Sacramento canals) or has actively sought water projects where customers are available (for example, the East Side project). By combining questionable practices in appraising the benefit-cost relation for its California projects (see Chapter 11) with statutory discretion in its pricing policies designed to favor irrigation, it has sought to push the use of water for agriculture well beyond the level justified by the value of the marginal product of water and the long-run marginal costs involved. The city of San Francisco has struggled with objections to its high prices in order to maintain a contribution of water department profits to city revenues. Other producer-wholesalers are spurred by the faith that abundant water supplies will encourage local economic growth.

[62] The problems of political viability in relation to the size of retailing water agencies, especially those serving agricultural users, were discussed in Chapter 9.

Local wholesaling agencies, themselves buying from large outside suppliers, also have assorted special objectives. The Kern County Water Agency has been formed to buy water from the Feather River Project aqueducts and resell it to several large water storage districts and other agencies in the county. The intermediary's primary role is to gain access to the tax base of industrial and municipal property in the county in order to subsidize agricultural water. Several other county-wide organizations have either undertaken or strongly considered this tactic.

The diversity of agencies and objectives helps explain why few generalizations are possible about the price or related contract terms reached in wholesaler-retailer negotiations. Even the critical matter of the availability of alternatives has had only weak effects on prices. To its various service areas in the Central Valley the Bureau of Reclamation has charged prices crudely proportional, but not equal, to ability to pay, but has made only minor concessions from its original terms. The complex rivalries in Santa Clara County have not produced any substantial adjustments of posted prices; and, in particular, the city of San Francisco was able to command its asking price despite the availability of possibly cheaper alternatives to its customers. On the other hand, East Bay Municipal Utility District was eventually forced to give a price concession to the Southwest Contra Costa County Water District when the latter demonstrated its determination to deal with an alternative wholesaler, the Bureau of Reclamation.[63] Most of the smaller wholesaling agencies, especially those not producing electric power along with water, have normally set contractual water payments to cover costs, occasionally with some assistance from general taxation over initial periods of development.

The availability of alternatives may not have affected price determination in a regular fashion,[64] but it certainly has altered the tone of wholesale-retail negotiations. In pressing individual retailers for decisions, wholesalers have clearly had an advantage when they could point to alternative customers for their available supply. This consideration appears in the Bureau of Reclamation's negotiations with the Friant-Kern districts, which suppressed their strong objections to the non-price terms of the Bureau's offer once they perceived that the Bureau could find alternative customers on these terms. Conversely, no amount of suasion to take clearly plentiful supplies has speeded contracting for water from the Sacramento canals. The state of California's contract with the Metropolitan Water District of Southern California gave it just the same bargaining card with prospective northern customers while that District held a residual option on all unsold water. The state pressed this point strongly both in Santa Clara County

[63] This case was discussed in Chapter 10. The tacit alliance between San Francisco and the Santa Clara Valley Water Conservation District explains much of the difference between these two cases.

[64] One exception to this proposition, not previously discussed, is competition during the 1950's between the Bureau of Reclamation and the Department of Water Resources over the San Luis dam site and local customers for irrigation service on the west side of the San Joaquin Valley. Before this rivalry ended with an agreement on the joint use of San Luis, the state had cut its tentatively announced price from $11 to $6 per acre-foot in response to the announcement of a $7.50 price by the Bureau. See U.S. Congress, House Committee on Interior and Insular Affairs, Subcommittee on Irrigation and Reclamation, *San Luis Unit, Central Valley Project, California,* 84 Cong. 2 sess. (1956), pp. 14, 22, 57.

and in the southern part of San Joaquin Valley. However, the evident availability of alternatives to the North Bay and South Bay aqueducts and for part of Kern County weakened the effect of the clause in the Metropolitan Water District contract.

If the presence of alternative customers has strengthened the position of wholesalers, their position has been weakened just as clearly in those cases where they could not withhold benefits. The study of the Bureau of Reclamation negotiations with the Sacramento channel users and the Kings River interests illustrates this effect, even though in the latter case the retail "customers" have had to endure a delay in planning a potentially profitable installation for the generation of electric power at Pine Flat.

When all is said and done, the main effect of rivalry at the wholesale level in water transactions remains the classic one of causing more alternatives to be considered and each to be examined more carefully. The chances of misallocation resulting from a lack of information about relevant alternatives are correspondingly reduced. It also reduces the chances of acrimonious and stalemated situations. The increased consideration of alternatives does not, however, guarantee that the economically preferable one will be chosen. Indeed, the special interests and policy preferences of the public agencies dominating these decisions often guarantee that it will not.[65] This harsh judgment should not be assumed to lead directly to sweeping conclusions about the proper organization of the water industry. If profit-maximizing enterprises negotiated these transactions, the inevitable fewness of participants would still make an outcome which was not optimal very likely. The more relevant question for policy would seem to be providing the government agencies involved with more appropriate economic guidance in making their allocative decisions.

The growth of wholesaling agencies in California's water industry guarantees a continued evolution of wholesaler-retailer relations, and particularly it assures an increase in the number of cases in which wholesale sellers or retail buyers enjoy practical alternatives. Even over a period of many decades, the emergent competitive forces will remain weak and the implied markets for water extremely thin. But against this thinness, the relative size and substantial demonstration effects of the typical water market transaction underline the importance of the trend. Various fragments of evidence, not previously discussed, suggest the forthcoming possibilities of rivalry and effective alternatives. One such element is the rapid increase in the number of retailing agencies with economical access to alternative sources of water. The populous areas north, east, and south of San Francisco Bay have already reached this stage, and within another decade almost the whole of the San Joaquin Valley and parts of the Sacramento will enjoy a similar status. In the northern half of the Central Valley, the complex of the Feather, Yuba, and Bear rivers will become a partly integrated arena of interagency rivalry with the construction of Oroville Dam by the California Department of Water

[65] Possible examples include the Bureau's Pine Flat negotiations and the old Madera versus Miller and Lux efforts. For another study of problems of stalemate in conditions of bilateral monopoly involving public agencies, see Robert E. Firth, *Public Power in Nebraska: A Report on State Ownership* (1962), especially chap. 12.

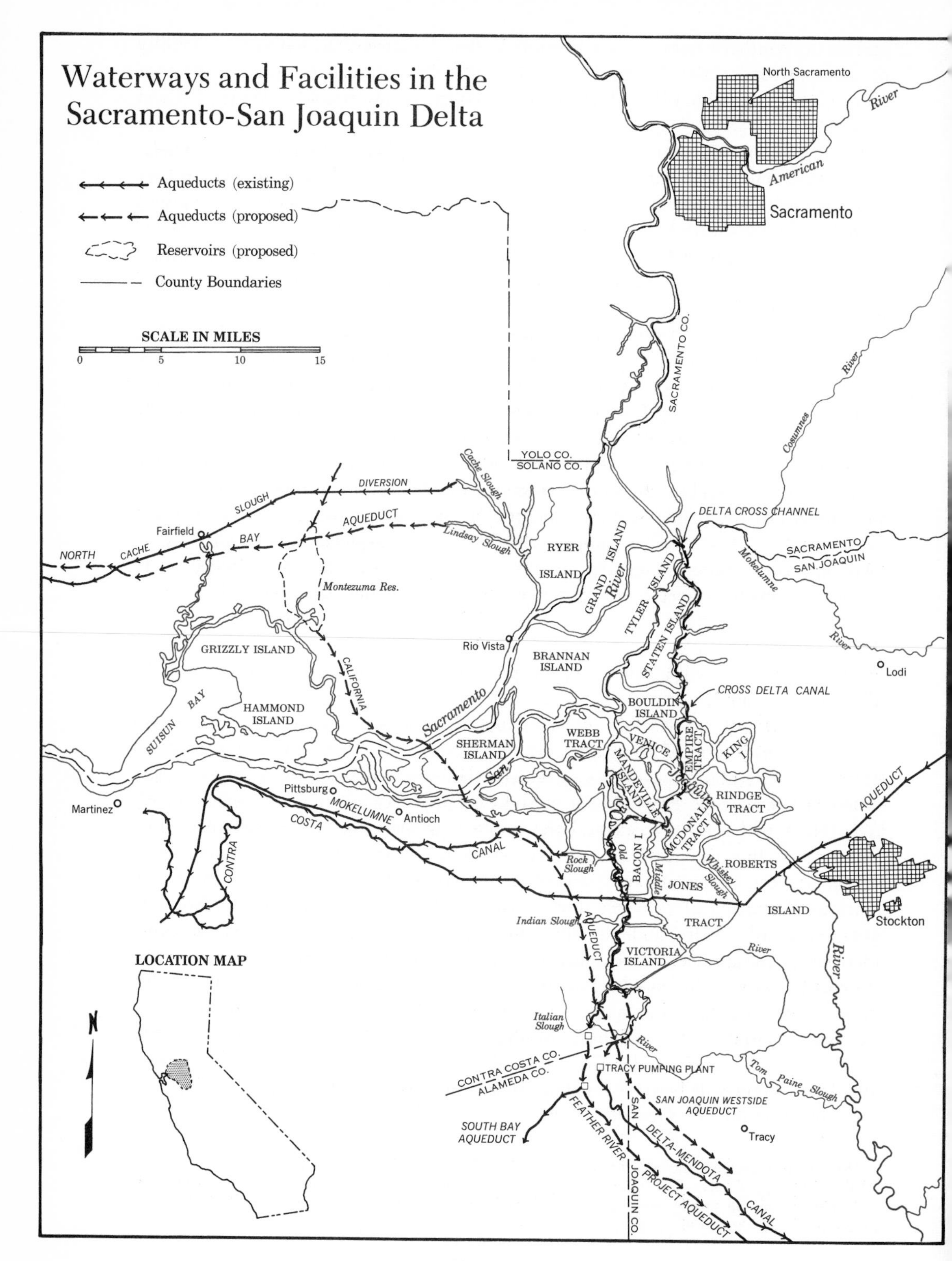

Waterways and Facilities in the Sacramento-San Joaquin Delta
Aqueducts (existing)
Aqueducts (proposed)
Reservoirs (proposed)
County Boundaries
SCALE IN MILES
0
5
10
15
North Sacramento
River
American
Sacramento
SACRAMENTO CO.
YOLO CO.
SOLANO CO.
Cosumnes
River
Cache Slough
DIVERSION
SLOUGH
NORTH
CACHE
BAY
AQUEDUCT
Fairfield
Lindsay Slough
RYER ISLAND
GRAND ISLAND
River
TYLER ISLAND
STATEN ISLAND
DELTA CROSS CHANNEL
SACRAMENTO
SAN JOAQUIN
Mokelumne
River
Lodi
Montezuma Res.
Rio Vista
GRIZZLY ISLAND
BRANNAN ISLAND
CALIFORNIA
SUISUN
BAY
HAMMOND ISLAND
Sacramento
CROSS DELTA CANAL
BOULDIN ISLAND
WEBB TRACT
SHERMAN ISLAND
San
VENICE
EMPIRE TRACT
KING I.
MANDEVILLE ISLAND
RINDGE TRACT
MCDONALD TRACT
AQUEDUCT
Pittsburg
MOKELUMNE
Antioch
Martinez
COSTA
CONTRA
CANAL
Rock Slough
Old
BACON I.
Middle
Whiskey Slough
ROBERTS
JONES
TRACT
ISLAND
Stockton
Indian Slough
AQUEDUCT
VICTORIA ISLAND
River
River
LOCATION MAP
N
Italian Slough
River
CONTRA COSTA CO.
ALAMEDA CO.
TRACY PUMPING PLANT
Tom Paine Slough
SAN JOAQUIN WESTSIDE AQUEDUCT
Tracy
SOUTH BAY AQUEDUCT
FEATHER RIVER
PROJECT AQUEDUCT
SAN JOAQUIN CO.
DELTA-MENDOTA
CANAL

Figure 29

Resources and of several lesser local projects. Under the authority of state legislation, the Department has stepped in as a potential customer for the water output of one Corps of Engineers project, Black Butte Dam on Stony Creek, where local users have not shown interest in the available irrigation water at the Bureau of Reclamation's asking price. Farther south, the Folsom South Canal and the East Side Division are planned to bring alternative sources to the whole east side of the San Joaquin Valley. South of the San Joaquin on the east side of the valley, the Friant-Kern Canal has already accomplished this to a degree, and the East Side Canal will augment the alternatives. On the west side of the valley, numerous districts lie within reach of both the Delta-Mendota Canal and the channel of the lower San Joaquin River. The Delta-Mendota service area also abuts on that of the San Luis project. The California Water Plan's Delta-Los Angeles aqueduct will add another alternative for the whole west side of the San Joaquin. In Kern County at the south end of the Valley, this aqueduct will come into rivalry with the Bureau's proposed East Side Canal—a rivalry that is already affecting local plans and negotiations.

Perhaps the most important physical facts of all for the future of water transfers and transactions are those concerning the Sacramento-San Joaquin Delta, shown in Figure 29. Into the Delta empty all rivers of the Central Valley except those of the Tulare Lake Basin. The Bureau of Reclamation now collects water from the Delta for transmission through its Delta-Mendota and Contra Costa canals, and the Department of Water Resources will use the Delta as a transfer point in its Feather River Project and possible future projects, using routes and conveyance facilities not yet fully determined. Not only can these direct diversions from the Delta potentially draw upon the water of any river emptying into it, but also exchanges of water are conceivable between users on different rivers through offsetting changes in storage releases and/or diversions. Against these potential transfers, however, must be placed the many factors discouraging them that have turned up in our investigation. Increased transfer and consumptive use of water within the Central Valley tends to reduce the quality of water along the lower San Joaquin River and in the Delta itself. Local water users have become acutely conscious that exports from the Delta detract to some extent from the quantity and quality of their supplies unless compensating imports to the Delta are made,[66] and complex legal actions may grow out of their concern. The lack of clearly defined water rights of existing users greatly complicates the negotiation of water transfers and exchanges, as the Bureau's difficulties on the Sacramento indicate. The potential for water transfers is thus increasing, but it will be realized slowly.

[66] *Western Water News,* September 1963, p. 2.

14

JOINT AND ALTERNATIVE USES OF WATER

This study has emphasized "consumptive" uses of water—its employment for irrigation and urban purposes in which a large part of the water diverted or pumped for use does not return directly to its source. Water in its natural state has many other beneficial uses. Its flow in streambeds turns the turbines of hydro-electric power stations. It sustains navigation and combats the intrusion of saline water into river estuaries. It is essential for the maintenance of recreational and other fisheries, and furnishes a habitat for migratory water fowl.

The in-stream uses of water which generate these benefits are in part complementary with each other and in part competitive, as these terms are defined in Chapter 8. This is true also of the relations of in-stream uses of water to consumptive uses. In some cases, at least to a degree, benefits from consumptive use may be realized consistently with the preservation or enhancement of benefits from the in-stream use of water. But in others, consumptive uses are enhanced at the expense of in-stream uses, and the two types of use are essentially competitors for the allocation of scarce water. The latter relationship between consumptive and other uses of water is perhaps of predominant importance.

A rather broad view of the character of joint (common) and alternative uses of water is appropriate in this chapter. Although the theoretical exposition of Chapter 8 assumed perfect complementarity among joint uses, and also supposed that independent net demand curves could be calculated for competing uses, actual behavioral relations in the water industry are not so clear-cut. A cooperative venture between a power company and an irrigation district to build a multiple purpose dam and power plant basically represents an exploitation between them of common facilities. Yet the most conspicuous feature of the partners' mutual relations may be a quarrel over the scheduling of water releases from the dam, for which substantial parts of their respective outputs stand in alternative relationship. Other pairs of utilities derived from water present the same problem of behavioral analysis: when two uses served by water can be said ultimately to stand in joint or alternative relation to each other, the organizational relations between the parties undertaking these uses may contain both complementary and rivalrous aspects.[1]

The fact that various pairs of uses of stream water are partly complementary

[1] We shall not distinguish between the pure case of joint products and the more general case of common costs or common facilities, and so shall use the term "joint uses" to cover both. By and large, the observed conduct pattern in the water industry has been concerned not with true joint products but with common costs or facilities.

and partly competitive leads to the generation of external benefits and disbenefits when different parties exploit different uses. That is, the value of water to a second user is increased or decreased with increases in the quantity of water employed by a first user, in a strict sense without the quantity of water available for the second user being enhanced or reduced.[2] Joint and alternative uses do not give rise to external effects if a single agency exploits all uses of a source and internalizes all externalities, but the same technical and value relationships of different water uses remain.

This chapter seeks to indicate the way in which relations between different types of uses of water—whether complementary or competitive—and various resulting external benefits and disbenefits influence the pricing and investment decisions of the water industry. This information, in turn, provides the basis for estimating the extent to which the allocation of water and of non-water resources in the industry properly takes account of all external effects. It may be said in advance of Part Three that the direct measurement of trade-offs and marginal opportunity costs to permit an appraisal of performance in these cases is a difficult matter. Since, in addition, a set of measurements undertaken with regard to one reservoir or river (given the insularity prevailing in the water industry) proves nothing about conditions elsewhere in the area, we have been forced to depend heavily upon inferences from conduct rather than direct measurements of allocative performance in regard to joint and alternative uses.

In part, our discussion will stress the elementary question of whether or not external effects are taken into account at all. Economic theory suggests that an allocative deficiency exists when externalities operating at the margin are ignored, but that their recognition by the parties creating and receiving them gives rise to the possibility of "trade" or compensation to attain a Pareto-optimal adjustment. Externalities with only inframarginal incidence (over the relevant range of activity levels) have no separate allocative significance, although they may give rise to questions of distributive equity.[3] Although in a setting of perfect private markets marginal externalities might thus be worked out in private negotiations (and require no market intervention), this requires that all affected parties perceive and correctly measure the effects involved and—especially—make an accurate distinction between marginal and inframarginal externalities. The state of market organization in the water industry is clearly not conducive to making such fine discriminations, and the hypotheses to be developed concerning the handling of externalities can be related to its imperfections.

[2] See discussion in Chapter 1 of the distinctive features of the water industry.

[3] J. M. Buchanan and W. C. Stubblebine, "Externality," *Economica*, n. s. XXIX (November 1962), 371–84. Consider an example of inframarginal external effects in the context of the water industry: damage done to anadromous fisheries by the construction of a dam that is independent of the scale of the dam. Assuming that the direct total net benefits of the dam justify constructing it at some scale, then the optimal scale is not affected by the existence of the external diseconomy because it does not enter into marginal benefits. On the other hand, if the external diseconomy to the fishery varies with the scale of the dam or the volume of water regulated, an "efficiency" argument is established for taking the externality into account in determining the best adjustment of the margin. (Most footnote references in this chapter are cited in brief form when they are also included in the Bibliography.)

First, action to reduce or gain compensation for external diseconomies seems much more likely than action to increase or pay compensation for external economies.[4] Second, less readily measurable externalities are obviously less likely to be taken into account. Third, an externality with total effects valued at a given amount is more likely to be taken into account if its impact concentrates upon a few parties than if it is dispersed over many. Fourth, an external effect that alights upon a "public good" is unlikely to be taken into account. Pure public goods are not common in the uses made of water in California, but we shall argue below that several important services provided by water are treated by public policy as if they were public goods. Finally, external effects that are difficult to measure, widely dispersed, or felt by public goods, may be allowed for in very imperfect ways. Broad legislative acts and crude regulatory procedures may force their consideration without requiring any careful appraisal of gains and costs.

To reduce it to a manageable body, the evidence on conduct regarding joint and alternative uses and externalities has been grouped into two sections. The first deals exclusively with electric power, since all the traits of its production and use of water make its role felt in pricing and output decisions relating to consumptive uses. The second considers a group of joint and alternative uses lacking some of these traits, with stream fisheries serving as the leading example.

Electric Power and Consumptive Uses of Water

The conspicuous conflict over the relation between water for consumptive uses and for power generation have concerned the terms under which common facilities will be exploited. The use of multiple purpose storage dams to produce power and transfer water for use in the summer season has been taken for granted. But the combination of outputs for which a given project should be designed and operated, the prices at which they should be sold, and the organization which should undertake the development have been bitterly contested.

These contests have centered on the marketing of electric power. Agencies oriented primarily toward securing water for consumptive use have constructed many multipurpose projects over the last half-century—the city of San Francisco, various large irrigation districts, and the Bureau of Reclamation. The retail distribution of this power output in each case has raised the question of competition with the privately owned electric utilities in Northern California—most now collected into the giant Pacific Gas and Electric Company (PG&E)—and thereby the marginal valuation of electric power and the combination of outputs yielded by multipurpose projects.

[4] Underlying this hypothesis is the assumption that effective discriminations are not made between marginal and inframarginal externalities: that an offer to "buy" a slight increase in an activity producing external economies at the margin is likely to lead to a stalemating demand for compensation for the inframarginal benefit; at the same time, opportunities are available for an injured party to collect for external diseconomies whether or not a marginal effect is involved.

Electric utilities and local water districts

Some of the older cases of relations between private electric utilities and local irrigation districts offer interesting evidence. The disputes among these parties raise issues primarily about the sale and retail valuation of electric power, rather than the design or operation of common facilities. In the interwar period, the most notable clash involving water and power distribution involved the Modesto and Turlock irrigation districts with the Pacific Gas and Electric Company and the San Joaquin Light and Power Company. The two districts jointly completed Don Pedro Dam on the Tuolumne River in 1923, deriving therefrom a large supply of electric power as well as irrigation water. Both districts decided to retail their output of power in the area, in direct competition with the established utilities. The Turlock Irrigation District soon reached an agreement with San Joaquin Light and Power under which the District agreed not to sell power outside its own boundaries and the Company agreed to buy the District's surplus power.[5] The Modesto Irrigation District, however, entered into active retail competition affecting electric rates in a substantial portion of the San Joaquin Valley during much of the interwar period, and an agreement similar to Turlock's came only in the 1940's.[6]

Several other irrigation districts which constructed multipurpose projects in the interwar period readily reached agreement on the sale of their power output to electric utilities, but experienced diverse results in the returns on their investments. The arrangement negotiated by the Nevada Irrigation District was designed to generate power revenues covering its capital and part of its operating costs, but by taking upon itself the risk of low power revenues in dry years the District was driven to refinancing.[7] The Merced Irrigation District negotiated a somewhat better arrangement in being able to regulate its own pattern of water releases subject only to daily load-factor requirements, but was also thrown into default during the 1930's.[8] By contrast, the Oakdale and South San Joaquin irrigation districts developed a contract covering power sales from their joint project which became the precedent for all subsequent arrangements of this type: a contractual series of payments by the electric utility set to cover the interest and repayment requirements for the districts' bonds.[9]

[5] California Department of Public Works, Division of Water Resources, *San Joaquin River Basin, 1931,* Bulletin No. 29 (1934), pp. 226–27. (Hereinafter cited as Bulletin No. 29.)

[6] J. Rupert Mason, "Single-Tax, Irrigation Districts, and Municipal Bankruptcy" (Typescript, 1958), pp. 126–30; California State Public Utilities Commission, *In the Matter of Application of Pacific Gas and Electric Company, and Modesto Irrigation District . . . Agreements,* transcript, Application No. 23,553, August 9, 1940.

[7] California State Department of Public Works, Division of Engineering and Irrigation, *Irrigation Districts in California, 1929,* by Frank Adams, Bulletin No. 21 (1930), pp. 123–33 [hereinafter cited as Bulletin No. 21 (Adams)]; William Durbrow, "William Durbrow, Irrigation District Leader" (Typescript, 1958), pp. 92–111; Charles F. Lambert, "Land Speculation and Irrigation Development in the Sacramento Valley, 1905–1957" (Typescript, 1957), pp. 198–99.

[8] Bulletin No. 21 (Adams), *op. cit.,* pp. 190–99; Bulletin No. 29, *op. cit.,* p. 234; Murray R. Benedict, *The Merced Irrigation District: An Economic Survey of Farm Incomes, Expenses, and Tax-paying Abilities* (1933).

[9] Bulletin No. 21 (Adams), *op. cit.,* pp. 168–77; Bulletin No. 29, *op. cit.,* pp. 218–19; Tudor-Goodenough Engineers, *Summary Report on the Tri-Dam Project, Stanislaus River, California* (1959), pp. 17–26.

These cases from the interwar years suggest that, in a political sense, joint ventures came off smoothly for those irrigation agencies with no power-marketing ambitions of their own. And the Oakdale-South San Joaquin arrangement innovated a method which seemed to avoid most of the incidence of capital rationing upon the local districts. The cases involving harmonious relations with the electric utilities, however, did nothing to provide a competitive test of the marginal valuation of electric power resulting from the utilities' pricing decisions (as filtered through the state's regulatory machinery).

The numerous cooperative investments developed by PG&E and local districts since World War II all fall into the "harmonious" pattern. We suggested in Chapter 11 that these agreements all take the same form and seem to rest on the same general investment criterion—one that may not result in the optimal scale of project or utilization of common facilities. Restricting these projects to the scale for which PG&E will pay the interest and amortization costs and assume all risks in return for the power output alone amounts to treating irrigation water as a by-product, apart from the contribution of the local district in paying for the costs of designing and promoting the project. This practice would yield investments of the correct scale only where the value of the marginal product of irrigation water as a joint product (net of operating and distribution costs) is approximately zero.

Here we shall supplement the discussion of these projects in Chapters 11 and 12 by considering the process by which these bargains are struck. Are the allocative results as uniform as the similar contract terms would suggest? Do the characteristics of the bargaining process add further information about the economic character of the results?

One important question in appraising these arrangements is the availability of alternatives to the bargainers. Pacific Gas and Electric can always develop new steam generation plants at relatively constant costs. The alternatives for the districts are less clear. They have often considered public power agencies as potential customers, but none of these has proved a feasible alternative to PG&E.[10] The bargaining process between PG&E and the local districts exerts a major influence on the determination of whether a proposed project shall be constructed, with what scale and design characteristics, and how its water yield will be divided between consumptive and power uses. As was shown in Chapter 11, negotiations with PG&E constitute but one of the hurdles facing a district desiring to undertake a project. The following discussion of the role of negotiations with the utility, then, extracts one thread out of a tangled web, with the objective of showing the impact of their conduct upon the performance of the water industry.

Contracts between the sponsoring district and the utility start with the beginning of the planning process and not after a fullfledged project has been drafted by the district. The refining of details of the project and negotiating of a contract with PG&E go hand in hand.[11] Given the standard form of agreement between PG&E

[10] U.S. Congress. Senate Committee on Interior and Insular Affairs, Subcommittee on Irrigation and Reclamation, *Tri-Dam Project,* 83 Cong. 2 sess. (1954), pp. 57, 61, 66–67; Tudor-Goodenough Engineers, *op. cit.,* pp. 24–25.

[11] See, for example, Ebasco Services, Incorporated, *Nevada Irrigation District—Water and Power Development Feasibility Report* (1960), p. 4; McCreary-Koretsky Engineers. *Feasibility Report, Placer County Water Agency, Middle Fork American River Project* (1961), p. S14.

and the sponsoring district, the two critical points for negotiation are what scale of project (if any) PG&E will support, and what pattern of water releases it will agree to.[12] In this bargaining, the utility seems to set as its standard securing power at costs no higher than those of additional steam generation capacity. It may possibly relax this standard to support local construction of projects as an alternative to construction by the Bureau of Reclamation or other agencies which might act as rivals in the markets for electric power. The districts make no such minimum demand in the bargaining, but clearly seek to gain the maximum quantity of irrigation water consistent with their making no contribution to the capital cost of the project. In the extreme, as noted in Chapter 11, a district may appear willing to accept a water release pattern geared entirely to the production of power and having relatively little utility for consumptive use, in order to have its nameplate on a project, or in anticipation of water or profits after the retirement of the bonded indebtedness for the project.

As the parties, guided by these motives, enter into negotiations over a proposed project, important types of uncertainty affect their bargaining strength, especially that of the local district. Both parties may face difficulty in planning projects for streams lacking long-standing gauge records, and estimates of the power output that can be generated from a known streamflow may diverge widely, since assumed operating criteria and efficiencies as well as methods of calculation can make a significant difference.[13] Prior rights of other claimants to the water source may add an element of uncertainty at this point. Finally, the deepest source of uncertainty for the district proposing a project is the value of any given pattern of power output to PG&E. A schedule of releases over the year implies a pattern of potential power output levels. The market value of power depends on its creation at a time when a firm demand exists for its service, the pattern of which is both variable and subject to uncertainty. Even more important, a given project stands not by itself but adds to the existing giant generating capacity of PG&E. Only complex studies by the utility itself determine how much firm power a project can add to PG&E's existing capacity, and thus what load factor it can attain; these studies are not normally available to the bargaining partner or the general public.[14] Many sources of information provide guesses on the cost of power produced through the alternative of steam generation, but these give only a rough check of PG&E's estimates.

[12] The current importance of release schedules is revealed by a comparison of recent contracts with older arrangements between PG&E and local districts. For example, the first contract between PG&E and Oakdale and South San Joaquin irrigation districts (Melones Dam, 1925) contained only general terms governing which party would control the release pattern at what time of year. A second contract involving these same parties (Tri-Dam Project, 1952) contains 3½ pages of minute specifications.

[13] As a sample, the California Department of Water Resources reviewed estimates of the annual power revenues of a Merced River project made by Tudor Engineering Company and found them excessive by from 11.1 to 19.6 per cent. See California Department of Water Resources, *Review of Report on Merced River Development Proposed by Merced Irrigation District* (1961), pp. 18–28. Without considering the question of which party is correct, this case gives an impression of the scale of disagreements that can arise even when one party is disinterested.

[14] This account simplifies considerably the economic problems encountered and the technical concepts normally employed in valuing the power output of a project. It also neglects such elements as transmission losses which affect the value of power to PG&E at the source.

What is the outcome of the bargaining process conditioned by the motives and surrounded by the uncertainties stated above? Unfortunately, only a few sketchy conclusions can be drawn. No district has recently succeeded in extracting payments from PG&E beyond the minimum needed to meet interest and amortization costs on the bonds issued to finance the project. Furthermore, in the negotiation of operating criteria for the project, some local agencies have had to forego water releases scheduled other than to maximize the power yield of the project, at least in the early years of its life. At first glance, such an outcome might seem to suggest that all the bargaining strength lies on the side of the utility. Such a conclusion is not supported, however, by the utility's clearly sincere interest in the good will of the irrigators or the copious circumstantial evidence of the marginal feasibility of many of these projects. Given their input-output relations and the present marginal value of power and irrigation water outputs, they may offer no significant slice of implicit profits to be haggled over. Both the local district and PG&E may receive benefits of a discounted present value that exceeds the value of their respective contributions to costs only by a small amount.

The public position of PG&E has been that it will participate in such ventures as these only if they yield power at costs competitive with steam generation. Indeed, the utility must make such a showing before the California State Public Utilities Commission. There is no doubt that this standard does control PG&E's participation to a substantial degree, and thus provides a partial market test of the feasibility of the resulting projects. Yet this test surely does not entirely control the utility's decisions. The Company's complex political embroilments, inevitable for a firm of its size and position, cannot be without significance for its investment decisions. Furthermore, the cooperative projects do not add significantly to PG&E's rate base, as would a steam plant constructed by the Company, and thus in theory do not increase the profits allowable to it under state public utility regulation. Therefore, any rationalization on these decisions on the basis of profit maximization by the utility is shaky from the start. While PG&E's participation in joint projects is pegged to the cost of alternative supplies for the utility, the variation of individual agreements from this norm may be quite wide.

Rivalry over wholesale power marketing

The continual sparring between PG&E and the Bureau of Reclamation during the past two decades—at the bargaining table and in the public forum—has been concerned with the same issues of the exploitation and pricing of joint outputs of electric power and irrigation water. Extremely inimical positions of the parties, however, have brought them into conflict on a number of particular issues. But despite the heat generated by this controversy, it probably has had less effect on the performance of the water industry, as such, than the cooperative arrangements with local agencies discussed above.

The Bureau's exact policy on the pricing of water and power as joint products is hard to define. It has often taken the position that its main function is to "put water on land." If so, its objectives relate to increasing irrigated acreage and reducing the cost of water to the irrigators. Given such motives, its interest would lie in maintaining the existing structure of retail electric power rates and its area of intrinsic conflict with private electric utilities would be sharply limited. However, the Bureau of Reclamation has always held a more general goal of income redistribution that is consistent with promoting low power rates. This, combined with a statutory preference for selling power to publicly owned distribution systems, brings it more into conflict with the private electric power industry. The Bureau enjoys substantial freedom in pricing the joint products of any project having a reasonably favorable benefit-cost ratio.[15] The familiar separable costs-remaining benefits method (SCRB) is now customarily used as a standard arbitrary method of assigning joint costs to such projects' several categories of benefits. Electric power, at a minimum, must be priced to return its allocated costs with interest. Irrigation prices and repayment obligations are determined without including interest charges, and the Bureau is free to apply "excess" revenues from power and from municipal and industrial water to reduce the repayment obligation for irrigation. In short, although the SCRB method tends to allot higher costs to power than would some other arbitrary allocation formulas,[16] the Bureau can vary its water and power prices widely in conformance with its policy goals.

Pacific Gas and Electric sees its far-flung, interconnected system of stream and hydroelectric generating plants as the logical source of power for the whole Northern California area. The large number of production and consumption points included in this network gives it great flexibility in meeting peak demands. Once largely a hydroelectric system, the relative exhaustion of feasible hydro sites and rapid postwar growth of demand for power have brought PG&E around to operating more than two-thirds of its capacity in steam plants. Both steam and hydro capacity are still being added, however, and incremental units of capacity of the two types are adjusted closely for the most efficient development of the system. In addition to a natural dislike of market rivals, the Company feels that the independent operation in the area of large generating facilities such as the Bureau's is manifestly inefficient. Such a competing system, unless fully interconnected with its own, must either operate at an inefficiently low load factor or develop its own complex of interconnected steam and hydro facilities. In the latter case, it would naturally prove an unwelcome competitor to the utility.

Spurred by these considerations, PG&E has followed a program of continued opposition to the Bureau's activities in power production and marketing. The Bureau's plans in the 1940's called not only for hydroelectric installations but also a federal interconnected system involving transmission lines and a large steam plant in the Sacramento Delta. Pacific Gas and Electric concentrated its opposition on the steam plant, which was authorized for construction but never built, and the transmission lines, which were substantially restricted and delayed. In 1954, when the Trinity Division of the Central Valley Project was under consideration for con-

[15] For a more complete discussion of pricing constraints upon the Bureau, see Chapter 13.

[16] U.S. Congress, House Committee on Interior and Insular Affairs, Subcommittee on Irrigation and Reclamation, *Water Resources Development Criteria,* 84 Cong. 2 sess. (1956), pp. 97, 105.

gressional authorization, PG&E expanded its position by seizing upon the announced "partnership" policy of the Eisenhower Administration. It offered to construct the generation equipment as well as the transmission lines for the project, making the same sort of fixed payments to the United States for "falling water" as it offered to the local districts in the Central Valley. After several years of maneuvering, the partnership policy was defeated.[17]

As the Bureau's generating facilities came into operation—first at Shasta and Keswick dams on the Sacramento River, later at Folsom and Nimbus on the American—the utility's strategy centered on controlling the distribution of this power and seeking to frustrate the Bureau's efforts to acquire customers for power generated beyond the pumping needs of the Central Valley Project. It accomplished this until 1951 by both refusing to transmit Bureau power over its own lines to Bureau customers and using its influence to prevent the Bureau from securing appropriations to construct its own lines. In 1951, a "wheeling" contract for the transport of power was finally reached,[18] and the Bureau was able to contract for the sale of its firm power output to several public agencies, particularly the Sacramento Municipal Utility District (SMUD). This and other Bureau contracts clearly had the effect of forcing special rate concessions by PG&E in the affected area.

A considerable controversy arose over the prices in the contracts entered into by the Bureau both with its retail customers and with PG&E for wheeling and for the sale of nonfirm power. The SMUD contract, which in effect offered the Utility District a very favorable price, was bitterly attacked by private power interests and also by irrigators. Some of the farmers were then mounting a campaign to get the state of California to buy the Central Valley Project from the federal government and thereby avoid the acreage-limitation law, and saw the feasibility of this move threatened by the SMUD contract; other irrigators merely feared it would reduce the Bureau's ability to provide subsidy to irrigation uses. On the other hand, the Bureau's contracts with PG&E were also attacked within the government for the unfavorable terms which the Bureau had been forced to accept, a clear reflection of its lack of alternatives.[19]

In conclusion, the Bureau has definitely found itself in a weak short-run bargaining position in marketing its output of electric power (beyond that used for pumping in its own operations). Paradoxically, however, considering the Bureau's practice of using power revenue to subsidize the sale of irrigation water below its long-run, and possibly short-run, marginal cost, the net effect of these marketing difficulties may if anything have been to reduce the misallocation of resources. Only if the PG&E appeared to be selling electricity in Northern California at a price substantially exceeding its marginal cost and, further, the Bureau were using correct

[17] U.S. Congress, House Committee on Interior and Insular Affairs, *Central Valley Project Documents, Part 1: Authorizing Documents,* H. Doc. 416, 84 Cong. 2 sess. (1956), pp. 871–961. (Hereinafter cited as *Central Valley-Project Documents, Part 1.*) Similar proposals for PG&E partnership in Folsom and Nimbus dams had received less attention.

[18] *Idem, Central Valley Project Documents, Part 2: Operating Documents,* H. Doc. 246, 85 Cong. 1 sess. (1957), chap. 14. (Hereinafter cited as *Central Valley Project Documents, Part 2.*) Also see House Appropriations Committee hearings on the Interior Department appropriations for the years in question.

[19] *Central Valley Project Documents, Part 2, op. cit.,* pp. 303–05, 337–43.

investment criteria—neither conjecture seems substantially correct—could this controversy be likely to depress the development of common facilities for water and power development below the optimum. Indeed, it may overextend them, so far as PG&E takes part in joint ventures with local districts in order to forestall additional construction by the Bureau. Certainly the controversy helps to becloud the efficient selection of hydro and steam generation projects to satisfy the increasing demand for electrical energy in the area. Finally, the power-marketing agreements eventually reached between PG&E and the Bureau seem to imply no serious short-run inefficiencies in the operating criteria used by the Bureau in producing power and other outputs from its common facilities, however equitable the prices involved may be.

Public Goods and External Effects

Other uses of water lack the tight behavioral connections to its use or diversion for consumptive purposes that we have found in the case of electric power, though they are alternative to or joint with consumptive and power uses, and may be externally affected by such uses. One such set of utilities falls into (or near) the economist's category of "public goods." No market exists for a public good, and hence no measure of market-determined value gained or foregone can be derived directly to guide planning in the water industry. True public goods seem scarce among the services provided by water in Northern California. However, several such services are treated by public policy as if they were public goods and, furthermore, are not subject to such a clearly fixed total supply that their "non-publicness" comes into conflict with the public policy. The best examples are flood control, stream fisheries, and navigation. Flood control on a river is a pure public good: in the absence of special flood-waterways, holding back floodwaters from one segment of a river valley will protect other portions as well. Navigation and stream fisheries are public goods in California by virtue of public policy. The privilege of fishing in a stream or towing a barge up a river obviously could be rationed by the price mechanism. However, the streams of the state are dedicated to the public and cannot be enclosed and rationed to fishermen by private owners. The federal constitution confers the same status upon navigable waterways, and no tolls are collected from shipping. Both stream fisheries and navigation have some traits of the pure public good: fisheries to the extent that today's unsuccessful fisherman does not reduce tomorrow's potential catch; navigation simply by virtue of the excess capacity which is common on navigable waterways. Thus in neither case is increased utility enjoyed by one user at substantial expense to others, except as fishing waters become overcrowded or over-fished.

Further utilities are also complementary or alternative to urban and rural water consumption, and are altered by true external effects rather than proportional gains and losses in associated water consumption or use. An example of such external effects would be that of changes in diversion for irrigation use in the Central Valley causing water downstream to become more or less saline from the intrusion of ocean water. The hypotheses discussed above suggested that whether the decision-making center that originates external effects will take them into account depends on the sign of the externality, the ease of measurement, and the like.

Fisheries and storage reservoirs

In effect, if not in substance, in-stream fisheries comprise a public good in California. When the construction of a storage dam and reservoir interferes with fish life on a stream, no property right of the fishermen, as individuals or as a group, need be purchased or compensated. No direct physical exclusion occurs, as when private land is taken for a highway. Furthermore, California law recognizes no strong right of fisheries to protection against adverse stream uses. This became strikingly clear in the controversy which arose following construction by the U.S. Bureau of Reclamation of Friant Dam, which in the dry water year of 1946 almost extinguished the salmon run on the San Joaquin River. It was determined that state law in effect required no provision to protect fish life below the Dam, while federal law referred only to the conservation of wildlife in waters impounded by the Dam.[20] There was no evidence that the Bureau had considered the fishery benefits lost by stopping all releases of water into the San Joaquin channel.

The story of interference with stream fisheries by the construction of dams goes back many years, especially for anadromous or migratory fish such as salmon and steelhead. Before World War II, the construction of dams by power companies and local water agencies had cut off the upstream spawning areas of many rivers flowing through the Central Valley, and major damage to runs of anadromous fish had already been done.[21] Since World War II, the tide has been partly turned through political action to demand, sometimes successfully, that agencies constructing new stream barriers make some type of compensating arrangement. Legislative and policy changes have improved the practices of the federal agencies. By the terms of the Wildlife Coordination Act of August 14, 1946 (62 Stat. 1080), the federal agencies that build dams are required to make "adequate provision" consistent with the primary purposes for the conservation of wildlife resources, and to consult the U.S. Fish and Wildlife Service and corresponding state agencies. While legal interpretations have limited the impact of this provision, considerable improvement in federal practice has followed. Within California, the Department of Fish and Game has come to play a much more successful role in securing the protection of fish life. This postwar evolution affords a case study of alternative uses of water guarded or promoted by different public agencies.

Economic interaction between fishing interests and users of water for consumptive purposes simply does not occur. When private fishermen unite to oppose in-stream construction adverse to their interests, they immediately take their case before public authorities. Their only weapons are political. They do not and cannot seek monetary compensation for benefits to be foregone. They can only protect the recreational benefits of stream fisheries by opposing projects in their entirety or insisting on conditions which avert or reduce the potential damage.

That fishery benefits gain even a political voice depends upon their presence among the elements of public interest considered by the several administrative

[20] Opinion of the State Attorney General, Opinion No. 50–89, July 23, 1951, summarized in *Central Valley Project Documents, Part 2, op. cit.*, p. 429.

[21] Donald A. Duerr, "Conflicts between Water Development Projects and Fish and Wildlife Conservation" (unpublished M.A. thesis, University of California, Berkeley, 1955), chap. 2; on early regulatory policies, see Gerald D. Nash, *State Government and Economic Development: A History of Administrative Policies in California, 1849–1933* (1964).

agencies which may act upon a new water project proposed for construction in California. Indeed, only recently has state legislation declared fish and wildlife maintenance to be officially a beneficial use of water.[22] Defending the interests of fish conservation before these bodies falls largely to other public agencies, the California Department of Fish and Game (and its bureaucratic ancestors) and the U.S. Fish and Wildlife Service. The federal agency tends to play a significant role only in Federal Power Commission license proceedings. It holds less importance for California, and will receive less attention here, than the state unit.

The legal powers of the California Department of Fish and Game are largely those of planning and consultation. It must review and comment on water resource projects of the state when they are submitted to the legislature. It reviews all applications for the appropriation of water and may file protests and recommendations when necessary. It reviews applications to construct dams and may recommend means for fish passage or substitute facilities such as traps or hatcheries.[23] In making use of these powers, the Department seeks to take an active role in the planning of water projects to protect and improve fish and wildlife habitats wherever possible. It also stresses research and study so that it can urge constructive alternatives to projects or project operations with adverse effects on wildlife.[24]

The Department of Fish and Game has now come to make effective, if limited, use of these powers. Such has not always been the case. Before World War II, a lack of money and personnel precluded any active policy. Virtually the only fish protection resulting from its activities was an occasional fish ladder for salmon and some gentlemen's agreements on water releases. In any case, the rivalry of irrigation and fish conservation for water had not then become strongly apparent. Only in 1945 did the (then) Division of Fish and Game begin to scrutinize the effect of every new dam by examining each application for a permit to appropriate water and to enter protests where necessary. It took the position that many applications are minor but that the aggregate cuts sharply into the total amount of water which can support game fish. Its reports took on a tone of urgency when viewing the prospect of dams cutting off more and more migratory salmon from their spawning beds. After the setback of Friant Dam,[25] the agency took an increasingly active role

[22] See Chapter 3, section on Public Regulation of the Use of Water.

[23] California *Water Code* (1963), §§ 223, 345.1, 12608; *Statement of California Department of Fish and Game on the California Anadromous Fish Development Program* (mimeo., n.d.), p. 5.

[24] See *Policy Statement of the California Department of Fish and Game,* adopted July 27, 1959 (mimeo.).

[25] The loss of the San Joaquin River salmon run was the result of many factors and not just capricious action by the Bureau of Reclamation. Considerable shrinkage of the run had occurred before Friant Dam went into operation, and the decline thereafter was due in part to two extremely dry years. The importance of the case lies partly in what it revealed about legal protection for stream fisheries. The Bureau had indeed rejected requests by the U.S. Fish and Wildlife Service and the California Department of Fish and Game for fish conservation, claiming that putting their suggestions into effect would require more than one-fourth of the capacity of Friant Dam. Later, the Rank suits (*Rank* vs. *Krug,* 90 Fed. Supp. 773-S.D. Calif., 1950; *Rank* vs. *Krug,* No. 685 N.D.-S.D. Calif., opinion dated February 1956) included fishery interests, among others, seeking to block or restrict storage at Friant, but the district court decision denied any legal basis for a private suit on behalf of stream fisheries. Later public action under state law was effectively blocked by Opinion No. 50–89 of the State Attorney General (cited above), which held that fishery interests had no claim upon scarce water as against the "higher uses" designated in the *Water Code.* (See Duerr, *op. cit.,* chap. 8, and works cited therein.)

in opposing projects and suggesting modifications, along with a stepped-up campaign to gather the information necessary to appraise the effect of new projects. Finally, in the 1950's, it gained enough prestige to carry some weight in influencing the design and operation of water development projects.[26] However, it still did not carry enough weight to secure drastic revisions in project designs and scales, much less abandonment of projects, on the ground that they appropriated water which should be reserved to maintain fisheries.

In the opinion of the Department, fish life can be maintained following the construction of a project in several ways. Operating procedures and facilities can be designed to preserve the fisheries resources both in kind and in place. Resources may be replaced in kind, though not in place, as when depleted flows in one portion of a river channel are replaced by augmented flows in another. Finally, resources may be maintained in place, but not in kind, as when warm-water reservoir fisheries replace cold-water stream fisheries. Many different types of modifications to projects may serve to gain these objectives. Most involve some significant cost to the entrepreneur of the project—either the capital cost of constructing additional facilities (fish ladders, hatcheries, and so on) or the operating costs of special water-release procedures or foregone power revenues. The Department of Fish and Game follows negotiating procedures to obtain such modifications which resemble those between competing water agencies described in Chapter 12. Its claim to a hearing can be exercised before the California Water Commission, the California State Water Rights Board, and the Federal Power Commission. But actual accommodations usually come about in negotiations behind the scenes with the entrepreneurial agency. Postponements of public hearings and other such devices are used to encourage such negotiated settlements.

The Department suffers certain prima facie drawbacks in gaining acceptance for its wishes to protect or enhance fish life. The first of these is uncertainty. Comprehensive data often do not exist to show the damage to fish life which may result from a proposed project. Even more uncertain are the results of various costly modifications of projects which the Department of Fish and Game seeks. The scientific knowledge involved essentially takes a pragmatic form, and what solves the problem of fish conservation in one case may fail entirely in another. A second factor weakening the Department's negotiating strength is the relatively high opportunity costs which its proposals seem to impose. The developers of a project can argue that modifying their release pattern to protect one more fish denies water on the average to a significant number of acres of land. In the controversy over the salmon run in the San Joaquin River, the California Division of Water Resources claimed that the releases for fish conservation proposed by the U.S. Fish and Wildlife Service would have an opportunity cost of about three crop-acres annually per fish.[27] Other cases seem to involve similar orders of magnitude. These figures often seem to embody comparisons of gross average costs in situations where net marginal opportunity costs might lead to quite different conclusions, but they have largely gone unchallenged. Another factor undercutting the bargaining

[26] This paragraph summarizes information from interviews and the biennial reports of the Department (previously the Division) of Fish and Game.

[27] Under some assumptions about project operations, the foregone revenue to the Bureau of Reclamation (a sum less than net productivity of water to the irrigators) could rise to $65 per fish. See *Central Valley Project Documents, Part 2, op. cit.*, pp. 432–33.

strength of the Department of Fish and Game is a view, widely held but seldom clearly expressed, that where wildlife protection facilities would make a marginally feasible project unfeasible, wildlife should take the hindmost.[28]

Despite its slow evolution as an effective defender of wildlife interests and its inherent bargaining disadvantages, the Department of Fish and Game finally has come to have a measurable effect on the design and operation of water projects in California. The following paragraphs discuss five recent cases which illustrate the impact of wildlife conservation interests on the investment process and the design of new projects. They illustrate the factors pointing toward success or failure in averting or limiting external diseconomies or adverse alternative use affecting in-stream fisheries.

Little trouble arose in connection with the American River project of Sacramento's electric power agency, the Sacramento Municipal Utility District. This system of relatively small dams and power diversions on the upper tributaries of the American posed some threat to trout fisheries by the substitution of reservoirs for flowing streams and by the effect of its water releases on streamflows and temperatures. Representatives of the Department of Fish and Game worked with the District during the planning phase of the project; and the substitution of reservoir for stream fisheries was acceptable to the Department. The Sacramento District, being interested solely in power generation and not diversion for consumptive use, without incurring higher costs could agree on minimum release patterns from its dams, the avoidance of sudden changes in flows released, and the construction of low-level intakes from its reservoirs to avoid raising stream temperatures excessively.[29]

The project designed by the Nevada Irrigation District for the Bear River included upstream diversions and powerhouses and a downstream storage reservoir, Rollins Reservoir. From Rollins, water stored for irrigation uses would be released into the Bear River channel for rediversion downstream. Fish life would suffer from two phases of the project—reduced flows upstream where water was diverted into conduits to pass through the project's power plants, and from inundation of several miles of the Bear River channel by Rollins Reservoir (a common composite of effects). The Department of Fish and Game at first proposed minimum releases into the upstream channel to maintain suitable water temperatures and food conditions for fish. This the Irrigation District flatly rejected, arguing that the revenue losses which would result from reduced output of power would wreck the feasibility of the project.[30] The District argued that its releases from Rollins Reservoir would

[28] California legislation and administrative agencies treat fish and wildlife conservation, like other beneficial uses of water, not by placing a quantitative value upon unit benefits but by implicitly ranking it in a hierarchy of types of benefit. This view is reflected in such statements as the following: "The Department of Fish and Game is handicapped because water for fish and game has been assigned an extremely low priority in comparison with the other legally recognized 'beneficial' uses." (California State Department of Natural Resources, Division of Fish and Game, *42nd Biennial Report, 1950–52,* p. 37.)

[29] The more valuable game fish require relatively low water temperatures in order to maintain their populations. If intakes from reservoirs are designed to draw relatively warm water from near the surface, the stream below the dam may be warmed to an excessive degree.

[30] The District placed the foregone revenue at $80,000 a year, on a project with capital costs of $60 million. (Interview with Edwin Koster, manager, Nevada Irrigation District, April 26, 1962.)

improve conditions for fish life in lower reaches of the stream and thus afford a "replacement in kind" for the upstream fishery. Since these releases would be later rediverted in part by the District, with power revenues much less affected, the project would remain feasible. Furthermore, Rollins Reservoir might enjoy some use as a fishery resource. This position was accepted by the Department of Fish and Game, which had requested releases below Rollins smaller than those offered by the Nevada District.[31]

The project of Richvale Irrigation District on the Middle Fork of the Feather River has forced the defenders of wildlife conservation to demand, not modifications and adjustments, but complete rejection of the project. The Richvale District proposes a series of dams and reservoirs in the canyon of the Middle Fork. These would destroy what the Department of Fish and Game has called "one of the finest resident trout streams in California." The trout habitat would be changed sharply and "rough fish" such as squawfish, suckers, and carp would drive out the trout. Also the U.S. Fish and Wildlife Service has protested "that the scenic values, the wilderness aspects, and the naturally propagated fish and wildlife resources can only be maintained by prohibiting development in the canyon."[32] The issue between Richvale and the conservation agencies has turned on whether the project should be permitted at all, since many, though not all, of the project's works would lie in the canyon. The canyon of the Middle Fork represents an unused wilderness resource. The trout stream owes its quality to its inaccessibility by automobiles; use of the area is estimated at only 5,000 visitor-days annually.[33]

The findings of the California Water Commission, in connection with Richvale's application for the release of the state's filings to water needed for the project, show the dilemma posed by the case. A subcommittee of the Commission held extended hearings on the fishery and related recreational issues of the case. Dividing the works of the proposed project into those in the critical canyon area and those upstream, the subcommittee found that the latter would actually enhance recreational facilities (a highly debatable finding). But "in the lower canyon area the evidence developed indicates that the existing trout fishery will be damaged to an extent that the subcommittee could not fix on the evidence adduced."[34] But it found the opportunity cost of protecting these benefits too great. Not only did the very quality of the resource depend on the fact that few members of the public could use it, but also the preservation of benefits of the canyon for a small number of fishermen might cost project benefits (gross, apparently) of "hundreds, if not thousands, of dollars for every fisherman day. If, on the other hand, the number

[31] See California Department of Fish and Game, *Existing and Proposed Water Developments on Yuba and Bear Rivers and Their Effects on Fish and Wildlife,* Water Projects Report No. 4 (1962), pp. 24–27; and letter from Assistant Secretary of the Interior to Chairman, Federal Power Commission, in the matter of Project No. 2266, Oct. 12, 1962.

[32] California Department of Fish and Game, *Effects on Fish and Wildlife Resources of Proposed Water Development on Middle Fork Feather River,* Water Projects Report No. 2 (1961), pp. 19–30; and letter of Assistant Secretary of the Interior to Chairman, Federal Power Commission, Aug. 30, 1960, p. 2.

[33] California Department of Fish and Game, *Effects on Fish and Wildlife Resources, op. cit.,* pp. 20–21.

[34] California Water Commission, *Report of Subcommittee designated to hear the request of Richvale Irrigation District for a release from priority of state applications to California Water Commission,* March 16, 1962 (mimeo.), p. 5.

of beneficiaries of the canyon fishery increases substantially, it appears inevitable that the high quality fishing will soon disappear."[35] The full Water Commission concurred with the subcommittee's recommendation that the state filings be released. The controversy then moved before the State Water Rights Board, where it has long been under study, with no compromise or other definite solution in sight.

Two of the most difficult cases for defending the interests of fish conservation have involved clashes between the interests of large urban water agencies and the maintenance of salmon runs. Anadromous fish are felt to present a much more critical conservation problem than the resident fish at issue in the Richvale case. But California law also classifies the municipal consumption of water as a "higher" use. One of these cases involved Camanche Dam, proposed by Oakland's East Bay Municipal Utility District (EBMUD) as a further development of its water supply from the Mokelumne River. The Department of Fish and Game could propose only limited alternatives to the Camanche project. The Mokelumne River is heavily utilized, and under existing rights EBMUD could divert the whole flow in dry periods. This fact, plus EBMUD's asserted need for the unappropriated balance in the foreseeable future, confined the discussion to means of preserving the salmon run on the River other than by maintaining the flow over the natural spawning beds. Additional water in the Mokelumne channel might be secured by exchange.[36] Fish hatcheries or spawning channels might be developed on the Mokelumne below Camanche Dam. A compensating hatchery might be developed on another stream, or at tidewater using fresh water flows piped by EBMUD. Or the District might draw its additional supplies not from the Mokelumne River but farther down in the Sacramento-San Joaquin Delta. Several of these solutions were ruled out at the start. Like other San Francisco Bay area agencies, EBMUD refused absolutely to supply its customers with "ditch water" from the Delta.[37]

When the parties reached agreement on major elements in 1959, under pressure of the terms of a permit issued by the State Engineer, EBMUD was obligated to release only a small fraction of the scarce Mokelumne water requested by the Department of Fish and Game. It did agree to construct a spawning channel and steelhead hatchery and a low-level outlet at Camanche Dam in order to provide cooler water for the fish. Of the total cost of this project of approximately $33 million, slightly over $1 million is allocable to the cost of fish conservation features.

In the final important case of conflict over fish conservation, the Department of Fish and Game was placed in its most disadvantageous bargaining position. The Modesto and Turlock irrigation districts propose to build New Don Pedro Dam on the Tuolumne River to increase their supplies of irrigation water and raise their power output. Standing with them as a silent partner is the city of San Francisco, which has long drawn its water supply from the Hetch Hetchy Project upstream,

[35] *Ibid.*, pp. 5–6. The report went on to argue that the recreational benefits of the project upstream were relatively certain, and that many recreation benefits of the canyon would not be lost.

[36] Woodbridge Irrigation District, another large claimant on the Mokelumne, might conceivably be served with American River water via the Folsom South canal of the U.S. Bureau of Reclamation.

[37] California Department of Fish and Game, *Report upon Negotiations and Suggestions for Settlement or Disposition of the Above Applications Prepared Pursuant to Notice of Hearing Dated April 25, 1956*, May 2, 1956 (mimeo.), pp. 4–6.

and which will contribute to the project's costs and gain more water by an exchange arrangement from New Don Pedro. The Tuolumne is an important stream for anadromous fish life[38] even though an older dam has long blocked access to upstream spawning areas. The operating schedule for the project outlined by the engineers would allegedly destroy such fish life due to an outright shortage of water in dry years and, over the longer run, flows inadequate to prevent the encroachment of vegetation upon the spawning riffles below the dam.[39]

In this case, the Department of Fish and Game suffered the same disadvantages as in dealing with EBMUD's Camanche project (over-all scarcity of water, having a say only after project plans had become firm, and dealing with an urban agency having many voter-beneficiaries). In addition, the parties already held all the necessary water rights. This fact denied the Department its usual chance to make a case before the state regulatory agencies—the State Water Rights Board and the California Water Commission. The project still required a license from the Federal Power Commission, however, and the fact that FPC hearings were pending brought the parties into their first lengthy round of negotiations. These eventually produced a compromise agreement which set minimum flows for maintaining fish life over the first twenty years of the project, varying with water-supply conditions and with the growth of San Francisco's diversions. After twenty years, the FPC was to reopen the issue of the fish releases and facilities. This "compromise" was not satisfactory to any party, and all filed petitions for review in the courts. Although the U.S. Court of Appeals, in May 1965, upheld the terms of the FPC license in all respects, it is uncertain at this writing whether or not Turlock and Modesto will accept the license. The ruling indicated that San Francisco, although not a party to the proceedings, might be expected to assist financially in the provision of fish facilities at the end of the twenty-year period. The Court stated that the FPC could order such releases though they "interfered" with the water rights of the districts and San Francisco established under state law and the Raker Act. Either an additional long delay will ensue, or the districts will undertake the project with uncertainty about future costs and rights.

These cases suggest the elements which make the position of the Department of Fish and Game either strong or weak in dealing with projects sponsored by local agencies. The protection of anadromous fish affords a greater problem than that of resident fish because the latter resource offers more possibilities for "replacement in kind," and protective provisions tend to be less costly to the project's sponsor. Coming into the picture early in the planning process also helps, for a sponsoring agency faced with problems of "momentum" in carrying a fully planned project past many obstacles is likely to be more truculent. Furthermore, changes in design and plans for operation at an advanced stage become more difficult. The Department of Fish and Game has trouble when dealing both with projects that are

[38] During 1953–59 the Tuolumne contributed 6 per cent of all salmon originating in California. See *Prepared Testimony of Donald H. Fry, Jr. before Federal Power Commission in Hearings on Project No. 2299*, n.d. (mimeo.), pp. 6, 7.

[39] *Prepared Testimony of Daniel P. Christenson before the Federal Power Commission in Hearings on Project No. 2299*, n.d. (mimeo.), p. 52; U.S. Department of the Interior, Fish and Wildlife Service, Bureau of Sport Fisheries and Wildlife, *A Proposed Development Program for Anadromous Fish in California* (1962), p. 30.

marginally feasible and those promising relatively high inframarginal benefits. In the first case, the prevailing ideology favoring construction and water development boggles at blocking a whole project to protect fish life; in the second, the fish seldom seem worth the sacrifice. The Department of Fish and Game seems less strong politically against large urban agencies with many voter-beneficiaries than against irrigation districts and other agricultural users. But this drawback may be directly offset by urban users' substantially greater "ability to pay" for fish protection facilities and operations. Existing procedures seem better adapted to forcing adjustments for the marginal externalities of dam construction than the inframarginal ones, although there is no evidence of careful balancing of values at the margin. No hard evidence can be developed, without exhaustive investigations into individual cases, to test the optimality of the fish conservation measures now demanded by the Department. It is clear, however, that suboptimal provision has been made in the past and that the Department can be expected to get its way only under especially favorable political circumstances.

To complete this discussion of the protection of fish life, we should note the relations of the Department of Fish and Game to dam-building agencies other than those of local government. One group is the large privately owned electric utilities—principally Pacific Gas and Electric Company, in the area of this study. In the past, PG&E and other utilities with numerous hydroelectric installations have followed practices seriously adverse to the interest of fisheries. Their existing systems of reservoirs and powerhouses on swift-flowing streams tend to dry up long stretches of stream channels and seriously impair resident fisheries, even when they lie far enough upstream not to interfere with anadromous fish. However, PG&E has modified its operations significantly in the interest of maintaining fish life, and the utility's chief engineer estimated in 1960 that roughly $1 million worth of power generation at market prices is foregone annually as a result of water releases to maintain fish life.

Apart from any sacrifice of cost minimization for protecting fisheries which a utility's management may see as lying in the public interest, the Department of Fish and Game has two sorts of leverage for gaining favorable release patterns. One is the force of public opinion; the other is the requirement of renewal of Federal Power Commission licenses. Evidence on the effect of both is highly conjectural. In one case before the State Water Rights Board involving PG&E's development of the McCloud River, an initial decision rejected the Department of Fish and Game request of a minimum release of 300 cubic feet per second for fish life in favor of a significantly lower figure offered by the utility, describing the Department's evidence as "vague and indefinite." But the decision was later reconsidered at the request of both parties; fish releases were revised upward according to an agreement between them, and appropriations from one creek were eliminated.[40] A concern with public relations may have induced this change in position by PG&E after a legal victory was in hand. The FPC licenses for hydroelectric projects require renewal after fifty years, and a number of older projects in California are approaching the critical age. The utilities normally desire renewal at a minimum, and often seek consolidation with newer projects. The FPC's will-

[40] California State Water Rights Board, Decision D 978, Aug. 25, 1960, p. 7; Decision D 989, Jan. 13, 1961, pp. 3–4; *Outdoor California*, July 1962, p. 10.

ingness to listen to wildlife conservation interests and the experience of several utilities outside the Northern California area in getting FPC renewals suggest that the federal agency affords a major opportunity for conditioning hydroelectric project operations.

Another major water development agency, the Bureau of Reclamation, has also taken an increasingly favorable view of expenditures favoring the maintenance of fish life. The effect of Friant Dam on the San Joaquin salmon run constituted a major blow to fish conservation, but the Bureau's policies have otherwise shown more consideration. The Bureau spent $2,230,000 on a salmon hatchery near Shasta Dam to offset its effect on the Sacramento River salmon run, and its other major dams provide minimum releases to maintain fish life. A fish screen of novel design was completed at a cost of $3,225,000 to protect small striped bass and salmon from being ingested by the Bureau's giant pumps at Tracy. Both Folsom and Trinity dams cut off major spawning areas for anadromous fish, and the Bureau has constructed fish hatcheries below these dams, to be operated by the California Department of Fish and Game. The congressional authorization for Trinity was unique in specifically directing the Secretary of the Interior to adopt measures to insure the preservation and propagation of fish life.[41] A generally favorable trend toward fish conservation has developed in other quarters as well. The California Department of Water Resources has recently taken a more friendly stand. It and the Department of Fish and Game are now both lodged in the State Resources Agency. This may insure an administrative reconciliation of interests as the construction of the California Water Plan approaches; but it is a reconciliation in which the public interest in the preservation of fisheries lacks a representative that is independent of the major agency committed to construction of dams to block wild rivers in order to support major interbasin transfers of water.

Of course, a trend toward increased recognition of fish benefits is one thing, but a precise marginal balancing with competing types of benefit is another.[42] Certainly no collective social judgment exists about the cash value to be placed—now or in the future—upon preserved fishery benefits. Nor do the operations of the Department of Fish and Game seem to rest on any attempt, conscious or unconscious, to estimate them. The ratios commonly presented of foregone crop-acres, power revenues, or acre-feet of water per protected fish give a starting point, but the next step of placing an appropriate marginal value on both the numerator and denominator of the ratio has not taken place.

Other external effects

The extent to which water development projects in California take external and competitive effects on fish life into account depends on the powers and vitality of the California Department of Fish and Game and the U.S. Fish and Wildlife

[41] California Department of Fish and Game, *44th Biennial Report, 1954–56,* pp. 15, 22.

[42] Methods for measuring the total value of recreational resources have made considerable headway, but not so the valuation of marginal externalities associated with variations in the scales of projects. See Jack L. Knetsch, "Economics of Including Recreation as a Purpose of Eastern Water Projects," *Journal of Farm Economics,* XLVI (December 1964), 1148–57.

Service, plus the unmeasurable influence of sportsmen's organizations in the political sphere. Other external effects of water projects show a similar dependence on political and administrative processes for gaining recognition in the planning process. The detailed results, however, differ in significant ways from one external effect to another. The interests of waterfowl conservation, the avoidance of water pollution, and the control of intrusion of saline water into the Delta are defended in varying ways, and with varying effectiveness. The resulting patterns give some idea of how fully the allocation of resources in the water industry takes external effects into account and which institutional arrangement may come closest to hitting the optimal mark.

The trough of the lower San Joaquin Valley contains extensive marshlands or grasslands which lie on a major flyway for migratory waterfowl. They have provided both natural food and shelter for the birds and a recreational facility for hunters. These grasslands historically received much of their water supply from the uncontrolled winter and spring floods of the San Joaquin River. Thus, the construction of Friant Dam by the Bureau of Reclamation, to store these flows and divert them into the Friant-Kern and Madera canals, meant a substantial cut in the water available to the grasslands and thus some loss of economic benefits.

As it turned out, the loss of these benefits was avoided, and their magnitude was put to an economic test, in a rather direct fashion. The area in question passed into the hands of private cooperative groups of sportsmen—"duck clubs"—which have contracted to buy water from the Bureau of Reclamation at a price matching its value in alternative uses in agriculture. The legal steps leading to this outcome are interesting. Miller and Lux, the giant enterprise which once controlled the San Joaquin grasslands, began selling them off in relatively small parcels in 1926, but retaining the water rights by reservation. These rights were bought by the United States in 1939 to permit the construction and operation of Friant Dam upstream on the San Joaquin. When Friant began to fill in 1944, the grasslands ceased to receive water from their original source—the high flows of the river in the winter and spring. After 1944, the duck clubs purchased "interim" water supplies from the Bureau of Reclamation through a mutual organization, Grasslands Mutual Water Association. At the same time, they sought to secure water from the Bureau on a permanent contractual basis, a course not legally open to the Bureau on the basis of existing reclamation law.[43]

The necessary legislation was secured in 1954,[44] partly through the efforts of the grasslands representatives, but with substantial assistance from the rice growers of the San Joaquin Valley. The latter presented evidence that, without wild pasture for waterfowl in the grasslands, the ducks consumed large quantities of rice in the fields and substantial expenditures had been made to drive them out.[45] One can hardly conceive of waterfowl recreation being handled optimally by an atomistic

[43] U.S. Congress, House Committee on Interior and Insular Affairs, Special Subcommittee, *Grasslands Water Problem, San Joaquin Valley, California,* 82 Cong. 1 sess. (1951); Duerr, *op. cit.,* chap. 9.

[44] P. L. 674, 83 Cong. 2 sess. (1954).

[45] One large association of Fresno County growers testified to having employed 30,000 rounds of shotgun ammunition, 12,000 rounds of rifle ammunition, 400 imitation hand grenades, more than 14 cases of star shells, and three airplanes to frighten off the ducks in one season. See *Central Valley Project Documents, Part 1, op. cit.,* p. 826.

market mechanism any more than fishery recreation, which has been turned into a quasi-public good by legislative action that precludes any such private cooperative group from denying any benefits of its actions to others. But the role of the duck clubs, acting as users' cooperatives in much the same fashion as do public water districts, at least supplies a direct economic test of the value of recreation benefits which is absent from the negotiations of the Department of Fish and Game.

The external effects of the construction of water projects on water pollution pose sharp contrasts to the cases of fish and waterfowl conservation. These effects are clearly of large magnitude, but a structure of institutions is only now emerging which may assure their consideration. Although the problem of water pollution plays a minor part in the California water industry when compared to the eastern United States, it has assumed major proportions on the lower San Joaquin River and in the Sacramento-San Joaquin Delta. Though logically similar, problems of pollution have taken technically and politically different forms in these two areas. Irrigation districts along the lower San Joaquin have no difficulty claiming the quantity of water to which their rights entitle them, but the steady development of irrigation upstream on the San Joaquin and its tributaries means that this water consists in the irrigation season mainly of return flows from other irrigation districts. The Delta likewise never faces a quantitative shortage of water because it lies at sea level, but inflows depleted by upstream consumption during the summer months fail to block the intrusion of salt water from San Francisco Bay. Salinity sometimes makes the water in the Delta sloughs unusable for most crops.

Of these two problems of external effects, more attention has centered on salinity. The intrusion of salt water to the Delta had long been a problem in dry years. As far back as 1920, the city of Antioch, acting on behalf of landowners in the Delta, brought suit to enjoin certain upstream diverters on the Sacramento River from cutting the flow into the Delta below 3,500 cubic feet per second. The State Supreme Court, however, found no sufficient cause for granting relief to the Delta interests.[46] One benefit expected and enjoyed after the construction of Shasta Dam on the Sacramento River was ample summer-time flows to protect most of the Delta farmlands from salinity. But, as irrigation developed rapidly along the Sacramento channel during and after World War II and irrigation depletions kept expanding on other streams emptying through the Delta, the problem returned. Indeed, it afforded a major issue in the long battle before the State Water Rights Board over the granting of the Bureau's water rights applications covering the operation of Shasta Dam.

The Delta landowners, well organized politically, have taken the position that the Central Valley Project was premised upon giving the Delta nearly complete protection against salinity intrusion. On the other hand, the landowners have resisted any efforts to bundle their lands into a district to collect for the benefits conferred.[47]

[46] *Antioch* vs. *Williams Irr. Dist.,* 188 Calif. 451 (1922). After noting the unprecedented character of the issue, the Court placed much weight upon the great curtailment of upstream irrigation that would be needed to give substantial relief to the Delta (pp. 460–61). It also noted the threat to further development of irrigation on any streams tributary to the Delta which would result from granting relief.

[47] U.S. Congress, House Committee on Interior and Insular Affairs, Special Subcommittee, *Central Valley Project, California: Water Rights, Supplies, and Uses,* 82 Cong. 1 sess. (1952), p. 241.

Everyone agrees that the project was to confer some benefits from salinity repulsion. The issue is how much, and what opportunity cost to tolerate in the form of other foregone benefits. The Bureau of Reclamation has made its own judgment on the basis of available information, and this judgment so far has stuck. The Bureau has allowed just enough outflow of water through the Delta to San Francisco Bay to keep salinity acceptably low at the intakes to its Delta-Mendota and Contra Costa canals. This criterion requires a rate of outflow to the Bay of approximately 1,500 cubic feet per second, less than half of what would be necessary to protect the lowest portion of the Delta during the critical summer period. In defending its actions the Bureau has argued that, if the whole of the Delta were protected, the releases required would reach the staggering maximum of 300 acre-feet annually per protected acre, enough per protected acre to irrigate perhaps 100 acres of crops elsewhere in the Central Valley.[48]

In short, the heed given to the benefits of salinity repulsion has been decided by administrative action and successfully defended against attack. The administrative decision rests on a conscious balancing of opportunity costs. The issue of external effects on the Delta is far from finally settled, however. As the Department of Water Resources develops the California Water Plan, the Delta will become even more crucial as a collection area for water to be exported to Kern County and Southern California. Representatives of Contra Costa County, one of the Delta areas irked by the Bureau's refusal to provide complete salinity protection, have promised to fight any future exports from the Delta until this protection is provided.

The controversy over the quantity of water to be exported from the Delta is aggravated by the proposal of the Bureau and the Department of Water Resources to improve the quality of exported water by constructing a peripheral canal to convey Sacramento River water around the Delta to the east, and then to the pumping plants located at its southwestern edge. At present, this transfer is accomplished for the Central Valley Project by the use of slightly modified natural sloughs, with the result that the pumps pick up water of whatever quality prevails in the Delta at that distance from the Pacific Ocean. The peripheral canal, while improving the quality of exported water, would at the same time reduce the average quality of water remaining in the natural sloughs and used for irrigation within the Delta. The U.S. Public Health Service estimates the 1970 annual equivalent value of the improvement of exported water at $5,282,000, the annual equivalent value of the degradation of Delta water at $1,800,000,[49] a favorable balance but one which is bound to strengthen the opposition of the Delta counties to further exports.

The other issue of water pollution, affecting the lower San Joaquin River irrigators, is also a salinity problem in large part, for dissolved chlorides that concentrate in reused return flows constitute the chief menace to crop productivity. So far, only two sorts of action have been taken by the affected irrigation districts. They have promoted an investigation by the state of California to establish the magnitude of the problem,[50] and they have begun entering protests against addi-

[48] U.S. Department of the Interior, Bureau of Reclamation, Region 2, Exhibits No. 154 and No. 155, Applications No. 5625 *et al.*, State Water Rights Board.

[49] U.S. Public Health Service, *Water Quality Control Study, Peripheral Canal, Sacramento-San Joaquin Delta, California, Summary Report* (1964), p. 27.

[50] California Department of Water Resources, Division of Resources Planning, *Lower San Joaquin Valley Water Quality Investigation,* Bulletin No. 89 (1960).

tional water storage projects on the tributaries of the San Joaquin. One was an objection to Merced Irrigation District's application in connection with its enlarged Exchequer project on the Merced River. Here the protestants made no headway, and indeed the Merced District contended that the net effect of its project, taking into account the increased quantity of water it would discharge to the San Joaquin River during the critical months, would be to improve water quality in the San Joaquin.[51]

As in the case of salinity in the Delta, one can see forerunners of greatly expanded controversies over the external effects of projects on water quality in the lower part of the Sacramento-San Joaquin system. The U.S. Department of the Interior brief before the Federal Power Commission in the New Don Pedro case turned mainly on the objections of the Fish and Wildlife Service to the threatened destruction of the salmon run on the Tuolumne River. But the brief also deplored the loss of an inflow of pure water to the Delta during the summer.[52] It rejected placing upon the Bureau of Reclamation or the state of California responsibility for making up for the net external diseconomies stemming from projects constructed by local agencies.[53] Likewise, the Department of the Interior intervened with the Federal Power Commission to request the attachment of a condition to the license issued to Nevada Irrigation District for its project on the Yuba and Bear rivers. The Bureau of Reclamation operates no projects on these rivers, but it was clearly concerned with the effect of depletions on the Delta and the federal interest therein. It proposed to subordinate the water diverted by the Nevada District to all future depletions upstream from it. Such a condition would not protect the Delta against Nevada's own diversions, but it would make the District bear the risk of any future increases of water consumption upstream by the counties of origin.[54]

Characteristically, a physical solution to these problems is currently proposed by the Bureau and the Department of Water Resources in the form of a San Joaquin Master Drain to collect waste waters throughout the Valley from Bakersfield north

[51] Whatever the truth of this assertion, the investigation by the Department of Water Resources shows the return flows from the large irrigation districts on the east side of the San Joaquin Valley to be much less contaminated than those coming from the west side, draining into the San Joaquin River between Mendota Pool and the mouth of the Merced River. See *Ibid.*, chap. 4, and Figure 21 in Chapter 12 above.

[52] "We wish to point out that . . . the project will have a substantial effect on the Central Valley project and the Feather River project. Water supply for the Central Valley project and the Feather River project as defined by agreement, dated May 16, 1960, between this Department and the State of California is predicated upon certain operational criteria and a general pattern of water use throughout the entire Central Valley. A part of this general pattern is the availability of multiple-use water from the Tuolumne River providing fish benefits on the Tuolumne River and water quality benefits on the Lower Tuolumne and Lower San Joaquin Rivers and the Delta. Investigations in progress involving the quality of water in the Delta point up the need for increased minimum flows on the tributaries to the San Joaquin . . . rather than decreased flows." See U.S. Department of the Interior, *Briefs to the Federal Power Commission in the Matter of Project No. 2299,* Jan. 14, 1963 and Feb. 20, 1963 (mimeo.). See also Exception and Motion filed by Department of the Interior with reference to the same project on July 22, 1963.

[53] "Salinity control has been recognized as a costly and necessary function of the Federal Central Valley Project. This does not mean, however, that total responsibility for such control has been assumed by this Federal project. That responsibility must be shared by other projects and developments including New Don Pedro." (*Ibid.*, p. 67.)

[54] Letters from Assistant Secretary of the Interior to Chairman, Federal Power Commission, in the matter of Project No. 2266, Oct. 12, 1961, and May 2, 1962.

and transport them to a point in the lower portion of the Delta (near Antioch, in Contra Costa County). This Drain would inevitably have adverse effects on the Delta and thus is under bitter attack. There are proposals to establish intermediate storage reservoirs along the Drain so as to allow the release of waste waters when they can do the least damage, and to extend it to a more westerly outfall below the Delta or to the Ocean at an entirely different point (such as Monterey Bay). The Bureau has resisted the pressures for alternative or extended routes for the Drain, since the costs of the proposed alternative routes are much higher, and extension of the canal farther west through the Bay area might more than double its cost.[55]

Conclusions

Although the evidence presented here has failed to show quantitatively the position of joint and alternative uses and external effects in the Northern California water industry, it has pointed to the general direction of their influence. It also may indicate what institutional arrangements or other conditions raise the likelihood of such effects gaining consideration in the investment process. The examples discussed above suggest, in a very tentative fashion, the following conclusions:

1) In practice, the coexistence of clear-cut joint or alternative relationships among two or more uses of water, the predominance of commercial interests in both uses, and relatively few users tends to assure recognition of these relationships and corresponding adaptations of water-using practices—whether or not the presence of more than one user gives rise also to external effects—although optimal coadjustment of uses is not assured. Conversely, where particular external disbenefits are not clearly related to particular adverse uses, where adverse users and those suffering disbenefits are numerous, or where the adversely affected uses are not commercial, adequate adjustments of water use to allow for externalities and the phenomena underlying them are less likely, and become increasingly so as the conditions enumerated become more severe.

2) Where external effects cannot be taken into account by private actions, for one reason or another, the burden shifts to legal and administrative mechanisms. In principle, these might work either well or badly. The Bureau of Reclamation's policy toward salinity repulsion in the Delta seems to rest on an effort at optimizing the distribution of benefits at the margin. By contrast, the increasingly successful efforts of the Department of Fish and Game apparently are not founded on such calculations of marginal benefit, leaving one unsure whether—in the few cases where the Department has its way—its efforts have been pushed too far or not far enough.

3) Where political decisions are operating, both legislation and the administrative preferences of different governmental units may exert separable influences on the final allocative outcome. When laws provide no basis for attaching marginal valuations to competing classes of benefits, the attitudes of different agencies take a dominant role. Little can be said in general about the results. A "selfish" local

[55] California Department of Water Resources, *San Joaquin Master Drain, San Joaquin Valley Drainage Investigation,* Bulletin No. 127 (1965), p. 25.

agency may push the solution in the direction that is economically correct; one sensitive to "public opinion" or some segment thereof may promote an inefficient solution.

4) A specific feature of the California Water Code which fails to advance the optimal allocation of water among joint and competing uses is the declaration ordering "higher" and "lower" uses. There is sense in such a declaration so far as it recognizes clear differences in the average values of water put to different uses and thereby deters actions or policies which systematically discriminate against or impede uses with higher values. The proper balancing of competing uses, however, requires attention to marginal values. A relatively high average value of a class of benefits can coexist with a zero marginal value, while for another the marginal value may equal the low but positive average.

5) When the benefits of a water resources development project are compared with its costs in external diseconomies or foregone alternative uses, California practice tends frequently to make inappropriate comparisons between the net opportunity cost of the project and its gross benefits or investment costs. The destruction of a migratory fishery with a present net value of $500,000 would generally be viewed as a trifling cost of the construction of a project yielding $100 million in present value of gross benefits. Yet if the present value of the project's other costs is $99.9 million this would be an incorrect allocative decision.

6) Private decision-making mechanisms, like those in the public sector, may work either well or badly in optimizing the distribution of benefits at the margin. The pricing of water and power as joint products in Northern California rests upon small numbers of decision-making units, and for that reason (among others) may not produce an optimal economic result. By contrast, the sale of San Joaquin water to the duck clubs for waterfowl conservations shows no structural traits ruling out an optimal allocation, although such a result has certainly not been demonstrated.

PART THREE: PERFORMANCE

15

THE LEVEL OF DEVELOPMENT

Evaluations of an industry's economic performance typically center upon the various facets of economic efficiency and the extent to which the industry achieves it. Sometimes, an industry's contribution to other major goals of the economy, such as progressiveness and equity, can be appraised. However, even the most thorough industry investigations stumble in dealing with these goals for lack both of reliable normative standards and of solid factual evidence. Our treatment of the performance of the Northern California water industry will be limited almost entirely to appraisals of its efficiency. In part, this limitation is placed on the scope of our discussion because of inadequacies of data bearing on other aspects of performance. In larger part, it is because efficiency in this industry has many intricately interrelated dimensions, and its evaluation poses difficult problems both at the conceptual level and at the level of empirical measurement.

The Analysis of Performance: Concepts and Methods

The numerous dimensions of efficiency in the Northern California water industry may be discussed under three broad headings: the level of development, the sequence of development, and the rationality of development of water resources. We first consider in turn the meaning of these interrelated dimensions of economic performance.

The level of development: two definitions

Two definitions of the level of development of water resources complement each other conveniently and facilitate the over-all appraisal of a crucial aspect of efficiency in a water industry.

According to the first definition, water development is the commitment of non-water resources to make water available for added or alternative uses, or (as in the case of flood control) to reduce economic losses inflicted by uncontrolled water. A general characteristic of water development so defined is that most of the non-water resources committed are durable goods or capital facilities, although some labor, land, and nondurable goods or materials are typically committed along with capital facilities. For purposes of brevity (and at the expense of a slight imprecision in nomenclature), we will refer to water development thus defined as water-facilities development. The corresponding level of development is the level of water-facilities development, and it is measured by the quantity or value of non-water resources committed to making water available for use (or to controlling floods).[1] It is this definition of the level of water development which most people probably have in mind when they think of water development.

According to the second definition, water development is the application of water to productive or want-satisfying uses. These include, in the case of rivers, not only consumptive uses but also in-stream uses for such things as power generation, navigation, and recreation. We will refer to water development thus defined as water-usage development (for want of a prettier term). Development in this sense is the use of water, regardless of the potentially variable extent to which use depends on the development of facilities. The corresponding level of development is the level of water-usage development. It is defined jointly by the proportion of available water which is applied to productive or want-satisfying uses, and by the relationship of total supply of available water to the aggregate of demands which are expressed for its use (such demands being based on its marginal productivity or marginal want-satisfying virtues).[2] The level of water-usage development can vary only between zero and the very definite ceiling of "full water-usage development." This ceiling is reached when all available water is applied to productive and want-satisfying use and, further, when the total demands for it are large enough relative to its supply that, if properly allocated, its net marginal value in every use exceeds zero. As full water-usage development is attained, water becomes a scarce good, and has a positive net economic value and shadow price. The ceiling of full water-usage development cannot be exceeded (we cannot put more than all available water to uses in which it has positive net marginal values), and in this particular sense "it is impossible to overdevelop scarce water" (to have an excessive level of usage of scarce water). Raising the level of water-facilities development only reallocates scarce water; its level of usage cannot be increased. If the level of full water-usage development of water has not been reached, water is a free good (without necessarily a positive net marginal value in any use). In the range of levels of water usage within which it is a free good, it can be overdeveloped or underdeveloped in the sense that the level of water usage may be excessive or deficient in the light of its potential productivity in use.[3]

[1] The quantity of non-water resources committed to making water available for use is determined primarily by the types and sizes of the tasks undertaken, but it also is influenced by the degree of technical efficiency attained in accomplishing these tasks. In the following discussion of changes in the level of water-facilities development, we will disregard possible changes in technical efficiency, and assume that technical efficiency remains at a constant level as the level of water-facilities development is varied.

[2] Our emphasis on this concept runs counter to the method of analysis normally employed in research on water problems in humid areas; the justification for our procedure was discussed in Chapter 1.

[3] It is conceivable that the level of water-usage development of free water could be excessive in some uses while deficient in others. The net excess or deficiency could then be determined only by finding if the total quantity being applied to use, if properly allocated among different uses, would have a net marginal value which differed from zero.

The levels of both water-facilities and water-usage development can be measured and evaluated either with reference to the total water supply of an area or region, or with respect to individual sources of water, such as rivers or ground-water basins. Our aim is an appraisal of these levels of development for the entire Northern California area. However, since water has reached full water-usage development in some water sources and not in others, we must center analysis initially on the levels of development of particular water sources, or on groups of water sources with similar scarcity or freedom conditions. Then attempts can be made to make area-wide evaluations of the levels of water development by appraising the combination of situations of the numerous individual sources.

With respect to any water source, the level of water-facilities development and the level of water-usage development are closely, but not uniquely, related over a certain range of water-usage development—namely, in the range over which water remains a free good. In this range, increases in the level of water-facilities development are generally accompanied by increases in the level of water-usage development. Once full water usage is attained for the source, however, and water is scarce, further increases in the level of water-facilities development cannot induce increases in the level of water usage, but can only reallocate water among uses. The determination of the level of water-facilities development thus requires separate appraisal, depending upon whether the water it makes available for added or alternative use is free or scarce.

Where the level of water-facilities development is determined for free water, it may be either excessive or deficient, and the level of water-usage development may also be excessive or deficient—the two sorts of excesses and deficiencies tending to go hand in hand. Determination of the gross level of facilities development imposes no necessary constraints on the allocation of water. But it may incorporate a specific allocation of the water developed among potential uses or users which is not ideal, which lowers the total and marginal values of water obtained, and which thus produces all the signs of an excess development (in the form, for example, of deficient rates of return on investment), when the same level of development with ideal allocation of developed water would not be excessive. (Similarly, poor allocation may result in depressed yields on investment which conceal a deficient level of development.) Thus, interpretations of data purporting to measure the appropriateness of attained levels of water-facilities development of sources in which water is free should make allowances for deficiencies in associated allocations of developed water which are not intrinsic and inseparable features of the developmental levels being examined.

Where the level of water-facilities development is determined for scarce water, it may again be either excessive or deficient, but its excess or deficiency is not reflected in the level of water-usage development, which is constant at the full-development level. The level of facilities development, however, will almost certainly (and especially when in-stream uses requiring no facilities are considered) influence the pattern of allocation of scarce water. One can imagine a situation of optimal water-facilities development which also embodies optimal allocation of water among uses. One can also imagine a situation of excessive water-facilities development in which the facilities serving all uses have been increased proportionally, and the optimality of the water allocation remains unchanged. The fact is, however, that shifts in the level of facilities development which do not disturb the pattern of allocation between uses—for good or ill—are most unlikely. Moreover, misallocation among uses tends to coincide with either too high or too low a general level of facilities development, although it may also occur along with a general level of facilities development which appears appropriate but nevertheless embodies a poor composition of types of facilities.

The preceding argument makes several things clear. First, in appraising a level of water-facilities development, it is essential at the outset to determine whether the water it is making available for added or alternative use is a free good or a scarce good in its source. Second, if the facilities development draws on free water, evaluations of the level of facilities development (and its composition) are essentially also evaluations of the level of water-usage development (and its composition), and we are really talking about the level of water development in a simple and unambiguous sense. Third, if the facilities development draws on scarce water, the evaluation of the level of facilities development becomes essentially an evaluation of the rationality of water allocation, with a connected evaluation of whether or not the proper amount of non-water resources has been devoted to making water available for added or alternative uses. At this point, appraisals of the composition of facilities becomes inseparable from appraisals of the level of water-facilities development, and equal in importance.

What aspects of performance will be emphasized as we discuss the level of development of water resources? Initially, we will inquire into how many and which water sources in Northern California are (1) below the level of full water-usage development, thus offering free water, and (2) at the level of full water-usage development, thus offering scarce water. In the case of sources of free water, we will ask two questions about the level of water-facilities development: whether it implements a deficient, correct, or excessive usage of free water; and whether the commitment of non-water resources is deficient, correct, or excessive, proper account being taken of the composition of the existing facilities development. In looking at sources of scarce water, we will evaluate the level of water-facilities development from the standpoint of its impact on the allocation of water among uses, users, sites, and times of use. We will then judge the allocational results in terms of certain accepted norms, and also ask whether, in the light of allocational impacts, the amount of non-water resources committed to water development has been deficient, correct, or excessive. Such evaluations will refer generally to individual sources or subregions; any over-all evaluation of the level of development of water resources in Northern California must rest on some sort of appraisal of the aggregate of individual excesses and deficiencies in various parts of the area.

The sequence of development

Some aspects of performance of the water industry are illuminated by the sequence or historical time pattern of development. The sequence of development involves the timing of particular accretions of development and the order in time in which mutually compatible accretions were undertaken. A theoretically ideal time pattern of water resource development can be defined for any area like Northern California with reference to the following criteria: developing contemporary supplies of water which will fulfill contemporary demands; providing for growing demands neither wastefully far in advance nor too late; adjusting water allocation in response to changing geographical and other patterns of demand; and crossing new developmental and allocative frontiers at the economically most desirable times. In discussing the actual sequence of development, these four criteria will be taken into account as we inquire generally into the extent to which the timing of water development in Northern California has conformed to, or diverged from, what would seem in retrospect to have been the best attainable time pattern.

The rationality of development

Our primary emphasis in appraising the rationality of development will be on evaluating the present allocation of water among uses, users, and sites and times of use in Northern California and within its various regions and localities. Applying theoretical criteria of optimal allocation developed in Chapter 8, we will attempt to appraise the extent of divergence from the optimum of allocation in the following respects: of surface water between natural in-stream use and competitive consumptive uses; of consumptively used water drawn from various local sources among different uses, users, and sites of use; of streamflows between winter and summer use through the operation of storage reservoirs; of water among regions and subregions through long-distance transportation of water; and of investments of non-water resources in water development among different places and developmental functions. Although the prior discussion of level of development will have referred to the allocative impacts of development, and that of the sequence of development necessarily to the historical development of current allocational patterns, our discussion of the rationality of development will center on the contemporary pattern of development itself, and evaluate it in as many of its aspects as available information permits.

Rationality of development, however, comprehends two types of phenomena in addition to the allocation of water among uses and of non-water resources among different water development opportunities. The first of these is the degree of technical efficiency attained in the development of water, primarily as this is affected by the scales or capacities of individual works or plant facilities such as reservoirs and canals or other aqueducts, and by the geographical relationships of the routes of individual canals or other aqueducts—the attained degree of efficiency being measured against the best attainable with the existing geography of water-using lands and water sources and existing hydrologic and topographic conditions.[4] The second involves the choice by agencies engaged in investing in water resource development among mutually exclusive alternative projects for performing about the

[4] Technical efficiency as affected by the rate of utilization of facilities, or the degree of excess capacity in facilities, may also be considered.

same functions, where the alternatives can be ranked in order of economic desirability. Although information on this aspect of performance is hard to come by, we should at least recognize the problem of whether or not investing agencies generally have tended to make socially optimal choices among mutually exclusive projects. In sum, our discussion of rationality of development will fall into two main parts which are analytically separable—a discussion of allocation of water, and one of technical efficiency in developing water—and be concluded with some comments on choices among mutually exclusive alternative water projects.

The concepts of the level, sequence, and rationality of development obviously supply closely interrelated criteria for the appraisal of performance. Thus, for example, changing the level of water-facilities development usually affects the rationality of allocation of water among alternative types of use; and the sequence of development refers essentially to the historical record of changes in the level of development, in the allocation of water among uses, and in the related allocation of non-water resources among alternative types of water development.

Grouping our discussion of performance under the three general headings of level, sequence, and rationality of development of water resources is thus no more than an expository device for dealing with a very complex maze of historical phenomena and their past and present consequences for economic efficiency. The device will enable us to view a single common group of such phenomena from three primary standpoints, or with primary emphasis on three general sorts of economic consequences they have had, each evaluated in terms of certain norms of performance. It will not enable us, however, to consider the current level of development of water resources in analytical isolation from current rationality of development, or to consider either of these in isolation from the timing of development and of changes in rationality of allocation.

Measuring the level of development

This classification of aspects of allocative performance leads directly to some propositions about the measurement of the level of development. A fundamental theoretical measure of the level of development of the use of scarce resources in any line of activity is the relation between their marginal value (either value of their marginal product or their marginal utility) and their long-run marginal cost. Equality between these two magnitudes in all lines of activity (or, possibly, a constant ratio in all lines) guarantees that no incremental transfer of resources from one use to another could increase the total value of output. For the very same reasons that we distinguish between the level of water-facilities and of water-usage development, however, we must expect that reported money costs in the industry will frequently not serve as an adequate basis for this traditional welfare test. Let us consider the theoretical problem at issue.

In interpreting a relation between long-run marginal cost and long-run marginal value as a test of resource allocation, one normally would assume that all of the inputs of the process in question—water, physical facilities, labor services, and others—were combined in optimal proportions. We would then conclude that the amount of all resources taken together, dedicated to a particular use, was either correct or incorrect. The possibility would be ruled out that an apparently correct marginal adjustment cloaked an excessive input of water combined with a deficient input of physical facilities. But if we drop this assumption of optimal input combination, the problem of appraising the level of development becomes much more complicated, because we must then test the appropriateness of the allocation of each input separately. Unfortunately, this is essentially what must be done in evaluating the performance of the water industry: the levels of water-facilities development and of water-usage development must be studied separately.

The whole body of evidence developed in Part Two has shown a steady growth over time of alternative uses for water which has tended to create water scarcities, and thus positive shadow prices for water (as these were defined in Chapter 8), at most of the sources of water supply which are being intensively used in Northern California. The evidence also showed, however, the near absence of any actual market prices for water or for water rights at the source; and it failed to reveal any substitute allocative mechanisms possessing more than rudimentary powers to equalize the net marginal value of water in different uses.[5] Agencies which have access to water normally pay either no unit price at all for it, or one somehow related to the cost of non-water inputs employed by a wholesale agency for its storage and transportation. Users thus have a virtual incentive to employ water to the point where its net marginal value is zero, unless prevented by rationing constraints or other limitations on its physical availability.

In those situations where the water supplied or used by an agency is scarce—and thus has a positive shadow price and an opportunity cost—any test of the relation of long-run marginal value to long-run marginal cost which uses a money measure of costs necessarily understates the true long-run marginal cost. The equality of marginal costs in money terms to marginal value for a water agency would actually indicate an excessive allocation of water to the use in question, an excessive level of water-facilities development, or both. Because of the pervasive presence of this problem of inference from money costs, we must consider what conclusions can be established concerning the level and rationality of development in particular submarkets—rivers, river segments, ground-water basins, and the like—on the basis of such cost information and of knowledge of the availability of water. We distinguish two cases:

1) Water sources in which water is not scarce—At times when, and places where, all uses of water can be satisfied to the point of zero net marginal value of water without exhausting the source of supply, the following conclusions apply to appraising the level of development of a water source: (*a*) The net marginal value of water should be zero in all uses, and misallocation of water can occur (independent of misallocation of non-water inputs) only from insufficient or excessive use of water for some purpose or purposes. (*b*) If water is correctly allocated to each use and user, so that its net marginal value everywhere equals zero, then the marginal value of delivered water in each water-using activity will equal its long-run marginal cost, where marginal cost is made up entirely of the costs of all

[5] A similar but less pronounced problem arises because of capital-market imperfections and tax legislation, which create sharp differences in the supply price of capital to different agencies that are unrelated to opportunity cost.

non-water inputs. If such a marginal cost exceeds marginal value in any use, the levels of water-facilities and water-usage development are excessive, and if marginal value exceeds marginal cost in any use, the two levels of development are deficient, unless the excess or deficiency results from poor allocation of developed water among actual and potential users. (*c*) The total amount of water available should not be exhausted by all competing uses. No primary question arises about the allocation of water inputs among competing uses, but the level of water-usage development can be either deficient or excessive for any or all of the uses supplied by the source.

2) Water sources in which water is scarce—At times when, and places where, not all competing uses of water can be satisfied to the point of zero net marginal value of water by the available supply, the following conclusions apply to appraising the level of development of a water source: (*a*) The net marginal value of water should be the same in all actual competing uses, and this common level of the net marginal value can be thought of as an ideal price. Any excessive use of water by one agency corresponds to deficient use by some other agency or agencies. (*b*) Comparisons of the level of development by individual water-using agencies in terms of long-run marginal value of delivered water and marginal cost should include in long-run marginal cost the prevailing ideal price or opportunity cost of water. If it is not included, we can generally establish an excessive level of water-facilities development by the agency (and misallocation of water) in those cases where marginal value falls short of or equals long-run marginal cost of the non-water inputs. However, excessive development of total facilities exploiting the same source can be inferred only if a reallocation of water among all competing actual and potential users from the source would not result in marginal values of delivered water in excess of the marginal costs of non-water inputs. When marginal value exceeds the marginal cost of non-water inputs for individual agencies, we can draw no definite conclusion about the level of water-facilities development. (*c*) All water available in the source should be devoted to one competing use or another; there is no problem of overdevelopment of water per se from the source as a whole, but there are problems of misallocation between economically competing uses, and of excessive or deficient use of non-water resources in development.

The prevalence of scarcity

These two cases present very different problems for organizing our appraisal of the performance of the water industry. Therefore, we need to make some rough preliminary judgment about the classes of water sources where scarcity is the prevailing rule. This can be done fairly readily from the evidence developed in Part Two.[6]

[6] Evidence of water scarcity based on the actions of local users and would-be users, of course, could give a deceptive impression about true scarcity in the sense of a positive ideal price prevailing. Such a case would arise where inefficient users of a river employ water far enough beyond the point where its net marginal value becomes zero that they could rationalize their operations and release enough water to satiate other users without emergence of a positive ideal price.

To keep the discussion manageable, we consider as water sources primarily the individual rivers in the Central Valley and the north coastal region, dividing the demands made upon their waters into summer and winter demands. We will also refer to ground-water basins in the Central Valley. The analysis will not be pressed to the detail of examining segments of rivers or to a more elaborate division among the seasons of the year.

At the present time, the large rivers of the north coastal region are little utilized except for recreation at any time of year. Even considering that the marginal productivity of water for stream fishery recreation may remain positive for very large quantities of water, nonetheless no other problems of scarcity emerge in this area. By the same token, it is clear that water becomes scarce in all of the Central Valley rivers during the summer months. There is abundant evidence that scarcity is felt on most of the individual streams. Furthermore, these rivers all have a common outlet through the Delta, where the pumping plants at the head of the Bureau of Reclamation's canals, plus the productivity of river water to repel saline ocean water from the Delta farmlands, guarantee a mutual scarcity affecting the whole supply of surface water in the Central Valley during the summer.

North of the American River, there is some chance that water during the winter months is scarce to a significant degree because in-stream use for navigation and (particularly) recreation creates some positive scarcity value.[7] Even if this winter scarcity value in the Sacramento Valley currently amounts to a small or negligible sum per acre-foot of water, its magnitude will undoubtedly grow rapidly in the near future. The San Luis project, under construction for joint state-federal operation, will create substantial new storage capacity to hold winter runoff from any streams debouching through the Delta for consumptive use in summer.[8] The proportional increase in the wintertime net demand for Sacramento Valley streamflow will be great. From the American River south through the San Joaquin Valley, nearly all river flows seem clearly scarce in the winter. Reservoir capacities on most streams can retain much of the winter and spring runoff for summer uses, and any winter runoff not so captured probably has some net marginal value through direct winter diversion to on-the-land uses, percolation to ground-water basins, or (for rivers north of the Tulare Lake Basin) in-stream uses for navigation or anadromous fisheries.[9]

Evaluating the performance to date in Sacramento Valley winter markets requires attention to the possibility of excessive use of the existing free water. In practice, close attention must be paid to one particular demand upon winter flows—

[7] Evidence of this scarcity value is found (given the burgeoning population of Northern and Southern California) in the ubiquitous heavy "fishing pressure" readily observed on all accessible streams in Northern California in the late spring, summer, and early fall seasons, and in an equally ubiquitous fishing pressure in the rest of the year on all streams flowing to the sea on which artificial interferences with stream channels have not decimated or eliminated the natural late fall, winter, and early spring runs of migratory salmon and steelhead trout.

[8] Water will be pumped from the Delta into the large off-stream San Luis Reservoir in the winter for release to various service areas in the summer. Potential service areas include the San Joaquin Valley, Santa Clara Valley, and Southern California.

[9] This judgment suggests a precision in classification that is difficult to support with evidence. It would be safer to distinguish between rivers south of and including the Mokelumne and north of but excluding the American, in the matter of scarcity of winter water, leaving the American and Cosumnes in an undesignated border category.

that for storage and subsequent transfer (including interbasin transfers) to uses in the summer season. Within summer markets throughout the Central Valley, however, water is a scarce commodity, and the efficiency with which it is used depends mainly upon the proper allocation among competing uses.[10]

It is useful to draw the implications of these findings for the major classes of agencies to be discussed below. Since projects implementing large-scale interseasonal and interbasin transfers of water usually draw upon a source in which water is a free good (or is provisionally viewed as one), appraisal of these projects will be concerned with excesses or deficiencies in the levels both of water usage and water facilities. Conceptually, at least, these present the simplest problem. For the many small-scale projects and agencies, the most prevalent situation is one in which water in the source exploited is scarce, but in which opportunity cost of water does not appear as a money cost of the user agencies. This warns that the relationship of marginal values to long-run marginal costs must be carefully interpreted if sound conclusions about the level of water-facilities development are to be reached.

One type of water source remains to be considered—the ground-water basin. Conjunctive use of surface and ground-water sources is so common in agriculture, the main consumptive user of water, that any tentative conclusions about the scarcity of surface supplies would have to be confirmed by a finding of scarcity of alternative ground-water supplies. In fact, they are generally confirmed.

The question of whether or not ground water is scarce actually turns on whether or not successive increments to its supply involve distinctly increasing marginal costs of pumping it to the surface. Like winter streamflows made available for summer use by storage reservoirs, ground water is only made available for use by incurring some costs of non-water productive factors. If, as the amount extracted per unit of time increases, the long-run marginal cost of pumping remains constant, it is in a sense a free good underground with an attached constant cost of delivery to the surface. If the supply of winter water made available for summer use were extensible at a constant marginal cost, it also would constitute a free source of supply which merely cost more to deliver than summer water. But if the extension of supply is made at a distinctly increasing marginal cost, the supply is, by definition, scarce and a crucial symptom of scarcity appears—inframarginal water supplies from the source, secured at lower costs than the going marginal cost, command a price in excess of non-water costs of supplying them, or have net opportunity costs to those who capture them. So far as the supply of winter water for summer use is generally extensible at increasing non-water marginal costs, it is scarce in the summer season for this, if for no other, reason. Most available evidence points to the fact that supplies of ground water are generally extensible at distinctly increasing marginal costs, and by this token they are generally scarce.

This scarcity is quite possible and evidently does exist, even in ground-water basins in which the water tables are holding at a constant average level over time, as a result of differential advantages among pumping locations, and especially as a result of seasonal declines of water tables during the course of each irrigation season. The fact that throughout the Central Valley there is a drawing down of

[10] The other influence on the efficiency of its use is the degree of technical efficiency attained in water storage and transport.

water tables in each summer season wherever agricultural users depend significantly on ground water for irrigation, tends to support the conclusion that ground-water supplies are scarce. A secular decline has not been observed in most areas north of the Merced River—that is, in the lower part of the San Joaquin River valley, the Delta, or the Sacramento River valley—and an historical decline in the water tables in the upper San Joaquin River valley and the Tulare Lake Basin may have been checked in large part by the importation of water by the Bureau of Reclamation. But these considerations do not suggest serious qualification of the observation that ground-water supplies are in a meaningful sense scarce in the main irrigation season in the Central Valley generally.

Marginal values, rates of return, and benefit-cost ratios

In addition to comparisons of marginal cost and marginal value, we have mentioned at various points other familiar forms of criteria for testing the appropriateness of the level of development. It is frequently easier, with available data, to test the correctness of the allocation of resources to a particular activity through these other types of measures—such as rates of return on investment and benefit-cost ratios—than through the direct comparison of long-run marginal values and marginal costs. Under some conditions, these expedient tests will provide evaluations of the level of development in a line of economic activity consistent with those based on comparisons of marginal values and marginal costs; under others, they will not. The substance of these conditions must be reviewed briefly, because of the frequency with which incorrectly stated conclusions are found.

In a market economy, rates of return on invested capital provide a common test for the correctness of resource allocation where input markets are sufficiently perfect to equate the money cost of an input to one firm with its opportunity cost in any other firm using the same type of input.[11] The average rate of return in an industry or line of economic activity will correctly indicate a relation between long-run marginal costs and marginal value if long-run marginal costs for the firms in the industry are constant. If they decline, then the equality of marginal costs and marginal value requires a rate of return below the applicable market interest rate; if they rise, a higher return (which may be captured by owners of some factor of production as a rent) is called for.

The fact that most water-supplying entities in Northern California are governmental units rather than business enterprises complicates, but does not preclude, the use of rate-of-return tests. One troublesome problem involves the accounting method that such entities use, generally "fund accounting," which fails to measure depreciation of physical facilities or count it as a current cost, and does not always distinguish clearly between capital and current expenditures. Since current costs, in the measurement of annual rates of return, must include depreciation but exclude

[11] For a general statement regarding the measurement of the current rate of return, see Joe S. Bain, ***Industrial Organization*** (1959), chap. 9. (This and other footnote references are cited in brief form when they are also included in the Bibliography.)

capital outlays, considerable manipulation of costs reported by public agencies is required in the calculation of rates of return. The other major difficulty arises because the public water agency in essential respects is generally a users' cooperative. There is thus an intrinsic vertical integration of the facilities acquired by the cooperative enterprise and the plants of its customer-members. Therefore, a calculation of the rate of return on a public agency's investment, independent of the investments of the member-customers in their own plants, would require (1) the measurement of any annual revenue in terms of the quantity of water supplied by the agency multiplied by net marginal value of the water as delivered to the members; (2) the deduction from this revenue total of depreciation and current costs other than interest incurred by the agency,[12] and (3) the determination of the ratio of the net revenue so calculated to the depreciated valuation of agency investment in facilities. But the public agency will show in its books as revenues only the payments it has received from members in return for water service (in the form of taxes and water charges). And the resulting implicit "transfer price" (which is total member payments divided by quantity of water delivered) may not be the same as the net marginal value of water delivered to the customer-members.

Instead of rates of return on capital investment, ratios of benefits to costs (including ratios of marginal benefits to marginal costs) can be employed with equivalent ease as criteria of whether a single investment, a project, a program, or an aggregation of projects is devoting the economically right amount of, or too many or too few, non-water resources to the development of water in a locality, region, or area. In Chapter 8, we defined such ratios and indicated how they should be used to determine the proper scale of an investment project (and thus by inference the proper quantity of resources committed to water development in a given sphere), to choose the best among several mutually exclusive investment opportunities, and so forth. Recalling the definitions of the present value of total benefits when the services of a project are priced at the marginal values (B) and when they are priced at their average values, including buyers' surpluses (B'), it may be noted that the condition that $B/C = 1$ is fulfilled when the average rate of return on investment equals the applicable interest rate, and that B/C respectively greater and less than unity signifies average rates of return on investment respectively greater and less than the interest rate. A ratio of B'/C for a project which is equal to or greater than unity tells us that building it to some scale is better than not building it at all, but does not indicate that its scale is correct (that is, that $\Delta B'/\Delta C = 1$). Similarly, a B'/C ratio which is less than unity can mean either that the development at any scale is undesirable, or only that the scale is excessive.

The use as investment and development criteria of benefit-cost ratios and first derivatives of total benefits (B') with respect to total costs, in lieu of rates of return on investment, does not really get rid of the two problems, mentioned above, that are encountered in ascertaining the relevant rates of return on investment by public agencies. When we calculate benefit-cost ratios instead of rates of return, we still face the problem of reconstructing the actual costs of agency operations when their books fail to show them. Also we face the problem of finding a net

[12] The costs incurred by the members on their own accounts having already been deducted in determining the net marginal value of water supplied to them by the agency.

marginal value (as well as the net average value) of water delivered if member payments to the agency per unit of water delivered do not accurately measure the marginal value. And the use of benefit-cost ratios instead of rates of return on investment does not really make any simpler the general task of assigning marginal or average values to services where no market prices exist to measure such values, or the comparable task of estimating opportunity costs of projects when there are no going market prices to serve as measures of such costs.

The Level of Water Development: Measurements and Conclusions

In spite of these complex restrictions on the interpretation of evidence, some conclusions can be drawn about the level of development in the Northern California water industry. Because water is a scarce good in most regions of the area, questions of the level of water-usage development tend to become secondary to questions of the level of water-facilities development and of water allocation. The evidence which follows immediately will focus upon this level of facilities development, but we will return later to the possibility of excessive water-usage development where water remains a free good.

Local public water agencies—behavior and level of development

To appraise the level of development in local public water agencies, we can draw upon two basic types of evidence. One is deductive inferences drawn from our examination of the conduct of agencies, extensions by logical reasoning which indicate that conduct patterns (if correctly observed) imply certain strengths or deficiencies in performance. The other type of evidence consists of objective measurements of the results of agency behavior—inductive measures of performance not dependent on the evidence relating to conduct.

Our investigation of the pricing objectives of agricultural water agencies, based on interviews and other types of direct observation, has suggested a quite general inclination to set financial receipts so as to cover financial outlays, with some tendency in good times to accumulate financial reserves against anticipated replacements or improvements. This operating rule holds in the context of accounting practices which treat bond or loan amortization, but not depreciation of capital assets, as a current cost. The pricing objectives of city water systems appear somewhat more diverse, sometimes focusing on covering current costs, sometimes seeking to accrue net revenues for transfer to the city's general fund. In both cases, accounting practices associated with fund accounting make it possible that a surplus of revenue over current financial obligations could easily coincide with a subnormal or even negative rate of return, were depreciation taken into account.

What do these patterns of pricing objectives imply for rates of return yielded by agency receipts on the depreciated value of the agencies' investments? The answer depends on the typical relation between bond or loan amortization and depreciation of the basic investments of water districts in plant and equipment. On the one hand, facilities such as dams and canals usually have very long physical lives. In many cases, even a depreciation period which takes the possibility of economic obsolescence into account might reasonably run beyond half a century. On the other hand, bond and loan amortization periods tend to be somewhat shorter. Irrigation districts contracting with the Bureau of Reclamation for the construction of distribution systems repay over a period of forty years after an initial ten-year development period, making a total of fifty years. However, agencies borrowing in the private capital market to finance dams and distribution facilities (with or without the assistance of power companies) usually plan to repay in a somewhat shorter period, with thirty or forty years being common. These repayment periods have changed little in past decades.

This pattern implies that older agencies, with their major indebtedness repaid, would show very low rates of return on depreciated investments. Indeed, returns after allowing for depreciation could easily be negative if an adjustment for price changes were made in the initial undepreciated value of the investments in question. Conversely, new agencies, or those with newly constructed major facilities, might show substantial rates of return resulting from a build-up of reserves to meet amortization requirements in excess of depreciation.

The century-long decline of private enterprises in the water industry suggests typically subnormal rates of return, past and present. The private firms have faced the twin hazards of vulnerable market positions and a hostile political climate. These have usually led to the transfer of the private facilities to a public district, whether or not preceded by actual bankruptcy of the enterprise in question. Those private enterprises which remain typically operate very old facilities, and if they earn a normal rate of return it is probably only after the deduction of depreciation allowances unadjusted for price changes.

Because of the legal nature of the public agencies or districts prevalent in the water industry, these behavioral inferences about probable rates of return earned by the agencies fall short of answering all the important questions. Sticking to the case of public agencies distributing irrigation water, what about the fact that they generally are parts of vertically integrated enterprises consisting of farms and the district plants which serve them? Could not the predicted low rates of return to the district (cooperative) plant reflect essentially an internal financial transfer sufficient to meet the financial obligations of the agency? Could the farmers themselves, and thus the whole vertically integrated bundle of resources, be earning significant positive profits?

Evidence, impressionistic or otherwise, on rates of return earned by farm enterprises within irrigation districts is even harder to gather than evidence on the districts themselves. In the 1930's, when large quantities of agricultural land reverted to local water districts for the nonpayment of taxes, as the districts were forced into default on their bonds, there was no question that the integrated bundles of resources were failing to earn a normal rate of return. During and since World War II, all such evidence of agricultural bankruptcy has disappeared, and the rapidly rising prices fetched by irrigated farm lands have suggested generally improved rates of return for the farm enterprises themselves. The same conclusion would follow from the rapidly rising price of shares of mutual water companies in those areas where they play an important role. But the judgment of agricultural experts suggests that many farmers and their capital in the area may still fail to earn a return equal to their respective costs inclusive of opportunity costs.[13]

The more optimistic picture is confirmed in some degree by studies made by the Bureau of Reclamation and other agencies of agricultural payment capacity for new water facilities. At least in the San Joaquin Valley, these studies have often shown that new irrigated farms at the margin of development could easily pay the full charges made for water distribution facilities without suffering subnormal rates of return.[14] However, the difficulty faced by the Bureau in promoting districts and selling water in a few regions—notably that of the Sacramento canals on the west side of the Sacramento Valley—indicates that in some regions both districts and farm enterprises may face prospective subnormal returns, at least at the margin of development. The same conclusion about the margin of development of new irrigated areas can be drawn from the problems of the few districts which have tried to develop new water storage facilities on their own, without the assistance of electric power revenues. Again, these bits of evidence do not prove that any agricultural water districts and their customer enterprises are jointly unprofitable under present conditions. But they certainly suggest that in some areas further development at the margin is unprofitable, and do not refute the possibility that the margin has already advanced too far.

This conclusion is strengthened when we recall that most irrigation districts utilize water having a scarcity value not included in recorded costs. Moreover, a deficient marginal rate of return on investment in the combined facilities of water districts and their customers is likely to be concealed by an average rate of profit (in the integrated enterprise combining water supply and farming) which includes the profits or rents gained by inframarginal investment on inframarginal farm lands. These considerations suggest that if marginal profit rates as measured do not appreciably exceed a reasonable interest rate, the level of water-facilities development is probably somewhat excessive.

We can also ask about behavioral evidence on the water storage projects constructed jointly by local districts and the Pacific Gas and Electric Company

[13] T. R. Hedges summarizes the pattern of returns earned by California farms in the late 1950's as follows: "Even the large highly commercialized farms in California are, for the most part, receiving unsatisfactory earnings compared with capital returns in alternative uses. The general situation is that smaller units fail to return the operator wages equal to those he might earn as unskilled labor, ignoring any profits to pay for his capital and management! At best, they return but a small margin over wage equivalent earnings. Larger farming operations can spread their fixed costs over a greater volume of production and obtain other economies that enable them to show positive returns, after allowing for the value of the operator's own labor at the going rate of farm wages. Most large farms, however, show profit percentages that compare unfavorably with alternative earnings on high grade securities." See California State Legislature, Assembly Water Committee, *Economic and Financial Policies for State Water Projects,* Vol. 26, No. 1 (1960), p. A-288.

[14] These impressions stem mainly from the Bureau of Reclamation's so-called *Factual Reports,* which are prepared before it contracts with a district for a supply of water (cited under "Government Documents" in the Bibliography). However, the Bureau's water distribution facilities are provided to the farmers at charges reduced by substantial subsidy elements. Whether integrated farm and water district enterprises could profitably pay an unsubsidized price for Bureau water is another question.

(PG&E). That which we have been able to organize reveals little about the margin of development for these projects, but it does permit a few inconclusive statements on the chances that this cooperative investment process either misses desirable projects or proceeds with some having deficient true benefit-cost ratios. The pervasive enthusiasm of local districts and county governments in the Central Valley and Sierra Nevada to take part in these projects rules out the possibility that financially feasible projects are being missed. No river has been overlooked except possibly in the north coastal region. The more difficult issue concerns the chances of excessive development.

One key fact is that PG&E finds the power yield of these projects sufficiently valuable to be willing to finance their capital costs. Since PG&E must justify these investments to the California State Public Utilities Commission as well as to its stockholders, the utility's commitments to finance them could hardly involve substantial losses. Furthermore, the projects convey other gross benefits to which revenues are not imputed in determining their financial feasibility—water transferred from the winter to the summer market for consumptive use by the local agencies, plus occasional recreational and flood control benefits.

Nevertheless, several other features of these projects suggest—rather convincingly, on balance—that they constitute excessive or premature investments. The exemption of local government securities from the federal personal income tax, and of the works themselves from local property taxes, suggests strongly that PG&E might be allocating its investment in generating plant too much toward these joint hydro projects as against facilities for steam generation. Does it also follow that these projects would prove both infeasible and undesirable without these biases affecting PG&E's participation? The argument requires several intermediate steps to reach that conclusion, but these steps can probably be negotiated. First, electric power has been in some sense the major output of all those projects constructed or seriously planned in the last decade. For them to have shown favorable benefit-cost relations after deleting biases tending to overvalue the power output of the projects (as compared to steam-generating facilities) would require either (1) a substantial excess of benefits over costs at the start or (2) discriminatory terms in the sharing of benefits whereby the utility was able to appropriate the benefits to itself through all-or-nothing offers. Neither condition seems likely from the historical record. The well-documented difficulties in designing financially feasible projects suggests that typically there is no great surplus of benefits over costs unless in the form of external economies—an unlikely possibility. The marginal productivities of water for the districts in question seem to be low, either because their existing supplies from other sources are relatively adequate, or because their soil qualities will not support high-productivity uses of irrigation water.[15] Assessment of the distribution of benefits between the utility and its water agency partners has proved difficult. The issue definitely arises in negotiations between them, especially in connection with the scale of the reservoir capacity and the scheduling of water

[15] Several types of evidence presented in Chapters 2 and 6 suggested that the average and marginal productivity of irrigation water in most parts of the Sacramento Valley area to be served by these projects lies below the corresponding magnitudes in average areas of the San Joaquin Valley.

releases over the year. The terms seem to vary considerably from one contract to another, with the projects often yielding only a small quantity of additional water for irrigation use. But the balance of forces still seems to suggest that the tax biases favoring investment by PG&E in joint-venture hydro facilities may be a critical element in committing excessive capital to this form of construction, whether or not they also result in too much water being transferred for use in the summer season.

Local public water agencies—statistical evidence on the level of development

Almost no published reports exist which contain properly calculated rates of return for agencies in the California water industry. Evidence dating before 1930 does document the unprofitability of public utility irrigation companies. During the period 1913-1926, 61 irrigation utilities reported to the California Railroad Commission an average annual net return of 0.38 per cent on the nominal value of their investment.[16] A study prepared by the state of California noted that the Commission permitted an 8 per cent return on the depreciated value of the irrigation utility's plant, valued at original cost, but "in practice public utility irrigation companies have seldom been able to obtain the maximum rate."[17]

Present water agencies in California must report their financial data to various units of the state and federal governments. These reports, however, do not come close to yielding data on the rate of return imputed to the local districts' investment. Because of the importance to our investigation of resource allocation within the water industry, we have carried out two sample investigations aimed at providing a limited answer to the questions raised above about the appropriateness of the level of development. The first of these seeks to construct figures for the rates of return earned on depreciated investments in recent years by a sample of irrigation districts, in the calculation of which revenues are counted as payments received by the agencies from their customers. The other goes directly to the more fundamental question of the relation of long-run marginal cost to the marginal value of water within selected districts, inquiring whether the imputed net average value product of the water consumed by the "marginal crop" is equal to its long-run marginal cost.

The measurement of rates of return on depreciated investment for irrigation districts in Northern California in recent years was undertaken for a random sample of those districts which in the period studied did not make appreciable urban water sales and did not produce and sell electric power. The sample included eighteen districts out of an eligible population of fifty-nine.[18] The basic rate of return sought for each district was an annual rate of return calculated for each

[16] U.S. Department of Agriculture, *Commercial Irrigation Companies,* by Wells A. Hutchins, Technical Bulletin No. 177 (1927).

[17] California State Department of Public Works, Division of Water Resources, *Cost of Irrigation Water in California,* by Harry F. Blaney and Martin R. Huberty, Bulletin No. 36 (1930), p. 21.

[18] The characteristics of the sample are described in greater detail in Chapter 6 in the subsection on water costs of irrigation districts.

district as the ratio of (1) a numerator representing annual district revenues (in the form of taxes plus water charges collected for water service) minus annual operating and general and administrative expenses (excluding interest payments on debt) and minus a depreciation charge on the district's capital assets to (2) a denominator representing a depreciated valuation of the district's investment in assets. (The resulting rate of return thus includes imputed interest returns on investment.) Such a rate was calculated for each district for each of the nine years from 1952 to 1960, and then a simple average of these nine annual rates was computed. It should be noted that revenues were measured by payment to the district by its member-customers (and not directly as the marginal value of water delivered to the customers) and that costs expressly do not include any opportunity cost or value of water other than payments to wholesalers. Depreciation charges were calculated on the basis of a series of rough estimates of the life spans of districts' facilities, the inflation of prices since the acquisition of these goods, and (in some cases) the dates of their original acquisition.[19] These estimates were adopted after weighing the relevant evidence that is available, but each nonetheless represents a rough guess stated in round numbers. The findings should be interpreted accordingly.

Because of the rough-and-ready nature of the procedures through which the findings were developed, we will present the annual average rates of return in Table 27 only as approximate ranges of numbers. The average rates of return on investment for the eighteen districts show a distinct modal tendency in the neighborhood of a zero return, with half the districts earning between minus 1 per cent and plus 1 per cent per annum on investment, and fourteen of the eighteen earning between minus 3 per cent and plus 3 per cent. Three districts show very high rates of return over the period in question. These high rates of return, however, result both from high taxes and water charges which were levied to pay off obligations to the Bureau of Reclamation for the construction of distribution systems, and from the fact that

TABLE 27
DISTRIBUTION OF AVERAGE ANNUAL RATES OF RETURN, EIGHTEEN IRRIGATION DISTRICTS, 1952–1960

Rate of return (per cent)	Number of districts
−3.1 to −5.0	1
−1.1 to −3.0	2
−1.0 to 1.0	9
1.1 to 3.0	3
3.1 to 5.0	0
5.1 to 10.0	0
Over 10.0	3

SOURCE: Calculated from data supplied by California Districts Securities Commission; California State Comptroller, *Annual Report of Financial Transactions Concerning Irrigation Districts of California for the Calendar Year 1952* and for calendar years *1953* through *1960* (1953 through 1961).

[19] The methods used are described in detail in Chapter 6, note 5. Table 16 presents other calculations making use of this same sample of districts.

the costs of the distribution systems except as paid off (which they were to only a minor extent) are not included in the reported valuation of district investment in capital assets. Apart from districts faced with special loan amortization requirements and having badly understated investment valuations, these findings suggest that irrigation districts in Northern California generally fail to earn normal rates of return on the depreciated values of their investments, and indeed are often engaged in capital consumption to a modest extent.

Do these findings tend to suggest an excessive level of water usage by such districts, accomplished either by an overallocation of scarce water to them (probably) or by excessive water usage from free sources (possibly), and a corresponding excessive level of water-facilities development by them for their own use? If the average revenues per acre-foot of water they receive in the form of payments from customers could be accepted as measures of the marginal values of water as delivered to the customers, the findings would indeed point in the direction indicated. They would, in fact, do so more strongly than the calculated rates of return per se indicate, because in no case is the opportunity cost or value of scarce water per se deducted in computing a rate of return. If such opportunity costs were deducted, rates which were either negative or barely positive would probably be more strongly the rule. Only if the marginal values of delivered water in use significantly exceed average revenues per unit of water received by the irrigation districts—as they might if water supplies available to customers are regularly rationed—might the conclusion of excessive water usage and water-facilities development be reversed; the evidence discussed in Chapter 10 fails to indicate the required incidence or prevalence of rationing.

This judgment of excessive water usage applies only to irrigation districts as a group, and not necessarily to the over-all level of development of the water sources on which they draw. So far as they depend on sources in which water is scarce, a definite misallocation of water is implicit in the judgment, but whether or not the total level of water-facilities development drawing on these sources is excessive depends on the non-water inputs or facilities requirements of undersupplied alternative uses or users. With proper allocation, either more or less or the same amount of total facilities might be devoted to optimal development of the sources. If the misallocation mainly involves shortening the supply of water available for in-stream uses like recreation and navigation, or the supply of winter water as opposed to summer water, the over-all level of facilities development on sources is very probably too great. If it involves shortening the supplies available to competing actual or potential irrigators drawing water from the source, the over-all level of facilities development on the sources may not be too great and could even be deficient. So far as they are drawing on sources in which water is free (free generally or free in the winter for transfer to the summer), both an excessive over-all level of water-facilities development and an excessive level of water usage for the source are probably implied. Considering that several allocative frontiers generally may be simultaneously involved, a net tendency toward an excessive over-all level of development of water facilities seems more likely than not to be implied.

To supplement the foregoing information on irrigation districts' rates of return on capital, we have investigated the possibility of estimating directly the relation of long-run marginal costs of supplying irrigation water to the net value of the marginal product of water delivered to users within irrigation districts. This is potentially a more meaningful test of the level of development than the rates of return on investment earned by public water agencies.

Marginal productivity functions are always difficult to derive empirically, and the best we have been able to do is to obtain a series of estimates of the net value of the average product of water for different crops and different soil qualities, derived on the assumption of a fixed land-water coefficient for each crop-land combination. The economically relevant range of a marginal productivity function is that lying below the average function. If it can be shown that water is put to uses such that its average product is less than its marginal cost, then the margin of use has been pushed too far. Conversely, no conclusions can be drawn about the significance of average productivity in excess of marginal cost at the margin of application unless the land-water coefficients are known to be fixed.

Data contained in reports of the Bureau of Reclamation provide a reasonably good measure of the net value of the average product of water applied to a projected pattern of crops in various Central Valley irrigation districts.[20] The net value of average product of water typically differs substantially among different crops grown within a district and even on a single farm. The growing of several different crops in a district or on a farm may result from acreage restrictions on preferred crops, so that one or more of them are grown (each to the allowed limit) along with unrestricted crops. Sometimes a rational crop mix contains crops of varying productivity because of economies in the staggered use of fixed facilities, including the supply of the farmer's own labor, or in gains from enrichment of the soil. At other times, crop patterns not explainable by these factors seem to reflect an absence of profit maximization. Whatever the cause, the typical district grows a range of crops differing widely in their apparent net values of average product per unit of water.[21]

However rational existing crop patterns and rates of water application may be, the reports of the Bureau of Reclamation which provide the basis for the following calculations forecast from, and reasonably well represent, current practice in the Central Valley. We have arranged the list of crops grown in each of twenty-four districts for which data were available (a nonrandom sample heavily weighted with actual purchasers of wholesale water supplies) in descending order of the reported net value of the average product of water. These were then plotted against the percentage of each district's land given over to crops of successively lower average product, as shown schematically in Figure 30, with the average-product figures expressed as ratios to an estimate of marginal (equals average) cost of water to the districts. This is a valid procedure if marginal costs are approximately constant as

[20] Almost all of the data used in the following calculations come from the *Factual Reports* described in note 14 above. For a discussion of the limitations of the data contained in these reports, see Appendix C.

[21] We concede that these empirical propositions are not fully consistent with the theoretical argument developed in Chapter 5 and Appendix A, suggesting that crop substitution provides a sensitive and potentially significant source of elasticity in the demand for irrigation water. In general, the bias injected into our present conclusions—if these theoretical conjectures about crop substitution are in fact correct—would be to overestimate the marginal productivity of water in certain ranges. The bias is thus in the same direction as that of substituting average for marginal values.

the size of a district is increased.[22] Consider the right-hand portion of the average productivity function in Figure 30. It suggests that the net value of average product of water for the crop with the lowest water productivity lies below long-run marginal cost. Since marginal productivity (at the intensive margin) is presumably no higher than average for this crop, the conclusion follows that under actual and foreseen cultivation processes water is being put to uses in which its marginal productivity lies below its marginal cost, representing either an inappropriate choice of crop or an excessive use of water at the extensive margin (that is, too much water irrigating too much land).

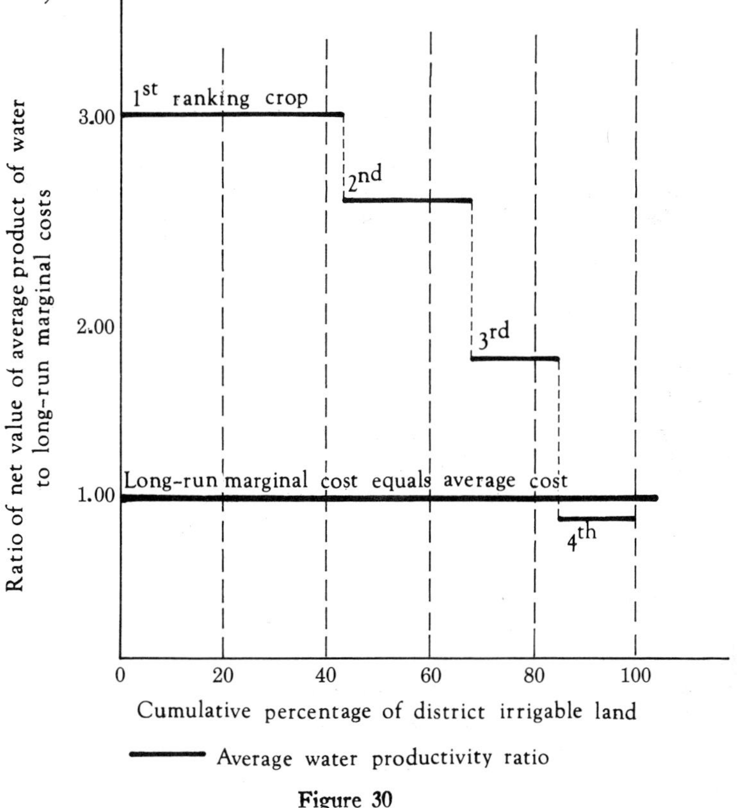

Figure 30

Rather than showing these distributions of the ratio of the net value of average product to average cost separately for twenty-four districts, we have summarized them in Table 28 by presenting the distribution of these relatives at the quintiles of the percentage distribution of the district's lands. Figure 30 should assist in giving an understanding of this presentation. We divided each district's land into quintiles, as shown along the horizontal axis of the diagram, and read off the ratios of

[22] This assumption largely agrees with evidence presented in Chapter 6 and Appendix B. The data, drawn from the same *Factual Reports* of the Bureau of Reclamation, include both average distribution costs to the districts and payments to the Bureau. Whether the latter component represents a correct measure of marginal social cost, as well as money cost to the district, depends on the appraisal of the Bureau's own facilities presented below.

TABLE 28
RELATION OF NET VALUE OF AVERAGE PRODUCT OF WATER TO MARGINAL COST IN TWENTY-FOUR SELECTED IRRIGATION AND WATER DISTRICTS

Range of ratio of average net productivity to marginal cost	Cumulative percentage of district acreage				
	20	40	60	80	100
Number of districts reporting ratios:					
Greater than 4.00	16	13	10	2	1
3.01 to 4.00	3	5	3	2	2
2.01 to 3.00	3	3	4	10	5
1.26 to 2.00	1	2	2	5	5
1.01 to 1.25	1	1	1	0	1
1.00 or less	0	0	4	5	10
Total	24	24	24	24	24

SOURCE: Computed primarily from data contained in U.S. Department of the Interior, Bureau of Reclamation, Region 2, *Factual Reports* for individual districts.

average water productivity to long-run marginal cost by districts at each quintile. Table 28 shows the distribution of these readings.

Of the twenty-four districts for which data could be obtained, ten were predicted to grow crops at the extensive margin (the 100 per cent quintile) where they had net values of average product of water below long-run marginal cost. In five of the ten cases, a fifth or more of the district's acreage is in crops of deficient productivity. For the other districts, because our evidence conveys no information on the intensive margin, we are unable to determine whether or not water-facilities development and the use of water has been carried far enough on the irrigated lands to which the productivity data refer, but there is nothing to indicate positively that this development in either sense has exceeded the optimal level. For these districts, there may have been a failure to reach the extensive margin by bringing adjacent unirrigated lands under irrigation, but we have no information on the existence or nonexistence of such lands or on their adaptability to growing profitable crops. These findings lend some support to the judgment formed previously, on the basis of district rates of return, that agricultural water agencies probably overinvest in facilities and receive an overallocation of water—at least for a substantial minority of twenty-four districts which are, or were, to become Bureau of Reclamation customers.

Like our earlier conclusions involving rates of return, these involving ratios of average value product to cost indicate nothing definite about the over-all level of water-facilities development for exploiting individual water sources. It is possible that this water could be differently allocated among more irrigators in such a way as to avert overdevelopment by a district, irrigator, or group of irrigators, with no decrease in the over-all quantity of water facilities employed, or with a desirable increase therein. Moreover, we cannot be certain whether for most of the numerous rivers feeding the Central Valley there is in general an overallocation of scarce surface water to irrigation or an overuse of free surface water in irrigation. This is because there is substantially no evidence on the relationships of the marginal cost of water for a body of self-supplying diverters of surface water, mutual water companies, and commercial water companies—or for potential users of surface water which have not gained access to its use. Such evidence might permit us to confirm or reject the hypothesis that the overallocation of water to irrigation and water districts, and a corresponding excess investment in their water facilities, is counterbalanced by an under-allocation to other actual or potential irrigators, so that the over-all level of development for irrigation is about right, or closer to right than the data examined suggest. If this were the case the major problem would be one of misallocation of water among users of irrigation water rather than overallocation of water to irrigation.

The evidence has other limitations as well. First, since we lack any measurements of the scarcity value of water in various surface sources, and even a precise indication of which sources do and do not have a water scarcity, such conclusions as we can draw are qualitative rather than quantitative. Second, we have substantially no statistical evidence on the propriety of the level of development of streams for power generation. Third, there is a similar lack of statistical evidence concerning the level of development of ground-water sources, though in this case behavioral evidence suggests an approximately appropriate level of development. Fourth, the levels of development achieved by suppliers of urban water have not been examined.

In the light of the preceding, we must certainly leave open the possibility that the general level of water-facilities development is excessive on some river sources, appropriate on others, and deficient on still others, so far as local public agencies, companies, and self-supplying users are primarily responsible for their development. And, also, there is the possibility that development for one use, such as irrigation, may be excessive while development for another use, such as power generation, is not.

The discussion of the level of local development of surface water resources for irrigation must be concluded by considering a rather interesting possibility concerning development. Users of irrigation water may very well generally be at or beyond the proper margin of development of water-facilities and of allocation of water to irrigation, *given the existing state of development of reservoir storage on many rivers and given corresponding constraints on the time pattern of availability of irrigation water.* But an increase in investment in reservoir storage on a number of rivers would, by reducing the constraints on the time pattern of water availability, increase the net value of the marginal product of irrigation water. And it might increase this value sufficiently that the added total and marginal costs of additional reservoir storage would be offset, or more than offset, by increases in the total and marginal values of water. Then, the present developmental situation would not be worsened and might be improved by further development in the form of investment in reservoir storage. The possibility is suggested by the fact that a majority of the principal rivers feeding the Central Valley are still some distance from reaching full physical development through the construction of dams to create storage reservoirs, as data presented in Table 3 have shown. It is a possibility worth careful investigation, though it may turn out to be a poor one if further increments to reservoir capacity would not support increased power generation, which has carried a good part of the cost of most major reservoir construction to date.

Large wholesale agencies—behavior and level of development

Further light may be cast on the level of development of water resources in Northern California by examining the performance of large-scale public agencies engaged in developing and wholesaling water in the area—the achieved performance of the main federal agencies, the Bureau of Reclamation and the Corps of Engineers, and the prospective performance of the California Department of Water Resources. For such agencies, we may again divide available evidence on the level of development into inferences from behavior and measurements of economic results.

Behavioral evidence on the construction activities of the Bureau of Reclamation and Corps of Engineers bears upon the volume of projects which they construct, on the scales of the particular projects, and on output combinations chosen. The patterns of conduct outlined in Chapter 11 raised several questions about the efficiency of the economic results. Whether or not these agencies choose the right project among exclusive alternatives, and whether or not they build it at the right time, are questions relating to the sequence and the rationality of development dealt with in later chapters. Here we are concerned only with the resulting level of development—whether whole projects, or their marginal units of capacity, represent an excessive use of resources.

Although the use of benefit-cost ratios provides a basic guard against gross economic error in the projects built by the major federal agencies, many defects in methods of calculation tending toward an overestimate of the ratios have persisted, at least until recently. The computations of benefit-cost ratios have now reached a point where the methods of the federal agencies would be economically appropriate under some assumptions, although economists differ sharply on whether these or alternative assumptions are more appropriate in planning government investments in water resource projects.

Rather than enter into a general evaluation of federal benefit-cost practices, we shall confine our discussion to a few remarks on the most significant features of actual practice, followed by extensive calculations of the benefit-cost relations of two major projects. Devoting attention to practice rather than theory seems fully warranted because of the divergence between the two uncovered in Chapter 11. Some federal projects have been constructed in California without any serious benefit-cost ratios being calculated prior to the decisions to undertake the projects. Major changes have been made in the scales of proposed facilities without any recomputed benefit-cost relations being made public. Single ratios have often been presented for bundles of clearly separable facilities. Benefits have apparently been grossly overstated in some cases, either directly or by measuring them in terms of inappropriate high-cost alternative sources of benefits. Indirect costs have been ignored, particularly lost recreational benefits from in-stream fisheries and assorted costs or losses stemming from induced or augmented water pollution or drainage problems. The California Department of Water Resources, in undertaking the Feather River Project has committed a comparable range of analytical and related sins in its evaluations.

Chapters 8 and 11 also suggested that many questionable practices remain in "official" federal procedures for calculating benefit-cost ratios. The two of greatest quantitative significance, at least for projects that include a large component of irrigation benefits, are surely the treatment of secondary benefits and the valuation of increased outputs of price-supported crops. The main type of secondary benefit counted by the Bureau of Reclamation—the additional profit accruing to processing and service industries—is widely felt to be illusory. If these increased profits actually represented rents imputed to fixed stocks of resources following the completion of a project, they would indeed measure virtual secondary or indirect benefits, but they might well be offset by reduced rents elsewhere. If they reflect normal returns earned by additional entrepreneurial capital drawn into these service and processing industries by the economic pull of the project, then they are linked with opportunity costs as large as the returns, and cannot be counted as a net addition to economic welfare at the national level. Most economists feel this is the case with such secondary benefits, except in conditions of general unemployment when the market prices of not just equity capital, but also all other factors of production, overstate their social opportunity cost. Projects constructed or authorized for construction in Northern California by the federal agencies in the past two decades have not depended on secondary benefits to bring their reported total benefit-cost ratios above 1.0, but some have just barely gone over the mark on the basis of ostensible direct benefits.

The other major questionable practice is counting the market value of any increased output of price-supported crops as a gross contribution to the national product. Customary practice in calculating benefit-cost ratios treats their excess of market price over all other input costs as a net benefit from the water project, just as with any other crop. We shall argue below, in examining the Central Valley Project, that these benefits should be substantially adjusted downward.

This review of the behavioral evidence on the level of development achieved by federal agencies has so far considered the issue of whether the right number of projects has been undertaken. A separate issue concerns the scale to which individual projects are constructed. The pure logic of using benefit-cost ratios as criteria for public investments calls for enlarging each separable feature or dimension of a project to the point where marginal benefits become just equal to marginal costs. In principle, this rule is now ostensibly followed in determining the size of projects for construction by the federal agencies, with marginal benefit and cost functions established for each separable feature. However, the behavioral evidence suggests that the Bureau of Reclamation and Corps of Engineers often have taken as given some output level desired by a group of beneficiaries, such as those in a territory to be served with irrigation water, and designed the most efficient project to produce that output. There is no reason to expect that expressions of public interest in the scale of project outputs reflect the shape of the marginal benefits function in any way. The direction of the bias in the typical case is not fully predictable. The prevalence of a concern with "full physical development" also leads to doubts about the proper sizing of projects.[23]

[23] Irving K. Fox and Orris C. Herfindahl, "Attainment of Efficiency in Satisfying Demands for Water Resources," *American Economic Review,* LIV (May 1964), 201–02. The authors cite Luna B. Leopold and Thomas Maddock, Jr., *The Flood Control Controversy* (1954), with regard to past policies of the Corps.

Retrospective Appraisal of the Level of Development in the Central Valley Project

As in the case of local public water agencies, we place our main emphasis in appraising the levels of development achieved or planned by the large-scale federal and state agencies on statistical measurements of results. Making inferences about performance from observable behavior suffers intrinsic limitations which stem from potential differences between what people do and what they say they do. On the other hand, the raw data needed to appraise the level of development can be gathered and processed only with difficulty. We have therefore confined our intensive efforts in statistical appraisal of levels of development achieved by the large-scale agencies to two main endeavors: (1) a full retrospective benefit-cost analysis of the so-called basic features of the Central Valley Project of the Bureau of Reclamation; and (2) a briefer prospective benefit-cost analysis of the first main undertaking of the state of California under its omnibus California Water Plan—the so-called Feather River Project.

In this section, we consider the basic features of the Central Valley Project (CVP). In the symbols used in Chapter 8, we shall be estimating the relation of total benefits including elements of surplus to total costs (B'/C) for a group of interrelated projects and also for the separable pieces. Much more briefly, we will consider the relation of the project's commercial revenues to its total costs (R/C). The features under consideration are shown in Figure 31, along with other constructed and currently proposed features of the Project. The facilities which we shall evaluate include Shasta and Keswick dams and reservoirs on the Sacramento River, two canals diverting water from the Sacramento-San Joaquin Delta for export to the south and west (the Delta-Mendota and Contra Costa canals), Friant Dam on the San Joaquin River, and the north-bound Madera and south-bound Friant-Kern canals. In the late 1930's, the Bureau of Reclamation arranged to buy a portion of the water rights to the San Joaquin River and compensate other San Joaquin users by imports from the Delta, permitting it to impound and divert nearly the whole flow of the San Joaquin River. Shasta Dam and power plant provide respectively the increased supply of water for diversion in the Delta and the electric power needed to pump it to the heads of the Delta-Mendota and Contra Costa canals.

In Appendix C we describe the large amount of relatively routine calculation required to produce the desired estimates of benefits and costs. Agricultural benefits, the dominant category, were estimated on the basis of the increase in income from farm operations, minus associated increases in other costs, for areas receiving supplemental supplies of water from the project. The availability of estimates of "payment capacity" made by the Bureau allowed these irrigation benefits to be computed in a relatively elaborate manner. The effects of CVP water supplies on the cost and availability of ground water were taken into account. No allowance was made for secondary benefits of the conventional type, since no such national benefits could be discerned in association with this Project.

The only controversial issue to arise in connection with establishing irrigation benefits of the Central Valley Project concerns the valuation of crops affected by

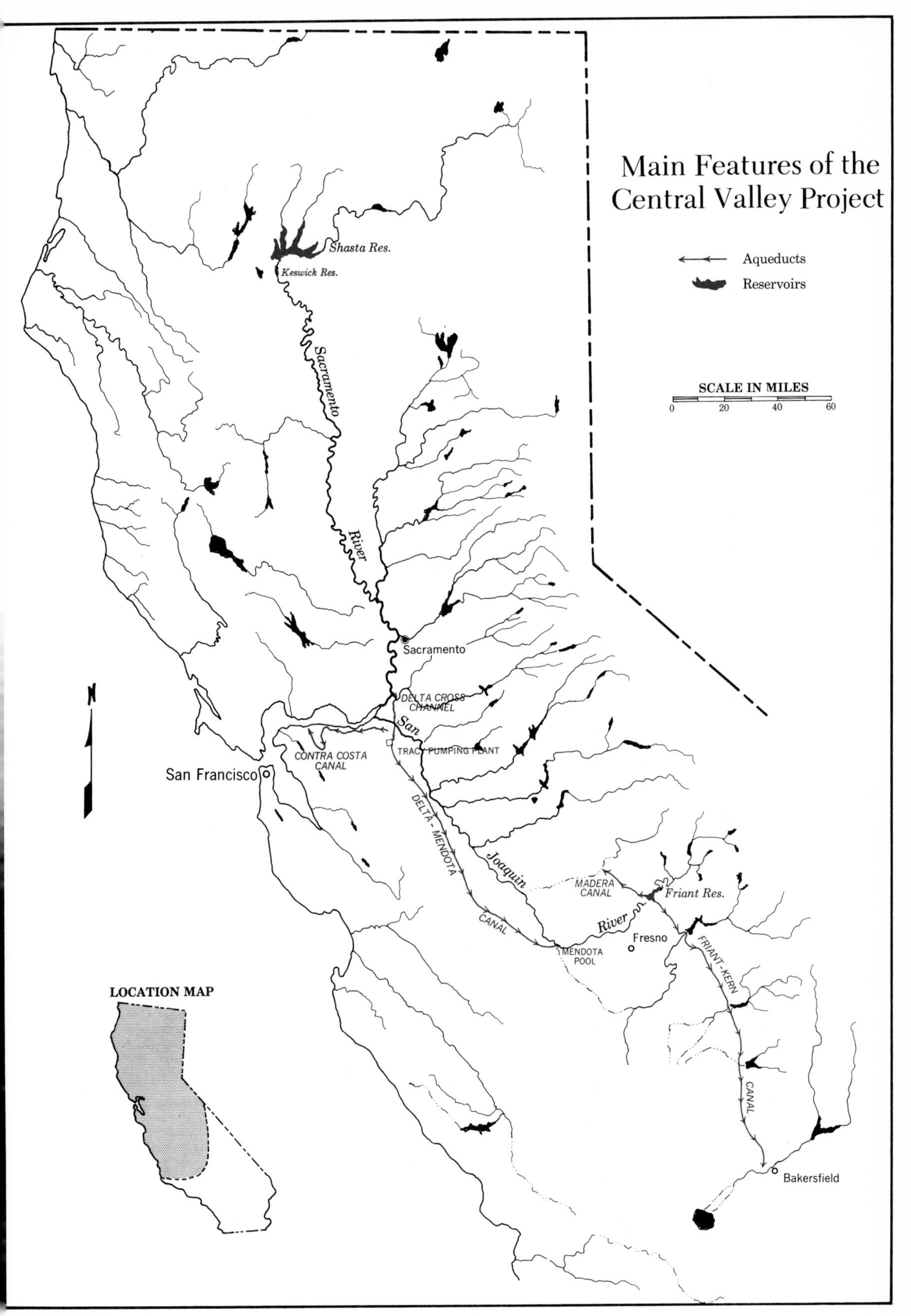
Main Features of the Central Valley Project
Aqueducts
Reservoirs
SCALE IN MILES
0
20
40
60
Shasta Res.
Keswick Res.
Sacramento
River
Sacramento
DELTA CROSS CHANNEL
San
TRACY PUMPING PLANT
CONTRA COSTA CANAL
San Francisco
DELTA - MENDOTA
CANAL
Joaquin
MADERA CANAL
Friant Res.
River
Fresno
MENDOTA POOL
FRIANT-KERN
CANAL
Bakersfield
LOCATION MAP

Figure 31

federal price-support programs. A substantial portion of CVP water is applied to cotton acreage, a minor part to sugar beets and field grains. When public policy holds the price of a crop above the marginal cost of supplying it (by restricting output), or when it puts the marginal value of the crop to consumers above that which the commercial supply would permit by purchasing and storing part of the crop, extra supplies of the crop produced in reclamation projects cannot be valued at the market price. Several alternative valuation procedures might be used, and we shall review these along with the reasons which led us to choose one for inclusion in our own calculations.

1) By gathering copious information about supply and demand conditions for a given crop in all parts of the country, including its production costs on lands affected by the reclamation project in question, one might estimate the competitive equilibrium price and the optimal output and its regional distribution in a free market agricultural economy. If, for example, it turned out that the Central Valley could produce cotton profitably at this shadow price, the cotton acreage and corresponding shadow price could be used to calculate irrigation benefits of the project. This procedure seems sound intellectually, and we investigated the possibility of using it. Despite the availability of a large part of the necessary data, especially on demand parameters,[24] information on costs and supplies turned out to be incomplete, and what purport to be estimates of the same parameter sometimes diverge widely.[25] The attempt had to be abandoned.

2) It could be argued that, when crops are subject to output-restriction schemes, or are either purchased and stored by the government or "dumped" overseas, any increases in their outputs associated with reclamation projects simply cause the wastage or suppression of equivalent outputs elsewhere. In that case, no benefits would be attributed to crops, and the total value (measured by alternative earnings) of factors of production lured into the growing of surplus crops by a new reclamation project should be charged as a cost against the project, for the country can be said to forgo the alternative outputs which these factors might have produced in order to gain something of no marginal value at all. This procedure is quite harsh, however; especially since, over the long run, crop "surpluses" associated with the federal farm programs eventually have either been put to some use within the country or disposed of on the world market.

3) One might calculate the agricultural benefits of an irrigation project on the assumption that its farm lands produce the most profitable mix of crops not subject to market interferences by the government or private cartel arrangements. Such an estimate would not only be difficult to develop empirically, but it also seems of little significance, since nobody proposes actually to forbid farmers to grow "sur-

[24] For example, George E. Brandow, *Interrelations Among Demands for Farm Products and Implications for Control of Market Supplies,* Bulletin No. 680, Pennsylvania Agricultural Experiment Station (1961).

[25] Among the more promising sources of information on agricultural supply relations are Marc Nerlove, *The Dynamics of Supply: Estimation of Farmers' Response to Price,* Johns Hopkins University Studies in Historical and Political Science, Series LXVI, No. 2 (1958); W. W. Cochrane, "Conceptualizing the Supply Relation in Agriculture," *Journal of Farm Economics,* XXXVII (December 1955), 1161–76; and W. A. Cromarty, "An Econometric Model for United States Agriculture," *Journal of the American Statistical Association,* LIV (September 1959), 556–74.

plus" crops on newly irrigated lands when they may do so under the terms of federal farm legislation.

4) Agricultural crops subject to government controls might be valued at their world prices, on the theory that present U.S. policy employs extensive disposal of surpluses on the world market, either through normal commercial channels or as foreign aid. Thus disposed, it seems fair to argue that the crops in question have a marginal value measured by the world price, reduced by the substantial administrative and storage costs which the federal government incurs for the farm programs. This procedure seems to have the advantages of being fairly simple empirically and of agreeing well with the alternatives actually available under present legislation. Thus, we have chosen to follow it.

When an output of a water project consists of a homogeneous addition to a large established output, as in the case of electric power, the distinction between benefits including and excluding surpluses (B' and B) disappears. Surplus elements are no longer traceable, as they are in the case of irrigation water. In the case of electric power (and also the small amount of municipal and industrial water supplied by the Central Valley Project), we have followed the customary procedure of valuing the power output of the project at its alternative cost. The generation of electricity in hydroelectric facilities is alternative to its production by steam plants,[26] and we have developed an estimate of the cost of producing the CVP's power output by this means.

Less elaborate procedures were employed to establish the value of the remaining classes of benefits. A very rough measure had to be used of benefits from the repulsion of saline intrusion to the Delta because of the lack of any precise measure of the physical association between the operation of the Bureau's works and the extent of the salinity problem. Similarly, recreation benefits and disbenefits could not be estimated formally on the basis of available data, and are covered by a simple assumption. Estimates of the Corps of Engineers for flood control and navigation benefits were used.

Calculating the costs of the Central Valley Project constituted largely a problem of organizing available data. All capital costs were converted to a comparable price level. The level of the different categories of operating costs could be estimated from their behavior over the early years of the Project's operation. The small number of observations did not permit any formal statistical analysis of these categories of variable costs, and a variety of simple functional relations, trends, and averages was employed to establish normal levels of operating costs.

In assembling these benefit and cost estimates, it was assumed that all the Central Valley Project works under analysis were built at the same time. Allowance was made, however, for the development of those classes of annual benefits deriving from Project outputs which would not be fully utilized at the start. Table 29 contains the main results of our analysis in the form of conventional benefit-cost ratios (B'/C, in the notation of Chapter 8) for the Project under various assumptions about interest rates, the life span of the project, agricultural prices, and the degree

[26] It has been pointed out that valuation of benefits by the cost of alternative sources of supply is not the same thing as an opportunity-cost approach and involves some pitfalls of its own. See Lawrence G. Hines, "The Hazards of Benefit-Cost Analysis as a Guide to Public Investment Policy," *Public Finance/Finances Publiques,* XVII (No. 2, 1962), 105.

of integration of CVP's various facilities, with present values calculated as of 1950.

The first item of the table shows the benefit-cost ratio of the Project for interest rates of from 3 through 6 per cent. As with many projects with such great capital requirements, the rate of interest makes a substantial difference. At 3 per cent the ratio is distinctly above unity over a fifty-year period. At 4 per cent it pales drastically, unless a longer pay-out period is used. At the rates of 5 to 6 per cent, the range found to be appropriate in our preceding discussion, it reflects an uneconomic use of resources.

Taking into account the fact that much of CVP's irrigation water nurtures crops in redundant supply at the present price support levels proves fatal to the Project's feasibility even at very low interest rates (item 2 of Table 29). Since this adjustment should in principle be made in evaluating reclamation projects, and since a discount rate of 5 to 6 per cent and a life span of fifty to a hundred years seem most appropriate, we can say that our best estimate of the ratio of total benefits (including elements of surplus) to total costs of the Project lies between 0.47 and 0.57.

TABLE 29
BENEFIT-COST RATIOS FOR THE CENTRAL VALLEY PROJECT AND SEPARABLE FEATURES

Item	Time period	Interest rate			
		3%	4%	5%	6%
1. "Basic" CVP features; without adjustment for surplus crops	50 years	1.21	1.03	0.89	0.77
	100 years	1.45	1.16	0.96	0.81
2. "Basic" CVP features; using adjusted world prices for price-supported crops	50 years	0.72	0.61	0.53	0.47
	100 years	0.85	0.69	0.57	0.49
3. Shasta Dam; including maximum net benefits attainable along Sacramento channel, but excluding all works south of the Delta	50 years	1.16	1.00	0.86	0.76
	100 years	1.38	1.11	0.93	0.80
4. Delta-Mendota and Contra Costa canals and Friant Division; without Shasta but including allowance for opportunity cost of water use foregone in the Delta	50 years	1.22	1.05	0.91	0.79
	100 years	1.47	1.18	0.99	0.84

SOURCE: See text.

The Central Valley Project would also prove definitely unattractive as a com mercial venture. Taking the figures for commercial revenues developed in Appendix C, Tables C-3 and C-4, plus an allowance for payments by the Sacramento channel users, the present value of commercial revenues discounted at 6 per cent over fifty years would be about $200 million, implying a revenue-cost ratio of 0.27 and a present value of minus $550 million. This dismal showing reflects the pricing policies actually chosen by the Bureau for water and power, and could be improved somewhat by profit-maximizing charges for these outputs.[27]

We have been unable to derive a direct measure of the marginal benefit-cost

[27] We may recall the demonstration in Chapter 6 that the Bureau's prices for irrigation water fail to cover the fixed charges directly allocable to them.

ratio for the Central Valley Project ($\triangle B'/\triangle C$)—the value of which is crucial in evaluating the scale of the project.[28] However, we may infer from the very low revenue-cost ratio (R/C) the probability that the marginal benefit-cost ratio for the Project is below unity, and that scale is thus excessive, according to the following reasoning: In the presence of economies of large scale (decreasing unit costs with increasing scale—assumed for the CVP), the ratio B/C[29] will in the realm of discounted-present-value calculations obviously be less than $\triangle B'/\triangle C$ by an amount depending on the steepness of decline of unit costs with increasing scale, for precisely the same reason that in the realm of statical analysis MV/AC (the ratio of marginal value to average cost) will be less than MV/MC (the ratio of marginal value to marginal cost). If B/C is far below unity, $\triangle B'/\triangle C$ will also be less than unity unless unit costs decline very steeply with increasing scale (a circumstance not evident in the case of the Central Valley Project). Now, we have not been able to derive a measure of B/C for the project because of lack of data, but we have a measure of R/C, and also an indication that R/C is somewhat below B/C (since CVP water is evidently sold for somewhat less than its marginal value to buyers). Since R/C is very far below unity, we estimate that B/C, though not so small, is far below unity, and that scale economies in the Project are not so important but that it may be deduced that $\triangle B'/\triangle C$ is also probably below unity by a significant amount. If this is the case, the basic features of the Central Valley Project are of excessive scale.

Apart from these basic conclusions about the Project, we can consider further the efficiency of the planning processes behind its construction by computing benefit-cost ratios for its major separable pieces. The position maintained by the Bureau of Reclamation has always been that Shasta Dam and the canals south of the Delta should be treated as a single unit because of the interrelation of water rights and financing. A merit of the Project is often found in the role of sales of electric power and municipal and industrial water in helping to cover the costs of providing irrigation water. The Bureau's periodic repayment analyses always show irrigation paying less than its fully allocated costs, with other reimbursable benefits furnishing enough revenue to make the total Project financially feasible.[30] One might suspect, as have friends of the Project, that the works south of the Delta could not pass the test of feasibility on their own.[31]

[28] $\triangle B'/\triangle C$ should be unity for a project of optimal scale; if it is above unity the project is of suboptimal scale, and if it is below unity the project is of excessive scale.

[29] B is the present value of benefits priced at marginal values.

[30] See, for example, U.S. Congress, House Committee on Interior and Insular Affairs, *Trinity River Division, Central Valley Project, California,* H. Doc. 53, 83 Cong. 1 sess. (1953), p. ix.

[31] This was the conclusion of a 1931 appraisal of the CVP, which proves to be extremely accurate in the light of our own calculations: "As to the [Shasta] reservoir, there does not seem to be room for much doubt. The power capabilities are such that, with contributions from the Federal government toward its cost reasonably equivalent to its benefits in the way of flood control and the improvement of navigation, and with the State bearing the cost of the necessary highway relocation and construction, its revenue from this source will approximately meet its operating expense plus interest at from 3 to 3½ per cent on its cost not covered by direct contributions and sinking fund payments sufficient to amortize this cost in fifty years.

"As to the Friant reservoir and canals, the situation is that its operating expense and the

Physically, the basic features of the Central Valley Project consist of three major separable pieces—Shasta and Keswick dams, the Delta-Mendota Canal, and Friant Dam and its canals.[32] Let us take Shasta Dam first by itself, assuming no Bureau-built canals removing water from the Delta. Because of the limited productivity of additional irrigation water along the Sacramento channel, no extra irrigation benefits can be imputed to Shasta's releases when operating alone instead of in conjunction with the Delta-Mendota Canal, nor would navigation or flood control benefits be augmented. We have, however, estimated that a proportionally large increase of salinity-repulsion benefits would be attainable in the Delta. While Shasta could probably be operated to produce a higher yield of firm power in these circumstances, we have no way to estimate the gain, and so must neglect it. Item 3 of Table 29 shows the resulting relation of benefits to costs. Looking at the appropriate range of interest rates, 5 and 6 per cent, the Shasta division of the CVP appears uneconomical by itself, as well as when teamed with the works lying south of the Delta.

Weighing the benefits and costs of the Shasta Dam alone poses no conceptual problems because Shasta's operations depend in no physical way upon the remaining works. When we turn to the separable features south of the Delta, however, we run into difficulties on this score. The discussion in Appendix C of the relation of Shasta's net releases during the irrigation season to the Bureau's diversions from the Delta shows that a wide range of interpretation could be placed on the relation between these releases and diversions. But in any case it is clear that the south-of-Delta works operating alone would incur significant opportunity costs by permitting saline intrusion to the Delta. This must be allowed for in appraising the benefit-cost relation of the south-of-Delta works.

In item 4 of Table 29 we present a benefit-cost calculation for all the Bureau's works south of the Delta—the Delta-Mendota and Contra Costa canals and the Friant Division. In order to allow for the net depletion of the Delta's water supplies which the operation of these works alone would entail, we have assumed a marginal opportunity cost for water taken from the Delta of $2 an acre-foot, a crude reflection of the increased crop damage from saline intrusion or other forms of foregone benefits. Under this assumption, the south-of-Delta works show a benefit-cost relation very similar to that of Shasta and of the project as a whole: slightly favorable at discount rates of 3 and 4 per cent, unfavorable at the more appropriate rates of 5 and 6 per cent. In view of the guesswork figure for the marginal opportunity costs of net depletions of Delta water, we should mention that even zero opportunity

---

charges for interest and sinking fund payments can not possibly be met out of the revenue it may make . . ., even by charging all that the lands benefited can afford to pay for the water. . . . In the way of what might be termed direct benefits, that is, benefits directly to the land receiving the water, the cost will exceed any increment of value it will bring." California Joint Federal-State Water Resources Commission, *Report to the President of the United States and the Governor of the State of California* (1931), pp. 10–11, quoted in U.S. Department of Agriculture, Bureau of Agricultural Economics, *History of Legislation and Policy Formation of the Central Valley Project,* by Mary Montgomery and Marion Clawson (1946).

[32] The Contra Costa Canal, a much smaller facility, is included with the Delta-Mendota and Friant works. We neglect the possibility of making further separations—for example, Friant Dam without its canals.

costs would not save the south-of-Delta works at discount rates of 5 and 6 per cent; and, of course, higher opportunity costs would render them still less economical.[33]

One might also wonder about the benefit-cost characteristics of the Friant works and of the Delta-Mendota Canal, taken separately from each other. To evaluate Friant Dam and its canals alone, we would have to allow for the opportunity cost of water use foregone along the lower San Joaquin River above its junction with its major tributaries (for example, the Merced River). As a matter of historical fact, the Bureau found it desirable to buy out a portion of the water rights to the San Joaquin held in this region, but to recognize the bulk of them by providing substitute flows through the Delta-Mendota Canal. The opportunity cost to assume for water use foregone along the lower San Joaquin is highly conjectural, but trial calculations have shown that even a very low opportunity cost would not serve to to justify the Friant Division by itself at discount rates of 5 and 6 per cent. The Delta-Mendota Canal cannot meaningfully be considered independent of the Friant Division, for the majority of its flows provide an exchange for San Joaquin River water diverted at Friant. Without this diversion, the marginal net productivity of additional discharges into the San Joaquin would be very low.

In summary, applying appropriate rates of discount and measures of benefit and cost, we have found the "basic features" of the Central Valley Project and its separable components to represent an uneconomic use of resources at their present scales. Either they should not have been built at all, or they should have been constructed to smaller scales. We have not attempted to estimate marginal benefit and cost functions for each of the separable features, but the various trial calculations suggest the following judgments. Shasta Dam would probably receive a favorable evaluation at some smaller scale. The same judgment would hold for the south-of-Delta works if the adjustment for surplus crops were ignored, but its inclusion raises substantial doubts about the wisdom of constructing these irrigation oriented works at any scale.

Prospective Appraisal of the Level of Development of the Feather River Project

The sort of benefit-cost analysis just applied to the Central Valley Project of the Bureau of Reclamation is also appropriately used in making an economic evaluation of the Feather River Project (FRP) of the California Department of Water Resources. This evaluation involves problems different from those encountered in appraising the CVP mainly in two ways: (1) It is a prospective appraisal of a project which, though by now more or less finally planned, is still under construction and thus has substantially no operating experience. (2) Because it will be devoted mainly to supplying water for urban use, an acceptable system of measuring marginal and average benefits derived from urban water must be devised.

[33] Omitting the influence of a few minor special features of the computation, one would expect the *B′/C* ratios for Shasta alone and for the south-of-Delta works alone to lie on opposite sides of the ratio for the Project as a whole. In our analysis, there is no economic interaction between them (the Bureau's view to the contrary).

The Feather River Project is the first large undertaking of the Department of Water Resources and comprises the first major unit of the California Water Plan.[34] At the present writing, it would appear that the schedule and timetable of project deliveries and their prices are sufficiently complete and firm, and the design and sizing of major project features sufficiently settled, that a meaningful prospective economic evaluation of the project can be made.[35] Indeed, several cost-benefit analyses of the FRP have previously been made on the basis of much more preliminary data, but their findings were generally vitiated by the use of inappropriate and unjustifiably high estimates of urban water benefits. We eliminate these sources of error in our analyses, but our findings will necessarily be plagued with uncertainty so far as we accept delivery schedules, mostly based on contracts already written, which are also implicitly based on regional population projections which are sometimes incredible.[36]

In making our analysis of the FRP, we necessarily assume as final both the latest available estimates of the design and size of numerous project features which could still be altered, and the latest estimated water and power delivery schedules supplied by the Department of Water Resources. We also must enter as costs estimates of expenditures yet to be made and as revenues estimated receipts yet to be collected from delivery areas in which service has not yet begun. With respect to costs and revenues, we have simplified matters by accepting all estimates made by the Department of Project costs and revenues, subject to interpretation in detail as set forth in Appendix D-3. In estimating benefits from FRP deliveries, however, we have rejected the valuation procedures employed by the Department (on grounds discussed in Appendix D-2), and have used instead valuations based on revised general criteria described below. Any benefit-cost ratio presented below will thus have as a denominator an estimate of costs taken directly from the Department of Water Resources, and as a numerator an estimate of benefits (aside from power benefits[37]) based on the Department's estimates of physical deliveries and on our own estimates of values per unit of water delivered.

Project features, service areas, and delivery schedules

The major purpose of the Feather River Project is to export about 4 million acre-feet of water annually from the Sacramento River basin to the southern San Joaquin Valley and to the South Coastal Basin of Southern California. Its "grand design" involves capturing "surplus" winter runoff in a major reservoir on the Feather River and a supplemental one on the Eel River; transporting the flow south to the Delta in the main channel of the Sacramento River; and carrying the bulk of it southward to and through the San Joaquin Valley and across the Tehachapi

[34] The general character of that Plan and the place of the FRP in it are summarized in Appendix D–1.

[35] See Appendix D–1.

[36] See Appendices D–2 and D–5 for further comment on this matter.

[37] Values of power benefits are taken directly from Department estimates, in a manner described in Appendix D–3, as equal to power revenues.

Mountains to the South Coastal Basin in a long aqueduct. Details of the design include minor spur aqueducts serving the northeastern and southern parts of the San Francisco Bay area, another minor spur aqueduct serving part of the central coastal area, and a terminal branching in the Tehachapis of the main aqueduct to lead Southern California water deliveries in part directly to the Los Angeles area and in part across the western Mojave Desert and thence to the eastern edge of South Coastal Basin. A spur aqueduct leading from the east branch of the main canal to the Palm Springs area is to be built by the agencies which will purchase water at canal-side from the east branch. In addition, the Project incorporates a drainage canal extending the length of the San Joaquin Valley to carry "agricultural sewage" northward to the Delta. The principal dam sites and canal routes of this Project, as just described, are shown in Figure 32.[38]

The scales of the principal features of the project as shown in Figure 32 are described in Table 30. Omitted from this table, as from the figure, are the locations and capacities of numerous pumping plants and in-transit holding reservoirs. grouped heavily at the southern end of the main Feather River Aqueduct (also known as the Southern California Aqueduct), where about 2,557,000 acre-feet of water annually are to be lifted to an altitude 3,615 feet above the sea level of the Delta source in order to cross the Tehachapi Mountains (at an energy cost in excess of the value of the entire power output of the project). Power generation facilities and appurtenant works are similarly not shown in the table; the main power facilities are at Oroville Dam and will have a dependable capacity of about 710,000 kilowatts. Shown in Figure 32, but not in Table 30, are San Luis Reservoir (capacity including forebay 2,154,000 acre-feet)—a joint FRP-Bureau facility for offstream storage on the main aqueduct route—and the facilities which will convey water from the Eel River reservoirs across or through the Coast Ranges to the Sacramento River (capacity not available).[39] Figure 32 does not show five minor Feather River reservoirs upstream from Oroville, or the Dos Rios reservoir (adjacent to the Spencer Reservoir) in the Eel River development listed in Table 30.

The projected distribution of ultimate project deliveries of water among service areas, with related data, is shown in Table 31. As indicated in Appendix D-3, practically all deliveries are by now contracted for. This table reveals notably that the bulk of FRP water is to go to the southern end of the San Joaquin Valley (for irrigation use primarily) and to Los Angeles and adjacent South Coastal Basin areas (for urban use). As read in conjunction with Table 30 and Figure 32, Table 31 also reveals that a substantial share of deliveries to the South Coastal Basin are to be made circuitously by way of the East Branch Aqueduct in order to be able to supply minor amounts of water en route to the western Mojave Desert area, and

[38] This figure does not show the San Joaquin drainage canal (still not finally located), power generation facilities at Oroville and on the aqueducts, or the numerous pumping stations and minor in-transit holding reservoirs on the aqueducts that are required mainly to effect the pump lifts which the delivery of Project water requires. The figure shows a spur canal leading to Palm Springs which is now to be built by purchasing agencies, and is thus not a feature of the Project.

[39] California Department of Water Resources, *The California State Water Project in 1964*, Bulletin No. 132-64 (1964), chap. 3. The water from the Eel River is evidently to be carried eastward through a tunnel about 20 miles long to a holding reservoir on the west side of the Sacramento Valley, and thence by local creek beds to the Sacramento River.

TABLE 30
Major Facilities of the Feather River Project, as Planned in 1964

Facilities	Location	Capacity (reservoir storage in acre-feet; aqueduct head flow in cubic feet per second)	Length (in miles)
On-stream storage and regulation facilities:			
Oroville Dam and Reservoir[a]	Lower Feather River	3,484,000 ac-f	—
Five Feather River reservoirs above Oroville	Forks of Feather River	187,900 ac-f	—
Spencer and Dos Rios reservoirs and conveyance facilities	Middle Fork of Eel River	800,000 ac-f[b]	
Delta facilities:			
Barriers, control works, and canals	Lower Delta	—	—
Delta pumping plant	Tracy	10,330 cfs	—
Aqueducts:			
North Bay Aqueduct	Delta west to Napa Valley	138 cfs	32
South Bay Aqueduct	Delta[c] south to Santa Clara Valley	363 cfs	44
Main Feather River Aqueduct[d]	Delta south to Tehachapi division point	10,000 cfs[e]	322
West branch of Feather River Aqueduct	Division point south to Castaic Reservoir	1,500 cfs	13
East branch of Feather River Aqueduct	Division point east and south to Perris Reservoir	1,842 cfs	118
Central Coastal Aqueduct	Main Southern California aqueduct west to Santa Maria River	329 cfs	110
San Joaquin drainage facilities[f]	South of Bakersfield north to Delta	1,100 cfs[g]	288

[a] With connected power plant and other facilities.
[b] Estimated annual yield of water; storage capacity not available.
[c] Strictly from elevated reservoir above the Delta pumping plant.
[d] 103 miles of this Aqueduct, from San Luis Reservoir south to Kettleman City, is a joint facility of the FRP and the Bureau of Reclamation, having a head capacity of 13,100 cfs of which the FRP share is 7,100 cfs.
[e] Capacity tapers to 3,800 cfs at the south end of the San Joaquin Valley.
[f] Joint facility of FRP and Bureau of Reclamation.
[g] Terminal capacity near Delta.

SOURCE: California Department of Water Resources, *The California State Water Project in 1964*, Bulletin No. 132–64 (1964), chap. 3.

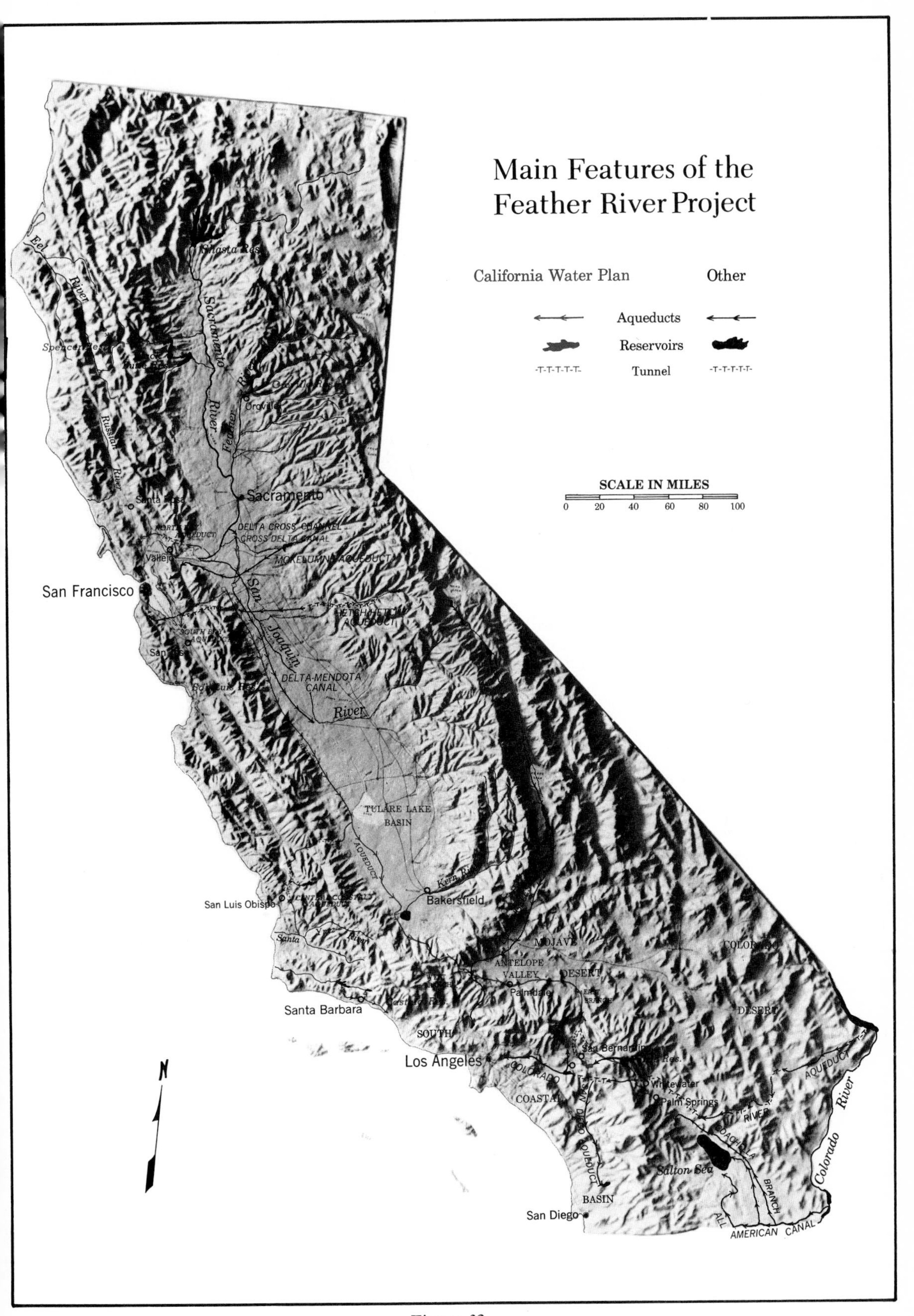

Main Features of the
Feather River Project
California Water Plan
Other
Aqueducts
Reservoirs
Tunnel
SCALE IN MILES
0
20
40
60
80
100
Eel River
Shasta Res.
Sacramento River
Feather River
Oroville
Russian River
Sacramento
DELTA CROSS CHANNEL
CROSS DELTA CANAL
MOKELUMNE AQUEDUCT
Vallejo
San Francisco
San Joaquin River
DELTA-MENDOTA CANAL
TULARE LAKE BASIN
AQUEDUCT
Bakersfield
San Luis Obispo
MOJAVE
ANTELOPE VALLEY
DESERT
Palmdale
Santa Barbara
SOUTH
Los Angeles
COASTAL
BASIN
San Diego
Whitewater
Palm Springs
Salton Sea
BRANCH
ALL AMERICAN CANAL
AQUEDUCT
Colorado River
N

Figure 32

TABLE 31
ESTIMATED ULTIMATE ANNUAL DELIVERIES OF FEATHER RIVER PROJECT WATER, BY SERVICE AREA

Service area	Aqueduct source	Ultimate annual deliveries (thousands of acre-feet)	Year in which deliveries scheduled to begin
Feather River area	Local canals	38.5	1967
San Francisco Bay area, northeast	North Bay Aqueduct	73.0	1980
San Francisco Bay area, south	South Bay Aqueduct	194.0	1962
San Luis Obispo and Santa Barbara	Central Coastal Aqueduct	75.0	1980
Southern San Joaquin Valley	Main Feather River Aqueduct	1,362.5	1968
South Coastal Basin	West and East branches of Feather River Aqueduct	1,925.0	1971
Antelope Valley-Mojave Desert	East Branch of Feather River Aqueduct[a]	264.0	1971
Coachella Valley-Palm Springs	Purchasers' aqueduct	68.0	1972
Total deliveries		4,000.0	

[a] And southern end of main Feather River Aqueduct just north of Tehachapi division point.
SOURCE: California Department of Water Resources, *The California State Water Project in 1964*, Bulletin No. 132–64 (1964), Table 7.

by a purchasers' spur aqueduct to the Palm Springs area of the Colorado Desert. Each ultimate delivery shown in Table 31 is of course underlain by a specific timetable of annual deliveries which increases from a smaller amount to the ultimate over a period of years following the first date of delivery.

The calculation of benefits

Our derivation of FRP water revenues, described above and in Appendix D-3, rests essentially on the application to a large number of individual time series of water deliveries to individual service areas and purchasing agencies an equal number of annual equivalent contract prices as calculated by the Department of Water Resources. As already noted, however, we find it necessary to reject corresponding Department estimates of water benefits, and to derive our own estimates by calculating appropriate benefit values per unit of water for all service areas and applying these to the same group of time series of water deliveries.[40]

Two types of measures of unit benefits have been calculated: (1) the marginal values of water, as supplied in every year through 2039; and (2) the corresponding average values of water supplied, inclusive of buyers' surpluses as appropriately

[40] In general, the same benefit values have been used for all purchasing agencies in any service area, since interagency differences in unit benefits are too small to estimate.

calculated. Analytical problems are encountered in the derivation of these benefit measures because most benefits of the FRP are those of water supplied for urban use, and because in all cases urban water to be delivered by the FRP could be obtained from alternative sources which are variously, in different service areas and at different points in time, below and above both the costs of FRP water and its probable marginal values in use. Two subproblems thus arise. First, lacking direct measures of the marginal and average value in use of FRP water, we must infer these values from other relevant data. Second, given these inferences, we must choose between value-in-use and alternative-cost-of-supply as the proper measure of benefits secured through using FRP water.

Our resolution of the second subproblem rests in part on the following propositions: (1) that a quantity of urban water imported to a service area by FRP in any year can have a marginal value no greater than the cost of securing the same amount of water from the marginal alternative source;[41] and (2) that the same quantity of imported urban water can have a marginal value no greater than its marginal value in use. Therefore, in any year in any service area, the marginal value of imported FRP water is either its marginal value in use or its cost of supply from the marginal alternative source, whichever is lower. We have applied this principle in measuring the marginal value of FRP water in each service area for each year, to arrive at benefits as measured by marginal values. This application requires inferring the marginal value in use of water in various areas at various times, in a manner described below, as well as securing data on costs of water from alternative sources.

The corresponding derivation of average values of FRP water for urban use, inclusive of buyers' surpluses, follows a familiar principle. The average value of a given quantity of water should be the simple average of the marginal value of the marginal unit delivered and of the higher marginal values of all inframarginal units, as determined generally by the price elasticity of demand for the water in question. Measurement of average values according to this principle, however, is subject to the constraint that no inframarginal unit of project water can have a higher marginal value than the cost of securing the quantity of water delivered from the marginal alternative source.[42] Calculation of the average value of project water in

[41] Supposing that alternative sources are tapped in order of their costs per unit of water, beginning with the lowest-cost source, the marginal alternative source is the most costly that would have to be tapped in order to secure for the service area the same quantity of water from alternative sources that is supplied by the project. This cost from the marginal alternative source may be either (1) the value in alternative uses of water from a nonproject source being put to alternative uses (such as irrigation) in the import area, or closer to the area than the project source, plus any costs of transporting it to the service area; or (2) the costs of producing fresh water by conversion of waste water or by demineralization of salt water in or for the service area, plus any costs of transporting it to the service area. The marginal value of imported project water cannot exceed this alternative cost even though the cost of imported project water may exceed it.

[42] Thus, if the cost of water from the marginal alternative source is somewhat higher than the marginal value of project water, the average value of a quantity of project-delivered water would be an average of the marginal values of a certain proportion of inframarginal units having inframarginal values below alternative cost and of the values of all remaining inframarginal units priced at alternative cost from the marginal alternative source. If the marginal value of project water is the cost from the marginal alternative source, inframarginal units have no higher values, and the average value of project water is the same as its marginal value.

cases where the cost of water from the marginal alternative source is above the marginal value of project water requires knowledge of, or an assumption concerning, the price elasticity of the demand for urban water. In our calculations, we have assumed this elasticity to be finite but at the lower limit of various estimates made of urban water demand elasticities, or −0.25. Accordingly, in cases where alternative cost lies above the marginal value of project water, average value is generally found at a level between marginal value and alternative cost, and closer to the latter than to the former.

Returning now to the problem of inferring the marginal values in use of FRP water delivered for urban use, we have assumed that the marginal value in use in each service area, as measured at points of delivery to local agencies,[43] is equal to the contract price at which the Department of Water Resources expects to sell water to the customer agencies.[44] This results in an adequately high estimate of marginal values in use, since customer agencies in general resell project water freely at prices no higher than the contract prices at which they purchase it, so that their buyers can purchase enough water at these resale prices (or at final delivered prices based on them) to bring the net marginal value of water in use at least down to equality with FRP contract prices.[45]

We thus pursue benefit calculations on the assumption that the marginal values in use of FRP water delivered for urban use equal contract prices in the various service areas. In addition, we have secured data for each area on the costs of water from marginal alternative costs of supply at all relevant points in time. Employing these measures in combination, we have derived for each urban service area annual estimates extending through the year 2039 of marginal and average values per unit of water delivered, applying the principles just outlined. These calculations, together with data on alternative costs, are described in Appendix D-4. For the one important service area in which FRP water is intended for irrigation (the southern San Joaquin Valley), we have calculated marginal and average values directly from estimates of the productivity of water as used in irrigation in that area, the costs of marginal alternative sources of supply generally lying above marginal values in use. This calculation is also described in Appendix D-4.

These calculated marginal and average values, in essence comprising time series of unit values of water deliveries for each service area through the year 2039, have been applied to the corresponding time series of estimated water deliveries for these service areas (by multiplying each annual delivery first by a corresponding marginal value and then by a corresponding average value) to produce two sets of time series of annual aggregate project benefits by service areas—one set valuing de-

[43] And thus net of distribution costs incurred thereafter.

[44] This price being derived as described in Appendix D–3.

[45] In fact, contract prices are probably overestimates of values in use in most service areas, since the customer agencies in these areas have stated their intentions to resell FRP water at prices in the neighborhood of from 55 to 70 per cent of the FRP contract prices at which they purchase, collecting the balance through property taxes, and thus inducing urban water use in a volume which will bring net marginal values in use below the FRP contract prices. The Department of Water Resources, moreover, has calculated delivery requirements on the assumption that these customer agencies will follow such pricing policies, or on the alternative nonsense assumption that the demand for urban water is iso-elastic with a price elasticity of zero.

liveries at marginal values and the other valuing them at average values. An aggregate of the series for all service areas in each set has then provided us with two corresponding total-project time series of aggregate annual benefits from water deliveries. The discounted present value of all water delivery benefits for the project as of 1960, using any of several alternative discount rates, is thus readily calculated—either as B_w (present value of water benefits as priced at marginal values), or as B'_w (present value of these benefits as priced at average values, or inclusive of buyers' surpluses). Either of these present values, plus the discounted present value of all future power benefits of the FRP (taken as equal to the present value of estimated power revenues), gives us a discounted present value—either B or B'—of all FRP benefits, other than those omitted along with the omission of federal contributions to the costs of state facilities. Such present values of project benefits (based alternatively on marginal and average values) have been computed for fifty- and eighty-year periods beginning with 1960, with discount rates alternatively at 3, 4, 5, and 6 per cent.

Benefit-cost and revenue-cost evaluation

To derive benefit-cost ratios for the Feather River Project, we of course divide present values of benefits, B or B', by the present values of Project costs, C, as discussed in Appendix D-3. Revenue-cost ratios are obtained by dividing the present values of estimated revenues, R (also discussed in Appendix D-3), by corresponding values of C.[46] All present values are calculated as of the beginning of 1960, with no adjustments for possible future price changes. The resulting ratios, which test the economic and commercial feasibility of the Project, are shown in Table 32.

TABLE 32
BENEFIT-COST AND REVENUE-COST RATIOS FOR THE FEATHER RIVER PROJECT, BASED ON 1964 ESTIMATED VALUES

Item	Time period	Rate of discount per annum			
		.03	.04	.05	.06
1. Revenue-cost ratios (R/C)[a]	50 years	0.95	0.83	0.72	0.63
	80 years	1.12	0.99	0.80	0.68
2. Benefit-cost ratios with benefits based on marginal values (B/C)	50 years	0.78	0.68	0.54	0.51
	80 years	0.95	0.86	0.62	0.56
3. Benefit-cost ratios with benefits based on average values (B'/C)	50 years	1.09	0.94	0.80	0.69
	80 years	1.32	1.11	0.90	0.75

[a] The revenues entering these ratios are calculated from uniform average annual equivalent contract prices (see Appendix D–3). If cash-flow revenues reflecting anticipated prepayments are used instead, the R/C ratios are altered slightly, as follows for eighty years: 1.07 at 3%; 0.97 at 4%; 0.82 at 5%; and 0.72 at 6%.
SOURCE: See text.

[46] In calculating C, all costs incurred prior to 1960 are entered at face without any interest charge.

Before interpreting this table, a few aggregate magnitudes may be mentioned. The discounted present values as of 1960 for eighty years of project operation, using a 4 per cent discount rate, are: for costs (C) $2,419 million; for revenues (R) $2,390 million; for benefits at marginal values (B) $2,077 million; and for benefits at average values (B') $2,685 million. These, of course, neglect federal shares of costs, revenues, and benefits for joint facilities; federal contributions to the costs of state facilities; and nonreimbursable benefits presumably supported by such contributions.

A first finding suggested by Table 33 concerns the "commercial feasibility" of the FRP. It promises approximately to pay for itself only if operated at least until about 2039 and only if capital investment is asked to bear an interest charge not appreciably in excess of 4 per cent. With higher interest charges (or a shorter life) it would definitely be a loser; for example, with a time horizon of eighty years and interest charge of 5 per cent the present value of its net deficit would be about $339 million. Four per cent is appreciably lower than the going marginal borrowing rate on private funds.

Second, the FRP rates much more poorly in terms of the ratio to costs of benefits priced at marginal values than in terms of the ratio to costs of revenues. This reflects the fact that the California Department of Water Resources has contracted to collect from customer agencies prices for water which are substantially above the marginal values of water delivered, and which include a part of the buyers' surpluses of water users. This is presumably a viable arrangement provided that the final buyers from customer agencies are denied access to alternative water supplies having lower costs, or that the customer agencies collect a significant share of their revenue in the form of general property taxes as distinguished from water charges (as San Joaquin and Southern California agencies evidently intend to do). There still is no definite answer to the question of how commercially feasible the Project will be if changes in price levels should elevate future construction and operating cost substantially.

Third, the relationship of "total benefits" inclusive of buyers' surpluses (B') to costs is marginally favorable in fifty-year calculations only at an interest rate below 4 per cent; in eighty-year calculations it is mildly favorable only at interest rates below 5 per cent. The fact that the B'/C ratio exceeds unity at 3 and 4 per cent rates of discount, moreover, does not indicate that the project is economically desirable in general or built to a proper scale—even if these interest rates are accepted. This is particularly so because it cannot be argued that the FRP is an indivisible unit, with no features which could economically be left out or scaled down. All features of the Project except Oroville Dam, the Delta Pumping Plant, and the main Aqueduct as extended only by its West Branch to Los Angeles clearly could be eliminated, and the slight excess of B' over C at low interest rates does not demonstrate economic feasibility of the Project as a whole.

Fourth, the marginal benefit-cost ratio for the Project as a whole ($\Delta B'/\Delta C$) is very probably below unity even at 3 and 4 per cent interest rates, and certainly so at rates of 5 or 6 per cent, as suggested both by C exceeding B' at these rates and by the low values at these rates of B/C—even if adequate mental allowance is made for decline of unit costs with increasing scale. This suggests that the FRP is generally oversized or includes large uneconomical segments, or both. Moreover, the use of 5 or 6 per cent rates of discount in evaluating the Project seems called for (if for no other reason) because of the need for discounting the sanguine estimates of future growth of water deliveries which rest on sanguine estimates of future population growth in Southern California. Questions concerning these estimates are raised in Appendix D-5.

Fifth, detailed analysis of benefits, revenues, and costs for individual segments (not presented here) suggests that the Feather River Project as now planned includes several distinctly uneconomic segments. It appears that the revenue-cost and benefit-cost ratios are as good as they are (or no worse than they are) because the Project is largely "carried" by South Coastal Basin benefits and revenues sufficiently in excess of costs to offset most losses in many other segments. An economically much more feasible or justifiable project would delete entirely the Eel River dams and transmission facilities, the North Bay Aqueduct, and the East Branch Aqueduct serving the Mojave Desert and the Palm Springs-Coachella Valley area.[47] And the Central Coastal Aqueduct would be a clearly marginal inclusion. So far as these deletions of delivery areas do not reduce demands sufficiently to permit dispensing with Eel River water, deliveries to the southern San Joaquin Valley should be reduced enough to permit fulfillment of estimated South Coastal Basin demands with Feather River water.[48] A straight-line delivery from the Delta to Los Angeles of water released from Oroville Dam, with a lateral delivery through the South Bay Aqueduct and the dropping off of surplus water for irrigation in Kern County might be close to economically feasible if the ratios in Table 33 are accepted at face value and if long payment periods and medium interest rates are used—though the Oroville development and the main Feather River Aqueduct might prove to be somewhat overscale from an economic standpoint.

A possibly feasible alternative would have been postponement of some version of the present FRP by two or three decades. The low benefit-cost ratios for the present FRP result from the long period of build-up of demand, the very heavy anticipatory construction costs, and the relatively inexpensive alternative sources of water to meet water demands for the near future in FRP service areas. Though an interbasin transfer of the sort embodied in the FRP may ultimately be needed, it would be more economical first to exploit less costly alternatives. It would also be more prudent, because several decades from now changes in technologies and developments in population patterns not presently anticipated may indicate the desirability of different solutions to any problem of water deficiency in the southern part of California. The unseemly haste which has marked the early undertaking of the Feather River Project can probably be attributed more to the desire of Southern

[47] The long East Branch Aqueduct appears to provide a relatively inefficient and expensive way of delivering a great deal of water to the South Coastal Basin, with its route chosen to facilitate supplying the Mojave Desert en route. The incremental costs of this route evidently far exceed any possible benefits provided in the Mojave Desert area.

[48] The productivity of irrigation water in the southern San Joaquin Valley is such that any marginal subtractions from scheduled water deliveries attributable to not tapping the Eel River would reduce benefits by less than the cost saving accomplished by not developing the Eel.

California interests to secure rights to Northern California water while they are still available than to any misapprehension on their part concerning the fact that the Project is being undertaken prematurely from an economic standpoint.

Comparing the performance of the California Department of Water Resources in its Feather River Project with that of the Bureau of Reclamation in the basic features of the Central Valley Project, it appears that the Department can be charged with somewhat grosser errors of overdevelopment of water facilities than the Bureau, if benefit-cost relationships are used as a criterion. However, subsequently added and presently planned features of the CVP indicate that the Bureau may be in the process of coming down to the level of the Department with late CVP developments. On the other hand, the Department of Water Resources evidently intends to collect a much larger proportion of the costs of its Project from direct beneficiaries than does the Bureau of Reclamation. This is a solace to the general taxpaying public, but not to the economist interested in the efficient allocation of resources and the avoidance of economic waste.

At this writing, it theoretically is not too late through drastic measures to improve the Feather River Project by deleting the several most wasteful segments now planned, although the Department of Water Resources has committed itself contractually to supply water to all of these segments, and perhaps implicitly to developing the Eel River. However this may be, the danger flags should fly with respect to the Department's long-range intention, within the California Water Plan, to undertake developments of the Klamath and Trinity rivers which would dwarf the Feather River Project and probably make it, by comparison, look like a sound investment.

The preceding findings might be attacked by parties at interest on the basis that, in determining benefits, we have been unwilling to accept their assumption that irrigation water now being used in FRP delivery areas, or more cheaply available to Project delivery areas, should not be considered transferable to urban uses. They might reject our analytically defensible estimates of project benefits in favor of concocted estimates which hinge mainly upon an insistence that gross misallocation of water among uses should be deliberately sought and is a desirable end. We are not ready to agree, supposing a supermarket 500 yards from the Columbia River in an irrigated plain were fenced and by state law denied access to the waters of the Columbia, that the benefits of water to the supermarket should be calculated by the state as the cost of flying it in by tanker planes from the nearest alternative water source.[49]

[49] For earlier critical analyses of the Feather River Project, see Bechtel Corporation, *Report on the Engineering, Economic, and Financial Aspects of the Feather River Project* (1956); and Jack Hirshleifer, James C. De Haven, and Jerome W. Milliman, *Water Supply: Economics, Technology, and Policy* (1960), chap. 11. Hirshleifer *et al.* did not make a benefit-cost analysis of the Feather River Project, or calculate project benefits, but instead analyzed the costs of supplying the Los Angeles area with the amount of water scheduled for delivery by the FRP by various alternative means, including several other than the FRP. They found that the FRP was the most expensive of the alternatives considered, if its costs included a large share of those for all facilities north of the Tehachapis and all those incurred solely for delivering water into the South Coastal Basin. Their emphasis was on the comparative value of the FRP to water users in Southern California rather than on the evaluation of the whole Project.

The Level of Development: Summary

In this chapter, we have been concerned primarily with one aspect of the performance of the water industry of Northern California. As we recognized at the outset, the level of development of water resources in the area may be taken to mean either the level of water-usage development (the extent to which available water is being put to want-satisfying uses) or the level of water-facilities development (the volume and value of non-water resources being used to make water available for various consumptive and in-stream uses).

It appears in general, as will be argued further in Chapter 17, that by the early 1960's the water resources of Northern California had reached the ceiling of full usage. That is, water from all sources was economically a scarce good, and water-facilities development at, within, and beyond the present margin tended mainly to reallocate scarce water supplies among types, places, and times of use. As a result, current interest centers mainly on the level of water-facilities development. This level is to be judged both by whether or not it is appropriate in terms of the positive economic yields obtained at the margin from investments of non-water resources for developing water, and by whether or not it is consistent with or implements an optimal allocation of water among uses. It is difficult to appraise the current level of water-facilities development without paying heed to at least its broad allocative impacts as well as to the ratio of positive returns to the costs of investments in facilities.

In attempting to appraise the level of water-facilities development in Northern California, we have drawn on such statistical evidence as was available, or could be produced, concerning (1) rates of return on investment earned by local agricultural water agencies; (2) relationships of the productivity of irrigation water to its costs at the extensive margin, and (3) ratios of benefits to costs obtained from, or predicted for, large-scale water development projects undertaken by the federal Bureau of Reclamation and by the California Department of Water Resources. This statistical evidence is clearly less than comprehensive and adequate as a basis for appraising all types of water development and all water development projects of a given type in the area. Therefore, we have also depended in our appraisals on inferences concerning attained levels of development which may be drawn from the detailed analyses of the water agencies' conduct presented in Part Two above.

The statistical evidence presented in this chapter refers mainly to water development of four types, as classified by developing agency and character of development: local irrigation districts that are primarily engaged in exploiting local water sources for local uses as integrated diverter-retailers (and in most instances not engaged in reservoir storage operations); local agricultural water agencies which purchase water at wholesale from the Bureau of Reclamation; the Bureau in its construction and operation of the basic features of the Central Valley Project; and the California Department of Water Resources in its on-going construction of the Feather River Project. Inferences drawn from the conduct of this roster of water agencies have tended to reinforce (or be reinforced by) conclusions drawn from the statistical evidence accumulated. They have also provided some basis for extending conclusions concerning the categories of local agricultural water agencies that we have subjected to statistical analysis to such agencies in general. In addition, they provide support for our conclusion that Northern California projects of the Bureau of Reclamation other than those which created the basic features of the Central Valley Project, including projects already built, under construction, and planned, embody in full or extended degree the same tendencies toward overdevelopment and misallocation found in the basic features of the CVP. Further, such inferences support the tentative conclusion that the U.S. Army Corps of Engineers shares, at least in part, the undesirable performance tendencies of the Bureau of Reclamation, and have given some indications concerning the performance of the Pacific Gas and Electric Company in developing water facilities so far as it has engaged in joint ventures with agricultural water agencies to build dual purpose storage reservoirs.

It would be fair to say, however, that the combined available evidence provides a somewhat deficient basis for appraising the net influence on the level of water-facilities development in Northern California of the operations of the Corps, of the two major electric utility companies (PG&E and the Southern California Edison Company), of private diverters of surface water, and of private pumpers of ground water. In addition, we have little in the way of firm findings concerning the comparable influence of urban water agencies, although this omission is minor so far as it affects the over-all development of water for use within Northern California.

The evidence accumulated on the level of water-facilities development in the area would appear to offer at least semiconclusive support to the following observations:

1) Local agricultural water districts in Northern California which are engaged in the integrated capture and retail delivery of irrigation water have tended to make investments in water facilities for their own use which are excessive for this use, at the same time tending to overallocate water to irrigation use within their own boundaries.
2) Agricultural water districts purchasing irrigation water at wholesale from the Bureau of Reclamation receive excessive allocations of scarce water and develop excessive investments in facilities to transport and apply it.
3) The Bureau of Reclamation, as the principal federal agency investing in water development in Northern California, has undertaken an excessive level of development of water facilities on certain major rivers of the area, which incorporates misallocations of water involving excessive transfers from winter to summer use, excessive interbasin transfers, and overallocations of water to irrigation as compared to other uses. This conclusion is quite firm with respect to the basic features of the Central Valley Project; and there is every general indication that it applies at least equally to the American River and Trinity River reservoir projects—either as so far completed or as considered in conjunction with planned projects for interbasin transfers of irrigation water which they have been designed to serve (the East Side Division, the Sacramento canals, and further south-of-the-Delta transfers).
4) The California Department of Water Resources, in its first major project, appears to be engaging in excessive development of water facilities and in connected interseasonal and interbasin misallocations of water in a degree at least as severe as, and probably more severe than, the Bureau of Reclamation; and is doing it on a much larger scale. The associated misallocations of water among types of use which the Department is in the process of developing involve in some degree

overallocation to agricultural use, and in comparable degree overallocations to urban use by hypothetical future urban populations, at the expense of in-stream uses of water. As the Department of Water Resources has entered the area of water development, additional major rivers of the area have become involved. Its proposed future projects would appear to be more seriously uneconomic than the Feather River Project.

The preceding findings refer to important segments of the industry engaged in developing water in Northern California. Firm conclusions on the over-all development of water facilities in the area and on the propriety of the pattern of allocation of water among types of use, including passive in-stream use, are difficult to draw. This is because of the lack of good evidence on the allocation of all developed water among all actual and potential irrigators and other consumptive users, on the status of current hydroelectric development relative to the proper economic margin, on actual values in use of streams for fishing and other recreation, and on the actual value of flood control benefits (and on alternative modes and costs of providing them) supplied by projects of the Corps of Engineers. The wind blows in the direction of an appreciable general overdevelopment of water facilities in Northern California at present, and of more substantial overdevelopment in the near future. This generalization holds even if present practices for valuing the benefits of irrigation water are accepted, and more strongly if the value of water used to grow price-supported crops is discounted. But, on the basis of available evidence, a sweeping conclusion that water facilities in the area are at present excessive in aggregate quantity, rather than merely maldistributed among streams and with respect to the specific water uses and users they supply, cannot be either affirmed or denied.

Leaving the Central Valley Project and the Feather River Project aside for the moment, our guess is that Northern California generally has either (a) a general overdevelopment of most sources of water in terms of facilities, together with connected misallocations of water including too much diverted to irrigation as opposed to most or all competing uses, or (b) about the correct level of total development of water facilities mixed with a significant misallocation of developed irrigation water as among all actual and potential irrigators. (This misallocation could also be associated with general overdevelopment.) This applies to a dominant proportion of the development of the water resources of Northern California to date.

As to the rest, we find an overdevelopment of the Sacramento River with a project of excessive scale, and a project underway to overdevelop the Feather and Eel rivers—not only with excessive reservoir facilities and interseasonal transfers of water, but also excessive aqueduct facilities and interbasin transfers of water. The same tendencies toward overdevelopment are evident on the American and Trinity rivers, and evidently less desirable projects are planned or proposed. These gross aberrations from optimal development are being or have been set in concrete mainly by the Bureau of Reclamation and the California Department of Water Resources. The state and federal projects in general look either "all bad," "too large," or "very premature." Their economic feasibility at reduced scales has not been fully analyzed, but postponement of the Feather River Project would certainly make it less unattractive economically. At their present accomplished and intended scales, the projects could hardly be made feasible by juggling allocations, but their economic rating might be improved.[50]

It is discouraging that the economic errors embodied in these overdevelopments of water facilities in large part are not economically reversible. Once the facilities are built and their costs are sunk, it is more economical to use them than to dynamite or abandon them, since their future operating costs are only a minor fraction of total costs. The significance for public policy of our appraisals of these facilities is thus largely as a warning for the future against repeating and compounding past errors. We will return to this theme in Chapter 17.

At the beginning of this chapter, we indicated that the three main aspects of efficiency in water resource development which we have distinguished—the level, sequence, and rationality of development—are closely interrelated, and none is fully appraised until all have been considered. We turn now to the sequence of development, and subsequently to two aspects of the rationality of development: efficiency in the allocation of water and technical efficiency in water storage and transport.

[50] Conclusions about the level of water development for irrigated agriculture consistent with those of this chapter, but reached by a different route, are presented by Vernon W. Ruttan, *The Economic Demand for Irrigated Acreage* (1965), chap. 3.

16

THE SEQUENCE OF DEVELOPMENT

As was stressed throughout the preceding chapter, any conclusions about the level of development in the Northern California water industry can be drawn only within the context of findings concerning the efficiency with which resources are allocated in storing, transporting, and using water. We now turn to the evidence bearing on the efficiency with which these allocations are made. In the interest of convenient exposition, we can divide our evidence on the efficiency of resource combinations in the water industry and present it in three separate chapters. The present chapter stresses empirical data concerning the historic development of the industry, which was outlined in Part Two; Chapter 17 deals with the efficiency of the contemporary pattern of water allocation; and Chapter 18, with the technical efficiency of existing water facilities, as affected by their sizes and their spatial relationships.

The theoretical analysis presented in Chapter 8 identified the major allocative frontiers in the water industry and the conditions which must prevail if they are to be adjusted optimally. The capacity and operation of storage reservoirs must just suffice to attain the proper allocation of streamflow among years and among seasons of the year. (We shall largely confine our investigation to the volume of storage reservoir capacity together with the associated volume of transfer of late winter and spring runoff to other seasons.) Interbasin transfers and the facilities permitting them must be constructed and operated at optimum scale, a condition which in practice is interrelated with the correctness of interseasonal transfers on the streams in question. Water from a given source must be allocated optimally among uses and user agencies at any given time, and the supply claimed by a given retailing agency must be distributed optimally among its member-customers.

We face the problem of appraising the extent to which actual allocation deviates from the optimum on each of these allocational frontiers, and of detecting the causes for the major deviations from the optimum. Because of these interrelated objectives and because, once more, of the limitations on available data, we shall attempt to use both behavioral evidence and outright measurements of returns at the appropriate margins. The behavioral evidence holds special importance because of its potential ability to show what institutions, laws, physical factors, or human attitudes seem to produce economically undesirable results. It is particularly important for appraising the efficiency of the historical sequence of development, for which elaborate objective measurements are impractical. Therefore this chapter reviews the evolution of the Northern California water industry, showing what the major patterns of behavior imply for performance in terms of allocation of available water.

Events in the water industry hardly move with breath-taking speed. Physical works a half-century old and prices and water allocations unchanged for many years are commonplace. Not only that, events and decisions many years past can influence contemporary allocations in an essential way. Water rights, for example, are perpetual in character, contingent upon continued beneficial use (a vague standard) by their holders.[1] Given the infrequency with which transfer of water rights between users takes place, current decisions affecting resource allocation may be critically affected by water rights perfected in the early years of California's statehood. Given the indivisibilities and physical durability of facilities for the storage and transportation of water, investment decisions of almost equal antiquity can strongly influence the payoffs which affect similar decisions made at the present time. These allocative forces operating in tandem—perpetual rights and nearly perpetual physical facilities—not only affect all of the allocative margins listed above at the time they are initially fixed; they also color the atmosphere of decision-making for many subsequent years. A "wrong" decision about water rights and facilities can bring a succession of other wrong decisions in its train over a period of decades.

In the light of these considerations, it is easy to see why the efficiency of the sequence of development in the industry holds more than antiquarian interest. We wish to know not only whether resources are now allocated efficiently within the industry, but also what may be the trend toward efficiency or inefficiency. We wish to possess not just a comparison between allocations in the actual industry and those in a hypothetical utopia where all margins are optimally adjusted; we also want to know about the apparent rationality of the series of steps which led to the present allocations. Contemporary misallocations may stem from past decisions (relating to investment, water rights, and so on) which looked right by economic tests at the time, but were subsequently negated by the emergence of unforeseen circumstances. Alternatively, present errors in allocation may reflect the allocative results of past decisions which were economically wrong at the time they were made. The former case gives rise to few policy conclusions, but exhorts prayer for greater foresight and more flexibility; the latter implies that poor allocative performance reflects systematic structural defects, whether curable or not. What follows is a schematic review of the development of the water industry, mostly summarizing information presented in Part Two, aimed at testing the efficiency of the historic sequence of development and paving the way for answering these questions about the contemporary allocative efficiency of the water industry and the causes of its deficiencies.

Formation of Agencies, Water Rights, and Scarce Summer Flows

The formation of public water agencies in most cases precedes any major action affecting the allocative margins in the water industry. The evidence reviewed in Chapter 9 suggested that the formation of local districts in an area responds

[1] Except for riparian and overlying ground-water rights, maintenance of which does not require continued use.

broadly to shifts in demand and cost factors, which would also tend to provide economic justification for the construction of water collection and distribution facilities to serve the area. For urban agencies, an obvious relation holds between the demand and cost conditions which favor the formation of agencies and those which justify such decisions to reallocate water. For agricultural agencies, the relation is much less direct. Irrigation districts have not arisen in response to objective demonstrations of the economic superiority of any resource complexes which they might erect over all alternative construction. Furthermore, the timing of interest of local landowners in forming a water district and developing a large-scale project has often suggested that they are "satisficers" rather than "maximizers." Unsatisfactory returns from previous land uses appear to create a stronger incentive for action to form agencies and invest in water projects than the availability of superior returns from an alternative land use after a district has been formed and a project constructed.

The early history of the Northern California water industry records the movement of late spring and summer flows of most Central Valley rivers into the category of a scarce resource. As water becomes scarce, temporal priority of water rights on each river plays a vital role in determining the efficiency of evolving allocations of water among consumptive uses which a given stream might satisfy. Allocations based on established water rights have normally remained permanently unchanged as to place of use. Partly this has been due to the terms of California water law, which render the transfer of a riparian right a legally difficult procedure and which threaten the holder of an appropriative right who sells water with the loss of that right. Partly it has been due to the users' co-operative structure of water agencies, which impedes any commercial water transactions between an agency and outsiders who might pay more for agency controlled water than it is worth at the margin to member-customers of the agency. The difficulties resulting from the inflexible assignment of water rights to agencies might have been rectified by adjusting the boundaries of the agencies, but such adjustment has also been uncommon. Again, certain reasons are apparent. Existing distribution systems are seldom easily extended to serve large new blocks of territory. Existing political control may be threatened. Existing bonded debt for the original district makes either the inclusion or exclusion of territory extremely complicated, although not impossible.

These conditions have generally meant that late-coming territories demanding summer flows from Central Valley rivers have had to accept residual claims on available supplies, independent of the comparative marginal productivities of water to them. The situation has never arisen in which existing retail agencies acted as rival sellers willing (much less eager) to supply water to new territory. Lands newly seeking water supplies have typically had only the option of forming new districts and competing as buyers or claimants for scarce supplies of water. A few large-scale transfers of water rights between agencies have occurred within particular subbasins, but very large and obvious differences in the productivity of water between groups of users have been necessary to bring these about. In some cases, negotiated settlements of water rights have improved water allocations somewhat, but relative marginal productivities obviously have held a minor place in the elements of bargaining strength which have typically determined such outcomes. The transfer of shares in mutual water companies provides a relatively efficient mechanism for local reallocations of water, but the mutuals have flourished in only a few areas of Northern California. Furthermore, the case of the Kaweah River basin shows that the reallocation of mutual shares does not preclude serious technical inefficiencies.

In both the Kings River and Kaweah River basins, substantial misallocations among user agencies arose in the past. An examination of their history suggests some of the reasons why such misallocations can persist in the face of sustained efforts by the have-not agencies to change them.[2] It also illustrates the way in which the complexity of interrelations among agencies increases more than proportionally as the number of agencies in a river basin increases. Much of the protracted Kaweah litigation turned on whether the current holders of water rights were making beneficial use of their full diversions from the river. Without trying to establish that their marginal products of water were typically zero or negative, it was certainly clear that they were less than the excluded Lindsay-Strathmore Irrigation District could attain. Among the factors which frustrated Lindsay-Strathmore's efforts were many inherent in the physical complexity of the situation and not related solely to water law. The network of diversion canals of the older users was patently inefficient, but the inefficiency seemed to be consistent with incremental rationality of the individual units taken one by one, and to a large degree reflected historic shifts of the Kaweah's flow between its two distributary channels. The Lindsay-Strathmore Irrigation District could not legalize pumping from its wellfield or shift the points of diversion of the water yields of its mutual water company shares, not only because the complex external effects of such transactions could not practicably be compensated, but also because the standing legal arrangements for dividing the waters of the Kaweah River would have been thrown into confusion by any such change.

The area of the Kings River, immediately north of the Kaweah, has undergone a similar sequence of attempted reallocations between agencies which came to nothing. Again, owners of territory near the foothills, which was developed later than that farther out in the floor of the valley, failed in a series of legal and market maneuvers to secure a water supply. Significant reallocations of claims to the summertime flow within the service area of the Kings River have come about only through transfers of mutual company shares and one large purchase of water rights in the nineteenth century. Similar problems, in varying degrees and at different times, have affected the Tule, Kern, San Joaquin, Merced, Tuolumne, Stanislaus, and Yuba rivers.

It is true that most of these, and other river basins within Northern California in which consumptive uses have long claimed the full natural surface flow during the summer months, fail to show such serious allocation problems as have the Kings and Kaweah rivers. Partly this reflects physical differences in terrain: land areas readily served from most San Joaquin Valley rivers lying between the San Joaquin and the American contain more homogeneous land than those at the south end of the San Joaquin Valley, so that greatest probable misallocations are

[2] This section draws upon the Gaffney-Trelease debate, mentioned above in Chapter 12, and upon the various court decisions in the Lindsay-Strathmore cases.

perhaps smaller. The directions of bias are clearly the same in all cases. Given the practical limitations on the transfer of water rights and the adjustment of district boundaries, older areas with perfected water rights have tended to claim too much water as against unorganized or more newly organized territory. So far as crops are tied to particular soil types and land areas, crops facing expanding demands have claimed too little water as against static crops. Local actions to alleviate these misallocations, furthermore, have tended to generate inefficiencies in the use of non-water inputs; new users in river basins have developed adjacent parallel-hauling canals and ground-water pumping systems at a long-run resource cost greater than that of rationalizing water allocations in the basins. Incremental rationalization has repeatedly failed because of the restraints of law and attitude on marginal adjustments by established agencies and the complexities associated with external effects.

Storage Works and Interseasonal Water Transfers

The full utilization of natural streamflow in the summer—which first occurred by the 1920's for much of the San Joaquin Valley and since World War II for most of the rest of the Central Valley—has regularly generated an interest in large-scale dams and reservoirs for the transfer of water from winter to summer use. These projects usually involve power generation and always affect in-stream uses of a river's flow to some extent. Thus they raise issues of allocative efficiency for at least three of the major frontiers listed above: between winter and summer uses, among classes of use, and among user agencies on a particular stream.

The entrepreneurship for such projects has come from three primary sources. The most important has been public agencies, including local agencies interested primarily in storing water for agricultural or municipal use, and federal and state agencies acting in the interest of such uses. Second, electric power companies have taken the initiative in constructing a substantial number of dams in Northern California. When acting on their own behalf they have most frequently constructed single purpose structures, which are capable of only relatively small interseasonal transfers and which also have relatively small net significance for the allocation of water among different types of uses. Nonetheless, they have built, on their own account, about 15 per cent of the major on-stream reservoir capacity in the area, which *nolens volens* accomplishes an important volume of interseasonal water transfers for consumptive use. Finally, some agencies have acted in the interest of flood control, notably the U.S. Army Corps of Engineers. Projects initiated out of an interest in flood control also frequently have served the purpose of interseasonal water storage for consumptive uses, despite the potentially incompatible release patterns which the two functions would indicate.

Before reviewing the conduct of these different types of agencies and their implications for performance, we can refer to some data showing the timing of the construction of storage reservoirs in Northern California and the class of entrepreneurial agencies responsible. Table 33 covers the construction of the sixty largest reservoirs in the area, comprising 84 per cent of all reservoir capacity at the present time. Over 90 per cent of this capacity in the largest sixty reservoirs was constructed in two periods, the 1920's and the years after World War II. Clearly, the transfer of water from winter to summer markets was not pushed very hard until after World War II. Table 34 shows that the types of agencies responsible for construction in each of these periods have shifted sharply over time. Private water companies predominated in the relatively small volume of construction before 1921, and electric utility companies in the even smaller volume between 1931 and 1941. In the 1920's, electric utility companies and local public districts serving consumptive users accounted for almost all construction. Since World War II, the great bulk of dam construction has been by the federal agencies, in substantial part to support not just interseasonal but also interbasin transfers of water. Thus a discussion of the behavior of different classes of entrepreneurial agencies is largely congruent with a discussion of the forces governing the determination of interseasonal transfers in different periods of time. This is especially true when we note that most projects currently planned or under construction by irrigation districts and other nonurban local agencies are cooperative ventures with electric utilities, and thus differ significantly from the sort of unilateral projects previously undertaken by these agencies.

TABLE 33
TIMING OF COMPLETION OF SIXTY LARGEST RESERVOIRS IN NORTHERN CALIFORNIA EXISTING IN 1962

Date of completion	Number of reservoirs	Total capacity (millions of acre-feet)	Per cent of total capacity of largest 60 in 1962
Before 1921	10	1.56	8.0
1921–1930	20	3.60	18.5
1931–1941	2	0.21	1.2
1947–1962	28	14.07	72.3
Total	60	19.44	100.0

SOURCE: California Department of Water Resources, *Dams within Jurisdiction of the State of California, January 1, 1962*, Bulletin No. 17 (1962).

TABLE 34
PERCENTAGE OF CAPACITY IN SIXTY LARGEST STORAGE RESERVOIRS OF NORTHERN CALIFORNIA IN 1962, BY TYPE OF AGENCY AND PERIOD OF COMPLETION

Date of completion	U.S. Bureau of Reclamation, Army Corps of Engineers	Electric utility companies	Irrigation districts	Municipal districts	Other public agencies	Private water companies
Before 1921	37.2	13.5	3.1	5.8	0	40.4
1921–1930	1.4	53.3	23.3	22.0	0	0
1931–1941	0	67.0	0	0	33.0	0
1947–1962	87.8	3.8	2.8	2.3	3.3	0

SOURCE: Same as Table 33.

Power companies can be disposed of first, since much of their construction activity before World War II involved the construction of reservoirs at relatively high altitudes to make falling water available for power generation. Despite their size, the operation of these reservoirs generally did not result in interseasonal transfers of water for consumptive use proportional to their capacities to effect such transfers. This was partly because of the power companies' seasonal demand patterns at that time and partly because much of their capacity was concentrated on a few rivers whose flows were fully utilized for consumptive purposes only at a later date. Only in minor cases did power companies undertake to sell water for consumptive use, and those were mainly in that part of the Sierra Nevada where their own works made use of old mining flumes. Thus they did not appropriate, and so probably did not take into account, many external benefits of their construction for other classes of users. By the same token, these other classes of users (most, irrigation water users) could freeload on the extra summer water supplies created by the operation of power company reservoirs. Presumably the rate and scale of construction of storage reservoirs by the power companies prior to World War II tended to be appropriate in the light of their own cost and revenue prospects, and probably it tended to be suboptimal with regard to the volume of storage capacity, its distribution among rivers, and the level of interseasonal transfers appropriate to water uses as a whole.[3]

Interest in the construction of projects to support interseasonal water transfers (or projects in general) by local public suppliers of irrigation water has almost always come about for the same reasons that such agencies are formed in the first place: an inadequacy of existing supplies felt by the final users. The same might be said of municipal water agencies, except that they tend to be more responsive to anticipated future shortages of supply. These local government units thus have tended to act on the basis of potential benefits for their own member-customers rather than on the basis of any broader criterion of economic welfare. And they have tended to take action when spurred by internal current or prospective shortages rather than from discerning an opportunity for a project having a favorable benefit-cost relation.

The process of project design and construction has always been affected by a number of elements which could result in incorrect allocations among classes of users. For example, the familiar phenomenon of capital rationing clearly afflicts local water agencies, each with its borrowing ability keyed to the size of its initial tax base rather than to the prospective payoff of its project. Also, local agencies tend to seek and design projects with a particular output or service area in mind, and not necessarily with a view to picking the optimal scale for any project contemplated.

The most common objective of retail water agencies considering storage projects to augment their supplies from natural streamflow is to satisfy demand within

[3] Interaction between the power companies and other agencies before World War II was less important than subsequently, but not entirely absent. The San Joaquin Light and Power Company sought a cooperative arrangement to build Pine Flat Dam on the Kings River, but was frustrated for various reasons. Some irrigation districts arranged to sell the power output of their own projects to the electric utilities.

their own territories. That means, of course, demand at whatever marginal cost per unit of water governs the demand decisions of their constituencies. Our study does not show any abundant evidence of marginal water pricing related to considerations of long-run marginal cost except in terms of ground-water management, but it does indicate that the customer-constituents of agricultural water agencies look beyond water charges to long-run water costs in determining their water demands. So far as they do not look at long-run water costs, there may be a tendency for agencies to design capacities to supply economically excessive water supplies for their own customers. (This tendency seems more likely in urban than in agricultural water agencies.) But, on the other hand, they tend not to consider the possibility of developing projects substantially larger than their own requirements would warrant and going into the business of wholesaling water. Important qualifications must be attached to this assertion: (1) Cities or water districts based in urban territory sometimes seek to enter the water wholesaling business in order to gratify political objectives. (2) In several important cases, pairs of districts have jointly undertaken large projects for agricultural water supply, or one large district has acted in trust for adjacent smaller ones. Nonetheless, the fealty of districts to their existing membership certainly exerts some influence on the extent to which the optimal scale and timing of a storage project are considered. The evidence cited in Chapter 2 (Table 3) of sharp differences in the degree of storage regulation of closely adjacent rivers in the Central Valley tends to confirm this implication.

This orientation of local districts to the requirements of their own members implies a bias toward inefficiently small project scales—although some biases run in the opposite direction. The critical difficulties which local districts have always had in financing their projects tell a tale of capital rationing. Without the participation of power companies, general-obligation bonds have usually been a necessary means of financing projects, testifying to the concern of lenders with the base payment capacity of the district rather than the payoff associated with its prospective project. This pressure could tend to restrict the scale of a project built by a district to serve its own lands, let alone block any inclination toward wholesaling water to other agencies. Another bias tending to induce insufficient scale for the projects of local districts has been their typical inability to appropriate to themselves the cash value of certain external economies, most notably flood control. In a few recent cases, the federal government has provided grants to compensate for flood control benefits, and the state of California can similarly provide funds covering recreational benefits under the Davis-Grunsky program. Not all external effects of local projects have been favorable, of course, with in-stream fisheries being the prominent loser, but large favorable externalities have clearly been ignored until recently.

Still another factor which has tended to produce an insufficient level of water transfers for use in the summer season through projects developed by local agencies has been the effect of tangled water rights and misallocation of natural flow within a river's service area. The Kings River and several lesser cases document the way in which unsettled water rights can create uncertainty about the claims to the water which any one local agency might undertake to store from the spring runoff for summer use; this was certainly one factor which precluded the construction of Pine Flat Dam in the 1920's. A water rights situation which causes the marginal productivities of water to differ sharply among agencies drawing on a river can also distort the timing and scale of the construction of storage works, although here the direction of bias is less evident. The greater incentive to bring about the transfer of more water to the summer market will tend to lie with districts having high marginal productivities, which would be lowered by any rationalization of the allocation of claims to the natural flow. Thus, misallocation might encourage excessive construction and transfers of water for use in the summer season. The effect of capital rationing on local agencies, however, seems historically to have offset this bias completely. The wealthier agencies (in terms of assessed valuation), less afflicted by capital rationing, have almost always been the older ones with well-entrenched rights to natural flow, not the newcomers with insufficient water supplies to irrigate all of their lands. Furthermore, most construction of storage has in fact been by agencies with relatively strong rights to natural flow, and marginal productivities of water probably lower than those of excluded would-be users. The net effect of misallocation, therefore, has probably been that transfers of water from the winter to the summer season have come too little and too late, with the effect of capital rationing more than offsetting the effect of differing marginal productivities.

These important historical factors creating a bias toward insufficient scale in the projects of local agencies may not, of course, have overwhelmed opposing forces sufficiently to create a net bias. Cutting the other way, besides external diseconomies, would be a tendency to overestimate future net returns from irrigated farming. This could be caused by estimating demand with reference to water prices charged to district customers which are less than long-run marginal cost, and by inflating the scale of projects for the sake of greater local glory. The historic evidence thus does not prove that local districts' transfers of winter water for use in the summer season have been too little and too late, but there is a moderately good chance that the bias has leaned in that direction, especially prior to World War II.

In the past decade, most of the important water storage projects constructed by local districts serving agricultural users have been cooperative ventures involving the Pacific Gas and Electric Company. The form of these projects substantially changes the biases involved, so that the conclusions suggested in the preceding paragraph well may not hold for them. First of all, PG&E essentially assumes the risk-bearing function associated with these projects, so that the problem of capital rationing largely disappears.[4] Second, the tax biases favoring the construction of these hydroelectric projects as against facilities for steam generation suggest that their timing may be premature rather than delayed.[5] Assuming them to be justifiable investments at some scale, however, their scales

[4] Other risk-bearers have also made themselves available lately. Several small-scale programs of the state and federal government can be used to cover project planning costs, and some engineering firms have been willing to work on a contingency basis in the planning of projects.

[5] See Chapter 14, the subsection on electric utilities and local water districts, and Chapter 15, the subsection on local public water agencies—behavior and level of development.

may be deficient rather than excessive, because of the use of a standardized form of joint participation whereby the irrigation district makes no contribution to the capital costs of the storage facilities. Furthermore, the sequence in which these joint projects are undertaken is somewhat random in relation to their economic justification, because the initiative lies with the local water agency and thus depends on the vagrant forces of local entrepreneurial zeal. Comparing the recent joint projects with those carried out previously by local districts acting on their own, both types share the features of a possible bias toward suboptimal scale and substantial random elements in the timing and sequence of constraint of capital rationing; and they are subject to the operation of some biases which might permit the construction of projects with deficient benefit-cost characteristics.

The story of investment in water storage and transport facilities by municipalities, both in the 1920's and since World War II, has been somewhat different from that of agricultural districts. In discussing their behavior, we immediately encounter the problem of generalizing from a very small sample, because in Northern California most cities outside of the San Francisco Bay area have developed water supplies from ground-water basins, a process which permits incremental adjustments in capacity and raises relatively less taxing problems of resource allocation. The major investment decisions by municipal agencies themselves have been those of the city of San Francisco and the East Bay Municipal Utility District. The main feature distinguishing their investment behavior from that of the local agricultural districts is a reluctance to take a chance that available supplies will be inadequate at the going price. As a result, substantial excess capacity is maintained at most times in all parts of their water systems. Several separate factors contribute to this overcapacity. The San Francisco Bay cities face the special threat of earthquakes, which in extreme cases might both sever their conduits and greatly increase water needs for fighting fires. They maintain substantial excess capacity in terminal storage and distribution facilities for that reason. But even apart from the problem of earthquakes, these and other cities typically maintain a good deal of excess capacity in their water systems for fire-fighting purposes. Still another cause of excess capacity is uncertainty about water rights and the market for water. San Francisco, operating under the peculiar terms of the Raker Act, has had to maintain a steady pace of development of its source of supply in the Tuolumne River in order to protect its continued access to water rights. Even without the Raker Act, however, the difficulty of depending on transfers of water rights would induce much the same behavior pattern. We have not, on the basis of this type of information, been able to reach an unqualified conclusion that municipalities tend to maintain excessive and premature investment in water storage and transfer. Once again, forces such as capital rationing cut in the opposite direction. But the bias toward excessive or premature investment is much stronger than for agricultural districts acting without the assistance of PG&E.

The federal agencies have been the dominant organizations in building water storage facilities in Northern California during the last two decades. Our evaluation in Chapter 11 of the project planning practices of the Bureau of Reclamation and the Corps of Engineers in California indicated a number of biases tending to cause nonoptimal allocation—a finding which agrees with those of other investigators who have focused on the national activities of these agencies. Before the past decade, in particular, numerous inappropriate practices entered into the calculation of benefit-cost ratios. Among these are the confusion of agricultural benefits with gross additions to farm income; and secondary benefits still seem inflated in most cases. The Bureau has largely ignored the additions resulting from its projects to the outputs of crops already in surplus under federal support programs.[6] Evidence suggests strongly that the Bureau and Corps tend to overestimate the benefits of their projects and underestimate the costs. Although they are now committed to examining incremental benefit-cost relations, they have as yet shown little sign of doing so;[7] indeed, the scales of projects seem frequently to be changed after the initial benefit-cost evaluations are issued, without any public revelation of revised calculations.

Outside of such difficulties with the technical planning practices lie the forces reflecting the political environment of the planning decisions of these agencies. Their activities respond to the expression of local interest much more than to the discernment of a favorable benefit-cost ratio, a fact which holds true even more for the congressional appropriations process once a project has been proposed by the Corps or the Bureau. This political responsiveness may tend to make the federal agencies sensitive to the plight of would-be water users excluded by the water rights situation from drawing upon the summertime natural flow of a river. Inefficient construction can result if the marginal products of water for agencies with established rights are substantially less than those for the excluded users whose activities set the measure for prospective benefits, for a more rational allocation of natural flow would place lower-value uses at the observed margin and lower the apparent benefits of storing spring runoff for transfer to summer use.[8] These facts, plus the lack of attention to incremental benefit-cost ratios, overstatement of benefits and underestimate of costs, seem to add up to the possibility of excessive construction and excessive transfers of water from winter

[6] For example, the U.S. Department of Agriculture, commenting on the feasibility report for the Sacramento canals projects of the Bureau, declared: "Many of the products of the specialized orchard industry of California are now being produced in quantities exceeding demands. In fact, Government programs have for some time been necessary to deal with surpluses of most of the fruits and nuts mentioned in your proposed reports. . . . It appears . . . that a considerable increase over present demands could be satisfied without expansion of the acreage now devoted to these crops. Should additional acreage be required, many established orchards could be economically and quickly expanded. Contrary to the impression given by the reports, there is little prospect that the United States growers can expect to compete successfully for foreign markets." Of the project's other major crop output, the Department remarked that "not even the best (irrigated) pasture can justify an investment" of the magnitude envisioned. U.S. Congress, House Committee on Interior and Insular Affairs, *Sacramento Canals Unit, Central Valley Project, California,* H. Doc. 73, 83 Cong. 1 sess. (1953), pp. 201–02. (This and other footnote references are cited in brief form when they are also included in the Bibliography.)

[7] I. K. Fox and O. C. Herfindahl, "Attainment of Efficiency in Satisfying Demands for Water Resources," *American Economic Review,* LIV (May 1964), 198–206.

[8] Of course, the Bureau's intervention can work the other way and force a rationalization of existing rights. It clearly did so in one very important case, the purchase of Miller & Lux rights to the San Joaquin River in order to permit its storage and diversion at Friant. But the troublesome political aftermath of this transaction suggests that it may prove unique.

to summer markets as a result of construction activities by the Bureau and the Corps.

Having reviewed the behavior patterns of the major groups of dam-building agencies, we can consider an important implication of the time sequence of their major periods of activity. The power companies and the local agencies representing consumptive users largely preceded the state and federal agencies in developing Northern California's water resources, with the joint projects of the districts and PG&E excepted. We get the impression (it could be converted to a certainty only by making a number of retrospective benefit-cost evaluations) that the sequence in which these projects were chosen was largely rational: the best projects were picked off first. Power company officials have affirmed this view with regard to hydroelectric projects. In the case of storage reservoirs built largely or entirely to support consumptive uses, the pre-World War II local projects not only refrained from overdeveloping the resources picked for exploitation (as we argued above), but also chose approximately the best bundles of resources available.

This predominant rationality of the sequence of reservoir construction means that in the last two decades the only water resource bundles available for development by the federal and state agencies have been inferior to those already exploited. That is, they have been inferior in the sense that efficiently designed projects to utilize them would offer lower benefit-cost ratios than would local projects already in existence, if evaluated for construction at the same time. The fact that the federal and state agencies have often had to choose among picked-over water resources helps, along with the biases previously identified, to explain their tendency toward excessive levels of development. There are two exceptions to this proposition that the cream of projects had previously been skimmed by local agencies: cases where water rights entanglements had precluded local development; and cases where large minimum scales of efficient construction had blocked local action because of capital rationing. Friant Dam on the San Joaquin River and Pine Flat Dam on the Kings River probably fall under the first exception. Shasta Dam on the Sacramento, Oroville Dam on the Feather, and possibly Folsom Dam on the American River may come under the second exception, with Folsom dependent largely on its flood control benefits. As suggested in Chapter 15, however, even these potentially justifiable projects actually have been overdeveloped, or designed for inefficient service areas. The other state and federal projects seem largely designed to exploit inferior bundles of resources—Trinity, Berryessa, Auburn, the smaller dams in the southern San Joaquin Valley, and a number of large projects now proposed or authorized for construction. Growing demands, of course, can eventually justify the exploitation of inferior resources at the extensive margin, but the fact that the unexploited resources are inferior compounds the chances of overdevelopment when the behavior of the agencies in question predisposes them toward this outcome in the first place.

Our review of the historical process of constructing storage reservoirs on Northern California rivers has centered on questions relating to the various extensive margins affected by the behavior of the agencies concerned. Interest also attaches to the internal margin of capital-intensity of the project designs developed by local districts, PG&E, and the federal agencies. Capital-intensity is partly a question of the discount rate employed in calculating the optimal design and partly a question of technical standards of safety or reliability in construction. We have only fragmentary evidence on both aspects. Those feasibility studies of projects for local agencies which specify the discount rate used in valuing future costs and revenues usually mention a figure between 3.0 and 4.5 per cent. The marginal borrowing rates for the agencies in question are typically higher, suggesting the possibility of designs which are excessively capital-intensive in terms of the agencies' own access to capital markets, but not necessarily in terms of an appropriate social rate of time preference. The Pacific Gas and Electric Company is widely believed to insist on more "conservative" engineering and design standards for projects than do other agencies, with the result of greater capital-intensity. Also when designs by the Bureau of Reclamation are compared with those for similar projects by local agencies, especially distribution systems, the Bureau's strongly tend to be more capital-intensive. It may be possible to rationalize the designs chosen by these different agencies in terms of differences in capital constraints and rates of time preference among them. Without trying to settle the very complex issues of optimal allocation which are involved, it is clear at the least that not everybody can be right from the viewpoint of general economic welfare.

The rivalries between agencies over the construction of storage reservoirs on Sierra Nevada rivers in the past few years also have implications for the performance of the industry in transferring winter water for use in the summer season. The biases are several, and the net effect is not clear. Rivalry over making such transfers could be desirable if it insured a vigorous pursuit of the best possible project design for a river. But the evidence presented in Chapter 12 suggests that the best project may not always win. First of all, temporal priority in water rights applications, the political strength and solidarity of the contestants, and the availability of financing—all of these play a powerful role, and none bears a conspicuously close relation to ideal project selection. Consistency with the California Water Plan (a test often invoked by the California Water Commission in assigning state filings) does not help much since the Plan itself constitutes a grand design with largely untested details. Second, the bargaining strength conferred by statute upon the counties of origin may be accepted as a valid expression of social policy; but the low productivity of large-scale water developments in most of these upland areas suggests that the role of these counties may be to delay otherwise desirable projects or force design changes which may reduce the present value of the projects in question. Third, the appearance of rivalry, actual or potential, for the interseasonal transfers encourages a race for scarce resources which may result in premature construction or excessive use of water in order to establish water rights to large quantities through a showing of "beneficial use." On balance, rivalry does not seem to produce more rational design of projects or reasoned consideration of the probable value of future benefits. Whether, on balance, it spurs or retards construction activity is impossible to tell.

The storage of water for consumptive use in the summer months has always had important effects upon other types of uses. Chapter 14 described ways in which uses such as power generation, recreation, navigation, and salinity repulsion can bear complex relations to the level and pattern of water use for consumptive purposes. These other uses are sometimes complementary, sometimes competing, depending on the particular circumstances. For example, they depend on both the winter and spring runoff in the case of water to sustain salmon runs, and upon summer levels of streamflow in the case of navigation. Although we shall not summarize here the whole history of the water industry as it has affected the optimal allocation of water to these uses, we can indicate to what degree the process of developing projects to transfer water to the summer market has resulted in incidental gains and losses in utilities derived from these other uses of water.

Until the end of World War II, it is fair to say that the only external effect upon other types of uses of the transfer and use of water for agricultural and municipal consumption which affected allocations to consumption was its impact upon power generation. Navigation had not been affected adversely. Problems of salinity and water pollution were recognized, but no feasible remedy directly[9] involving other uses was under discussion. Dams constructed before World War II had been seen to affect stream fisheries adversely, particularly salmon runs. However, the California Department of Fish and Game possessed neither statutory authority nor appropriations to secure more than minor concurrence of the water users with the interests of fisheries conservation.

Since World War II, and especially in the past decade, the situation has changed somewhat. Construction of the major dams has had the effect of ameliorating the salinity problem considerably, although marginal adjustments between this and other beneficial uses of water have remained a matter of controversy. Nothing substantial has been done about pollution of the lower San Joaquin by irrigation runoff upstream, but the problem and some physical approaches to solving it have at least been studied. The Department of Fish and Game has taken a more active role before state and federal regulatory agencies in demanding that conditions be imposed on the operation of projects to protect fisheries resources. Its success seems to have been limited, mainly on account of a prevailing bias that the construction of projects should be allowed to proceed; that if wildlife protection and the project itself are incompatible, the fish must take the hindmost. Therefore, the Department has had poorer results in dealing with agricultural than with municipal projects, because the latter more often possess a sufficient margin of feasibility to afford the costs of protective arrangements. Although the situations in individual river basins differ significantly, in-stream uses have probably been insufficiently served as a result of the construction and operation of storage projects, and too much water has been transferred for use in the summer season.

In short, the general impression emerges that, through the end of World War II, the water industry had probably not attained a high enough level of transfers of water from the winter runoff to summer uses. Since the War, however, that deficiency has been made up and quite possibly has been substantially over-compensated.

[9] The main solution put forth to deal with salinity problems had been the grandiose Biemond Plan for a barrier to be built across San Francisco Bay to keep out saline ocean water.

Water Transfers between River Basins

A new development in the water industry since World War II is the large-scale transfer of water between basins or subbasins. Two of these began in the interwar period on behalf of the cities of the San Francisco Bay area. The same years saw the development of the basic concept of the Central Valley Project, a complex transfer from the northern to the southern part of the Central Valley, and the California Water Plan, a more grandiose project for the transfer of water from as far as the north coastal region to the southern part of the San Joaquin Valley and to both the coastal and interior desert regions of Southern California. The so-called "basic features" of the Central Valley Project are in operation, with more works to come; the first project unit of the California Water Plan is under construction; and the Plan and its implementation will be a dominant issue in the state for decades to come. Figure 33 shows the major interbasin transfers which have been completed, planned for construction, or seriously proposed by the California Department of Water Resources, the Bureau of Reclamation, and certain local agencies. It illustrates the extensive interconnections of river basin water supplies that have been at least contemplated in the plans of agencies empowered to carry out such construction.

Technical economies of scale insure that interbasin transfers, if they occur at all, will be made at a very large scale. This fact consigns their undertaking to agencies of the state or federal governments or to large cities. They become subject to all the influences discussed in the preceding section which can affect allocative decisions by such agencies.

The basic design of the Central Valley Project illustrated these problems clearly enough. It was influenced strongly by misallocations existing in the regions to be served by the interbasin transfers. One such critical area was the lands now comprising the Arvin-Edison Water Storage District, located south of the Kern River and to the east of territory served by irrigation from the Kern itself. The Kern service area is clearly one in which the allocation of irrigation water has responded poorly to differences in marginal productivities. The basic agreement governing its allocation dates back to the 1880's and has not been changed substantially since. (A major effort to rationalize it in the 1920's met with failure.) There seems a strong possibility that the productivity of water in the Arvin-Edison area is higher than in adjacent areas served by the Kern, but the failure to produce this rationalization gave rise to a substantial amount of the pressure for constructing the Friant-Kern Canal in its present location. Other misallocations of the waters of rivers north of the Kern had a similar influence. The "citrus belt" along the east side of the San Joaquin Valley consists mostly of lands developed too late to gain rights to the Kings, Kaweah, or Tule rivers, but with significantly higher water productivities than many areas possessing such rights. These lands to the east, which had resorted extensively to ground-water mining, could make a strong case on the basis of equity for large-scale public action to import water from other areas. Overlapping the problem of lands too newly developed to possess water rights was the problem of declining ground-water resources. Especially during and after World War II, the expanded rate of agricultural activity in the

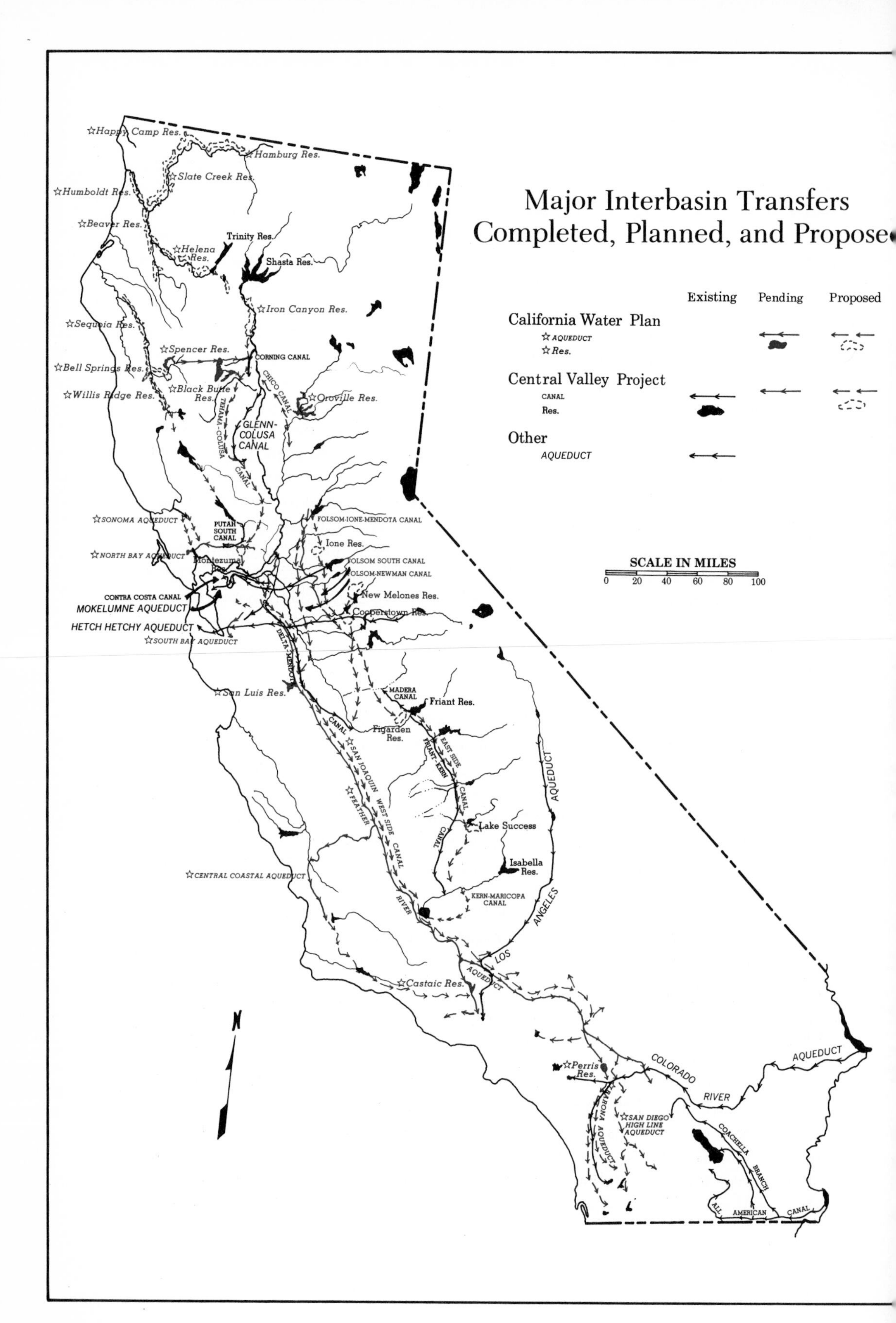
Major Interbasin Transfers
Completed, Planned, and Propose
Existing
Pending
Proposed
California Water Plan
☆ AQUEDUCT
☆ Res.
Central Valley Project
CANAL
Res.
Other
AQUEDUCT
SCALE IN MILES
0
20
40
60
80
100
☆Happy Camp Res.
☆Hamburg Res.
☆Slate Creek Res.
☆Humboldt Res.
☆Beaver Res.
☆Helena Res.
Trinity Res.
Shasta Res.
☆Iron Canyon Res.
☆Sequoia Res.
☆Spencer Res.
CORNING CANAL
☆Bell Springs Res.
☆Black Butte Res.
☆Willis Ridge Res.
CHICO CANAL
☆Oroville Res.
TEHAMA-COLUSA CANAL
GLENN-COLUSA CANAL
☆SONOMA AQUEDUCT
PUTAH SOUTH CANAL
FOLSOM-IONE-MENDOTA CANAL
Ione Res.
☆NORTH BAY AQUEDUCT
Montezuma
FOLSOM SOUTH CANAL
FOLSOM-NEWMAN CANAL
CONTRA COSTA CANAL
MOKELUMNE AQUEDUCT
New Melones Res.
HETCH HETCHY AQUEDUCT
Cooperstown Res.
☆SOUTH BAY AQUEDUCT
DELTA-MENDOTA CANAL
☆San Luis Res.
MADERA CANAL
Friant Res.
Figarden Res.
☆SAN JOAQUIN
FRIANT-KERN CANAL
EAST SIDE CANAL
AQUEDUCT
☆FEATHER
WEST SIDE CANAL
RIVER
Lake Success
Isabella Res.
☆CENTRAL COASTAL AQUEDUCT
KERN-MARICOPA CANAL
LOS ANGELES AQUEDUCT
☆Castaic Res.
N
☆Perris Res.
COLORADO RIVER AQUEDUCT
☆SAN DIEGO HIGH LINE AQUEDUCT
COACHELLA BRANCH
ALL AMERICAN CANAL

Figure 33

San Joaquin Valley depended heavily upon the mining of ground-water resources by irrigators in areas lacking a surface supply which would itself cover the increased demand and maintain ground-water reserves. Ground-water extraction throughout the area is a competitive process, mainly engaged in by individual farmers. The adjustment process implied is one of water tables declining until lower productivity uses are driven out. But this tends to involve the abandonment of irrigated farm lands and the displacement of farm families, a prospect which understandably bestirs political sentiment to take remedial measures.

Even in areas having less claim to relief than portions of the San Joaquin Valley, the importation of substantial outside supplies of water has often been seen as the logical alternative to the legal imbroglio required definitively to settle rights of current users of a river. The campaigns for both the initial and subsequent features of the Central Valley Project were strongly motivated by the idea that importing substantial supplies of water from outside sources constituted a highly desirable alternative to the legal endeavor of deciding conflicting claims to presently available supplies.

In short, the misallocations of surface flows within river basins, the unpleasant prospect of approaching competitive equilibrium in ground-water extraction, and the costly and time-consuming process of reaching a definitive determination of water rights on a river by standard legal procedures have all contributed political strength to the demand for government action to bring about large-scale interbasin transfers of water. Once unleashed in the 1930's, these motives have tended to become cumulative. When the idea of interbasin transfers was accepted by the Bureau of Reclamation and propounded in its major planning document of 1949, *Central Valley Basin,*[10] water users on all rivers in the area began to examine their own situations for possibilities that, in the eyes of the Bureau of Reclamation, an "exportable surplus" might be flowing in their streambeds. A powerful incentive was immediately created for expanded use within each basin, encouraging full utilization of the summer natural flow if that had not been accomplished before, or local storage projects to forestall construction by the Bureau of Reclamation if these could be financed and promoted.

In the midst of these pressures for and against interbasin transfers of water, the decision processes employed by the major construction agencies, the Bureau of Reclamation and the California Department of Water Resources, came to take on great importance. Unfortunately, such agencies are ill-equipped for the Olympian contemplation of benefits and costs in the face of such complex and far-reaching political pressures. No evidence suggests that a wide range of alternatives were considered in the design of these giant projects, either in the form of scale of construction or location of service area. For instance, interchanges of water between the Friant-Kern Canal, running south from the San Joaquin River, and the Kings River, whose channel it crosses, might logically have increased the average firm output of water in both sources during the summer season, but

[10] U.S. Department of the Interior, Bureau of Reclamation, *Central Valley Basin: A Comprehensive Departmental Report on the Development of the Water and Related Resources of the Central Valley Basin, and Comments from the State of California and Federal Agencies,* S. Doc. 113, 81 Cong. 1 sess. (1949).

political hostility to the Bureau among irrigators in the Kings River service area made this impossible. At a more fundamental level, one can wonder about areas of irrigable land, still unirrigated or served only from limited ground-water sources, which might have provided alternative service areas for supplies imported from the Sacramento River to the San Joaquin Valley. As an example, soil maps show the lands in the western and southwestern parts of the San Joaquin Valley comparing favorably in quality for irrigated farming with large parts of the Valley actually irrigated with water from the Central Valley Project.[11] An extension of the Delta-Mendota Canal to the south, into the so-called federal service area of the San Luis project, might possibly have possessed a higher benefit-cost ratio than Friant Dam and its canals. The point is that no serious study of this or other possibilities seems to have been made: the orientation of the Bureau's efforts in designing the Central Valley Project was toward responding to demand voiced with considerable political force.

The doubts which beset us in appraising the planning process of the Bureau of Reclamation remain when the effects of rivalry among wholesalers engaging in interbasin transfers are examined. As in the case of rival designs for projects to transfer water to the summer season within particular basins, it seems possible or even likely in principle that the presence of alternatives might increase the chances of the best design being sought and found. The examination of cases in Chapter 12 showed that some gains clearly do occur, such as a meaningful choice for retail agency customers as to the quality of water which they receive. But when all of the wholesale rivals are afflicted by a diverse assortment of political motives, the assurance evaporates. Furthermore, the thrust of bargaining over wholesale water transactions is not to preserve the flexibility of allocation inherent in the existence of alternatives, but to tie natural sources of final uses with the sinews of traditional water law. Much of the Bureau's difficulty in negotiating contracts for the sale of Central Valley Project water, apart from friction over the acreage limitation provisions of reclamation law, has resulted from the Bureau's effort to employ a so-called utility service contract rather than to sell the wholesale facilities to their current retail customers on the installment plan. So far as the appearance of rival wholesalers has increased the availability of alternative allocations within the water industry—and this has certainly been accomplished—the result was not welcomed by many of the participants.

In any case, there is probably little point in complaining about the lack of flexibility in transactions between wholesale and retail agencies. It is bound to be limited, at best. One adverse pressure lies in the dependence of water rights upon beneficial use of the supplies claimed, a requirement which tends to put the wholesaler in a difficult bargaining position except when a network of long-term commitments has been established. Water law is, of course, mutable. Less changeable is the uncertainty afflicting the marketing of water in a continuously adjusting market, a strong and sufficient force impelling long-term contracts and a slow turnover in water market transactions. The passing of private enterprise from

[11] R. Earl Storie and Walter W. Weir, *Generalized Soil Map of California,* Manual No. 6, Agricultural Experiment Station and Extension Service, College of Agriculture, University of California, Berkeley (n.d.).

the water industry a half-century ago or more testifies to the fruitlessness of seeing a sufficient way out of the industry's allocative difficulties through a massive increase in the use of market transactions, whatever kinds of legal entities populate the market.

The brief review of the conduct of the water industry over the course of its development has shown some of the violations of particular allocative frontiers which have at times assumed significant proportions. These allocations have been important not only for their own time, but even more for their cumulative impact over time. Physical capital lasts for a long time in the storage and distribution of water, and water rights tend to last forever. For many reasons these elements, once firmly set, affect decisions for years to come.

The following two chapters continue the examination of marginal allocations in the water industry, emphasizing detailed evidence and measurements relating to the contemporary situation. That evidence, placed beside the evolutionary process which brought present-day conditions into being, allows finally an appraisal of the causes of defects in the industry's performance and some conclusions about what remedial measures might prove effective.

17

EFFICIENCY IN THE ALLOCATION OF WATER

This third phase of our appraisal of efficiency in the Northern California water industry involves the rationality of the contemporary allocation of water among uses.

For any scarce resource, there is a definable optimum in allocation, such that the greatest total addition to economic welfare, as measured by value of products and services, will be secured from the use of the resource. Such an optimum for a homogeneous resource, which is transferable without cost among types, locations, and times of use and among individual users, requires that in every use and for every user the resource should have the same net value of marginal product. For a resource which is fundamentally nonhomogeneous as regards its own location in space and time (and perhaps also nonhomogeneous in quality), which is used at various different locations and at various different times, and which is transferable only at appreciable costs, optimal allocation requires attainment of a somewhat more complex set of relations among its marginal productivities. The form of the relations, familiar from general economic theory, was discussed in Chapter 8.

As we consider water as a resource in Northern California, the initial simple question regarding its allocation is how closely it conforms to the optimum. Water is a resource which is fundamentally nonhomogeneous in location in space and time and is used at a variety of sites and times, in a context where interlocational and intertemporal transfers are costly. Thus, not only is a simple criterion of optimal allocation replaced by a complex of related criteria, but the simple question is necessarily elaborated into a series of subquestions about the various allocative frontiers mentioned at the beginning of Chapter 16. How closely does the allocation of water from various individual sources among types of use—such as irrigation, power generation, and recreation—conform to optimum allocation among such uses? What degree of conformance to the optimum is found in allocation of water for use among the seasons of the year? Is there a significant divergence from optimal allocation of water for use among the regions, subregions, and river basins of the area? In individual localities wherein various users and potential users of water for a given purpose, such as irrigation, have access to a common source of supply, to what extent does the allocation of water from the source among users or groups of users conform to or diverge from the optimum? And within groups of users served by single water agencies, how appropriate economically is the typical allocation of water among the numerous customers of an individual agency?

Although we may take up, in turn, the propriety of the contemporary allocation of Northern California water at each of these five allocational margins or frontiers, they cannot all be analyzed separately and independently. This is because the determination of allocation on one frontier frequently involves either codetermining or strongly influencing allocation on another, either as a matter of logical necessity or as a matter of practice as particular water projects are constructed. Thus, determination of the interseasonal allocation of water unavoidably influences the allocation of water among types of use, and vice versa. As a result, allocational optima on the two frontiers must be codetermined, and appraisal of actual allocation on either frontier must involve an appraisal of unavoidably interconnected actual allocation on the other. Or, a given interseasonal allocation may be properly appraised only in the light of interbasin water transfers it has been designed to implement. In that case, the actual interseasonal allocation and actual interregional allocation of water really requires a joint appraisal, as a sort of indivisible package of allocations. In other cases, practically interconnected allocations, such as the allocation of water between exporting and importing regions and of imported water among localities of use and users in the importing region, may be evaluated semiseparately. Determination of the scale of the interbasin transfer could have been linked with any of a variety of allocations of the imported water, of which one was chosen as an option.[1] In sum, as we appraise allocation on each of several frontiers, we must continually take account of the fact that a given allocation on any one frontier must be judged in the light of both its logically necessary impact and its *ad hoc* impact on allocation on other frontiers.

Before we proceed to an appraisal of contemporary water allocation, several comments are in order concerning limitations on the sort of appraisal undertaken and of the data available as a basis for appraisals.

The first limitation has to do with the standards employed in determining whether or not a contemporary misallocation exists. Consider testing the propriety of various sorts of contemporary water allocation arrived at by the erection of man-made facilities, such as dams creating storage reservoirs, major long canals for interbasin transport of water, diversion dams, and local main canals. This generally can be done by comparing (1) the contemporary marginal value of delivered water—delivered for summer instead of winter use, to an importing area, or to a certain group of local users—with (2) the marginal cost of delivery measured in terms of the value of non-water inputs plus the marginal opportunity cost of the water delivered in the source from which it was drawn. But which marginal costs of non-water inputs should be counted—both past and future marginal costs, including sunk costs of investment in fixed facilities, or the *ex ante* marginal costs of operating and maintaining facilities which are already built? The answer depends on whether we are attempting to arrive at an appraisal of the extent of historically developed contemporary misallocations of water, or

[1] In this sort of case, the allocation on the first frontier can properly be judged both in terms of the results obtained with the chosen option on the second frontier, and in terms of the results which could have been attained if a superior option had been chosen on the second frontier, though the actual justifiability of accomplished allocations on the prior frontier is in fact conditioned by irrevocable choices of options on the second frontier once these choices are made and have hardened in concrete.

at a set of recommendations as to which of such misallocations should now be corrected by cutting the rate of utilization of, abandoning, redesigning, relocating, or destroying existing fixed facilities.

Since our primary aim is to determine the degree of historically developed contemporary misallocations, we will base this part of our appraisal on comparisons of long-run marginal costs (inclusive of presently sunk costs as well as of contemporary opportunity costs of water) with contemporary marginal values of water. Tests based on long-run marginal costs so defined are the only ones that give us valid appraisals of contemporary allocations; tests based on short-run or *ex ante* marginal costs only provide criteria of whether living with existing misallocations contributes more to economic welfare than correcting them. Since we will adhere to the standard of long-run cost-benefit comparisons in judging contemporary allocation, we must warn that the finding of a serious misallocation does not necessarily provide the basis for inferring that it should forthwith be corrected with dynamite or reconstruction. Correction is warranted only if the resulting excess of total benefits over total costs, including any new capital costs, would be greater after the correction than the excess of total benefits over the future costs of using existing facilities without correction. Where expensive facilities with long useful lives remaining are intrinsically involved in a misallocation, the capital costs of correction are not likely to be warranted. In other instances, where such facilities are less involved (as where reallocation would require only differential adjustments in the rates of use of existing canals plus some new canal construction), correction may be warranted, but only after a more detailed examination of the facts than we will present here.

A second and related limitation can be explained much more briefly. If contemporary misallocations viewed in retrospect are the result of past investments made in fixed facilities, we are not going to pause here to inquire whether on the one hand the investments undertaken were "right" at the time they were made from the standpoint of their allocative impact, and have subsequently become "wrong" because of unanticipated changes in demands for water, in costs of alternative supplies, and so forth, or whether on the other hand the investments were wrong when undertaken and are still wrong. This question is important, especially as we turn to consider forward-looking public policy measures designed to improve future performance in the industry. But it has been explored in sufficient detail in Part Two to suggest the importance of the role of *ex ante* errors in bringing about contemporary misallocations as well as the character of, and reasons for, such errors.

A third possible limitation of the following appraisals could result from the fact that some apparent misallocations (to summer use at the expense of winter supply, for example, or to irrigation at the expense of in-stream uses) might reflect excessive usage of free water rather than misallocation of scarce water.[2] If this were the case, we might be treating a combination of excessive usage and misallocation as if it were all misallocation of scarce water. Since, as we argued

[2] This appears as a possibility, at least with respect to transfers of water from winter availability in rivers feeding the Sacramento Valley to summer use there or in other subregions, and also to proposed future transfers to the south from rivers in the north coastal region.

in Chapter 15, however, winter flows are probably scarce (and growing scarcer) throughout the Central Valley, this possibility can be largely dismissed. Because this dismissal rests heavily on the value of water for recreational uses, it is regrettable that no reliable data exist on the height of the marginal value of streamflow to sports fishermen in various locations and at various seasons. (The surrogative measures of recreational benefits usually included by federal water agencies for reservoir recreation provide no valid clue to the scale of disbenefits to in-stream recreation ignored in these calculations.) We are thus lacking in any quantitative data on marginal values in one of the uses which competes for an allocation of water, and are forestalled from making more than qualitative judgments about the propriety of allocation on some of the principal allocative frontiers.

A final and very serious limitation on our appraisals is that we also lack statistical data bearing directly on the propriety of allocation at the interrelated frontiers of interseasonal transfer and of allocation between power generation and irrigation uses of water; or data on allocation between navigation together with salinity repulsion and pollution control uses and all other uses. Some statistical evidence bears indirectly on the propriety of allocation at these interrelated frontiers, but otherwise we must rely on behavioral evidence which was largely recounted in the preceding chapter. Most of the available statistical evidence that has a direct bearing on allocations concerns the distribution of irrigation water among users from various common sources and among subregions or river basins.

The reader may thus anticipate a "constructed" evaluation of water allocation in Northern California that depends on echoes as well as original sounds, shadows as well as the substances that cast them, and impressions as well as solid findings. With this caveat, we turn to the appraisal of water allocation.

Allocation of Surface Water among Seasons of the Year

The part of the winter-spring runoff captured in storage for interseasonal transfer varies widely among rivers, ranging from substantially less than the excess of this runoff over the annual average weekly or monthly runoff of the river to substantially more. The time pattern of the releases of stored water during the year after the normal flow has dwindled from the winter peak also varies considerably among rivers, and among different reservoirs on the same river.

In principle, the optimization of a pattern of reservoir storage and release could be refined to equate net marginal productivities in any number of time periods within the year. In practice, pursuit of this refinement is limited by our inability to detect and measure changes in the marginal productivity of water for all relevant uses over very short time periods, and perhaps to solve the problems of temporal interdependence that are likely to arise. Whatever refinement of time periods can be made, the over-all optimization basically requires an appropriate reconciliation of the (correctly measured) patterns of marginal productivity at different times for the various competing uses, with all complementarities and substitutabilities taken into account. As if the problem were not complex enough at this stage, the optimal pattern of water storage and release must be codetermined with the optimal volume of storage capacity. Thus redefined, the over-all optimization becomes rather analogous to the peak-load pricing problem: the storage and release pattern is optimal only if no change would increase the total net value of product; the storage capacity is optimal only if a small increase (or decrease) of capacity and its cost would result in a smaller increase (or larger decrease) in the total net value of product.

We shall ignore these difficulties to the extent that they could be dealt with only in elaborate simulation or programming studies of each of Northern California's many rivers, and reduce them to two major interrelated questions which can be answered to some degree from the quantitative and qualitative evidence developed above:

1) Is the quantity of winter-spring water in various rivers which is stored for transfer by release to use outside of that period deficient, optimal, or excessive in the light of the non-water costs of storage, the gross benefits gained from released water, and the gross losses of benefits attributable to the quantity transferred, given the time pattern of releases actually adopted?

2) Is the time pattern of releases of the quantity of water stored from the peak runoff optimal from the standpoint of maximizing benefits from released water when the virtual losses and gains in different uses associated with each alternative time pattern are considered?

The second question will be simplified by considering mainly two limiting alternative types of time pattern of releases plus all types that lie between them. The first is a "power pattern" which may be characterized as releases in a shallow double cycle annually, with a broad peak in the summer and a sharper one in winter, separated by not very deep troughs in spring and fall (possibly combined with an unregulated spillage at times during the winter peak runoff). The second is an "irrigation pattern," featuring heavy peak releases from the time of diminution of natural flow below some critical level to the end of the irrigation season, with releases of minimal flows in the autumn and possibly during the early spring (again possibly combined with an unregulated spillage of some winter floodwater).[3] This problem will be simplified further by supposing that regulatory agencies impose given minimal-release requirements in off seasons of water needed for in-stream uses as well as maintenance-of-flow requirements to the river mouth in cases where navigation and salinity repulsion are involved.

Counterposing these two questions, it would appear logically possible to find cases in which the volume of storage and transfer was excessive, given the time pattern of releases chosen, but which would not be excessive with an improved time pattern. The data available to us, however, will hardly support judgments of this order.

Before attempting to answer these questions with respect to Northern California rivers, some brief comments about the general impact of different volumes of

[3] The irrigation pattern naturally varies somewhat from river to river due to variations in local crop mixes. By and large, its peak passes before the termination of the summer power peak, and it may also begin earlier.

storage and different patterns of releases on benefits in various uses may be in order. The storage of winter runoff for later release has an unequivocally deleterious effect on the value of benefits received in only one type of use of the rivers—sports fishing for the anadromous species, salmon and steelhead trout. Dams tend to cut off the migratory runs of these fish from their spawning grounds, and more dams and higher dams do so progressively, to the point where the runs dwindle drastically or are eliminated. Dams well into the mountains (usually powerplant dams) do the least damage, and those at or near the edges of valley floors do the most; but an extensive system of dams on all major rivers feeding a basin (such as the combined basins of the Sacramento and San Joaquin rivers) can effectively exterminate a great natural sports fishery. And they place the belated efforts to maintain the ghosts of historically great migratory fish runs with artificial spawning beds in much the same category as measures to prevent extinction of the whooping crane.[4]

Development of reservoir storage for interseasonal water transfers, therefore, must initially be charged with a significant, but unmeasured, opportunity cost in terms of lost benefits from fall and winter fishing for anadromous species. These statements refer primarily to the presence or absence of dams as stream impediments, and to their number, character, and location; given their presence, small modifications in the amount of winter flow intercepted may or may not further reduce the value of water for anadromous fisheries. The competitive relation between anadromous fisheries and other uses thus results because significant increases in the volume of interseasonal transfers of water generally require the construction of more and higher dams.

Aside from this, if a convenient though not necessarily optimal time pattern of releases is chosen, increases in reservoir storage relative to annual runoff do not necessarily take water away from one major type of use at the expense of another. They do so, however, if the volume of winter storage becomes so great as to prevent a pattern of winter releases or unchecked flows consistent with maintaining the desired winter bulge in the shallow double cycle associated with the power pattern of releases. This is to say that no major use suffers if storage volume permits a power pattern of releases (as well as an irrigation pattern and a range of patterns in between) which maintains considerable flow in the river upstream of irrigation and other diversions throughout the year. With such a power pattern, recreational benefits, including the bulk of fishing for nonmigratory trout species, are probably in the net enhanced, since good fish habitat is maintained in the mountain areas throughout the year, and flowing rivers are maintained for general enjoyment for a very long recreational season.[5] Further, with

[4] The maintenance of a severely reduced salmon fishery on the Sacramento River after its channel was blocked by Shasta Dam at the point of entry of the river into the Sacramento Valley is attributable to the topographical happenstance that the Sacramento runs a very long course through its valley from Shasta Dam to the Delta on which no further dams have been built.

[5] This generalization is subject to qualification with respect to the effect of some individual reservoirs on strategic stretches of particular rivers, even when the reservoirs are operated by utility companies for power generation alone; especially, if individual reservoirs are parts of a coordinated reservoir system on a river and if the system, but not each reservoir, is operated in a typical power pattern.

such a pattern, the summer supply of irrigation water is increased; and with diversions restricted so that river flow to the sea will permit navigation and repulse salinity, there need be no loss of these benefits either. But if winter storage becomes so great as to cut off the desired winter peak in the power pattern of releases, benefits in power production are sacrificed as the summer supply of irrigation water is further increased.

It is true, of course, that with the power pattern or other patterns of release, there can be such a thing as economically excessive storage well before full physical control of the river is reached, because of declining marginal values of added irrigation water in the irrigation season and rising marginal reservoir costs of added year-round power production and of added summer irrigation water. (The same general argument applies to urban water supplies as increased by storage.) In fact, it would appear that "full physical development" of any major rivers in the Central Valley north of the San Joaquin River would be distinctly uneconomic at the present time; and that such development was, and currently remains, uneconomic on the Sacramento River. For the Central Valley rivers from the San Joaquin south, an economic justification of the relatively full physical development that has been accomplished through dam structures hinges crucially on estimates of flood control benefits and of the costs of alternative devices for flood control.

Leaving volume of storage for the moment, let us consider time patterns of release. Here we tend to encounter a definite conflict between a power pattern and an irrigation pattern of releases. A power pattern (that is, the double cycle with only a modest summer peak and sustained releases at a substantial level between low summer and winter peaks), as noted, will be ideal for power production and not be generally inimical to recreational uses upstream of diversions or to in-stream uses downstream of diversions—if regulations to protect them are imposed. But the power pattern will definitely tend to reduce the supply of water in the irrigation season relative to what could be had with an irrigation pattern of releases; and will very possibly sacrifice positive irrigation benefits in order to augment or preserve power and other benefits. And it possibly could do so to the extent of attaining a level of aggregate net benefits less than the optimum.

An irrigation pattern of releases, on the other hand, will augment the summer supply of irrigation water, very possibly adding appreciable benefits thereby. However, it will reduce power benefits to the extent that it is associated with insufficient releases for power generation in the fall, in the winter, and possibly in part of the spring (reducing the annual load factor on the quantity of power-generating facilities which a power pattern of releases would justify, and thus tending to reduce the quantity of facilities installed). Furthermore, the irrigation pattern will tend to cause a deterioration of fish habitat upstream from diversions and below reservoirs, particularly because of insufficient autumn flows and heightened autumn water temperatures. Fish habitat will be protected only so far as governmental authorities succeed in requiring minimal releases as a means to preserve habitat and, perhaps, to serve navigation and salinity repulsion. The irrigation pattern also means a much greater relative drawdown of reservoir levels during the summer season than does the power pattern, and usually demands a more widely fluctuating reservoir water level and a less attractive shoreline for recreational use. For that reason, the power pattern in general is consistent with a higher level of benefits from reservoir recreation (boating, swimming, and the like). Finally, the criteria for flood control operation of California reservoirs typically require that reservoirs not be filled until the end of the spring runoff, a condition which does not interfere much with benefits of either power or irrigation, since neither use peaks at that time. Thus, unless very large quantities of summer irrigation water have substantial positive marginal values, the offsetting losses in power, recreation, and other benefits which are imposed by an irrigation pattern of releases may make that pattern also nonoptimal, and increasingly nonoptimal as the volume of storage on a river increases.

The preceding argument, stated in strictly qualitative terms, suggests that a pattern of releases which represents some compromise lying between a power and an irrigation pattern is likely to be optimal. It appears that, other things being equal, the compromise should tend to be a bit nearer to the power pattern pole than to the irrigation pattern pole; and, as the volume of storage on a river increases, the optimum tends to shift toward the power pattern pole, largely because the elasticity of demand for water tends to be substantially greater for power generation than for irrigation water. This is probably about as far as it is profitable to carry our qualitative argument.

Based on this background, we can now consider available evidence bearing on the quantity and pattern of seasonal reallocation of water attained to date on Northern California rivers. Two inexpensive but large-scale reservoir developments were built by commercial water companies prior to the first World War. Aside from these, nearly all of the major on-stream storage reservoir capacity within or serving the Central Valley region today which was not built by the two large federal agencies (or about 30 per cent of it) was constructed by two public utility companies, eight irrigation districts plus two state agencies, and four urban water agencies.[6] Their shares in this nonfederal fraction of such capacity are a bit over half to the electric utility companies, about 30 per cent to agencies primarily supplying irrigation water, and roughly 20 per cent to the four urban water agencies. The large utility company reservoirs are rather heavily concentrated on the Feather and San Joaquin rivers, although the Pacific Gas and Electric Company (PG&E) has appreciable reservoir capacity on the Yuba, Kings, and Mokelumne rivers.[7] Reservoirs of irrigation districts are also of some importance on the Feather and Yuba, but are otherwise largely concentrated on three major northerly tributaries of the San Joaquin River—the Stanislaus, Merced, and Tuolumne rivers. The dominant reservoir development by the urban agencies is also on the Tuolumne, whereas much lesser ones are on the Mokelumne, Calaveras, and American rivers.

The scope of river coverage of these nonfederal agencies is emphasized in order to show that whatever tendencies they display as a group in interseasonal alloca-

[6] See Chapter 4, the section on Integration and Concentration in Wholesaling, Streamflow Regulation, and Power Generation.

[7] In speaking only of major reservoir capacity (individual reservoirs with storage capacities above 40,000 acre-feet), we omit smaller storage reservoirs and powerplant reservoirs, of which PG&E has many, including a cluster on the Pit River.

tion of water will have strong effects mainly on seven major rivers from the San Joaquin River north—the San Joaquin, Merced, Tuolumne, Stanislaus, Mokelumne, Yuba, and Feather rivers. Their reservoir operations do not importantly affect the Tulare Lake Basin rivers (the Kings, Kaweah, Tule, and Kern), the American River, or the Sacramento River. It may be noted further that of the rivers on which the operations of nonfederal agencies are quite important, the Feather and the San Joaquin are predominantly electrical utility or "power company" rivers (except for Friant Dam on the San Joaquin); the Stanislaus, Tuolumne, and Merced rivers are predominantly regulated by public water agencies supplying irrigation or urban water for consumptive use; and the Mokelumne and Yuba have flows regulated in important part by both power companies and such public agencies.

About these nonfederal agencies, as a group, several things pertinent to their operations in interseasonal allocation of streamflows may be said. First, a number of considerations taken together make it unlikely that they have tended to make appreciably excessive transfers of water from the winter to other seasons, although they may have overallocated transferred winter water to their own service areas for consumptive use. All of them build storage reservoirs generally subject to the requirement that they be commercially feasible—that revenues (exclusive of nonrecompensible benefits) may reasonably be expected to exceed costs. There is thus a sort of inherent check on their overinvesting in reservoir storage and overallocating water from the winter to other seasons; but it perhaps is not a sufficient check since there is a general tendency to disregard the opportunity costs of their storage projects in terms of lost recreational and similar benefits. The fact that electric utility companies, in operating reservoirs for their own use, typically tend to ignore the resulting incidental irrigation benefits and do not collect for them serves as a further check. Public agencies supplying irrigation water which have built reservoirs "on their own account" (without cooperative arrangements with an electric utility company) usually have been subject to budgetary constraints and have been motivated to serve predesignated and limited areas rather than all of the areas that their reservoir projects might economically serve. This circumstance, though consistent with overallocation of water to their own service areas, is not conducive to excessive interseasonal transfers of water in the aggregate. Against these tendencies, we must count a possible inclination of large urban water agencies to engage in somewhat excessive transfers, for a variety of reasons discussed in Chapter 11,[8] but they are relatively unimportant in terms of volume of interseasonal transfers involved. As a group, therefore, the nonfederal agencies would not appear to tend significantly toward overallocating water from winter to other seasons.[9]

Second, the patterns of interseasonal allocation vary between electric utility companies and all the other agencies, and thus vary among rivers so far as the regulation of the flows of given rivers may be dominated by the utilities. In

[8] Section on Water Investments by Urban Agencies.

[9] There is the possibility that, so far as storage capacity is built jointly by irrigation districts and PG&E under contracts whereby the utility company pays all capital costs of the reservoir, PG&E may have a qualified inducement to engage in excessive interseasonal transfers, but offsetting considerations appear to make this possibility rather faint.

building and operating reservoirs on their own account, utility companies naturally tend to favor a "power pattern" of seasonal releases; and while the power pattern, as described above, is optimal for power production, and probably acceptable for recreation, it is distinctly suboptimal from the standpoint of irrigation. This utility dominance is really notable, however, only on the Feather River, which largely "belongs" to the Pacific Gas and Electric Company; the effects of utility dominance on the San Joaquin River upstream from the Valley are largely canceled by the operation downstream of the Reservoir at Friant Dam.[10] As to the public agencies, including irrigation districts and urban water agencies, practically all of their storage reservoirs make interseasonal transfers of water not only for irrigation or urban consumptive use, but also for electric power generation. This power generation has either been undertaken by the public agencies on their own account (the usual practice prior to World War II), or under cooperative arrangements whereby PG&E agrees to pay the capital costs of reservoirs to the public agencies (the usual postwar practice). In either case, the irrigation districts have had strong incentives or obligations not to adopt an unmitigated "irrigation pattern" of releases of stored water, and good reasons to adopt release patterns representing compromises between the power pattern and irrigation pattern. Though numerical data are not available which would permit us to characterize their release patterns more precisely, it would appear that their dual interest in power and irrigation tends to favor adopting release patterns closer to the optimum than would be attained if they operated single purpose reservoirs. The same general argument seems applicable to the urban water agencies involved.

Viewing the nonfederal operators of storage reservoirs as a group, it would appear that, on the rivers where their reservoir operations are dominant, interseasonal transfers of water are probably optimal or slightly less than optimal, in terms of both volumes of water transferred from the winter to other seasons and of the time pattern or releases—though transfers to summer use are probably misallocated among the irrigation users. This judgment is generally consistent with our finding in Chapter 15 concerning rates of return on investment in distribution systems earned by irrigation districts, and with observed rates of return earned by utility companies. The most appreciable divergence from the optimum would appear to arise from the fact that compromise release patterns from reservoirs impose marginal disbenefits on fisheries which are less than fully offset by marginal benefits in irrigation and other consumptive uses. So far as this is the case, it is not apparent that interventions by the Department of Fish and Game have been expressly aimed at securing, or have secured, approximately optimal marginal adjustments in release patterns.

About 70 per cent of the present major reservoir capacity serving or located in the Central Valley region, however, has been built by the Bureau of Reclamation and the Corps of Engineers, with most of it completed since World War II. The Bureau accounts for about four-fifths of the total. As suggested in the preceding chapter, this huge increment to reservoir capacity has evidently carried interseasonal transfer of water too far on the average. But it is noteworthy that

[10] This will also be the case on the Feather River when Oroville Dam, near the entrance of the Feather to the Valley, is completed by the California Department of Water Resources.

the overallocation to summer use so far has been selective among rivers. Excessive seasonal transfers by the Bureau of Reclamation occur mainly with respect to the waters of the Sacramento, American, and San Joaquin rivers within the Central Valley, and of the Trinity River as dammed and tapped for the transfer of water to the Central Valley. There are strong general indications (not fully confirmed by detailed study) that at least two of the four major reservoirs of the Corps on the Kings, Kaweah, Tule, and Kern rivers of the Tulare Lake Basin region accomplish similarly excessive seasonal transfers. This combined list of rivers excludes the major rivers with appreciable developments by local public agencies and private utilities, with the exception of the San Joaquin River.

It seems likely that many of the more opportune river developments for irrigation were undertaken by irrigation districts before the large-scale arrival of the federal agencies in California. The federal agencies are generally reluctant to undertake projects on a river afflicted with serious water rights complications or entrenched positions, often the case when such a local development has occurred. For these reasons, the thought occurs that the rivers lately developed by the large federal agencies may have been selected not only because their development could involve grandiose projects beyond the contemplation of local agencies, but also because they offered the marginal developmental opportunities that were left after the cream had been skimmed by local agencies. However this may be, any tendencies to overdevelopment involving excessive interseasonal transfer through federal projects appears to involve mainly a group of rivers distinct from the group largely developed by local agencies.

Statistical evidence on the excess of interseasonal transfer involved in the basic features of the Central Valley Project of the Bureau of Reclamation has been presented in Chapter 15. The data presented there, from which marginal benefit-cost ratios substantially below unity may be inferred even before adjusting for surplus price-supported crops, provide a basis for inferring large excessive interseasonal transfers of the waters of the Sacramento and San Joaquin rivers. Although these transfers are intermixed, of course, with excessive interbasin transfers, they would still be excessive if interbasin transfers were smaller or in different patterns. In Chapter 11, we discussed several types of defects apparent in the published economic justifications of the Bureau's projects. Our rough adjustments to correct for these suggested that a number of Northern California projects (in addition to the basic features of the Central Valley Project) constitute both excessive levels of water-facilities development and of interseasonal transfers.

The reservoir projects of the Corps of Engineers in the Central Valley have not been subjected to such a detailed appraisal as have those of the Bureau of Reclamation. Nor is such an appraisal easy in view of the propensity of the Corps to measure added irrigation water supplies in a rather bizarre fashion and to concoct numbers representing the assumed values of irrigation water and of flood control benefits. A moderately thorough examination of available documents, however, supports a strong, though tentative, conclusion about two of the five major Corps reservoirs in the Central Valley (Success and Terminus on the Tule and Kaweah rivers): If the cost of added summer irrigation water supply were counted as the excess of the cost of building these two dams and reservoirs over the cost of alternative facilities which would have accomplished comparable flood control results, then the winter-summer transfers of irrigation water are excessive in the light of marginal benefit-cost ratios. For at least one other Corps reservoir, Isabella on the Kern River, there is the same strong possibility.

Although the federal projects seem clearly excessive in scale, the seasonal time patterns of releases from their reservoirs ordinarily do not appear to involve serious departures from the optimum. The Bureau in the operation of its major dams affecting Sacramento Valley flows appears to follow a balanced pattern of multipurpose releases which is probably not far from optimal, and is related to comparative marginal benefit calculations. However, some question arises as to whether a pattern with a lower summer peak might not facilitate the increase of over-all benefits, if adopted in conjunction with a charge for irrigation diversions from the Sacramento of water produced by the Bureau. The efficiency of the rules governing release patterns of the Corps' dams (involving the conditions under which off-season spillages of floodwaters will be undertaken) has not been appraised, but they sound sensible as they are stated. Data on intended release patterns from the new Trinity Dam, which are potentially important from the standpoint of a great anadromous fishery of the Trinity and Klamath rivers, have not been appraised; it is significant that in no calculation has the Bureau counted disbenefits to this fishery as a cost of the Trinity project.

Viewing the Central Valley as a whole, we find something like a two-part world, made up of one group of rivers primarily developed by local public agencies and private utility companies, and of another group developed mainly by federal agencies. In the first, quantities of interseasonal water transfer are optimal or less than optimal; and on most of the rivers, time patterns of seasonal releases from storage would appear to be somewhere within sight of the optimum (depending on the extent of multipurpose operation). In the second, or federal-agency world, excessive interseasonal transfers seem to be the general rule, subject to minor exceptions for some operations of the Corps, so that there is a misallocation of water toward summer uses. Seasonal release patterns in this world, however, are not demonstrably nonoptimal in serious degree among the seasons and months which are outside the winter season.

The performance record of the California Department of Water Resources at this writing still must be predicted, as the agency is in the earlier stages of constructing its first major water project, the Feather River Project. However, our analysis in Chapter 15 of the Department's detailed plans, to which it has been largely committed through advance contracting to supply water, suggests that this state agency is paralleling the performance of the Bureau of Reclamation (if not outdoing it) by undertaking excessive interseasonal transfers of water from the Feather and Eel rivers in order to support excessive interbasin transfers to the southern San Joaquin Valley, to the South Coastal Basin of which Los Angeles is the hub, and to the Mojave and Colorado deserts of Southern California. We may thus extend the federal-agency world of Northern California water development to include the California state agency; and designate it, for purposes of future reference, as a federal-and-state agency segment, the membership of which shares many common tendencies of conduct and performance.

Since the primary problems of interseasonal allocation of water in Northern California arise in the Central Valley, we have confined this discussion almost entirely to rivers originating in, or serving, the Central Valley region. There is not a great deal of interest to be said about interseasonal allocations in other regions of the area.

Allocation of Water among Types of Use

Most of what we can say about the propriety of the contemporary allocation of water among different types of use has been stated or implied in the preceding section, since allocation among most uses at the margin is generally the consequence of the volume and time pattern of interseasonal transfers of water. Several tentative conclusions concerning allocation among uses, however, may be drawn from our appraisal of interseasonal allocations.

First, the over-all allocation between power and irrigation uses of streamflows, so far as these are competitive, appears to lie within a range of reasonableness in the Central Valley. The general use of dual purpose reservoirs (including power generation as a purpose, wherever such generation is feasible) accounts for this tendency, which persists except on rivers where reservoirs of utility companies are dominant, such as the Feather River. It has further been suggested that there may be some tendency toward release patterns which in effect allocate a bit too much water to irrigation and a bit too little to power generation in the operation of Shasta Dam on the Sacramento River. On the other hand, the standard form of participation in the joint projects of PG&E and local districts may result to a minor extent in releases excessively oriented toward power generation. The preceding conclusions are based largely on circumstantial evidence rather than on quantitative measurements, other than indicators of the low productivity of Bureau-produced water diverted for irrigation from the Sacramento.

Second, on rivers primarily developed by the federal and state agencies, there is a distinct tendency to allocate too much water either to summer irrigation alone or to summer irrigation plus power generation, and correspondingly too little to other in-stream uses, including sports fishing for nonmigratory species in all cases, and pollution control in the lower San Joaquin River. (In contrast, the Bureau has been sensitive in its flow regulation policies to the need to repulse salinity in the Delta, and navigation is well protected by statute and by activities of the Corps.) This conclusion is based on the observation that the marginal benefit-cost ratio for irrigation plus power uses of seasonally transferred water supplied by the Bureau and the Department of Water Resources is very evidently below unity, and that the excess water devoted to these uses would certainly have appreciable marginal values in the preservation of fish habitat and in controlling pollution. The same tendency is probably present also on rivers primarily developed by local public agencies: their release policies reduce in-stream recreational values by damaging fish habitat and, in the lower San Joaquin Valley, their diversions for irrigation appear to be excessive in the light of pollution created by return flows.

These deficiencies reflect the broader problems created by the biases in planning that predispose the federal and state agencies toward heeding benefits which call for physical works or construction as against those which do not, and benefits accruing to specific and vocal groups of beneficiaries as against (paradoxically) "public goods." The predisposition toward physical solutions appears in the lack of interest of the Corps of Engineers in flood control measures which do not involve the construction of large-scale dams; and in the general practice of the federal agencies to include allowances for benefits from reservoir recreation in their planning without allowing for the disbenefits to in-stream recreational activities. It also appears in the emphasis upon the benefits of additional storage reservoir construction for salinity repulsion in the Delta, in contrast to the lack of timely attention to the additional problems of polluted irrigation return flows created by such projects as San Luis.

Demands for water for competing uses which are not matched by evident commercial impacts and are characterized as public goods are likely to receive the least, and last, voluntary attention from water developing agencies (whether federal, state, or local) ; appreciable concern with these demands must be expressed by regulatory agencies such as the Department of Fish and Game. (This tendency is confirmed by the differentially favorable attention given by the Bureau of Reclamation to the preservation of waterfowl as compared to fisheries habitat as noted in Chapter 14.) In California, administrative protection of fisheries only recently has become at all effective, and the protection sought and secured, in the absence of substantive law providing standards for protection, has been of an *ad hoc* variety not based on marginal benefit considerations, and usually not adequate or optimally directed. As to control of pollution resulting from return flows from irrigation, the multitude of "adverse users" collectively responsible for this pollution has stood in the way of private resolution of the problem of excessive irrigation diversions, and public interference to resolve the problem is only now being considered.

The adverse relation between in-stream recreation relating to anadromous fisheries and those uses of water dependent on reservoir construction illustrates the point made at the beginning of this chapter about the difficulty of moving from a finding of misallocation to a conclusion about the appropriate remedy. Because the adversity in this case relates much more to the existence of dams than to the amount of streamflow regulation which they perform, marginal adjustments in the functions performed by existing reservoirs in most situations will work little improvement. Indeed, many major runs of anadromous fish were killed off by reservoirs constructed long before the wave of federal construction during and after World War II. The operative issue for policy concerns the appropriate consideration of in-stream recreational effects when future projects are planned. The streams of the north coastal region are as yet substantially undeveloped for power or consumptive uses of water, and they support anadromous fisheries of substantial value as well as nonmigratory fisheries at higher elevations. The only major infringement on the value of these fisheries to date has been the construction of two large dams on the middle-upper reaches of the Trinity River, for the diversion of water into the Sacramento Valley for use there or further south. (This reallocation does not appear to be economically justified, with or without counting the loss to the anadromous fishery of the Trinity.) But the long-range California Water Plan (as well as alternative federal regional plans for which trial balloons are appearing) contemplates severe future interference on all of the three chief rivers of the north coastal region—the Klamath, Trinity, and Eel—with large dams at locations guaranteed to exterminate one of the few great anadromous sports fisheries of the Pacific Coast.

The principal message of our findings is that the benefits of the fisheries, which grow apace with the population of California, must be considered against correctly measured benefits of construction if these proposed projects are not to cause even further misallocations among in-stream and other uses of water. In view of our finding in Chapter 15 that the first project of the Department of Water Resources—the Feather River Project—constitutes premature and excessive construction, and also biases the allocation of water against various in-stream uses, it becomes a matter of particular concern that the appropriate changes be made in project evaluation practices before further damage is done in the north coastal region.

Another allocational frontier between uses within Northern California involves agricultural and urban uses of water. In this area, where only about 6 per cent of all water used consumptively goes to urban uses, and the remainder to irrigation, the frontier is perhaps not a very exciting one. A significant incremental supply of irrigation water is provided by the federal government in the Central Valley under deficient marginal benefit-cost conditions; and this supply is affected by various forms of subsidy. Urban water supplies drawn from the same or easily substitutable sources, for use both in the San Francisco Bay region and in the Central Valley, are in general not so subsidized, although the large urban water agencies themselves probably tend toward some economic excess of water development for their own needs as we noted in Chapter 11. Since Chapter 5 showed that urban demands in the area appear to have appreciable price elasticities, especially in urban industrial uses, some net misallocation of water toward excessive irrigation use at the expense of a deficient comparative use for urban purposes may be fostered by Bureau of Reclamation policies. The special terms of the Raker Act and other settlements between the Bay area cities and their agricultural water rivals have the same effect, as was shown in Chapter 12. Furthermore, the Feather River Project—which can be characterized in part on the basis of our appraisal in Chapter 15 as developing excessive interregional transfers to avoid an agriculture-to-urban transfer of water—will by design contribute further toward an excessive allocation of water to agricultural uses relative to urban uses.

Allocation of Water among Subregions and River Basins

Interbasin transfers of water are not as yet very highly developed within Northern California. The major transfer is from the Sacramento River and the Delta into the San Joaquin Valley, in the complex operation involving the Shasta and Friant dams, and the Delta-Mendota, Friant-Kern, and Madera canals. The net effect of this operation in terms of interbasin transfers is the shift of about a million acre-feet of water annually from the Sacramento River basin to the southern part of the east side of the San Joaquin Valley—primarily to the Tulare Lake Basin region. Lesser transfers involve the movement of about 50,000 acre-feet annually from the Delta to the San Francisco Bay region in the Contra Costa Canal, and about 200,000 acre-feet annually from rivers on the west slope of the Sierra Nevada to the Bay region by aqueducts of the two principal agencies purveying urban water in that region. Many more interbasin transfers, however, are imminent, including the transfer of water from the Trinity River into the Sacramento Valley (for the support of which the major dams are already built), and further transfers of Sacramento Valley water southward through the Feather River Project of the California Department of Water Resources and the East Side Project of the Bureau of Reclamation.[11]

The major existing transfers undertaken by the Bureau of Reclamation are from the Delta to the Tulare Lake Basin and to the San Francisco Bay region. These involve, as has been shown in Chapter 15, clearly excessive interbasin transfers, and thus a misallocation jointly of water among basins and water among seasons (the latter so far as the transfer is supported by increased reservoir storage capacity). A marginal benefit-cost ratio on transferred water less than unity adequately reveals this misallocation. The amount of benefits generated in the import areas has simply not justified the non-water costs of making the transfer, or at any rate of the costs of appreciable inframarginal increments of the transfer, even if we neglect opportunity costs of the water in the area of origin. In fact, even if the marginal benefit-cost ratio were as good as unity, the transfer to the Kaweah-Tule Basin would be excessive, since local water as delivered there yields lower marginal values than imported water with comparable local delivery costs. The import volume should be shortened until the marginal value of reallocated local water as delivered equals the marginal costs as delivered of imported water having comparable local delivery costs.

The main possible qualification to the preceding judgments is that the water transferred to the San Joaquin might have yielded benefits sufficient to justify the transfer if it had been allocated to a different area within the San Joaquin Valley. The major alternative destination which would have seemed at all promising would have been at the south end of the San Joaquin Valley, in parts of the Kern River Basin receiving little local surface runoff, and along the west side of the southern part of the Valley—principally at the expense of large deliveries to the Mendota Pool to serve low-grade lands bordering the San Joaquin River. Whether the quantity of transfer undertaken would have been economically justified if shifted entirely, or in considerable part, to this other area of the San Joaquin Valley remains in doubt. Although considerable land areas of high potential productivity lie in the neglected area, the transmission costs of carrying water to them would have been significantly greater than those presently incurred, and the required volumes of surface water per acre would have been greater because of relatively deficient ground-water supplies.[12] On the other hand, in view

[11] See Figures 12, 31, 32, and 33.

[12] Appraisals of the payment capacity for water in Kern County made in connection with the Feather River Project suggest that this shift, given the added transmission costs, would probably not have changed net benefits enough to justify the Bureau's interbasin transfer in the volume undertaken. See Appendix D.

of the political pressures which were influential in selecting the present destination of the transferred water, we have no assurance that the relative economic desirability of alternative destinations of the imported water was adequately evaluated, or that a rational economic choice was made among alternative destinations.

The other major transfer involves the importation of water from the Tuolumne and Mokelumne rivers in the Central Valley to the San Francisco Bay region by the water department of the city of San Francisco and by the East Bay Municipal Utility District. This transfer is hard to evaluate (aside from noting that San Francisco has tended toward premature development, largely because such development was strategic in establishing long-term water rights sufficient to assure meeting anticipated future demands). The difficulty in evaluation results from the existence of competition for water from local sources in the San Francisco Bay region for irrigation, and from the importance attached to a pure and potable water supply by the urban water agencies and their constituencies. Serving urban needs of the Bay region wholly from local sources would have involved drying up most of the local irrigation water supply, and if this had been legally feasible, would have led to the importation of water for irrigation needs, probably at a somewhat lower cost than that of the urban imports. But, legal difficulties aside, the urban supply over time would not have remained exceptionally pure and potable. Tapping the rivers of the Sierra, therefore, was probably a fairly rational solution to the problem of meeting all water demands in the Bay area, provided that purity and potability of the urban supply are assigned appreciable value weights (as they may well be, considering the low treatment costs involved with these as compared to alternative supplies). The major inefficiency involved, therefore, apparently was not one of irrational interbasin allocation. Rather, it is possible that San Francisco's choice of a river source, the Tuolumne, and the tapping of this source very deep in the mountains—actions which were influenced by political considerations and undertaken subject to severe constraints imposed by existing water rights to reasonably accessible Sierra rivers—was economically irrational and unduly costly.

We will not consider here the pending interbasin transfer from the American River southward under the proposed East Side Project of the Bureau of Reclamation, except to comment that it has not been demonstrated to be, and from all superficial evidence does not promise to be, an economically justifiable regional reallocation of water. The Feather River Project, as suggested in the preceding section and in Chapter 15, under present plans will undertake a clearly excessive aggregate interbasin transfer. Not only is the Project excessive in aggregate scale; it also includes segments that could be eliminated, which now drag down its overall economic rating. In general, the proposed transfers to the North Bay region, to the Mojave Desert, and to the Palm Springs area for urban use lack any visible economic justification *in toto;* the proposed transfer to Kern County for irrigation is at best overly large; and any transfer from the Eel to feed these dubious delivery areas is economically unsupportable. It is conceivable that a scaled down project designed mainly to carry Feather River water to the South Coastal Basin might have economic justification.

A final question involving interregional transfers concerns whether any good possibilities for reallocation of water among river basins have been overlooked. These would involve in large part transfers between the "natural service areas" of adjacent rivers. Such transfers would be either (1) a persistent one-directional sort, because of the relative abundance of the flow of one river and the relative scarcity of flow in an adjacent one, or (2) an alternating two-directional transfer, the direction of which was changed from year to year because the annual flows of the rivers did not fluctuate over time in a closely coordinated fashion. As to the latter possibility, an investigation of the statistical correlation of changes in the annual flows for six adjacent pairs of rivers (involving a total of eight major rivers) in the Central Valley, for the period 1895 to 1947, has showed such high correlations of fluctuations in the flows of adjacent rivers that building facilities for alternating two-directional transfers could hardly be economical.[13] As to the former possibility—regular one-directional transfer from one river to the natural service area of another—our investigations suggest that possibility in the case of at least one complex of adjacent rivers, the Stanislaus, Tuolumne, and Merced. Some shifts of irrigation water from the Merced and the Stanislaus rivers toward the Tuolumne, which lies between them, would improve the geographical allocation of water in an important agricultural subregion, but these shifts would mainly involve redefining the service areas of the rivers so that the definition would be more rational than at present. This apparent misallocation is thus considered in the following section, under the general heading of interagency allocations from a common source or complex of rather closely adjacent sources.[14]

The alternative possibility that transfers between adjacent river basins might be justified because reservoir storage could economically be heavily loaded on one river and lightly loaded on a neighbor, with the storage on the highly developed river supplying summer water to the service area of the other has also been investigated. Such transfers might be economic either because of the existence of superior or lower cost reservoir sites on one river or because of economies of scale in reservoir size attainable subject to topographic constraints. Our conclusions on this point are generally negative or neutral, since systematic differentials in

[13] The pairs of rivers compared were Feather-Yuba, Yuba-American, Feather-American, Stanislaus-Tuolumne, Tuolumne-Merced, and San Joaquin-Kings, with the comparisons covering the major possibilities for short-distance transfers between individual river basins. (See Figure 5.) The squares of the coefficients of correlation of paired annual flows fell between 0.94 and 0.98 for all but one pair (the Feather and American) where the corresponding number was 0.84. Flow data were taken from California State Water Resources Board, *Water Resources of California,* Bulletin No. 1 (1951), Table 62. (This and other footnote references are cited in brief form when they are also included in the Bibliography.)

[14] One comparatively minor but absolutely quite important local misallocation of water among river basins is worthy of note. This involves the Friant-Kern Canal, which carries water south from the San Joaquin River to the Kaweah-Tule Basin and en route crosses the Kings River on its east-west course about twenty miles south of Friant Dam on the San Joaquin. The misallocation arises from the fact that about one-third of a million acre-feet of Kings River water annually is carried north to the edge of the San Joaquin River to serve the Fresno Irrigation District. If this District were served instead from the San Joaquin River (which it could be quite feasibly), and a corresponding amount of Kings River water were diverted south in the Friant-Kern Canal to the Kaweah-Tule Basin, a good deal of water haulage would be eliminated and the capacity of the Friant-Kern Canal could have been reduced by at least one-third over the twenty miles between Friant Dam and the crossing of the Kings. This matter is considered further in the following chapter, in connection with the appraisal of technical efficiency in water transportation, under the general heading of crosshauls.

the adaptability of adjacent rivers to reservoir storage do not appear to be present and since, subject to topographic constraints, any attainable economies of scale in reservoirs realized by loading reservoir storage on some rivers and developing others less intensively are generally slight, both absolutely and as compared to the extra water transmission costs which such a plan would involve. This conclusion applies to completed reservoirs as well as to a long roster of proposed reservoirs under consideration by the Bureau of Reclamation in its long-term development of the Central Valley Project.[15]

Allocation of Water among Users from a Common Source

We turn now to the way water devoted to a given type of use is allocated among actual and potential users having economic access to given surface sources or complexes of related sources. Our discussion will be confined to allocation of irrigation water in some of the principal river basins of the Central Valley.

As suggested in previous chapters,[16] the water industry of Northern California has undergone a historical process in which first comers secured prime water rights to natural summer flows in amounts which subsequently have resulted in allocating too much scarce water to them and too little to late-comers. Moreover, when the late-comers were able to secure comparable amounts of water, it was usually secured only at substantially higher costs than the early users, because they generally had to pay for their costs of reservoir storage to create added summer supplies of water, whereas the early comers were entitled to natural summer flows without paying for storage costs. It would have been economically rational for the early arrivals to reallocate rights to natural summer flow by selling water rights to others until the marginal value in use of water to them was as high as the marginal cost of summer water produced by storage. But in the substantial absence of water markets this opportunity for profitable trade was ignored. Given the numerous legal and institutional impediments to the transfer of surface water rights, accidents of temporal priority in agricultural development are today responsible for a complex pattern of misallocations of irrigation water among users and their lands in a number of river basins.

The resulting misallocations were made more severe by the circumstance that the early comers often occupied and secured prior water rights for use on valley bottom lands along main river courses, and that these lands were generally inferior to valley lands which were occupied later and which secured less water or water at higher costs.[17] Despite the fact that even a rough equality in allocation of water between valley bottom lands and adjacent valley lands is uneconomic since more should go to the adjacent valley lands, the valley bottom lands frequently secured more water. The perpetuation of this misallocation was made possible by the

[15] U.S. Department of the Interior, Bureau of Reclamation, *Central Valley Basin,* S. Doc. 113, 81 Cong. 1 sess. (1949).

[16] In Chapter 3, where the economic implications of the operation of the law of water rights were discussed; in Chapter 12, where agencies' rivalries for water were considered, and again in Chapter 16.

[17] The general inferiority of valley bottom as compared to valley lands in the Central Valley has been discussed in Chapter 5.

disregard of opportunity costs, by differentials in non-water costs between valley bottom and adjacent valley land users, and by the iron grip of established water rights.

The sort of phenomenon is quite notable in the San Joaquin River valley, and has continued even after the replacement of the San Joaquin flow (between Friant Dam and the Merced-Tuolumne-Stanislaus confluences with the San Joaquin) by water from the Delta-Mendota Canal. Old riparian rights appurtenant to lands bordering the San Joaquin River still afford holders of these generally inferior lands access at a very low non-water cost to about as much water per acre as is used on better adjacent valley lands. On this basis, it might be argued that if San Joaquin River water were diverted south to the Tule-Kaweah Basin through a Friant-Kern Canal, it would have been economically more rational for landholders on the edge of the San Joaquin River to sell off a substantial part of their rights to summer water in order to supply the Kaweah-Tule Basin than for the Bureau to replace this part of their water, pursuant to exchange agreements, through such large imports to the Mendota Pool via the Delta-Mendota Canal. Officials in the Bureau of Reclamation must have thought of this; in the event this solution was preferred as an alternative to the one chosen (as it should have been), the existing water rights situation probably forestalled this optimal (and economically feasible) choice by the Bureau.

A somewhat comparable situation developed in the areas served by the Kings River. The valley bottom lands just north of the Tulare Lake Basin, which are served by the Kings, were occupied early and owners secured prior and superior water rights for use on soils which were clearly inferior to subsequently occupied valley lands upstream which were serviceable from the Kings. Though some holders of the better upstream lands subsequently secured good water rights, others did not; at the same time, some but not all of the holders of poorer downstream lands sold their superior rights. In the present situation, excessive water is put to low valued uses at low non-water costs on part of the downstream lands, while part of the upstream landholders receive too little water, considering the differential in soil quality, and at a higher non-water cost. Perpetuation of this situation (which was ameliorated by some transfers of rights) can be explained in the same terms as the situation on the San Joaquin. And a somewhat similar situation is repeated in the basin of the Kern River, though differences in soil quality there do not play a major role.[18]

The preceding description of some general historical tendencies in allocation among users leaves out of account the extent to which good lands in various river basins have secured practically no surface water at all. This is a matter with respect to which it is exceedingly difficult to obtain any adequate data. Thus, we

[18] It may be noted that the same sort of rigidities inhibit ground-water transfers between agencies or others holding rights as block inter-agency transfers of surface water. The cumbersome legal procedure for making a definitive determination of ground-water rights in an area discourages transfers and encourages negotiated settlements which tend to allocate water more according to the relative strength of the negotiators than according to the principles of efficient allocation. Difficulties in resolving conflicting ground-water claims have served as a primary basis for organized efforts to induce a wholesaler to import surface water. (See Chapter 12, section on Rivalry for Ground Water.)

are able to offer no general judgments, other than that there is probably some degree of such deprivation in most subregions; that it is evident in the Kern River Basin and was in the Kaweah-Tule Basin prior to the introduction of Friant-Kern imports; and that landholders, to a considerable extent, have compensated for the deprivation by a heavy reliance on ground-water pumping at elevated marginal costs. As a result, the allocation of ground and surface water combined has been seriously distorted—again because of the lack of economically appropriate transfers of surface water rights.

The meaningful statistical evidence we have on allocations among users of surface water for irrigation largely concerns quantities of water per irrigated acre secured from common or potentially common sources by irrigation districts and by mutual ditch companies in various river basins and subregions. It must be interpreted in the light of preceding comments on differentials of soil quality where these are relevant, and the fact that serious inequalities in allocation of surface water in a locality generally, though only roughly, indicate a misallocation of water from surface and ground-water sources combined.

Beginning with the southerly part of the Central Valley, we note first a rather remarkable variance in the quantities of water per acre secured annually by mutual ditch companies (generally not eligible for Bureau water) drawing upon the Kaweah River. Data showing acre-feet per irrigated acre of surface water secured from the Kaweah River (uniformly the only significant source of surface water) by sixteen mutual ditch companies are arranged in Table 35 in order of quantity

TABLE 35
RANGE OF GROSS DIVERSIONS PER IRRIGATED ACRE MADE BY SIXTEEN MUTUAL DITCH COMPANIES FROM KAWEAH RIVER, 1955

Company[a]	Diversions (acre-feet per irrigated acre)	Irrigated acreage
1)	12.0	595
2)	11.0	500
3)	8.0	1,000
4)	4.7	1,130
5)	4.5	1,550
6)	4.0	13,800
7)	3.5	23,000
8)	3.2	7,200
9)	3.2	8,050
10)	2.9	4,500
11)	2.7	3,100
12)	2.6	1,290
13)	2.1	9,600
14)	2.1	170
15)	1.7	175
16)	1.5	1,120

[a] Some of the ditch company units represent combinations of interdependent companies.
SOURCE: California State Department of Public Works, Division of Water Resources, *Kaweah Flows, Diversions and Service Areas, 1949–1955*, Bulletin No. 49–b (Sacramento, 1956); California Department of Water Resources, Division of Resources Planning, *Report on Irrigation and Water Storage Districts in California, 1956–58*, Bulletin No. 21 (1960); California State Water Resources Board, *Water Utilization and Requirements of California*, Bulletin No. 2 (1955), Appendix B; and James F. Sorenson, *Report on Water Resources and Water Needs of Tulare County, California* (1959).

of diversions per acre in the year 1955; the irrigated acreage served by each company is also shown. These data, which indicate a very wide range of availability of surface water among companies in general, and a substantial range among those serving appreciable acreages, must of course be interpreted in the light of the existence of unmeasured differences in soil quality and in cost of delivering water. (Losses between diversion and delivery are substantial in some cases.) But an examination of the differences in delivery distance and in soil quality suggest that the disparities in allocation are great enough so that, after allowing for such differences, there is a substantial general misallocation among irrigators of surface water from the Kaweah. Furthermore, the misallocation is most marked among mutual companies with relatively small individual service areas. Considering the implications of this misallocation for relative dependence on ground-water pumping, a distinct general misallocation of water from all sources is indicated.

Some rather appreciable disparities in surface water diversions per acre are also noted in the service area of the Kings River. For four large irrigation districts and five mutual or commercial water companies depending primarily on Kings River diversions,[19] the "average year" allotments per irrigated acre arrived at under a settlement of rights in 1957 are shown in Table 36 (the average year is higher than a true annual average in runoff). Here again, the disparity of allotments (direct measures of established water rights) among agencies and companies is substantially greater than is explicable by soil differences or differences in transport costs. This applies even to the three large irrigation districts (Fresno, Consolidated, and Alta), which are contiguous and closely grouped in the upper service area of the Kings. Interagency misallocations of some importance appear to be indicated.

Continuing northward along the east side of the San Joaquin Valley, we come

TABLE 36
RANGE OF GROSS ALLOTTED DIVERSIONS PER IRRIGATED ACRE, KINGS RIVER RETAILING AGENCIES, AVERAGE YEAR

Retailing agency	Allotment of Kings River water (acre-feet per irrigated acre)	Irrigated acreage
Laguna Irrigation District	4.07	35,000
Fresno Irrigation District	3.14	169,900
Liberty Canal Co.	3.02	4,000
Consolidated Irrigation District	2.78	210,300
Peoples Ditch Co.	2.69	72,070
Lemoore Canal & Irrigation Co.	2.68	52,700
Last Chance Water Ditch Co.	2.39	38,000
Alta Irrigation District	2.04	100,000
Crescent Canal & Irrigation Co.	1.81	12,500

SOURCE: Kings River Water Association, *Water Master Report for Year 1957: Pine Flat Reservoir Operation Schedule, Administration and Canal Diversion*, by C. H. Smith (1958); California State Water Resources Board, *Water Utilization and Requirements of California*, Bulletin No. 2 (1955), Appendix B.

[19] All of these agencies can be located in Figure 20, Chapter 12.

upon the overlapping basins of the Merced, Tuolumne, and Stanislaus rivers, which flow parallel on east-west courses to enter the San Joaquin River.[20] The span between the Stanislaus and the Merced is roughly 35 miles, with the Tuolumne lying between them about 12 miles south of the Stanislaus. Their combined service area is about 50 miles long from north to south and 20 miles deep, with its western border at or close to the San Joaquin River, and it consists of overlapping alluvial fans containing high-grade valley soils of relatively uniform quality. Almost the entire service area is supplied by six irrigation districts (five large and one small), but in a peculiar and seemingly quite arbitrary pattern so far as the relation of lands served to the sources that serve them is concerned. Nearly all diversions from the Merced River (95 per cent of them) are made by the Merced Irrigation District, but it serves land almost entirely to the south of the Merced River. The waters of the Tuolumne River are diverted mainly by the Turlock Irrigation District and the Modesto Irrigation District (which account for about 90 per cent of all Tuolumne irrigation diversions), with the Turlock District serving an area entirely south of the River and the Modesto District an area entirely north of it. Moreover, the Turlock District carries Tuolumne water southward all the way to the banks of the Merced River, over a broad band about as long as the depth of the District's service area; and the Modesto District carries Tuolumne water north all the way to the banks of the Stanislaus River, over a similarly broad band. The only other Tuolumne diverter of consequence is the Waterford Irrigation District, which serves a small area along the Tuolumne upstream from the areas of the Turlock and Modesto districts.

From the Stanislaus River, the South San Joaquin Irrigation District serves an area entirely north of the River. The Oakdale Irrigation District delivers water on both sides of the Stanislaus River, its service area lying east of, or uphill from, the areas of the South San Joaquin District (on the north side of the Stanislaus) and of the Modesto District (on the south side of the River). That water from the Tuolumne River should serve most of the area between the Stanislaus and Merced rivers, which lie north and south of it, seems a little strange. And this impression is confirmed in a degree when the surface water diversions per irrigated acre of the irrigation districts involved are compared in Table 37, which lists the districts in north-to-south order. Detailed examination of the area suggests that allocation of surface water is probably significantly nonoptimal, mainly in that the Turlock Irrigation District receives a short quota of surface water which does not appear justified in the light of soil quality, topographic, or ground-water conditions. Allocation could evidently be improved by rearranging service areas in a somewhat more natural pattern, with (1) some Merced River water being shifted to serve land just north of it (in the Turlock District) now served from the Tuolumne, (2) some shifting of Tuolumne water from the area now served on its north side to land on its south side, and (3) some shifting of Stanislaus water to serve lands just south of it now served from the Tuolumne.

While examining the lower San Joaquin Valley, passing attention may be paid to five irrigation districts whose narrow service areas, generally made up of low-grade land in the valley bottom, border the San Joaquin River below the Mendota

[20] The area is shown in Figure 21.

TABLE 37
RANGE OF GROSS DIVERSIONS PER IRRIGATED ACRE MADE BY IRRIGATION DISTRICTS FROM STANISLAUS, TUOLUMNE, AND MERCED RIVERS, 1957

Irrigation district	Diversions (acre-feet per irrigated acre)	River source	Irrigated acreage
South San Joaquin	4.7	Stanislaus	62,200
Oakdale	4.8	Stanislaus	56,400
Modesto	4.3	Tuolumne	68,300
Waterford	4.5	Tuolumne	6,900
Turlock	3.3	Tuolumne	168,900
Merced	4.7	Merced	116,500

SOURCE: California Department of Water Resources, Division of Resources Planning, *Report on Irrigation and Water Storage Districts in California, 1956–58*, Bulletin No. 21 (1960); *idem, Surface Water Flow for 1957*, Bulletin No. 23–57 (1958); *idem, Lower San Joaquin Valley Water Quality Investigation*, Bulletin No. 89 (1960); California State Water Resources Board, *Water Utilization and Requirements of California*, Bulletin No. 2 (1955), Appendix B; *idem, San Joaquin County Investigation*, Bulletin No. 11 (1955); Tudor-Goodenough Engineers, *Feasibility Report on Merced River Development for Merced Irrigation District* (1958); Stanislaus County Planning Department, *A Water Need Study for Stanislaus County for the Year 2050* (1957).

Pool.[21] Listed in series from south to north in Table 38, the figures for these districts suggest no serious interdistrict misallocation. However, the larger Central California Irrigation District probably receives a relative overallocation of water compared to the four other districts, largely because of ancient water rights.

Viewing the showings for four basins in the San Joaquin Valley as a group, the general indications relative to the possibility of interbasin misallocation are that, differences in land quality considered, some reallocation of San Joaquin River water from the valley bottom districts to the Kings and Kaweah-Tule service areas would probably be desirable. This would very possibly have been a preferable alternative to substantial inframarginal increments in existing water

TABLE 38
RANGE OF GROSS DIVERSIONS PER IRRIGATED ACRE MADE BY IRRIGATION DISTRICTS FROM LOWER SAN JOAQUIN RIVER, 1957

Irrigation district	Diversions (acre-feet per irrigated acre)	Irrigated acreage
Central California	4.4	122,447
West Stanislaus	3.7	23,228
Banta-Carbona	3.7	14,628
West Side	3.6	9,647
Byron-Bethany	3.9	9,627

SOURCE: California Department of Water Resources, Division of Resources Planning, *Report on Irrigation and Water Storage Districts in California, 1956–58*, Bulletin No. 21 (1960); *idem, Surface Water Flow for 1959*, Bulletin No. 23–59 (1960); *idem, Lower San Joaquin Valley Water Quality Investigation*, Bulletin No. 89 (1960); California State Water Resources Board, *Water Utilization and Requirements of California*, Bulletin No. 2 (1955), Appendix B.

[21] All of these irrigation districts except the northernmost, Byron-Bethany, are shown in Figure 21, Chapter 12.

transfers through the Delta-Mendota Canal, assuming a Friant-Kern Canal were employed roughly as at present. Lacking the Friant-Kern transfer to the Kaweah-Tule Basin, some reallocation of Kings River water serving valley bottom lands in the Kings service area to better land in the Kaweah-Tule Basin would have improved allocation. In view of the distances involved and the opportunity costs, reallocation of Stanislaus, Tuolumne, and Merced water southward to the Kings and Kaweah-Tule areas would not appear to have been economically desirable even before the construction of the Friant-Kern Canal; and reallocations southward to the valley land area north and east of the San Joaquin appear to be of dubious desirability because of differences in land quality.

We find it much more difficult to make evaluations of interdistrict water allocations in the Sacramento Valley, because of the disparities in location and in soil type and quality among districts drawing on common sources, and because of considerable ambiguities in the distinction between total acreages and irrigated acreages as reported. There is a substantial variance among the larger agencies diverting from the Sacramento River with respect to apparent acre-feet of water diverted per irrigated acre (the range was from 4.3 to 13.6 acre-feet per acre in 1957 for four large irrigation districts, a large mutual company, and two very large farm companies).[22] However, the evident disparities in soil type and topography among agencies is such that we hesitate to draw conclusions about allocations. The same applies to findings concerning interdistrict allocations from the Feather and the Yuba rivers, considered either separately or as a single water source complex.[23] The possibility, or probability, of interagency misallocations of water in this region is certainly not barred, but we are not in a position to make semisolid evaluations of existing allocational patterns.

Our general investigation of interdistrict allocations of surface water from common sources in the Central Valley suggest that nonoptimal allocation or misallocation is probably pervasive in all river basins, the deviations from the optimum varying from mild to fairly severe. In addition, there is an unmeasured quantum of probable misallocation as between organized and unorganized territory in the various basins, although we do not have data which would confirm or reject this suspicion. The general hypothesis developed earlier in this volume concerning the probability that the historical process of acquisition of water rights in Northern California would tend to lead to appreciable misallocations of water among users from a common source seems generally to be supported by our findings.

Allocation among Member-Customers of Individual Public Agencies

A good deal of potential misallocation of irrigation water among users has been averted by the formation in most subregions of the Central Valley of very large individual irrigation districts, each serving many users and a large area of

[22] California Department of Water Resources, Division of Resources Planning, *Report on Irrigation and Water Storage Districts in California, 1956–58,* Bulletin No. 21 (1960); *idem, Surface Water Flow for 1957,* Bulletin No. 23–57 (1958); and information provided by Bureau of Reclamation.

[23] *Ibid.* See also California State Water Resources Board, *The California Water Plan,* Bulletin No. 3 (1957); *idem, Sutter-Yuba Counties Investigation,* Bulletin No. 6 (1952).

land. And there is the further fact that within any large district all member-customers have more or less equal access to water obtained under rights held by the district, so that gross misallocations among users within large total acreages of irrigable land are avoided. Eleven of over sixty active districts in Northern California account for nearly 40 per cent of all surface diversions of water in the Central Valley. Their territories are interspersed with numerous smaller territories served by fairly small and very small public agencies, mutual companies, commercial water companies, and self-supplying users; for their combined territory, the possibilities of misallocations among individual users or small groups of users are much greater. Such possibilities of misallocations evidently are fully realized in the Kaweah Delta, and are realized at least in some degree throughout the Central Valley.

As the existence of large districts tends to reduce the incidence of interdistrict misallocations, there is a contrary—though by no means fully offsetting—tendency for them to foster intradistrict misallocations of water among their customer-members. The principal reason for intradistrict misallocations within large districts stems from the large size of their service areas. Transportation distances and costs for different member-users vary significantly (most large districts have main canals from 20 to 60 miles long, from which diversions are made along their entire courses into lateral canals), but the districts generally do not vary the charge for water according to the distance over which it is delivered. Thus, there is a tendency to promote intradistrict patterns of water use such that the net marginal value of water (net of definitely allocable transportation costs) varies appreciably among users within districts according to their distances from the main water source; and this results in a misallocation which could be eliminated if relatively more water were supplied to users closer to the source and relatively less to users farther from the source. These misallocations may not be large, especially if water-land coefficients are relatively inflexible for given crops and if transport-cost differences are insufficient to induce shifts in crop patterns, but they are probably appreciable enough to deserve mention.

A second, and less pervasive, source of intradistrict misallocations is that some agencies, in effect, charge different rates for water to grow different crops. This practice is clearly conducive to misallocation of water among uses and users, though total misallocations of this sort may not be very great.

Against these possible intradistrict misallocations should be placed some behavioral evidence mentioned in Chapter 10. There it was shown that the use of improvement districts, special zones of benefit, and structures of charges which take district pumping costs into account avoid some inefficiencies which might otherwise creep into water districts' pricing and allocations.

Water Allocation—Some Summary Remarks

In Northern California, there are evidently existing or growing four fairly serious sorts of misallocation of water among types of uses, users, and places and times of use. The first three misallocations are interrelated, and involve generally excessive interseasonal transfer of water on a part of the rivers of the area, over-allocation of water to power, irrigation, and urban uses at the expense of recreational and pollution control uses on the same group of rivers, and excessive interbasin transfers from the Sacramento Valley southward. All of these misallocations can be charged in preponderant part to excessive scale or inefficient design of river development and interbasin transfer on the part of the Bureau of Reclamation and the California Department of Water Resources since World War II. However, some of the misallocations that under-supply in-stream uses of water are chargeable to the activities of local public agencies, and the Corps of Engineers is responsible for some excessive interseasonal transfers. Further, local public agencies are partly responsible for misallocations of water from common sources among individual basins, in that they have failed to make intrabasin transfers that were economic, and in that their errors of omission provided an incentive for the federal agencies to undertake excessive long-distance interbasin transfers. The main culprits in this latter aspect of misallocation are clearly the law of water rights, the law governing water agencies, the integrated structure of local agencies, and the connected failure of markets in water and water rights to develop and be used.

The fourth sort of important misallocation, among water agencies drawing on common sources, has resulted mainly from the actions and inactions of local public agencies, and is explained again by water law, agency law, agency integration, and the lack of water markets.

Unfortunately, most of the allocational errors apparent at present are in large part economically irreversible. For many of these mistakes, given the connected commitments already made in long-term investments in facilities, it would be uneconomic—because of the comparative costs of operating these facilities and of destroying or relocating them or of reducing their scales—to impose a significantly different allocational pattern at this time. The findings of such misallocations are thus of policy significance mainly in providing a warning that federal and state agencies should be discouraged from compounding their economic felonies by making further allocational and developmental errors, many of which are now on the drawing boards. Some of the errors, however, are economically reversible at least in a degree, such as those involving interdistrict and intradistrict misallocations of irrigation water. Even interseasonal misallocations could economically be somewhat ameliorated in the short term by modifying the rate of use of water and the pattern of water releases from existing storage reservoir facilities.

18

TECHNICAL EFFICIENCY IN WATER STORAGE AND TRANSPORT

When we evaluate the "degree of technical efficiency" attained in the Northern California water industry, we start by accepting as given both the level of development of water resources attained in the area generally and with respect to individual water sources, and the existing pattern of allocation of water. Then we inquire how closely the industry has approached the goal of minimizing the non-water costs of the development and allocation it has accomplished. How efficient or inefficient has it been, in terms of non-water costs, in performing the specified tasks?

This is a broad and complex problem if considered in all of its dimensions. We will simplify our inquiry here first by centering attention on the two major functions involved in developing and allocating water—storing it in on-stream reservoirs and transporting it from sources to localities of use. Have the quantities of reservoir storage on the various rivers in the area been provided at the minimum attainable total non-water cost? If not, what is the general magnitude of the difference between attained and attainable storage costs? Is water being transported from sources to localities of use at the minimum attainable total transport costs? If not, what is the rough size of the excess of attained over attainable transport costs? The efficiency of scale and location of canals and reservoirs thus will comprise our main concern. We shall be forced to neglect other aspects of efficiency in long-run design and construction as well as all questions of short-run utilization.

In appraising technical efficiency we encounter again the choice between standards of appraisal identified in Chapter 17—that is, between long-run past and future costs, including sunk costs of past investments in facilities, on the one hand, and future costs only (disregarding sunk costs), on the other, as measures of efficiency. We shall stick to the position previously taken that a valid contemporary retrospective appraisal of efficiency should consider all long-run costs as the criterion, and inquire into the extent to which such costs, in the present situation, are higher than the minimum costs attainable if all facilities were designed and built anew to serve the requirements of the current situation. We also face again the problem of whether or not contemporary inefficiency, as viewed *ex post,* has resulted from past investment decisions which were wrong at the time they were made, and are still wrong, or whether it has resulted from past decisions which were correct when made, but became wrong because of unanticipated changes. This issue, brushed aside in the preceding chapter, poses more difficulty here. In the case of canal systems, we find that a contemporary inefficiency as appraised *ex post* often resulted from past investment commitments each of which seemed correct *ex ante.* The investment commitments made at later stages in development may have been frequently justified *ex ante* as consistent with minimizing future costs as then counted, given the pre-existence of the non-optimal facilities resulting from earlier investments in which fixed costs were then sunk. This possibility certainly limits the policy significance of *ex post* inefficiencies.

Inefficiences of Small Scale and Crosshauls in Transport

The costs of water transportation are the major non-water costs of water consumed, other than costs of reservoir storage. This is true usually of the costs of both irrigation water and water supplied for urban uses. Because a preponderant share of all consumptively used water in Northern California goes to irrigation, we will focus our attention here primarily on technical efficiency in transporting irrigation water, commenting only briefly on efficiency in the transport of water to the major metropolitan region of Northern California.

With respect to irrigation water, we intend to pursue two general questions. First, defining the "task" of irrigation water transport as that of carrying predetermined quantities of water to given localities of use, and holding constant the source now supplying each destination we ask: are the number of canals and their capacities optimal in the sense that they perform the transportation task at a minimal cost? If not, how great is the deviation from the optimum? Second, accepting the same definition of the task, but allowing the source of water to vary: are there technical inefficiencies (excesses of cost over the minimum attainable) resulting from an uneconomic pairing of sources and destinations that result in wasteful crosshauls of water? In answering these questions, minimization of costs will be taken primarily to mean minimization of long-run past and future costs, but we will also comment on the efficiency of existing canal systems in terms of their advantage or disadvantage over alternative systems in terms of future costs alone. A full appraisal of how closely the optimum is approached is substantially impossible here because of the huge volume of data which would have to be assembled and analyzed; the most that we can attempt here is to identify and appraise, primarily for the Central Valley, the more obvious deviations from optimal water transport efficiency as of the present time.

In Chapter 6 we analyzed the complex problem of co-determining the number and capacities of canals used to perform a given task of local water transportation (see also Appendix B). On the one hand, there are distinct economies of scale in canals up to the largest relevant capacities, in the sense that the cost of carrying capacity per acre-foot per mile decreases as carrying capacity increases. Thus, the unit cost of water transport should decrease as the capacity of a canal is enlarged, the rate of utilization and length of the canal remaining constant. This tendency suggests the virtual advantages of consolidating main-canal capacity in a given locality and drawing on a given source or closely adjacent sources in a relatively few large-capacity canals. On the other hand, we now know that in several types of geographical situation consolidating main-canal capacity drawing on a given source may entail increases in the distance over which the average acre-foot of water is carried. This increase in delivery distance, requiring a larger total volume of canal capacity than with more and smaller canals, comprises an offset to the gains from providing a given total capacity in larger canals with lower costs per unit of capacity. Optimization clearly requires a balancing of these forces.

The complexity of this optimization problem precludes our reaching finely drawn conclusions about the efficiencies of actual canal systems without making elaborate calculations for each particular case. There are two sorts of discrepancies from optimal efficiency, however, which we can more or less unambiguously identify. The first is that of parallel hauls. Such a discrepancy occurs when two or more canals carry water from the same (or different) sources along the same general route and in the same direction to a common area of destination (or to areas of destination which lie at different places along the same route), and where the canals are quite close together or gain no significant advantage from the distance which separates them. This discrepancy involves both the scale and number of canals. The second discrepancy does not involve scale economies per se but rather crosshauls, a clearly wasteful procedure in the absence of special topographic conditions.

Parallel hauls of irrigation water

In developing conservative, but rough, rules for detecting inefficient parallel hauls of irrigation water, we have purposely excluded some which might seem questionable. We have not counted as parallel hauls those involving a canal and a natural river channel, on the theory that the addition of the canal was probably justified economically. We have overlooked parallel hauling in main canals more than three miles apart, if lateral diversions are made from the canals over the distance where they are parallel, because of the possibility that increased lateral canal costs might well offset the virtual savings that would result from merging the main canals. (The three-mile limit is an arbitrary average, since the limit should vary with the length of the outhaul from the source in main canals, but it is generally a conservative one.) And, we have overlooked parallel hauls involving differences in canal elevations in excess of 20 feet because of the possibility that the feasible route for a single canal would not be the high route, and excessive pumping costs might result from merging the canals on the low route.

Our analysis, centering primarily on the Central Valley, involved a much more intensive evaluation of the San Joaquin Valley than of the Sacramento Valley, largely because there were more adequate maps and other information on canal routes in the former region. We will thus begin with a summary of findings referring to various river basins within the San Joaquin Valley.[1]

[1] We will not present here a full list of the very numerous sources consulted in one way or another in developing these findings. The major sources are: (1) a set of detailed large-scale working maps drawn for purposes of this study by C. E. Erickson & Associates, Berkeley (on file at the Water Resources Center Archives, University of California, Berkeley);

There is no apparent evidence of significant parallel hauls in the area on the east side of the San Joaquin River north of Friant Dam, including the alluvial fans of the Stanislaus, Tuolumne, and Merced rivers, as well as lands south of the Merced to Friant and those served by the Madera Canal from Friant. The dominance in this important subregion of a few very large irrigation districts, each (with minor exceptions) served either from a different river or other source or from a different side of a shared river, probably has been mainly responsible for this result.

In the service area of the lower San Joaquin River proper (mainly lands bordering the River between Mendota Pool and the Delta), there is one *ex post* inefficiency of parallel hauling which is distinctly important. The Central California Irrigation District has a service area along the San Joaquin north of the Mendota Pool. It carries water through most of the area in two south-to-north main canals that parallel the River on its west side, and parallel each other at distances from 1 to 3 miles apart, over a common distance of about 55 miles. The two canals—the "Main" and the "Outside," have intake capacities respectively of about 1,000 and 500 cubic feet per second (cfs), and together carry about half a million acre-feet of water annually. It would appear that their service could have been provided more efficiently by a single canal with a total capacity equal to their combined capacities, on the general route of the Outside Canal, since scale economies on the long outhaul should readily outweigh any increased capacity requirements for lateral canals.

Shifting south to the Kings River service area,[2] we note first at its northerly extreme some evidence of significant parallel hauling within the large Fresno Irrigation District. The district uses three roughly parallel main canals—the Gould, Enterprise, and Fresno canals—which divert from the north bank of the Kings River. The Fresno Canal seems justified as a separate facility because it diverges to serve a separate area within the District. But the Gould and Enterprise canals, with intake capacities respectively of about 155 and 315 cfs, are parallel and only about 3 miles apart over a common distance of about 23 miles. Though some complexities arise because of the relationship of diversion points, it would appear that a single canal would more efficiently provide the services of the Gould and Enterprise canals over the 23 miles in question, with scale economies substantially outweighing increases of costs due to added capacity in lateral canals. A very

(2) maps printed by the Bureau of Reclamation covering the San Joaquin River basin, the Tulare Lake Basin, and the Kern River basin (undated but referring to the middle or late 1950's); (3) California Department of Water Resources, Division of Resources Planning, *Surface Water Flow for 1960,* Bulletin No. 23–60 (1961); *idem, Report on Irrigation and Water Storage Districts in California, 1960,* Bulletin No. 21 (1961); (4) California State Department of Public Works, Division of Engineering and Irrigation, *Irrigation Districts in California, 1929,* by Frank Adams, Bulletin No. 21 (1930); (5) California State Department of Engineering, *Water Resources of the Kern River and Adjacent Streams and Their Utilization, 1920,* Bulletin No. 9 (1921). (These and other footnote references are cited in brief form when they are also included in the Bibliography.)

[2] All except one agency mentioned here in connection with the Kings River service area can be located in Figure 20, Chapter 12. That one agency, Lakeside Ditch Company, lies at the southern border of the Kings River service area, being within the northern edge of the adjacent Kaweah River service area; the Company appears in Figure 22, Chapter 12.

similar pattern occurs in the Consolidated Irrigation District, another large district, which adjoins the Fresno District on the south and diverts from the Kings River.

The Alta Irrigation District adjoins the Consolidated District on the east or uphill side, and lies just south of the Kings River. Its main canal diverts from the south bank of the Kings at about the point where the Friant-Kern Canal (carrying water south from the San Joaquin River) crosses the Kings, and it parallels the Friant-Kern Canal for a distance of about 25 miles, 2 to 3 miles west of the Friant-Kern, with an intake capacity about one-third that of the Friant-Kern. It seems apparent that a single canal (the Friant-Kern with a bulge added at the crossing of the Kings) could provide the service now rendered by the two canals over the 25-mile stretch much more efficiently than the present two; there would be scale economies, with relatively minor offsets in the form of costs of added lateral mileage.

South of the Consolidated Irrigation District, west of the Alta District, and beginning at the south bank of the Kings River, there is a "vertical stack" of adjoining agencies running roughly from north to south—the People's Ditch Company, the Lakeside Ditch Company, and the Corcoran Irrigation District (listed in north to south order).[3] Their main canals run in the same direction (south) and are roughly parallel, and a single large canal for the most part could largely replace the three now employed.

In the Kaweah River delta, where an extremely complicated and evidently quite inefficient network of large and small canals is found, the most significant inefficiency involves the Tulare Irrigation District, the Consolidated People's Ditch Company, and the Farmers Ditch Company, which together serve most of the irrigated land in the Kaweah delta—a roughly rectangular area about 4 by 12 miles on its sides, and southwest of the Friant-Kern Canal crossing of the Kaweah River. The three agencies maintain separate, parallel-radial canals, with the canals of the Tulare District and the Farmers Ditch Company running through the service area of the Consolidated People's Ditch Company. All divert from the Kaweah River, which has two terminal branches that, together with its main stem, are used for diversions by these agencies. These and other complexities can be noted generally in Figure 22. Our own analysis, not presented here in detail, suggests that a single main canal from the Kaweah, used both to distribute water and pick up added diversions en route, would be more efficient. Its operation would be facilitated by appropriate transfers between the terminal forks of the Kaweah River and, with a length of about 13 miles, would do the duty of about 34 miles of existing canal segments of various capacities, at a substantial net saving to the Tulare, Consolidated People's, and Farmers agencies.

Since parallel hauls do not constitute a primary problem in the Kern River basin, we shift our attention northward to the Sacramento Valley. In the service areas of the Sacramento River and of the Feather and Yuba rivers, few significant parallel hauls can be noted from available maps and other evidence, although this may partly result from a lack of the sort of detailed information which was available for the San Joaquin Valley. We observed one case of a probably ineffi-

[3] People's Ditch Company and Corcoran Irrigation District are shown in Figure 20, Chapter 12; Lakeside Ditch Company appears in Figure 22, Chapter 12. See note 2 above.

cient parallel haul, over a distance of 10 to 12 miles, in two canals carrying water west from the Feather River. These are the Biggs Extension Canal, which supplies the Richvale Irrigation District, and the Western Canal belonging to the Pacific Gas and Electric Company. However, a single canal performing their combined functions over this stretch might possibly fail to be more economical, because it would involve lifting costs into laterals which are not incurred with the use of two canals.

Would it pay now to undertake construction to eliminate the inefficiencies in the cases we have described? Probably not. In terms of costs from now on, it is at present cheaper to operate the existing inefficient systems than to replace them with "ideal" alternative systems. It will become efficient to do so in the future mainly so far as changes in the physical or economic environment render existing facilities inoperative or greatly alter their economic productivity. Do these inefficiencies embody the results of investment decisions which were rational when they were made? They no doubt seemed rational to the agencies which undertook them, and often were, but in some cases insularity, rivalry for ill-defined water rights, or the institutional inflexibility of water allocations and transfers probably precluded alternative plans that would have been more profitable for all parties. The pre-World War I rivalries for San Joaquin Valley water and the post-World War II hostility between the Bureau of Reclamation and many local agencies could account for much of the inefficient construction.

The magnitude of the total inefficiencies attributable to parallel hauls of irrigation water in the Central Valley would be very difficult to estimate. Considering the apparent frequency of their incidence (moderate but not extreme) and the implicit cost effects, it seems improbable that they could be responsible for elevating all irrigation water transport costs in the Central Valley by as much as 10 per cent; and it further seems that any such elevation was in large part "economically unavoidable."

Parallel hauls of urban water

A few comments are in order on the character of the parallel-haul problem involved in the operation of the main agencies supplying urban water to the San Francisco Bay region—the water department of the city and county of San Francisco and the East Bay Municipal Utility District. Both districts import water from the Sierra Nevada on the east side of the Central Valley through long aqueducts, each, at present, in amounts of about 100,000 acre-feet annually, and these amounts are growing. They divert from river sources about 45 miles apart in a north-south direction; and given this selection of sources, a common long-distance transport facility evidently would never have been economical. However, with each system undertaking about a 100-mile haul from the lower reaches of the Sierra to the Bay area, and in four aqueducts with individual capacities of about 250 cubic feet per second, it is worth noting that one aqueduct with a capacity of 1,000 cfs would do the same job at about one-half the cost per acre-foot per mile of transport, given available scale economies in hard-surface lined canals and in pipelines. This would be a large saving in costs of Bay area water, and would not be seriously offset by the costs of necessary rearrangements in water distribution within the Bay area. Its accomplishment, of course, would have required a change in the selection of sources, with the two systems drawing on a single river or on two adjacent rivers, such as the Mokelumne and Stanislaus or the Stanislaus and Tuolumne. Legal barriers involving water rights, insularity of agency actions, and the somewhat different timing of the growth of urban water demands on the west and east sides of the San Francisco Bay all contributed to the failure to take advantage of available economies of large-scale transportation. The implicit inefficiency of what was done is certainly not economically remediable now.

Within each of the agencies, there has been a further development of parallel hauling by using essentially two (or for the East Bay Municipal Utility District, eventually three) long parallel aqueducts to carry water from the Sierra, at the expense of quite appreciable added costs per unit of water delivered resulting from the use of inefficiently small aqueducts. This may be explicable in terms of safety factors, or of sequenced responses to growing demands in a context where the rate of growth was badly underestimated. Had the estimates been correct, construction of substantially larger single aqueducts at an early stage would probably have been economically justified.

Crosshauls on the Bureau's canals

From our analysis of existing canal systems, the incidence of crosshauling of water appears to be negligible among the canals of local water agencies in Northern California. We are inclined to attribute this to the fact that local agencies have not in the past generally made investment decisions which at the time were grossly erroneous, except occasionally under the influence of irrationalities inherent in the law of water rights. The principal crosshauling which has developed in the area's water industry has resulted from the superimposition of the two major long-distance canals of the Bureau of Reclamation—the Delta-Mendota and Friant-Kern canals—on a pre-existing network of canals which had been developed when the origin of some water supplies and the availability of others had not been altered by the Bureau through its canal building, and when such alterations were not anticipated.

Three cases of significant crosshauls (one really an out-and-back haul) have emerged as a consequence of canal developments by the Bureau. In the case involving an out-and-back haul, water is carried south to the Mendota Pool in the Delta-Mendota Canal and then north by the users of this water; the second is an essential crosshaul of San Joaquin River water in the Friant-Kern Canal against Kings River water, as the latter supplies the Fresno Irrigation District; and the third is a crosshaul of Kern River and Friant-Kern water at the southern end of the Friant-Kern Canal.

With respect to the Delta-Mendota out-and-back haul, several major agencies were traditionally dependent on diversions from the natural flow of the San Joaquin River to irrigate an area lying along the river course north of what is now the Mendota Pool; to do so, they carried it northward in canals for a distance of about 55 miles. The main agencies worth mentioning in a brief discussion are the Central California Irrigation District, the Firebaugh Canal Company, and the San Luis Canal Company. Firebaugh irrigates an area extending about 12 miles north of the Mendota Pool on the west side of the River, diverting before and after the Delta-Mendota Canal was built from the San Joaquin in the vicinity of Mendota Pool. Central California Irrigation District (CCID) irrigates an area beginning about 6 miles north of Mendota Pool and extending north about 40 air-line miles, or 50 miles as its canals run, on the west side of the River, and also traditionally diverted from the San Joaquin in the vicinity of Mendota Pool. The San Luis Company serves an area along the river about 22 miles north of Mendota Pool, diverting from the San Joaquin at that point (Temple Slough).

Prior to the cutting off of the natural San Joaquin River flow by Friant Dam, all of these districts had developed economically sensible canal systems predicated on the supposition that they would divert from water flowing from the east to Mendota Pool in the San Joaquin River. (They were sensible, at least, except for internal parallel hauling in two canals by CCID, mentioned above.) With the cutting off of the San Joaquin flow at Friant Dam, the Bureau replaced this flow by bringing Delta water southward in the Delta-Mendota Canal all the way to Mendota Pool, for diversion therefrom by the agencies mentioned. This arrangement introduced a gigantic out-and-back haul of Delta-Mendota Canal water, with about 745,000 acre-feet annually carried in the Delta-Mendota well south of its points of use and then back north through the established local canals that generally were parallel and close to the Delta-Mendota Canal. That imposition of this out-and-back haul was the most economical thing to do, given the pre-existing local canals, is not entirely obvious, but it may have been and we will give it the benefit of the doubt. However, an ideal system designed to supply the area and Delta-Mendota water would utilize a much more tapered Delta-Mendota Canal tapped directly by south-bound laterals comprising a much less expensive local distribution system.

The Friant-Kern Canal became the source of one crosshaul when it was built because it carried water south from the San Joaquin River alongside territory already served by the Kings River and north of the Kings, and then crossed the Kings and carried San Joaquin water further southward to the Tulare Lake Basin area. The main service area involved was that of the large Fresno Irrigation District, which lies north of the Kings River and has traditionally secured its water supply from the Kings—diverting about 340,000 acre-feet per year and carrying it north as far as the south bank of the San Joaquin River. Prior to the construction of the Friant-Kern Canal, the Fresno District might have been supplied either from the Kings or the San Joaquin, and possibly more cheaply from the latter, but drawing its supply from the Kings involved no crosshaul. (The original selection of source was probably mainly determined by water rights availability.) With the construction of the Friant-Kern Canal, however, a situation was introduced in which San Joaquin River water sufficient to irrigate the Fresno District was hauled south to and past the Kings, against the north haul of Kings River water in the canals of the District.

The Friant-Kern Canal becomes involved in its second crosshaul at its southern end where it enters the Kern River basin. There two parallel local canals, the Calloway and Beardsley-Lerdo canals, divert water from the north bank of the Kern River and carry it north for about 30 miles. In the last 20 miles of this haul, the two canals parallel the Friant-Kern Canal, which is carrying water from the San Joaquin River (133 to 153 miles away) southward. The two local canals serve the North Kern Water Storage District with about 90,000 to 100,000 acre-feet of water per year. The Friant-Kern Canal crosshauls them through the territory of the North Kern District and delivers water south and west of that District and south of the Kern River. The Friant-Kern has a terminal capacity of 2,000 cubic feet per second (half its intake capacity). Unless more water is found to feed into the Friant-Kern Canal, it has serious excess capacity at its southern end, since the Bureau of Reclamation has contracted for the delivery a considerable distance north of the Kern River basin of the bulk of the water available for carriage in the Canal.

All three canals (Friant-Kern, Calloway, and Beardsley-Lerdo) lie within a strip of land from 1 to 5½ miles wide where they are parallel. Lerdo, the smaller of the two local canals, is east of and upslope from the Friant-Kern at an elevation 35 to 40 feet higher; Calloway (four times larger than the Lerdo) is downslope from the Friant-Kern.

An "ideal" canal system would be predicated on exchanging Friant-Kern water now delivered south of the North Kern Water Storage District for Kern River water now supplying that District; supplying that District from the Friant-Kern except for water carried in the Lerdo Canal; not building the Calloway Canal at all; supplying the present Friant-Kern service area in the Kern River basin largely from the Kern River; and reducing the terminal capacity of the Friant-Kern by at least half (1,000 cfs), with a tapering reduction beginning 20 miles north of its southern end. This alternative system would be substantially more economical than the present one, since it would eliminate one large local canal and reduce the end size of the Friant-Kern substantially, with only a relatively small offset in added lateral capacity.

In this case, it seems that there was a good chance that if the necessary exchange of water rights could have been negotiated a more efficient alternative could have been chosen at the time of the construction of the Friant-Kern Canal. There could have been a net saving in having the Friant-Kern serve the North Kern Water Storage District even if the sunk cost of the Calloway Canal is neglected. In fact, the extension of the Friant-Kern Canal to the Kern River was originally justified on the basis of an anticipated exchange of Friant-Kern water for Kern River water in the area south of the Water Storage District, but this exchange could not be arranged. Plans have now been announced to crosshaul Friant-Kern water uphill for 14 miles against the downhill flow of the Kern River, in order to serve the Arvin-Edison Water Storage District.[4]

Taking an overview of technical inefficiencies in canal systems in the Central Valley, it would appear that those attributable to crosshauls by Bureau canals are of appreciable importance, but less important in the aggregate than those of all parallel hauls by local canals.

[4] *Western Water News,* July 1962, pp. 1–2.

Efficiency of Scale in Reservoir Storage

Of the various aspects of the efficiency of on-stream reservoirs in Northern California we shall examine one: whether or not they have been built to optimal scales in the sense that they performed given water storage tasks at the lowest possible cost in the light of constraints imposed by available site characteristics. We wish to inquire not only whether individual reservoirs on a given river are of optimal size, but also if efficiency could have been increased by consolidating a given total reservoir capacity on the river in fewer and larger reservoirs, without sacrificing much in terms of their ability to perform designated functions.

This appraisal, however, is not very easy to make. We have, of course, information on the actual capacities of the larger reservoirs in the area. In addition, we have some rather clear indications that on a given site or for the "average" site, there are distinct economies of scale in larger reservoirs, in the sense that as reservoir capacity is increased from 20,000 or 50,000 acre-feet to as much as 5 million acre-feet, there is a significant progressive decline in reservoir construction cost per acre-foot of storage capacity.[5] However, a constraint on exploiting these scale economies is the fact that few reservoir sites in Northern California will support very large reservoirs; optimal reservoir scales for them are much smaller than an "average experience" chart would indicate. This stems in large part from the fact that most available on-stream reservoir sites are on numerous rivers that are not very large, and that the rivers run through the rugged Sierra terrain. When these considerations are combined with the fact that the most economic reservoirs will generally be built either for power generation, or for irrigation plus power generation, and that power generation is ordinarily not very well facilitated by low-elevation reservoir sites, a tendency to select sites which impose fairly severe limitations on reservoir scale is readily understood.[6]

Furthermore, it is quite evident that among the developed rivers of Northern California, and on individual rivers of the area, differences in site characteristics exert a more powerful influence on the construction costs per acre-foot of reservoir storage than does the scale of reservoirs. This finding is clearly supported by the empirical findings of the Bureau of Reclamation: whereas, for all regions within which it operates there is a steady decline in construction costs per acre-foot of storage as reservoir capacities are increased from 20,000 to 500,000 acre-feet, in the Central Pacific region there is almost no decline in unit costs of storage over

[5] See Chapter 6, subsection on economies of large-scale reservoirs, where cost-scale relationships found empirically by the Corps of Engineers and the Bureau of Reclamation are presented and discussed.

[6] Low-elevation sites which are good for power generation, such as the Shasta Dam site, are rare on the developed rivers of Northern California. A very large high-elevation dam on the Trinity was possible because of the river's unusually large run-off and of special terrain conditions. It is, of course, possible to build very large reservoirs at low elevations on very small rivers or creeks at a low cost per acre-foot of storage—such as Monticello Reservoir, with a capacity of 1.6 million acre-feet on a creek with a mean annual flow of less than half a million acre-feet. But such projects evidently are not inexpensive in terms of the benefits of interseasonal transfers of negligible streamflows—if, in fact, they are economically justifiable at all.

this range of capacities.[7] Further sustenance is lent to the finding by the fact that there is practically no correlation between reservoir scales and reservoir costs for on-stream reservoirs with individual reservoir capacities above 40,000 acre-feet in Northern California. This is true both when such cheap and large lowland puddles as Monticello Reservoir and Clear Lake are included, and when they are omitted.[8]

The dominant influence of reservoir site on reservoir costs in Northern California, and the practical statistical impossibility of isolating this influence from the influence of reservoir capacity, makes it very difficult for us to offer any real appraisal of the extent to which available economies of scale have been exploited in reservoir construction in the area. We are thus reduced to offering some rather general observations.

One notable fact is that about half of the fifty-six largest on-stream reservoirs in Northern California have individual capacities between 40,000 and 100,000 acre-feet, generally a "suspect" range of scales on the basis of evidence drawn from numerous regions combined. And another one-fourth of them have individual capacities below 300,000 acre-feet, also a moderately suspect range of scales from the same standpoint. In spite of moderately pervasive limitation in some degree on reservoir scales by available site characteristics, especially when sites suitable for power generation must generally be favored, there is room for suspicion that at least a part of the smaller three-fourths of these reservoirs were built at inefficiently small individual scales. Furthermore, there is reason to suspect that this inefficiency could have been eliminated in large part by consolidating the capacity on individual rivers in fewer and larger reservoirs, using only the best sites.

This suspicion is lent some support by the finding that about one-third of the reservoirs with capacities below 300,000 acre-feet, or one-fourth of all large on-stream reservoirs, were built by local water agencies, either agricultural or urban. The bulk of these agencies may reasonably be expected to have been operating subject to significant budgetary constraints which may have prevented them from financing reservoirs of optimal-scale on the sites they selected (and pre-empted). Also the agencies would probably have limited the scale alternatives from which they selected the capacity of reservoirs to those appropriate to serve their own arbitrarily defined service areas, rather than to supply water economically to unlimited or elastically defined service areas. General behavioral and structural evidence thus suggests that, for perhaps a fourth of the largest reservoirs in the area, there may have been good reasons for building to inefficiently small scales.

Neither sort of constraint—budgetary or those connected with an arbitrarily limited service area—seems to have affected the public agencies and private firms which built most of the other three-quarters of the large on-stream reservoirs in the area. But seventeen of the large on-stream reservoirs out of the largest fifty-six (another 30 per cent of them) were built by Pacific Gas and Electric Company

[7] See Chapter 6, *loc. cit.*

[8] This conclusion is drawn from our scatter diagrams plotting reservoir capacities against unit construction costs of storage, using data drawn from the California Department of Water Resources, *Dams within Jurisdiction of State of California, January 1, 1962,* Bulletin No. 17 (1962), and from other plottings including planned dams and their estimated costs and capacities.

and Southern California Edison Company "on their own account"—not under cooperative arrangements with irrigation districts or other agencies representing consumptive users of water. With respect to most of the seventeen, it would appear that their general failure or inability either to build the dams under cooperative and cost-sharing arrangements with such agencies, or to collect for irrigation benefits that their reservoir operations might provide, tended to induce them to construct reservoirs which were smaller than they would have built in the absence of these failures and disabilities, and smaller than the most efficient scales that reservoir sites permitted and joint demands for water justified. This tendency is predictable, at any rate, except where site limitations were such that sites would be fully exploited for power purposes alone.

About 55 per cent of the fifty-six largest on-stream reservoirs were thus built subject to structural conditions and behavioral tendencies which generally favored individual reservoirs of inefficiently small scale (though not as much as 55 per cent of all large-reservoir capacity). Most of the other 45 per cent plus of large reservoirs, on the other hand, were built by public agencies (most by the federal agencies) which were neither structurally nor behaviorally influenced toward building reservoirs of inefficiently small scale. On the contrary, they have probably in general realized available scale economies of large reservoirs up to the hilt, actually pursuing them so far that inframarginal increments of capacity were economically unjustified.

If we view Northern California reservoir development as a whole, the evidence just discussed casts a noticeable shadow of doubt on the proposition that reservoirs in the area have generally been built to optimal scales. It seems probable that a substantial share of the large reservoirs—from perhaps 30 to 50 per cent of them —have been built to inefficiently small scales; that many of the more intensively developed rivers have been developed with too many reservoirs of inefficiently small scale; and that a corresponding elevation in cost of reservoir storage is attributable both to inefficiently small scales and to a failure to concentrate reservoir capacity sufficiently on the most efficient sites on various rivers. Ours is an unproved suspicion, and the circumstantial evidence supporting it, while significant, is not overwhelmingly strong. This seems to be about as far as we can proceed in appraising technical efficiency in reservoir storage in Northern California.

If this probable, or possible, inefficiency were combined with the more firmly documented inefficiency in water transport, the following conclusions might seem reasonable. The costs of supplying water, using it for power generation, and regulating streamflows are probably 10 or 15 per cent above minimal costs for performing designated developmental, allocational, and transportation functions. There is a corresponding overcommitment of non-water resources to developing Northern California water, in addition to the overcommitments associated with overdevelopment and misallocation, as discussed in the three preceding chapters. However, some of this technical inefficiency (most of that involving canals) was historically unavoidable; and practically all of it is irreversible, in the sense that, when the fixed costs of existing facilities are sunk, it is cheaper now to operate existing facilities than to replace them with better ones.

PART FOUR: SUMMARY AND POLICY PROPOSALS

19

SUMMARY: STRUCTURE, CONDUCT, AND PERFORMANCE IN THE WATER INDUSTRY

Studies of the economic problems relating to water in the humid regions of the United States often center upon external effects and the degree to which they are recognized and allowed for. In Northern California, by contrast, these problems can more fruitfully be identified with competition for a scarce natural resource and the efficiency of the allocations resulting from this rivalry. In most of the region, streamflow and the "safe yield" of ground-water basins are inadequate to satiate all uses to the point of zero net marginal productivity. Only in certain clearly defined segments—the lower San Joaquin Valley and the Sacramento-San Joaquin Delta—does the water problem become primarily one of the externalities involving pollution. Only in the north coastal region in the winter season is surface runoff both a free good and largely free of pressing problems of externalities. Not only are the economic tests for scarcity satisfied when applied to most of the region's sources of water, but also the behavior of the members of the water industry reflects their overt concern for their access to water in the face of demands made by competing users.

If water has a positive opportunity cost in most uses, then the familiar corpus of the economic theory of markets becomes applicable to explaining the resulting competition and evaluating its results. This study has sought to apply the techniques of economic analysis developed for conventional markets and industries to this markedly unconventional industry. In this chapter, we seek first to recapitulate the method used to adapt the industry study technique to this case, and then to summarize the results of testing our predictions about the quality of the market performance of the industry and our conclusions about the causes of its deficiencies. Finally, we consider what the industry's behavior tells about how it would perform if its economic structure were different. This summary paves the way for Chapter 20, in which we make suggestions for changes in the legal structure of the industry and consider their consequences.

The Users' Cooperative Hypothesis and Predictions of Conduct and Performance

The most critical assumption employed in adapting the traditional industry study methodology to the water industry is that most entities in the water industry other than self-supplying users can be regarded as if they were cooperative organizations formed to supply water to fixed groups of uses or users. Developed inductively from a large number of observations about the industry, this central hypothesis substitutes for the conventional master hypothesis of price theory that members of an industry seek to maximize their profits. Most water supply organizations take the legal form of special local government agencies or departments of general local governments, and the hypothesis seems to hold well for them as a class. Federal and state agencies resemble users' cooperatives to some degree, but they are sufficiently few and important that we have considered their motivation largely on a case-by-case basis. The hypothesis naturally does not alter the normative principles governing the optimal allocation of water and associated inputs in relation to their productivities for final uses. We stated in Chapters 3 and 8, however, that in association with other features of the industry's environment it generates a set of distinctive, testable predictions about conduct and performance. We shall argue that these predictions have been largely confirmed, and thus that both the hypothesis and the general methodology within which it has been embedded possess significant explanatory power. In short, a collection of interacting governmental units performing the same economic function can be usefully studied as an industry.

To indicate the fundamental role of the users' cooperative hypothesis in this study, we shall first summarize the direct evidence supporting its validity, then indicate how it was combined with other information on the structure or environment of the industry to yield testable predictions. The following are among the major pieces of evidence supporting the hypothesis directly:

1) The review of the law of water organizations in Chapter 3 showed that the legal process of forming most types of special purpose water organizations is usually initiated by a prospective group of member-customers. In the drawing of the boundaries of most agricultural retailing districts, landowners have a considerable—but not unfettered—opportunity to opt in or out. Effective political control over the district's management and major managerial decisions lies with the electorate. Where city water agencies function as departments of general municipal governments, this sovereignty lies one step removed, but retains the same general form.

2) Chapter 9, in exploring the circumstances under which local public agencies are formed, showed that they arise in response to pressures and problems felt by their prospective member-customers rather than to profit opportunities scented by a conventional entrepreneur or promoter. Delineations of service areas contain important arbitrary elements explained by members' private preferences.

3) Our examination of the pricing practices employed by local water agencies (Chapter 10) revealed an emphasis on setting charges to cover money costs and providing irrigation service thriftily and without frills. Price discrimination is employed against outsiders, and a major concern in agricultural pricing (but a minor one in urban pricing) is to provide equitable treatment to an agency's differently situated member-customers. These traits were all found consistent with the users' cooperative hypothesis.

4) The theory and practice of the urban agency's investment decision, studied in Chapters 8 and 11, possess a number of traits that we can associate with the hypothesis. The ardent desire to avoid uncertainty in the agency's ability to supply its customers provides a good example. So do the efforts of agricultural

districts to take part in joint water and power projects that might provide "free water" to their member-customers.

5) Chapters 9 and 12 documented the usual lack of interest of local districts in any entrepreneurial transactions with outsiders. New member-customers are sought and new territory is included only when these actions are incidental to serving the interests of previous members.[1]

These are some of the principal pieces of direct evidence supporting the employment of the users' cooperative hypothesis. In order to develop operational hypotheses to forecast or explain the behavior or performance of the industry, we generally sought to deduce how cooperatives could be expected to act in the structural and environmental setting of the water industry. Evidence on the strategic features of this structure was developed in Part One.

Among the chief components of the industry's structure are certain features of the law of water rights and the law of water agencies. California statutes have offered several routes for the establishment of rights to water for power generation and for the several uses requiring diversion onto the land, but generally none for creating rights relating to other (in-stream) uses. The transfer of each type of right from one use or user to another (except by the purchase of land to which it is appurtenant) is restricted in varying ways and degrees. The law of water agencies also impedes the transfer of water or rights. The appurtenance of rights to land makes any sale of water rights by a district a complex process; temporary outside sales can cause rights complications because of the possibility of developing public service responsibilities. Changes in agencies' service areas encounter difficulties such as the adjustment of existing bonded indebtedness.

These legal features combine to predict the absence of continuous markets for water and rights, and a corresponding focus of water agencies upon the defense of rights and their acquisition well in advance of anticipated needs. For performance, they predict excessive applications of water to uses allowed to establish rights (as against other uses) and to users who established rights to a given source early (as against those seeking access to it later). Somewhat less definitely, they also predict an economically excessive volume of water development facilities put in place to serve uses capable of gaining water rights; those in strong positions tend to build heavily to establish the "beneficial use" required by law, while those in weak positions may build heavily to overcome their underprivileged access to water or water rights.

Other important traits of the industry's environment were described in Part One and give rise to further hypotheses. The agricultural and urban demands for water were shown (Chapter 5) to be sufficiently elastic that the choice between correct and incorrect water prices should make a significant difference for the allocation of water.[2] Numerous aspects of the structure of costs of water storage and distribution facilities discussed in Chapter 6 could influence the industry's behavior and performance substantially. Moderate economies of scale prevail in the con-

[1] This proposition fails to hold true for some urban suppliers and local wholesalers, but applies strictly to agricultural retailers.

[2] To the extent that competing demands for a scarce resource are absolutely insensitive to price, the level of the price holds only distributional or equity significance.

struction of storage reservoirs (in terms of costs per unit of capacity), and moderate to extreme scale economies in the construction of canals. The presence of scale economies in canal construction, however, cannot be taken to imply that efficiency can always be increased by serving a given territory through a smaller number of retail distribution systems. Enlarging the scale of water transport facilities entails an increase in the distance traveled by the average unit of water delivered, a substantial offset to the scale economies of consolidating canal capacity in units of larger scale. Our analysis of costs also revealed that the proportion of fixed costs in water distribution is much higher than in most conventional industries. Finally, the estimated unit costs of water distribution organizations in various parts of Northern California were shown to vary substantially.

Adding in these structural elements of demand and cost provides us with more hypotheses about the behavior and performance of the industry. The scale economies in water storage and transport facilities, coupled with the rigidity of agency boundaries, implies that a relatively large number of agencies may be formed within a given area or basin and may construct dams and canals of suboptimal scale. For behavior, these scale economies (coupled with the relative lack of scale economies to the geographic expansion of retail agencies) imply a pressure for the formation of separate layers of retail and wholesale organizations, especially as the relative growth of demand for water raises the productivity of interseasonal storage and long-distance transport. The evidence of high fixed costs suggests that agencies' abilities to meet fixed charges are sensitive to fluctuations of their revenues. Considering the cooperative's concern with avoiding uncertainty, a prevailing preference for long-term contracts becomes likely. Also, one might expect stalemates and related difficulties in arm's-length bargaining over the sale of water analogous to the problems of price warfare or collusion sometimes found in conventional industries with high fixed costs. Finally, the large interagency cost differences, in addition to reflecting the lack of markets, may imply significant intrabasin and interbasin differences in the average and marginal productivity of water, particularly water for agricultural use.[3] If retail agencies on the short end of local misallocations can induce someone to undertake interarea imports on their behalf, then long-distance transfers might result that are excessive in the light of what would be appropriate with correct intrabasin water allocations and cost adjustments.

Two more blocks of information on the structure of the industry can now be added, along with the related hypotheses. Our examination of concentration patterns (Chapter 4) was guided by the implication of the users' cooperative hypothesis that seller concentration would hold little significance. Buyer or user concentration might, however, as could the degree of vertical integration. Our measurements indicated a high degree of vertical integration in consumptive uses, although the amount of wholesaling activity is increasing rapidly. The concentration of users

[3] These differences do not per se imply inefficiencies in the construction of facilities or the allocation of water, since they may reflect real cost differences in supplying water to different parcels of land, and be offset by differential Ricardian land rents. Furthermore, an experimental analysis of the variance of irrigation districts' reported average costs showed significantly greater variation among basins or local areas than within them. Both of these considerations warn against drawing strong conclusions about the significance of interagency cost differences, but do not justify ignoring them entirely.

diverting from the major surface-water sources in Northern California is generally high, although it varies enough from river to river to raise the possibility of testing its significance by cross-sectional inference. Also variable from area to area is the concentration of different types of water agencies, offering the possibility of testing hypotheses about the significance of differences in their legal powers. Shifting from the form to the substance of hypotheses generated in Chapter 4, we argued that relatively low concentration in fully integrated segments of the industry might augment the problems of inefficiencies of small scale. It might also increase the amount of uncertainty and rigidity in the tenure of water rights, because the character of legal restrictions on such transfers suggests that large transfers might be much less costly per unit than small ones, and transfers where a small number of parties might be incidentally affected easier than those in which the number of third parties is large.

Finally, Chapter 2 outlined the general geographic and hydrographic characteristics of Northern California and suggested some additional cross-area or cross-basin hypotheses. For instance, the relatively wide distribution of major rivers through the Central Valley implies that local agencies may undertake substantial development of water resources and also that interbasin transfers between adjacent areas could be carried out at relatively moderate transport cost. The distribution of precipitation and surface runoff shows that such developments for consumptive use, if carried beyond a modest level, must involve the construction of storage. There are important interbasin differences in both the absolute and relative size of surface-water resources: the Sacramento Valley has more large rivers, and more water relative to agricultural land, than the San Joaquin Valley, implying a predominance of wholesaling activity and the origination of interbasin transfers in the Sacramento Valley. Finally, Chapter 2 also surveyed the prevailing extent and scale of water storage and transport facilities. A substantial portion of reservoir capacity appeared to be designed and operated to serve (that is, to optimize in relation to) fewer purposes than it should. Scale inefficiencies as well as a misallocation of water among types of use was suggested.

Part Two, dealing with revealed patterns of conduct in the water industry, supplied information on a limited number of additional structural elements in the form of standard decision rules used by water agencies and conditions in markets one step removed from the water industry itself. These factors are structural in the sense of comprising stable forces affecting, and not affected by, the conduct and performance of the water industry. The major structural influence stemming from other markets is capital rationing, limiting the borrowing power of local districts (when operating on their own) in relation to their initial assessed valuation. A number of decision rules of local districts assume importance. Some concerning retail water pricing can be deduced from the users' cooperative hypothesis, notably the setting of agricultural water prices to cover costs; others concerning investment decisions are seemingly arbitrary, such as the choice of low interest rates for discounting and the employment of a "requirements" approach to evaluating future benefits from incremental urban water supplies. These structural elements add yet another layer of hypotheses concerning performance—hypotheses which unfortunately cut in opposite directions. The pricing rules, choice of discount rates in project evaluation, and use of a requirements approach to benefits imply excessive scales of construction and use of water; the first two factors operate especially, the third exclusively, on urban districts. On the other hand, capital rationing tends to restrict the scale of projects or delay construction. Finally, the statutes and policies governing the actions of federal and state water wholesalers comprise another vitally important set of decision rules. In California, as at the national level, these tend to imply excessive investment in water development facilities and misallocation of water toward irrigation and away from in-stream uses.

The Quality of Performance and Sources of Deficiencies

So far, we have set forth the main outlines of the network of hypotheses we developed concerning the relation between the legal, economic, and physical environment of the water industry and its conduct and performance. The analysis of conduct within the framework of these hypotheses sought to accomplish two broad purposes, aside from testing our hypotheses concerning conduct per se. It organized a portion of the evidence needed for drawing inferences about the quality of performance; and in its depiction of behavioral patterns, it provided some basis for anticipating how the industry would perform if strategic (and malleable) aspects of its structure were altered. In summarizing, we shall reverse the original order of presentation and discuss, first, the measurements made of performance and their relation to a priori structural hypotheses about its quality. Then we can discern what aspects of structure might be profitably altered, and return to the evidence on conduct with greater insight into its value for predicting the effect of alternative arrangements.

Some preliminary evaluations of selected aspects of performance were made in Part Two, but most of the relevant measurements were made, and appraisals assembled, in Part Three. We developed a special series of categories of performance norms to cover the many dimensions of correct allocation in the water industry. It was necessary to explore separately the level, sequence, and rationality of the industry's development, referring respectively to the appropriateness of the over-all quantity of resources dedicated to satisfying utilities relating to water, the efficiency of historic patterns of adjustment of this quantity, and the efficiency of the allocation of these resources among various users, uses, and places of use of water. Furthermore, we distinguished between the level of water-usage development and the level of water-facilities development. The quantity of either input may be either excessive or deficient in a particular case, independent of the level of use of the other.

In Chapter 15, we concluded from benefit-cost appraisals of the Central Valley Project and Feather River Project, along with other assorted statistical and behavioral evidence, that the levels of interbasin transfers and of distribution-system facilities for local agricultural use in Northern California are generally excessive. In the case of interbasin transfers (excluding those made by the cities of the San Francisco Bay area), this conclusion seems relatively unambiguous for both extant and pending transfers. In the case of local agricultural districts, however, the evidence of local (intrabasin) misallocations leads us to suspect that the appearance of excessive water-facilities development may merely reflect misallocations favoring low-value uses of facilities and water; if local distributions of the water and facilities presently devoted to irrigation uses were rationalized, their total amounts might not prove excessive.

These results seem consistent with the thrust of our major hypotheses about the quality of performance. The copious restraints upon interagency transactions in water and rights and the incentives created for inflating water use in some situations in order to assure future access to supplies imply strong pressures to push the level of water usage and of transport facilities beyond the optimum. Conversely, capital rationing deters the construction of dams by local districts for interseasonal transfer of water, although perhaps not the building of distribution systems.[4] So deficient interseasonal transfers from some surface sources may also contribute to making the return on distribution facilities look subnormal.

The evidence of excessive development by state and federal agencies relates to a different set of hypothesized causes. These are the direct statutory motives of the agencies in question; their decision rules for investment and pricing; and the impact of local water misallocations and uncertainties concerning rights upon the apparent marginal productivity of interseasonal and interbasin transfers. Some of these sources of inefficient project development—such as the errors in the formal criteria for project evaluation previously used by the Bureau of Reclamation and the Corps of Engineers—have been thoroughly studied before at the national level. Our evidence, developed in Parts Two and Three, supports an enlarged and reshaped view about the significance of this and other sources of deficient performance by the large agencies. First of all, the defects in formal criteria for project evaluation seem minor compared to the simple abuses found in their applications: gross overstatements of benefits, omissions of allowances for associated costs or disbenefits, and the like. Second, while the state and federal agencies are often, and properly, flayed for undertaking excessive investments or preferring physical to nonphysical solutions in response to bureaucratic motives, it should also be emphasized that their actions are ultimately controlled and approved by the political process. The Bureau, the Corps, and the California Department of Water Resources have all been shown to plan their projects in close liaison with local interest groups, operating both through and outside of the U.S. Congress and California State Legislature; these groups are able both to promote projects and to shape their designs to their own interests.[5] Finally, the successful promotional campaigns of these interest groups are motivated importantly (although not exclusively) by their desires to overcome local misallocations or protect themselves against anticipated future misallocations of water and rights. Therefore, these deficiencies in local allocations must take a significant part of the blame for the defects in the large agencies' performance.

[4] A dam must be built all at once, while a distribution system need not. Furthermore, numerous forms of public assistance are now available to local districts seeking to finance investments in distribution systems.

[5] A general inclination of legislatures to subsidize agriculture should be mentioned as an obvious reason why local campaigns can score such successes in this field, as should the equally general faith within California in the efficacy of water supply projects to promote general economic (especially urban) growth.

Chapters 16 and 17 presented evidence on the past and present rationality of the allocation of water at various economic frontiers. With regard to the volume of interseasonal transfers, we found broadly contrasting patterns of performance between the local organizations and the state and federal agencies. By and large, local agencies have accomplished no more than an optimal volume of interseasonal transfers and have chosen reasonable release patterns in those cases where storage is operated for both irrigation and power generation—and these cases are in the majority. However, facilities operated either exclusively for irrigation or exclusively for power do not employ ideal release patterns, and the power group probably makes a suboptimal volume of interseasonal transfers. Federal and state agencies have carried out excessive interseasonal transfers but, given the volume of transfers, have chosen largely appropriate release patterns. These conclusions about interseasonal transfers also largely cover our findings about allocations among uses, except they do not note the substantial damage done to in-stream anadromous fisheries by the construction of dams. In general, all of the public agencies engaged in reservoir construction tend to choose allocations biased against "public good" uses not represented by definite customer or interest groups.

These biases once more largely confirm the hypotheses previously developed in our study. The limitation of the power to acquire water rights to certain uses of water has tended to prejudice water allocations against the excluded uses. The fact that these uses assume the traits of "public goods" (for this and other reasons) seals their fate. The effectiveness of state and federal agencies appointed to look after these interests naturally varies, and they tend to lack the political support needed for the pursuit of decisive policies. The federal agencies by statute and tradition are not neutral in their attitudes toward the various productive uses of water: The Bureau leans toward irrigation and, perhaps, power generation; the Corps, toward flood control. The state regulatory bodies—the California Water Commission and State Water Rights Board—have shown a preference for compromise solutions which permit proposed projects to be built in some form, with the benefit-cost aspects of the compromise and its relative marginal productivity for various types of water uses receiving no explicit attention. Thus, the misallocation of water among uses and among seasons of the year results basically from the asymmetries of water law and the parochial interests of local organizations of water users. It is compounded by the statutory and administrative preferences of the large-scale wholesalers, and state and federal regulatory agencies designated to protect the "public interest" do not offset these biases effectively.

Other aspects of the rationality of development appraised in Chapters 16 and 17 included allocations of water among and within local basins. Our benefit-cost analysis showed actual interbasin transfers to involve excessive amounts of water and also some misdirection of imports within the receiving basins. Significant and long-lasting misallocations of agricultural water supplies drawn from individual rivers were detected in the San Joaquin Valley. These misallocations, in some instances, could be associated with the existence of large numbers of agencies competing for a particular source of supply, and the resulting complexity of the process of defining or of transferring rights. The durability of these intrabasin misallocations is related to the durability of fixed assets (particular canal systems), and a normative assessment of their significance runs into the problem raised in Chapters 17 and 18 concerning whether we evaluate actual arrangements against an ideal system rebuilt from scratch, or against the best attainable on the basis of future costs, ignoring those already sunk into durable fixed assets.[6] The durability of intrabasin misallocations also reflects, in some cases at least, the power of distortions at certain points in time to spoil the chances of making subsequent optimal allocative and investment decisions. Water rights settlements and agreements (as in the Kings, Kaweah, and Kern basins) and canal systems (as in the Feather-Yuba-Bear area) have demonstrated this power to initiate inefficient sequences of development. Construction of dams and reservoirs seems less culpable in this regard, since numerous, obsolete facilities have been enlarged or inundated by new works without any serious trouble among the parties in reaching agreement.

A final category refers to allocation among the member-customers of particular districts or agencies. Most of our evidence relating to this type of allocation takes the form of behavioral inferences drawn from Chapter 10. The surprising thing about agricultural retailers, in a sense, is the extent to which they employ relatively efficient pricing systems for insuring correct allocations among their customers: not that they allocate perfectly, but that they allocate well at all. Perhaps the only systematic lack is the absence of pump taxes in managing the conjunctive use of ground water and surface supplies. The presence of largely correct approaches to retail pricing and allocation in the agricultural sector should not, however, obscure our conclusion that many districts either fail to use the proper pricing techniques or use them incorrectly. Incorrect usage in some instances stems from a concern with "fairness" operating through the users' cooperative organizational form; by and large, however, the organizational pressures arising within these agencies probably have a favorable effect on pricing and allocative efficiency. Misallocations within the agency resulting from the pricing system are more apparent in the case of urban systems, where the same inefficient types of conventional pricing systems are employed by the California cities as by those elsewhere. To a minor extent, these represent the political structure and objectives of general city governments; to a major extent, they are merely conventional.

Chapter 18 reviewed the performance of the water industry in attaining optimal technical efficiency in the construction of dams and canals. Some portion of the inefficiencies of major canal layouts can be attributed to the familiar culprits of water rights uncertainty and agency fragmentation, since they turn up predominantly in those basins where such defects are, or have been, present. Power companies and local water agencies predominate among the builders of reservoirs in those ranges of capacity where inefficiencies of small scale may be suspected. The scales of many no doubt can be justified by the characteristics of the site or the magnitude of discounted marginal benefits at the time of construction. Nonetheless the adverse influence of two factors mentioned above—capital rationing and the

[6] Conclusions similar to ours about the effects of fragmented investment decisions and the *ex post* fruitlessness of rebuilding canal systems to remove inefficiencies are reached by George S. Tolley and V. S. Hastings. "Optimal Water Allocation: The North Platte River," *Quarterly Journal of Economics*, LXXIV (May 1960), 279–95. (Most footnote references in this chapter are cited in brief form when they are also included in the Bibliography.)

insularity of agencies in neglecting potential project outputs or service areas outside of their prime interest—seems to be confirmed.

Patterns of Conduct and Effects of Structural Changes

One of the major findings desired from a study of the behavior of the water industry is evidence about how it might respond to various changes in its structural environment. We argued in Chapters 1 and 2 that the manifest absence of a single market for water in Northern California can be turned to a methodological advantage so far as differences from area to area within the region permit cross-sectional comparisons and evaluations. Here we draw together the inferences reached by this and other methods of studying the industry's conduct about the viability and efficiency of changes in its structure.

Changing the structure of an industry is, of course, accomplished by public policy measures, and the effect on conduct and performance of measures likely to improve performance will be discussed in Chapter 20. These turn out to be principally alterations in water law and the framework of regulation. In this section, however, we offer speculations on the effect of variations in nonlegal features of market structure. These do not relate directly to public policy changes in most cases, but they assist in displaying our conclusions on the determinants of some aspects of market conduct in the industry, and shed light on policy proposals that are sometimes put forward.

The logic of the public enterprise organization of the water industry provides a useful starting point. Why has private enterprise shriveled so much? Could it be revived, and, if so, would it improve upon the rather unsatisfactory record chronicled above? Chapter 9 and other portions of Part Two indicated the historical reasons for the retreat of private firms from retail water distribution, and various data from Part One supplemented these conclusions. Some factors deterring a private enterprise organization are economic. The extremely high capital intensity of most facilities in the industry, coupled with scale economies (relative to the absorptive capacity of local market areas), guarantee that serious problems of uncertainty would face private arm's-length sellers. Continuous alternative sources of supply or customers can be made available in the water market only at the cost of significant technical inefficiencies. With only a few parties present in the market, the range of possible bargaining outcomes grows very wide, and private water sellers necessarily face substantial market risks about the deviation of an actual from an expected rate of return. These economic barriers, which historically prevented viable private markets from persisting, are supplemented by other deterrents stemming from water law and political attitudes in California. Various sources of uncertainty in water rights have augmented the market uncertainty just mentioned.[7] Hostile attitudes and interests include the municipal objectives unrelated to water that can be served by the actions of a municipal water department and the antipathy

[7] For analysis of types of uncertainty relating to water rights, see S. V. Ciriacy-Wantrup, "Concepts Used as Economic Criteria for a System of Water Rights," *Land Economics,* XXXII (November 1956), 295–312.

of irrigators to the earning of a positive rate of return in supplying water. Historically, the operation of the state's public utilities regulation machinery also proved inimical to private water categories.

In short, our historically based argument does not hold that private organization of the industry would necessarily be inefficient, although many cards are stacked against it, but rather that it could hardly prove viable. This is an assessment based on economic and political dynamics, not comparative statics. The publicly organized users' cooperative (and also the mutual company) performs what is thereby marked as a necessary function in eliminating one layer of market uncertainty to the enterprise unit and transferring the corresponding economic uncertainty to the cooperative's member-customers, where it seems to rest somewhat more easily. Making water rights appurtenant to land and dependent on beneficial use serve to shift uncertainty, removing from water users a market uncertainty in the acquisition of water but leaving them with whatever degree of natural or physical uncertainty may exist. It does so at the cost of some misallocation—that is, leaving would-be users without rights perfectly certain that they will get no surface water.

This analysis of the reasons for the prevalence of public enterprise in the water industry and the placement or absorption of uncertainty leads into several other types of conclusions which can be drawn from the conduct of the industry discussed in Part Two. Very important structural features of the conventional industry, moderately significant in the water industry, are the prevailing degrees of vertical and horizontal integration. We use the latter term here in place of the more conventional notions of buyer or seller concentration for reasons which will become apparent below. We shall recall, first, the hypotheses about various patterns of vertical and horizontal integration developed in Chapter 4, then try to weigh the desirability of various types of changes in the prevailing structural patterns.

Noting the variety of legal forms which retailing water organizations can take in California, we suggested that behavior patterns might vary with the types of districts found in a particular basin or latent market, other things held constant. The evidence of Chapters 9 and 12 undermined this hypothesis by showing the absence of legal entry barriers to the formation of new types of districts. Not only do the important economic powers of the major types of districts overlap substantially in the first place, but also the appearance of any need for changing the form of a district or creating a new one leads to prompt action.[8] The concentration of districts by types is more a determined factor than a determining factor.[9]

We suggested in Chapter 4 that decreasing the concentration of retail agencies in a particular basin tends to affect performance unfavorably. Because the law of water agencies tends to force them to operate as closed-membership cooperatives, increasing the actual number of agencies raises the alternatives effectively available to would-be final users of water very little, if at all. But it may affect technical efficiency adversely, and certainly complicates the process of defining and

[8] Indeed, the legal forms of districts themselves evolve in response to other factors. See Albert T. Henley, "The Evolution of Forms of Water Users Organizations in California," *California Law Review,* XLV (December 1957), 665–75.

[9] In agricultural water supply, mutual water companies comprise an exception to this proposition; the effects of their presence in the Kings and Kaweah areas were discussed in Chapters 10 and 12.

administering water rights. Each of these predictions was strongly confirmed in Parts Two, Three, or both.

Regarding vertical integration, we hypothesized that the existence of independent wholesaling organizations could make considerable difference for the behavior and performance of the industry. The differing legal and financial powers of the state and federal wholesalers documented in Chapters 3 and 11 increase the potential flexibility of allocations. Vertical disintegration comports well with the sharp differences in efficient operating scales found in Chapter 6 between retail water distribution, on the one hand, and reservoir storage, electric power generation, and bulk water transport, on the other. Partly because of this scale advantage and often partly on account of their status as state or federal government agencies, wholesalers can potentially effect various swaps and rationalizations in allocations of water and water development facilities among retailers which the latter could not arrive at themselves. Finally, decreases in the concentration of independent wholesalers (consistent with scale efficiency) seemed likely to improve performance for the conventional reason of offering to buyers (in this case, retailing agencies) a greater number of actual or potential alternatives.

Our behavioral findings on vertical integration and wholesaler concentration were somewhat mixed. The potential gains from wholesaler rivalry, particularly rivalry in the development of competing plans for the construction of reservoirs and transport facilities, seem plain enough. However, the special motives affecting the federal, state, and local wholesalers actually operating in Northern California make it clear that, although more wholesalers cause more alternatives to be considered, the right one is not necessarily picked. The cases discussed in Chapter 13, although limited in number, seem to point strongly to this conclusion.

As to the gains from vertical disintegration per se, Part Two suggests that those of scale efficiency and legal flexibility are real enough. Northern California's wholesalers have had little luck in rationalizing local misallocations (and in some situations have shown no inclination to do so), but the evidence seems to suggest that they could assist with this objective. Furthermore, present arm's-length wholesaling carried out by large public organizations seems to lead to viable (if not optimal) bargaining in the market, something that was found lacking among the private enterprises which predominated in the industry's early years. This change has come about through the removal of some of the uncertainty associated with water rights by the development of state administrative procedures (especially the state filings and the process of assigning them), and by the universal use of long-term contracts by the large wholesalers. These run twenty to forty years in most cases, and some wholesalers effectively require vertical integration with their customers. Wholesalers with limited powers to tax and borrow tend to secure long-term contracts in advance of the construction of physical facilities, thus protecting the solvency of their operation against most contingencies. Wholesalers with better potential access to finance, such as the state and federal agencies, have been able occasionally to pursue speculative construction in anticipation of contracts to come. The retail customers of the wholesalers share this preference for long-term arrangements, and so all pressures tend to bring them about. Thus the development of wholesaling in the industry, with its potential for attaining scale economies and reducing interregional differences in the marginal productivity of water, is advanced significantly by long-term arrangements. Some additional economic and physical uncertainty in most cases is passed on to the final users of water, but considerable pooling of risks is generally achieved at the same time. This putative gain in performance must be placed against the misallocations that result directly from the rigidity of the long-term arrangements, essential as these may be in some cases to induce large investments in very durable facilities.

To conclude this discussion of vertical and horizontal integration, the gains from vertical disintegration seem, on balance, quite compelling. Our sharp criticisms of the decision rules and policies actually employed by major state and federal wholesalers should not obscure the major advantages which independent wholesalers can potentially provide. Furthermore, the discussion of Chapters 12 and 13 suggests that, as the demand for water grows relative to the physically fixed rate of long-run natural supply and latent markets are increasingly linked throughout the region, the potential advantages of disintegrated wholesaling will grow more than proportionally because of its potential role in basin-wide rationalization and inter-basin transfers. The existence of competing wholesalers would clearly be desirable if the problems concerning their policies and decision rules could be straightened out. Finally, certain local wholesalers, such as county-wide flood control and water conservation districts, provide the advantages of horizontal integration as well as vertical disintegration so far as they can force the rationalization of external effects, manage conjunctive ground-water use, and handle other allocative problems lying outside the scope of action of individual retailing organizations.

The desirability and feasibility of horizontal integration at the retailing level (or in vertically integrated sectors) of the water industry cannot be so neatly summarized. Part Two suggests at least three senses in which horizontal integration may be defined and measured in the industry: (1) the number of organizations actually or potentially supplying water to a given group of on-the-land users; (2) the number of organizations actually or potentially drawing water from a particular source; (3) the number of different types of water use served or administered by a particular organization. Our conclusions differ sharply about the apparent desirability of horizontal integration (that is, high concentration) in these various senses.[10] Since integration is often put forward as a panacea for cases of governmental fragmentation (in order to internalize external effects and bring them under the benevolent hand of administrative discretion), we must distinguish carefully. Retaining the three concepts of integration listed above, our evidence provides a weak favorable case for integration in the first sense—service to a given territory by a single agency. Reducing the number of agencies providing a given volume of water to a given territory makes the appurtenance of water to land, in a sense, less specific. It enlarges the scope for long-run or short-run transfers of water use that do not become tangled in the complications of water law. It also increases the area in which externalities directly relating to consumptive use can be taken into account by administrative processes, such as the control of drainage and the conjunctive

[10] Compare Stephen C. Smith, "The Role of the Public District in the Integrated Management of Ground and Surface Water," *Economics and Public Policy in Water Resource Development*, eds. Stephen C. Smith and Emery N. Castle (1964), chap. 19.

management of surface supplies and ground-water basins. These tasks can all be performed relatively well by administrative decisions.

In Chapter 12, we argued that horizontal disintegration in the second sense—the number of agencies competing for a given source of water—has been clearly undesirable in the setting of certain patterns of water rights determination in California. The atrocity stories concerning the Kings and other rivers in the 1920's and earlier are now somewhat dated, and the case for integration disappears once all existing rights are fully defined and an orderly procedure is established for creating new ones. Not too much comfort should be taken from this comfortable sounding conclusion, however. Although the procedures for creating new rights are indeed orderly, existing rights are anything but well-defined. The difficulties of the Bureau of Reclamation over the Sacramento River in the last decade provide a convincing illustration. Even more important, the successive joining of latent markets for water to cover most, if not all, of the Central Valley steadily creates new situations of rivalry in which rights turn out not to be fully defined against one another. In Part Two, we identified the crucial role of the Sacramento-San Joaquin Delta as the common focus of this incipient general rivalry. Some types of rights, such as those of the counties of origin, can exert imprecisely defined claims against existing users, and the present unsettled status of the federal government's water rights may comprise a similar uncertainty. This is not to argue that horizontal integration of all water rivals in the Central Valley is needed, but only that the problems associated with horizontal disintegration in this sense will continue to appear.

Our third and final concept of horizontal integration—over different types of uses or utilities relating to water—is conventionally viewed with favor in policy discussions. Unfortunately, the evidence developed in Part Two (especially Chapter 14) provides little support for this form of integration except in the obvious case of the joint production of electric power and interseasonal water transfers for consumptive use. No population of water supply organizations—whether organs of federal, state, or local government—has shown itself able to behave neutrally in allocating water at the margin to the different types of benefits or utilities which it serves. Interest group relations, statutory or otherwise, and bureaucratic pressures come into operation; we noted above the paradox of public goods failing to claim the public interest. Without considering alternatives here (this is done in Chapter 20), the chances of effective performance through functional horizontal integration look rather poor.

Part Two thus provides some basis for forecasting the changes in the behavior and performance that would come about following changes in the economic dimensions of the industry's environment. It also supplies a basis for weighing, as a prelude to Chapter 20, the relative significance of features of water law and other structural elements discouraging the creation of water markets. In Chapter 3, we identified numerous features of the law of water rights and water agencies which tend to restrict transfers of water or rights between users or organizations. These constitute, however, only one among many explanations uncovered in our study for the failure of continuous markets to emerge. Since the restrictive features of water law have been stressed and heavily blamed for poor performance by "Chicago school" writers,[11] we should ask what our research indicates about their importance as against other sources of restrictions on transactions. One other is the prominence of external effects in the use of water, such that any transfer from one primary user to another involves relatively large incidental gains and losses for third parties. A third restriction lies in the technological traits of water enterprises: their relatively high fixed costs and typically low short-run marginal costs permit great differences in marginal productivities before the discounted present value of a new project (at optimum scale) exceeds the discounted present value of an existing one, ignoring its sunk capital costs. A fourth explanation lies in the attitudes governing decision-making in the California water industry, only partly embodied in law.

While no quantitative statement can be made, these explanations seem very important as against the influence of water law per se. The magnitude of fixed costs was established in Chapter 6 and its effects discussed in Chapter 17. Various cases mentioned in Chapters 12 and 13 showed the organizational complexities created for water transactions by external effects. And Chapters 9, 10, and 12 documented the attitudes of water agencies (and their relation to the legal structures of public water districts) which serve to discourage transactions in water and rights, switches of customers, expansions and contractions of territory and functions, and other activities which would increase the allocative flexibility of the water industry. This evidence gives some indication of the relative gains one can expect from various types of policy recommendation aimed at improving allocative flexibility.

[11] For example, J. W. Milliman, "Water Law and Private Decision-Making: A Critique," *Journal of Law and Economics,* II (October 1959), 41–63.

20 

CHANGES IN THE LEGAL FRAMEWORK OF THE INDUSTRY: SUGGESTED REVISIONS IN PUBLIC POLICY

The first of two main sorts of structural changes in the Northern California water industry which might affect its performance—those which do not involve changing the legal framework of the industry—were discussed in the last section of the preceding chapter. We have reserved for treatment in this final chapter the second major aspect of possible structural changes and their effects, generally embracing changes in the legal framework.

Of these latter changes, two things are notable. First, they may be accomplished or imposed by the electorate and its representatives directly and deliberately through the process of amending or repealing old laws and writing new ones; they are not simply structural changes which may or may not evolve under existing law with or without some encouragement from public authorities. Second, these changes would thus generically embody changes in public policy toward the industry, and in discussing them we are in essence considering the probable effects of changes in public policy toward the California water industry on its conduct and performance.

Here we shall not, in treating changes in public policy, indulge in an academic consideration of all reasonably conceivable changes in the legal framework of the industry and of their putative effects. Instead, we confine our attention only to a few types of change in public policy toward the industry which are more or less suggested by the foregoing study and which we will thus describe and offer for consideration. This shift of attitude from analysis per se to the suggestion of possible revisions in law based on analysis seems entirely consistent with the role of political economists, and even demanded from them on the ground that any normatively oriented analysis of actual economic affairs is, or should be, capable of generating constructive advice concerning public policy.

Existing public policies toward the California water industry, as Chapter 3 showed, are embodied partly in the law of water rights, partly in law establishing the powers and responsibilities of water agencies, and partly in regulatory law as administered by a number of state and federal departments, boards, and commissions. Our analysis of the conduct and performance of water agencies in Parts Two and Three clearly suggested that the existing complex of public policies has not been efficacious in securing from the industry conduct and performance which is reasonably close to the optimum from the standpoint of over-all economic efficiency, or which comes tolerably close to "best serving the public interest." Major deficiencies in performance have been reviewed at length in Chapters 15 through

18, and recapitulated in the second section of Chapter 19. What alterations in existing public policy might bring forth in the California water industry substantially superior conduct and performance?

Because this is a large question which might be answered in a variety of ways and could entail many detailed suggestions, it is not practicable in a study of this nature to assess every alternative possibility or to describe a unique and definitive solution. Instead we will roughly and briefly outline a few crucial types of change in public policy which our analysis has suggested. Our suggestions thus will not be comprehensive in that they will not touch on all evident avenues for policy reform, nor detailed in that they will stop short of describing specific possible changes in statutes or administrative arrangements. Four major areas for policy reform are considered: (1) regulation governing the authorization of water projects; (2) law governing the policies of federal water agencies and of agencies which purchase water from the California state agency; (3) law affecting the marketability of water and water rights; and (4) law dealing with the external effects of various water uses. Our suggestions are described and analyzed in four corresponding sections of this chapter.

Regulation Governing the Authorization of Water Projects

The regulations under which water projects are authorized in California presently operate through the attachment of conditions for the release of water rights by California authorities and through the federal licensing of nonfederal projects. The major indictment of the present regulatory system must include the facts that:

1) It imposes only nominal and imprecise economic conditions for the approval of water projects generally.

2) No binding economic conditions for project approval are effectively imposed on the U.S. Bureau of Reclamation or Army Corps of Engineers, which are not subject to the licensing authority of the Federal Power Commission and are either *de facto* or *de jure*[1] immune from meaningful regulation by California authorities.

3) Both California and federal regulatory agencies, operating subject to existing statutory instructions, almost necessarily emphasize the function of compromising or arbitrating conflicts among competing claimants for water (and their projects), or between project proponents and injured third parties, in a context in which the desirable aim of securing the economically most desirable or efficient project is not effectively pursued.

4) California regulatory authorities are required, or induced by statute or by institutional circumstances, to apply some conditions or decision rules which are not economically sensible.

[1] The Bureau of Reclamation apparently enjoys *de facto* immunity from even the rather nominal regulation of California authorities, in the light of Supreme Court decisions discussed in Chapter 3 and also because of the general reluctance of California authorities in any way to discourage federal building of projects in and for California; the Corps of Engineers is by law immune from state regulation.

None of these facts except the last provides in itself a prima facie ground for indicting existing regulation of project authorization, since adequate self-regulation by federal, state, and local water agencies could conceivably secure an economically optimal water development program under the lightest and most nominal sort of regulation by independent commissions, or under no such regulation at all. Actually, the first three facts just enumerated amount to serious deficiencies in the independent regulation of project authorizations in major part because the self-regulated conduct of the federal agencies and of the California Department of Water Resources (subject to legislative and executive control and approval) has led, and promises in the future to lead further, to gross overdevelopment of water resources and to numerous connected misallocations in the use of water. In less part, regulatory deficiencies stem from the fact that similarly self-regulated conduct of local water agencies has tended to generate performance that diverges in several ways from economic optima. A system of regulation governing water project authorizations which is loose and permissive, which does not invoke adequate economic criteria in determining whether or not water projects should be authorized, and which effectively exempts the federal water agencies from regulation thus turns out to be seriously deficient.

Rebuttal of the argument for no radical policy change

Under the existing law, the unsatisfactory conduct of the federal and state water agencies results in large part from the imprudent exercise of broad discretionary powers within these agencies and from misguided or careless legislative actions in promoting, authorizing, and granting appropriations for projects of questionable economic merit.[2] In support of the view that these deficiencies are likely to be remedied only by imposing a strong independent control of federal and state project authorizations, we must contest the view that whatever projects these agencies undertake are not open to question. This point of view which we are contesting is based on the observation that the agencies in question are all instruments of central governments operating under the general directions of popularly elected chief executives, and dependent both for authorizations and appropriations on popularly elected legislative bodies (or even on popular referenda). To us, these considerations appear insufficient either to guarantee that the public will be supplied with economically optimal water development programs, or to exempt these programs from scrutiny of their economic merits.

Various economists over the years have pressed with some success for reforms of the project evaluation criteria employed by the federal agencies (although the Department of Water Resources has been substantially immune to such pressures). Desirable as this trend may be, results of our analyses suggest that it fails to go to

[2] Relative to projects undertaken by the California Department of Water Resources, the general electorate of the state has shared the responsibility for misguided action by approving through referendum the financing of projects proposed by the Department and the state legislature.

the heart of the problem. The real problem is that the combined effect of the bureaucratic motives of the federal and state agencies and of the pressures of certain interest groups is unopposed by any systematic counterpressure for the application of dispassionate economic analysis.[3] This combination of forces underlies the sorry record of project planning and evaluation. As was suggested in Chapter 11, agencies bend the interpretation of substantive rules concerning project justifications so as to produce project evaluations based on unjustifiably optimistic estimates of project benefits, revenues, and costs. They internalize project evaluation to a degree that reports requesting authorizations of and appropriations for specific project "packages," laid before legislative bodies, provide neither the legislators nor the impartial observer with enough information to evaluate the proposed projects as against alternatives.

Our political system also renders the legislative and executive levels of higher government undependable for seeking to insure the preservation of the general public interest (as distinct from the interests of limited water-using groups) in the field of water resource projects. Water is a political football, as is every major water project. Executive and legislative support of federal projects demonstrably tends to turn a good deal on the desires of congressmen to secure federal expenditures within their districts, on the desires of party members at executive and legislative levels to curry favor in forthcoming elections, and on the mechanism of the legislative log-rolling process.[4] In this context, a bureaucratic project evaluation is not a document to be objectively scrutinized but a necessary bit of armor in a political struggle. At the state level, the situation in California differs only in degree. Coalitions of pressure groups, bureaucracies, legislators, and executives form to secure approval of projects within a process in which project evaluations are flexible instruments of questionable validity.

Even when elements of the legislature or executive would resist the practice of authorizing projects because of these pressures by interest groups, they are poorly equipped to do so. Politicians themselves generally do not possess the specialized training required to make adequate critical analyses of project proposals and justifications submitted by the water agencies, nor have they often chosen to avail themselves of skilled specialists with this capacity—and, when they have done so, often have not chosen to accept and defend the specialists' judgment. At the federal level, the U.S. Bureau of the Budget could potentially develop into this role, though experience has shown that it is probably too sensitive politically; no existing counterpart seems available in the California state government.

In short, the flaws in project planning, evaluation, and selection at the federal and state levels do not rest narrowly upon particular institutional features of agency

[3] Political scientists have correctly identified this combination of forces but generally have not pressed on to deduce the sort of institutional arrangements which might reduce the resulting amount of resource misallocation. See Charles McKinley, *Uncle Sam in the Pacific Northwest* (1952), chap. 18. (This and other footnote references are cited in brief form when they are also included in the Bibliography.)

[4] The predominance of congressmen from the West on the U.S. House and Senate committees which authorize water projects has often been identified as an important channel for building into the legislative process the expression of a client-centered interest rather than an objective appraisal of proposed projects.

bias, legislative organization, and the like. Rather, they reflect a whole system of relations among interest groups inside and outside of the public sector. Because the difficulties are all of a piece, it does not appear that a sufficient means of securing appreciably better future performance from the federal and state water agencies will be found in exhorting the agencies in question to improve their processes of project evaluation or their ways of thinking. Nor will it lie in exhorting legislatures to pass statutes giving more rigorous and adequate substantive instructions to the water agencies regarding the evaluation of the same projects that legislators want to have approved on grounds having little to do with such instructions or rules. And, finally, better performance cannot be attained by exhorting the executive branch to be more prudent, to seek and pay heed to dispassionate and expert economic counsel, or otherwise to change its ways. Exhortations by economists—particularly those directed to the agencies urging that they develop improved methods of project analysis and evaluation—have apparently wrought some improvements in agency conduct, and may accomplish more, but the net improvements are minor. This being so, it becomes clear that, in addition to developing better sets of substantive rules which might be adopted by the federal and state agencies, it is the function of the political economist to view the water policy problems as a governmental as well as an economic problem, and to consider what legal and governmental changes would actually result in the adoption and pursuit of better economic policies. If we undertake this responsibility, we apparently must recognize that appreciably better performance in the case of federal and state water agencies is likely to be secured only through radical legal reform. Such reform would be directed in general at curtailing the discretionary powers of executives, executive departments, legislatures, and the bureaucratic agencies with regard to making final decisions on water development projects, and at providing for an independent and objective appraisal of projects that the agencies propose to undertake.

The preceding argument is most convincing as applied to regulation of the authorization of federal and state water projects. Nonetheless, it is also applicable to regulation as applied to local water agencies, especially on the ground that if an independent regulatory agency does not conduct an adequate economic analysis and appraisal of most local agency projects, no one ever will.

A suggestion for fundamental change in policies for project authorization

In a broad sense, the most basic deficiency in the present system of regulating authorizations is found in the failure to establish, in federal statutes and California law, adequate substantive rules and adequate procedures of review, public hearing, and adjudication which would (1) apply alike to water projects proposed by federal, state, and local agencies, and (2) greatly limit the present discretionary powers of these agencies (and of the executives of higher government that control them). Although the political forces responsible for the unsatisfactory performance of these agencies extend well beyond the agencies themselves, the way that seems best to us of cutting into the circle of relations described above would be to establish a strong and completely independent check or evaluation upon their proposals. The general public seems to need the protection of a requirement that every project proposed by these agencies could be authorized only after detached and extensive public scrutiny, and after demonstration before a commission of arbiters entirely independent of the agencies and of the executive and legislative branches of federal, state, and local governments that the project fulfilled an adequate body of substantive statutory requirements which defined and protected the public interest.

The general aims of legal reform just outlined might be implemented in the following fashion. First, two independent commissions with extended powers over the authorization of water projects would be established, one at the state and one at the federal level. The suggested continuation of the clumsiness inherent in overlapping federal and state jurisdictions over the same projects is perhaps regrettable, but it seems unavoidable as a practical matter because: (a) given the present Supreme Court interpretation of federal and state water laws, the federal water agencies could conceivably be brought under the full authority only of a federal commission; (b) there is no likelihood that Congress would surrender (or the Court permit it to) the overriding federal control over all projects affecting navigable waters and waters on reserved public lands; and (c) having any state such as California vacate the field of state and local project authorization is so unlikely and also questionable a prospect that it may be dismissed. Under the system about to be described, the criteria of project evaluation employed by the federal and the state commission respectively would ideally be so similar that the second screening by the federal commission of a project already approved by the state commission typically would be only ministerial.

Second, the federal water agencies would by federal legislation be made subject to the supervision of the federal commission. Furthermore, and very important, the U.S. Congress by its own legislation would divorce itself from the authorization of (as distinct from appropriation for) federal water projects. It would subordinate this power to the federal commission and consider for appropriations only projects which were duly authorized, after review and appraisal, by that commission. Authorization of federal water projects would thus be made subject to the approval of an independent federal commission.

Third, and comparably, the California legislature would divorce itself from the authorization of state water projects by subordinating this power to the independent California commission and by considering for appropriations only state projects (a) duly authorized by that commission and (b) also duly licensed by the federal commission. (The federal commission, it is implied, would authorize federal projects and license state and local projects.) Added substantive legislation would not be needed to make the California Department of Water Resources *de jure* subject to the regulation of any California water commission.

Fourth, approximately the same provisions of substantive and procedural law would establish, define the powers of, and instruct both the federal and the California state commission. As to composition and tenure of membership, each commission would be made "nonpolitical" by providing for an appointed membership of a few (perhaps five) persons with long terms of office expiring serially, and by providing that the membership included a qualified member of the bar, a qualified professional engineer, and at least one member not identified with commercial water-using interests. Each commission would be provided with an adequate technical staff including qualified engineers, economists, and lawyers, and would in no way be dependent for staff assistance on any federal or state water agency. The sole function of each commission would be to receive, evaluate, and pass judgment on applications for the authorization or licensing of water projects under its jurisdiction. As to procedure, each commission would be instructed to investigate and, after due notice, to hold hearings as appropriate on every application for project authorization or licensing presented to it, and finally to approve or deny each application (either as originally submitted or as amended before final commission action). One essential part of the procedure would be the requirement that every applicant present a detailed formal justification for its project, including all data pertinent to determining whether or not granting of its application would be in the public interest, this information including a full economic analysis as well as a full engineering analysis of the project. Each commission would be instructed to invite the participation of every party at interest in all hearings on applications, and to require both the consultation and the participation of every interested public agency (including public health, water pollution, fish and wildlife, and recreational agencies), in line with the present practice of the Federal Power Commission. Associated procedural requirements are obvious enough not to require discussion. The jurisdiction of the federal commission would cover authorization of all federal water projects and licensing of all state and local water projects affecting navigable waters or reserved public lands. That of the state commission would cover authorization (and state licensing) of all local and state water projects, including those of the California Department of Water Resources.

The more novel part of possible new regulations would be substantive; laws would instruct each commission by specifying the criteria to be observed in determining whether or not proposed projects were in the public interest and should be authorized or licensed. In general, it would be specified that in order to be in the public interest, and thus eligible for authorization or licensing, any project should fulfill the following conditions (with the terms used being fully defined in the legislation):

1) The project's aggregate primary benefits should exceed its aggregate direct costs, both benefits and costs being measured as discounted present values computed with a rate of discount no lower than the lowest going rate on long-term debt the interest on which is taxable.

2) The project's marginal or incremental primary benefits should be no less than its marginal or incremental direct costs for the project as a whole and for each separable segment thereof, when such marginal or incremental amounts are calculated as discounted present values at the same interest rate.

3) The excess of the aggregate primary benefits of the project over its aggregate direct cost should clearly exceed the sum of (a) all net losses in recreational values imposed by the project (as valued by the best available means)—including losses of fisheries, wild game, scenic assets, availability of "wild rivers," and so forth, as

assessed in the context of the recreational needs and desires of the whole population of California or other subject state—and (b) the value of all disbenefits to be suffered by water users other than the applicant or by affected third parties, as a result of the proposed project (such disbenefits including those stemming from pollution, impaired drainage, saline intrusion, and so forth).

4) The project should be defensible as economically superior to any mutually exclusive alternative project or projects which parties contesting authorization or licensing might wish to support with evidence, or which the staff of the commission might propose.

These substantive provisions could be included indentically in legislation establishing both the new federal commission and the new state commission, and would be implemented by intensive analyses of all proposed projects by the commissions, except so far as the federal commission might wish to accept after summary review the prior findings of a state commission. No project would be eligible for final authorization and supporting appropriations by legislative bodies until it had been found by the commissions to meet the several tests just listed.

The basic suggestions just presented concerning criteria to be applied and procedures to be followed by the commissions in reviewing project applications would require some detailed supplementation, including the following: First, the commissions would be instructed to continue protection of vested prior rights against infringement by new appropriations, although there would be advantages in encouraging the sale of such prior rights to applicants where such sale would enhance over-all economic welfare. Second, present rules covering temporal priority of applications would be revised to subordinate the rule of seniority of filings to all of the more important rules suggested above. The rule of seniority would govern only choices between competing projects which are equally desirable and in the public interest. Third, though "out of court" settlements of conflicting claims for water or of protests against applications by agreements involving project modifications or payoffs in water, power, or cash would still be countenanced, the commissions would take an active role in the negotiation of these agreements. And they would have and exercise the power to declare invalid any agreement on the ground that the compromise project or the payoff agreed upon would result in the construction of a project which was not economically desirable or not as desirable as an alternative. Competing and mutually exclusive projects would be subject to revision to satisfy contesting applicants, but the commissions would reserve and exercise the right to choose one project over another and to reject economically less desirable compromise projects.[5]

Fifth, some revisions in existing law would be desirable to implement the creation of the new federal and state commissions. We will consider them only briefly. On the federal level, the Federal Power Commission, already overburdened with

[5] Since it is possible that some projects may be undertaken to exploit previously established water rights, the powers of the commissions would properly be extended to cover review of every new water project incorporating on-stream facilities, even if the project were intended to exploit existing water rights. Agencies or other parties proposing to undertake such projects would be required to file applications for construction permits with the commissions, and would have to fulfill the same procedural and substantive requirements that would apply to applicants for new water rights in order to secure commission approval of their projects.

many other tasks, would be fully relieved of its powers and responsibilities with respect to the licensing of water projects, and the powers and duties described above would be assigned to a newly created body, possibly designated a Federal Water Development Commission. On the state level, the present California Water Commission and the California State Water Rights Board would be eliminated or combined into a single new body which might be called a California Water Development Commission, having the membership, powers, and duties outlined above. Also it would have the right to assign state filings of applications to appropriate water to approved projects, to issue permits and licenses, and to perform other functions now carried out by the State Water Rights Board. Such a California Water Development Commission would be in every way, legally and factually, independent of the California Department of Water Resources and of the State Resources Agency and its other departments.

Remaining aspects of the suggested reform of regulation of the water project authorization would involve striking of some "nuisance" provisions in existing law. A prime candidate for elimination would be the California Water Code provision which specifies an absolute preference ordering of different uses of water—namely urban, agricultural and other.[6] All types of use, including in-stream public use, would be equally privileged competitors for water. A second provision which is a candidate for striking comprises all references in California law to the California Water Plan as a model with which proposed water projects should be consistent. Although a close textual reading reveals that the law does not instruct existing regulatory agencies to regard this plan as a definitive model for general and coordinated development, it apparently is often so considered. The Plan would not appear in any guise among the substantive statutory criteria which would guide a new California Water Development Commission. It seems sufficient that the engineering plans which the California Water Plan contains are available to all interested agencies for reference purposes, and it is not evident that a complex of proposals which have never been analyzed with respect to economic feasibility or desirability qualifies as a legitimate source of criteria for evaluating various individual water projects.

A final matter concerns county-of-origin and watershed-of-origin protections embodied in existing California law regulating the authorization of water projects. It is our tentative, but not entirely firm judgment, that the main justification for these protections at the present time is that they comprise an offset to existing allocative biases which would be eliminated if the reform described above were adopted, as well as a defense against the rigidities restricting the transfer of established water rights from one party to another. On the other hand, they can themselves cause performance deficiencies in the industry. Since their desirability is uncertain and depends upon the acceptance or rejection of other reforms, we shall not attempt to consider them further.

The preceding complex of suggested changes in the regulation of water project authorization and licensing may seem not only radical but in some crucial respects impractical. A widely prevalent view among water lawyers today is that all water

[6] California *Water Code* (1962), § 1254.

law is turning out to be in the main just what federal and state legislatures make it—an observation embracing water rights as well as project authorizations. Recognizing this, we have in our suggestions initially struck at the heart of the problem by advancing the notion that the U.S. Congress and the California State Legislature might effectively delegate their powers of water project authorization to independent and nonpolitical federal and state commissions, properly and fully instructed by statute, to the extent of declining to consider appropriations for water projects until they have been approved by these commissions. This is not the most politically salable idea ever advanced. But we believe that it has substantial merit, and could be worth a substantial sales effort.

Law Governing Policies of Federal and Certain Local Agencies

A closely connected kind of public policy reform might involve some changes in the federal laws which give statutory instructions to federal water agencies, and other changes in state laws limiting the powers of classes of local agencies which are typically the direct or indirect customers of the California Department of Water Resources. The major problems of agency conduct with which we are concerned here generally involve "unholy alliances" between federal and state producer-wholesaler agencies and the customer agencies they serve. Such alliances generate powerful political leverage for undertaking uneconomic projects. Some undermining of the bases of these alliances might seem in order, even if a radically changed system of regulating project authorizations were put into effect.

Two fairly distinct sorts of alliance between a major federal or state agency and a beneficiary group or customer agency are important. The older and more common type is between the major agency and beneficiaries who expect to receive water from a project at subsidized prices which do not cover the costs of supplying it. The typical example involves the Bureau of Reclamation and agricultural water users and their local districts, although in some instances the Corps of Engineers assumes the same role as the Bureau. Considerable legal encouragement is given to this sort of alliance (a) by statutory provisions instructing the Bureau to give agricultural water preferential pricing treatment, (b) by the use of a project's surplus power revenues further to subsidize irrigation water customers of the Bureau, (c) by the ability of the Corps to dispose of irrigation water at cut rates as a by-product of "flood control" projects which are really dual purpose in function, and (d) by the Corps' treatment of flood control benefits as nonreimbursable. Alliances of this sort could be substantially discouraged by revision of federal statutes.

Since subsidizing irrigation to encourage the settlement of the West is an anachronism as well as being in conflict with federal programs to limit farm outputs, all parts of federal reclamation and land laws providing for preferred treatment to agricultural water users by the Bureau might well be repealed forthwith. At the same time, the amended legislation could prohibit the Bureau from price discrimination in favor of agricultural water users in allocating project joint costs, and could encourage for every class of customer service collection of its non-water costs inclusive of interest, plus feasible amounts to defray the costs of non-reimbursable benefits. (Surplus revenues from project power outputs might be earmarked for defraying the costs of nonreimbursable benefits.) This complex of measures would tend in large part to strip uneconomic projects of local political support. Eliminating subsidization of agricultural water users by Corps projects would pose a somewhat more difficult problem. It is suggested tentatively here that the Corps might be instructed in legislation to count as the cost of agricultural water output from its projects the incremental costs of supplying it (over and above the costs of supplying flood control alone), and could then collect either all such incremental costs from agricultural water beneficiaries, or as large a proportion as the market will bear. As regards flood control benefits, the law could provide for repayment to the Corps of part or all of their costs by local flood control districts which could be delineated and created under state legislation for this purpose.

Some students of federal policy suggest the need for a thoroughgoing legislative and administrative reform of reimbursement policies employed for water projects of the Bureau of Reclamation, and perhaps Corps of Engineers, to require that all possible classes of project beneficiaries pay their full shares of project costs. They feel that this would be an efficacious single measure for aborting economically undesirable projects and securing improved project selection from the agencies and from Congress. A number of these students would further feel that such a reimbursement reform would render a radical reform of the project authorization system unnecessary. Although we favor reimbursement reform and suggest it as a supplement to reform of project authorization, we do not think that undertaken alone it would be entirely efficacious—if only because of the demonstrated or potential ingenuity of customer agencies which purchase state or federal water to increase repayments without placing an extra financial burden on final water users and thus depriving them of subsidies.

This leads us to consider a second sort of alliance which has so far appeared full-fledged in California in connection with the Feather River Project. It involves a major supplier (the California Department of Water Resources) and customer districts which are willing to contract to "overpay" for water in order to get it delivered. They overpay, that is, in the sense that they pay the wholesale supplier substantially more for water than they sell it for to local water users—and more than they could sell it for in the quantities they take—and collect the difference in the form of substantial taxes on all real property in their districts. Through the taxing device, they finance excessive investment in water development and excessive interbasin transfers, and promote a misallocation of water among classes and places of use, at the same time lending a patina of financial feasibility to the projects they support. Local districts supplying urban water in Southern California are principally involved, but some large county water agencies are using the same device (of taxing urban and industrial real property) to finance the importation of irrigation water to be resold at a discount.

The place to undermine this sort of alliance, which usurps the taxing power of governments to finance uneconomic water development, is apparently at the buyers' end. A possible restrictive measure in California would be a statute which provided that no water agency or municipality could assess taxes to finance the purchase of water from wholesale or re-wholesale agencies, or to retire or service indebtedness incurred to secure water supplies, except on land alone. Real property other than land would then be exempt from taxation for the purposes mentioned. This would place some restriction on the effective taxing power of the local water agencies in question, and have the advantage of resting more of the tax burden on land speculators who supported projects to import water and who stood to gain most from its importation. A further restriction which at least deserves consideration would require all agencies and municipalities selling water to collect no more in taxes to finance water development or purchase than is required to service and retire bonded indebtedness incurred for this purpose.

Law Affecting the Marketability of Water and Water Rights

Throughout our study, we have noted that a striking attribute of the California water industry is its consistent failure to develop continuous markets for water and water rights. And this failure, we have stressed, is in significant part responsible for the failure of agencies in the industry to correct historical misallocations of water among uses, users, and sites of use or to reallocate water when changing economic conditions made such reallocation desirable. We also have noted—at length in Chapter 3—that various attributes of the California law of water rights and of the law governing the powers of local water agencies are among the principal deterrents to the development of water markets. Although these characteristics of the law are not the only reasons for the failure of water markets to emerge—and perhaps not the most important ones, as suggested in Chapter 19—they seem important enough that possibilities for the alteration of state law to encourage the development of water markets seem worth considering.

We will not repeat here the detailed discussion, presented in Chapter 3, of the various ways in which the laws of water rights and water agencies evidently tend to retard economically beneficial transfers of water among users and user groups. But taking that discussion as a starting point, we will consider a complex of minimal changes in the relevant laws which would facilitate the development of water markets.

As regards the California law of water rights, we suggest for study the following specific and selective changes:

1) The barriers of uncertainty as to the extent of individual ground-water rights in most basins, which clearly deter transfers, might be removed either (a) by instructing the California State Water Rights Board or a successor agency to determine the safe yield of each basin and also the specific rights of each overlaying rights holder and each appropriator, or (b) by establishing in all basins ground-water management units, through or with the assistance of the Water Rights Board or a successor, which could levy pumping taxes based on the cost of replenishment. In either case, every ground-water pumper would be enabled to sell a definite amount of water or right thereto, with clouds on title substantially dissipated.

2) The holders of riparian rights might be permitted by statute (or by state constitutional amendment) to sell water as if they were appropriators, their present

specific disabilities in this regard being stricken. Since the quantities of water to which many riparians have rights from many river flows have been determined through adjudication, this permission would in these instances remove the major barrier to water transfers. Where riparian rights have not yet been adjudicated, the State Water Rights Board or a successor might be instructed to promulgate agreements on the extent of riparian rights; where this proved impossible, the state agency could press for adjudication of such rights.

3) Principal changes in water law affecting appropriative rights to surface water (and also of riparian rights once they were comparably treated) might (a) relieve the appropriator of the requirement of filing for a new license when changing the place of use of his water by means of sale of water or of rights thereto, and (b) provide that the making of year-to-year sales by the appropriator (and similarly treated riparian), even if continued for a period of years to one party, did not create any public service responsibility (to continue service) on the part of the seller. These changes, plus the equalization of the position of the riparian, would remove the major barriers in water law to transfers of surface water and rights thereto.

4) Where water sales impair the rights of parties external to the transaction (such as those diverting return flows), the law could provide for compensation in water or in money upon the showing of loss.

If these alterations in the law of water rights were made, the need for changes in the law of water agencies would be minimal. However, it might be desirable to provide that local public agencies and governments which hold water rights in trust for their constituent-customers could sell these rights or water secured under them to outsiders freely upon approval by two-thirds of the electors who control the agency or government. And it might be provided further that, failing such an endorsement, the agency or government could "split the trust" and sell such water or rights as individual customers were willing to release as their prorated shares of the trust, such customers being compensated accordingly. Perhaps a more important change in the law could permit every variety of local water agency to apply to the State Water Rights Board or successor agency for rights to water to be sold without limit to nonmembers of the applying agency, so that local agencies could have flexible service areas and become entrepreneurs in water development. Such a provision of law would assist in severing the umbilical cord between the water agency and its water rights on the one hand, and its specific constituency on the other.

It is not argued that the legal changes just considered would necessarily bring water markets into being on a broad scale, because there are many other impediments to the development of such markets, but they would remove selectively the major legal barriers, for the perpetuation of which little good can be said. Some commentators have suggested that in addition the State Water Rights Board or successor agency might undertake to create, and the Department of Water Resources should participate in, numerous regional or subregional water-exchange pools. Through these pools, bids for and offers of water could be made by all agencies, firms, and other potential water buyers and sellers, with an emphasis primarily on single-year sales contracts, and with a complex set of rules governing the pricing policies of the state as it participated in these pools (particularly in its role as a water importer). The suggestion would appear to have some merit, but we have not developed it in detail.

Law Dealing with the External Effects of Water Uses

Not only are water industries full of externalities; also governmental efforts to force or induce individual water agencies to take them into account (other than by internalization in large multipurpose developments) have not been notably successful. Both statements are true in California, the second perhaps truer there than elsewhere. Without probing our way into the subject with a full taxonomy of externalities, we will consider here policies dealing with three types of external effects of water: (1) water pollution; (2) impairment of streamflows for public recreational use; and (3) other external effects generated by water users and felt by others.

Water pollution

Serious water pollution problems have been encountered in Northern California mainly in the lower San Joaquin River, in the Sacramento-San Joaquin River estuary, and in the bay system into which these rivers empty, including Suisun, San Pablo, and San Francisco bays. Polluted return flows from irrigation, industrial water, and treated and untreated sewage contribute to the problem, which is becoming acute. The present California system for regulating or abating pollution (as distinct from contamination of urban water supplies, which is well controlled) is either a severe disappointment or a farce, both on paper and in action, as our discussion of the system of regional water pollution control boards in Chapter 3 may have suggested. It is thus a matter of some concern that possible legal reforms affecting this aspect of state water problems should be seriously studied.

We submit for consideration, as an alternative to the present regulatory system, the vesting of broad and direct regulatory powers over pollution in the California State Water Quality Control Board. This could be done through a law which would provide, first, for the establishment (on the basis of an extended initial study) of strict standards for the abatement of all types of pollution; and, second, for the establishment (after legislative study and approval) of a schedule of penalties or taxes which would be payable to the state by various classes of water users for unabated or nonabatable pollution. Such taxes might be set so far as possible to equate the marginal private cost of contributing to pollution to the marginal public and private disbenefits generated by this contribution.[7] Separate tax schedules could be devised to apply to various classes of industrial water users (whose effluent

[7] If it were preferred on distributive grounds, a subsidy contingent upon the abatement of pollution to this same degree could be employed instead of a tax designed to achieve the same result.

discharges would so far as feasible be metered), to municipalities and urban water agencies (with heavy penalties on untreated or incompletely treated sewage effluents), and to irrigators who generate polluted return flows to rivers. Contributing to pollution might thus be made taxable and hence costly in an appropriate amount.

Although the State Water Quality Control Board could be appropriately instructed to implement the regulations proposed and provided with the necessary expert staff and force of investigators, consideration should also be given to changing the present law specifying the composition of its membership.[8] At present, seven of its nine members must be chosen from seven designated fields of interest in water by reason of their occupations; and six of these fields represent groups of firms or public agencies which are major contributors to pollution. This membership requirement might be stricken, and a substitute requirement could require a smaller membership (perhaps seven instead of nine) dominated by "disinterested" but qualified persons, including a lawyer and a professional engineer, with the heads of the California State Department of Public Health and of the California Department of Fish and Game designated as ex officio members of the Board.

The foregoing comprises the major part of our suggestions of changes in public policy toward pollution control in California; one additional part will be considered separately.

Impairment of streamflows for public recreational use

As noted in Chapters 14 and 17 and elsewhere above, public in-stream uses of water for fishing and other recreation generally tend to be inadequately or weakly protected in the approved designs of water projects, as well as by the criteria which are applied in determining whether or not various water projects should be authorized. Our suggestions of changes in the system of regulating the authorization of water projects, as outlined above, could remedy the crucial imbalance in criteria of project evaluation to a considerable extent. Nonetheless, added measures might be required, either to buttress or to supplement these suggested changes, if undue impairment of streamflows for public recreational use is to be reduced and held in check.

An initial suggestion which bears indirectly on the preservation of streamflows for public recreational use, would be for establishment of a new state Division of Recreational Resources, as an agency entirely independent of the Department of Water Resources, the State Resources Agency, or any other superior agency of the state. For this Division, a three-man governing board appointed to staggered nine-year terms by the Governor with the consent of the state Senate might seem desirable. Qualifications for appointment to the governing board would include lack of engagement, direct or indirect, in agricultural enterprises; in agricultural or urban landholding, other than on a nominal scale; in development of urban residential, commercial, or industrial tracts; in the real estate business; in industrial

[8] California *Water Code* (1963), § 13010.

enterprises which are large water users; in the management of water agencies; in electric utility companies; or in the management of banks or other financial institutions appreciably engaged in serving agricultural areas or communities. Such a Division of Recreational Resources would appropriately include the Department of Fish and Game as one of its departments.[9]

One of the primary responsibilities of this Division—in addition to formulating long-run regional plans for balanced preservation and development of recreational resources, including streams and lakes—would be to participate actively as a representative of public recreational interests in all hearings before the suggested federal and state water development commissions. It should assume the role now taken in water rights hearings by the California Department of Fish and Game, and the broader total role of representing all public recreational uses of water.

Under recent California legislation, as described in Chapter 3, the uses of surface waters as fisheries and for other recreation have been recognized as beneficial uses for which water may be appropriated. And it instructs the Department of Fish and Game to take into account the amount of water required for these uses when "determining" the amounts of unappropriated water which are available for other beneficial uses, and with making the enhancement of fish, wildlife, and recreational resources part of the conditions for proper multipurpose water use in state water projects. The legislative mandate seems broad, but it has been timidly applied by the Department of Fish and Game as a participant in hearings before the present California Water Commission and State Water Rights Board. An independent Division of Recreational Resources might replace this basic timidity in asserting powers to reserve and appropriate water for fish, wildlife, and recreation, with a more vigorous assertion of these powers. It might also have added powers, as provided by statute and subject to statutory instructions, to "insist" in some cases that basic project features should be drastically redesigned, relocated, or reduced in scale, and in others that certain rivers should remain substantially undeveloped or wild, within the framework of a statewide plan for prudent preservation of recreational resources. All of these suggestions, of course, would be subject to final decision by a State Water Development Commission and by a corresponding federal commission as necessary.

Consideration might be given also to state legislation which would substantially strengthen the powers of this new Division to reduce pollution as it affects stream and bay fisheries and swimming and boating waters. It might be empowered (1) to secure greater reservations of water diversion on principal and minor rivers in order to reduce and dilute the pollution of these rivers (and the bays into which they empty) sufficiently to maintain specified standards of quality and quantity of water used for recreation generally and serving as fish habitat; and (2) similarly to secure more adequate all-season maintenance of flows below on-stream reservoirs

[9] It would seem particularly desirable for the California Department of Fish and Game to be removed from its present position of subordination to the State Resources Agency and of forced companionship with the Department of Water Resources, where it is fated to occupy a subordinate status and a subordination of its actions to dominant commercial motivations of the Department of Water Resources.

in general (no classes of reservoirs or agencies being exempted).[10] In this connection, it could be empowered to make administrative determinations of required reservations and releases, pursuant to fairly specific statutory instructions and subject to review by a properly instructed State Water Quality Control Board.

Other external effects

Other externalities still to be considered comprise in the main external disbenefits other than pollution and impairment of water for public use, and also external benefits generated by some water users and damaging or aiding other water users or third parties. A typical external disbenefit of the sort in question involves one irrigator who creates a drainage problem for another irrigator or other landowner. A typical external benefit is generated when an electric utility operating a reservoir for power generation incidentally increases the summer flow of downstream water available to irrigators. It is generally accepted that a better allocation and more productive over-all use of water would be secured if water users generating such external disbenefits were discouraged from doing so in some appropriate degree, and if water users generating external benefits were encouraged to generate more of them in some appropriate degree. How should public policy in California deal with these problems?

For practical purposes, we would suggest enunciating in law the right of parties damaged by external disbenefits to proceed in the courts for relief or compensation, in normal civil litigations. Although a direct tax treatment of the external disbenefits of pollution has already been suggested, as well as increased direct regulation of the quantity of diversions and of release flows from reservoirs, we do not deem it practicable to establish regulation by commission of remaining types of external disbenefits. Such regulation would, or should, involve extremely complicated problems of economic analysis which would emerge endlessly; and the predictable accomplishments of commission regulation would probably not be worth its cost, supposing that the major problem of pollution control had already been taken care of.

Nor, for similar reasons, do we suggest determination of external benefits by a commission and the payment of "bonuses" to the generators of these benefits in order to attain optimal allocative results. What we do suggest is that the Department of Water Resources might be instructed actively to use its good offices (with the assistance of appropriate staff additions) to arrange negotiations between water users generating external benefits and the beneficiary parties or agencies. Such negotiations would be designed to arrive at private agreements whereby the bene-

[10] In this connection, also, we must strongly oppose the current federal-state plan to locate the large San Joaquin Drainage Canal (a feature of the combined Feather River and San Luis projects), which is designed to carry a large volume of agricultural sewage from Bakersfield to the sea, so that it empties into the San Joaquin River estuary just above the bays of the San Francisco area.

ficiaries would pay those generating external benefits for expansions or alterations of their operations such as would increase the external benefits in question. It does not seem very likely that (equitable as it might be) external beneficiaries can generally be induced to pay for spillover benefits which their generators cannot profitably withhold.

Conclusion

The preceding list of policy suggestions certainly is not exhaustive. Most of the limitations on the list result from the fact that, as a practical matter, we believe that new public policy measures should be aimed at revising and remedying the legal and other structural framework within which entities in the water industry operate, and at imposing only a necessary minimum of direct governmental interference or direct regulation of water agencies. This is a sound principle in dealing with private industry, and it appears comparably sound in an industry made up largely of public enterprises.

Thus, we have not suggested the imposition by higher governmental authority of maximum or minimum price regulations, of forced sales or transfers of water or water rights, or extensive governmental intervention in general. Similarly, we have not attempted to rewrite the operating rule books for the federal and state water agencies, or to exhort them voluntarily to follow revised rule books.

Emphasis, instead, has been placed mainly on study and consideration of a radical change in the regulation of water project authorizations; of some revisions in legislation setting policy for federal agencies and limiting powers of local purchasers of wholesaled water; of a selective revision of water-rights and agency law aimed at facilitating the development of water markets; and of a considerable extension of the regulatory and taxing powers of the state to deal with pollution and related problems and with the preservation of waters for public recreational uses. These suggestions, of course, could be elaborated at length. Elaboration, however, seems to belong properly in another volume.

APPENDICES

A.

A "Pure" Theory of the Demand-Price Relationship for Irrigation Water

B.

The Determination of Optimal Capacities of Main Irrigation Canals

C.

Retrospective Benefit-Cost Evaluation of the Central Valley Project

D.

The Feather River Project—Measurement of Benefits and Costs

Appendix A

A "PURE" THEORY OF THE DEMAND-PRICE RELATIONSHIP FOR IRRIGATION WATER

A pure theory of the relationship of demand for irrigation water to water price may be developed on the following assumptions:

1) Any potential or actual user of irrigation water (hereinafter referred to simply as a "user") controls a tract of land with given and homogeneous topography, soil type, climate, and so forth—these determining the range of crops which may be grown on the land and those crops which, other things being equal, may most advantageously be grown.

2) Each user has available a given and unchanging technology for growing crops generally and each particular crop which he may consider. But, within the limits of such technologies, he may as feasible vary methods of production in response to variations in the price of irrigation water or other inputs, usually by varying the intensity of irrigation and the proportions in which water and other variable factors are used to grow crops.

3) The price per unit at which the individual water user can sell each possible crop is given, and is invariant to any variation in the quantity of the crop that he may grow.

4) The prices of all factors other than land and water used in crop production are given and unchanging to any single user.

5) There are no legal or other institutional constraints which limit the proportion of acreage the user may plant to any crop, or the output for any crop he may produce or market at its going price.

6) Any user has water available to him in any quantity at any time he desires it, paying for it a given and invariant amount per unit (per acre-foot) used.[1] Thus we rule out rationing of water at any going price as well as any price variation within the year.

Given these general assumptions, we proceed with our simplified analysis. First, any potential user of irrigation water with a given tract of land to whom a water supply is made available can use this water to grow one or more alternative or complementary irrigated crops. In addition, he may have the alternative of making

[1] We shall refer throughout to the price of, and demand for, water at the point of delivery to the farm ("at the headgate"). In so doing, we will refer to a price which reflects the cost of transmitting water from its natural source and any costs of local distribution, including allowance for any water losses incurred in such transmission and distribution. Also, the demand-price relationship for irrigation water as calculated at the point of delivery to the farm will necessarily be influenced by or reflect any water losses incurred beyond that delivery point.

productive use of his land without irrigation—for example, dry farming, unirrigated pasturage, and so on.

Second, calculating at the headgate, the potential user can ascertain a production function for each possible crop grown on land such as his, and from each crop production function he can derive—for his total area of land—an average productivity function and a related marginal productivity function.[2] These will show the response of the physical yield of the crop per year, or per growing season, to successive increments of all non-land factors, including irrigation water applied to the homogeneous acreage involved. (The composition of the incremental unit "dose" of the different non-land factors applied may be influenced somewhat by their relative prices.) The *net values* of crop yields attributable separately to alternative amounts of water applied to a given acreage for growing a given crop (either average or marginal net values) may be calculated by deducting from the successive values attributable to water with other non-land factors the costs of the other non-land factors employed in conjunction with water. The result can be thought of as a net value of average product (*VAP*) curve and its corresponding net value of marginal product (*VMP*) curve.

The potential user can calculate a pair of net value of water curves (functions) for each potential crop. The several pairs emerging for comparison will tend to differ among crops (1) in terms of the quantity of water applied per acre to reach the maximum net value of average product per unit of water, (2) in terms of the height or size of this maximum net value, and (3) in terms of the shapes of the *VAP* and *VMP* curves over a range of larger quantities of water applied (larger than required to maximize *VAP*). In general, a crop which to maximize *VAP* uses the same quantity of water per acre as another *and has a lower maximum net value of average product of water* will tend to be absolutely inferior,[3] and if so, under unconstrained conditions and a perfectly elastic supply of water at a given price will not be grown, unless necessary for crop rotation purposes. The same, in general, tends to apply to any crop which uses a smaller quantity of water per acre than another *and does not have a higher maximum net value of average product* than the other.[4] All crops having either of these characteristics will tend to be eliminated from the list of primary crop possibilities. The primary possibilities then tend to fall naturally into an array of crops with *successively decreasing water requirements per acre* to reach maximum net value of average product, and *successively increasing maximum net values of average product*. Graphically such an array would be represented by a series of *VAP* curves with the maximum *VAP* lying progressively further to the left (toward zero water) on the horizontal scale and progressively higher on the vertical scale.

[2] For convenience of exposition, we shall suppose that the production functions of all crops are linearly homogeneous, so that the problem of proportions of inputs can be separated from that of scale of output. Thus we can indifferently compare the productivity functions of water in growing various crops on one acre of land or on the whole of an unspecified homogeneous tract.

[3] Except when the difference in maximum net value of average product is quite small and, in addition, (a) the crop with the lower maximum has a substantially more elastic *VAP* curve as larger quantities of water are applied, and (b) the price of water is appreciably below the maximum *VAP*.

[4] Subject to the same exceptions described in the preceding footnote.

This argument is illustrated in Figure A-1, the lower portion of which shows four *VAP* curves and their corresponding *VMP* functions. The upper portion of the diagram contains the four total net product functions (TNP_1, etc.) from which the functions in the lower portion (VAP_1, VMP_1, etc.) are derived. The solid-line portions of the *TNP* curves constitute an envelope total net product function. The solid-line portions of the *VAP* and *VMP* curves indicate the possible choices of crop and quantity of water purchased that would be made by a profit-maximizing farm enterprise at various prices for water. At prices higher than p_1, the crop corresponding to TNP_1 would be grown, and the solid portion of VMP_1 constitutes

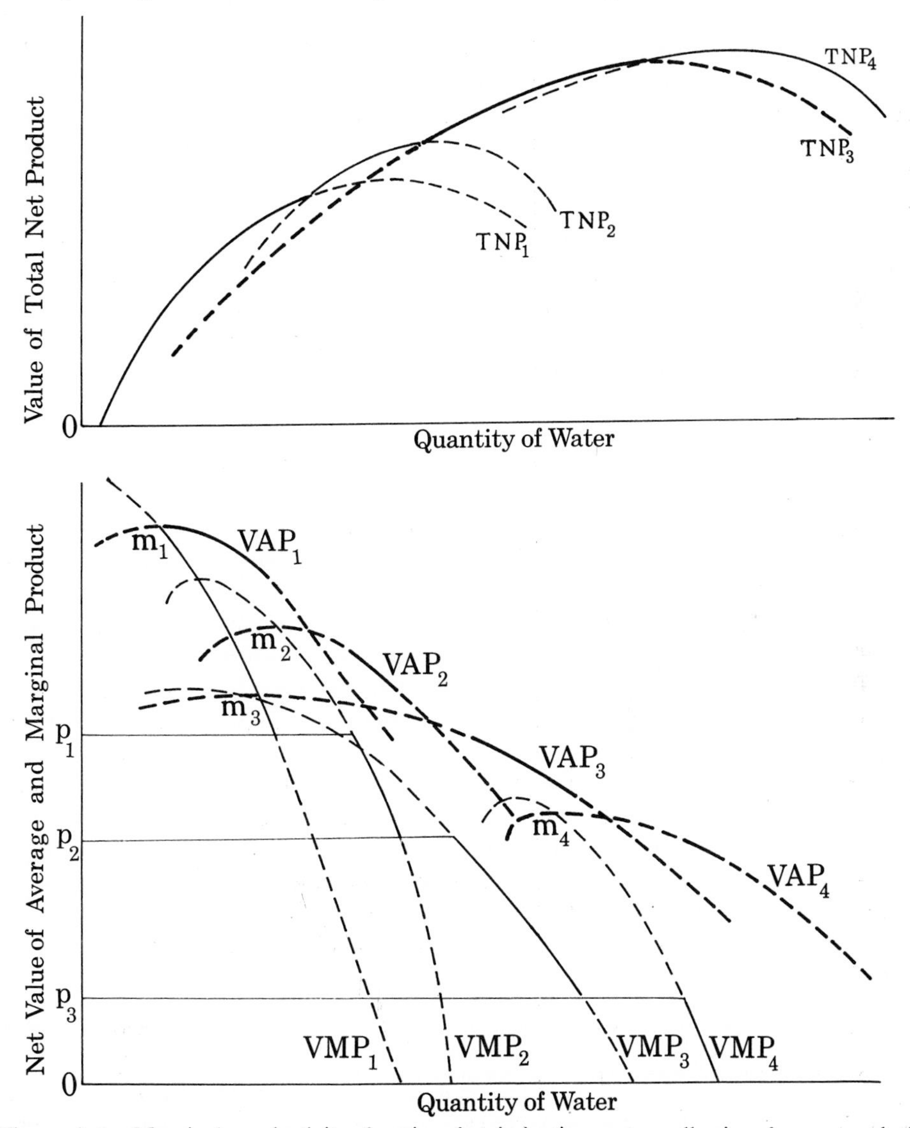

Figure A-1. Marginal productivity function for irrigation water, allowing for crop substitution.

a demand curve for irrigation water over that range of prices. If the price is lowered below p_1, profits are maximized by shifting to the crop corresponding to TNP_2, and the solid portion of VMP_2 indicates the quantity of water demanded. Thus, the demand function for water consists of the solid-line segments of the four *VMP* functions. The solid-line portions of the *VAP* curves lie directly above the solid segments of the *VMP* curves and show those ranges of net value of average product of water which might be observed. The points m_1, m_2, m_3, and m_4 are the maximum values of the respective *VAP* functions, and they can be seen to progress from upper left to lower right with the exception of m_3, illustrating the case mentioned in footnote 3.

Given a certain price for irrigation water and a perfectly elastic supply to the user at that price, the potential user must first decide if it would be profitable to grow any irrigated crop on his land. For this to be true, the price of water must be below the maximum net value of average product for one or more possible crops. He must then decide if growing any of the possible irrigated crops will yield a greater profit than the use of the land without irrigation. If, and only if, both conditions are met, irrigation will be undertaken.

If the potential user becomes an actual one, he will generally select for any area of roughly homogeneous land that one crop which will yield the greatest aggregate profit, or excess of aggregate yield over aggregate water and other non-land costs. Over time, this decision pattern may be modified if it is necessary to rotate crops or periodically to let land lie fallow to preserve the soil quality. Thus, a less than maximally profitable crop may be grown, and land may be left idle intermittently for the sake of the soil and of long-run profits. Subject to this qualification, however, there is generally under the assumed conditions one best crop for any area of homogeneous land served by water at the same price, and all of the area should be planted to it by any individual user (unless two or more crops are equally profitable).[5]

To secure a maximum profit from the best crop, the user will purchase and apply water in such quantity per acre in each year or crop season that the net value of the marginal product of water is made equal to the price of water.[6] Thus, the quantity of irrigation water per acre used on given land at any given water price is determined by deciding whether or not to irrigate, and if irrigation is undertaken, by co-determining the crop to be grown (or possibly crops, if two or more land areas of different quality are involved or if crop rotation is needed) and the intensity with which irrigation water will be applied in growing the crop.

The question now arises as to how increases over time in the price of irrigation water to a given user will affect the rate of use of water for irrigation. The reactions of irrigation water users to increased or higher water prices should be of three general sorts:

[5] If the land controlled by a given farm enterprise is not homogeneous, but consists instead of several differing tracts, each internally homogeneous, then the calculations described up to this point must be performed separately for each tract. Significant differences among tracts would in this instance amount to different positions for the *VAP* and *VMP* functions of various crops relative to one another or relative to the profitability of dry farming or both.

[6] This generally implies a quantity of water at least slightly in excess of that at which the maximum net value of the average product per unit of water is reached.

1) If the crop which is, or would be, most profitable for designated lands at a relatively low water price remains profitable and in addition is still the most profitable crop opportunity at a given higher water price,[7] the same crop will be grown at that water price, but use of irrigation water per acre will be restricted to the point where the net value of the marginal product of water equals the higher price of water. This restriction of water use will be accomplished by some restriction of crop output and some reduction in the quantity of water used per unit of crop yield.[8] The restriction will not be great if the net value of marginal product curve for the crop is quite inelastic, as predicted for the bulk of cases by the empirical evidence discussed in Chapter 5. These reaction patterns point to some negative price elasticity of demand for irrigation water, though to a rather low elasticity. Given users will react to an increase in the price of water by using somewhat less water per acre to grow a given crop.

2) At a higher water price, the same crop may not remain the most profitable alternative, and the user may shift to another crop that requires less irrigation water per acre and yields a larger net value of average product per unit of water used. (This net value must, of course, be sufficiently higher per unit of water to more than compensate for the reduced number of units of water used.) Consider the following example (referring to a given hypothetical tract of homogeneous land), which assumes fixed production coefficients for water:

Item	*Crop A*	*Crop B*
Net yield per acre (crop value minus non-water variable costs, in dollars)	$40	$60
Annual irrigation water use per acre, in acre-feet	2	5
(Net value of average product per acre-foot of water, in dollars)	($20)	($12)
Water cost at $4 per acre-foot	$ 8	$20
Profit per acre with water at $4 per acre-foot	$32	$40
Water cost at $8 per acre-foot	$16	$40
Profit per acre with water at $8 per acre-foot	$24	$20
Water cost at $12 per acre-foot	$24	$60
Profit per acre with water at $12 per acre-foot	$16	0

It will be noted that Crop *B*, though having a smaller net value of average product per acre-foot of water, is the crop of choice if water is priced at $4 per acre-foot. But Crop *A* becomes the more profitable one if the water price moves to $8 per acre-foot. Further, Crop *B* becomes unprofitable with a water price of $12 per acre-foot, though Crop *A* remains profitable. It is significant, moreover, that for a shift to a crop using less water per acre to be induced by a higher water price, it is not necessary that the profit on a crop which is a heavier water user become zero or very small with the higher water price in effect. As the preceding example shows, a shift from Crop *B* to Crop *A* should occur when the price of

[7] Water price remains below the net value of the average product of water if the crop is to be grown, in addition to its remaining more profitable than alternative crops.

[8] The latter resulting in part, possibly, from some substitution of other non-land factors for water.

water goes from $4 to $8 per acre-foot, even though at the higher water price Crop *B* would yield a substantial profit. At this point, Crop *B* has a "payment capacity" for water of $60 per acre and $12 per acre-foot, and a water cost only two-thirds as large, but Crop *A* should be grown instead. Substantial surplus payment capacities for water on crops using water heavily offer no firm assurance that making water prices higher, but not high enough to erase profits on these crops, will not cause a reduction in demand for irrigation water.

Under unconstrained conditions, the crop-shift phenomenon may be expected to contribute significantly to the price-elasticity of demand for irrigation water, and probably much more so than the varying intensity of the use of water in growing given crops. The crop substitution giving rise to this appreciable negative elasticity of water demand can contribute importantly to explaining the existence of different crop patterns on differently located lands of similar quality but having different conditions of water supply. And it also can contribute importantly to predicting the response of potential water users on presently unwatered lands to the offer of irrigation water at prices two or three times as high as those prevailing in adjacent areas or regions. When certain constraints are applied to planting crops, as we will see below, the effects of crop shifts on the price elasticity of demand for irrigation water may be significantly altered, although by no means entirely suppressed.

Even under unconstrained conditions, however, there may be exceptions in particular localities to the tendency toward shifting crops in response to changes in the price of irrigation water. It may be that a single crop would be the most profitable choice at any of a relevant range of alternative water prices, so that the array of primary crop possibilities was reduced to one item. A one-crop economy would then tend to emerge in the locality or area in question so far as soil, climatic, and topographic conditions permitted and except as crop rotation was required. This is substantially the case in some limited areas of the Central Valley and in some coastal valleys of Northern California.

3) A third effect of raising the price of irrigation water to a given user may be to induce the withdrawal of marginal irrigated land from irrigation. Land will be withdrawn from irrigation when at a given water price no irrigated crop will yield a positive profit and as much profit as will nonirrigated use of the land. The appreciable sensitivity of the quantity of land irrigated to the price of irrigation water appears as a major factor contributing to an appreciable negative price elasticity of the demand for irrigation water, at least in some price ranges. This sensitivity may be increased when artificial constraints on planting given crops impede or dampen natural tendencies to accommodate to changing water prices by choosing crop patterns unrestrainedly.

At least under unconstrained conditions, an appreciable negative price elasticity of the demand for irrigation water seems likely to be reflected in the responses of individual users or limited groups thereof to changes in water prices, and to differences in water prices as among localities. Let us consider the aggregated response of a very large number of users, growing a major share of some crop or crops going to a national or quasi-insular regional market, to a general change in prices of irrigation water. The probable response would show noticeably less elasticity of the aggregate demand for irrigation water than that of individual user's demands because of crop-price changes resulting from changes in the aggregate outputs of the crop or crops which are associated with changes in the aggregate quantity of water used and in the proportions in which it is devoted to growing specific crops. This sort of adjustment for induced crop-price changes entailed in estimating large-scale aggregations of water demands, however, is not very important when we consider the water demands of most local or subregional groups of users of irrigation water.

In analyzing the demand-price relationship for irrigation water in Northern California (as in other agricultural regions depending on irrigation), several assumptions of the preceding "pure theory" should be modified. We need to recognize the effect of certain constraints that are assumed away in the pure model, but which exist and are significant in the agricultural region we are studying. Perhaps the most important of these are limitations on the proportions of their acreages which water users may plant to some crops, or the outputs of some crops they may produce or market.

In fact, there are in various regions and localities of Northern California legal and other institutional constraints which directly or indirectly limit the proportion of his acreage which the user of irrigation water is allowed or induced to use for growing each of a number of important crops. These deter the user from making the single-best-crop choice for given land that corresponds to any given price of irrigation water. These constraints may be direct—as they are in the case of acreage allotments for cotton under the federal price support program, or in the case of beet-sugar processors' contracts with growers for limited amounts of acreage to be planted to sugar beets. They may also be indirect—as in the case of perishable crops, with respect to which producers' marketing agreements, backed by either federal or state authority, directly determine crop prices and/or crop quantities marketed, and indirectly influence crop outputs and acreages planted to the growing of given crops. A more elusive constraint may be a limitation on handling and processing facilities for given crops. This may, at least in the short run, encourage limitations for certain crops of marketings, output, and acreage planted. Thus it frequently happens that the individual user of irrigation water is required, or has strong institutionally derived incentives, to limit his planting of a certain crop (or of each of several crops among his primary alternatives) to a fraction of his available acreage, although he will generally have some crop opportunities to which no direct or indirect acreage limitations apply.

The imposition of such a system of acreage limitations may result in substantial differences in the behavior of the user of irrigation water in co-determining the amount of land to be irrigated at a given water price, the crops to be grown, the quantity of water to be used in growing them, and the shifts in all three of these things in response to changes or differences in water prices—all as compared to his behavior along these lines in the absence of acreage limitations. Such a shift in behavior may considerably influence his demand-price relationship for irrigation water. The major differences in behavior include the following:

1) He may, when unrestrictedly supplied with water at a uniform unit price, irrigate and grow crops on only a part rather than all of a tract of land of uniform

quality, over a certain range of alternative water prices. (Without constraints, he would irrigate all or none, depending on the water price.)

2) At a given water price, he may not (considerations of crop rotation being put aside) plant all of a land area of uniform quality which he irrigated to one "best" crop; rather he may plant several crops, some being inferior to others from the standpoint of profit per acre.

3) He may include in his crop pattern some crops which would never be grown in the absence of acreage limitations, given the set of crop prices which prevail with acreage limitations in effect.

4) The crop-shift reaction to upward or downward movements in water price may be considerably subdued, though in general not entirely eliminated.

Although the imposition of acreage limitations may have an appreciable effect on the demand-price relationship for irrigation water in the usual case, a systematic net influence on the price elasticity of demand for irrigation water at various water prices is not in general predictable. This is because the influence depends on the character of the array of primary crop possibilities, on crop prices, and on the nature and extensiveness of the constraints. Therefore, no generalizations are offered on this point.

Without purporting to represent any generalizations concerning the direction of the effects of acreage restrictions on the demand-price relationship in question, the following example may illustrate the rather bizarre development of a demand schedule for irrigation water under such constraints. In this example, we include as crop possibilities Crops *A, B, C,* and *D,* all under specified acreage limitations, and Crop *E* to which no acreage limitations apply. (Crop *E* is arbitrarily supposed to be the heaviest user of irrigation water.) The acreage limitations on *A, B, C,* and *D* are supposed to be 100 acres each for a user with a total acreage of 350 acres of uniform quality. The supposed essential data are as follows:

First, a more or less usual array of assumed crop possibilities (with no one crop included which is absolutely superior, regardless of price) is set forth in Table A-1.[9] For this set of crops, with 350 acres of land to be used, the total acreage planted, the crop selection, the acreage planted to each crop, and the demand for water at various alternative water prices appear in Table A-2.

TABLE A-1
HYPOTHETICAL WATER PRODUCTIVITIES IN PRODUCTION OF ACREAGE-RESTRICTED CROPS

Item	Crop *A*	Crop *B*	Crop *C*	Crop *D*	Crop *E*
Net value of average product per acre-foot of water (in dollars)	$ 40	$ 30	$ 25	$ 20	$ 12.50
Annual water use per acre (in acre-feet)	2	3	4	6	10
Net value of average product of water per acre (in dollars)	$ 80	$ 90	$100	$120	$125
Acreage allowed (in acres)	100	100	100	100	Unlimited

[9] Fixed water-land coefficients are assumed.

TABLE A–2
WATER DEMAND AND CROP PATTERN IN RELATION TO WATER PRICE ON 350-ACRE TRACT, HYPOTHETICAL EXAMPLE OF ACREAGE-RESTRICTED CROPS

Price of water per acre-foot	Number acres planted to various crops					Total acreage planted	Total water demand (acre-feet)[a]
	Crop *A*	Crop *B*	Crop *C*	Crop *D*	Crop *E*		
$35.00	100	0	0	0	0	100	200
27.50	100	100	0	0	0	200	500
22.50	100	100	100	0	0	300	900
17.50	100	100	100	50	0	350	1,200
10.00	100	100	100	50	0	350	1,200
7.50	50	100	100	100	0	350	1,400
5.50	0	100	100	100	50	350	1,800
4.50	0	0	100	100	150	350	2,500
1.00	0	0	0	0	350	350	3,500

[a] See Table A–1 for acre-feet required for Crops *A*, *B*, *C*, *D*, and *E*.

Over the progression of water prices downward from $35 to $17.50, we observe a reaction to water price involving entirely the movement of land, of uniform quality and receiving water at a uniform price, into production by adopting crops as water price falls. At a price of $7.50 per acre-foot for water, a crop-shift reaction comes into effect as the order of the crops in terms of net profits per acre has become *D, C, B, A, E* ($75, $70, $69.50, $65 and $50 per acre respectively). Thus, with all 350 acres already in use, the planting of *D* is expanded to 100 acres at the expense of a corresponding reduction in the planting of *A*. At a water price of $5.50, the crop shift proceeds further, as *E* becomes slightly more profitable per acre than *A* (though still less profitable than *B, C,* and *D*), and 50 acres of *E* are planted at the expense of abandoning *A* entirely. At a water price of $4.50 per acre-foot, *E* also displaces *B* (though not *C* and *D*) in terms of profitability per acre, and we arrive at a planting of the allowed 100 acres apiece of *C* and *D* and of 150 acres of unrestricted *E*. With water at $1.00 per acre-foot, it would pay to plant the entire acreage to *E*.

The connected effects on the total demand for water for the 350 acres are shown in the last column of Table A-2. The implied price elasticities of demand for irrigation water at most points, resulting from the arbitrary figures shown, are probably somewhat greater than found in practice. It may be noted that the sort of reaction pattern presented would be altered moderately in degree if one crop subject to acreage limitations were absolutely superior to all others—that is, more profitable per acre at any water price. If, for example, Crop *A* had a net value of average product per acre-foot of $70—thus yielding $140 per acre before water costs—it would always be planted to the limit of 100 acres (at any price below $70 per acre-foot for water) and would not be displaced by any of the other crops as a result of any declines in the price of water, even to a zero price. The reaction pattern of crop choice and water demand would otherwise be roughly the same, except that Crop *D* would be substituted for *B* instead of *A* (to the extent of 50 acres) at a water price of $7.50; Crop *E* would not be brought into production at a water price of $5.50; at a water price of $4.50, 50 acres of *E* would be substituted for the remaining 50 acres of *B*; and at lower prices E would additionally displace only *C* and *D*. The large possible variety of patterns of demand reaction to price changes for irrigation water under a broad range of conceivable acreage constraints is obvious.

Returning to our initial suppositions concerning the net values of average products per acre-foot of water for the given crops (Table A-1), it may be noted that in the absence of acreage limitations, *and assuming that the same crop prices still rule despite their absence,* the reaction pattern to water-price change (crop rotation being put aside) would be very simple. None of the land would be irrigated if water cost over $40 per acre-foot. All 350 acres would be planted to Crop *A* at water prices from $10 to $40 per acre-foot; all of the acreage to Crop *D* at water prices between $10 and $1.25; and all of the acreage to *E* at water prices below $1.25. (Crops *B* and *C* would never be planted.) The corresponding demand schedule for irrigation water would show the following:

Price of water per acre-foot	*Quantity of water demanded (acre-feet)*
$10 -$40	700
$ 1.25-$10	2,100
$ 0.00-$ 1.25	3,500

The comparison of the preceding with Table A-2 is not very meaningful, since crop prices and net values of water used in growing given crops could hardly be expected to remain unchanged if acreage restrictions were removed.

In the preceding simplified example of the development of water demand under acreage restrictions, we have not considered a water user with two or more parcels of land of different quality (that is, in fertility or susceptibility to water losses). Elaboration of the example to recognize this phenomenon would add little to the basic generalizations concerning the effects of acreage restrictions in demand for irrigation water, but they could reveal such possibilities not explored here as the planting of an unrestricted crop on second-grade land (once a favorable water price was reached) without displacing the planting of restricted crops on first-grade land, the displacement of one restricted crop by another on first-grade land accompanied by transferring the planting of the displaced crop to second-grade land, etc.[10]

A somewhat similar modification of our results occurs when we drop the implicit assumption that the expected profitability (per acre) of growing a given crop is

[10] The calculation for individual farms (and aggregates thereof) of demand-price relationships for irrigation water subject to various acreage constraints has been undertaken by Trimble R. Hedges and Charles V. Moore for the Giannini Foundation at the University of California, and drew our attention to the possible significance of acreage constraints in Northern California as influences on the price elasticity of demand for irrigation water. See especially Hedges and Moore, *Economics of On-Farm Irrigation, Water Availability and Costs, and Related Farm Adjustments* (in 3 pts.), Giannini Foundation Research Report No. 257 (1962), pp. 52–58, and No. 261 (1963). (For full citation, see the Bibliography.) The example presented here is based on imaginary data but, in a very simplified form, illustrates their technique in calculating irrigation-water demand schedules or curves subject to acreage constraints. Some of their statistical findings are reviewed in Chapter 5, the section on Price Elasticity of Demand for Irrigation Water.

independent of the total acreage of that crop planted and the mixture of other crops also under cultivation. For example, the farmer's labor and the services of the machinery that he owns constitute fixed inputs to the farm enterprise. Because different crops require these inputs at different times during the growing season, they may be more efficiently utilized by cultivating a mixture of crops rather than the one that would, in the absence of temporal constraints, produce the highest return (at any going price of water and other inputs and outputs). By the same token, the avoidance of uncertainty about crop or input prices may call for a mixture of crops rather than the production of the one with the highest expected profitability. These and many other factors[11] may cause the opportunity costs of substituting one crop for another to increase at the margin as substitution proceeds. The sensitivity of the crop mix to the price of water, and thus the virtual elasticity of the derived demand for water, are reduced.

Another assumption of the pure model which may be relaxed in calculating demand-price relationships for irrigation water is that at whatever price he is charged per unit of water, the user obtains the water not only in any desired quantity but at any desired time. There frequently may be constraints on the quantity of irrigation water available to the user at given times during the growing season for crops generally or for particular crops. Then, although his total annual water supply at the going price is in a sense unrestricted, he is unable to accomplish the ideal in time pattern and frequency of application of various alternative annual quantities of water applied to a given acreage in growing specific crops or crops in general.

The general effect of this sort of constraint will be to alter the positions and elasticities of the average and marginal product curves of any crops affected by the constraint. The net value of average product of water curve and the net value of marginal product of water curve will shift and change elasticity correspondingly for any affected crop, and for all possible crops—though in different degrees. These constrained value-of-product functions, moreover, will be analytically meaningful if the constraints on water availability are sufficiently limited that users are offered unrestricted quantities of water at the going price during substantial and crucial parts of the irrigation season, as would seem usually to be the case.

If this is the case, there is introduced a revised set of individual crop productivity functions as determinants of irrigation water demand.[12] This is likely to result in some reordering of the array of crop possibilities, as ranked in terms of decreasing water use per acre and increasing maximum net value of average product of water. Given this revision of the array, the analysis of the determination of the demand-price relationship for irrigation water may be applied without revision, either in the pure case or in the case in which acreage limitations are imposed. A general tendency to favor crops which are more tolerant of a shortage of irrigation during the times of short water supply—or of revisions in the time pattern, frequency, and size of individual applications of irrigation water—should

[11] See, for example, Earl O. Heady and Harald R. Jensen, *Farm Management Economics* (New York: Prentice-Hall, 1954), chap. 6.

[12] The revisions should generally involve shifting of the functions leftward and downward, and a reduction of their elasticities.

be present. The ordering of crop shifts as the price of water changes under otherwise unconstrained conditions, and of additions and withdrawals of given crops when acreage limitations are in effect, should tend to be altered. And the prices at which demand will be reduced by the withdrawal of given marginal lands from irrigation should be reduced. Periods of water shortage during growing seasons will in general tend to decrease the total annual demands for irrigation water at given prices, but the over-all effect on the price elasticity of these demands is difficult to predict a priori.

All of the preceding refers to constrained demands determined where the pattern of constraints is not associated with the level of water price so, for example, that as the price of water is raised the constraints on water availability do not become less (or more) severe. Only by assuming this to be the case can we derive a true price elasticity of constrained water demands. If the level of price and the degree of constraints on water availability were correlated—that is, negatively correlated because higher prices reflected higher costs incurred to reduce the constraints—then the total response of water demand to price change would not reflect a true price elasticity of demand. Instead it would reflect the composite effects on demand of price elasticity and of shifts in the demand curve induced by the change in constraints which was associated with the price change. We can readily eschew this sort of confusion in treating the price elasticity of water demand on a theoretical level. But as we turn to a statistical anlysis of the relationship of actual demands to prices, we must keep in mind the possibility that there is in the data some correlation of price and the degree of constraints on water availability. Such a correlation would produce a bias in the measurement of the price elasticity of demand for irrigation water.

Appendix B

THE DETERMINATION OF OPTIMAL CAPACITIES OF MAIN IRRIGATION CANALS

We assume that the distribution of irrigation water is through main canals, then into laterals, then into sublaterals for delivery to individual plots of land. All flows are actuated by gravity. The spacing of laterals (assumed straight and parallel to each other) is taken as given, although we will take into account variations in the carrying capacity of laterals warranted by changes in the number of main canals. The location and capacity of sublaterals is assumed fixed, and optimizing changes in them are not taken into account in the following discussion. Also, we will adhere to simple cases of single main canals tapped by laterals, and will not consider more complex cases wherein a main canal divides into distributary branches, some with laterals, though the principles of optimizing canal systems in the simpler cases are readily adaptable to the more complex ones.

The general solution of the problem of determining the optimal size of territory to be served by a single main canal, or the optimal degree of consolidation of total main-canal capacity in fewer and larger (as opposed to more and smaller) main canals, is so complex, when all possibly relevant considerations are taken into account, that its full development is not justified here. Rather than building a general solution, and then deducing its corollaries applicable to a variety of specific situations, we will first suggest that the interplay of two principal countervailing influences on cost determine the net advantage in enlarging the territory served by a main canal (or in consolidating main-canal capacity). We will then illustrate the application of this system of determination in four general cases which comprehend most situations actually encountered in transporting irrigation water.

On the general level, we can be brief. First, consider main canal capacity that serves to carry water *away from a source* toward and through a service area *all of which* may be served either by laterals running downhill from a single main canal, or by an extension of the single main canal which after the outhaul from the source turns to run parallel to source (this extension being tapped by laterals). For such canal capacity, the costs per unit of water delivered *incurred for the outhaul* may be reduced by concentrating all of the main-canal capacity for the service area in one main canal. This follows from the general principle that a *given* aggregate outhaul capacity is most economically provided by a single main canal which exploits to the maximum feasible extent the economies of large-capacity canals; aggregate outhaul capacity is not increased, and the cost of supplying it is reduced. This generalization applies even though the single main canal effectively combines the capacities of alternative smaller canals which would have outhauled water different distances from the source. The single main canal can have a capacity which tapers downward as it proceeds away from the source, sustaining at each point only enough capacity to carry water to be delivered beyond that point. The only significant constraint is that there be a suitable and economic diversion point on the source to accommodate the single main canal in its proper location.

Second, so far as either lateral canals tapping main canals, or extensions of main canals, are used to carry water more or less parallel to the source (if it is a river), or in roughly concentric arcs around the source (if it is a point), the *average distance that each unit of water delivered is carried* in lateral and main canals increases as the number of main canals drawing on a source decreases and the distances between main canals increase; the average distance of carriage per unit of water reaches a maximum with a single main canal serving the maximum physically feasible area. Therefore, reducing the number of main canals (toward the limit of one) and increasing the distances between them increases the amount of lateral or main-canal capacity required to perform a given water-delivery task, and this tends to increase the transportation cost per unit of water delivered.

Taking these two tendencies together, we see that as we move from more numerous, smaller, and more closely spaced main canals toward fewer, larger, and more widely spaced main canals drawing on a given source to serve a given territory, we find operative both a cost-reducing and a cost-increasing tendency. The optimal number, individual size, and spacing of main canals will be established at that point where increases in the cost of hauling parallel to or around the source outweigh decreases in the cost of outhauling water from the source. (The availability and relative economic merits of numerous alternative diversion points from a river will of course affect the character of the optimal solution.)

The preceding may be clarified by considering our four simplified examples of water transport situations. Consider first Case I, in which there are several service areas, each economically serviceable (lateral canal costs being taken into account) only from a single diversion point on a single source, and in which the service areas lie progressively farther from the source. Their relationship to the source is suggested in Figure B-1. Each area needs a single main canal running from the diversion point *a* to a point slightly east of its western (lower) boundary along its southern (right) border, with four laterals tapping its main canal and running north more or less parallel to the source. It is assumed that the distance of the haul in laterals is given and that over-all costs could not be reduced in any area by using two main canals (the second bisecting the area) instead of one. Problems of excessive capacity for hauling water parallel to the source are thus assumed away. Now the required main-canal capacity might be provided by three main canals, one serving area *X* and running from *a* to *b*, one serving area *Y* and running from *a* to *c*, and a third serving area *Z* and running from *a* to *d*. But it would clearly be most economical for the three areas to be served by a single main canal from *a* to *d*, with the combined capacity of the alternative three canals. This is because all the outhaul from the source could be accomplished with the same total capacity, because this capacity could be furnished most cheaply in a single canal, and because there are no offsetting losses of increased lateral capacity, which by assumption would remain the same.

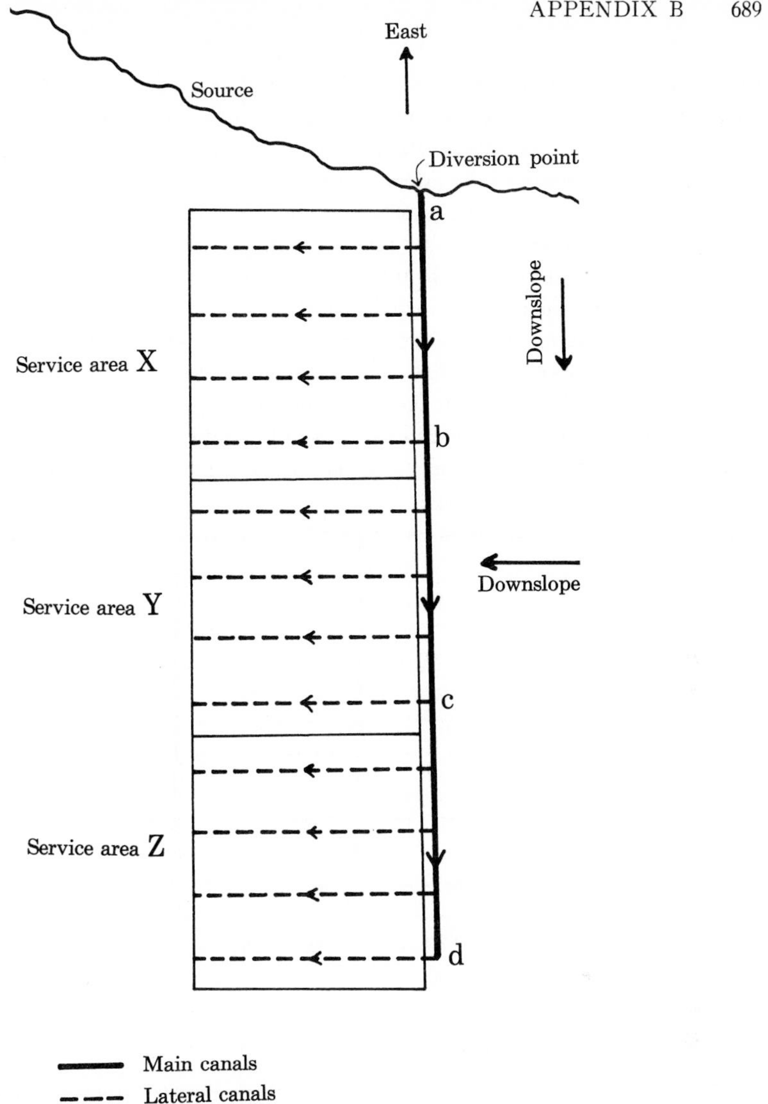

Figure B-1. Schematic map of water service areas supplied from a single origin on a single source, and of canal alternatives, Case I.

Suppose that each of the three areas uses water requiring 100 cubic feet per second of flow into the main canal or canal sector serving it, and that the distances *ab, bc,* and *cd* are each 12 miles. With separate main canals, we would require 12 miles of main canal with a constant capacity of 100 cfs for 3 miles and a capacity tapering from 100 to 25 cfs for 9 miles; 24 miles of canal with a constant capacity of 100 cfs for the first 15 miles and a capacity tapering from 100 cfs to 25 cfs for 9 miles; and 36 miles of canal with a constant capacity of 100 cfs for the first 27 miles and a capacity tapering from 100 to 25 cfs for the last 9 miles. It would certainly be economical to replace these three with a single main canal 36 miles long on the same route with a head capacity of 300 cfs, tapering steadily (after the first three miles) to a terminal capacity of 25 cfs. (The choice is between 36 miles of main canal with an average capacity of about 150 cfs and 72 miles of main canal with an average capacity of about 75 cfs but divided among 3 canals of inefficiently small capacity.) Requirements of lateral canals with either three or one main canals would be identical—twelve laterals of given length with head capacities of 25 cfs apiece, each tapering to zero terminal capacity. Case I, of course, illustrates the unadulterated advantages of consolidating outhauls from a source in the smallest feasible number of canals to serve a given area.

Consider now Case II, in which there are several service areas which lie equidistant from a river source, and together form a continuous band of land parallel to the river. Suppose also they are to be served by a main canal or canals which haul water directly out from the river to and through them, and by laterals which tap the main canal or canals and carry water parallel to the river. Their relationship to the source, and the general canal pattern, are shown in Figure B-2. We assume

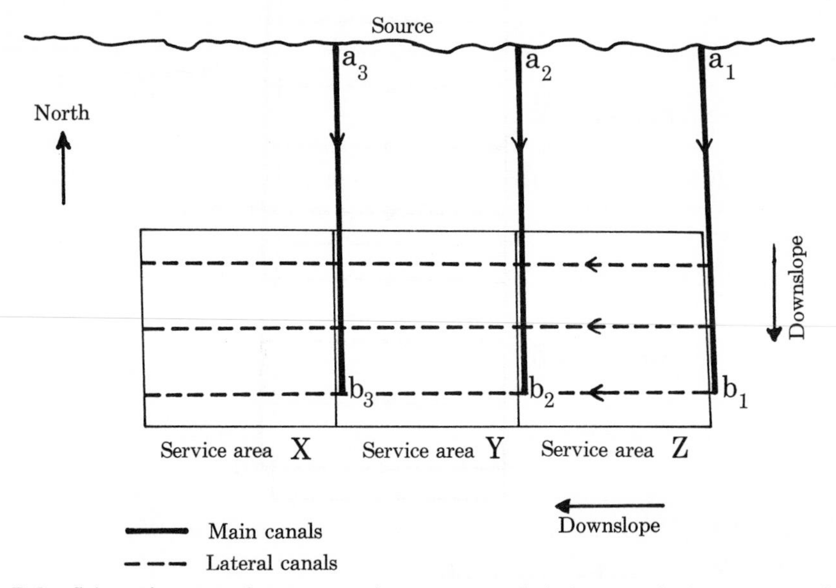

Figure B-2. Schematic map of water service areas supplied from a single source, and of canal alternatives, Case II.

that each service area is square with 6 miles to a side, that the northern border of each is 6 miles from the river, and that the length of any main canal leading from the source to the outside lateral in any area is 11 miles, the distance *ab*. Suppose further that each area uses water requiring 1,200 cfs of flow into the main canal serving it, for diversion into its own laterals. Let us now compare the relative merits of serving the areas with three separate main canals and connected laterals and with one main canal and connected laterals.

With three main canals, located at a_1b_1, a_2b_2, and a_3b_3, the total main-canal requirement is for three main canals, each 11 miles long; and each with a head capacity of 1,200 cfs, maintained over the first 7 miles, and tapering to a terminal capacity of 400 cfs over the last 4 miles. This is a total main-canal requirement of 33 miles at an average capacity of about 982 cfs. The corresponding lateral requirement is for nine segments of lateral canal each 6 miles long and each with a head capacity of 400 cfs, tapering to zero terminal capacity. The total lateral-canal requirement is thus for 54 miles of laterals with an average capacity of 200 cfs.

The alternative of one main canal, located at a_1b_1, to provide all main-canal service, would require a single main canal 11 miles long, with a head capacity of 3,600 cfs, maintained over the first 7 miles, and tapering to a terminal capacity of 1,200 cfs over the last 4 miles. This is a total main-canal requirement of 11 miles at an average capacity of about 2,945 cfs. Since the same total capacity is thus provided as would be in three smaller canals, substantial scale economies of the large capacity canal should appreciably reduce main-canal costs for the system. To this saving, however, there is an offset. The average length of haul for water reaching service areas X and Y, through laterals from the single main canal at a_1b_1, would be substantially increased, and the capacities of the laterals would have to be increased correspondingly. With one main canal, we would require three lateral canals, each 18 miles long and each with a head capacity of 1,200 cfs and a terminal capacity of zero—or 54 miles of laterals with an average capacity of 600 cfs. The lateral-capacity requirement is thus trebled, and it seems very likely that building 54 miles of laterals to an average capacity 400 cfs greater than their capacity with three main canals would add more to costs than the saving resulting from carrying 3,600 cfs of head flow 11 miles in a single main canal of more efficient size.

The spacing of main canals 6 miles apart on the river is probably not too narrow. Any wider spacing (including one every 18 miles, just considered) would evidently be less economical because it would add enough to total canal-capacity requirements for hauling parallel to the source to more than offset the economies of consolidating the outhaul from the river in fewer canals. Is the 6-mile spacing too wide? If we compare a 6-mile with a 3-mile spacing (serving each service area with two main canals), the decision becomes close. For any one area, there would be these two choices: one 11-mile main canal, at an average capacity of about 982 cfs with 18 miles of laterals at an average capacity of 200 cfs; and 22 miles of main canal at an average capacity of about 491 cfs with 18 miles of laterals at an average capacity of 100 cfs. Detailed calculations of the extent of scale economies in the main and lateral canals would be required to determine if the 3-mile spacing would be preferable to the 6-mile spacing of main canals. A 1-mile spacing of main canals certainly would not be economical.

By now, we have pursued this analysis far enough to perceive the interplay of cost reductions through consolidated outhauls from a river and of cost increases due to associated increases in the average distance water is carried, and to corresponding increases in canal-capacity requirements. This interplay determines the optimal service areas and capacities of main canals where hauls parallel to the source are involved. It may be noted that a consolidation of main-canal capacity into fewer canals may be uneconomical, even though it does not increase or decrease total main and lateral canal mileage, because it increases capacity requirements in lateral or other parallel-hauling canal mileage. It should further be noted that (site considerations for diversions aside) the optimal spacing of main canals drawing on a river will depend on the length of the outhaul from the river, and that the optimal spacing will tend to become wider as the outhaul becomes longer. In Case II, for example, a 40-mile outhaul would very probably justify a 12-mile spacing of main canals.

Related Case III involves main canals which radiate from a "point" source such as a pool or the end of river running into a closed basin. Such points are usually established or selected where there is some downslope outward toward irrigable lands over a range of directions covering a considerable arc on the compass. Main canals can be run outward over much of the arc with a sufficient canal downgrade, plus a side-hill slope which permits the use of laterals which also have downgrades, so that gravity can be used to move water throughout. Where terrain permits, the main-canal outhaul serving land covering a considerable arc of directions can be provided in a single main canal—that is, if over this arc the grade downward from the source point progressively increases, permitting the use of long laterals which "circle" the source point concentrically at various distances from it. Again, the problem of optimal spacing of main canals (here radial canals) arises. If we regard the radial main canals as spokes of a wheel, how close together should the spokes be for lowest-cost water transport? The same considerations govern as did in Case II, which involved spacing of outhauls from a river. Wider spacing of main canals reduces outhaul costs by consolidating outhaul capacity in canals of more efficient size (which provide a given total capacity at lower costs); but the wider spacing also increases the average distance of haul per unit of water delivered and the required capacities of lateral canals. An optimum compromise can be struck, and the optimal spacing of radial main canals will be wider as the length of the outhaul from the source point is greater.

The final case to be considered, Case IV, involves the service of several areas which (1) form a band of land parallel to and bordering a river, and (2) are served by a main canal or canals which first pull water away from the river and then carry it parallel to the river, with the laterals which tap them carrying water back toward the river. This sort of arrangement is illustrated in Figure B-3. The total service area might be served by three main canals "in series"—*abc, def,* and *ghi,* with laterals tapping each to carry water through the service area back toward the river. Or the total area might be served by a single main canal with the route *abcefhi,* involving only one combined outhaul, *ab,* and one long stretch of main canal, *bi,* parallel to the river. With one, instead of three main canals, neither length nor the capacity of lateral canals would be appreciably changed. There would be a saving from consolidating all outhaul capacity in one canal, at *ab.* But again there would be offsets, because the average distance of delivery per unit of water in the main canal parallel to the river would be roughly trebled, and the average capacity of the canal stretch from *b* to *i* would also be trebled. Therefore, a very substantial outhaul (or special limitations on diversion points or canal routes) would evidently be required to justify any wider spacing of main canals than that shown in Figure B-3. Here we encounter the same sort of check on the optimum size of service area of a main canal as was encountered in Case II, the only difference being that the increased canal-capacity requirement which goes with enlarging the service area occurs in main rather than lateral canals.

These cases, taken together, tend to suggest that there are very definite limits on the optimal service areas of individual main canals and on the degree to which

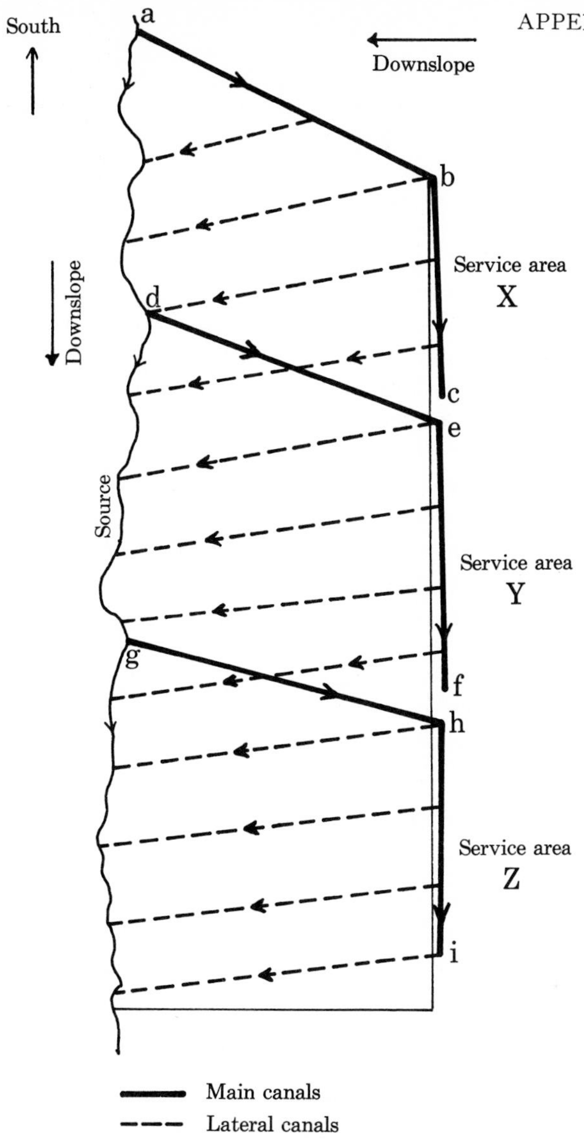

Figure B-3. Schematic map of water service areas supplied from a single source, and of canal alternatives, Case IV.

it pays to concentrate main-canal capacity in fewer and larger canals, in spite of the obvious economies of large-capacity canals in terms of cost per unit of capacity per mile. Long outhauls from sources to service areas generally favor the use of somewhat fewer and larger main canals, but very long outhauls (longer than generally experienced), or special terrain conditions or limitations on diversion sites would be required to justify any very considerable concentration of main-canal capacity in a relatively few canals per river basin. The major opportunity for economical extension of the service areas of main canals arises when a canal can be lengthened to reach irrigable service areas farther and farther from the source (from the river or the point source), up to the limit where water from another source is closer or cheaper or where land farther away is of insufficient quality.

Appendix C 

RETROSPECTIVE BENEFIT-COST EVALUATION OF THE CENTRAL VALLEY PROJECT

Here we describe in detail the capital and operating costs of the features of the Central Valley Project of the U.S. Bureau of Reclamation described in Chapter 15, then their commercial revenues, and finally we develop measures of their total benefits and of the relation of benefits to costs.

Capital and Operating Costs

Since the features of the Central Valley Project (CVP) under consideration here have been fully constructed, stating their capital cost becomes a relatively simple matter compared to estimating their operating expense in a typical year. The Bureau of Reclamation's property accounts for the Project seem to be relatively complete, so that the only problem of adjustment comes in converting original costs to a price-level base consistent with that of related costs and benefits. There are two ways in which the capital costs, presented in Table C-1, might be incomplete. First, some initial exploratory expenses involving surveying and planning were incurred by the state of California in the 1930's, before the Project became a federal undertaking; and these were never transferred to the Bureau's books. No basis has been found for estimating these costs, and so they have been excluded. Another cost category conventionally omitted in such investigations is the appropriation and supervisory costs of the United States Congress. Also excluded, for the present, are complementary investments built by other agencies in order to use CVP water (these expenditures are indicated below in Table C-6).

We have adjusted the reported capital costs of the Central Valley Project to 1959 prices, using special indexes constructed by the Bureau. A small amount of guesswork was necessary concerning the relative amounts of expenditures on a particular facility which took place in a given year.

All major features of the so-called initial stage of the Central Valley Project have been in at least partial operation for a decade or more. Thus we have at least a few years' experience with CVP's operating costs from which to estimate the expected normal experience over its span of life. In these years, nature has provided significant variations in the runoff of the Sacramento and San Joaquin rivers and thus in the water delivered and power generated by the Project. Some slender basis thereby exists for making simple associations between these inputs or outputs

TABLE C-1
INVESTMENT ACCOUNTS OF THE CENTRAL VALLEY PROJECT, SHASTA, DELTA, AND FRIANT DIVISIONS, INCLUDING CONSTRUCTION THROUGH THE FISCAL YEAR 1961

Item	Adjusted cost (1959 prices)
Shasta and Keswick dams, reservoirs	$242,581,414
Shasta and Keswick power plants, switchyards	81,733,810
Shasta and Keswick transmission lines	20,599,815
Shasta and Keswick general property[a]	3,475,259
Tracy pumping plant	18,271,916
Delta fish protective facilities	3,625,625
Contra Costa Canal	8,861,650
Delta Cross Channel	2,448,058
Delta-Mendota Canal	52,566,286
Tracy switchyard	8,060,000
Delta general property[a]	1,562,662
Friant Dam, Reservoir	34,829,352
Madera Canal	4,891,990
Friant-Kern Canal	65,528,117
Friant general property[a]	1,280,907
Sacramento and San Joaquin rivers water rights[b]	21,557,250
Central Valley waterfowl conservation	448,000
Preference customer metering facilities	359,107
Central Valley radio network	363,376
Total	$573,044,594

[a] Prices of general property accounts were adjusted by the index for the primary facility (dam or canal) of each division.
[b] For want of a better solution, the original value of the water rights settlements was multiplied by the increase of the U.S. Department of Agriculture's index of prices received by farmers.
SOURCE: Calculated from U.S. Department of the Interior, Bureau of Reclamation, Commissioner's Office, *Analysis of Cost Changes, Authorizations, and Benefits of Reclamation Projects* (1960), Table 1; *idem, Construction Cost Trends, January 1961* (1961), Table 12.

of the Project and categories of its reported operating costs. No appropriate price indexes exist to help remove the influence of unit-value changes in the Bureau's reported current costs. Pacific Gas and Electric Company sometimes uses the assumption of a 5 per cent annual increase, which seems excessive for years in the 1950's even considering the high labor content of operation and maintenance expenditures. We have assumed a 3 per cent annual price increase during that decade for those cost categories in which labor costs seemed to represent a large fraction of the total. In adjusting replacement costs, indexes developed by the Bureau for hydroelectric plants and switchyards and for transmission lines were employed.[1]

Three different methods have been used to establish normal values for the various categories of operation and maintenance costs for the basic features of the Central Valley Project. In some cases, such as the operation of power plants and diversion canals, it has proved possible to establish a relation between the physical level of activity (watt-hours generated or acre-feet diverted) and the reported cost.

[1] Their source is U.S. Department of the Interior, Bureau of Reclamation, Commissioner's Office, *Construction Cost Trends, January 1961* (1961), Table 12. (This and other footnote references are cited in brief form when they are also included in the Bibliography.)

In others, such as certain categories of maintenance, a trend over CVP's early years affords the basis for a crude guess about a long-term normal or average value. In still other cases, where neither trends nor functional relations could be developed, an average was taken of the price-adjusted values for whatever run of recent years seemed appropriate. Table C-2 presents a list of current-cost categories for the Central Valley Project, the basis for estimating each category, and the numerical result.[2]

Except for the cost of replacements, practically all of the major cost categories for canals could be estimated on the basis of functional relations. The character of these relations merits some discussion. The operating costs of CVP's major canals have borne, as one would expect, a relatively close relation to the amount of water diverted through them. The resulting functions could be used in connection with an estimate of water diversions in a normal year to give an estimate of costs in a normal year. A study of runoff patterns and diversions in the past decade suggests that, in a year of normal runoff for the San Joaquin River, diversions would be 900,000 acre-feet through the Friant-Kern Canal and 230,000 acre-feet through the Madera Canal.[3] Normal use of the Delta-Mendota Canal is harder to estimate because of its greater flexibility in collecting water and reaching customers. The bulk of this water is delivered to San Joaquin River users in exchange for the flow of that River now intercepted at Friant. The exchange amounts to 855,000 acre-feet in a normal year, but in years of critical subnormal runoff into Shasta Dam it may be reduced to 665,000 acre-feet.[4] On the basis of the past four decades, about one year in four would be classed as critical, suggesting an average delivery of 800,000 acre-feet annually under the exchange contract. The Bureau has also entered into or is negotiating contracts which would commit it eventually to deliver a maximum firm amount of 419,860 acre-feet annually, not counting a temporary delivery of 80,000 acre-feet to the state's South Bay Aqueduct. Since the Delta-Mendota Canal's potential service area has not been entirely "saturated," water marketing developments suggest an ultimate level of deliveries of perhaps 1,300,000 acre-feet. The final major canal, the Contra Costa, is also subject to steadily growing demand which, under a pending contract, might reach a level of 185,000 acre-feet annually.[5] Such a volume of demand will develop quite slowly from the recent flow of about 65,000 acre-feet. Thus a normal value of 100,000 acre-feet would seem reasonable as representing the average diversion over the life of the project.

[2] Sources of data and information underlying these calculations included the following: U.S. Department of the Interior, Bureau of Reclamation, Region 2, *Annual Project History, Central Valley Project, 1936–1961,* 26 vols. (various years); and Bureau of Reclamation, *Annual Financial Report* (various years).

[3] The Bureau's completed and pending contracts for maximum deliveries of firm (Class 1) water through these canals total 591,100 and 140,000 acre-feet respectively. Undoubtedly most of the remaining San Joaquin water subject to diversion at Friant Dam will be sold, in the future as now, as an uncertain supply (Class 2). See U.S. Department of the Interior, Bureau of Reclamation, Region 2, *Water Service Repayment—Review Statement, 1960* (1961), pp. 63 ff. (Hereinafter cited as *Water Service Repayment—Review Statement.*)

[4] U.S. Congress, House Committee on Interior and Insular Affairs, *Central Valley Project Documents, Part 2: Operating Documents,* H. Doc. 246, 85 Cong. 1 sess. (1957), p. 606. (Hereinafter cited as *Central Valley Project Documents, Part 2.*)

[5] *Water Service Repayment—Review Statement, op. cit.,* p. 68.

TABLE C–2
NORMAL ANNUAL OPERATING COSTS OF THE CENTRAL VALLEY PROJECT, SHASTA, DELTA, AND FRIANT DIVISIONS

Cost category	Basis of estimate	Annual cost (1959 prices)
Shasta Division:		
Shasta power plant	1,987,000 mwh @ 0.12 mills/kwh	$ 238,440
Keswick power plant	413,000 mwh @ 0.22 mills/kwh	90,860
Shasta Dam, Reservoir	Avg. of adjusted values, 1955–59[a]	209,300
Kewsick Dam, Reservoir	Avg. of adjusted values, 1955–59	19,800
Shasta switchyard	Avg. of adjusted values, 1955–59	59,000
Keswick switchyard	Avg. of adjusted values, 1955–59	31,000
Transmission lines, west side	Trend	57,000
Transmission lines, east side	Trend	109,000
Sacramento Channel	Avg. of adjusted values, 1955–59	28,000
Toyon pipeline	Avg. of adjusted values, 1955–59	2,600
General expense	Avg. of adjusted values, 1955–59	86,800
Replacements	Adjusted trend	425,000
Subtotal		$1,356,800
Tracy Division:		
Tracy switchyard	Trend	125,000
Tracy transmission lines	Trend	5,500
Tracy pumping plant[b]	1,430,000 ac-f @ $1.14/ac-f	1,630,200
Contra Costa pumping plant[b]	112,000 ac-f @ $1.44/ac-f	161,300
Delta-Mendota Canal	1,200,000 ac-f @ $0.40/ac-f	480,000
Contra Costa Canal	100,000 ac-f @ $2.55/ac-f	255,000
Delta Cross Channel	Trend	25,600
Delta fish screen	Trend	97,700
Water marketing	Avg. of adjusted values, 1955–59	17,900
Power accounting, collecting	Avg. of adjusted values, 1955–59	2,700
General expense	Trend	167,800
Replacements	Avg. of values, 1956–59	210,000
Subtotal		$3,178,700
Friant Division:		
Madera Canal	230,000 ac-f @ $0.32/ac-f	73,600
Friant-Kern Canal	900,000 ac-f @ $0.45/ac-f	405,000
Friant Dam, Reservoir	Avg. of adjusted values, 1953–59	104,200
San Joaquin River	Adjusted trend	65,000
Columbia-Mowry system	Avg. of adjusted values, 1957–59	3,800
Water marketing	Avg. of adjusted values, 1956–59	121,300
General expense	Avg. of adjusted values, 1955–59	132,200
Replacements	Avg. of adjusted values, 1955–59	137,000
Subtotal		$1,042,100
General and Unallocated:		
Purchased power	Avg. purchases @ 2.875 mills/kwh	115,000
Customer metering	Avg. of adjusted values, 1956–59	5,800
Rent, wheeling expense	Avg. of values, 1954–59	874,400
Meter rentals	Trend	9,000
Power accounting, collecting	Avg. of adjusted values, 1953–59	28,800
Power marketing	Avg. of adjusted values, 1955–59	5,700
Water marketing	Avg. of adjusted values, 1956–59	45,900
General expense	Avg. of adjusted values, 1953–59	339,000
Replacements	Avg. of values, 1956–59	51,500
Total		$7,046,700

[a] In this and most of the following items, the adjustment consists of assuming a 3 per cent annual price increase, treating 1959 as the base year.
[b] Most of the operating costs of these facilities consist of charges for electric power, which in the Bureau's accounts is valued at an arbitrary transfer price. We have adjusted these reported costs to value the power at the benefits it would provide if disposed of externally by the Bureau.
SOURCE: See text.

The preceding paragraph has covered the estimation of operation and maintenance costs for the Bureau's major canals, but not the pumping costs incurred by the Contra Costa and Delta-Mendota canals. These annual average costs decline with the scale of operations, but do not reflect such relatively clear functional relations as operation and maintenance costs. The figures in Table C-2 are estimated from historical functional relations. In the Bureau's published accounts these pumping costs rest upon an arbitrary charge placed by the Bureau upon electric power generated at its hydro installations and transferred to the pumps. We have adjusted this transfer price to set it equal to the benefits of comparable power provided to outside users; this benefit estimate is discussed below.

The operating costs of the power plants at Shasta Dam and its afterbay dam, Keswick, are hard to estimate because of inadequate data. This information is available for even fewer years than that relating to operation of the canals, although power generation at Shasta and Keswick has been going on longer. The data suggest that the average flow of the Sacramento River in Shasta Reservoir of 6,110,000 acre-feet (based on 1938-59) will generate approximately 2,400,000 megawatt-hours of electric power, of which about 500,000 mwh would be classed as nonfirm under the Bureau's prevailing interconnections and marketing practices. In reaching these estimates, an attempt has been made to allow for the influence of the Bureau's Folsom and Nimbus dams on the American River after they came into operation in 1956; they are not included in the present benefit-cost study, although their completion significantly influenced the operation of the basic CVP features under examination. At this level of generation, the limited data available on Shasta and Keswick generating costs suggest 0.12 mills per kilowatt-hour for Shasta and 0.22 mills per kwh for Keswick.[6] These low values, of course, do not include all components of short-run marginal cost for these facilities.

Only one more category of CVP costs requires explicit discussion—the purchase of electric power from Pacific Gas and Electric Company (PG&E). In a *normal* year the Bureau's basic electrical system is self-sufficient and requires no purchases. In dry years, however, purchases are required to fulfill existing commitments, so that, in the *average* year, the Bureau incurs some cash cost for the purchase of power. The purchase price shown in Table C-2 is based upon a contractual rate of 1.15 times the price paid to the Bureau by PG&E for nonfirm power.

Commercial Revenues

Although the main focus of this study of the initial features of the Central Valley Project lies upon its benefits, some interest attaches to its performance in terms of commercial standards of profitability. These commercial revenues arise almost entirely from two types of benefit—water and electric power.[7]

The Bureau's power revenues in years of normal operation of CVP arise from

[6] Prior to fiscal 1955, the Bureau's statistics fail to segregate costs relating to Keswick Dam and Keswick Reservoir. For the years since then, no relation between average costs and scale of operation is apparent, and the figures in the text represent little more than averages.

[7] The Bureau's accounts show cumulative revenue from other sources through 1960 totaling only $125,000 (*Water Service Repayment—Review Statement, op. cit.*, p. 60). Such revenues will be ignored in the following calculations.

the sale of the average amount of nonfirm power and of whatever firm power remains after satisfying the pumping requirements of the Delta-Mendota and Contra Costa canals. From the estimate of power generation at Shasta and Keswick in a year of typical runoff we must subtract an estimate of the power requirements of the canals when operating at their normal rate of diversion. When operating at anything near full capacity in the 1950's, both sets of pumps consumed power at a highly consistent rate in kilowatt-hours per acre-foot pumped. The figure for Contra Costa is about 205 kwh, that for Delta-Mendota about 225 kwh. When multiplied by the expected normal rates of diversion,[8] these pumps consume 345,000 megawatt-hours of the estimated normal generation of 1,900,000 mwh of firm power. A small allowance for other interdepartmental uses brings the total to 355,000 mwh. Thus, in a normal year, the Bureau would produce for commercial sale 1,545,000 mwh of firm power and 500,000 mwh of nonfirm power.

The most direct approach to determining sale prices for this power is to examine the revenue yield of the contracts in force between the Bureau and power users. Revenue received from sales of nonfirm power (to Pacific Gas and Electric Company) has fluctuated narrowly around an average receipt of 2.5 mills per kilowatt-hour, rendering it clearly the appropriate price to assume. The proper price for firm power involves somewhat greater complications. The average price received by the Bureau for its firm power fell steadily over the 1950's due to a major shift in the composition of its customers. These customers include PG&E, which has paid a relatively high price for firm power (6 mills/kwh or more in most years), and a small number of public districts having the status of "preference customers" under federal reclamation policies. The smaller public agencies have paid between 4.5 and 5 mills/kwh while the largest preference customer, Sacramento Municipal Utility District (SMUD), has paid only a little over 4 mills/kwh. During the past decade, SMUD's purchases of firm power have risen sharply as a share of the total and PG&E's have dropped, causing the reduction of average unit revenue. Unless the Bureau changes its basic pricing decisions, this trend will continue, and so a net unit revenue of 4.35 mills/kwh would be appropriate for an average year over the economic life of the Project. These estimates of power generation and prices received are summarized in Table C-3 along with the implied annual revenue from commercial power sales.[9]

It should be noted that taking the Bureau's prices for power as a measure of potential commercial revenue may involve a conservative bias. The price given to Sacramento Municipal Utility District is widely regarded as a low one (renegotiable by the terms of the contract), and the PG&E sales contract has often been attacked in Congress as lacking in mutuality.[10]

[8] On the basis of experience to date, the Delta-Mendota Canal is assumed to experience transmission losses of 10 per cent of all water delivered, the Contra Costa Canal 12 per cent of all deliveries.

[9] The preceding analysis has run entirely in terms of power deliveries rather than generation, thus containing an assumption that losses are proportional to deliveries—an assumption which appears to be relatively accurate. In fiscal 1960, unaccounted losses amounted to about 5.5 per cent of total generation. See U.S. Department of the Interior, Bureau of Reclamation, Region 2, *Central Valley Project, Annual Report to the Federal Power Commission for the Year Ending June 30, 1960,* pp. 85, 86.

[10] See *Central Valley Project Documents, Part 2, op. cit.,* pp. 286–348, 352–53.

TABLE C–3
POWER GENERATION AND SALES, SHASTA AND KESWICK POWER PLANTS, NORMAL YEAR

Type of customer	Firm or nonfirm	Price (mills/kwh)	Quantity (mwh)	Revenue
Commercial customers	Firm	4.35	1,545,000	$6,720,750
Interdepartmental, total	Firm	0	355,000	
Tracy pumping plant	Firm		322,000	
Contra Costa Canal	Firm		23,000	
Other	Firm		10,000	
Pacific Gas and Electric Co.	Nonfirm	2.5	500,000	1,250,000
Total			2,400,000	$7,970,750

SOURCE: See text.

Estimating project revenues from water service raises a question of greater difficulty than estimating those for electric power. The power output of the Central Valley Project in a normal year can be crudely estimated without too much difficulty on the basis of past experience. The water output of Shasta Dam during the months of heaviest consumption, however, is a more controversial and difficult matter. The question of how much water is the Bureau's to sell has been fought over at length in hearings before the California State Water Rights Board, during which a mountain of evidence has been accumulated. Prospective revenue is easy enough to calculate for those contractual arrangements already in effect. Table C-4 shows the expected revenue under these contracts in a year of normal deliveries. For most irrigation contracts, the contractual maximum quantities of water can be assumed to approximate closely annual deliveries over the economic life of the Project, except for an initial period of development. The maximums contained in contracts for municipal and industrial water, however, allow substantial room for the growth of demand. We have followed the same procedure in estimating both revenues and benefits from agricultural and municipal and industrial water supplies. We have assumed a steady growth over an initial period of ten years to an "ultimate" value. The ultimate value for agriculture clearly corresponds to a stage of maximum development. For the much smaller municipal and industrial demand, however, it represents something of a guess concerning the average level likely to prevail for several decades following the initial ten years of operation.

All water deliveries covered in Table C-4 are estimated from contracts presently in force with two exceptions: the city of Fresno is assumed to reach a contract for municipal water which will eliminate the overdraft on its ground-water supplies;[11] additional contracts in the Delta-Mendota service are assumed for the quantity of water discussed above.

Now we turn to the more fundamental question of estimating the water output of Shasta Dam during the dry summer months relative to the quantity of water captured and sold by the Bureau. This problem bears not only on the potential

[11] The Fresno contract will also clearly claim the last of the Bureau's firm supply of water from the San Joaquin River.

TABLE C–4
CENTRAL VALLEY PROJECT REVENUES FROM WATER SERVICE CONTRACTS, SHASTA, DELTA, AND FRIANT DIVISIONS

Service area	Type of service	Price per acre-foot	Normal quantity (acre-feet)	Total revenue
Shasta Dam	M&I[a]	$20.00	2,000	$ 40,000
Delta-Mendota Canal	Class 1	3.50	431,100	1,508,850
	Waterfowl conservation	1.50	68,900	103,350
	Exchange	0	800,000	0
Subtotal			1,302,000	1,652,200
Contra Costa Canal	M&I	10.00	95,000	950,000
	Class 1	3.50	5,000	17,500
Subtotal			100,000	967,500
Friant Dam	Class 1	3.50	710,000	2,485,000
	Class 2	1.50	389,900	584,850
	M&I	10.00	31,000	310,000
	M&I	20.00	100	2,000
Subtotal			1,131,000	3,381,850
Total			2,533,000	$6,001,550

[a] Municipal and industrial.
SOURCE: See text.

commercial water service revenues of the Bureau, but also on many other questions. Do the Bureau's water sales from the Delta equal, exceed, or fall short of its increment to Delta supplies during critical months? How much could the Delta export using "surplus" water and without any increased storage at all? How does Shasta's net contribution to usable flows in the Sacramento River compare to the increased demand of long-time Sacramento diverters since Shasta's construction, and to the demand of newly irrigated areas along the Sacramento? The answers to these questions underlie an issue of great importance to the benefit-cost evaluation of CVP's basic features as well as to the estimation of its revenues: the economic separability of the works south of the Delta from Shasta Dam. Would the south-of-Delta works have been feasible without Shasta? Assuming Shasta's feasibility, were the south-of-Delta works a wise increment to it?

Numerous reports prepared by the Bureau and the California Department of Water Resources bear upon these issues. Each, however, was prepared for its own purposes and based on whatever assumptions seemed appropriate. Manipulation of these studies to answer different questions has raised grave problems, and the reader should keep in mind that, at best, the following estimates may be based upon some set of operating rules for the Project which are optimal for an objective other than that at hand.

Shasta Dam's primary function is to augment the flow of the Sacramento River during months of the year when water demands along the channel and in the Delta would otherwise exceed supply.[12] What has been the size of its contribution? Table C-5 contains some estimates of the size of Shasta's net releases during the critical five months (June through October) of the irrigation season and of certain competing demands which might be viewed as drawing upon Shasta's releases. The first of these competing demands (line 2 in Table C-5) is net diversions from the Sacramento River between Shasta Dam and the Sacramento-San Joaquin Delta. They increased on the average by more than a half-million acre-feet annually in the fifteen-year period after Shasta's construction (1943-57), and can at a maximum be interpreted as intercepting Shasta's releases to this extent. Furthermore, net depletions reduced the average inflows to the Delta from other rivers during the same critical months by an average of 374,000 acre-feet (line 3), and Shasta can be viewed as making up the difference in Delta water supplies caused by these depletions. Charging both of these items against Shasta's net releases leads to the conclusion (line 5) that, at a minimum, the reservoir contributes only 66,000 acre-feet per year to Delta supplies after intervening demands are taken into account. The maximum imputable contribution would be Shasta's actual net releases at the dam site (line 4).

Depending upon the interpretation chosen, Shasta's contribution to Delta water supplies appears either clearly adequate or clearly inadequate to support the diversions made by the Bureau via the Delta-Mendota and Contra Costa pumps. Because

TABLE C-5

EFFECT OF SHASTA RESERVOIR OPERATION AND CHANGES IN DIVERSIONS ON SACRAMENTO RIVER AND DELTA WATER SUPPLIES, JUNE-OCTOBER, 1922–1957

(Thousands of acre-feet)

Item	Average of annual total flows, June-October		Difference
	1922–1942 (before Shasta)	1943–1957 (after Shasta)	
1) Net release from Shasta (addition to flow of Sacramento River)	0	967	+967
2) Net diversions from Sacramento River, Shasta to city of Sacramento[a]	798	1,325	+527
3) Net inflow to Delta, all rivers except Sacramento	1,326	925	−374
4) Maximum addition to Delta supplies imputable to operation of Shasta (line 1)			+967
5) Minimum addition to Delta supplies imputable to operation of Shasta (1 − 2 + 3)			+66

[a] The city of Sacramento lies below all points of substantial diversion from the Sacramento River channel and just above the Delta and the Sacramento's junction with many other rivers.

SOURCE: Computed from California Department of Water Resources, *1957 Joint Hydrology Study, Sacramento River and Sacramento-San Joaquin Delta* (1958), Tables 10, 40, 88, 128; *idem*, Division of Resources Planning, *Surface Water Flow*, Bulletins No. 23–54 through 23–57 (1955–1958); U.S. Department of the Interior, Geological Survey, *Surface Water Supply of the United States*, Water Supply Papers (various numbers).

[12] The consequence of excess demand in the Delta, lying at sea level, is not a dry channel, but rather excessively saline water caused by the intrusion of salt water through San Francisco Bay.

of a lack of statistical information developed consistently over time, we can make a comparison based on historical data for only two years, 1953 and 1954. Interpreted by the method presented in Table C-5, Shasta's maximum contributions were 991,000 and 1,405,000 acre-feet respectively in those years, and its minimum contributions were zero in each of them. The Bureau diverted an average of 618,000 acre-feet in the critical months of those two years through the Delta-Mendota Canal and 35,000 acre-feet through the Contra Costa Canal, a total of 653,800 acre-feet. Since the diversions from the Sacramento channel and from other rivers emptying into the Delta in fact intervene between Shasta Dam and the Bureau's Delta pumps, the most realistic physical interpretation of these data would hold that the Bureau does not succeed in delivering to the Delta, the central transfer point in its operations, water supplies equal to its gross diversions therefrom.

To explore the connection between Shasta and the Delta diversions over a longer period of time, we must turn from historical facts to an extensive hypothetical study prepared by the Bureau showing the effect of operation of the main Central Valley Project features over the rainfall sequence actually experienced from 1921 to 1954.[13] This study unfortunately includes many more factors than would be desirable for the purpose at hand, and, in removing them, some ambiguities enter into the amended results. For example, the Bureau's study includes not only Shasta but also Folsom and Trinity dams. Their net releases can be subtracted readily enough, but the release pattern assumed for Shasta, presumably optimal when all three major storage reservoirs operate as a team, becomes evidently inefficient for the operation of Shasta alone. Nonetheless, this operation study is the only source for long-term estimates of water demand and availability relating to the Central Valley Project. The study also assumes full development of CVP's uncompleted Sacramento canals unit, drawing 740,000 acre-feet annually from the river between Shasta and the city of Sacramento, and allows for further increases in diversions by historic users of the channel. Finally, it assumes a continuous outflow of water from the Delta toward San Francisco Bay of 1,500 cubic feet per second, enough to protect the Bureau's pump intakes and the bulk of the Delta farm lands from significant damage by the intrusion of saline water.

Over the three decades covered by this hypothetical study, Shasta's storage was necessary to supply an average of 109,000 acre-feet per year of the Bureau's exports through the Delta-Mendota Canal. These exports averaged 1,041,000 acre-feet to satisfy the exchange contract (including conveyance losses) and 625,000 acre-feet of water sold under contract to users along the canal. This estimate of Shasta's supplemental effect takes into account the contractual agreement of the Delta-Mendota customers to accept short deliveries in dry years; that is, Shasta's average contribution of 109,000 acre-feet goes to meet the Bureau's contractual obligations but does not give a constant supply from year to year.[14]

[13] U.S. Department of the Interior, Bureau of Reclamation, Region 2, *Central Valley Project Operation Study, Shasta Reservoir Operation, for Hydrologic Period 1921–22 through 1953–54,* USBR Exhibits No. 164 and 164A, Applications 5625 *et al.,* California State Water Rights Board (1959).

[14] During a year of normal runoff, the Bureau would transmit 1,070,000 acre-feet under the exchange contract and 647,000 acre-feet under sale contracts. The excess of these figures over those given in the text indicates the average shortage due to subnormal runoff—2.7 and 3.4 per cent respectively.

To indicate the variation of Shasta's net contributions from year to year, the values for the thirty-three water years between 1921-22 and 1953-54 lay below 50,000 acre-feet in nine years; 50,000 to 100,000 in five; 100,000 to 150,000 in eight; 150,000 to 200,000 in eight; and over 200,000 in three years. The need for Shasta's contribution always falls in about the same months—July through October in all years, June about half of the time, and, during very dry years, in April and May.

To summarize the calculations of the preceding paragraphs, both actual experience with CVP operations and the Bureau's hypothetical operations study show that, in terms of water supply, there is little connection between the operation of Shasta Dam and the Bureau's works south of the Delta. The historical data show that most of Shasta's flows are in fact intercepted short of the Tracy pumps and put to other uses. The hypothetical operation study suggests that only a small fraction of the annual export through the Delta-Mendota Canal depends on Shasta releases to augment the surplus of other sources of water to the Delta over other uses within the Delta and along the Sacramento channel.

These findings place a wide band of uncertainty about the conclusions which can reasonably be drawn about the potential commercial revenues of the Central Valley Project. Ignoring for the moment the legal aspects of the matter, one could say that the Bureau has captured for sale *both* the water which it diverts and exports from the Delta and that which it stores and subsequently releases from Shasta Dam (the two overlapping only slightly). At the other extreme, one might hold that the Bureau should get credit for the sale only of that water which it shepherds from Shasta to the Delta pumps and then to southern users (plus perhaps a charge for transport services for the Delta surplus not resulting from Shasta). Many intermediate interpretations could be constructed. As a matter of legal fact, the Bureau has an apparently firm right to divert and collect for its Delta exports, and has also reached agreements whereby the channel users will pay for diversions in excess of the average natural flow.

Considering these legal and economic conditions, a reasonable minimum for water service revenues from the Bureau's Delta-Mendota Canal and Contra Costa Canal would seem to be the full amount which the Bureau has actively and prospectively under sales contract (shown above in Table C-4) plus an allowance for revenues from Sacramento channel users. The natural flow of the Sacramento during the irrigation season, May through September, was 1,393,000 acre-feet on the average between 1921 and 1954—412,000 acre-feet less than average post-Shasta diversions.[15] At the recently agreed price of $2 an acre-foot, collecting for this increase of diversions over natural flow would yield the Bureau $824,000 per year, in addition to revenues shown in Table C-4.

Agricultural Benefits

The Bureau of Reclamation compiles large quantities of data on the actual and prospective farm output in the service areas of its irrigation projects which serve, when supplemented from other sources, to show the Central Valley Project's net

[15] Computed from California Department of Water Resources, *1957 Joint Hydrology Study, Sacramento River and Sacramento-San Joaquin Delta* (1958), Tables 3 and 88.

benefits from irrigation uses. The Bureau estimates the *payment capacity* of each district with which it contracts, this capacity being the excess of revenues from farm crops over the costs of all other inputs but water, once the district has come to utilize fully the supply of surface water. Neglecting for the moment how the Bureau estimates these costs and revenues, the basic concept is closely related to that of net value of average product for the water in question. Total benefits are thus measured *inclusive* of producers' surpluses (B'), rather than as a quantity of water supplied multiplied by marginal value of water (B).

A complication arises at the start, for the Central Valley Project was built to serve largely as a supplemental source of water to areas already partly developed for irrigated agriculture, using water pumped from underground aquifers or diverted from local streams. The CVP should obviously be credited at most with the average net productivity of the extra water supplied to an already partly developed economy. Added to previous supplies, the Project's water certainly confers benefits where it permits additional acres to be devoted to irrigated crops. It may permit larger quantities of water to be applied to presently irrigated lands in order to increase crop yields, or more profitable crops to be grown. Finally, it may lower the cost of obtaining previous native water supplies from the underground basins, since CVP water permanently sunk into the basins raises the water table and reduces pumping costs.

Many issues arise about the quality and appropriateness of data available for measuring the net benefits which should be credited to the Central Valley Project. The Bureau's method of estimating the costs of other inputs has not changed drastically since the first CVP contracts were executed and it proves reasonably satisfactory for the present calculations. The approach taken in its *Factual Report* series (in which a study is published for each contracting district) combines information on land classifications and productivities, farm and crop budget studies, and forecasts of the crop mix and the scale of farm enterprises under full irrigation development. Each of these links has its weaknesses. The farm budget studies raise problems common to all small nonrandom samples. Forecasts of the future crop mixes derive from current trends and the judgment of local observers rather than, say, an estimate of those which would maximize farmers' profits. Similarly, the forecasts of the scale of farm enterprises rest upon local judgment and comparison to similar areas under full irrigation development. No easy method exists for improving on any of these forecasts, however. To the farm budget studies there is simply no alternative. Crop patterns in some areas seem subject to many degrees of freedom; a long lag may occur before farmers are willing to try a profitable crop not previously grown in an area, but it may be adopted widely once grown successfully. Thus, available data afford no simple method for improving on the Bureau's forecasts of crop patterns. Finally, the size of farm enterprises does not seem subject to any very precise set of determinants, despite the fact that heavy fixed costs associated with the individual farm enterprise cause average unit costs per crop to vary sensitively with the size of farm.

The Bureau's methods of handling individual input costs are largely acceptable. Debt service costs to the farm enterprise are based upon land prices prevailing before the Project, but property taxes are assumed to increase in proportion to the probable increase of land values. Reasonable depreciation schedules cover fixed inputs other than land, and the Bureau estimates local prices for both fixed and current input items. In most investigations an allowance has been made for implicit wages to members of the farm family.[16] The Bureau's reports continually suggest that these calculations are made with care so as not to understate costs. The assumption about the size of the typical farm and the assumed crop yields have been described as conservative.[17] Apparently an allowance of 5 per cent is often added to the costs reported in farm budget or crop budget studies "to cover the numerous small items of expense which are not included in any of the other costs of production,"[18] but this practice is probably well justified by underreporting.

In addition to the actual and imputed costs of current farm operation and depreciation, the Bureau includes a "farm family living allowance" as a cost in estimating payment capacity. This practice is acceptable for the present study if the allowance can be designated as an imputed entrepreneurial return. The Bureau used $1,600 for the living allowance measured in World War II prices and $2,250 in the prices of the 1950's. These sums, added to imputed family labor income, have been described as meeting basic family needs or as bringing family income to the level where saving becomes possible. The resulting family incomes correspond reasonably well to those actually prevailing in comparable sectors of California agriculture. The living allowance, then, should be allowed as a cost to reflect the opportunity cost of farm families in reclamation service areas. This decision does not, however, justify the Bureau's practice of counting the family living allowance for new families on a project as a benefit when computing benefit-cost ratios.[19]

More serious difficulties arise when the Bureau estimates prices to be received by farmers in determining payment capacity for water. The earliest of the Bureau's repayment studies for the Central Valley Project took both the prices paid and received by farmers in the years 1939-1944 as a basis for projecting prices, costs, and payment capacity. The prices of certain specialty crops, however, were assumed to fall to 10 to 25 per cent below their uncontrolled wartime levels. In the early 1950's, the Bureau changed its assumptions about farm prices received as part of its general effort to bring its practices into line with those recommended by the Federal Inter-Agency River Basin Committee in the so-called "Green Book."[20] As

[16] See F. S. Scott, Jr., "Some Weaknesses in the Use of Imputed Values for Unpaid Family Labor and Family Living Allowance in Determining Payment Capacity," *Journal of Farm Economics,* XXXVI (August 1954), 526–29.

[17] See, for example, U.S. Department of the Interior, Bureau of Reclamation, Region 2, *Factual Report, Panoche Water District* (1954), p. 17, and *Factual Report, Porterville Irrigation District* (1954), p. 12. (All reports in this series are hereinafter cited as *Factual Report,* followed by the name of the agency studied.)

[18] *Factual Report, Solano Irrigation District* (1950), p. 42.

[19] See Otto Eckstein, *Water-Resource Development: The Economics of Project Evaluation* (1958), pp. 197–200. In at least some studies of payment capacity, the Bureau has allowed as a cost of farm operations the accumulation each year of a 1 per cent equity in the farm itself. Such an inclusion is not proper unless this can be justified as an addition to the family living allowance. But since the living allowance itself is not conspicuously low as a measure of opportunity cost, this equity allowance has not been removed. See *Factual Report, Eagle Field Water District* (1958), p. 8.

[20] Federal Inter-Agency River Basin Committee, *Proposed Practices for Economic Analysis of River Basin Projects,* Report by Subcommittee on Benefits and Costs (1950).

a result of this effort to standardize practice among the federal agencies, the Bureau of Agricultural Economics (BAE) began issuing forecasts of farm prices paid and received. In 1951, BAE recommended the use of an index of 215 (1910-1914 = 100) for both prices received and paid by farmers. This assumption, which was adopted by the Bureau of Reclamation, extrapolated the parity ratio between prices received and paid then prevailing, but predicted levels for both of them would settle much lower. It indicated payment capacities for the San Joaquin Valley about 30 per cent higher than those calculated on the 1939-1944 base.[21] In 1956, the BAE recommended a change to an index of 235 and 265 for prices received and paid respectively, implying a fall of the parity ratio to 89.[22] The Bureau of Reclamation, however, chose to assume a value of 250 for prices received and thus a parity ratio of 94.[23] The data on farm prices paid and received in California during the late 1950's suggest that the Bureau of Reclamation's calculations based on index values of 250 and 265 lie right on the mark for that period. Consequently, studies computed on this basis have been taken over without any price adjustment. Those done on other price bases have been converted by the use of index values provided by the Bureau of Reclamation.[24]

The Bureau's estimates for each contracting district's "payment capacity"—the amount of revenue the farmers have left over to pay costs relating to water after meeting all other expenses, including the family living allowance—furnishes the starting point for our adjustments. From the payment capacity of a district with its use of CVP water fully developed, we first subtracted an estimate of the payment capacity which would have prevailed in the absence of the Project. This deletion could not be based simply on economic conditions prevailing at the time CVP began. Through most of the east side of the San Joaquin Valley, ground-water levels had declined on the average for several decades. Without CVP water, the existing irrigated acreage could not have been sustained. Rising water costs would have forced marginal enterprises out of existence, reducing the annual ground-water draft, until the water table eventually stabilized. We have made a crude allowance for the reduced payment capacity in this alternative equilibrium by subtracting from the irrigated acreage before CVP the portion irrigated by what the Bureau calculated to be the prevailing annual overdraft of the ground-water basin. This allowance neglects the higher pumping costs which the remaining farm enterprises would have faced without CVP and is, in any case, no better than the Bureau's estimates of overdraft. But it seemed the best which could be done with available resources.

In many parts of the Friant service area and a few portions of the land served by the Delta-Mendota Canal, a significant benefit of the Central Valley Project will come in the form of higher ground-water levels (and lower pumping costs) sup-

[21] *Factual Report, Shafter-Wasco Irrigation District* (1953), p. 33.

[22] The 215 index implied a parity index of 100, the 1939–1944 base a parity index of approximately 96.

[23] U.S. Department of the Interior, Bureau of Reclamation, Region 2, *Projected Agricultural Prices, Region 2* (1957), pp. i–ii; also see Eckstein, *op. cit.*, pp. 104–08, 197–201.

[24] Several of the Bureau's studies of individual districts contain computations on the basis of more than one set of price assumptions. The ratio between the results of different assumptions could be used to convert the calculations for similar districts.

ported by CVP water permanently sunk into the underground aquifers. Since these areas will continue to pump significant supplies from underground in connection with the use of the ground-water basin for cyclical storage, the reduction in pumping costs constitutes a significant gain. We have estimated the probable recovery of ground-water levels from information given by the Bureau and valued the benefit by the reduction in variable pumping costs.

Still other subtractions must be made from the Bureau's information on payment capacity to convert it to an estimate of the total net productivity of CVP water. Payment capacity refers to the ability of irrigators to pay most or all water costs, not just the wholesale charge for CVP water itself. Operating costs of the local water district must be taken into account—all of the district's costs in the case of those districts formed exclusively to receive CVP supplies, and a portion in districts having partial surface supplies from other sources. The Bureau's estimate of payment capacity is calculated without deducting the costs of a distribution system for surface water in those instances where the district plans to construct one, and in some cases the costs of pumping water from underground also are excluded. Both of these classes of costs had to be included—pumping costs to the extent that they would be higher than without the CVP, and distribution system costs to the extent that their construction is associated with the utilization of CVP supplies.[25]

The basic numerical results for the service areas of the Delta-Mendota Canal and Friant-Kern and Madera canals appear in Table C-6. The computation includes an allowance for additional contracts in the Delta-Mendota service area, taking into account the expectation that these lands will be significantly less productive than those already under contract. To explain the evident differences between the two service areas, the Delta-Mendota area will generally enjoy no benefits from ground-

TABLE C–6

IRRIGATION BENEFITS AND ASSOCIATED COSTS FOR SERVICE AREAS OF THE DELTA-MENDOTA CANAL AND FRIANT-KERN AND MADERA CANALS[a]

Item	Delta-Mendota area	Friant-Kern and Madera area
1) Allocated distribution system capital costs	$14,484,030	$88,993,100
2) Increment in annual payment capacity	7,132,364	22,637,011
3) Annual ground-water recovery benefits	0	705,310
4) Allocated annual district operating costs	1,423,030	6,940,397
5) Increments to annual payment capacity, future contracts	500,000	0
Annual net benefits (2 + 3 + 5 − 4)	$ 6,209,334	$16,401,944

[a] Values expressed in prices of the late 1950's.
SOURCE: See text.

[25] The Bureau's studies of the individual districts contain the numerical basis for all of these estimates. However, in many cases, we have used instead the actual costs of distribution systems constructed and operated after the CVP canals went into operation.

water replenishment because the basins are confined through much of the area and thus do not benefit from local percolation. The quality of any ground-water supplies developed from shallow depths will be in doubt. Operating and capital costs of the district appear relatively much lower in the Delta-Mendota area because, in many small districts, farmers pump or divert directly from the Canal and provide their own distribution systems. This substantially reduces reported costs of the distribution system and district operation, since the corresponding real costs are subtracted before reaching the estimates of payment capacity.

Benefits accruing along the Sacramento channel from the consumptive agricultural use of CVP water remain to be considered. We have shown above that a large portion of the increased summertime flow of the Sacramento resulting from releases by Shasta Dam has not gone to feed the pumps of the Bureau's canals in the Delta but, instead, has been diverted for various users along the Sacramento River. These gross diversions seem to have risen to an average of 412,000 acre-feet more than the natural (unregulated) flow of the Sacramento would support, and to an average of 735,000 acre-feet more than the level prevailing before Shasta's construction. No reliable basis exists for estimating the benefits from these increased diversions, such as the Bureau's extensive investigations of its service area in the San Joaquin Valley. Sacramento Valley benefits, however, will clearly be much less per annual acre-foot than those in the San Joaquin—partly because of lower values per acre and larger water requirements for the typical crops, and even more because supplies before Shasta was constructed served the area relatively fully. To make the roughest of guesses, the benefits per acre-foot must lie somewhere between the sum of $1.50 which the Sacramento users initially offered to pay and the average net benefit levels of $15.80 and $14.90 per acre-foot calculated for the Delta-Mendota (present contracts only) and Friant areas respectively. A net benefit level of $2 per acre-foot would seem a reasonable estimate, taking into account probable low efficiencies of irrigation operations in the area and the fact that this is the agreed price. This level implies a net annual benefit in the Sacramento of $824,000 for the 412,000 acre-feet of average annual use beyond the Sacramento's natural flow, equal to CVP revenues calculated above from the sale of this water.

For reasons indicated in Chapter 15, we have chosen to value the output of price-supported crops at their world prices, adjusted for the costs of the U.S. support machinery, as the best practicable measure of their marginal value. In 1959, a total of 315,885 acres of land in CVP service areas was devoted to the production of such crops—the majority (196,261 acres) to cotton, the balance to sugar beets and a few field crops. The Project provides only supplemental water to many districts, however, and our calculations suggest that the equilibrium irrigated acreage of all crops in the CVP service areas without the Project would be 47.2 per cent of that under full development with CVP water. Making the crude assumption that price-supported crops are distributed proportionally as between acreages dependent on CVP water and upon other sources, 178,159 acres of supported crops would be attributed to the Central Valley Project.

Estimates of the world prices of these crops and of the adjustment to be made for federal costs of storage and administration might be made on a very elaborate basis, but we have chosen to employ only very rough estimates. For cotton, the world price is a relatively meaningful concept, and has been approximately three-fourths of that maintained in the past under domestic support schemes. For field grains and sugar, control programs are sufficiently widespread in other countries that the existence of a meaningful world price is open to doubt, and we have taken what seemed to be the most appropriate price series for commercial export values. To allow for the costs of the federal control programs, we have arbitrarily reduced these world price values by one-third. The resulting total annual deduction from CVP agricultural benefits to allow for farm price support programs thus comes to $19,429,000.

Electric Power Benefits

Benefits from the production of electric power by the Central Valley Project will be measured by the costs of alternative generation facilities. The need to base this measurement upon the alternative costs of power generation in steam plants rather than in other hydro facilities seems clear enough. All measurements of costs of hydroelectric generation must disentangle joint costs and benefits, and so cannot be readily compared from project to project. More important, California does not now have an abundant supply of sites for hydro generation that can produce at lower costs than the most efficient steam plants.[26]

Federal agency practice generally involves calculating the alternative cost of power generation in a plant operating at the average load factor of the common system to which the public facility will be linked. Allowance is made for the greater transmission losses of the hydroelectric plant if it is located farther from load centers, and some other operational differences are taken into account on an *ad hoc* basis. Since about 1953, consistent tax rates have been used in calculating the costs of public and private projects, but the lower federal interest rates are often applied to public projects while the higher borrowing costs of private utilities are employed to calculate the interest costs of private developments.[27]

Within the framework of this generally acceptable procedure, certain specific questions arise in the setting of the Central Valley Project and the power market in which it operates. The power generated at Shasta and Keswick dams (as well as by subsequent units of the Project, Folsom and Trinity) is fully integrated into the Northern California power grid, meaning primarily the system of the Pacific Gas and Electric Company. The Bureau of Reclamation supplies firm power to several public distribution systems and to its own pumping plants and also sells both firm and nonfirm power to PG&E. In abnormally dry years, it buys power from PG&E to make up its deficiencies. These extensive marketing arrangements,

[26] Northern California's principal private electric utility has moved from a system capacity of 63 per cent in hydroelectric installations at the end of World War II to 32 per cent in hydroelectric installations in 1957.

[27] Eckstein, *op. cit.*, chap. 8. For an example of the calculation of power benefits (not entirely by the alternative-cost method), see U.S. Congress, House Committee on Interior and Insular Affairs, *Columbia River and Its Tributaries, Northwestern United States*, H. Doc. 531, 81 Cong. 2 sess. (1950), Vol. VIII, Appendix O.

the load curves of the various uses, and the physical interconnections underlying them determine the load factor which can be achieved for the Bureau's generating plants and the relative amounts of firm and nonfirm power which the Bureau can generate from the average year's flow of the Sacramento River. That load factor is about 59 per cent for firm power, and the ratio of firm to nonfirm power is about 5.5 to 1.[28] This load factor closely approximates the figure of 60 per cent commonly used in alternative-cost calculations of electric power benefits and presumably takes full account of any beneficial role which the Shasta-Keswick generators play as short-term peaking capacity for the rest of the Northern California power system. Thus the alternative cost to the Bureau's firm power would be that of an efficiently located steam plant in the Sacramento-San Joaquin Delta operating at about a 60 per cent load factor. The alternative cost of the Bureau's nonfirm power also can be taken as the variable or short-run marginal cost of producing power in such a steam plant.

Lacking the resources to make an independent engineering estimate, we have considered several available sources of information on the alternative costs of steam generation of electric power. The Federal Power Commission (FPC) annually publishes standardized figures on the operating costs of individual plants throughout the United States, from which those presently operating in California can be identified. Also available is a comprehensive estimate prepared by the California Department of Water Resources of the costs of a large 975,000 kilowatt plant located in the Delta.[29] And Pacific Gas and Electric has provided additional figures on the estimated costs of its Pittsburg plant beyond those reported to the Federal Power Commission.

Of these three sources, the FPC figures prove to be the least promising. They exclude depreciation, taxes, interest charges on debt, other return charges, and general and administrative expenses. Even for those categories of costs included, a national sample would obviously be inappropriate. The use of figures reported by large plants in California founders on the sharp differences in fuel costs stemming from locational factors.[30]

This leaves the California Department of Water Resources and the PG&E estimates, which are summarized in Table C-7. Fortunately, they give relatively similar results when adjusted for differences in assumed load factors and assumed cost of fuel, although some differences remain. The PG&E estimate assumes that all costs except fuel are independent of the plant's level of operation, while the Department's calculation assumes that 35 per cent of annual operation and maintenance cost is variable with output. The Department's assumed plant is fired by two parts gas to one part oil, while the PG&E plant is assumed to use only oil, although the Pittsburg plant in fact also burns gas.

As an initial check on the reasonableness of these figures, the costs estimated for the Department's plant were converted as nearly as possible to the same basis as

[28] The basis of these estimates is explained below.

[29] Figures supplied in letter from Maynard M. Hufschmidt, Harvard University, to J. Margolis and J. Krutilla, April 21, 1961.

[30] See Federal Power Commission, *Steam-Electric Plant Construction Cost and Annual Production Expenses* (annual supplements, 1959–1962).

costs reported to the Federal Power Commission. At its assumed fuel cost, the Department's plant probably would have reported a cost of about 3.75 mills per kilowatt-hour. In 1959, PG&E's Pittsburg plant actually reported 3.82 mills/kwh, and ten steam-electric plants in various parts of California having a nameplate capacity of 300 megawatts or more reported an average of 3.96 mills/kwh. This difference could be the result of different plant capacities or design, the large scale of the assumed plant,[31] load factors, fuel prices, or any of a number of other features. The spread is small enough, however, to make the estimate of the Department of Water Resources look quite reasonable.

TABLE C–7
COMPARISON OF COSTS OF STEAM GENERATING PLANTS IN SACRAMENTO DELTA ESTIMATED BY THE CALIFORNIA DEPARTMENT OF WATER RESOURCES AND PACIFIC GAS AND ELECTRIC COMPANY

Item	Department of Water Resources	Pacific Gas and Electric
Installed capacity (mw)	975	660
Gross generation (mwh)	4,387.4	3,469.0
Plant factor (%)	51.369	60
Cost of plant (land, structures, equipment) ($000)	131,508	70,882
Cost of plant/kw capacity ($)	134.88	107.40
Annual production costs ($000):		
Fuel	12,811	13,828
Other "variable"	658	0
Total "variable"	13,469	13,828
Fixed capacity charge	17,716	8,293
Fuel inventory cost	566	148
No-load fuel	1,170	947
Fixed operation and maintenance	1,219	1,339
General and administration	305	214
Total "fixed" costs	20,976	10,941
Total annual costs	34,445	24,769
Average costs (mills/kwh):		
Variable cost less fuel	0.15	0
Variable fuel cost	2.92	3.986
Variable cost	3.07	3.986
Fixed cost	4.78	3.154
Total fuel cost	(3.32)	(4.302)
Total variable and fixed cost	7.85	7.14

SOURCE: See text.

[31] PG&E's own studies indicate that the 325 MW generating units assumed by the department would be more efficient than the smaller ones which the utility has typically built. See B. W. Shackelford and F. F. Mautz, "An Approach to the Selection of Steam Unit Size for a Large Hydro-Steam System," American Society of Mechanical Engineers, Paper No. 57–SA–99, 1957.

Several adjustments were made to the Department's and PG&E's figures to render them fully comparable and to secure the proper cost inclusions. The first adjustment involved the price of fuel. The Department's estimate places a delivered price of $2.38 a barrel on fuel oil and $0.356 per thousand cubic feet (Mcf) on natural gas. The PG&E study, which was prepared as a five-year forecast, assumed a higher delivered price of $2.87. Fuel oil prices over the 1950's behaved in uncertain fashion with no definite trend. In view of the enormously complex factors which determine the prices of petroleum products, there seems little hope of predicting the course of California fuel oil prices over a half-century span. Therefore, the Department's assumption, representing the actual level of recent years, was accepted.[32] Another adjustment involved the load factor to be assumed for the hypothetical plant. The Department's estimate is 4,500 hours a year, or a load factor of 51.37 per cent; PG&E shows values for both 60 and 80 per cent. New plants, in fact, often operate at factors greater than 80 per cent, but also the addition of a new plant to a going system means the downgrading of some older capacity to reserve status. There is typically no corresponding gain in the load factor for the whole system. Thus the load factor of 60 per cent—that actually achieved by the Bureau's Shasta and Keswick units and typical of the larger Northern California power system—seemed the appropriate one.

Taxes and interest rates must be treated consistently for federal projects and assumed private alternatives in calculating benefits. This can be done either by omitting taxes and interest in excess of the federal rate from the private alternative or adding in-lieu charges to the cost of the public project. The latter procedure raises difficult questions about the amount of property taxes to be assumed, which is yet another phase of the joint-costs problem. So we omitted taxes from the alternative costs of steam generation and used the interest-rate value of 3 per cent commonly applied to the power features of reclamation projects. With this adjustment, the Department's estimate of total cost per kilowatt-hour would drop from 7.85 to 5.16 mills. Adjusting the Department figures further, the total cost per kwh would be 4.88 mills at a load factor of 60 per cent, 5.21 mills at 50 per cent, and 4.64 mills at 70 per cent. The figure of 4.88 mills was chosen to value firm power delivered in the Delta region. The average variable cost of the Department's plant, 3.07 mills per kwh, provided a value for nonfirm power delivered in the same area.

Other Classes of Benefits

In addition to the major classes of benefits discussed in the two preceding sections, many other classes of potential benefits exist which were not studied in such detail. They include municipal and industrial uses, flood control, navigation, recreation, and the repulsion of salinity from the Delta sloughs.

Municipal and industrial water deliveries serve only a little more than 3 per cent

[32] In unofficial estimates (letter from Lesher S. Wing, regional engineer, July 6, 1960), the San Francisco regional office of the Federal Power Commission uses a fuel cost figure which, when adjusted for taxes and transportation costs, almost exactly equals that of the California Department of Water Resources.

of the consumptive demands upon the Central Valley Project. Most of this service takes place through the Contra Costa Canal to urban and industrial areas lying along the series of bays running northeast from San Francisco Bay. Such benefits are customarily valued like those from the generation of electric power—by the next most costly source of supply. That procedure appears quite suitable in the present case. For the Contra Costa service area, more than the usual amount of evidence exists on the costs of alternative supplies because of the active search of some of the industrial customers for the cheapest possible source.[33] Both the Bureau's investigations and the offer of a potentially competitive supplier, East Bay Municipal Utility District, indicated a cost of around $38 an acre-foot for single purpose facilities to serve the city of Richmond. Since Richmond lies farther from the source of water in the Delta than any other portions of the Contra Costa service area, a figure of approximately $30 would more properly resemble an average for the area. An allowance is also made for a small amount of irrigation benefits, based on figures from the Bureau's study of the payment capacity of the area.[34] The sum of these benefits amounts to $3,650,000 annually under conditions of full development.

The basic features of the CVP provide small amounts of municipal and industrial water in the immediate area of Shasta and Friant dams and, prospectively, to the city of Fresno. Benefits from the negligible quantities served to towns in the Shasta and Friant area are assumed equal to the sale price, itself somewhat high in comparison to the costs of pumping ground water in the general area. In the case of Fresno, pumping costs clearly are less than the Bureau's price for municipal and industrial water; and, to generalize broadly, only legal factors are compelling Fresno to strike a bargain with the Bureau rather than outbidding marginal rivals for the local ground-water supply. Alternative pumping costs are thus used to measure benefits. If the water deliveries estimated in Table C-4 are so valued, municipal and industrial benefits outside of the Contra Costa service area would amount to $150,000 annually. Adding the figure for the Contra Costa service area indicated in the preceding paragraph, annual municipal and industrial benefits under full development will come to $3,800,000.

Flood control benefits conferred annually by Shasta and Friant dams and navigation benefits in the Sacramento River associated with Shasta's regulation are estimated by the U.S. Army Corps of Engineers. Lacking the resources for an independent calculation, we have simply taken over a revised estimate provided by the Corps in 1959 and, fortunately, expressed in that year's prices.[35] The Corps' estimate of flood control benefits provides what is presumably an average for two different time periods, 1941-1991 and 1959-2009. Since our interest rests on the fifty-year period 1950-2000, following the completion of the main features of the CVP, we have taken a simple average of these figures, giving $3,280,000 annually. Of this sum, $960,000 is associated with Friant Dam, and $2,320,000 with Shasta. The Corps' estimate of navigation benefits rests on the savings stemming from the

[33] See Chapter 10.
[34] *Factual Report, Contra Costa County Water District* (1950).
[35] Letter from U.S. Army Corps of Engineers District, Sacramento, to Regional Director, U.S. Bureau of Reclamation, Sacramento, Sept. 2, 1959.

use of water transport where otherwise a more expensive means would have been necessary. To this annual saving is added the annual maintenance saving on existing channel facilities below the city of Sacramento permitted by Shasta's operation; the sum is reduced by the annual cost of associated supplemental channel works above Sacramento. The resulting figure for annual navigation benefits is $1,260,000.

The effect of the basic features of the CVP on recreational opportunities in California could be studied at great length, but the resources available for this study have permitted only a casual review. Three types of recreational activities have been principally affected—water sports associated with Shasta and Millerton (Friant) lakes, channel fishing for stream fish and ocean fishing for anadromous fish, and hunting migratory waterfowl. The project appears to have had a favorable effect on the water sports and an unfavorable effect on the fishing and hunting.

Only for the two major dams can any meaningful statistics on recreational use be assembled. Bureau of Reclamation figures reveal an average of 309,000 visitors annually at Shasta Dam in the years 1956 and 1960, an average of 89,000 at Friant Dam. In neither case has the trend been strongly upward. Visitors have certainly made substantial recreational use of the lakes, but the statistics do not permit calculations of the types now employed to evaluate such benefits.

Stream fishing and the propagation of anadromous fish, on the other hand, have clearly suffered from the construction of large dams despite the adherence to minimum releases for fish conservation and efforts to establish artificial salmon hatcheries. Again, the precise deterioration defies any close measurement. Other streams exist for recreational uses, but as the supply grows more limited, the intensity of use on each remaining stream increases. The utility derived by the typical angler presumably falls. Increasing expenditures by the California Department of Fish and Game and changes in its stream-stocking practices reflect these changes.

The Bureau's works affect migratory waterfowl in the extensive grasslands of the lower San Joaquin River. The water rights purchased by the Bureau to permit storage behind Friant Dam covered water that once flooded unconfined over these lands in the winter and spring, supporting native pasture grasses which in turn provided livestock food and a habitat for waterfowl. The termination of winter floods on the San Joaquin threatened to eliminate this important waterfowl sanctuary on the Pacific flyways and led to legislation (P.L. 674, 83rd Congress) authorizing the delivery of water to the Grasslands Water District and to agencies of the state of California for wildfowl conservation. The costs of these operations represent a charge against CVP's worth, since no evidence seems to suggest a significant net improvement of wildfowl conditions from pre-Project days. Furthermore, the reduced grassland acreages have led ducks to take refuge in San Joaquin rice fields, imposing on farmers additional costs to control the depredation of their crops.[36]

[36] See U.S. Congress, House Committee on Interior and Insular Affairs, *Central Valley Project Documents, Part 1: Authorizing Documents,* H. Doc. 416, 84 Cong. 2 sess. (1956), pp. 815–47.

When the effects of the Central Valley Project on lake sports, fishing, and migratory waterfowl are considered together, a casual examination certainly gives no impression of any positive net benefit. We shall assume no net benefits or losses, despite the existence of a substantial possibility that losses on balance have occurred.

The final class of benefits derived from the Central Valley Project relates to controlling the intrusion of saline water to the sloughs of the Delta during the summer months. Prior to the construction of the CVP, salinity intrusion had threatened or actually impaired the yields of the westernmost of the reclaimed islands comprising the Delta's agricultural lands. A good deal of evidence has been prepared concerning the relation between changes in the outflow of water from the Delta and the resulting changes in salinity intrusion, in the course of testing the efficiency of different operational patterns for releases from Shasta Dam. Setting an average level of benefit based on a comparison of salinity conditions with and without CVP, however, poses a difficult problem. In its 1949 report on the large group of features proposed for ultimate incorporation in the CVP, the Bureau placed an annual value of $1,600,000 on salinity-repulsion benefits through enabling "increased crop production on 360,000 acres of irrigated land in the Delta area."[37] No explanation is provided of the basis for this calculation.

As a matter of historic fact, the first two decades of operation of the Central Valley Project have furnished significant benefits to the Delta. The intrusion of water containing more than 1,000 parts per million of chlorides (unfit for irrigation) past the city of Antioch and into the Delta has become much less frequent and extensive. But this gain resulted in large part from special circumstances which did not match those assumed in the present benefit-cost calculation. For most of the first decade of Shasta's operation, the Delta-Mendota Canal was not in operation, and the releases from Shasta during the critical summer months served only to allow increased diversions along the Sacramento River and to aid in repelling salinity from the Delta. Delta-Mendota exports had hardly become substantial before the Bureau's Folsom Dam on the American River came into operation in the mid-1950's, raising American River flows in the critical months without substantial associated increases in diversions. The question becomes, then, whether Shasta Dam alone can support the fully developed Delta export, increased use along the Sacramento channel, and other benefits already imputed to Shasta releases, and still provide a significant improvement in the salinity protection given to some parts of the Delta.

The Bureau currently seeks to maintain an outflow of water from the Delta to the ocean which is only sufficient to keep salinity acceptably low at its diversion pumps at the heads of the Delta-Mendota and Contra Costa canals. These pumps are located some distance from the outlet of the Delta, and an outflow which protects them may fail to protect the lower part of the Delta, an area of some

[37] U.S. Department of the Interior, Bureau of Reclamation, *Central Valley Basin,* S. Doc. 113, 81 Cong. 1 sess. (1949), p. 61. For extensive background on the problem of salinity repulsion, see California State Water Rights Board, *Opinion by Board Member W. P. Rowe concurring in part with, and dissenting in part from, Decision D 990,* Applications 5625 *et al.* (1961).

20,000 cultivated acres.[38] It seems unlikely that under conditions assumed in our investigation the Bureau could achieve much more than that on the average. Since no reliable figures exist to provide a functional relation between salinity intrusion and net returns per acre of the affected agricultural lands, any economic estimate of salinity benefits would seem to be a pure guess. Since the salinity invasion, except for extremely dry years, comes only relatively late in the summer in any case, the impairment of farm income and net returns is probably seldom a total one in the affected areas. Considering the acreage primarily protected by Shasta's releases and the potential net productivity of this land when irrigated with water of acceptable quality, a crude guess of $1,500,000 annually might serve to indicate salinity-repulsion benefits of the basic CVP features.

Benefits and Costs

We have now come to the stage of assembling the preceding estimates of the benefits and costs of basic features of the Central Valley Project to test its retrospective benefit-cost relationships and the efficiency of the release pattern in use. The calculation of greatest interest, the over-all benefit-cost ratio for the project, appears in Table 29, Chapter 15, and its computation from the preceding material was routine, subject to the following comments.

It was clear that some benefits and operating costs of the Project would, soon after its construction, settle down to some normal average level (in real terms) related only to the scale of the Project. Other benefits and their directly associated costs, principally those involving the consumptive use of water, would develop at varying speeds over time. To give some reflection to this comparative behavior, without entering into the purely speculative complexities of diverse fifty-year time trends, we assumed that some of the benefits and costs would require a development period of ten years, after which they would settle down to their long-term level. This assumption reflects closely the Project's actual experience with agricultural water demand; and, while urban water demand is developing at a slower and more prolonged pace, its role in the Project's benefits is too small to warrant separate treatment. Another question which arose in combining our estimates was the proper starting point to assume for the Project. The construction of Shasta Dam was completed in 1949 and of Friant Dam in 1947, but both had long construction periods and began to store water earlier. The canals were not completed until the early 1950's. The prolonged construction period for the basic features of the Central Valley Project did not seem intrinsic to the Project, and so we assumed that all of its physical works were completed simultaneously in the early 1950's. (The price level throughout, however, is that of the late 1950's, 1959 wherever possible.) The levels of the benefits of the Project can also be thought of as associated with general economic conditions from the early 1950's on, but it should be noted that the estimates of levels of benefit are not tied in any narrow way to trends or levels of general economic activity.

[38] The Bureau holds that giving full protection to these lands would involve such high costs in terms of water released to the ocean and such high opportunity cost in terms of other benefits foregone as to be unjustified. This view seems to be fully borne out by the present study. See U.S. Department of the Interior, Bureau of Reclamation, Exhibits No. USBR 154 and 155, Sacramento River Case, State Water Rights Board, Decision D 990.

Appendix D

THE FEATHER RIVER PROJECT—MEASUREMENT OF BENEFITS AND COSTS

1. The California Water Plan and the Feather River Project

The California Water Plan (CWP) is a grandiose, but detailed, engineering plan for developing practically all previously undeveloped surface water in Northern California, distributing some of it in areas of origin, and exporting the bulk of it to areas of anticipated need. It embraces major projects which would capture and store about 21 million acre-feet per year of surplus river runoff in the Sacramento Valley and north coastal region. From there it would transport water southward, in minor proportion to the San Francisco Bay and central coastal regions; in somewhat greater proportion to the South Coastal Basin of Southern California; in still larger proportion to the interior desert areas of Southern California; and in greatest proportion to the San Joaquin Valley. The CWP contemplates diverting about 10.7 million acre-feet annually from the Klamath, Trinity, and Eel river systems from the extreme north part of the state, and about 10.2 million acre-feet per year from rivers feeding the Sacramento Valley. Projected annual deliveries include about 2.3 million acre-feet to the San Francisco Bay region, 1.1 million acre-feet to the central coastal region, 2.9 million acre-feet to the South Coastal Basin of California, 5.2 million acre-feet to the Mojave and Colorado deserts, and 7.6 million acre-feet to the San Joaquin Valley.[1] These estimates are subject to revision with the passage of time, particularly since they rest on very long-range estimates of the growth of urban population in existing urban and farming areas and in desert regions which are now only sparsely populated. (They refer almost entirely to additions to existing water transfers made under the federal Central Valley Project, which could be considered the initial phase of the CWP.) The CWP is strictly an engineer's detailed plan, dealing with demand in terms of "requirements" and not incorporating any appraisal of the relationship of benefits to costs for the numerous projects proposed, even though the economic feasibility of most of them is strongly suspect.

The Feather River Project (FRP), as the first unit of the California Water Plan to be undertaken, draws primarily on that major source of surplus water for export which is by far the least expensive in terms of transport costs to destinations—the Feather River at its entrance to the lower Sacramento Valley. Designed

[1] California State Water Resources Board, *The California Water Plan,* Bulletin No. 3 (1957), especially Plate 8. (This and other footnote references are cited in brief form when they are also included in the Bibliography.)

to deliver an ultimate 4 million acre-feet of water annually, it is predominantly oriented toward supplying urban water to the South Coastal Basin (with about 48 per cent of ultimate estimated deliveries under the FRP), and irrigation water to the southern part of the San Joaquin Valley (with about 34 per cent of ultimate estimated deliveries under the FRP). Correspondingly, it is scheduled to supply much smaller proportions of estimated ultimate FRP deliveries to the San Francisco Bay, central coastal, and Southern California desert regions (areas where a medium-term future need for very much added water is not at all apparent), though it is designed to provide aqueduct capacities to parts of some of these regions which could in the future carry more water than the FRP is scheduled to deliver.

The FRP has undergone a number of revisions in design since it received legislative approval in the 1950's and its first legislative appropriation in 1957. These include a last round of revisions since 1963, and not all design features are yet finally determined, as the following quotation from the latest published report on the Project suggests:

> While major construction proceeds, many facilities are still in various stages of formulation and sizing. Certain features cannot be finally sized until the entire minimum project yield has been committed. The Delta facilities and the San Joaquin Drainage facilities are currently under intensive study in cooperation with agencies of the federal government and with local agencies, and no final decisions have been reached with respect to the nature of the projects and agencies that will construct components of each.[2]

By June of 1964, however, 87 per cent of ultimate total Project deliveries had been contracted for by specific purchasing agencies in specific locations. Thus it appears that the design and size of all major features except the San Joaquin Drainage Facilities (in which the state's share does not importantly affect the costs, revenues, or benefits of FRP) as now described by the Department of Water Resources are approximately fixed, unless the federal government implements the projected Pacific Southwest plan in such a way as to expand the volume of water transportation through California.[3]

2. Official Economic Appraisals of the Feather River Project

Economic analyses of the feasibility of the FRP by the California Department of Water Resources and by outside consultants were generally made after the Department and the State Legislature had become committed to supporting construction of the principal features of the Project. Thus they were made in a setting where objective appraisal was difficult to obtain. Economists within the Department of Water Resources and outside consultants in effect were presented with decisions

[2] California Department of Water Resources, *The California State Water Project in 1964*, Bulletin No. 132–64 (1964), p. 154. (Hereinafter cited as Bulletin No. 132–64.)

[3] The planned features and delivery schedules of the FRP are discussed in Chapter 15 and later in this Appendix.

to evaluate rather than with a range of proposals which depended for adoption on the results of their scrutiny. Under these conditions, it is not surprising that some rather bizarre expedients were employed to arrive at estimates of benefits high enough to "justify" the project on economic grounds.

The most notable overestimate of benefits involved pricing FRP water deliveries to various areas for urban use at or substantially above the artificial scarcity values in urban use which they would have if substantial amounts of irrigation water in the same areas, having much lower values in agricultural use, were prevented from being transferred to higher valued urban uses. This estimating procedure was justified on the grounds that the FRP should have the "merit" of not disturbing existing agricultural patterns of water use. It resulted at the extreme in valuing Project-supplied urban water in a desert area at $150 per acre-foot at canal-side when abundant irrigation water in the area could be transferred to urban use at an opportunity cost of no more than $30 per acre-foot without significantly affecting the supply of irrigation water. For service areas in which local irrigation water was not available as an alternative supply at the margin, a related aberration in estimating procedure involved both (1) valuing a large volume of anticipated FRP water deliveries, at the cost of replacing them with demineralized ocean water (at $150 per acre-foot), and (2) assuming the demands for water scheduled for delivery to be based on much lower predicted resale prices to be charged by the re-wholesalers of FRP water (about $32 in the South Coastal Basin). Much lower contract prices were also assumed to be paid by the re-wholesalers for FRP water (about $63 in the same area).

After the legislature and Department had made commitments, a highly questionable economic analysis of the aqueduct features of FRP (exclusive of reservoir facilities or water sources), incorporating all the aberrations in benefit estimation just mentioned, was submitted by the Department of Water Resources to the State Legislature in 1959. This was prior to passage of the bond act which placed a proposal for a $1.75 billion bond issue to finance the Project on the ballot for referendum.[4] This analysis produced for the aqueduct system a fantastic benefit-cost ratio in excess of 2.5. Subsequently the Department (after passage of the bond act by the Legislature and before the bond issue was approved in the referendum of November 1960) prepared for internal use, but did not make public, three editions of an office report which arrived at an estimated benefit-cost ratio for the entire Feather River Project.[5] This ratio, again derived from very questionable estimates of urban water benefits, was placed at 1.3 for an eighty-year period and with a discount rate of 4 per cent.

Though the main basis of error in Department estimates of benefit-cost ratios for FRP is found in the principles applied in calculating urban water benefits, there has been a further general difficulty with the process of making economic appraisals. Anything resembling firm information on prospective water demands in

[4] California Department of Water Resources, *Investigation of Alternative Aqueduct Systems to Serve Southern California—Feather River and Delta Diversion Projects,* Bulletin No. 78 (preliminary edition; 1959). (Hereinafter cited as Bulletin No. 78.)

[5] Office reports of April, May, and June of 1960 entitled "Information and Data on Proposed Program for Financing and Constructing State Water Facilities."

most prospective service areas began to become available only after construction was under way. (The first feasibility report on a service area appeared in November 1962.)[6] Since then, several more feasibility reports on contracting agencies have become available, but a number of service areas have not yet been covered, and the available feasibility reports are frequently marked by reliance on flimsy shreds of evidence.

3. Notes on Data Concerning Project Costs, Revenues, and Water Deliveries

The data which we employ directly in analyzing the Feather River Project refer to costs, revenues, and benefits. As noted in Chapter 15, we rely on the latest information published by the California Department of Water Resources for data concerning project costs and revenues, and for underlying data concerning physical volumes of water deliveries (used in our own calculations of FRP benefits). We will comment here on the sources and characteristics of these data, and on any special problems of computation we have encountered other than those involved in evaluating benefits.

The costs of the Project comprise a time series of annual outlays for both capital equipment and operation, with the bulk of capital costs and nearly all operating costs to be incurred subsequent to this writing. (Capital costs began in 1952 and are scheduled to be incurred through 1989, with the bulk of them falling between 1963 and 1983, and the peak period of expenditure extending from 1963 to 1971.) The Department has prepared all of the essential components of such a time series of outlays for the whole FRP through the year 2039 (the end of the "project repayment period") in the form of component time series referring to individual project functions and service areas. In these it records past costs as incurred and projected costs as estimated for the design and sizing of project features as currently defined, and on the assumption of water delivery schedules by service areas as currently projected. It has also supplied a parallel time series of actual and projected federal participation in project costs.[7] From these component series, we have compiled a time series of total annual FRP costs net of federal participation in costs,[8] extending through the year 2039 (or for eighty years from the base date of 1960 for which benefit-cost ratios for the Project are computed), as well as accumulating the aggregate of Project cost incurred prior to 1960. Our estimates of the time series of total FRP costs are thus essentially those of the Department as of 1964; it may be noted that no future costs have been adjusted for anticipated

[6] California Department of Water Resources, *Feasibility of Serving the Desert Water Agency Service Area from the State Water Facilities,* Bulletin No. 119–1 (1962).

[7] All cost data referred to are summarized in Bulletin No. 132–64, *op. cit.,* Tables 14 to 22 and Appendix Tables C–6 to C–10.

[8] The federal share of costs in facilities jointly constructed by the federal government and the state is omitted because the corresponding federal shares of benefits and of revenues are not shown or included in our calculations. Federal contributions to the cost of state facilities are omitted from costs to counterbalance the corresponding omission of nonreimbursable benefits in support of which such contributions are made (thus assuming rough equality of the value of these nonreimbursable benefits and the federal contribution to costs).

changes in input prices. The resultant time series has been reduced to a present value of total costs as of 1960 by conventional methods of discounting at various interest rates, with a time horizon of eighty years.[9]

The revenues from the Project comprise a similar time series, beginning in 1962 and extending through the year 2039. The revenue series has one minor and two major functional components: receipts for use of the San Joaquin Drainage Facilities; receipts from sales of hydroelectric power to be generated by the Project; and receipts from water deliveries. Drainage revenues (comprising only about 2 per cent of FRP revenues) have been estimated by the Department on the basis of contemplated provisions of contracts with local water agencies which they intend to execute. The corresponding time series of expected revenues, increasing from 1968 through 2039, is accepted for purposes of our calculations.[10] Electric power receipts as calculated are based on the Department's estimated time series of physical outputs of Project power to be sold (running from 1969 through 2039) and on a calculated unit price for power. The Department has to date made a high and a low estimate of this price;[11] in calculating a power revenue series we have applied the mean of these two prices to the physical output series (or equivalently taken the mean of two power revenues calculated by the Department for each year)[12] to arrive at the time series of FRP power revenues used in our calculations.

The calculation of revenues from FRP water deliveries is fundamentally based on a large group of time series of anticipated physical deliveries of water to each of a large number of purchasing agencies located in the several service areas to which the Project will transport water. Each such series begins in some given year of planned first delivery and registers annual water quantities which increase over time to the level of maximum entitlement, and thereafter remain constant at that level through 2039. (These delivery series are fundamental to our calculations of FRP's benefits as well as to those of its revenues.) As noted above, 87 per cent of ultimate total Project deliveries (a total of 4 million acre-feet per annum) had been placed under contract with purchasing agencies by 1964 (each contract providing a basis for estimating each annual delivery as well as ultimate or maximum-entitlement delivery); and the remainder of deliveries had been allocated among service areas and stated in terms of time series of deliveries by estimates of the Department.[13] (As of May 1965 practically all Project water was reported to be contracted for, with the added contracts generally conforming to the 1964 estimates.) Each of these many time series of estimated water deliveries can be converted into a revenue series by multiplying each quantity by a uniform annual contract price per unit of water applicable to the service area and purchasing agency in question. This price is calculated according to a formula provided in each contract, as applied to estimated costs of supplying the agency, and is designed to amortize all allocable capital costs by 2039 and pay all allocable operating costs until then. Such "annual equivalent unit water charges" have been calculated by the

[9] Certain data essential for projecting the time horizon to 100 years (past the end of the "project repayment period") are unavailable.

[10] Bulletin No. 132–64, *op. cit.,* Table 24.

[11] *Ibid.,* pp. 190–92.

[12] *Ibid.,* Table 26.

[13] *Ibid.,* Table 7.

Department, and we have used them to arrive at our corresponding revenue time series, before aggregating all individual revenue series to arrive at a time series of total water delivery revenues for the FRP as a whole, extending from 1963 through 2039.

The annual equivalent unit water prices for various purchasers in fact have two components: one a transportation charge and the other a "Delta water charge" for water made available in the Delta by the Feather River and Eel River reservoirs via the Sacramento River. The transportation component of each contract price (the size of this component varies widely among destinations) has been taken for use in our calculations from the latest estimates of the Department.[14] The "Delta water charge" component (also an "annual equivalent unit charge") is the same per unit of water for all purchasers, but has been estimated at two alternative levels by the Department, corresponding to the two alternate levels of power revenues mentioned above.[15] In our calculations, we have used the mean of the high and low Department estimates of the Delta water charge, consistently with our use of a similar mean of high and low estimates of power revenues, mentioned above.

The constructed time series of total revenues for all FRP water deliveries has, like the similar series for power and drainage revenues, been reduced to a present value as of 1960 at various interest rates for an eighty-year period extending to 2039, to provide one of the three components of an estimate of the present value of all Project revenues as of 1960.

An alternate measure of revenues from water deliveries is available for this use in the form of an estimated series of annual cash receipts from water purchasers. This series reflects some anticipated annual "prepayments" in excess of annual deliveries multiplied by annual equivalent unit prices, and some anticipated "deferments" of payment as defined by the same standard (the present worth of each payment series being supposedly unchanged as discounted at 4 per cent).[16] We have also computed the aggregate present values of these "cash-flow" series for water deliveries, as presented by the Department, for comparison with the aggregate present value of such revenues calculated from delivery schedules and unit contract prices.

The calculation of benefits will be discussed in the following section of this Appendix. Such a calculation necessarily rests on the multiple time series of water deliveries to service areas and purchasing agencies described above, and also rests in part on the annual equivalent unit contract prices, the derivation of which we have just discussed.

4. Calculations of Marginal and Average Benefits of FRP Water by Service Areas

Our calculations, outlined below, of the marginal and average benefits of FRP water deliveries follow the principles outlined in Chapter 15.

[14] Preliminary release of Table 19 of the Department's Bulletin No. 132–65.

[15] Bulletin No. 132–64, *op. cit.*, pp. 195–96.

[16] *Ibid.*, pp. 187–90 and Tables 24, 27, and 28. Again, we have used the mean of high and low estimates of revenues based on "Delta water charges."

As regards the marginal values of these deliveries by service areas from date of first delivery through the year 2039:

1) For the North Bay Aqueduct area, FRP water is assigned a marginal value equal to the estimated contract price for all years, in a situation where the cost from alternative sources is about the same or lower.

2) For the South Bay Aqueduct area, local irrigation water provides an alternative source of supply from 1962 to 1995, and for this interval the marginal value of FRP water is set at the average payment capacity (net value of average product) at canal-side or wellhead of local irrigation water, below the FRP contract price. From 1996 through 2039, the marginal value of Project water in each year is set at a marginal value in use equal to the estimated FRP contract price (which is only slightly below the cost from alternative sources).

3) For the Central Coastal Aqueduct area, local irrigation water provides a source of supply alternative to scheduled deliveries from 1980 through 2039, so that the marginal value of Project water is set at the average payment capacity (at the farm headgate) of this irrigation water for all years, this value being below the FRP contract price.

4) For the Coachella Valley-Palm Springs area, where there is abundant local irrigation water, the marginal value of Project water is set at the average payment capacity at canal-side of this irrigation water, plus local transport costs, for all years from 1972 through 2039, this value being below the FRP contract price. This value is probably overstated, since the purchasing agencies in the area are to provide their own transportation facilities from the East Branch Aqueduct, and if the costs of these are deducted a more reasonable marginal benefit figure would be zero.

5) For the Antelope Valley-Mojave Desert area, local irrigation water provides an alternative source of supply from 1971 to 1990, and for this period the marginal value of Project water is set at the average payment capacity for this irrigation water (at the farm headgate), this value being below the FRP contract price. From 1991 through 2039, the marginal value of Project water is set at the estimated FRP contract price.

6) For the South Coastal Basin area, the computation of marginal values is a bit more complex. From 1971 to 1974, local irrigation water plus reclaimed waste water provide an alternative source for 413,000 acre-feet of water per year if local irrigation deliveries are cut by 173,000 acre-feet annually from the current 393,000 and reclaimed waste water is supplied in the annual amount of 240,000 acre-feet.[17] For this short interval, the marginal value of Project water is set at an average of the average payment capacity for local irrigation water and of the cost of reclaimed water, at $25 per acre-foot and well below the FRP contract price. From 1975 to 1984, the shift of Colorado River water from use in the Imperial Valley

[17] The supposed potential cut in use of irrigation water exceeds the Department of Water Resources estimate by 60,000 acre-feet, the Department estimate referring to automatic elimination of irrigation because of encroachment of urban uses of land. In our estimate, we have left enough irrigation water hypothetically untransferred that the net value of its marginal product would be well below the marginal value attributed to urban water. Thus, in a sense, we have unreasonably advanced by a short time interval the date at which more expensive alternative sources must be considered.

and adjacent areas in amounts rising to a maximum of 1 million acre-feet annually provides a further source of water alternative to the FRP. This water is assigned a cost of $60 per acre-foot, including $45 per acre-foot for transportation through an aqueduct from the existing Coachella Valley Canal to the eastern part of the South Coastal Basin. Thus, $60 is taken as the marginal value of FRP water from 1975 to 1984.[18] From 1985 through 2039, lower-cost alternative sources no longer sufficing to supply as much water as the FRP is scheduled to deliver (given arbitrary limits we have placed on shifts of alternative water from irrigation to urban uses), the marginal value of FRP water is set at the estimated contract price of $61.35 per acre-foot.

7) For the southern San Joaquin Valley area (principally in Kern County), the relevant measure of the marginal value of FRP water is the net value of its marginal product in irrigation, for which nearly all deliveries are to be used. In calculating this value we have relied on basic estimates developed by David Weeks for Kern County,[19] as applied under the suppositions that Project water will be used principally on previously unirrigated acreage, which is brought under use progressively over time, and that the water will be in comparatively abundant supply relative to developed land in the earlier years beginning with 1968 and reach a stable scarcity level in about the year 2020. Given these suppositions and Weeks' data, we have derived for each year during which water will be supplied by the Project through 2039 a marginal value equal to the average payment capacity at canal-side for lands and crops at the extensive margin. This marginal value rises from a low figure with the beginning of service to $8.50 per acre-foot (a very liberal estimate given Weeks' figures) in the year 2020.[20]

8) For the Feather River area, with very unimportant scheduled deliveries, we have assumed that the marginal value of Project water is equal to the estimated FRP contract price, which appears to constitute a maximal estimate of marginal value in use.

[18] The potential shift of 1 million acre-feet per year is out of a present diversion of Colorado River water for irrigation in the Imperial Valley area of from 6 million to 7 million acre-feet annually. The $60 cost per acre-foot is composed of an estimated $15 value per acre-foot in irrigation use (a generous estimate, given all conditions of irrigation water use in the Imperial Valley) and a $45 per acre-foot transportation cost from the Coachella Valley to the system of the Metropolitan Water District in the South Coastal Basin. This transportation cost is the same as that estimated by the California Department of Water Resources for transporting water from the Salton Sea in Imperial Valley to Perris Reservoir in the northeast corner of the South Coastal Basin. (Bulletin No. 78, *op. cit.*, Appendix D, p. 44.) The hypothetical shift of water from the Imperial Valley to the South Coastal Basin is actually stopped well short of the economically optimal shift, thus arbitrarily elevating the total benefits attributed to FRP water appreciably.

[19] Leeds, Hill and Jewett, Inc., *Report on the Capacity of Kern County Agriculture to Pay for Irrigation Water at the Farm Headgate* (1962), Section C.

[20] The payment capacities for the sample of farms studied by Weeks was greater than the average for the service area of the Kern County Water Agency, and therefore our assumption that added acres to be irrigated by FRP water have equally productive lands is generous. Cost of replacing Project water by pumping would generally exceed the marginal values of irrigation water in use, though not the average values (to be discussed below), according to estimates by Weeks and by the state (see Department of Water Resources office report, "Information and Data on Proposed Program for Financing and Constructing State Water Facilities," June 1960, Supplement, Table C–VI–18).

Before discussion of computation of the average values of the same deliveries, it should be noted that in calculating average values of urban water, the alternative cost of demineralized ocean water is one of the determinants of these values for considerable spans of years in two areas—the South Coastal Basin and the Antelope Valley-Mojave Desert area—though this cost is in no case relevant to the determination of marginal values of Project water. Some interest, therefore, attaches to the probable cost of demineralized ocean water at the earliest date that it becomes relevant in our calculations—that is, in 1985. The Department of Water Resources has generally used a figure of $150 per acre-foot as the cost of such water in its calculations (and misused it, whatever its magnitude). However, recent reports on technological progress with a process of demineralization by reverse osmosis under pressure suggest that by 1985 we can reasonably expect to supply demineralized ocean water for adjacent urban use at a cost not in excess of (and very possibly below) $100 per acre-foot. We have thus assumed this to be the relevant cost of converted salt water in the South Coastal Basin by 1985; and have assumed this cost, plus $40 per acre-foot transportation, to be the cost of alternative water supplies in the Antelope Valley-Mojave Desert area after the same date. Given this, let us review our findings on average values of FRP water in the several delivery districts:

1) For the North Bay Aqueduct area, the average value of Project water for all years is set at the estimated FRP contract price, since that price is as high as the alternative cost of the quantities of water scheduled for delivery, and the average value of Project water cannot exceed cost from the marginal alternative source.

2) From the South Bay Aqueduct area, the average value of Project water, from 1962 to 1995, is set at the alternative cost of water which could be shifted from irrigation (equal to marginal value); and, from 1996 through 2039, it is set at the alternative cost of water from San Francisco's Hetch-Hetchy Aqueduct, minus treatment costs incurred for FRP but not for Hetch-Hetchy water.

3) For the Central Coastal Aqueduct area, the average value of Project water for all years is set at the alternative value of local water in irrigation use, or equal to marginal value as described above.

4) For the Coachella Valley-Palm Springs area, the average value of Project water is similarly determined, on the same grounds that the cost of local irrigation water sets not only marginal value but also a ceiling on the average of FRP water.[21]

5) For the Antelope Valley-Mojave Desert area, the average value of Project water is set equal to the alternative cost of local irrigation water until 1990, and thus equal to marginal value. For the period 1991 through 2039, calculations of average value are based on a marginal value of Project water of about $60 per acre-foot and an alternative cost of demineralized ocean water of $140 per acre-foot including transport. Since average value rises from $60 to somewhat less than $140 by the year 2039, a constant average value of $110 per acre-foot in all years from 1991 through 2039, as registered in present values discounted to 1960,

[21] This value is evidently overstated for the same reason that the marginal value of the same water is overstated—see p. 725, item (4).

represents a very liberal estimate of the average value of Project water in the years involved. Average value of Project water from 1991 through 2039 is therefore uniformly set at $110 per acre-foot.

6) For the South Coastal Basin area, the average value of Project water is set at the level of alternative costs (equal to marginal values) from 1971 to 1984, which is to say at $25 per acre-foot from 1971 to 1974 (local alternative supplies) and at $60 per acre-foot from 1975 to 1984 (alternative cost of Colorado River water). From 1985 through 2039, the marginal value has been set at $61.35 (the FRP contract price) and the cost of demineralized ocean water at $100. Our calculations suggest that assignment of a uniform average value of $90 per acre-foot to all Project water delivered from 1991 through 2039 will adequately reflect the full average value of such water for that group of years, and the $90 uniform average value has thus been adopted.

7) For the southern San Joaquin Valley area, the average value of Project water devoted to irrigation has been set year by year at the average payment capacity for water (net value of average product) at canal-side for all lands irrigated by Project water, including inframarginal lands, using the Weeks estimates.[22]

8) For the Feather River area, the FRP contract price has been accepted as a maximal measure of average value, given the availability of alternative sources and the relatively low average payment capacity for irrigation water in the area.

5. Population and Demand Estimates Made by the Department of Water Resources

It has been suggested in Chapter 15 that rates of discount of at least 5 or 6 per cent should be used in evaluating the Feather River Project because the official estimates of demands for water reflect rather sanguine estimates of future population in Southern California. These estimates, and related unit benefit and revenue estimates, refer to periods of time as long as seventy-three years from now (eighty years from the evaluation date of 1960), and a span of seventy or more years is so long a time that no present estimate of any magnitudes referring to years past 1990 or 2000 could be characterized as "reliable."

More specifically, the crucial long-run population estimates for the South Coastal Basin area appear to be mildly sanguine. This is particularly true so far as they rest in part on the supposition that Southern California will maintain its present proportion of national defense contracts and on the assumption that accumulating smog (already severe) will not be a deterrent to population growth. The population estimates for the Antelope Valley-Mojave Desert area are unbelievably optimistic, predicting a population growth from about 157,000 in 1960 to between about 700,000 (called "conservative") and 1,200,000 in 1990. This growth is predicted for a desert plateau well removed from the Los Angeles metropolitan area, with broiling summer temperatures and without an acceptable winter-resort climate. Yet

[22] Leeds, Hill and Jewett, Inc., *op. cit.*

the predicted growth of the Antelope Valley-Mojave Desert area is based on good climate, advances in air-conditioning, "proximity" to Los Angeles, cheap land, and the opportunities it offers to escape from Los Angeles smog (the future existence of which is denied in analyzing Los Angeles population growth).[23] It is difficult to believe that those making the population estimate in question were intimately acquainted with the geography and climate of the various parts of Southern California. A field survey which we undertook in 1960 of the Antelope Valley and adjacent Mojave Desert area failed to reveal any substantial basis for a rapidly expanding population, and indicated that the major economic potential was for a maintained or expanded Air Force installation, for installations for testing advanced aircraft and rockets, for a strictly limited agriculture, and for a modest expansion of residences—second or primary—by aficionados of rugged desert plateaus.

[23] Bulletin No. 78, *op. cit.,* and California Department of Water Resources, *Feasibility of Serving the Palmdale Irrigation District and the Pearland Area from the State Water Facilities,* Bulletin No. 119-4 (1963).

BIBLIOGRAPHY

Note on Bibliography

This bibliography includes materials in the following categories:

(1) Books and Pamphlets
(2) Articles in Periodicals and Conference Proceedings
(3) Unpublished Dissertations, Memoirs, Papers, and Addresses
(4) Government Documents: Local, State, and Federal

Within the first three categories, items are listed in the alphabetical order of authors' names, these including private firms and other nongovernmental organizations as well as individual persons. In the fourth category, documents are listed in the alphabetical order of the names of the issuing agencies.

Arbitrary decisions had to be made as to whether some entries should be listed under "books and pamphlets" or "government documents." Several reports published by governmental agencies have become classics in the relevant literature, and are often identified mainly with the names of their individual authors. For these, we have generally listed full citations under "government documents" but have inserted the authors' names under "books and pamphlets," with cross-references to the issuing governmental agencies. More numerous reports have been prepared by individuals or private organizations under contracts with government agencies. These have been listed under "government documents" if they were published and distributed by the contracting governmental bodies, and under "books and pamphlets" if published by those who authored the reports.

We have omitted from the bibliography a large number of "legal" citations that appear in footnotes to the text, because they would not be of much interest to the general reader. Omitted are references to provisions of the State Constitution, Statutes, Water Code, Fish and Game Code, Public Utilities Code, Health and Safety Code, and Civil Code of California; to provisions of U.S. Statutes and Code; to decisions and opinions rendered in cases before the California and federal courts; to decisions, orders, regulations, and opinions of California and federal regulatory commissions and boards; to briefs and petitions filed with such bodies; and so forth. The footnotes to Chapter 3 constitute a sort of supplemental bibliography covering most but by no means all such citations. Further, the bibliography does not list numerous newspaper articles and other fugitive materials that are cited in the footnotes. The intensive research scholar should thus not depend entirely on the bibliography for a listing of source materials.

All references aside from those just mentioned appear in the bibliography. For the sake of brevity, footnotes to the text have cited these sources in abbreviated forms.

BIBLIOGRAPHY

1. *Books and Pamphlets*

Ackerman, Edward A., and George O. G. Löf. *Technology in American Water Development.* Baltimore: The Johns Hopkins Press for Resources for the Future, Inc., 1959.

Adams, Frank. See Government Documents: California State Department of Engineering and California State Department of Public Works.

——, and Martin R. Huberty. See Government Documents: California State Department of Public Works.

Alexander, B. S., George Davidson, and G. H. Mendell. See Government Documents: U.S. Congress, House of Representatives.

Alexander, William A. See Government Documents: Lower Tule River Irrigation District.

Bailey, Richard C. *Explorations in Kern.* Twenty-second Annual Publication of the Kern County Historical Society. Bakersfield: 1950.

Bain, Joe S. *The Economics of the Pacific Coast Petroleum Industry.* 3 vols. Berkeley: University of California Press, 1944–47.

——. *Industrial Organization.* New York: John Wiley & Sons, Inc., 1959.

Barnes, Harry. See Government Documents: California State Department of Engineering.

Bechtel Corporation. *New Don Pedro Project: Report on Project Operation Studies.* San Francisco: 1961.

——. *Preliminary Feasibility Report on Yuba River Development.* San Francisco: For Board of Supervisors, County of Yuba, California, 1959.

——. *Report on Economic Feasibility of Pardee Turbine Uprating, East Bay Municipal Utility District, Oakland, California.* San Francisco: 1960.

——. *Report on the Engineering, Economic, and Financial Aspects of the Feather River Project.* Sacramento: 1956.

——. *Report on Mokelumne River Development Investigations, East Bay Municipal Utility District.* San Francisco: 1960.

Benedict, Murray R. *The Merced Irrigation District: An Economic Survey of Farm Incomes, Expenses, and Tax-Paying Abilities.* Berkeley: California Agricultural Experiment Station, College of Agriculture, University of California, 1933.

Beringer, Christopher. *An Economic Model for Determining the Production Function for Water in Agriculture.* Giannini Foundation Research Report No. 240. Berkeley: California Agricultural Experiment Station, Giannini Foundation of Agricultural Economics, University of California, 1961.

Blaney, Harry F., and Martin R. Huberty. See Government Documents: California State Department of Public Works.

Bonner, Frank E., Consulting Engineer. *Report for Oroville-Wyandotte Irrigation District on Proposed Water and Power Development of South Fork of Feather River, California.* San Francisco: 1950 and 1958.

——. *Report for Sacramento Municipal Utility District on Upper American River Project.* San Francisco: 1955.

Bookman, Edmonston, and Gianelli. *Investigation of Supplemental Water Supplies for Modesto Irrigation District.* Glendale and Sacramento: 1961.

Boyce, Ronald R. (ed.). *Regional Development and the Wabash Basin.* Urbana: University of Illinois Press, 1964.

Brandow, George E. *Interrelations Among Demands for Farm Products and Implications for Control of Market Supply.* Bulletin No. 680. University Park: Agricultural Experiment Station, Pennsylvania State University, 1961.

Brewer, Michael F. *Water Pricing and Allocation with Particular Reference to California Irrigation Districts.* Mimeographed Report No. 235. Berkeley: California Agricultural Experiment Station, Giannini Foundation of Agricultural Economics, 1960.

Brinkley, T. C. See Government Documents: North Marin County Water District.

Brown and Caldwell. *Study of Water System Improvements: A Report Prepared for the City of Palo Alto, California.* San Francisco: 1957.

——. *Water System Improvement Program, Thermalito Irrigation District, Oroville, California.* San Francisco: 1955.

Buchanan, J. M., and Gordon Tullock. *The Calculus of Consent: Logical Foundations of Constitutional Democracy.* Ann Arbor: University of Michigan Press, 1962.

Carlson, Sune. *A Study on the Pure Theory of Production.* New York: Kelley & Millman, 1956.

Chamberlin, Edward H. *The Theory of Monopolistic Competition: A Re-orientation of the Theory of Value.* 8th ed. Cambridge: Harvard University Press, 1962.

Chambers, Clarke A. *California Farm Organizations: A Historical Study of the Grange, the Farm Bureau, and the Associated Farmers, 1929–1941.* Berkeley and Los Angeles: University of California Press, 1952.

Ciriacy-Wantrup, S. V. *Resource Conservation: Economics and Policies.* Berkeley and Los Angeles: University of California Press, 1952.

Comfort, Herbert C. *Where Rolls the Kern: A History of Kern County, California.* Moorpark: The Enterprise Press, 1934.

Committee on the Economics of Water Resources Development, Western Agricultural Economics Research Council. *Water Transfer Problems: International River Basin Development.* "Water Resources and Economic Development of the West," Report No. 10, Conference Proceedings, Portland, Oregon, Dec. 4–5, 1961. Berkeley: 1962.

Committee on Public Administration Cases. *The Kings River Project in the Basin of the Great Central Valley.* Washington: 1949.

Conkling, Harold, and Charles L. Kaupke. See Government Documents: California State Department of Public Works.

Creegan and d'Angelo. *Comparison of Cost of Importing Water to North Santa Clara Valley from Hetch Hetchy, South Bay Aqueduct and/or Pacheco Aqueduct.* San Jose: 1961.

——. *North Santa Clara Valley Demand Study, Prepared for Santa Clara-Alameda-San Benito Water Authority.* San Jose: 1960.

Davidson, Ralph K. *Price Discrimination in Selling Gas and Electricity.* Johns Hopkins University Studies in Historical and Political Science, Series LXXII, No. 1. Baltimore: The Johns Hopkins Press, 1955.

Davis, Arthur P. *Additional Water Supply of East Bay Municipal Utility District: Report to the Board of Directors.* Oakland: 1924.

De Roos, Robert. *The Thirsty Land.* Palo Alto: Stanford University Press, 1948.

Dillon, Read & Co., Inc. *Interim Report of Financial Consultants to State of California Department of Water Resources on Financial Aspects of Program for State Water Resources Development System.* New York: 1960.

Dorfman, Robert (ed.). *Measuring Benefits of Government Investments.* Washington: The Brookings Institution, 1965.

Downey, Sheridan. *They Would Rule the Valley.* San Francisco: Privately printed, 1947.

Ebasco Services, Incorporated. *Nevada Irrigation District—Study of Water System and Future Requirements.* New York: 1958.

——. *Nevada Irrigation District—Water and Power Development Feasibility Report.* New York: 1960.

Eckstein, Otto. *Water-Resource Development: The Economics of Project Evaluation.* Harvard Economic Studies, Vol. CIV. Cambridge: Harvard University Press, 1958.

Elias, Sol P. *Stories of Stanislaus.* Modesto: Privately printed, 1924.

Engineering Science, Inc. *Water Requirements of the City of Fremont, California.* Oakland: 1960.

Erlich, Harry, and P. H. McGauhey. *Economic Evaluation of Water, Part II. Jurisdictional Considerations in Water Resources Management.* Sanitary Engineering Research Laboratory, University of California, Contribution No. 42. Berkeley: Water Resources Center, 1964. [See also McGauhey and Erlich.]

Etcheverry, B. A. *Progress Report on Water Supply from Central Valley Project Required for Lands in Kern County.* Berkeley: "Made to Kern County Water Committee," 1938.

Firth, Robert E. *Public Power in Nebraska: A Report on State Ownership.* Lincoln: University of Nebraska Press, 1962.

Gillett-Harris & Associates, and Woodward-Clyde-Sherard & Associates. *Feasibility Studies of Extensions to Irrigation Facilities for Browns Valley Irrigation District.* Yuba City and Oakland: 1959.

Golzé, Alfred R. *Reclamation in the United States.* 2nd ed. Caldwell, Idaho: Caxton Printers, 1961.

Goodenough, Sudman and Overholser, Inc., Tudor Engineering, Inc., and R. E. Hartley, Civil Engineer. *Report and Development Plan, Stanislaus River Basin Area For Stanislaus River Basin Group.* Oakdale: 1961.

Graham, Leland O. *Some Aspects of Federal-State Relationships in California Water Resources Development.* Sacramento: Privately printed, 1961.

Hall, William H. See Government Documents: California State Department of Engineering.

Harding, S. T. *Water in California.* Palo Alto: N-P Publications, 1960. [See also Government Documents: California State Department of Public Works.]

Heady, Earl O., and Harald R. Jensen. *Farm Management Economics.* New York: Prentice-Hall, 1954.

——, and Luther G. Tweeten. *Resource Demand and Structure of the Agricultural Industry.* Ames: Iowa State University Press, 1963.

Hedges, Trimble R., and Charles V. Moore. *Economics of On-Farm Irrigation, Water Availability and Costs, and Related Farm Adjustments.* 3 pts. Giannini Foundation Research Report Nos. 257, 263, and 261. Berkeley: California Agricultural Experiment Station, Giannini Foundation of Agricultural Economics, University of California, 1962 and 1963. *1. Enterprise Choices, Resource Allocations, and Earnings on 640-Acre General Crop Farms on the San Joaquin Valley Eastside.* No. 257. 1962.

——, and ——. *Ibid. 2. Farm Size in Relation to Resources Use, Earnings and Adjustments on the San Joaquin Valley Eastside.* No. 263. 1963.

——, and ——. *Ibid. 3. Some Aggregate Aspects of Farmer Demand for Irrigation Water and Production Response on the San Joaquin Valley Eastside.* No. 261. 1963.

——, and ——. *Some Characteristics of Farm Irrigation Water Supplies in the San Joaquin Valley.* Giannini Foundation Research Report No. 258. Berkeley: California Agricultural Experiment Station, Giannini Foundation of Agricultural Economics, University of California, 1962.

Hirshleifer, Jack, James C. De Haven, and Jerome W. Milliman. *Water Supply: Economics, Technology, and Policy.* Chicago: University of Chicago Press, 1960.

Houk, Ivan E. *Irrigation Engineering.* 2 vols. New York: John Wiley & Sons, Inc., 1951 and 1956.

Hurley, Charles S. *The San Joaquin Valley Water Story. Fresno Bee,* 1958.

Hurst, James Willard. *Law and Economic Growth: The Legal History of the Lumber Industry in Wisconsin, 1836–1915.* Cambridge: Belknap Press of Harvard University Press, 1964.

Hutchins, Wells A. *The California Law of Water Rights.* Sacramento: State Printing Office, 1956. [See also Government Documents: U.S. Department of Agriculture and U.S. Farm Credit Administration.]

International Engineering Company, Inc. *Preliminary Report on Irrigation and Hydroelectric Developments, Upper Yuba and Bear Rivers.* San Francisco: 1957.

——. *Report on Development of Water Resources of Yuba River.* San Francisco: 1961.

Irrigation Districts Association of California. *Minutes of Semiannual Convention* (for various years, 1957 through 1962). San Francisco: 1958–1963.

——. *Water Use and Water Costs in Some Typical Irrigation Districts in California.* San Francisco: 1960.

Jones, Burton, and H. S. Crowe. See Government Documents: Turlock Irrigation District.

Kaiser Engineers. *Engineering Review of Yuba River Development for Johnson Rancho County Water District.* Oakland: 1961.

Kaupke, Charles L. See Government Documents: Kings River Water Association.

Kaysen, Carl, and Turner, D. F. *Antitrust Policy: An Economic and Legal Analysis.* Cambridge: Harvard University Press, 1959.

Kennedy, Clyde C., Engineering Office of. *Report on Water Development Phase I, Supply and Storage for the Paradise Irrigation District, Paradise, California.* San Francisco: 1954.

Kneese, Allen V. *The Economics of Regional Water Quality Management.* Baltimore: The Johns Hopkins Press for Resources for the Future, Inc., 1964.

——. *Water Pollution: Economic Aspects and Research Needs.* Washingon: Resources for the Future, Inc., 1962.

Knight, Frank H. *Risk, Uncertainty, and Profit.* Boston: Houghton, Mifflin, 1921.

Krutilla, John V., and Otto Eckstein. *Multiple Purpose River Development.* Baltimore: The Johns Hopkins Press for Resources for the Future, Inc., 1958.

Lee, Charles H., and Koebig and Koebig, Consulting Engineers. *Feasibility Report for Surface Water Supply, Fresno Metropolitan Area, Fresno, California.* San Francisco and Los Angeles: 1958.

Lee, Ivan M. *Optimum Water Resource Development.* Giannini Foundation Report No. 206. Berkeley: California Agricultural Experiment Station, Giannini Foundation of Agricultural Economics, University of California, 1958.

Lee, Robert R. *Local Government Public Works Decision-Making.* Project on Engineering-Economic Planning, Report No. EEP-9. Stanford: Institute in Engineering-Economic Systems, Stanford University, 1964.

——. *The Santa Clara Water Controversy.* Stanford University, Project on Engineering, Economic Planning Case Study No. 1. Palo Alto: 1961.

Leeds, Hill, and Jewett, Inc. *Report on the Capacity of Kern County Agriculture to Pay for Irrigation Water at the Farm Headgate.* San Francisco and Los Angeles: 1962.

Leopold, Luna B., and Thomas Maddock, Jr. *The Flood Control Controversy: Big Dams, Little Dams, and Land Management.* New York: Ronald Press, 1954.

Lerner, Abba P. *The Economics of Control.* New York: Macmillan, 1944.

Leuchtenburg, William E. *Flood Control Politics: The Connecticut River Valley Problem, 1927–1950.* Cambridge: Harvard University Press, 1953.

Maass, Arthur. *Muddy Waters: The Army Engineers and the Nation's Rivers.* Harvard Political Studies. Cambridge: Harvard University Press, 1951.

——, *et al. Design of Water-Resource Systems.* Cambridge: Harvard University Press, 1962.

Macabee, L. Cedric, Consulting Engineer. *Feasibility Report, Small South Yuba Canal Project for the Wheatland Water District, Yuba County, Calif.* Palo Alto: 1954.

——. *Feasibility Report on the Yuba River Development for the Wheatland Water District, Yuba County, Calif.* Palo Alto: 1954.

McCreary-Koretsky Engineers. *Feasibility Report, Placer County Water Agency, Middle Fork American River Project.* San Francisco: 1961.

——, and T. H. McGuire & Son, Consulting Engineers. *South Sutter Water District, East Nicolaus, California, Camp Far West Project.* San Francisco: 1962.

McGauhey, P. H., and Harry Erlich. *Economic Evaluation of Water. Part I: A Search for Criteria.* Sanitary Engineering Research Laboratory, College of Engineering and School of Public Health, University of California, Technical Bulletin No. 14, IER Series 37. Berkeley: 1960.

McGuire, T. H., and Son, Consulting Engineers. *Camp Far West Project, Feasibility Report.* Grass Valley: 1958.

McKean, Roland N. *Efficiency in Government Through Systems Analysis, With Emphasis on Water Resources Development.* New York: John Wiley & Sons, Inc., 1958.

McKinley, Charles. *Uncle Sam in the Pacific Northwest: Federal Management of Natural Resources in the Columbia River Valley.* Publications of the Bureau of Business and Economic Research, University of California. Berkeley and Los Angeles: University of California Press, 1952.

Main, Charles T., Inc. *General Evaluation of the Proposed Program for Financing and Constructing the State Water Resources Development System of the State of California Department of Water Resources.* Final Report. Boston: 1960.

Mann, Dean E. *The Politics of Water in Arizona.* Tucson: University of Arizona Press, 1963.

Marglin, Stephen A. *Approaches to Dynamic Investment Planning.* Amsterdam: North Holland Publishing Co., 1963.

Mead, Elwood, *et al.* See Government Documents: U.S. Department of Agriculture.

Montgomery, Mary, and Marion Clawson. See Government Documents: U.S. Department of Agriculture.

Nadeau, R. A. *The Water Seekers.* New York: Doubleday, 1950.

Nash, Gerald D. *State Government and Economic Development: A History of Administrative Policies in California, 1849–1933.* Berkeley: Institute of Governmental Studies, University of California, 1964.

Nerlove, Marc. *The Dynamics of Supply: Estimation of Farmers' Response to Price.* Johns Hopkins University Studies in Historical and Political Science, Series LXVI, No. 2. Baltimore: The Johns Hopkins Press, 1958.

Nolte, George S., Consulting Civil Engineers. *Milpitas County Water District Study, Milpitas, California.* Palo Alto: 1960.

O'Shaughnessy, M. M. *Hetch Hetchy: Its Origin and History.* San Francisco: Recorder Printing and Publishing Co., 1934.

Ostrom, Vincent. *Water and Politics.* Los Angeles: Haynes Foundation, 1953.

Pacific Gas and Electric Co., *Annual Report to the Public Utilities Commission.* San Francisco: various years.

Palmer, Charles L. *The Story of the Kings River.* Fresno: "Prepared for Publicity and Advertising Department, Pacific Gas and Electric Company," 1955.

Porter, Urquhart, McCreary & O'Brien, Consulting Engineers. *Feather-Yuba River Development, Preliminary Plan and Feasibility Report for County of Yuba and Yuba County Water District.* San Francisco: 1958.

——. *Placer County Water Agency, General Plan For Proposed Development of the Water Resources of Placer County.* San Francisco: 1959.

Renshaw, Edward F. *Toward Responsible Government: An Economic Appraisal of Federal Investment in Water Resource Programs.* Chicago: Idyia Press, 1957.

Robinson, Joan. *The Economics of Imperfect Competition.* London: Macmillan, 1933.

Ruttan, Vernon W. *The Economic Demand for Irrigated Acreage: New Methodology and Some Preliminary Projections, 1954–1980.* Baltimore: The Johns Hopkins Press for Resources for the Future, Inc., 1965.

San Jose Water Works Co. *Annual Report, 1959,* and *1964.* San Jose: 1960 and 1965.

Smith, C. H. See Government Documents: Kings River Water Association.

Smith, Stephen C. *The Public District in Integrating Ground and Surface Water Management: A Case Study in Santa Clara County.* Giannini Foundation Research Report No. 252. Berkeley: California Agricultural Experiment Station, Giannini Foundation of Agricultural Economics, University of California, 1962.

——, and Emery N. Castle. (eds.). *Economics and Public Policy in Water Resource Development.* Ames: Iowa State University Press, 1964.

Snyder, J. Herbert. *Ground Water in California: The Experience of Antelope Valley.* Giannini Foundation Ground Water Studies No. 21. Berkeley: California Agricultural Experiment Station, Division of Agricultural Sciences, University of California, 1955.

Sorenson, James F., *Report on Water Resources and Water Needs of Tulare County, California, to the Board of Supervisors, Tulare County, California.* Visalia: 1959.

Southern California Edison Co. *Annual Report to Stockholders, 1961.* Los Angeles: 1962.

Spengler, Joseph J. (ed.). *Natural Resources and Economic Growth.* Washington: Jointly published by Resources for the Future, Inc., and Committee on Economic Growth of the Social Science Research Council, 1961.

Stanford Research Institute. *Economic Considerations in the Formulation and Repayment of California Water Plan Projects.* Menlo Park: 1958.

Stoddard & Karrer. *Solano County Water Resources and Requirements.* 2nd ed. Los Banos: 1962.

Stone and Youngberg. *Control and Use of Russian River Water: A Report on the Financial Feasibility of the Proposed Coyote Valley Reservoir and Utilization of Russian River Water in Sonoma County.* San Francisco: 1954.

——. *An Evaluation of the Proposed Joint Contract Approach to a Water Service Contract for the South Bay Aqueduct.* San Francisco: 1960.

——. *Financial Analysis, Camp Far West Project, South Sutter Water District.* San Francisco: 1958.

——. *Financing Report, Water System Acquisition, City of Petaluma.* San Francisco: 1958.

——. *Ibid., City of San Jose.* San Francisco: 1961.

——. *Ibid., City of Stockton.* San Francisco: 1960.

——. *Ibid., Contra Costa County Water District.* San Francisco: 1959.

——, and Charles H. West. *An Economic and Financial Analysis of the Solano County Project (Monticello Dam) and Certain Alternate Sources of Water.* San Francisco: 1951.

Storie, R. Earl, and Walter W. Weir. *Generalized Soil Map of California.* Manual No. 6. Berkeley: California Agricultural Experiment Station Extension Service, College of Agriculture, University of California, n.d.

Taylor, Ray W. *Hetch Hetchy: The Story of San Francisco's Struggle to Provide a Water Supply for Her Future Needs.* San Francisco: R. J. Orozco, 1926.

Teilman, I., and W. H. Shafer. *The Historical Story of Irrigation in Fresno and Kings Counties in Central California.* Fresno: Williams & Son, 1943.

Thorne, Wynne (ed.). *Land and Water Use, A Symposium Presented at the Denver Meeting of the American Association for the Advancement of Science, 27–29*

December 1961. Publication No. 73. Washington: American Association for the Advancement of Science, 1963.

Todd, David K., *Ground Water Hydrology.* New York: John Wiley & Sons, Inc., 1959.

Treadwell, Edward F. *The Cattle King.* 2nd ed. Boston: Christopher, 1951.

Tudor Engineering Co. *Feasibility Report and Plan, Calaveras County Water Development for Calaveras County Water District, San Andreas, California.* 2 vols. San Francisco: 1961.

——. *Merced River Development.* San Francisco: 1960.

——. *Preliminary Report and Plan, Calaveras County Water Development for Calaveras County Water District, San Andreas, California.* San Francisco: 1959.

Tudor-Goodenough Engineers. *Feasibility Report on Merced River Development for Merced Irrigation District, Merced, California.* San Francisco: 1958.

——. *Summary Report on the Tri-Dam Project, Stanislaus River, California.* San Francisco: 1959.

University of California, Bureau of Public Administration. *Irrigation District Movement in California: A Summary,* by J. F. McCarty. A report prepared for the California State Legislature, Assembly Interim Committee on Conservation, Planning, and Public Works. Interim Committee Reports, Vol. 13, No. 5. Sacramento: State Planning Office, 1955. [See Government Documents: California State Legislature, Assembly Water Committee, for other Interim Committee Reports.]

Water Resources Engineers, Inc. *An Interagency System for Water Quality Management.* Berkeley: 1961.

Webb, Sidney and Beatrice. *English Local Government: Statutory Authorities for Special Purposes.* London: Longmans, Green and Co., 1922.

Wehe, Roy A., Consulting Engineer. *Cost and Rate Analysis, Hetch Hetchy Water and Power Divisions, for City and County of San Francisco.* San Francisco: 1958.

——. *Cost and Rate Analysis, San Francisco Water Department, for City and County of San Francisco.* San Francisco: 1958.

——. *Hetch Hetchy Water and Power Division: Separation Study and Power Division, Cost and Rate Analysis for City and County of San Francisco.* San Francisco: 1955.

Wollman, Nathaniel (ed.). *The Value of Water in Alternative Uses.* Albuquerque: University of New Mexico Press, 1962.

Woodward, Guy O. (ed.). *Sprinkler Irrigation.* 2nd ed. Washington: Sprinkler Irrigation Association, 1959.

2. *Articles in Periodicals and Conference Proceedings*

Anderson, Raymond L. "Operation of the Irrigation Water Rental Market in the South Platte Basin," *Journal of Farm Economics,* XLII (December 1960), 1501–03.

Angel, Arthur D. "Who Will Pay for the Central Valley Project of California?" *Journal of Land and Public Utility Economics,* XXII (August 1946), 266–72.

Bain, Joe S. "Criteria for Undertaking Water-Resource Developments," *American Economic Review,* L (May 1960), 310–20.

——. "*The Theory of Monopolistic Competition* after Thirty Years: The Impact on Industrial Organization," *American Economic Review,* LIV (May 1964), 28–32.

Blaney, Harry F. "Use of Water by Irrigated Crops in California," *Journal of the American Water Works Association,* XLIII (March 1951), 189–200.

Brewer, C. Marvin. "Taxation of Water Rights in California," *Journal of the American Water Works Association,* LIII (May 1961), 619–24.

Brewer, Michael F. "The Economics of Water Transfer," *Natural Resources Journal,* IV (January 1965), 522–36.

——. "Local Government Assessment: Its Impact on Land and Water Use," *Land Economics,* XXXVII (August 1961), 207–17.

——. "Public Pricing of Natural Resources," *Journal of Farm Economics,* XLIV (February 1962), 35–49.

Buchanan, J. M., and W. C. Stubblebine. "Externality," *Economica,* n.s. XXIX (November 1962), 371–84.

Castle, Emery, Maurice Kelso, and Delworth Gardner. "Water Resources Development: A Review of the New Federal Evaluation Procedures," *Journal of Farm Economics,* XLV (November 1963), 693–704.

——, and Karl H. Lindeborg. "The Economics of Ground Water Allocation: A Case Study," *Journal of Farm Economics,* XLII (February 1960), 150–60.

Ciriacy-Wantrup, S. V. "Benefit-Cost Analysis and Public Resource Development," *Journal of Farm Economics,* XXXVII (November 1955), 676–89.

——. "Concepts Used as Economic Criteria for a System of Water Rights," *Land Economics,* XXXII (November 1956), 295–312.

——. "Cost Allocation in Relation to Western Water Policies," *Journal of Farm Economics,* XXXVI (February 1954), 108–29.

——. "Some Economic Issues in Water Rights," *Journal of Farm Economics,* XXXVII (December 1955), 875–85.

Cochrane, W. W. "Conceptualizing the Supply Relation in Agriculture," *Journal of Farm Economics,* XXXVII (December 1955), 1161–76.

Craig, Gavin M. "Prescriptive Water Rights in California and the Necessity for a Valid Statutory Appropriation," *California Law Review,* XLII (May 1954), 219–42.

Cromarty, W. A. "An Econometric Model for United States Agriculture," *Journal of the American Statistical Association,* LIV (September 1959), 556–74.

Dawson, John A. "The Productivity of Water in Agriculture," *Journal of Farm Economics,* XXXIX (December 1957), 1244–53.

Durbrow, R. T. "Use of Irrigation Water for Domestic Purposes," *Journal of the American Water Works Association,* XLI (September 1949), 771–76.

Eckstein, Otto. "A Survey of the Theory of Public Expenditure Criteria," National Bureau of Economic Research, Universities-National Bureau Committee for Economic Research, *Public Finances: Needs, Sources, and Utilization.* Special Conference Series 12. Princeton: Princeton University Press, 1961.

Fisher, H. Buford. "Problems of System Expansion by Annexation," *Journal of the American Water Works Association,* LIII (April 1961), 388–96.

Fox, Irving K., and Lyle E. Craine. "Organizational Arrangements for Water Development," *Natural Resources Journal,* II (April 1962), 1–44.

——, and O. C. Herfindahl. "Attainment of Efficiency in Satisfying Demands for Water Resources," *American Economic Review,* LIV (May 1964), 198–206.

Gaffney, Mason. "Diseconomies Inherent in Western Water Laws: A California Case Study," *Economic Analysis of Multiple Use.* ("Water and Range Resources and Economic Development of the West," Report No. 9.) Proceedings of Western Agricultural Economics Research Council, Tucson, Arizona, January 23, 1961, 55–81.

——. "Water Law and Economic Transfers of Water: A Reply," *Journal of Farm Economics,* XLIV (May 1962), 427–34.

Gertel, L., and N. Wollman. "Price and Assessment Guides to Western Water Allocation," *Journal of Farm Economics,* XLII (December 1960), 1332–44.

Goodall, M. R. "Land and Power Administration of the Central Valley Project," *Journal of Land and Public Utility Economics,* XVIII (August 1942), 299–311.

Gottlieb, Manuel. "Urban Domestic Demand for Water: A Kansas Case Study," *Land Economics,* XXXIX (May 1963), 204–10.
Gramm, Warren S. "Limitations of the Theory of the Firm for Water Resource Analysis," *Land Economics,* XXXIV (May 1958), 113–21.
——. "Water Resource Analysis: Private Investment Criteria and Social Priorities," *Journal of Farm Economics,* XLV (November 1963), 705–12.

Hallock, Richard J., and W. F. Van Woert. "A Survey of Anadromous Fish Losses in Irrigation Diversions from the Sacramento and San Joaquin Rivers," *California Fish and Game,* XLV (No. 4, 1959), 227–96.
Harding, S. T. "Background of California Water and Power Problems," *California Law Review,* XXXVIII (October 1950), 547–71.
Headley, J. Charles. "The Relation of Family Income and Use of Water for Residential and Commercial Purposes in the San Francisco-Oakland Metropolitan Area," *Land Economics,* XXXIX (November 1963), 441–49.
Heim, Peggy. "Financing the Federal Reclamation Program: Reimbursement Arrangements and Cost Allocations," *National Tax Journal,* IX (March 1956), 35–45.
Helmberger, Peter G. "Cooperative Enterprise as a Structural Dimension of Farm Markets," *Journal of Farm Economics,* XLVI (August 1964), 603–17.
——, and Sidney Hoos. "Cooperative Enterprise and Organization Theory," *Journal of Farm Economics,* XLIV (May 1962), 275–90.
Henley, Albert T. "The Evolution of Forms of Water Users Organizations in California," *California Law Review,* XLV (December 1957), 665–75.
Hicks, J. R. "The Foundations of Welfare Economics," *Economic Journal,* XLIX (December 1939), 696–712.
Hines, Lawrence G. "The Hazards of Benefit-Cost Analysis as a Guide to Public Investment Policy," *Public Finance/Finances Publiques,* XVII (No. 2, 1962), 101–17.
Hirshleifer, Jack. "On the Theory of Optimal Investment Decision," *Journal of Political Economy,* LXVI (August 1958), 329–52.
Hutchins, Wells A. "California Ground Water: Legal Problems," *California Law Review,* XLV (December 1957), 688–97.

Kaarlehto, Paavo. "On the Economic Nature of Cooperation," *Acta Agriculturae Scandinavica,* VI (No. 4, 1956), 3–114.
Kessel, Reuben A., and Armen A. Alchian. "Effects of Inflation," *Journal of Political Economy,* LXX (December 1962), 521–37.
Kletzig, Russell R. "Prescriptive Water Rights in California: Is Application a Prerequisite?" *California Law Review,* XXXIX (September 1951), 369–76.
Knetsch, Jack L. "Economics of Including Recreation as a Purpose of Eastern Water Projects," *Journal of Farm Economics,* XLVI (December 1964), 1148–57.
——. "The Influence of Reservoir Projects on Land Values," *Journal of Farm Economics,* XLVI (February 1964), 231–43.
Kristjanson, Kris. "Institutional Arrangements in Water Resources Development," *Land Economics,* XXX (November 1954), 347–62.

Maass, Arthur A. "Congress and Water Resources," *American Political Science Review,* XLIV (September 1950), 576–93.
Manne, Alan S. "Product-Mix Alternatives: Flood Control, Electric Power, and Irrigation," *International Economic Review,* III (January 1962), 30–59.
Margolis, Julius. "The Evaluation of Water Resource Development," *American Economic Review,* XLIX (March 1959), 96–111.
Metcalf, L. "Effect of Water Rates and Growth in Population upon Per Capita Consumption," *Journal of the American Water Works Association,* XV (January 1926), 1–22.
Milliman, J. W. "Commonality, the Price System, and Use of Water Supplies," *Southern Economic Journal,* XXII (April 1956), 426–37.

——. "Land Values as Measures of Primary Irrigation Benefits," *Journal of Farm Economics,* XLI (May 1959), 234–43.
——. "Policy Horizons for Future Urban Water Supply," *Land Economics,* XXXIX (May 1963), 109–32.
——. "Water Law and Private Decision-Making: A Critique," *Journal of Law and Economics,* II (October 1959), 41–63.
Moore, Charles V. "Economics of Water Demand in Commercialized Agriculture," *Journal of the American Water Works Association,* LIV (August 1962), 913–20.
——. "A General Analytical Framework for Estimating the Production Function for Crops Using Irrigation Water," *Journal of Farm Economics,* XLIII (November 1961), 876–88.
——. "Value of Storing Stream Runoff for Irrigation Use," *Natural Resources Journal,* III (May 1963), 98–102.
——, and Trimble R. Hedges. "Irrigation Costs of Pumping in the San Joaquin Valley," *California Agriculture,* XIV (October 1960), 3–4.

Orlob, Gerald T., and Marvin R. Lindorf. "Cost of Water Treatment in California," *Journal of the American Water Works Association,* L (January 1958), 45–55.
O'Shaughnessy, M. M. "Present Status of Hetch Hetchy," *Transactions of the Commonwealth Club of California,* XVII (May 1922).
Ostrom, Vincent. "The Political Economy of Water Development," *American Economic Review,* LII (May 1962), 450–58.
——. "The Water Economy and Its Organization," *Natural Resources Journal,* II (April 1962), 55–73.

Phillips, Richard. "Economic Nature of the Cooperative Association," *Journal of Farm Economics,* XXXV (February 1953), 74–87.

Renshaw, Edward F. "The Management of Ground Water Reservoirs," *Journal of Farm Economics,* XLV (May 1963), 285–95.

Scitovsky, Tibor. "Two Concepts of External Economies," *Journal of Political Economy,* LXII (April 1954), 143–51.
Scott, F. S., Jr. "Some Weaknesses in the Use of Imputed Values for Unpaid Family Labor and Family Living Allowance in Determining Payment Capacity," *Journal of Farm Economics,* XXXVI (August 1954), 526–29.
Seastone, D. A., and L. M. Hartman, "Alternative Institutions for Water Transfers: Colorado and New Mexico," *Land Economics,* XXXIX (February 1963), 31–44.
Shaw, Lucien. "The Development of the Law of Waters in the West," *California Law Review,* X (September 1922), 443–60.
Smith, Stephen C. "Legal and Institutional Controls in Water Allocation," *Journal of Farm Economics,* XLII (December 1960), 1345–58.
——. "Problems in the Use of the Public District for Ground-Water Management," *Land Economics,* XXXII (August 1956), 259–69.
——. "The Rural-Urban Transfer of Water in California," *Natural Resources Journal,* I (March 1961), 64–75.
Snyder, J. Herbert. "Institutions, Ground Water, and Overdraft—An Aspect of Irrigated Agriculture," *Land Economics,* XXXI (May 1955), 120–30.
——. "On the Economics of Ground-Water Mining—A Case Study in an Arid Area," *Journal of Farm Economics,* XXXVI (November 1954), 600–10.
Steiner, Peter O. "Peak Loads and Efficient Pricing," *Quarterly Journal of Economics,* LXXI (November 1957), 585–610.

Taylor, Paul S. "Excess Land Law: Execution of a Public Policy," *Yale Law Journal,* LXIV (February 1955), 477–514.

——. "Excess Land Law on the Kern?", *California Law Review,* XLVI (May 1958), 153–84.
——. "The Excess Land Law: Legislative Erosion of a Public Policy," *Rocky Mountain Law Review,* XXX (June 1958), 480–504.
——. "The Excess Land Law: Pressure vs. Principle," *California Law Review,* XLVII (August 1959), 499–541.
Teilmann, Henrik. "The Role of Irrigation Districts in California's Water Development," *American Journal of Economics and Sociology,* XXII (July 1963), 409–15.
Timmons, John F. "Theoretical Considerations of Water Allocation among Competing Uses and Users," *Journal of Farm Economics,* XXXVIII (December 1956), 1244–58.
Tolley, George S., and V. S. Hastings. "Optimal Water Allocation: The North Platte River," *Quarterly Journal of Economics,* LXXIV (May 1960), 279–95.
Trelease, Frank J. "Government Ownership and Trusteeship of Water," *California Law Review,* XLV (December 1957), 638–54.
——. "Water Law and Economic Transfers of Water," *Journal of Farm Economics,* XLIII (December 1961), 1147–52; "Rejoinder," *ibid.,* XLIV (May 1962), 435–43.

Walsh, Philip F. "Problems of Service Extension to Fringe Areas," *Journal of the American Water Works Association,* LI (March 1959), 348–53.
"Water Rates in California Cities," Parts I and II, *Western City Magazine,* XXXI (October and November 1955).
Weeks, David, and J. Herbert Snyder. "Soil Variables for Use in Economic Analysis," *Hilgardia* (April 1957), 497–520.
Worcester, D. A., Jr. "Justifiable Price 'Discrimination' under Conditions of Natural Monopoly: A Diagrammatic Representation," *American Economic Review,* XXXVIII (June 1948), 382–88.

3. *Unpublished Dissertations, Memoirs, Papers, and Addresses*

Angel, Arthur D. "Political and Administrative Aspects of the Central Valley Project of California." Unpublished Ph.D. dissertation, University of California, Los Angeles, 1944.

Bartlett, Louis. "Memoirs." Typescript, Regional Cultural History Project, University of California General Library, Berkeley, 1957.
Blaney, Harry F. "Determining Irrigation Requirements from Consumptive Use Water Rates," Paper read at the Fifth International Conference of Agricultural Engineers, Brussels, 1958.
Boone, W. P. "Kings River Water Rights History, Litigation and Mutual Agreement of Settlement." Unpublished manuscript, *ca.* 1935.

Duerr, Donald A. "Conflicts between Water Development Projects and Fish and Wildlife Conservation in the Central Valley Basin, California." Unpublished M.A. thesis, University of California, Berkeley, 1955.
Durbrow, William. "William Durbrow, Irrigation District Leader." Typescript, Regional Cultural History Project, University of California General Library, Berkeley, 1958.

Fourt, Louis. "Forecasting the Urban Residential Demand for Water." Unpublished seminar paper, University of Chicago, 1958.

Gottlieb, Manuel. "Some Characteristics of the Urban Demand for Domestic Water." Unpublished paper, University of Wisconsin, 1961.

Hohenthal, H. A. "A History of the Turlock District." Unpublished M.A. thesis, University of California, Berkeley, 1930.

Lambert, Charles F. "Land Speculation and Irrigation Development in the Sacramento Valley, 1905–1957." Typescript, Regional Cultural History Project, University of California General Library, Berkeley, 1957.

Martin, Richard G. "Water Conservation in the Santa Clara Valley." Unpublished M.A. thesis, University of California, Berkeley, 1949.

Mason, J. Rupert. "Single-Tax, Irrigation Districts, and Municipal Bankruptcy." Typescript, Regional Cultural History Project, University of California General Library, Berkeley, 1958.

Renshaw, Edward F. "The Demand for Municipal Water." Unpublished paper, University of Chicago, 1958.

Rhodes, Benjamin Franklin, Jr. "Thirsty Land: The Modesto Irrigation District, a Case Study of Irrigation Under the Wright Law." Unpublished Ph.D. dissertation, University of California, Berkeley, 1943.

Shackelford, B. W., and F. F. Mautz. "An Approach to the Selection of Steam Unit Size for a Large Hydro-Steam System." American Society of Mechanical Engineers, Paper No. 57-SA-99, 1957.

Smirnovsky, V. F. "A Report on the Effect of Canal Capacities on Cost of Canals on Irrigation Systems." Unpublished B.S. thesis, College of Civil Engineering, University of California, Berkeley, 1930.

4. *Government Documents: Local, State, and Federal*

Alameda County Water District. *Annual Report, 1957–1958.* Fremont: 1958.

——, Engineering Staff. *Comparison of Supplemental Sources of Water Supply.* Fremont: 1961.

——, ——. *Engineering Report on Ground Water Supplies in the Alameda County Water District, 1962, and Report on Financing South Bay Aqueduct Costs, Fiscal Year 1962–63.* Fremont: 1962.

——, ——. *Report on Bond Sale No. II (1960) for Improvement District No. 1 Bonds Authorized March 1956.* Fremont: 1960.

California Conservation Commission of 1911. *Report, January 1, 1913.* Sacramento: 1912.

California Department of Fish and Game. *Effects on Fish and Wildlife Resources of Proposed Water Development on Middle Fork Feather River.* Water Projects Report No. 2. Sacramento: 1961.

——. *Existing and Proposed Water Developments on Yuba and Bear Rivers and Their Effects on Fish and Wildlife.* Water Projects Report No. 4. Sacramento: 1962.

——. *44th Biennial Report, 1954–56.* Sacramento: 1956. [for earlier reports, see California State Department of Natural Resources, Division of Fish and Game.]

—— and Department of Water Resources. *Annual Report (1961–62), Delta Fish and Wildlife Protection Study.* Report No. 1. Sacramento: 1962.

California Department of Water Resources. *Activities and Transactions of the Department of Water Resources Under the Davis-Grunsky Act: 1962 Report to the Legislature.* Sacramento: 1962.

——. *The California State Water Project in 1964.* Bulletin No. 132–64. Sacramento: 1964.

——. *The California Water Plan.* Bulletin No. 3. [See citation under California State Water Resources Board.]

——. *Colusa Basin Investigation.* Bulletin No. 109. Sacramento: 1962.

——. *Dams Within Jurisdiction of State of California, January 1, 1962.* Bulletin No. 17. Sacramento: 1962.

——. *Directory of Water Service Agencies in California.* Bulletin No. 114. Sacramento: 1962.

——. *Feasibility of Serving the Desert Water Agency Service Area from the State Water Facilities.* Bulletin No. 119–1. Sacramento: 1962.
——. *Feasibility of Serving the Palmdale Irrigation District and the Pearland Area from the State Water Facilities.* Bulletin No. 119–4. Sacramento: 1963.
——. *General Comparison of California Water District Acts.* Sacramento: 1958.
——. *Ground Water Conditions in Central and Northern California, 1957–58.* Bulletin No. 77–58. Sacramento: 1960.
——. *Interim Report to the California State Legislature on the Salinity Control Barrier Investigation.* Bulletin No. 60. Sacramento: 1957.
——. *Investigation of Alternative Aqueduct Systems to Serve Southern California—Feather River and Delta Diversion Projects.* Bulletin No. 78, Preliminary Edition. Sacramento: 1959.
——. *Land and Water Use in the Tule River Hydrographic Unit.* Bulletin No. 94–1. Sacramento: 1962.
——. *1957 Joint Hydrology Study, Sacramento River and Sacramento-San Joaquin Delta.* Sacramento: 1958.
——. *North Bay Aqueduct.* Bulletin No. 110. Sacramento: 1961.
——. *Northeastern Counties Investigation.* Bulletin No. 58. Sacramento: 1960.
——. *Report of Findings on Formal Application for a State Loan for Camp Far West Project.* Sacramento: 1962.
——. *Report on Proposed Oroville-Wyandotte Irrigation District Water and Power Development on South Fork of Feather River.* Prepared for California District Securities Commission. Sacramento: 1958.
——. *Report on Proposed Semitropic Water Storage District, Kern County.* Sacramento: 1958.
——. *Report on Proposed Wheeler Ridge-Maricopa Water Storage District, Kern County.* Sacramento: 1959.
——. *Review of Report on Merced River Development, Proposed by Merced Irrigation District.* Prepared for California Districts Securities Commission. Sacramento: 1961.
——. *San Joaquin Master Drain, San Joaquin Valley Drainage Investigation.* Bulletin No. 127. Sacramento: 1965.
——. *Water Conditions in California: California Cooperative Snow Surveys.* Bulletin No. 120. Sacramento: 1962.
——. *Water Use by Manufacturing Industries in California, 1957–59.* Bulletin No. 124. Sacramento: 1964.
——, Division of Resources Planning. *Kaweah River: Flows, Diversions, and Service Areas, 1955–60.* Bulletin No. 49–C. Sacramento: 1961.
——, ——. *Lower San Joaquin Valley Water Quality Investigation.* Bulletin No. 89. Sacramento: 1960.
——, ——. *Report on Irrigation and Water Storage Districts in California, 1951–55,* and *1956–58, 1959,* and *1960.* Bulletin No. 21. Sacramento: 1956, 1959, 1960, and 1961. [For earlier issues, see entries under California State Department of Public Works, Division of Water Resources and Division of Engineering and Irrigation.]
——, ——. *Surface Water Flow for 1954,* and *1955, 1956, 1957, 1958, 1959,* and *1960.* Bulletins No. 23–54 through No. 23–60. Sacramento: 1955 through 1961.
——, Policy and Programs Office. *Information and Basic Data Concerning the Construction, Cost Allocation, and Financing of the South Bay Aqueduct Project.* Sacramento: 1960.
California Districts Securities Commission. *Report on Activities and Actions of the California Districts Securities Commission and the State Engineer, with Particular Reference to Contracts Entered into Between Public Districts and the United States.* San Francisco: 1952.
——. *Supplemental Staff Report on Merced River Development Proposed by Merced Irrigation District.* San Francisco: 1961.

California Irrigation District Bond Commission. *Report on Modesto Irrigation District.* Sacramento: 1914.

——. *Report on Oakdale Irrigation District.* Sacramento: 1914.

California Joint Federal-State Water Resources Commission. *Report to the President of the United States and the Governor of the State of California.* Sacramento: 1931.

California State Comptroller. *Annual Report of Financial Transactions Concerning Cities of California, Fiscal Year 1955–56,* and fiscal years *1956–57, 1957–58, 1958–59,* and *1959–60.* Sacramento: 1957–1961.

——. *Annual Report of Financial Transactions Concerning Irrigation Districts of California for the Calendar Year 1951,* and calendar years *1952* through *1960.* Sacramento: 1952 through 1961.

California State Department of Engineering. *Investigations of the Economical Duty of Water for Alfalfa in Sacramento Valley, California, 1910–1915.* Bulletin No. 3. Sacramento: 1917.

——. *Irrigation in California. (Southern.) The Field, Water-supply, and Works, Organization and Operation, in San Diego, San Bernardino, and Los Angeles Counties. The Second Part of the Report of the State Engineer of California on Irrigation and the Irrigation Question,* by William H. Hall. Sacramento: 1888.

——. *Irrigation Districts in California, 1887–1915,* by Frank Adams. Bulletin No. 2. Sacramento: 1916.

——. *Use of Water From Kings River, California, 1918,* by Harry Barnes. Bulletin No. 7. Sacramento: 1920.

——. *Water Resources of the Kern River and Adjacent Streams and Their Utilization, 1920.* Bulletin No. 9. Sacramento: 1921.

California State Department of Natural Resources. Division of Fish and Game. *Biennial Report.* Sacramento: 1936 through 1952.

California State Department of Public Health. *California Domestic Water Supply Statistics.* Sacramento: 1958.

California State Department of Public Works, Division of Engineering and Irrigation. *Irrigation Districts in California, 1929,* by Frank Adams. Bulletin No. 21. Sacramento: 1930.

——, Division of Water Resources. *Analysis of Plans for Development and Utilization of Water Resources of the South Fork of Feather River.* Sacramento: 1954.

——, ——. *Cost of Irrigation Water in California,* by Harry F. Blaney and Martin R. Huberty. Bulletin No. 36. Sacramento: 1930.

——, ——. *Engineering Report on Tri-Dam Project on Stanislaus River of Oakdale and South San Joaquin Irrigation Districts.* Prepared for California Districts Securities Commission. Sacramento: 1952.

——, ——. *Kaweah River: Flows, Diversions and Service Areas.* Bulletin No. 49. Sacramento: 1940.

——, ——. *Kaweah River: Flows, Diversions and Service Areas, 1949–1955.* Bulletin No. 49–B. Sacramento: 1956.

——, ——. *Permissible Annual Charges for Irrigation Water in Upper San Joaquin Valley,* by Frank Adams and Martin R. Huberty. Bulletin No. 34. Sacramento: 1930.

——, ——. *Program for Financing and Constructing the Feather River Project as the Initial Unit of the California Water Plan.* Sacramento: 1955.

——, ——. *Report on Feasibility of the Feather River Project.* Sacramento: 1951.

——, ——. *Report on Irrigation Districts in California for the Year 1929.* Bulletin No. 21–A. Sacramento: 1931. [Bulletins No. 21–B through 21–O cover the years 1930 through 1943; Bulletin No. 21–P covers 1944–1950. These are part of a series which began with issuance of the Department of Engineering's Bulletin No. 2 by Adams (above) and the Division of Engineering and Irrigation's Bulletin No. 21 by Adams (above). For subsequent reports in the series, see California Department of Water Resources, Division of Resources Planning (above).]

——, ——. *Report of the Kings River Water Master for the Period 1918–30.* Bulletin No. 38. Sacramento: 1931.
——, ——. *Report to the Legislature of 1931 on State Water Plan.* Bulletin No. 25. Sacramento: 1930.
——, ——. *Report on 1956 Cooperative Study Program, Vol. I: Water Use and Water Rights Along the Sacramento River and in the Sacramento-San Joaquin River Delta.* Sacramento: 1957.
——, ——. *Sacramento River and Sacramento-San Joaquin Delta: Trial Water Distribution, 1955; Summary Report of Data.* Sacramento: 1956.
——, ——. *Sacramento River Basin, 1931.* Bulletin No. 26. Sacramento: 1933.
——, ——. *San Joaquin River Basin, 1931.* Bulletin No. 29. Sacramento: 1934.
——, ——. *Some Economic and Agricultural Aspects of the Proposed Solano Unit, Central Valley Irrigation Development,* by Frank Adams. Sacramento: 1948.
——, Division of Water Rights. *Kings River Investigation, Present and Proposed Use of Water for Irrigation and Power Development: Water Master's Report 1918–23,* by Harold Conkling and Charles L. Kaupke. Bulletin No. 2. Sacramento: 1923.
——, Divisions of Engineering and Irrigation and Water Rights. *Ground Water Resources of the Southern San Joaquin Valley,* by S. T. Harding. Bulletin No. 11. Sacramento: 1927.
California State Legislature, Assembly Interim Committee on Water. *Study of Water District Laws.* Sacramento: 1962.
——, Assembly Water Committee. *Economic and Financial Policies for State Water Projects.* Assembly Interim Committee Reports, 1959–1961, Vol. 26, No. 1. Sacramento: 1960.
——, ——. *Water District Laws of California: An Analysis, Report Prepared for Assembly Interim Committee on Conservation, Planning, and Public Works.* Assembly Interim Committee Reports, 1953–1955, Vol. 13, No. 5A. Sacramento: 1955. [See Books and Pamphlets: University of California, for Interim Committee Report No. 5.]
——, Joint Legislative Committee on Water Problems. *Report of the Counties of Origin Subcommittee.* Ninth Partial Report. Sacramento: 1957.
——, ——. *Report on Water Problems of the State of California.* In the 1947 and 1949 regular sessions. Sacramento: 1947 and 1949.
——, Senate Committee on Water Resources. *Feasibility of State Ownership and Operation of the Central Valley Project of California.* Report prepared pursuant to S.C.R. No. 48, Legislature of 1951. Sacramento: 1952.
——, Senate Fact Finding Committee on Water. *Budgets, Reports, Local Assistance for State Water Development.* A Partial Report. Report No. 2. Sacramento: 1961.
——, ——. *Contracts, Cost Allocations, Financing for State Water Developments.* Partial Report. Sacramento: 1960.
California State Public Utilities Commission. *Annual Report, 1959–1960,* and *1962–1963* and *1963–1964.* San Francisco: 1960, 1963, and 1964.
——. *General Report on the Results of Operation of California Water Service Company, 1959 Adjusted and 1960 Estimated.* San Francisco: 1960.
——. *Report on the Results of Operation of Buena Vista Canal, Inc., Year 1959 Recorded and Adjusted, Year 1960 Estimates.* Applications No. 41402–41407 for Authority to Increase Rates for Irrigation Service Near Bakersfield, County of Kern. San Francisco: 1960.
California State Water Resources Board. *The California Water Plan.* Bulletin No. 3. Sacramento: 1957.
——. *San Joaquin County Investigation.* Bulletin No. 11. Sacramento: 1955.
——. *Sutter-Yuba Counties Investigation.* Bulletin No. 6. Sacramento: 1952.
——. *Water Resources of California.* Bulletin No. 1. Sacramento: 1951.
——. *Water Utilization and Requirements of California.* 2 vols. Bulletin No. 2. Sacramento: 1955.

California State Water Rights Board. *Second Annual Report, Covering Period July 1, 1957–June 30, 1958.* Sacramento: 1958.

——. *Third Annual Report, Covering Period July 1, 1958–June 30, 1959.* Sacramento: 1959.

California Water Commission. *Agenda and Data for Meetings.* Various monthly issues. Sacramento: 1960–1963.

East Bay Municipal Utility District. *Official Statement of the East Bay Municipal Utility District: Alameda and Contra Costa Counties, Water Development Project for the East Bay Area Bonds.* Oakland: Jan. 16, 1959.

——. *Ibid., Water Development Project for the East Bay Area Bonds (General Obligation), $25,000,000 Series A.* Oakland: 1959.

——. *Ibid., Water Development Project for the East Bay Area Bonds, Series D.* Oakland: 1962.

——, Water Resources and Planning Division. *Mokelumne Aqueduct No. 3: Determination of Size of Future Water Supply.* Oakland: 1957.

Federal Inter-Agency River Basin Committee. *Proposed Practices for Economic Analysis of River Basin Projects.* Report to the Committee prepared by the Subcommittee on Benefits and Costs. Washington: May 1950.

Federal Power Commission. *Hydroelectric Power Resources of the United States, Developed and Undeveloped.* Washington: 1960.

——. *Steam-Electric Plant Construction Cost and Annual Production Expenses.* Annual Supplements. Washington: 1959–1962.

Fresno Irrigation District. *Annual Report, 1959,* and *1960.* Fresno: 1960 and 1961.

Humboldt Bay Municipal Water District. *Official Statement Concerning $10,700,000 General Obligation Bonds, 1959 Series A.* Eureka: 1959.

Kern River Water Storage District. *Digest of Report on Modified Plan of Development Recommended by Board of Directors.* Bakersfield: 1928.

——. *Report to State Engineer on Feasibility of Project.* Bakersfield: 1928.

Kings River Water Association. *Forty Years on Kings River, 1917–1957,* by Charles L. Kaupke. Fresno: 1957.

——. *Water Master Report for Year 1957: Pine Flat Reservoir Operation Schedule, Administration and Canal Diversion,* by C. H. Smith. Fresno: 1958.

Los Altos, City of, Mayor's Water Study Committee. *Water for Los Altos.* Los Altos: 1960.

Los Angeles, City of, Department of Water and Power. *Statistical Reports, Fiscal Years 1950–59.* Los Angeles: 1959.

Lower Tule River Irrigation District. *Lower Tule River Irrigation District: History and Operational Report, 1950 to 1957,* by William A. Alexander. Woodville: 1958.

Madera Irrigation District. *History of Madera Irrigation District.* Mimeographed. Madera: n.d.

Modesto Irrigation District. *Annual Report, 1962.* Modesto: 1963.

Nevada Irrigation District. *Charges for Water Service Established by Board of Directors Effective April 1, 1961.* Grass Valley: 1961.

North Marin County Water District. *Water Supply and Distribution Report,* by T. C. Brinkley. Novato: 1960.

Redding, City of, Engineering Department. *A Survey of Water Rates and Related Data for 86 Municipal Systems in California as of January 1, 1960.* Redding: 1960.

Sacramento Municipal Utility District. *Report on Substitute Plan, American River Basin.* Sacramento: 1956.

San Francisco, City and County of, Board of Supervisors. *Report on the Water Supply of San Francisco.* San Francisco: 1908.

——, City and County of, Public Utilities Commission. *Annual Report, Fiscal Year 1961–62.* San Francisco: 1962.

——, ——. *Rate Schedule for Water Service.* San Francisco: 1960.

——, City and County of, Water Department. *Annual Report, Commercial Division, Fiscal Year 1958–59.* San Francisco: 1959.

Santa Clara-Alameda-San Benito Water Authority. *Report of Progress.* San Jose: 1958.

—— and Santa Clara County Flood Control and Water Conservation District, Board of Review. *Materials Supporting Report on Supplemental Water Supplies for North Santa Clara Valley.* San Jose: 1960.

—— and ——, *idem. Report on Supplemental Water Supplies for North Santa Clara Valley and Related Service in San Benito and Santa Cruz Counties.* San Jose: 1960.

Santa Clara County Flood Control and Water Conservation District, District Engineer. *Engineer's Report: Zone W–1, Proposed Water Treatment and Distribution System.* San Jose: 1962.

——, Special Water Committee of the Board of Supervisors. *Unified County Water Plan: Report to the Board of Supervisors.* San Jose: 1961.

Santa Clara Valley Water Conservation District. *Annual Report, 1959.* San Jose: 1960.

——. *Report to the Honorable Board of Directors on Additional Conservation and Distribution Facilities.* San Jose: 1960.

Sonoma County Flood Control and Water Conservation District. *Official Statement in Connection with the Sale of $5,650,000 1955 Coyote Valley Dam Bonds.* Santa Rosa: 1955.

Southwest Contra Costa County Water District. *Reply to Statement of East Bay Municipal Utility District, Before the California Districts Securities Commission.* Typescript. Concord: Jan. 28, 1952.

Stanislaus County Planning Department. *A Water Need Study for Stanislaus County for the Year 2050.* Modesto: 1957.

Turlock Irrigation District. *Seventy-First Annual Report—Year of 1959.* Turlock: 1960.

—— and Modesto Irrigation District. *Report of the Turlock and Modesto Irrigation Districts, Stanislaus County, California, in Reply to Reports on the Proposed Use of Tuolumne River on Behalf of San Francisco, California, and Neighboring Cities,* by Burton Jones and H. S. Crowe. Turlock: 1912.

U.S. Army Corps of Engineers, South Pacific Division. *Appendix C to the Technical Report on San Francisco Bay Barriers.* San Francisco: 1963.

——, ——. *Water Resources Development in California.* San Francisco: 1961.

U.S. Bureau of the Budget. *Reports and Budget Estimates Relating to Federal Programs and Projects for Conservation, Development, or Use of Water and Related Land Resources.* Circular No. A–47. Washington: 1952.

——, Panel of Consultants to the Bureau of the Budget. *Standards and Criteria for Formulating and Evaluating Federal Water Resources Development.* Washington: 1961.

U.S. Congress, House of Representatives. *Camanche Reservoir, Mokelumne River, California.* H. Doc. 436. 87 Cong. 2 sess. Washington: 1962.

——, ——. *Report on Irrigation in the San Joaquin, Tulare and Sacramento Valleys of the State of California,* by B. S. Alexander, George Davidson, and G. H. Mendell. H. Ex. Doc. 290. 43 Cong. 1 sess. Washington: 1874.

——, House Appropriations Committee, Subcommittee on Interior Department. *Interior Department Appropriations for 1951.* Hearings. 81 Cong. 2 sess. Washington: 1950.

——, ——, *idem. Interior Department Appropriations for 1953, Part 3 (Bureau of Reclamation).* Hearings. 82 Cong. 2 sess. Washington: 1952.

——, ——, *idem. Interior Department Appropriations for 1954.* Hearings. 83 Cong. 1 sess. Washington: 1953.

——, House Committee on Government Operations. *Effect of Department of Interior and REA Policies on Public Power Preference Customers.* H. Rep. 2279. 84 Cong. 2 sess. Washington: 1956.

——, House Committee on Interior and Insular Affairs. *Central Valley Project Documents, Part 1: Authorizing Documents.* H. Doc. 416. 84 Cong. 2 sess. Washington: 1956.

——, ——. *Central Valley Project Documents, Part 2: Operating Documents.* H. Doc. 246. 85 Cong. 1 sess. Washington: 1957.

——, ——. *Columbia River and Its Tributaries, Northwestern United States.* H. Doc. 531. 81 Cong. 2 sess. Washington: 1950.

——, ——. *Russian River, Dry Creek Basin, California.* H. Doc. 547. 87 Cong. 2 sess. Washington: 1962.

——, ——. *Sacramento Canals Unit, Central Valley Project, California.* H. Doc. 73. 83 Cong. 1 sess. Washington: 1953.

——, ——. *Trinity River Division, Central Valley Project, California.* H. Doc. 53. 83 Cong. 1 sess. Washington: 1953.

——, ——, Special Subcommittee on Irrigation and Reclamation. *Central Valley Project, California: Water Rights, Supplies and Uses.* Hearings. 82 Cong. 1 sess. Washington: 1952.

——, ——, *idem. Federal Assistance for Small Reclamation Projects.* Hearings on H.R. 104, H.R. 384, and H.R. 3817. 84 Cong. 1 sess. Washington: 1955.

——, ——, *idem. Grasslands Water Problem, San Joaquin Valley, California.* Hearings. 82 Cong. 1 sess. Washington: 1951.

——, ——, *idem. Report on Central Valley Project, California.* 82 Cong. 1 sess. Washington: 1952.

——, ——, *idem. San Luis Project, California.* Hearings on H.R. 6035, H.R. 7295, H.R. 2452, H.R. 2521, and H.R. 4969. 85 Cong. 2 sess. Washington: 1958.

——, ——, *idem. San Luis Unit, Central Valley Project, California.* Hearings on H.R. 10915 and H.R. 10952. 84 Cong. 2 sess. Washington: 1956.

——, ——, *idem. San Luis Unit, Central Valley Project, California.* Hearings on H.R. 301, H.R. 302, H.R. 5681, H.R. 5684, and H.R. 5687. 86 Cong. 1 sess. Washington: 1959.

——, ——, *idem. Trinity River Development.* Hearings on H.R. 123. 83 Cong. 2 sess. Washington: 1954.

——, ——, *idem. Water Resources Development Criteria.* Hearings on H.R. 7362. 84 Cong. 2 sess. Washington: 1956.

——, House Committee on Public Lands, Subcommittee on Irrigation and Reclamation. *To Amend the Reclamation Projects Act of 1939.* Hearings on H.R. 1772, H.R. 1886, H.R. 1977, H.R. 2583, H.R. 2873, and H.R. 2874. 80 Cong. 1 sess. Washington: 1947.

——, ——, *idem. To Amend the Reclamation Projects Act of 1939.* Hearings on H.R. 830, H.R. 1762, H.R. 1770, H.R. 1999, and H.R. 2000. 81 Cong. 1 sess. Washington: 1949.

——, ——, *idem. The American River Basin Project.* Hearings on H.R. 4152 and H.R. 4157. 80 Cong. 2 sess. Washington: 1948.

——, ——, *idem. The American River Basin Project.* Hearings on H.R. 93, H.R. 165, H.R. 310, H.R. 1223, H.R. 1336, and H.R. 1738. 81 Cong. 1 sess. Washington: 1949.

——, ——, *idem. Authorize Sacramento Valley Canals, Central Valley Project, California.* Hearings on H.R. 163. 81 Cong. 1 sess. Washington: 1949.

——, ——, *idem. The Solano County Project, California.* Hearings on H.R. 5927. 80 Cong. 2 sess. Washington: 1948.

——, Senate Appropriations Committee, Subcommittee. *Interior Department Appropriations for 1953.* Hearings on H.R. 7176. 82 Cong. 2 sess. Washington: 1952.

——, Senate Committee on Interior and Insular Affairs, Subcommittee on Irrigation and Reclamation. *Acreage Limitation (Reclamation Law) Review*. Hearings on S. 1425, S. 2541, and S. 3448. 85 Cong. 2 sess. Washington: 1958.
——, ——, *idem. San Luis Unit—Central Valley Project, California*. Hearings on S. 1887. 85 Cong. 2 sess. Washington: 1958.
——, ——, *idem. San Luis Unit, Central Valley Project, California*. Hearings on S. 44. 86 Cong. 1 sess. Washington: 1959.
——, ——, *idem. Tri-Dam Project*. Hearings on S. 3040. 83 Cong. 2 sess. Washington: 1954.
——, ——, *idem. Trinity River Division, Central Valley Project, California*. Hearings on H.R. 4633. 84 Cong. 1 sess. Washington: 1955.
——, Senate Committee on Public Lands, Subcommittee. *Exemption of Certain Projects from Land-Limitation Provisions of Federal Reclamation Laws*. Hearings on S. 912. 80 Cong. 1 sess. Washington: 1947.
——, Senate, Joint Subcommittee of Committee on Appropriations and Committee on Interior and Insular Affairs. *Bureau of Reclamation, Interior Department*. Hearings on the Solano Project in California. 82 Cong. 2 sess. Washington: 1953.
——, ——, Select Committee on National Water Resources. *Floods and Flood Control*. Committee Print 15. 86 Cong. 2 sess. Washington: 1960.
——, ——, *idem. Water Resources Activities in the United States: Water Supply and Demand*. Pursuant to S. Res. 48. Committee Print 32. 86 Cong. 2 sess. Washington: 1960.
U.S. Department of Agriculture. *Commercial Irrigation Companies*, by Wells A. Hutchins. Technical Bulletin No. 177. Washington: 1930.
——, Bureau of Agricultural Economics. *History of Legislation and Policy Formation of the Central Valley Project*, by Mary Montgomery and Marion Clawson. Berkeley: 1946.
——, ——. *A Wartime Facilities Plan for Rehabilitation and Utilization of Irrigation Works for Food and Fibre Production, Southern Portion of the Central Valley of California*. Washington: 1943.
——, Office of Experiment Stations. *Report of Irrigation Investigations in California*, by Elwood Mead *et al.* Bulletin No. 100. Washington: 1901.
U.S. Department of Commerce, Bureau of the Census. *Census of Governments, 1957*. Washington: 1958–59.
——, ——. *County and City Data Book*. Washington: 1961.
——, Office of Area Development. *Future Development of the San Francisco Bay Area, 1960–2020*. Washington: 1959.
——, Weather Bureau. *Climatological Data*. Vols. LIX and LX. Asheville, Ky.: 1955 and 1956.
U.S. Department of Health, Education, and Welfare, Public Health Service. *Water Quality Control Study, Peripheral Canal, Sacramento-San Joaquin Delta, California, Summary Report*. Sacramento: 1964.
U.S. Department of the Interior, Bureau of Reclamation. *Annual Financial Report*. Washington: various years.
——, ——. "Canals and Related Structures," *Reclamation Manual*. Vol. X, Supp. 3. Washington: 1952.
——, ——. *Central Valley Basin: A Comprehensive Departmental Report on the Development of the Water and Related Resources of the Central Valley Basin, and Comments from the State of California and Federal Agencies*. S. Doc. 113. 81 Cong. 1 sess. Washington: 1949.
——, ——. *Delta-Mendota Canal, Technical Record of Design and Construction*. Denver: 1959.
——, ——. *Estimates of Appropriations, Fiscal Year Ending June 30, 1962*. Part 1. N.d. and n.p.
——, ——. *Friant-Kern Canal, Technical Record of Design and Construction*. Denver: 1958.

——, ——. *Hydraulic and Excavation Tables*. 10th ed. Washington: 1950.
——, ——. *Reclamation Repayments and Payout Schedules, 1902–1957*. Washington: 1959.
——, ——. *Report on the Feasibility and Estimated Cost of the Southwest Contra Costa County Water District System*. Washington: 1953.
——, ——, Commissioner's Office. *Analysis of Cost Changes, Authorizations, and Benefits of Reclamation Projects*. Denver: 1960.
——, ——, *idem*. *Construction and Cost Trends, January 1961*. Denver: 1961.
——, ——, Region 2. *Annual Project History, Central Valley Project, 1936–1961*. 26 vols. Sacramento: 1937–1962.
——, ——, *idem*. *Central Valley Project, Annual Report to the Federal Power Commission*. Sacramento: various years.
——, ——, *idem*. *Central Valley Project Operation Study, Shasta Reservoir Operation for Hydrologic Period 1921–22 Through 1953–54*. USBR Exhibits No. 154, 155, 164, and 164A, Applications 5625 *et al.*, California State Water Rights Board. Sacramento: 1959.
——, ——, *idem*. *East Side Division, Central Valley Project, California: A Discussion of the Need for a Supplemental Water Supply and Facilities for Providing It*. Sacramento: 1960.
——, ——, *idem*. *Factual Report, Broadview Water District, Central Valley Project*. Tracy: 1958. [Although exact titles and places of publication vary, this series includes reports on the districts listed below.]
Contra Costa County Water District
Davis Water District
Del Puerto Water District
Eagle Field Water District
El Dorado Irrigation District
Foothill Water District
Garfield Water District
Lindmore Irrigation District
Lindsay-Strathmore Irrigation District
Lower Tule River Irrigation District
Main Prairie Water District
Mustang Water District
Orestimba Water District
Orland-Artois Water District
Oro Loma Water District
Panoche Water District
Plain View Water District
Porterville Irrigation District
Quinto Water District
Romero Water District
San Luis Water District
Saucelito Irrigation District
Shafter-Wasco Irrigation District
Solano Irrigation District
Stone Corral Irrigation District
Sunflower Water District
Terra Bella Irrigation District
Westside Water District
——, ——, *idem*. *Folsom South Unit, Central Valley Project, California: A Report on the Feasibility of Water Supply Development*. Sacramento: 1960.
——, ——, *idem*. *Kings River Project, California: Verbatim Transcript of Public Meeting Called by Bureau of Reclamation*. Fresno: 1946.
——, ——, *idem*. *Projected Agricultural Prices, Region 2*. Sacramento: 1957.

——, ——, *idem. A Report on the Feasibility of Water Supply Development: San Felipe Division, Central Valley Project.* Sacramento: 1963.

——, ——, *idem. A Report on the Feasibility of Water Supply Development: San Luis Unit, Central Valley Project, California.* Sacramento: 1955.

——, ——, *idem. Sacramento River Service Area: Investigations of Glenn-Colusa, Jacinto, Provident, Compton-Delevan, Maxwell Irrigation Districts and Related Areas.* Sacramento: 1953.

——, ——, *idem. Water Deliveries and Revenues, Central Valley Project, Calendar Year 1957.* Sacramento: 1958.

——, ——, *idem. Water Service Repayment—Review Statement, 1957,* and *1959* and *1960.* Sacramento: 1958, 1960, and 1961.

——, Fish and Wildlife Service, Bureau of Sport Fisheries and Wildlife. *A Proposed Development Program for Anadromous Fish in California.* Portland, Ore.: 1962.

——, Geological Survey. *Geologic Features of Ground Water Storage Capacity of the Sacramento Valley, California.* Washington: 1959, 1961.

——, ——. *Ground Water Conditions and Storage Capacity in the San Joaquin Valley, California.* Washington: 1959.

——, ——. *Surface Water Supply of the United States.* Water Supply Papers, various numbers. Washington: 1923–1960.

——, ——. *Water Resources of the San Francisco Bay Area.* Circular No. 378. Washington: 1957.

——, Office of the Secretary. *Excess Land Provisions of the Federal Reclamation Laws and the Payment of Charges.* 2 vols. Washington: 1956.

——, ——. *Proceedings in Re: Use of Hetch Hetchy Reservoir Site in the Yosemite National Park by the City of San Francisco.* Washington: 1910.

——, Pacific Southwest Field Committee. *Natural Resources of Northwestern California, Preliminary Report.* Washington: 1958.

U.S. Farm Credit Administration, Cooperative Division. *Mutual Irrigation Companies in California and Utah,* by Wells A. Hutchins. Bulletin No. 8. Washington: 1936.

U.S. Interagency Committee on Water Resources. *Proposed Practices for Economic Analysis of River Basin Projects.* Washington: 1958.

U.S. President's Water Resources Council. *Policies, Standards, and Procedures in the Formulation, Evaluation, and Review of Plans for Use and Development of Water and Related Land Resources.* S. Doc. 97. 87 Cong. 2 sess. Washington: 1962.

U.S. President's Water Resources Policy Commission. *Water Resource Law.* Washington: 1950.

INDEX